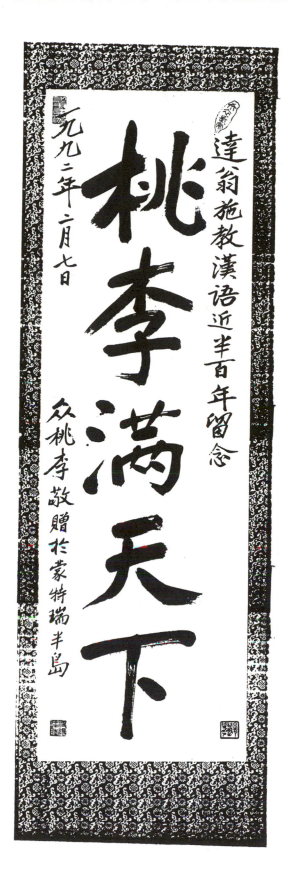

桃李滿天下

達翁施教漢語近半百年留念

一九九三年二月七日

眾桃李敬贈於蒙特瑞半島

Calligraphy by Chang Ta-mu

Provincial Map of China

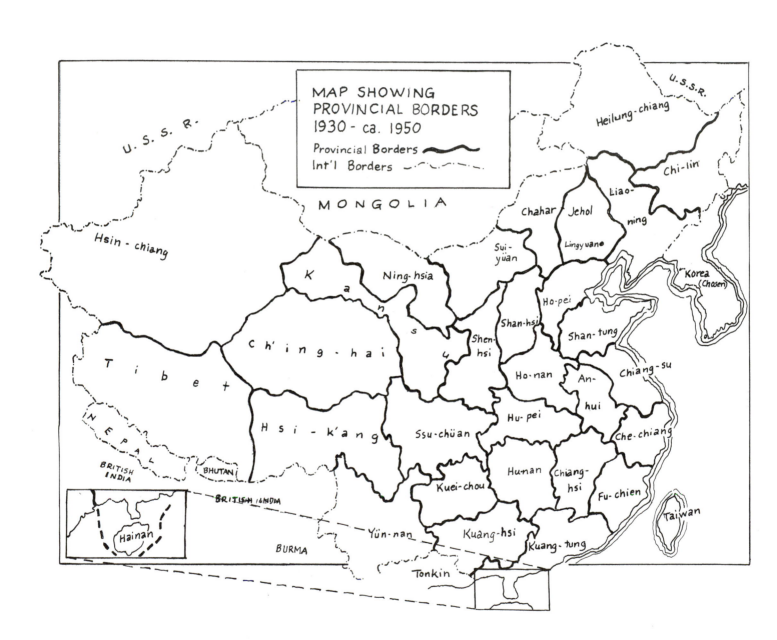

MAP SHOWING
PROVINCIAL BORDERS
1930 - ca. 1950
Provincial Borders
Int'l Borders

Cities and Towns

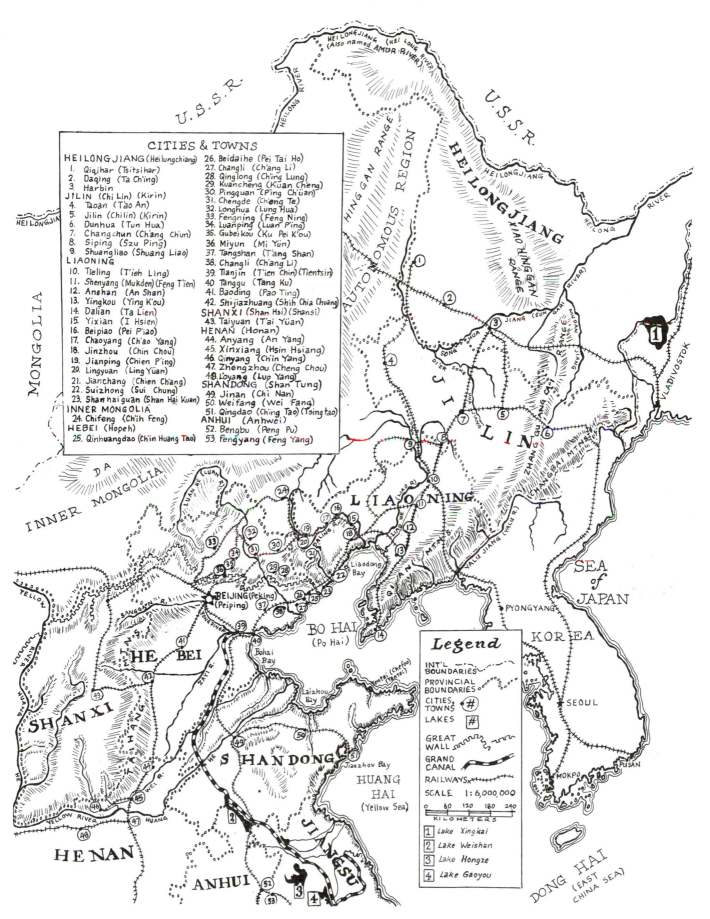

CITIES & TOWNS

HEILONGJIANG (Heilungchiang)
1. Qiqihar (Tsitsihar)
2. Daqing (Ta Ch'ing)
3. Harbin

JILIN (Chi Lin) (Kirin)
4. Taoan (T'ao An)
5. Jilin (Chilin) (Kirin)
6. Dunhua (Tun Hua)
7. Changchun (Ch'ang Ch'un)
8. Siping (Szu Ping)
9. Shuangliao (Shuang Liao)

LIAONING
10. Tieling (T'ieh Ling)
11. Shenyang (Mukden) (Feng T'ien)
12. Anshan (An Shan)
13. Yingkou (Ying K'ou)
14. Dalian (Ta Lien)
15. Yixian (I Hsien)
16. Beipiao (Pei P'iao)
17. Chaoyang (Ch'ao Yang)
18. Jinzhou (Chin Chou)
19. Jianping (Chien P'ing)
20. Lingyuan (Ling Yüan)
21. Jianchang (Chien Ch'ang)
22. Suizhong (Sui Chung)
23. Shanhaiguan (Shan Hai Kuan)

INNER MONGOLIA
24. Chifeng (Ch'ih Feng)

HEBEI (Hopeh)
25. Qinhuangdao (Ch'in Huang Tao)

26. Beidaihe (Pei Tai Ho)
27. Changli (Ch'ang Li)
28. Qinglong (Ch'ing Lung)
29. Kuancheng (Kuan Cheng)
30. Pingquan (P'ing Ch'üan)
31. Chengde (Ch'eng Te)
32. Longhua (Lung Hua)
33. Fengning (Feng Ning)
34. Luanping (Luan P'ing)
35. Gubeikou (Ku Pei K'ou)
36. Miyun (Mi Yün)
37. Tangshan (T'ang Shan)
38. Changli (Ch'ang Li)
39. Tianjin (T'ien Chin) (Tientsin)
40. Tanggu (Tang Ku)
41. Baoding (Pao Ting)
42. Shijiazhuang (Shih Chia Chuang)

SHANXI (Shan Hsi) (Shansi)
43. Taiyuan (T'ai Yüan)

HENAN (Honan)
44. Anyang (An Yang)
45. Xinxiang (Hsin Hsiang)
46. Qinyang (Ch'in Yang)
47. Zhengzhou (Cheng Chou)
48. Loyang (Luo Yang)

SHANDONG (Shan Tung)
49. Jinan (Chi Nan)
50. Weifang (Wei Fang)
51. Qingdao (Ch'ing Tao) (Tsing tao)

ANHUI (Anhwei)
52. Bengbu (Peng Pu)
53. Fengyang (Feng Yang)

Legend

INT'L BOUNDARIES

PROVINCIAL BOUNDARIES

CITIES, TOWNS (#)

LAKES [#]

GREAT WALL

GRAND CANAL

RAILWAYS

SCALE 1: 6,000,000

0 60 120 180 240
KILOMETERS

1 Lake Xingkai
2 Lake Weishan
3 Lake Hongze
4 Lake Gaoyou

Lingyuan and Vicinity

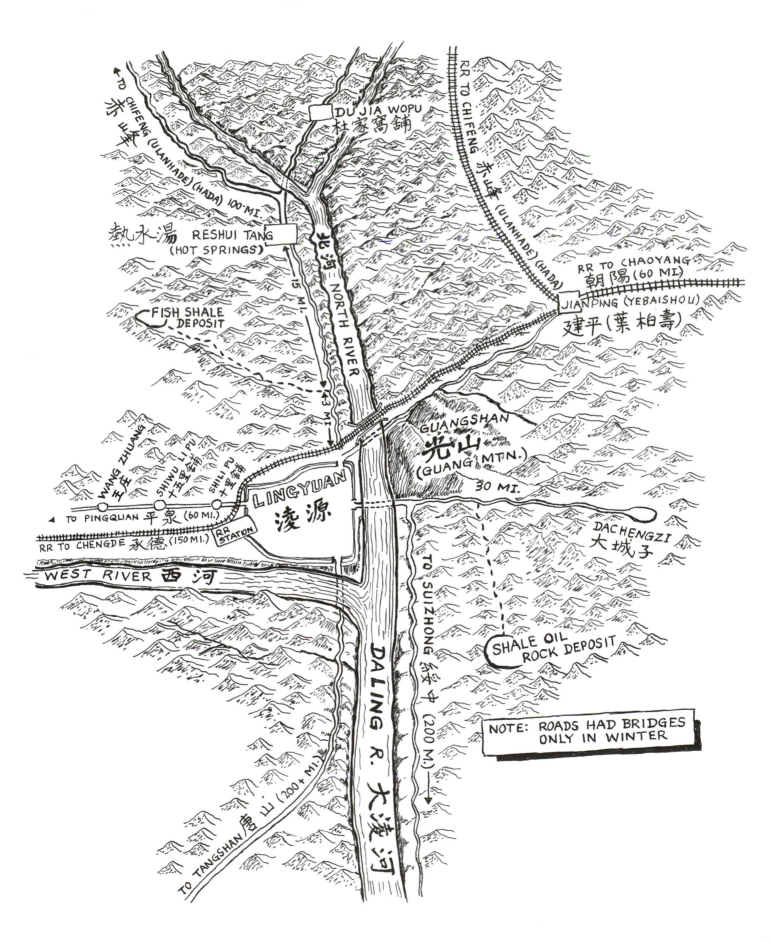

Detail of Lingyuan

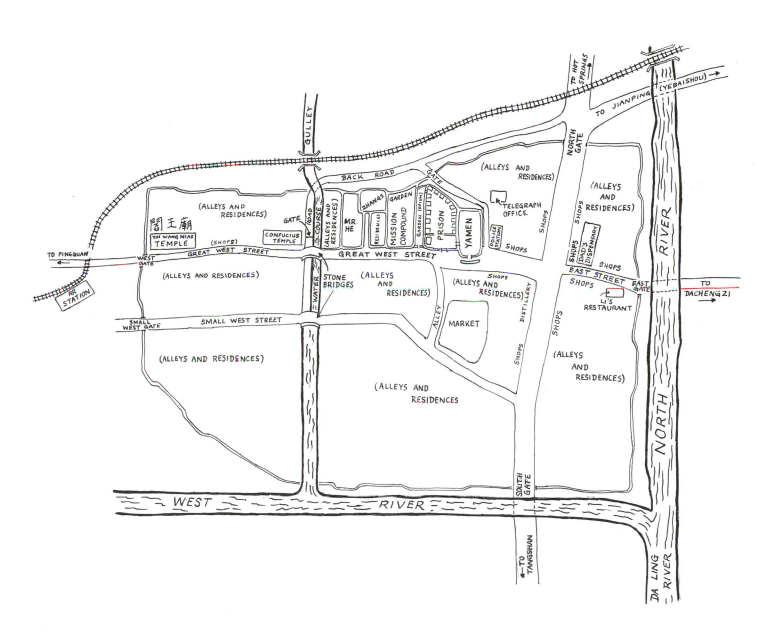

They Called Us
White Chinese

"The Story of a Lifetime of Service to God and Mankind"

BY

Robert N. Tharp

They Called Us White Chinese
Copyright © 1994
Eva E. Tharp Publications

Library of Congress Cataloging-in-Publication Data
Publisher's Cataloging in Publication
(Prepared by Quality Books Inc.)
Tharp, Robert N.
    They called us White Chinese: the story of a lifetime of service to God and mankind / by Robert N. Tharp.
    p. cm.
    Preassigned LCCN: 93-95018
    ISBN 0-9639425-0-6

    1. Tharp, Robert N. 2. Missionaries--China--Biography. 3. China--Description and travel--1901-1948. 4. China--History--20th century. I. Title.

BV33427.T43T43 1994   266'.0092
                             QBI94-989

First Edition
Printed in the United States by
Delmar Printing & Publishing
Charlotte, North Carolina

This book was typeset using Times Roman for the body copy and Present for the headings. It was designed by Bob, with the help of his loving wife, Eva, her publishing assistant, Kathleen Biersteker, a team of 17 friends, and Ed Bohannon at Delmar. Eva selected and captioned the photographs.

For information about purchasing this book, please write to:
Eva E. Tharp Publications
c/o Ed Bohannon
Delmar Printing & Publishing Co.
P.O. Box 1013
Charlotte, NC 28210-1013
704—845-3345 or FAX 704—845-1218

Preface

This story is dedicated to God, family, and those named and unnamed who, in their large and small roles, made the telling possible.

It is a tapestry woven largely from the experiences and reflections of Bob and Eva Tharp, their families and their colleagues; a tapestry spanning nearly a century. Its effect is to take the reader on an adventure, to reintroduce the reader to large world events and personalities while providing the smaller events and voices their important places in the tenuous fabric of history. It encompasses the old and new China — the China of the Empress Dowager and the end of the dynasties, of the warlords, of the Japanese occupation of Manchuria and war against China, of the Second World War, and finally, of the era of Mao, the Great Helmsman, and Red China.

The tapestry is vibrant with broad, rich colors woven with threads of individual challenge, faith, courage, and often heroism. It is dulled by wars, small and large, by national, factional, and individual acts of terror, cruelty and inhumanity. It is glorified by acts of great sacrifice by people whose names have either been lost in the mists of passing time or not known at the beginning.

If, at the beginning of the 1900s, one had attempted to predict China at the end of the century, one probably would have erred. The land known as China has been in turmoil and change from antiquity. Where shall this giant go and what further impacts will she have on her people and the world? God knows. That is sufficient — but perhaps this story will add to the reader's perspective and to increased understanding of that land and her magnificent people.

Reader, go in time. Visit with the people in this tapestry. Live their lives, meet their challenges, endure their pain, and rejoice — for their beliefs and ideas have prevailed and will continue undiminished.

Reader, this is your adventure . . . God bless.

J.E. Pauley
National Security Agency
USAFSS/IFEL 1953-54

Table of Contents

Foreword

My wife, Evangeline, and I were born in China, on opposite sides of that huge country. She was born in the extreme Southwest in the shadows of the Himalayas, and I in the Northeast, about as far north as one could go without getting into Mongolia.

That we were born there is not particularly unusual because many Westerners, both British and American, were born there either of missionary parents or business people. What is perhaps somewhat more rare is that both of us stayed in China for approximately thirty years and, but for the unusual circumstances that overwhelmed China in 1949 when Communism took over, we would still be there.

This is the story of how our parents came to be there, how my wife and I first met as youngsters at a seaside resort not far from Peking, and where many years later we were married, and is basically the story of our lives during that thirty-year span that was one of the most turbulent, chaotic and momentous periods in China's history. It was a time of internal uprisings among the peasants, fighting between a dozen or more warlords who were greedy for power and territory, and later the brutal occupation of Manchuria by the Japanese Army and their subsequent war against China as a whole.

I started writing this book in 1987 at the urging of my many friends who had heard my stories about China and felt they should be preserved for posterity, but the book was never intended to be a historical account per se, nor did I wish to comment at length on the political situation in China at the time. This has already been done by others much more qualified than I. However, elements of both the politics and history of the period have inevitably crept into the account, primarily as they affected us personally. As to dates and times, and because of the fact that almost all of our letters and family records were lost when we left China, I have had to rely almost completely on my memory for the dates of certain happenings, although members of the family, my sister and brother in particular, have contributed their recollections as well from time to time. However, any errors in dates are purely mine.

In addition to being the story of our lives this book is also a tribute to my parents who served God in China for almost forty years, working under the harshest and most primitive conditions one can imagine, being on call literally 24 hours of the day. They neither asked for nor received any recognition during their lifetimes, but I've felt their story should also be known.

The book is also a tribute to the many dear Chinese friends I grew up with and the great number who came to know Christ through the efforts of my parents and fellow missionaries we worked with. These were the people who exerted a very great influence on my life and character as a young lad and whose names would otherwise fade into oblivion.

Finally this book is also the story of my later years in this country, where I had the privilege of teaching Chinese to thousands of young American servicemen, whom I wish to honor with this book. Many through the years have corresponded and have become close friends. Among them, I especially wish to pay tribute to Adrian Johnston, who spent many years in the Far East and traveled several times extensively through

China. So not only did he become my good friend, he was also my dependable observer of conditions in the land that we both loved. His passing in December 1992 was a great loss to me.

Most Americans know very little about the geography of China, but many of those who think about China at all and who know a little about China in the old days have formed the opinion that China has changed all of its place names. The familiar names such as Peking, Tientsin, Canton, Chungking, Tsingtao and Nanking seem to have disappeared and been replaced by Beijing, Tianjin, Guangzhou, Chongqing, Qingdao and Nanjing. In actuality this is one area in which there has been very little change. In a few places, particularly in areas bordering on Mongolia, familiar Chinese names have given way to Mongolian names. But the vast majority of Chinese place names are exactly the same as they have been for as long as most people can remember. The difference for Americans is that these places are now being called by the names the Chinese themselves have always used and not the anglicized forms that for so many years have been used by Westerners.

Peking, as it has always been known to Westerners, has always been known to the Chinese by the Chinese name Beijing. The old romanized spelling of this for Westerners was Pei Ching. When the Nationalists under Chiang Kai-shek moved the capital to Nanjing (also known as Nanking) for a relatively brief period between 1928 and 1937, Beijing was changed to Beiping, which, to the Chinese, had a dual meaning. The intended meaning was that "Bei," the north, had been pacified, since "ping" means peace. However, "ping" also means level or flattened out, and the residents of Beijing felt quite strongly that a slight had been cast on their city by saying it had been flattened. Despite the official change of name, the locals went on calling it by its old name and only in official documents and newspapers did one see the new name. Beijing, as it is now getting to be known worldwide, is simply the new official Pinyin spelling of the old name. "Bei" means north and "jing" means capital. Nanjing means southern capital, and for the Chinese there is an eastern capital, Dongjing, which is their way of pronoucing the Japanese name for Tokyo.

Usage of these Chinese Pinyin (a phonetic alphabet system used in place of Chinese characters) spellings of place names is just another reflection of the Chinese government's endeavor to get away from any Western taint in identifying Chinese city names. A seeming exception is Shanghai, which is spelled just as it always was, but that is simply because the Pinyin spelling happens to be identical. The present pronunciation of the name, however, is purely Chinese, and as it has always been for the Chinese. Westerners called it Shanghai, with the syllable "Shang" pronounced to rhyme with "hang." The Chinese say it to rhyme more closely with "long," as though it were spelled Shonghai.

While on the subject of Chinese place names, I am at the same time both amused and annoyed by the careless habit of many American newscasters on TV and radio mispronouncing the name Beijing. The proper pronunciation is ridiculously simple. "Bei" is pronounced just like the English word "bay," and "jing" is pronounced just like the "jing" in "jingle bells."

However, that apparently was too easy for some of our more sophisticated broadcasters. Back a few years ago when China began to open up again, one of our distinguished TV anchormen, while broadcasting from China, kept pronouncing the name Beijing with a "zzh" sound preceding the "jing," and it came out "Beizzzhing." Perhaps he had a tin ear and couldn't hear the way the Chinese pronounced it, but in any case, other announcers promptly took his lead and followed suit, and far too many still pronounce it that way.

Numerous Chinese words and phrases appear throughout the text. For the Western reader these have been written phonetically in what is known as romanization or latinization. There are numerous forms of romanization, but I decided to use the most modern form, Pinyin, the form officially adopted by the People's Republic of China. However, since my story covers the China of 80 years ago, when Westerners had their own names for the large cities, in most cases I have used the Western form of that time, but on the map in the front of my book, both the old name and the traditional Chinese names are shown. For those individuals familiar with other forms of Chinese romanization, a conversion chart is given in the back of the book.

February 1993

Prologue

My birth in China in 1913, was the direct result of momentous happenings exactly thirteen years before.

On a very hot day in early June 1900, exciting events were taking place in the city of Baoding, some eighty miles south of Peking in Hebei province. It was the time of year when the farmers had normally finished planting their fields and the seeds should have long since begun to sprout, with weeds everywhere that needed to be hoed. But 1900 was an unusual year. The fields instead of being green and lush were, for the most part, dry and barren because of a severe drought. The people were frightened, and uneasy. Thousands of farmers had gone into the city carrying branches of willow trees, to march in processions, carrying the rain god exposed to the hot sun and appealing to him to end the drought. At the same time everyone wanted to attend an outdoor opera performance in honor of that deity, held in front of one of the largest temples in the city. They hoped that he would be so pleasured by the performances that he would supply the much-needed rain.

The huge dusty square in front of the temple was packed solidly with people. No breeze disturbed the hot air that was filled with dust stirred up by the constantly moving mass of people. The sun beat down mercilessly on the crowd, most of whom were peasants wearing their large conical-shaped straw hats, but none complained. This was a grand celebration for them. Nothing could spoil it.

Chinese opera performances consist usually of a series of plays performed by one or more actors. Despite the fact that ostensibly these plays were being performed for the benefit of the temple gods, the stage, (a crudely built platform about five feet high, constructed from light wooden poles and rough-sawn boards loosely placed on top), was set on the far side of the square opposite the temple. The gods presumably had better eyesight than people, and there had to be room for the crowd to see the show as well. Since the show was for a good cause, the local businessmen had readily contributed to the collection that had been taken up to pay the actors, though as usual, much of the money taken in had found its way into the pockets of the local magistrate and his staff, and of the police who stood around the outer edges of the square.

The majority of the crowd stood, although a few had brought along their small stools, and some, their six-inch-wide sawhorse-type benches. Off to one side the women and children sat atop the farm carts. Most of the carts had temporary mat coverings to shield the women from the sun, other women carried oiled-paper umbrellas, and a few were sitting in the shade under their carts. All in the square were having a wonderful time enjoying the traditional plays that they knew by heart but loved to see over and over again. As they watched, hour after hour, some wandered off here and there to the ring of booths that encircled the outer perimeter of the square where they could buy from a wide choice of foods. At the same time vendors circulated through the crowd hawking their own variety of foodstuffs, together with hot tea. Others supplied towels dipped in hot water and wrung out, for people to wipe the sweat and dust off their faces. These men stood at the outer edges of the crowd and deftly threw the rolled-up towels to anyone who raised their hand and shouted for one. Payment was rolled inside the used towel and thrown back, or passed from hand to hand. For all it was a monstrous outdoor picnic that lasted for six days. Everyone intended to enjoy it to the fullest.

The constant movement and noise of the crowd, the cloud of dust they stirred up, and their apparent inattention in no way bothered the actors. This was quite normal in Chinese theaters. Playing a leading role on the stage was a young actor named Zhang Lan-fang, whose given name Lan-fang meant "keep harm away." His appearance seemed to justify the name because he was an evil-looking young fellow, his face showing the years of leading a dissolute life. He had all the characteristic signs of a dissipated opium sot. However, he had a good voice, and was popular with the crowd.

The stage, covered with a matting roof, had an orchestra of four men with stringed instruments on the front left corner. Otherwise it was empty except for Zhang, and no props of any sort were in sight. As Zhang strode around the stage dressed in all his finery, with two crossed flags on his back identifying him as a famous general of the Third Kingdom, he sensed that somehow, the crowd's attention seemed to be lagging. As he sang he was disturbed by something he had noticed happening on the far side of the square near the temple entrance. It bothered him and greatly aroused his curiosity, since many in the crowd were moving in that direction.

What he had seen was a group of men carrying what appeared to be a large wooden cage which they set down near the temple gate. But it then immediately disappeared from sight as a huge mob of people surged around it. Zhang was determined to find out what it was all about as soon as his part in the play ended.

The city of Baoding where Zhang was performing was a prosperous place within a hundred miles of his birthplace. He had been born in a small village just beyond the nearby mountains, across the border in neighboring Shanxi province. Mandarin Chinese was spoken there but with an appalling provincial dialect

that immediately identified him to other Chinese. At his birth the midwife had given him the "milk name" of *Wutou* or black head, because of his mop of jet black hair. He had been a sickly child, an "opium baby," addicted to the drug at birth because his mother had been an inveterate user, and the only way she could keep him from howling all day was to keep him stupefied with the occasional pellet of opium under his tongue each time she herself lay down to smoke it.

As he grew older his need for the drug became more acute. Even though his father grew the opium poppies, it was too valuable a crop to keep, and it was enough that the mother had to be kept supplied, so as soon as the boy was ten and old enough to work, his father used him in the fields by day, but encouraged him at night to go to the nearby town where he readily found work in an opium den. His job there was to prepare the small pellets of opium that fed the pipes of the habitue's. As he went around from one man to the next to supply their pipes, he deftly appropriated for himself as much as he would need for the following day.

One night, amongst the addicts frequenting the den, he met several actors who took a fancy to him, and recognizing a fellow-user of the drug, they assured him he would be able to get plenty of opium wherever they went. They told him if he would join them as an apprentice, they would teach him their art, and without consulting his parents, he joined the troupe. For several years he had been on a circuit of the various towns and villages within a couple of hundred miles of his home, without ever going back or letting his parents know where he was.

The rear part of the stage was enclosed with straw mats and that area served both as a backdrop and a changing room for the actors. It had a door at the left from which the actors emerged onto the stage, and one at the right where they exited. At the back of it was a set of steps so they could leave the stage without the crowd noticing. When Zhang finished his act, he quietly disappeared into the changing room, changed his clothes and disappeared down the back steps into the crowd.

Making his way across the square through the press of people, Zhang reached the temple gate, and with great difficulty managed to squeeze his way through the tightly packed throng to the area where he had last seen the wooden cage. As he got closer he could distinguish the words the mob shouted: *Sha yang guizi, sha yang guizi* (kill the foreign devils, kill the foreign devils.) His interest was piqued because he had never seen a foreigner.

A number of men were standing around the cage each dressed in a sort of black uniform, and wearing turbans of red or yellow, with bright red leggings, and each carried a huge wide sword, Zhang had heard of the *Da Dao Hui* (Great Sword Society) movement as they were commonly known, so named because of the huge swords with which they beheaded the foreigners. The society was an anti-imperialist movement that had started to the south, in Shandong province, some few months before, and its members called themselves *Yi He Quan* meaning Righteous United Fists. Because of that name they came to be known by the rest of the world as the "Boxers," and the whole infamous incident that followed, tearing the country apart, was known as the "Boxer Uprising" or "Boxer Rebellion." They had gradually worked their way north, killing every foreigner they could find, mostly missionaries, and countless numbers of Chinese converts as well.

The Boxers' intent had been to rid their country of all foreigners and everywhere they went they found great sympathy among the local people in their cause against the Westerners, so they had no difficulty enlisting supporters. Their leaders practiced the occult. They also stuffed heavy two-inch-thick pads of paper inside their shirt-fronts and with considerable mumbo-jumbo allowed themselves to be shot at from point-blank range in order to demonstrate how impervious they were to bullets. The peasants in particular were much impressed. It was easy to convince them to hate the foreign missionaries because, as the Boxers told everyone, the "Jesus Church" people had defamed all Chinese gods by claiming they were only made of mud and paper, and were not real gods, and that there was only one true God in heaven above. This, the Boxers claimed, was what had made the gods angry, and was the reason why there had been no rain.

Openly enjoying the support of the Empress Dowager, Ci Xi, the Boxers swarmed into Peking in the early part of June and laid siege to the foreign quarter where the diplomats of various nationalities lived and had their legations. The fighting went on for weeks until an allied army of soldiers from the United States, Great Britain, France, Russia and Japan stormed Peking on August 14, 1900, and raised the Boxer siege, and thereupon looted the city, killing many Chinese in the process. The Empress Dowager, seeing her cause was lost, fled to the west and established a temporary capital in the city of Xi'an, where she remained for nearly two years until a peace treaty was signed with the Western powers.

As Zhang neared the cage, roughly constructed of green willow poles bound together with straw rope, and not much larger than a telephone booth, he saw squeezed inside a white man and woman, and their little boy of about six. Their clothes were torn and dirty, their faces filthy from the billowing dust and streaked with sweat. Peasants and young boys prodded them with sticks and spat on them.

It was the little boy who held Zhang's attention. His face was streaked from tears, and Zhang, who had no particular sympathy for the two adults, and had never had compassion for anyone, suddenly found himself filled with a deep pity for the boy. He drew closer to the cage, and bending down peered at the boy, who looked directly at him and smiled faintly. As Zhang told of this in later years, he said "That smile melted my heart."

Zhang went to a nearby food stand and bought some hard boiled eggs and a few wheat cakes, then sidling up close to the cage, he managed to slip them into the boy's hands without the Boxer guards seeing him. A strange feeling came over him as he looked at the three foreigners, and he had a strong desire to get away from that place where something terribly evil was about to happen. That evening just before dusk, after being pulled out of the cage and manhandled by the crowd, the missionary and his wife were beheaded, but the little boy disappeared, smuggled away somewhere, probably to be sold or given to one of the officials. To this day the fate of that child is not known. Zhang, after seeing the execution of the two missionaries and the disappearance of the small boy, was so emotionally overwrought that he never went back to join the theatrical troupe. He wandered off into the countryside with no definite destination in mind, and as he left the city, he met an old man with white hair and a shaggy beard who accosted him and said, "Young man, you ought to believe in the only living and true God." Zhang was also much shaken by this second incident, which seemed to him to be some kind of omen. But try as he could to shrug it off, the thought kept coming back to him, "What kind of a god could these foreigners believe in that would make them leave their own country and come across the seas to China, only to be killed?"

This incident was only one of the many killings all over China during the Boxer Rebellion. It is estimated that during the previous 230 years in the entire world, only 130 Protestant missionaries had suffered martyrdom, while in those few months of 1900 in China alone, 136 Protestant missionaries were killed, together with 53 of their children, for a total of 189. The final count, including Catholic missionaries, was well over 200 Westerners murdered. During the Baoding incident that Zhang witnessed, less than 100 miles away across the border in Shanxi province, quite near his home, 88 members of the China Inland Mission were trying to escape the Boxers. Some tried fleeing north to Peking and Tientsin, while others went south toward Shanghai. Only 41 escaped. Of these, one small party of five, a Miss Caroline Gates, with Mr. and Mrs. Archibald Glover and their little boy and girl managed to make their way from their home in the small town of Luanfu, to Shanghai. They were on the road for ten weeks during the hottest part of the year, covering more than 1000 miles on foot, in litters, on mule back, by wheelbarrow, and finally river boat, suffering imprisonment several times, and daily under the threat of death. They were beaten, spat upon, and stripped of much of their clothing. The women were pulled around by their hair, tossed out of their mule litters by the mobs, and starved for days on end. They were threatened with death numerous times by government officials as well as the Boxers, and on more than one occasion, their children were temporarily taken from them by officials who coveted them. Nevertheless they finally escaped to Hankow on the Yangtse River, where Mrs. Flora Glover gave birth to a little girl who died ten days later.

The group proceeded from there by river boat to Shanghai, but Mrs. Glover was in such poor health that she died shortly after their arrival. Many years later as a small boy I came to know Miss Gates very well indeed, and from time to time she would tell us stories of God's wonderful deliverance of them from certain death during that horrendous flight.

Another group of 44 of their fellow missionaries in Shanxi province were summoned to Taiyuan, capital of the province, by Yu Xian, the infamous Manchu governor, who was secretly in league with the Boxers. He had promised to protect them from the Boxers, but no sooner had they arrived than he ordered all forty-four men, women and children to be beheaded. For that he paid with his own life some few weeks later, either by suicide or by being beheaded, according to whichever account one reads, because he had caused the Empress Dowager to lose face in front of the Western nations.

Meanwhile, after weeks on the road, singing operatic parts for his meals, and living much like a beggar, Zhang Lan-fang returned to Shanxi province where he felt more comfortable, because of his very pronounced local dialect.

As events turned out, his arrival in Taiyuan coincided with that of the Empress Dowager who was passing through on her way to Xi'an, farther south in the Wei River valley. Many Americans are somewhat familiar with the Empress Dowager because of the recent film "The Last Emperor," in which she was shown as a benign old lady dying a dignified death. Books of the period describe her somewhat differently. She has been variously called a vain, complex and able woman, but tough-minded and ruthless when she thought it necessary. Some described her as a despotic tyrant. When her son, the emperor Tong Zhi, died in 1875 at the age of 28, she immediately assumed the position of regent. The young Empress, who was pregnant at the time, was left out of the picture entirely. Shortly afterward the young woman committed suicide and disputed reports attribute that to extreme pressure from Ci Xi, who struggled to stay in power and ensure there was no direct heir to the throne. Her next act was to appoint her three-year-old nephew, Guang Xu, as emperor while she remained as regent.

Three days after the entry of the allied forces into Peking, a diary of some considerable length, covering the period from January to August 1900, was reportedly found by an Englishman in one of the buildings being sacked. The diary had been written by Ching Shan, a Manchu noble and kinsman to the empress, who had died at the hands of his eldest son just three days before. In the diary, which covered all the news of the imperial court, he detailed the Boxer's slaughter of foreigners in Peking and that of hundreds of Chinese, Christians or otherwise, who were accused of being associated with the foreigners.

Writing of the Empress Dowager's flight from the city as the allied troops entered from the southeast, he reported that the Empress ordered her nephew Guang Xu, (now around 18 years of age), to accompany her. Hearing that, Guang Xu's favorite concubine, known as "The Pearl," had the temerity to challenge the decision by the "Old Buddha," as everyone in the court called her, and demanded that the Emperor be allowed to remain in Peking. Ci Xi was so enraged she told her eunuchs to throw the woman down the nearest well, which they did.

From that point on the diary becomes somewhat murky because presumably the diarist had reportedly died (at the hands of his eldest son) three days after the Empress Dowager had fled southwest from Peking. But in any case, the diary continues that when she finally reached Taiyuan, in Shanxi province, the governor Yu Xian met her some distance outside the city. As he came up to her palanquin, she is said to have gently chided him for having been so overly confident as to the invulnerability of the Boxers when she had last seen him in Peking, (and he took that as a rebuke), but then, supposedly in the words of the same diarist, she went on to say: "...but you did splendidly in carrying out my orders in ridding Shanxi of the whole brood of foreign devils...." She went on to tell him that, because the allies were now loudly calling for vengeance upon him she might have to dismiss him from office. However, she assured him, he should not be disturbed because the move was only "...to throw dust in the eyes of the barbarians, for our own ends."

Yu Xian housed her in the same quarters in which he had held the 44 hapless missionaries some six weeks previously, and the same writer of the diary supposedly reported that the "Old Buddha" appeared delighted when Yu Xian showed her the blood-spattered courtyard where the missionaries had met their fate, and walked around cross-examining him on every detail of the butchery.

While she was doing that, the young Emperor Guang Xu was "...swaggering noisily up and down the courtyard, brandishing the huge sword given him by Yu Xian, with which his devil's work had been done..." The writer concluded: "No better example could be cited of this remarkable woman's primitive instincts and elemental passion of vindictiveness."

The Empress had been accompanied on her journey by a small army under the command of General Ma Gong-bao, which acted as a rear guard to protect her from the allied troops. When Zhang Lan-fang saw the soldiers, he decided to enlist. Next to actors, soldiering was considered to be the basest form of occupation that a man could have, but he would at least be fed and clothed. Accepted into the army, he became part of the Empress's personal bodyguard and followed her south to Xi'an, where she set up her temporary court.

In the meantime, Miss Caroline Gates, after a short period of rest in Shanghai, had returned to her missionary work in Shanxi. Two years later, in 1902, the Empress Dowager returned to Peking and re-established herself in the palace, Zhang accompanying her in her immediate bodyguard. A year later, in 1903, Miss Gates decided to move about 300 miles north to Jehol Province, where she briefly visited the Barnett family in Chengde, capital of the province, and site of the Imperial summer palace. Chengde is outside the Great Wall and a small company of Christians lived there. The city was originally named Jehol, (pronounced "Re He" meaning "Hot River"), because of a small stream that started there in a large pool, just outside the Imperial palace. A large engraved stone marks the spot. The water wasn't actually hot, or even warm, but had some chemical content that prevented it from freezing in the coldest of weather.

That same year, 1903, the Empress decided to spend the summer in Chengde in the sumptuous palace there, where the Emperors had been going for years to escape the summer heat of Peking. Again, Zhang accompanied her.

A short time later in Chengde, Zhang, now a low-ranking officer, was walking down the main street when he saw a small crowd gathered around an elderly Chinese man who was preaching. Zhang stopped to listen and found himself compelled to purchase a set of the four Gospel portions and a copy of Acts, which the man, Wu Yong-sheng, was selling for a few coppers each.

Returning to his barracks Zhang showed the books to his fellow officers, who glanced at them, laughed uproariously, and tore the books apart to use the paper to repair holes in the paper windows and ceilings. Zhang managed to save the Gospel of John, and upon reading it was drawn to the mission compound to learn more about the Christian religion. It was there that he and Miss Gates came to be in the same room during Sunday services, although they didn't speak to each other. And another person was present in church that morning: Edwin J. Tharp, soon to become my father, who had just arrived in China and had been brought there by circumstances difficult to imagine. Zhang didn't speak to Father, either, but it is remarkable that three people previously unknown to each other, from widely scattered points, were together in one room for a short period of time and their lives were to be closely linked from that moment on.

Oddly enough, it was the Boxer Rebellion that had taken my father to China. Born Edwin James Tharp, in Canterbury, England, on February 10, 1877, one of a family of 13 children, he was a successful business-man, manager of a prosperous haberdashery estab-lishment in St. Neots, Huntingdonshire, England. He was only 23, but had been offered an equal partner-ship and the future looked bright for him. He was a dedicated Christian, very active in church work, but had never given a thought to the possibility of becom-ing a missionary until one day in June 1900, he opened a copy of the London Daily Telegraph and saw dozens of photographs of missionaries massacred by the Chinese. At that moment, he felt God calling him to go to China to take the place of one of those murdered victims. However, he wavered, and for two years resisted the call, struggling with the decision to give up his prosperous and attractive business career and go to faraway China. However, one day an inci-dent occurred that helped him make up his mind to leave the business, and when I was a small boy I remember him telling me about it.

One day an elderly lady went into the store to pur-chase some dress material. She had arrived in a car with a chauffeur and was obviously well-to-do, and my father waited on her. After looking at all the mate-rials available, she found one bolt of cloth that appealed to her, but she wasn't completely happy with it, and asked my father if he hadn't something better. The owner of the store, who had offered my father a partnership, overheard the conversation and called Father into the back office where he told him to simply wrap that particular bolt of cloth in tissue paper, take it back out to her, and tell her it was twice the price of what he had shown her previously. My father did as he was told and the lady bought the entire bolt. However, my father felt that it was unethi-cal and he began to have second thoughts about stay-ing in the business world.

A few weeks later he was in London buying new stock and decided to attend a businessmen's breakfast prayer-meeting. As he climbed the stairs to the meet-ing room he heard the group singing the well-known hymn, "He leadeth me." The speaker that morning was a veteran China missionary named Edward Eagger. He told a dramatic story of his deliverance from certain death at the hands of the Boxers through the intervention of a Chinese army officer. At the risk of his own life the officer had taken the Eagger and Stephen families from the mission station in Chengde and smuggled them to the headwaters of the Luan River, a short distance away. From there, hidden under the deck-boards of a river boat, they had been carried downriver to Luanxian, where they had been able to board a train to safety. As a result of the stir-ring message and the hymn Father had heard on his way in, he could not resist any longer and made his decision then and there to go to China as soon as pos-sible. Later he was to write: "It was a decision I never regretted."

Mr. Eagger was about to return to China, and my father decided to go with him. Together they sailed from Liverpool for Boston in May 1903, aboard the *S.S. Mayflower* of the Dominion Lines, not the origi-nal ship with that name, but a very old ship nonethe-less. Incidentally, that was her last trip under that name.

The first day aboard ship my father met a young woman named Margaret Hankey. She, with her two younger sisters and parents, was emigrating to Canada. My father got into a conversation with Miss Hankey, and discovered that she, too, was a born-again Christian. He told her of his call to China as a missionary. By the end of the voyage they were engaged. In telling the story years later, my mother told us children that she knew immediately that her life to that point had been unfulfilled. She said she knew at that instant, when talking to my father, that going to China with him was what God had planned for her all along.

Father was a member of a Christian group known variously as "Brethren" or "Plymouth Brethren," who met not in churches, but in storefronts or modified buildings that they called Gospel Halls or

"Assemblies." (Not to be confused with "Assemblies of God.") The Brethren were (and still are), a highly missionary-oriented group, very active not only in England, Canada and the United States, but also in Australia and New Zealand, as well as in many other countries. The missionaries who went abroad under their auspices did so without any promise of financial support and with no salary. They went in the simple faith that God would supply their every need as promised in His Word.

My father spent three months in Canada and the United States visiting various Assemblies of Christians, then sailed for Shanghai together with Edward Eagger aboard the Canadian Pacific liner, *Empress of Japan.*

Mother, a very pragmatic woman, decided that before joining him, she should first take some training in nursing. She enrolled at Chicago's Michael Reese Hospital Nursing School. Upon graduating, two years later in 1905, she too left for China, where she and my father were married in Tientsin.

At that time there were no recognized Chinese language schools in China. However, there was a Chinese language textbook, the *"Mandarin Primer,"* written by an F.W. Baller, which was used by everyone who wanted to learn Chinese. My father, arriving in China, followed the practice of that time of going to live with a senior missionary while learning the language, and joined Eagger at his mission station in Bagou (Eight Gullies), in the province of Jehol in northeast China, known as Manchuria. There for a year he laboriously studied Chinese, using the *"Mandarin Primer"* with a locally hired Chinese teacher. After that he opened up his own mission station in the tiny town of Kuancheng, two days' journey to the south, where Mother joined him after their marriage.

They stayed there for two years, then, following tragic circumstances, moved back to Bagou, where they relieved Eagger so he could go on furlough. It was in Bagou that they stayed for the next ten years, and it was there that I was born.

My parents had a most difficult time while in Kuancheng. It was just five years after the Boxer Rebellion, and feelings against foreigners still ran high. They had great difficulty finding a place to live until a Moslem businessman who had been helped earlier by another missionary rented them some space. At that time Western missionaries all wore Chinese clothing. The people of Kuancheng, having never before seen a white woman, refused to believe mother actually was a woman, and thought she was a man dressed in a woman's clothes. A year after they got there, my oldest sister Eleanor was born, the birth actually taking place in Weihaiwei, a British naval port established on the northern side of the Shandong peninsula. Just why they went there for Eleanor's birth I never learned, but it was not until the Chinese women in Kuancheng saw Mother feeding the child that they hesitantly approached, and ultimately became sufficiently confident as to allow Mother to treat their illnesses, and a few Chinese women were won to Christianity, but none of the men in the town.

As children, we all knew that Eleanor had died an early death, but we never really took in the complete details. It wasn't until recently that I came across a graphic account hand-written by my father, and it is such an astounding story I have excerpted the following. He wrote:

In July 1906 our firstborn, Eleanor Avenell, at the age of eleven months, was suddenly stricken with infantile cholera...and in the short space of six hours she literally melted away and went to be with Him who said, "Suffer little children to come unto me, and forbid them not."

It was in the middle of the rainy season, and it was most necessary that the precious little body should be buried at once. Our heathen Chinese servant let it be known in the town that the "foreign devil's" little child had died. Almost immediately the whole place was in an uproar, for all the people were superstitiously afraid that the spirit of the little "foreign devil" would be roaming around and take possession of one of the babies in the neighborhood and thus cause it to die!

We begged and pleaded with the officials and leading men in the town to allow us to bury the little one in our own garden, or else allow us to purchase a piece of ground outside the town and inter her there. Instead of obtaining permission to do either, we were ordered to take the little corpse out of the district at once.

It was an exceedingly hot day and was threatening to rain and we were in a dilemma; not knowing whether to go south four days, where some Belgian and Russian engineers and soldiers were buried, or go north two days where there was a small burial ground belonging to a Chinese Assembly of Believers. We...decided to go north.

We tried in vain for some time to hire animals to carry us, and men to carry the "Sunlight Soap" box, which served as a casket for the precious remains of our little one. No amount of money or persuasion would move any of the Chinese Buddhists...By now it was raining tropical rain and flies were beginning to swarm around the body. Although it was inside our little home, the ill-fitting windows and doors with no screens allowed a horrible type of green fly to enter. Whilst we were praying, three Chinese Mohammedans came into the compound, two of whom offered to carry the box. The third offered us three mules for hire...No saddles were provided with the animals so we were obliged to throw some padded quilts over their bony backs. My wife had never ridden on the back of an animal and Chinese mules are not the most tractable of steeds. Torrential rain was now falling, turning the road into quagmires, and the thermometer stood at 84 degrees...

Before starting forth on our sad journey, we knelt down and committed ourselves to the Lord. We knew there were several streams to be crossed, one of which was a wide and deep river. Whilst on our knees, the Lord gave us His promise, "When thou passest through the waters, I will be with thee, and through the rivers they shall not overflow thee." (Isaiah 43:2). The two Mohammedans, carrying the little casket swinging on a pole between them, went a little ahead of us; a very fine young Australian brother, Mr. Merrington, was living with us at the time, he followed; then my wife with our faithful cook leading her mule; and I brought up the rear of the saddest procession I've ever been in.

To get out of the town we were obliged to pass through the main street and both merchants and residents stood in the doorways. Most of them were hostile, for Kuancheng was a very wicked place, and all and sundry had bitterly resented our settling there with the Gospel.

Some of the women had received medical treatment from my wife and their mother-sympathy went out to her, but (we later learned) they were careful not to tell their children why the Foreign Devils were leaving the town at a time when no one ever thought of traveling even short distances. We passed through many villages, but fortunately the deluging rain kept most folk indoors. However, whenever we were seen, the men called out, "What have you in that box?" or, "What is the reason for your traveling on such a day as this?"

Hour after hour the rain fell...thoughts of our little one constantly passed through our minds and we could still picture her facial contortions while she was suffering....Toward sundown we came near to the wide river we knew to be ahead of us. As we approached a village leading to it, the folk came to their doors and offered us hospitality, warning us of the danger of trying to ford the turbulent stream...They had done the same to the Mohammedan carriers who were still ahead of us, although suspicious of what they were carrying...Their suspicions were further aroused by the odor being given off from the rapidly decomposing body, so the burden bearers had been told to proceed quickly on their way.

We found the river a swirling flood, and it was impossible to know where the brink of the stream was, but we were encouraged to see the carriers had already crossed the angry waters. We realized however, that they must have had a terrific struggle, for their clothing and the little container were covered with silt. We were all young and strong in those days, but we were all pretty much exhausted after riding for many hours in the warm enervating tropical downpour, and it was only with the greatest difficulty that my wife could keep her seat on her razor-back animal.

Mr. Merrington was riding the largest and (as we thought) the strongest mule, so it was decided that he should lead the way. Our cook followed, leading my wife's mule, and I brought up the rear. We had not gone far before we came to the brink of the stream and Mr. Merrington's animal was carried off its feet and both man and mule were rapidly swept down the stream. The Moslem carriers were strapping young men, and on seeing the danger to both man and beast, they rushed into the boiling waters and allowed themselves to be carried by the current beyond, then linked hands and managed to stop him and gradually drag him to the bank. Fortunately our mules could swim and for a time breasted the waters. Then I saw my wife's animal almost on its side...I managed to grab hold of the tail of my wife's mule and at the same time was able to put my left hand under my wife's armpit. The cook still held fast to the bridle and we were both lying flat on the water, but I could feel we were being rapidly taken downstream, for it was utterly impossible for animals to swim in such silt-laden waters. We had been carried down almost to where the carriers had rescued Mr. Merrington, and once more they plunged into the wicked-looking waters and were able to drag my wife and the cook to safety. I still clung to the tail of my wife's mule and after being washed down to a bend in the stream, he managed to regain his feet and pull me ashore.

The account continues by telling how they reached an inn after dark. That was fortunate, because the Moslem carriers were able to hide the coffin in a stable before the innkeeper could become aware of its contents. Otherwise, they would not have been permitted to stay. They had no change of clothing, and had to wear their wet clothes all night. They kept their shoes on to prevent shrinkage, but Mr. Merrington, who put his shoes near a charcoal fire, found them charred and useless in the morning.

They continued their journey the next day in brilliant sunshine, feeling no ill effects from their soaking. By early afternoon they reached the town of Bagou, where two Chinese Christians dug a small grave for the coffin. My sister Eleanor was buried as the sun set. My father concluded his narrative: "...Baby Eleanor Avenell Tharp was the first and only baby girl to be buried in the Bagou cemetery. However, our beloved brother, Alfred Merrington, was laid quite near to her less than two years afterwards."

In the meantime Zhang Lan-fang had not immediately accepted Christianity, although his interest continued. But as the days passed, this opium sot, ex-actor, professional soldier, bodyguard to the Empress Dowager, and self-confessed reprobate, who admitted having participated in every conceivable crime, apart from murder, began to slowly show himself a changed man as God began to work in his life.

In 1907, his brigade was transferred to the city of Bagou, (now called Pingquan) 60 miles to the east of Chengde. There he visited the mission and for the first time actually met my father. One day Zhang approached my father and asked for a job, any kind of a job, without pay, just food and a place to sleep because he wanted to "study the doctrine." He seemed so sincere my father offered him the job of cook, since they were badly in need of one. However, within two weeks my parents regretted that decision, because Zhang broke so many dishes and burned so many meals that they decided he had to go. Instead, my father offered him the job of all-purpose man around the compound, drawing water, chopping wood, cleaning, and doing the buying, as well as baby-sitting when the children (including me) came along. Zhang took his demotion in good grace, and when, in 1913, three months after my birth, the family moved 60 miles east to the city of Tazigou (Little Pagoda Ravine), he went with us.

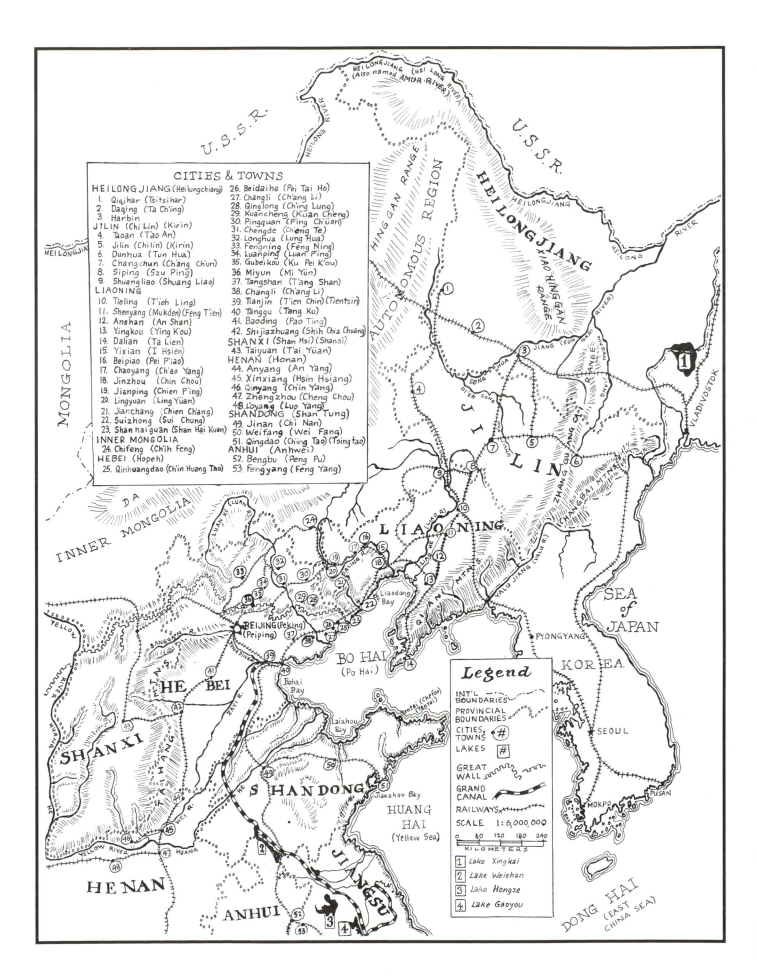

CITIES & TOWNS

HEILONGJIANG (Heilungchiang)
1. Qiqihar (Tsitsihar)
2. Daqing (Ta Ch'ing)
3. Harbin

JILIN (Chi Lin) (Kirin)
4. Taoan (T'ao An)
5. Jilin (Chilin) (Kirin)
6. Dunhua (Tun Hua)
7. Changchun (Ch'ang Ch'un)
8. Siping (Szu P'ing)
9. Shuangliao (Shuang Liao)

LIAONING
10. Tieling (T'ieh Ling)
11. Shenyang (Mukden) (Feng T'ien)
12. Anshan (An Shan)
13. Yingkou (Ying K'ou)
14. Dalian (Ta Lien)
15. Yixian (I Hsien)
16. Beipiao (Pei P'iao)
17. Chaoyang (Ch'ao Yang)
18. Jinzhou (Chin Chou)
19. Jianping (Chien P'ing)
20. Lingyuan (Ling Yüan)
21. Jianchang (Chien Ch'ang)
22. Suizhong (Sui Chung)
23. Shanhaiguan (Shan Hai Kuan)

INNER MONGOLIA
24. Chifeng (Ch'ih Feng)

HEBEI (Hopeh)
25. Qinhuangdao (Ch'in Huang Tao)

26. Beidaihe (Pei Tai Ho)
27. Changli (Ch'ang Li)
28. Qinglong (Ch'ing Lung)
29. Kuancheng (Kuan Ch'eng)
30. Pingquan (P'ing Ch'üan)
31. Chengde (Ch'eng Te)
32. Longhua (Lung Hua)
33. Fengning (Feng Ning)
34. Luanping (Luan P'ing)
35. Gubeikou (Ku Pei K'ou)
36. Miyun (Mi Yün)
37. Tangshan (T'ang Shan)
38. Changli (Ch'ang Li)
39. Tianjin (T'ien Chin) (Tientsin)
40. Tanggu (Tang Ku)
41. Baoding (Pao Ting)
42. Shijiazhuang (Shih Chia Chuang)

SHANXI (Shan Hsi) (Shansi)
43. Taiyuan (T'ai Yüan)

HENAN (Honan)
44. Anyang (An Yang)
45. Xinxiang (Hsin Hsiang)
46. Qinyang (Ch'in Yang)
47. Zhengzhou (Cheng Chou)
48. Loyang (Luo Yang)

SHANDONG (Shan Tung)
49. Jinan (Chi Nan)
50. Weifang (Wei Fang)
51. Qingdao (Ch'ing Tao) (Tsingtao)

ANHUI (Anhwei)
52. Bengbu (Peng Pu)
53. Fengyang (Feng Yang)

Legend

INT'L BOUNDARIES
PROVINCIAL BOUNDARIES
CITIES, TOWNS #
LAKES #
GREAT WALL
GRAND CANAL
RAILWAYS
SCALE 1 : 6,000,000

0   60   120   180   240
KILOMETERS

1 Lake Xingkai
2 Lake Weishan
3 Lake Hongze
4 Lake Gaoyou

Po jia zhi wan guan.

The poorest home
is worth ten thousand 'guan.'
(Ancient Chinese coinage).
- Chinese Peasant Saying.

Book One
1913 - 1932
Chapter One
"Our Town" Manchuria

I think that our family's move to Tazigou in 1913 was occasioned by the fact that Miss Gates and Mrs. Merrington, who had been working there for several years, had decided to move some thirty miles north to a large village called Dujiawopu (shack of the family Du), thus leaving the city with no missionary presence. In the years that followed, and as I grew up, I visited that village many times and came to know it very well indeed.

While the name Tazigou had reference to a small pagoda, in all the years we were there, we never found a trace of the pagoda from which it supposedly got its name. In fact, the nearest pagoda of any size was more than fifty miles away. However, the fact that there was no pagoda was unimportant because the city didn't retain its name for very long after we moved there.

First the name was changed to Jianchang, and then a few years later it was again changed, this time to Lingyuan (source of the Ling river), and that is the

name shown on present-day maps.

What was the province of Jehol at that time is now part of Liaoning Province. It was extremely mountainous and barren, with little open space for cities or towns. Where they were built, usually about fifty or sixty miles apart (two days' journey by horse-drawn cart), the terrain often demanded that the town be crammed into a narrow valley. That had been the case with Bagou, and, as a result, the place tended to be a very long, one-street town.

That was not the case with Lingyuan, with its estimated population of 30,000. High mountains surrounded it, but the valley in which it lay was at the confluence of two rivers, one flowing down from the north, and the other coming in from the west. Neither river had been given any particular name, they were simply referred to as the north or west river, but both had water even in the driest of years. Normally they were quiet streams, easily fordable except past the point where they joined to become the Ling, from which the city of Lingyuan got its name. The two rivers joined just a half-mile south of the city, and from that point on cut through high rocky cliffs, with a lot of whitewater rapids and much run-off from the mountains around.

Approaching from the west as we did, the city was not visible from any great distance. The road for many miles had followed the river and wound through barren hills devoid of vegetation. About four miles out from Lingyuan the valley widened a bit, and small villages occurred at intervals measured in "*li*," about one-third of a mile. All were named with a "*pu*" ending, meaning "shop." There was 15 *li pu*, then 10 *li pu*, and finally 5 *li pu*. Each village had a small shop of some sort, usually selling sesame seed bread, candies, peanuts, etc., or simply hot tea; something for the wayfarer as he started on a trip or ended a tiring journey.

Just past the 5 "*li*" point approaching the city was a low hill topped by a large temple. The temple was not named for any particular deity; it was simply called the *Xi Liang Miao* or "Temple of the Western Pass," even though the low hill on which it stood in no way resembled a mountain pass. The temple was the temporary repository for hundreds of coffins, each above ground and enclosed in a brick structure, awaiting such time as the relatives of the deceased could transport them back to their native towns or provinces. Some had been there for many years, and possibly would remain there forever, as relatives had died or moved away. Just past the temple, the city of Lingyuan came into view.

Although in Chinese, Lingyuan was called a *cheng*, which denoted a walled city, there was actually no wall, only the irregular back walls of the residences, which composed what passed for a city enclosure. In fact, our own back garden wall was part of the "city wall."

There were somewhat imposing gates at most entrances to the city. They were not the huge brick structures of Peking, but simply hollow towers on each side of the road, built of mud bricks. Each stood about fifteen feet high, and had a ladder inside leading up to an enclosure at the top from which gunports faced outward. Huge wooden gates were mounted on each side closing toward the center, with a crude wooden wheel at the outer end of each gate to carry the weight and enable them to be closed quick-

ly. The gates themselves weren't solid, just roughly cut wooden bars about six inches apart, and six or eight inches square, Thus, even with the gates closed it was possible to look down the length of the street (or at least to the first bend), and, on many occasions, attacking bandits or invading armies would simply shoot their rifles through the gates' apertures.

Just outside the west gate the road was lined on each side with a number of makeshift houses, a sort of overflow from the city itself. They housed primarily farmers or laborers, and mixed in with them were beggars' shacks. The hills and mountains surrounding Lingyuan dictated the shape of the city, which was roughly triangular. Dominating the city, a huge, craggy mountain stood directly to the east, just across the river and about a mile away. A sheer rock wall faced the city. It was known as Guang Shan or "bright mountain." Standing some four thousand feet high it was visible from miles away. We climbed it a number of times over the years, each time approaching it from the back, where the slope was more gradual. From the top, the view of the city and its surroundings was spectacular.

The main north-south street was about two miles long, wide and fairly straight. Two-thirds of the distance down, it was bisected by the main west-to-east street, also wide, but only something over a mile in length and with a number of bends in it. Some smaller streets ran parallel to both the main streets, but no sizable cross streets between, just *hutong* or alleys. Some of them could take vehicular traffic but were not wide enough for two vehicles to pass, and most of them were for pedestrians alone. A few were wide enough for carrying in a bridal chair or carrying out a coffin, but others were barely wide enough for two people to pass each other and had so many sharp angles that funerals and weddings were usually conducted at the mouth of the alley. Within each alley there were dozens of family residences, each with an obscure entrance, each teeming with people, yet most knew their neighbors and lived in relative harmony despite the close quarters.

There were, of course, no sewage facilities whatsoever in the city except for open drains along some of the main streets and the alleys all had a fearful odor, and particularly in the rainy season were simply mud holes for their entire length, with little or no drainage. At night they were completely dark, in fact there were no street lights anywhere in the city. The only lighting at night was on the main streets and was from lighted storefronts or the dim lighting showing through paper windows. Here and there before midnight were food stalls, illuminated with a single lantern, or vendors carrying snacks for the night gamblers and opium smokers, shouting their wares as they moved about the city.

Before dawn the night soil collectors roamed the city emptying the latrines and carrying their loads to be deposited in dumps outside their respective houses, where it was readied for fertilizing the fields and gardens, thus the odors were simply removed from one place to another. But these were some of the sights, sounds and smells we grew up with. They were part of our daily lives and we gave them little or no thought.

Entering the west gate, the first place on the immediate left was a very large and imposing temple dedicated to the god of death, the *Yanwangmiao*, with two huge and frightening terra-cotta images, one on each side just inside the front entrance. They were two or three times life-sized, and were supposed to guard against intruders. The one on the left was called *heng,* the one on the right, *ha* (both of these words are simply exclamations).

This temple was a very busy place, since all departed spirits were called together by the god of death, and scarcely a day passed that one or more processions from some part of the city did not approach this temple and pass directly in front of our gate. They were simple processions: four men carrying a chair between them in which the departed spirit was supposedly seated. Mourners surrounded the chair, and a band headed the procession, playing mournful music. After the burning of incense at the temple, the procession would break up, and, to demonstrate that the spirit of the departed had been left behind where it belonged, the empty chair would be carried upside down over one man's shoulder. The mourners — many simply hired for the occasion — were now cheerful and divested of their white mourning attire as they walked back to the residence of the deceased to join in the bountiful feast that always marked such occasions.

Except after rain, when the streets were usually mud holes, most of the time a thick layer of dust covered the streets, where the heavy iron-bound wheels of the carts had cut deep ruts over the centuries, and the hooves of the passing animals had also dug into the surface of the road. Our street was no exception and its width — 60 feet or so to the west of us — was deceptive because the actual roadway was five to six feet below the level of the houses on each side, and the vehicular roadway at the bottom of this declivity was often only wide enough for two vehicles to pass each other. In front of the houses was a twenty-foot-wide dirt embankment with gradually sloping sides, and the embankment had, at one time, undoubtedly been the actual street level; however, the annual flooding of the street and the cutting edges of the cart wheels had done their share in lowering the actual level of the roadway. To try and stop further erosion, every hundred yards of so down the street, large boulders had been sunk into the roadway forming a low barrier across the street. It was a good idea, but it also proved somewhat of a hazard to vehicular traffic, which had to bump its way across.

On the embankments on both sides of the street, householders piled their annual collection of manure for fertilizer, or stored a cart when it was not in use. In some places there was room for a threshing floor and a community grindstone that saw daily use.

Three hundred yards or so past this first temple, the street bent slightly to the right. Our house was another three or four hundred yards past the bend, and we frequently had reason to be thankful for that in later years, when, even with the city gates closed, attackers shot through the bars. Since our back garden was in a direct line from the city gate, we were often able to hear stray bullets whistling overhead.

Just past the first bend, another large temple stood on the left. The outer walls were painted a bright red and it was known as the Confucian temple, even though Confucianism was not really a religion and it was not a place of worship, just a meeting place. Alongside the temple was a narrow road leading north, also protected by a gate. After a few hundred yards, it was out in open country and then it circled around behind our compound's back garden wall.

Alongside the road, and parallel with the Confucian temple wall, ran a watercourse about fifteen feet wide and eight feet deep. It was a continuation of a deep gully flowing down from the nearby mountains to the north, cutting deeply through the fields on its way, and completely bisecting the city at that point all the way down to the south river. Most of the year it was dry, but during the rainy season it was a raging torrent that frequently overflowed its banks and sent water pouring down the main street in front of our house, carrying everything before it. Right by the Confucian temple the watercourse was crossed by an ancient, very narrow, and slightly hump-backed bridge made entirely of huge slabs of stone. The slabs were deeply indented with dual ruts where, for centuries, the wheels of the carts had cut into them. Profusely carved with images of Chinese deities, heavy stone balustrades on each side "protected" travelers. The bridge, less than ten feet wide, was about twenty feet in length and was reputed to be more than 500 years old. It certainly looked it.

Our street — the Great West Street — had up to the point of crossing the bridge been about sixty feet wide. East of the bridge it widened out to a hundred feet or so, and it was a mere hundred yards or so to our house, on the left, or north side. That, in China, was the most desirable location because all entrances to houses were supposed to face the south. For that reason, mostly blank walls and backs of houses lined the south side of the street, with only rarely a door or a window showing because of the bitter north winds in winter. Entrances to those houses were almost always down narrow, winding alleys with barred doors opening to the various yards. At the point where our house stood, the road took a noticeable downward slope, and from there for a short distance it widened out to about three hundred feet or more. That was the "civic center" of the city, and the Yamen, or official residence of the magistrate, stood at that point.

Our home in Lingyuan was a paradise for us children, but for my parents, when they first moved there, it must have been very difficult and discouraging, and I am sure it was particularly true for my mother. By that time she had three small children, my brother Gilbert, who was around five, my older sister, Ruth, around three, and I was the baby, just three months old. It was her third home since coming to China. I know she was not unhappy about moving away from Kuancheng; it held too many sad memories for her. However, Bagou had been her home for ten years, and although the mission station there was small, it was well established and relatively comfortable. There Gilbert had been born, and I, too, five years

later. For our births a missionary doctor, Dr. Robson, had traveled seven days to attend Mother. Between our births, Mother gave birth to my older sister, Margaret Ruth, but for that occasion, the doctor apparently was unable to make the trip and Mother traveled by mule litter the seven days to the coastal town where Dr. Robson lived. That was a place called Yongpingfu, a town not far from Tangshan on the railroad line.

Buying a piece of property in China in those days was not a simple matter. There were no Realtors to consult and no "For Sale" signs out in front. What one did was to discreetly let it be known that a "certain party" was in the market to buy a place and then see what developed. At no time could it be revealed that a foreigner wanted to buy the property; that would have caused the price to skyrocket. Word-of-mouth in China was, and always will be, a wonderful medium of communication. In Lingyuan, in the years we lived there, nothing happened in the town that wasn't known everywhere and to everyone within a few minutes of its occurrence, so it probably was not long before my father learned of our place, just diagonally across the street from the existing mission compound, which was much too small for our needs. The church was growing and my father had the faith to believe that it would continue to grow, so he wanted a larger place where he could have schools as well as the church meeting place.

The property eventually decided upon was, in Chinese terms, a mansion, and it had originally belonged to an upper-class family who, because of addiction to opium, had been forced to sell. I was born on January 31, 1913, and we moved there in April 1913. I can well imagine Mother's first view of the compound. The houses were all built of gray brick and needed repair. The windows were not glass, but paper, and the doors were the standard Chinese two-leaved type, opening inward with a cross-bolt on the inside for security at night. By the time I was old enough to notice things, Father had already made numerous alterations, including glass windows and Western-type doors. However, the local carpenters were unfamiliar with what was required and the results were somewhat crude and ill-fitting. Later I shall describe the compound in greater detail, but first a brief description of the city of Lingyuan itself as my family must have seen it that first day in 1913.

Looking down the street to the left from our doorstep, the Yamen with all its buildings was only a hundred yards away. Following the usual pattern of such structures, they were extensive and very ornate, though usually in considerable disrepair. The entrance of the Yamen itself extended out into the street about two hundred feet or more, with a low, semi-circular wall enclosing the area, and an elaborate archway on each side, one facing east and another directly opposite facing west. Well out in the street itself, and facing the main entrance into the Yamen, was a high blank wall, part of the semi-circle. It was called a "spirit screen." All Chinese houses had them, but in all cases except the Yamen, the screens were just inside the main entrance, or, in some cases, further into the compound. The Chinese believed that evil spirits could only travel in a straight line. So when they reached the spirit screen, they were unable to turn left or right, but strangely enough were able to turn around and go back the way they came.

Although wide enough for vehicular traffic, the two archways through the enclosed area were usually only used by pedestrians, pack animals, or anyone riding on horses, mules or donkeys. All carts and other vehicles were supposed to go around on the outside, in effect, behind the spirit wall. That was no problem most of the year, but when the rains came, that particular spot by the wall, being the lowest section of the street, became a nearly impassable quagmire and many unsuspecting drivers found their vehicles bogged down there. But then, that was all part of the street entertainment. Both of the ornamental archways were guarded by police, but they seldom objected when someone wanted to drive a cart or other vehicle through.

Although the purpose of the enclosure was nothing more than to add dignity to the Yamen, it did serve another purpose. It was the gathering place for spectators, who stood to watch trial proceedings held just inside the Yamen gates. The brave ventured inside, but most people were content to stand at a distance so as not to risk a possible run-in with the feared Yamen runners known as *yayi*. The *yayi* really ran the place; they were the enforcers, the torturers of prisoners during trials, and the people who had to be paid off before an audience could be gained with the magistrate. They were also the people to be contended with if any preferential treatment could be accorded a pris-

oner. There was a common saying: "The Yamen gate is open wide; with right, but no money, don't go inside." Another frequently quoted one was: "All Yamen gates face to the south. Whether in the right or in the wrong, bring money in your mouth." Justice was bought and sold like any other commodity.

Impressive as the Yamen itself was, with its fancy buildings and gates, it was overshadowed, literally, by the huge prison structure that stood between it and our family compound to the west. The prison was no more than three hundred feet from our front gate. On the street, we were separated from the prison by a row of residences. At the rear, our back garden was separated from it by an eight-foot wall between our property and the garden next door. However, the garden next door extended to the very foot of the prison wall. As children we would climb the trees next to our wall and watch groups of prisoners coming to draw water from the common well next door, each wearing leg irons and manacles and accompanied by guards.

The prison itself was unique, nothing more than a very large enclosure surrounded by brick walls forty feet high and about ten feet thick at the base. My father frequently went in to preach to the prisoners and attend to their many illnesses, but he would never allow me to accompany him. Nevertheless I had many a glimpse of the interior through the single narrow entrance that was often left open. I was able to see a large courtyard surrounded by one-story buildings backing right up to the wall, with roofs sloping up toward it. The buildings were little better than what we would consider suitable as cow sheds or pig pens, and the prisoners lived in utter squalor. There was a constant stench emanating from the prison, and when the wind was right, we could smell it from our house.

Above the entrance to the prison was a huge wooden plaque inscribed with three large Chinese characters: *Hou Hui Chi*. The actual meaning was, "Pool of Remorse." However, since Chinese is a tonal language, one similar sounding word can carry an entirely different meaning. The word *chi* meant "pool," but another word, written differently but sounding exactly the same, meant "too late." Thus the prison was aptly named. It was not only a pool of remorse, but once in there, it was too late for remorse.

Once incarcerated, a prisoner had little hope of getting out or even surviving to serve his full sentence unless he had access to a considerable amount of money. Even then, negotiating with the *yayi* and prison guards could be a lengthy process. Inside the prison, disease was rampant and vermin of all types abounded. Most of the magistrates permitted my father inside to preach to the men on a fairly regular basis. Usually he went in alone, but occasionally he was permitted to take a Chinese helper in with him. He did what he could to help the sick and injured, but tuberculosis was common, and in those days there was little that could be done for patients with the disease. All too many of the prisoners expired before their sentences did. As a result, scarcely a week went by that we didn't see a dead prisoner being carried out for burial. They all passed our front gate, since the dead always traveled west. Most were simply carried out by the *yayi*, rolled up in a sorghum-stalk mat, but some magistrates opted for a cheap coffin made of extremely thin boards, so thin that the Chinese gave it the name *gou peng tou*, meaning "dog bumps his head," implying that the coffin would break open if a dog bumped into it. The dead prisoners were buried in the gully just behind our compound. The yayi were lazy and seldom dug a grave, particularly in the winter when the ground was frozen. More than once we came upon them burying a corpse. They simply placed the wrapped-up body at the foot of the nearest cliff and pulled some loose earth down over it. In the winter we often took our weekly walks up these gullies to avoid the bitter north wind, and not infrequently we would find corpses that dogs had dug out and partially consumed. It was astonishing that any of the prisoners survived the appalling conditions in the prison, but some did, and in a later chapter, I shall tell the extraordinary story of two young men who did, and the reason they were in there in the first place.

One of Lingyuan's more elaborate city gates.

One of the main streets in Lingyuan.

Bob's parents with their first-born, Eleanor Avenell (b. July 1906), who died before she was one.

Zhang Lan-fang
Former opium sot, actor, soldier, body-guard to the Empress Dowager, repro-bate and criminal. He became a bright Christian and colporteur.

Street in front of our Mission Compound.

眼見為實

Yan jian wei shi.

What the eye sees, that is the real thing.

- Chinese Proverb.

Chapter Two

"Our House" In Lingyuan

The front entrance to our compound in Lingyuan was unique. Outside the entrance was a platform of large stone slabs, measuring about ten feet wide by twenty feet long. Three steps on each side led up to it. No one knew the original purpose of the platform, but it effectively prohibited access by any wheeled vehicles into the compound.

From the platform itself two more steps led to the front gate, set back about six feet into a recess. The gate was the traditional two-leaved type, both leaves opening inward from the middle, each about five feet wide by ten or twelve feet high, and each door well over two inches thick. Painted jet black, the doors were heavily studded with huge iron nails, with heads two inches across. Other than the nails and two ornamental brass handles, the exterior of the doors was blank.

The doors didn't reach to the brick flooring because there was a high "coaming," or sill, that one had to step over. It stood about sixteen inches high, and when I was a small boy it formed quite an obsta-

cle for me. All Chinese entrances had these sills in varying heights. Most were fitted into slots or grooves in the stone supports for the door frames and were removable, but this one wasn't.

On the inside of the doors were two heavy horizontal cross bolts for security, as well as a short heavy chain with links about four inches in length. To lock the doors the chain was looped over a large eye-bolt and then secured with an antique lock. For additional security, the two cross bolts had grooves cut into them on the upper surface. When slid crosswise into holes cut in the two upright, permanently mounted bars on the back of each door, a secret hardwood "stick-lock" concealed inside each of the uprights would drop down into the grooves on the crossbars, preventing them from being pulled back. That was to prevent anyone on the outside from using a knife blade through the crack of the door to manipulate the bolts and open the gates. To open the bolts, one had to know the location of a secret hole where a finger inserted could raise the stick inside and thus release the bolt. The lock itself, independent of the stick locks, was a genuine antique made of heavy brass. It measured about a foot in length and had a key almost twice as long. The key, unlike anything I have seen anywhere else, had a series of bends in it that defied copying. How many years the lock had been in use before we bought the place I have no way of knowing, but it served us well for the thirty years we lived there.

Our compound in Lingyuan, from the street front to the back wall — which, as I mentioned earlier was, in effect, part of the city wall — covered about an acre or perhaps slightly more. A good half of the expanse was taken up with courtyards and buildings, but the back garden, a very large open area surrounded by various kinds of trees, date, willow, elm, and cedar, as well as some fruit trees, was where we children spent a great deal of our time.

Lingyuan was built on a gradual downward slope from north to south, so that as one went in the front entrance, each of the three main courtyards of our compound was at a slightly higher level, with a series of steps at the entrance to each. The back garden itself was then almost another five feet higher than the third courtyard, and was in the shape of an upside-down "L." Eight-foot-high walls lined the two sides adjoining our neighbors, and the backs of the neighbors' houses also formed part of the wall in places. At the extreme north end, or back of the garden, the walls were twelve feet high on the inside, but on the outside only eight feet, because the land outside there consisted of soil that had washed down over the years from the fields above and gradually had built up. Ancient graves covered most of the land immediately outside our back wall for a distance of almost two hundred feet. Beyond that a one-lane road ran parallel with our back wall. From that point both north and west to the hills about a mile away, it was all farmland.

The original compound that my father bought consisted of some seven buildings with 29 rooms, but we quickly outgrew the place. We needed a larger meeting hall as the church grew, so when the neighboring compound was up for sale a few years later, my father bought that as well, adding another thirty or so rooms, all of which were fully utilized.

Speaking of the number of "rooms," however, is somewhat misleading, because what I am referring to is in Chinese called a *jian*. The Chinese always use a numerative to classify everything, and the numerative *jian* used in regard to Chinese houses in a general sense means "room," but at the same time it also specifically means a division in the structure, determined by the length of the timbers used in the roof. In any given building, these would be of a uniform length, thus making all the rooms in that building the same size. In North China, the houses for the very poor were built of mud brick or of mud mixed with straw, packed into a wall by using boards on each side to determine the thickness. When the desired height of the wall was reached, beams were laid across from back to front, resting on the tops of the walls, then horizontal beams were added, and the mud or thatched roof was placed atop those. That sort of building was very susceptible to either flood or earthquake. In a bad flood the walls simply dissolved and in an earthquake they collapsed.

Houses for the better-class families who could afford them were unique, and very different from anything in America. Built either with stone, mud bricks, kiln-fired bricks, or a combination of all, the roofs were quite independent of the walls, and in the entire building no wall was what we know as a "bearing wall." For that reason, it was theoretically possible to take down all the walls and still have the roof standing intact.

The reason for this was that the roof framework was the first thing to be constructed and put into place. In the old days, no building was started without first consulting a necromancer to select the "lucky day" for beginning work on a house. In fact, most people consulted the necromancers for a wedding date, a burial site, or any really important event in their lives. These men would, for a price, go through a long and tedious procedure and come up with a time or day that was considered fortuitous. Oddly enough, for reasons of his own, it was quite common for the necromancer to select a day in mid-winter as the auspicious day on which to start building, when in actuality, starting a building was quite impossible, the ground being frozen to a depth of three or four feet. Nonetheless, the building would be "started," or bad luck would ensue. The wooden frame for the roof structure would be fabricated and assembled and would stand until spring, when it would be partially and temporarily dismantled so that the footings could be dug and walls could be built up around it.

The way the buildings were designed is shown in the accompanying drawing. Sturdy, upright wooden pillars were used on all four corners of the house, each about the diameter of a telephone pole. The same sort of upright would be used for each division, or *jian*. As the roof frame was constructed, the pillars would first be put in place and held upright by four supporting poles "tented" around them, then huge lengths of timber, usually a complete tree, with a girth more than that of a man, would be laid atop them from front to back. The large timbers were called *to*, and it didn't matter how crookedly the tree might have grown, a Chinese carpenter could still use it.

On top of the cross beams, a second short *to* would be mounted on short uprights of about four feet in length, and in the middle of the second *to* would be a final upright of the same height. That was done for each *jian* of the building, and would determine the slope of the roof.

Most Chinese buildings were either a basic three *jian*, five *jian* or seven *jian*, all built in a straight line abreast, but on occasion they were even longer. There was no standard size for a *jian*; it was determined by whatever cross timbers were available. However, in most cases a *jian* measured anywhere from twelve to twenty feet from front to back and might be ten to fifteen feet from side to side.

When the front-to-back beams were in place, cross beams called *linzi* would be laid between them, and there would be five in all for each *jian*; one at the eaves back and front, one for the ridge pole, and one in the middle on each side back and front. Finally, atop those, from the ridgepole downward, much smaller poles were used for rafters. Those were called *chuanzi* and were usually at least three inches in diameter, sometimes more.

The roof framework was assembled atop a very substantial footing which, in our area of North China, had to be over three feet deep to get below the frost line. Built entirely of stones laid in mortar, the footings were frequently three feet or more in width. At the four corners and where the *jian* dividing upright pillars were placed, large square blocks of stone were laid. All of them were neatly chiseled by hand and provided a round, flat surface on top for the base of the pillar. When in position, they would be brought to a uniform level using an ingenious time-honored method, which, while crude, was nonetheless completely foolproof. With no theodolite nor spirit level to work with, this was how it was done:

A basin of water was placed on a low table on a level spot a short distance from the building site. On the surface of the water in the basin was floated a second, smaller basin of water. A short square stick of wood was then floated in the smaller basin, the stick having two shallow saw cuts on the upper face, about six inches apart. Into those cuts were placed two stiff pieces of paper, usually calling cards. Care was taken that they were exactly the same height.

The chief carpenter would then bend down and sight across the top of the two calling cards, while an assistant took a pole with inches and feet marked on it, and held it upright atop each of the stone footings in turn. As the master carpenter shouted his commands, the masons moved the rocks as required to find the exact level. The system was extremely effective, but it had to be carried out on a windless day; otherwise ripples on the surface of the water could throw the whole thing off.

Many years later I built two houses here in America using this method to find the level. In Connecticut my wife and I built a house of cinder blocks, and the walls, including the basement, were sixteen feet high. When I reached the top, I was pleased to find there was less than a one-eighth inch difference between the height at the four corners. The second house was built in California using wood, and calculating levels with the same method.

After the base rocks on the footings had been set and leveled, the entire roof assembly (with the exception of the rafters) would be put in place, then the outside walls would be built. The walls, usually around two feet thick, as was the case in the buildings in our compound, had kiln-fired brick on the outside and mud bricks inside. The space between was filled with rubble and provided a measure of insulation from the heat and cold. The end walls of each building were called *shan chiang* or "mountain walls" because of their peaked shape. They extended to the very top of the ridgepole, and when all the outer walls were completed, the wooden supporting pillars were entirely enclosed within the walls, where they lasted for centuries. I've never seen nor heard of any termites in China, although doubtless they exist in parts other than the north; nor was there much incidence of dry rot. In fact, this type of building was so effective in preserving the wood used in it that, when planning a new building, my father would search the town for some large, old building that was near collapse and ready to be torn down, and would then buy it just for the wood that could be salvaged from it.

The Chinese have a saying for everything, and in regard to their roofs they say *li mu ding qian jin* — "an upright post will support one thousand pounds." Their roofs are indeed so heavy that the supporting pillars have to be exceptionally sturdy.

After the rafters are in place — usually about eight inches apart — a strip of wood is nailed along the front edge. That is to hold in place the large and very heavy "mats" that will be laid first. The mats are woven from willow tree branches or twigs, and the weavers were an exclusive group who did nothing else. Living usually near a stream, they harvested the willow branches, tied them in bundles, then soaked them in the river or stream, weighted down with large rocks. The bundles remained there until the willow branches turned black, which usually took a month or so. The material was then sufficiently pliable to be woven freely.

The mats were always made to order, the men coming to the site and carefully measuring the roof to be covered. Completed, the mats usually came in six- to eight-foot widths and could be fifty feet or longer. Rolled up, they were moved to the site on a cart, but then had to be manhandled onto the roofs, and that was always quite a feat.

The men leaned two long poles at an angle against the eaves. Then two long ropes were used, one end of each being tied to the top of each pole, while the other end was fed under and around the rolled-up mat. The loose ends were then passed up to a group of men on the roof, who pulled in unison, and in that way slowly rolled the bundled mat up the poles onto the roof. It was a simple but nonetheless effective method of raising such a heavy load. It usually worked well, unless one or both of the supporting poles broke, as I saw happen from time to time. When that occurred, they patiently started over again.

Once the mats were up, they were unrolled and nailed into position, but they formed a very slippery and dangerous surface to walk on because of the steepness of the roof. The Chinese have an ingenious method of dealing with the problem. They take short

lengths of wood, about two feet long, and nail them together in the form of a crude "T." A large, square Chinese nail is then driven through the ends of the horizontal portion, with about two inches exposed on the lower side. Those, with the cross-part of the T at the top, are banged down hard onto the mats, where they hold fast and serve as supports for the men climbing around and working on the roof. The Chinese call them *hama*, "frogs."

After installing the mats the next step is to spread a thin layer of mud onto the mats. When that was dry, they started to lay the tiles. However, instead of starting from the bottom and working to the top, as we would do, they start at the top, working first on the peak, or ridge. For such a pragmatic people, it seems strange that the Chinese should do this, but here on the ridgepole they construct a totally useless and highly ornamental peak to the roof, which is anywhere from twelve to eighteen inches in height, adding a lot of unnecessary weight.

First they take sausage-like rolls of mud and lay them along the top of the ridgepole. Into that they feed tiles at the requisite intervals to start each downward row. When the "sausage-roll" mud is sufficiently dried, they then build it up with tiles of different shapes set into new mud. Sometimes the result is a solid and unbroken "wall" and at other times it will be constructed with tiles in an openwork pattern. Only when the ridge peak is completed is the actual tiling begun. From that point on they work from the bottom up, each tile overlapping the preceding one. The tile at the very bottom of the row is called a "drip tile" and has a bent-over, pointed tip so that water will not run backward onto the woodwork underneath.

All the tiles are set into a thick base of mud, usually three to four inches thick. One might think of mud as something fairly simple to make. However, it is not that straightforward. A Chinese mason prepares his mud several days in advance. It is first roughly mixed using shovels and a mattock, then allowed to "cure" for a day or two. It is then stirred once again, this time with short lengths of straw mixed in with it. This stage is often accomplished by workers tramping in the mixture with their bare feet. The straw helps to prevent cracking and also carries off any water that might leak through the tiles. When the mud has reached a proper consistency and is considered to be "ripe," it is pliable and not too wet; otherwise, it would slide down the roof before the tiles could be placed.

To get the mud up onto the roof (sometimes twelve or fifteen feet high), they again have an ingenious method. From the roof they hang a rope with a big knot on the end. On the ground, the helpers take pieces of cloth about sixteen inches square and tie short lengths of rope to each of the corners, so that when brought together, the ropes form a handle. The cloth is then wetted down and filled with a shovel or two of mud. The rope handles are then hung over the knot on the end of the long rope reaching up to the roof. A man at the top pulls it up, dumps it, then throws the cloth "bag" down onto the ground for another load. As can be imagined, it takes many days to tile a big roof.

Of course, getting the tiles up onto the roof is another massive job, but handled with ease by the Chinese, who have had centuries of practice. Rather than climb up ladders with a load, they stack the tiles six or eight in a pile, then deftly throw them up to a "catcher" on the roof. Surprisingly, very few get broken. When the roof is extra high, an "intermediate" man stands on a platform partway up to catch them first, then throws them higher.

The roof peak ridge is finished at each end with a specially designed tile that projects upward and out at a sharp angle. That is because the Chinese believe that evil spirits land on roof ridges at night, and when they run to either end, they'll run up the sloped tile and fall off into space, landing in a neighbor's yard.

All the buildings in our compound were gray in color. The brickwork was gray, the roof tiles were gray, and the bricks covering the walks and the interior courtyard were gray. The only touches of color on a Chinese house in those days were the ends of the rafters, each of which was usually brightly painted with a peach framed in green leaves. The peach denotes longevity. Other than that, the door and window frames were usually painted black. However, by the time I was old enough to remember things, my father had painted the doors red with black trim, adding a bit more color to the yard.

By the time Mother arrived with me, Father had fixed the place up a bit, but, as he would have found it initially, the interiors of all the buildings would have been typical of a Chinese house, and the layout of the courtyards would also have been traditional. In North China, all houses are built facing south wherever possible, particularly those that are considered the main buildings. Not only is that considered to be lucky, but it is also practical, because of the persistent north winds. The fronts always had papered windows atop a four foot wall, the upper section of each being hinged to open upward to admit air in summer. Most buildings had only one entrance.

I mentioned that the houses came in combinations of three, five, or seven *jian*. Rarely did one see a house of only one room unless it was a shack. Two *jian* was considered the absolute minimum for a small family. The three-room grouping was the most common, and what the Chinese consider the most practical. The middle room was a combination front entrance, joint kitchen, and all-purpose room for the two families, each of whom occupied one of the side rooms. Grandparents usually shared one room with their son and family. When a grandson was old enough to marry, he brought his wife into the second room, both families sharing the central kitchen, but each had their own cooking facilities.

Left and right, just inside the front entrance to the middle room, one would find two-foot-high platforms made of mud bricks. They were about four feet square. Those were the cooking stoves, and into each of them was inserted, flush with the top, a large wok, as it is called in Cantonese (and the name most familiar to Americans). In North China it is called a *guo*. The *guo*, still used everywhere in China, are usually quite large, measuring about thirty-six inches or so across.

The cooking stoves were fueled through an opening at floor level, on the side away from the front entrance to the room, the fuel usually being brush or grass roots, sorghum stalks, and, for the wealthier, coal. On the side of the cooking stand there is a small hole at floor level, and against that is placed a *feng xiang* or "wind box." That is an ingenious contraption that acts as a bellows to create a forced draft for the cook stove. It is a long and narrow rectangular box, about eighteen inches in height and ten to twelve inches in width. A handle attached to a shaft protrudes from the front end. It is connected to a moving baffle inside, which is simply a piece of board placed upright and attached to the end of the shaft, and measuring an inch or so smaller in all dimensions than the interior of the box. All around the edges of the baffle is woven a thick belt of chicken feathers. As the shaft and baffle are pulled toward the operator, then pushed away again, air is sucked in through a side hole — covered by a moveable flap — and is discharged out through an opposite hole into the fire chamber under the *guo*. Apart from the baffle, there are no moving parts to break down and the feathers can be readily replaced as often as necessary. On top of the box there is a small sliding lid that can be opened to inspect the baffle, and through which it can be removed when the feathers need to be replaced.

In the kitchen area, the only other furniture is usually a long, sideboard-type table against the back wall. On that, and on a shelf below, are stored bowls and other utensils. Each family also has a large ceramic earthenware water pot, from one and a half to two inches in thickness, varying from three to four feet or more in height, and some thirty inches or so across the top opening. They hold anywhere from twenty to fifty gallons of water and are the water supply for all purposes, both cooking and washing. The water, of course, is carried in from the nearest well, which frequently may be a mile or more away. Sometimes the two families will share one water jar between them to save space.

In most houses similar large earthenware jars (called *gang*) are used in the inner rooms as secure places for storing food grains against the foraging rats and mice that abound in Chinese homes, despite the usual presence of one or more cats. All of the earthenware pots are covered with flat lids made from the thin, topmost parts of sorghum stalks. The dried stalks are called *shujie*, and I'll say more about that versatile product in a later chapter.

Doors to the inner rooms on each side of the central room are usually placed, not in the center of the dividing wall, but a little toward the back. That allows room inside for the *kang* or brick bed that is used throughout North China. Standing about thirty inches high, it extends across the entire front of any Chinese room. The height is just a bit too high to sit with your feet on the floor. One must hike oneself up onto the bed and once there, sit cross-legged, or with legs hanging over the side. At night it is a sleeping platform for the entire family. In the daytime it is cleared and all bedding is neatly piled against the far wall, while a low table, roughly about two feet square

and eight to ten inches high is placed in the center. It occupies the space during the day and the *kang* becomes the dining-room. When not in use, the table stands against the wall and provides a work space for the womenfolk to do their sewing or becomes a sitting-room for visitors.

Apart from the *kang*, there is little in the way of furniture in a Chinese home. There might be a straight-backed chair, but that is rare. In every home, along the back wall, and sometimes along the side wall also, there will be a large, box-like sideboard on six-inch legs, standing about four feet in height. They are always covered with red lacquer, and with lift-up lids on top, using just half of the surface. Divided into two or three compartments, these sideboards are used to hold either food, grains, or clothing. Back of the lids, and decorating the top, are usually two very large vases, about two or three feet in height. They are not merely for decoration, however, but also hold the traditional feather dusters, without which a Chinese home would not be complete. The feather dusters in themselves are works of art. They may be completely black or white, or a combination of both, or, more frequently, made with a rooster's brightly colored tail feathers. The feather dusters and the vases that hold them are always part of the dowry brought along by the bride.

The floors of 99 percent of the lower-class Chinese homes are hard-packed bare earth, the same level as the ground outside. Under the kitchen sideboard there is always a washbasin, often made of brass, but more commonly a cheap enameled metal basin, usually brightly decorated with flowers. That is the only bathing convenience for the entire household. After use, the water is not wasted. It is used to dampen the interior dirt floors of the house to keep down the dust and maintain a hard-packed surface. On the dirt floor under the kitchen sideboard are usually two other bowls, both somewhat larger than a washbasin and made of cheap, often un-baked earthenware. One of them is used at night as a chamberpot and the other is for washing feet. No self-respecting Chinese would ever wash their feet in the same basin used to wash their faces.

The Chinese are probably the most practical people on earth. No matter what they do, it has to be done in one certain way, the way it has always been done, for a very good and pragmatic reason. Superstition has always played a large part in their lives, and still does. However, when it comes to practical matters, superstition yields to practicality where any waste or unnecessary expense might result.

Take the sleeping *kang* for example. Built of adobe or mud bricks, it is ingeniously constructed with the interior built according to a specific pattern of wind flow developed over the centuries. Smoke from the cooking pot in the outer room is fed through a hole in the wall into flues built in a very specific pattern under the *kang*. Directed by a series of baffles, the smoke travels back and forth under every square inch of the *kang*, giving off heat as it goes, until it reaches the chimney, built into the far wall. Since in private homes the *kang* can vary in size from at least ten to twelve feet long, and a minimum of six feet wide, (in the inns I have seen them 50 to 60 feet in length, but with fire openings at intervals along the length), the smoke has to travel a tremendous distance before going up the chimney, and for that reason, the draft has to be just right. The heated brick beds provide the only source of heating in winter, except for an occasional charcoal brazier made of iron or brass sitting on the *kang*, for those who can afford it.

In the course of a year a great amount of soot collects in the flues inside the *kang*, and the mud bricks with which it is constructed become heavily impregnated with creosote from the wood and brush fuel used. This is where the extreme practicality of the *kang* comes in. At least once a year, usually in early spring, the entire top and interior of the *kang* is removed. The old mud bricks are taken out, pulverized, and then thrown onto the manure pile, which is always most evident out in the street in front of every Chinese home. There they form a valuable addition to the fertilizer supply. Then, with new mud bricks, which everyone can make in his own yard or out on the street, the *kang* is rebuilt.

The rebuilding of a *kang* is another work of art, yet every householder seems to know just how to do it. A three- to four-inch layer of soft earth is placed in the bottom of the empty shell of the *kang*. Into that layer of earth the new mud bricks are placed upright, standing on their ends, forming a series of walls about a foot apart. At the end of each alternate row, one or two bricks are left out. The result is much like a maze, leading toward the distant chimney. Then comes the tricky part. Onto the upright bricks, other bricks are laid flat to form the surface of the *kang*. Extreme care must be taken to balance them perfectly and avoid knocking down any of the upright bricks. To do so would cause a blockage of the airflow, a disaster.

When the surface bricks are all laid, a two-inch layer of mud mixed with straw is spread across the entire surface, and the *kang* is complete. It is immediately fired to dry the mud, and by the end of the day is ready for use.

Despite the elaborate back-and-forth smoke channels, most *kang* work perfectly. But when there is an adverse wind, the smoke frequently refuses to go up the chimney, and backing up, fills the rooms. Consequently, almost every Chinese house where the *kang* exist is blackened with the smoke and soot of generations.

Of course, the end of the *kang* nearest the cookstove is the warmest spot, and, naturally, that is reserved for the family elders. Grandpa and grandma have that space for sleeping. Then, in descending order of age, come the other members of the family, although, for a time, the youngest get to sleep next to their parents.

The bedding is very practical as well. Each individual has his or her own, and it consists of a padded coverlet in which they roll themselves and an underlying mat on which they lie. The latter may be a simple cloth-padded thing, a woven wool carpet, or, most prized of all, a dog-skin mattress. Of dog skins, black is the favorite color and is reputed to be much warmer than any other color. I was quite skeptical about that theory until I happened to notice, over a period of time, that during the coldest months of the year, although the white or brown dogs would prefer to lie in the sun, the black dogs seemed to prefer to lie on the ice, or, where no ice was available, to lie in the shade. So perhaps there was some truth to the theory. Of course, in the United States we have long known that a black roof attracts and holds the heat of the sun, while a white roof reflects it.

Quite naturally, under those living conditions, there is no such thing as privacy. Indeed, the Chinese language has no word to convey the meaning of privacy. The concept is neither considered nor expected.

As I mentioned above, there were no facilities for bathing in the average home, especially for the poorer class. A wash basin served for the face and hands, and since those are the only parts of the body visible to others, that usually sufficed until, perhaps once a year or so, a visit could be made to a public bath-house, where, in some cases, for one day or part of a day, the place would be made available for women only. In summer, men would bathe in any river or stream nearby. Children could be given a stand-up bath out in the yard, or in summer they were often seen in the pond that generally existed outside each village, where the earth had been excavated to make bricks to build the houses.

Most Westerners who have visited China have had occasion to remark on the noises that Chinese make: clearing their throats, hawking and spitting, coughing, or blowing their noses. While that may have become a habit with some, it was not an accidental thing, but was quite deliberate on the part of an individual approaching someone's home. The purpose was to alert the homeowner to their coming. Through the paper windows, the noises can easily be heard, and one was given time to prepare one's self so as not to be caught in a possibly embarrassing situation.

In that connection, the story is told that, in the southern city of Ningbo, not far from Shanghai, which is known as the birthplace of many of China's famous people, including Chiang Kai-shek, there lived a wealthy family whose son married an aston-ishingly beautiful young woman. The young man was very much in love with his bride, and at the same time insanely jealous and afraid that she had eyes for others.

One morning the young man said goodbye to his wife and headed off for his place of business. He had not gone far before he remembered something he had forgotten to take along with him, and returned to the house. When he entered their room, he found his wife standing nude, in the act of bathing herself. Furious, he accused her of indecency and exposing herself for others to see, and proceeded to give her a sound thrashing.

His mother, in an adjoining room, heard the ruckus and the loud cries of the girl, and went to investigate. When told by her son the reason for the beating, the mother roundly scolded him, telling him that it was he who was to blame, not the wife. She spoke six words that have become immortalized in Chinese his-tory, and have been passed down from one generation to the next:

Jun sheng tang, sheng bi yang - "When a gentle-man approaches the house, it is imperative he make some noise." Hence the origin of those noises that Americans so dislike is merely a matter of cultural differences.

People have frequently asked me how my parents, who had no salary nor even any definite source of income, were able to afford the large compound they bought. While the groups of Christians calling them-selves "Brethren" that my parents were associated with in England, Canada and the United States could in no sense be called a "mission" nor a denomination, they nonetheless organized themselves to some extent to facilitate sending funds from various sources to the missionaries in the field. It soon became apparent to them that those same missionaries had to frequently lay out sizable expenditures either to rent or buy property for mission premises, and for that purpose a fund was established called the Steward's Fund, and it was from that source that all monies for property were acquired, and the same was true for money needed to make necessary repairs.

Mother used to tell us children how, in those first weeks and months, when we first moved into our new home in Lingyuan back in 1913, the rooms, originally filthy, had already had most of the walls whitewashed by my father and the floors swept. However, for a considerable period of time, everyone slept on the hard brick *kang* that every room had. The floors were loose brick, the cracks between them filled with sand, and so somewhat cleaner than a plain dirt floor, but Mother soon had them covered with sorghum-stalk mats, which helped keep down the dust. Some of the mud-plastered walls were papered, and all the rooms we lived in had paper ceilings, ten feet above the floor. The ceilings were always full of rats and mice, which we could hear running around during the night.

The only toilet facility was an outdoor privy behind the main building, the typical hole in the ground, behind a low wall or fence. None of the priv-ies ever had a roof, and it wasn't long before my father moved the privy to another part of the front yard, putting it under a roof and making it more like the traditional American "outhouse" with a bench and a cut-out hole with a lid. Underneath was a five-gal-lon can, and alongside the bench, a box containing a mixture of coal ash and quicklime, together with a small shovel. Use of that helped to reduce the odor and keep the flies away. We used that or a similar type of outhouse for the first thirty years of my life, since we never had any running water. In summer it wasn't bad, but in the cold winters it was brutal. American-style toilet paper would have had to be brought in from the coast, so we never used it. Instead, we used cut-up Montgomery Ward catalogues, no comfort either. The Chinese used a very rough and crude type of paper, or, more often, because few could afford even that small luxury, old corncobs or a handy smooth stone.

As time went on, my father set about converting the rearmost rooms of the compound to something resembling Western style. At first we used a middle-aged carpenter named Wang, but later Father found a jewel of a young man, a most talented carpenter, who became, over the next several years, more a part of the family than someone hired to do a job. The young man was named Sun, and, craftsman that he was, he was always addressed by the title *shifu*, which means

"master worker." He was a delightful fellow. With a slight build, and not very tall for a Northerner, he always appeared impeccably dressed in black clothing, his head clean shaven, and a broad smile on his face. In the many years I knew him, I never saw him anything but cheerful and good-natured, even when pestered with the million and one questions with which I, as a little boy, bombarded him, and which he always meticulously answered, never pausing in his work. Sun Shifu taught me many of the tricks of the skilled carpenter, and, unlike most of his kind, let me use his tools without stint. Even though we employed him on a regular basis over a period of perhaps fifteen years or more, we never learned a great deal about him because of his reticence about himself. We did know that at first he was unmarried, but that changed, and, some time later, he proudly brought his first son to be vaccinated by Mother. This remarkable young man will play a big part in my story.

courtesy of Kathleen Bennett Biersteker

Front gate to compound.

The "Bug" House and Wash House. The "Bug" House was so named because it was always full of bugs.

Cowsheds and chicken runs, behind what later became Bob and Eva's home.

Remodelling one of the houses.

The carpenters at work.

Stage 1
Lay large cubical stones to support uprights. Use these stones to find level for the foundation. Lay foundation (large rocks sunk about 3 feet into ground). Erect 6 uprights, with the main supports being round logs about the diameter of telephone poles.

Stage 2
Install crossbeams (round poles). Begin laying bricks. Install window and door frames where required.

Stage 3
Install rafters (round poles) as shown. Nail board across bottom part of rafters to support willow-twig matting.

Stages 4 and 5
Lay willow-twig matting over rafters. (This matting came pre-manufactured in large rolls.) Plaster a layer of mud over the matting. Install oil-paper windows and door.

Stage 6
Install fireplace, stove, chimney and *kang*. Install tile roof.

This is a five-*jian* house.

1 *jian*

Chapter Three
Earliest Memories

In 1916, at the age of three, I was abandoned by my mother, or so I thought, and there's nothing quite so traumatic to a three-year-old. I wasn't left by the roadside or anything like that. But it was nonetheless real to me.

Woodrow Wilson was president of the United States at the time, and Yuan Shih-kai was the first president of the new Republic of China, which had come into existence just five years previously, in 1911, following the successful revolution led by Dr. Sun Yat-sen.

What actually happened to me was basically attributable to my younger sister, Barbara, who was only a few weeks old at the time and therefore cannot be held accountable. Still, she was quite innocently the cause of the incident. Barbara's birth had not made very much of an impression on me, but I do have a clear memory of the doctor who rode in on a horse to take care of Mother. He was a short, stocky little man named Robson. He'd ridden all the way from Yongpingfu, where Ruth had been born, taking six or seven days for the trip. I remember he had a long, very bushy, and very red beard. Since few Chinese had beards, and if they did they were generally little wispy things, Dr. Robson's beard impressed me greatly, but didn't scare me. He was such a kindly man, we all fell in love with him.

In early June, right after Barbara's birth, our whole family started out on a trip to Beidaihe (Peitaiho), a summer resort for Westerners that lies on the coast of a gulf in the Yellow Sea called Bohai. There we would escape the intense heat of our home in Lingyuan, in the interior of China, and it would give Mother a chance to recuperate.

Traveling in China in those days was never easy. It required a great deal of advance work and preparation. Lingyuan was about 200 miles by road northeast of Peking, and due to the very mountainous terrain, the most direct route to Peking from Lingyuan was actually a very roundabout way. The journey took seven days because, traveling in horse-drawn vehicles, one was unable to cover more than 30 miles a day. After reaching Peking, Beidaihe was still 180 miles farther along the coast, but that part of the trip could be covered by train.

Even though Peking was some 90 miles inland, everyone who lived inland, as we did, spoke of it as the "coast." There were other ways for us to get from Lingyuan to Beidaihe and the coastal cities, and over the years we tried all of them. However, one way or another, they all ended up taking just about the same length of time. The very fastest any of us ever made the trip was in six days, and that was on horseback.

One route that we used frequently when heading for Beidaihe was to start out due southeast from Lingyuan, in what was basically the wrong direction. Our initial destination was the small town of Suizhong, on the famous Peking-Mukden railroad, which paralleled the coast of the Bohai gulf for some 300 miles or more.

On the map, Lingyuan and Suizhong appear to be only around 100 miles apart, but it was such a twisting, mountainous, and dangerous road that in actual mileage it was closer to 200 miles, and it usually took five and a half days to reach Suizhong. From that point it was a ten-hour journey by train, in a southwesterly direction, to Beidaihe. Even though we have no record of it, I am quite sure this was the route we took that time.

In those days journeys always started very early in the morning, long before daybreak. A day's journey was measured in *li,* and in one day the most one could hope to cover was 90 *li,* or 30 miles. In fact, one had to travel at least that distance each day, as the inns where one spent the nights were all spaced about that distance apart. Even to accomplish that meant a twelve-hour day at the very least, even without any delays en route. Hence the very early morning departures.

Starting a journey in the early morning darkness was something of a paradox. The Chinese hated to travel in the dark. More specifically, they feared traveling in the late evenings after dark, because supposedly evil spirits and ghosts were out in force. Perhaps more significantly, that was also the time when bandits — less afraid of the dark — were most active and ready to intercept the tired and less wary traveler. However, from the point of view of the Chinese, leaving in the early morning darkness was quite another thing. Although it was just as dark, perhaps even more so, there was the promise of light before too long, and bandits, one hoped, never got up that early. Then, too, it was well-known that come cockcrow, evil spirits all disappeared.

Leaving home in the early mornings was always more involved than leaving from an inn. At an inn one unpacked just what was needed for the night, so it was quite simple to repack and get started. However, the departure from home always involved a lot of last-minute packing, then closing up the house for the three months that we would be away.

The vehicles hired for the trip always arrived at the house the afternoon before we left, so the heavy boxes and trunks could be roped onto the freight carts. Nevertheless when morning came, there was much confusion, a great deal of shouting and running around, and last-minute instructions to be given to those remaining to look after the place. Add to that the arrival of the numerous horses and mules, and the job of harnessing them up that had to be accomplished, all by the light of a few flickering lanterns. Finally, the time came for everyone to take their allotted places, either in one of the horse-drawn carts or in the mule litters that were for the ladies in the party.

The mule litter was unique to North China, and quite different from the litters found in other parts of the country. They are now doubtless extinct. Since it is quite unlikely that something so prosaic would ever end up in a museum, they are worthy of a brief description. Looking back, I have to say that unquestionably they would head the list for the most confining, phobia-inducing, and ungainly contraptions ever devised by man as a form of transportation. Yet the mule litter was first-class travel in North China in those days, and, when the occupants got over their initial fears, they could be quite tolerable.

Essentially the litter was a box or cage-like affair suspended on two sturdy shafts, which extended six or seven feet back and front and were borne by two mules, one in front and one behind.

The bottom of the passenger compartment extended about two feet below the shafts and was made of very light wooden boards, set in a sturdy frame that could withstand considerable abuse. That part was always painted red or covered with red cloth. The top was of much lighter construction. Sturdy posts at the four corners held a wooden lattice framework on three sides, and supported a slightly domed roof made of reed matting, spread over a bamboo framework. The entire exterior was covered with blue cloth, the roof having a six-inch overhang all around, with another six inches of cloth hanging down from it on all sides, much like the early English "surrey with the fringe on top."

The front of the litter was open, so the passenger had a good view of all that was ahead. In winter a padded cloth curtain was dropped down to keep out the cold wind, and in summer, a temporary cloth "tent" was extended out on two poles over the back of the mule in front in order to keep the sun off of the passenger riding inside. In a few cases there was a swinging door to cover the front opening.

The passenger sat on a platform of removable boards laid across the interior at the approximate height of the shafts. The storage space under these boards was primarily reserved for the driver. Here he kept his bedding roll and personal effects. Sometimes the driver would have a donkey, which he rode alongside the litter, but most of the time the men walked and thought little of it. On the return journey, usually traveling empty, they could ride in style with a pocketful of money.

The overall space inside the litter was approximately three feet wide by four deep. The roof was just a few inches above the passenger's head as he or she sat cross-legged in what is sometimes called the "Lotus Position." For a Chinese this is quite natural and most comfortable, and a Chinese can maintain this position for many hours. For a Westerner, however, sitting in this position for a minimum of six hours at a stretch is a near impossibility.

Fortunately, it was possible to remove two or three of the boards at the front of the seating platform, thus providing space for the non-Chinese person's legs and feet. With a roll of bedding and some pillows behind, sitting there was not uncomfortable, but one's knees were usually close to, if not touching, the six-inch coaming, or sill, that extended across the front opening. Little space was left for any personal belongings, and litters were strictly one-passenger vehicles.

It's not hard to imagine that getting into a litter before it left the ground required considerable dexterity. One had to walk between the forward shafts,

climb through the three-foot by three-foot front opening, head well down, and bent well over forwards. Once inside on the platform, the passenger had to somehow manage to twist legs and feet around, and fit them into the ten- or twelve-inch-wide well, where the boards had been removed. Over-sized European feet seldom had enough room for comfort.

Once aloft and in motion, one was a prisoner for a minimum of six hours, or until the noon stop was reached, or the inn at night. If one was thin and very athletic, it was possible to crawl over the front sill, and, supported on one's arms, slide down behind the mule's rump; then, dodging the swishing tail, duck out underneath the shafts and so reach freedom. Of course, climbing back in was even more difficult, and, for the average Western woman wearing voluminous skirts, next to impossible. Consequently, the experienced traveler drank very little when traveling by litter. Answering a call of nature was not even to be considered.

Even though space inside a litter was limited, the muleteers never objected to a woman having one or two small children in there with her. After all, they didn't weigh that much. When Mother crawled into the litter that morning, and baby Barbara was handed in to her, I started to follow, fully expecting to ride in there with them. I quickly found out otherwise. I was ignominiously carried — kicking and screaming — to the second litter, where a young woman by the name of Carrie Brixton was already ensconced. Miss Brixton had been staying with us for some months, learning Chinese. She had assisted at Barbara's birth and was now accompanying us to the seaside. Short and slight of figure, she took up little space, and there was a reasonable amount of standing room for me in the area where her legs were, and that's where I spent most of my time for the next several hours.

Litter travel was not for the faint-hearted, and that first time for me has never been forgotten. I felt totally abandoned. It was the first time I had been separated from my mother, and I loudly let the whole world know about it. I can remember that morning vividly. In the darkness just ahead of us, I saw a bunch of men lifting Mother's litter onto the backs of the two mules. Then came our turn. Lifting the loaded litter onto the mules' backs is no small project. Empty, a litter probably weighed around 200 pounds. Add a person, and her belongings, and it is well over 300 pounds. Usually it took four men to lift the shafts to the height of the mule's back, two men to a side.

For the first-time passenger, the whole procedure was quite a shock. The rear mule was harnessed first. From inside, one could hear a great commotion going on behind the litter, but nothing could be seen. Then, without any warning, the litter suddenly tilted forwards until the ends of the front shafts were on the ground, and the passenger felt it necessary to grab onto the sides to keep from falling out of the front opening, as the back rose jerkily into the air.

The harness used was, by our standards, makeshift and crude, yet it was simple and very effective. On the mule's back was a padded saddle, on top of which rested a wooden framework with a smaller, inverted V-shaped wooden rack inside that rode freely on top of the first one. On each side of this smaller rack was a strong metal hook, about the thickness of one's little finger. On the end of each shaft was a four-inch-wide strap made of rawhide, several layers thick, one end of which was wrapped around the tip of the shaft and extending about twelve inches in length. Into the free end of this strap was threaded a triangular metal loop. As the men lifting the litter got the shafts level with the mule's back, it was the responsibility of the man at the front end of the shaft to place the triangular loop over the hook on the saddle.

It rarely happened that the two men at the ends of the shafts managed to synchronize their movements and get the two sides hooked up at the same time. More often than not, when one man got his loop onto the hook, he naturally felt that his job was done, and would thereupon duck out from under the shaft. If the other side was not yet hooked, the weight on the already hooked side caused the small wooden saddle to slide over, and the hook on the opposite side would then be out of reach, with the litter tilting ominously. When this was going on at the back, the poor passenger could see nothing of what was happening, and when it was the front end that was being hooked up, he or she wished they couldn't see it. When things did go wrong, it usually meant that everything had to be done over again. The saddle had to be put straight, the mule pacified, and each man tried once again to get his loop over the hook.

Harnessing the rear mule was easy compared to the one in front. That was a different matter altogether! In their stubbornness Chinese mules are no different

from American mules. One thing they don't lack is intelligence, and those front mules were well aware that being backed between those shafts meant a heavy load was about to be placed on their backs, with a full day's work ahead. As a result, they displayed an individuality that would be hard to beat. It usually took three or four men to push and cajole the mule into position, one man to hold it there, and four men to lift the litter and hook up the straps.

Litters were always harnessed up last of all, just before departure, because with all that weight on their backs, the mules didn't like standing around. For some reason the back mules usually seemed fairly docile, but not so the front ones. Once the final loop was in place, the front mule wanted to be off and on his way and that's exactly what he did. The resulting violent jerk forward was, for the passenger, a terrifying "lift-off," and that was only the beginning. As the front mule started off, the one at the back found himself being pulled violently forward, and with his nose almost up against the back of the litter, he couldn't see where he was going. He naturally resisted and stood his ground, and a tug-of-war ensued. The driver meanwhile seemed to be anywhere but where he should have been, or certainly, seldom where he could be seen by the passenger.

Once started, the gait of the two mules usually differed, and they seldom walked in step. As a result, the motion varied: one minute the litter swayed from side to side; the next, it was bouncing up and down or jerking back and forth. If there was a strong side wind, the litter might tilt at a sharp angle. There were constant surprises. The rear mules generally seemed content to go where the front mules led, but that wasn't always the case. Now and then each mule would decide to walk on different sides of the cart ruts, resulting in a crab-like motion over which the poor passenger had no control whatsoever, and frequently it was some time before the driver would notice and take corrective action.

As we moved out of the courtyard, I could see Mother's litter up ahead. I knew she was in there, and for most of that morning I tried to scramble out over the mule's back to get to her. Poor Miss Brixton. For the next six hours she had to contend with a little boy climbing over her feet as he roamed back and forth in the tiny space at the front of the litter.

When daylight came, my father suddenly appeared

beside the litter and lifted me out. On most of the litters, the side panels had a section that could slide back in a shallow trough to allow air to blow through, so it was easy for him to reach me. I was delighted to be able to walk beside him awhile, and he even lifted me up to let me look into Mother's litter to assure myself that she was still there. But why I was not permitted to join her was beyond me. However, resilient as children are, it wasn't long before I was actually enjoying the journey. Whether that was the case for Carrie Brixton is another matter entirely. Thinking back, I feel I most certainly owe her my deepest apologies.

I don't remember much else of that journey by litter, but on subsequent occasions years later, I found a litter to be a very comfortable way to travel. Riding in a mule litter was unlike anything else on earth. It was somewhat like riding a camel, but at the same time it also resembled a small boat in rough seas.

On that first trip I distinctly remember crossing many rivers. Our route roughly followed the course of the Ling River, *ling* meaning icy or cold. That was the river from which Lingyuan got its name. Although I didn't know it at the time, it was mainly that river that we crossed and re-crossed over those five and a half days. In some places the Ling was wide and shallow with a sandy bottom; other times, it was narrow and deep with a rocky bottom and the water reaching the mules' bellies. At most crossings the driver would take off his shoes, roll up his pant legs, and wade through alongside the litter. But when the river crossing happened to be near a village, the villagers often maintained a small footbridge for their own convenience that was available to travelers. Unfortunately, the bridge seldom was immediately adjacent to the crossing. It was usually several hundred yards upstream or downstream. Naturally, when there was such a bridge, the litter driver wanted to use it rather than wade through the river. When that occurred, his usual procedure was to get the litter to the water's edge, shout at the mules, perhaps throw a rock or two after them, then run for the bridge and hope that the mules would cross on their own. It seldom happened as planned; the mules seemed to know that driver was no longer present. Most times, immediately upon reaching the water, the front mule would decide it wanted a drink and would stop abruptly, and naturally the rear mule, sensing there was water

ahead, wanted a drink also, and would keep on pushing. There would be a few moments of a most disconcerting bucking motion, and the passenger would feel certain that one or other of the saddles would be pushed off the mules' backs. Standing its ground to finish its drink, the front mule would then suddenly lunge forward, paying no attention to the other mule's desire for a drink. When that one stopped to get its share, more pulling and bucking resulted. All that while the litter swayed dangerously over a rushing river was, to say the least, unnerving.

When the water was very deep, both mules often would stop in the middle of the stream just to enjoy the feel of the water on their legs or bellies. That could drive the muleteer and the passenger to desperation. The passenger would shout and attempt to smack the lead mule on its rump to get it going, but to no avail. The driver, already on the far bank, would join in the shouting and deftly throw stones at the balky mules. Sometimes it worked and sometimes not. Often enough, the driver had to wade in and lead the reluctant mules to the bank. The mules were no dummies.

The lead mule on those litters always wore a string of bells around its neck. The bells were audible some distance ahead and were intended primarily to warn pedestrians to get out of the way. But they were useful at other times as well. Most of the roads in North China had been there for many centuries, and the track would often be so deeply cut into the land that there were high banks, frequently twelve to fifteen feet in height on either side. Since there was never room for two vehicles to pass in those narrow defiles, the bells were useful in warning oncoming traffic to wait. The experienced drivers, knowing of the long defiles, would walk along the top of the bank, the better to hear any oncoming vehicles, or even to see the tips of the drivers' whips in the distance. In such cases, a lot of shouting would occur, and one or the other would wait. But when that didn't work, and one met another vehicle in those narrow cuts, the ensuing action was always interesting and frustrating to watch.

First there would be a long argument as to which vehicle would have to turn around. Fortunately, mule litters usually got the right of way, simply because they couldn't be turned around in such a narrow space. With the carts, unless they were military or government vehicles, usually the lighter vehicle would have to give way. That would result in unharnessing the mules, unloading the vehicle, lifting it off its wheels, upending it and turning it around, and reloading it. All that could take an hour or two. Having had that kind of experience more than once, my father would usually walk far ahead when reaching that type of road situation, and in that way stop any oncoming traffic before a problem resulted.

Since much of our route on that trip was over mountain ranges, we met constant surprises. The roads for wheeled vehicles, such as they were, tended to follow more gradual inclines, often winding back and forth on the mountain slopes, or following the bed of a stream. Pack animals, pedestrian traffic, and horseback riders were not always confined to those roads. Over the years, many shortcuts had been carved out, and it seemed to be the general rule that, where a man could climb, a pack animal could follow. Those shortcuts could often save travelers considerable mileage, but seldom were they easy to negotiate. It was a common occurrence to see packs sliding off the backs of the mules or donkeys as they scrambled up the steep slopes. It could be extremely disconcerting if one happened to be following those same pack animals in a mule-borne litter. There was often great physical danger in taking the shortcuts — many of the paths were just narrow ledges with a steep drop-off into a gorge or ravine — so my father would not permit the litter drivers to use them when we traveled in a caravan or when ladies occupied the litters. Moreover, apart from the danger of the roads themselves, if the litters used the shortcut, they saved so much time they could get far ahead of the wheeled vehicles, and, being alone, could fall easy prey to bandits. It was just not worth the risk, but it didn't make the drivers any happier.

In later years, when on those several occasions I traveled in a litter, we were usually in a hurry and used every shortcut possible. Each was an unforgettable experience. More than once, as the mules literally bounded up steep slopes, the saddles would slide off and the litter crashed to the ground. Usually no great damage resulted since the distance of the fall was only about three feet. However, finding the necessary manpower to reset the litter back onto the mules' backs often meant a long delay as we waited for someone to come along to lend a hand. The

Chinese, never at a loss for an apt proverb, would mutter: *Bu pa man, jiu pa zhan* — going slowly is not to be feared, it is the stops that one must fear.

That first trip of mine held another memorable experience — my first sight of a railroad train. I clearly recall reaching the end of our journey late one afternoon. All the vehicles had been unpacked, but instead of going into an inn as usual, we went into a strange-looking building standing all by itself, the railroad station. I remember seeing the railroad tracks outside and not knowing what they were. The station master evidently let us use his office, because I can remember a lot of ringing bells, probably telephones, and watching men handle huge levers which probably moved switches and signals. I must have fallen asleep quickly because I don't remember any trains going by. My next recollection is being awakened and carried out into the dark night. Hundreds of people seemed to be milling around in the dark, with only a few hand-held lanterns giving off some feeble light. As we stood close to the railroad tracks, suddenly, far in the distance, I could see a bright light. It grew larger and brighter by the minute and was accompanied by a horrendous noise. Out of the darkness roared this colossal black monster belching smoke, sparks and steam, and making a fearful clanking noise. It was quite logical that the Chinese had named trains *huo che*, "fire carts." Standing at track level, it towered above us as it went by. Desperately, I clung to Mother until it had passed. Behind it were moving houses, with windows and lights, and people looking out. Suddenly all was quiet and my father carried me up some steps and I can remember the inside of what must have been the third-class coach. Packed with people, filled with smoke and strange smells, it started to move and suddenly, without warning, the floor under me started to shake. That was my introduction to a train.

On our return from the seaside, we made the same journey in reverse, but by then the train was "old hat" to me, and I remember nothing of the trip. I do remember, though, that when we got off the train in Suizhong we stayed the night in a small, Western-style hotel. In later years I learned that it was called Sanborn's Hotel, and it was operated by an expatriate American named Sanborn who had a Chinese wife and several small children. We stayed there a number of times in later years. The hotel was small but very well kept. It was a typical Chinese building near the railroad station, but in the several small rooms, Mr. Sanborn had installed wooden floors and Western-style furniture, all of it obviously locally made, and quite functional. But what I remember most are the wonderful meals he provided.

Aside from running the hotel, Mr. Sanborn also conducted a forwarding business, although perhaps that was a private arrangement my father had set up with him. In any case, I know that in subsequent years he accepted shipments for us that came in on the trains, and forwarded them to us by mule-pack train. I've often wondered who he was and how he got there initially. He was apparently very contented with his lot. Most certainly he was a good friend to us, and over the years he helped us very much.

As Barbara grew older, she and I were constant companions and our back garden was our playground. We had a makeshift seesaw there. An old pear tree had rotted at the base and toppled over. We found a board to lay across it and that served us well for several years, although we had our minor accidents with it. On one occasion, when Barbara was certainly no more than a year old, my older brother Gil was on one end of the board, holding Barbara in front of him. Ruth and I were on the other end and we were merrily seesawing. But Barbara was sitting too close to the center, and somehow she managed to get her thumb under the board, where it got squashed. Barbara screamed so long and so loudly that my father heard her from our schoolroom, where he was conducting a prayer meeting. He hastened out to see what was wrong. Fortunately, no serious injury resulted.

Most adults have a recollection of some favorite toy they had as a young child. There were no toy stores in Lingyuan, and as children we had very few playthings, but I remember well those we did have. Among them were Chinese toys that either were sold at stalls downtown or were brought around to our front gate by traveling salesmen. One toy we all liked was called a *ban bu dao*, "it can't be tipped over." They were crudely fashioned dolls, garishly painted, and about eight or ten inches in height. They had a rounded base made of mud. Push them over and they always bounced back up.

Another Chinese toy that was extremely popular and cost only a few pennies was called a *duga*, because to their ears, one sound it made was *du*,

while the other was *ga*. (To the Western ear, it would be "ping" and "pong"). They were made of extremely thin glass, blown on the spot as one watched. The glassblower worked with a little charcoal stove on one end of his carrying pole. His stool was on the other end. He used a thin brass tube to blow a steady blue flame from the glowing charcoal and in the flame he melted the glass. He picked up the molten glass with another tube and blew multicolored bottles about the size of a half-gallon ice cream container. The bottles were bulbous in shape with a neck about six inches long and the diameter of a pencil. The bottoms were so thin that when one breathed into the neck the bottom would bulge out with a "pong" sound. When one drew a breath the bottom snapped back in with a "ping" sound.

Such a toy would have given American parents apoplexy, or at least gray hairs, had they seen their children playing with it. We played with them often, as a matter of course, as did the Chinese children, and saw nothing wrong with them. Of course they didn't last very long, and the danger of cutting oneself on the broken glass was always present, as was the possibility of sucking broken glass into one's lungs. However, I never heard of any child getting hurt with one of them, nor did we.

Since we had few toys, we usually invented our own games. For me, a stick held between my legs was a huge and powerful horse. I would ride my horse round and round the periphery of the garden, hugging the wall. I was always on a journey somewhere. Certain points were the noon-time stops, where I would feed my horse; others were night stops, where I would pretend to sleep on a *kang*. The drains that crisscrossed our garden for watering the vegetable beds were deep rivers that had to be crossed, and the raised mound at the bend of the inverted L of our garden, where the well was located, was a high mountain pass. Barbara joined me in this game with her own "horse," and we traveled on wonderful adventures together.

Later, someone gave me a tiny horse and cart made of metal. That toy opened up a whole new world for us and kept us occupied for hours as we made roads for it. I drove, while Barbara pretended to be the passenger. Unfortunately, I left it out one night and apparently someone stole it. Most likely it was a neighbor or one of the numerous people who from time to time came into the garden on some pretext or another just to see how the foreigners lived. Possibly one of our dogs carried it off somewhere and buried it, as happened to other things of mine. In any event, it was a big disappointment in my young life.

As children we spent much of our time in that back garden. It was, to us, a wonderful place. The grandeur of the mountains immediately behind was visible over the top of the back wall. In the garden, immediately to the right, was a small fenced-in courtyard with a row of open sheds facing south. We called it the "cow yard" and there, in two of the white-washed sheds, we always had two cows to keep us supplied with fresh milk. It was necessary to have two because they only gave milk while their calves were young, and throughout the year we had to buy new cows as calves were weaned. Chinese visitors seeing the white-washed sheds for the cows remarked that the cows were "in heaven." Next to the cow sheds was a shed where the straw fodder for the cows was cut and stored, and the last shed on the left was the chicken run. We also usually kept a half-dozen ducks in that fenced-in yard, and at one time had a flock of large white geese, which were remarkable "watch dogs."

The garden stretched northward for seven or eight hundred feet, and a four-foot-wide path hugged the left-hand side. That path was raised about a foot higher than the garden and had a stone border. It was surfaced with powdered coal ash to keep it dry in summer, something that was necessary because of the amount of traffic on it each day. It was the direct route to the back well, the focal point of the garden. Actually, we had three wells on the property, but two of them were very shallow and the water wasn't fit to drink.

Our neighbors' houses formed most of the left-hand wall along the path. At the corner of the inverted "L," where the garden spread out to the left, there was a small one-room building made of mud bricks, but with a tiled roof. At one time it most probably housed the gardener, because it had a brick bed in it and a cooking stove with a large cauldron. That was our "wash house," where each Monday morning You Wang, our house-boy, did the laundry. Immediately adjacent to the well, it was an ideal spot for washing. We children named it the "bug house" because of all the insects that infested it. Behind it were the clothes lines where the wash was hung out.

All around the garden grew a variety of trees, most of them planted a few feet away from the walls to conserve the rest of the space for the planting of vegetables. Most of the trees were native date trees, which had a fruit much smaller than the American date. Also known as the jujube, it had a pit so large that there was very little meat, but what there was of it was most delicious. The fruit as it ripened first turned brown, and although very hard, at that point it was quite edible. Left a few days longer on the tree, it would turn red and become wrinkled, and then it was at its best.

Additionally, there were a number of gnarled old pear trees at various points around the garden. Again, they were near the walls, and we liked them best because they were so easy to climb. On a hot summer's day, to sit on a high branch in the shade of the leaves and watch what went on next-door was a good way to spend a few hours. However, we frequently would find ourselves looking at some of our neighbor's children who were up in the trees on their side of the wall, looking over at us.

We also had some crab-apple trees and several very tall elm trees, each standing around sixty feet in height. Early in the springtime, before the leaves came out, the elm seeds would form in big bunches. They were edible and much prized both by us and by the Chinese. Then, too, we had some acacia trees that delighted us each spring with their fragrant white flowers, and a short distance from the well there was a row of rose bushes that flowered each May with bright yellow blooms, so fragrant we could smell them from clear across the garden.

But the well was our favorite spot. With the well mouth raised on a mound about three feet high to provide gravity flow for watering the garden, it had rock retaining walls on the southern and eastern sides, and on the other two sides it tapered off to the level of the garden nearby. The mouth of the well was about four feet square, surrounded with hewn rock slabs, and it was never covered. As children we were warned not to go too close, but we still occasionally crawled on our stomachs to the edge to look down into it.

Extending out over the mouth was a wooden Chinese windlass about sixteen inches in diameter. Over one hundred feet of one-inch rope was wound around it, all of it needed, because the well was one of the deepest in the city, and everyone claimed it was the sweetest water to be found. Even during the worst droughts the well never ran dry, and we were able to provide water for those who couldn't get it elsewhere. The inside walls of the well were rock, and it was probably two or three hundred years old, from the look of it.

Summer and winter, the well was in constant use, either for watering the garden or providing drinking water for the entire compound and for some of our neighbors as well. Around the well stood a half-dozen ancient cedar trees, each with a trunk larger than the girth of a man and standing forty or fifty feet in height. Additionally there were two or three very old fir trees. We particularly prized these trees because they remained green all year round.

Drawing water from the well was hard work. The bucket, woven from willow twigs, weighed about ten pounds when dry, and twice that when thoroughly soaked, as it usually was. It held about five gallons of water, and that, together with the long hemp rope, was a sizable weight. Drawing the full bucket up took several minutes, but the empty bucket and rope falling back down the well took only seconds. In fact, the combined weight of bucket and rope caused the windlass to revolve so fast that it was in danger of flying apart. For that reason, a crude but effective brake was provided by using a rawhide strap that was held firmly against the revolving windlass.

At the lip of the well was a huge stone slab about three feet wide and six feet or more in length. It looked as though it had been there for centuries. The center had been hollowed out into a deep trough to form a drain. It was for irrigating the garden. As the windlass was turned, and the full bucket came up to the lip of the well, the operator used his left hand to deftly flip the bucket into the trough, allowing a gush of water to pour down into the network of shallow drains that covered the entire garden.

The garden itself was symmetrically laid out into neatly arranged beds approximately four feet wide by ten feet long with a drain between each row. When watering the beds, one yard man drew the water, while a second person controlled the flow into the various beds by making a small opening in the side of the drain and blocking the flow of water in the drain so the water was diverted into the bed. When sufficiently full, the opening was blocked, and another opening created farther down the drain. Watering the

entire garden always took several hours.

Spring was a joyous time of the year after the long winters. The very first fresh vegetable on the market was spinach, which usually came in April, and we all loved it. The Chinese lunar calendar is much more interesting than ours. Divided like ours into twelve months to a year, the months are either "small" months of twenty-nine days, or "large" months of thirty days, with an additional intercalary month inserted seven times in every nineteen years to make up the deficiency between the solar and lunar years.

Of course, the Chinese followed their lunar calendar, and we found ourselves doing the same to a very large extent. Each month there are two special days when one can watch for a change in the weather. For example, in the 12th month, which usually comes in our January, you get first, "slight cold" and then two weeks later comes "great cold." Chinese New Year's Day is either in late January or in February, and in that month you get "beginning of spring," then, two weeks later "rain water," (although, since we were very far north, with us most often it was a light snowfall). All through the year there are those special days that the Chinese farmers watch for to judge the time to plant or harvest their crops.

Our favorite day was in the second lunar month, usually in March, when there was a day called *jingzhe* which meant "waking of insects." On that day we children would run around turning over rocks to see who could find the first insect of the year. Unfailingly we'd always find several, no matter how cold the weather might be.

Father started planting the garden each year in May with a crop of vegetables that not only fed us all summer long, but lasted almost through the winter. We had a big potato patch, also cabbages, carrots, turnips, parsnips, chard, broccoli, onions, beets, rhubarb, and even asparagus, and, of course, sweet corn. Each of us children was given a bed quite near the well where we were encouraged by our parents to grow our own garden. Mine never did very well. I was always too impatient. Every second day I would dig up the seeds to see why they weren't coming up.

We thoroughly enjoyed those summers that we spent in Lingyuan, although the heat and humidity made it very uncomfortable most of the time. We generally stayed there every second year, but because it was such a busy time for the farmers, and because the rainy season made travel impossible, there was not much that could be done in evangelistic work. As a result most of our parents' time was spent in curing the sick.

Fall was always a delightful time of the year with pleasant warm days and no mosquitoes. Sad as we always were to see the summer end, there was great satisfaction in watching the harvesting all around us, and unless it was a particularly bad year, people were happy and optimistic. Threshing floors appeared on every flat space along the city streets and just outside the city's walls; there were always three or four of them in the immediate vicinity of our house and a big one just outside the back garden gate. The latter was used during the summer to grow a particularly delicious, thin-skinned melon tasting something like the cantaloupe, or muskmelon. We all loved them. When they were in season, we only had to climb up on the wall early in the morning and shout to the owner, who spent the nights there in a small shack guarding the patch, and he would bring over a bunch of them and put them into a basket that we would let down on a rope. We simply peeled them like apples and cut them into slices.

We enjoyed watching the farmers bring in the harvest then crush the grain out of the heavy heads with a roller pulled by a donkey, and finally by throwing the grain into the air and letting the wind blow the chaff away, the winnowing. Some of the threshing floors used an ancient type of winnowing machine. It was a large box on legs, with a funnel on top into which the grain was poured, and it was powered by a handle on the side that turned a large fan made with a series of paddles on a revolving wheel on the inside. Grain was shoveled into the top, then it came sliding out of a chute while the chaff was blown away.

Some of our happiest memories were those fall days when harvest time came, and we helped Father dig up the potatoes, carrots and other root vegetables for storage in the winter vegetable pit that the yard boy would dig. Each winter it was dug in a different spot to ensure that the ground was hard and that there would be no cave-in of the walls. The pit was the size of a small room, about eight to ten feet wide, and twelve to fourteen feet long. It always took over a week to dig, and it had to be at least eight or nine feet deep to get well below the frost line.

We had an elderly man named Qiu Li who did the outdoor work, our "yard boy." He was a kindly old chap who fussed over us whenever we went out in the garden. If the weather was cold he always made sure we were wrapped up warmly, and in the summertime he made sure we didn't stay out in the sun too long. I remember Qiu Li for one incident in particular. He was in charge of the cows, and when one of them got sick, Qiu Li took it down to the vet for treatment. The vet diagnosed the illness, gave Qiu Li a big pill to give the cow, and told him to be sure and walk the cow after administering the pill. Qui Li followed these instructions, but the cow's condition didn't improve, so he took it back to the vet and demanded another pill. The vet asked if he had followed the instructions, and if the cow had been walked. Qiu Li assured him this had been done. The vet wanted to know exactly where the walk had taken place. When Qiu Li told him, the vet exclaimed: "That's where you went wrong. You were walking her downhill. The sickness is in the cow's rear end. You must walk her uphill for an hour or two. That will make the medicine go to the point where it is needed." Qiu Li followed these instructions and the cow eventually recovered, but how much of that was due to the walking uphill, or even to the pill, is debatable.

In any case, Qiu Li began to find the work a little too heavy for him, so he asked Father if he could have an apprentice helper. That seemed like a reasonable request, and a few days later a gangly young fellow appeared, thin as a rake, and so shy and scared of the foreigners he was seeing for the first time that we couldn't get a word out of him. Asked his name, he finally told us it was Sirrr. That could either mean a cork or the slurred form of the number three. It was the latter. From then on we called him Lao San, but that wasn't his real name. It merely meant that he was "Old Three," the third son. His surname was Hu, and he was the youngest son of an elderly woman who was one of Mother's "Bible Women" who did visitation work among women throughout the city. For some reason that I have now forgotten, we had called her "Peter" from the very beginning. For a very good reason that I will explain later we had nicknames for all the servants, and everyone else in the compound.

As time passed, Lao San became like an older brother to us. He was around seventeen when he first came, and, where we were concerned, he took over where Qiu Li left off. He watched us with an eagle eye, comforted us when we got hurt, and kept us from doing many of the dangerous things kids tend to do. We were all deeply fond of him. Ultimately, when Qiu Li retired, Lao San assumed responsibility for all the outdoor work.

As Lao San dug the vegetable pit, the earth was thrown higher and higher along the sides. For me and my Chinese playmates, that was a wonderful opportunity to wage battles with clods of dirt. We would form up on the two opposite sides of the pit, behind the mounds of dirt, and throw the clods across at each other. Frequently, two clods from opposite sides would collide in midair and shower poor Lao San below, but he never complained.

When he reached the right depth, Lao San would very carefully trim the walls until they were smooth and perfectly straight up and down. Then he would dig a four-foot-wide trench at one end, about a foot deeper than the rest of the pit's floor. That was for the potatoes. When the digging was completed he laid heavy beams across the top, covered them with a thick layer of *shujie* (dried sorghum stalks), and piled earth on top to a depth of about three feet. A two-foot-square trap door was left at the southern end. It was heavily insulated with woven straw, and the whole thing effectively kept the cold out. As the winter progressed we could watch the frost line creeping down the walls to a depth of four feet or so, while heavy hoarfrost collected in a thick layer on the ceiling, but it didn't change the inside temperature, which remained a constant 40 degrees Fahrenheit, or thereabouts, and the vegetables kept perfectly.

As Lao San dug the pits each year, he frequently came across ancient bits of colorful pottery, which he would save for us. On one or two occasions he found some tiny bronze human figurines, about two inches high, and on one occasion one made of white jade. They were called *hu xin fo*, heart-protecting Buddhas, and were charms to be hung around the neck to protect the wearer against illness. Many years later I managed to bring two of them out of China to the U.S., and when in New York City, I took them to a world-famous appraiser of antiques to get his opinion of their value and age. However, the man had never seen anything like them before and would not believe that they were authentic Chinese antiques. My own estimate, and that of my Chinese friends, was that they had probably lain in the ground in our back garden for a couple of hundred years before Lao San found them.

Each morning our cook, Gao Cai, would go to the pit to select vegetables for that day's meals. Sometimes he would let us climb down with him. We weren't supposed to go down there alone because of the danger of falling off the ladder. However, on very cold winter days we frequently did, sometimes taking our Chinese playmates down with us. It was a grand place to keep warm and, at the same time, chew on raw carrots or turnips. Naturally, beyond casually wiping off the most obvious dirt on the vegetables, we never gave hygiene a second thought.

I well remember one cold morning when my older brother Gil and I climbed down there. After eating some carrots, Gil, for no apparent reason and without saying a word, suddenly climbed up the ladder, pulled it up after him, and closed the trapdoor, leaving me in utter darkness. At first I thought it was fun, but then, as the hours crept by, I knew he had forgotten about me and no one else knew where I was. At noontime, I could dimly hear You Wang, our house boy, ringing the bell for lunch. He always rang the bell ten minutes before mealtime to give everyone a chance to wash up, then he rang it again just as the meal was to be served. That ensured that we were all in place at the table when the food came. After I heard the second bell I knew it wouldn't be long before Mother would begin to worry about me and to start asking questions. A search was begun, and Gil, suddenly remembering what he had done, was too scared to confess. Fortunately, someone discovered the ladder for the pit lying on the top outside, became suspicious, and decided to look inside. I became the celebrity of the day. I don't know what punishment Gil suffered, but I, at least, didn't hold a grudge. For me it had been a lot of fun, even though I had been a bit frightened at first, and I certainly received a lot of attention and commiseration from it.

Getting attention also had its drawbacks. Mother had taught Gao Cai how to salt down a roast of beef for corned beef, and corned beef and cabbage was frequently a winter's day meal, and I loved the stuff. Without question it was one of my favorites. One day we were having it for lunch, always our big meal of the day, and I got sick for some reason. That brought me so much attention that I conceived a brilliant idea! From then on, whenever we had corned beef on the menu I would refuse it on the grounds that it made me sick. For years I deprived myself of that delicious favorite of mine just because of the attention it brought me. I was about six at the time and only realized years later how stupid I had been!

A millstone being moved.

A typical Chinese well.

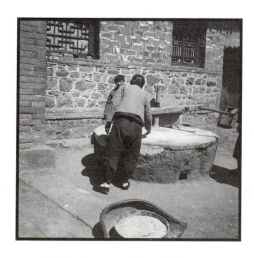

Grinding at the millstone.   Feeding livestock.

Jim Lance's Litter Sketch

Jing yi shi, zhang yi zhi.

Experience something,
and gain knowledge.

- Chinese Proverb.

Chapter Four
The Third Courtyard & Second Compound

The farther toward the back one lives in a Chinese compound, the more prestigious it is for the owner or resident, and, as a result, the buildings toward the rear are more ornate and better built than those toward the front.

In any Chinese compound, buildings that face south are called *zheng fang*, the word *zheng* being an auspicious word with a variety of meanings, all of them good. It not only translates as "main" but also means correct, straight, proper, right, honest, upright, and more. Just to write the character is considered a lucky or auspicious act. The written character for *zheng* has five strokes and is considered so auspicious that it is used by the Chinese as a counter in their tally system.

Our first compound had three of these main buildings, one for each courtyard, and each had five *jian*. However, in each case, only four *jian* were actually usable because the fifth was used as a passageway. The main building that fronted directly onto the

street, for security reasons, had only one entrance on the southern side, the main gate, which was exactly in the middle. The rest of the wall facing the street was blank except for some very small windows, high up under the eaves and quite inaccessible from the ground.

Once inside the front gate, the first courtyard actually consisted of two small courtyards behind eight-foot-high walls, one on each side of a wide, paved path leading toward the back. Each of those courtyards had its own two-leaved gate and its own privy. Both yards were vegetable gardens in the summer and sources of dust in winter. The two rooms to the right of the front gate were for the gatekeeper, a Mr. Hu (no relation to Lao San). One room was the kitchen and the other was living quarters for himself, his wife and small son. The two *jian* to the left of the main gate were one large open space, with two quite large *kang* on each side, and a narrow alleyway between. Both were large enough to sleep six or eight people, and there were cooking facilities at the other end of the large room.

Because the floors were all dirt, the area presumably had been the servants' quarters when the compound was first built. For our purposes, however, it was utilized as the home for a group of orphan girls whom Mother had taken in off the streets and "adopted." They were taught to cook and sew, how to make shoes and also how to read and write. When they were old enough, Mother, following the Chinese custom, helped find husbands for them if they so wished. The gate into their area was originally very close to the street-front entrance. However, Chinese soldiers had a habit of forcing their way in, and the entrance to the girls' quarters was the first one that caught their eye. After the girls had been frightened several times, Father blocked up that gate and opened another from the north end of the courtyard, placing it inside the second courtyard, where it was less visible.

The high walls on each side of the pathway leading toward that second courtyard at the back were plastered smoothly with lime, and were white with a gray edging, so the courtyard actually was not unattractive. The entrance to the second courtyard was a large and very ornately decorated gateway. It had two big doors, very much the same as those on the front gate. These could be closed, but I can remember only two or three occasions when that was done: once when there was fighting in the streets and we anticipated troops breaking in, and another time when hostile mobs had gathered outside, as happened occasionally. That particular gateway was essentially for ornamentation. It was mounted on a heavy stone base, which was elaborately carved. At the base of each door, the stone was carved in the shape of a large drum, with an ornamental border.

Once past that gate and inside the second courtyard, on the left and right were side buildings, which the Chinese called *xiang fang* or "wing" buildings, even though in every case they were independent and not attached to the main buildings. Those originally had housed lesser members of the family, sons and daughters-in-law. For our use, the one on the left was Mother's dispensary. It was a three-*jian* building, divided into one large and one small room. The large room had a big *kang* and a cook stove. The smaller room also had a *kang* and space for Mother's medicine cabinets.

Every day as many as 60 to 100 women and children came in for treatment of a variety of diseases. Mother had the help of two Chinese Christian "Bible Women" as they were known, who taught the waiting women short choruses, gave them lessons in reading and writing, and preached the gospel to them.

In China, where women in reality ruled the home, it was they who decided what religion the family should adopt, and if these women could be won over to Christianity, in almost every case they later brought their husbands along.

Directly across from that building was an identical one. Its larger room was used for church services until a few years later, when we outgrew it and Father purchased the next-door property. The smaller room was used for overnight or weekend visitors.

The main building at the rear of the second courtyard stood on a platform of stone, about three feet higher than the rest of the yard. The center *jian*, in a direct line with the front street gate, was a passageway through to the third courtyard. On each side of it were two single-*jian* rooms. The first one on the left was Father's study, and the second was our kitchen for a number of years.

Just outside the kitchen Father had built a large shed, between the kitchen and an adjoining side building, which was at a right angle to it. It was used to store coal. The first room on the right side of the passageway was a guest room, and the second was used for storage. We called this our "cold room." In winter the sides of beef that hung there would remain solidly frozen for several months.

Originally, entrances to the rooms in the second main building had all been on the south side. However, Father wanted the building to be part of the third courtyard, so he bricked up the doors facing south, leaving windows for each room, and cut doors in the northern walls. Added to that, Father felt that the wide corridor through the building was a waste of space, so, since the side walls were not bearing walls, he had them moved outward several feet into the passageway, thus enlarging the rooms on each side.

Entrance to the third courtyard from that passageway was blocked at the north end by a "spirit screen" standing in the way. That was a seven-foot-high wall, about five feet out from the passageway exit, and originally one had to go either left or right to get around it to enter the third courtyard. Although we had no fear of evil spirits trying to make their way into the courtyard, Father decided to keep the screen in place in order to gain some privacy. Without it, people outside in the street would have been able to peep through the crack between the front gates and see all the way up into our residence. Father even improved the screen concept. He blocked off the right-hand side so that everyone had to go left around the screen to gain access to the third courtyard. That took a couple of seconds longer, but gave us a couple of seconds more in preparation time when undesirable visitors entered the yard. In later years when the Japanese army occupied Lingyuan, and we became part of the new country of Manchukuo, we frequently had reason to be very grateful for the few seconds gained through that slight diversion.

Going around the spirit screen into the third courtyard, the first thing noticeable was the much higher and more imposing main building to the north. Like the other two, it also had five *jian*, but it was the extreme left-hand *jian* that was the passageway leading through to the rear and eventually, by way of an alley, to the back garden. That building was also built on a stone platform, about four feet higher than the yard itself.

The approach to the passageway was around the corner and up a flight of very wide brick steps, built in an "L" shape. In front of the passageway stood an ancient white lilac tree. We loved that tree with its thick twisted trunk and gnarled branches. In all probability it had been there for 100 years. In early spring, because of its protected location, it was one of the first trees to come into leaf, and then it would burst out in a profusion of large bunches of the most fragrant flowers. When the tree was in bloom, the entire courtyard was filled with the fragrance.

At the right-hand end of the main building was the entrance to our living quarters. Seven wide stone steps led up to the fourth *jian*. At the top of the steps was a small porch, about five feet deep and the width of the *jian*. On the left was a door that led into the two bedrooms, and on the right, a door opened into the dining room, which also served as our living room. It was a two-*jian* room and quite large, measuring about twenty by twenty-five feet on the right-hand side, and slightly smaller in the center, where a large window looked out onto the small porch and the courtyard.

The brick-paved courtyard was most unusual in that part of China, and signified the unusual wealth of the original owners. In the center, a rectangular patch about ten feet by twenty feet had been left as a flower garden. At the northern end of that garden stood two stately spruce trees standing about fifteen feet high, and they, together with the lilac tree, added a little color to an otherwise very drab view from the windows. In fact, the yard was so tightly enclosed that we were unable to see the surrounding mountains from any window.

The flower garden was Mother's special preserve. Each year she selected the seeds to be planted, and Lao San took special pains to plant and weed the garden for her. A profusion of varicolored flowers bloomed throughout the summer and it was You Wang's self-appointed job to cut flowers for the vases in the dining-room. At each meal he would put a vase of flowers on the table and make sure that the flowers pointed toward Mother.

Mother's flower garden was watered from two large earthenware pots, or *gang*, just like the ones used in kitchens. They were about two inches thick and stood almost four feet high. Each contained about fifty gallons of water, which Lao San carried from the back well, and standing as they did close to the wall under the bedroom windows of the main building, they caught some of the rainwater from the roof. To us as children they were a constant source of fascination and interest. They were too high for us to look into when we stood on the ground, but that didn't deter us. The stone platform beneath the main building extended outward about a foot along the entire front of the building, with a ledge of heavy stone slabs. When we were small, we would either walk or crawl along that ledge until we got to the water vats, and there we would spend hours playing with the water. We sailed our "boats," of leaves or twigs, or, using the tubular leaves of the large Chinese onion as "straws," we siphoned out water by drawing it up into our mouths. We supposedly knew enough not to drink the water (Mother had told us enough times), but we saw no harm in getting it into our mouths and then spitting it out. But we did drink it at times. I well remember our sitting on the front steps having "tea parties," using a toy tea set belonging to one of the girls. We would dip water out of the *gang* with the tiny teapot, and then in our minds it became "tea" and was thus fit to drink. During the rainy season the water was coated with green slime and algae, but we drank our "tea" anyway until Mother discovered our "party" one day. Why we never got sick from it is a mystery; we must have built up an extraordinary tolerance.

As in the second courtyard, there were two side buildings of approximately the same size. Both had three *jian*, with one large and one smaller room. The large room in the building on the left was a guest room. The smaller one was our sewing room, although from time to time it, too, had been used as a bedroom for one or another of us. As the sewing room, it was occupied daily by a dear little old lady, Mrs. Wu. She was so bent and deformed by arthritis that she walked with her head down nearly touching her knees, and unless she turned her head, it was impossible to see her face. She sat all day on a mat on the brick floor of the room and sewed clothes and bedding for the orphans, as well as making things for Mother when needed. She and her husband lived across the street from our compound in a house that was approached through one of the narrowest alleys in the city. Two people could not pass in it, but that made it less visible and more secure.

Our schoolroom occupied the larger room in the building across from the sewing room, while Gil and I had the smaller room for our bedroom. There was just enough space for two single beds and a desk for Gil to use for his studies. The only other furniture was a washbasin stand originally made from a packing case, but later, Sun Shifu, the carpenter, made little commodes for each of the bedrooms, complete with a cupboard below for the ubiquitous chinaware chamber pot that everyone used at night rather than go out to the outdoor privy in the dark.

Because the side buildings, like all the others, stood independently of the main building, it was at first awkward for Mother to have to go out of the dining room, down the steps to the yard, then up another set of steps into the schoolroom, and in bad weather it was particularly unpleasant. That gave Father another of his good ideas. He had workmen build a flat-roofed shed between the dining room area and the side building, cutting a door from the dining room into the shed, and then one through the end wall of the wing building into the schoolroom. Consequently,

we could all get to the schoolroom without having to go outdoors.

The shed also served as a pantry for Mother. Two large cupboards standing ceiling high occupied the back wall of the shed, with windows facing them. The cupboards contained the canned goods and other foodstuffs that Mother ordered once a year from England and occasionally from the coast. As children we were always intrigued when Mother unlocked the cupboards, unleashing the fragrant odors of spices and dried fruits as she took something out for the cook to use for one of the meals. To this day I can smell it.

At the other end of the dining room was another doorway leading into the first of the two bedrooms. It had a door that could be closed, but usually, to conserve heat in the winter, a heavy red cloth curtain hung in the doorway. I remember that particularly well, because one day when I was carrying a kettle of hot water into the bedroom, I brushed through the curtain and ran into Barbara coming from the other direction. The spout of the kettle caught her in the forehead, leaving a permanent scar.

Furniture in all the rooms was sparse to begin with. However, after Father discovered Sun Shifu, things changed. A Western-style house was completely new to Sun, and he had never seen anything but Chinese furniture. However, after he was shown pictures of furniture in a Montgomery Ward catalogue, Sun copied them remarkably well. He built a four-poster double bed for my parents, and single beds for us kids and our guests. Instead of springs, holes were drilled in the frame on all four sides, and quarter-inch rope was strung through the holes and woven across. Mrs. Wu made the mattresses, using washed horsehair and cotton wool, and the beds were remarkably comfortable. The rope "springs" stood up well, except when three or four of us kids climbed onto the bed and bounced wildly in horseplay. On more than one occasion the ropes broke and deposited us on the floor.

Sun also made chests of drawers for the bedrooms, stand-up closets, and some so-called "easy chairs," but the latter didn't turn out to be terribly comfortable. For the dining room Sun built a Morris chair from a picture. He got the sloping adjustable back just right, but the dimensions were too large. It was almost wide enough for two adults to sit in, and easily held two of us kids, but the arms were too high for comfort. The only other comfortable chairs in the dining room were two or three folding chairs, like deck chairs, but with heavy brocade cloth instead of the usual canvas.

We had a large dining table that would easily seat eight, and I remember we always had that many and sometimes more at the table because of the young missionaries staying with us. I don't think that table had been made by Sun. It looked too old. It could easily have been a Chinese table, as was another, smaller one that stood just inside the front entrance. The second table was used as a serving table by You Wang. He brought the food from the kitchen on a large tray, and heavily laden as it always was, he balanced it neatly on one upraised hand and carried it across the courtyard, regardless of the weather. Not once did he drop it or spill any of the food. We had a very large soup tureen that was frequently used. It alone, empty, was quite heavy.

On the serving table sat a large earthenware pot filled with water that had been boiled and allowed to cool. We could drink from it any time we wished. The pot was unglazed, and the water seeped through the porous inner surface and then evaporated on the outside. As a result, the water inside was always cool, regardless of how hot the weather was.

At the dining table there were only four or five straight-back chairs, which Sun had made. We kids were given stools to sit on at the table. Father assured us that it was better for our backs. And there were two other pieces of furniture I remember well. One was a low sideboard with two smallish cupboards underneath, and on top, a glassed-in bookcase filled with wonderful books that Dad had bought at second-hand stalls in either Peking or Tientsin. We had an Encyclopedia Britannica in twelve volumes, each of which I read from cover to cover, some more than once. He also had a whole set of Charles Dickens' books, The Swiss Family Robinson, Penrod, Robinson Crusoe, a set of all of Shakespeare's plays, and a lot of wonderful stories by the noted American novelist, Zane Grey. In addition we had numerous other books whose titles I no longer remember.

In the corner near the door that led to the schoolroom stood an old secondhand pump organ that Dad had picked up somewhere. It had numerous stops on it that Mother pulled out when she played it, and we

always marvelled at her knowing of which ones to pull. That organ was Mother's joy and delight.

Although both my parents had extensive medical knowledge, neither of them were doctors, so when any of us got sick, as occasionally happened, I know they became greatly worried and wished that a doctor lived nearby. Not infrequently people around us became severely ill. I recall one occasion when a young Australian missionary living with us while he studied the language suddenly fell ill with extreme pain in his side, appearing to have all the symptoms of appendicitis. Our nearest doctors and hospitals were seven days' journey away, and no doctor could reach us in time to operate. We sent telegrams to Dr. Robson, giving the symptoms, and his replies seemed to confirm the diagnosis. But all we could do was pray, and the young man recovered completely within a matter of days.

The very worst occasions for us as children were when Mother herself fell ill. That was always a disaster. I vividly recall one time when I was about six. We were confined to the schoolroom and were forbidden to go in and see her.

A few days before, Father had preached a sermon on the "unforgivable sin," something that we didn't quite understand, but we were quite sure that, whatever it was, we had committed it, and Mother's illness was God's punishment on us. We spent hours on our knees in the schoolroom praying for Mother and ourselves, for forgiveness for we knew not what. Gil, as the oldest, was the only one permitted near Mother's room, and his reports of "buckets of blood" being carried out were all we needed to convince us that Mother was dying. Mother got well in time, but for months she wasn't herself, and as I grew older I learned that she had had a miscarriage and that we had lost a baby brother.

Speaking of sickness, the Chinese were firm believers in always keeping the stomach covered and warm to prevent illness of any kind, and cholera in particular. In cold weather it was not uncommon to see men working bare-chested, but always with their stomachs well protected by their heavily padded pant tops, so perhaps there was something to the theory of the "cholera belt" which was widely used by Westerners in the summer when cholera was prevalent. They were knitted woolen belts about a foot wide, which fit tightly around the middle and were worn at night in case one became uncovered. We as children wore them all the time during the summer months regardless of how hot the night. Cold on the stomach, of course was not the cause of cholera, which is unknown in the United States. It comes about through poor sanitation and polluted water, but the Chinese did not know that. For some reason late July was the worst time for it, when plums were in season. That brought about a saying among the Chinese that, "apricots are harmful to you, peaches are most nourishing, but under plum trees, dead people are buried."

One aspect of Chinese life that we all found fascinating was what to us seemed their casualness in giving names to their children. Surnames were never changed, and the Chinese prided themselves on being able to look back for generations and trace their heritage. However, the giving of personal or given names was somewhat of a haphazard affair. At birth, children were all given what was called a "milk name," and that they kept until they went to school or reached marriageable age. When and if they attended school, the teacher always gave them a school name, something that was done after careful thought. In most cases that name was then used for life. However, many young men, either going into business or some sort of official career, would decide, while keeping their old name, to give themselves a new name that they considered more fitting to their status in life, and that they did at will, without any official interference. In fact, they usually came up with two names for themselves, one as their official or honorific name, and the other for close friends and acquaintances. Their old names would still be used by the family.

Children's "milk" names were decidedly odd by our standards, but made sense to the Chinese. There was so much sickness among children and such a high rate of child mortality that the Chinese gave them names that they thought might ward off the attention of evil spirits or the god of death. Boys were often given girl's names, and were even dressed as girls until they were three or four years of age, the principle being that, since a girl was worth much less than a boy, the evil spirits might be fooled by the name and thus leave the boy alone. Girls being considered of little value, they were usually given disparaging names: brick head; ugly; slave girl; what the dog wouldn't eat. Others were given names intended to be auspicious, such as *ling xiao* (bring a boy), which meant bring a boy when pregnant. Very few girls outside of the large cities were sent to school, in fact in Lingyuan there were no schools for girls apart from the one my Mother established. As girls approached a marriageable age their names would be changed to something sweet-sounding and attractive, such as jade blossom, lotus flower, rose, or beautiful lotus, all with the hope of attracting the attention of some marriage broker who would find a husband for them.

From early childhood I had been called Bobbie by the family. To the Chinese hearing, it sounded like the Chinese words *bao bei*, which meant "treasured object" or "darling baby." That didn't matter to me for the first few years, but then I became aware that it was hardly the name for a boy, so I asked everyone to call me Bob. That still didn't work, as to the Chinese it sounded like the first word of *bao bei*, which now meant "precious," so I wasn't much better off. Later I was very happy when one of our Chinese teachers eventually gave me my school name, *Da En* which meant "great grace."

Our Chinese surname is Da, which has the connotation of having arrived at, reached, or attained a certain goal. It is not a common Chinese surname; in fact, it doesn't appear in the Book of 100 Family Surnames, the *Bai Jia Xing*, but nevertheless it was quite acceptable. When my father arrived in Shanghai in 1903 and was asked what his English name was, the Chinese tried to give him a surname that sounded somewhat similar to his English surname, but was not necessarily a translation of it. In fact, seldom was it possible to come up with a translation of Western surnames, except with a name such as White. When Father told them his name was Tharp, a difficulty arose. The Chinese have no "th" sound in their language, and the closest they can come to pronouncing Tharp is *"sa pu"* which would not be fitting as a surname. As Dad pronounced his name, it sounded to the people of Shanghai like "da," so that was the name they gave him. However, they compromised on his given name, Edwin, by giving him the Chinese name *Yi Wen* which sounds something like it, and meant "righteous and refined."

In China, the surname always comes first, followed by the given name. Americans often have difficulty remembering that. There was a famous incident when President Truman forgot it, and in a radio speech, referring to Generalissimo Chiang Kai-shek of China, Truman spoke of him as: "...my good friend Mr. Shek..."

When it came to naming us children when we reached school age, our head teacher You Bichen, older brother of You Wang our houseboy, was consulted and he named my brother Gil, *Tian En*, which means "heavenly grace." "Grace" is considered a fully appropriate name for boys in China, as witness the well-known and much-admired first premier of the People's Republic of China from 1949 to 1976, Chou En-lai. His name, "grace comes," was the name given him when he first attended a missionary school. He kept it throughout his life.

My older sister Ruth's name in Chinese was *Bao En*, meaning "precious grace," and mine, of course, was *Da En*, "great grace." When it came to naming Barbara, for some reason our teacher called her *Ping An*, "peace." Barbara wasn't overly fond of that, however, and later gave herself the name of *Yu Mei*, which meant "jade plum blossom." As I grew older I felt that my name "great grace" was less than appropriate, so when I was eleven or twelve, I asked an elderly Chinese Christian gentleman to give me a different name.

Mr. Wei was a kindly old man and very well educated. In China, to be asked to do that was considered a great honor, and the old gentleman felt extremely flattered by being consulted. He asked for a few days to think it over.

Taking into consideration my Chinese surname of *Da*, Mr. Wei gave me the name *Fu Tian*, which means "field of good fortune, blessing, or happiness." Thus, combined with my surname *Da*, it means that I have "arrived at the field of happiness." Mr. Wei told me that he had studied my personality and had arrived at that name because of my "outgoing and happy disposition." I certainly found the name much more appropriate than "precious," or "great grace."

While I was still a small child and had barely gotten to know our first compound well, my father bought the one next door. The second compound was equally as large in square footage, if not larger, and had approximately the same number of *jian* in the various buildings. However, the layout was somewhat different. The main building, which fronted onto the street and was practically joined to our own front building, consisted of seven *jian*, the middle one being an entrance for wheeled vehicles. The main entrance was narrower than our original front gate because the size of the *jian* was smaller. Between the large, squared-off stone footings that held the two gates, there was ample room for a Chinese cart to enter, because the axles of the carts were higher than the stone blocks, and thus readily cleared them. When, some years later, I had an automobile and used that gate, the clearance between the two footing blocks was not more than an inch and a half on each side.

From the street, a very short and steep slope led up to the gate. It had the regular eighteen-inch sill, against which the gates were closed, but the sill fitted into slots in the stone footings and was removable. Behind the gate, was a fairly narrow corridor with seven-foot mud walls on each side. These walls enclosed yards for the three *jian* on each side. The three on the left became the residence for two Christian families, and the three *jian* on the right were turned into a girls' school, which my sister Ruth operated with the help of one or two young Chinese women.

Daily, some forty to fifty girls of all ages came there to learn to read and write and to learn about the Christian faith. It was, as I said above, the only girls' school in the city, and at first occasioned considerable criticism on the part of the populace, which held that girls had no business being educated. However, in time, as they realized that an educated girl was much more marriageable, and it was much more likely that a wealthy home could be found for her, the parents were happy to send their girls to the school. After the Japanese took over in 1932, there was even a little Japanese girl who came. All instruction was, of course, in Chinese, but that little girl spoke Chinese quite well when she first came, and very much better when she left.

Father's primary purpose in purchasing the second compound was to have more space for church activities. What had caught his eye was the very large main building, in what could be considered the second courtyard. It was only a three-*jian* building, but the *jian* were exceptionally large and it easily held around three hundred people when it was made into the chapel or meeting hall.

Like the main buildings in the first compound, that building also stood on a platform higher than the courtyard, but in this case, the platform, entirely paved with bricks and with a stone slab border, was not only the full length of the building, but extended out into the courtyard some twenty feet or more. In front of it stood a large old elm tree some seventy feet high and about four feet in diameter at its base. In summer it not only provided shade for the platform, but for the front of the church building as well.

Unlike the buildings in our original compound, all buildings in the second compound were in a very bad state of repair. A crop of grass and weeds grew from between the rows of tiles on the roofs, a sure indicator of leaks. All the roofs had to be replaced, and several of the buildings were so dilapidated that they had to be demolished and rebuilt. One side building at right angles to the large main building in the second courtyard was a case in point. It was a five-*jian* building, and when it was rebuilt it was used as a small meeting hall on weekdays. It required less coal to heat in winter, but it was very hot in the summer because it got all the western sun.

With the main building, Father first tore out the front wall and put in large glass windows and a door at each end. The right-hand door was for the women's side, and the other for the men. Inside they were separated down the middle of the hall by a high wooden partition, the upper part of which was open woodwork and papered. The pulpit was built into the back, or north wall, by cutting through it and building a small shed-roofed building there. From that point the preacher could readily see the entire audience on both sides of the screen, and they in turn could see the preacher, but not each other. Audiences in China had to be segregated in those days.

With the front gates open on Sundays, people could look directly up from the street to the building and could hear the singing. The openness of the place encouraged people to come in and investigate. From Montgomery Ward Father had purchased a large school bell that he had mounted on a tall pole in front of the building next to the tree. When rung on Sunday mornings, it could be heard over most of the city, and had considerable drawing power. We never failed to have big crowds in church on Sundays, and gradually more and more of the people turned to Christianity, although there were problems along the way.

Alongside the main building, which we now called The Hall, and in line with it, was a smaller building on each side. Each consisted of two *jian*, and both were badly in need of repair. Eventually, the one on the left became a room for male visitors (and many years later was turned into the garage for my van). The one on the right was left as it was, with only minimal work done on the roof, and it was used as a storeroom for lumber and a place where Sun Shifu could work when it rained and during the winter months.

Three entrances were cut through the dividing wall from our first compound into the second compound. One of them was right next to the gatekeeper's rooms, the second was in the second courtyard, next to the well, and the third was in the third courtyard right next to our privy, which from that point on had heavy traffic going by it throughout the day, but it was something that couldn't be avoided as there was no other place to cut through.

The third and rearmost courtyard of the second compound was larger than the one we lived in. But there was no main building there, just two, three-*jian* buildings facing south, which stood apart from each other and backed onto the cow yard in our back garden. They were joined by a wall between them. That very quickly came down, and the main route to the back garden was then through that aperture instead of through the original passageway at the far end of our third courtyard main building. Father's next move was to close in that original passageway to the back garden at both ends, making another bedroom out of it. That became my room, and Gil got his own room in the "new" third courtyard, where he got part of the right-hand building when it was renovated, while Father moved his study over to the building on the left, after it, too, had been torn down and completely rebuilt. It was not only in very bad shape, but Father felt that it was so filthy that it possibly harbored diseases.

All that took some time, and as a result of all the remodeling and repair work, we had workmen everywhere for the next several summers. I was delighted, totally fascinated by all that was going on and terribly disappointed when winter came and all work had to stop except for Sun Shifu working away by himself on some project or another.

One of the biggest jobs that Sun Shifu had to undertake was making pews for the new meeting hall. Prior to that, only eight-inch wide, backless benches had been available, but Father felt that the people coming to church deserved more comfort than that, so, from Father's description, Sun Shifu devised a long, narrow pew with a straight back and arm rests at each end. Each would seat six to eight people, depending on the amount of clothing they were wearing in summer or winter. The pews were made of heavy elm wood, and the fact that the seats were two inches thick added to the weight. However, they were not easily moved about.

Sun spent several months making and painting the pews, The only real improvement over the old, backless benches was that they were a bit wider and had a straight back to lean against, but it was very straight and not particularly comfortable. Apart from that, there was no pretense of providing comfort, such as a padded cushion. They were just as hard as the old benches. I didn't particularly like them, because at my age they were too high for me and my feet didn't quite reach the floor. They were, however, certainly an improvement over the old benches in one way. Previously, when people fell asleep on them, they frequently tumbled backward onto the floor or into someone else's lap. The Chinese church members all thought the new pews were grand. Nothing like them had ever been seen in Lingyuan, and people from all over town came to try them out.

With so much construction and repair work going on and all the strange workmen coming into the compound day after day, Father worried about their getting to know the place too well, and that the dogs, several of which we always had around the place, would grow so accustomed to them that they would allow one of them to climb over one of the walls some night and rob us. But it never happened. In all the years that we lived there, we never had a single case of robbery. Not only that, even though all the newly installed Western-style doors had locks and keys, never once did we lock our doors at night. We did have one or two cases of minor theft, but those were committed by one of the servants who got into debt and stole a few things. But the culprits were soon discovered and restitution was quickly made.

Hiring the workmen to rebuild or repair the buildings was always a most interesting procedure.

Usually Father would get two or three well-known masons to come in and bid on the jobs to be done. That was a great deal more satisfactory than hiring the men on a daily wage basis. Just as in America, when a job is on a contract basis, the work is done much faster and there is little sitting around wasting time. While it became the chief mason's job to keep everyone working, it was our responsibility to maintain a close watch to make sure everything was done properly, and for that job, our gatekeeper, old Mr. Hu, was always there.

As a small boy, one of my very best friends was Mr. Hu (pronounced "who"). He and I got along wonderfully well together, probably because he had a boy of just about my own age. Mr. Hu was a tall, extremely dignified gentleman who always had a somber look on his face and rarely smiled. He always dressed in the traditional long blue gown of the gentleman, with a short black coat worn over it. I very rarely saw him without that badge of his primary position as a teacher. His job as gatekeeper was secondary.

Mr. Hu took his responsibilities very seriously indeed. Not only was he gatekeeper, he was also our chief buyer of any commodities we needed to buy in bulk. It was he who watched for the farmers coming into town with fresh eggs or food grains, both of which we used a great deal. He bought all the straw that we needed for the cows. He would watch for the carts hauling coal into the city, or the pack animals carrying charcoal, and it was always he who would stop them and bargain with them, then eventually, when a satisfactory price was arrived at, would bring them into the yard to be weighed with the big "steelyard" kept for that purpose.

All in all, Mr. Hu was a very busy man, and I spent long hours as a little boy following him around, watching him while he watched over me. When we had workmen on the job, he was always there to keep an eye on them while his wife took over the job of watching the front gate. The exception was Sun Shifu, who never needed watching. We always trusted him to work conscientiously on his own, and he never let us down.

Once a head mason had been found and a contract price had been agreed upon, it was up to the mason to provide the men for the job. Usually, when the Chinese hired someone to do a job for them, meals were a part of the bargain, but we always made the head mason assume that responsibility, feeding his men at his own house, but at our expense.

Seldom did one of the masons have more than one or two regular assistants or apprentices, nor were more than that needed. They did, on the other hand, require a considerable number of temporary day laborers. There were many jobs for those unskilled men: mixing the mud, carrying the dirt, chopping up the straw that was mixed in the mud, digging the trenches for footings, and carrying the bricks, tiles and mortar, as well as cleaning off the old bricks from a torn-down house or wall.

Hiring day laborers was in itself an interesting procedure. Every town had what was called a *renshi* or "human market," In Lingyuan it was on Small West Street, which ran parallel to the street on which we lived. There was a large open area at one point, where, early in the morning before daybreak, various groups would assemble. Among others one could find a vegetable market, a grain market, an animal market, and the human market. There, on any given morning in the darkness before dawn, dozens, and sometimes hundreds of men of all ages would line up hoping someone would come along and hire them for the day. Many were farmers who had walked for miles from their homes in the countryside. The market was in pitch darkness, and the head mason would walk up and down the line carrying his flickering lantern. Those who were familiar to him, or whom he had used before and found to be satisfactory, he would pull out of the line. He would then go back and look them all over once again, looking for men who appeared sufficiently strong for the job, even checking their hands for calluses to make sure they were used to manual labor, or checking their arm or leg muscles. If a good man was needed for carrying, his shoulder would be checked to see if he had the callous there caused by the carrying pole.

Finally, when he had all the men he wanted, he would lead them back to his home, where his wife had cooked up a big breakfast. When the men had eaten their fill, they were brought to our place to start work, and by that time it would be just barely daylight.

At noon they would all troop back to the head mason's house for the noon meal, and again at dusk, when the day's work ended. If a man had proved himself well that first day, he would be told to come back again in the morning; otherwise, the whole procedure of hiring would be repeated.

During the day there were two regular breaks for tea, one in mid-morning and another in the afternoon. At those times Mr. Hu would bring around huge quantities of a good quality tea for the men to drink. In order to keep the men in a good mood and ensure quality work, Father would frequently have Mr. Hu go out and buy a few pounds of cakes for the men to enjoy at their breaks. In addition to the rest periods, the workmen took a noontime siesta when they came back from their noon meal. For an hour or so, everyone would find a shady spot and drop off to sleep.

As a footnote it is of interest to comment that while in old China the siesta period was a nationwide practice for workmen and laborers, when the Communist regime came along in 1949 it became part of the way of life for every member of society, "all men and women being equal." The practice was so widely in effect that at times trains would stop for an hour so the crew could rest, and plane schedules were so arranged that they would land for an hour for the same reason. The Chinese government finally came to its senses and abolished the practice in 1984, but from what I hear from Chinese coming here recently from the mainland, they achieved only minimal success.

Another of Mr. Hu's jobs was to waylay and bring in the itinerant "tinkers" we employed several times a year. I call them "tinkers" for want of a better word. Their job wasn't repairing pots and pans; rather it was repairing broken chinaware, glassware, or crockery of any sort. Paul Theroux in his recent book "Riding the Iron Rooster," writes that China is "...a great society for mending things..." and nothing could be closer to the truth. The Chinese throw nothing away. Except in the large cities, you won't see trash piles as we know them. In the rural areas, everything is saved either to be mended or to be used again in some other form. The only things we knew of that were thrown away were the short handles to the large straw brushes the Chinese used for sweeping their floors. They believed that evil spirits were swept up and lodged in the handle. For that reason, when the brush was worn down and only the handle was left, it was thrown out rather than burned under the cooking pot, as burning might release the bad spirits into the room. Of course, when someone else not connected with the family found the brush handle, there was no reason why they couldn't use it for fuel. Any evil spirits that might be in it belonged to someone else.

We employed the tinkers only two or three times a year. For months prior to their arrival, everyone in the compound would save his broken chinaware or glassware. Every little chip was saved, and it was a rare piece of crockery that those men couldn't salvage.

They arrived carrying a small stool on one end of their carrying pole and on the other end a miniature "chest of drawers." Tiny drawers and larger drawers, and in them an assortment of small and large cramps or "staples" made of either brass or iron that ranged in size from approximately one-quarter of an inch up to an inch or more. They had a flattened back, about one-eighth of an inch wide, and short, stubby, but sharply pointed "legs" approximately one-sixteenth or one-thirty-second of an inch in length.

Each man carried with him a tiny anvil, a variety of small hammers, and a manual drill operated by leather thongs wrapped around the body of the drill and attached to a bow that was moved back and forth.

Setting to work, they would painstakingly piece the broken article together, using a cement that they mixed from a white powder, the ingredients of which were a trade secret. When that was accomplished, they bound everything in position with string.

The next step was to drill tiny holes on each side of the cracks, spacing them the exact distance apart to accommodate the staples. The staples would be placed about an inch or so apart. When all holes were drilled, the tiny staples would be hammered into place and the job was complete.

The staples only cost a few coppers each, a copper at that time being worth probably one-tenth of a U.S. cent or even less. We always had the men use brass staples because the iron ones, although cheaper, would eventually rust out after repeated washings. Very large staples were used to mend the huge water gang, which burst if not emptied when the weather got cold and ice formed inside. In addition there were other large pottery bowls the size of the old American galvanized washtub. Occasionally those needed repair, and thanks to the tinkers, they could be repaired and used indefinitely. The tinkers' skill wasn't limited to pottery. On more than one occasion they repaired iron stove lids which either broke from the heat or from being dropped. Repaired with the iron staples, they usually held up for several years.

At least once a year we hired a sheet-metal man. He, too, carried all his tools and a stool on a carrying pole. He usually came with a small supply of sheet metal, consisting of flattened tin cans or five-gallon oil cans. From those he would make a large variety of cooking pots or other utensils.

We needed him primarily to make stovepipes. For years they were made from empty five-gallon kerosene cans. They usually rusted out within a year. Later my father managed to buy a roll of galvanized sheet metal at the coast. After that the stove pipes lasted considerably longer. In the compound there were some twenty-five or thirty stoves. Some of the stovepipes were fifteen or more feet long to take advantage of every bit of heat. Those men were so good they could fabricate a stovepipe that was in every way comparable to one made by machinery, with tight joints and tapered to fit one to the next. Even elbows were no problem. They did it all with a pair of shears, a short pole over which to bend the metal, and a flat piece of wood used to pound the joints.

One of their specialties was the making of what the Chinese called a *kuaihu*, or "fast kettle." They were universally used to heat water for tea and practically every home had one. They were much faster than any gas or electric kettle that I've ever seen.

The principle of the kettle was very simple. A base made of sheet metal, cut and crimped together to form an inverted cone with a flat bottom and an opening in the side at the bottom to admit air, with a grate about three inches from the bottom. The top, or small end of the cone, was open and was approximately two inches across. The cone was the "fire box." The kettle itself was even more ingenious. Made in a double layer, the outer layer had perpendicular sides, but the inside layer was also conically shaped to fit over the fire box. Tapering from a soldered seam at the bottom, the two sides of the water compartment ended at the top, less than an inch apart. The kettles held just enough water to fill a teapot, and although made in larger sizes, the smaller one was by far the most popular. They came complete with a lid to keep out the ash and smoke, a spout, and a handle. Filled with water, the kettle was placed over the fire box, and a fire of either twigs or grass would be started. The draft was so good and the heat generated so intense, even a couple of sheets of tightly rolled-up newspaper were sufficient to bring the water to a boil in seconds. The only disadvantage of the ingenious contraption was that because of the smoke it had to be used out-doors. However, when it was raining, the Chinese thought nothing of lighting the kettles indoors. Who cared about a little smoke? Were it not for that slight drawback, I am sure these "fast kettles" would be a big hit even in the Western world.

As a child, I would watch intently as the men practiced their trade. Itinerant barbers also came by once or twice a month as the men in the compound got their haircuts, or rather, got their heads shaved. There was one barber in the city who claimed to be able to give Western-style haircuts. He would come once a month and give Father and us boys a haircut, although in the hot summer months, we, too, had our heads shaved for comfort. Because of the many skin diseases around, Father would be sure to have him disinfect his tools before starting to work. The man had a little shop in the center of town, but thought nothing of closing up shop to come when "invited" to do so. He was a very pleasant sort of fellow and just as garrulous as most barbers seem to be in America and elsewhere.

That was the world of my early years, and although largely confined to the compounds and back garden, there were at any given moment anywhere from twenty to forty people in the two compounds and always some sort of activity going on. There was plenty for a little boy to watch and wonder at. When bored with the compound or the garden, I would stand outside the front gate, under the watchful eye of Mr. Hu, watching the world go by. Frequently I became the object of curiosity and a small crowd would gather to look at the little fair-haired foreigner. When that happened, Mr. Hu would take the opportunity to preach to them and invite them in to sit down on the bench he had just inside the gate.

Dozens of beggars came by each day. Many of them were professionals who chose that way of life rather than working. Although the majority of them were very deserving of help, to start feeding them would have been a bad mistake. There were literally hundreds in the city, and once the word got around, we would have been besieged, so it was our policy to welcome them in to the church services, especially on cold days, but not to hand out food or money.

Mr. Hu, though, was very tender-hearted and gentle. He had a practiced eye for the truly sad and deserving cases. Many times I watched him surreptitiously hand out food from his own meager larder, particularly if the recipients were a family or a widow with several small children. Mrs. Hu would remonstrate with him when he did so, but he would simply smile (the few times that I saw him do so), and quietly go on sharing again the next time he saw someone he felt was truly worthy of help. I loved Mr. Hu deeply, and it was a very sad day when he died. For those few years that I knew him, I was proud to have him as a friend.

Minted in 1375, this Ming dynasty coin apparently played a role in the tribute system. Characters on the obverse side center translate as "8th Year of (the reign of Emperor) Hung Wu," and the characters on the outside translate as "Annual Tribute (offered by a vassal state or protectorate). Bestowed by Imperial Order." Minted in both copper and silver.

Going from one courtyard to another.

One of the courtyards.

Vendors on the street in front of the gate for vehicles into the compound.

The Gospel Hall yard. The hole into the room in the center is used to stoke up a fire to heat up the "kang."

Barbara's chicken run.

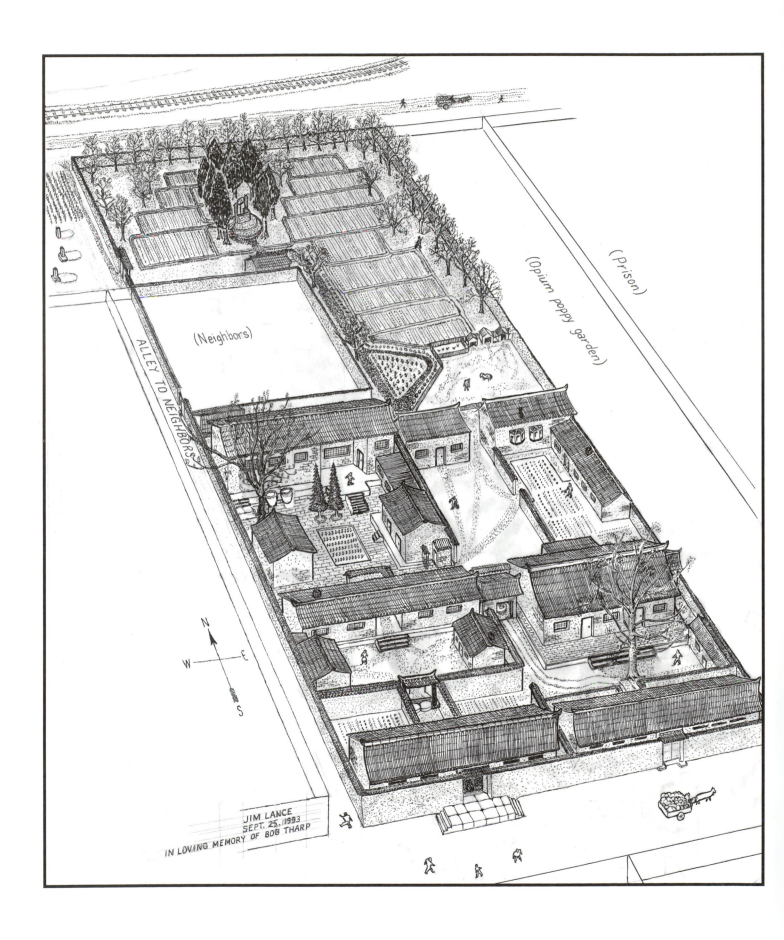

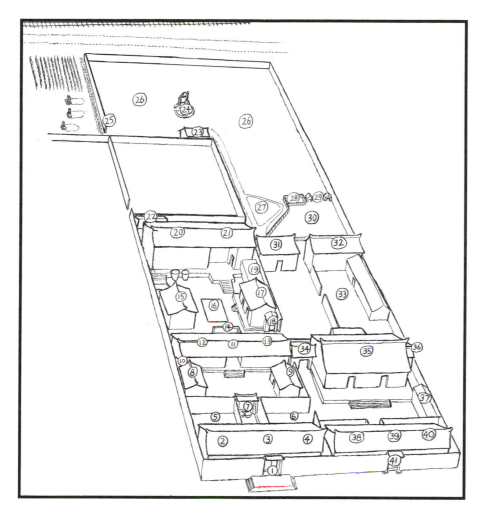

This drawing shows the compound approximately as it was when we last saw it.

1: The front gate of the original compound.

2, 3, 4: These are parts of a 5-jian building. No. 2 was housing for orphan girls. No. 3 was a covered passageway to the front gate; actually, it is the middle jian of the 5-jian building. No. 4 was living quarters for the gatekeeper and his wife.

5 and 6: Vegetable gardens.

7: Ornate gateway between the first and second courtyards. It was mounted on a heavy stone base which was elaborately carved. Where the base of each door stood, the stone was carved in the shape of two large drums with ornamental borders.

8: The south end of this building was a waiting room for people visiting Mother's dispensary. The doorway to the building was through its east wall, and the doorway to the dispensary itself was through a wall between the waiting room and the dispensary. In the dispensary along the north wall were Mother's medicine cabinets.

9: The doorway shown led into a kitchen on the south side. A doorway in the kitchen led to another waiting room on the north side of this building.

10: Coal shed.

11, 12, 13: This was originally a conventional 5-jian building. Dad had the middle jian (No. 11) made into a covered passageway. The room on the west end was our kitchen, and Dad's study occupied the next room, between the kitchen and the passageway. The first jian on the right side of the passageway was a guest room and the other jian was used for storage. At one point, Dad had the passageway made more narrow than shown here, adding space to the rooms on either side of it.

14: The spirit screen.

15: The first two jian on the south side of this 3-jian building contained a guestroom, and one jian on the north end is what was usually our "sewing room" occupied daily by Mrs. Wu. Doors from outside to both rooms were through the east wall.

16: Mother's flower garden.

17: Two jian on the north end of this 3-jian building was our schoolroom when we were children. Gil's and my bedroom occupied one jian on the south end. Later, after acquiring the second compound, Dad added an additional bedroom to the main house, which became mine, and added a bedroom for Gil in No. 32.

18: Toilet. An outhouse, actually.

19: Covered passageway between the main house and the schoolroom, something Dad added to make life more pleasant. Mother's pantry for spices, dried fruits, and so on, lined the wall on one side, and windows looking out to the courtyard were on the other side.

20 and 21: The main house. This building originally was a conventional 5-jian building, but Dad's remodeling changed it a lot. At first, Dad converted the jian on the west side into a covered passageway to the garden area in back. Later he changed this to an addi-

tional bedroom. In the end, there were three bedrooms on the west end (No. 20), and the dining and living rooms (No. 21) occupied the rest (from where the front porch begins behind the spruce trees all the way east to the wall of the first compound). Shown in front of the house are the two vats for storing water used on Mother's flower garden.

22: Shed with alleyway to and from the garden area.

23: The wash house.

24: The well.

25: Our back gate. Outside the gate was a footpath going to the road in back, several graves, a sorghum field, and a small shrine.

26: Vegetable gardens.

27: A flower garden.

28: The chicken run.

29: Two cow sheds and a shed for fodder.

30: Cow yard.

31: A 3-jian building divided into a covered passageway in the middle and two storage rooms at each end. Dad moved his study to this building at one point.

32: This became Eva's and my living quarters after we were married. The north end of No. 31 originally was a 3-jian building, two jian of which was another guest room and which served as Gil's bedroom just before he left China in 1928; the remaining jian was used for grain storage. We remodeled this building and attached new rooms to it southward along the compound wall.

33: Vegetable garden.

34: This was a 2-jian building, used most of the period as a room for male visitors. Later, I used it as a garage for the van.

35: This 3-jian building, larger than most 3-jian buildings, was our church meeting hall. We called it simply, "The Hall." The addition in back held the pulpit. This was necessary so that both sexes in the congregation (they were divided by a wall between them) could see the person speaking.

36: This was a 2-jian building, used for storing lumber and as a carpentry shop for Sun Shifu.

37: We called this the "Small Hall." It was used for prayer meetings and other small meetings during the week. At one time it was used as sleeping quarters for refugees during one of China's revolutions.

38, 39, and 40: This building originally was a conventional 7-jian building, but the middle jian (No. 38) was used as a covered passageway for as long as I know. This middle jian probably served as a covered passageway from the time the building was first built, as this was the entrance to this compound. Most of the time over the years Nos. 37 and 39 were guest rooms, but in later years we used them as a school for girls.

41: The front gate of the second compound.

Lumber Saw

Sawing Lumber

Chinese Carpenter's Chalk Line Box

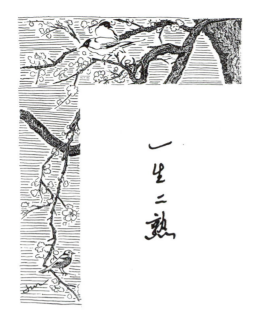

一生二熟

Yi sheng er shu.

The first time all is strange,
the second time it is familiar.

- Chinese Peasant Saying.

Chapter Five
Paper Ceilings, Wooden Floors – and Buried Babies?

Something had to be done about the paper ceilings and the brick floors in our living quarters. Father decided to tackle the floors first, but that turned out to be a mistake. In any event, he and everyone else was thoroughly fed up with the brick floors, because the bricks, although kiln-fired, were relatively soft and were badly worn where traffic was heaviest. Walking on them created a lot of unpleasant dust, even though, up to that time, the floors had been covered with mats woven from dried and flattened sorghum stalks, a truly remarkable and versatile material.

Sorghum is grown in the United States and is described in my dictionary as: "A cereal grass, having broad, corn-like leaves and a tall, pithy stem bearing the grain in a dense terminal cluster." The description is quite apt. However, the sorghum I've seen in America grows only to a height of about three or four feet. Sorghum is extremely hardy, and not subject to blight. It also does well with a minimum of rainfall, although, in those circumstances it doesn't grow quite

as tall, nor are the heads quite as full. In North China, in a good year, it may grow anywhere from ten to fifteen feet, and is appropriately called by the Chinese, *gaoliang* or "tall grain."

It is used widely throughout Northern China as food both for humans and animals. It came in two varieties, white and red. The white was mainly used for cereal by the middle and poorer classes and the red for animal feed. However, in times of famine or food shortages of any kind, the red sorghum was consumed readily by humans, and we used both often as a breakfast cereal. Another use for sorghum was, of course, the making of a very potent wine with high alcoholic content.

Growing as it does to such a height, sorghum changes the landscape completely in summer. When traveling, where the main road wound between sorghum fields, one might as well have been in a jungle; all familiar landmarks were obliterated.

As children, our greatest delight was to take walks

through those fields, following the little paths the farmers used as shortcuts. We would walk in semi-darkness, unable to see the sun, hearing only the sound of the wind blowing through the leaves. There was always a sense of delightful terror until that moment when we came to the edge of the field and stepped into brilliant sunshine. However, sorghum fields were the perfect hiding place for bandits, and travelers always felt uneasy when the sorghum was tall in late July and August. That, coincidentally, was also the rainy season, so for both reasons travel was usually minimal during that period.

Since the sorghum stalks were almost as highly prized as the grain, the taller they grew the more valuable they were. For that reason, the farmers stripped off the lower leaves, believing it improved growth. The stripped leaves were not wasted; they made wonderful fodder for domestic animals. In fact, along the roadsides, the leaves were so tempting to passing horses and mules that farmers invariably grew a crop of castor oil plants as a buffer zone. Animals won't eat the leaves of the castor oil plant, perhaps instinctively knowing what it would do to them. However, the crude black oil produced from the plants was widely used by the peasants as lamp oil, even though it produced very little light, was very smoky, and had a strong odor. Additionally, it was used as a lubricant for cart wheels and the axles of wheelbarrows. Sometimes the farmers used it in cooking. I've often eaten food cooked with castor oil in farmers' homes. The food tasted terrible, but it was all they had, and of course, the expected results inevitably followed.

When the sorghum was harvested, it was the custom to cut the green stalks about eight inches above the ground. The stubble left behind, with its bushy roots, is prized by the poorer class as fuel and is meticulously gleaned. That was a job usually carried out by women and children. When we saw them doing that, we were inevitably reminded of the Biblical story of Ruth gleaning in the fields of Boaz. (Ruth, chapter 2.)

Usually the stubble was left in the fields to dry before it was dug up, thus reducing the weight. However, the slanted cut made by the harvesters, left a dangerously sharp point that was a real hazard to pedestrians. As children, we were warned to avoid the fields when the stubble was drying. Each year my parents had to treat any number of injuries caused by people who had fallen onto the sharp points.

In the past thirty-plus years, much has been said by the Communist regime in China about the rapaciousness and greed of the Chinese landowners in the "old days" and of their callous disregard for the poor, particularly the tenants on their lands. However, at harvest time it was our experience that the big landowners deliberately left the stubble in the fields for the poor to glean. It must be said, however, that was not entirely from an altruistic motive. To dig up the stubble and knock out the dirt from the roots is a back-breaking and extremely time-consuming job, and hired laborers had the habit of making that kind of work last indefinitely.

When sorghum stalks are cut down, the heavy heads of grain are removed, and the stalks are tied in bundles of about fifty or so, using a flattened stalk as a tie. Since they are very heavy, they, too, are left in the fields to dry in the hot sun. When dry, they become a new product, which the Chinese call *shujie*, *shu* being the generic name for sorghum and *jie* simply meaning "stalk."

While neither as tough or hard as bamboo, nor as versatile, sorghum is nevertheless to the Northern Chinese what bamboo is to the Southerners, an invaluable asset with multitudinous uses. One of the most common of those uses was for fencing. Every farmhouse or village building had its *shujie* fence; standing high and thick, it was impenetrable to animals and impervious to the highest winds. Any thief trying to cut his way through the hard and brittle stalks during the night would readily be heard by the householder. Unfortunately, the material tended to rot in the summer rains and the fences never lasted more than a couple of years. Even then, however, the discarded fencing material was valuable as fuel, or, in the worst case, as fertilizer, something not possible with bamboo.

Shujie was a marvelous product in more ways than one. In the fall, when the stalks were first brought in from the fields in cart-loads, the price was at its lowest, and Father used to buy at least five or ten loads, since we used so much of it. It was much valued for fuel in cooking, and Lao San always used a lot on top of the vegetable pit for insulation before piling on a thick layer of earth. For us children, the arrival of the *shujie* carts was a momentous occasion because of all the fun we had with it.

The stalks, tied in large bundles, were stored out-doors in an upright position, leaning at an angle against a blank wall. At the base, this formed at the back a most challenging and delightfully intriguing tunnel that we found irresistible, and which would keep us occupied for hours. It was not without its hazards, though, because the dried leaves had extremely sharp edges, and many were the small cuts that we received as we crawled through in the near-total darkness, but it was worth it.

When we tired of that game there were always others. The topmost piece of the stalk was long, straight and slender, about the thickness of a pencil, and often almost three feet in length. Like bamboo, the sorghum stalk is divided into segments at about one foot intervals, with a sort of knuckle. At the "knuckles" (unlike bamboo) the stalks could be broken off quite cleanly. We used to break off a quantity of those slender topmost stems (if they hadn't already been taken by the farmers for other uses), picking the ones that were the straightest. We then took a segment near the base of the stalk, where it was thicker and broke it off. With a sharp knife we would cut off a piece about two inches long, near the knuckle. Inside was a pithy substance, and when the long, slender piece was inserted into the short piece, one had a perfectly straight arrow with a head on it. Unless it hit a child in the eye, it was perfectly safe and guaranteed to fly true. We were taught that trick by Lao San, who also made us bows. We became expert in shooting at still targets, such as trees. Cats, dogs and birds in the area were all fair game, I am ashamed to say. However, we never managed to kill anything.

But *shujie* wasn't merely useful for making toys. Far from it. What the peasants didn't sell, they used for a variety of purposes in addition to fencing and fuel. Before the stalks became too dry and brittle, they broke off the topmost piece from each stalk. When dry, those were made into large, circular lids to cover not only the cooking pots, but also the water *gang*. That was done by weaving the sticks together with fine hemp string in a crisscross pattern. The lids, when finished, were ideal for keeping steam in the cooking pots and for keeping dirt out of the water vats.

The long, thicker stalks had many uses. For one of them the peasants stripped off the leaves, carefully cleaned each stalk, then split them lengthwise, flat-tening each half with either a stone roller or heavy mallet, then scraped off the pulp from the inner side.

The flattened stalks would then be woven into large rectangular mats, usually about six feet wide, and varying in length from ten to twelve or even fifteen feet or more. They were called *kangxi* and were specifically made to fit on top of the dried mud on the *kang*, or brick beds. Rolled into a tight roll, they were light and easily carried, and every fall one would see the farmers coming to market, carrying several of them for sale. Each New Year's Day everyone put a new one on the *kang*, so sales were always good. Spread on the *kang*, they made a smooth, hard, and shiny surface, fairly readily cleaned and for the most part devoid of sharp edges that could hurt tiny hands or feet. Making the *kangxi* was an early winter home-craft activity for most farmers, and everyone seemed to know how to make them.

It was *kangxi* that we used extensively on our brick floors for a number of years. They concealed the bricks, which were just loosely set in sand, and, because the bricks were porous and gave off a lot of dust as we walked over them with our leather-soled shoes, the mats helped to keep down the dust. At the same time, their bright reflective surface helped to brighten the rooms. However, they, too, had their drawbacks. They tended to break down under heavy traffic, particularly with our leather-soled shoes constantly pounding them, and that made them dangerous to walk on with bare feet. They were easy to sweep, but at the same time, with their open weave, they tended to collect the dirt that was being swept up, only to later re-distribute it as they were walked on. It was an endless cycle, and we had to change them frequently.

To a large extent we covered the floors with throw rugs and carpets, but they didn't keep out the cold and damp from the bricks underneath. So my Father's dream was to install wooden floors throughout. That, however, was easier said than done, and nothing like it had even been heard of before in Lingyuan.

Buying wood in China in those days was no easy task. There were no convenient lumberyards with pre-sawn boards and no forests in the area from which to select and cut down suitable trees. Again, like buying a house, one had to spread the word about being in the market to buy logs and await the results.

Father first consulted Sun Shifu about it. To Sun, that was a whole new ball game. Wooden floors? He had never heard of them, and I am sure he was unable to conceive of such a wasteful use of lumber. However, he was very enthusiastic as he set about measuring the rooms and estimating the amount of board feet that would be needed. Soon after, he followed up on reports of logs available in the surrounding villages, going in person to make his purchases and bringing back the logs on farm carts.

Good quality wood was almost impossible to find in China a few years after the revolution of 1911. When Father arrived there in 1903, the mountains and hills of Jehol Province were heavily forested with pine and cedar. But after the revolution of 1911, not only were transportation and government administration badly disrupted, but also law and order broke down for such a considerable period of time that the populace began to cut down the forests for fuel. By the time I was five or six and began to notice such things, some sixteen years had elapsed, and the mountainsides were completely devoid of vegetation. When traveling, the few trees of any kind that we saw usually signaled either a village or a graveyard, and the only pine or cedar trees were in the occasional burial plots, temple grounds, or in people's back yards.

Other than those, the most common trees were the elm, which grew quite large and had relatively hard wood, or the poplar and willow, both of which were soft woods and usually grew extensively only in proximity to a stream or river, and then only if there was a village or farm hamlet nearby with people to protect them.

Sun told Father that elm wood was too expensive for such a large project, and suggested *yangshu* (poplar). It's a very soft wood, hardly suitable for flooring, but since there was little in the way of an alternative, that was what he bought, and the cartloads that came in bore logs in all shapes, sizes and lengths, most of them green and recently cut.

Sun brought in a couple of helpers and they stripped the bark from the logs. Next, the logs had to be marked for saw cuts. The Chinese equivalent of a chalk-line is an open, shoe-shaped wooden container with a small section at one end filled with chopped-up hemp shreds, saturated with lamp-black, mixed with water and glue. A thin cord was run from the outside through this mixture to the other end of the "shoe," where a small windlass or spool, with a metal handle on the outside, was used to wind up the excess cord. The devices couldn't be purchased anywhere. Rather, each was hand-crafted by the individual carpenter, and each was a work of art. Although the same basic design was used, each man tried to outdo his competitors either in the overall size and shape or in the intricacy of the carving that appeared on the sides. The one Sun had made was so beautiful and unique it could have been a museum piece.

With that marking device, the carpenters very carefully snapped black longitudinal lines approximately one inch apart on each of the logs. They then set up an A-frame, standing about seven feet high, and hoisting the logs onto it one at a time, one end in the air and the other on the ground, commenced sawing the boards.

It was a long and tedious process. Sun balanced himself on the top of the sloping log, and his chief helper, Liu, stood underneath. The saw was approximately seven feet in length, and like all Chinese saws, it had a frame shaped like a horizontally stretched-out "H." The two end pieces and the middle cross-piece were of wood. The narrow saw blade was at the bottom of the "H," and across the top of the "H," a length of thin rope was strung back and forth. A short length of wood was stuck between the strands of rope to twist it as tightly as necessary in order to produce further tension on the blade.

The blade had teeth pointing both ways from the middle. In that way, regardless of the direction in which it was pulled or pushed, it was sawing. That general type of saw, in a variety of sizes, was not only common to China but also to some other Far Eastern countries, as well as the Middle East, and they didn't look too different from saws used in the early days of America. The Japanese were different. Their version of the saw had a wide, tapering blade, about two feet in length, with saw teeth on both edges, usually different sizes. The saw was always pulled toward the operator. Although most people found it clumsy, the Japanese were satisfied with it.

As the two men sawed the logs, it was a toss-up as to which man had the better deal. Sun on top, besides having to constantly maintain his balance, had to pull the saw toward him in an upward direction, and that was hard work. Liu, on the bottom, pulled downward, a much easier task, but all the sawdust fell onto his head and upturned face. Of course, there were no such things as goggles in those days available for him to use. Liu had my greatest sympathy over those several weeks that it took to saw out the boards, but I never heard him complain.

Liu, incidentally, was an interesting individual. Much taller than Sun Shifu, he still wore his hair long and braided into a queue, or "pigtail" in the manner of the old Manchu Empire days of China. Originally, the queue had been imposed on all Chinese men by the Manchus as a sign of subservience, but in time they had become comfortable with it and found it to be fashionable. Although with the coming of the revolution, most younger men shaved their heads, many men, especially the more conservative ones, retained the style. They had never known anything different. Liu's "pigtail" reached below his waist, but when he was working, he always kept it coiled around the top of his head like an open-topped cap. It always fascinated me how much sawdust would collect on the crown of his head as he sawed those logs.

Unfortunately, Liu suffered from leprosy. It was still in the early stages, but nonetheless his face, hands and arms showed large areas of white scaly growth. It was apparently quite painless, and like many other diseases, there was so much of it around that none of the Chinese gave it a second thought. My parents, however, were at first very much concerned, thinking it might be contagious. But after reading about leprosy in their medical books, they concluded that if we avoided touching any of his tools and had no actual physical contact with him, we were relatively safe, and we were so warned.

I got to know Liu very well over the next few years since he frequently came as Sun's helper. A most gracious and dignified man, very self-assured, proud of his trade and aware that he was good at it. He also had an excellent sense of humor. During the tea and rest breaks he would entertain me with stories or teach me Chinese songs. In those days, little was known about leprosy and there was no place he could be sent for treatment. As the disease became worse, he began to lose parts of his fingers and toes. Eventually, he died, while still a relatively young man. I was about ten at the time and grieved over the loss of a very good friend.

When the boards had all been sawn, they had to be planed on one side and on both edges. The wood was far from dry, so each board had to be dried over a bed of hot embers, a painstaking and time-consuming process. Finally, the day came when they actually were ready to be put in place.

Father decided to start with our main living room, which was always called the "dining room." All furniture was moved into an adjoining room while the brick floor was torn up, and about six or eight inches of soil was removed from underneath. During that process, we found a number of artifacts, mostly small shards of pottery, but there were also a few ancient coins. They meant nothing to me at the time, but years later, when I began to collect coins, I wished I had kept them; they might have been both rare and valuable.

Father had to show the men how to lay rough-hewn cross beams to support the floor. Strings were drawn across the room in both directions to find the proper level, and the beams were placed on rocks to avoid contact with the earth and help prevent rot. All that was very new to Sun and his helpers, but they set to work enthusiastically. Nailing down the boards turned out to be a work of art, and a study in patience at which the Chinese excelled. Father had purchased a keg of ordinary Western-style box nails in Tientsin, and those were also quite new to the carpenters. The standard Chinese nail was square, about one-quarter of an inch square at the top and tapering to a blunt point. Each was individually hand-made using the poorest of iron, with no two exactly alike, and they bent or broke easily. In fact, the Chinese have a saying: *"Hao tie bu nian ding, hao ren bu dang bing,"* which translates as: "Good iron is never used for nails, and a good man never becomes a soldier." To their way of thinking, why use good metal for a nail which, after being pounded into the wood, won't be seen again.

The Chinese never waste anything that could be saved for some other use. So, rather than saw the boards all to one specific length and width — as we would have done and with considerable waste — they sawed the boards in the shapes of the original logs. Not only were the boards of varying lengths, they also varied greatly in width, and to make things more difficult, a great many of them were wide at one end and narrow at the other. Each board that was nailed down had to be planed and re-planed to fit to the one before it. For an impatient little boy watching, it was a long and tedious process. Putting down that floor could be compared to working out a most difficult jigsaw puzzle without a picture for reference. For my Father, who was paying for the carpenters' time, it must have been an equally trying period, even though their pay was much less than one American dollar per day.

Finally, after several weeks of work, the floor was finished and I shall never forget the thrill of running around with bare feet on what seemed to me a huge expanse of flooring, so clean and level. The nail heads had all been sunk, the holes filled with a putty-like mixture made from pipe clay and glue. All knot-holes had been similarly filled, so the floor was actually a mosaic, not only of various-sized boards, with seams running at different angles, some even curved back to back, but also was a patchwork of white spots of varying sizes that forever showed through the tung oil varnish that was later applied. But who cared! We had a beautiful wooden floor, the first of its kind in Lingyuan. People came from all over town to look and admire, and everyone had to remove their shoes before being allowed to walk on it. Sun and Liu stood proudly by their handiwork, but as the strangers paced about, stamping their feet to hear the unusual hollow sound, disaster struck.

Up to that point in our life in Lingyuan, the people had been friendly to the missionaries in their midst, or, if not exactly friendly, had at least been tolerant of us foreigners. No one showed real opposition to the preaching of Christianity, and crowds thronged daily to the meeting hall that we had downtown on East Street, where Father conducted a daily medical dispensary for the men, while Mother operated her own for the women and children in our West Street compound. However, it was still only a few years after the Boxer "trouble" as it was then referred to, and the stiff punishments that had been imposed on the Chinese Empire by the allied troops who put down the rebellion still rankled with many Chinese.

No one knows how the rumor started. Perhaps it was started by some petty official who felt he had been wronged by the foreigners. In any case, suddenly the word was out that women in great numbers had been seen going into the "Gospel Church" on West Street with their babies, but no babies had been seen when the women came out. Obviously, the babies had

somehow been disposed of, and where else but under the new floor? In their thinking, that had to be the reason the foreigners had installed the unheard-of contraption.

Events quickly took a very ugly turn. The people who had laughed and exclaimed with pleasure as they first viewed the floor now looked at us with hatred in their eyes. Huge crowds assembled outside our front gate shouting: "Death to the Foreign Devils." Rocks were thrown at the closed and tightly barred front doors and some through the gatekeeper's windows. Fortunately, no one attempted to batter their way in, although there was a great deal of banging on the door with fists and sticks. Nevertheless the trouble persisted for almost an entire day. At one point we closed and barred the doors for the gateway to the second courtyard when the battering on the front gate became too insistent. Finally, Father climbed over our back wall and then our neighbor's wall, and secretly made his way out to see the magistrate in the Yamen to ask for help.

The magistrate, fully aware of what was going on, was at first less than friendly and was obviously not willing to become involved. However, since by that time the crowds had backed up to the very doors of the Yamen itself, Father eventually was able to convince him that, if the riot continued, our lives were in danger, and in the end he would be held responsible. Father suggested that the magistrate should form a small committee of leading citizens and bring them in to view the floor. He offered to tear up any portion of it for their inspection, or, for that matter, to tear up the whole floor so they could look underneath.

The noise continued all that night and into the second day. Finally the magistrate arrived in his sedan chair, accompanied by his bodyguards and followed by about twenty town elders and dignitaries who solemnly (and somewhat sheepishly) paraded around the dining room floor, stamping their feet and muttering under their breath.

The magistrate himself, an educated man who had traveled outside the province and had seen wooden floors before, knew that it was all a farce, but to maintain "face" for himself and his people, he finally pointed to a certain spot on the floor and asked that the boards be removed.

Poor Sun and Liu, who had stood by terrified throughout the incident, hurriedly tore up a section of the boards. A spade was produced and a token hole was dug to prove that no babies were buried there, and the incident seemed to be closed. However, for months thereafter and even years later, when Mother, for some reason or other brought one of the Chinese women up into our quarters to visit or for some medical treatment, it was not uncommon to have the woman suddenly get down on her knees, crawl under the bed, and pound on the floor just to make sure there were no babies buried there.

After several months, all the floors of the other rooms in the third courtyard were boarded without further incident, and the "buried babies" affair was apparently forgotten by everyone except us. Thereafter, whenever we were about to start some project that might be considered unusual or different, we made certain it was well publicized beforehand, and that a number of influential and well-informed citizens knew about it.

Up to that point we had had paper ceilings in all the rooms and they were the bane of our lives. The paper was pasted onto a *shujie* framework using a paste made of ordinary flour and water. That was very attractive to rats and mice, and every ceiling had its colony of rodents. How they got up there in the first place was anyone's guess, but at night they often kept us awake, running around squealing as they bit each other's tails or gnawed on the paste. Each day we awoke to see new holes in the ceilings, and almost every day the ceilings had to be patched because we were afraid the rats or mice would fall through the holes onto us. As it was, it was not uncommon to find a dead rodent on the floor. On one occasion, when my brother Gil and I were sharing a room, about ten baby mice fell through a hole directly onto my bed. They all survived the fall, and the two of us spent the next hour trying to round them up. Occasionally hornets would also make their nests in the ceilings and find their way through holes into our rooms, and it was not uncommon to hear a bird flying around inside at times. As for the rats and mice, on one occasion Father thought he had the solution. When a new ceiling was put up, he mixed strychnine into the paste. It was instantly effective, and all noise ceased within a day or so. However, the stench from the dead animals was so intense that the ceiling had to be torn down and done over.

Another annoying feature of the ceilings was the fact that because there were air vents under the eaves of the house, which allowed air to penetrate into the area above the ceilings, every time the wind blew, the ceilings heaved up and down, often depositing a cloud of dust onto everything below. It happened also when doors were opened or closed, so when Father decided to replace the ceilings with ones covered with plaster, everyone was delighted.

While the dining room was free of furniture, Father decided it would be a good idea to experiment first with the dining room ceiling. He called in the men who specialized in putting up the *shujie* framework for paper ceilings, and called in our regular mason. Father asked them if it would be possible to put up a framework of *shujie* that would be strong enough to hold a plaster ceiling. Spreading mud and plaster on a wall was easy, but on a ceiling? Such a thing had never been heard of. However, they talked it over and decided that it could be done, and a day or so later they set to work.

Strong supports consisting of several stalks of *shujie* were hung vertically from the rafters, then instead of the widely spaced horizontal sticks that normally would have been tied to them to form the surface for a paper ceiling, the *shujie* sticks were laid close together and tied side by side with hemp to form a flat surface, but with minimal cracks between, so the first layer of mud would ooze through and stick. The surface of the sticks was roughened somewhat to ensure that the mud would adhere to them. It seemed like a good idea.

When the framework was finished, the masons, who doubled as plasterers, spread a thin layer of mud as a base for the plaster. It was an entirely new and unfamiliar process for them. Initially, amid much laughter, while spreading the mud above their heads, they dropped a lot onto the floor below, as well as onto their own heads and faces, and since we had nothing to cover the floor with, the nicely varnished surface was soon a mess. At the same time it was badly scratched by the scaffolding that they had erected to reach the ten-foot-high ceiling. However, that was nothing compared with what followed.

The rainy season had started and the weather was extremely humid. When the masons finally got the hang of it, and the first coat of mud was on, all windows and doors were left open so the circulating air could dry the mud. But that was not the case. In fact, the circulating damp air, instead of drying the mud, simply softened it further, and all through that night, poor Father lay awake listening to the loud "plops" as great sheets of mud fell onto the floor. In the morning when we went to look at it, we could hardly believe our eyes. The entire floor was covered with mud, and there was not a bit left on the ceiling.

Father was discouraged, but he didn't give up, and the whole process was repeated. The second time, however, the masons used a much drier mud and spread it more thinly. Also, all doors and windows were shut. After a day or so, the mud had dried sufficiently for the plaster to be put on, and after two coats of that, we had a gorgeous white ceiling that astounded all who saw it. Unfortunately, it took days of cleaning before the floor regained anything like its original beauty. From then on the lesson was well learned, and in the remaining rooms, plaster ceilings were put up first, before the wooden floors were installed.

While the furniture was still out of the dining room, Father had another idea. Apart from the original papering of the walls, most of which had a plastered surface underneath, only whitewash had been used where the paper had been removed. Father thought it would be nice to get some color onto the walls and he decided to experiment.

He bought buckets of soybean milk, a staple of the Chinese diet in North China. It is the liquid that results when the soybeans are ground and processed for tofu, (the Japanese name for bean-curd) or *doufu*, as it is known in North China. Using that as a base, Father mixed in red ocher, a natural red earth that was readily available in large blocks, but which had to be smashed, then finely powdered. For the powdering process, the Chinese had long had a sort of mortar and pestle contraption that was highly ingenious and very effective. The mortar was a narrow, boat-like, trough sort of receptacle about sixteen inches in length, made of cast iron, curved and rising at both ends. The pestle was a narrow iron wheel about nine or ten inches in diameter with a blunt, narrow rim that fit the base of the trough. It had a handle through the middle, extending about five inches on each side. When grinding any substance to powder, a man grasped the two extended handles of the wheel, one in each hand, and rolled the wheel back and forth in the mortar. Since the handle was of solid wood, it was

hard on the hands, so the Chinese, never at a loss for a better way of doing things, had learned to sit on a low stool and roll the pestle with their feet, while wearing shoes of course.

When the red ocher was ground to the fineness of talcum powder, Father mixed it into the soybean milk, then brushed it onto the walls. By adjusting the amount of red ocher, he developed a pleasing pink color that became our favorite.

Other colors were tried: a blue made from the blue indigo dye the Chinese used for dyeing their white cotton cloth, but none of us particularly liked it; it was too dreary. A green proved very attractive, and everyone liked that until Father discovered that the only green coloring available was arsenic, so that was discarded. Then there was a yellow that, no matter how much color was added, always looked rather sickly. So pink it was, and we used it widely thereafter. The only problem with that wall coloring was that the soybean milk turned rancid very quickly and gave off a very strong and disagreeable odor that lasted for several days after it was applied to the walls. However, in time the smell went away. In any case, that was a small price to pay for the pleasure of getting away from white walls everywhere.

With that experiment, and the gradual installation of wooden floors and plaster ceilings in all of the living quarters, Father's Westernization of our house took a breather for a short while. However, he had a lively imagination, which seemed to work overtime during the winter months, and which led to trying out something new when spring came around.

One thing that bothered Father considerably was that the location of the kitchen required that the food had to be carried across the courtyard in all kinds of bad weather. He finally thought of making Gil's and my old bedroom into a new kitchen. To provide indoor access to it he had a long, low, shed-like structure built along the back of that building, extending from the pantry corridor he had earlier built to the schoolroom. A door was cut in the back of that first corridor into the new "shed" structure, and another door was cut in the back of our old bedroom, while the original front door was bricked up.

The "shed" was roofed with a new product that Father had discovered on one of his trips to the coast, and which caused great excitement when he imported a cartload of it. It was galvanized, corrugated iron roofing — sheets of metal about three feet wide by eight feet long, with alternating valleys and ridges. It was ideal for covering sheds, and it wasn't long before the cow sheds and the chicken run were all covered with it instead of the earlier mud-and-plaster roofs, which leaked badly after a year or so.

The new corridor to the new kitchen delighted everyone, particularly You Wang, who had been soaked to the skin so many times over the years. In addition, the food now arrived at the table hotter than before. Mother could now get to the kitchen without going outdoors. Even Lao San was happier. A door from the shed corridor led out into the back third courtyard, which saved him quite a few steps when he was carrying water from the well to the kitchen.

Another thing Father introduced to Lingyuan was cement. He'd brought back a few bags of it from the coast and used it sparingly for a few things such as steps and window sills. In the new kitchen he tried another experiment - a sink for our cook Gao Cai to use when washing dishes. It was a brick structure, three feet high with a large, rectangular bowl about six inches deep, which Father lined with a mixture of cement and sand. It even had a drain leading out to a dry well out back.

It was not possible to buy any sort of pipe locally, but some years before, Father had bought a well pump with ten-foot lengths of three-inch pipe from Montgomery Ward. It had been installed in the back well, and there were twelve lengths of pipe. That's how I knew the back well was 120 feet deep. Father had originally bought the pump because he felt sorry for the men having to work so hard on the windlass, drawing water. However, the Chinese didn't really accept the pump. At first it was a novelty, but the nuisance of having to prime it, and the fact that it froze up badly in winter, caused it to fall into disuse.

The drain from the kitchen was one length of that well pipe. Another length was out in the back garden stretched between two date trees. It was used to hang out the rugs and carpets so You Wang could beat out the dust. Gil and I found it a great exercise bar where we could chin ourselves or hang upside down by our knees. Each piece of pipe found a use somewhere. All those changes took several years. Life was never dull in Lingyuan.

The family in the back yard. From left to right, Ruth, Mr. Tharp, Bob, Mrs. Tharp with Barbara on her lap, Gil.

Bob and Gil's room.

Huide bu nan, nande bu hui.

That which you know how to do
is not difficult.
That which is difficult,
you don't know how to do.

- Chinese Proverb.

Chapter Six
The Magistrate Comes To Dinner

After the "buried babies" incident, Father decided to wait a few months before flooring the bedrooms. In the meantime he felt that some furniture for the dining room was the most pressing need. Although it was winter Sun Shifu had a place indoors where he could work.

What we most needed, Father felt, was a traditional sideboard with plenty of space below to store condiment bottles, a cruet set, toast rack, sugar bowls, and things of that sort. Also it should have some drawers for table silver and linens. At the time we used linen serviettes, as the British called them, or table napkins. They had to last a full week. Consequently, after each meal we folded and rolled our napkins tightly and fitted them into individual serviette rings. All of those things required storage space.

Father found a picture of a sideboard in some magazine or catalog, and showed it to Sun Shifu and asked him if he could copy it. Sun took one look at it and replied "*mei shemma*," the Chinese equivalent of

"it's a piece of cake," or "nothing to it."

Father gave him a free hand, and Sun decided that a piece of furniture such as that needed quality wood, so he set about finding some thoroughly dry elm wood with a nice grain. Without drawing any sort of plan, he proceeded to cut and plane and chisel and fit pieces together. In a very short time the sideboard began to take shape. For the back piece that stood against the wall on top of the sideboard, Father had envisaged a simple plain board. Sun had quite different ideas.

Without saying anything to anyone, he turned up one morning with a piece of board approximately a foot wide, an inch thick, and about seven feet in length. It was the smoothest wood I had ever seen and I've seen nothing like it since. Sun told me it was called *duan mu*, or "satin wood" (related to Bosswood). There were no knots in it and absolutely no grain. It was unbelievably smooth to the touch.

Sun took a short piece of bamboo, split it lengthwise, cut one end to a diagonal slant, then sharpened that to a knife-like edge. He then proceeded to cut a series of very fine teeth in that slanted portion. I watched with the greatest of interest as he dipped that "comb" into his lampblack marking-line "shoe," then without the slightest hesitation, used it to draw free-hand on the board, producing a most remarkable scenic design.

In a very short time a fascinating picture emerged. Trees and flowers of all kinds abounded. Tiny, lifelike human figures stood around in a variety of poses and activities. There were various animals and birds, and, what most amazed me, a mule-drawn cart complete in every detail: the driver with a whip in his hand sat on the outside left front shaft, and a passenger was ensconced inside. There was even baggage tied on behind. There were many other details that don't come to mind now, but I do recall the realistic clouds in the sky, birds flying around, and tiny houses with smoke curling out of the chimneys. All of it was drawn unhesitatingly, with not one single erasure or change. Everything came straight out of his head. I couldn't believe my eyes.

When almost every square inch on the board had been filled in, he drew a detailed and intricate border around the whole thing. Then, looking at me, he gave a self-deprecatory smile and stood the board in a corner, facing the wall. In a conspiratorial tone of voice, he told me very firmly that I was to tell no one about it. Not only that, but he wouldn't tell me why, nor would he tell me what the board was intended for. At the end of the day he wrapped the board up in a piece of sacking and took it home with him, and that was the last I saw of it for several weeks. In fact, I forgot all about it.

Eventually, he brought it back, but it was unrecognizable. In his own time, and working nights by pitifully inadequate lamplight, he had carved the entire surface, everything standing out in bold relief. The carving was exquisite. The detail was so fine, the proportions so accurate, that the whole thing was almost like a photograph: the leaves on the trees, the petals on the flowers, the smiles on the faces of the men, women, and particularly the children; the nails in the cart wheels standing out sharply; the braided whip in the hand of the driver. Everything was unbelievably realistic.

Sun painstakingly rubbed it down until it was

smooth and silky to the touch, and only then did he tell me that it was to be the back of the sideboard. At the same time, he released me from my promise not to tell anyone about it. I raced to the house to get my parents to come and look at it. Both they, and everyone else who saw it, were astonished at the beauty of Sun's workmanship. Of course, Father wanted to pay Sun for his time, but Sun adamantly refused. His masterpiece was his gift to the family, and especially to Mother. He wanted everyone to know it was out of appreciation for what Mother had done for him.

In the meantime, the sideboard had been completely assembled. It stood on four carved legs, perhaps four feet high, its bottom about six inches from the floor. There were three drawers across the front, each with carved wooden drawer-pulls. Below there were three cupboards. The two side cupboards were fitted with doors, and somewhere Sun had managed to find some fancy brass knobs and hinges. The middle compartment was left open but fitted with shelves.

On top, there were two posts toward the back, one at each end. Both were intricately carved, but where they faced each other, a deep groove had been cut into the face of each. Into those grooves Sun fitted the board he had so meticulously carved, and the sideboard was complete.

Before moving the sideboard to the dining room Sun came up with a stain of his own making, one of which he alone seemed to know the secret. With that he stained it to a rich walnut color and finished it to a high gloss with numerous coats of tung oil. Unquestionably a beautiful piece of furniture, it occupied the place of honor against the north wall of the dining room. My place at the table faced it, and I never tired of looking at that lifelike picture of China that Sun had so miraculously produced.

It was just about that time that the magistrate invited Father to a banquet. The invitation was written on a large red card that came in a big red envelope about two feet long and ten inches wide. It was presented with a great deal of ceremony by the messenger, and on an accompanying sheet of paper, Father put his "chop" to indicate his acknowledgment of the invitation. Usually, affairs of that sort were held in a restaurant, but in this case, the magistrate decided to show Father a very special honor by inviting him to his home. By giving the banquet he was following the traditional Chinese way of giving himself some "face" after the "buried babies" incident, and since he also invited a large number of the leading citizens of Lingyuan, it was his way of showing that all was now well between himself and the foreigners. Father was the guest of honor, and the custom in those days — strange as it may seem — was always for the guest of honor to be the last one to arrive.

We employed at the time a language teacher by the name of Wu, husband of the little old lady who was Mother's sewing woman. Mr. Wu was a short, very compact little man. I guess he could best be described as very dapper in his dress, which was always formal although obviously well-worn, and he always wore a skullcap with a brass button on top. The brass button indicated that he was a Scholar of the First Degree, a *xiu cai*. He was one of those few individuals who had passed one of the imperial examinations at the county level given in the Ming and Qing dynasties. Although the *xiu cai* was the lowest level of the scholar class, the degree carried with it a tremendous amount of prestige, and there were only two other scholars of the same rank in Lingyuan. He was therefore a person very highly respected in the community. The fact that a man of his caliber had accepted the Christian faith created quite a sensation at the time, and his employment by Father as a language teacher added to his prestige, as well as to Father's for having the perspicacity to hire such a very distinguished person.

In the China of those days the entire population fell into four categories: *shi, nong, gong* and *shang*. They were in order: scholars, peasants, laborers or working class, and merchants. All others, of any profession, such as barbers, priests, soldiers, actors, butchers, or whatever, were all considered to be outside the pale and thus not to be mentioned. The rankings implied that the scholar was the most respected and the greatest asset to the country. The peasant came next, because he fed the scholar. The laborer, or working man, helped the peasant in the fields and brought the food to the scholar, so he came next, and the merchant supplied the needs of all of them in one way or another.

To attain the rank of *xiu cai*, an aspiring student had to undergo many years of exhausting study followed by rigid examinations given by a representative of the Emperor. The examinations were held once every four or five years at a number of sites designated by the Emperor. The sites were scattered throughout the country, where examinations were held simultaneously. Some were in large cities, but others in rural settings. Even so, most students had to travel great distances to reach the nearest one.

Wu's examination was held in the city of Yongpingfu, the town in which my sister Ruth had been born. Yongpingfu is not far from the coast and is near the mouth of the Luan river. It was six days' journey from Lingyuan by horseback, but Wu had walked the entire distance and back when he had gone some years before to take the examination. When I was a small boy, Wu was one of my heroes, and I loved to hear him tell stories of his experiences and the rigorous and demanding life of a scholar-to-be.

Of particular interest was his account of the examinations. Years later I visited Yongpingfu. The original site of the examinations was still intact and of intense interest to me even though, with the coming of the revolution, that type of higher learning had been changed to a more modern form.

The examination site lay just outside the city on a hillside thickly covered by short, scrubby, wild date trees. It consisted of a series of perhaps fifty small stone buildings, each separated from the other by some twenty or thirty feet to discourage any communication between the student candidates. Each of the tiny houses faced south, and was designed to hold a single scholar. Each was only slightly larger than the old rural "outhouse" common in early America before indoor plumbing came into general use. Each building had a low wooden door with a bolt on the outside. In front was a small opening facing south to admit light and air. The interior held no furniture whatsoever, but simply contained a raised stone slab, which served as a desk, and a stone seat. That was all there was.

The student taking the examination was shut into the little hut, the door was bolted behind him, and there he stayed for several weeks. His scanty meals were brought to him twice a day, and twice a day he was allowed out for a brief period when he was escorted to and from the latrine. He was given a container of water, but nothing else. At night, a small, smoky lamp was provided — just a wick floating in a dish of castor oil — and such sleep as he got was in a sitting position.

However, Wu told me that sleep was something

farthest from his thoughts while he was there. Each day at daybreak, a new theme, on some subject specifically designated by the emperor, was brought to the hut, and the essay written on the previous day's theme was collected, finished or not. As a result, most of the students spent their entire time, day and night, writing. The students were judged on the beauty of their calligraphy, their interpretation of the theme given by the emperor, and the length of their essay.

Keeping awake was the trick, and Wu told me they accomplished that in different ways. In those days all the men wore queues, and one trick was to tie the end of the queue to an overhead beam. When their heads fell forward in sleep, they were painfully jerked awake. Another way was to collect the half-inch thorns from the wild date trees on the hillside. They would insert one of the thorns between the eyelids on each eye, and then do their best not to fall asleep.

The successful graduate, after being formally designated a *xiu cai*, was given a pewter button to wear on the top of his skullcap, but he was permitted to substitute a plain brass one if he preferred. Those obviously were more conspicuous, and that was why Wu wore one on his cap.

Wu was our protocol expert, so Father consulted him on how to respond to the magistrate's invitation, and also how to behave at the banquet. The banquet was to begin at four in the afternoon; however, Wu told Father that it was most important that he, as the guest of honor, ignore the stipulated time and wait until a runner came up from the Yamen to press him to attend. Not only that, but Father was to wait for that to happen three times. That was traditionally known as *cui qing*, or "urgent invitation," and was accorded to all but the lowliest of guests invited to a formal meal. However, only the guest of honor got three of them. One call would come about an hour or so before the meal, to give time for one to change one's clothes; the second call was at or about the designated time; and the third, for the most honored guest, would be after everyone else had arrived. Only then could the banquet begin.

The Chinese as a whole, and particularly those in the North, have a marvelous sense of humor. There is nothing about their daily life or the lives of those around them that is exempt from gentle ridicule, and they are the first to joke about their superstitions and antiquated customs as well as their frailties. Regarding the custom of the guest of honor arriving late, they tell a humorous story that points up the farce that it was.

It seems that at one time there was a leading citizen who received an invitation to a banquet from the local magistrate, and he was designated as the guest of honor. He was a somewhat impatient individual and, upon receiving the invitation, tore open one end of the envelope. Knowing from whom the invitation came, he was only concerned with the date. Withdrawing the enclosed card only partially, he saw a single horizontal stroke, which indicated "one." "Aha!" he said to himself, "it is to be on the first of the month. Today is the 29th of this month and, this being a long month of thirty days, that's only two days away. I'll starve myself for the next two days and in that way thoroughly enjoy the meal."

Two days went by, and the first of the new moon came. Near the appointed time he dressed in his best clothes and sat down to await the coming of the messenger. However, as the day wore on, no messenger came to press him to go to the banquet.

Puzzled, he wondered if he had somehow misread the date, so again he pulled out the card, again only part way, but a little farther than the time before. This time he discovered a second stroke under the first. That made it the second of the month. "Well," he said, "that's tomorrow, and since I've starved myself this long, I might as well starve another day, then I'll really have a good meal."

The next day, on the second day of the month, he again dressed himself in all his finery. Once again the same thing happened. The day passed with no messenger coming to urge him to go to the feast. When it was long past the usual hour for a banquet, he flew into a rage, knowing that now there was no question but that he had been deliberately insulted. There was not, and never had been, any intention of inviting him to the banquet. He reached for the invitation card, pulled it out of the envelope and spat on it, then, when just about to tear it to shreds, he saw a third stroke. That meant that all along the invitation had been for the third of the month, not the first or the second.

"Ah, well," he said, "I'm not going to let a little thing like this bother me. I've waited and starved this long. What's one more day?" Sad to say, when on the third day the messenger finally arrived to urge him to attend, he found the poor man lying there fully dressed and ready, but unfortunately dead from starvation.

In Father's case, he had read the invitation correctly and nothing so drastic occurred. Sure enough, on the appointed day the messengers arrived, just as Wu had said they would. Father, who was a most punctual man, didn't like delaying at all, and felt he should go, but Wu convinced him that it was important he abide by the custom to give the magistrate "face." Finally, after the third urging, Father, accompanied by Wu, walked the short distance to the Yamen. There, with a great deal of pomp and ceremony, Wu took Father's visiting card, and preceding Father by about fifty paces, carried his card above his head, held high in both hands with Father's name on the card facing forward, and marched toward the rear courtyard, where the magistrate resided.

Father approached to within a hundred yards of the residence, waited until a servant came out and accepted the card, then watched, as that man in turn held the card high over his head, this time with Father's name facing toward the rear. When all had been done in the prescribed manner, the magistrate himself came out in person to welcome Father. The banquet began and lasted for several hours.

The honor of inviting Father to his home for the banquet was a singular one in many respects. It was an honor generally accorded only to very special friends, and the only honor greater would have been to have a "simple" meal of six or eight courses cooked personally by his wife, and then have Father come either alone or with his family. The magistrate by his gesture was indicating to all Father's fellow guests, and through them to the town as a whole, that Father, this strange foreigner, was a very special friend of his and should be accorded the same respect with which he, as magistrate, was treated.

Following the banquet, the atmosphere for both the church and for the small group of foreigners in Lingyuan improved greatly. There was less fear and suspicion evident on the part of visitors, and more friendliness on the streets as we moved about among the people. As a result, Father not only felt that we owed a lot to the magistrate, at the same time he had taken a strong liking to the old gentleman. A few weeks later, Father suggested to Mother that we reci-

procate by inviting the magistrate for a meal. What better way could there be of honoring him than by inviting him to a Western-style meal in our own house?

Mother was enthusiastic, now that the dining room with its brand new floor and marvelous sideboard was a very presentable place. Where better to have the meal? A date was fixed, and an invitation, written in both Chinese and English, was sent to and accepted by the magistrate. We children were very excited as the momentous day approached, and Mother carefully schooled us as to our behavior when the great man came.

Although by protocol, the magistrate never went anywhere without his deputy and his bodyguards, it was made clear to him through Mr. Wu that this was to be a very private meal for the magistrate alone, and it would be served in Western fashion with the entire Tharp family present at the table. For a Chinese, it would be a highly unusual event. Customarily, when they invited someone to their homes, even close friends, it was rare indeed that the womenfolk would sit at the same table. Usually the women in the family were nowhere within sight or else, if included in the function, they were seated at a separate table and more likely in a separate room. I can remember only two or three occasions in the thirty years I spent in China that, when invited to a meal in a Chinese home, the wife joined us at the same table. Instead, the wife would cook and serve the meal and the guests would make sure that they ate sparingly so enough was left for the women to eat later. That was why, in China, one left as soon as the meal was over, so the women could eat the food while it was still hot.

For the magistrate, it was to be a historic occasion. Apart from the fact that it was to be foreign food in a foreign setting, I am sure also that it would be a first for him to sit down at a table with foreign women present, not to mention the children, who in a Chinese home never sat at the table with guests. But we wanted him to see just how we lived.

I've mentioned that it was customary in those days for missionary families to have younger "apprentice" missionaries staying with them while they learned the Chinese language. During my entire childhood, I cannot remember a time when we did not have at least one younger missionary living with us, either a young man or young lady. Quite often there were several. At that particular time, I recall that we had a young American woman staying with us. She was Harriet Minns from Buffalo, New York. She had just joined us. That would make it 1919, and I was six years old. She traveled out with us from America when my family returned to China from a furlough, and she remained with us for many years thereafter.

As a six-year-old I was brash and very talkative, and probably very precocious, and I certainly wasn't afraid of strangers. Probably for those reasons, Mother decided to sit me next to the magistrate so that with my chatter I could help keep the conversation going.

Our dining table could seat eight comfortably, and ten in a pinch. In China, the guest of honor sits to the left of his host, but Father wanted the magistrate to see how we did it in England, so he put him on his right. I was moved from my customary seat, which faced our new sideboard, to a position with my back to it, and to the magistrate's right. Father, of course, was at one end of the table, and Mother at the other, with Barbara in a high chair beside her. Gil and Ruth were opposite me, with Miss Minns next to Barbara. Since that left one extra place to my right, I feel sure that there must have been at least one other person staying with us at the time, but who it was I cannot now remember. In any case, I mention the seating because of what followed.

The magistrate had been diplomatically informed in advance that he would be the only guest, and because Western meals, unlike Chinese food, had to be cooked ahead of time, he would be expected at the exact hour indicated. We would follow the Western custom, rather than the Chinese. No messenger would be sent to urge him to come.

As the hour approached, I was so excited that I had to go down to the front gate to see if the magistrate was coming. Looking down the street to my left, I could see the entrance to the Yamen less than three hundred yards away, where a crowd was forming outside, indicating that something was happening inside. Then a troop of mounted police came out of the gate and drew up outside in two opposing columns. That was immediately followed by the magistrate's ornate sedan chair, carried by four men and surrounded by his immediate bodyguard of ten men heavily armed with big Mauser pistols. Behind the bodyguard marched a small detachment of police, all carrying

rifles. The impressive procession was followed by a crowd of curious onlookers. As it started up the street the short distance to our front gate, I dashed back inside to tell Father and Mother that the magistrate was coming.

All the panoply was in no way intended, nor needed, as protection for his august personage. It was simply to show that the individual he was visiting was very important and that the honor was due him. I need not have hurried inside to warn Father of his coming. There was plenty of time.

The mounted police formed up in a half circle outside our front entrance. The foot patrolmen rushed inside and lined up along each side of the passage to the second courtyard, then, with much ceremony, the sedan chair was carried in and deposited just in front of the entrance to the third courtyard facing the "spirit screen."

Mr. Wu stood there awaiting the magistrate's arrival. The guest produced his visiting card and handed it to one of his bodyguards, who carried it high over his head to Mr. Wu. Wu, in turn, holding it in both hands high over his own head, and walking with his peculiar little strut, proceeded toward the third courtyard, where he handed it to Father, who was waiting out of sight behind the spirit screen. Father then walked back with Mr. Wu and ushered the magistrate out of his sedan chair and together they walked up to the house, followed by the bodyguards and all the policemen.

When the entire group attempted to follow their master into our dining room, Father gently suggested to the magistrate that perhaps four of his guards would be sufficient. The rest were told to wait outside. Inside, the four men lined themselves up against the wall for the duration of the meal.

Even at that point, eight years after the overthrow of the Imperial Empire, the magistrate still usually wore his Imperial-style robes of office on formal occasions. On that day he was dressed in civilian attire: a long gray gown of flowered silk, lined with fur, covered with a short jacket of black satin. On his head he wore a black silk skullcap with a red topknot. Our dining room was well heated, but, over-dressed as he was, he didn't show any sign of discomfort during the entire meal.

Mother had decided to serve a typical English meal: a soup, followed by roast beef, very well cooked to conform to Chinese tastes, and accompanied by Yorkshire pudding, which Gao Cai had learned to make to perfection, and vegetables from our own garden. The dessert had proved to be something of a problem for Mother. It was in the middle of winter and there were no fresh fruits available, so rather than make some kind of a pudding, Mother decided to use the only thing she had in the house: dried prunes. They were served as a stewed compote. That, in turn, raised another problem. The prunes had pits in them, and pits, when removed from the mouth, had to be disposed of somewhere. We, of course, would normally put them on the sides of our plates, but not so a Chinese, and that is where Mother anticipated trouble.

In the traditional Chinese way, where the floors in those days were either brick-covered or simply plain earth, the floor was the accepted place to deposit all unwanted table debris. Bones, pits, skins, anything one wanted to discard, was spit out or dropped to the floor. The wandering dogs, pigs or cats ate it or it was later swept up. The Chinese abhorred putting anything like that on the sides of their plates, and definitely not on the table itself.

Since disposing of his prune pits might prove to be a problem for the visitor, Mother decided to put several saucers on the table when the dessert was served. She carefully told us children what we were to do with our prune pits so that the visitor might see the way a Westerner did it and follow suit. We were supposed to take them out of our mouths with a spoon, then put them onto the nearest saucer. At the same time Mother urged us to be sure to gently tap the saucer with our spoons as we got rid of the pits, to attract the attention of the magistrate, while not embarrassing him by telling him what to do. We had held a short rehearsal the day before, and since it worked well, Mother felt it was an excellent idea. So much for careful planning.

The soup and meat courses went off well, the magistrate handling his knife and fork uncommonly well despite the fact that it was the first time he had used them. He talked a blue streak the entire time and seemed to be most thoroughly enjoying himself. When dessert was served, the magistrate found the prunes very much to his liking and took several helpings. However, from the minute he started on his first prune, I saw trouble ahead. He was not getting rid of

his pits: he was storing them up in one cheek and the bulge was getting bigger and bigger.

Feverishly, I ate my own prunes, and as ostentatiously as I could, I put my pits on the saucer just in front of the magistrate, tapping the saucer loudly with my spoon as I did so. Then everyone else at the table, seeing what was about to happen, joined in and did the same thing. It didn't do a bit of good. The magistrate completely ignored what we were doing and kept on eating his prunes and storing up the pits as he continued his conversation with Father. Apparently it just went too much against the grain for him to deposit his pits on the table in any form at all, even if the uncouth foreigners did so.

When the bulge in his cheek nearest to me appeared to be about the size of a tennis ball, I noticed his eyes casting about the floor for a suitable place to get rid of the pits. There was a carpet right under his feet, so he didn't want to spit onto that. Then he spotted the sideboard behind him, sitting on its six-inch legs. The space underneath was the perfect spot. Without anything but a momentary pause in his conversation, he turned his head very slightly to the right, and, with unerring aim, spat out a stream of pits which, like machine-gun bullets, flew past my ear and over my shoulder, landing out of sight under the sideboard. Not a single one missed! He then, without the slightest change of expression, turned his head and resumed his talk with Father as though nothing at all had happened.

For us children, it was the most difficult thing in the world not to burst out laughing, particularly when I caught the eye of You Wang, our house boy, standing at the back of the room grinning broadly and with a twinkle in his eye. Somehow we managed to keep our composure and not cause the magistrate to lose face. After all, from his point of view, he did the right thing under the circumstances, and he probably felt very superior to the oafish barbarians who dirtied their own table. It is all in the point of view. The four bodyguards meanwhile had stolidly looked on throughout the entire episode, blank expressions on their faces that nothing could change, and, with their unwashed bodies, smelling up the room to an extraordinary degree.

From that time on, we were very close friends with that particular magistrate. In those days, no gentleman of any position in the community would be seen walking anywhere. One had to take a sedan chair or ride on a horse or mule, and always be accompanied by a retinue of retainers. In time, however, that more enlightened man got away from such formality, and he took to dropping in on us unexpectedly, walking the short distance between the Yamen and our house, accompanied by only one retainer instead of his usual entourage. Father also frequently dropped in to pay him a visit and often took me with him.

It was that magistrate, Yang Shu-ping, who made it possible for Father to visit men in the prison whenever he liked. His obvious sympathy toward what the missionaries were trying to do helped us greatly during the several years that he was in office. Unlike most of the magistrates who held that position, he became known as a benevolent man, very fair in his judgments and not subject to bribery or corruption. He was indeed a rare individual. Unfortunately, he didn't last very long. Three years later the governor appointed another man to the job.

The magistrates of those days held immense power.

Appointed by the governor of the province, they were usually relatives or close friends of the governor. They were charged not only with keeping the peace in the county over which they presided — an area of hundreds of square miles — but also collected taxes and ran the police forces, both the city force and a special county police force. They were also charged with putting down banditry and acted as judge and jury in all trials held at the Yamen. They had the power of life and death over the entire populace. As a general rule, they exercised that power ruthlessly. Over the years, we saw many of them come and go as the tides of civil war swept back and forth over the province and power changed hands. Since, through the actions of that one magistrate, Father had been accepted as one of the gentry, from that time on he was always invited to official functions and was made a part of any group welcoming a new magistrate or seeing one off when he left office. In later years that led to some extremely interesting situations.

Cut Paper Art.   富 貴 有 餘 (魚)   "Fùguì You Yú"—
a charm to provide a surplus of wealth. 餘 (Yú), meaning "surplus," is pronounced exactly the same way as 魚 (Yú), meaning "fish." The language provides many opportunities for such plays on words, and the Chinese love to use them.

Left to right: back row, Mrs. Tharp, Ruth, Gilbert, Mr. Tharp; front row, Barbara, Bob.

The family at a meal. On left you see Bob and Miss Minns next to him. Mrs. Tharp is at the end, then Gil, Ruth and Barbara.

Magistrate's residence.

Magistrate's attendants.

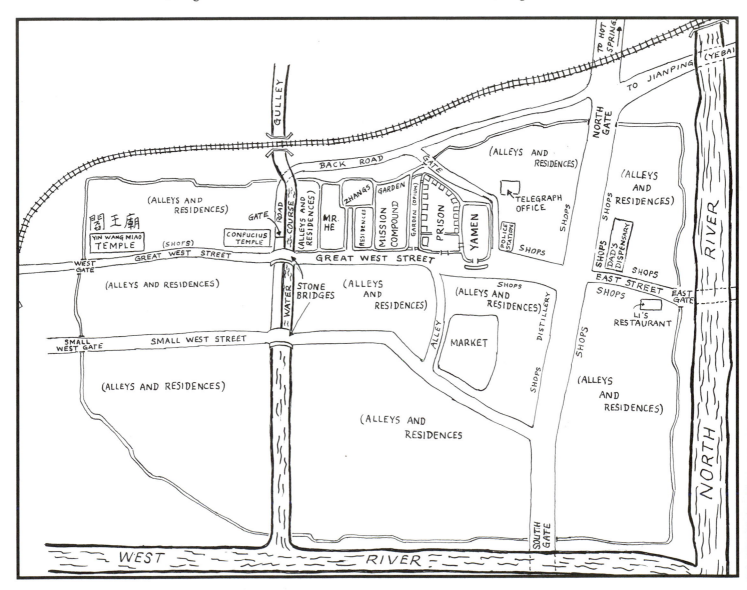

Lingyuan

Chi shei xiang shei.

The one whose food you eat
is the one to whom you are loyal.

- Chinese Proverb.

Chapter Seven
"Family" – Not Servants

Missionaries in China, or for that matter in any part of the world, have often been criticized by fellow Christians as well as by non-Christians for employing servants. The general feeling expressed seemed to be: "Why should these individuals, who supposedly were dedicated to a life of austerity and sacrifice, surround themselves with servants to do their every bidding?" We often heard that criticism, and people in America would sometimes bluntly ask us why we were entitled to live the "high life," while they had to do their own work at home and support us at the same time.

The answer is actually very simple. In China, servants were not a luxury for missionaries; they were a necessity. Just as necessary as one's housing, food, and clothing. Being a missionary was a twenty-four-hour-a-day job, and the missionary was always on call. Because of living conditions, without servants nothing could be accomplished as far as missionary work was concerned.

It is true, some missionaries tried to get along with-out servants, but they failed miserably. I knew of one or two who tried. They hoped by example to show what Christianity was. Like the Apostle Paul, who lived as a tent-maker while he preached, they believed they could work for a living and preach at the same time. In China it didn't work out that way.

In the previous chapter I mentioned the four categories under which everyone in China was placed. Missionaries were "teachers," and teachers fell under the category of scholars. As such they were in a class where at least one servant was expected unless one was very poor. Missionaries, in addition to being "teachers," were foreigners, and all foreigners were thought to have money. Anyone in China with money had servants. If they didn't, something was wrong and they were heartily despised, even by the poor.

But quite apart from that, consider the circumstances under which we lived as a missionary family — and we were typical of most such families. We lived in a Chinese house, with no central heating, no piped-in water, no electricity or gas, no insulation, no indoor bathrooms, and no sewage disposal. Every drop of water had to be brought from a well, and although we had three wells on the property, only one had water that was potable, and that one was farthest from the house. It took Lao San, the yard boy, at least two hours each day to fill the various water containers: in the kitchen, the bedrooms, to supply the girls' school and the orphans, to say nothing of the water necessary for the vegetable garden and the flower garden in the third courtyard.

We had only two household servants, a cook and a table-boy, or house-boy, as they were often called. Gao Cai was the cook, and we had him as cook for as long as I can remember. I can remember Father telling us how Gao Cai came to work for him while still a boy. He then accompanied us when we moved from Bagou, where I was born. Gao Cai had an older brother named Gao Zun, an opium addict. He tagged along, and for a number of years caused us a great deal of trouble. But more of him later.

We had pet names or nicknames for everyone around the place, servants and teachers included. Although they never knew it, and we always addressed them by their proper names, there was a basic and, we felt, very sound reason for the nicknames. We found from experience that when, for some reason or other, it became necessary to talk about one or another of them when conversing among ourselves in English, the table-boy You Wang or anyone else within hearing would pick up on any Chinese name that we used and later would ask us children what had been said about that particular individual. Not being able to understand anything of what was being said, they were nevertheless very conscious of any Chinese word or name spoken, and were both sensitive and curious as to why so-and-so was being discussed. From that source, numerous rumors had been started, and more than once, as young children, when asked by someone as to what had been said concerning someone else, we inadvertently let slip some information that caused trouble when passed on. Primarily for that reason, Father came up with some of the nicknames, and we children supplied others.

The names were in no way meant to be disparaging. They were essentially utilitarian, and we used them as lovingly as any of the nicknames we had for

each other. Gao Cai, our cook, was known to us as "K.O." — an abbreviation of the first part of his name, Kao Ts'ai in the romanization used at that time. His brother was called "Katie," because of the first two letters of his name, Kao Tsun, as it was then spelled. For the table-boy, You Wang, we again abbreviated and called him "Y.U."

Those men, and a number of others around the compound, were never thought of as servants. They were simply members of our household, as much a part of the family as we were. Their daily lives and their individual problems were of as much concern to us as our own, and we loved them as brothers and sisters, or, in some cases as uncles and aunts, and in turn we were loved by them.

Gao Cai was an extremely intelligent young man. He was a natural cook. Mother had only to show him something once and he mastered it immediately. He learned to bake bread, cook all the traditional English foods that Mother taught him, and, like all Chinese master chefs, he never wrote down a recipe but kept them all in his head. He was, of course, an expert on cooking Chinese food, and at least two or three times a week we ate Chinese dishes of one kind or another. If we children could have had our way, we would have eaten them more frequently than that.

Like most northern Chinese, Gao Cai was tall. He had a slim build, a bright, open face, and a cheerful disposition. He had an excellent sense of humor, and one seldom saw him without a smile on his face. He was devoted to us as children and probably spoiled us rotten. When it came time for him to find a wife, Father helped with the arrangements, and although it was a typically Chinese arranged marriage, they were happy together and had two sons.

With no refrigeration whatsoever, it was necessary to buy all meats on a daily basis, and that was Gao Cai's job. It usually took him about two hours each day to walk downtown, scour the meat stalls, find what he needed and bring it home. Most of our vegetables came from our own garden, but there were other things, such as rice and flour, which we had to buy on the local market.

Another of Gao Cai's jobs was to milk the cows and pasteurize the milk. The only place we could keep things cool was down the well at the end of the alley behind our dining room. The well wasn't very deep, but it was relatively cool under the shed roof that Father had built over it. Things we wanted to keep cool were placed inside a large earthenware bowl, inside a basket, which we let down into the well on a rope. The first bowl was covered by an inverted bowl of the same size, and to provide additional insulation, Father had rigged up a system of suspending another larger bowl above it. That one was kept full of water, which dripped slowly from a stick protruding from a hole in the bottom. Evaporation helped cool things, and most of the time it proved very effective. The only times the system failed were when we had severe thunderstorms, whereupon the milk invariably curdled. We never did learn why that was so, but it always happened.

You Wang, our table-boy, came to us also when quite a young lad. He was an ignorant country boy who had never had any education. His village was only about five miles from Lingyuan, and his father, a farmer, had been a Christian for a number of years. In addition to You Wang, he had another son named You Bichen. Their mother had died when the boys were quite young, but the father had brought up the boys quite rigidly, teaching them what he knew of Christianity and walking the five miles to church each Sunday with the boys.

As was common in those days, the older son, Bichen was sent to school, while the younger was kept at home to help with the farm work until he was old enough for a job and marriage. Bichen was the first to come to work with us as a language teacher for the younger missionaries, and at the same time he helped Father a great deal at the downtown hall. He had become a Christian while still a young lad in school and was a born preacher who could keep an audience enthralled for hours. Not too long afterward, You Wang came to work for us, and in his case, too, Father helped in making the arrangements for his marriage to a farm girl from a nearby village. During their lifetime they had three children.

Poor You Wang was just the opposite of his brother. He was a natural "klutz" and a more apt nickname for him would have been "clumsy." He was terribly shy and totally inept at anything Mother tried to teach him. Despite all that, and although at times Mother despaired of his ever being able to learn anything properly, he endeared himself to us with his total sense of honesty, his willingness to learn, his patience, and his gentleness with us children. But for

a long time it seemed that he broke everything he touched.

In time, a very long time, he became quite proficient in all the household chores: washing, ironing with a charcoal iron, setting the table and serving the meals, cleaning the house, and tending the stoves in winter. Another of his jobs was to keep all the oil lamps clean. The glass chimneys needed polishing daily because of the lampblack that collected on them. For that he devised a tool of his own design. He broke off a branch from one of the cherry trees, and with some old rags formed a soft knob at the end of the stick. That he would push back and forth through the narrow necks of the lamp chimneys. Every day each lamp had to be filled with kerosene, coal had to be carried in for the stoves and the ashes carried out, and once a week all the carpets had to be carried out and beaten, which took him half the day. Another weekly job in winter was taking down stove pipes and taking them outdoors to knock the soot out of them. With 15 or 20 of those coal stoves around the compound, that was a major job, but Lao San helped him with it since it required two men, The soft coal we burned caused a heavy buildup of soot in the chimneys as well, which meant constant cleaning to avoid chimney fires, and Lao San also climbed on the roofs and swept the many chimneys several times each winter.

You Wang and Gao Cai started their day around five in the morning, You Wang's first job in the winter being to start fires in all the stoves. They both worked through the day until after we had eaten our supper and the dishes were washed. Both performed their duties cheerfully and diligently and without too much prompting. Everyone, including the servants, had a two-hour siesta at noon, although we, as children, rebelled against it and always tried to get out of it in one way or another.

In the early days we used to tease You Wang for his forgetfulness. The two words of his name, when said in Chinese with a slightly different tonal expression, meant "forgotten again," and for quite some time we used to call him that when he had forgotten something important. But he took it all very good-naturedly.

Apart from Gao Cai and You Wang, none of the other "retainers" worked inside the house itself. As I mentioned in a previous chapter, we had two yard boys, Qiu Li, and later, young Lao San. Their jobs were very diverse and primarily involved keeping all the yards clean, carrying water to everyone in the compound, feeding and grooming the cows, and tending the back vegetable garden. They also emptied all the outdoor latrines each day. However, for them, that was a bonus to their pay rather than a requirement of their job. Human waste was much prized for use as fertilizer on the land, and in order to collect the waste, Lao San, whose home was almost a mile from ours, would get up at three o'clock each morning and make several trips back and forth, carrying the waste to his house before he came to work. Since there were some six or eight latrines in the compound, it kept him pretty busy. Lao San didn't have any land of his own, but the impressive manure pile that he built up outside his house each year sold for a tidy sum when planting time came.

Qiu Li was the yardman when we were very small. Both Barbara and I watched in awe as he ate chickens' heads, legs, and feet, which he cadged off Gao Cai every time we had chicken. He baked them in the hot coals of the kitchen stove, then gnawed off every bit of skin and meat. When Lao San came, although just a young lad, he'd lived such a hard life that he was more like a little old man. Soon after he came he was given a proper "school name" when he started to learn to read. However, very few of us ever bothered to use it. He was always "Lao San" (Old Three) to us. A few years older than I, he was very knowledgeable about farming. He had an inquiring mind and a natural ability to learn. Very quickly he proved himself expert at handling tools and soon became our all-around repairman.

Before coming to us, Lao San had never seen a foreign coal stove. We had a large number of them, most of them shipped from Montgomery Ward in Oakland, California. They were fed coal through a door in the upper part and had a cast-iron grating on which the coals sat. The grating was movable, and could be shaken from the outside by attaching a temporary handle. The severe shaking several times a day caused considerable wear and tear, so the gratings frequently broke. Lao San, without any prompting from us, drilled holes in the iron bars and patched them together with wire or large staples he had made from scrap iron, making them like new.

As the years went by and we got bicycles, he learned very quickly how to repair them, though he never learned to ride one. Still later, when I got an automobile, he adapted himself to that form of locomotion, not only learning all I could teach him about mechanics, but also learning to improvise where I would tend to give up on something in utter despair. Lao San worked so hard he literally burned himself out, and he died when still in his early thirties. He was a dedicated and loyal friend, and I missed him greatly.

Undoubtedly, the oddest but perhaps most endearing member of our extended family in Lingyuan was another "yard-boy" named Chang Yin. How he got that name or what it meant, no one knew. Neither word was an accepted surname or given name, and he himself knew nothing whatsoever about his background, where he was from, or where he was born. He didn't even have the slightest idea as to his age.

The Chinese wrote him off as an *Er Bai Wu*, a "Two Hundred and Fifty" person, that is, half of five hundred and thus "not all there." However, even though it was evident he didn't have all his marbles — as they so aptly say in the United States — he was far from stupid. In his own way he was really a most intelligent person.

Somehow, he reminded us of Dickens' character Barnaby Rudge, and that became his nickname. He'd been with us almost from the first day of our move to Lingyuan, and we kids all grew up with him, but somehow he never aged, and he always seemed the same as when we first met him.

He had come from Dujiawopu, the village thirty miles or a day's journey to the north of us, where Miss Gates and Mrs. Merrington had started a mission. They had found him there and adopted him.

So far as we could learn from Chang Yin, he had come from a very poor family. His parents had either died or abandoned him. When Miss Gates found him, he was a beggar boy, barely scraping out a living by such wits as he had, and was the butt of everyone's humor. A pathetic figure of a boy, he was little more than four feet tall, and he never grew any taller. When first found, his entire body and head were a mass of sores. He was emaciated from malnutrition to the point that it seemed a puff of wind could blow him away.

Dujiawopu was a large market village of perhaps two or three thousand people, and was the center for the surrounding agricultural area. An open market was held there every five days, and hundreds of farmers would come in from the surrounding area to sell their produce or livestock, and return home with the daily necessities they had bought.

In one area of that marketplace were set up a number of makeshift sheds for eating places. Each of them had a mud-brick cooking stove that was left there between market days. Only the metal wok was removed. When he wasn't begging around the village, Chang Yin spent most of his time during the winter months hanging around those sheds. He found some degree of shelter in the sheds, and on cold winter nights would crawl inside one of the empty cooking stoves and curl up on top of the still-hot embers. As a result, he had been burned severely, and his entire back and legs were scarred for life. On those nights when the cooking stoves were cold, he burrowed into one of the convenient manure piles where, with the fermentation, there was always some degree of warmth.

Miss Gates took pity on him, took him in, fed and clothed him, and over a period of time was able to cure his sores. He had, however, lost most of his hair and it never grew back. His head was a mass of ugly, hairless patches. He was quite sensitive about it, and for as long as I knew him, he always wore a hat to conceal them except when in church. In addition, he was so bowlegged he waddled duck-like. He appeared to walk on the sides of his feet, scuffing his shoes badly with each step, his head swinging from side to side. In spite of all that, he was one of the most lovable individuals I have ever known.

Because of his lack of physical strength there were not too many things Chang Yin could do. However, he could look after us as children, and when we were small that was his main job, but only when we were outdoors. In that he was most faithful. He was gentle, full of patience and understanding, and although we teased him unmercifully about his almost unintelligible speech and his peculiar walk, it never seemed to bother him. Mother told us in later years that she had taught him a song, which he had to sing all the time he was with us in the yard so she would know where we were. When Mother could no longer hear the singing, she would check through the window to see if all was as it should be.

Later Chang Yin learned to make himself useful in a number of other ways. He was charged with sweeping the various courtyards, collecting rubbish, sweeping out the Meeting Hall, and servicing the cooking stoves for the girl orphans, keeping them supplied with fuel and raking out the ashes. At first he ate with the orphaned girls, taking his turn learning to cook. He became so good at it that he asked if he could cook his own food. Since there was a cook stove attached to the *kang* in his room, Father agreed. From then on he was most proud of being given the job of cooking millet gruel for the several dogs we always had around the place.

Chang Yin never forgot the habits of his beggar days, and when he swept up the yards, anything he found lying loose, he saved and stashed away in a stack of small wooden boxes he kept in his tiny room, boxes he had nailed together from bits and pieces of used lumber. Extremely neat in his habits, he had a special box for every conceivable kind of thing he found. He kept old rusty nails, bits of string, pieces of wire, colorful pieces of broken crockery, oddments of sticks, rounded stones — everything one could imagine. Despite the fact that he had been an inveterate thief before being rescued by Miss Gates, we never caught him stealing anything. However, whenever anything was missing, something perhaps that we had inadvertently left lying around in the yard or back garden, Chang Yin would inevitably find it and stash it away in his room. When looking for it, we always went first to his room, and on almost every occasion, that was where we would find what we were looking for. With a grin on his face, Chang Yin would cheerfully hand it over without a murmur.

I've already mentioned that, because of the size of the compound, we were always called to meals by You Wang ringing a hand bell outside the dining room. One bell was rung ten minutes before the meal to give everyone time to get into the house to wash up, and a second bell was rung just before the meal was served. Chang Yin loved that idea! Somewhere he found himself a small hand bell, and just as he was about to eat his own meals, he would stand outside his front door and ring it vigorously, much to everyone's amusement. With him, however, it was serious business.

Chang Yin wanted to learn to read like everyone else. At the time, no one believed it would be possible, but dear, patient Mr. Hu, the gatekeeper, took him in hand, and each morning for an hour he would seat Chang Yin on the bench just inside the front gate and teach him a few characters. To everyone's surprise Chang Yin did extremely well. In no time at all, during morning prayers that Father held each morning right after breakfast for the servants and everyone else in the compound, he was taking his turn at reading a verse of Scripture, albeit with a little help from time to time. Although he couldn't carry a tune, he loved to sing, and he learned the words of many of the hymns by heart. When he was in his room or working around the yard, he sang to himself. He sang only one tune, and that in a monotone, but it was the sheer spirit of the thing that counted.

Most Westerners who were born in China can look back with very fond memories to the faithful "amah," or Chinese nurse, who took care of them when they were children. However, Mother and Father did not believe in using amahs and never had one for us. Mother, who from the beginning had been very close to the Chinese women wherever she had been, had noticed that when caring for their children, no matter how often the child cried, they would immediately breast-feed them to keep them quiet. At the same time, the women would fondle the children's genitals whenever they fussed or cried. When that didn't work, they would sometimes feed the child a little opium milk to quieten them. Having seen that, Mother had no intention of taking that kind of risk with us.

That fondling of the children was also the practice of the Chinese amahs and was apparently not known to the foreign nationals in the coastal cities who hired them. Even when warned, they usually adamantly refused to believe it. However, when at Beidaihe Beach or other coastal spots, I frequently observed the amahs intimately fondling their little Western charges to keep them quiet. I sometimes remonstrated with them, telling them it wasn't the proper thing to do. They usually replied that they didn't do it just with children of foreigners that they were caring for, it was common practice with their own children, and what was wrong with it anyway?

In America it would likely be considered sexual molestation or abuse. However, among Chinese men as well, the habit of fondling children's genitals, particularly boy's genitals, was extremely common. No Chinese children ever wore diapers. Instead, the Chinese had a very practical solution. The children's pants had neither seat nor crotch, and thus nothing to wet or soil. Children were early taught what we call "potty training," which in China meant squatting wherever they might be, on the floor indoors or outside on the ground, after which the family dog would be called over not only to clean up the mess, but also to lick the child's bottom clean.

Chinese are doting parents, and fathers love to carry their children — especially their boys — wherever they go, to show them off to their friends. When the father met a friend in the street and stopped to chat, the child would naturally fuss after a while, whereupon the friend would immediately thrust his hand into the open crotch between the child's legs and fondle his penis until he quieted down. It was very effective, and as far as I know from personal observation, the habit never led to trauma of any sort with the child.

Chinese considered it a very friendly and intimate gesture when friends met each other with their children. As a very small child I experienced it on many occasions. Of course, I wore trousers, and that baffled the efforts of the men or women who attempted to fondle me. Nonetheless, they would then thrust their hands into my trouser pockets, and try to reach my genitals that way. I would try to squirm out of their reach and Father would at once, and very politely, tell them that we, as Westerners, did not have that custom. Even when I was five or six and walking around on my own, I experienced the same thing on numerous occasions when casual Chinese acquaintances, or even strangers, attempted to fondle me. To them it was the most natural thing in the world, a purely friendly gesture, with nothing of a salacious or sexual intent whatsoever.

I have no doubt that that early practice led to widespread masturbation by the boys themselves in later life, because we witnessed much of that among young boys. But we saw no indication that it led to homosexuality, which, although not unknown in China, was extremely rare. In Lingyuan, for example, we had only one known homosexual. He was an outgoing person, very effeminate in his walk, talk, and behavior, and he was widely ridiculed. He went by the name of Wang Niangzi, or "Wang the Woman." Although he knew he was called that, it didn't seem to bother him.

All those "servant" friends of ours were wonderful people, and we loved them dearly. Of all of them, with the exception perhaps of Lao San, I think Mr. Hu, our gatekeeper, was the one I spent most of my time with as a young lad. In addition to being gate-keeper, Mr. Hu was also considered to be a teacher, a category of people greatly respected. In China, one uses the word *gu* to mean "to hire" a servant, but in the case of an educated man like Mr. Hu, the term used was to *qing* or "invite" him aboard. In most cases watching over the gate would be considered a demeaning job, but Mr. Hu was a devout Christian, and he loved to tell others of the Christ he had found and loved. When Father first explained the job to him, and asked him if he would take it, Mr. Hu welcomed it as a golden opportunity to speak of Christ to the many people who came each day into the mission compound.

I've spoken of Mr. Hu as our chief buyer. I'm reminded that he wasn't always too successful when buying coal. A number of small coal mines were in the area, all of them operated by private individuals. Some of the mines produced a superior quality anthracite, others a soft coal that smoked a lot but still gave off a reasonable amount of heat. To Mr. Hu, anything black was coal, and he couldn't tell the difference between the different kinds. Several mines produced beautiful shiny-looking "coal," but it was nothing but black shale, was extremely difficult to light, and would produce very little heat. It also left huge clinkers that stopped up the grates. Eventually, after suffering through a number of loads of that poor quality stuff, Father had to tell Mr. Hu to bring him a sample before making a purchase.

Eggs were another thing that Mr. Hu purchased for us. We kept our own laying hens, and for many years, all were Chinese hens, which were somewhat erratic and temperamental about laying. Later, on one of his trips to the coast, Father brought back some fertile eggs from Leghorns and Rhode Island Reds. When they hatched, we gradually developed a nice flock of hens that produced eggs for a good part of the year. At first, looking after the hens was my job, but when one of the hens hanged itself on a loop of string that I had used to tie up a bunch of lettuce for them, Father decided to let my younger sister, Barbara, take over. She, in fact, did a much better job than I ever could have. She not only fed and petted them, she knew each one by name and kept meticulous and detailed records of each hen's egg production. When any one of her hens turned up on the dining table, poor Barbara grieved sorely, and it is not surprising that she never developed a taste for chicken.

Even with our own hens, though, there were times during the winter months when it was too cold for them to lay, and Mr. Hu would watch out for farmers bringing eggs to market. Many of the peasants kept their hens inside their houses, where it was warmer, and so they had eggs the year-round. But the Chinese also had the trick of storing eggs in boxes of grain, where they kept relatively fresh for a time. Unfortunately, on several occasions Mr. Hu bought eggs that turned out to be rotten, so Father devised a method of testing them in cold water. If the eggs sank to the bottom they were good, but if they floated, they were bad. That worked well for a time, but one or two of the more avaricious peasants caught on to the idea and hard-boiled their eggs before coming in and offering them to Mr. Hu. Naturally, they all sank to the bottom, and Mr. Hu bought them. However, Mr. Hu was no dummy, and he very soon came to recognize the individuals who pulled that trick and refused to deal with them.

Generally we found most Chinese businessmen to be scrupulously honest in their dealings with us, but there were always exceptions. Father used to tell the story of an Englishwoman in Tientsin who had a great love for birds, particularly finches and wild canaries, which the Chinese caught and sold in small cages. The lady didn't want to see them caged, so she would buy up all she could find and free them. The bird-sellers quickly caught on to what she was doing and came to her daily with trained sparrows they had dyed either yellow or red. The lady bought them as usual and freed them, whereupon the birds would return to their owners, who re-caged them, and the cycle would be repeated. It took many months before the lady learned what was happening.

Those then were the men-servants with whom we grew up as children. However, we thought of them only as friends. They tended to spoil us, and my parents had to remind them constantly to let us stand on our own two feet.

Although we never used amahs, there were several Chinese women on the payroll, because we always had young, unmarried women missionaries living with us, and we had to exercise extreme caution and observe all the proprieties of Chinese custom. It was not proper for men servants to go into those ladies' rooms under any circumstances either to deliver water, or to service the coal stoves, etc., without a Chinese woman present. For that reason, Lao San's mother, (also surnamed Hu, but no relation to the gatekeeper) and to whom we had given the unlikely nickname Peter, had the dual role of taking care of the single missionary ladies, as well as being Mother's Bible Woman.

Bible Women were Christian women who could read, and they went from house to house teaching the Bible to all who wanted to listen. Mrs. Hu was a lovely person. She lived with Lao San until he married, then she moved in with the orphan girls and became their chaperone. A dedicated Christian, by her gentle manner, soft speech, and genuine interest in all with whom she came in touch, she, over the years, led many Chinese women to Christ.

And then, of course, there was the sewing woman, Mrs. Wu. Her year-round job was primarily sewing for the orphans. Their clothing, bedding, and shoes all had to be hand made, and although for the most part she worked in the little room in the third courtyard, she also spent a good part of her time demonstrating sewing techniques to the orphan girls and teaching them her tricks.

Their winter clothing was the most time-consuming job for her. Most Chinese of the peasant class had only one suit of winter clothes, and their children were frequently sewn into their clothing for the duration of the winter. However, Mother insisted that the orphans should have two sets each. One was for everyday wear, one for Sundays. Each spring, all padded clothing had to be made over, and all Chinese housewives became involved in that task after spring planting. Each item of clothing had to be taken apart, the inner and outer layers washed, and the cotton-wool padding had to be painstakingly picked apart, fluffed out for re-use, and mixed each year with some new cotton-wool. The same thing was done with their winter bedding.

All those dear people who worked with us were paid, but in terms of U.S. dollars, the sum total of all their salaries was a pittance. When I was a child, the old Imperial currency of brass "cash" and silver "taels" was still in use, particularly in the back coun-

try where we lived. In the cities, the government was struggling to do away with the unwieldy strings of "cash" and the awkward silver tael, slices or chunks of which had to be cut off with a knife and then weighed. When I was very small, I watched Father do that, weighing it on a tiny "steelyard." After the 1911 revolution the new currency was a silver dollar, much like the United States dollar in size and appearance, but far less in value. But it was a long time before they started circulating up our way in any quantity.

At first, the Chinese government had no facilities for minting the coin, and purchased millions of silver dollars from Mexico. From that came the name "Mex Dollar," which was widely used for many years, and which was even applied to the silver dollars that the Chinese finally began minting themselves carrying the likeness of Yuan Shih-kai, their first president.

There were also no banks in Lingyuan in those early years, so most missionaries did their banking in either Peking or Tientsin. The larger missionary societies all had regional headquarters in those cities, and, in our case, the China Inland Mission in Tientsin graciously accorded us the privilege of using their facilities whenever we visited Tientsin. At the same time they handled our funds for us.

Father kept an account with the British-owned Hong Kong and Shanghai Banking Corporation in Tientsin for funds originating in the United Kingdom, and had another account with a branch of the National City Bank of New York for funds coming from the United States. However, there was no way to cash checks from those banks in Lingyuan. Rather than have to make the long journey to Tientsin, then carry back relatively large sums in silver dollars to Lingyuan, Father worked out a convenient arrangement with local merchants of repute, and started accounts in silver dollars with them.

The merchants, who made regular trips to Tientsin to buy more stock, were also reluctant to carry large amounts of silver dollars with them because of so many bandits on the roads. Therefore, when they needed cash to spend in Tientsin, Father would give them a check to cash there, and they in turn would credit the same amount to his account with them. The system worked for years without a hitch. But after one or two incidents where the merchants were robbed of their checks by bandits, another method was devised. A note would be written to the business manager of the China Inland Mission in Tientsin, asking him to give the bearer whose "chop" appeared on the note a certain sum of money. The merchant would carry a copy and the original would be sent to Tientsin by mail. Thus, if the merchant lost his copy, he could still get his money by presenting his "chop," or personal seal at the mission in Tientsin.

After the Japanese occupied Jehol Province in 1933, when severe penalties were meted out to anyone transferring large sums of cash across the borders, the system played an even more important part in enabling us to keep going. We simply modified it so no sum of money was mentioned in the note carried by the merchant. Instead, we resorted to the subterfuge of asking that the bearer be given some quantity of "butter," or some other commodity to indicate the sums in tens, hundreds, or thousands.

Lingyuan merchants kept their accounts in small, accordion-pleated booklets with a hard cover at each end. The whole thing was housed in a slipcase about the size of a package of cigarettes, bound in blue cloth. On the face of each booklet was a bright red label with the name of the client. When Father wanted to withdraw money from his account, Mr. Hu would be entrusted with this *zhezi*, as it was called, a name which simply meant something that folded up, and would go to the particular merchant who held that account, returning with a bag full of silver dollars from which all were paid.

The average pay for all the people who worked for us was six Mex dollars per month. The rate of exchange at that time was somewhere around seven Mex dollars for one U.S. dollar. Consequently they were each earning something less than one U.S. dollar per month and the monthly payroll for everyone, including Sun Shifu the carpenter, and any workmen who happened to be working on the buildings, seldom exceeded US $40 in any given month.

On those seemingly infinitesimal sums of money, a Chinese family could live quite well. Of course, their housing was in most cases provided for, and Father did many other things to help them make ends meet. Most of them never had enough ready cash to buy large supplies of grain or fuel at harvest time, when they were least expensive. As we had ample storage space, Father would buy cartloads of grain and *shujie*, and by purchasing in such large quantities, he could get a much better price.

Another of Mr. Hu's responsibilities was distributing those supplies each month to those who needed them. We had a large Chinese bushel measure, a *dou*, shaped like a trapezoid, with all four sides tapering to the top — a shape favored by the Chinese — and bound with iron at all the corners. Filled, and with the top leveled off with a flat stick, it was an exact measurement. Smaller quantities were measured out with cylindrical containers equivalent to our "peck."

The Chinese term for a servant is *yong ren*, which literally means "use person." Our *yong ren*, after trips to Beidaihe with us, where they came into contact with servants who worked for other foreigners, frequently told us that of all the Westerners, it was the Americans who knew least how to "use" or deal with their servants. Whether that was due to a desire to demonstrate "democracy" or from a feeling of guilt at using the services of a fellow human being, I don't pretend to know. What I do know is that many American business people treated their servants as part of the family, inviting them to sit down with them when talking to them, and even eating meals together. On the other hand, there were others who treated their servants as non-persons, with total disregard for their welfare, and frequently acted as though their servants were not human. Either way, what that often resulted in was their servants taking advantage of them at every turn, while robbing them blind when making purchases for them, and thoroughly despising them in the process.

We knew one American missionary who had at one time been a carpenter in the United States. He had felt the call to go to China as a missionary, but strictly as a working missionary in his capacity as a carpenter. His objective was to build houses for other American missionaries, not to preach. However, after he had built several houses, he developed such a love for the Chinese that he learned the language and turned to evangelistic work, spending most of his time traveling in the countryside on horseback, accompanied by a single servant, who rode on a mule. The servant, acting also as his cook, had the primary job of caring for the animals at night in the inns. The practice was to get up several times during the night to feed them, and our American friend was so democratic that he set his alarm clock and got up to feed the animals himself, leaving his servant to sleep. As a result, he was the laughing-stock of everyone wherever he went.

Our own staff, close as we were to them, always respected the fact that we were their employers. They always stood when being spoken to, head down and eyes averted in true Chinese fashion. Even though as Christians, we treated them in church as fellow brothers and sisters, they never took advantage of that intimacy in their serving capacity. Those wonderful people with whom I grew up greatly enriched my life. I look back now on all of them with a great sense of nostalgia and deep appreciation, and feel a need to let the world know what remarkable people they really were.

Making shoes for the girls in the school.

Helpers in the compound with two happy children.

Stoking the charcoal in the iron.

Cutting up ice for the vegetable pit.

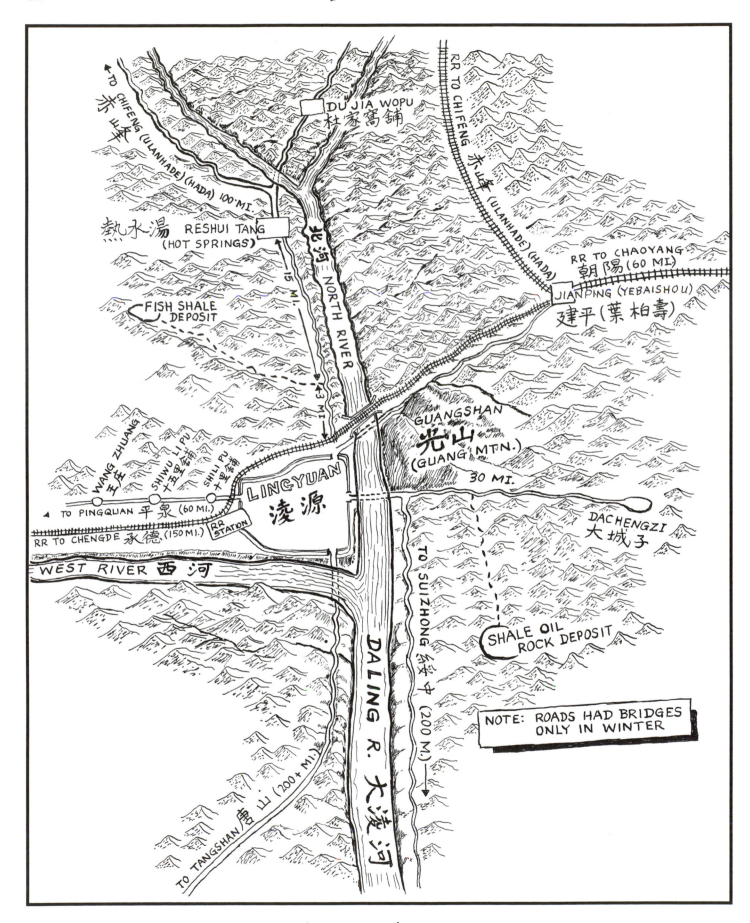

Lingyuan and vicinity.

由浅入深

You qian ru shen

(Lit. From the shallow enter the deep,
i.e., from the easy,
proceed to the difficult.)

- Chinese Saying.

Chapter Eight
Schooling and Holidays

My brother, two sisters and I were the only white children in Lingyuan for most of my childhood. When I was four or five years old I became aware of a Scottish family there with a boy and a girl about our own ages. Their name was McAlpine, but a year or so later they were gone. They lived across the street and down a few doors from us, but strangely enough, I have no recollection of our ever going to their house to play, nor of their coming over to ours. I remember going over there one Christmas morning to take them some presents, and Mrs. McAlpine served us some cookies she had made, but they were filled with caraway seeds, which were new to me, and which I've disliked ever since. Although other missionaries in the province had children, we seldom saw them, or any other white children, except when we went to Beidaihe Beach every three years or so. Despite that, we never felt isolated.

There was a minimum three-year age difference among the four of us, so our play habits differed considerably. Yet we got along wonderfully well together. Barbara and I in particular were inseparable companions, and we had many adventures together. As she learned to walk, Chang Yin and I were the ones charged with looking after her. I felt proud of my part in the job and took the responsibility very seriously.

At that time Chinese boys had much more freedom than girls. To the ages of eight or ten, boys and girls played together, particularly in the rural areas where they were usually stark naked in the hot summer months. After that, and as they entered puberty, the girls were rigidly segregated. Boys and girls were never seen together, except in the company of adults. We largely ignored that taboo, and as I grew older and was allowed to go pretty much where I pleased, Barbara accompanied me much of the time, particularly after we were old enough to have bicycles.

With the large number of American and British nationals in China, it was natural that a number of good schools were established in various coastal cities. Most of the missionaries in China sent their children to those good boarding schools and, because of the distances involved and the poor transportation, they seldom saw their children for more than short periods once or twice a year. In our case, because of general unrest and the danger and difficulties of travel, my parents decided against that policy and elected to educate us at home. They doubtless believed that a good normal home life, even though it meant separation from other white children of our own age, was more important in the long run. I guess they also wanted to enjoy their children for as long as possible.

For a short time an exception was made with my older brother, Gilbert. In 1919, when we returned from a furlough in the United States and England, Gil was dropped off at a coastal city then known as Chefoo by foreigners. Its Chinese name is Yantai. At that time it was a United States naval base. The China Inland Mission had established a school there specifically for the children of missionaries.

A coastal port on the Shandong peninsula, Chefoo could best be reached by coastal steamer from Tientsin, or from Dairen in Manchuria. Gil, who was around twelve, went there in May 1919 or thereabouts, and at Christmastime Father made the long journey, first by cart and railway to Tientsin, then by ship to Chefoo, to bring him home for the holidays. The round trip took almost a month. When the time came for Gil to return, Mother decided against it. I don't know the reason for the decision, but I suspect that, although the unsettled conditions with civil war all around us played a part, my parents simply did not want to break up the family. They missed him greatly, as we all did.

Before Gil went to Chefoo, he and my older sister, Ruth, had been taught at home. So it was with me when I became old enough. In her younger days in England, Mother had been a teacher in a public school for some years. She was well experienced and both she and my father were well educated and, more importantly, knew how to pass on their knowledge to others.

A large two-*jian* room in our third courtyard was set up as a schoolroom, complete with desks and blackboard made by Sun Shifu. There each morning and afternoon we studied the "Three R's" as in any other school. Mother was a strict disciplinarian. Very early she taught us the meaning of the honor system.

We started school after our early breakfast, and for the first hour or two Mother would go over our lessons with us, give us assignments, and then for two or three hours she went down to the dispensary to tend the sick. When she returned just before lunch time, she expected to find the work done. If it wasn't done to her satisfaction, she wanted to know why. Any serious misbehavior or failure to finish an assignment meant standing in the corner for a period as punishment. We even had a dunce cap, which each of us wore from time to time.

Those school days were among the happiest of my life. As a small boy, I couldn't wait until it was my turn to have my own desk in the schoolroom. I had watched the desks being made. Each desk had its inkwell and a lift-up top with space inside for our books. Typically, we sat on backless stools — just like the Chinese — and were expected to sit up straight, without slouching.

As all schoolwork does, from time to time our studies became tedious, and, like all children, we sometimes took advantage of the fact that we were alone and got into mischief of one sort or the other. Whenever we heard some activity outside in the yard, we were tempted to run to the window to see what it was, and when workmen were busy on some project outside, it was very hard to keep one's attention on lessons.

In general, I think we did as well as could be expected. Gil, being the eldest, was given the unenviable job of being "prefect," as classroom monitors were called in those days, and the rest of us were expected to obey him. He took his duties very seriously but did not abuse his authority over us. However, where I as the little brother was concerned, he developed his own unique form of discipline for various "offenses," both inside the classroom and out. Serious misbehavior earned me a clout — a sidelong swipe with the flat of his hand to the back of my head. It was painless, but drew my attention. For lesser offenses he gave me a "clicket," which was an upward swipe with his palm over my forehead. They well served their purpose, but his ultimate punishment was informing Mother of our misdeeds. Mother, on the other hand, was an understanding person, and although she had a paddle that was supposed to be used on our backsides when necessary, I do not recall an incident where she used it in the schoolroom.

However, my parents believed in corporal punishment in moderation. The Chinese have a saying: "*gunzi tour chu xiao zi*," — "out of the end of a stick comes a filial son." Father didn't use a stick or a paddle, but the flat of his trouser belt. In the worst cases, it was the threat of using the buckle end. I can recall times when I deserved and got a belting on my bare backside, but he never did use the buckle. In any case, all such punishment was delivered in love, and I have only the fondest memories of my parents.

Our school day lasted about six hours, as I recall. Mother covered all the usual subjects. Geography in particular was a subject I enjoyed. With all our travels, I was always interested in maps and places. World history was another subject I liked. However, I abhorred grammar, particularly "parsing," when one had to take a sentence, dissect it, minutely describe each word, and name its grammatical part of speech. I never did well, and to this day grammar and punctuation are my weakest points.

I loved doing "sums" as we called arithmetic, but algebra was another thing entirely. I would have been most happy if this, and later geometry, had been left out of the curriculum. Foreign languages were included. Mother was fluent in French and gave us a good grounding in that language. Of course, we took Latin, and much in the same way as Chinese students did, we loudly shouted the Latin declensions in the approved manner. Unfortunately, for all the good it did me, the only thing I seem to remember about Latin is that "mensa" meant "table," and I am not entirely sure about that.

There was talk at one time of sending me to the Chefoo school when I reached the age of twelve. However, civil wars and the general unrest prevented it. Instead, when Mother felt I was ready, I was enrolled in a correspondence course from Wolsey Hall in Oxford, England. For a number of years thereafter, I studied alone, although Mother was always near when I ran into difficulties. The correspondence course had been set up many years before by alumni of Oxford University to serve the children of the British Empire's overseas diplomats and businessmen, but anyone with the money for tuition was welcome to join.

The curriculum was tailored to the student. One selected the subjects and indicated how many hours per week were available for study, and the school did the rest. Individual tutors were assigned to each student for every subject, and the lesson materials were mailed from England at staggered intervals, with the intention that they should reach the student every second week, and with enough content to last until the next one arrived. In principle that was fine. However, at the time, mail was sent from England either by sea, a very long trip that took some six weeks or more even by the fastest mail steamers, or by the Trans-Siberian Railroad, which was supposed to take between two and three weeks from the time the letters left London.

Then, mail service in China was among the most reliable in the world. But frequently, because of civil disturbances, bandits, or other causes, mail deliveries were erratic. Sometimes mail from England even by the "fast" route might not reach us for six weeks or more. That meant that on occasion, several weeks would go by with no correspondence course materials reaching me. Then two or three of the large manila envelopes would arrive at once. It was very frustrating at first, but I learned to live with it.

The lessons were all mimeographed with purple ink on legal-sized sheets of light blue paper. I can see them now. Instructions were very detailed, requiring a great deal of reading, together with much practice work. The course was designed very systematically, and, if one followed the instructions, one couldn't go wrong. In addition, each lesson covering each subject was usually accompanied by a hand-written letter from the individual tutor assigned to that subject. In the letter, he or she discussed the student's progress and invited a letter in response if there were any further questions about the work. The method led to a very close and friendly relationship between tutor and student. All along I felt I was working with friends.

I had no problem with the reading part. From the time I had learned to read I devoured every book we had. Father managed to create a very diversified library for us. He unearthed books in the large second-hand markets in Tientsin and Peking, where he always found large numbers of English-language books. In addition to the ones mentioned in a previous chapter, Father got us Sir Walter Scott's books and a considerable number of others on a variety of more general topics.

We also had a large number of religious books, which Father kept in his study. We primarily read them on Sundays when no other reading material was permitted. My parents also made sure that we kept up with current affairs — as much as was possible with the somewhat erratic mail service. In addition to the English-language newspapers obtained in Tientsin and Peking, always a week or two late, Father subscribed to the famous English weekly, the Illustrated London News. It was much like Life, which someone sent us from America.

The latter however, with its somewhat graphic display of female anatomy in advertisements and news stories, was usually censored by Father before we ever saw it. That was not so much because of any improper impressions it might give us children, but rather so that, when left lying around, the pictures would not offend the morals of the extremely puritanical and conservative Chinese. On the other hand, the precautionary measure was perhaps superfluous. Pornography was nothing new to the Chinese. They've had their own forms of explicit pornography for centuries, not only in their literature, but also in their art. As a very small boy I recall going with Father to a county fair where, on the counter of a food stall, I saw two-foot-high nude figures of a man and a woman made of fine porcelain. The figures were hollow, and the proportions exquisite. The man's figure, in a standing position, contained tea, which was dispensed as he urinated when a lever was pressed. The woman, depicted in a squatting position, "gave birth" to meat balls at the touch of a handle. Strangely enough, the figures attracted no special attention from the crowds of Chinese milling around. To them, the figurines were simply a pragmatic use of pottery.

But getting back to my correspondence course. With each two weeks' work there was a fairly long and comprehensive test on that batch of work. That had to be completed and mailed back to Oxford. The answers were always contained in the next package, so, in theory, I did not have long to wait to see what mistakes I had made. However, the test paper itself, graded and with notations made by the tutor, seldom got back to me in less than three or four months. After that length of time, it was tedious to go back and look at something that had become history.

On those occasions when several thick envelopes of study material had arrived in one batch, it was most difficult to work on those tests, and it took a great deal of will power not to peek into one of them

to see the answers. Often, when I had completed the test to the best of my ability and had sealed it in the return envelope, I would hastily tear open the next set of lessons, to see how well I had done. Too often I was frustrated to see the stupid mistakes that I had made, but it was too late to rectify them.

All in all, it was an excellent course, and certainly, if nothing else, it built character. One subject I took was Biblical interpretation. The subject matter they sent me often differed greatly in its theology from the teachings I heard from my father. At first, when answering the test questions, I gave my own views and interpretations. As a result, I got very poor grades from my tutor in Oxford. After one or two such papers, he wrote me a personal letter. In it he said it was quite obvious to him that my religious viewpoint and beliefs differed greatly from his, and that was, of course, my privilege. However, he reminded me that what I was working on was an educational program, and he suggested that I should take the broad view and learn as much as possible about what other people believed. He added very kindly that I should answer the test questions according to the textual materials he had assigned, then state my own divergent views on a separate sheet of paper, and he would be glad to debate them with me. That I did, and an interesting theological correspondence developed between us that lasted for a year or more. At the same time, my grades improved.

So much for my formal education. I've not spent a day in a regular school in my entire life; however, I am hesitant to recommend that form of education to others. I have often been asked by parents here in America who are concerned with the deteriorating conditions in our public schools whether I would recommend their teaching their children at home or using correspondence courses as I did. I have difficulty in answering the question. It worked for me, but the circumstances and times were very different. I had no peers of my own age and race, so I could not compare my progress with others. In many years of teaching the Chinese language in the United States, I have found much evidence suggesting that healthy competition among fellow classmates leads to greater achievement by all. With that line of thought, had I had competition in my studies, I might have done much better than I did, but this is pure speculation. Although working alone so many hours a day for those several years of my youth was unquestionably character building, without the constant support and encouragement of my parents I could never have succeeded.

At the end of each phase in the Wolsey Hall correspondence course, I was supposed to take written and oral tests in the presence of some British Consular or Embassy representative in order to qualify for a certificate of satisfactory completion. The political situation, however, was so volatile, and the country in such a state of upheaval, that I was never able to make the necessary trips to Tientsin to meet the requirements. In the worldwide experience of the school that was not unusual. When I explained it to the registrar at Wolsey Hall, he agreed that my grades had been such to entitle me to certification, so each step of the way I was given a certificate without even asking for it.

How proud I was of those grandiloquent and often quaintly phrased certificates. Unfortunately, all were lost among our other papers and belongings at the outbreak of hostilities with Japan in World War II. Many years later, when it came time to apply for U.S. citizenship, and later for employment at Yale University and the Army Language School, those educational records were sorely needed. Fortunately, a letter explaining their loss to Wolsey Hall elicited a letter certifying that I had indeed earned diplomas for College of Preceptors, Junior and Senior Oxford, and Matriculation, the equivalent of more than two years of college in the United States. In every case, that letter was accepted without further question.

During those school days in China, my Chinese education had not been neglected. Father believed it important that, in addition to speaking the language fluently, I should also learn to read and write Chinese. Late each afternoon I had a Chinese tutor for an hour or more. I remember that young man with great fondness and we became fast friends.

He was a fine Christian lad named Zhang Yao-ting. He was a year or two older than I, but I always felt he was a great deal more mature. He had certainly undergone many more hardships. Not only did I read the Chinese classics with him, but we spent part of every hour reading the Bible in Chinese, and he spent some of the time teaching me to write Chinese characters with the conventional Chinese brush pen.

Chinese calligraphy is considered by all to be an art in itself, In fact, a really good Chinese calligrapher earns as much respect as any renowned artist. The uninitiated and casual observer may think that all Chinese handwriting is alike. The fact is that each individual's "brushmanship" is as distinctive and unique as the whorls of his fingerprints.

The method Zhang Yao-ting used in teaching me writing was as old as writing on paper itself. The Chinese invented it, and that's a long time back. Beginning with the simplest of characters consisting of one or two strokes, I was given a printed master sheet covered with characters written by an expert, each fitted in a neat frame approximately one inch square. Over it I was required to lay a very thin sheet of rice paper, blank except for the same size of neatly ruled squares, with the printed characters showing through.

After mixing the ink on a stone slab, using a stick of ink dipped in water, I was to copy the characters. Zhang Yao-ting taught me to hold the pen firmly upright between the thumb and first two fingers, the right wrist supported by the left wrist, which was resting on the desk in front of me. That permitted a freedom of wrist motion.

In copying the characters, it wasn't enough to get the initial outline. Every stroke had to match the one underneath: wide or narrow, thick or thin, tapering from a broad slash to a fine point, and so on. At no time was it permissible to touch one of the ruled lines of the squares.

Regretfully, despite the conscientious efforts of Zhang Yao-ting, I never became an accomplished calligrapher, possibly because I have no artistic talent. Another reason may be that at an early age I suffered an injury to my right hand that deprived me of its use for many months. Because of that, I resorted to using a typewriter and never regained my penmanship, even after the hand healed. Furthermore, and much to my regret, I neglected to maintain such ability in writing in Chinese as I had achieved, simply because there always seemed to be other more important things. If you don't use it, you lose it, and I lost it. What I did learn, however, stood me in good stead on many occasions in later life when it became necessary to communicate with Chinese from other parts of China who could not understand Mandarin. With such a variety of dialects across that huge land, most of them so different that people from even a few miles away cannot understand their neighbors, it is most fortunate that the Chinese character is universally the same in meaning. With people whose dialect I couldn't understand, I could still communicate by using the Chinese method of fingertip writing of the characters on my palm. What was much more important to me happened during World War II when we were interned by the Japanese. Unable to write to my wife in English, I was able to write her in Chinese. That, however, is an event that comes later in this narrative.

One thing that came from those daily lessons with Zhang Yao-ting was that I taught him not only to read and write English, but to a limited extent to speak it. That he could communicate in English was later to prove of immense help to us when, on furlough in the United States, we were able to receive letters from him, reporting on the ever-changing situation in Jehol, as the Japanese took over.

Those school days in China weren't always all work and no play. On Saturdays and Sundays, my parents always found time to spend with us. Every Saturday afternoon Father would take a long walk in the country to prepare and practice his sermons for the next day, and I would tag along. Usually he took along his shotgun, hoping that we might run across a hare or a pheasant somewhere on the hills, and occasionally we did. But I always realized that it was also protection against bandits. Fortunately, we never met any of them. Over the years we must have covered every square inch of the hills within a five-mile radius of Lingyuan, and I treasure the memory of those long walks with my father.

We frequently saw foxes, and an occasional wolf. The Chinese hunted them ruthlessly for their furs, and in time they disappeared. One hunting method the Chinese used was to scatter small, golf-ball-sized homemade grenades, coated with pig fat. When a fox or wolf bit into one of the grenades, the explosion killed it. We often saw those lethal objects lying around on the hills. Most of the shepherd boys knew what they were and avoided them, but occasionally one of the lads would be tempted to play with one, attempting to explode it by smashing it with a stone. Several young boys were killed playing with them, and on numerous occasions, Mother had to treat one of the boys for serious injuries.

Summer and winter I went on those walks with Father, Barbara joining us on numerous occasions as she got older. Father, always thoughtful, managed to carry some baker's chocolate, which he would produce at the moment when we were beginning to tire, when it was most needed. In later years, when we got bicycles, we roamed farther afield, and I accompanied Father on his preaching tours into the countryside villages.

Between the ages of six and ten I was famous for my affinity with water — not to drink, but to fall into. On more occasions than I can count, as Father and I walked in the countryside, we would ford a small mountain stream on stepping stones, or cross one of the two nearby rivers on makeshift footbridges. The footbridges were made of inch-thick boards about eight to ten inches in width, laid on A-frame trestles in the river, with no side rails or hand holds. When walking on them, the boards bounced up and down. My mistake was to either look down into the water flowing below, which caused vertigo, or to follow too closely behind Father's heels and get bounced off.

It wasn't serious in summer, since my clothes dried quickly, but in the winter, before the rivers froze solid, it always terminated our walk, much to my father's frustration, and I was hustled home for a change of clothing. But my falling into water wasn't limited to outdoor streams. Even after I mastered the art of crossing the footbridges — primarily by not following the person in front of me too closely — I had been known to fall into the bathtubs of water in the wash-house when You Wang was doing the laundry or into the baptistry when it was being filled for a baptismal service. I lost a lot of "face" with that distressing habit, but like everything else, I outgrew it, and presumably everyone except for me has forgotten it.

As a youngster I wanted to try everything. I envied Mother her skill with her hand-operated Pfaff sewing machine and her deftness with a needle. I, too, wanted to learn how to make clothes. When I was tall enough to reach it, I helped her turn the handle on the sewing machine, studying every move she made. One year for Christmas someone gave me a boy-doll. That winter, under Mother's directions, I spent many long and happy hours hand-sewing a variety of clothes for the doll. However, that activity came to a sudden and unexpected end one day when Barbara found the outdoors much more inviting than watching me sew. When I refused to go out and play with her in the garden, she picked up the scissors and snipped one of my ear lobes. The resulting copious bleeding scared everyone, but no great harm was done. Barbara shed a lot of tears and was inconsolable, and I had a hard time convincing her that she hadn't killed me.

Mother also taught all of us how to knit, and another winter I took to knitting with a great deal of enthusiasm, making my own gloves and scarves.

In the long winter evenings we sat around the green-shaded oil lamp in the dining room, and Mother or Father read to us, or we played Parcheesi while Father and Gil played chess. Other times Mother played the organ and we sang songs and hymns together, Mother teaching us how to take parts. I enjoyed the singing most of all, and to this day my eyes tear when I hear the hymn that begins: "I come to the garden alone, while the dew was still on the roses." That was Mother's favorite hymn and she sang it frequently, with great feeling.

One day while we were singing I got a bit bored and decided to simply mouth the words without singing them. I was astonished when, amidst the noise of all the others singing, Mother turned to me and told me to sing out loud. I never could understand how she had detected that I wasn't singing. Although Barbara at first was too small to enjoy the singing, the elaborate cloth-covered cut-out openings on the organ through which the sound came thoroughly intrigued her. One day while we were singing, she got a sharp piece of wood from the wood box next to the stove and punched out all the openings she could reach. She managed to take care of quite a few before any one of us noticed what she was doing. Naturally, a spanking followed.

While Saturday was the day that Father took us walking, Mother took us out on Sunday afternoons. However, Mother usually limited our walks to the area immediately behind our back garden, in winter going up the gullies to get out of the cold wind, and in summer walking through the tall sorghum.

One walk we very much enjoyed was visiting a fellow missionary, Miss Ada Blackmore, whose house was just about a mile north of our back garden wall and within sight of our garden. Now that I look back, I guess she was a bit on the eccentric side, but she didn't seem so to us then. She didn't want to live inside the city, so, against the advice of my father and the Chinese elders, she bought a piece of land at the very foot of the hills that came down close to the city. On that bit of land, between two deep gullies, she built a three-*jian* house for herself, and two more *jian* for a man and his wife who looked after her. She also built some sheds for a cart and horse that she bought. Her primary interest was visiting the womenfolk in the many villages that surrounded Lingyuan.

Unfortunately, Miss Blackmore chose her first horse by color, without getting the advice of someone who knew about horses. It wasn't until she got it home, and later bought the cart and harnessed the horse to it, that she discovered the horse was blind. Even so, she used that horse for several years. With a man leading it, the horse pulled the cart without any problem.

Because the ground rose up behind our garden, Miss Blackmore's place was in full view just above the garden wall. On Christmas Day, Miss Blackmore always came to spend the day with us, bringing us presents, and nothing would start until she arrived. As children, we used to stand out in the cold looking toward her place, waiting for her horse and cart to come out of the gate and head toward us. After that it was a good half-hour wait before she finally arrived, but at least we knew she was on the way.

Some years later, after the Japanese had taken over in Jehol Province and built what passed for motor roads, Miss Blackmore made the mistake of buying an automobile, but I'm getting ahead of myself in the story. In any case, it was quite a surprise to everyone, to say the least.

For vacations, we went to Beidaihe Beach every two or three years to escape the intense summer heat in Lingyuan. It was one of the Northern seaside resorts that had been developed by foreigners for the foreign community. However, a few wealthy Chinese had residences there, and there were a couple of small hotels.

Beidaihe was 180 miles northeast of Peking. Many years before some far-sighted individuals had purchased large areas of barren, rocky, and, to the Chinese, worthless land on that section of the Chinese coast. The main Peking-Mukden railroad passed about five miles inland from the beach, and the station stop was the small village called Peitaiho (now spelled Beidaihe), which meant "North Dai River." In the very early years when we first went there, it was necessary to detrain at that village and then hire local transport to the beach area. However, as the Chinese government saw the popularity of the place increasing, they built a branch line of the railroad to service the beach.

Part of the fun in going to Beidaihe was the ride on that special branch-line train. The equipment was new, kept scrupulously clean, and was only used for the few summer months each year by those going on holiday. Getting off the crowded mainline train and transferring to this local beach train was always exciting. Not only was one likely to meet old friends, but there were always other children our age.

After nearly a half hour's ride through an ocean of sorghum fields, with an almost unbroken line of tall willow trees on each side of the track, we would arrive at the Beach Station and the end of the line. There, after all the baggage was assembled, we would face the clamor of dozens of rickshaw pullers competing to attract our attention and get our trade.

The railroad station was in a part of the beach area called Rocky Point. It was an extension of a Chinese fishing village that had been there for many centuries. It was composed of one street, lined with Western-style shops, most of them branches of stores in Tientsin and Peking that catered to the foreign population. Behind the stores were villas and summer cottages all the way down to the ocean, most owned and used by business people.

The majority of the missionaries spent the summer months in a more remote area called East Cliff. That area had a mixed population, and was by no means limited to missionaries. East Cliff, four or five miles to the east of Rocky Point, was reached by a narrow, winding road over the rolling terrain, lined on both sides by flourishing acacia trees, cultivated fields of sorghum, millet and sweet potatoes, and for most of the distance, within sight of the ocean.

All the roads in the area, with hard all-weather surfaces made from decomposed granite, were well kept, but most of them were barely wide enough for two rickshaws to pass. Hearing them called "macadamized roads" sounded most impressive to me as a small boy, and that was one of the first English words I learned how to spell. There were no automobiles in the entire area, only bicycles, rickshaws and donkeys. The donkeys were equipped with a white cloth cover over a padded cloth saddle (quite often not too clean), but they were fun to ride, and a favorite of most everyone.

East Cliff itself was on a hilly and very rocky peninsula that jutted into the Gulf of North Chili, as it was then known. The gulf was an extension of the famous Yellow Sea of China, colored by the silt carried down by the great rivers running into it.

Flying to China nowadays, I doubt that, from the high altitude at which modern planes fly, the astonishing change in the color of the ocean can be seen as we used to see it in the old days of the steamships. In those days approaching the Yellow Sea, the Captain would notify the passengers as the ship neared the line of demarcation. From the deep brilliant blue of the Pacific, a clearly delineated line suddenly crossed the ocean where the color instantly changed to a muddy yellow and the water appeared quite opaque. One had the sensation, in crossing that line, that the ship was about to run aground, or at the very least bump into something, and that was some two or three hundred miles at sea.

A few miles later, and still a day or so away from port, came the all-pervading odor that is China, a smell that many have tried to describe, but which, unless one has experienced it and met it many miles at sea, can never be truly appreciated — if that is the right word.

The smell of China is totally different from the smell of Africa, which is one of rotting vegetation. China's smell has been described by some authors as the smell of the "unwashed millions." But that is not the origin of the smell, and it is a totally inadequate description. Strangely enough, once ashore, one becomes quite accustomed to the odor in a very short time. The nose tends to notice and appreciate other and more pleasant things, or so it was with us. It was only when we approached the land by sea after a trip abroad that we once again identified that unique aroma and felt were home again.

While technically a part of the Yellow Sea, the water at Beidaihe Beach wasn't yellow. It always seemed to us a marvelously clear blue, like the brilliant crisp blue of the kingfisher's wing, the normal color of the sky in North China in those days before pollution. Each year when we went to the beach, we reveled in the first sight of the ocean. It was always breathtaking, no matter how many times we had seen it.

But Beidaihe with all its beauty was simply a vacation spot for a few months. It wasn't home, but we had many wonderful adventures there, and on the beach one day, I met the girl who was eventually to become my wife. However, as much as we enjoyed the three months or so we spent at the seashore, we were always happy to go back to Lingyuan and the warm welcome that always awaited us there.

Cooling off at Beidaihe. Barbara, Mr. Tharp, Ruth, Mrs. Tharp (partially hidden behind Ruth), Gil and Bob.

Out for a walk on a cold day. Bob, Barbara, Ruth.

Bob's teacher on the left and good friend on the right.

左家靠非父母，
出外靠非朋友

Zai jia kao fu mu, chu wai kao pengyou.

At home one depends on parents,
abroad one relies on friends.

- Chinese Proverb.

Chapter Nine
Mostly About Neighbors

For us as children, our back garden was a place of total safety and privacy most of the time. On rare occasions one of the cows would break its halter and in joyous abandon come galumphing around the garden, tearing up the vegetable beds and enjoying mouthfuls of the various vegetable leaves. They were no real danger, but we were always terrified. More dangerous were the stray dogs that occasionally found their way into the garden. That happened sometimes during the rainy season, when one or the other of the back walls would become waterlogged and topple inside our garden or into our neighbor's. Again, perhaps there was no great danger from the dogs, but we liked to think there was and took no chances. We were all adept at climbing trees to avoid them, and sooner or later someone would come and catch the cow or chase the dogs away.

One of our favorite pastimes on a hot summer's day was to sit on a branch among the leaves in one of the trees near the wall and watch our neighbors' com-

ings and goings. To the east, between us and the prison, was a garden even bigger than ours but with very few trees. In summer it was always planted with opium poppies, and we would watch from day to day as the crop was sown, watered, hoed, and tended carefully until the flowers bloomed. It was a beautiful sight then: over an acre of red, pink, purple, blue, and white flowers which lasted for about ten days until the harvesting.

The well in that garden was more or less public, and a constant stream of water carriers passed back and forth in front of us. Every morning and afternoon a group of prisoners carried water for the prison, all of them with chains clanking on their wrists and ankles. We pitied them greatly as they shuffled by, guarded by one or two policemen. Seeing us watching, they would often call to us. There was no short-cut to the prison. Several times each day the prisoners had to travel the full length of the garden, out into the street, and down to the Yamen, and then into the prison. They weren't the most dangerous criminals, but were the fittest of the crowd and possibly it provided them a bit of variation from the monotony of prison life.

When the opium poppies were being watered, two water buckets were used on the same windlass with two men operating it, standing opposite each other. As an empty bucket went down, a full one came up. The men, paid by the number of buckets they drew, sang aloud the numbers of buckets drawn. They didn't like being interrupted by people coming for water, even though it gave them a bit of rest, and there were frequent altercations.

After the petals fell off, harvesting the opium began. The work was done chiefly by women, many with children strapped on their backs. Each woman was equipped with a tiny curved knife on a ring that was placed on the first finger of her right hand. With it she would make an incision around the green and as yet unripened seed pod. Each pod had to be cut once or twice each day for about ten days, until they were completely dried out. The pods were about an inch or more in diameter, and an inch and a half high. As the incision was made, a thick, somewhat whitish-colored juice would ooze out. The women would wipe it up and in a circular motion with another finger smear it into a small tin cup held in their left hands.

At any given time there might be a hundred or so women working in that one garden, cutting the thousands upon thousands of poppy heads. Every now and then the women licked some of the poppy juice off their fingers, and, if the baby was fussing, they would smear some on the baby's lips. Bitter and acrid to the taste in that form, it was unlikely to be addictive. When asked about it, the women said that it helped relieve their tiredness. The babies, although usually making a face when they tasted it, seemed to quiet down for a time. The high morphine content was dangerous if consumed in a sizable quantity, but none of the women seemed to suffer from the small amounts they took. Minuscule as the amount of juice gleaned from a single poppy plant was, the overall harvest from that one garden was immense and very profitable to the owner.

When the poppy heads were completely dry, and no further juice could be gleaned from them, they were harvested for their tiny black seeds, seeds that are so familiar to Americans on their seeded buns.

Even in the raw form the seeds were quite tasty. We tried them occasionally, but our parents didn't like us to do so. They weren't harmful, but the association of those pods, with their multitudinous ugly brown cuts, was too strong a reminder of the vicious opium drug that was the end result when the juice had undergone the "cooking" process, as was the crime, degradation, poverty and death that followed in its wake for the users and addicts.

Although much has been written about the widespread use of opium in China in those days, it certainly wasn't the case in that part of China in which we lived. In all the years we were there, we saw relatively little use by those who produced it; it was too valuable a commodity to be lightly treated. The producers used opium only in cases of severe pain or illness. More often than not, when taken for pain relief, addiction resulted. I knew a number of individuals who had started the habit in that way. One of them was our near neighbor to the west, Mr. He. He had come down with a severe case of hemorrhoids, and like so many in similar situations, started smoking opium to relieve the pain. In a very short time he became enslaved.

According to many popular novels, opium dens were to be found on every street in China. I knew of only two or three public opium "dens" in Lingyuan where one could go and be provided with a pipe, a young lad to tend it, and a place on the *kang* to spend a few blissful hours. I've been into many such places in North China (to look, not to smoke) and they were quite unlike the "dens" that novelists or movie makers like to depict in their stories about China. Girls or women were never present and the places were purely functional. One went there for one purpose only — to relieve the craving that was a part of addiction or to relieve pain.

Opium smoking was primarily limited to the middle class or the wealthy. Of course, much was smoked also in private homes or in places of business where the entire staff lived on the premises. We often recognized the smell of opium smoke as we walked on the streets, particularly at night. Nevertheless, I would estimate that less than 1 percent, or even half of 1 percent, of the population could afford to smoke it.

The opium growers seldom sold their product in its raw form directly from the field. Everyone seemed to be an expert in preparing it for market. In the process of curing or "cooking" it, the Chinese were adept at adulterating it with a variety of other things, one of the most common being a concoction produced from uncured animal skins — particularly goat skins — and certain plant leaves that had been boiled in water for many hours. The adulteration was done in much the same way that glue was made. The resulting "broth" was then cooked with the raw opium, resulting in a brownish-colored paste.

Most of the paste was exported from the province. In the years of Japanese occupation, when the area was known as Manchukuo, it was a highly prized government monopoly, and many Japanese became addicts. Despite the quantity exported, there was always enough remaining for the local addicts, and unfortunately, it was always readily available for those wishing to take their own lives. It was, in fact, the most common way to commit suicide. Swallowed in a sufficiently large quantity, it was invariably fatal. However, if detected in time, a strong emetic to produce copious vomiting would usually save the victim.

Suicides or attempted suicides were extremely common among young wives in North China, and it was one of the most common topics of conversation. That was one of the main reasons Mother had such a loathing for the drug. From her earliest experience in treating the sick, she had developed a strong emetic just for the purpose of saving attempted suicides. However, I often heard my parents wondering aloud whether the fact that the young wives knew of the availability of the "cure" was, in some cases, a contributing factor in the suicide attempt. Sometimes the victims only took a token amount of opium, just to scare those who were mistreating them or with whom they had had a fight. Of course, many of the young women who took opium had been miserably treated, either by their husbands or by their mothers-in-law, and genuinely wanted to die. But we also knew of many cases where a fight between married couples, or between a young wife and her mother-in-law, or even a fight between neighbors, resulted in a suicide attempt simply to gain "face" and cause extreme embarrassment to the other party.

The emetic to save lives was the only medicine that Mother supplied from her dispensary for which she charged a fee; everything else was free. I can well remember as a small boy how all of us helped Mother prepare those life-saving doses. Once or twice a month we would gather around the dining room table, where one of us would be given the job of cutting up newspapers into tiny sheets about four inches square. Mother would carefully measure out the required dosage, weighing each dose on a small pair of scales, then mix it with either flour or crudely refined Chinese sugar, and transfer it to the small sheet of paper, which we would then fold in the traditional Chinese "envelope" shape. We achieved that by folding one corner over the pile of white powder. That fold was turned over frontward, and after that, both sides would be folded in toward the middle and the fourth corner would be tucked into the pocket thus formed.

The resulting packets were kept in a big tin container that was placed where all of us could find it in an emergency. Another tin was placed beside it to hold the money we collected. Mother taught each of us the urgency of getting the cure to the victim as quickly as possible. In the event we were absent, the gatekeeper, Mr. Hu, the cook, Gao Cai, and You Wang, the houseboy, all knew where to go for those little life-saving packages.

It seemed that 90 percent of the suicide attempts happened at night, usually in the early hours of the morning. They occurred at least two or three times a month, sometimes more frequently, depending upon the time of the year. Most of those coming for the "opium medicine," as they called it, were distraught and embarrassed husbands or fathers-in-law. Knowing through hearsay of the price, they brought money, but when they didn't, we would either insist they return to get the money or we sent someone along with them to collect it before we released the medicine to them. No one received it for free. The charge of Mex. $1, while only a fraction of a U.S. dollar, was equivalent, in most cases, to a week's wages and thus a considerable sum of money, particularly for the poor. Mother made the charge simply as a deterrent, in the hope that it might discourage a future or repeated attempt. To make a higher charge might have tempted a cost-conscious father-in-law or husband to consider letting the girl die and replacing her with a new wife, despite the loss of face and the cost and embarrassment of a funeral.

Adjoining our compound to the west was a regular warren of houses where, at any given time, eight or nine different extended families lived. Each family had its own walled-in compound, all reached through a narrow alley connecting with the front street. The activities of these neighbors were of the greatest of interest to us as children. In turn, our daily lives were under frequent scrutiny from them as they surreptitiously gazed at us over the dividing wall from time to time. Often we would see a row of heads showing just above the wall as men, women, and most particularly children, would watch us by the hour as we played in the garden.

I had my own vantage point from which I could overlook three different courtyards. In the alley just behind our dining room was the shed where we had the well used for keeping our milk cool. The roof of that shed was almost flat, and lay a foot or so below the tops of the two adjoining walls. For most of the morning the roof would be in the shadow of our main building, and on a hot summer's day it made a great place to lie and watch the happenings below.

I lay on my stomach there by the hour with my head just above the top of the wall and watched unobserved (or so I thought) as our neighbors went about their daily lives. I watched the children at play, usually stark naked, the adults grinding their grain, preparing food, working on clothing or shoes, feeding their animals, and engaging in every other aspect of their daily lives. Even when they saw me, as they frequently did, it didn't bother them one whit. Chinese are not used to privacy.

Each household in those three courtyards had as many as three or four generations living together. I knew as much about them as they did about us. Neither they, nor I, thought of it as "spying." It was just natural curiosity and no one resented it.

It certainly gave me an insight into the lives of the Chinese that few others have had. I am often amused when reading some of the best-selling novels written about China to see how little they actually knew of what they were writing about. Too often what is written is either pure surmise or wishful thinking on the part of the writer. Many writers have never set foot in China, depending solely on researching other writers' materials. Others are like a young Canadian I once knew. He visited China for three weeks, returned to Canada, and wrote a novel that sold extremely well. Unfortunately it was a mass of misinformation. Personally, even after spending almost thirty years there, I am still reluctant to write about anything other than what I actually observed, and even then I know that because much of what I saw was so commonplace and ordinary to me, I saw it only superficially and often missed the details. Furthermore, China is such a vast land that to speak in generalities regarding its customs is dangerous, since frequently a distance of only a few miles may make a considerable difference.

Our neighbors to the rear were the Zhangs. They were typical of the townspeople around us, and their daily life and habits were full of interest to a young boy. Four generations lived there: the elderly grandparents, two sons with their wives and children, and one young married grandson with a newborn baby. They were representative of middle-class families, owning their own house and a few acres of land outside the city. They kept a mule and a donkey in their back yard, and pigs and chickens roamed the property, going in and out of the houses at will.

Early in the morning the womenfolk rose first and made breakfast. In the summer, towering Mount Guang hid the rising sun for nearly an hour after sunrise, casting a long shadow over the city that kept us cool and refreshed. All over the city one could see wisps of smoke rising from hundreds of chimneys as the people prepared their breakfasts. The streets resounded to the cries of hawkers selling tasty breakfast snacks for those who either were too lazy to make their own or who didn't want to heat up the house with a fire under the cooking pot and *kang*.

Beancurd (*doufu*) was part of breakfast for almost everyone each day, and usually the other meals as well. It was bought fresh from salesmen who came around just after dawn with their highly distinctive and long-drawn-out cry: "*doooou fuuuuu*" starting on a high note, then falling and rising again.

The Chinese tell an amusing story concerning beancurd sellers. They tell of one man who sold only the skin of the beancurd. His cry was *doufu pi* (beancurd skin). However, he was an extremely lazy individual, and thought of a way to save himself a lot of effort. Each morning he followed immediately behind the man selling the *doufu* blocks. Instantly, after the first man had made his cry "*doooou fuuuuu*," the lazy man would simply shout the one word "*pi*," thus saving himself the effort, and at the same time getting all the business.

The fresh white *doufu* squares were carried on the

salesman's shoulder on a long narrow tray, covered by a dirty, gray-colored cloth that had once been white. *Doufu* comes in a variety of forms, but each salesman sold only one type of the product. Some handled only the most common "block" form, others sold the skin that rises to the surface when the product is forming (a delicacy much enjoyed by the Chinese), and still others carried only the milk, which is highly prized as a morning drink. In addition, there was a deep-fried form that, sliced and sauteed with meat, was delicious.

Nothing was wasted. Even the crushed skins of the yellow soya beans, with very little nutritional value left in them, were saved and, with a crude press, formed into large circular cakes the size of a small bicycle wheel about three inches in thickness. Those were used primarily for animal feed, but in famine years, or as in the 1930s, when the Japanese completely monopolized the soya bean crops and no *doufu* was available for the ordinary individual, these cakes were eaten for protein.

Every day we heard around us distinctive cries of one vendor or another. Most were from salesmen with a huge variety of products that were carried from door to door to tempt the housewives. One after another they approached the gate of the Zhangs' residence as I watched.

Peddlers sold everything one could imagine: foodstuffs, both cooked and raw, cloth and threads of all colors, notions, bolts of silk, satin, and plain cotton cloth. There were also knife and scissor sharpeners who did a good business, and even a traveling barber. In late afternoon, along came the man selling kerosene for lamps.

Perhaps the most unusual of all was the man who bought, not sold, common rags of any size or shape regardless of their condition. The rags were for the shoe shops, which made shoe soles from them, but since the housewives made shoes for their own families, the man had a hard time finding people who would sell their scrap rags.

Every salesman had either a special call or some noise-making device, such as a small drum mounted on a stick with leather thongs on each side and a bead on the end of each thong. Another man might have the same device, but in addition would have a small brass cymbal mounted on the same stick. When the sticks were twirled either quickly, or slowly, they gave off a most distinctive sound that clearly identified the product being sold and could be heard for a considerable distance.

Even the householders around us used characteristic cries of their own for calling their children or their various domestic animals. For each there was a specific call. The ones called each knew the calls and would come running. Calling pigs was "Ga, ga, ga," dogs answered to "Ber, ber, ber," the donkey and mule that the Zhangs owned answered to "Der, der, der," and the chickens knew they would be fed when they heard "Sa, sa, sa."

The Zhangs had a big watchdog and several cats. They were not pets, nor did they have names. As a general rule, the Chinese did not make pets of any of their household animals, nor did they give them names as we do. The only exception I knew of were camels; every camel had its name and responded to it. Dogs occasionally might be called by some distinctive marking, such as "Four Eyes" for a common type that had a white tuft of hair above each eye. Pekingese dogs were often called *"Ber Tou,"* (protruding head), referring to the prominent, overhanging forehead typical of this breed. The same nickname was given to some people with the same prominent forehead. Generally, the Chinese attached no sentiment to the keeping of domestic animals. Animals were purely utilitarian. If they did not properly perform their functions, they were replaced. Dogs were watchdogs, pure and simple. Cats were kept around simply to get rid of rats and mice. The children naturally played with these animals, but only the very well-to-do kept a dog purely as a pet, such as the Pekingese, or "Lion dog," as they called them, or the rarer "Sleeve dog," a tiny creature so named because it could sit up in the dangling sleeve of its owner, with room to spare.

The relationship and rapport between the various members of the Zhang family were what I liked watching most of all. The elders were always treated with extreme deference by young and old alike. The old grandfather was waited on hand and foot and usually sat somewhere in the shade all day smoking his pipe and drinking endless cups of tea, when he wasn't napping. The grandmother, on the other hand, was in the forefront constantly, getting more than her share of attention from all the young wives as she watched their every activity from her seat near the front door or by an open window. She criticized the younger women unmercifully. Nothing they ever did was just the way she would have done it. All her comments and commands were shouted in a voice that could be heard all over the entire neighborhood. From time to time, one or another of the younger women would be in tears; but more often there were sly glances of amusement among them, and they merely made a pretense of doing what the old lady commanded, hoping that her failing eyesight would not detect their disobedience.

Chinese women are extremely modest in public, but in their own homes they think nothing of baring the upper body. On very hot days, the Zhang women all went around "topless" except for a tiny apron-like upper garment called a "*dou dou*." It was shaped roughly like an elongated diamond, with one point extending in a narrow strip between the breasts to a loop around the neck, covering the point at the base of the throat that is considered by Chinese males to be the most erotic point on a woman. The opposite point hung down over their trouser tops, and the two other points were tied around the waist. It was when a stranger came to the door that they put on a jacket; otherwise, with their own menfolk and people they knew, there was no embarrassment whatsoever.

The grandfather was the only man who stayed at home. The other men all went to work daily, most to their land, some distance out of town, coming home just before dark. The older son, who had been well educated, was a businessman with a very popular photography studio. He specialized in group and individual photographs, and had a supply of spectacle frames without lenses, which his customers favored when their pictures were taken so that they might appear for posterity as having been educated and, therefore as intellectuals. The older son always dressed formally in a long gown when he left each morning. His position in the family assured him of a great deal of deference from the womenfolk. When he left in the mornings they escorted him to the front gate as a group and bowed him out. His call at the barred gate when he returned for lunch brought everyone running to meet him, including his wife. But I never saw the slightest sign of affection between the two of them. His first action upon entering the gate was to divest himself of his hat and outer clothing, which his wife dutifully carried indoors.

Then they brought hot water for him to wash his face and hands, (which he did outdoors), then tea to drink, and finally his lunch was served in solitary splendor. Most of the time, just to show his authority, he complained about one thing or another. Now and then he would give the children a cuff on the back of the head whether they deserved it or not. The Chinese have a somewhat humorous reference to this sort of thing. They say: "*Yintian da haizi*," ("Smack the children on a cloudy day"), the inference being that since there is nothing else to do with the threat of rain, give the children a whacking. If they don't deserve it then, they will later on.

By and large, the Zhang family lived a very harmonious life, although occasionally a fight would break out with a lot of cursing and shouting, usually among the sisters-in-law. Most Chinese fights were more show than action, and rarely did the participants resort to fisticuffs. A fight normally started with a lot of verbal abuse, which got louder and louder, each participant trying to out-shout and out-swear the other. When all members of the family had gathered, the fight would more often than not move from the yard to the front doorstep and then out into the front street to gain maximum attention, and neighbors would gleefully drop everything to watch the fun. When a sufficiently large crowd had gathered, and when either party began to run out of epithets, then and only then was there a show of blows about to be struck, but few if any ever landed. Invariably, someone would grab the individuals and hold them back. Gesturing would then become fiercer and the language fouler until someone, usually an older person, would step in and "talk peace." Every street had its "*shuo he ren*" or mediator, (literally, "talk peace person") and they were always well respected. "Face" having been saved, the combatants usually walked away with heads held high.

Fights between husbands and wives were an exception. Here no one interfered, not even the official mediators. A husband was permitted to beat his wife for just cause, and a father-in-law could beat his daughters-in-law, and their "causes" were always "just." There was, of course, the usual crowd of spectators, but only when and if the woman's life appeared in danger would an attempt be made to break up the fight. We saw many sad cases of such abuse of women, and many were the cases of severe injury that Mother had to treat. Both my parents experienced occasions when they tried to step between a husband and his wife to stop a fight. Sometimes they succeeded. However, on more than one occasion when Mother tried to stop two women from fighting, they stopped, only to turn on her and butt her from both sides with their heads and stomachs. Father also had the same experience on several occasions. I tried to stop fights numerous times, but I took the Chinese approach, using verbal persuasion rather than physical contact. When I could determine who was the aggressor, a judicious use of humor and ridicule usually did the trick by making the spectators participants in supporting my efforts.

We were on good terms with all our neighbors, and Mother made a point of frequently visiting the womenfolk. The Zhangs were particularly friendly, but the friendship became strained at one point quite by accident because of Gil's high spirits and his dislike of cats. I guess Gil was about twelve at the time. When the cats came out to play in the evening, they roamed the tops of our walls, making wonderful targets. Gil, who had excellent aim with a clod of earth, would throw clods at the cats with no intention of harming them, but simply wanting to discourage their nocturnal yowling. Unfortunately, the clods of earth would scatter on impact, and the paper windows in the Zhang house took a severe beating.

The Zhangs said nothing to us directly. That was not the way it was done. Through a third party the problem was discreetly brought to Father's attention and Gil was urged to desist from his nightly cat hunts. Instead, he found a new and much more satisfying hobby, one that proved quite profitable as well.

Father encouraged all of us kids to keep pets if we wished. My first pets were pigeons that I trapped with a big shallow basket made to sieve the dirt and dust from the straw we fed to the cows. I propped up one side of the basket with a short stick to which a string was attached, and scattered grain underneath. In no time at all, pigeons walked under the basket, I yanked out the stick, and I had several pigeons that not only became quite tame but also supplied the table. Later, I also kept a number of rabbits.

The Chinese polecat, a vicious predator that usually came out at night or very early in the morning was the natural enemy of all our pets. Unlike its European cousin, the Chinese polecat has a small and very pointed head, short fur, and a beautiful golden-yellow color. The bones of its head are quite flexible, and any hole that it could get its head through, the body could follow. As a result, we found it almost impossible to protect our pets. We used fine chicken wire, and boards sunken into the ground at the base of the wire surrounding the pens, but neither did any good. The polecat could climb like a cat and never failed to find a way to get in.

Apart from its obnoxious odor, much like that of the skunk, the despicable animal, like all the weasel family to which it belongs, kills for the pure joy of killing, biting the throat of anything it attacks, and then leaving the body uneaten.

Our hen house was equipped with roosts that were high enough off the ground to protect the hens, or so we thought. However, polecats often got in and destroyed every single hen, killing twenty-five on one occasion. Apparently the hens panicked when the polecat got in, and in their efforts to escape, flew down to the ground, where the polecat systematically slaughtered them. On several occasions it happened early enough in the evening for us to hear the noise and one of us would go out and drive the polecat off before any serious damage could be done. I was not so lucky with my pigeons and rabbits. One morning I found all my pigeons dead, and despite all precautions, it wasn't long thereafter that my rabbits suffered the same fate. Always a very early riser, Barbara actually saw the polecat running away over the roof after having bitten off the head of a pigeon, which a moment or so before she had seen alive, its head protruding from the pen.

Things got so bad that Father bought a half-dozen steel traps for Gil to set, and that became Gil's new hobby. Between our compound and neighboring properties there were a number of drains through the base of the walls. By judiciously smelling each of them for the telltale odor of the polecat, Gil found just the right places for his traps, and we didn't have to wait long for results. With high hopes I went with him the next morning and each morning thereafter to see if anything had been caught.

Few of us had ever seen a live polecat close up, although we'd seen many dead ones in the marketplaces. The Chinese hunt them, not only for the skin, but primarily for the long bushy tail, which comes to a fine point. At the tip of the tail are a number of long hairs, highly prized for making brush pens. A few of those hairs placed in the center of a brush pen attract the surrounding hairs to them, and that makes for a perfectly shaped pen, which keeps its shape even when wet.

The first polecat we caught was a somewhat unnerving experience for all of us. The famous explorer Roy Chapman Andrews, in his book *Across Mongolian Plains*, described the first one he caught: "I have never seen such an incarnation of fury as this animal presented. It might have been the original of the Chinese dragon, except for its small size. Its long, slender body twisted and turned with incredible swiftness, every hair was bristling, and its snarling little face emitted horrible squeaks and spitting squeals. It seemed to be cursing us in every language of the polecat tribe." That description aptly fitted the ones that we caught, and handling them — caught usually by one leg in the trap — was always dangerous.

Once they were caught, killing them without damaging the pelt was a problem. Nearly all of them had attempted to bite through their own leg in order to free themselves, and occasionally one succeeded before we got there. To shoot them in the head with a .22-caliber bullet was expensive and also dangerous. Bashing them on the head was not always immediately effective. We finally found that drowning them was the most expeditious way to kill them, but even that took a surprisingly long time. On occasion, after they had been immersed in the big water *gang* out by the back well until no further bubbles came to the surface, we would pull them out, only to have them revive just as Gil was about to release them from the trap. Once or twice Gil narrowly escaped being bitten.

The place where we caught most of them was a drain at the extreme rear of the garden in the north wall. A drain Father had put in to get rid of the laundry water, it was about four feet up on the wall on the inside, which brought it to the level of the outside ground. Numerous small animals came through the drain in addition to the polecats. One morning Barbara found a baby fox in the garden. She fed it and petted it for several days before setting it free through the same drain. Occasionally a hedgehog made its way in.

I seem to remember that we caught one or two polecats a week on the average. After Lao San had most skillfully skinned them, there was a ready market for the skin, and the tails in particular. Aside from our joy in seeing ourselves rid of those pests, there was the satisfaction, for Gil at least, of adding to his pocket money each time one was caught, and it made it that much safer for our neighbors' chickens, so it made them happy as well.

While thinking of that particular drain at the back of the garden, I am reminded that right next to it we had a small walled-in enclosure where there was an extraordinarily lush growth of peonies. They had to be protected from the winter cold, so the enclosure was roofed over with the first frost each year. The peonies had been there for many years, and Father told us that the reason they were so lush and healthy was because it was inside that enclosure that we buried all of our pets when they died.

As the years rolled by, the womenfolk of the Zhang family became increasingly friendly as Mother continued to visit them. They occasionally attended Sunday services and, of course, they brought their children to Mother when they were sick. In all Chinese families, the man may be the breadwinner and nominal head of the house, but it is the woman who makes the big decisions where money or religion are concerned. The Zhang family was no exception. My parents knew very well that, if the wife could be won over to Christianity, there was little question but that later the husband would follow suit, hopefully out of conviction, rather than just by giving in to the wife's demands. After the death of the grandparents, Mrs. Zhang, wife of the older son, made no open profession of faith at first, but while attending church services herself, she quietly encouraged her husband to attend as well. By that time our gatekeeper's son, Hu Wen-rui, my playmate from childhood, had grown up and become a Christian like his father, and he and Mr. Zhang had gone into business together.

One Chinese New Year Mrs. Zhang made the decision for the family that they were to burn their heathen gods. Up to that point the Zhangs, like all families throughout that part of Manchuria, erected what was called a *deng long ganzi* or "lantern pole," two weeks before the Chinese New Year. It was a pole about twenty-five or thirty feet in height, topped by a shallow square box with tapered sides, painted a bright red with black markings, decorated with flags at the four corners and bells that chimed in the wind.

On the more elaborate ones, there were also small "windmills" that turned and rattled in the slightest breeze. The whole affair was topped with a short branch from a fir tree, and below the box was a bracket with a pulley and rope. At dusk each evening a red lantern was lighted and raised to the top of the pole and left to burn all night.

All of it was part of the process of replacing the kitchen god each year, a "god" that was simply a poorly printed reproduction of a benign-looking bearded old man dressed in garish-colored robes. Shortly before New Year's Day the kitchen god would "ascend" to heaven by being ceremoniously burned, after first having had his lips wiped with sugar or some type of sweetmeat to make sure he would report only good things about the family's doings. The lighted pole was erected to provide a landing place for his successor to alight, either by day or night. Although it was supposed to happen on the eve of New Year's Day, the Chinese took no chances, erecting the pole two weeks early in case he mistook the date, and keeping it up for another two weeks just to make certain that any late-arriving god would find his way to the right household. What actually occurred was that on or before the last day of the year, a new paper god would be purchased, and with much burning of incense and exploding of firecrackers, he would, on the first day of the new year, be pasted up on the wall behind the kitchen cauldron. In theory, the "spirit" of the new god arrived at the same time.

The lantern poles added a picturesque touch at night to the otherwise darkened city. All over town the red lanterns glowed above the rooftops. Not all the poles were as grandiose as that of the Zhangs, but even the poorest families made an effort to put up a pole of some sort, even if it only had a small branch of fir at the top and nothing but the lantern hanging below.

When the Zhangs turned to Christianity they burned all their idols, along with their ancestral tablets and their lantern pole. Instead of doing it in the privacy of their own backyard, as many might have been tempted to do, they made a public ceremony of it. They did it on the common threshing floor adjoining the front street near their alley entrance, and drew a big crowd of onlookers. Such a public testimony took a great deal of courage and it had a great

effect. It wasn't many months later that the Yang family, who lived right next door to the Zhangs, also converted to Christianity, and before we left Lingyuan for the final time in 1947, several other neighbors on both sides had joined the church. They'd all come to the conclusion that the Christian God was better able to help and protect them than their own gods of paper and mud.

Next door but one to the west was the He family, one of the wealthiest families in Lingyuan. Mr. He was a large landowner. He counted his land not by the Chinese *mu*, which we spoke of roughly as a Chinese "acre" although it was much less than that, but by the *qing*, each of which was one hundred *mu*, or about 15 acres, and he had several hundred *qing*. However, he lived very modestly, even by Chinese standards, although he had a big compound nearly as large as ours, and a huge extended family occupying the place.

Mr. He was a very good friend of my father and frequently came over to visit with us. I never saw him dressed in anything but long blue or light gray silk or satin gowns, but that was his only outward show of wealth. Although he could well afford it, he did not keep a private cart to use in the city, but walked everywhere he went. It was he that I mentioned earlier as having become addicted to opium after using it to cure the pain of hemorrhoids.

Mother and Miss Minns, the young American missionary who lived with us, often visited the womenfolk in his home. Although none of his family came out openly and accepted Christianity, they always welcomed those visits and a number of them regularly attended church services.

I well remember one occasion when Mr. He invited our entire family over to a sumptuous feast with about twenty different dishes. Remarkably, his wife and children all ate at the same table with us, which, for a conservative Chinese like Mr. He, demonstrated an extremely close family friendship. After a variety of tasty meat and vegetable dishes, when the rice was brought to the table, we all had a very hard time keeping a straight face. Instead of the usual rice pot, the container used was a large ceramic Western-style chamber pot decorated with flowers on the outside. The young son proudly told us that he had been to Peking a short time before and had bought the pot in one of the open-air secondhand markets, where, most likely, it had first been sold by some servant who had stolen it from one of the foreigners. Mr. He's son, not having the slightest idea of what it was for, thought it would be an ideal container for steamed rice. We didn't have the heart to disillusion him, although any one of our servants could have told him what it was designed for.

We and our neighbors all felt indebted to Mr. He because he employed a night watchman who supposedly patrolled his compound all night long, beating out the night watches on a hand-held, hollow wooden gadget, called a *bangzi*, which could be heard for a considerable distance.

Each watch was two hours long and had a name, and was identifiable by a specific tattoo of a certain number of strokes on the "sounding box." Waking to the sound at any time during the night, one could tell what time it was without looking at a clock. The night watch I liked best, especially in the summertime, was the one shortly before dawn. It was the period between 1 and 3 a.m. and was known for some reason as *chou shi*, the "ugly period." To me it signaled the beginning of a new day. When we talked with Mr. He about his watchman, he laughingly told us it was difficult to get a man who was truly responsible and who didn't sleep on the job. He said that most of the men had a way of keeping time with lighted sticks of incense. The sticks were cut to a certain length, and after completing the circuit of the compound once or twice in a watch, the men would find a corner out of the wind and light a stick of incense. Grasping it tightly in one hand, they would go to sleep, trusting that when the stick burned down to the point where it reached their hand, they would awaken and go out and sound the next watch. Mr. He said that he regularly inspected the men's hands for burn marks, and if any showed, the man was summarily fired.

Mr. He was the epitome of a gentleman and was known throughout the city as a *shan ren* or philanthropist. Daily, his servants cooked up a huge quantity of food to feed the beggars who came to his door, never fewer than a hundred each day. He didn't do it merely for show. He was a truly good man at heart. While not an elderly man, he was yet considered one of the leading gentry, a status in China usually given to the older generation. A genial person, he treated his numerous land tenants with a generosity that few others matched. Regularly we would see his tenant farmers coming to visit him, and twice a year he held a big feast for them, setting up a large temporary mat shed outside the front gate of his compound. Yet, kind man that he was, when the Communists took over in Lingyuan in 1947, he was among the first to be slaughtered, simply because of the amount of land that he owned and his great wealth. It was true, as the Communists said, that some of the great landowners did exploit their tenants and were extremely cruel, but killing the landowners was also a convenient excuse for the Communists to confiscate land and subdivide it to the poor and the peasant class, thus gaining favor for themselves. It was a tragedy that Mr. He lost his life; he was the last to deserve that kind of fate.

Those, then, were our immediate neighbors to the left and right. We saw little of those across the street from us, and the neighbors behind our compound, out behind the back garden wall, were all in their graves. Even so, there was much of interest to us as children when funerals took place and more neighbors were buried there.

Near the very large elm tree against the back wall was an old date tree that we climbed. We often sat in the high branches watching the world outside. In addition to the traffic on the road, there was always some kind of activity in the fields except in the dead of winter. In late winter, as the sun began to warm the earth, the dye shops sent their men out with cartloads of huge rolls of cotton cloth that had been dyed various colors (sometimes green or gray, but chiefly blue or black), to be draped across the hills to dry, providing a truly magnificent sight from a distance. While it was tedious and time-consuming work, it was better than hanging the cloth on the high racks they had built in their yards, where it simply froze stiff as a board and took days to dry. For us, it was always another welcome sign that spring was near.

To the right, about half a mile from our tree, stood a sizable grove of trees: some firs, but mostly elms and poplars. It marked the local Muslim burial ground and was one of the places we visited quite often on our Sunday afternoon walks. In the summertime we could enjoy both the shade and a degree of privacy, because it was shunned by most Chinese. In the spring we found violets and vetch there. Even in winter it was pleasant to walk among the trees, although there was less privacy because the fuel gatherers were there scratching the ground with their bamboo rakes for every tuft of grass and fallen leaf. Superstition kept them from any desecration of the trees.

Winter burials were always difficult, since the ground was frozen to a depth of three or four feet. Many Chinese families could not afford the cost of digging a grave, a job that might take several days. An alternative was to place the coffin in a nearby temple courtyard, enclosing it with a brick structure until the spring thaw. But not for Muslims. Regardless of the cold, they buried their dead in the ground, and it became a communal effort to do so as expeditiously as possible.

In the winter we always knew when there was to be a Muslim burial. From our perch in the date tree we could see a temporary tent erected for shelter from the cold. Then anywhere from fifty to a hundred men would congregate, build a fire over the grave site to thaw the ground, and then furiously dig away before it froze again. They worked day and night, digging down an inch or two at a time, then building another fire to thaw it some more and repeating the process until the grave was deep enough.

When it came time for the actual burial, the deceased was not placed in a coffin as was the case with the Han race, as the ethnic Chinese were called. The dead were, instead, wrapped in cloth and brought to the grave site in a monstrous ornate catafalque carried by fifty or more men, with mourners in white preceding and following the procession, but without the funeral music and the burning of paper images so common in Chinese Buddhist funerals. At the grave site, the catafalque was placed over the open grave, and the body was dropped into it by means of a sliding panel.

As the church enrollment grew larger and we had, from time to time, deaths among the Christians, it became increasingly difficult to find burial places for them. Many were without land, and although other Christians offered their land as burial sites, that was only a temporary solution.

On our walks, Father and I had discovered a delightful spot about two miles from our house, where a spur from the hills formed a V-shaped valley and a spring gushed out mid-way up. A lot of trees and brush grew on the hillsides near the spring. We could find no explanation as to why it had remained that way, untouched by the fuel-gatherers. Some said

it was because of what the Chinese called *feng shui*, literally "wind and water." That was something that the geomancers decided upon as being a good omen, and which nothing earthly could change. The Chinese paid close attention to anything the geomancers told them when it came to selecting a location to build a house or buy a piece of land, but it meant little to Westerners. Father thought the valley would be an ideal place to establish a Christian burial site, since only a tiny portion of the land could be tilled. The price was right, and it soon became ours. Over the years before we left China, some twenty or more Christians had been buried there, in addition to a number of babies.

The site covered about five or six acres and included a small two-*jian* building close to the spring. Father invited one of the poorer Christians from a distant country village to come and live there to care for the place. His name was Nai. He was a quiet-spoken, modest little man who smiled a great deal but seldom said a word unless directly spoken to. He had eight children at the time he moved in, and four more were to follow. One day he told me that, in all, he and his wife had had twenty-two children, but only the twelve survived. Old Nai was a hard-working man, and very quickly he started to build terraces on the lower slopes of the hill. Soon he had crops growing sufficient to feed his family and enough left over to sell and enable him to become self-supporting.

Because the place was near and we visited there so frequently, Father decided to cut a gate in the far left corner of our back garden wall so we could slip out the back way unobserved and without having to walk through the city streets. We made our own path between and around the graves outside, and many a weekend we spent in that lovely spot having picnics or just roaming the hillsides.

From the top of the hill we had a magnificent view of the city. I remember the very first time we climbed to the top. Barbara happened to be with us, and we had to laugh over her great disappointment when reaching the top, only to find more mountains on the other side, and not a whole new world as she had expected.

Lao Nai protected the place well, and the woodcutters respected the property. It wasn't long before there was a fairly heavy growth of underbrush, which encouraged what little wildlife there was around. We saw an occasional fox, and Lao Nai said he'd seen wolves at night. Once there was a rumor of a tiger having been seen in the area, but it was probably wishful thinking. There were, however, many grouse and partridge, together with numerous hares, and an occasional hedgehog. Our main pleasure there was the spring that flowed, even in drought years, and the tiny brook that gushed down from it. In summer the place was cool and pleasant, a little paradise on earth.

Summers in our back garden were one long delight; there was always something to do. As we grew older we enjoyed helping the yard boys water the garden. In those usually dry summers with only an occasional thunderstorm until the rains came in late July or early August, that was a near-daily job. Because the garden was so large, only part of it could be watered on any one day. Usually the two yard boys would spell each other at the well: while one worked the windlass, the other would direct the water into the network of drains. We, as children, got the hang of this while still quite small, and we loved to use a spade to dig out a six-inch entranceway from the drain into each dry bed to let the water in, using the dirt dug out to block the drain itself and prevent the water from going farther until the bed was full. As we stood there watching the gently rippling flow of water, every few minutes showing a surge as another bucketful was dumped into the drain, we saw the twigs, leaves, and an occasional beetle or other insect carried along in the water, and to us, each drain-full of water was a mighty river boiling along through a narrow canyon, carrying everything before it, but over which we had absolute control.

One year when the schoolroom became intolerably hot, Father had another of his endless ideas. In the rear of the back garden he had a temporary mat shed built for us, just a few poles forming a framework, with the ubiquitous *shujie* sorghum-stalk mats covering it. A couple of crude tables and benches were all we needed in the way of furniture, and out there we did our schoolwork in absolute bliss; birds sang in the trees and the leaves rustled as the breeze blew through the corn patch nearby. The mats having a fairly loose weave also allowed cooler air to circulate, but it wasn't rainproof, and although we loved the place so much we wanted to sleep out there, it wasn't possible. But it gave Father still another idea.

The next spring, a camel appeared in the front yard with a huge package on its back. It turned out to be a large army-style tent Father had ordered from Montgomery Ward. White, with sidewalls and a khaki-colored fly covering the roof for added protection, it measured about ten by fourteen feet. We set it up in the far right-hand corner of the garden, after first constructing an eight-inch raised earthen platform for it and digging a one-foot-deep ditch all around to keep the water out during the rainy season. At each end a small footbridge covered the ditch.

For a number of years, the tent went up at the first sign of spring and didn't come down until the cold nights of October. Gil and I slept out there until he left for Canada in 1928. After that I had the tent to myself, except for the occasional visiting missionary or traveler who wanted to join me. Since it was so spacious inside, there was plenty of room for two beds, a washstand and a small table and chair, and the roof was high enough for us to hang mosquito nets.

Nights out there weren't always peaceful. Usually we were lulled to sleep by the distant sounds of the city: barking dogs and night watchmen making their rounds, beating out the watches on their hollowed-out wooden blocks. Occasionally we heard some late traveler passing by on the road behind the wall, always singing some chant or opera at the top of his voice to build up his courage and scare away any evil spirits that might be around. On quiet nights when there was no breeze at all we also heard the clanking of chains as the prisoners moved around in the prison just a stone's throw away, a sound that we always found disturbing.

And there were other sounds as well. Many were the times in the wee hours of the morning when we were awakened by a sudden thunderstorm and had to rush out into the rain to loosen the ropes, drive in the stakes, and tie down the sidewalls and the fly. But that was all part of the fun, and we always stripped off our pajamas to enjoy the rain on our naked bodies. We even had our own shower out there, a crude, raised platform on four poles, a galvanized tub on top, with a makeshift spray formed from a small tin can punched with holes and soldered onto a short length of pipe. It worked, and a shower at night and in the morning was a lot better than dunking ourselves in the water *gang* by the well.

And as I write of our neighbors, I mustn't forget the inmates of the prison so close to us. One dark night we had a visit from some of them, but no one heard or saw them.

Usually one or more of our dogs would be in the tent to keep us company at night. But one night in particular, when I was sleeping alone in the tent, the dogs were somewhere else. I was normally a very heavy sleeper. Often even a thunderstorm wouldn't awaken me until I was thoroughly soaked by the driving rain. Each morning at daybreak You Wang would come to wake me, always having to shake me thoroughly to bring me to life. He often told me I slept like a dead man.

But that one morning was quite different. Some time before daybreak, instead of You Wang waking me, it was Katie (Gao Zun), who had taken the job of gatekeeper after Mr. Hu's death. I could hardly believe my eyes. There were eight or ten heavily armed policemen with him, with revolvers drawn, wanting to know if I had heard anything during the night. Naturally, I hadn't. They then told me that eight former bandits had escaped from the prison during the night. The men were considered very dangerous and the police suspected they had made their way out toward our garden, so they wanted permission to search the place.

I hurriedly threw on some clothes and accompanied them, as one of them told me they had identified the point on the prison wall where the men had climbed out. They had then tracked them across our neighbor's garden to our wall, the leg manacles they were wearing having left a wide swath of damaged opium plants. We went directly to a point just behind the cow sheds, and sure enough, there were distinct marks on the top of the wall across which their chains had been dragged. That was at the opposite end of the garden from my tent. The police suspected they were still in the garden.

Few people possessed flashlights in those days, and, since it was still pitch dark, the feeble light from their lanterns was little help in searching the garden. However, they started to look around the place, and we saw marks on the path where the chains had dragged — and the marks led almost directly to my tent.

Less than thirty feet from the tent, where we had a fairly large boulder next to the path, we suddenly stumbled across several piles of chains, some on the edge of the path and others thrown into the vegeta-

tion. We concluded that the men had made their way up the path until they reached the boulder, and had used it and a piece of rock that they had torn from the base of the wall to hammer off the manacles from their ankles and wrists. It was obvious they must have made a fair amount of noise, but I hadn't heard a sound.

By that time one of our dogs had joined us, and I noticed him sniffing the ground between the chains and the tent. It seemed fairly apparent from his excitement that one or more of the men must have approached the tent and perhaps even entered it to see if anyone was there. It wasn't a pleasant feeling to think of someone standing over me in the dark.

From that point on, we had no success in tracking them, but after daylight, upon careful examination of the top of the wall, we finally found the spot on the far side of the garden where they had climbed one of the date trees, dropped to the top of the wall, and then jumped the eight feet or so to the ground outside. To my knowledge, none of the men were ever recaptured.

Despite the forty-foot-high wall around the prison, an escape by an individual prisoner was not unknown; however, the mass escape of eight men together was unheard of and created quite a sensation. To everyone, it indicated conclusively that they must have had inside help from one or more of the guards. From the roofs of the prison buildings, it was a thirty-foot climb to the top of the wall, and for that, as well as for the forty-foot drop outside, a good length of rope would have been needed. However, it was well known that captured bandits had good support from their gang leaders outside. Most of the time, payments to the guards only resulted in better food and living conditions. But on that particular occasion the bribery paid off better than usual, for the guards had not only turned their heads while the escape was in progress, but had plugged their ears as well. However, it did them little good. The magistrate was so incensed that he interrogated the prison guards, and all who were on duty that night were put on trial. After being forced to confess their part in the escape, they were fortunate that they weren't shot. Instead, for many months thereafter, they found themselves a part of the prison population being guarded, rather than doing the guarding.

Mr. Tharp Sr. with some of the family's pet dogs.

The tent in the backyard.

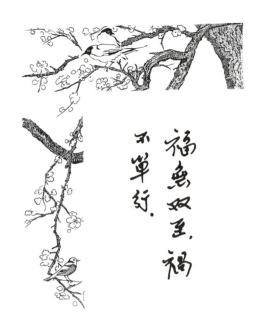

福无双至，
祸不单行.

Fu wu shuang zhi, huo bu dan xing.

Good fortune never comes in pairs.
Disasters never come singly.

- Chinese Proverb.

Chapter Ten
Nature's Famines

Life in Manchuria wasn't only schooling, play, and hard work while growing up — at least not for us. What with droughts, famines, civil wars and peasant uprisings, not to mention travel both in the country and abroad, life for a lad lucky enough to be growing up in Manchuria was a constant series of exciting and sometimes frightening events.

When I write of Manchuria, I am reminded that it is not generally known by Westerners that, insofar as the Chinese are concerned, there is no such place as "Manchuria." They neither know nor use the word. As a matter of fact, it is also astonishing how many Americans do not know where Manchuria is located. There have been many times when I have told people where I was born (including some officials of the U.S. Immigration Service), only to have them ask me, "In which state is that city?"

That area of northeastern China that we call Manchuria was so named by early Western visitors, who called it that because it was ruled by the Manchus. To the Chinese, however, it was outside the Great Wall and thus considered to be a barbarian country, commonly called *kou wai* (or "outside the mouth," the mouth being any one of the openings in the Wall), or *guan wai* ("outside the pass, or gate"). The formal Chinese name for Manchuria is Dong San Sheng, Three Eastern Provinces. However, the Chinese, who abbreviate wherever possible, simply call it Dong Bei, the Northeast. Since Jehol was a fourth province added to the original three, that latter name made more sense.

The population of Manchuria, fairly sparse at the turn of the century, was at one time predominantly Manchu. Over the years it has become more and more dominated by the Han race, the pure ethnic Chinese. Due to that and to intermarriage, there are now probably fewer than 10 percent who are of original Manchu blood, although Manchu surnames are still fairly frequently found. Initially, Chinese immigrants from Shandong, Henan and other more southerly provinces heard of that land of promise, where good farm land was available, and came by the thousands. Later, when drought and floods destroyed crops and caused very severe famines in those and other provinces, hundreds of thousands of destitute and hungry people came surging northward in search of food.

The great famine of 1920 in Henan brought countless thousands of refugees through Lingyuan. While to begin with there was no famine in our province, a subsequent drought caused an extreme shortage of food, and we suffered from exactly the same conditions that had earlier prevailed in the south.

Much has been written of the aid given by America and other countries at the time, and of the International Famine Relief Commission that was set up to administer and distribute funds and food grains throughout the stricken areas. Huge sums of money were given to the Chinese government, and grain was purchased in vast quantities from those areas where it was still plentiful and shipped to where it was most needed. But it all took time to arrive, and many thousands perished before help could reach them.

As a boy of seven, I watched the first trickle of those refugees, or *nan min* ("Calamity People"), as they came in from the west and passed our front gate. At first they came in groups of tens and twenties. As each day passed, the numbers grew until an unbroken mass of humanity was passing in front of us, shuffling silently along, looking neither right nor left. Most were walking, carrying their pitifully few possessions on their backs or on the ends of carrying poles. Occasionally there would be a wheelbarrow carrying children on one side and an elderly parent on the other, or a scrawny donkey, so thin and emaciated that it could scarcely walk, yet carrying its load of some elderly or sick person unable to walk. And those were only the ones coming in from the west. An equal number came in through the south gate.

The people weren't beggars; they had no experience in asking for food. They were just simple farmers and middle-class people with no idea of where they were going, trudging along, following the crowd and hoping for a miracle. They ate what grain they could glean from the fields (wherever there was any grain standing), or the leaves and bark from trees. They reminded me of a swarm of locusts, a phenomenon we had often seen. Most striking was their total silence. Not one of them seemed to have the strength to speak, and all one could hear was the shuffle of their feet, day and night, as they passed in an unending stream.

My parents had been somewhat forewarned from the newspapers that almost the entire population of whole provinces was on the march northward, so they became heavily involved from the very start of the disaster. But it was hard to believe, even when it we saw it with our own eyes.

One of the first things Father did was to build a number of temporary cookstoves on each side of the alleyway between our first and second courtyards. We cooked grains from our own stock, and later from that which we had begged and borrowed from the magistrate and local businesses. Christians and other volunteers cooked it into a semi-liquid gruel and doled it out to those starving families as they went by. Two doors away from us up the street, Mr. He also set up some cookstoves in the street, and fed hundreds more.

Chinese crowds, or crowds of any nationality for that matter, can be very unruly, particularly when they are hungry. However, the police provided by the magistrate for crowd control were quite unneeded. These people were quiet and docile. Like so many sheep, they lined the roadways as they came into town, collapsing on the ground at nightfall until all places were taken and no more could be accommodated, and still more kept coming. Hurriedly, other feeding places were set up throughout the city, and for weeks thereafter the thousands were fed, then encouraged to move on to make way for still more.

They were at their peak in May 1920, and fortunately the weather was favorable. Because of the size of the crowds on the street, in groups of thirty to fifty they were admitted through the front gate to our compound, fed, and their places taken by others. It kept two people busy just washing the food bowls and chopsticks. That continued day and night. Dear, softhearted Mother couldn't bear to send the women and children away when night fell, so space was made for them in the other courtyards, and hundreds spent the night there before moving on. But even after they were fed, the overall silence was quite eerie. Not even the children cried. The adults had nothing to talk about with each other and appeared totally exhausted and numb. Even when we talked directly with them, they answered in monosyllables, often unable to tell us where they were from and unable to say where they were going.

Many of them had been on the road for months and had traveled for hundreds of miles. How they had lasted so long was a mystery to us. In recent years the world has seen many such scenes on television, with similar happenings in Africa, so I need not try to describe the appearance of those walking skeletons. Hunger does the same thing to people the world over.

As the influx continued, local food supplies fast became exhausted, so it was a most welcome sight when long caravans of grain-carrying carts escorted by government troops began to arrive from the nearest railhead. The carts came by the hundreds, passing our front gate for days on end. Despite the protection of soldiers, it was common to see young boys make a mad dash toward the back of a cart where, with a piece of glass or a broken pottery shard, they slashed at one of the grain bags, then collected the grain that spewed out onto the roadway, running behind the cart to catch as much as they could before being driven off by the soldiers. Even then, the women sifted through the dust of the roadway for what they could find after the carts had passed.

My parents were greatly concerned about the possibility of disease, and the magistrate was urged to organize street-cleaning parties, to set up public latrines, and to carry out the burial of the many who died. The Famine Relief Commission encouraged public works projects, and Father was in the forefront in suggesting roads that needed repairing or dikes that could be built along the riverfront. Thousands were employed for months on those projects, fed, and given a small amount of money at the same time. Gradually a semblance of order was restored and the numbers began to thin out, but the population of Lingyuan had increased considerably with the many who stayed on, building their little shacks on the outskirts or living in deserted temples.

One incident stands out vividly in my memory. One late afternoon a family with four small children arrived in our compound. With them they had a very tall and extremely emaciated donkey, which staggered as it walked and was too weak to carry any load at all. The parents were in very bad shape, particularly the mother, and they had obviously given the children what little food they had been able to find. After feeding them, Mother wanted them to stay at least overnight because two of the children were sick and

needed treatment. The donkey attracted my attention in particular, but it seemed too weak to eat, although it did accept some cabbage leaves from me. It was so frail, Father didn't expect it to live, so in order to help the man, he offered to buy the donkey, though the man seemed very reluctant to sell. Father felt, however, that the money would be more beneficial to the family than a dead donkey.

We children were delighted at the purchase of a donkey. Despite her emaciated condition, she looked beautiful to us, and we named her "May." She was moved to the cow yard and left free there, and Lao San took over and fed her mouthful by mouthful. Father told us we had to let her rest for a month before we could ride her, but I was impatient and couldn't wait that long. I wanted to be able to boast that I had been the first to have a ride on her.

One afternoon a few days later, when Father was having his usual nap after lunch, I sneaked out into the cow yard and led May out into the back garden with the intention of riding her. She was so tall I could barely reach her back with my out-stretched hands. The problem became how to climb up onto her, particularly as we had no saddle. Finally, I led her to a large rock at the edge of the path, mounted the rock, and placing both hands on her back, I leaped up, intending to land on my stomach. But I had miscalculated and promptly went clear over the top, slid off head first on the other side, and landed on the top of my head on the hard path. I was quite sure that I was dead, and remember feeling that I well deserved to be. Fortunately, apart from a sizable lump on the top of my head and a sore neck, I suffered no damage except to my dignity, and never told a soul about the incident.

Toward evening each day the grain carts continued to come in from the west. I remember standing at the front gate with Mr. Hu watching them: big freight carts pulled by seven mules, and smaller carts pulled by three. The grain was packed in long brown bags, tied with a short piece of thin rope with a red tassel on each end. The carts were always escorted by a troop of soldiers to preclude interference by bandits or theft of the grain by the many unscrupulous officials en route who might seek to make money at the expense of the suffering poor. Following behind the carts was always a small crowd of men, women and children, all hoping one of the bags would spring a leak and spill some of the precious grain onto the ground.

It was fortunate indeed that the grain continued to arrive, because we, too, had had a long period of drought, and it wasn't long until the famine reached our own area. Father helped organize the setting up of huge storehouses in the city, and started a systematic distribution of millet and sorghum for the refugees and for local villagers as well. A census of families in the nearby stricken villages was taken, with the intent that each family would get a quota of grain consistent with the number of mouths they had to feed. Officials of the Famine Relief Commission made trips through the countryside and asked Father to help make a survey of the villages that most needed help and to supervise distribution of the grain. He was gone sometimes for weeks at a time, and I remember him returning tired, dirty, totally exhausted, and usually very discouraged and heartbroken, not only because of the appalling sights he had seen, but also with the seeming impossibility of the task. Everywhere people were dying from hunger, and unfortunately nearly all of the survivors were too weak to walk the few miles from their homes to Lingyuan, where grain was available. Many came, but many more couldn't.

I wanted badly to go with Father on one of his trips, so he finally agreed to take me with him to an area not many miles from the city, but remote and almost inaccessible because of the mountains. Looking back, I think his reason for taking me was not so much to satisfy my pleas, but that he thought the presence of a young foreign lad in the group of officials and soldiers might help calm the fears of the isolated village people when we arrived among them.

The weather was still very hot when we set off on our trip early one morning. It was probably August or September, and the fields should have been green and golden with ripening crops. Near Lingyuan, where the two rivers flowed by the city, there was some vegetation, but when we got away from the city, there was nothing. We'd had no rain for almost two years, and everywhere the fields were brown and deserted. Not a vestige of any sort of vegetation, not even weeds. We were quite a large party, a number of Chinese officials and an escort of soldiers, all of us on horseback or riding mules. We took a shortcut over the mountains, the carts carrying the grain having been sent to the area two days previously by a very roundabout route.

We didn't reach our destination till mid-afternoon. In many places the paths we followed over the mountains were so steep that everyone had to dismount and lead the animals, which consumed a lot of time. An advance party had gone several days earlier to each of the villages we were to visit. The members of the party told the headman of each village to prepare a list of all the families in his village and the number of "mouths" in each family. When we came within sight of the first village, in a rocky gorge surrounded on all sides by high mountains, we saw a few terraced fields nearby. There wasn't a blade of grass to be seen, nor a leaf on any of the trees, and most of the trees had even been denuded of their bark, all of it eaten by the populace. Usually when approaching a Chinese village, the sound of barking dogs was the first thing one heard. That day there was not a dog or a cat to be seen. All had been eaten, and all the horses, mules, donkeys, and other livestock had either been eaten or sold.

The grain carts had already arrived and were standing off to one side, guarded by soldiers to discourage hungry crowds from mobbing them, but as it turned out, the precautions were completely unnecessary. No one in the villages had the strength to move more than a few feet at a time, and many were lying in their homes awaiting death.

At each village, the headman, or a survivor who had taken his place, would be outside to meet us, accompanied by only a handful of villagers. Sometimes there would be a list of the inhabitants, but most often, since they were illiterates, the spokesman would reel off a list of names and the number of people in each house, and one of the Chinese officials with us would laboriously copy it down.

After that we fanned out, checking each household to make sure of the exact number of people inside and whether that tallied with the list we had been given. It seldom did; there were usually too many names and too few people. A long and vociferous discussion would ensue as we tried to locate the missing, and invariably non-existent, people. It was, of course, an understandable effort to get a larger handout of grain. In many cases it also reflected the numbers who unfortunately had already perished.

When everyone had been accounted for, all the

premises were thoroughly searched to determine that there were no foodstuffs hidden. We looked into every jar and container. Piles of brush in the yards were turned over, and long metal spikes were driven into the ground around each house to see if anything had been buried. When Father was finally satisfied that a family was truly needy, he would produce a white card, and with a ticket punch, would punch out a series of holes designating the amount of grain to be given to that family. The number of holes did not correspond to the number of people in a given family, but indicated the number of bushels of grain they would get. Pathetically, some of the people had picked up the tiny bits of paper that had been punched out and stuck them back in, in the belief that would get them more grain, thus unknowingly short-changing themselves. Fortunately most of those were very obvious.

As the cards were given out, the distribution of grain began, but many were too weakened by hunger to even move off their brick beds to get the life-saving food. I saw sights that day that have lived with me ever since. The people all appeared to be walking dead with lifeless eyes. It barely seemed to register with them that we had brought them food, and the effort of cooking and eating it was almost too much for them to contemplate.

In one village Father had an experience that was both amusing and sad. Approaching a fairly large residence, he saw a middle-aged woman turn around and run into one of the rooms as fast as her bound feet would carry her. Father followed at once with the thought that she was about to conceal a stock of grain. Instead, she climbed onto the *kang* and hurriedly reaching up onto the wall, turned a hanging picture so that the previously exposed side faced inward, and it now displayed a picture of the virgin Mary. Out of curiosity Father got up onto the *kang* and looked at the other side: it showed a likeness of Buddha. The family purported to be Catholics, and the woman had mistaken Father for a priest; hence her panic. But it was obvious they were not missing any bets. If one religion didn't help them, perhaps the other would. As it turned out, the family was well supplied with food and didn't need any help.

Father told us of one village he had visited a few days previously where he had come upon a house with the doors and windows all bricked up, and it was obvious the door had been sealed from the inside. The village headman told Father that the family that lived there was inside, and that was their coffin. The mud was dry, and it was apparent it had been done some days before. However, Father broke in to see if there might possibly be any survivors, but there weren't. He found a number of bodies, all of them adults. He learned that the family had exchanged their children with others from another family, then eaten the children — as they expected the other family to eat theirs — and had closed themselves in and settled down to die. That was not an isolated incident; we heard of numerous such cases. It was not cannibalism to prolong their own lives, but a pathetic effort to save their children from the agonies of dying from starvation. None of them could face eating their own children; someone else had to do it.

Fattened donkey "May" making friends with Barbara's dog.

Washing clothes by a brook.

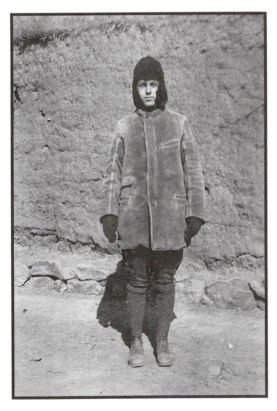

Gil all dressed for cold weather.

Getting water from a well.

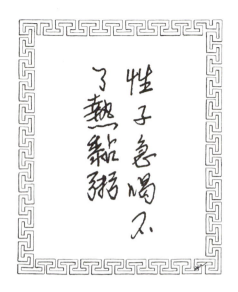

Xingzi ji hebuliao re nian zhou.

*One who is impatient
cannot drink hot glutinous gruel.*

- Chinese Peasant Saying.

Chapter Eleven
Man's Wars

Not only was the year 1920 a year of great famines, but, as if that weren't enough for the poor Chinese, the summer of that year also saw the beginning of the so-called "Warlord Era," which lasted until about 1931.

A great many of the journalists who covered that period, and other writers who have since written about the civil wars of China, saw those wars primarily from positions in one of the larger coastal cities. They probably didn't stray too far from the nearest club bar. The strongest impression conveyed by most of the writers was that China's internal wars were "comic-opera," not to be taken seriously. Much was made of the so-called "Silver Bullet" diplomacy purportedly used by one side to bribe commanders and troops of another, in an attempt to induce them to change their allegiance and thus avoid actual fighting. Unquestionably, some of that did occur, but it was far from being the whole truth.

From our vantage point in Lingyuan, the wars were all too real. Not only were they real to the innocent population of the region, who suffered and died by the thousands, but also to the equally large numbers of soldiers who perished or were maimed for life in the many battles that we witnessed. It is not my intention to attempt to write a historical account of that chaotic period; that has already been done by others. I was very young at the time, and my memories of our varied experiences — many and vivid though they be — are altogether too confused and jumbled for me to make any attempt to form a clear picture of just who was fighting whom and why. Even at the time, when we were right in the middle of it, we sometimes didn't know what was going on.

Lingyuan lay on one of the two-centuries-old, main east-west trade routes from northern Manchuria to Peking. The other route was the Peking-Mukden rail line, which was about two hundred miles south of us. As the struggle for power continued between those warring generals, it was along those two routes that they surged back and forth, much like the ocean tides, except that unlike the tides, the timing was wholly unpredictable.

We lost count very early of the number of times Lingyuan was besieged and occupied by armies that approached from the east, from the west, and occasionally even from the south and north. Judging, however, from the number of warlords whom I met over those years, it was, as the Chinese say, "a few tens" of times, or so it seemed.

Chang Tso-lin, perhaps the most widely known of those many warlords, was the undisputed ruler of Manchuria at the time, and he remained so for many years until he died on June 4, 1928, when his train was bombed, an act attributed to the Japanese, who were attempting to take over the country. Had he been agreeable to cooperating with them, they might have used him as a puppet, as they did others, but perhaps he was too powerful for their liking.

Although I never met Chang Tso-lin personally, I saw him on several occasions at his big villa in Beidaihe. I knew his two sons well, and I played tennis with them on occasion. The elder son, Chang Hsueh-liang, took over after his father's death, and while he was never as powerful as his father, he is perhaps more famous in a way. It was he who in 1936 kidnapped Chiang Kai-shek, and was under house arrest for about 55 years, first in China and later in Taiwan. He was finally released in March of 1991. The younger son came to America and became a translator at the United Nations in New York City, and I met him there a number of times when I took students to the U.N. to hear the Chinese translations.

The first of numerous battles of the civil war that I can remember was in 1924, when I was eleven. Gen. Chang Tso-lin's authority in our part of the world was challenged by General Wu P'ei-fu, whose armies advanced on Lingyuan from the west and south. General Wu, who accompanied his troops, was in Lingyuan for some weeks, and I met him several times. He was a big burly fellow, not at all soldierly in his bearing and very dissolute in appearance. He was reputed to have had 500 wives, whom he kept in a hotel he had taken over in Yantai (also known as Chefoo) on the coast in Shandong Province. To begin with, Wu's troops surprised the garrison in Lingyuan and forced them out, then Chang's forces re-grouped and pushed Wu's troops back.

The man who succeeded in driving Wu back was a general under Chang Tso-lin named Chang Tsung-ch'ang (no relation to Chang Tso-lin). When his troops came into Lingyuan, it was obvious they were a well-disciplined bunch, and well paid. Father took me with him when he went to visit the general and we found him studying his maps, planning his next offensive. He was a tall man with wide shoulders, and probably weighed around 250 lbs. Dressed in a very smart uniform, with a shiny Sam Browne belt and a Mauser pistol at his side, he looked the part of a real soldier. He was most affable, and asked Father some questions about the area and about how best he could maintain the peace. He showed us his maps. The one of the city of Lingyuan was so complete in every detail that it even showed the small footpath leading from our back gate out to the back road. We asked where he had got the maps and he told us he had bought them from the Japanese for $5,000. Even in Chinese dollars that was a lot of money in those days. As we walked home after seeing the general Father told me a story of his early days in Bagou in 1903, when he was studying Chinese.

Father used to take his books with him and walk the nearby hills as he tried to memorize Chinese phrases. One day he had noticed two Japanese in the town selling medicine, but thought nothing further about it. A day or so later on his usual walk, he came up from behind a hill, and as he topped the ridge, with just his head appearing over the top, he saw in front of him the two Japanese sitting on a large rock with their backs to him. As he approached them he saw they had a large sheet of paper spread in front of them and Father realized they were mapping the town below. The instant they noticed Father, they crumpled the sheet of paper into a ball and started to walk away. That was almost twenty years before General Chang Tsung-ch'ang showed us his maps, and it was entirely likely that it was those two men who had drawn at least part of them back in 1903.

Over the next ten years, numerous other warlords entered the wars. One army would come in and occupy the city, and just as we had become accustomed to them, we would find ourselves taken over by an entirely different group. Yet through all those battles the city suffered very little damage. Frequently there was fighting in the streets, but for the most part the generals did not use their artillery on the city, doubtless because it was too important a base for them and they wanted to keep it intact. But we always felt that God had a hand in it.

Another reason, perhaps, that we fared so well was the dexterity of our local Chinese gentry, whose practice of diplomacy was honed to a fine art. In times of peace, it was the practice of the Chinese to always go outside the city for some considerable distance to welcome any incoming visitor of importance, be he a new magistrate or a newly assigned military commander. The degree of the man's importance determined the distance the welcoming party would travel out to meet him. Sometimes, when prior notice had been given by telegram, the distance might be as much as a full day's journey, and it was seldom less than five or ten miles outside the city.

It was somewhat ironical that the same courtesy was accorded, although to a lesser extent, to any departing official, even if he was leaving in defeat or disgrace. Perhaps it was only an "honor" on the face of it, and they simply wanted to make certain the departing official was really gone for good. In any case, when the civil war reached us, the same practice was carried out whenever possible. Each time a conquering army approached the city, there would be a period of hectic activity as the defeated occupying general was gently persuaded that it was in his best interest to leave, and he would be politely escorted out of town. Then the town fathers would hustle out to the other side of the city to welcome the incoming — and at least temporarily — victorious general and his army.

On occasion, depending upon the stubbornness of the defeated general or the enthusiasm and aggressiveness of the incoming man, the time between seeing the first man out of one gate and welcoming the second through a different gate, could be quite short, or non-existent. In the latter case, fighting in the streets resulted.

Any welcoming party would be made up of the local magistrate and his entourage, with such local dignitaries as the head of the telegraph office; a Mr. Chen, who was a Christian; the postmaster; the chief of police; a group of local scholars and intelligentsia; and, for good measure, the head priests of some of the larger temples. Dating back to the "buried babies" incident, and the subsequent good relations established with that particular magistrate, Father was

inevitably invited to be a part of the welcoming or send-off parties, though it was unclear as to whether he was considered one of the gentry, a scholar, or simply the leader of a church. Most likely it was simply because he was a foreigner. Although there were always one or two Caucasian Catholic priests in Lingyuan, usually Belgians, they were seldom asked to participate. Father used to feel that it was simply the fact that he was a Britisher that made him so desirable at those functions, and that his presence lent a certain degree of prestige to the magistrate and possibly at the same time helped guarantee his safety. Whatever the reason, Father was certainly popular with nearly every magistrate we had. Maybe it was due in part to the fact that Father never imposed on his friendship with them. He, unlike the Catholic Fathers, never invoked his extraterritorial rights with the magistrates, even though the latter were very well aware of those rights for foreigners, which had been imposed on China by the allies as punishment following the Boxer Uprising of 1900.

When the first of the civil wars came to Lingyuan, one of the first things Father did was to make up some large Union Jacks, and since Harriet Minns was living with us, a facsimile of the Stars and Stripes. Mrs. Wu, our delightful and much beloved resident seamstress was pressed into service to make up the flags, copied from colored pictures in the encyclopedia. Perhaps the colors might have been a bit off, and the size of the stars somewhat out of proportion, but there was no mistaking what they represented. In addition, since there was no Red Cross, and no doctor in town, Father had been unanimously appointed as head of the local Red Cross. He had a large number of those flags made up as well, together with dozens of armbands bearing the red cross.

Well before the arrival of any incoming army, our flags were prominently displayed outside the front gate. That was not with any real expectancy that they would be recognized and respected for what they were by the mostly illiterate soldiers, and certainly not because we felt or looked for any degree of protection that such flags would give us. They were essentially used as simple markers to indicate that that was a building used by foreigners as a residence. They were hung primarily to discourage a most distressing habit of the Chinese armies, arbitrarily billeting their troops in every available house, particularly in places that looked as spacious and imposing as ours. The Chinese armies had a practice known euphemistically as "marking houses" or "numbering houses" (*hao fangzi*). The advance guard of an occupying army would enter the city first with a pot of paste, then slap small strips of paper on any likely looking house indicating how many men were to be billeted there, without first ascertaining from the owners whether there was sufficient room or whether they would be welcome.

As troops entered the city from the west, our house was one of the first large houses to be encountered: therefore we always got more than our share of those unwelcome visitors. However, Mr. Hu would point to the flags indicating that it was where foreigners lived, and usually the soldiers would leave without too much fuss. In the event that they insisted on pasting a sticker onto our gates, it was always possible to remove it surreptitiously before troops tried to take up residence. However, once or twice they succeeded in gaining entrance and setting up their bivouacs, but Father countered by later paying a visit to their commanding general and getting the order countermanded.

In almost every case as the fighting approached our city, we had plenty of warning. Initially there would be the usual spate of rumors. In each army of occupation there were usually one or two Christian soldiers who were able to give us more or less authentic news of the war and tell us of any opposition army approaching. Then, too, long before we began to hear the sound of distant gunfire, the pathetic sights common to all warfare were very much in evidence: the fleeing refugees, the constant flow of wounded soldiers and civilians being carried past our front gate, and, so characteristic of broken and disorganized armies in retreat, the straggling lines of spent and weary soldiers, usually barefooted and mostly without their weapons.

In addition to what might happen when the fighting came close to the city, our very real fear was the possibility of wholesale looting, which was expected from an army in retreat, accompanied by the raping of women and the burning of houses. To try to prevent that, Father usually paid a courtesy visit to the headquarters of the general then occupying the city, if he hadn't already fled, and on numerous occasions he took me with him. Those visits were always very

exciting for me. Father felt that my presence might make it seem less of a political call and more like a casual visit. In any case, the generals were always gracious enough to receive us, despite the urgency of the moment for him. Father was always treated with extreme courtesy. as he explained to the generals that the welfare and safety of the citizens of Lingyuan was of paramount importance, and, while in that moment of defeat it might have seemed somewhat undiplomatic, Father would ask them to do all in their power to ensure that as their troops left the city they behaved in the same exemplary manner as they had when occupying it in the first place.

The generals invariably assured us that all would be well, as it turned out to be. In fact, although time and again we had the same set of circumstances, Father's seemingly casual visits to the departing generals always paid off. He had given them the all-important "face" so crucial to a Chinese. Apart from a very few minor incidents, we never saw any of the raping and looting that was so much a part of warfare elsewhere in China where, with few exceptions, the soldiers were paid a pitifully small sum of money, or none at all, and looting was an accepted way of life.

I recall one occasion when an incoming army followed so closely on the heels of the retreating forces, that the outgoing group were still within sight as they crossed the south river, when the new general took up residence. It so happened that one of our Christian farmers was coming in to market, and told Father that the retreating army had taken up offensive positions just behind the hills south of the river. Their big guns were pointed at the city. Father hurried down to visit the general, taking me with him as usual, and with Mr. Wu, our protocol expert, carrying Father's card in advance.

The general was Li Ching-lin, not as well known as some of the warlords, but with a large and well-disciplined army, mostly cavalry. General Li had arrived in a French Citroen halftrack, the first motorized vehicle we had ever seen in Lingyuan. However, he was more an intellectual than a soldier. When we met him he was not in uniform, but dressed in the long silk gown of a scholar. Father didn't wish to get involved in politics, but after chatting with him for a bit, Father diplomatically asked the general if he had sent out any scouts to the south to see where the retreating army might be. General Li took the hint and immediately dispatched a company of men. Within the half hour we could hear heavy gunfire south of the river as the forces there were surprised before they were ready to make their counterattack. General Li was so grateful for Father's roundabout suggestion that he personally wrote a pair of scrolls and gave them to us, a significant gesture on the part of a Chinese, showing great friendship.

In October 1924, when the weather was already very cold, we were surprised one morning by an incoming army from the north. That one traveled by night and entered the city at dawn. The first we knew of it was when we discovered the entire city was overrun by white men in Chinese army uniforms. We couldn't believe our eyes, nor could the Chinese. Without the slightest warning that army of five or six hundred men had approached the city under cover of darkness, and the opposing army had managed to flee ahead of them out of the south gate, leaving everything behind.

Shortly after dawn Father was alerted by the magistrate, who was in a panic, and a group was hurriedly formed to go and pay a courtesy visit on the commanding officer. We then discovered it was part of an army of White Russians who had been recruited by General Chang Tso-lin. It was an artillery unit with horse-drawn, French 75-mm guns. The man in command was a former colonel under the Tsar, who had fled to Manchuria when the Bolsheviks took over Russia in 1917. Father asked him with some of his staff officers to dinner that night, and left him to rest up after his all-night march.

On the way home Father saw a White Russian girl sitting by the roadside looking absolutely exhausted. He approached her and spoke to her in English, but like the colonel, she could only communicate in Chinese. Father invited her to accompany him to the house, where she would be fed and given a place to sleep. We were all astounded when Father walked in with a pretty young woman in her early twenties, dressed in the usual gray cotton-padded uniform, exactly like a Chinese soldier. She wore a Red Cross armband, and told us her younger brother had signed up with the army, so since he was the only family she had, she had joined up, too. She was the only female among all those men, acting officially as the "medical corps" for the entire force, even though the only medical supplies she had were some iodine and a few bandages.

She must have been nearly starved, because she ate a huge breakfast. Over the meal she told us her parents had been murdered by the Bolsheviks, and that only she and her brother had survived and escaped to Manchuria as young children. She had taken care of her brother since then, and she told us, and it was later confirmed by the colonel, that Chang Tso-lin in recruiting them had promised them that if they fought their way down to Shanghai, he would then use his entire army to help them fight the Bolsheviks and get back to their beloved Russia. Of course he never made good on his promise. When they eventually fought their way to Shanghai, Chang disowned them and left them to their own devices.

While the girl slept the entire day — and I remember being bitterly disappointed that we didn't see anything of her — Father was busy taking care of Russian soldiers with frozen feet. Although their uniforms were warm enough, they had been issued only ordinary Chinese cloth shoes to which they were not accustomed, and many had suffered frostbite. Father did what he could for them, but it was pathetic to see so many of them walking around with sacking tied around their feet.

That evening the colonel and his staff officers were due for dinner at six o'clock, but the time came and went with no sign of them. We waited for half an hour and then Dad sent Mr. Hu to the colonel's headquarters to urge him to come to dinner. In the darkness, and carrying only an oil lantern, Mr. Hu mistook every Russian private he met for the colonel, and since all of them were white men, he ended up bringing back some twenty or more of them. However, in the meantime, the colonel finally showed up, and after Gao Cai had done what he could to feed the soldiers, they were sent away.

The colonel and his staff thoroughly enjoyed the meal and the next day a Russian private delivered a note written by the Colonel's adjutant, a Captain Gregory Gonelin. At the same time the colonel gave Father two empty brass shell casings, which we used for umbrella stands. The Russian troops stayed in Lingyuan for just two days and then headed south.

Where the young girl was concerned, Father gave her the address of a friend in Tientsin for her to contact. We later heard that she was fed there and then went on to Shanghai, where she got a job. The

Russian troops did not fare so well. Months later we read in the newspaper that they had been forced to evacuate Shanghai, after which they were surrounded by Chinese troops, who shot all of them. I think the Chinese resented them.

The next big surprise was in early 1925, when one of the northern armies arrived with airplanes. It caused a tremendous sensation. They built an airstrip on the opposite side of the river, outside the north gate, simply by selecting a fairly level spot in the fields, then commandeering hundreds of people from the city to go out there and walk up and down until the ground was hard and level. The planes were there for several weeks. Each morning they would fly west to drop bombs on the enemy. As soon as they were heard in the distance, everyone would rush out to watch them fly over, and when the wind was right we could hear the bombs exploding, although reports were that the bombs did very little damage. As I remember there were two or three twin-engined bombers and two fighters, all of them ancient Handley Paige biplanes, and very slow moving, but they created a great deal of excitement.

Old Mrs. Wu, the seamstress, had heard a lot about them from others, but being so bent over she had been unable to see them. She asked me to let her know the next time they came over, so when I heard them in the distance, I got her out in the yard and sat her down so she could look up. When they finally came into sight she looked at them for a minute or two and then said, with a tone of disgust, *"He! Namege dongxi"* ("Huh! A thing like that.") With that she got up and walked away, completely unimpressed.

In the early 1920s, when it became obvious that hostilities between the warring generals were fast approaching our area, Father anticipated that in all likelihood there would be many civilian and military wounded. Apart from our two small dispensaries, there was nothing even resembling a clinic or hospital in the city. Father advised the magistrate of his concerns and made some suggestions. The magistrate agreed, and to provide some sort of medical facility, he commandeered a very large temple on a back street in the northwestern part of the town, actually not very far from where we lived. The temple, like many others around the place, was no longer in use, and apart from the many idols, was vacant. It was in a pretty dilapidated condition, with very little in the way of facilities for either cooking or sanitation, but at least it had lots of space.

The magistrate, chamber of commerce, and leading citizens were all asked to contribute money and labor to clean the place. Then food for the wounded and bedding and tables were requisitioned, and Father organized squads of men as litter-bearers, carriers of water, cooks, and so on. All were provided with Red Cross armbands, which made them not a little proud. Certainly it gave them a feeling of security as they moved about the city, where the soldiers were grabbing every available man for forced labor in digging trenches and carrying supplies to the front lines.

In every battle, long before we could hear the sound of distant gunfire, we would see wounded being carried in, soldiers mainly, but occasionally some civilians. That kept both my parents very busy. Mother had organized the orphan girls and a group of women to help make up bandages. Coarse Chinese cotton cloth was torn into strips, boiled to sterilize it, and rolled. My parents had some limited previous experience in treating gunshot wounds, since the occasional shot-up bandit would come in surreptitiously, or a wounded soldier or policeman would be brought in for treatment. And of course there were many accidental injuries on a day-to-day basis over the years, but that hardly prepared them for what we were to see.

The battle injuries were for the most part quite different. Apart from gunshot wounds, many of the men had severe shrapnel wounds from exploding hand grenades, or worse still, from artillery shells, with limbs frequently blown off or terribly mutilated. And the wounds, although severe, were only part of the problem. The men themselves were usually in very bad shape. Frequently they had been lying out in the field for a considerable length of time before being picked up, and had suffered great loss of blood, and since it was already early winter, they had all suffered from exposure. Most of the armies themselves had only a skeleton medical corps, so there was not much help available from that source. Apart from the somewhat limited resources of my parents' dispensaries, there was nothing at all in the way of medical supplies, and nothing could be purchased locally. For use as a disinfectant, Father got in supplies of native wine from the local distilleries. The owners somewhat reluctantly acceded to Father's demands that it be pure and undiluted in any way, and since it was nearly 100 proof, it met the need. In those days there was no such thing as penicillin, sulfa powder or antibiotics of any kind. To stop bleeding, the Chinese practice was either to use a handful of dust or cobwebs to plaster the injury. It was surprisingly effective. However, the possibility of infection was enormous. When the injured men were brought in, few of the wounds were bound with anything but a dirty piece of cloth. Infection was a real problem, and we had nothing with which to treat the injuries apart from small quantities of iodine, permanganate of potash, and Epsom Salts.

Initially, since I was only around eleven at the time, Father wouldn't let me go anywhere near this "hospital" he had set up. Later, however, as the numbers of wounded became more numerous, he finally agreed to my accompanying him. In a limited way I was able to give some help. I remember that on one side of the big temple compound there was one very long building with an open porch-like front. The larger-than-human-sized idols had all been pushed to the rear, against the back wall, and the wounded men were laid out in rows on the straw-covered brick floor. Apart from a few charcoal braziers here and there, there was no heat in the building, but at least the wounded were under cover and out of the wind. In that one building there must have been around three hundred men. I walked among them with tea and cakes that the merchants had donated, and did my best to cheer them up, joking about their injuries and kidding them about the way they were goofing off from their jobs as soldiers. They took it all in good heart.

The Chinese are very fatalistic and, for the most part, are not only used to discomfort, but have developed a very high tolerance for pain. Sores and wounds that we would consider critical, they tend to ignore until they are almost incapacitated. There were many with limbs blown off, but they, too, seemed quite cheerful, and I think that seeing a small foreign boy, probably for the first time, helped them forget their suffering. I was not at all surprised that the majority of the wounded were in relatively good spirits. For one thing, they were out of the fighting, and even though there was little in the way of heat, that wasn't at all unusual because it would have been the same in their homes. The only difference was that they were sleeping on the cold floor, but at least we had straw on the brick floors and cotton-padded mattresses for them, and they were being given three hot meals a day.

They were quite excited when they found I could speak their language. The majority of them were from southern or central provinces, because they were mostly Gen. Wu's troops, and for them that was very far from home. The dialects they spoke were quite different from our local speech, but we had little difficulty in understanding each other. Most had been away from home for months, some for years, and had had no news from home. When I offered to get letters written to their families, they were overjoyed, and for that I enlisted the services of Mr. Wu, Mr. You Bi-chen and my tutor, Zhang Yao-ting. Soldiers from opposing armies were lying side by side, but they demonstrated not the slightest animosity toward each other; in fact, they showed great friendliness.

Incoming wounded were treated first in a large building at the rear of the temple compound. When not busy with the men who were recuperating, I would go in and watch Father at work on the new arrivals. With the hundreds of wounded men that I saw (there were never fewer than 300 in the temple) I can recall no screams or loud cries from even the most severely wounded. The most one would hear were groans or the constant use of the common Chinese phrase used when in pain or in trouble: "Wode ma ya, wode ma ya!" ("Oh my mother, my mother!") It wasn't a question of pride or machismo. Those men were stoical and extremely grateful for the attention they were being given.

Father was not a doctor, and prior to going to China had not had any medical training whatsoever. However, he, like most missionaries when faced with the need, quickly learned the rudiments of medicine. Among the business community in the coastal cities there was a standing joke that missionaries had only two ways of treating the sick: aspirin for pain above the waist, and Epsom Salts for pain below the waist. However, my parents had provided themselves with the latest available medical journals and it was common for us as children to see them consulting them late into the night. There was also a very thick volume that I learned was called the "pharmacopoeia," one of the first words I learned to pronounce and spell correctly. "Astigmatism," was another word I learned from watching Mother thread the needle of her sewing machine. She wore pince-nez eyeglasses and had to take them off and peer closely at the eye of the needle as she was threading it. When I asked her why, she told me she had astigmatism, which I thought was a really neat word. Around the same time, Barbara, who was probably around four, astounded us all one morning at breakfast by suddenly saying to Miss Minns: "You have a very raucous voice." Miss Minns, of course, couldn't believe what she was hearing, and then it turned out that the previous day Mother had been telling Father about one of the patients having a very raucous voice. Barbara, hearing the phrase, liked it and thought she'd try it out on Miss Minns.

Although Father had spent a lot of time reading up on battle injuries, he had pitifully inadequate implements and medical supplies. To dig out the numerous bullets and pieces of shrapnel, his only "surgical" tools were Mother's knitting needles to use as probes to find the bullets and a crochet needle or a small pair of tweezers to lift them out when found. To make incisions, or when lancing a wound, he used his straight-razor, and for sewing up wounds there were only ordinary needles and heavy cotton thread, which was first boiled in a pot of water over charcoal. Of course, there was nothing in the way of an anesthetic. Father doubtless could have used opium, or possibly morphine, but I don't recall him doing so. Perhaps that was because they were such viciously addictive drugs that he wanted no responsibility for administering something for which we had all learned an abhorrence, but that is purely conjecture on my part. I do know we had nothing as sophisticated as syringes with which to give injections. During one of the big battles that brought in many wounded, and before Father had let me go with him to the "hospital," a surprise attack early one morning brought severe fighting in the streets. I well remember Father leaving for the "hospital" carrying a large Red Cross flag and telling us children not to stand outside the front gate to watch the retreating troops. We peeked through the crack between the front gates, but could see little except glimpses of marching men: first the retreating army, then, after a lot of shooting, the incoming troops rounding up stragglers.

When the shooting died down, we went to the back garden and climbed to the top of a ladder leaning against the wall. Peering through the grass that grew on top of the wall, we could see the incoming troops making their way across the fields in small groups, and later we saw a lot of horse-drawn artillery go by. It wasn't long after that we could hear a pitched battle taking place out to the west of the city. Gradually the battle sounds moved away from us, and then the streams of wounded were carried in by men wearing Red Cross armbands and by farmers who had been enlisted for the job. It was a pitiful sight.

As each occupying army took over and solidified its gains, the fighting moved steadily farther away from Lingyuan, and there was a gradual lessening in the number of wounded being brought in. However, those that were carried in came from greater distances, and they were often in much worse shape. Also we saw more civilian wounded, both men and women. Mother took care of the women in our own compound, but the men were put in with the soldiers. One day we were greatly shocked when the elderly father of our table boy, You Wang, was brought in on a makeshift stretcher, a door, carried by four men. He had been hit by a ricocheting bullet when he stepped out of his house to see what was going on as the fighting went through his village. He had lost a great deal of blood, and though conscious, was far gone. The bullet, damaged as it was by impact with the stone wall of his gate, had made a huge wound in his chest and lodged in one lung. There was little that Father could do for him, and he expired a few hours later.

Doors, by the way, were frequently used as stretchers. That was only one of the many uses to which a Chinese door could be put. Unlike our doors, Chinese doors had no hinges. Instead of hinges, on what we would call the hinge side, the side post of the door protruded both top and bottom for several inches. At the top it was extended about three inches in a round, post-like form which fit into a metal loop inserted into the frame above. The bottom, which extended only about two inches and was ball-shaped on the bottom, was frequently bound with a loop of iron to take the wear. That rounded end acted as a pivot where it fit into a "cup" cut either into a wooden or stone block that was used as a base for the door frame.

When a door was to be removed, it was a simple

matter to lift it up slightly from the inside and pull it toward you. From the outside, because of the high step, or coaming, against which the doors closed, it was impossible to lift the doors upward, so they actually were quite secure. The Chinese used their doors for a dozen different purposes. When there was a wedding or funeral feast, the doors were taken down and used as trellis tables. When housewives wanted to make shoe soles, the doors were used as a base on which to paste down layer after layer of small bits of cloth. After being dried in the sun, the sheets of cloth were peeled off, cut into shape and sewn with heavy string. When a wall needed repairing, two doors were used as a form, one on each side of the wall, and into the form was packed a heavy, semi-dry mud and straw mix, which was then pounded solid, first by barefooted men, then with heavy wooden blocks. And there were other uses as well.

One very real problem with the wounded being carried in from great distances was the shock and exposure they had suffered. More and more frequently men were carried in who had been lying out in the fields for a week or ten days before being found by a woodcutter or shepherd boy. Some told us that they had been seen by numerous people, but that no one wanted to get involved in case they died on their hands. On the other hand perhaps it was because the finder was either afraid or did not know whom to tell. Many of the injured had developed gangrene for which, in most cases, nothing could be done. In any case, the individual was usually near death from both the extreme cold and lack of nourishment. I recall one man in particular who was brought in after lying in a gully for more than two weeks. He had a bullet through the leg, and although he had managed to crawl for some distance, he had been unable to crawl up the sides of the gully. That may have saved his life, because in the bottom of the gully he had been less exposed to the cold. Surprisingly, he was not only conscious when brought in, but quite alert. Unfortunately, his leg wound had become badly infected and severe gangrene had set in. Father felt that the man was young enough, and quite possibly sufficiently hardy, to tolerate amputation of the leg. Although Father had never done anything like that before, he knew it had to be performed to save the man's life.

Father didn't approach it lightly or with any enthu-

siasm, but it was something he felt was necessary. First the man had to be fed for a day or so to restore his strength, and that gave Father some time to read up on amputations and prepare as well as he could. When it came time to perform the operation, the man understood why he had to lose his leg and was quite agreeable. Father told him that it would be very painful and that no anesthetic was available. The man merely grinned and said he was used to pain.

As an assistant, Father had a young Chinese who had had one year of medical school in Peking and had assisted in amputations. First Father gave the patient a sizable drink of straight alcohol. Then his body was tied securely to the top of a narrow table, and with a man holding down each shoulder and arm, and two other men assigned each to hold down one of his legs, Father commenced work.

Father had no scalpels, only his straight-razor and a nearly new American-style carpenter's saw. As Father told us later, apart from groaning, the poor man never cried out once, and he remained conscious throughout, with sweat pouring from his brow even though the room was freezing cold. All in all it was an extraordinary example of fortitude. Father had to amputate the leg above the knee, tying off the blood vessels with ordinary sewing thread and leaving a flap of skin, which he later sewed over the stump. Sawing through the bone was the hardest part, both for Father and the patient, but that, too, was eventually accomplished, and at the end, the man smiled and thanked Father for saving his life. He recovered well and for months thereafter was a familiar sight around town as he hobbled about on one crude crutch. From time to time he attended church services, and professed to be a Christian. Father urged him to go to one of the coastal cities where he could get fitted with a wooden leg, and some time later he left Lingyuan and we lost touch with him.

Looking back on all of this, I can remember the incidents so well, but have no recollection of any sort of shock or horror at seeing so much blood and suffering. I suspect that from early childhood, having been exposed to seeing diseases of all kinds and people carried into the dispensary with serious injuries, it was more or less commonplace to me. There just happened to be more of it than before. However, before I leave the gruesome subject, there was one more incident that I shall never forget, and which did shock me greatly.

A young soldier was carried in one day with only a relatively minor bullet wound in one leg, but he, too, had lain out in the open for more than two weeks before being found and had developed lockjaw, a form of tetanus where muscular contraction locks the jaws firmly together. I happened to be there when he was carried in, and Father immediately diagnosed what was wrong with him, even though he had never before seen lockjaw and had only read about it. The wound could be treated, but there was no possible way the man could be fed, nor was there any known treatment for lockjaw. Certainly none was available to us so far from civilization.

Still, Father couldn't bear to watch that young man die without trying something. In spite of his long exposure and not having had anything to eat or drink for two weeks, he was conscious, so Father decided on extraordinary measures to feed him. After making preparations, he told the man what he had in mind. Unable to speak, the man nodded in agreement and Father started to work.

The man was in his early twenties, and had a perfect set of teeth. It was Father's intention to pull out a couple of teeth so that he could insert a makeshift feeding tube. Unfortunately, the jaws were so tightly locked together it was quite impossible to insert anything between the clenched teeth, so pulling teeth was out of the question. Trying to pry open the jaws with a metal bar would probably break his jaws, so Father didn't want to try that. There was only one other alternative, and that was to knock out some teeth.

We had a blunt cold chisel at home, used for cutting or chipping metal or stone, and Father had me run home and fetch it, together with a carpenter's hammer. At the same time, I was to ask Mother for the rubber tube from the enema bottle. When I brought them back, Father commenced working on the teeth. He intended to simply knock out one tooth in the top jaw and one opposite it in the lower. However, the chisel was too wide, which meant it took out two teeth at a time. Father tried to do it with a single blow, in order to lessen the pain, but it took several blows before he was able to knock two of the top teeth inward. Like the first soldier who had his leg amputated, the man never cried out; he simply lay perfectly still until the teeth were removed. In fact, he was even able to spit one of them out through the hole.

Father fashioned a crude funnel, inserted it into one end of the rubber tube, and pushed the other end through the gap in the man's teeth. With that crude method Father managed to feed him some thin millet gruel and soup. The man was pathetically grateful.

Although the feedings over several days temporarily restored his strength, the tetanus continued to take over and his entire body gradually became paralyzed. I visited him every day, as did Father and our Chinese preachers, and together we told him about Christ and the way of salvation. He tried to talk, but it was mostly unintelligible, and he died about ten days later. I think Father felt more saddened by the death of that young man than by any of the many patients he had. I never saw him so tired and dispirited as after the young man's death. I remember that in subsequent months and years, as the fighting went on, we had at least five more cases of lockjaw, but that was the only time I can remember Father attempting to do anything for the patient. There just seemed to be nothing at all that could be done for anyone with that dreadful complication from what was sometimes a very minor wound.

I cannot leave the subject of Chinese warlords without mentioning the colorful "Christian General" Feng Yu-hsiang, who was probably better known to the outside world than any of the others, and about whom several books have been written. His troops never actually entered Lingyuan, but they came very close to us one time. They were known for being the best behaved and most rigidly disciplined men of any army. Many stories are told about General Feng, such as his baptizing whole companies of men with a fire hose, and assuring his troops that they had no need to fear bombs dropped by enemy planes. "After all," as he said: "How many times have you been hit by bird droppings as they fly over?"

One story about him concerned his dislike of the Western habit of shaking hands. Although he was a very big man, his hands were soft and flabby, but he was proud of them as being the hands of an intellectual and a writer. When some enthusiastic Westerner gripped his hand firmly to shake hands, he felt pain and resolved to do something about it. Feng ordered a brick to be brought to him, and using the brick, he practiced squeezing it day after day until eventually he was able to crush it to small pieces. He was then able to take on any foreigner that came along.

Feng's troops were widely respected by the populace for their high morality and honesty. Wherever they went, all brothels, gambling houses and opium dens were closed down while Feng's troops were there. His troops were billeted in people's houses, but unlike other troops, they paid for everything they ate. Like all other armies on the march, they were known for helping themselves to fruits or vegetables that they found growing in gardens along their route, but unlike the others, they always left money behind to pay for what they took. On one occasion two of Feng's men were caught not leaving money in the holes in the ground after they had helped themselves to two turnips. Their superior officer who saw it immediately shot them as an example to the rest of the men.

General Feng himself was a professing Christian and there can be no doubt that many of his troops were born-again Christians. However, others were Christians in name only. In one of the armies that occupied Lingyuan, one feature was quite different from any other Chinese army we'd seen. One brigade stationed in Lingyuan consisted of men who were expert in *Qi gong*, a somewhat mystical system of deep-breathing exercises. Among other things the practitioners are reputed to be able to cure illnesses, both for themselves and others, and perform astonishing feats not only of endurance but of different forms of levitation for which there is no logical explanation. In speaking of it, Chinese frequently use the term *xie shu* or sorcery, or *xie fa*, trickery. Whatever it may be, I saw some truly remarkable demonstrations of their prowess, much of which smacked of the occult. Small groups within the brigade had their own specialities in purely physical prowess, one group concentrating on the use of swords, another on long spears and a third using lengthy chains. The latter could throw the chains to encircle an enemy's neck and drag him down. The swordsmen flashed their swords around at an incredible speed, and the spear wielders used their spears in a jabbing motion at the "enemy" so fast and furious that on the camera films of that period it appeared simply as a blur.

However, it was the various forms of levitation I witnessed that really astonished me. For Chinese New Year the men put on a demonstration where a telegraph pole was embedded upright in the ground, and at intervals of eight or ten inches on opposing sides of the pole, holes were cut out large enough to take the handles of swords that were placed there with the blade facing upward. The idea was much like the metal spikes one sees on both sides of telephone poles in the United States. Each sword had been sharpened to the point where a feather dropped onto it fell in two parts. Despite the extremely cold weather, one of the men stripped down to his pants, and barechested and barefoot, he commenced a routine of deep breathing, and then appeared to go into some sort of a trance. Then, taking a short run toward the pole, he climbed the swords barefooted to the top of the pole and came down again, all within a matter of seconds, and showed the soles of his feet to be entirely whole and with no cuts on them. Had I not seen it with my own eyes I would never have believed it possible.

They performed another inexplicable feat. A troop of perhaps fifty or more men, loaded down with all their combat gear, trotted in perfect formation of four abreast, directly toward a ten-foot wall. Without any pause or hesitation, the entire group appeared to "float" up and over the wall with no apparent effort. To this day I cannot explain how it was done. I can only tell what I saw, and the Chinese I asked told me it was all a matter of *qi*, which is variously described as breath, air, morale, vital energy, energy of life, gas, spirit, and a number of other things.

For a considerable period of time during the past thirty years the practice of *qi gong* was prohibited by the Chinese Communist government as superstition, but of late it has had a tremendous revival in China, and is being taught in many cities by master practitioners.

Following the famines, the International Famine Relief Commission and a grateful Chinese government struck off some medals, which they awarded to the many volunteers who had worked so tirelessly in the famine areas, and who had without any doubt helped save hundreds, if not thousands, of lives. The International Red Cross also awarded medals to those who had worked with the wounded during the wars, and those were formally handed out by the local authorities. Father received several of the medals, a number of scrolls and numerous congratulatory banners from several of the warlords, who were grateful for the medical help he gave to their men. However, much as Father appreciated all of them, I know that his greatest satisfaction was in knowing that he had helped save many lives. But even more important to him was the satisfaction of having been able to do his primary work as a missionary. That many of the soldiers on their death beds did profess to having accepted Christ as their Saviour meant more to Father than any material awards.

October 10th 1924.

Dear Doctor
                    all officers of
Russian detachement present you and
your familly the sentiments of their
high regarding and best compliments.
We remember with great pleasure
the evening at your home and kindness of you and all your familly.
And I remember you every day, on
reading presented by your son Holy
gospel. Our humble petition - to sent
you, if you be so kind a little of
iodoform and creolin and my petition
to sent some newspapers or journal.
We beg pardon for the trouble
of fulfilling our petition.

            Respectfully yours

                    Captain Gonelin.

Letter from Russian officer, Capt. Gregory Gonelin, mentioned in this chapter (see page 117). Note: Smudges on letter are red ink from his name chop ink pad.

Chapter Twelve
Sights, Sounds, Smells & Other Trivia

When we were children, our day started at 5:30 when we had to practice our music — Gil on the organ (and later the trombone) and I on the violin, in separate rooms, of course — and then each of us had to memorize a verse of Scripture and be able to repeat it letter-perfect at breakfast. Looking back on it now, seventy-some years later, it was excellent discipline and what we learned then, we've never forgotten. At first Father let us choose our own verses, but after each of us in turn had tried to get away with the shortest verse in the Bible, John 11:35, "Jesus wept," he decided that enough was enough. After that he made the decision for us. I was given the assignment of Paul's two epistles to the Corinthians, which, memorized verse by verse, covered many months. To this day the thirteenth chapter of I Corinthians is still one of my favorites. I loved the opening verse, where I could practically hear Paul's sonorous voice: "Though I speak with the tongues of men and of angels, and have not charity, I am become as a sound-

ing brass, or a tinkling cymbal..." We repeated our verses between courses at breakfast, then, after the breakfast table was cleared, we all sat down for morning prayers, each one in turn reading a verse from a passage of Scripture that Father selected. In this way, all of us were reading at a very early age.

Every weekday after breakfast, Father held morning prayers with the entire staff in the compound, and then around ten o'clock, he walked to the downtown preaching hall on Great East Street to open his dispensary and treat the sick for two hours. He usually went there again for another hour or two in the afternoon. Before I started school I often went with him. Then, as I grew older and school kept me busy until around eleven o'clock, I frequently walked down on my own after school to meet him so we could walk back together. I would have been around ten at the time.

Great East Street was a continuation of Great West Street on which we lived, the name changing where it crossed the main north-south street, technically the center of the city. The downtown hall was about a mile from our house and just past this main intersection, on the left, or north, side of the street.

Each time I made the trip I found something new to stop and look at, and never tired of the many activities and distractions that were a part of the day in an average Chinese town. The Yamen, where the magistrate lived and held court every day, was usually my first stopping place. I was always curious about what went on there. My parents had forbidden me to go inside. However, nothing was said about my going to the gate and looking in, which I often did, and the guards there got to know me quite well. There were always several policemen there with rifles, and on each side of the gate there was always one of the *yayi*, or Yamen runners. They dressed in black and always carried their "badge of office," a three-foot club with a short rounded handle, and a three-sided "blade" with three very sharp corners. The clubs were painted a bright red with black trim, and the men were all adept at using them to beat prisoners, which was what they were for, using the flat sides when they were bribed sufficiently well, but otherwise using the sharply pointed corners to inflict maximum pain and damage to the poor victims.

Almost every morning when I went by, "court" would be in session with the magistrate sitting on a platform several feet high, his advisers around him, and the prisoners brought for trial standing or kneeling in front of him, depending on the crime with which they were charged. A Chinese prisoner in those days was always presumed guilty, and he had to prove his innocence before he could be released. If he denied his guilt, he was normally beaten or tortured until he confessed to whatever he was accused of, and then and only then would the magistrate pass judgment.

The *yayi* were the most hated and most feared individuals around because once a person fell into their hands, there was no escape. Police could be bought off when they made their arrests, and they often settled for a substantial payment, whereupon they would set the individual free after administering a beating. But the *yayi* were not so readily bribed. They were certainly the cruelest people in the "justice" system, adept at torturing their victims and sadistically enjoying what they did.

Regarding the *yayi* the Chinese had a little rhyme:
Che, chuan, dian, jiao, ya
Wu zui ye gai sha.
Literally: "Carts, boats, inns, chair-bearers, yamen runners, even if guilty of no crime, all of them ought to be slaughtered," the implication being that cart drivers, boatmen, innkeepers, chair-bearers and yamen runners all took advantage of people in adversity, making their money by charging excessive prices, and for that reason didn't deserve to live.

There was always a crowd watching the trial proceedings. In order that the maximum number of people could see the magistrate at his supreme best, the crowd was made to stand on each side of the courtyard, leaving the magistrate in full view from the entrance to the Yamen. For this reason, I could see what was going on without entering the place. I had mixed feelings whenever I saw a prisoner being tried. Most often they were captured bandits or someone accused of being a bandit. Common thieves were the next most common cases, and there were the occasional murderers. But there were also many civil cases tried there, and even in those cases, the accused was frequently beaten by order of the magistrate in order to have him confess his crime. Of course, if he could manage through a third party to make a sufficiently large payment to all concerned, he could get off with a light sentence.

Having seen firsthand the cruelty and inhumane treatment the bandits inflicted on their own prisoners, I didn't feel particularly sorry for them when they were tried and being tortured. Most of them were pretty tough individuals, and, because in most cases the penalty was death, they quite naturally suffered considerably before they would admit their guilt. However, if enough money changed hands, they often avoided the death penalty, endured the torture and ended up in prison for what might be months, years, or even life. Prison was for most of them a living death, although here again, some of the better known bandits lived quite well in the prison, having their food brought in from outside restaurants. There was one well-known case of a bandit chieftain who had been accidentally captured while attending a wedding. He was tried and convicted, but the magistrate had not dared to have him beheaded because he feared repercussions from his very powerful gang, which numbered over a thousand, so he was simply confined to the prison from where he continued to run his gang, bribing the guards to carry messages out for him.

I learned a lot about Chinese torture methods as a boy, and still more in later years. Apart from the beatings administered at the command of the magistrate, there were methods of torture that looked innocent enough but caused immense suffering over a period of time. In one of them the victim was condemned to kneel and hold a stick of *shujie* (dried sorghum stalk) in both hands high over his head with both arms outstretched. The stick weighed only a matter of an ounce or so, but the strain of holding both arms above one's head for hours on end is tremendous. Another was being forced to kneel on jagged pieces of glass, or rough coal-ash clinkers. Then there was the most painful of all, and this was the ultimate torture administered by the court. It was called *ya gun gang*, which literally meant: "press with the rolling pole." The prisoner was forced to kneel, then two men would take a stout pole about three or four inches in diameter, and with a man at each end of the pole, they would roll it back and forth. up and down the calves of the man's legs. When the pressure from two men didn't make the man confess, two more men were added, and if that didn't work, there was room on the end of the pole to add more men, until finally the pressure would be so great that the prisoner's calves simply split wide open or his lower leg bones were crushed. I've seen men maimed for life from the torture.

That prisoners would suffer torture for long periods of time always intrigued me. When they knew they were going to be convicted anyway, why not confess and get it over with. However, hope lives eternal, and I guess they hoped they could endure it and perhaps be freed. But it seldom happened. When they confessed, prison or death by beheading was the normal sentence, and very few, once accused, were ever freed.

Leaving the Yamen I would continue my walk downtown, always walking on the sunny side of the street in winter to get out of the wind. Not only that, but there was little to see on the south side until one reached the very center of town. Just past the Yamen was the police station, and next door to that I always stopped to watch the blacksmith at work. He was always making something of interest, either a special

tool for some farmer, iron tires for the carts, or shoes for horses. Out on the street in front of his place were two sturdy posts set into the ground about six feet apart, with a cross pole joining them at the top, and just room enough underneath for a horse to stand. There he shod the horses, tying their front and back legs securely to the posts, with other ropes under the belly of the animal tied securely to the cross bar. They took no chances of being kicked. One leg at a time would be released while he attached the horseshoes. It was always exciting to watch a horse being shod because they were feisty creatures, always bucking and protesting and biting anyone that came too close to their heads.

Next door to the blacksmith was the rope shop. It was marked by two odd-looking contraptions out in front on the street. Every time I see American football players at practice, using their shoulders to push at a padded and heavily weighted sled, I am reminded of the sled-like, L-shaped frames the ropemakers used. They were about six feet wide, heavily weighted down with large rocks. Each had a row of some eight or ten iron hooks along the outer top edge of the "L," each with a handle protruding on the inner side of the wooden frame, the handles all tied in together by a wooden bar into which the handles were inserted. Thus, by standing on the bottom of the "L" and revolving the wooden bar, the operators could make all the hooks turn in unison. To form the rope, long strings of hemp were strung from the hooks on one frame to the corresponding hooks on the other frame, the two frames set about thirty feet apart. As a man stood on the back of each of the frames and turned the bar in a clockwise direction, the hemp was twisted, and as the strands got tighter and tighter, they got shorter, and it slowly pulled the sleds toward each other, the hemp being constantly kept wet as they worked. When the small strands of rope were complete, they combined two or three to make a thicker rope, repeating the process again. When they were not making rope outside, I would go inside and watch them preparing the hemp; soaking it in water, shredding it and carding it to get out any lumps, the entire process ending up with ropes of all sizes, from about an inch or more in diameter to very fine rope about the diameter of the common American laundry line.

The next shop down the street was a small food shop selling sesame-seed buns baked in an inverted oven. I would stop sometimes to watch the baker kneading the dough, forming the cakes and slapping them inside the oven onto a concave metal plate, which was the roof of the oven. I particularly liked the kind of buns that were filled with unrefined brown sugar, and I often bought one to munch as I walked along.

Beyond the food shop was the barber shop, just a small hole in the wall with one chair, but always busy. Oftimes he would have his assistant or apprentice working out in the street just shaving heads, but what most interested me was watching the head barber manipulate his customers' heads and necks when he had finished shaving them. He would twist their heads until the neck bones cracked, then pummel their shoulders and backs, causing the bones of their arms and shoulders to make a cracking sound, and doing it so deftly and quickly that the customers suffered no pain and ended up feeling wonderful. These men were the forerunners of chiropractors.

At about this point on the street I could smell wine mash from a big distillery on the south side of the street. The smell became ever stronger until I was well past the place. There were few retail sales there; it was mainly wholesale. I used to watch them bring the wine out in large earthenware jars and load them onto carts for shipment, either for local consumption or to be taken to nearby villages. Also of great interest to me were the distillery vehicles. They always had excellently maintained equipment: freight carts with a seven-mule team, or, actually, six mules and always one horse, the latter between the shafts. That, I had been told, was because the mules tended to be more skittish than horses, and the horse provided a stabilizing influence. The harness was always of the finest quality with red tassels on it and on the drivers' whips. The owner had his own private passenger cart with a rounded roof covered with blue cloth that was changed several times a year. The wood was always varnished and polished to a high gloss, and the carts, for use around town only, had extra slim wheels. They also had a pull-down curtain in front for use when the women in the family went shopping or to visit friends. The two animals that pulled it were a perfectly matched pair.

Just across from the distillery was a harness shop. I enjoyed going in there to smell the odor of leather being tanned and to admire the variety of leather equipment they sold. Much of it was rawhide and untanned, because the Chinese believed it to be stronger and longer lasting. However, if any harness made of rawhide was accidentally left outdoors, it was usually pretty well chewed up by dogs before the owner discovered it.

Whether by accident or design, the shop next door to the harness shop was a fur store. I don't know if the two stores had the same owners or not, and I never thought to ask. In winter especially I liked to go in and admire the big variety of furs they displayed. Much of it was just the cured skins hanging in bunches, but they also had fur hats of all kinds. One was a very simple skull-cap made of brown or white felt, with fur-covered ear flaps that folded up inside the cap when not needed. That cap was favored by the working class. They also had a large choice of fancy hats made of a large variety of furs, with dog, cat and rabbit furs predominating, and there were wolf and fox furs as well. They also had better quality imported furs, and most conveniently, right next door was a tailor shop where they would sew the furs into fur gowns or short fur coats, always with the fur on the inside rather than on the outside, as is the custom in the West. The Chinese believe that having the fur on the outside is a classic misuse of the fur, because having the fur close to the skin gives much greater warmth.

Beyond the tailor shop was a carpenter shop. It made a variety of things to order: cupboards, storage boxes, counters for shops, tables and chairs and other assorted furniture, including the low eight-inch-high dining tables for use on the *kang*. It was a big shop, employing about fifteen or more carpenters, and when not occupied making furniture, they made coffins, always in demand. In a back room was a stack of them, and some were always being built out in front. Quite often I would find my old friend, carpenter Liu, working there.

Across the street from that carpenter shop was a totally different kind of carpenter shop. It manufactured carts, both the small passenger type and the big freight carts. I found that place particularly fascinating, and it was no accident that they were positioned near another blacksmith who made all the metal parts for them. The passenger carts, often called Peking carts, had wheels about three and a half feet in diameter, with a large hub in the center, and some twenty rounded spokes. The outer edges of the wheels were about six or seven inches wide and were heavily studded with large-headed nails to cut down on the wear and tear from the rocky roads, and there was an iron "tire" on the very narrow outer rim. The axle on those small carts was a fixed axle made of very hard wood, and where the wheels were mounted, strips of iron were inlaid to prevent wear on the axle. The wheels were so mounted that there was approximately an inch of play, which caused a lot of noise as the cart rocked back and forth on the uneven roads, but the advantage was that it gave the carter room above the axle to insert a brush dipped in castor oil inside the hub to lubricate the axle.

The freight carts used a different principle. The main frame of the cart itself was similar to that of the smaller carts, except that everything was much stronger and heavier. However, the wheels of those carts were solidly affixed to the axle and the entire axle turned, held in place by two inverted U-shaped sockets built under the frame of the cart. The wheels themselves were also of an entirely different construction. They were somewhat smaller in diameter and much thicker, with one very heavy "spoke" about a foot in width, and another smaller one crossing it at right angles to make a cross. Those wheels could take an immense amount of wear and tear. Unfortunately, the fixed axle made it difficult for the cart to turn in a short radius. When making a tight turn, the wheels stayed in place and were simply dragged around, which was very hard on any poor horse that had the misfortune to be between the shafts.

After the two carpenter shops was a shoe store on the left side of the street. The front room was simply a showroom with various kinds of shoes on display, most of them the native Chinese "slipper" type, with cloth soles and a bit of leather at the toe and heel. But they also imported a quantity of leather shoes from the coast for the more well-to-do, and business was always good. In winter they put out an impressive display of felt shoes and boots, primarily worn by shopkeepers who had to stand a lot. The shoes were an inch or more thick, their soles even thicker. They looked much like the Dutch wooden shoe, but were at least twice the size, and were definitely not made for walking. In the back of the store were the rooms where elderly women made the cloth shoes. Out in the back yard were boards covered with pasted-on layers of rags, drying in the sun. After drying, the sheet was peeled off and cut up for soles, and used, layer upon layer, sewn together with fine string.

From the back yard of the shoe store one could see to the dye shop next door. In their back yard were the twenty-foot-high racks built of slim poles on which the lengths of dyed cloth were hung to dry. I didn't like the dye shop much because of the obnoxious smell coming from it, something to do with the kind of dyes they used. I went in their shop a couple of times, but it was too easy to get splashed with dye, which reminds me of a Chinese saying. To warn young people to avoid getting involved with criminals, or getting hooked on opium by associating with opium smokers, the Chinese have a saying: *ran fang chubuliao bai bu*, ("You can't get white cloth out of a dyehouse"). In other words, any white cloth carried into a dye shop will come out contaminated, and if you associate with the wrong kind of people, some of it will inevitably rub off on you.

Near the crossroads were a series of foodshops and a couple of fairly large restaurants. My mouth watered from the wonderful tempting smells of food cooking. Not only was food sold in the shops, where one could eat either standing up or sitting at a small table, but also outside in the street were a dozen or more food stalls catering to the visiting farmers and the poorer class. The food was cooked on the spot on charcoal stoves carried on one end of a carrying pole. The food available varied tremendously.

Across the intersection, the first shop on the left was a sweet cake shop. I found watching the cakes being made fascinating. Some were molded by hand; others, the dough was pressed into carved wooden forms. All the cakes were baked in the same kind of inverted oven. The cakes were made of white flour, different kinds of bean flour, and also buckwheat flour, with different kinds of stuffing. Next door to that was a medicine shop, and then came the Gospel Hall. I haven't covered all the shops that lined the route, but those that I've mentioned were the ones that interested me most, and where I most frequently stopped to visit.

When I was early at the hall and Father was still busy in the dispensary, I would either go in and try to help him or sit out in the hall and listen to one of the Chinese preachers, or simply chat with the visitors who dropped in. Quite often I would stop in next door at the herbal medicine shop to watch the shop assistants making up prescriptions. Chinese herbal medicine is literally called "grass medicine" (*cao yao*) and the term used for filling a prescription was *zhua yao*, which means, "grab medicine."

The shop's owner or manager would read through the prescription when it was brought in, then shout the various ingredients to his assistants. The walls of the store were lined with tiny drawers containing a bewildering variety of powders, shredded herbal leaves, grasses, dried roots, and animal parts: claws of various kinds, bear's feet or powdered bones, horns, or animal skins, and many other items, some recognizable but most not. Most were designed to cure illnesses, but others, such as the bear claws, were supposed to impart virility.

As each ingredient was called, the assistant would "grab" a handful or a pinch, place it on a tiny steelyard scale, then dump it on a sheet of paper in front of the manager, who would closely inspect it to see if it was correct. When the prescription was complete, the purchaser would be told in explicit detail just how it was to be taken, either on an empty or full stomach, with or without water, dry or soaked in water, and so on. Sometimes the patient would take the dose then and there, and unless it tasted abominable they usually felt they hadn't got their money's worth and would complain loudly. That was one of the problems with the Western medicine that my parents dispensed. The patients often complained that it tasted too good and, therefore couldn't be of much value. As a result, with some of the more bland powders that my parents gave out, they would frequently add a pinch of quinine or Epsom Salts, just to make it taste bad and thus satisfy the patient. The psychological factor of a foul-tasting medicine sometimes seemed to work wonders.

Quite naturally, the Chinese would try everything that their own doctors could prescribe before they would, as a last resort, reluctantly come to the foreigner. And, strange to say, we knew many Western-trained Chinese doctors who, when their own elderly parents or family members got sick, would inevitably first call in a native practitioner before administering Western medicine. That was not necessarily because they believed in it, but because they knew their parents or relatives preferred it that way. Nowadays in China, both types of medicine seem to be equally well received, but it is not the case with all overseas Chinese. For example, in the Chinatowns of America, Chinese herbal medicine is still frequently chosen ahead of Western medicine.

Not all the people who came into the medicine shop were there to buy medicine. Many came to sell raw ingredients. Some brought herbs they had found in the mountains, others brought animal parts. Snakes and snake skins were popular items, as were frogs. Several times I saw nests of live baby rats and mice brought in. The medicine shop owner bargained with these people, but usually he bought all they had to offer. Although right next door my father was giving away medicine and taking business from him, the manager of that shop never showed the slightest annoyance or displeasure. It was characteristic of the Chinese that similar places of business invariably chose to locate next to another of the same kind. Thus, several restaurants might be close together, as would medicine shops; in fact, there was another medicine shop diagonally opposite the downtown hall. It was the same with pawnshops. Two were close by us, one right next door to the hall and the other across the street. The Chinese have a saying: *Tong hang shi yuan jia*, (people of the same trade or organization are enemies). However, they never showed any hostility toward each other; in practice it was quite the opposite. They visited together, discussed business, and freely borrowed money or goods from each other as necessity arose. The principle seemed to be: if the spot was good for someone else, it will be good for me also. That pattern of "flocking together" also suited the Chinese proclivity toward bargaining, allowing prospective buyers to go from one store to another with a minimum of trouble, and seeing that, the salesmen were more inclined to lower their prices.

When I was about eleven I had an illness that could easily have cost me my life. While playing with some carpentering tools that Sun Shifu had been using, I cut my right hand. It healed at first, but then it began to fester, and very nearly turned into blood poisoning. My hand and arm swelled up to an astonishing degree overnight, and my pajama sleeve became so tight it had to be cut off. When, after several days, and despite all medication, my temperature rose to 104 degrees, my parents became deeply worried. Finally Father decided the only recourse was to lance the hand to drain the poison.

We had nothing in the house in the way of an anesthetic except some brandy, which was kept around in case of an emergency. Father gave me a hefty swig of it, then, using a brand-new safety razor blade, made several deep cuts lengthwise in the palm of my hand, avoiding the tendons. As the wound drained, the relief was immediate, and my temperature started to drop. However, the damage had been done. The tendons in my hand had all been seriously damaged and after the swelling went down, I found I was unable to straighten my fingers. By the time the wound had healed, my fingers had collapsed into a tight fist and my hand remained that way for many weeks.

It had happened in early spring while the weather was still very cold. It was obvious that I needed medical attention as soon as possible if I were to regain the use of my hand, so my parents decided we should go to the coastal port city of Chinhuangtao (usually called Chinwangtao, *huang* and *wang* both meaning the same thing, "king" or "emperor"), where there was a small hospital run by a Dr. Muir, whom we had met a year or two earlier.

We started off for the railroad town of Suizhong probably some time in April, with our usual cavalcade of a litter for Mother and several carts. Barbara and I shared one of the latter with Barbara's Airedale terrier, Mike, to keep us company. All the cart drivers were Moslems. We never used any others, and I think the reason was that not only did Father find them to be most reliable, he also had a very warm spot in his heart for the Moslems because of the incident when my older sister Eleanor died in Kuancheng and no one but Mohammedans came to their aid. Moreover, the Mohammedans carried their own food with them and didn't demand extra payment for food at the inns as did the Han drivers.

Underneath the front of each cart hung a large, square, shallow basket in which the drivers kept their personal effects, including their food. On our second day out, Mike smelled the food, and, escaping from Barbara's arms, jumped out of the cart and made a bee-line for the basket underneath. No one noticed it at the time, and the next thing we heard was Mike howling in agony as his left back leg slipped into the rut and the wheel ran over it and broke it. For us it was a major calamity, and Barbara was heartbroken. However, Mike settled down quietly in the cart with scarcely a whimper. At the noon stop

when we got down from the cart, Mike was carried off the cart and when put on the ground, to our utter astonishment, he proceeded to walk around on his two front legs with his back legs elevated in the air, just like a circus performer, and acted as though nothing at all had happened.

For the rest of the five-and-a-half-day journey, Mike gave us no trouble at all. We eventually took him to Dr. Muir, the old doctor who ran a hospital for the mining company that operated the port of Chinhuangtao. Dr. Muir gave Mike an anesthetic and did some work on the leg, and the bone knitted well. Although that back leg always had a very large "bump" on it, Mike recovered complete use of it in a very short period of time.

My own injury was quite another matter. We thought it would require an operation, but Dr. Muir, with his ever-present cigar stuck in his mouth, took one look at my clenched fist, and with no advance warning whatsoever, proceeded to pry open the fingers one at a time causing me excruciating pain. I could see the tendons rising under the skin as he pulled each finger up, even though he could only move the fingers very slightly. That was exactly what he wanted to see. He told us that even though the tendons had been badly damaged initially, in the collapsed hand they had grown together again, although considerably shortened. It was his opinion that since I was young, there would be no need to operate. The fingers only needed to be stretched. He simply inserted a pad of cotton under the fingers, each day enlarging the pad until he could insert a golf ball, then later a larger rubber ball, and finally a tennis ball. For weeks he stretched the fingers until he was ultimately able to straighten them completely, and my hand was practically back to normal.

That, of course, took a considerable length of time, and I went to the hospital on a near-daily basis for Dr. Muir to work on my hand. Often I waited for hours as he operated on a patient, and sometimes he would let me watch him work (invariably with an unlighted cigar in his mouth). On one visit I waited so long, that time in the operating room itself, that I got bored, and like most small boys, I became inquisitive about the inviting handles and gadgets on the operating table in front of me. I pressed various buttons and pulled on the different levers to see what they would do. Suddenly, one of them collapsed the entire table onto the floor with a resounding crash, breaking the plate-glass top. I envisaged some dreadful punishment for my crime, but Dr. Muir took it all in stride and simply laughed it off. He was a wonderful man and I shall always remember his great kindness, all of it without demanding a penny from us. Although my hand recovered almost completely, I never recovered my penmanship, such as it was. To this day my handwriting is illegible, even to me, and I have depended on a typewriter, which I learned to use during those months when my hand was out of commission. Altogether our stay in Chinhuangtao was most pleasurable. The mining people were extremely kind to us and provided us as a family with a nice house, close to the hospital.

* * * * *

With our daily close association with the Chinese we learned many things that might be considered trivia, but when the occasion demanded, they often proved useful. For example: How do you stop a dogfight? The Chinese have found that you get instantaneous results when you throw a handful of dust into the dogs' eyes. Of course, in America a handful of dust is not always readily available, but in China it was everywhere. Another thing: How do you pry something out of a cat's mouth? A live bird, for example? Simply blow in the cat's ear and it will immediately drop whatever is in its mouth. And how would you go about taming an obstreperous or wild horse? At the county fairs I would watch the Chinese cowboys (yes, they had them) capture a wild pony from a herd that had been brought in from the Mongolian steppes. As the prospective buyer watched, the cowboy would pacify the horse in a matter of seconds. They simply bit on its ear. Of course, you naturally don't want to stand close to its head while you do that or you could end up being the one bitten. Those Chinese cowboys would leap up onto the horse bareback, slide forward onto its shoulders with their legs around its neck, hang onto the mane, then lean forward along the horse's neck and bite into the ear, hard. The results were magical. In seconds the horse would stop bucking and become absolutely docile. If the cowboy let go of the ear briefly, the horse might act up again, but another bite, and once more he would subside. After a few such "treatments" the horse would in time associate someone

getting on its back with severe pain in its ear if it didn't remain still, and you'd have no further trouble with it.

In every country elderly men frequently have trouble urinating, and that is particularly true when they first get up in the morning. It is due to pressure on the urethra which carries off urine from the bladder. In America, doctors will tell you to sip some cold water, or put your hand onto a cold water pipe, or run the faucet. Faucets and running water were impossible to find in the interior of China, but cold water was readily available, and the Chinese have found that the most effective way to induce urination is to take a mouthful of water — the colder the better — and let it circulate around the back molars. Try it sometime if you should ever have this difficulty.

And some hints for mothers. Have you ever wanted to make the baby urinate just before putting him or her down for the night? Try whistling. The Chinese do, and the babies respond to it like magic, and with the open-crotch pants that all Chinese babies wear, there were never any diapers to wash. In fact, they were unknown except in the cities. Cloth was much too valuable to use for that purpose.

Then there is the matter of unwanted hair on the body or face. Small tweezers are hard to find in rural China, and only in the coastal cities have they heard of depilatories. However, for centuries Chinese women have used a very clean and effective method to remove unwanted hair. Take a length of thread and double it, then, placing the two threads on different sides of the hair(s) you want removed, twist the two ends of the threads in opposite directions, and presto, out they come. Painful? Of course, but what's a little pain in the interest of beauty?

And home remedies — what we might call old wives' tales. The Chinese had hundreds of them, some most efficacious. They were not to be confused with what the medicine shops sold, which is a whole different story. Take, for example, broken bones. There were two schools of thought on that subject in the old days in China. One theory for helping bones knit concerned a certain ancient coin called *ban liang* (half ounce), a coin with the usual square hole in the center which had a slightly rounded face and just the two characters for "half ounce" on it, the back being completely flat and blank. The theory was that that coin, when crushed into powder and swallowed, would cause the bones to knit quickly. The coin, although out of circulation for many, many years, was so much in demand that it was extremely rare to find one.

The other school held to a different theory. I first heard of it when we were on the road and staying overnight in an inn. Suddenly there was a tremendous commotion. I went to investigate, and saw a man with a broken leg being carried in on a makeshift stretcher. He'd been run over by a cart and his leg was badly fractured. Someone immediately called the village barber to set the broken bones, something he did quickly and effectively. In old China it was always the barbers who knew everything there was to know about bone structure.

When one had a sore back, the Chinese barber would have you lie face down on a hard *kang* or on a board trestle. He would then find the location on your back where it needed adjustment and would call in his small assistant, a little boy of around four of five, whom he would have stand on your back. Then the barber would put his finger on the sore spot, the little boy would raise his foot and stamp down, heel first with a rapid movement, and the bones would fall nicely into place. It never seemed to fail.

At the inn, where the man had his broken leg set, the barber wanted to make sure that the break mended properly, so he called for the prescribed remedy. He summoned the innkeeper's wife, and asked if there were any pregnant young women in the inn. Presently, we heard much giggling and whispering in the adjoining room, then a large bowl of steaming urine from one of the pregnant women was brought out and given to the injured man to drink. It sounds preposterous and revolting, but I've told this story to a number of American doctors, including orthopedic surgeons, and each of them confirmed that the urine of a pregnant woman contains the hormones estrogen and progesterone that aid in the formation of bones in the fetus, and the Chinese have known about it for centuries. What it will do for a baby it will apparently also do for an adult.

Apart from the Chinese doctors who prescribed herbal medicine, there were those who practiced acupuncture, which is now well-known in the United States, where many American doctors have studied it and agree with the principle. Most patients who have submitted to this "needling" swear by its effective-ness. But there are two other Chinese ways of treating illnesses that are not so widely known. One is called "cupping," which, as far as I know, has not made its way to Western countries, although in ancient times it was used in England. Cupping is a counter-irritant used to relieve internal congestion or pain by drawing blood to just under the surface of the skin. In China it was widely used for headaches, sore throats, congestion in the chest due to a bad cold or pneumonia, and also to relieve sore backs or in fact, sore muscles anywhere in the body. The English used to use a "cupping glass," but the Chinese use their small wine cups, which are about an inch deep and measure a little over an inch across the mouth.

A small amount of alcohol or native wine is poured into the cup and ignited. When it has burned off, the cup is immediately inverted over the sore spot and then tightly pressed to the skin. The resulting strong vacuum instantly draws the blood up toward the surface, leaving a bright-red round spot, which later turns almost purple and lasts for days. In most cases the Chinese felt that that has the desired effect, although my parents didn't think too much of it.

Another method to accomplish the same result was still more common in North China. That was the practice of what the Chinese call *jiu* or "pinching." Using the first two fingers in a bent position, the practitioner grips a portion of flesh in the affected area between the first and second joints of the fingers, then tightly squeezes it for a few seconds. The pinching is usually done in vertical lines down the forehead for a headache, or down and sometimes across the chest for inflammation and congestion. It, too, brings the blood up near the surface and leaves a bright-red patch, which later turns purple just like the cupped spot. All the Chinese we knew used it extensively, and although painful, all agreed that it was most effective, and in fact it was apparently instrumental in reducing some fevers. Most Western-trained doctors I have talked with on the subject agree there is some merit to these systems in relieving superficial pain, but that they do little or nothing to take care of deep-seated ailments.

I've mentioned that Mother took great care of us as children to avoid our contracting the many diseases that were so prevalent and that we saw around us on a daily basis. We seemed to have developed an immunity to most of them, but there was one ailment to which we were not immune, and that was internal parasites, commonly called tapeworms.

Mother used a specific remedy for that, called Santonin, which was administered to us regularly once a month, and inevitably we saw the desired results within a few hours. Acquiring those undesirable parasitic worms in the intestines was in our case not necessarily due to the food we ate, as great care was taken in its preparation. All vegetables were carefully washed in a solution of permanganate of potash (which we always abbreviated to "permang") and very few things were eaten raw, even from our own garden. All meats, which were thought to be the source of some of the parasites, were very thoroughly cooked. Where the Chinese were concerned, the average Chinese ate meat not more than once or twice a year, so that was an unlikely source for them. Most of the doctors with whom I have discussed this subject thought probably that we got the parasite eggs from the dust in the air that we breathed. The Chinese had very little conception of sanitation, and human and animal feces were everywhere abundant and became part of the soil around us, which blew in constant clouds of dust wherever we went.

Santonin was probably the most frequently dispensed medication handed out by my parents. Regularly, one evening would be spent with us helping my parents as they measured out doses of the powder, mixing it with a little flour or sugar to give it some bulk, then packaging it in the same small envelopes made from pieces of newspaper, just as we did for the opium antidote, Almost everyone seemed to be afflicted with the parasites, which, if left untreated, attained the length of eight to twenty inches and were thicker in diameter than the common garden worms with which we are all so familiar. I've seen them as thick as a pencil. One medical book that I read stated they have been known to grow to a length of thirty feet. Even before they reach anything like that size they can cause extreme abdominal pain and, as I know all too well in my own case, one may get rid of the worms themselves and still have the eggs left in the system to reproduce again. When we left China for the last time in 1947, it was over two years before I finally rid my intestines of those pests and I had great difficulty in convincing my doctor in Monterey to give me the medication I needed. He simply refused to believe that I still had them.

The Chinese were frequently unaware of what was causing their stomach pains. Because of the severity of the pain, and the gnawing, griping cramps that pervaded the entire length of the intestines, they would ascribe it to a snake, which they insisted had entered them at some point when they were defecating. That theory was widely believed, and at many of the country fairs that I visited, we frequently saw the quack doctors playing on that superstitious belief. One man in particular was a real master of showmanship. He was most adept in using sleight-of-hand to prove to the unsuspecting farmers that he could cure them. He would give the patient a pill of some sort, wait a few minutes, then have the man drop his pants and squat. The "doctor" would then miraculously produce a live snake from one of his pockets as evidence of the efficacy of his pills, and the poor farmer would happily go his way, only to be struck with the same pains shortly thereafter.

I have no idea what the incidence of the problem may be in China currently. However, many of my Western friends who have visited there in recent years have returned with stories of the same kind of outdoor privies with which I was so familiar, and tell of much the same crude conditions in general sanitation, even in the cities, and particularly in some restaurants. So I would imagine that it is much the same as it always was. In any event, since so many American travelers are going to visit China, it is not unlikely that some of them may come away with the parasitic eggs in their systems. Should you, the reader, be one of them, and should you have felt some strange and unusual pains in your bowels, or itching of the anus, I suggest you see your doctor, tell him of your visit to China and your suspicion that it might just be plain, ordinary parasitic worms. If he is anything like the doctors I met back in 1947, he'll express disbelief, since the malady is relatively rare in the United States. Still, insist on a dose of Santonin. I have never known it to do any harm.

I am reminded of another Chinese "doctor" whom I used to watch at those country fairs. He had a much more drastic method of curing worms. I have not the slightest idea what the concoction was that he used, but it was an extremely powerful laxative of some sort, which he administered in a pill almost the size of a walnut. He called the pill a *tie shuazi* or "iron brush." To make it more realistic, the pill was black in color with a number of short horsehairs protruding from it, and time and time again, I watched as he gave the pill to gullible sufferers, who, much like ourselves, wanted instant results for their money. In that case they certainly got it.

That "doctor" was quite a showman as well. He had dug a latrine trench near his stand, and after much hocus-pocus, and a display of his horrendous pill, he had the patient swallow the pill. He then allowed a few minutes to elapse, at which point the patient would be seized with severe stomach cramps, whereupon he would be sent to the trench. Within seconds the gaping crowd who were watching the proceedings would see a mass of worms produced, many of considerable length, but along with them quantities of blood and mucus. Some of the patients vomited, and worms came out of their mouths and noses. A doctor friend of mine, Dr. Matt Kaufman, tells me that the tapeworms will do that when excited. What intestinal damage was done can only be imagined. However, the "doctor's" patients all went away perfectly satisfied that they had got their money's worth, and immediately other suckers would step forward for the same treatment. I remonstrated with the man on several occasions, telling him he was probably doing great harm to his patients. His response was that he had never had any complaints and didn't expect to have any.

As a family we kept remarkably well in spite of the many forms of illness to which we were exposed each day. We had our share of childhood diseases such as chicken pox, measles and mumps, but were spared anything worse. None of us ever had any broken bones, despite our frequent falls from trees or into the deep gullies where we went to take our walks. Mother did worry a great deal about our eyes because of trachoma, which was prevalent everywhere and is extremely contagious. We were given eye drops regularly and were taught to wash our hands faithfully after touching tools that the workmen left around.

There were many deaths each summer from cholera and three or four times I can remember Mr. Hu opening the front gate in the morning to find a dead body lying on the front steps, a victim of cholera. Whether the individual had come there for treatment but arrived too late, or had been carried there after death, we never knew. No one claimed any of the bodies and it became our responsibility to bury

them. We suspected that was why they were placed there.

Among other things I remember about my father were the times when he definitely seemed to have psychic powers. Mother would become quite disturbed when he would forecast events or solve seemingly impossible situations. When I was quite a young boy, we were at breakfast one morning when Father suddenly turned quite pale and told Mother that his old friend and mentor, Mr. Eagger, had just died, and that we would shortly receive word of it. Before we had finished breakfast, a telegram was brought in announcing Mr. Eagger's death. When we wanted to know how Father could have possibly known of it, he said that as the telegram passed through the wires behind our house, the information somehow had been imparted to him, but he didn't know how.

There were numerous other incidents, none of them perhaps quite as dramatic, but each of them astounded us at the time. On one occasion, on the day before payday for the compound staff, Father sent Mr. Hu to the merchant who did banking for us to withdraw a couple hundred silver dollars. Mr. Hu used an old leather bag that could be locked. When Mr. Hu brought it back with the money in it, he left it in Father's study where it lay overnight.

Lao San's brother, whom we called Lily Root, had just been hired. One of his jobs was to clean the study and take out the ashes from the stove each morning. The next morning Lily Root cleaned the study before breakfast, but while we were having breakfast, Father, who had not yet been down to his study, told us he had had a dream during the night that someone had stolen the money from the bag, that he had clearly seen Lily Root as the culprit, and that he had seen how it had been done — by cutting a hole in the bottom of the bag. Later, when Father went to his study after breakfast, the money was gone, and sure enough, a hole had been cut in the bottom of the leather bag.

Father didn't accuse Lily Root immediately. He talked with Mr. Hu and told him of his suspicions, suggesting that Mr. Hu pick up some of the dog chains we used to tie up the dogs. Mr. Hu was then to wait around the corner, behind the "spirit screen," until he saw Lily Root called in. When Mr. Hu saw him enter the study, he was to wait just a minute or so, and then he was to stand outside the door and shake the chains violently, then drop them on the ground. It all went off as planned. Lily Root was called in. Without saying a word, Father simply held up the bag and showed him the hole cut in the bottom. At that moment Mr. Hu rattled the chains outside the door. Lily Root thought it was the police who had come to arrest him, and confessed at once to what he had done and brought the money back. There had been some minor cases of theft before that. Bundles of *shujie* and light wooden poles that had been stacked against one of the walls had mysteriously disappeared — obviously thrown over the wall by someone and then retrieved on the other side — and Lily Root had been the suspect. However, after the incident of the stolen dollars we never again had any trouble with him, nor any further cases of theft, and eventually he became one of the most honest and trusted individuals one could hope to find. His name will enter into my story on numerous occasions in future chapters.

While writing of Chinese doctors I mustn't leave out the Chinese dentists of the time. Often I would either walk or ride my bicycle down to the temple of the god of riches on Small West Street, where there was a big open square. That was the same square where the various early morning markets were held, including the labor market I wrote about earlier. After sunup, the entire area became a different kind of market. Small stalls sold every conceivable kind of commodity, new and used. There were also areas where fresh produce was sold, and another part of the market was devoted entirely to various grains. In addition to the stalls people with just a blanket spread on the ground, sold odd bits of pottery, old coins, pieces of metal, and assorted oddments of clothing. There was a place for fortune tellers, and in a section up against one of the temple walls, the various kinds of doctors had their stalls, and among them there was usually a dentist.

I watched one of those men from time to time. There was no such thing as filling cavities then: he primarily pulled teeth and fitted false teeth in their place, — except that the teeth he fitted in were not false, but teeth that had been pulled from someone else's mouth. To fill a gap in the teeth, he would select a suitable tooth from his stock, drill holes in the adjoining good teeth, then deftly string the "new"

tooth in with wire, a very painful process.

In an earlier chapter I briefly mentioned Mr. Hu's son, who was around my own age, and who was a constant playmate of mine. His "milk" name was Dong, which could mean either "east" or "winter." We never quite knew which, but I suspect it was the latter, and they named him that because he was born in the cold weather. When Dong finished his schooling he was an extremely bright young man, and one who looked to the future. He had talked with me about taking up dentistry, and when he was around seventeen he went to Tientsin for a few months, took a course, and returned a full-fledged dentist, complete with all the most modern equipment of the period: a foot-treadle drill and some heavy-duty pots in which to "cook" the upper and lower dental plates that he had learned to make.

With a small loan from Father, he went into business for himself, renting a shop just across the street from the police station, on the other side of the Yamen. Later, it was in that same shop that our neighbor, the older Zhang son, joined him in a combined photographic studio and dental parlor. Young Hu became very well-known for his good dentistry, but he made most of his money in fitting people with gold teeth — capping perfectly good teeth with a gold cap, purely and simply for cosmetic purposes and the suggestion of wealth that it imparted. Most often, the patient wanted a cap that could be removed at will, so that it could be stored away at night and not be stolen during his or her sleep.

When Dong went into business he changed his name to Hu Wen-rui, with, as was common then, an additional name of Zi-bin for his special friends and acquaintances. Shortly after he went into business, he married a young country girl, who had never heard the gospel, and knew nothing of Christianity, but who whole-heartedly adopted her husband's religion immediately upon their marriage and became one of the most dedicated and earnest young Christian women we had ever met. Over succeeding years she proved a wonderful help to Mother, and later to my wife, and was used by God in a remarkable manner to win other Chinese women to Christ.

Although like all marriages of that time it was an arranged marriage, Zi-bin and his new bride fell deeply in love from the first moment they met. In all the years that I was in China, theirs was one of just two or three cases I knew of where the man and wife were deeply in love with each other in the sense that we as Westerners know it.

For some reason she was unable to bear any children, a source of immense grief to her, and in the early days of their marriage she constantly begged him to get rid of her and marry someone who could give him a son, but Zi-bin would have none of it. He loved her for herself and wanted no one else.

The young couple were singularly fortunate in that the gatehouse where the older Mr. Hu and his wife lived had no room for the married pair, so they lived in a two-*jian* house diagonally across the street, down one of the narrow alleys. For the young bride that was ideal, because she didn't have to slave day and night for her mother-in-law in the usual Chinese fashion. She only came to our compound once or twice a day to see how the old lady was doing. That helped make it a happier marriage than most.

As we were growing up together Dong and I constantly played practical jokes on each other, and it didn't stop after he got married. A few weeks after the wedding he invited me and our other good friend Zhang Yao-ting, my Chinese-language tutor, to a meal, the object being to meet his new bride.

For the occasion she had prepared *jiaozi*, meat-filled dumplings, which are famous in North China. Because of the time and effort taken to prepare them, it is always considered to be a very great honor when one is invited over and those dumplings are served.

I went over to the young couple's little house and was treated like a royal guest. The young Mrs. Hu was shy, and at first was reticent to talk with me, a foreigner, but she very soon thawed. When the meal was served, I, as the guest of honor, was helped first from the top of the huge plate of *jiaozi*. Then Zi-bin and Yao-ting took their portions. After saying a short grace, we started to eat. I was immensely embarrassed for the young bride peeping around the door-

way to see if I liked them, because at first taste I thought she had put too much pepper into them, but then I noticed that instead of the usual Chinese cabbage they seemed to be filled with the hottest kind of Chinese red peppers. However, I thought perhaps that was something native to her village, and not wanting to embarrass her by showing I didn't like them, I valiantly swallowed the first one or two although I dislike food that is too peppery hot. Then I noticed that both Zi-bin and Yao-ting were looking at me and grinning, and I realized the whole thing was a put-up job, and that only the two or three that had been put on my plate contained the peppers. I laughed with them, but vowed to get even with Zi-bin even if it took me a lifetime.

My opportunity came a few weeks later. I invited Zi-bin and his wife over to our house for a Western-style meal to let her discover what we ate. Of course Zhang Yao-ting was invited as well. We happened to have a ham in the house at the time, one that Father himself had smoked out in a smokehouse he had built in the back garden, and it had turned out to be extraordinarily good. Gao Cai had baked fresh bread that day, and I served my guests ham sandwiches, something they had never eaten before.

When the plateful of sandwiches was carried in, the two or three top ones I gave to Zi-bin as the guest of honor, and then served his wife and Yao-ting, and we all started to eat. Poor Zi-bin: his sandwich meat seemed to be exceptionally tough, and bite as he would, he was unable to separate his mouthful from the sandwich. That was not surprising, because I had made some sandwiches specially for him, using a pink-colored inner tube from my bicycle, which looked identical to the ham in the rest of the sandwiches. Young Mrs. Hu laughed so hard I thought she was going to fall off her chair, but Zi-bin took it all with a big grin, and started planning his next joke on me.

This was taken when Bob got his first van.

Bob and some little friends.

The characters are: Xuan Chuan Fuyin, meaning: Preaching the Gospel.

Traveling on a very narrow road.

Town's general store.

Druggist weighing out a prescription.

Repairing broken china.

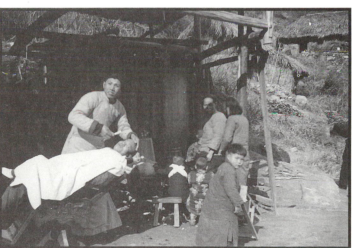

The Barber Shop.

Dried-up gourds cut in half and used for dipping water.

Typical idol in a Temple.

Street scene: Note sewage ditch running in front of stores.

Gift Shop.

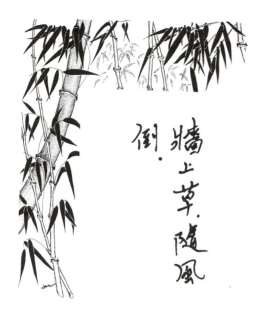

倒牆上草．隨風

Qiangshang cao sui feng dao.

Grass that grows on top of
a wall bends with every wind.

- Chinese Saying.

Chapter Thirteen
Furloughs Were Not Vacations

Aside from their use of servants, other criticisms leveled at missionaries were that not only did they take long summer vacations at the seaside, but also that every seven years or so, they had a one-year paid vacation back in their homeland. Western business-men in China were particularly antagonistic on that issue.

It is true that most missionaries did indeed go on furlough every seven years or so, but to call it a vaca-tion would be stretching the truth. Most of the mis-sionaries that I knew awaited those "home" trips with something approaching dread rather than joyful antic-ipation. It was always nice to go back and see rela-tives and friends once again, but at the same time it always meant tearing up well-established roots in China, living out of suitcases and trunks for about a year on the average, and being constantly on the move.

When I was four years old, in the latter part of 1917, we had taken a furlough. I remember very little of it, but my brother Gil has filled in some of the details. We sailed from Shanghai on a Japanese liner, the Nippon Yusen Kaisha Line's *Nippon Maru*, and probably landed in Vancouver, British Columbia.

World War I was in progress, and that is doubtless the reason we did not go on to England. In any event, we first traveled across Canada to Nova Scotia and ended up in a small town called Sackville, where Mother's family had settled in 1903. We stayed there with uncles and aunts and got to know some of our cousins. I have some very vague memories of that time, mainly events on their farm, and the various animals.

From there we moved to Sea Cliff, Long Island, for a short period while my father traveled extensively around the eastern part of the United States visiting assemblies of Christians with whom we were associ-ated. Later that same year, we went to Chicago, and then rode the Sante Fe train to California where Mother and we four children settled into a rented house in a small town called Monrovia, some considerable distance from Los Angeles but now part of the greater L.A. area. With Monrovia as a base, my father continued his travels through the Midwest and the western states, and we very seldom saw him at home that entire year.

The Plymouth Brethren group with which we were affiliated was not one of the better-known overseas mission boards, but was simply a non-denominational group that believed in the Bible literally, which met in modest quarters called "Gospel Halls," and held a firm belief in the Biblical injunction: "Go ye into all the world and preach the Gospel..." From these relatively small groups in various countries, hundreds had gone abroad as missionaries to almost every country in the world.

The members of these "assemblies" were just ordinary people from every walk of life who contributed what they could to their representatives overseas, none of whom received a stipulated salary, but lived in faith that God would provide, as indeed He did. From time to time they liked to see their missionaries and hear their reports of the work in their various fields. This traveling around "at home" was known as "deputation work," and it was in many ways similar to the campaigns undertaken by American political candidates, and was just as grueling, perhaps even more so.

The visiting missionary was not only expected to speak about his work — often two or three times on Sundays — to large and small groups in the regular meeting places, but was on demand almost every night of the week for meetings in homes and to participate in visits to jails, hospitals, insane asylums, schools and downtown "missions" for the down-and-outs — in fact, anywhere the local Christians had a testimony.

That was usually fine as far as the individual missionary was concerned, and it was done happily. However, it didn't end there. Very rarely was the missionary put up in a hotel where he could get some undisturbed rest at the end of a very long day. Instead, usually, he was lodged with some generous and loving souls who happened to have a spare room or a fold-down couch in their living room. Always they were delightful and warm-hearted people, but more often than not they had small children who needed to be entertained while their mother made the meals.

After the meal came the usual evening service somewhere. Later, the children were put to bed, but the missionary was expected to talk for long hours with his hosts about his travels and experiences abroad. When he finally got to bed it was more than likely at a very late hour, and he would likely be awakened very early the next morning to catch a train to his next stop.

I know the routine well and speak from experience, because I found myself in the same position in later years when I, too, became a missionary, but I'll get to that later. To return to that first furlough in my young life, I have lively memories of train trips: exciting experiences of nights spent in the sleeping cars with the berths being made up at night, and eating in the bustling dining cars. There were also occasions where the train stopped at mealtimes, and just about everyone got off and ate in what were known as "Harvey Houses," a sort of cafeteria operated by the railroads.

Most clearly of all I remember my first ride in a taxi. We got off the ship and stepped into it, my first automobile. It was a shiny Yellow Cab with real leather seats, and, most fascinating of all, my own little fold-down jump seat, where I sat just behind the driver with his shiny leather cap.

There was a certain degree of culture shock coming to America where everything was so different. Another vivid memory was my first introduction to the wonders and "shocks" of electricity. In another home in which we stayed, some little friends taught me how to wet two fingers and put them up against the two holes in the wall sockets. I survived that, to learn how to play with the light switch, which somehow most mysteriously made the overhead light go on and off. I toyed with that for such a long time that I learned another lesson: that doing it too fast and too often would blow what was called a fuse, but that could be remedied by putting a shiny brass penny under it. Those kids were sophisticated to a degree that I had so far not encountered. From them I also learned that it was a lot of fun to slide down an outside cellar door, but it left me with a butt full of slivers.

While crossing the country we stopped in another city where our hosts had a fine car parked out by the front curb. Gil and Ruth climbed in and sat there demurely, but I wanted to play with the knobs and dials and blow the horn. When my brother kicked me out I started walking down the street in a huff and ended up six blocks away in a small park, tired out and ready for a nap. I sat down on a convenient bench and was shortly joined there by a very nice lady who started to talk to me. Realizing I was all alone and probably lost, she had me lie down with my head in her lap and take a nap. My anxious parents found me there a short time later, and I well remember the spanking I got.

Our best friends in Monrovia were the Jacksons. There was Grandma (and since I never knew my own grandparents, she became as real to me as my own Grandma) and George and Lydia, who had three children much the same ages as ourselves. The youngest, Helen, was Barbara's age. Walter was a year older than I and had a tricycle on which he gave me rides standing on the axle behind him, and later he generously let me learn to ride it myself. Then there was an older sister, Frances, who grew up to become a missionary to Colombia, South America, where for a lifetime she worked with the Wycliffe Translators. She retired only recently, and she has been generous enough to share with me some of the letters my mother wrote to Lydia, her mother, and letters from my sisters to her, from which I've been able to glean a few details to fill out my story here. She also passed on to me photographs which my mother sent to them.

The Jacksons lived near the Sante Fe tracks and had a small ranch and nursery called the "Pioneer Nursery." It sat among the orange groves near a dry creek that had water only during the winter months. On the ranch they had rabbits and several domestic animals. Best of all they had a real horse and buggy in which Lydia rode us around an area that was then largely open countryside, but is now so heavily populated that it is unrecognizable. The only sight I found familiar on a recent visit through that area was Mount Baldy, which Gil climbed on several occasions.

Seven years later, in 1925, we were back from China on another furlough and renewed our acquaintance with this wonderful family. But Grandma was no longer living and the horse and buggy had given way to an equally exciting Model T Ford, in which Lydia again drove us all around the countryside and up into the canyons of the nearby mountains.

By that time I was twelve, and our trip across the Pacific on the pride of the Canadian Pacific "White Fleet," the *Empress of Australia*, is something I'll never forget. Aboard ship we made a number of friends. Jimmy Braga, known as "Sparks," who ran the radio shack, and a young lad just a few years older than I, whose name I have forgotten, who had the most glamorous job I could conceive of. Ocean liners in those days had a number of youngsters working as bellboys, and he was one of them, dressed in his smart uniform with a little pill-box cap. We became very good friends, and when we reached Vancouver, his home town, he, as a crew member, went ashore without the formalities we had to go through. To my astonishment, he returned to the docks a short time later, before we had even gotten off the ship. He was driving his very own convertible, in which he subsequently took us on a tour of that beautiful city, including Stanley Park, with its acres of trees and flowers, and the scenic shoreline. It was an introduction to a whole new world for me.

Again we traveled across Canada by train, and I can still relive every moment of that ride from Vancouver to Montreal. First, up through the Frazer Canyon, where the Canadian Pacific Railroad had its tracks on one side and the Canadian National Railroad on the other, with the broiling river in between. There was much competition at that time between the two lines and they ran their trains on almost the same schedules. From our train we could watch another one just a few hundred yards away across the river. At times our train pulled ahead, then the other train would catch up and it would get ahead. Eventually the tracks diverged and we lost sight of it.

We were traveling coach that time, possibly because my father did not have enough money for Pullman berths, but it was a real thrill for us kids to sit up all night and follow the printed train schedule. We reveled in the glamorous strange-sounding names of the many small stations through which we passed: Port Coquitlam, Mission, Agassiz, Yale, North Bend, Ashcroft, Kamloops, Salmon Arm, Sicamous, and so on. Finally, after nearly ten hours we stopped at a place called Revelstoke, where the Rockies really begin.

The stop there was lengthy, and we were able to get off for a meal. We watched with the utmost interest as three more huge steam locomotives were attached to the train, two at the front and one behind to push. That was around noon of the second day. Then followed an unforgettable experience as our train wound its way through those majestic peaks, many still topped with snow. We chugged in and out of tunnels, back and forth across rushing torrents and deep ravines, catching exciting glimpses of deer, bears, and other animals, and all the time the sound of the engines puffing away up ahead, their exhaust echoing back from the mountains as they belched clouds of smoke and steam.

In mid-afternoon the train stopped at a small way-side station for the engines to take on water, and the conductor invited us to get off and take a stroll on the platform. The scenery was awe-inspiring, with mountains on all sides of us. Apart from the water towers, nothing was there except a station platform built out over the edge of a huge ravine, seemingly only a couple of hundred feet wide, but so deep we could not see the bottom. Placed at intervals along the platform were large barrels filled with small rocks and signs inviting the passengers to try and throw a rock to the other side of the ravine. It looked so easy, and everyone tried, but no one was successful. The ravine that appeared so narrow was actually nearly a mile wide. Distances were most deceptive.

Just as the sun was setting we came in to Lake Louise, and on the spur of the moment, Father, stricken with the beauty of the place, decided it would be a lot of fun to get off and spend the night there. It is possible, too, that he thought another night of sitting up on those not-too-comfortable coach seats would be just too much. At any rate, the conductor obligingly punched our tickets valid for the next day's train, and after we hurriedly gathered our stuff together, we got off.

The train wasn't out of sight before we knew we had made a serious mistake. Swarms of mosquitoes descended on us, apparently sensing new blood, because the locals seemed in no way affected. The mosquitoes whirled around us as we rode to the hotel in an open jitney, and even in our hotel room we couldn't get rid of them. Finally a hotel employee told us that the only safe place was in a boat out in the middle of the lake.

By that time it was pitch dark, but Father rented a small boat with an outboard motor, and out into the center of the lake we putted, staying there undisturbed until well after midnight. When my parents finally decided it was time to go to bed, the young man who was operating the boat was unable to start the engine, and, to our dismay, he unscrewed the cap on the gasoline tank, lit a match and peered inside. Fortunately, the tank was apparently completely dry, so there was no explosion, even though there must have been some gasoline fumes. I recall Father lecturing him on the dangers of such behavior. We had to sit there for another hour or more until a second boat came and towed us in.

The following day we had the entire day to wait for the next train heading East, but despite the beauty of the lake, I think Father decided that if we stayed any longer we might run out of blood. In any case, he rented a car to drive us the short distance to Banff, where we were told there would be fewer mosquitoes. As I sat in the car, for want of something else to do, I counted the bites on just one of my badly swollen legs and stopped counting when I had reached two hundred. The experience, however, apparently somehow gave me total immunity to the bites of any kind of insect. In subsequent years I was never again bothered in the same way, and neither the vicious black flies of northern Canada nor the voracious bedbugs and fleas of China had the slightest effect on me. Unfortunately, I am hesitant to recommend the same form of immunization to others who might be tempted to try it, because I had an inflamed leg for days thereafter.

From beautiful Banff we went to Calgary, where we broke our journey for a day or so, then made stops at Regina, Edmonton and Winnipeg. In each place we stayed with friends for a few days while Father talked to interested audiences on his work in China. From there we proceeded to Halifax, where Mother's only surviving sister lived. Aunt Gertie was our favorite aunt, but our visit was short, and it was then on to St. John, New Brunswick, to board the Canadian Pacific liner *Montcalm* for Liverpool, England.

We stayed in England for several months, but saw little of Father as he traveled around visiting the Brethren Assemblies. We met a number of his relatives, including Uncle Jack, who had a big farm in Kent that we found fascinating, particularly his huge Percheron horses, which he let us ride. They were so wide across the back that I was unable to straddle them, and it was more like sitting on a moving floor than riding a horse. Another uncle lived in nearby Sturry, where my Father had been born. He had a small country store that sold just about everything one could imagine. What most appealed to me were the thick leather shoe soles he sold to the farmers and he gave me a boxfull to take back to China.

It is said that travel is educational, and I am sure my parents felt it was good for us kids to see as much of the world as possible. However, all that traveling played havoc with our studies, so we settled for a few months in a small town called Deal, right on the English Channel coast. There we stayed with another uncle who ran a large haberdashery shop and I immediately fell in love with my oldest cousin, Margaret, who was at least twice my age. I spent what spare time I had between home studies "helping" in the shop just to be near her, until events of greater importance came along.

Deal, and the nearby coastal towns of Ramsgate, Margate and Dover, were full of interest to a boy of twelve and I never tired of watching the ferries leaving for the French ports across the Channel and standing watching the many ships passing to and fro in the Channel itself. One night we watched for hours as a large freighter burned several miles out at sea, and were thrilled to watch the local lifeboat go out and bring back the crew from the stricken ship. Deal seemed to be a great place for thunderstorms. I had seen many in China, but somehow, the storms over the Channel were much more spectacular, and it was there that I learned the dangers of lightning. One stormy evening a seaman walking along the top of the chalk cliffs near Deal was struck by lightning and killed. The gold chain-link belt that he was wearing around his waist, which probably represented his life-savings, was fused into a solid band of gold that had to be sawn off before they could bury him.

It was also in Deal that I met the unforgettable Miss Pugh (pronounced "pew"). She gave me violin lessons three evenings a week. I rode a local tram to a large schoolhouse on the outskirts of Deal just as school was letting out, and she would painstakingly teach me the mysteries of the violin. She was a dear and lovely little old lady, but, I regret to say, I never became very proficient in playing the instrument. I finally abandoned the violin entirely in favor of first, a cornet, and then a trumpet, both of which I found much more to my liking.

Somewhere about that time my parents must have decided it would be a good experience for me to go by myself and visit another uncle for a few weeks.

That was my Uncle Lewis, my Father's younger brother. He and his wife, with a son of around seventeen or so, lived in a small village just ten miles from the original London airport of Croydon. That was my first time away from home, and I was utterly miserable for the entire period. The weeks dragged by, and with no one of my own age to play with, I amused myself with long walks and writing a daily letter to my mother. I am sure those letters consisted of little more than complaints. Even a simple thing like posting a letter turned into a near disaster for me on one occasion. The local post office was in a candy shop, what the English call a "sweet store." The owner, a most forbidding lady, was postmistress as well. One day as I dropped my letter into the outside slot, I noticed at the instant it left my fingers that I had forgotten to put a stamp on it. For what seemed like hours I walked up and down outside, trying to screw up enough courage to go in and talk to the lady. Finally, when I did approach her, she was most suspicious and her reaction was to lecture me on the sanctity of His Majesty's mails and insist that something once put into the box could not be taken out again. However, she finally relented and retrieved the letter so that I could put a stamp on it.

I am sure that my uncle and aunt tried their best to make me feel at home. He was a salesman of sorts, driving around to the neighboring towns in a small van, visiting various shops and making his sales. On many occasions he took me with him, and that I enjoyed. Unlike my father, he was a very dour man who seldom smiled, nor did he have much to say to me as we rode around. It seemed to me at the time that he spent as much time chasing after his son, who was chasing after girls, as he did in conducting his business.

Our visit to England was shortly after the end of World War I, and the country was still in a pretty bad way, but the countryside was beautiful. On one of the trips with my Uncle Lewis, we went to Croydon airfield, where I was fascinated to watch all the planes flying around. I made a note of the route my uncle used, and from that point on, I frequently spent an entire day walking over there and back. At one point there was an extremely long and steep hill that my uncle told me was the steepest in all of England and was used by the Morris Car Company in testing their vehicles. Indeed, walking it on several occasions I saw them testing new cars, and quite often some of them couldn't make the grade.

At one point on my walk, I passed through a small village, where I was always joined by a small and very nondescript dog, which attached itself to me for the rest of the trip to Croydon and back. I never learned its name, nor to whom it belonged, but it was most friendly, and I found it good company. At the airfield I had a favorite spot under a big hedge, at the exact end of the main runway, where for hours I would sit and watch flights of fighter planes practicing their takeoffs and landings. They were the same type of biplanes that a few years before had filled the skies over Germany. As a flight of planes approached, the little dog would sit up with his ears cocked and watch them intently until they were directly overhead, raising his head and then his whole body on his hind legs as he did so, then falling over backward as the planes passed behind him. He did that unfailingly every time and greatly brightened my day with his antics.

Uncle Lewis was quite generous in giving me pocket money to spend, and on my way home in the late afternoons, it was my habit to stop regularly at one of the small village tearooms to have some sandwiches and a cup of tea. One day as I sat there having my tea, the little dog disgraced himself by stealing a plate of sandwiches from a neighboring table. When the proprietress wanted to put it on my bill, I vociferously denied ownership of the dog, but dared not return to the place again.

Finally the time came to rejoin the family, and together we traveled by train down to Wales, where we settled in Cardiff for several months as Father visited the various towns in that area. In Cardiff I got my first bicycle. We didn't have the money to buy one, but one day when out on a walk, I saw a discarded bike on a trash heap and asked permission from my father to take it home with me. It was a Raleigh, in very sorry condition, with bent wheels and many spokes missing. However, the frame was good, and after purchasing a few spare parts, I proceeded to completely strip and rebuild it, and when through sanding and repainting, it looked to me almost as though it had just come out of the factory.

Cardiff was a miserably dirty and smoky city and we didn't really enjoy our time there. It was a wonderful day when we finally left there and boarded the S.S. *Montcalm* once again and headed back to the United States, the first step in our journey home to our beloved China. Gil had left some months earlier to go by himself to New York to pursue his studies, and he met us at the dock. We spent that winter in Brooklyn, living in a house on Prospect Place, just off the famous Flatbush Avenue.

The house was one of a pair of two identical brownstones owned by Sam Pirie of the big Chicago department store, Carson, Pirie and Scott. The family lent it to us for as long as we needed it, and they sometimes used the one next door. Most of the time they were in their summer home out on Long Island, in a small town called Sea Cliff. The two houses jointly shared a huge back yard enclosed by a high fence, and there was a big garage there that housed several large and very impressive automobiles that appealed to me greatly. I became good friends with their chauffeur, who lived above the garage, and his young black helper who came in every day to wash and polish the cars. However, the friendship cooled considerably one day when I heard the chauffeur talking about someone "looking as red as a live lobster." The young black man corrected him, telling him that only cooked lobsters were red in color, and that live ones were green. When I supported his statement, the chauffeur told me to stay out of it. From that point on he would have little to do with me, but I had learned another lesson, that of diplomacy.

Those months in Brooklyn passed very slowly and we saw very little of my father except at Christmas. Mother, too, was kept busy several days each week going around to various women's groups to tell them about her work in China. I was always Mother's escort on those trips as we visited places in all the different boroughs, and in Manhattan itself. In time I became completely familiar with the New York subway system, where for a nickel you could ride forever, as many seemed to do. As Mother talked to the ladies' groups, I would patiently sit in the rear of the room until it was time to go home, often falling asleep, since they were, for the most part, evening meetings and we seldom got home before midnight. On one subway trip I found a miniature domino set made of celluloid, packed in a small leather case. It became one of my most prized possessions until one evening Mother found me playing with it in the back of the meeting hall while she was addressing the ladies. Mother confiscated it at once, and after that I never saw it again. I think Mother associated it somehow with gambling.

Our schooling was undoubtedly somewhat haphazard during all that time, but Mother wanted to be sure that at least culturally we were not deprived, and we visited many of the museums in New York. A favorite place was the huge department store, Wannamakers in Manhattan, where free symphony concerts were held frequently in their large auditorium. Those were very special treats and were usually accompanied by a much anticipated lunch at one of the nearby automats, where for a nickel you could have your choice of a tremendous variety of foods.

Another great treat for me was visiting the giant Cunard liners at their Manhattan docks when they came in from their Atlantic runs. The pier captain, a man by the name of Barlow, was a member of one of the small Assemblies in Brooklyn, and when he learned of my interest in ships, he gave me an open invitation to go down to the Cunard piers any time I wanted. Mother let me go on numerous occasions, and Captain Barlow gave me a pass that allowed me free run of any one of the several ships that were usually docked there. Those were indeed happy hours as I roamed the famous *Mauretania* and other great ships of the line, and invariably I was invited to lunch by the captain.

It was in Brooklyn that I first tried to earn some pocket money, but it ended in disaster. Nearby on Flatbush Avenue, there was a large grocery store that catered to the immediate area. Each week the owner hired several boys to distribute crudely printed fliers to every house within a ten- to twelve-block radius. One day I asked him if I could help, and he gave me a big packet of fliers and told me which streets I had to cover.

I took the matter very seriously and felt extremely important as I marched up and down those dozens of brownstone steps and pushed the fliers through the mail slots. An hour or so later, when I had completed my route and meticulously handed out every single sheet, I went back to the store to get my quarter in payment, only to have the owner become extremely angry with me, telling me that there was no way in which I could have properly done the job in so short a time and accusing me of having thrown the papers into a trash bin. He told me to go at once and retrieve

them and finish the job before I could get paid. No amount of protestation on my part was of any avail, and I left there very crestfallen. After walking disconsolately around the area for some time, I came across some of the regular delivery boys and screwed up enough courage to ask one of them what I should do. They thought it was a huge joke and told me they ordinarily distributed only twenty or thirty each and then threw the rest away, and the secret was not to go back and get paid for at least two or three hours.

Such blatant dishonesty was totally alien to everything my parents had taught me, and later, after I finally collected my quarter and got another tongue-lashing from the owner, I decided that a life in business was not for me. On my way home, out of curiosity, I looked into several trash bins and sure enough, found the discarded fliers. I toyed with the idea of telling the store owner, but felt certain he would never believe me, even if I took the fliers back to him, and I didn't relish the thought of what the other boys might do to me if I squealed on them.

Like most youngsters our age, we weren't little angels by any means, and being left alone quite often, we got into trouble of one form or another from time to time. One winter day when it was too cold to play out in the back yard, we discovered the attic, and while exploring that, found a "secret" door that led into the attic of the adjoining house. Of course, we had to explore further, and spent some hours going through the empty Pirie home next door. Sam Pirie was an avid hunter, and the walls of the downstairs rooms were adorned with dozens of animal heads that at first scared the wits out of us, but later proved fascinating and highly educational. Most had been shot in Africa. When later Mother learned of what we had done, we were properly reprimanded and forbidden to ever go back into the other house, except by invitation.

While speaking of Mr. Pirie, I am reminded of a story my father once told me. On one of his trips through Chicago he had gone to Carson, Pirie and Scott to visit Mr. Pirie, and while waiting for a luncheon date, had wandered into that section of the huge department store that sold oriental art and antiques. Father was very much struck by a beautifully carved ivory box that was purported to be many hundreds of years old and was priced at several thousand dollars. However, my father immediately recognized it as a fake, and he drew Mr. Pirie's attention to it. While it was, in fact, carved with an authentic Chinese scene on the lid and the sides were covered with genuine Chinese characters, all the characters were in reverse and in many cases upside down. On closer inspection the characters proved to have been taken from newspapers of a fairly recent date, and since even the most illiterate Chinese recognize whether a character is written backward or upside down, it had obviously not been carved by a Chinese or any other oriental. Mr. Pirie was intrigued by the mystery and had one of his men track down the history of the piece. Some time later he informed my father that they had traced the purchase to a little old Italian man in a back street in Chicago. Somewhere he had located some abandoned Chinese newspapers, had pasted sections of them onto the ivory box, then carved out the characters. The scene on the top had been taken from an old Chinese fan.

Our time in Brooklyn eventually came to an end, and Mother took the four of us children by train directly to California to wait for Father as he slowly worked his way across the country. Again we settled in Monrovia, and the time passed quickly with our old friends the Jacksons, as well as a new family named Tyler that we got to know. They had three girls and a boy all approximately our ages. To show how fickle I was, when I saw the girls, I promptly forgot my cousin Margaret and fell head-over-heels in love with the middle one, and liked to think my feelings were reciprocated until I noticed that she paid just as much attention to other boys my age as she did to me.

The family lived clear across town from where we were, but I made that long walk many times just to be able to stand and gaze at her. That is as far as it went, because I could never think of anything clever to say. However, she always accepted the small gifts of candy or fruit that I took to her, and I felt encouraged. Then one day I saw a four-wheeled hand-pulled toy wagon for sale in the local Piggly-Wiggly supermarket. I simply had to have one, but the price of five dollars was beyond our means, and all I could do was look at it. Despite my unhappy "business" experience in Brooklyn when I distributed fliers, I still had inclinations toward making money, and told Mother that if she'd lend me the money for the wagon, I would go into the business of selling oranges and in no time would be able to repay my debt.

I guess Mother realized how important it was to me, so the wagon soon became mine, and each afternoon after finishing our schoolwork at home I would proudly — kneeling on one knee in the wagon and pushing with the other foot — make my way down to an orange packing plant near the Sante Fe tracks, and there sort through the piles of seconds that they had thrown out. Each day I would find several wagon-loads of beautiful, near-perfect navel oranges with barely a mark on them, and had no difficulty whatsoever in selling them as I went door-to-door around the neighborhood. In no time at all I had repaid my debt to Mother. In the meantime I had forgotten all about my newly found girlfriend.

It was in Monrovia that I went for my very first haircut on my own. Mother had given me a quarter and told me what to do, and although very nervous, I bravely climbed up into the chair and asked for a haircut. The price in those days was twenty cents, and I was to give the man a nickel as a tip. When he finished cutting my hair, he asked if I wanted the ends of my hair singed. I had no idea what he meant, but told him to go ahead. He then asked if I wanted a shampoo. Thinking it was all part of the twenty-cent price, I agreed to that as well. He asked if I wanted hair lotion, and I thought, why not? If all that was part of a haircut, then I wanted it. I seem to remember there were some other things he suggested, but the bottom line was that when he finally flicked the hairs off my shoulders and I got out of the chair, the price had now risen to the horrendous figure of three dollars. With visions of jail ahead of me, since I only had a quarter in my pocket, I told the man I had to go home and get some more money, and poor dear mother had to fork it out. What a difference that was from the haircuts I was used to getting in Lingyuan, but it was another lesson learned.

We have some very happy memories of those days in Monrovia. For the first time we had American playmates with whom we felt at home. And an occasional ride into Los Angeles on one of the huge red trolley cars of the famous Pacific Electric line which so efficiently served the entire Los Angeles area and its outskirts was a momentous and unforgettable occasion. Miss Harriet Minns had by that time joined us, preparing to return with us to China. I recall one occasion, when returning from Los Angeles on a hot afternoon, she was wearing a brand-new hat, and as the trolley sped along, all windows wide open to the breeze, her hat was sucked out the window, much to her dismay and to our very unsympathetic laughter.

From my association with boys my own age there, I learned some rhymes that I've never forgotten. They're not particularly edifying, but I quote them because perhaps children of this generation might be interested to know what youngsters seventy years ago were saying. One was a poem called the "Dirty Old Man." I went:

"Sam, Sam was a dirty old man
He washed his face in a frying pan
He combed his hair with the leg of a chair
And died with a toothache in his ear."

Also, because of my having come from China, the children in Sunday School liked to quote another perfectly useless poem about "Chinamen," emphasizing the difficulty that Chinese supposedly have with the letter "r." It went:

"Chin, chin Chinaman, velly velly sad
Me aflaid, evely tlade velly velly bad
Noyi joke stoney bloke, makee shutee shop
Chin, chin Chinaman, chop, chop, chop."

In those days it was considered quite the proper thing to call all Chinese "Chinamen," just as we use the term "Englishmen" and "Frenchmen." No one gave it a second thought. Nowadays the Chinese consider the term an insult. It seems rather peculiar because it is an exact translation of their own term for themselves. Their word for "Chinese" is "Zhongguo ren," which literally means "China man" or "China person." Of course it was understandable that they objected to the obviously offensive epithets "chink" and "slant-eyes," used so often in movies and literature of the period. Strangely enough, although one frequently hears and reads the term "round eyes," as supposedly a contrasting expression the Chinese use when disparaging Westerners, I never once heard it used all the time we were in China. Where it originated, I don't know. Probably in the fertile brain of some writer.

One little piece of doggerel I learned as a young boy on that furlough was of intense interest to me because the Chinese had something that was almost an exact counterpart of it. It was a crazy collection of opposites, and ran like this:

"One fine day in the middle of the night

Two dead men got up to fight
One blind man to see fair play, and
Two dumb men to shout 'Hooray,'
A paralyzed donkey standing by
Kicked the blind man in the eye,
Kicked him through a twelve-inch wall
Into a dry ditch and drowned them all."

The Chinese equivalent rhymes in Chinese, but not in English, and starts out as follows:

"If you want me to fabricate a story then I will.
On the first day of the New Year, autumn began,
And on the fifteenth of the first month there came a
 great flood
Which washed out a whole field of sorghum heads.
What I tell you now you won't believe,
My white horse gave birth to a big black cow.
An eighteen-year-old girl picking beans nearby
Was so frightened, her hair turned white..."

and it goes on ad infinitum. The humor involves the fact that in North China the Chinese New Year comes at the coldest time of the year, and thus the whole situation is quite preposterous. However, it does illustrate the fact that there are some similarities between Chinese culture and our own. For those interested in the Chinese version it goes as follows: *Rang wo zhou wo jiu zhou, da nian chu yi li liao qiu. Zheng yue shi wu fa da shui, chung daole yi di gao-liang tou. Wo shuozhe hua ni bu xin, bai ma xialege da qing niu. Shibade guniang zhai doujiaor, xiade bailiao tou...*

While in Monrovia during furlough, on one of my father's brief visits home he asked me one day to take his pocket watch to be cleaned. I left it at the watch repair shop, and later that day Father got a phone call from the owner asking if he would drop in to see him at his convenience. Father was a little surprised, but later stopped by to see the man, who asked if the watch had ever been repaired before. My father remembered that it had at one time stopped on him when in China, and he had given it to a Chinese watchmaker to repair, and he had had no trouble with it since. The Monrovia man then took a large magnifying glass and asked Father to look at the hairspring on the watch. There, totally invisible to the naked eye, he pointed out a spot where the Chinese crafts-man had snipped off two small pieces from an old hairspring, and, after drilling small holes on both sides of the broken spring, had ingeniously riveted the two patches onto the broken spring, thus mending the break. The Monrovia businessman offered my father a brand-new quality watch in exchange for the old one, which he wanted to use as a window display, and Father agreed. When we left Monrovia, the watch was still on display in the window with a magnifying glass focused on the repaired spring and a card describing the repair that no one in this country would have thought possible. Mind you, it was the hairspring, not the mainspring. I've always regretted Father giving the watch away: it was unique, and it would have been a nice keepsake. I've not been back to Monrovia since, and don't know what happened to the watch. Possibly it is in some museum, or in some proud owner's collection of old watches. Should any-one reading this have seen such a watch, I would like very much to hear about it.

Toward the end of that second furlough, conditions in China were very bad. Civil war raged everywhere, and letters from Lingyuan discouraged us from returning because travel conditions were so unsafe. However, there seemed to be indications that peace might be in the offing, so my parents decided to leave for Shanghai, hoping that conditions would have improved by the time we arrived. Consequently, we made our way to Vancouver, British Columbia, intending to board a ship for Shanghai. On arrival in Vancouver, we were dismayed to read in the newspa-pers of a fresh outbreak of fighting in Jehol Province, and friends in Vancouver urged us to wait. Some very kind folk put us up in the Elysium Hotel, a stately old place that sadly is no longer there. We stayed there for about four months, waiting for the situation in China to clarify.

One could not have asked for a more delightful spot to stay, and with so much to see and do, the days passed quickly. It was summertime and there were trolley trips to the beach at Kitsilano, where we swam in the ocean, and a fish-and-chips lunch there was not the least of the anticipated pleasures. Other days we took a ferry trip across the bay to the famous Capilano Suspension Bridge, where we could watch the salmon leaping upstream in the river, two hundred feet below us. From the hotel it was a very short walk to the world-famous Stanley Park, where we also spent a lot of time enjoying not only the beaches, but the trees, flowers and animals.

Living in the hotel became somewhat boring at times, and as children will, from time to time we got into some mischief that caused Mother some grief and embarrassment. For one thing, we found an end-less supply of hotel stationery in the lobby, and those sheets of paper made wonderful airplanes, which we sailed out the upper-story windows into the street or onto a neighboring lot. One day we made the mistake of sailing them down the stairwell into the lobby, where they came to the attention of the manager, and that was the end of that game. Mother was courteous-ly asked to make sure that we never did it again.

The self-service elevators were a great discovery, particularly when we found that watching down the stairwell, we could see people approaching the eleva-tor and then, by pressing the button, we could pull the elevator away from them.

My brother Gil and I had a number of adventures on our own that any boy would envy us for. One day we were invited by the captain of an ocean-going tug-boat to go with him on a trip across the sound to Vancouver Island. Captain McFarland was a member of the local Christian group with whom we met on Sundays, and we had gotten to know him really well. His regular run each night was to leave Vancouver around nine o'clock, towing a large barge loaded with railroad freight cars, and head for Nanaimo, then come back the next morning with a return load. The night that we went with him was very stormy — or at least it seemed so to us — and it was one of the roughest sea voyages I can recall. However, that didn't prevent us from enjoying every minute of it. We spent most of the night on the bridge with the captain, even though we could see very little around us except for the flashing navigation beacons on both shores and the lights of an occasional passing ship. The huge ferries that are currently used on that route make the trip in about three or four hours, but it must have taken us eight or nine hours, because we didn't arrive in Nanaimo until well after daylight, and once there, we saw little except the unloading and re-load-ing of a new batch of cars. I remember nothing of the trip back. I suspect that we slept most of the way after having been up all night, but the whole experience at that very impressionable age lives more vividly in my memory than any of the many other ocean voyages I have made.

One other experience that Gil and I enjoyed while in Vancouver is perhaps worth recounting. Stanley Park had a place where one could rent rowboats for fishing, or just for pleasure. One day we decided it would be fun to do some fishing. We got ourselves some rods, fishhooks and bait, and, with a sackful of sandwiches, we sallied forth to make a full day of it, filled with the grandest expectations of returning that evening with more fish than we could eat. It was not to be.

We fished the entire day without a single bite, even though we moved from one spot to another around the bay; and most frustrating of all, people around us seemed to be having considerable success. Apparently we had the wrong kind of bait.

In the late afternoon, we were thinking of giving up when an "old man" in an adjoining boat (he was perhaps in his late forties) rowed over near us and asked if we knew the time. Gil was wearing a wristwatch and politely told him the time, and we gave the matter no further thought. Perhaps a half hour later, much to our surprise, the same man rowed over to where we were and, pulling alongside, asked us what bait we were using and if we had had any luck. Somewhat shamefacedly, we told him of our lack of success. He then showed us his own catch which, to our astonishment, seemed like hundreds of fish. He told us that, because unlike most kids our age we had been very polite to him in telling him the time, he would tell us the secret of his own success, the kind of bait he used.

In great detail he told us how to find the right bait. He pointed out a small cove, told us to get there at low tide the next morning, and to creep as silently as we could down to the waterline, where we would see some finger-like objects sticking up out of the shallow water. They would look like tubes, about six or eight inches long, with a purple tassel showing on top. We were told to quietly reach out and pinch those tubes at the base, then pull them up as quickly as we could. If we were quick enough we would find a thick fat sea worm inside. However, if we made any noise, or weren't quick enough, we would simply get an empty tube.

It all sounded pretty farfetched, but he seemed a very sincere and friendly man, and, after all, he had shown us the fish to prove what he was saying. We thanked him and told him we would try it the next day. We booked the boat again for the following morning, and shortly before daylight, when the tide was its lowest, we approached the designated cove where, with some skepticism, we set out to find the "purple" worms. Sure enough, in the dim light we could see those finger-like objects he'd spoken of, waving back and forth in the gentle ripples. Our first attempts were unsuccessful; we were not quick enough or made some noise, and so we simply pulled up an empty casing. But in time we learned the trick and soon had a good supply of those fat, juicy and ugly-looking tubeworms.

That day our fishing was a huge success. We pulled in fish almost as fast as we could bait the hooks. In fact, we caught more kinds than we could name, and we even pulled in a couple of small, two-foot-long sharks. We threw those back, but one fellow persisted in getting caught several times over, so we had to change our position and find another spot. By early afternoon we had more fish than we thought we could handle, and didn't quite know what to do with them.

Back at the dock we borrowed a couple of gunnysacks and took the fish back to the hotel kitchen. The cook was delighted to have them, but he offered us nothing in exchange. Then, with such an inexhaustible supply of bait and fish to be had, we got the bright idea of going into business and selling our catch to restaurants.

The next day we had the same kind of success. Every day thereafter for the next ten days or so, we caught as many fish as the two of us could carry. We even became quite sophisticated when we found that rock cod brought a better price than anything else, and discovered the best place where those could be found. The spot happened to be in the very swift-flowing and dangerous waters of the Narrows of Burrard Inlet, which was the main shipping channel into Vancouver Bay. There, we had to constantly keep an eye out for ships going by in both directions; not that there was any danger of their hitting us, but in that narrow channel the wash of their passing created quite sizable waves, which several times nearly swamped us. Particularly fearsome were the very fast Canadian Pacific "Princess" ships, which ran a regular ferry schedule to Vancouver Island. Not only were they absolutely silent in their approach, but also were always traveling very fast. Frequently they were past us before we noticed, and we had to hustle to get our boat turned around and headed into the big waves they created.

Another hazard we discovered was the tremendous tidal surge for which the Narrows was justly famous. That happened twice each day when the tide changed, but no one had told us about it. The first time we experienced it, we found it hard to believe our eyes. Quite suddenly, and without the slightest warning, a monstrous wave approached us. From our position in the rowboat, it appeared to be about eight feet high and extended the full width of the narrows. It was coming fast, and because we were frozen into immobility, we almost met with disaster. At the last minute we managed to turn the boat head-on into the wave and rode it out. Only later did we learn what it was.

Apart from a good scare, a thorough wetting, and a lot of water to bail out of the boat, we came through it unscathed, but from then on we made a note of the tidal changes and kept a sharp eye out for that six- to eight-foot wall of water as it came roaring through with each change of the tide, first from one direction and then from the other. By the third day we became quite blasé about it. It was all part of the fun.

At the end of each day after carrying our catch into town, my job was to approach the back doors of various restaurants, where we tried to sell our fish. Gil thought that since I looked "kinda cute," I would be the most logical one to be the salesman. Whatever it was, we sold every fish we could catch, and we not only made enough money to pay for our boat, we had plenty left over for pocket money. Those were indeed happy, carefree days.

With my share of the money I went to Woolworth's and bought a large quantity of spectacles in a variety of different strengths. I had remembered the many Chinese I knew who had bad eyesight, and wanted to take something back to help them. I must have purchased several dozen in a wide range of strengths, and when we later got back to Lingyuan, I had no difficulty in disposing of them. Everyone with poor eyesight wanted to try out a pair, and I charged them just what I had paid for them in Vancouver. But I had forgotten that there was a difference in the exchange rate, so actually I was charging them in Chinese money only about a third of what I had paid. But it didn't matter. It was good to be able to help a lot of people who were in great need.

From our windows in the hotel, we could watch the harbor entrance and never tired of the constant parade of ships of all kinds and sizes. Our favorites were the famous Canadian Pacific "White Fleet," the "Empresses" which plied the Pacific. With their distinctive yellow funnels and the house flag of three red and three white squares, they were unmistakable, and we came to recognize each of the different ships on sight and were near enough to the pier to be down there before they docked. Our special favorites were the *Empress of Russia* and *Empress of Australia*, on which we had crossed the ocean, and we always got passes to go aboard to visit with both crews, some of whom remembered us. The *Empress of Australia* was formerly a German ship and was a prize of war from World War I. We found it of great interest that the water faucets or "taps" in the staterooms were all marked in German, and there were brass plaques throughout the ship giving instructions or directions in German. We also boarded the newer *Empress of Japan* and *Empress of Canada*, both of which were larger and much more opulent. On one occasion, when the *Empress of Canada* was docking, a sudden surge of the tide caused the ship to go out of control and it headed straight in for the pier, just where we were standing. We saw it coming, and amid loud shouts from the police, "Run for your lives," and cries and screams from the crowd who were on the pier, we managed to make it to safety just before the ship crashed into the pier and took out a hefty twenty-foot bite from the concrete dock, with little or no damage to the stem of the ship. Sad to say, all, or most of those wonderful ships, were sunk during World War II when they were being used as troopships, but they will be long remembered by all who traveled on them.

Finally, one day in August we received an optimistic letter from Zhang Yao-ting in Lingyuan telling us that the situation had stabilized and it was safe for us to return. Father immediately booked passage for us on the *Empress of Russia*, which sailed in mid-September with all of us aboard, and some two weeks or more later we left Vancouver, with a stop in Honolulu, then in Japan at Yokohama and Kobe. We finally arrived in Shanghai, happy to once again smell the distinctive "aroma" of the Orient, and glad to be near home again. However, there were still to be some surprises in store for us.

Going "home" on furlough. Person at far left in picture is a friend.

Bob's love of ships and the sea started very early in life.

Being greeted at one of the fairs we visited.

Fortune teller at the fair.

Getting ready for the dragon parade.

Infant in coffin, dressed and ready for burial.

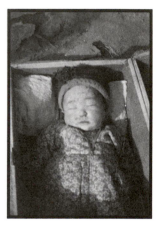

A Christian wedding, with the bride and groom in the front row.

Litter bearers take a break.

好事不出門壞
事傳千里。

Hao shi bu chu men,
huai shi chuan qian li.

The good things one does
don't go out of the door,
but the bad things you do
are talked about a thousand miles away.

- Chinese Proverb.

Chapter Fourteen
A Little Of This And A Little Of That

Shanghai was not the kind of city where we wanted to spend any great length of time: the dialect there was strange to us and, although we were in China, it was a different China from the one we were familiar with. We were glad to get aboard the small coastal steamer and be heading north to Tientsin. By that time we all had our sea legs and the rough trip didn't bother us at all.

There weren't a great many passengers: a few missionaries, business people, and some military officers belonging to various foreign embassies in Peking. One of the civilians in particular interested me greatly. He was a Scotsman, and it was by no means his first trip to China. He told us he worked for a large coal-mining company in Scotland, and was going to Peking to buy soybeans for the pit ponies they used in the mines in Scotland. That they used ponies in the mines was news to me.

From what he told us, it seems that for many years they had loaded coal wagons at the working face of the mine, then used small ponies to pull the wagons on tracks to the high-speed hoists, which raised them to the surface. The ponies, for as long as he could remember, had been stabled down in the mines and were born and raised there without ever seeing daylight.

Over a period of time, they discovered that the ponies, living and working in constant semi-darkness, were gradually going blind, so a remedy had to be found. After trial and error, it was found that a diet of the yellow soybean from China restored the ponies' eyesight, and for a number of years they had no further trouble.

Then one day they suddenly realized that the ponies had started going blind again. The diet was the same, the beans appeared to be the same and were coming from the same source, but something was terribly wrong. Someone had the bright idea of washing the beans, fearing that perhaps they had been exposed to some kind of contamination. When the beans were put into the water, to the consternation of the mine owners, they discovered that almost half of them immediately dissolved, leaving a yellow clay deposit behind. On close examination of the unwashed beans they discovered that as many as half of them were man-made from yellow clay, and were not genuine beans at all.

Our Scottish friend had thereupon been sent to Peking to find the source of the fake beans. Unannounced, he quietly visited the villages where the beans were grown and discovered an active and thriving cottage industry with numerous women and girls using yellow clay and rolling tiny balls of mud on horsehair screens until they were the correct size. After being dried in the sun, those fake beans, at a casual glance, were indistinguishable from the real thing.

It then became our friend's job to make an annual trip to China to carefully examine each purchase of beans before they were bagged and loaded aboard a ship for Scotland, and to water-test random batches to make sure the Chinese remained honest. He told us that once the purity of the beans had been re-established, the pit ponies' eyesight immediately improved, but whole villages of Chinese had to find some other source of income.

When we reached Tientsin, disappointment awaited us. Telegrams from Lingyuan told of renewed fighting while the fall harvest was in full swing, and our Chinese friends advised us against returning. We had to winter somewhere, and although it would be possible to rent quarters in Tientsin, it would be prohibitively expensive, and living in such a large city did not appeal to my parents. At Beidaihe, the beach resort where we sometimes spent our summers, we now had two houses that had been purchased some years earlier for the use of all the missionaries in Jehol Province, but they were not winterized and were not acceptable alternatives, so Father started looking elsewhere.

Just down the coast about ten miles from Beidaihe was the small railroad town called Chinhuangtao, "Island of the Emperor Ch'in," which I have mentioned in a previous chapter, and where we spent some time when my hand was being treated. It was the site of an island, originally a quarter of a mile or so off the coast. Ch'in was the emperor famous for having built the 1500-mile-long Great Wall, the sea-

ward end of which was just a little farther along the coast at the frontier town of Shanhaiguan.

In the late 1800s, a Belgian coal-mining company called the Kailan Mining Administration (KMA for short) had purchased the island and a sizable area of the mainland. The KMA then built a deep-water harbor off the tip of the island, after which it filled in most of the water between the island and the mainland nearby so that it was no longer an actual island. The company operated the Kaiping mines in the city of Tangshan, about 90 miles to the southwest, halfway between Chinhuangtao and Tientsin. At the mines they employed some 50,000 miners, who worked in shifts twenty-four hours a day, producing a very high quality coal which was then carried in their own fleet of coal cars and modern locomotives to Chinhuangtao, where it was loaded aboard ships from various parts of the world. One of their best customers was Japan.

The KMA later came under British ownership, and the port was run by a small community of Englishmen, with thousands of coolies employed in first unloading the trains, then loading the coal aboard the many colliers that called at the port.

Someone in Tientsin suggested to my father that it might be possible to find an empty house in Chinhuangtao that could be rented, just as we had done a year or two earlier. Father thereupon approached the KMA representatives in Tientsin and explained our dilemma and found them to be most cooperative. It appeared that there was, indeed, an available house belonging to the British and American Tobacco Company (BAT), which was only used in the summer months, and we could have it for the winter for a very modest rental. That was certainly a godsend. Father made a quick trip down there by train, found the house fully furnished and with plenty of space for us as a family, and shortly thereafter we moved in.

The "island" part of Chinhuangtao covered an area of only a few square miles and it was heavily forested with acacia trees, which held the sand in place. At the southern, or harbor end of the island there was a high rocky bluff with a steep drop-off on the harbor side but tapering gradually off to the north. The mainland portion of the KMA property was used to store the coal awaiting shipment, and it also had extensive repair facilities for the company's locomotives and rolling stock. Apart from the harbor and the two piers the company had built, which could handle four or five colliers simultaneously, the remainder of the island was used exclusively for company houses for the British staff. No Chinese lived on the island portion at all, and company police were stationed at the two main entrances to ensure the privacy of the Westerners who lived there.

The company housing had been built primarily northward along the bluff and the adjoining beach leading away from the harbor. It housed a permanent year-round staff of perhaps some twenty or thirty people including wives and children. In addition, there were a number of houses that were used only in the summer for KMA staff from Tientsin and Tangshan. The permanent staff included a few single men, as I remember, and one or two single women from time to time, but most of the residents were families.

At first we were in some doubt as to how we would be accepted by the English KMA staff, since to most of the "foreign" business people at the coast, missionaries were anathema and "beyond the pale." However, we needn't have worried. Those year-round "regulars" gave us a warm welcome and made us feel very much at home, extending to us all the amenities of their clubhouse and recreational facilities, not only at the club, but also at the nine-hole golf course on a flat part of the mainland about a five-minute walk from our house.

The house stood a little way back from the beach, surrounded by woods, and it backed onto a nearby tidal creek only a few hundred yards away that separated us from the mainland. The creek was about a hundred yards wide and was spanned nearby with a modern concrete bridge with huge movable "gates" that served as a flood-control barrier in times of heavy flooding from the marshes above the bridge or the occasional extra high tides from the seaward side.

Just across the bridge was the golf course, and it was there, on a bitterly cold day that winter, that I played my first game of golf. Father had been loaned a set of clubs by one of the KMA staff, and one afternoon he took me out with him to try them out. The course was unquestionably unique; certainly I have never seen one quite like it. The tees were something like a baseball pitcher's mound, except they were clay platforms, about six feet square, and about eighteen inches or more in height. The "greens" had a hard surface and were covered with finely crushed granite, rolled smooth so that they had a very fast surface, and the "fairways" — if they could be called that — were barely distinguishable from the surrounding countryside. They were completely bare, either hard-baked mud in spots, or covered with short tufts of grass, and there was low brush everywhere. Of course, there were the mandatory sand traps, some natural and some man-made, and the natural water hazards were the marshes on two sides of the course. But it was a fun place to go. It was almost completely flat, and in winter nearly always had a biting cold wind sweeping down from the high mountain range just a few miles to the north. Yet it was a delightful spot, with all the fresh air one could want and almost complete solitude.

That first day Father took me there, he handed me one of the irons and gave me a short lesson on how to tee up the ball and hold the club, then how to aim and swing. He then drove his own ball well down the fairway and told me to wait until he got near the first hole before hitting my ball. But as usual, I was young and impatient and didn't want to be left too far behind, and Father looked so far away that I felt it was safe to make my drive. I put everything I had into that first swing and my club connected with the ball with a most satisfying "thwack" and away the ball went. Unfortunately, the instant the ball left my club I knew exactly where it was going, and that it was going to hit Father. He had told me to shout "fore" when I hit, and that I did, but somewhat belatedly. Hearing my shout, he turned part-way around toward me and the ball struck him exactly on the right temple, knocking him flat to the ground.

I was certain I had killed him, but as I rushed toward him, he was on his feet waving his club and running in my direction with fire in his eyes and with the obvious intent of giving me a sound thrashing, which, at that moment, I knew I deserved and would have welcomed simply out of relief at seeing that he was unharmed. But as we got near each other, Father suddenly stopped short and convulsed with laughter. The irony of my very first shot traveling that distance and hitting him on the head struck him as unbelievably funny. It was most fortunate that he was wearing a thick fur cap, with the ear flap protecting his temple and taking most of the force of the ball's impact.

Apart from a fairly large lump there, he suffered no ill effects.

The nearby marshes were the winter feeding ground for large flocks of bustards, huge birds weighing thirty pounds or more and with a wingspan of seven feet or so. The Chinese found they very good eating, and so did we. Every time we played golf out there that winter, there were always hunters on the other side of the marshes, hiding behind their blinds and banging away at the birds with their ancient muzzle loaders. They were not very often successful because the bustard is a difficult bird to shoot, particularly when sitting on water or on the ground. The wing feathers are thick and very hard, and even a .22-caliber long bullet just bounced off without doing any damage, as I discovered when I got a .22 rifle and started hunting them myself. The only way to get one was either a shot in the head or under the wings as they took off or landed.

One afternoon on the golf course my father was just teeing up when we heard a shot in the near distance and saw a large bustard rise from the water and head in our direction. It was obvious the bird had been wounded, because it was unable to gain any altitude and was flying no more than eight feet above the ground, with the Chinese hunter — who had waded through the marsh — running close behind in hot pursuit. The bird continued to fly in a beeline directly toward us and I was transfixed by the sight of that immense creature coming straight at us. But Father remained perfectly calm and as the bustard flew just a foot or so above our heads, he took a mighty swing with his driver and brought it down. As it turned out, the bird had a head injury and would not have survived, so we were glad to be able to put it out of its misery, and of course the Chinese hunter was all smiles at getting his bird. That was one "birdie" shot for the history books!

We missed Lingyuan and our friends there very much, but Chinhuangtao proved to be a most pleasant place to stay. There were a few children our own ages, but most lived some distance from us. I found a friend in Dennis Donahue, whose father was the harbor pilot and whose house was the closest one to ours. I spent many happy hours playing with him.

The "island" being a restricted area, the only Chinese we ever saw there were those employed by the KMA. The company had its own very efficient and well-trained police force, which patrolled the area day and night, so it was very secure, and for all the Chinese that one might see during the day, it might just as well have been someplace in England or the United States. One lost the feeling of being in China completely.

There were probably not more than fifteen or twenty miles of paved roads in the entire area owned by the KMA, including the mainland part, but almost all of the Europeans had motor vehicles of one sort or another that they used primarily for commuting the mile or so to work or to go to the club. Apart from rickshaws, there was no form of public transportation at all, and the rickshaws were not allowed to go looking for fares but were restricted to one or two stands where they waited until called. As a result, nearly everyone who didn't have a car used a bicycle, and we acquired several for ourselves. The KMA club was not used very much during the day, and was not far from where we lived, so we children, when not doing our schoolwork, would go there to play badminton on their large indoor court and had a marvelous time on cold winter days.

That winter of 1927 that we spent in Chinhuangtao was the coldest that had been experienced there in anyone's memory. The creek behind our house froze solid to a thickness of six or seven feet, the ice being constantly broken up by the tide and piled in huge hummocks along both sides of the shore as well as up against the bridge. Before long the open ocean itself began to freeze and continued to do so until the solid ice extended out for a distance of five miles or more. It was an extraordinary sight; the ice wasn't a smooth expanse, but a succession of uneven hummocks, many rising to heights of eight or ten feet, formed as the waves pushed the huge irregular floes of ice up onto the already hardened pack during the freezing process. The sea was frozen like that for many weeks and a number of ships were stalled out beyond the ice with no hope of gaining the harbor. One fairly large ship had attempted to push through the ice at the very beginning of the freeze, but had been caught about two or three miles out and became stuck fast there and unable to move.

The small hospital the KMA maintained on the island not far from where we lived, was primarily for the treatment of injured or sick coolies. Incidentally, the word "coolie" comes from the Chinese name for laborers, *ku li*, and means "bitter strength," a reference to the bitter lives those men lived and the strength necessary to do their job. Dr. Muir, who ran the hospital, was an old friend of mine, having treated my hand a year or more before.

One day during that great freeze, I was out riding my bike when Dr. Muir passed me in his little Morris Cowley, perhaps the best-known car on the roads there. Seeing me, he stopped and told me they had received a wireless message from the ship that was stuck in the ice that there was a man on board urgently in need of medical assistance, who might have to be brought to the hospital. He told me he was going to drive out over the ice, and would I like to go along and help. What an experience that would be, and who could possibly refuse an invitation like that? Without giving it further thought, or even thinking about what my parents would say, I pushed my bike into the woods and jumped into the car with him.

From the top of the bluff, the ship was visible and didn't appear to be very far away. However, when we got down to the beach and finally out onto the ice, from that low vantage point, the ship was a distant speck and at times, because of the ice hummocks, completely invisible. Dr. Muir drove slowly and most carefully, threading his way around the huge mounds of ice, and constantly on the watch for open water, but we needn't have worried. The ice — as it turned out later — was at least four feet thick, and after an hour or so of very slow progress, we were within about a hundred yards of the ship. Dr. Muir decided that was close enough. Thinking that perhaps the ice might be thin up close to the ship, he decided to stop there and walk the rest of the way. He suggested that I stay with the car and keep the engine running lest the car freeze up.

By that time the sailors aboard the ship had seen us approaching and had let down a ladder, and one of them came to meet Dr. Muir to help carry his bag. He was gone for almost an hour, and I sat there waiting in the car. It was an eerie experience; it was a windless day, and the sun glared off the ice making it difficult to see anything at any distance. There was a constant, low rumbling sound of the ocean moving under the ice, reminding me that there was nothing between me and that very deep water except the layer of ice which, minute by minute, seemed in my imagination to be getting thinner and thinner, and which I momen-

tarily expected would open up and swallow me, car and all. Every few minutes I heard loud booming, cracking sounds as the ice was moved by the waves beneath. I don't think I moved a muscle until, with considerable relief, I finally saw Dr. Muir returning. He told me the man was not as ill as had been reported and would not require further care, so we proceeded home.

I am sure Dr. Muir had never done that before, because although the sea froze to a certain extent every winter, it had never been known to freeze that far out before, but the way he had gone about it was so casual that it might all have been just an ordinary day's work, and he apparently saw nothing unusual about it. However, to me it was a most extraordinary experience, and one that not many boys my age could boast about. In the sixty-odd years since then, no winter has been so severe, and to my knowledge, no recurrence of that unusual phenomenon. Someone on shore took a photograph of the event, and later I saw the picture, where the car appeared as but a tiny black dot a short distance from the ship. When I faced Mother she had a lot to say about my long absence, and I remember being punished in some way. But it was well worth it.

The ice disappeared much more suddenly that it had formed. One day shortly after the above incident, the wind began to blow very strongly, and by nightfall it had become a real storm. Throughout the night we could hear the loud booming noises of the ice breaking up, and by morning the entire shoreline was a mountain of ice: huge blocks piled up one on top of another, so that from the beach, the ocean itself was completely obscured. In places it must have been piled twenty feet high, and it was some weeks before it had entirely melted or been broken up by the waves.

After any storm along that beach, it was an exciting place to go and collect coal. I had often been down to the wharf to watch the coolies as they loaded the ships. It was all manual labor. Railway trucks would dump huge piles of coal on the pier, then hundreds of coal-blackened coolies shoveled it into large wicker baskets, which, hung on a pole carried on the shoulders between two men, would be carried up a narrow gangplank onto the ship. At the foot of the gangplank, one of the two men would collect a bamboo "tally" stick, which at the end of the day would be presented for payment. On the way up the gangplank it was a common sight to see large lumps of coal roll off the top of the load, falling into the harbor. Not infrequently I would notice the coolie at the rear give a helping hand to one of the larger lumps. Not only did that lighten the load for them, but it was these same men who later, after a storm, would scour the beach for the coal that eventually washed up. I am sure the supervisors knew about it, but nothing was done about it.

The KMA had a large dredge that dredged some part of the harbor every day of the week, and every day, a lengthy barge loaded with sand, mud, and lumps of coal, was towed out a mile or more to sea and dumped. I have no idea how long it took for those lumps of coal to get washed up on the beach, but it could have been months or even years. The lumps we found, some of them weighing twenty pounds or more, were completely rounded at the edges and many looked like huge footballs. They were a much-prized commodity because not only were they the finest coal obtainable, but they cost us nothing. In addition, they burned with a fierce heat and gave off almost no smoke. Perhaps because of the long soaking in salt water, they burned with a bright blue flame that in an open fireplace was most attractive. Living as close to the beach as we did, we youngsters were always among the first to pick up coal after a storm and it helped considerably to cut down our fuel bills that winter. But it always meant we had to hustle, because of the intense competition from a horde of coolies who showed up as well, and who, perhaps rightly, felt that they had first claim on it since they had been responsible for its getting there in the first place.

During Chinese New Year celebrations that year, I had the new experience of being allowed to play with firecrackers for the first time. Back in Lingyuan, all the Chinese kids we played with had a wide choice of firecrackers but, since their use was associated with idol worship and the driving away of evil spirits, my parents would not allow us to have any. But in Chinhuangtao it was different. We were in an isolated area, away from any Chinese community, and Father could see no harm in letting me have a few — just to get it out of my system, I guess.

Among those noisemakers, my favorites were what were known by the Chinese as *Ertijiao*, which loosely

translates as a "Two Kicker." They were so named because when lit they exploded with a tremendous bang on the ground, then shot a hundred feet or more into the air, where they burst once again with an even louder bang. After firing off a few of those I became inventive, and thought they would make a fine mortar shell just like I had seen the Chinese soldiers use. I found an old piece of stovepipe, and after setting it up at an angle in the sand, I tried shooting the firecrackers across the frozen creek. I would light the fuse, drop the firecracker into the stovepipe, and quickly step back out of the way. After a satisfyingly loud bang inside the stovepipe, the firecracker would sail away in the direction I wanted it to go, bursting on the far shore. It was unquestionably a dangerous pastime, but at that age, who knew anything about danger? When I tired of that, an obvious variation was to use the firecracker as a bomb. I wondered if I could crack the ice in the creek, so I chipped out a hole, put the firecracker in with a long fuse, then poured water around it and waited for it to freeze solidly. After a few minutes I lit the fuse and ran. The loud explosion and the cracking of the ice in all directions was heard some distance away, and brought so many people running that I was dissuaded from doing it again.

My father was away from home a good part of that winter. It wasn't long after we got to Chinhuangtao that he decided to pay a visit to Lingyuan to see for himself what the political situation was like, and he set off in a locally hired two-mule cart with only the driver as a companion. Mother was deeply worried about him, because he would have to cross the lines between the two warring armies up north, but Father seemed unconcerned and the driver assured him that he frequently made the trip without any trouble.

That was one of the surprising yet quite typically Chinese aspects of those years of civil warfare, where, during lulls in the fighting, the opposing armies interfered very little with civilian foot traffic or normal commerce. They allowed people to pass with only a minimum of inspection and usually only a token demand in the way of some sort of commodity or money changing hands. Seven days later we were greatly relieved to get a telegram from Father saying he had arrived safely, and a letter followed soon after.

He had experienced no trouble passing through the very vaguely defined lines between the two armies. He'd been stopped and questioned a number of times, but since he was going "home," his business was considered to be legitimate, and they eventually let him through. In the eight or ten miles of no man's land, it became a little touchy. When it became apparent, because of outposts on the hilltops, that he was approaching the opposing line, he decided to get out and walk, and proceeded forward carrying a white flag. The soldiers had barricades across the road at a mountain pass, but when Father approached on foot they were quite civil and let him through. Once in Lingyuan, he visited the commanding general and from him received a pass for his return trip by another route, which proved quite uneventful.

From the Chinese Christians Father learned that during our absence on furlough the city had changed hands a number of times. Despite the scares, all had gone well. Father was away about a month, and when he returned, he brought with him Gao Cai, our cook, and You Wang, the table boy, both of whom had expressed a strong desire to come to Chinhuangtao to look after us. We were overjoyed to see them, because although up to that time we had been "making do" with a couple of locally hired men, it was not the same as having our own people around us. Gao Cai and You Wang had left families behind but were confident that all would be well with them.

Some weeks later Father made a second trip to Lingyuan and on that occasion, at my insistence, he took me with him. The trip up was cold but uneventful, and again we passed through the opposing army lines without trouble. Once there, since it was the Chinese New Year season, we were kept busy with a flood of visitors and several feasts. At one of the latter I apparently ate something that disagreed with me and became quite ill. I was unable to eat or keep anything down and began to run a high temperature. Father became worried about me and decided it would be best to get me back to Chinhuangtao as soon as possible. I traveled in the luxury of a mule litter while Father rode behind on a mule, and the driver — an old friend of ours — was urged to take the quickest route possible.

I remember nothing of the first two days because I lay on my back feeling pretty rotten, and sleeping most of the time, lulled by the motion and by the jangling bells around the neck of the lead mule. By the third day I was able to sit up, and I began to enjoy the trip. We were deep in the mountains, following a track that was normally used only by pack animals, and much of the going was rugged and spectacular. On the fourth morning we were on our way long before daylight and caught up to a long camel train with over 100 camels. Usually camels traveled only at night, mainly because they were slower than other traffic, and mules and horses seeing them tended to shy away from them. Therefore, the drivers normally found a wide spot in the road before daylight and "parked" for the day, feeding the camels and sleeping the hours away. In that case, the mountain valleys through which we were passing were so narrow and with such steep sides that the lead driver had been unable to find a spot large enough for so many camels, so for hours we were forced to follow behind them. The lead mule in my litter was impatient to get ahead, and, once it had gotten used to the presence of the camels, it kept pushing up close to the last camel in line only to have the camel turn its head and spit and kick out furiously to one side or the other when my mule started to pass. Fortunately none of the kicks connected.

At one point we came to a small village high in the hills. Several children came out with wicker baskets slung over their shoulders and carrying hooked bamboo scrapers with which they were trying to pick up the camel droppings. One boy of about eleven was especially daring and dodged in and out among the camels without the slightest fear. Suddenly he got too close to the rearmost camel, which evidently had a particularly bad temper. It spat at the boy, then as the boy came closer, it kicked out sideways. Fortunately, the boy was so close that the kick had not gained momentum before it connected with him; still, it lifted him some ten feet into the air and threw him about twenty feet away. The surprised look on the boy's face as he sailed through the air was hilarious. Fortunately he landed on all fours and was unhurt, but I am certain he learned a lesson about camels.

Ultimately we were able to pass the camels, and then, as the road continued to climb upward, we entered an area that was heavily wooded for miles, a most remarkable sight in North China, where completely barren hills were the norm. Just why the trees in that area had not been cut down for fuel we were unable to learn, but we presumed it was due to some superstitious beliefs by the sparse local population. In any case, we saw a lot of small game: hare, foxes, and most surprising of all, dozens of beautifully colored long-tailed pheasants, either alongside the road or walking the road ahead of us and at times flying overhead.

We stopped that night at a tiny inn high in the mountains and the next morning joined a main cart route leading to a pass through the Great Wall at a point where we had never crossed before. For several hours, as we approached it, we could see the wall in the distance, winding its way up and down the mountains like a huge serpent, with lookout towers on the highest peaks all around. Then came a particularly long and very steep climb where we were constantly delayed by the heavy cart traffic coming down the pass and by equally heavily laden carts going in the same direction as we were. As the ones coming down had the right of way, everyone else tried to get as close to the shoulder of the mountain as possible to let them pass. The technique used to brake the heavy carts was unique and cruel. Two of the mules usually used in the forward team were taken from harness, a rope was loosely tied around their necks, and the other end was tied to the back of the cart. As the cart started down the steep slope, a man walked backward in front of the two mules, hitting them on their noses with a stick, which caused them to rear up and drag backwards, thus providing braking action for the cart. In addition, a stout green pole was tied firmly across the back of the two wheels, rubbing against the rim, and it was kept tight by constantly twisting the rope that held it in position. Even so, it was well known that not infrequently a heavy cart would go out of control and over the edge, with a drop of anywhere from several hundred to several thousand feet.

We didn't know quite what to expect as we finally reached the top of the pass and came under the shadow of the Great Wall. After a few moments, the road made a sharp turn, and the sight was dramatic and without doubt the most spectacular of any of the several *kou* ("mouths") in the famous barrier, through which we had passed so many times over the years. Perched in a narrow cleft in the mountains, the "gate" was actually a series of three huge adjoining towers built roughly in the shape of a squared off "S". At first, as we approached the wall, which towered on each side to a height of forty feet or more, there seemed to be no way to get through. Then the road again made a sharp right turn directly under the wall,

and we entered the first gate, which looked like a long narrow tunnel some fifty feet or more in length, with a beautifully rounded archway some twenty-five feet above our heads providing a loud echo as we went through. Just inside we came to a small square courtyard with just enough room for one vehicle at a time. We then made a sharp left turn through another gateway exactly like the first one, and then entered another small courtyard, and finally made a sharp right-hand turn through an identical third gateway. All around and above us were the battlements with stone embrasures at intervals of ten feet or so, and it was easy to imagine the defenders in ancient times being able to hold this entry secure from any invaders from the north. From above they could throw their spears, fire their arrows, or drop boulders or boiling oil directly onto the heads of anyone trying to get through. For that reason the gateways, even without gates to close, were easy enough to defend.

Once we were through the last of the gates, it wasn't long before we looked from a height of five or six thousand feet directly out onto a vast expanse to the left and right as far as the eye could see. Immediately in front of us the ocean extended to the far horizon. Looking straight down in the near distance we could see distinctly the "island" of Chinhuangtao, with tiny ships tied up at the pier. However, near as it looked, because of the tortuous trail down the mountains and the roundabout route we had to take through the villages between us and the shore, it was not until late that evening that we arrived back at the house, and of course by that time I felt completely well again.

It was that winter in Chinhuangtao when we began to notice that my older sister, Ruth, was showing signs of an illness that later was to become most severe and that was to dog her throughout her adult life. She was about seventeen at the time, and up to that point had been perfectly normal in every way, but that winter she seemed to want to do little other than sleep. During the day it was common to see her fast asleep on the couch and I would overhear my parents worrying as to whether she had in some way contracted some form of sleeping sickness. However, when awake she seemed to be perfectly normal, and Dr. Muir could not find a single thing wrong. It was not until some years later that a doctor in Toronto diagnosed her illness as Parkinson's disease, but little was known about the disease at the time and many years after that we were to find out the diagnosis had been incorrect.

That winter of 1927 passed quickly. There were occasional visits from British warships "showing the flag," and parties aboard them to which we were invited. When Father was at home, between trips back to Lingyuan, he took us out to various places. Once, it was down to the KMA workshops to see where they repaired and rebuilt railway cars and locomotives. There was also a large glass factory near the railway station, not operated by the KMA. We visited there a couple of times and it was fascinating to watch the molten liquid pouring out at one end of the production line and long, wide sheets of clear glass emerging at the other. We also watched the cutting and packing process, but my most lasting memory was that of a group of workmen sitting around a huge block of red-hot glass slag, warming themselves with their tea kettles sitting on top of it, heating water for their tea.

On another interesting trip we visited the nearby U.S. Marine encampment. It was primarily a summer camp for the Marines stationed in China. However there was a small year-round contingent based there. They made us feel very welcome, treating us to an American lunch and giving us a ride in one of their shiny, olive-colored sedans. We made a number of friends among the Marines and had the pleasure of having them visit us at our house on a number of occasions.

One of my favorite pastimes that winter was following the many trails through the acacia forest on the island where the local KMA residents rode their horses. On one occasion I heard a horse galloping toward me, and a character right out of a Zane Grey novel appeared. I thought I was dreaming, but there was a magnificent chestnut horse, and astride it a most beautiful young woman with black hair streaming out behind her. I fell in love with her instantly, and for days thereafter would haunt that trail in the hope of seeing her again. I later learned she was the wife of one of the KMA executives. Tragically, not too long afterward she was thrown from her horse and broke her neck. The death of that beautiful young woman cast a pall over the Christmas celebrations in that small, tightly knit community, and everyone mourned her passing — I not the least of all.

Shortly after our arrival in Chinhuangtao I made friends with a young Chinese lad my own age whom everyone called Xiao Liu (Little Six.) His father held a position in one of the KMA offices, and he was the sixth and last son in the family. Being the same age, we had much the same interests. I taught him English, and he taught me a great deal about Chinese life in an environment different from that of Lingyuan, some of it good, and some not so good.

Despite the civil war going on in the interior, it was relatively peaceful along the coast, and large cruise ships began calling at Chinhuangtao that winter, with the passengers debarking and boarding special luxury trains to Peking for a couple of days of sightseeing. The ships flew the flags of many different nations and were all too large to moor alongside the wharf, so they were anchored a mile or so offshore and were tended by a large ocean-going tug operated by the KMA.

Xiao Liu and I enjoyed going down to the wharf to watch the tourists come ashore on the tug, then board their luxurious train for Peking. It was a train that was never used for any other purpose, and it was kept spick and span to make the best possible impression. Some of the passengers, for a variety of reasons, elected to stay on the ship rather than face the long train trip to Peking. When I noticed that, I conceived the idea that perhaps they might enjoy a shorter trip to visit the Great Wall at a point along the coast some ten or twelve miles north of Chinhuangtao, in the town of Shanhaiguan, which means "mountain sea pass." There the wall had originally started, not merely on the beach, but actually some distance out in the water, from where it went a short distance overland to the nearby mountain range.

Xiao Liu and I went aboard one of the ships and talked with some of the passengers, who could see the Great Wall from the ship through binoculars. They showed a great interest in the idea of a sightseeing trip, so I contacted the agents in Tientsin who represented the various cruise lines and proposed the idea to them. They were quite enthusiastic, so I hustled around and organized one-day trips for future tour ships.

I first had to talk to the railway people and arrange for a special car, but that proved exceptionally easy to accomplish. The railway agreed that when a cruise ship came in they would shunt the car down to the wharf to pick up the Shanhaiguan passengers after the special train to Peking had left, then hook the car onto the morning northbound passenger train at around ten o'clock, for the half-hour trip to Shanhaiguan.

Shanhaiguan itself held little of interest to foreign visitors, apart from the fact that it was a typical Chinese town. However, the wall passed right through the middle of the town, and was the site of a huge, ornate gate that has been much photographed. It had a very large wooden plaque above the rounded archway, which read: "*Tian xia diyi guan*," usually translated as "The First Gate Under Heaven." That translation is not incorrect, but the word *guan*, rather than meaning only a "gate," conveys more the meaning of a pass, or barrier, and was the term used for all the openings through the wall, most of which were in the mountains. In that instance it was used even though there was no pass and it was on flat ground. Near the gate was the railway station, and immediately past the station was a huge gap that had been cut through the wall for the railway line to pass through.

All the tourists wanted to photograph the gate, but the most scenic part of the wall was about two or three miles inland. Before each trip, I would learn from the tour agency when the ship was due, have them contact the ship by radio to ascertain how many people wanted to make the trip, then go to Shanhaiguan a few days in advance to hire a "fleet" of donkeys to carry them up to the most spectacular part of the wall, where it began its climb almost straight up the side of a mountain.

Hiring the donkeys proved to be great fun, but frequently resulted in a lot of headaches. Sometimes as many as 100 passengers wanted to make the trip, and it was hard to find that many donkeys. Fortunately, I found a man who owned quite a number of donkeys himself, so I gave him the job of finding the rest, and each time it turned out pretty well, with only the minimum of confusion.

The ships' passengers always enjoyed the novelty of the trip, even though on several occasions it was extremely cold. For my part, I was always greatly amused by the fact that so many of them wanted to carry away a souvenir of the wall, even to the point that some tried to pry out one of the huge bricks, each the size of a small suitcase. I had to firmly dissuade them from that because if the Chinese authorities had gotten wind of it they would have become incensed and more likely than not would have terminated further trips.

Part of the fun was going aboard those big ships, and usually I was able to spend three or four hours aboard. Most of the ships needed to take on fresh water, and the KMA tug I went out on was equipped with huge tanks for that purpose, but it took time to pump it into the ship. On one occasion, however, things turned out quite differently. As my young Chinese friend, Xiao Liu, and I attempted to board the ship we were stopped at the gangway by the master at arms. I was told that I could go aboard, but not my "chink" friend. I protested, but to no avail, so I refused to go on board without Xiao Liu, and for the next four hours or so we were confined to the tug alongside.

When the tug had finished pumping all the water and was ready to head back to shore, the captain of the ship and several of his officers came aboard the tug to go ashore for a dinner given in their honor by Mr. Chilton, the KMA superintendent in charge of the station. Seeing me on the tug, the captain asked me how I liked his ship. I told him that what I had seen from the outside looked just fine, but since my Chinese friend had not been allowed to go on board, we had stayed on the tug. Hearing that, he became extremely annoyed and invited me back the following day to spend the entire day on the ship as his guest, and to have lunch with him. He told me to be sure and bring Xiao Liu with me, and he assured me that the master at arms would be properly rebuked.

The ship in question was the *Resolute* of the Hamburg America Line, a really beautiful ship. The following day we went out early on the tug's first trip and were given a complete tour of the ship by one of the officers, covering everything from the bridge to the engine room. We were then given shotguns and allowed to shoot skeet from the stern, an activity that kept us busy for a couple of hours. Our lunch with the captain in his private quarters was one of the most elaborate I have ever had, and altogether it proved to be a memorable day, particularly for Xiao Liu, who had never seen or done anything like that.

Chinhuangtao was also a frequent port of call for warships of different nationalities, British and American in particular. On one occasion, a whole fleet of Japanese warships came in and anchored offshore for several days. There must have been nearly a dozen ships, and we managed to go aboard several of them, including a submarine and a large battleship. We'd been aboard many of the British and American warships, including submarines, and what struck us most about the Japanese ships was how filthy they seemed in comparison to the spit and polish of the British and American navies. In those days the Japanese paid little attention to appearance, and not only were the ships covered with rust in many places, but the decks both above and below were littered with debris and filth.

Between the arrivals of ships, one of our haunts after school was the tiny lookout station on the highest point of the cliff overlooking the harbor. There, in a small glassed-in enclosure, worked an elderly Chinese man who had the job of scanning the horizon for incoming ships. From that height he could spot them with his telescope when they were fifteen or twenty miles out. He would read the flags to determine the identity of the ship and would then notify the KMA offices and the ship's agents, so that preparation could be made for its arrival, and, if it was a collier, coal trains could be moved up to the dock so there would be a minimum of delay in loading it. We spent many happy hours there "helping" the old gentleman. He was a friendly man and seemed to enjoy our company, and perhaps our being there helped relieve his boredom.

Numerous Japanese colliers and freighters came into Chinhuangtao. All Japanese ships apart from naval vessels carry the word "Maru" after their names. It has no particular meaning for them, it is just something that the Japanese have always done with ship's names, and the names were always written on the prow in Chinese characters. What interested the Chinese was the fact that the ideogram used for Maru is identical to a Chinese character pronounced *wan*, meaning pill or small ball, such as a meatball. But Chinese being a tonal language, and with a limited number of sounds, there is much duplication of similar-sounding words, though each has a different meaning and is represented by a different character. So another Chinese word pronounced in exactly the same way, and with the same exact tone as *wan*, has the meaning of "finished" or "the end." As a result, the Chinese had a lot of fun with Japanese ships' names at the expense of the Japanese, who were none the wiser.

There has never been much love lost between the Chinese and their Japanese neighbors, and at that particular time, Japanese aggressiveness was showing in relations with China, so the Chinese took every opportunity to show their feelings in return. Many of the ships bore the names of well-known Japanese cities. When, for example, the *Kobe Maru* came in, as the Chinese pronounced it, it meant "the end of Kobe" which caused a lot of merriment and gave the Chinese no little satisfaction.

One day when we were up at the signal station, a Japanese ship called the *Tokyo Maru* arrived in Chinhuangtao for the first time. That was too good an opportunity for the Chinese to miss. When the old man in the lookout tower first spotted the ship, he turned to me with a broad grin and told me to watch what was going to happen. With great excitement he made a number of telephone calls, and in the time it took for the ship to come alongside, a tremendous crowd of Chinese officials and curious spectators had gathered to watch the fun. They carried flags and banners, and, to the sound of beating drums, they fired off hundreds of firecrackers, as the crowd cheered and hooted. The Japanese crew stood dumbfounded, not knowing why they deserved such a monumental welcome and unaware that the crowd were cheering the "end of Tokyo."

When spring of 1928 came we had to vacate the house to make way for the original owners, who wanted to use it for the summer. By that time Father had made quite a few trips inland to Lingyuan and felt that the situation had stabilized to a point where it was safe enough to move the family there. So in late March we left by train for Suizhong, spending the night at the small hotel owned by the American, Mr. Sanborn, and found the litters and carts that had come from Lingyuan to fetch us there awaiting our arrival. All the drivers were old friends and seeing them once again made us feel we were already almost home.

We arrived back home in Lingyuan five and a half days later to a very emotional welcome. As a family we'd been gone almost two years, and it seemed as though the whole town had turned out to greet us. There was a welcoming party that met us several miles out. A runner went ahead to alert the folks back at the compound, and many of them were at the city gate to greet us. As we proceeded up the south street, people lined the streets, bowing and waving. When we finally reached the house, a big meal awaited us, and a joyful reunion with friends we had not seen for many months. Included were the two lady missionaries, Harriet Minns and Anna Fischer, who had carried on the work during our absence.

There followed a period of relative peace with the army of occupation behaving themselves in an exemplary manner, and although it was a very hot summer, we enjoyed every minute of it. That fall, on the first of August, we said goodbye to my brother Gilbert, who left for America to find a job. We were all sorry to see him go and missed him greatly. He went first to Kansas City, where he spent a few months, then to Toronto, where he joined the Manufacturers Life Insurance Company, a job he held for the next sixty years.

We took our bicycles back with us to Lingyuan, and at the age of fifteen I felt very grown up, so when I had finished my studies, I frequently rode my bike around town, and soon everyone in town got to know me. Outside the city there were a wealth of places of overwhelming interest to a young lad, and from time to time on my trips out of town my younger sister, Barbara, accompanied me.

In the introduction I wrote about Zhang Lan-fang, ex-actor and soldier who became converted to Christianity and who followed us from Bagou to Lingyuan. After coming to Lingyuan he became a colporteur. That is a word not often heard now, but it describes a person who travels about to sell or publicize the Bible or religious tracts. Zhang, while working under my father's direction, was actually employed by the British and Foreign Bible Society. His year-round job was to go out into the country villages and isolated homes, to distribute Bibles and portions of the Scriptures printed in small booklet form. They were not given away, but were sold for a few coppers each, because to the Chinese, anything that was free was immediately suspect and by definition had to be worthless. Otherwise, why would anyone be giving it away? On the other hand, something purchased, for however small a sum of money, was obviously of some value.

Zhang Lan-fang went everywhere on foot, wearing out countless pairs of shoes during the course of a year. Since he could only carry a limited number of books with him, packages were mailed ahead to strategic spots on his route, so that he frequently stayed away from home for six to eight weeks at a time. A few years earlier his wife had died, leaving him with a small girl whom Mother took care of with the orphan girls. Zhang loved all children, and on every trip, he always managed to bring back something of interest for us youngsters. Usually, they were semi-precious stones of unusual color or markings that he had found in some river or stream he had waded or on one of the mountains he had crossed. By rolling them around against each other in his hand as he walked, he smoothed them into either round or elliptical balls. Balls of that sort were commonly rolled in the hand by artists or writers to keep their fingers supple, and as the men walked around town, they always had a pair of those stone balls in their right hands. Even during Sunday services we could hear the clicking of those balls as their owners turned them around and around. After Zhang's many trips, we had quite a collection of them.

On one of Zhang's trips he had picked up a piece of white shale which he brought me, thinking I would like it. It was about two feet long and some eight or ten inches wide, and I was astonished to find it had the imprint of a large fish skeleton on it, mouth wide open, large eye sockets very prominent, and every single bone in fine detail. Having never seen anything like it before, I thought at first it was a drawing or engraving of some kind that had then been baked somehow in a kiln, but Father told me it was a fossil that was possibly hundreds, if not thousands, of years old. Zhang told me where he had picked it up, and I simply had to go and see the place for myself.

The fossil deposit was about twenty miles northwest of Lingyuan in a narrow valley walled in by high mountains. Although Zhang's directions were easy to follow, the road was hardly suitable for a bicycle, so I found myself walking more than riding. It could be reached only by a small footpath that led first to an isolated little village, and when I finally reached the spot, I found it at first highly disappointing. It looked as though a mountain had turned on its side, and the shale deposit was lying in vertical layers that peeled off readily. But once I made my first find, I became fascinated and spent several hours peeling off layers of stone, finding fossilized fish of many kinds and shapes and various other kinds of aquatic creatures in abundance, more than I could carry with me.

I returned there several more times until I had what I thought was a representative collection, which I then photographed, sending the pictures to the *Illustrated London News*, where they were published. When I received my copy in the mail, I was naturally very gratified and proud. That issue of the pictorial became a most prized possession. But like everything else we owned, it was eventually lost when the Japanese deported us after the outbreak of war in the Pacific in 1941.

When the Japanese army first occupied our area of Jehol Province in 1933, they, too, quickly found that place and "mined" great quantities of those fish fossils, which they framed and sold as souvenirs to visiting Japanese. In fact, they could be found in Japanese gift shops all over Manchuria, and many tons of the raw shale were exported to Japan. To them it was the kind of unique natural art they greatly appreciated, and the area became "off limits" to any but Japanese, so I was never able to go back there.

However, in 1928 Father and I one day went on a hike to the top of Guang Shan, the huge mountain that dominated Lingyuan to the east, mentioned in an earlier chapter. Since the side of the mountain facing the city was a sheer rock surface that only a skilled mountaineer could climb, we had to approach it from the back, where the ascent was more gradual. We rode our bicycles to a point about six miles out, left them in a village, and began our climb to reach the top. It took us several hours, but it was well worth it. The view from the top was magnificent and we could easily make out our own house in the distance because of the distinctive high prison walls almost next door.

While on the mountain top, Father happened to peel off a flat piece of shale, and astonishingly we found the perfect imprint of what looked like a large lobster or crayfish. The mountain peak was well over four thousand feet above sea level, and we wondered if that deposit could date back perhaps to the time of Noah and the great flood. That the area had at one time been subjected to tremendous earthquakes and land upheavals was obvious everywhere because of the jumbled strata of the rocks. That was true not only on that particular mountain, but on all the other mountains nearby, almost every square foot of which Father and I had covered on our Saturday walks.

In another direction from Lingyuan, about fifteen miles to the northeast, some other great disaster had struck in ages past because there was an expanse of petrified logs and stumps of trees, many feet in diameter. The area was quite similar to such places that exist in the United States and elsewhere. It was an eerie place to visit and one could readily visualize what a huge forest it had been at one time.

In still another direction, about 15 miles to the southeast, I found another favorite spot. There, again along a narrow mountain trail where I walked my bike more than I rode it, was a tiny village in a remote valley high in the mountains, completely isolated and otherwise totally inaccessible. Thinking back, in every way it reminded me of the famed Shangrila of movie fame, originally from James Hilton's novel, *Lost Horizon*. That was a movie that I didn't see until many years later. Most of the people I met there had never been out of the village and all told me they had never before seen or met a foreigner. They were curious about me, but friendly and most polite. I was immediately invited into their homes and given tea to drink and later a meal.

That place, much like the mountain pass near the Great Wall that I described earlier in this chapter, was equally unique for that part of China in that the hillsides were heavily covered with trees and brush. I found it hard to believe my eyes the first time I went there. Remote as it was, the people evidently understood the principle of conservation and reforestation, because I saw many newly planted trees everywhere replacing those cut down by the villagers to make charcoal, which they carried out to the city on pack animals over the mountain trail. In fact, I had met a number of them on my way in on that first trip. But there had to be another reason why the brush remained so thick and untouched, and I found out why soon enough.

On my first visit, the village headman thought I would like to see their local temple, of which they were very proud, built as it was on the nearly vertical side of the mountain. He took me there, and on the way told me that I would see something I had never seen before. For such a small village the temple was remarkably large and ornate. There were about fifty lama priests in residence, and they eagerly took me on a tour of the place.

Their proudest possession turned out to be the entire and completely intact skin of a human being, which they said had belonged to a very holy lama who had died some five hundred years before. It was hung in the center of one of the large temple rooms, and although I was unable to get close enough to touch it, it certainly looked like authentically dried human skin. However, on later reflection, I suspected that although originally they unquestionably had such an artifact — if one can call human skin an artifact — that particular exhibit was more likely a replacement made of cloth. In that climate, hot and humid in summer and very cold and dry in winter, openly exposed as it was, it seems extremely doubtful that human skin — even had it been cured like leather, which it was not — could have lasted that long. To the locals, however, it was nonetheless real and greatly revered.

The headman of the village insisted I eat with him, and while waiting for the food to be served, he told me that I was only the second foreigner to have visited their village. I came to the conclusion that the first foreigner must have been my father, who had been there some years before when carrying out famine relief. Later, Father confirmed that.

While the meal was being prepared I noticed the lady of the house was using a peculiar kind of fuel that I had never seen before. It was black and looked like coal, but it burned like no coal I had ever seen. They brought me a piece to examine and demonstrated how it could be readily lit, simply by applying a match to it. The texture was not at all like ordinary coal; it seemed soft and oily to the touch, but it gave off very little smoke, and burned completely to a very fine powder.

They later took me about half a mile down the valley and showed me the source of the fuel. There on the face of the mountain was a vein of the black, coal-like substance, about twelve or fourteen feet thick and extending upward as far as the eye could see. It was apparent that over the years the people had dug into it extensively; there was a deep overhang of rock at ground level, but the vein appeared to have been barely touched, and obviously there were thousands of tons remaining to be mined. With a mattock they showed me how easily one could hack off large pieces with little or no effort. I wondered why the entire mountain had not caught fire long before on its own. There were several other places in Jehol Province where coal mines had been burning for years, having been set afire deliberately by someone

out of spite or having caught fire accidentally.

They told me it was the only fuel they used, and that explained why the brush on the mountain sides was untouched. I asked why they did not mine it in quantity and sell it in Lingyuan, and the answer was that, apart from the narrow foot track over which I had reached the village, there was no other way to get to the place, and without carts, it was not economical to transport any quantity on pack animals, although from time to time they said they did so. On the other hand, charcoal, they told me, was their main source of income, and was a great deal lighter to transport and a much more lucrative product.

When I left, I took a large lump of the stuff with me on the back of my bicycle and showed it to the family when I got home, lighting it with a match to demonstrate how it burned. Father told me it was probably some kind of oil shale, although it did not resemble shale in appearance. I wished then, and many times thereafter, as I saw other remarkable rock formations, that I had had some training in geology.

In the mid 1930s, after the Japanese had taken over the entire area, they used local manpower to hack out a crude track over the mountains to that delightful spot, primarily so that their police vehicles could get in there in search of bandits. However, on the first and only occasion they took a truck in, it overturned and several of the Japanese lost their lives. I think that deterred them from going back in again.

On a subsequent occasion when I went back there around 1936 or so, the headman told me that on no other occasion had he seen any Japanese vehicles, and that was the only time he had seen any Japanese at all. He told me that four of them had been killed in the truck accident, and that was confirmed by the Chinese driver of the truck, whom I knew quite well. He told me the truck had overturned down a steep cliff when the roadway had given way under the weight of the vehicle. When they righted the truck and pulled it back up to the road, he found that all the oil had been drained from the engine, and he had nothing with which to replace it. One of the surviving Japanese told him to get some oil from the villagers, any kind of oil, even cooking oil. He had subsequently filled the engine with the crude lighting oil the villagers used, made from castor oil plants. As a result, they were able to get the truck back to Lingyuan, but the engine bearings were entirely burned out from lack of proper lubrication. I might add that although some of the villagers, from their appearance, very likely were bandits, I saw no proof of it. Each time I returned they treated me as an old and much respected friend.

From the time I was a very young boy, my lifetime ambition was to follow in my Father's footsteps and be a missionary. As I grew older I used every opportunity to carry the Gospel message wherever I went. On each occasion as I visited those villages on my bicycle, I always carried with me portions of the Bible and religious tracts, and preached to the crowds that gathered around me. Rarely did I find a place that Zhang Lan-fang had not visited before me. Wherever I went they told me they knew him and had books they had bought from him. Nevertheless they were still most receptive to what I had to tell them about Christ, and were happy to get the books that I provided.

Another place I had a lot of fun visiting on my Saturday jaunts was a small village almost due north of Lingyuan called *Reshuitang*, or "Hot water springs or baths." It was the midday stopping point on our regular trips to our out-station, Dujiawopu, and was notable for the hot mineral springs from which it took its name. The village lay at the foot of a high mountain range. Just beyond the village the road branched, the main road turning northwest following a small watercourse up into the mountains and over a tortuous pass through rocky defiles that were noted for bandit activity. The right branch went due north and climbed almost straight up the sides of the mountains for about four miles, and was always a challenge to anyone trying to negotiate it. I had been over that road to Dujiawopu on several trips with Father, but in the years that followed I made the trip many times on my bicycle, and still later by car. For the present, though, at age fifteen, my jaunts would stop at the village, where I would eat my lunch and visit the hot springs.

I was never able to learn anything of the history of those springs. Everyone I asked simply told me they had been there for hundreds of years and that the baths had been built by monks from a nearby temple that was now all but abandoned. The village, consisting of the one fairly large inn and a dozen or so houses, hugged the hillside on one side of the valley, which at that point was barely a quarter of a mile wide.

Immediately in front of the village was a narrow branch of the river, with a footbridge leading across to the springs. The springs were spread over a considerably wide area of solid rock a few feet higher than the river bed. In summer weather the entire surface of the rock-pan appeared wet, as everywhere the waters bubbled up through cracks. In winter it was covered by a cloud of steam, with thick ice at the two extreme outside edges. On the far side of the rock-pan was the main river course running up against the mountain wall.

Scattered randomly over the large expanse of flat rock were small huts built entirely of stone, with even the roofs covered with thick rock slabs. Each hut had an open doorway facing south, but no windows. Inside, the huts measured about eight feet long by six wide, and each had a small space where one could stand and remove clothing, and there were even wooden pegs driven into the rock walls on which to hang belongings. The remainder of the space was taken up with a four-foot-deep bath that had been cut into the solid rock, the sides and edges worn to a glass-like smoothness over hundreds of years of use. The baths were particularly impressive because the rock was almost jet black in color, with very little striation showing. There were upward of fifty huts, a few in a tumbled-down state of disrepair. Downstream and off to one side, at a distance of a hundred yards or so, were some ten or more that were reserved for women.

I bathed there at Reshuitang a number of times and always found the baths extraordinarily clean, in contrast to most such places in China. The people who centuries before had so painstakingly chipped out the baths had designed them well; they were so constructed as to be self-cleaning, with fresh hot water coming in from the bottom and the top, then flowing out of a drain at the bottom end. I had been curious about that and on one trip took some soap with me to test out the flow of water.

Many of the huts were occupied — seemingly on a permanent basis — by beggars, male and female, whose livelihood depended on the great number of annual visitors. They were places to keep warm, but where and how they slept, I have no idea. Visitors came from great distances and lodged at the inn, sometimes for weeks at a time, because of the supposedly curative powers of the water, which gave off an almost overpowering sulfuric odor. I had no means of measuring the temperature of the water, but it was so hot that one had to enter it very slowly and carefully. For me, just a few minutes were enough, but many of the people would lie in the water for hours on end. There was no charge for the use of the baths, and what little maintenance they required was carried out by the owners of the inn. There were also several boys and young men who, for a small fee of a few coppers, would locate a hut that was unoccupied and would when requested, bring tea and food from the inn.

After several visits I made a friend of one of the boys. One day he took me to a place that was of extreme interest. On the far side of the valley was a sheer rock cliff. At one point, at the foot, was a long, horizontal rock overhang that extended outward and downward from the rock face to within about two feet of the valley floor. The main river channel passed between that rock face and the springs, and when in spate, the water covered the entire rock-pan, swirling around the huts, and it had obviously undercut that particular rock overhang. As I approached it from a distance, there appeared to be nothing more than a shallow, cavernous-like space carved out underneath the rock wall by the river. However, at a certain point, the young lad who was showing it to me lay face down on the sand, rolled in under the overhang for a few feet and disappeared in the darkness. I followed him in and found myself able to stand up inside. Four feet or so from where we had entered, the roof sloped upward at a very steep angle, as did the floor of the cavern. He scrambled upward over the slippery rock with me in pursuit, and I found myself in a low-roofed cavern extending some twenty or thirty feet into the mountain and about thirty feet in width. The air inside was stuffy and damp. The floor, walls and roof were all of a light cream-colored, clay-like substance that reflected what little light came from the opening through which we had crawled. Once my eyes got used to the dimness inside, it was surprising how much light there actually was.

The young lad reached up on the wall of the cave and grabbed a handful of the clay, molded it into a crude saucer shape, and headed for the entrance, telling me to follow. We slid down the slope, rolled out from under the overhang, and then handed me the dish he had made. To my utter astonishment, it was solid and hard as if it had been baked in a pottery kiln. In those few seconds it had turned from a rubbery-like consistency (very much like "Silly Putty"), to something completely solid. I thought he had somehow pulled a trick on me, and crawled in again and got myself a handful, which I rolled into a ball and brought outside. By the time I stood up, it, too, was as solid as a rock. I have discussed the phenomenon with several different geologists, none of whom had ever seen anything quite like it, but their explanation seemed to make sense. They theorized that the overhanging rock somehow formed a natural air-lock that kept the outside air from the cavern and thus kept the material soft.

Reshuitang is such a small place that it appears on no map that I am aware of. However, it was a place where I visited or passed through many many times. Frequently there were incidents, some humorous, and some dangerous and life-threatening, which I will write of in later chapters.

Reshuitang was one of the first places that attracted the Japanese when they took over the province in 1933. The Japanese are particularly fond of hot springs, and at Reshuitang they built a very large bathhouse and entertainment center upstream from the existing baths, carving out a large and deep pool in the rock, and built a sizable brick structure around it, roofing the whole thing in. They also built a single-lane, gravel-surfaced road to it from Lingyuan that cut the trip from five hours by horse-drawn cart to around thirty minutes by car when the weather was good and the river not running high. In that bathhouse in that remote mountain village, they set up a geisha house that was to be the scene of many wild parties, perhaps the wildest of which occurred on the night preceding Pearl Harbor when, due to an unusual set of circumstances, I found myself in the midst of it and came within a hairsbreadth of losing my life.

"Tian Xia Di Yi Guan" Gate, see page 164.

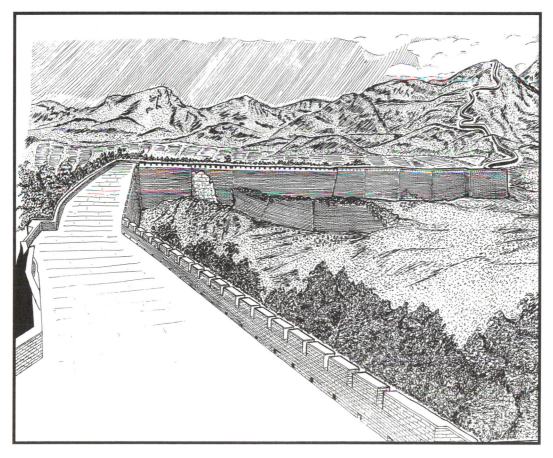

The Great Wall as sketched by Jim Lance.

A portion of the Great Wall seldom photographed.

Where the Great Wall meets the sea.   A bus going through one of the gates
                                              of the Great Wall.

Zhei shan wangzhe nei shan qing.

From this mountain,
that mountain looks greener.

- Chinese Proverb.

Chapter Fifteen
Westerners In China

The winter of 1928, after my brother left for America, passed uneventfully except for the death of a very good boyhood friend of mine, the son of You Bi-chen, our head teacher. His name was You Bin. Although he had been in apparently good health, he, like so many others we knew, had suddenly started coughing and spitting blood. My parents knew at once that he had developed tuberculosis, and in a very short time he faded away. He and I had spent many happy hours playing together over the years, and his death was a tremendous shock to me. One of the experiences we shared together, and which had brought us very close, was an occasion when I had been shooting rats in our grain room with my .22 rifle. I had run into the house for a drink and carelessly left the loaded gun lying on the ground just outside the door. When I came out, You Bin had shown up, and picking up the rifle, he playfully pointed it point-blank at my chest and pulled the trigger. It happened so quickly that I was helpless to stop him, but my guardian angel was watching over me and the bullet misfired. I took the bullet out and looked at it. On the bottom of the casing was the mark where the firing pin had made an indentation, so I turned it around and reinserted it, then, pointing the gun at the ground, I pulled the trigger, and this time the shell fired. Both You Bin and I were very much shaken by the incident and were much more careful with the gun after that. I resumed my shooting of rats, however, and was greatly elated when, with one shot, I managed to kill two rats at the same time. I had aimed at one, and, as I fired, a second rat had run out from behind a storage bin directly into the line of fire.

In the summer of 1929 we again went to Beidaihe, where we stayed in one of the two houses that had been acquired for members of our Jehol missions. One day in mid-July, just before the rains came, I was asked by several of the young women missionaries if I would organize a one-day trip for them from Beidaihe to Chinhuangtao by sampan. I was all for it.

The trip across the bay in a straight line was only about ten miles and for a few Chinese dollars, I hired one of the local fishing boats with three men to spell each other on the large sculling oar on the stern.

The name "sampan" comes from the Chinese name *san ban*, which means "three planks." The boats are usually about twelve to fifteen feet in length with a beam of five or six feet at the widest point, and have a blunt prow and stern, a completely flat bottom, and tapering sides. The "three planks" refers to the flat bottom and the two sides.

It was a gorgeous summer's morning at about 6:30, just after sunrise, when we left. Barbara and a young friend of hers named Doreen, and the three young missionary ladies and myself made a party of six, not counting the three fishermen. There was not sufficient wind to use the sail, so the trip across took about three hours. It was pleasant enough even for the most queasy stomachs once they got used to the oscillating motion of the boat caused by our crossing the swells of the sea at an angle, and to the back-and-forth motion of the big sweep oar at the stern.

Arriving in Chinhuangtao, I gave the fishermen some money for their lunch and told them to wait for us. We then toured the area, shopped, ate a picnic lunch in the shade of the acacia trees, then headed back to the dock shortly after noon for the journey home. However, when we came within sight of the bay, it became apparent that our return trip was going to be very different from what it had been in the morning. A strong wind had risen and was blowing directly in our faces, and the bay was covered with whitecaps with breakers crashing along the beachfront near the harbor entrance.

I knew that someone was definitely going to be seasick, so I suggested that perhaps it would be advisable to pay off the fishermen and return to Beidaihe by train. However, the ladies, after talking it over among themselves, decided that if the fishermen thought it was safe, they were game to make the trip by boat, so off we started.

No sooner had we left the dock than the wind, which had been blowing in our faces, swung to the east, blowing directly onshore, which meant that the waves were coming at a right angle to our line of progress, and we wallowed through every trough and over every crest in a corkscrew motion that was most unsettling. The men tried to use the sail, but with the

flat bottom, we were drifting relentlessly toward the shore instead of holding to a direct line across the bay. After about three miles, all of us were soaked from the spray, and with one of the men kept busy bailing water out of the boat, it became apparent that our trip home was going to be an exceedingly long one.

To add to our problems, the oldest of the ladies, Carrie Brixton, became violently seasick, developing a severe case of diarrhea as well. Carrie was in the front of the sampan, and one of the fishermen pulled out the sail and very considerately used it as a makeshift screen to give her some privacy, but her condition seemed to worsen by the minute, and I decided it was time to abandon the trip and head for shore.

To return to Chinhuangtao would have taken too long, and since we were much closer to the beach, I told the fishermen to head for a point on the shore where the U.S. Marine Corps had a summer camp. From there I knew we would be able to get transportation to the railroad station. However, it was easier said than done. The wind was directly at our backs and we made good time toward the shore, but a strong current deflected us away from the point where I wanted to land. We found ourselves being carried to a deserted strip of shore about a mile south of the camp and on the wrong side of a deep river that ran down into the sea at that point, a river that could only be crossed at very low tide because of its depth and strong currents, and in our case the tide was just beginning to turn. To cross the river any other way meant a long hike upstream to the nearest bridge.

The closer we got to the beach, the more nervous the fishermen became, and one of them told me that it was a bad area, with bandits in the nearby village who had killed two Americans there some months previously. However, we had no other alternative.

When we touched land we were nearly swamped by the huge waves pounding the beach, but hot as the weather was, getting wet was merely refreshing. I hurriedly paid off the fishermen and helped them turn the boat around and push it out into deep water. They were three very frightened men and doubtless happy to see the last of us as they headed home.

With the high tide, the strip of beach was only about twenty feet wide, backed by a high bank of sand, which was topped at that point by a dense stand of poplar trees. I waited until Miss Brixton was made as comfortable as possible, then headed into the trees toward a village that I knew to be about a mile or so inland from that point, hoping to find some sort of transportation for her. I hadn't gone more than fifty feet into the trees when I saw a Chinese standing with his back to me, holding a rifle. In the distance I also saw several other men disappearing through the trees, and I knew immediately that we were in big trouble.

I surmised that the man with the gun was one of the local part-time bandits who had seen our boat heading for shore and was now waiting for his friends to go and get their own weapons before attacking us. He hadn't heard my approach through the trees, so I had the option of turning around and heading back to the beach to make a run for it or bluffing it out with him. I decided on the latter.

I approached him quietly from the rear as he stood watching for his companions. When I was almost touching his back I greeted him in a friendly manner, asking him in the usual Chinese way if he had eaten. Startled, he turned to find me pressing so close to his chest that he hadn't the chance to raise his gun, even if he had wanted to. I pretended not to notice the gun at first, and, as the Chinese do, I asked him what he was doing there. He stuttered for a second or two, then muttered that he was there to "guard the crops." That would have explained the gun, except for the fact that it was almost two months before harvest time and the wrong time of year to be guarding any crops.

I pretended to accept his explanation and asked if there was a village nearby where I could hire a cart, or, failing that, a donkey or mule that could be ridden. I told him that we had a sick person who couldn't walk, then I pulled out a five-dollar bill and asked him if he would be good enough to go to the village and see if he could hire a cart for us.

He turned momentarily and looked behind him, and not seeing any of his friends, he decided to pretend to humor me. Taking the money, he started off in the direction of the village. He kept going in a straight line, looking back every few minutes to see if I was watching. I concealed myself behind one of the trees as best I could and waited to see what he would do. When he next looked back and couldn't see me, he ducked down into a hollow and didn't reappear. I knew then that my suspicions were well founded, and

that he hadn't the slightest intention of going to the village to find a cart. There was only one thing left for us to do.

I raced back to the beach and told the ladies there was no village within sight, that we had better try and walk home along the beach. We would have to leave at once because the afternoon was well along and in another few hours it would be dark. I knew that to head back toward the U.S. Marine camp would be fatal, because the bandits, should they chase us, could easily catch us at the river, which we would be unable to ford or swim because of the falling tide. And they could certainly head us off before we could walk upstream to the nearest bridge.

Fortunately, in the fifteen or twenty minutes that I had been absent, Carrie Brixton had recovered considerably. She was sitting up and was apparently strong enough to walk. I insisted that we leave at once and with the two other ladies supporting her, we started off. They must have thought me most inconsiderate, but my excuse was that we had almost twelve miles to walk, and it would be dark long before we could arrive home.

We started off along the waterline in a tight group, and I managed to fall behind a few paces and to beckon Barbara to my side. I told her the true situation and urged her to get up ahead and set as fast a pace as she could, keeping as close to the water as possible to take advantage of the hard sand. I would deliberately lag behind to distract the bandits should they attack, because I was certain they would follow us. Barbara, although only twelve, appeared quite unconcerned, and with her friend Doreen, she briskly moved ahead, pretending to be casually looking for shells as she went.

I figured we had about fifteen or twenty minutes' head start, because I knew the general location of the village and estimated it would take at least that length of time for the other men to get their weapons. As a precaution, I ripped off a branch from one of the trees and fashioned a crude club. It was not so much for possible protection, but to use as a prop. I held it over my shoulder to give the impression from a distance that I, too, was carrying a rifle, and gradually I fell back until I was about twenty or thirty yards behind the rest of the party.

The ladies up ahead remained completely unaware of what was going on. I kept looking backward, watching behind me until we had covered about two miles, and when no one seemed to be following us, I thought that perhaps I had been mistaken. Suddenly the growth of trees and the sand dunes petered out, replaced by tall sorghum growing almost to the beach line. It was only a few minutes after that that I spotted three men with guns trotting through the sorghum stalks, about half a mile behind us, with the obvious intention of getting in front of us to head us off.

Since we were walking on hard sand we had some slight advantage, but I knew it was going to be close. Then, about half a mile ahead of us and slightly inland, I spotted a Japanese flag flying from a pole and remembered there was a Japanese army summer camp there in an isolated area near the beach. On a previous trip along the beach I had spotted it when we had come across a number of Japanese soldiers bathing in the sea, but that was the closest I had been to it. I feared the Japanese might be unfriendly, but I decided to head there anyway, and take our chances with the Japanese rather than face the certainty of having the bandits catch us on the beach.

I ran up the incline of the beach to the sorghum field. Then, while momentarily hidden from the bandits, I shouted to Barbara and the ladies and beckoned them toward me. I told them there was a village nearby where we might be able to hire donkeys and kept them in line ahead of me, in among the sorghum stalks, to make us less visible to the bandits following. Within a very short time, as I knew we would, we came across a footpath leading inland through the sorghum and in the general direction of the Japanese flag.

Before long we came to the barbed-wire fence enclosing the Japanese camp, but we continued to skirt it. At one point I spotted several Japanese soldiers under some trees. They looked at us with curiosity but didn't interfere, and after a short time we arrived at the village. I asked the first man I met where I could find the village headman. When we found him, he showed not the slightest surprise at seeing me, and in the usual courteous Chinese manner, invited me into his home. After the mandatory pleasantries I told him I needed six donkeys to take us back to Beidaihe, which was about five or six miles from there. He protested that it was getting dark, that no one wanted to go at that time of the evening, that in the dark they would be unable to find their way, et

cetera, and he urged us to stay the night with him. But I wouldn't accept his reluctance, and promised we would pay them well.

He finally agreed to round up six donkeys for us, and when three men finally appeared with them, we mounted and started off through the village. I made certain that none of the three men was carrying any weapons, and, as an added precaution, in case he took it into his head to organize a group to follow us and "hijack" us, I persuaded the village headman to accompany us as well. I needed to do that. He protested, saying he was too old, but I was adamant, and in a friendly manner I flattered him by saying we needed his experience to find the way and to be sure we were on the right track. After about a mile or so I quietly told him that he had been most helpful, and thanking him profusely, gave him something for his trouble and told him he could return to the village now that we were well on our way. He turned back and the three men up front were unaware that he was no longer with us. We had been traveling on small footpaths through high grain for most of the time, but as we got closer to the shore, it became sparse shrubs and tall reeds with a considerable amount of swampy ground. At one point the donkey Barbara was riding got stuck in the mud and needed the efforts of all three men to get it out. Finally, well after dark, in the distance we could see the welcome lights of the houses in Beidaihe. When we reached the first hard-packed road near a promontory known as Eagle Rock, I sighed with relief. We still had some distance to go before reaching our homes, but I had to dismiss the men, since they were not licensed to operate their donkeys at the beach resort and I didn't want them to get into any trouble. I thanked them and paid them off, and they happily went their way.

Up to that point, although I'm sure the ladies were puzzled by my unusually peremptory manner, they had looked upon the whole jaunt as a lot of fun. I hated to disillusion them, but standing there in the dark I told them of our near run-in with the bandits. One of the young ladies said: "I'm glad I didn't know anything about it, for I'm sure I wouldn't have been able to walk another step for fear."

All in all that was a busy summer for me at Beidaihe. For a number of years my parents had given me a subscription to a British monthly for boys called *The Boys' Own Paper*. I've never seen anything quite like it in the United States, and don't know if it is still published in England. However, it was a wonderful source of information on every possible subject for boys.

Among other things, each issue had detailed instructions and pictures on how to build something or other. One of the articles told how to build a ten-foot canvas kayak. That was something I wanted badly. I worked every spare moment over a period of several weeks and finally had a boat of my own. Some years earlier Father had found a local carpenter and had him build a small rowboat, but it was a complete failure. It floated, but was too heavy and quite impossible to row. But my kayak was an instant success. Unable to obtain canvas, I improvised by substituting coarse Chinese cotton cloth, which I stretched over the frame and oiled heavily with linseed oil to waterproof it, and, when that was dry, I painted it bright red. The boat only drew a couple of inches of water, and in it I could skim over the water at what I felt to be a breakneck pace. Unfortunately, it only seated one person. Envious as all the other boys were of me, I was unable to take any of them for a ride and was reluctant to let them use it. A couple of years later the magazine came out with a revised version of the boat: a sixteen-footer that would seat two, and I promptly built one of those, painting that one white with a blue deck. By that time I was very girl-conscious and managed to impress a number of them by taking them out on rides — thrilling them, or so I hoped.

Each year that we were at the beach, different talented individuals would organize some constructive activity for the young people, both boys and girls, and I got involved in as many of those as I could find time for. Among other things there was a choral society, where we learned to sing in harmony. Mother had taught us all to read music, and for years we had stood around the organ at home singing hymns and songs of the period, but I hadn't learned any particular part. By that time, however, my voice had changed, and in the choral group, the director found I had a moderately good bass voice, which is what I have sung ever since. Over the weeks, we practiced two or three times a week, and at the end of the season gave a public performance where we sang several numbers, including the Hallelujah Chorus. I thoroughly enjoyed the whole thing. One thing I enjoyed

most of all was that on the way to practice I had to pass the tent of Dr. Robson, the doctor who 15 years before had been at Mother's bedside when I was born. His wife had died some years earlier, and he had brought up their only daughter who was then around eighteen. I thought it most glamorous that they lived in a tent, and Molly Robson was a very beautiful girl. Each time I went by I hoped to catch a glimpse of her, but that was as far as it went. I hadn't the courage to speak to her.

Another class I joined was star-gazing and I learned a lot about the various stars and planets. But the activity I enjoyed most was a course in life-saving. When I graduated from the life-saving course I was given a certificate and a patch to wear on my swimming trunks and was then assigned daily duty as the lifeguard at what we called East Cliff Beach. The beach was immediately in front of our house, and about five minutes' walk down the hill. Because of the sloping land, the beach was clearly in sight from our house.

It was a relatively small and curving stretch of beach, bounded at each end by a rocky promontory stretching out into the sea, the two points being about a third of a mile apart. A few Chinese fishermen used the beach and kept their boats up on the beach at the south end, but the middle portion was reserved exclusively for swimming. The beach was covered with a very fine sand, and sloped gradually down into the water, so that one could walk out a fair distance, even at high tide, before it dropped off into deep water. Along the beach stood numerous temporary sheds, built with thin wooden poles and the ubiquitous *kang xi*, or sorghum-stalk mats. Some were used simply for shade, while others were used for changing clothes and were equipped with doors.

About four or five hundred yards offshore, in quite deep water, a diving raft was anchored. It had been a gift from a wonderful old gentleman, Mr. Baldwin, a near neighbor of ours. A retired businessman, Mr. Baldwin was (we felt) quite elderly and something of a recluse. He had a Chinese wife, lived the year-round in a very large house with a high stone wall around it, and had a large number of servants. He was rarely seen outside except when he went for an occasional ride in his private and quite luxurious black-lacquered rickshaw with a liveried puller, or when he went fishing in his Western-style motor boat with an inboard engine — the only one of its kind in the entire area.

I am unable to recall ever seeing Mr. Baldwin swimming at the beach or using the raft he so generously provided, but his annual maintenance and launching of the raft was very much appreciated by everyone. Only one or two of the other beaches had a raft, and none so well constructed as ours. It measured approximately ten feet wide by twelve to fourteen feet long, was very solidly constructed with a sturdy wooden frame, covered with wooden slats, and was mounted on about a dozen empty fifty-five-gallon oil drums. At one end stood a diving tower, about six or eight feet high, and at the other, a diving board covered with sacking. About fifteen or twenty people could use the raft simultaneously, and during swimming hours it was a very busy place.

My job was to watch the swimmers from around nine in the morning until noon. Most people swam during that period, and on sunny days there would be as many as two or three hundred people there. The beach was not segregated, and quite a few Chinese went down to swim as well: most of them wealthy and with their own Western-style houses in the area. Promptly at noon, everyone went home to lunch, and I was off duty. I guess we were all pretty well regimented in our behavior. In the early afternoons, the beach was used by the many Chinese servants in the area while their employers took afternoon naps. However, very few of the servants were swimmers, and rarely did I see any one of them out on the raft.

No lifeguard's tower was provided for me. My primary job was to patrol the area around the raft to ensure there was no horseplay among the young people that might endanger themselves or others, and to keep an eye on the swimmers going back and forth from shore. Most of the time I spent in the water, although at times I patrolled in my kayak. From time to time people overestimated their swimming abilities and got into trouble. That was particularly true on days when the water was rough, as happened quite frequently, and when the undertow was strong. I remember one such day quite vividly.

I was swimming near the raft when a middle-aged gentleman beckoned me over to him, and in a very conspiratorial manner, leaned down from the raft and in a whisper asked me to discreetly follow his wife as she swam back to shore. He told me she wasn't a strong swimmer and might not make it. I kept an eye on them, and when both dived off the raft and headed for shore, I followed a few yards behind.

To my surprise, the wife turned out to be a very strong swimmer, and she quickly forged ahead, leaving her husband behind. Still, fearing that it might be just a burst of speed, and that she might falter, I followed her closely, passing the husband, who never said a word to me as I went by. A few minutes later when she safely reached the shore, I turned to look for the husband and discovered he had disappeared. It turned out that it was actually he who was the poor swimmer, but he had been too embarrassed to tell me and it had very nearly cost him his life. He had become exhausted, and without any outcry at all had gone under. I knew the general area in which I had last seen him, and after diving repeatedly, I located him and pulled him to shore. After working on him for some minutes, I managed to pump all the water out of him, and he regained consciousness. When he confessed the truth, he was a very embarrassed man.

My job as lifeguard was unpaid, but I still took it very seriously and never left the beach until everyone else had done so, but it was rare for anyone to dawdle much past twelve o'clock. One day, however, a few minutes after twelve, I was already on my way back up the hill heading for home when, on a nearby path, I saw a young Caucasian girl in her swimsuit heading for the beach, obviously intending to swim. I recall feeling some annoyance that she didn't swim when everyone else did, but much as I wanted my lunch, I felt that duty called for me to keep an eye on her, and so I did.

I had never seen her before, but that was not unusual since foreigners were there from all over North China, and many came only for a week or two. She had to have noticed me, but she completely ignored my presence and without any hesitation, dived into the ocean and promptly swam out to the raft, with me in pursuit. I need not have had any concern for her safety, because she was obviously a strong swimmer. However, it was one of those windy days when the water was quite rough, so I hung around the raft as she dived and swam, then dived and swam some more. Finally, in the same businesslike manner, she returned to the beach and headed off toward wherever it was that she lived, all the time without giving me even a glance. She appeared to me to be a very sophisticated young woman, undoubtedly several years older than I, although in fact, as it later turned out, she was actually a year younger.

To my increasing annoyance, the same thing happened on three successive days, Thursday, Friday and Saturday. Even Mother became annoyed at my repeatedly late arrivals home for lunch. Sunday was my day off, and as far as I was concerned, people swam at their own risk on that day, although after church, we always went down for a quick dip before lunch. But that particular Sunday the mystery of the young lady was solved.

As was the case with most of the houses at Beidaihe, we had quite a large semi-enclosed porch, where we spent a good part of our daytime hours, particularly on rainy days; some even slept out there at night. On Sundays, though, we brought out all the chairs we could muster, and Father conducted church services there in English, for twenty or thirty people from the immediate neighborhood. That Sunday, during the singing of the second or third hymn, I saw my mysterious young lady raise the bamboo screen that covered the entrance and quietly slip in and take a seat.

After the service, my older sister, Ruth, got acquainted with her, and although I don't remember actually speaking to her, I learned all I needed to know about her. Evangeline Elsje Kok was staying only three or four houses from us. It also turned out that she swam so late in the morning because she had a temporary summer job as tutor for the young son of a colonel in the U.S. Marine Corps, Colonel (later General, and Commandant) Holcomb. The young lad had been seriously ill with polio, I believe, and had lost a lot of time at school in Peking, where his father was stationed in charge of the U.S. Marine detachment at the American Legation, or Embassy. Evangeline, whose father was First Chancellor of the Netherlands Legation, became known to the colonel who, impressed with her achievements in school, had invited her to Beidaihe for the summer to tutor his son and thus help the boy keep up. Evangeline was very conscientious and kept the boy at his studies all morning right up to twelve o'clock, hence her late swimming habits.

Throughout the rest of the summer I saw Evangeline again on numerous occasions. She frequently visited our home and became good friends with Ruth, but other than casually greeting her, I had little further interest in her because I thought she was much older than I was, and from then on I didn't bother to continue watching over her at the beach. It was two years after that before I saw her once again under quite different circumstances.

I never could get enough of the water at Beidaihe, and swam as often as I could. Before sunup every morning I went down for a quick dip, and rain or shine, I swam at least twice a day, frequently in the evening as well, before or after dark. On the morning swims, I often ran into a group of White Russians who apparently lived somewhere in the neighborhood. There was quite a large community of White Russians living in an area on the far side of the railroad station but it was unusual to see them in our area. Perhaps the group were just renting a place there that particular summer. There were three or four women and two men, together with several children. The women usually swam topless, and sometimes totally nude. That behavior shocked the rather prudish Chinese, who frequently talked about it among themselves and to our servants. When Chinese women went into the water they were dressed completely in their usual daily garb.

Western women in general had never been thought of very highly by the Chinese, and they were frequently heard speaking disparagingly about them. That was partly due to the European style of low-necked dresses and knee-length skirts that showed of a lot of leg. To the Chinese of that era, the hollow at the base of a woman's throat was the sexiest part of her, and next was the leg. To show either of those parts was considered very vulgar.

With the behavior of the White Russians, who were noted for their freedom on the beach, and the scandalous activities of many of the other Western women there, the attitude of the local Chinese toward Western women in general was one of utter contempt. They thought of them as being little better than prostitutes, giving them the name *ye ji*, which meant pheasants, but was a euphemism for prostitutes.

Not all Western women merited the criticism by the Chinese. Most of them lived normal lives and were most circumspect. However, enough of them misbehaved to give all Western woman a bad name. Our servants told me many stories that they had heard from servants of nearby houses: stories of drunken orgies, wife swapping, and blatant nudity around the house by their employers. It frequently made me feel ashamed to be a Westerner, and I had no way of making any excuses for the women's actions. That most of those stories were true I have no doubt, because of a number of incidents that I personally witnessed.

It was commonly known that many of the Western business people and visitors looked upon the Chinese as non-persons, i.e., as if they just did not exist, and cared nothing for what the Chinese might think about them. On one occasion I went into a Chinese tailor's shop at Rocky Point at the beach to pick up a suit being made for me, and I found a young Western woman standing there completely nude while the tailor measured her for a bathing suit. The front door was wide open, and she was in full view of a small crowd standing outside on the street. I had noticed them looking in, but I had no idea what they were looking at until I entered the place. On another occasion I entered another tailor's shop and found an older Western woman in the nude being measured for some underwear. I later asked both tailors if that was a common happening, and both told me that most of the Western women who patronized their shops thought nothing of stripping to the buff to be measured. In the case of the two I saw, neither seemed in any way embarrassed by my presence.

That year, for some reason, seemed to be the year for nudity at the beach. The two houses we lived in were in a row of four on our little street, which actually was like a little island, with a field of sorghum in front and a field of corn behind. Both of our houses were two-story buildings: the ones on either side were single-story. The house on our far right belonged to another mission group, and was occupied each year by missionaries. But the one on the left-hand end was owned by some businessman in Tientsin who rented it out each summer. Every year there were different tenants, some renting for just a few weeks at a time. Frequently during the course of a summer there would be a succession of different tenants, from either Peking or Tientsin, and often from as far away as Shanghai and Nanking.

That year the house was occupied for a two-week period by two youngish German women, both blonde, extremely well endowed, and avid nudists. Their house was less than thirty feet from ours, with a porch on the front side and also on the side facing us.

From morning to night, the two women gamboled on the two porches entirely in the nude, without the slightest pretense of modesty or concealment, fully aware that they could be seen not only from our front porch and side windows, but from the street as well. The two women might as well have been living in a world all by themselves for all they cared about being seen.

They were not alone in giving foreign women a bad name. A few years before that, while we were up in Lingyuan, a widely known and highly respected American woman journalist paid a visit to Chengde, the capital city of Jehol. The English-language newspapers carried stories about her trip and highlighted the fact that she was, supposedly, the first white woman to venture into the wilds of Jehol Province. To give her credit, she traveled the hard way (and the only way possible at the time), in the highly uncomfortable small Peking cart, but she was accompanied by two larger carts, carrying her cook, her No. 1 houseboy and a coolie, together with a mass of paraphernalia to make her trip more comfortable.

As I recall, she spent around two weeks on the trip, taking five days to get to Chengde, and the word quickly spread throughout the province about the wild doings of that foreign woman. She was the subject of conversation for months, and even years, thereafter. I did not actually see her, so I won't name her, but from dozens of individuals I had reports of her shameless behavior, and the details were so similar in detail that I haven't the slightest doubt that it happened just as I was told.

She stopped each night at one of the regular inns, but instead of spending her nights inside the buildings, she had a tent set up for herself in the yard, with a folding cot and mosquito netting to keep away flies and bugs. She had a kerosene-fueled cookstove on which her cook prepared her meals; those she ate at a small folding table set up outdoors, but all that was the least of it. What stirred up the people was her daily bath in public. As soon as she arrived at the inn each evening, her coolie dragged out her tin bathtub and set it down in the yard. After heating water, he filled the tub, and she took her bath in full view of the crowd of villagers who had gathered to watch, seemingly totally oblivious to their presence. I was told that such a large crowd gathered each day, that the yard was not only full, but even the roofs of the surrounding buildings were covered with people, and I can believe it. She also carried with her a portable commode, which she used out in the open, to the astonishment of the onlookers. When she reached Chengde, she stayed with missionary friends of ours and was the epitome of propriety. But for years thereafter her scandalous behavior was talked about throughout the province, and everywhere I went, much to my embarrassment, I was often asked if that kind of conduct was common to Western women, because, to the Chinese, such displays of nudity by a woman were inconceivable. Their own prostitutes, lowest of the low, were despite their heavily made-up faces, almost always demure and chastely dressed when out in public, and they wouldn't dream of showing any flesh.

I recall an incident around 1930 when I was making one of my regular trips by bicycle to Dujiawopu. I had reached a point approaching bandit territory, and in one of the small villages I saw an old man sitting in the shade of a tree and decided to stop and chat with him. I parked my bike and sat down on a rock near him, and addressing him as honorable grandfather, I asked him if he had eaten, and his surname and age, and what family he had. When the pleasantries were over, I asked him if there was news of any bandits in the area, using the euphemism "bad persons." The old gentleman misunderstood me and thought I was asking if there were any prostitutes in the village. After a little thought, he told me there weren't any, but that if I needed a woman badly he would ask around among the young women of the village to see if one of them would oblige me. I hastened to tell him that that wasn't my meaning at all, and that I was referring to bandits.

By that time several other Chinese men had joined us, and after I'd been assured that the road was perfectly safe, the old question of differences between Westerners and Chinese came up. They first made some comparisons about me, then spoke of the woman journalist I mentioned above, and I heard the whole story once again. But at least her actions had cleared up some of the misconceptions the Chinese had about Western women, and they no longer asked me if our women were built the same as theirs and conceived children in the same manner. In that case, one man who claimed to have seen the journalist told the group in considerable detail that she was exactly like a Chinese woman in every respect except that she was white.

One of the men there turned out to have been a coolie on the Western Front in World War I, when thousands of Chinese coolies had been taken by the allies to France to work behind the lines. He was obviously something of a celebrity in the village, and everyone listened when he spoke. In all probability while in France he had not seen a single Frenchwoman, so when he started elaborating on the extraordinary physical features of French women, such as their having three breasts and other extraordinary physical characteristics, I had to step in and enlighten them all. He didn't take it well, though, and started another story about a fictitious country he claimed to have visited where all the inhabitants looked, he said, exactly like me. Each was said to have two arms and two legs, and a head, but the difference, he claimed, was that they were unable to use their legs to walk. He elaborated by saying that each individual had a hole extending from front to back through the middle of their bodies, the size of a grapefruit. When they went anywhere, two other people had to carry them by using a pole thrust through the hole in their middle, and then hoisting the pole onto their shoulders. The several peasants sitting around listened in awe to the story, accepting it as gospel truth until I asked the man if everyone in that country had been exactly the same. He said they were. I then asked if each of them had to be carried in the same way everywhere they went, and he got in deeper and deeper by replying in the affirmative. I then drew a picture in the dust on the ground showing the first person being carried on a pole by two others, then the two carriers of the first person in turn being carried by two additional people, and so on, making a pyramid, and within seconds the entire group broke up into uproarious laughter at the obvious fallacy of the story, and the poor storyteller lost a lot of face.

Bob and his kayak.

Bob, about the age when he first saw
Eva.

Enjoying the beach at Beidaihe.

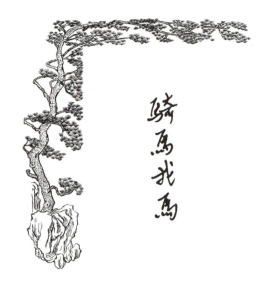

Qi ma zhao ma.

Riding one's horse
while searching for it.

- Chinese Saying.

(Said of someone who is absent-
minded, e.g., looking for one's
spectacles while wearing them.
Modern China usage: Holding onto a
job while looking for a better one.)

Chapter Sixteen
Living Among Bandits

Bandits have plagued China for as far back as any-one can remember. Almost every book written about China mentions them, and this one will be no exception. During the forty-year period between 1900 and 1941, there were a number of incidents reported in the international press where Westerners had been captured and killed by Chinese bandits, or were held over long periods for ransom. Notorious among those bandits was the well-publicized chieftain who called himself White Wolf. With his thousands of followers he terrorized a fair-sized portion of North China for several years until he was killed in 1914. Also there was the holdup of the famous *Blue Express* train between Peking and Shanghai sometime around 1923. A number of Europeans, including some Americans, were captured and held for ransom. It at once became an international incident. Among random killings of Westerners elsewhere, there was the infamous murder of the Rev. John W. Vinson in the fall of 1931 in North Jiangsu, followed two and a half

years later by the tragic slaying of a young American missionary couple, John and Betty Stam, of the China Inland Mission in a little town in Anhui Province. There was also the case of Father Gerard A. Donovan, a Maryknoll missioner who was slain by bandits in Manchuria in 1938, as well as other isolated incidents over the years.

Almost everyone who lived in any part of China outside the large coastal cities in those days had some kind of hair-raising story to tell of narrow escapes from bandits. But in my case, in thirty years there, during which I more or less "rubbed shoulders" with them on a day-to-day basis every time we traveled anywhere, I never really felt in danger of being captured by them.

Very early I lost count of the number of contacts we had with bandits. A number of them I got to know personally, on occasion even eating in their homes, although at the time I didn't know they were bandits. But all of those meetings were friendly and characterized by what — for want of a better expression — could be called an attitude of mutual respect.

It was not that I in any way respected them as individuals or for their way of life. Far from it. Our respect for them was more in deference to the fact that, armed with guns as they were and almost a part of the scenery, we had to accept their ubiquitous presence and cautiously "live" with them every time we went on the road. Their respect for us was due to the fact that we were classified as *shanren*, or "doers of good," and healers of the sick. It was widely known among them that we would cure their sick and tend to their wounded without asking any questions, and for those reasons we were able to travel widely with little fear of harm if we happened to meet up with them. Of course, we never deliberately sought an encounter, just in case they happened to be a group who didn't know us. If we knew of their whereabouts, we tried to avoid them, lest we come on them unawares and frighten them into taking action against us unintentionally.

From babyhood I grew up hearing about bandits and the atrocities they committed. The Chinese had numerous names for them; among them *hong huzi*, or "red beards" (where and how that name originated I have never been able to find out, but it is often credited to Russian invaders from the north). Then there were the names *tufei*, "earth bandits," *qiangdao*, "strong-arm bandits," and the most feared type, the *bang piaode*, or "kidnappers," literally meaning "tie up for ticket." There was a constant running battle between bandits of all kinds and the local authorities. From the time I was a very young child, and then over the years afterward, I saw numerous unlucky losers being taken past our front gate as prisoners to be shot, if their bribe had been large enough, or beheaded if not.

To this day I still have vivid recollections of those condemned men so frequently being transported past our front gate. Always they were seated in an open cart, tightly bound and shackled, police squatting around them in the cart, and often because of their fear, having to support them and hold them upright, and each of them with a stick shoved down inside the backs of their neck collars, carrying a placard proclaiming their names and crimes.

As our house was almost next door to the Yamen and the prison, we were always among the first to know when an execution was about to take place. I wasn't supposed to go down to the front gate to *kan renao*, "to see the excitement," as the Chinese expressed it, but the temptation was too great and I invariably did so. Although I knew of the terrible crimes they were alleged to have committed, it was always with a deep feeling of horror and pity that I watched those terror-stricken wretches pass by just a few feet away from me.

It was their eyes that I still cannot forget. Some would look at me unseeingly; in other cases there would be a sudden flash of interest as for the first time the man saw a small foreign boy standing there watching. Some would even involuntarily turn their heads to look back at me, and as I looked at their trembling chins and ashen faces, it was always the eyes that I noticed most. Each of those individuals, although at that moment still a living and breathing human being, was to me already a dead man, and looking like one.

Public executions were a very popular spectacle with the Chinese, who felt that the death of those men was well deserved. Large crowds of people would gather outside the Yamen to watch as the condemned were brought out and placed into carts, then follow the procession as it moved toward the execution ground outside the south gate. The procession would form with a squad of police at the front, then behind them came the executioner with his huge six-inch-wide sword on his back. He was followed by the carts with the prisoners, sometimes two or three men in one cart, and on some occasions when there was a mass execution, there might be several carts. More police walked alongside the carts to deter any possible attempts at rescue, and finally there was always a mob of people surrounding them.

In an earlier chapter I wrote of the dead in China always being carried out through the west gate; so it was with the executions. Because the men were already considered to be dead, the procession always started out past our front door toward the west gate. In most cases it would proceed only as far as just across the stone bridge to the west of us. There it would turn south down a narrow street alongside the watercourse, then through back streets toward the south gate. Just outside that gate by the river, there was a large open space that could readily accommodate thousands of people, and by the time the procession reached there, hundreds of people would be in place, having traveled there by a more direct route.

In certain cases, where the condemned man was a notorious bandit with a large following, the police feared there might be an attempt by fellow gang members to try and effect a rescue at the regular execution ground, so they would announce that the execution was to take place there, but instead they would simply take their prisoners directly through the west gate and carry out the execution at the first open space they came to. I even remember occasions when for the same reason the executions were carried out directly in front of the Yamen or sometimes inside the prison itself, and more than once just outside our back garden wall.

Although it was the usual practice to execute bandits as soon as possible after capture and trial, there were exceptions. Many of those I saw on their way to the execution ground had been in prison for months. They were unshaven, their hair unkempt, matted and sometimes down to their shoulders, while their clothing was filthy. Some would be in a state of total shock — slumped down with their heads on their chests and unable to sit up, being held erect by the police around them. Others were weeping and offering bribes to the police to let them go free. However, the majority were quite arrogant to the last minute, cursing the crowds who pressed close and milled around them, and vilifying the police and the magistrate.

From the Chinese point of view the executions were carried out humanely, and although the men had usually been subjected to torture during their trial, and often showed signs of it, they were treated fairly well during their last moments. Generally the police would ignore their outbursts and let them have their say, but on more than one occasion I saw men who were too vociferous and vindictive, so the police had gagged them by tying a chopstick between their jaws.

When the procession followed its usual route, it was standard procedure to stop near the south gate in front of a large wine distillery, where the owners would give the victim all the wine he could drink. It was something like the last meal given to condemned prisoners in the United States, and most took advantage of the free liquor, which was always the most potent that could be had. On the part of the distillery owners, it was considered a humanitarian act that would bring them much merit, and it usually resulted in the prisoners arriving at the execution ground in such a befuddled and drunken state that at the last moment they were hardly aware of what was happening to them.

I was never allowed to follow the processions, nor had I any inclination to do so, but many of our near neighbors would go and witness the final moments of the bandits and come back with gruesome and detailed stories of blood spurting high into the air, and how, when the head was lopped off, the man's jaws would crush the small rocks onto which the head fell, and would tell of muscular reflexes that would cause the body to leap into the air in some cases, just like a chicken when its head is cut off.

Decapitation was the usual method, because it was considered much more degrading than shooting. Our local executioner was widely known for his skill in taking the head off with one stroke. However, to the Chinese, who are strong believers in the afterlife, going to the nether world without a head is a monumental catastrophe, so in many cases, relatives (if he had any) of the dying man would pay the executioner to avoid complete severance of the head, leaving it slightly attached so that afterward it could be sewn back on before burial.

Another gruesome detail I was frequently told about was a custom carried out by the executioners themselves when the victim was a bandit renowned for his great daring and bravery. The Chinese word for bravery is *dan*, and the same character is the word for "gall." There is a belief among the Chinese that the gall bladder is the seat of bravery in a man, so it often happened that after the prisoner was either beheaded or shot, the executioner would cut open the body, remove the gall bladder, and drink the gall, so that some of the bravery of the deceased would be passed on to him. That often made me wonder if the origin of our own expression that someone "has a lot of gall," while not exactly meaning bravery, but impudence or effrontery, might have originated in China.

Of course, executions were not limited to bandits. The Chinese had the death penalty for a number of different crimes, and sometimes an individual was condemned to death simply on the whim of a presiding magistrate. When caught, murderers were almost always executed, and occasionally one would be a woman who in a fit of rage had killed her husband.

Such executions always drew the largest crowds. The greatest crime was when a woman had killed her husband because she had taken a lover. In those cases the punishment for the woman — still quite common when I was a boy — was "death by a thousand knives" (*qian dao sha*). The victim was tied naked to an upright post and the executioner would endeavor to kill her by degrees, keeping her conscious as long as possible by slicing away small portions of her body in non-vital spots as each stroke of his sword was counted aloud, and the goal was one thousand slices.

That method of punishment was officially done away with by the Chinese government after the 1911 revolution, but occasional incidents of its use persisted in remote areas, including where we lived.

In 1931 the League of Nations ordered an investigation into the Japanese takeover of Manchuria and various atrocities in China, and dispatched a commission led by the British statesman Lord Lytton to examine the situation. I happened to be in Tientsin when Lord Lytton passed through, and I met the group at their hotel. When Lord Lytton learned that I was China-born, he asked me if I had ever witnessed such a killing as the "death by a thousand knives" or had ever heard of such killings. I told him of incidents that had occurred in our area, and he asked me if it were at all possible to secure photographs of such an execution. I told him I would do my best, and for two days I searched every photography studio in the native city of Tientsin, an area that very few foreigners dared enter. After I visited about twenty such shops, one man reluctantly produced a set of pictures and sold them to me. I passed them on to Lord Lytton, and they are probably in some government archives in London to the present day. Never have I seen anything so grotesque or bestial as those thirty or forty pictures of a young woman being hacked to pieces bit by bit, and although I have consciously tried to forget them, the details are still vivid in my mind. Fortunately for the young woman concerned, it was obvious from the pictures that, after the first ten or fifteen cuts, she had lapsed into unconsciousness, although cold water was constantly thrown over her in an attempt to revive her.

As I've mentioned before, in Chinese law courts a prisoner had to confess before the magistrate could pronounce a judgment on him, and since most prisoners were reluctant to admit to a crime, torture was the accepted practice. Since the forms of torture were so many and varied, few individuals could hold out without confessing, so there was often doubt as to whether the condemned person was the actual perpetrator. That was particularly true in cases of murder, where quite often witnesses were simply carrying out a grudge against an enemy.

As a boy, I talked frequently with old-timers in Lingyuan who had been eyewitnesses to a case that had occurred a year or two before I was born, but which was still very fresh in their memories. A young woman had been accused of murdering her husband in a particularly brutal manner, reputedly because she had taken a lover. She was tried, but persisted in proclaiming her innocence despite torture, and many believed her. However, ultimately she was forced to confess to the crime and was condemned to death by the "thousand knives" method.

It was a very hot day in mid-July when she was taken out to the execution ground and tied naked to an upright post. A heavy summer storm was coming in over the mountains, which all present took to be an omen that the gods were also showing their anger, and the executioner was in a hurry to get it over with before everyone got wet. However, just as he was about to make the first slice, instead of the expected downpour of rain, it began to snow heavily. That phenomenon convinced the magistrate and everyone else present that the gods were telling them that the woman was indeed innocent of the crime. She was thereupon untied from the post, but imprisoned while the case was further examined. Subsequently, the real murderer was found to be the man who had been her chief accuser. He knew of her adultery with another man, had wanted her for himself, but she rejected him. To punish her he had killed her husband and thrown the blame on her, knowing she would be the chief suspect.

After that "divine" intervention, the magistrate decided that the woman had been punished enough and her acknowledged adultery was overlooked. She continued to live in Lingyuan and became a well-known figure. I know the story seems fanciful, but I heard it from so many different sources, always with the same details, and the several oldsters I talked with who claimed to have been eyewitnesses were so convincing that I have no reason to believe the story was untrue. The Chinese are very well aware of the difference between hail and snow, and I would ask if it conceivably could have been a hail storm, but all made a very clear distinction in the term they used. It was definitely snow and not hail. I have told the story to several American and British meteorologists, some of whom pooh-poohed the whole thing, but others conceded that, given the right atmospheric conditions, such a phenomenon could indeed occur. Having seen so many unusual things in China, I personally have no doubt but that it happened just as I have reported.

Military executions of deserters were equally common in the days of the warlords. Those, too, were always witnessed by large crowds, but were not always so popularly accepted. The Chinese well knew that soldiers were not always in the army by choice and that many had been forcibly drafted against their will, so it was not surprising that desertions were extremely common, and usually the deserter had the sympathy of the common man. However, when caught, as they most often were, the man was always shot or beheaded as an example to the other men. On each occasion, the entire garrison would be marched out to witness the event. I recall several instances where, in one or two of the more well-disciplined armies, such as that of the Christian general, Feng Yu-hsiang, some of his men were shot for stealing from civilians, for rape, and for even lesser crimes. Another general whose troops were neither well-disciplined nor well-paid became notorious for his harshness in dealing with the many deserters. It was his practice to execute the men when they were caught by feeding them alive, inch by inch, under the blade of a straw-cutting knife. Those knives are about six inches wide by approximately four feet in length, and are fastened with a large pin at the tip to a heavy five-foot-long wooden block with a deep slot down the length of it, and a strip of metal on each side of the slot, with small upright pins every few inches to prevent the straw from sliding away under the pressure of the knife as it is being cut. When cutting straw for animal feed, two men operate the knife. One man stands, and using both hands, raises the knife, while the second man, sitting alongside the knife, feeds the straw in six-inch-thick bundles, under the knife blade inch by inch as the first man cuts it. The knife is in principle much like the paper-cutting shear on the side of a board, with which most Americans are familiar. When used to chop up a human being, two men were needed on the handle of the knife, and two to feed the victim under the blade, the man, of course, being alive and conscious.

After several such executions, desertions from that particular army fell off noticeably, but one day word was spread around town that three men had deserted, and the hunt was on for them. Before the day was out they had been captured, and their execution was set for the following morning. However, the case stirred up quite a controversy because the three so-called men were only boys. The oldest was nineteen, and he alone had carried a weapon when they ran away. The other two were seventeen and sixteen, respectively.

The Chinese are normally quite indifferent when it comes to a question of someone else's life and death, but in that case the whole town of Lingyuan was literally in an uproar when the ages of the three became known. Because the general was not greatly liked or respected, crowds formed at the Yamen demanding that the magistrate intercede with him for the boys' lives. The magistrate paid a courtesy visit to the general but was rebuffed, and lost a lot of face, so he came to see my father to ask if he would go and see the general. Father agreed and took me with him. The general, a ruffianly type, was nevertheless very polite and received us most courteously, but when the subject of the boys' youth came up, and my father requested that he reconsider his decision to have them executed, he merely smiled and said: "I'll think it over," (*wo kaolu kaolu*). He then added that it was his opinion that the three must die as an example to their fellow soldiers, but with a smile he added that since they were so young, they deserved a more humane execution than the "straw-knife," so they would be shot. And with that we had to be satisfied.

The next morning before daybreak a tremendous crowd had gathered in front of the garrison headquarters. The small hill just outside the West Gate was the site where the executions were to be carried out, and by sunrise almost the entire garrison had been marched out there, not only to witness the execution, but also to prevent any attempt at rescue on the part of the populace. The troops were followed by crowds of people surging past our front gate for two or three hours, all in a very angry mood.

I was about eleven at the time, and the imminent death of those three boys not much older than I was affected me very deeply. Nearly in tears and feeling greatly depressed, I went out to our back garden and climbed high up in our favorite date tree, overlooking the open countryside, just to be able to get away from it all, but I could still hear the buzz of the crowds passing in the street out front.

Suddenly I was astonished to see a small group of six or seven soldiers passing on the road below me heading west escorting a one-horse cart carrying a coffin. Just one coffin, not three. It was just too much of a coincidence, and the conclusion was obvious. With tremendous relief and excitement I rushed back to the front gate to tell everyone the news that the general had relented and that only one man was to be shot.

But my joy was to be short lived. Before long we heard trumpets and saw a column of troops approaching from the other side of the Yamen with literally hundreds of civilians surrounding them. In the middle was a cart with the three boys bound hand and foot, their heads bowed, and shaking in abject fear. I couldn't stand it, and back to my tree I went, and sat there listening for the distant shots that I knew I would hear.

In the distance I could hear the roar of the crowd expressing its anger, then suddenly an ominous silence fell, and I distinctly heard the shots: I counted one, then a second, and finally a third. The quiet continued for a few seconds and then an extraordinarily loud and sustained roar from the huge crowd puzzled me. What had happened? I had to go and find out.

I rushed back down to the front gate and looked toward the west. I didn't have long to wait. The crowd started to trickle back, and all seemed to be in a laughing and joyous mood. We couldn't understand it. Finally I went down into the street and accosted one of the passersby and asked what had happened. He told me that only the oldest of the three had been shot and the two younger boys had been spared. Indeed, shortly thereafter back came the cart with the two boys aboard, both in a state of collapse but definitely alive.

Later we learned the details of the three shots. The three young fellows had been taken off the cart at the execution site and made to kneel facing the big temple. Then, three shots had been fired, but the first two shots had been deliberately fired just past the ears of the two youngest boys, while the third shot killed the older lad, who had deserted with his weapon. The terror that filled the minds of the two lads as they each listened and counted the shots being fired, believing that each one was the last thing they would ever hear, and that the next shot would be for him is not difficult to imagine.

Father was so gratified at the outcome that he immediately went down and got together with the magistrate, and together they gathered a group of the local gentry and paid a courtesy call on the general to thank him for his leniency. The general was thus given a great deal of "face," and he told Father that had it not been for him, the two boys would not be alive. He added, however, that despite their youth, they could not be pardoned but would have to serve a life sentence in prison.

The story doesn't end here. Father was still making regular visits to the prison at that time and came to know the two young lads very well. Sad to say, he found that the shock of their experience had affected both of them in the same manner. Both were completely paralyzed from the waist down and remained, for the rest of their lives, in the kneeling position they were in when the shots were fired past their ears. Father tried everything he could think of to help them, but to no avail.

About nine years later, in 1933, when the Japanese took over Jehol Province and captured Lingyuan, the first thing they did was to throw open the prison gates and release all the prisoners. The two lads, now young men and free, were still paralyzed. Far from their original homes, they had no alternative but to join the ranks of the many beggars of Lingyuan. I came to know them well in the years that followed, as they dragged themselves around the city on little makeshift wooden carts they had fashioned for themselves. They regularly stopped at our house, not so much for a handout as simply to greet us and express their thanks. We did what we could for them, even trying to get them some kind of employment, but that proved impossible. The labor market was so crowded and competitive at the time that even the healthy had a hard time finding jobs. But neither of the young men showed any bitterness at their lot and both worshipped my father, whom they never ceased to thank for saving their lives.

Apart from the different names for bandits, there also were three basic categories into which they were divided. There were the very large gangs, which at times could be as big as a small army, numbering a thousand men or more, most of them deserters from one of the warlord's armies or troops who had suffered defeat and wanted no more of the army. These gangs specialized in terrorizing small, undefended villages and the strongholds of wealthy landowners, and they would also occasionally attack a city. They made their headquarters in some mountain fastness where they could readily defend themselves from the police, and they carried out their raids at intervals without any prior warning. Fortunately, however, that type was in the minority.

A second type were smaller groups, usually fewer than twenty in number, who frequented the highways and specialized in kidnapping for ransom. Those men, like the first group, were usually mounted on horseback and were by far the most ruthless and most feared. They roved the countryside and seldom had a known base or hangout. They frequently took over a village, capturing a police outpost in the process to replenish their weapons and ammunition, then staying a few weeks until pressure from the police forced them to move on. Like the larger gangs, they were usually composed of deserters from one or another of the armies, usually having defected after a defeat in battle, but, unlike the larger groups, they were totally without discipline and often fought among themselves.

The third and most common type was the oft-met small-time bandit who, working either singly or in groups of three or four, would operate on foot in proximity to their homes. Some were farmers part of the time and bandits only by choice or necessity at other times. Their specialty was to set up an ambush in a nearby mountain pass or in one of the deep canyons through which the roads passed. They seldom actually used their guns, nor, as a general rule, did they harm their victims beyond perhaps roughing one up when he failed to produce on demand. They concentrated simply on taking money and valuables from travelers and rarely got involved in kidnapping, unless by accident.

I saw all those different types from time to time, and each time we set out on a journey we were well aware that we might encounter bandits at some point. We were not in any real sense fearful of them, but there was always some degree of apprehension lest one or other of them might be trigger-happy and, not recognizing us, might let loose with a weapon. So we always took the precaution of making inquiries when entering a known area of bandit activity, and when warned in advance we usually stopped and waited until an "all clear" message came through from other travelers. In a very real way our trust was in God: from my very earliest childhood I can remember just before leaving on a trip, my father would get us all together and in the candlelight would read to us Psalm 91, which to us will always be the "Traveler's Psalm." How well I remember Father's calm voice reading God's timeless promises: "....Thou shalt not be afraid for the terror by night; for the arrow that flieth by day; ...a thousand shall fall at thy side, and ten thousand at thy right hand; but it shall not come nigh thee....There shall no evil befall thee...for He shall give His angels charge over thee to keep thee in all thy ways." The promise over all those years was never broken.

About midway on the regular route we took to the railroad at Suizhong, we had to pass very close to a place with the appropriate name of *heishan ke* or "black mountain burrow." That mountain fastness was well known as the headquarters for a very large gang of bandits, said to number in the thousands. The bandits were constantly being attacked by the police or by army forces, but seldom with any degree of success. It was customary when we came near the area to approach the local militia and report our intention of passing through and ask about the situation. The militia were there ostensibly to protect the population against the bandits, but being vastly outnumbered, they never took any action against them. The bandits, whose stronghold could only be reached by a narrow footpath through the mountains nearby, never molested the local villagers, nor bothered the militia, much as birds don't foul their nests.

Not only that, the bandits depended on the locals for much of their food and intelligence. Therefore, our purpose in approaching the militia was to ensure that word would get to the real bandits about our passing and hopefully, knowing who we were, they would leave us alone. Despite that precaution, we always breathed a sigh of relief when we were well past that point.

Occasionally the militia would make a show of "escorting" us through the danger zone by assigning a couple of men on horseback armed with ancient muzzle-loaders to travel with us. That, for them, was an additional source of income, since we had to reimburse them for their time and trouble. However, most times the militia simply smiled at us, told us it was safe to travel, and let us go by. But there were times when the gang happened to be operating on the road up ahead, and we would be asked most courteously to stop awhile at the inn and rest. Taking the hint we would stop for an hour or two, giving them time to clear the road ahead of us.

The chief of that particular gang, which was variously reported to number anywhere from five hundred to two thousand men, was known far and wide by the name he had given himself, Bai She, or "White Serpent." People who claimed to have seen him described him as a giant of a man. He was renowned for being a crack shot with his Mauser pistol — a weapon the bandits seem to have had in abundance — and was said to be able to shoot eggs off a fence at a distance of 500 feet and to be able to drill a hole thorough a coin flung into the air. In addition, he had a rather warped sense of humor, which made him shoot the hats off the heads of people who happened to come anywhere near his headquarters unannounced.

In addition to the city police, the Chinese in Lingyuan county had a mobile force of very well-trained county police whose sole job was fighting the bandits, and if possible, rooting them out and getting rid of them for good. In that they did not have a great deal of success, but they did succeed in keeping the bandits on the move. The county force consisted of around three hundred well-armed men mounted on horses, who depended very largely on informants to tell them the location of active bandits. While not a sufficiently large force to attack the bandits in their mountain lairs, they were not afraid to do battle with them if they could find them in the open, away from home. On one memorable occasion the police were victorious and managed to take Bai She alive, along with a small number of his men. It was widely reported to have been a furious battle, but privately I was told that the police had been tipped off in advance as to his whereabouts on a given day when he went incognito to attend the wedding of a relative, accompanied by only a handful of his bodyguards, and that the police were there waiting for him when he

arrived.

The capture of Bai She created a great deal of excitement in Lingyuan, and his imminent execution was both expected and felt by everyone to be well deserved. However, there was a sudden and totally unexpected development: his "army" of several hundred men — or several thousand, depending upon to whom one listened — appeared overnight and encamped a mile or two south of Lingyuan, sending in an emissary to tell the magistrate that in the event any harm came to White Serpent, they would burn the city and massacre everyone in it. The magistrate was given two days in which to release his prisoner unharmed.

That was a scary two days. The size of the bandit army was probably greatly exaggerated, but the magistrate, having only a handful of police at his command, and there being only a token force of soldiers in the city at the time, knew he could not take the risk. He capitulated after having given the bandit chief a sound drubbing.

Of course, the news was all over town. Hearing that the man had been released, I rushed down to our front gate to see if I could catch a glimpse of the fearsome giant. All was peaceful and I saw no sign of him even though I stood out there for a couple of hours. Later I was told he had left the city to rejoin his men.

In the afternoon of the same day I was again down at the front gate with our gatekeeper, Mr. Hu, beside me, when I saw a diminutive little man, somewhat less than five feet tall, come limping up the street from the direction of the Yamen. He was meticulously dressed in obviously brand new clothing, a long, blue brocade gown with a short satin jacket over it in the style of the local gentry or educated class. He approached me with a broad smile on his face, bowed deeply, then produced his visiting card and presented it to me. I was about twelve at the time and hadn't the slightest idea what was going on, nor did I know who he was. Mr. Hu whispered in my ear that it was Bai She, the bandit chief. I was completely flabbergasted. That was the much-feared giant? Not knowing what else to do, I politely invited him to come inside and sit awhile and have some refreshment, but he smilingly declined. Then, after chatting with me for a few minutes, and asking me my age and nationality, he went on his way up the street, making another stop at our neighbor Mr. He's house. From there he went across the street to the alley, where our old teacher Mr. Wu the Scholar lived, likewise leaving him a card. I was astonished that he knew exactly where to go.

I learned that he had apparently been released from prison very quietly that morning, but instead of sneaking out of town with his men, he had gone to a tailor to have a new suit of clothes made, and then had had several hundred name cards printed. By openly declaring his name as Bai She, giving his rank as "General of the Peace Army," and by visiting the various officials and gentry of the town, he had, in effect, placed himself on a par with them and had thus restored his lost "face."

That wasn't the last we saw of Bai She. A year or so later our city came under attack again by an army belonging to one of the warlords, coming in from the north, and the city was again captured without loss of any civilian lives. The occupying army, although quite well-behaved, was badly undermanned. As the fighting progressed westward, the commanding general decided he had to send every possible man to the front and hadn't enough men to garrison the city. That meant the city, being entirely undefended, was open to attack by any bandit gang that had the inclination.

But the general was a wily old man. He sent an emissary to Bai She, inviting him to bring his army to Lingyuan to join up with his own army, promising that he would not only give amnesty to all, but would give Bai She command of the city.

When news of the development got out, there was a tremendous outcry from the inhabitants of the city, and everyone feared the worst. Father thought it was preposterous and went to see the general, suggesting that he reconsider his decision. However, the old general knew what he was doing and assured Father that all would turn out for the best, and so it did. Bai She was so flattered by the invitation and the chance to become legitimate that he promptly accepted the invitation.

The one man in the city who was most terrified was the magistrate who had ordered the beating of Bai She when he had been a captive. He was certain Bai She would wreak vengeance on him as soon as he entered the city, so he decided to flee. But Father talked him out of it and suggested that instead, they honor the incoming bandit army just as they had

every other army of occupation. In fear and trembling the magistrate went along with the idea.

When the last of the regular army had left the city, it was several hours before word came that Bai She and his men were coming in from the south. Father went out as usual with a group of the town officials and met him a few miles outside of town. The incoming "army" consisted of about a thousand men, and they proved to be a scruffy-looking bunch, without uniforms but well armed, and all mounted on well-fed horses. Bai She himself was quite affable when he spoke to the welcoming party, and after he was installed in his commandeered headquarters, Father paid him the usual official courtesy visit. He took me along with him since I had already met Bai She before.

Bai She gave us a very warm reception and recognized me at once, plying me with cakes and sweetmeats. It was difficult to believe that that little man was the same man who had terrorized the countryside for several years. To the surprise of everyone, he and his men occupied the city for almost a year and were one of the best-behaved armies we had ever "entertained." It wasn't long before they were all dressed in new uniforms — courtesy of the city's inhabitants, from whom money for the uniforms had been collected — and naturally, they lived off the people in whose homes they were billeted, but that was no different from any other army that had occupied the city. In time, we all forgot that they were ex-bandits and I got to know many of them, as a number showed up on Sundays for the church services, as well as attending the daily services in our downtown hall. As far as the magistrate was concerned, Bai She gained himself more "face" by completely ignoring the magistrate's earlier treatment of him and working with him as a friend instead.

The second type of bandit I mentioned were the small, roving groups who specialized in kidnapping for ransom. I ran into a bunch of them one Saturday quite unexpectedly when I was on my way to Dujiawopu, our out-station. That was some years later, when I was about sixteen and had been making the trip frequently to visit the Christians in that small, out-of-the-way place, and preaching the Sunday sermon.

I was riding my bicycle at the time, and as I approached the inn at the noontime stop at

Reshuitang, I noticed about a dozen well-groomed saddle horses tied up outside the inn. Thinking they belonged to a police patrol on one of their regular bandit-suppression forays, I gave it no further thought and entered the inn with my bicycle to have my lunch.

As I mentioned earlier, the road just north of Reshuitang branched into two roads. That was in an area known as *san buguan*, "Three don't control." It was a point on the map where the borders of three counties met. Since it was so remote from each of the county seats, the area was seldom patrolled by police and had thus earned its nickname. It was well known that when bandits were being chased by the police in any of the three counties, they would head for that point, then skip over the border and be safe from pursuit. Apparently that is what had happened on that day.

When I entered the inn, all appeared normal. The old cook in his greasy clothing was working over his cooking pot. A good friend of mine, he gave me a warm welcome and took my order for a lunch of noodles, but then, smiling, he bent low over the pot, and jerking his chin in the direction of a group of men sitting on one of the *kang* drinking wine, he mouthed the words *tufei*, "bandits." I hadn't even given them a glance, thinking they were police. When I saw the cook's expression, I looked at them closely and immediately recognized them for what they were. They were a highly disreputable-looking bunch, loud-mouthed and noisy, heavily armed with rifles and bandoliers full of bullets slung across their chests, and each with the ever-present Mauser pistol that no bandit would be seen without. I decided the only thing to do was to bluff it out. When they noticed me looking at them, I nodded courteously and turned to work on my bicycle, ostentatiously pumping air into the tires and oiling the chain, trying to appear very nonchalant.

They didn't know I understood Chinese, and I clearly overheard their conversation, speculating as to who I might be. Then, after some whispering, there were suddenly two very loud bangs behind me as one of them fired his pistol. The two bullets hit the floor an inch or so apart, right between my feet, no more than a couple of inches from my heels. Apparently that was their way of gaining my attention, or more probably they wanted to scare me into leaving. Not

knowing what else to do, I simply looked around at them and gave them a big grin, waved my dustcloth at them and went on with what I was doing. The rest of the men broke out into loud derisive laughter at their companion who had fired the shots.

The poor old cook was terrified and quite ashen, but when I had finished working on my bike, in an effort to show I was in no way intimidated by them, I walked over to the *kang* opposite theirs and sat down to await my lunch. The bandits, now only a few feet away from me, apparently decided, after having had their bit of fun, to show some civility, and very courteously invited me to join them at their meal. Just as courteously I declined, saying that I had already ordered food. Then I asked them what they did for a living and where they were going. They probably were now well aware that I knew, or at least suspected, that they were bandits, but they replied that they were "businessmen" and were headed "north." Then they wanted to know who I was and what I was doing there.

For me that was a grand opportunity, and for the next half hour or so I preached to them of the God I served who was all-knowing and who knew the hearts of all men, and who were good and who were evil. But I added that He was a God who was all-forgiving and would forgive the worst of sinners, if they but repented of their wicked ways and acknowledged Him. They all appeared to be men who had received at least some schooling, and they listened attentively and asked some intelligent questions. It was obvious that it was their first exposure to Christianity, although they acknowledged they had heard of the "Jesus Church." They seemed in no hurry to leave, nor was I. I continued to talk with them for over an hour and we parted friends after exchanging names and the ubiquitous visiting cards that all Chinese of the educated class carried with them. I also gave them some Christian literature, and a warm invitation to come and visit me any time they wished when they came to Lingyuan. With that I proceeded on my way.

Some months after that encounter, Lingyuan got a new magistrate who, from his first day in office, earned the hearty dislike of everyone. He was a very arrogant individual who had little time for missionaries, and without giving any reason, abruptly stopped Father's visits to the prison. He was a dissolute man, given to drunken orgies in the Yamen that were the talk of the city. He had three wives and numerous concubines, his favorite being one who was extraordinarily beautiful by any standard. He became renowned for his excessive and brutal torture of all the prisoners brought before him, regardless of their alleged crimes. That, together with his excessive zealousness in collecting taxes, incensed the general populace, who very much wanted to see him removed from office. Numerous complaints were lodged against him with the governor of the province, but his downfall and subsequent departure came about in a totally unrelated and unexpected manner.

His favorite concubine liked to go on shopping expeditions downtown, usually to buy silks and satins at one of the stores specializing in those materials. When she went, she was accompanied only by a serving woman. A group of the kidnapping bandits learned of it, either through their spies in the city or, as it was rumored, through the connivance and help of the local populace. The bandits apparently kept a watch on her movements, and one afternoon in broad daylight they snatched her and carried her off into the mountains, leaving a demand with the magistrate for a ransom of Chinese $40,000, an excessively large sum of money.

The magistrate ignored their demands and sent out a small army of police to try and rescue her. The police, who were not very enthusiastic about it in the first place, were deliberately misled by informants who wanted to get back at the magistrate in that way. The woman was not found.

The kidnappers continued to make their demands and threatened to disfigure the young woman if the magistrate didn't pay the ransom at once. He contemptuously refused to have anything to do with them. A day or so later, the tip of one of her little fingers was delivered to him. He continued to refuse and it was followed by her left ear. The magistrate remained adamant until one day a larger package was delivered. That time he found it was his concubine's left buttock which had been sliced off. That caused him such a loss of face that he capitulated and paid the ransom. The poor woman was left lying on the ground outside one of the city gates the next night.

There being no doctor in the city, the magistrate had to come to the much-despised missionaries to plead for help. The young woman was in a severe state of shock and the huge wound was already badly infected, as were her finger and the side of her head, where her ear had been sliced off. Mother took her in and with several weeks of day-and-night nursing managed to save her life and get her back on her feet. But she walked with a bad limp that probably stayed with her the rest of her life.

The magistrate showed his appreciation by inviting Father to a banquet although Mother had done all the work. Father, however, declined to attend. Having lost so much face in the incident and having become the laughingstock of the town, it was not long afterward that he quietly left, and we got a new and more acceptable magistrate. I've often wondered if the bandits who kidnapped that woman were of the same group I had run into at Reshuitang not long before. Those men had been rough and uncouth, but having talked with them, it was hard to imagine that they could be so cruel. Fortunately the young woman was spared her eyesight. To prevent their victims from identifying them the common practice with the bandits in those days was to blind the kidnapped victim by taking small wine cups filled with unslaked lime, which they bound over the victim's eyes, burning the eyeball out of its socket and leaving great gaping holes. I'd seen the results of that many a time.

Despite the prevalence of those bandits, the various missionaries in Jehol Province traveled freely without any molestation, except for one case that I knew of. One of our colleagues, James Duthie, was captured by a band on one of his trips and held for three days, but it was evidently a case of mistaken identity. They had mistaken him at first for a Chinese, and when they discovered he was a foreigner, they were very embarrassed and most apologetic, letting him go as soon as they considered he was no longer a threat to them.

The third type of casual, part-time bandit was by far the most commonly encountered. Their stamping grounds were very hard to predict; they could be almost anywhere. That was particularly true in the late summer and fall when the *gaoliang* (sorghum) was high. With no warning one or two of those men might suddenly step out from the sorghum fields where they had been hiding. They tended to attack only lone travelers, and for that reason, most people tried to travel in groups, and, when possible, foot-travelers would join a column of carts for safety.

We met with such bandits on many occasions but

never had any trouble with them. They were more embarrassed than we were scared, and usually tried to pass themselves off as soldiers. I remember my first encounter with them quite vividly. I was probably six at the time and on a trip with Father over the Dujiawopu road.

Father made regular trips to that out-station at least once a month, usually traveling on horseback, except in the winter months. I had long badgered him to let me go with him, so on that occasion he took me, and what a wonderful treat it was. Our trip up in a two-mule cart was quite uneventful but very cold, heading as we were directly into the north wind blowing down over the mountains, but it was a gorgeous day and all very exciting for me. When we got there, the two lady missionaries there, Miss Gates and Mrs. Merrington, fussed over me, and I felt quite important and very grown up.

On the return trip on Monday, about half-way through the morning, we were crossing a high plateau and approaching a deep rocky defile that led to the four-mile, very steep downhill pass to Reshuitang. Suddenly a solitary figure stepped out into the road from behind a large boulder about three hundred yards ahead of us. He had a gun over his shoulder, and the driver, recognizing him immediately as a bandit, wanted to stop and turn around. Father, however, suggested we should keep going and see what happened.

Ours was the only vehicle on the road, but behind us there were six or seven foot travelers keeping us company. When they saw the bandit, all but one of them disappeared into the nearby rocks. As we got closer to the man, Father thought it would be a good idea if we got out of the cart and approached him on foot. As we were stopped and getting out of the cart, I noticed that the one remaining foot traveler behind us was standing up close against the back of the cart. I thought he was hiding there, and paid him no further attention, and later he, too, disappeared.

Since it was rare for bandits to work singly, Father surmised the man to be a lookout, so he was not greatly concerned. But I remember I was very apprehensive, having heard so much about the *hong huzi*, or "red beards," and I found myself very surprised as we got closer to the man to find that he had no beard at all, let alone a red one, and looked just like everyone else. With that, my fear of him disappeared.

As we neared him, with the cart following slowly behind, he began to walk toward us. To our surprise he bowed deeply and very apologetically, and asked if we would mind "resting" there for a short time because, as he said, there were some people up ahead who were "busy" and it would be more "convenient" that way.

Father understood that to mean that his colleagues were working the pass, and indeed, since no traffic whatsoever was approaching from the opposite direction, that appeared to be the case. So we calmly sat down beside the road and Father engaged the man in conversation, telling him who we were and asking him what he did for a living. He said he was a farmer. Father asked him why he was carrying a gun, and the man laughed and said that it wasn't safe in the mountains and that he carried it for protection.

It was cold out there in the open although we were partly sheltered by the rocks behind us. We must have sat there for an hour while Father took the opportunity to preach to the man, who listened attentively and asked a lot of questions. It was obvious it was the first time he had heard about the "One and only true God." Father asked him if he could read, and he said he could, and then he told us that he was not a farmer at all. He said he had formerly been a soldier but couldn't stand the army and had run away the year before and taken up with some bandits who lived nearby.

Father gave him some Bible literature to read and urged him to consider another way of life. The man admitted that he knew what he was doing was "not good" and that he would think about it. Shortly thereafter we saw a couple of carts and a number of people on foot coming up over the brow of the hill ahead of us. The bandit stood up, bowed low again, and asked Father to please excuse him for the delay and then he scurried up into a nearby gully and disappeared, and we proceeded on our way. The approaching people told us there had been five bandits in the pass, and they had been robbed of all their money, but that it was now safe to go on through.

When we reached the inn at Reshuitang at the bottom of the pass an hour or two later, as we were getting out of the cart, a man ran up behind us quite breathless and exhausted. I recognized him as the same man who had been standing behind the cart at the top of the pass when we had been stopped by the bandit. He came up close behind the cart, where a two-foot-wide ledge extended outward on which the cart driver had tied on some sacks of feed. The man fumbled behind the sacks for a few seconds, then took out a roll of about two hundred silver dollars, which, with great presence of mind, he had secreted there when we first stopped on the pass. He then bowed to us and thanked us for taking care of his money for him.

In the years that followed, we must have covered that same route at least a hundred times. On numerous occasions, we met or saw bandits in the distance, but never once did they molest us. They recognized us then as what the Chinese call *shanren*, or "doers of good," and in their code of conduct such people were left alone.

The rest of the day was pleasant as our cart faced into the sun and our backs were to the wind. Late that afternoon we got back to Lingyuan, and following our usual route, we avoided going in the north gate and through the city streets. Instead we took a short-cut through the fields around to the back of our compound. As we passed the back wall of our garden, I spotted Gil and Ruth standing on a ladder watching for us, their heads just showing over the wall. I yelled to them my big news of our having met bandits on the pass, but when they yelled back that Mother had given them canned peaches for dessert the previous evening, I felt thoroughly deflated and wondered if the trip to Dujiawopu, with all its excitement, had really been worth losing out on a treat that we got only once or twice a year.

Perhaps my fondness for canned peaches needs a bit of explanation. When living in Lingyuan, for the most part we lived off the economy. We bought flour, beans, rice and other grains locally, and of course our fresh meats. However, there being long periods during the year when no vegetables or fruits were available apart from what we were able to store from our own garden, once a year Mother used to send out an order to wholesale houses either to London, or Shanghai, buying a quantity of canned vegetables of various kinds, together with some canned fruits, including peaches, to tide us over. In addition she bought coffee, sugar, and a few other kinds of foodstuffs including condiments. The Shanghai order was placed with an Indian firm called Vicagee & Co., but I have forgotten the name of the firm in London. Both firms sent the stuff securely packaged in wooden boxes, and rarely were there any losses en route.

On one occasion, sometime during that unsettled period, we experienced an instance of basic Chinese honesty and ingenuity that is worth recounting. Mother had sent in her annual order, and had received notification that the goods had been shipped. Later, word was received that the shipment had been forwarded from the railhead by our agent, and was on its way to us by pack train. However, weeks went by and it never arrived. So much time elapsed that eventually my parents wrote it off as having either been stolen or else confiscated by one or other of the armies through whose lines it had to pass, or by bandits. We settled down to try and make do without it.

However, late one afternoon, some six months or more after we had given up all hope of ever seeing the shipment, a train of pack mules arrived at the compound gate, and the owner of the mules told Mr. Hu that the boxes they carried were for us. It was the "lost" shipment, but it was hardly recognizable. All the boxes were caked with mud, the stencilled names and addresses on them were illegible, and many had split open from dampness of some kind. When Father questioned the owner of the pack train about it, he told Father that months before he had been caught in the fighting between two of the opposing armies, and not wanting his shipment of freight to be lost, he had buried it in a field under cover of darkness. Then he and his mules had been able to escape through the lines and return home.

The man went on to tell us that it had not been possible for him to get back to the spot where he had buried the boxes until months later when the fighting had moved on and it was safe to travel once again, and he apologized for the condition of the boxes, which had gone through part of the rainy season underground. We found it indeed remarkable that the man had demonstrated such trustworthiness in a situation where most people would probably have abandoned the load and forgotten about it. It was further amazing that after all that time he had been able to find the spot where he had buried the boxes. When we opened them, everything was there, although some of the cans showed a considerable amount of rust. Naturally, Father rewarded the man handsomely and recommended the agent use him for future shipments.

On another occasion, a shipment of a small box of tea didn't fare so well. The box the tea had been packed in reached us safely, but the moment Father lifted the box he knew something was wrong because it felt too heavy. When opened, it turned out to contain coal, the tea having been stolen somewhere en route. Father made a very careful study of the coal and thought he recognized it as some that came from Tangshan. Father was sure that someone in the post office in Tangshan had made the switch. Knowing full well that our postcards were always read by the postal clerks, who took every opportunity to practice their English, Father wrote a postcard and addressed it to the Postmaster General in Tientsin, stating what had happened, and where he thought the theft had occurred. Then, to make sure that the postal clerks in Tangshan would see it, Father asked one of the merchants to mail the card there on his next trip down on the railway.

The ploy was effective. Within a matter of days, the tea arrived in Lingyuan in a crudely fashioned wooden box, somewhat short of the original amount. Father's postcard was inside, with a note from the culprit attached, begging that Father not report the matter further. It was obvious that here were white-collar bandits as well as those we met on the road.

Cut Paper Art. "Sì Jì Fa Cái" — A charm to provide good fortune in the four seasons.

The van finally out of the ice. Eva is on right and Harry Bishop on the left (with Chinese helper right behind him).

A cart in trouble.

Bob changing a tire. He is jacking the van up. Characters on the van are John 3:16 in Chinese.

Room for only one car.

Crossing a pass in a snowstorm.

Stuck in a bad gully.

Close quarters.

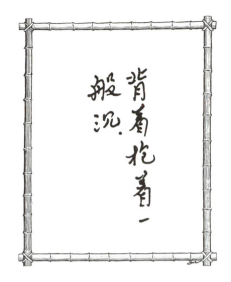

Beizhe baozhe yibanr chen.

It weighs the same whether you carry
it on your back or in your arms.

- Chinese Peasant Saying.

(Equivalent of our "Six of one and
half a dozen of the other")

Chapter Seventeen
Our Family Grows Larger

Lingyuan was a small backwater town where little happened that was exciting or newsworthy. I well remember the first bicycle that appeared in Lingyuan. It was ridden by some traveling salesman, and it created quite a stir. The populace followed the man everywhere, amazed that the machine could stand up straight and move by itself. For want of a better name they called it a *yang luzi* or "foreign donkey," and the name stuck for a number of years, until so many of them appeared that the official name *zixing che* "self move vehicle" became common, although some people called it *jiaota che* or "foot press vehicle." Some months after that, the first motorcycle came into town. That created an even greater commotion, and the people immediately named it "ground flea" or "ground jumper." But the arrival of the first automobiles was, by comparison, an earth-shaking event that had everyone bug-eyed and for days had the whole town awash with excitement, with crowds following the vehicles wherever they went. The first cars and trucks to pass through Lingyuan were in 1924. Some belonged to White Russian merchants, others to one or more expeditions that came through, and I recall a Citroen half-track belonging to a French expedition to Mongolia that broke down in Lingyuan and was abandoned on a back street for many months before it was repaired and taken away.

It wasn't until 1925 that one of the more enterprising merchants in Lingyuan decided that he could inaugurate and run a successful passenger "bus" and freight line to Suizhong on the railroad, and for that purpose he purchased a Dodge touring car and two light Dodge trucks, forerunners of the pickup.

They chugged into Lingyuan one evening just before dark and created an immediate sensation when their owner parked them out in the street in front of our compound. He wanted Father to be the first to see and ride in them. A huge crowd gathered to stare and to wonder as the drivers deliberately revved the engines and blinked the lights on and off. The trucks were about the size of the present-day pickup trucks but the load-carrying area was closed in with wire-mesh screening under a roof.

The merchant, a very good friend of my father's, insisted that we all take a ride immediately in the touring car, so we all piled in for a hair-raising ride through the darkened streets of Lingyuan, dust billowing in all directions and the blazing lights scaring the wits out of the bewildered citizens. Of course the horn blared the whole time, and the two empty trucks followed us everywhere we went.

The business venture proved moderately successful. The trip to Suizhong that normally took five days was now accomplished in one, with an overnight turn-around and a return trip the next day. Eventually the three vehicles became such a common sight on the streets that any sense of novelty was lost.

In 1929, the civil war still continued sporadically, but Jehol became relatively peaceful when one of the warlords installed a new governor for the province, one of his generals, with a large army of his own. The man's name was Tang Yu-lin, and before becoming a minor warlord, he had been a bandit chieftain with an army renowned for its cruelty and savagery. For a number of years thereafter, the entire province suffered the tyrannical and despotic rule of this man, who was called a *dujun*, meaning military governor. Tang was completely illiterate, and in the usual Chinese manner, for his personal protection, he surrounded himself with relatives and close friends, most of whom were equally uneducated but avaricious to a degree previously unknown and unheard of.

Among Tang's rascally cronies who were put into power as magistrates we had the misfortune to get a relative of his named Zhou, who was unquestionably the worst magistrate that we had ever seen, and his regime was characterized by every conceivable kind of graft and corruption known to mankind. With Tang's blessing he bled the populace with endless taxation, collecting land taxes many years in advance and inventing new taxes every few weeks. It would have been difficult to find anything that went untaxed, and his army, which was seldom paid, was billeted in large contingents in every city, living entirely off the people and treating them abominably.

When Tang and his cohorts started collecting land taxes ten years in advance, the peasants in our area became so incensed they rose in revolt, banding together in small armies, and advanced on the cities throughout the province. Armed only with crude homemade spears, decorated with red tassels, they called themselves the *Hong Qiang Hui*, or "Red Spear Society." The men wore no uniforms, were badly organized, but like the Boxers some twenty-odd years earlier, they, too, padded their chests with thick wads of a coarse grade of paper, believing that would make them immune to bullets. With a bravery born from hunger and desperation, they surrounded Lingyuan, shouting as their slogan, "We'll drink soup and eat porridge." That was a classic example of the Chinese being able to inject some humor into a serious situation, and was a play on the surnames of Tang Yu-lin and magistrate Zhou. The word for soup is also pronounced "tang" and the word for porridge is pronounced "zhou," with the two words sounding exactly the same as the names of the two hated individuals.

The rebellion however, was short lived, lasting only a few days. In their first encounters with Tang's troops the people were ruthlessly mowed down by the scores, and their situation was worse than it had been before. An indication of the cruelty of Tang's soldiers can be seen in the fact that in the Lingyuan area very few of the injured survived to come to the mission compound for treatment. Most were killed where they lay on the battlefield by Tang's men. Under the circumstances, it was not surprising that, when a few years later the Japanese occupied the province, they were generally welcomed by the peasants as saviors. For them, the unknown Japanese, albeit foreigners, couldn't be any worse than Tang's troops had been, and any changes they might bring were infinitely preferable to the vile conditions under which the people had lived while Tang was in power.

The bus and truck venture by our Chinese businessman friend was not very long-lived either. Wear and tear on the vehicles made them very expensive to operate. Breakdowns were frequent and the schedule erratic, and, like everything else, the operation was so heavily taxed that it soon became unprofitable. After a few months the vehicles disappeared from the streets and languished in a shed in the merchant's compound, but not before we had an opportunity to use them, but I'll get to that shortly.

Whether it was that little vehicular venture that gave Tang Yu-lin his idea I don't know, but that same winter and spring of 1929, Tang used his ill-gotten funds from opium and taxation to buy himself a large fleet of Chevrolet trucks. It was ostensibly to move his troops around, but actually it was to establish his own truck and "bus" line from the provincial capital in Jehol Province (Chengde), clear across the province, through Bagou and Lingyuan, then on to our neighboring city of Chaoyang, terminating in Beipiao, which was then the end of a branch line of the railroad from Jinzhou, on the main Peking-Mukden railroad. It was also the site of one of the largest and most profitable coal mines in the country, a coal that was of such high quality that it was greatly in demand in Japan, as well as in other foreign countries.

Tang's new venture with his bus line was an instant success. He ran a somewhat irregular "daily" service along that East-West corridor through the province, touching all the main cities. Where the original travel time had been at least eight or nine days, it was now cut down to two, and by using forced peasant labor, Tang improved the roads to the extent that they were vastly superior to the route used by the other bus line to Suizhong. Business was so good that Tang bought more trucks and ran them in convoys of three or more in each direction, with Lingyuan as the overnight stop. All the trucks were driven and guarded by soldiers. Civilian goods were only a minor part of the loads they carried. He made his greatest gains from the transport of opium, and the carrying of passengers was usually quite incidental, usually at the whim of the drivers. Although theoretically tickets were sold, most of the money went into the pockets of the drivers, because twice as many people rode on top of the loads as held tickets, and one of their dodges was to pick up people just outside of the towns, then drop them off before arriving at the official stops.

In the spring of 1929, we suddenly had a most interesting development in our lives. Earlier in March, we had been deeply saddened to hear the news that Mrs. Margaret Sturt, wife of one of our most beloved colleagues, Reginald Sturt, had died as the result of complications from an operation shortly after giving birth to a baby boy in Peking. (Incidentally, the Sturts were staying in the home of my future wife, who was about 15 years old then.) Reginald Sturt was a veteran missionary who had been in Jehol Province since 1907 and had established a mission station in Hada, later known as

Chifeng, or "Red Mountain," a town about 100 miles or three days' journey by road to the north of us, right on the border of Mongolia. From there Sturt made extensive journeys into Mongolia, mapping that little-known area and pioneering routes that later were to be covered by well-known explorer-writers such as Owen Lattimore and Roy Chapman Andrews. At the same time, Sturt compiled a dictionary of the Mongolian language and translated the Bible and portions of Scripture into that language.

The Sturt family were well known to us. My father, whose arrival in China had preceded that of Sturt by four years, had been the one to meet him at the coast in 1907 when he got off the boat from England, and to escort him on the overland trip back up into Jehol Province. Afterward they spent a year or more together, as Sturt learned the language. Of that first overland trip from the coast, Father used to tell the story that Sturt, on his first experience in a Chinese inn, was horrified at the filth of the place, and especially at the appearance of the cook. When the table was set for lunch, the crockery and chopsticks looked so filthy to him that he asked for a bowl of boiling water so he could wash his chopsticks and food bowl before eating. That he continued to do at every stop for the rest of the journey. However, one particular evening after an extremely tiring day, Sturt fell asleep after washing his utensils while waiting for the meal to be served. When the meal arrived and he was awakened, he was extremely thirsty and drank the bowl of water he had used to wash his chopsticks and bowl, thus getting a concentrated dose of the "poison" and germs, which he had so studiously sought to avoid. Father twitted him about it, and after that he took his chopsticks and bowl just as they came, the way the rest of us did.

Reg Sturt had experienced more than his share of troubles and sorrow since going to China. His first wife, Truda, who had followed him to China in 1912, had died just six years before in 1923, leaving three girls and a boy, all of whom were about the same ages as ourselves. Now the same tragedy had befallen him once again, leaving him with a motherless baby only a month or two old. The four older children were away at school in Chefoo, so there was no immediate problem with them, but knowing the difficulties Reg would face with the baby, Mother immediately sent him a telegram offering to take baby John for as long as might be necessary.

My parents made plans to leave at once for Chinhuangtao, feeling that, with the baby so young, it was desirable to be near a doctor, but our departure was delayed for several weeks when my sister Ruth and I both caught the measles.

We now had two new ways to get to the railroad: taking the Dodge touring car to Suizhong or riding on top of one of Tang Yu-lin's trucks to Beipiao. Either way would take a full day of travel, but going to Beipiao meant a change of trains in the middle of the night and many more hours on the train, so Father opted for the Dodge sedan, thinking it would probably be more comfortable for Mother. At the same time it would give our Chinese business friend a boost, by putting a little business his way.

Since we had to take a large supply of clothing and bedding with us for the entire summer, we needed more space than the open touring car could provide; besides, we were taking three servants as well. Consequently, Father asked for exclusive use of one of the trucks in addition to the sedan. That trip was one of the most momentous and exciting in our entire lives; certainly for me, possibly because it was our first by motorcar in China. We started off early one morning, the truck piled to the roof with boxes and bundles, and with Gao Cai, our cook, You Wang, our table boy, and Katie, Gao Cai's brother, sitting on the back end of the truck and going along as a general helper. The sedan was equally heavily loaded, with our family of five, the driver, and boxes and bags roped on wherever possible; in addition, there were several spare tires on each vehicle.

The first few miles the road followed the east bank of the Ling River as it wound its way south, the road being cut out of the cliff and barely wide enough for one vehicle. Fortunately, we could usually see far enough ahead to spot any oncoming traffic. However there was very little at that time of the morning. Even so, we had frequent delays as we caught up to slow-moving vehicles, or had to wait where the road was wide enough for carts and pack animals coming from the opposite direction. I would guess that for the first three hours we averaged no more than five miles an hour, if indeed we went that fast.

As we progressed, the valley widened and the road then dropped down into the riverbed itself as we got out of that particular range of mountains, but that brought problems, too. There we had to cross and recross the river a number of times and each time was an experience in itself.

The two drivers had traversed the road many times and knew it well, so apart from a blown tire or two the morning passed fairly uneventfully. But the afternoon was a different story. After we left the inn where we had stopped for lunch, the road started to climb a very high mountain range, one that we knew well from previous trips by cart and mule litter, but it was a different experience traveling by car. The narrow mountain defiles were barely wide enough for our vehicles and in many places the running boards scraped the rock walls on each side. Numerous places were so steep that all of us had to get out and walk while the two heavily loaded vehicles made a rush up the steep slopes, and in some cases, we even had to unload some of the stuff. The drivers told us that was routine, but it certainly slowed our progress.

Later, on the other side of the mountains, we came to another deep river that we had to cross numerous times. It had a very treacherous bottom at several of the crossings, by then quite familiar to the drivers, yet they approached each crossing with trepidation. One time the sedan got bogged down in the middle of the stream, and all of us except Mother had to get out while the truck pulled it out. At another crossing the truck blew a tire in midstream and had to be completely unloaded before it could be pulled out. Finally, there was one last crossing where the bottom was very similar to quicksand, and to get across both vehicles had to be completely unloaded and everything had to be carried across by hand. I was quite fascinated to watch the drivers wind lengths of rope around the rear tires to give added traction, something they had obviously done many times before, but even then, just before starting across, each driver got down in front of his vehicle and performed a "kowtow" by bumping his forehead on the sand a number of times, begging the vehicles to behave themselves and carry them safely across. All the passengers, of course, had to wade the river, though Mother was carried on Gao Cai's back. The rest of us thought it was great fun, even though the water was quite cold at that time of the year.

We reached Suizhong long after dark, after some twelve or more hours on a journey of something less than 200 miles, and were actually there in time to catch the night train, had we so wished. However, we were all so weary that my parents decided to stay the night at an inn. I remember the inn clearly, therefore Sanborn's Hotel, where we had previously stayed, must have closed down by then.

In the morning, while on the station platform waiting for the train, Barbara suddenly keeled over in a dead faint, giving all of us a bad scare. Some weeks before she had been exposed to the measles when we had it, but she had eaten a lot of dandelion greens, which the doctor later told us had probably given her a degree of immunity. However, fainting was the prelude to her belatedly coming down with measles, which meant that we had to be in quarantine for some time after we arrived in Chinhuangtao, thus causing a further delay in the arrival of baby John, who was to be delivered to Mother there. When he finally did arrive, he remained with us as part of our family for well over three years. Later, Reg Sturt married for a third time and young John was able to rejoin his own family.

That June, as in previous years, we moved over to our own house in Beidaihe, and the four other Sturt children came up from Chefoo when school closed for the summer and spent their holiday with us. When the Chefoo school reopened in the fall, the older Sturt children went back and we returned to Lingyuan, taking John with us.

Our trip back to Lingyuan was another new experience. Father decided that the trip down by car and truck had been too hazardous and the service too undependable to attempt to return the same way. Further, there was no knowing on which day the vehicles might be there to meet the train. So for a change, he decided that we would try out the truck line run by Governor Tang. It could not be any worse, and conceivably it might be better.

Beipiao, the small mining town at the head of the branch line from the main north-south railway, was to be our starting point, and Father telegraphed a request to a good Chinese friend there, a Dr. Lu, asking him to book an entire truck for us on a given date. Our train arrived there in the late afternoon and we received a very warm welcome from Dr. Lu and his wife, who most graciously put us up for the night.

Dr. Lu was a highly qualified Western-trained physician and surgeon who had been hired by the mining company to run a well-equipped hospital for the mining staff and the several thousand miners, all of whom were Chinese. He and his wife were born-again Christians, very active in Christian work, and entirely on their own initiative and without any outside help they had established a small Christian church there. That was the first truly indigenous church that we had ever seen or heard of, at least in that part of China.

While Dr. Lu was a gifted orator and dedicated preacher, he was kept very busy with his medical work and was unable to devote as much time to church work as he would have liked. Therefore, from time to time, he invited foreign missionaries, as well as Chinese lay preachers from other cities, to visit Beipiao and conduct special services. That was how my father had first gotten to know him a year or so before, when he had been invited there to conduct a week of evangelistic meetings.

Here I will digress for a moment and jump ahead a few years. Over the next four or five years, we saw the Lu family on many occasions as we continued to use the truck route to travel to the coast. However, after the Japanese took over Jehol Province in 1933, they very quickly built a railroad across the entire province, touching all the major cities, including Lingyuan. The starting point for that railroad should logically have been Beipiao, the end of the line. However, in order to save some mileage, the Japanese started the new line from a point some twenty or thirty miles before Beipiao. Thus the town became isolated, and in a very short time changed from a bustling railroad terminus and jumping-off point to the small, backwater town that it was originally, with the mines as the only major activity.

Father continued to visit there from time to time over the next year or so, but one night Dr. Lu suddenly disappeared and was never heard from again. That happened around 1936 or 1937, when Communist guerrillas were very active in that area. It was generally assumed that, as their forces grew, they needed medical help, so they had simply walked in and kidnapped Dr. Lu. A year or so later, his wife and four children also mysteriously disappeared one night, in the same manner. They, too, were never heard from again. Everyone assumed that the guerrillas had carried them off to rejoin Dr. Lu, wherever he was, and we hoped that was the case, but we were never able to have it confirmed. We made a number of efforts to ascertain his whereabouts, but the only unsubstantiated word we ever got about someone who might have been Dr. Lu came some ten years later, when I met a large group of Chinese soldiers who had been prisoners of the Communist guerrillas. On their release, they talked of a hospital in the mountain camp where they had been held. They were unable to confirm that it was Dr. Lu who was in charge, but their description of the man certainly gave us reason to believe it was he. Dr. Lu's kidnapping was a great shock to all of us, and we mourned the loss of that truly great man. However, knowing Dr. Lu as we did, we were certain that although the Communists might have held him captive physically, they would have been unable to control his mind, and he would have continued to testify for Christ wherever he was. Whatever his fate might have been after 1949, when the Communists took over the whole country and would have had no further need of his services, we can only surmise, but we fear the worst as many Chinese Christians died at that time.

But on our trip back to Lingyuan in 1929, Dr. Lu and his wife were wonderful hosts, and they treated us like royalty. Mrs. Lu was a remarkably fine cook, and she served us a sumptuous meal that night that few restaurants could have equaled, and she added a hearty breakfast the following morning.

The military truck that Dr. Lu had hired for us was late in coming, but when it finally arrived, it was manned by two soldiers: one very young man behind the wheel and an older man beside him who appeared to be his assistant. That was common practice, but we were disappointed because we had wanted Mother and baby John to be able to sit up front in the cab. It was not to be. Both men were quite surly and uncooperative, and neither lifted a finger to help load the truck, but we eventually got all our stuff aboard and climbed in on top of it, arranging ourselves as comfortably as we could. It was around nine o'clock in the morning, and after a rather jerky start, we were finally under way.

It had rained heavily during the night, so the road was very muddy for a considerable distance, and the truck slid around considerably. Fortunately the land was fairly level, so we encountered no difficulty. Then we came to a narrow defile where some carts were bogged down in deep mud and there was no way to pass. Our young driver, impatient over the

delay, elected to try and bypass the spot by simply driving through the plowed fields beside the defile. As the truck was not heavily loaded, that proved to be no great problem, although it was a bone-rattling experience as we bumped over the furrows with mud flying in all directions.

Although we had hired the truck for our own exclusive use, the drivers had picked up several other passengers in order to make a few extra dollars, but Father had not protested. However, that made the body of the truck very crowded. To give the others a little more room I had perched myself on the roof of the cab, facing backward, with my feet down in the body of the truck. As a result, in my cramped and somewhat stooped-over position, I never noticed a low-hanging telephone wire that stretched across the fields over which we were traveling, and apparently the driver didn't notice it either. As we passed under it, the telephone wire caught me in the back of the neck, and before I realized what was happening, I was neatly lifted — still in a sitting position — and carried cleanly over the top of the truck body and the heads of its startled occupants, and then deposited in the mud behind the truck. Fortunately, apart from a slightly sore and lacerated neck, I was unhurt, but from that point on, I, too, squeezed into the body of the truck with the others, finding a spot just behind the cab.

Shortly thereafter, the terrain began to rise as we approached a mountain range, and the road wound back and forth as we started to climb toward a steep pass. I noticed our driver was having some difficulty down-shifting gears, but I thought little of it until, at one point, the road narrowed into a twisting track cut into the side of a cliff, with a deep ravine on our left. After a particularly sharp outside curve, where he had to slow down, the road rose abruptly, and in attempting to shift down to a lower gear the driver suddenly stalled the engine; the truck stopped and then started to roll backward, toward the curve.

As with all motor vehicles in China, the truck had a right-hand drive, and positioned as I was immediately behind the driver, I was on the cliff side of the road. After we started to roll backward and the driver hadn't applied the brakes, I knew something was desperately wrong. I leaped down onto the running board beside the driver, yelling to him to step on the brakes, but I found him sitting there panic-stricken. His hands, instead of being on the wheel, were over his mouth, and when I looked down at his feet to see why he wasn't using the brake I saw his foot on the brake pedal pressed flat against the floor, and it was obvious the truck brakes had failed. As the truck picked up speed, held back only by the compression of the engine, it was evident, with the bend in the road behind us, we were headed for disaster unless something was done immediately. Without a second thought, and at the risk of the off-side front wheel going over the cliff, I reached into the cab and pulled hard on the steering wheel, yanking it over sharply toward me, thus causing the back end of the truck to veer left and smash into the bank behind us. We ended up tilted at a sharp angle, the off-side front wheel only a matter of inches from the edge of the precipice, and the truck itself less than ten feet from where the bend in the road began.

Shaken by that close brush with death, we all climbed out of the truck and stood around trying to calm our nerves. When Father berated the driver for his cowardice and ineptitude, he discovered that he wasn't the proper driver at all but merely an apprentice, and the older man was the assigned driver. That was the first time the young man had been permitted to handle the truck on his own. It also turned out that both of them knew there were no brakes and they had simply depended on engine compression to slow the truck when going downhill, and when coming to a stop, they down-shifted and then stalled the engine.

From that point on, we insisted that the older man drive, but we had lost confidence in the truck, and apart from Mother and young John, everyone else stayed out of the truck and walked to the top of the pass, repeating the process with each hill of any size for the rest of that morning. Each time, as an added precaution, I ran behind the truck carrying a large block of wood that had been aboard the truck for just such a purpose, ready to shove it behind the rear wheel should the engine stall again.

Fortunately, the rest of the morning passed with no further problems and we made our noon stop in Chaoyang, the only town of any major size on our route. We lunched there with our good friends and neighbors, J. Herbert and Heather Brewster, of whom you'll hear more later. The Brewsters were from Australia, and a finer couple I have never met. In the years that followed, we shared many long trips together, and their house to me was always an extension of my own home. I owe them both a deep debt of gratitude for their example of selfless devotion and their friendship and advice to a young man who was eager and self-confident, but doubtless at times impetuous and lacking in good judgment.

By the time we had finished lunch, the hot September sun had dried the surface of the roads, and except for the occasional mud holes, we had an uneventful journey to Lingyuan. The older man was obviously a more experienced driver, and as we gained confidence in him we had fewer delays with the mountain climbs, since we stayed in the truck. We reached Lingyuan just before dusk.

A short time later I had reason to make the same trip again on one of Tang's trucks, and on the same pass where we had had brake failure, we had another frightening experience. That time we were climbing from the other side, and the truck, after negotiating an inside turn, failed to straighten out and kept on turning out toward the edge of the precipice, stopping only inches from the edge. I got out to see what was wrong and found the driver spinning the steering wheel helplessly. Obviously something had broken down, so I crawled under the truck and discovered that a cotter pin had come out and the large nut at the bottom of the steering column shaft had been lost, leaving the vehicle with no steering. The fourteen of us riding on the truck all got out and searched through the dust for the lost nut, eventually finding it about twenty feet from the curve. After putting it back on and replacing the cotter pin with a bent nail that we were able to pull out of the wooden side of the truck body, we resumed our journey.

That winter, those military trucks on their daily runs through the city were a very common sight. Lingyuan being the overnight stop, the soldiers had taken over one of the big inns on North Street as their headquarters, and several partially dismantled trucks were always there as they took parts from one truck to keep other trucks running. The Chinese call that practice "Taking bricks from the east wall to repair the west wall," *(chai dong qiang bu xi qiang)*, something like our expression, "Robbing Peter to pay Paul."

One very cold morning, Lao San told me that the townsfolk were all talking about an extraordinary sight at the "bus" station: a man with a beard eight feet long and fingernails eighteen inches long. That I had to see for myself, and grabbing my box camera, I climbed on my bike and sped up North Street to get a picture. Sure enough, when I got there, sitting on top of one of the trucks I saw an elderly gentleman with his beard rolled up into a tight roll, and encased in a black silk bag that covered his entire chin, and that was suspended from his ears. The fingernails of his left hand were encased in neat leather pouches, the longest of which was at least eighteen inches in length. I greeted him politely and asked if I could take his picture, and he obligingly removed the leather pouches from his fingers so I could photograph his fingernails, but when I asked him to unroll his beard, he smiled and declined, saying it was too difficult to roll up again while seated on the truck. But he assured me it was indeed over eight feet in length. The little vermilion button on top of his skullcap showed that he was a scholar of the first rank, and the long beard and fingernails were to demonstrate that he was a man of leisure and did not engage in any menial tasks. Unfortunately, although the picture came out well, like everything else we owned, it was lost when World War II erupted in the Pacific.

The old saying, "It never rains but it pours," seemed to apply that winter as far as motor vehicles were concerned. Soon after the first one came to Lingyuan the place was swarming with trucks, and then one afternoon a Chevrolet sedan arrived, towing a small, two-wheel trailer. That was the arrival of Francis Grubb and his wife, a missionary couple who had just come from America with their three children.

Actually, they had arrived in China some months before and had stopped off in Peking, where they enrolled in a newly established Chinese language school to learn the language. Their stuff, however, had been sent on to Lingyuan before them and had arrived months before on a string of pack animals: wooden boxes of all shapes and sizes, which made quite a pile when placed in our old kitchen, by then a storeroom. As curious as children are, we were intrigued by the strange noises coming from one of the boxes. It turned out to be a clock, which struck the hours faithfully night and day and continued to do so until the Grubb family arrived to stay with us for some months before opening up a mission station of their own. They had two boys and a girl. Arthur was the oldest, Miriam came in the middle, and Royal was

the youngest. Royal was several years younger than I, but we had a lot in common and became good friends. After they left Lingyuan, I was not to see him again for eleven or twelve years. I met him again in India, where he was a pilot in the Army Air Corps, flying planes to China over the Himalayan "Hump." He had some marvelous stories to tell, some of which I shall relate later.

That winter and the following year, as I worked on my correspondence course and actively participated in missionary work as often as I could, I gave a lot of thought to my future and had long discussions with my parents on the subject. My brother Gil was in Canada, successfully established in the insurance field, and although I had many times assured my parents that I had no greater goal in life than to become a missionary like them and continue to work with the people I loved, they wisely decided I should first have an opportunity of at least experiencing something of the outside world before making a final decision. So the idea was born that when I turned seventeen I should go to Tientsin for a few months and try my hand at a business career of some sort in any area that I might choose.

Those were still very troubled times in China, and although we in Jehol Province were somewhat in a quiet backwater at the moment, there were storm clouds on the horizon. In the south of China the Communists were growing very active. For the first time we began to hear the name: *Gongchandang*, meaning "Communal Property Society" (that is, Communist Party).

In northern Manchuria, the Japanese were also a cause for concern, as their army was showing a great deal of restiveness. The Japanese had long had a very strong influence in the areas adjoining the South Manchurian Railway, and although in theory the railway was privately owned, it was in fact an arm of the Japanese government. They had their own very strong police force, as well as a large army. For some years they had had an understanding with Marshal Chang Tso-lin, the supreme warlord of Manchuria, and had allowed him great latitude, but he was becoming too powerful for their liking. In June 1928, a group of young Japanese officers who disagreed with the policies laid down in Tokyo decided to take things into their own hands. As Chang was returning by train from Peking on June 4, his train ran over a bomb they had placed on the track and he was killed. Although Chang's son, Chang Hsueh-liang, took over, he was never as dynamic as his father had been, and that incident marked the beginning of the end of a free Manchuria. From that time on, the situation deteriorated badly, and it was obvious that greater trouble was brewing.

It was in that atmosphere that, in June 1930, we as a family again went to Beidaihe for the summer, and later, partly because of the extremely delicate situation in Jehol Province, and partly because it seemed advisable that Ruth and young John be nearer to a doctor, my parents again decided to spend the winter in Chinhuangtao.

That summer, since I was then seventeen, I began to explore the possibilities of getting into some kind of business activity in Tientsin, a city we had visited numerous times. A place to stay was the first prob-

lem. We discussed it with our good friends Mr. and Mrs. Joseph Toop, and without hesitation they invited me to stay with them. Mr. and Mrs. Toop were parents of my closest friends, the twins John and Billy. They, however, had left for school in England, and only their younger sister Peggy remained behind. Both John and Billy later became missionary doctors, spending years in China until the communists took over, then went to Thailand.

Mr. Toop, the North China representative of the British and Foreign Bible Society, had his office and storehouse on a quiet back street next door to their residence. I spent a number of very happy months there with them. They were most gracious hosts, and much as I missed my own family, they made me feel very much at home and a part of their household for as long as I was there.

Beizhe baozhe yibanr chen.

It weighs the same whether you carry it on your back or in your arms.

- Chinese Peasant Saying.

The first Dodge to be seen in Lingyuan—this is not Bob's.

A footbridge.

Bob carrying baby John in Beidaihe. In the background (from left to right) Mr. Tharp polishing shoe, Miss Fischer and Ruth. "Mike," Barbara's dog, is there too.

A break in the journey during a bus trip
home from Tientsin.

Almost home — 22 km more.

Chaoyang Road — home in sight.

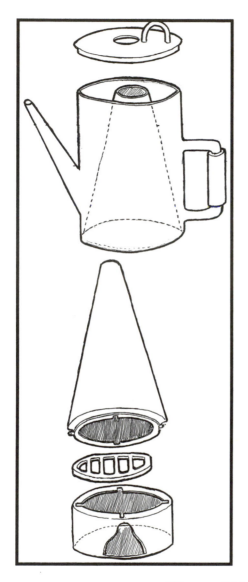

"Instant" Hot Water Kettle

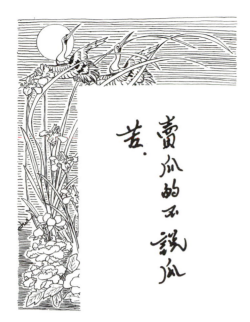

賣瓜的不說瓜
苦。

Mai guade bu shuo gua ku.

A seller of melons will never say his melons are bitter.

- Chinese Peasant Saying.

Chapter Eighteen
My Short Business Career

I went to Tientsin at the end of that summer of 1930, a few days after the Toop family had returned home. The second day after my arrival in Tientsin ("Tinsin" as most Westerners called it), I found employment. Since I had always loved to read, I had decided that working among books would be the most satisfying kind of job, so I went straight to the largest English-language bookstore in the British concession, approached the owner, told him I wanted to work for him, and was hired immediately.

The owner of the store was a delightful person, a Eurasian, part English and part Chinese. Sadly, he was one of a group of individuals who were actually non-persons, both as regards the Chinese, who despised them, and the Westerners, who generally shunned them. However, I found him to be pleasant to deal with and always gracious, both to his staff and customers.

The first job he gave me was as stock boy. I was responsible for opening the packages of books that arrived daily, sorting them, pricing them, and placing them on the proper shelves. That wasn't work for me, it was pure pleasure. As I studied the titles, browsed through the contents, and looked at the illustrations, I found myself in a whole new world. The owner allowed me to borrow whatever books I wanted, and I reveled in them, taking some home with me every night.

The weeks sped by, and in time I was promoted to part-time salesman, replacing the two Chinese salesmen when they went on leave. Thus I got to know many of the local Westerners of different nationalities, of whom there were several thousand in Tientsin. At the same time I met a great many English-speaking Chinese who came in to buy books, and not infrequently, sought my advice on what to buy.

Like most English boys, I always had very ruddy cheeks. That led to an amusing experience one day, or at least I found it amusing. I happened to be in the stockroom when the boss called me into his office next door to meet a visitor and to find a particular book that the visitor wanted. When I left the room, I inadvertently left the door slightly ajar behind me, and I overheard the visitor say: "That poor lad, he's obviously in the last stages of TB and doesn't know it." Bright red spots on the cheeks were, of course, just one of the indications of tuberculosis, which was so prevalent in those days and took so many lives, including a number of my close friends. I was very familiar with TB and its symptoms and knew that I didn't have it, so I was quite unconcerned, but it struck me as very amusing at the time. However, for days after that I often saw the owner looking at me with a somewhat pensive look on his face, and I wondered if he was worrying about my health.

Each Western-owned business in China in those days employed two Chinese, both considered essential to the effectiveness of their concerns. One was called a "comprador," and his job was primarily to act as a native agent and liaison between the foreign businessmen and the Chinese. The second man was called a "shroff," and he was concerned only with money.

Originally, the shroff was the expert employed to test the silver coins, which were often counterfeit. Being made of pure silver, the dollars were increasingly worth more than their face value, and not only were some found to be made of lead and covered with a light coat of silver, but others had their centers bored out and were filled with lead, and still others had the knurled edges filed off. It was very common to pass a Chinese place of business and see the coins being tested by flicking two together, then listening to hear if the coin had the right ringing sound.

In time, with Western business concerns, the shroff became a sort of assistant to the bookkeeper, and was chiefly responsible for collecting outstanding bills. The Chinese who worked for the bookstore in that capacity was a very mild-mannered man, middle-aged, very quiet and unassuming, and not very aggressive in his job. As a result, many thousands of dollars remained uncollected, and the vast majority of those owing money were Westerners.

Few of the Westerners buying books paid cash. Everyone had an account, and both bills and statements were mailed out every month, but an inordinate number remained unpaid, and usually they were for very large amounts and in many cases extended over a period of years. After a certain period of time the shroff was sent out to call in person to collect the money. However, in many cases, he professed himself quite unable to contact the individuals responsible, and the bills remained unpaid.

One day I overheard a particularly heated encounter between the store owner and the shroff when the latter came in empty-handed as usual. I knew right away what the problem was and how to get around it, so later I went in and talked with the boss, and without giving him any details, I confidently assured him that if he would let me go and collect the bills, I would guarantee he would get his money immediately. He thought it was a huge joke, but told me to go ahead and give it a try, and if successful, he promised me that I would get 10 percent of everything I got back for him. The problem was actually quite simple. Every Western household in Tientsin had a No. 1 houseboy who, in most cases, had complete control over all the other servants and supervised the running of the house down to the last detail. It was he who answered the door and admitted visitors or refused them entry if he thought it judicious to do so. All those men were hired for their ability to speak English, or any of the other languages of the foreign community. They acted like little emperors in their own kingdoms, having daily opportunities for making extra money in what was known as "squeeze," either from purchases made by the cook or other servants or from kickbacks from the rest of the staff, whom they had been responsible for hiring.

The same sort of arrangement was also true of the business concerns. Thus, when a shroff or bill-collector came and wanted to see the owner of the business or the individual responsible for the debt, the No. 1 "boy" would demand his "squeeze" in advance, and if it was not forthcoming in a sufficiently large amount to satisfy his greed, the visitor never got beyond the front door. That was what had happened to our poor shroff, although he would never dare admit it. Such "squeeze" as he paid out had to come out of his own pocket, and he had to make up for it by getting some "squeeze" himself from the monies he collected, and that wasn't easy to do. Even had the boss himself gone to collect the money owed him, it wouldn't have been possible. In the first place, as the owner of the store, he wouldn't want to offend his customers by going in person, but moreover, as a Eurasian, there wasn't the slightest possibility of the No. 1 "boy" letting him in, no matter where he went. And, of course, the individuals to whom the bills were sent never even saw the bills. The No. 1 "boys" were all wily enough to sort the incoming mail as it arrived each day and to extract whatever bills they felt would be beneficial to them, so the designated recipient knew nothing about it.

My plan was very simple and completely successful. I went to a nearby print shop and had some calling cards printed, with just my name, not showing my connection with the bookstore. Then, choosing the time of day when I knew the person I wanted to meet would either be home or in his office, I went directly to his residence or place of business, handed my card to the No. 1 "boy," and, as a visiting Westerner, was immediately admitted. I thereupon presented the bill to the person I had gone to see, or to his wife if he happened to be absent. In every case I got the money at once, and in every single case they told me they had never seen a bill in the mail and, although aware they owed the bookstore money, they had been surprised not to have been notified.

In three days I managed to collect well over $50,000 in Chinese money, most of it from accounts that had been outstanding for a year or two, and all of them owed by extremely distinguished people in the community: bank managers, consular officials, lawyers, doctors, and leading businessmen. For me, it was a most satisfying and exhilarating experience, and it led to my getting to know people whom otherwise I would never have met.

When I took the money to my boss, he was dumbfounded and couldn't believe the speed with which I had obtained the money for him. When he recovered from the shock, he asked how I had done it (which I didn't tell him), then expressed his gratitude. But he reneged on his promise to give me 10 percent and ended up giving me only $100. I wasn't happy with his decision, but there was nothing I could do about it; furthermore, when the shroff learned what I had done, he was naturally unhappy, as he had lost a lot of "face" in front of the other employees, and he became quite surly toward me. Since I had long before the incident made up my mind that a business career was not for me, that act of dishonesty on the part of my boss further convinced me that in business it is hard to be a Christian and do the right thing. So I decided

to quit, but I hadn't done so before something else quite unusual came along.

While working in the store one day I had met a most interesting man, a Mr. Allen Jones, who was, in effect, the unofficial "mayor" of the British concession. Tientsin in those days was divided into a number of concessions, which had been granted to the allied powers following the Boxer Rebellion when the allies had demanded reparations and had acquired quite sizable pieces of territory from the Chinese government. On them the various governments had built enclaves for their own people. In addition to the British concession, there was one for the French, the Germans, the Japanese, and, across the river, one called the Russian concession, even though it had been handed back to the Chinese some years earlier.

Mr. Jones was editor of the local English-language newspaper, *The Peking and Tientsin Times*, which, in every way, was the counterpart of its London namesake. Mr. Jones was a diminutive man, but a giant in intellect and a man full of energy. Not only was he a great sportsman, he was active in every aspect of the British concession's community life.

Overhearing me talking with one of the Chinese salesmen in the store one day, Mr. Jones asked if I would be interested in discussing a business proposition with him. He invited me to his office and showed me over the entire newspaper plant and all its operations, including the linotype machines, where Chinese men were typing from English copy at an extraordinary speed. He assured me that not one of them could read or understand a word of English, nevertheless, they were so unfailingly accurate that he had a policy of awarding $5 to anyone who could find a typographical error in the paper.

After showing me the plant, he invited me into his office and sat me down by his desk, treating me at all times like an equal and not like the teenager that I was. He told me something I already knew: that almost every Westerner in Tientsin could speak only a few words of Chinese. It was his very strong conviction that all Westerners doing business in China should know at least a little of the language, and he confessed to me that it was his dream to establish a school for British nationals where they could learn Chinese in their off hours. He would provide the facilities and the staff, but he wanted me to take over responsibility for running the place and hiring any teachers I might need. For me, a mere seventeen-year-old, it was extremely flattering, but I thought it was a great idea and confidently told him that I fully agreed and would be glad to do the job.

For several weeks Mr. Jones worked on the idea, promoting it through his paper and contacting the British chamber of commerce, together with a number of British businessmen. But he had very few takers, and although he had found suitable quarters, the school project eventually died. However, one of those businessmen he had contacted agreed entirely with Mr. Jones and felt strongly that the British members of his staff ought to be able to speak at least a smattering of Chinese, and he asked Mr. Jones to have me meet with him.

The offices of his concern were alongside the Hai River, quite some distance from the center of the British concession. It was a half-hour bike ride to get there, and it was huge, covering many acres of land. Tremendous warehouses, or "godowns" as they were called then, were everywhere, and Chinese men and women by the score moved around in every direction. In the center was a three-story building that housed the offices, and that was where I found the owner, whose name, unfortunately, I am unable to recall. He welcomed me warmly and I was much impressed by his large and palatial office.

Despite my youth, he, too, treated me like an equal, just as Mr. Jones had. He was a big man, a typical Englishman, bluff in manner but jovial, and with an excellent sense of humor. In no time, I felt like I had known him for years. He explained his business to me, that of purchasing eggs, not only from the surrounding counties but from a number of neighboring provinces. The key to his success in the handling of the delicate commodity was the fact that each of his sources could be reached by water, and all the eggs were transported to his plant by boat, either on the canals, rivers or by sea. After telling me that, he took me on a tour of the plant, showing me every aspect of the process in great detail.

He had his own private dock on the river where dozens of small craft arrived daily, laden with eggs packed in buckwheat husks inside huge wicker baskets that required several men to handle. He assured me that although some of the boats took several weeks to reach Tientsin, the eggs, insulated as they were in the buckwheat husks, remained fresh and could be transported in that manner year-round.

He then took me inside the godowns, where I saw what appeared to be hundreds of Chinese women and girls, sitting in rows on small stools, over a vast expanse of open floor space. Each had large, flat baskets of eggs on either side of them, and in front of each were two brand new, square-shaped five-gallon metal cans. They were deftly breaking the eggs into the cans, meanwhile separating the contents of the shells: yolks into one can and egg whites into the other. When the cans were full, they were whisked away by men who replaced them with new, empty cans, at the same time giving each woman or girl a bamboo "tally stick" for each of the filled cans. At the end of the day, she could collect her pay based on the number of sticks she had. Other men kept replenishing the egg baskets, while at the same time removing the empty shells.

I was astonished at the speed and precision with which the women worked. Each of them grabbed two eggs simultaneously in each hand, cracked them on the edges of the cans in a single motion, and then emptied the contents into the appropriate can. There was no rushing around, no smell, no waste, and even the empty shells were used. I was told that they were crushed and packed in containers for the boatmen to take back home to be fed to the hens to help produce better eggs.

I was then shown the fast-freezing process and the cans being sealed. When a sufficient number of cans had been collected, they were transported downriver by barge to Taku Bar (*Dagu*) at the mouth of the river, where, in deep water outside the sand bar that blocked the entrance to the river for the larger ships, a large refrigerator ship was always lying offshore to take the eggs to England. After reaching England, they were further processed into powdered form, the greater part being shipped to the United States for use by bakeries. I was told that that was necessary because it was illegal in the United States to buy eggs from China, but not from England. It was as true then, some sixty years ago, as it is now, that we know very little about what we eat.

The owner told me he employed more than 1000 Chinese, and that the women were paid by piecework, based on the number of cans they filled each day, while the men were given daily wages. Then, back in the office, he told me why he had asked me out there.

Even though he employed a large number of English-speaking Chinese, he also had a sizable British staff, both men and women, and he wanted them to at least be able to communicate with the Chinese personnel to a limited extent. It was for that reason that he had asked me to visit him. He wanted me to teach them Chinese, conducting classes for them at the office, on company time, or at home if the individuals so wished.

After I agreed to his proposal, he called his British staff together and introduced me, telling them in no uncertain terms that they were all expected to learn Chinese, period, and that I was to be the teacher. He left it to them to decide when and how they would go about it. I was inwardly amused to see the expressions on their faces as he talked with them and as they looked at me sitting there. After a show of hands, most of them elected to have a daily class on company time; however, a few of the more senior men wanted to be taught at home. I had no objection to that arrangement. I suspected that the older men were in all probability somewhat embarrassed to be part of a general class, and I respected their reticence.

For several months I conducted a daily class at the plant, and in the late afternoons and evenings, I went to private residences for two hours of work with individuals. Although I had previously had only limited experience in helping fellow missionaries with the language, the new challenge was exciting, and I thoroughly enjoyed the entire experience even though, at times, several of the older men who found the language difficult tended to put the blame for their own shortcoming onto me: my youth, my methodology, and my inexperience. However, I had the full backing of the owner and he supported me in any decisions I made.

At the time, there was only one standard language text available for the teaching of Chinese to English-speaking people, and I wasn't happy with that at all, so I wrote my own material and made up my own tests as I went along. We were only concerned with the spoken language, and primarily the language of business and daily life, and only a very few of my students wanted to learn written Chinese.

It wasn't long after the classes started that the owner called me into his office with another proposition. He explained that he had Chinese regional supervisors and agents who came to Tientsin from time to time with the loaded boats, and when they were in town, he liked to interview them in person and discuss any problems they might have and at the same time make suggestions to them on how to improve their output. He further explained that, although he had his own interpreters, he was not satisfied that they were always getting his ideas across, nor did he fully trust their honesty, so he wanted me to consider tackling the job.

I was nothing if not confident in those days, and I readily agreed, but with one stipulation. I told the owner that his meetings would be much more successful if he first allowed me to give the supervisors a good Chinese meal, after which they would be in a more receptive mood, and that the insignificant cost would be offset by much better results. It was quite true, but I didn't tell the boss my real reason. I was canny enough not to want to meet the men "cold" without knowing first what dialect they spoke, and I knew that over a meal, I could get to know them, break down any antagonism they might have toward a foreigner, and at the same time familiarize myself with their local dialects.

The owner had no objection to my terms, and from then on I was assured of regular and excellent Chinese meals at a nearby restaurant as I met these men. They came in all ages and spoke a variety of provincial and regional dialects, but I never ran into any major problems. I estimated that in all I handled some dozen or more different regional dialects during the months I worked for that organization. I enjoyed both the teaching and the contacts with the supervisory personnel, and most of all I had great satisfaction in getting my regular paycheck. However, although I worked at it for almost a year, I never lost sight of my ultimate goal of becoming a missionary and felt that all I was doing was simply preparation and good experience for what I eventually planned to do.

In the meantime I had become fairly well known to the English-speaking community of Tientsin. A by-product of that was an incident that I found most amusing. In Tientsin, a British-owned tugboat concern serviced the various steamers plying the river and towed barges up and down the river from Taku Bar, where the larger steamers had to anchor and unload. One night, one of their tugs ran down and sank a heavily laden Chinese junk that allegedly was showing no lights. The junk was the much larger, seagoing version of the sampan, with sometimes three or four masts, square sails, a very high stern, and usually a flat bottom. It could carry a sizable amount of cargo and usually had an entire family aboard as crew. On that occasion, even though the accident occurred in the narrow confines of the river, there was considerable loss of life because none of the crew could swim, and, of course, the boat and its cargo were lost. The owners of the boat decided to sue.

Since the accident happened in that part of the river that ran through the British concession, and with extraterritoriality for the British then in force (immunity from the jurisdiction of the Chinese courts), the case was to be tried in the British concession court, and the boat's owners had to hire a Western lawyer. The boat owners were from the province of Hunan, and I was asked by the lawyer for the defense (the tugboat owners) to be the official interpreter in court, because their own man could not handle the Hunan dialect. I brashly agreed and looked forward to the challenge just as I did everything else that was new and different.

The lawyer hired by the boat owners was an American, Mr. R. T. Evans, well known to everyone on the China coast. He was a close neighbor of ours at Beidaihe, where his house was immediately behind ours. and his children had been our playmates at the beach for years. He was known as a most able and aggressive attorney, and he had a pleasing personality and a ready smile for everyone, although at times some people thought him a bit eccentric.

When Mr. Evans heard that I was to be the official interpreter for the court, he loudly and strongly objected to the court officials. He told them that I was so much a Chinese in my outlook and thinking that there was no way I could be impartial during the trial, and that he was afraid that his Chinese client would suffer as a result. He requested that someone else be appointed. I thought his argument was nonsense, not only because I had every intention of simply doing my duty and interpreting or translating only what I was told or heard, but also, at the same time, I couldn't understand why, if he was afraid I would be partial toward the Chinese, he thought his client would suffer. Furthermore, I was a bit miffed at losing the court fee, which was the munificent sum of 10 pounds sterling a day, quite a small fortune in those days. In any case, I was excused and they looked for

another interpreter.

After some delay in finding an interpreter, the trial went forward, and I sat in daily for as long as I could, listening to the proceedings. The interpreter was a young Chinese whose English was fair, but he had extreme difficulty with the Hunan dialect, and much time was lost while he had the boat owners repeat their testimony over and over again so that he could understand it. They, in turn, had difficulty understanding him. I, in the meantime, sat there gloating, because it was costing the plaintiffs a great deal more each day than it would have had I been the interpreter. Although I was sorry for the boatmen, I took some satisfaction in the fact that Mr. Evans lost his case. It seemed quite evident from all the testimony of various witnesses on shore that the junk had indeed been traveling on the river without lights, something that most of them did all the time.

The months passed quickly and pleasantly enough in Tientsin, although I missed my family. At Christmas, however, I took time off to go and visit them in Chinhuangtao, taking along a stack of presents for everyone. I was most proud of a bunch of old 78-rpm records that I had purchased at a second-hand market, about a hundred of them for a mere pittance. Most of them were contemporary music, but a number were classical. They were heavy and awkward to carry, and I was glad when I got them onto the train and into the first-class sleeping compartment I had booked for the night run up the coast.

Because I had so much baggage and the compartment was small, I looked for space to store everything, soon spotting what appeared to me to be an overhead rack, above the two large plate-glass windows and folded toward the ceiling. It had a handle in the middle, and I gave it a half turn and was shocked when the whole thing came crashing down against the windows, which were covered by drawn blinds. I discovered it was not a rack, but an extra berth. I pushed it up again, crawled into my own made-up berth, and promptly went to sleep.

I was awakened around five the next morning by the porter as we were nearing Chinhuangtao, and after dressing, I raised the window blind to see where we were and discovered that one of the plate-glass windows was completely gone. Why on that cold winter night I had not noticed the cold air coming in, I shall never know. They kept the cars very hot, and I was a very sound sleeper, but I certainly ought to have noticed something. I called the porter, and he in turn called the conductor, but the latter showed little surprise and told me it must have been broken by someone throwing a stone at the train. It was only later that I began to wonder if I had not been the actual culprit, and if it wasn't the falling upper berth that had caused the damage. I have had a guilty conscience about that ever since.

That Christmas was a joyous occasion, and among other things, we had a lot of fun playing the old records and selecting the ones we liked. Many were scratched and damaged, but out of the hundred or more, we found some that we really treasured, and they were to give us much pleasure in the years that followed. We discarded quite a number, and I recall the fun we had skimming those out over the creek to see if we could land them on the other side. When we tired of that, we skimmed them into the oncoming waves in the open sea.

When I went back to Tientsin, I still had my job at the egg plant. Through that spring and early summer I taught my classes and made many friends, but I had made up my mind to work only until June and then quit. I wanted to get back to Lingyuan as soon as I could. Tragically, shortly before I was to resign my job, the owner went to his dentist for a routine checkup and was told he needed to have a tooth pulled. During the extraction, his jaw was accidentally broken, infection set in, and within a few days he was dead. I was deeply grieved to lose such a good friend, and his death was a great loss to the community. His successor, one of the senior men whom I had been teaching, did not share his views on the need to learn Chinese, and the whole project was terminated at just the time when I was planning to leave anyway.

On Sundays in Tientsin I attended church with the Toops at the Union Church in the British concession, and there I got to know a young man named Eric Liddell. Born in Tientsin, China, in 1902, he grew up in England and Scotland, but returned to China in 1925 to do missionary work. He taught the Sunday School class in which I was enrolled, and I got to know him well and spent much time with him in his various activities with young Chinese as well as with the foreign youths of the church. When first introduced to him I had been told that he was a former Olympic champion, and he was, in fact, the world-renowned young Olympic runner made famous in the United States with the award-winning film, *Chariots of Fire*. Over the years since those days in Tientsin I had completely forgotten about him, until one day in Monterey, California, almost fifty years later, my brother-in-law and his wife asked if my wife and I wanted to go and see a film with them. I heard the title of the film, but hadn't the slightest idea as to what it was about, but we went along anyway to a theater in nearby Carmel where it was being shown. When the credits appeared on the screen, giving Eric Liddell's name, I was completely dumbfounded, and when the young man playing the part of Eric first appeared, he was so very much like the real Eric that I was at once transported back in time to relive my memories of that dedicated young man, then in his prime.

His untimely death during World War II when he was interned by the Japanese in Weihsien in Shandong Province (now known as *Weifang*), saddened all who knew him. I didn't know it at the time, but have learned since from written accounts and from personal friends and fellow missionaries who were also interned there of the wonderful example he set for the young people of the camp and of his dedicated service to his fellow internees. He died from a brain tumor, on February 21, 1945, in the camp where little in the way of medical help was available, and nothing could be done for him, not even to help alleviate the severe pain he suffered. But he was never heard to make any complaint.

The river and docks of Tientsin were always an attraction to me, and one way or another, a good part of my spare time was spent there. Once a week I took one of the small sampan ferries across the river to the former Russian concession to take my violin lesson from an elderly White Russian man, and it was always an enjoyable trip, regardless of the weather. In the coldest part of the winter the river was frozen, and we crossed on sleds, with the operator standing at the back and poling the sled across with a long, spike-tipped pole. On the many canals that surrounded Tientsin, those sleds were commonly used for transporting produce and various other goods. A number had been fitted with benches, and on weekends many of the foreigners went out and took rides on them, as I also did on several occasions. It was a lot of fun, and the sleds skimmed along at a very respectable pace.

I have always had a great fondness for steamships, and although the ones that could navigate the Hai River to Tientsin were all very small and of a very shallow draft, they were still steamships and full of interest to me. One thing that always fascinated me was the coolies loading the ships. The coolies of Tientsin were a breed apart. Northern Chinese are, for the most part, taller and stronger than southern Chinese, and the men that worked the docks in Tientsin were exceptionally strong. It never ceased to amaze me what heavy loads they could carry and could continue to carry hour after hour. Flour was a major export from Tientsin, and all of it was loaded onto the ships manually. The coolies would line up beside a huge stack of flour, or alongside a freight car load, and two other coolies would place sacks on each coolie's back. Each sack weighed 50 pounds and a coolie wasn't worth his salt unless he could carry six or eight bags, and a number of them could carry as many as ten. The coolie would bend slightly forward, and the bags were first placed crosswise over his lower back and hips, then stacked crisscross up his back and shoulders, and finally, the load would protrude over the man's head. In that somewhat bent position, he would trot up the gangplank, the muscles of his legs bulging, and at the head of the gangplank he would stop while his load was counted and pick up the bamboo "tally sticks" that would later be exchanged for his meager day's earnings.

Those Tientsin coolies were renowned for their strength and endurance. I frequently saw them carrying an upright piano on their backs, and on one occasion I even saw one man carrying a baby grand piano. Refrigerators were routinely carried the same way and were considered a light load, and it was all done on a simple diet of grain, wheat-flour noodles, and steamed buns (with corn flour substituted at times), and a sprinkling of vegetables, mostly cabbage. Meat was a luxury they enjoyed not more than once or twice a year.

The Tientsin rickshaw coolies also were, for the most part, a highly individualized group. I got to know many of them during the months I lived there, and each summer a number who owned their own rickshaws and who could afford it would put their rickshaws on the train and migrate to Beidaihe for the summer trade, following the foreigners who went there by the hundreds.

To those men, pulling a rickshaw was an honorable profession, and they considered themselves to be businessmen, not laborers, and certainly not coolies like the dockworkers and load carriers. I used to be amused, and still am, when Westerners speak and write of the rickshaw coolie's job as demeaning or degrading, simply because as a means of livelihood he spent his time pulling fellow human beings around. The rickshaw men that I talked with certainly didn't think of themselves in those terms. The fact is, or was, that the professional rickshaw puller was, by Chinese standards, a relatively well-off, self-employed businessman, one who either owned his own rickshaw or hoped to earn enough to eventually buy one, and in time, own his own fleet of rickshaws to rent out to others. Many of them attained that goal. I have often read in novels or documentaries on China where rickshaw men were described as being "sickly," "emaciated," and "exploited," scarcely able to pull their passengers around and coughing their lives away. That indeed was the case with some, but for the most part, those were the amateur pullers: peasants who had come in from the countryside, or opium sots, or even beggars who, for a small sum, could rent a rickshaw by the day and who often had to pay an exorbitant fee to get into line at the designated "stands" where rickshaws could be hired. Most of them were unfamiliar with the proper techniques for pulling a rickshaw, or balancing the load, and that made life much harder for them.

In the early years, when rickshaws with rubber-tired wheels were first introduced, it was not uncommon to see them tip over backward, spilling the passenger or whatever other load they might have been carrying, and frequently taking the puller over with them as well. It was because of that problem that it became mandatory for all rickshaws to be equipped with a tripod-like tailpiece, something like the skid that airplanes used to have under their tails. That prevented the rickshaw from tipping over backward, but even with that device, an amateur puller could still come to grief at times. Incidentally, the rickshaw first appeared in Japan, where in Japanese it was known as *jinrikisha*, meaning literally "man strength cart." My brother-in-law, John Brady, who was born in Japan, tells me that rickshaws were introduced to Japan by a Baptist missionary, Jonathan Goble, sometime in the late 1870s. Goble had originally gone to Japan as a

Marine attached to the expedition led by Commodore Matthew Perry in 1853, then returned some years later as a missionary. He did not invent the rickshaw, and its origin is not clearly known, but pictures of a similar vehicle appeared in Europe some years before.

When the rickshaw came to China in the 1860s the Chinese adopted the same name the Japanese used, but in Chinese it was pronounced *renli-che*. It wasn't long, however, before the Chinese gave it other names. Most common was *yang-che* or foreign cart, and later in the Tientsin-Peking area it simply became known as *jiaopi*, meaning "rubber," referring to the rubber tires. It was Westerners who gave the vehicle the name "rickshaw."

The true professional rickshaw puller knew the dynamics of using his load to good advantage on level ground. He would find the exact balance by shifting his position between the shafts, either forward or backward, until he had practically achieved a sort of negative buoyancy, where the load was actually lifting approximately 99 percent of his weight as he ran, and all he had to do was raise his feet and move his legs, and where the ground was level, the weight of the rickshaw could actually be pushing him along. However, it was only the old-timers and experts who could do that; an amateur attempting to do it could easily tip the rickshaw over backward. Pulling the rickshaw up a hill was a different matter, of course, but most of the large cities in Northern China were completely flat, with no hills to speak of.

The Chinese police in Tientsin were especially rough on the amateur rickshaw men who didn't conform to the rules of the road. Coming in from the country as they did, they knew nothing about keeping to the left, as was the rule in China. The police used to beat them with nightsticks and kick them unmercifully. A time came when the authorities got so much flak about it from foreigners and tourists who witnessed the incidents that they tried to change the image of the police, and an order went out that no more of the rickshaw men were to be beaten for infractions of traffic rules. That didn't faze the police, though; they immediately invented new ways to take care of anyone not obeying the rules. I frequently saw policemen stop a rickshaw that had committed some offense, but instead of cuffing or beating the puller, the policemen simply confiscated the cushion from the seat, thus making it impossible for the man to get a rider.

It was not uncommon to see a policeman in the middle of an intersection directing traffic, a small pile of rickshaw cushions at his feet, and the disconsolate pullers standing nearby waiting for him to relent and return their cushions. When any of the men became too importunate in their begging to get their cushions back, the policeman would oblige, but first he would spit a thick wad of phlegm onto the cushion or stamp on it with his dirty boots. There were always ways of disciplining the unruly or ignorant.

On one of our early visits to Beidaihe, a rickshaw puller had come to the house one morning and been hired by Mother for a trip into town to do some shopping. Thereafter, he considered himself to be Mother's own personal rickshaw man, stopping at the house early every morning to see if he was needed that day. He was a charming rascal — we called him Lao Zhang — "old Zhang," and he was unquestionably one of the strongest and healthiest men I have ever seen. I recall one instance during the summer rains when the road was flooded at one place and the water was too deep to negotiate. Lao Zhang wasn't about to let that stop him. He put down the rickshaw shafts, then scouted the area for a way around, and discovered that on the other side of a three-foot-high wall, the ground was hard enough to make a detour. Without a second thought, he picked up the entire rickshaw with Mother sitting in it, stepped over the wall, and continued on his way as though nothing unusual had happened.

Beidaihe, of course, was quite hilly, and most of the rickshaw men had difficulty in pulling their rickshaws up the hills, but not Lao Zhang. He despised the assistance of small boys, who would station themselves at the foot of the hills and, for a few coppers, push the rickshaws from behind. Lao Zhang would run up the hills without even puffing, and frequently would show off by pulling up behind some other rickshaw that was having a hard time of it, and, with one hand push the other fellow, meanwhile pulling his own load with the other hand.

The winter of 1930 my being in Tientsin coincided with an outbreak of anti-Japanese demonstrations by Chinese college students, most of which turned into riots. For a number of weeks the infuriated students rampaged through what was known as the "native" or

Chinese quarter of Tientsin, with the police powerless to control them. Japanese businesses and any Chinese stores selling Japanese goods were fair targets, and many were looted and sometimes burned. On several occasions I, together with other foreigners, stood at the gates of the French concession, which bordered the Chinese city, and watched the battles just a few yards away. Every battle ended with a lot of broken heads, the Chinese police mercilessly battering everyone who got in their way. The fiercest battles were at the gates of the Japanese concession.

Police in the various concessions were also kept busy guarding the entrances against the refugees that flooded in. One night as I was returning home on my bicycle after a late class with one of my English "egg plant" students, I had a run-in with some of those police and found myself in a very sticky situation.

My usual route from that particular man's house was along paved and lighted streets, but that night I was in a hurry to get home to bed, so I took a shortcut on a footpath through the fields that bordered part of the British concession. Suddenly, out of the darkness, several policemen jumped up and confronted me and took me into custody, accusing me of being a Chinese student trying to sneak into the concession. My vociferous denials in Chinese were to no avail, nor would they believe that I was a foreigner, and I was dragged off toward the nearest police post. Only when we came to a street light and they saw that I was indeed the foreigner I claimed to be was I released with abject apologies, but also with a few bruises from the punches and blows from nightsticks that had been liberally applied to my back and head. Needless to say, I didn't use that route again at night.

Before leaving Tientsin in the late summer of 1931, I had my very first formal date with a girl, and it was a total disaster. I am embarrassed to admit that I don't recall her name, but I think she was the sister of friend whose name I seem to remember was Norman. She was a year older than I was, and a very beautiful girl who, on the various occasions when I had visited Norman at his house, had appeared to show some interest in me. One day, on an impulse, I invited her to go out with me for lunch. To my surprise she accepted, and asked me to wait while she changed her dress.

When she finally emerged, I was struck speechless. Where before she had merely been my friend's sister, casually dressed in whatever it was that girls wore, she was suddenly transformed into a most glamorous and sophisticated young woman, and I had difficulty in believing she was the same person.

We walked the short distance to a small, English-style cafe in the concession that was quite popular. Since we had not made a reservation, the Chinese headwaiter, seeing me as a callow youth with little or no money to spend, seated us at a table close to the front entrance, where we were buffeted by everyone coming past.

She was a charming girl, but I felt completely out of place and ill at ease. I don't remember what we ate; however, I do remember it was she who carried almost all the conversation. Hers was a whole different world from mine, and she chattered away about her daily life and friends, and all her different social activities, and I could think of little to say that could possibly be of any interest to her. I was glad when the meal ended and I was able to drop her off at her home. I never saw her again, as I left Tientsin soon after that, and a year or two later I was greatly saddened to learn she had tragically died of what I seem to remember was meningitis — a tragic end for one so young and beautiful.

A week or two before I left Tientsin another incident occurred. I was always an early riser, and one morning I went downstairs just as dawn was breaking. I turned on the lights in the dining room and was surprised to see a cloth laid on the table, and on it, in neat bunches, was all of Mrs. Toop's silver. I remember thinking that perhaps Mrs. Toop had laid it out to polish it. I then went into the sitting room to do some reading, and found a similar cloth laid out on the carpet, also with neat piles of various things on it, knick-knacks from the various shelves, vases and ornaments, and just about everything movable except books. I suddenly realized I had disturbed a burglary. There was so much stuff laid out that it had to have been the work of more than one man, and apparently they had heard my movements upstairs and had fled without taking a thing.

It was on that note that, at the age of eighteen, my brief career in business ended. I had saved what for me was a quite sizable amount of money, and that gave me a good feeling of independence, but my heart was back in Lingyuan, and I was more than ever convinced that my future would be to serve God as a missionary. I know that had always been my parents' greatest hope and prayer, although they had never in any way pressured me. I had been named "Robert" after the famous Dr. Robert Morrison, first Protestant missionary to China, and "Norman" after Dr. Norman Case, another veteran China missionary, so my destiny was laid out for me, and my parents were well satisfied that I had given business life a fair trial, and they did nothing further to try and dissuade me from my chosen goal in life.

The day I left Tientsin for Beidaihe to rejoin my family, I arrived at the Tientsin East Station rather late, and when I got out onto the platform, my train was already standing there. Tientsin East, the station closest to the concessions, had been the scene of many tragedies over the years. A few years previously, during a period of strife between two of the warring armies, an entire trainload of horses belonging to one of the cavalry regiments had been stranded in the station for some weeks as the fighting surged around the place, and every single horse had died of starvation or thirst. The photographs later published in the English-language papers had spoken volumes about the suffering endured by those poor animals, many of which had managed to kick out the sides of the freight cars in which they were held, but had still been unable to escape.

That day I left, there was another tragic scene. As I rushed along the platform to my train, I noticed a train that had just come in from the north on the opposite platform, and around one car in particular, a large crowd had gathered and was peering into one of the windows. Filled with curiosity, I went over, squeezed my way through the crowd and looked in the window. What I saw shocked me as few things ever have done. The entire car was empty except for one man, and he was sitting on the seat next to the window, just inches from me, with his legs cut off at the middle of his thighs, the raw ends sticking out over the edge of the seat. More bizarre, his two cut-off legs, with the bottom part of his trousers still on them, and with shoes on the feet, were standing neatly against the back of the seat beside him.

The man was obviously in shock, his eyes staring blankly at the crowd peering through the open win-

dow at him. They were making remarks, such as, "Why doesn't he die quickly so we can get on the train?" and, "He can't possibly live with that kind of injury; he'll be dead in minutes." Whether he could hear or understand, I don't know, but there he sat, upright, not saying a word, his eyes not moving, and supporting himself with one hand on the seat on each side of him, waiting for whatever might come. Apparently he had been run over by the train — a common happening — and the train had stopped to pick him up, which didn't happen too frequently. Oddly, the stumps had stopped bleeding. Apparently the weight of the train wheels had somehow cauterized the stumps of his legs and sealed off the blood vessels. I asked the people in the crowd if anyone had sent for an ambulance, and they told me the police had been there, and that help was on its way. When his eyes met mine I had a terrible feeling of helplessness. I whispered a few words of comfort to him, told him that he would soon be in the hospital, and told him that God had watched over him so that he had not been killed. I then had to run for my train, so I never saw what happened to the man and never learned whether he survived.

That was only one of many such incidents I had seen where people had been run over by the trains. The Chinese weren't speed conscious, and seeing a train in the distance, they often thought they could beat it across the tracks, having no idea how quickly it could approach. I saw one case in which an entire family of six, the parents and four children, were all crushed by a train. The circumstances were particularly sad, because they had waited while a train went by, then walked across the track behind it, directly into the path of a second train coming from the opposite direction on the adjoining track. China was indeed a land filled with sorrow, and we were to see much more of it as the years rolled by.

I rejoined my family in Beidaihe, had a week or two of swimming, fishing, and just generally enjoying the ocean in my kayak, and then we returned as a family to Lingyuan. I had been away almost a year and was happy indeed to get back and to get to work in the job I loved best, that of telling others about Christ.

Sled on ice in Tientsin.

Repairing a road.

A tiny and very poor village we often visited.

三句話不離
本行。

San ju hua bu li ben hang.

One cannot say three sentences
without revealing one's occupation.

- Chinese Saying

Chapter Nineteen
Preparation For Service

With the conviction that it was God's will for me to enter missionary service, I spent the next several months of 1931 "practicing" preaching as often as I had the opportunity. I daily visited our downtown hall and took my turn preaching to the ever-changing audiences we had each day, and at the same time helped my father with his dispensary work. In a large building in the back yard at the downtown hall, my good friend and tutor Zhang Yao-ting had a school for boys from around six to fifteen or so. There were usually some fifty or more enrolled, and in the classic "one room schoolhouse" situation, Zhang conducted classes at several levels all at the same time. In typical Chinese fashion, the boys chanted their lessons at the tops of their voices, but despite the bedlam, Zhang's ear was attuned to every boy's voice, and he knew when they were studying or merely faking it. I frequently visited Zhang there, and at the same time took the opportunity to talk to the boys as a group.

Our out-station at Dujiawopu, thirty miles to the north, was also a good place to practice preaching, and I went up there every other week on my bicycle and spent the weekend. The place was actually a very large village rather than a town, and every five days a big outdoor market-fair was held there. Quite often that coincided with my visits, and that particularly pleased me. The event gave me the opportunity to set up a stand out in the market place and preach to the hundreds of farmers and their wives who came in either to buy or sell produce, grain, livestock, or their handiwork. The group of Christians who met in the small church there each Sunday was quite small, but they were a faithful few, always ready to give me support, and I enjoyed those visits immensely.

On the way there much of the road was so mountainous that I pushed the bicycle almost as much as I rode it. Once or twice Father joined me, also riding a bicycle. But he found cycling a bit too strenuous, and usually when he went it was by cart or on horseback.

I well remember one trip in 1929 when I had

another companion. A young man from Australia had joined us in Lingyuan a few months previously, spending time with us as he learned the language. His name was Herbert Witheridge. As he became more proficient in Chinese, he was ever more eager to practice what he had learned, and he asked if he could accompany me to Dujiawopu on my next trip. He had memorized a prayer in Chinese and how to announce a hymn, and he had also memorized two or three verses of Scripture. His goal was to practice it before a small audience rather than with the much bigger crowd we had each Sunday in Lingyuan. I was all for it.

Although he and I had been out for numerous short bicycle rides together on the outskirts of Lingyuan, it was his first trip of any length, and since he had come originally from the coast by train and truck, it was also his first experience at "roughing" it in a Chinese inn. For him, our noon stop at the hot springs inn in Reshuitang turned out to be quite an experience and one he was not likely to forget.

After we entered the inn and ordered lunch, he asked me where the bathroom was. I took him outside and around to the back and showed him the narrow alley and open latrine, and I left him there. Almost half an hour went by without him reappearing, and I began to wonder what had happened to him. I went back there and to my astonishment, saw him with his coat off, his shirt sleeve rolled up to his shoulder, kneeling beside the hole with his arm stretched down into it as far as he could reach.

I asked him what in the world he was doing, and rather shamefacedly he told me he had accidentally dropped his pocket watch down into the hole and was trying to retrieve it. I looked down and found that the watch was not only out of reach, it was also out of sight, with only a small section of the chain showing. But there was an easy way to get it out, and I showed him an ingenious trick that Lao San had taught me years before.

From the *shujie* (sorghum-stalk) fence that protected the entrance, I pulled out a long stalk, split the thin end down about eight inches, carefully separated the two parts, and inserted a small twig into the crotch to keep the two ends apart. I then used the stick and reached down into the hole, straddled the watch chain, and twisted the stick until a few lengths of the chain were wound around the ends. I then took a sec-

ond stick and dislodged the twig, which caused the two open ends to snap together, thus holding the chain securely, and the watch was pulled up without further difficulty. For the young Australian, though, it was an introduction to life in China that he could well have done without.

While my bicycle was a vast improvement in travel over the Chinese carts and litters, it was the automobile that intrigued me most. After seeing the successful widespread use of trucks by Governor Tang, I was convinced that if only I could have a motor vehicle of some sort, I would be able to cover much more ground, and I was absolutely determined to acquire one somehow. Only with a car, I felt, could I reach the hundreds of small villages and hamlets dotting the countryside, most of them never visited by a missionary, and where, apart from perhaps a visit by colporteur Zhang Lan-fang, the residents had never had an opportunity to hear the Gospel. To purchase a car or truck in China was out of the question. The cost was prohibitive, so all I could do was pray a lot about it, and in the meantime use every opportunity to study the workings of any motor vehicle I could get my hands on.

Up to that point my only experience behind the wheel of a car had been an hour or so in a new Model A Ford, and that had almost ended in disaster. A year or so earlier, at Beidaihe, I had met a Mr. Dewey of the Methodist Missionary Society who had a mission in a place called Changli, on the railway, halfway between Beidaihe and Tientsin. One weekend he and his wife had invited me up there to see their work, and I was only too happy to visit them.

Mr. Dewey was an American, a trained agronomist. He was teaching the latest American methods in agriculture with considerable success and had numerous projects going in the Changli area. His Model A was the first that I had seen close up, and one of the first to have been imported into China. I was thrilled when he offered to teach me how to drive it.

Unlike the Model T Ford, the Model A had a stick shift, a clutch, and a foot accelerator, but like the Model T it retained a lever on the steering wheel column that controlled the throttle. The lever had to be manually adjusted to keep the engine running at a respectable idling speed, and when slowing down, one had to pull the lever back and lift the foot off the accelerator at the same time.

After a brief lesson and full of confidence, I thought I had it licked. After tooling around a bit on some open ground, Mr. Dewey suggested we try it out on one of the nearby cart tracks leading into town. That was fine with me, and away we buzzed in great style at possibly fifteen miles an hour, the horn tooting constantly to alert the many pedestrians heading for town and farmers driving their livestock to market.

All went well until we came to a canal that was crossed by an extremely narrow, excessively steep, and ancient hump-backed stone bridge. Like most such bridges, it was narrow and unprotected with any balustrades on the sides. As I neared it, I took my foot off the accelerator to slow down, but nothing happened. I had completely forgotten to retard the lever on the steering column, and we continued our approach to the bridge at the same headlong pace. We hit the bridge, going up and over it in what seemed like a flash, with a bare six inches of clearance on each side and no view of what was on the other side until we reached the top. After that episode I was happy to relinquish the wheel to Mr. Dewey, but driving a car was now in my blood and I couldn't wait to get my own.

I took every possible opportunity to watch the Chinese soldier-drivers of Tang's trucks when they worked on their vehicles, learning as much as I could about the engines and how they ran. Generally speaking, the Chinese were good drivers, but they had undergone little or no training in the mechanical aspects of motor vehicles, and the trucks took a severe beating on the rough and almost impassable roads. Most of the trucks were driven in a condition that would horrify any American driver.

I went on one trip where the driver invited me to sit up front with him in the cab, and I was intrigued by a number of flat sticks that he had on the seat beside him, each a different length and each notched at both ends. I soon learned their purpose: the gear shift was so loose that it would not remain in position, so the driver used the sticks to prop it in place. When he shifted into first gear, one stick would be jammed against the dash; another stick of a different length jammed against the seat held it in second gear, and so on. He was so adept with his sticks that he made it seem as though that was the normal thing to do.

On another trip, something had gone wrong with the carburetor and the driver was unable to fix it. However, that didn't faze him. He simply took the engine hood off and threw it into the back, then seated his young assistant on the side of the engine with a five-gallon can of gasoline balanced beside him and a thin rubber tube running out of the can. To get the truck started, the lad siphoned gasoline out of the can, then, pinching the hose between thumb and forefinger, he dribbled just the right amount of gasoline into the engine to get it running, then added more or reduced the amount as the driver directed him through shouted commands. We traveled some fifty miles or more in that manner until we reached his base where he could steal a carburetor from another truck. But, as can be imagined, it was a very jerky trip, to say the least.

In January 1932, I made my first trip to Peking with two good friends of mine, David Parry and Adrian Smith. It was the coldest time of the year but it didn't bother us. We took the train from Tientsin, traveling third class, as we usually did, and had much fun on the train with the Chinese passengers.

Friends had told us of an inexpensive place to stay, so when the train arrived at the bustling Peking station just outside the imposing city wall, we already knew the approximate cost of a rickshaw ride to our destination. Showing more confidence than we actually felt, we bargained with the rickshaw men to take us to *Xiaobaofang Hutong*, "Alley of the Small Newspaper Building," and set off in great style, each in his own rickshaw.

Instead of entering the city through the huge gate called *Qianmen*, which led in a straight line to the Imperial Palace, our rickshaw men ducked around behind the station and entered by the Water Gate, so named because of a canal that ran under the wall at that point. Once inside the wall, we found ourselves in the Legation Quarter, where the diplomatic corps of a dozen or more nations lived and worked. We first passed the prestigious Wagon Lits Hotel then turned right onto Legation Street and traversed the entire length of the Legation Quarter until we came out on the wide Hatamen Street (now re-named Chongwenmen Street), and a few minutes later we arrived at the alley we were looking for.

Peking was famous for its *hutong* (alleys) in which most of the populace live. Most are just narrow streets, unpaved and barely wide enough for two cars to squeeze past each other, but others are much narrower with many twists and turns. All of them, without exception, seemed to be littered with refuse and strewn with ashes to help conquer the mud. On each side were high brick walls or the backs of houses, broken here and there by modest and unassuming double-doored entrances. The appearance of those alleys was most deceiving. Behind those walls and gates were some of the most palatial residences in Peking, many occupied by foreigners who had converted the old Chinese buildings to Western-style homes.

The gate at which we finally stopped bore a small sign: "Home of Rest." Upon entering, we found ourselves in a typical Chinese courtyard surrounded by the usual, gray brick Chinese houses, but that was the only Chinese aspect of the place. When we were ushered into the reception room, we found ourselves in a delightful Western-style home. We waited a few minutes while the old gatekeeper called the lady of the house, and to my utter astonishment, who should appear but the mystery girl of Beidaihe beach, Evangeline Kok. I was dumbfounded, to say the least, but delighted to see her, and I suddenly felt terribly awkward in her presence. Here, after four years, I had again run across her, and now, at the age of eighteen, she was even more a self-assured young lady, in charge of what was to us nothing short of a small, modest hotel, although it was called a hostel.

Evangeline recognized me and seemed in no way surprised to have three young boys walk in on her, asking for room and board for several days. With great efficiency she assigned us rooms, and told us lunch would be served as soon as we were ready.

The Home of Rest, as we later learned, was actually run by her parents, but she was in temporary charge of the place while her mother was undergoing medical treatment. Her father, Arie Kok, whom I was to come to know very well in later years, had gone to China in the early 1900s as a missionary and settled in Yunnan Province in the extreme southwest of China. Their home had been in Lijiang, a small town nestling within the shadows of the great Himalayan Range close to the borders of Burma and Tibet. It was in Yunnan that Evangeline had been born under circumstances that were highly unusual, but I was not to learn about that until many years later.

In 1918, when Evangeline was four, her father had been asked by the Netherlands government to go to Peking and join their foreign service as First Chancellor in the Netherlands Legation, where his excellent knowledge of Chinese was much needed at the end World War I. As a result, Evangeline had grown up in Peking, and the city was as familiar to her as was Lingyuan to me.

The Kok family actually had their residence in the Legation Quarter, but Mr. Kok, although a diplomat, still held his missionary work foremost in his mind. Not only was he very active in church activities in Peking, both with the Chinese and with other nationals, but for years he and his wife had used their home to entertain the many missionaries who visited Peking from time to time for medical reasons or for dental work or even just for shopping at the Western-style stores there. Over the years, as the numbers of visitors increased, Mr. Kok purchased the property that became known as the Home of Rest and made it into a haven for visiting missionaries of any denomination, and there, for a token charge, they could stay as long as was necessary. The Home of Rest was ideally situated from the standpoint of visiting missionaries. It was near all the different legations, dentists, doctors, the hospital, and also close to the Western-style stores where the foreigners in Peking made their purchases. However, we were there to see the ancient city, and after lunch, Evangeline drew a map of the city, showing all the places we ought to visit, then found us rickshaws we could use for the entire day, and directed them where to take us.

Adrian Smith kept a diary of our five days in Peking and now, 60 years later, I am indebted to him for a copy of the diary and an account of all the places we visited. Among them were the Imperial Palace, concentrating on the museum there; the Temple of Heaven, the Winter Palace, the large man-made lakes in the center of the city, one of them the Summer Palace where at the edge of the lake there stood a monumental barge built of marble that the Empress Dowager had built using money that was supposed to have been used to build a navy. We took time to climb Coal Hill, which the Chinese told us was truly solid coal underneath, covered with earth, but there are conflicting theories about that. From the top we had a marvelous overall view of the city. We climbed the city wall, now completely torn down, and then spent some happy hours in the famous Dongan

Shichang (Eastern Peace Market), an indoor market covering several acres, and the forerunner of America's malls. It was a place where one could find dozens of restaurants and hundreds of shops and stalls selling every conceivable kind of commodity, new and old. There were also pet shops containing animals and birds that had never seen the light of day, and the place was thronged with people day and night.

We were in Peking for five days. On our fourth day we visited the Hill Murray Memorial Blind School. From Lingyuan we had sent Gao Zun's (Katie's) eldest son there to learn a trade. He had been blinded when his father had been a heavy opium smoker who had neglected to take him for treatment of trachoma. At the school there were 30 boys and 19 girls, in a three-year course learning everything from weaving, carpentry, wickerwork, sewing and knitting. At noon we ate a Chinese lunch with them, and that evening went to a feast at the famous indoor market by invitation of Evangeline's parents, and of course she was there as well. On our last day in Peking we visited a large rug factory run by a Chinese Christian to give work to poor Chinese boys. In addition to giving them work they also attended school, and daily were exposed to Bible teaching. A very high grade of rugs were produced at that factory.

When we said goodbye to Evangeline the next morning, I was not to see he her again for another year, but I couldn't forget her. At the time, though, never for an instant did the thought occur to me that one day she would become my wife. For one thing, I was not thinking in those terms at the time, and secondly, even had I thought of it, she was so different from any of the other girls that I knew, with her poise and completely adult bearing, that she would have seemed unattainable.

In the spring of 1932, it was time for another furlough, and as a family we headed for Canada, traveling on the Canadian Pacific liner, *Empress of Asia*, one of the fastest in their fleet. Our journey from Japan was made more interesting by the fact that, whereas on most trips across the Pacific, one never saw another ship for days on end, on this trip we kept company for the first several days with the brand new Nippon Yusen Kaisha liner, the *Asama Maru*, which ran parallel to us just a few miles away. We were told by our captain that it was her maiden voyage, and that

the Japanese had deliberately picked the occasion to challenge the *Empress of Asia* in a race to Honolulu. At night, her lights on the near horizon were a comforting presence, but noticeably, after a few days, she began to fall behind and soon disappeared from sight. At the time we didn't know why, and it wasn't until our return trip to China in 1934 that we learned the reason. A fellow passenger, an engineer from the famous Scottish ship-building firm of John Brown and Sons, on the Clyde, told us the story.

He told us that for many years his firm had been building ships for the Japanese, and the *Asama Maru*, and her sister ship, the *Tatuta Maru*, had been designed by them. However, after the plans had been submitted, the Japanese had secretly copied them, then had returned the plans as unsatisfactory. They then proceeded to use the pilfered plans and built the ships themselves. Unfortunately, their greed and overconfidence in being able to build more cheaply got the better of them, and in the long run it cost them a great deal more.

The Japanese had decided that the original plans called for far too many rivets in the hull, and they therefore spaced them more widely, putting one rivet where two were called for, and thus thought they had saved themselves a lot of money. However, on the maiden voyage of the *Asama Maru*, when it was racing against the *Empress of Asia*, the vibration caused by the high speed was too much of a strain on the hull; seams opened up and the ship began to take on so much water that they had been forced to cut the trip short and return to Japan for repairs. Instead of the original number of rivets called for in the plans, they had to put in twice as many to strengthen the hull and bring it back to what it should have been in the original specifications.

That same engineer told us that that wasn't the only time the Japanese had stolen plans submitted to them. When they did the same thing on several other occasions, the John Brown shipyard people finally got revenge. The canny Scots, when asked to prepare a set of plans for a different type of ship, did so, knowing all the time that the Japanese would probably steal the plans. Sure enough, they did. However, when the ship was finally built and launched, it immediately turned turtle and sank. The plans had deliberately been drawn so that the center of gravity was off, and the unsuspecting Japanese had failed to discover it.

The engineer chap regaled us with many more stories about Japanese perfidy. He told us of an instance in which the famous Imperial Hotel in Tokyo had placed a very large order with a British firm for thousands of pieces of fine English china, each piece embossed with the hotel's crest. The order was accompanied by extremely detailed specifications, and when the china was delivered to them, the Japanese used a micrometer-caliper to meticulously measure each plate, dish, cup, and saucer. As was to be expected, they found quite a few pieces that were off by a few millimeters, so they rejected the entire shipment as being unsatisfactory and not conforming to their specifications. The agent for the British company who had accompanied the shipment to Tokyo cabled his London headquarters with the bad news, and was told to do his best to auction off the china and hurry back to London. The Imperial Hotel was the only bidder, and they got their china for a fraction of the original price.

When we reached Vancouver, we at once boarded the train for Toronto, where my brother Gil met us, and for a few days I shared his room while we looked for a house to rent. Eventually we found one where we lived for some months. Then Gil's company sent him to Shanghai in September 1932, so there was no further point in our staying on in Toronto. Mother and the girls moved to Brooklyn, where they again took up residence in the Pirie house that had been lent to us some years before, and I joined them there when my year at the Bible College was completed.

In the meantime, however, immediately on our arrival in Toronto I had enrolled at the Toronto Bible College and spent the best part of a year there in Bible study and practical training in public speaking. Apart from daily classroom instruction in theology, we had practice sessions speaking to fellow students in assembly — one of the most difficult things to do — together with many assignments in outdoor street preaching, mission hall services, and Sunday services at small churches in outlying areas. We also conducted services during the week for the aged and poor in insane asylums and prisons, in hospitals and nursing homes. It was good practical experience, and I greatly benefitted from the time I spent in that very well-run school.

I made some wonderful friends among my classmates, and the following June, six or seven of us got hold of an old bus from somewhere and set off for a trip into the United States to do some field work in the small towns and villages along the border. When we crossed the Niagara Falls bridge and stopped at the U.S. Immigration station, the first question I was asked by one of the immigration officers was where I had been born. When I told them China, they immediately shut me up in a little lockup for an hour or so, then held an inquiry as to whether I should be admitted.

The others, all being American-born, had not carried passports with them, nor had I thought to do so, not knowing one would be needed for such a short visit. Ultimately, the rest of the group vouched for me and guaranteed my return to Canada within the two-week allotted period, and I was free to go. We spent the two weeks mainly in small communities, usually parking the bus on some farmer's property and working either in one of the small churches or out in the open air. One night we found ourselves parked in the middle of a large strawberry patch. The farmer's wife gave us permission to pick as many strawberries as we wished and we picked basins full, after which she most generously brought out a crock of fresh cream. That night we ate nothing but strawberries and cream.

We were no sooner back in Toronto than we were asked by the school authorities if we would consider a request made to them by two elderly ladies who wanted two students to drive them up into the backwoods of northern Ontario, where they wanted to spend a few weeks in missionary work among the "natives." Only one of our group owned a car; I only remember his first name was Jim. He agreed to take them and asked me to go along. I jumped at the opportunity. We set off a few days later in an old two-door Plymouth, towing a small trailer that was heavily loaded with sufficient food and camping gear to last several months.

We headed due north on graveled roads, traveling for several days through the dense forests for which Ontario is so famous. Coming from the barrenness of North China, it was an extraordinary experience for me. For days on end, the only sky we could see was the narrow strip above the winding gravel road. It seemed that every few miles we would come across a delightful little lake, and on several occasions we stopped and Jim and I went in for a swim. However, the water was always so cold we could only stay in for a few minutes. The two ladies refused to even consider taking off their shoes and paddling on the edge of the lakes, and it turned out that both were terrified of water. We had a number of rainstorms en route, which left large puddles in the road. Each time we approached one of them, the ladies would insist that we stop and get out to find out how deep the water was before driving through.

In those days, motels or tourist cabins were few and far between, and most nights we stopped in a clearing and set up a tent for the ladies, while Jim and I slept in the car. We had known in advance the route we would be taking, so I had studied the map and had given Mother the name of a small town about halfway to our intended destination so she could send mail to me there in care of general delivery. However, when we neared the place, we discovered it was actually several miles off our direct route and the two ladies were very reluctant to make the small detour just on the off chance that there might be a letter waiting for me.

I was keenly disappointed, but fortuitously, as we were approaching the turn-off point, we heard a loud squealing and rattling sound coming from one of the wheels on the trailer. Upon checking, we found some nuts missing from the clamps that held the old split-rim used in those days. That made it too dangerous to proceed further without making repairs, and the nearest garage was, of course, in the small town where I hoped to find my letter.

Rather than risk towing the trailer the extra miles and having the wheel come off, we decided to leave it at the junction point, and the two ladies volunteered to stay there and guard it. We pulled out a couple of folding chairs for them, ensconced them in the shade of the trees, and Jim and I happily tooled off in the direction of the small town, carrying with us the trailer wheel. I felt quite confident that a letter would be awaiting me.

We had experienced several thunder showers that morning, but at the moment the sky was clear in all directions and the sun was hot, so we were puzzled when, after a few miles, we saw what looked like snow in the fields alongside the road. As we approached the town there were large areas of the same white stuff on the road, and here and there dead cows lay in the fields nearby.

Getting out to investigate, we found not snow, but large hailstones, some the size of tennis balls, and when we arrived at the tiny, one-street town, the severity of the storm was even more apparent. On one side of the street the hailstones were piled up in drifts, obstructing the doors to the shops, and townspeople were out inspecting their broken windows and damaged cars. Had we arrived even fifteen minutes earlier we probably would have been caught in the middle of it.

The post office, however, was intact, and to my delight there was indeed a letter there awaiting me. We also found a garage where the wheel was fixed, and after picking up some cold drinks for the ladies, we headed back to the junction only to find the two of them very annoyed with us. In our absence they had been almost eaten alive by swarms of mosquitoes and both were extremely upset with us for not having foreseen that possibility. They were equally convinced that we had somehow deliberately brought about the wheel problem just for an excuse to go into town. It was some time before they would even talk civilly to us.

That night we stopped at a fairly large community called Kirkland Lake, where there was a well-known gold mine. A visit to the mine appealed to the two ladies. The next morning we joined a small tour group and had an unforgettable experience.

We were first asked to sign papers absolving the company from any liability in case we were injured in any way. We were then given rain slickers and hats and ushered into a large, cage-like, open-sided elevator that was to take us down into the mine. The elevator hung beneath a high tower surmounted by a huge wheel that carried the cable supporting the elevator. The cage was so huge, it could easily have held forty or fifty people. Before we started our descent, the guide warned us to hold on securely to the handrails and to keep our legs and knees flexible; otherwise, he told us, with the sudden acceleration of the cage, we could easily end up with broken legs.

As is the case in most mines, the cages were operated remotely, and because of the extreme depth of the mine — more than two miles straight down — the guide told us that we would actually be pulled down by a cable attached to the bottom of the cage and would travel faster than gravity.

The cage started off like no elevator I have ever

ridden in either before or since. The acceleration was so rapid it took my breath away, and because of the lengthy cables and the stretch in them, there was an up and down bouncing motion that had my heart in my throat one minute, and in my boots the next. In seconds, all we could hear was the sound of air rushing past the cage as the sides of the shaft passed in a blur.

The shaft was well lit, but we passed the lights so fast they looked like one single bar of light, and to our complete amazement the guide pointed out to us drops of water that, defying the laws of gravity, appeared to be going up instead of down. We were moving so much faster than gravity that the dripping water in the shaft could be clearly seen as we seemingly passed it in slow motion and left the drops behind.

We were not taken to the actual working faces of the mine because of the inherent danger, but stopped several levels above, and we were then guided through tunnels, where we could clearly see the veins of gold. We were invited to break off small bits of gold-laden rock as souvenirs. The extreme heat and humidity, together with the dripping water, made us very aware of the appalling conditions in which the miners worked for hours each day, and we were relieved when we finally reached the surface again.

We were next shown the various processes of crushing the ore and smelting, and at the very end of the tour we were taken to a storeroom where hundreds of the rough gold bars were stacked like cordwood. One of those bars was laid in the middle of the floor, and we were told that if we could lift it, we could take it with us. The bar was so heavy that even Jim and I together were unable to move it a fraction of an inch. It seemed as though it was nailed there, and perhaps it was.

A day or so later we reached our destination, a small farming community not far from James Bay, the southern arm of Hudson Bay. Jim and I busied ourselves building a wooden platform for the ladies' tent, setting up smaller tents for cooking and dining and one for ourselves, where we finally had folding cots to sleep on. Our campsite was near the village, and close by was a rushing stream of clear, cold water in which we bathed when the sun was out. Unfortunately, it was a very wet year, and we had so much rain that sunny days were few and far between.

The farmer folk were so busy in the daytime that there was not much we could do, so every evening we held services in the schoolhouse, and quite a large crowd gathered there. For them, it was a big event in that lonely part of the country, and they welcomed our coming. Apart from us, their only entertainment was the arrival and departure of the one train a day heading south, just before sundown, and the one heading north, which passed before dawn. My participation in the services consisted largely of providing music for the singing with a cornet I had learned to play, and showing slides of China and telling of our life out there. We had no electricity, so the slide-projector used a smoky kerosene lantern.

We had a couple of forest fires nearby while there, despite the frequent rains. It was the rains that eventually got the best of us, and to Jim's and my relief, our two elderly ladies decided to cut short the visit and return to Toronto. Both Jim and I were tired of getting out of bed in the morning and stepping into the mud and water that had oozed into our tent. We packed the car and trailer with alacrity and started back.

Study hours at the Bible Institute were so arranged that students got out of classes in the early afternoons to enable them to work at jobs that helped with their tuition fees. I, too, found a number of different places of employment while there. Among the many friends we made in Toronto was a Mr. George Brown, who headed one of the largest bakeries in Canada. He was a devout Christian, very active in the local Assembly we attended, and we were frequently invited to his home to meet with his wife and children.

At one point he came out with a new and very tasty bread, which he wanted to publicize. He packaged it two slices to a package, and hired me, together with a number of other young people, to deliver samples door to door throughout the city. That kept me well occupied and footsore for several weeks.

At one point Mr. Brown took me off the job for a day to drive his car to a place about 100 miles north of Toronto, where he had a summer cottage. I was to leave the car there and return by train. Even though I still held no driver's license, I welcomed the chance to practice driving. Since in those days the rules were not strictly enforced in rural areas, Mr. Brown was sure that I wouldn't be stopped, and so it turned out. The car was a very large and heavy 16-cylinder Cadillac that consumed fuel so voraciously that all I can remember about the trip was stopping at every gasoline pump on the way to fill the tank and worrying that I would run out of gasoline before the next station came along. But I can still remember the thrill of driving that powerful car, even though on the graveled roads I seldom attained a speed of more than thirty miles an hour.

Sadly, it wasn't long after that that Mr. Brown passed away very suddenly. He had felt somewhat out of sorts one morning on arising, and reaching into his medicine cabinet, had taken out an old bottle of medicine that unfortunately had been there so long that most of the liquid had evaporated. What was left in the bottle was so concentrated that the dose he took killed him within a matter of minutes. His death was a great loss to all of us.

My next job was with the Timothy Eaton department store in downtown Toronto. As an advertising gimmick, they hired an artist who specialized in "instant" landscape paintings, and they needed someone to act as a sort of barker, to peddle the paintings as he produced them, and I got the job.

The artist set up his easel in a corner of a landing on the broad staircase that led to the basement, and there, in a matter of minutes, he would produce an astonishingly good landscape or, for that matter, a painting on any subject the purchaser wanted, but he drew the line at portraits. He was an elderly man, very shy, and he sat with his back to the audience that gathered to watch him work, which also made it possible for people to watch his skillful hands and deft handling of the brush. I enjoyed working with him, and in time I developed quite a spiel to describe both the artist and his paintings. For me it was another great opportunity for practicing public speaking and facing crowds. My line of patter, however, appeared to amuse the old man because, from time to time, he would turn and grin at me and give me a broad wink.

Within sight of where I stood on the stairs was a section of the basement devoted to Chinese artware, mainly of the cheaper sort bought by tourists, but being Chinese, it appealed very much to me. During my lunch breaks I would haunt the area, delighting in the sight and feel of the vases, chinaware, wood carvings, bronzes and ceramic figures that reminded me so much of home. One day I got the idea that it would be fun to work in that section, so I screwed up my courage and approached the personnel manager. He

asked what experience I had in selling that kind of merchandise, and I had to tell him none, but that I had been born in China, and the ware — none of it of museum quality — was very familiar to me. He suggested I take some time to study what they had, then write him a paper outlining what I would tell prospective buyers.

After spending several noon-hours studying the entire stock, I wrote a three-page report giving a general description of various pieces, their original usage, probable origin, the meanings of the patterns, and so on. As an afterthought, I volunteered the opinion that, judging by the original cost of the pieces in Chinese money as marked on the bottoms of each item, they were either vastly overpriced, or their agent in China had not told them the truth in billing them.

I submitted the report to the personnel manager, and his reaction was instantaneous. I was called into the office of the general manager and asked to explain what I meant by the postscript. I went out onto the floor with him and showed him the small paper stickers that Chinese put on the bottoms of their wares, each marked with the original cost in a sort of commercial "code." I spelled out the price to him in Mexican dollars, and the equivalent in Canadian money, and it was amusing to see the expression on his face when he compared what I told him to what he had been charged by the agent on the original invoices. The agent's mistake was in leaving the stickers on, in the belief perhaps that they added authenticity to the items, and probably he didn't know what they were. In any case, he had not anticipated that someone like me would come along to spoil his little game. The upshot was that he was fired and, since the old artist had by that time served his purpose and was no longer a novelty, I was transferred to the Chinese artware section, where I worked part-time for several months as a salesman. I quite enjoyed both the atmosphere of the place and the opportunity of talking to people about things Chinese.

One day while on the job I was approached by a young man who told me he had just returned from a six-week trip to China and that he had opened a shop selling Chinese imports. He was impressed by my salesmanship and asked if I would like to work for him, since he wanted to devote his time to writing a book about China. It struck me as amusing that someone who had spent only six weeks in China could write a book about it, but he is not the only one to do so. In my own case, even after thirty years there, because of the huge size and diversity of the country, I am still hesitant at times to express an opinion.

In any event, I took his offer and agreed to work for him. He in turn produced a book that sold quite well, but I couldn't bring myself to read it. His shop was upstairs in a small, out-of-the-way building on a side street in Toronto, but surprisingly it was quite popular with tourists who somehow managed to find it. I was kept reasonably busy, but still I had plenty of time to spend on my studies for the Bible college assignments. Most of the things he sold were the usual cheap Chinese product made for tourists, but among the items of most interest to prospective buyers were some lithographs of Chinese paintings, for which he had paid about ten cents apiece and sold for one dollar.

An incident occurred one day which I will never forget, mainly, I suppose, because I still have somewhat of a guilty conscience about it. A very elderly American woman walked in one evening with her chauffeur and, after looking around, asked to be shown some reproductions of paintings, each of which she wanted described to her in detail. After going through a pile of perhaps fifty of them, she indicated that while she liked them, she wasn't fully satisfied, and she asked if I didn't have any others, perhaps a little better quality? I suddenly remembered that a week or two earlier a customer had gone through the pile and selected a dozen or more that he asked me to put aside for him, saying he would return for them in a few days, but he had never shown up again. I had them in the back room wrapped in paper, and by that time, being quite certain the lady wasn't really about to buy anything, and more to get rid of her than anything else, I went for the paintings. To make sure she wouldn't buy them, I told her they were priced at ten dollars each. She went through them carefully, told me they were exactly what she was looking for, and to my dismay, bought the entire lot.

I was worried about the boss's reaction and what the previous customer would say if he returned, but I needn't have had any concerns. The boss was so pleased by the windfall that he gave no thought to the man who had asked that the pictures be kept for him,

and indeed, he never did return. However, I didn't come out well in the deal. I was working on a 10 percent commission on everything I sold, but instead of giving me what I felt was my due, the boss figured the paintings at their stipulated price of one dollar each instead of the ten that I had gotten for them, and gave me 10 percent of that figure. For that I couldn't forgive him. It reminded me of my first job in the Tientsin bookstore, and being cheated of my proper commission on the debts I had collected. I consoled myself with the thought that my action was not intentional.

My year at the Toronto Bible College was drawing to an end, and I was making plans to leave the city, but before I did so, there was another incident with my boss that to me somewhat evened the score between us.

He owned a small, two-seater car that was old and dilapidated, but he was very proud of it. His father owned a carpet store; one day he had been asked by his father to make an emergency delivery of a roll of carpeting, but he was too busy, so he asked me to make the delivery. I told him I had no license to drive, but he assured me that I wouldn't be stopped. He tied the rolled-up carpet onto the car roof and told me to go ahead. However, he warned me in advance to be careful because the brakes weren't too good, and he cautioned me to take it easy.

Nothing loathe, I started off. I had barely gone a mile when I saw a motorcycle policeman standing by the side of the street. Instinctively I knew that I would be stopped for a brake check. Sure enough, the policeman held up his hand, and I stopped. In those days a brake check was made by clamping a clock-like device on the running board of the car. The officer would then stand on the running board, tell you to accelerate to thirty miles an hour or whatever, then, without any warning would tell you to put on the brakes, and the device would register whether the brakes were satisfactory or not.

When the officer shouted to me to put on my brakes, I did so, but nothing significant happened. He yelled at me again, and I shouted back that the brake pedal was fully depressed. He then told me to stop and proceeded to write me a ticket.

Fortunately for me, I had spotted my boss's license hanging in a glassine case with the ignition key, so when the policeman asked for my license, without giving it a second thought I handed that to him, and after writing the ticket, the policeman addressed me by my boss's name, telling me to come back the next day at the same time, to the same spot, with my brakes fixed.

When I returned to the shop I told the boss what had occurred, but he merely laughed and told me to take the car down to a garage to have the brakes tightened up, but not to spend any money on having anything further done to them. At the garage, the mechanic looked at the brakes and told me there was nothing he could do: the brakes had already been tightened to the limit, the shoes were worn out, and the only solution was to replace them. I called the boss and told him, but he refused to have a proper brake job done and told me to return to the shop.

Before I left the next morning for my appointment with the traffic officer, my boss told me he would show me a trick that would accomplish the job. He simply let air out of the tires until they were quite soft, and he assured me I would pass the inspection without any trouble, and so it turned out, but only just so. The officer told me I had only marginal brakes and needed to get them properly fixed.

I reported that to the boss, but he did nothing about it. However, to my immense satisfaction, two days later he was driving the car down a steep hill when another car emerged from a side street. He tried to make a sudden stop, but was unable to do so, and slammed into the other car. He suffered no injury, but his much beloved car was a mess. With perhaps some justification I felt that without my having had to do or say anything, he had gotten what he deserved.

Before leaving his employ, there was one thing more I felt I had to do, and that was to get a driver's license. After the car had been repaired, I asked the boss one day if I could borrow it to get my license, and he agreed. I made an appointment with the motor vehicle department and confidently set off to take my test. One thing I should mention is that the car had no starter and had to be cranked by hand. Unfortunately, in the accident, the engine had been knocked slightly out of line, and during the repairs that had not been rectified, so it was difficult to insert the crank so that it would engage the engine drive shaft. I had no difficulty when I first started the car in the morning, but later, with the inspector sitting beside me, I drove into the middle of one of the busiest intersections in Toronto, where the engine died on me.

I got out to crank the engine, but with horns blowing on every side, streetcar bells clanging, and people shouting at me to get out of the way, I simply panicked, and for the life of me I couldn't get the crank into place to start the car. Finally, giving it up as a bad job, I decided to push the car to the side of the road, and it was then I discovered that I was completely alone. The inspector had given up in disgust and had walked back to his office. Getting my license had to wait for another time and a better car.

Leaving Toronto I joined the family in Brooklyn and shortly afterward Mrs. Pirie telephoned from her place in Sea Cliff, Long Island, inviting Mother to go out there for the weekend. Mother asked the best way to get there, and Mrs. Pirie suggested that I use one of her cars to drive Mother out. I thought that was pretty neat, and asked the resident chauffeur which car I should drive. He said to use the station wagon and he also told me the best route to take.

We started off in fine style, but I was nervous and very conscious of the fact that I still had no license to drive, so I kept a wary eye out for policemen and drove very circumspectly. We reached the outskirts of Brooklyn without mishap, and as I was crawling along behind a slow-moving streetcar, I spotted a policeman directing traffic. Worst of all, he was looking directly at me and beckoning me in his direction. I had no way of knowing that the streetcar had reached the end of the line and the officer merely wanted me to drive around it to the left. Without warning, the streetcar suddenly stopped, and in my confusion I bumped into the back end of it, denting the front right fender of the station wagon.

The police officer saw that the damage was slight and understood the circumstances, and he waved me on without asking for my license, but I felt terrible about the damage I had done to such a fine-looking car. Later, as we got out to Long Island, I kept thinking about it and about what I would say to Mrs. Pirie when I saw her.

Long Island was a very different place in 1933 from what it is now. The highway for miles passed through lush green fields and market gardens, with only an occasional little town or village. The roads were all blacktop, and very narrow, with two-way traffic, and very little at that. As we drove along, I happened to notice a barn standing back off the highway in the middle of a field, and a dirt road leading to it, with a sign at the entrance: "Fenders Fixed $1.00." I pulled in immediately, and in a few minutes a very efficient young fellow had hammered out the dents and painted it with a coat of black paint so that it was impossible to tell that any damage had been done. When we reached Sea Cliff, I told Mrs. Pirie about it. She was most gracious and thought it a big joke, and told me to forget the whole thing.

I spent the rest of that year traveling around speaking to small and large groups of people, first in and around the greater New York area, then moved north to New England. Everywhere I went, my message was the same: I felt called to serve God in China, it was a land I knew well, and I knew the needs of the Chinese better than most. Everywhere I went people were receptive and wanted to help. But that was in 1933, and the great depression was still not over. President Hoover was ending his term in office, and on March 4, 1933, Franklin D. Roosevelt was inaugurated. With more than 12 million unemployed in the United States, every large city had bread lines and men standing on street corners selling pencils or apples. Few people had money enough for themselves, let alone to help the needy in China or finance a young missionary heading out there. Despite all that, I found people generous with what little they had, and I was given a dollar here and five dollars there by individuals and groups of people, some of whom knew my parents well and were overjoyed to see their son following in their footsteps.

In early summer of 1933 I found myself in the Chicago area visiting all the small assemblies in and around that city. I stayed with a delightfully warm-hearted couple named Barnes who graciously drove me everywhere in their car, listening time and again to what was essentially my standard message in each of the places where I spoke.

The 1933-34 World's Fair was open at the time, and one day Mr. and Mrs. Barnes suggested taking me there. My sister Ruth had told me that Evangeline Kok was in Chicago, studying at the Moody Bible Institute, and on a sudden impulse I decided to look her up, just for old times' sake. I suggested to my hosts that it would be nice to invite her to go along. They quickly agreed. I imagine they scented a romance in the offing.

We went to the Moody Bible Institute only to find that Evangeline was not there, but was at work at a large cafeteria some distance away. Since it was lunchtime, the natural thing was to go there for lunch.

The minute we entered the place I spotted Evangeline across the room, wearing an apron, working as a busgirl. As I approached her, she obviously recognized me, but her face showed no surprise, only pleasure. However, when I started to speak, she told me in a low voice that she was not permitted to talk with customers and that appeared to be the end of it.

But I was not easily discouraged. As we ate our lunch I watched her move around the room and noticed that her job was to go to various tables to pick up dirty plates. A brilliant thought occurred! On a tiny slip of paper I wrote her a note asking her to join us for a trip out to the fair when she got off work, then I slipped it under a lettuce leaf on my plate. When she next came past our table, I beckoned to her, and without a word handed her the dirty plate. She took it, and although at the time I didn't know it, she promptly went into the kitchen and dumped it into the garbage can.

What I did notice was that although she came out of the kitchen very quickly, she immediately went back in again. Later she told me that after she had dumped my lettuce leaf into the trash bin she had been puzzled as to why I would call her over just to get rid of a single lettuce leaf, and had hurried back to look through the garbage and had found my note. Even then I guess she was reading my mind. Having found the note, when she next passed our table she whispered that she got off work at 2 o'clock, and we told her we would meet her outside.

We spent a delightful afternoon at the fair, and Evangeline was a most charming companion, although I was still very much in awe of her. Without asking her permission, I started calling her Eva, which seemed much more natural to me, and it wasn't until years later that I learned she hated being called Eva and wouldn't let anyone use the name. Looking back, I would like to be able to say that it was that afternoon I fell in love with her, and perhaps that was the case, though I didn't recognize it at the time. However, I did begin to take more than just a passing interest in her as an old friend from China.

The highlight of our visit to the fair was when we noticed several people carrying short bamboo sticks from which hung tiny colorful figures made from rice-flour dough. Eva and I both recognized at once that they could only have been made by someone from Peking, and we stopped one of the individuals carrying a couple of them to ask where they could be purchased.

We finally located a small booth with a Chinese man working with his back to the crowd and watched him for a few minutes without saying a word. Then I said something to him in Chinese, and for a few seconds he froze, then looked around at the crowd behind him, searching for a Chinese face. Not seeing anyone, he went on with his work, but I noticed his forehead begin to perspire. I spoke again, and that time his head whipped around so quickly he caught my lips moving. He at first showed astonishment, but then as I continued to talk to him, he beamed. He told us he had been in Chicago for several months and had not found a single person who could speak Mandarin, and he was very homesick for Peking because he could speak no more than a few words of English. He promptly closed up his booth and spent the rest of the afternoon walking around the fair, chatting with the two of us, while Dr. and Mrs. Barnes discreetly stayed a short distance behind.

Later we took Eva back to Moody's and said good-bye, and I resumed my travels, gradually working my way east again. It wasn't many months before I had enough money to pay my fare back to China, which was the most important thing. But I needed a little more money as a cushion to support myself after I got there, and above all, there was one thing I felt I must have — a motor vehicle of some kind. With a car I felt I could accomplish so much more in a shorter time and visit places that otherwise could never be reached. I prayed, and made the need known in all the meetings I conducted, but during the depression no one was buying cars either new or old, even though it was possible to buy a new one for less than $1,000.

In a previous chapter I mentioned that our affiliation as missionaries was with a loosely knit group of Christians known as Plymouth Brethren. They were non-denominational, in that they had members who were firm believers in the Bible and all that it taught, and they carried on their beliefs without benefit of pastors or church buildings. Some groups met in converted storefronts, others pooled their resources and constructed modest buildings they called Gospel Halls, or Assemblies of Believers. Services were usu-

ally conducted by the elders in each group or by a visitor from some nearby group. They were all strong on local testimony and overseas missionaries, whom they lovingly and enthusiastically supported within their somewhat limited means. Of course, it was necessary that they first know who those missionaries were and what needs they might have, and it was for that reason one had to visit each group in person in what was then called "deputation work."

To aid the missionaries once they were abroad, in each of the "home" countries from which the missionaries departed, a group of highly dedicated people conducted an organization to correspond with the missionaries overseas and publish a monthly magazine that printed letters from the missionaries, reporting on their work, and, where possible, publishing pictures of aspects of the work as well as of the workers themselves. In the United States, for purposes of registering with the government as a non-profit organization, that group called itself "Christian Missions in Many Lands" (CMML), and was based in New York City. In England a similar entity went by the name of "Echoes of Service," and other such organizations existed in Australia and New Zealand. The groups still exist, each still manned by dedicated men and women who year-round freely give of their time and expertise. At the same time the groups act as a clearing-house for funds sent to them, designated either for a specific missionary in some country or to be put in a "pool" from which gifts are sent to various missionaries wherever there is the greatest need.

In general terms we were known as a "Faith Mission," one where every individual went abroad with no stipulated salary and no assurance whatsoever that any specific amount of money would be forthcoming monthly. Each held the simple faith that God, who knew their needs, would supply whatever money was required. I had grown up knowing all that and living it, so I went into it with my eyes open and with plenty of personal experience with the many occasions when my parents had suffered lean times and literally had to count pennies.

I vividly recall one occasion when, due to the civil wars going on around us, mails were held up and for many weeks nothing got through. My father brought it up in the weekly prayer meeting with the Chinese believers and asked them all to pray that monies would soon be forthcoming. Zhang Lan-fang at that time had six sheep farmed out with a peasant in the country as an investment. After the prayer meeting, he came to Father and offered him the sheep to tide us over, but Father refused and said God would provide. The very next morning we saw our prayers answered. We had a tear-off calendar, and it was Mother's practice to tear off the sheet each morning and bring it to the breakfast table, where she read the daily devotional reading. That morning, as she tore off the sheet something fell to the floor. When she bent to pick it up she discovered it was a U.S. $50 bill someone had stuck inside the calendar. Mother remembered the people who had sent the calendar and wrote them, but they said they had not put the money in. However, they remembered that when they were packing the box to mail it, a man had come and asked what they were doing. When they told him, they saw him flip the calendar pages and slip something inside, but they had thought nothing further about it. How true are the words of Christ to his disciples in Matthew 6:8: "...your Father knoweth what things ye have need of, before ye ask Him." I can truthfully say that, in all the years of my childhood and growing up, we never lacked, never went hungry, and never had to borrow.

For the record, once I was launched on my chosen pathway, I never looked back, and for the next ten years or so while China remained open to missionaries, God met all my needs and allowed me to conduct a wide range of activities. I recently came across a little account book in which I kept a record of all funds sent to us — one of the few things I managed to smuggle out in my belongings in 1942 when we had to leave China — and I discovered that, when added up, my receipts for those years averaged only U.S. $40 per month. It was the low cost of living in China and the favorable rate of exchange that enabled us to spread the money to cover so many needs.

Because of my overwhelming conviction that I needed to have an automobile for my work in China, I started to put aside money specifically for that purpose. As an initial act of faith and a concrete symbol for myself that I knew God would supply the car, I one day saw a tire pump on sale and bought it to carry with me as a constant reminder that the car would soon follow.

In the fall of 1933 I again spent a number of weeks in the general Boston area and other parts of New England, visiting assemblies both small and large. For part of the time I joined forces with Donald Hunter, a young fellow from New Bedford who had heard my father speak on numerous occasions and had felt the call to serve God in China. He was employed by the post office as a mail carrier on a rural route, and I accompanied him on several trips in his Chevrolet van as he delivered bulk mail to outlying towns during the last week of his job. With each trip, my mind went back to China as I studied the van and its performance and I mentally put myself in China and wondered how well a van of that type would stand up to the rough roads there.

I was to see much of Don Hunter in succeeding weeks as we visited town after town together, sharing rooms at night and the platforms in the halls in which we spoke. He was a year or two older than I, but we formed a strong friendship that continued until he eventually joined us on the ship to China and then spent many months with us in Lingyuan learning Chinese. Don was a deeply dedicated young man, but not physically strong. He worried a great deal about his health, and I'm afraid I kidded him unmercifully about the vitamin pills he always carried with him. I was in excellent health and had never felt the need for extra vitamins, but I guess he did. In the harsh conditions of northern China his health deteriorated badly, and a year or so later he had to go to the coast, where medical help was available, and then return to the United States, where he passed away while still a relatively young man.

Methuen and Lawrence are two adjoining cities not far from Boston, and there I spent over a week, meeting with some of the most aggressively "missionary-minded" people it has been my joy to know. In each town there was a very active assembly, and the depression had hit them with less severity than elsewhere, partly because of the presence of the large Bolta Rubber Co. factory nearby. It was operated by a German-American named Bolten who was a dedicated Christian with a great heart and an immense love for God's people. He and his delightful wife and young daughter welcomed Don and me into their home and treated us like royalty. Mr. Bolten took us on a tour of his factory, where I was particularly intrigued by some cafeteria trays he had invented and manufactured. They were made of some sort of solidly pressed hard-rubber composition, and were produced in vast quantities for cafeterias and self-service restaurants. But it hadn't always been so.

Mr. Bolten told me he had initially experienced a considerable lack of interest in the product. Everywhere his salesmen went, restaurant owners seemed well-satisfied with the heavy metal trays then in vogue, despite their weight and the difficulty in keeping them clean and free of grease. Everyone seemed to distrust the new lightweight alternative. Mr. Bolten told me his breakthrough came one day when one of his young salesmen had just completed what he felt to have been a convincing presentation, only to be turned down. In utter frustration, the young man had thrown his demonstration trays onto the floor, then jumped up and down on them. The restaurant owner he had been interviewing was so impressed by the evidence of the indestructibility of the trays that he immediately placed a very large order. Thereafter, sales of the trays took off and the "smash and jump" routine became standard procedure in all sales presentations. I personally can attest to the indestructibility of the trays. Mr. Bolten gave me one of them, and my wife and I have used it daily for the past 60 years, and it is still as good as new.

A day or two after meeting those wonderful people in Methuen, they took me aside and told me that God had answered my prayers through them, and that they would pay for a motor vehicle of my choice. What good news that was to me! Over the years in China I had seen the performance of Dodge cars and how well they stood up to the punishment of the almost nonexistent roads, and a Dodge product was my obvious choice.

In either 1932 or 1933, Dodge had come out with an all-metal, half-ton, six-cylinder commercial panel van that I had immediately spotted as being, with a few minor modifications, ideal for my purposes. The very next day Mr. Bolten accompanied me to the local Dodge dealer, where a contract was signed for a new van to be delivered to me at the factory in Detroit on a given date, just a few weeks later. For me there was no further reason to delay my return to China, and from that minute on, I was "homeward bound." But it was to be a very different China to which I would return. Much had been happening during our absence, and I was to find many changes, few of them pleasant. Our plans were to return together as a family to China late in the year. However, the news

from China had been all bad and everything was on hold until the situation cleared somewhat.

As I mentioned in an earlier chapter, just before we had left China for the United States, the Japanese military had, on the night of September 18, 1931, murdered the famous Chinese warlord Zhang Tso-lin by bombing his train as he returned from a trip to the south. The spot they had chosen to destroy the train was just outside the city of Mukden, immediately adjacent to the largest Chinese military barracks in the area. The spot for the attack had been deliberately chosen so they could lay the blame on Chinese troops. In the confusion that followed the bomb blast, fighting broke out between the Japanese and Chinese, and the Japanese launched a massive attack on the Chinese barracks, captured it, and then occupied the walled city of Mukden itself.

That was the beginning of the takeover of Manchuria by the Japanese, and by March 1932, they had occupied every part of Manchuria except the province of Jehol. At the same time they announced the establishment of a new country, which they called *Manchukuo* (more correctly spelled Manchoukuo), which meant "Country of the Manchus."

That was quickly followed by the installation of an "Emperor" in the person of the young ex-emperor Puyi of China. He had been living in retirement in Tientsin since he had been dethroned in 1925. Somewhat reluctant at first to accept the position, Puyi was finally persuaded to assume the throne, and he headed for Manchuria, taking with him some of his former court ministers, nobles and retainers from Peking to help his new regime look authentic. A palace was built for him in the city of Changchun, which the Japanese had renamed Hsinching or "New Capital."

While moving around in America that year we had followed the daily newspaper accounts and radio reports on the tragic events of the Manchuria takeover by Japan. Letters from Lingyuan from the Sturts and others who had taken over the work in our absence kept us up-to-date on happenings there. So far, they had been spared any fighting, but we felt certain it was only temporary, and that Jehol would not long be left alone, and we could only wonder just what the future would hold for us. We didn't have long to wait.

In February 1933, we heard the devastating news that the Japanese had invaded Jehol province. Daily we listened with dread to bulletins reporting their rapid advance. Lowell Thomas was the man we listened to most frequently. In Chinese, Jehol is pronounced *re he* which sounds something like "Ruh Huh," but Lowell Thomas confidently pronounced it "Ray Hol," and for the first time in history that little-known part of the world was very much in the international spotlight. In a matter of seven days the Japanese overran the entire province, using their mechanized artillery, planes and tanks, and moving their infantry by trucks.

Tang Yu-lin's poorly armed and badly disciplined troops made little effort to stop them and fled even from what could have been nearly impregnable positions in the mountain passes without making the slightest pretense of digging in. Most of the soldiers melted into the countryside to swell the ranks of the bandits, while Tang, who had valiantly shouted to the world that his troops would defend the province to the last man, fled the capital of Chengde a few hours before the triumphant entry of the Japanese. It was only a few months later, though, that he was reinstated under Japanese pay as the puppet governor in an apparent attempt to minimize the havoc being wrought on the long-suffering populace by his defeated army.

Letters from Lingyuan became few and far between and very slow in reaching us in the United States. Mr. and Mrs. Sturt, together with the Misses Fischer and Minns, had been holding the fort for us in our absence. They were forced to write in the most carefully guarded language because of strict censorship by the Japanese. So while we looked forward to getting back to Lingyuan, we knew very little of what had actually happened or of what might await us.

Japan was, of course, the first nation to recognize the new country of Manchukuo, but other countries held off while the League of Nations debated the issue, forming commissions to study what Japan had done. El Salvador was actually the first foreign nation to give Manchukuo recognition, but it was purely by accident. A Japanese in the Manchukuo government had decided to send out a batch of cables to every country in the world, extending New Year's greetings from the "Emperor" of Manchukuo, but all except one of the cablegrams were ignored. In El Salvador, an official greeting was regarded as an official greeting to be answered, so a cablegram was sent back saying: "The president of El Salvador extends felicitations to the Emperor of Manchukuo." That was all Japan needed to trumpet the fact that Manchukuo had been recognized by one of the "great countries of the world." Later, the Vatican, Germany, Italy, Hungary and Franco's Spain all recognized the new empire, but they were the only ones to do so.

In early December 1933, before leaving the east coast for Detroit to pick up the Dodge van, there remained one major appointment for me to fill. The Plymouth Brethren held an annual conference each year, and that year it was to be in New York. I had been invited to share the platform with a number of other speakers and was allotted twenty minutes to make my presentation; the anticipation of it was quite an ordeal. The conference was held in a huge hall in the Fulton Street Fish Market area which seated 4,000 people. It was by far the largest group I had ever addressed. However, much as I dreaded it in advance, when it came my turn to speak I felt completely at ease. After all, I had a real message to give: not merely what I, with God's help, intended to do in China, but how, despite the great depression, God had answered my prayers and made possible a much greater field of work with the van that I had been given. As I left for Detroit shortly thereafter, I had the confidence that the prayers of those 4,000 people would follow me in support. With God on my side, the future looked very bright, despite the dark clouds that loomed over our beloved home in Manchuria.

Countryside around Lingyuan. At that time Bob went to markets and outlying churches by bicycle.

Dujiawopu market — Bob was wanting a car so he could visit more such markets.

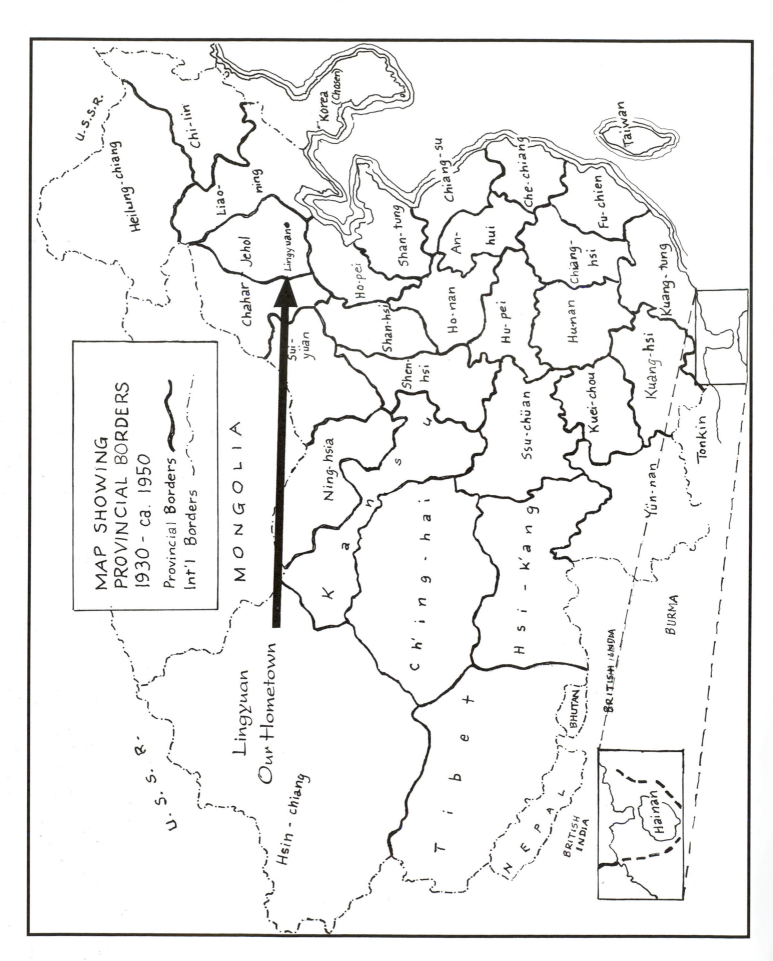

MAP SHOWING
PROVINCIAL BORDERS
1930 - ca. 1950

Provincial Borders
Int'l Borders

U.S.S.R.

Heilung-chiang

Chi-lin

Liao-ning

Korea (Chosen)

Taiwan

Chahar

Jehol

Lingyuan

Shan-tung

Chiang-su

Che-chiang

An-hui

Fu-chien

Ho-pei

Ho-nan

Chiang-hsi

Hunan

Kuang-tung

MONGOLIA

Sui-yuan

Shan-hsi

Shen-hsi

Hu-pei

Kuang-hsi

Kan s u

Ning-hsia

Ssu-chüan

Kuei-chou

Tonkin

Lingyuan
Our Hometown

Ch'ing-hai

Hsi-k'ang

Yün-nan

BURMA

Hsin-chiang

Tibet

NEPAL

BHUTAN

BRITISH INDIA

BRITISH INDIA

Hainan

口蜜腹劍

Kou mi fu jian.

Honey-mouthed and dagger-hearted.
(Honey on one's lips
and murder in one's heart).

- Chinese Proverb.

Book Two
1933 - 1941

Chapter Twenty
The New Manchuria

Early in December 1933, I arrived in Detroit two days before the scheduled delivery of my new Dodge van. I was so eager to see it, I immediately went over to the factory and found the people there most understanding, particularly when I told them I was taking it with me to China. They showed great interest and asked me if I would like to follow the step-by-step building of my van on the production line. Of course I was delighted, and as a result I had the unique opportunity of watching my much-awaited vehicle actually take form before my eyes as I followed it along the assembly line. It was a valuable experience, particularly when it came to carrying out repairs later in Lingyuan. I knew just where everything was, what it did, and how to take it apart and put it together again.

Just before I took delivery of the finished vehicle they took me into the office to sign some papers and I noticed the cost to the dealer was around $600, with an additional $300 or so added for his profit. In those days that seemed like a tremendous sum of money. The factory manager and his staff shook hands with me, escorted me out to the finished van, and handed over the keys while the staff applauded. I was so filled with pride and excitement as I climbed into my first beautiful car I could scarcely contain myself, but my first drive was a mere two blocks to a body shop, where I had arranged for them to modify it by cutting large windows in the panel sides and installing two rows of seats in the back. I also had them put in a rail on each side the length of the van, onto which the seats and seat backs could be laid to form a bed, while the boxes that provided a base for the seats allowed ample storage for tools and extra parts. My hand pump was the first item to go into one of the boxes.

Nowadays we are accustomed to seeing vans that have been "customized" with fancy side windows, plush carpeting, and comfortable armchairs, etc., but I like to think that mine was the very first one to have been altered in this way in the United States. Certainly, judging by the attention and comments it attracted wherever I went, that would seem to have been the case. The alterations to the van took about three or four days. and I spent the time watching the work being done, impatient to be on my way. I finally got away late one afternoon, and headed for Chicago, where I was to pick up Mother and the girls, who were going there by train. From there we would drive to California. I had the choice of going by road direct to Chicago and spending a night on the way in a motel, or taking the ferry across Lake Michigan to Milwaukee. I chose the latter because I could spend the night in a comfortable cabin and still be on the move.

In 1933, car heaters were a luxury, not standard equipment, nor were they supplied by the car manufacturer. At the body shop I had asked for the best possible heater that was available, telling them I needed as much heat as possible because of the cold Manchurian winters. The Arvin heater they installed certainly gave off plenty of heat during those first few miles on the way to Muskegon to catch the ferry, but it wasn't long before I noticed water dripping onto the floor mat, and soon it became a trickle that quickly turned into a miniature flood. I stopped and tried to tighten the clamps on the hoses to the heater but to no avail; the water kept pouring out, so I finally had to cut the heater off altogether.

In Milwaukee, I went to the first Arvin dealership I could find and asked them to repair it for me. Astonishingly, they told me it was a three-year-old model that had been patched up with plaster of Paris and that there was nothing they could do to repair it — all the inside pipes were rotted through. With their help I composed an angry telegram to the Detroit body shop demanding a new heater be delivered to me in Chicago. I continued on my way, but it was a cold and snowy trip. Two days later in Chicago I was given a brand-new heater, but the Detroit firm denied having tampered in any way with the first one, insisting it had been right out of the box and in first-class condition when they installed it. I imagine one of the service men had made the substitution, thinking that it would last me until I got to China and then it would be too late for me to do anything about it.

Having been to Chicago earlier in the year, I was fairly familiar with the layout of the city and drove around with confidence. I had two days to wait until Mother and the girls arrived, and now that I was back there with my brand-new van, I had a compulsion to show it off to Eva. I phoned her and without mentioning the car, made a date to take her out that evening. So it was that Eva was the very first person to ride in the car, and I proudly drove her around the city as she told me about the various places we passed.

Not knowing any particularly good restaurant, I was nonetheless determined to find a really "classy" place for dinner on that, our first date. For some reason I wanted to properly impress her, and as I drove, I looked for a place that might have proper table linen and silver, and deferential waiters who would make the evening a real success. On one of the main streets I finally saw the place I was looking for: it had an imposing front of green tile and lots of chrome, but the front windows were tinted glass, and I couldn't see the interior. However, I felt certain it had to be expensive. We parked and walked in the front door, passing immediately through some turnstiles, and to my utter dismay I discovered too late that it was just another fancy cafeteria. However, it didn't seem to matter to Eva and we enjoyed our evening together, talking over old times in the China that we both loved. Eva told me she was jealous that I was returning there so soon, while she still had several more years to wait until she finished her courses at Moody's.

Later I delivered her to the door of her rooming house and said goodbye. I was not to see her again for three years, and although she and my sister Ruth kept in touch by mail, I must frankly admit that I had very little time to give her much thought during the busy months that followed. Again, I can honestly say that never for one single moment did it occur to me that one day she would become my wife. As far as I was concerned, that was not in the realm of the possible.

From Chicago, with Mother and the girls aboard, we drove the famous old Route 66 to California, a two-lane blacktop road in those days. Christmas Day found us in Arizona, in beautiful, stark desert country. We had a picnic lunch just off the highway under a cactus, and there opened our gifts as the sun beat down upon us, and from there went on to spend the night in a tiny town called Globe.

Crossing the Mojave Desert in 1933 was very different from what it is now. Because gas stations were many miles apart, every car that crossed the desert then took along water in canvas bags, hung from either the radiator ornament or the back bumper. In some of the sandier places we traveled for miles on the old log road, which was still in use. It was a narrow single track about eight feet wide, with occasional "turnouts," where one waited if a car was spotted coming from the opposite direction. At one such turnout we spotted an old rusty spike, one of those used to hold the logs in place, and we picked it up and took it along as a souvenir. It is unlikely that many of those could be found today. We took it to China, where it possibly still is, left there with everything else that we owned.

When we reached California, I decided to take the coast road, Route 1, to avoid traffic, but it was a mistake. It was in the middle of the rainy season, and we got only as far as a place called Point Dana, where, in the torrential rains, an entire cliff had slid down and wiped out the highway. For two or three days we were stranded in that small community, where there was only one motel and little else. As the rains poured down unceasingly, we became fearful that we would miss our ship's sailing, but we finally got away, and after a brief stop in Monrovia to visit our old friends the Jacksons, we headed north again to San Francisco, arriving in plenty of time to find Father there awaiting us. Before sailing we had a big send-off by friends from both sides of the bay.

Our ship was the *Asama Maru*, the same one we had "raced" on our trip across two years before. She had been modified, was quite seaworthy, and with two other ships of the same NYK line was running scheduled trips across the Pacific. Her sister ship the *Tatuta Maru* (mispronounced Tatsuta) was later to be involved with an exchange of prisoners after Pearl Harbor, and we came to know her very well, too. The third ship, built later, was much larger and more modern, and was first named the *Chichibu Maru* in honor of a Japanese prince. That ship, however, seemed destined to have troubles. After becoming fairly well known to the American public by that name, the Japanese government decided to change their system of romanizing Japanese words, and the new spelling of the ship's name became *Titibu Maru*. The first time she sailed into San Francisco harbor, the new name occasioned such a storm of hilarity and offbeat jokes that the name was immediately changed to *Kamakura*

Maru. In early 1942, right after Japan's conquest of Indonesia and Singapore, the *Kamakura Maru* was torpedoed off Java by an American submarine. She split in two and sank immediately with a great loss of life. She was carrying high-ranking Japanese military and civilian officials who were on their way to take over administrative duties in the newly conquered territories. Few, if any, survived.

The day before we sailed I drove the Dodge van down to the pier and watched with considerable concern as the stevedores put a sling underneath it and swung it aboard to be stowed in one of the lower holds. Surprisingly they didn't even drain the gasoline from the tank, and nothing was done to protect the engine against the damp sea air, something that caused me a considerable amount of trouble once we arrived in Manchuria.

As we sailed through the Golden Gate we could see preparations being made on both shores for construction of what is now perhaps the most famous bridge in the world. It was to be eleven years before I was to see the shores of America again.

Our trip across the Pacific — with a brief stop in Honolulu, as was common with most trans-Pacific ships at the time — was uneventful and enjoyable. We were impressed by the excellent service given by the entire Japanese crew and the deference they showed to passengers. There were probably 200 fellow passengers with us in second class, but apart from us and Don Hunter, there were only a dozen or so other "civilians," including the mining engineer whom I wrote about in a previous chapter. The rest of the passengers were all members of a colorful vaudeville troupe composed of several different nationalities en route to perform in both Japan and China. Our days and evenings were kept lively by those very versatile men and women who were continuously rehearsing their acts. Of particular interest was a group of Arabian jugglers and acrobats who performed daily on deck, and a number of singers could be heard practicing day and night. We were somewhat amused by their constant concern for their throats. All of them wore woolen scarves when on deck, and they were never seen without a bottle of medicinal spray to ward off colds. And, of course, there was a sizable chorus line of very attractive young women, who, however, were kept very much in their place by an older woman in charge who happened to sit at our table. None of the girls was permitted to come into the dining room dressed in shorts, but almost every day one or more of them would defy the rule and try to sneak in unseen by the boss lady. We found it very amusing.

Arriving in Japan, our China visas were declared invalid, and it was a new experience for us to have to get visas for the new country of Manchukuo. It proved to be a relatively easy procedure because the Japanese were anxious to gain recognition from the Western powers and therefore treated us with deference. However, it was a nuisance we could have done without. We transferred to a small Japanese ship that took us (and the van) through the Inland Sea of Japan, and across the straits to Dairen (*Dalian*) on the tip of the Liaotong Peninsula of Manchuria, a very modern port that had long been under Japanese domination and that was the southern terminus of the South Manchurian Railway (SMR).

In Dairen it took two days to clear the van through customs, even with considerable assistance from a Japanese Christian gentleman in the customs service. Through his good efforts, and because the van had been used, we didn't have to pay any duty. Through the local Dodge agency I arranged to have them ship the van by railway to Beipiao, which they did, although due to moisture in the engine they had considerable difficulty in getting the engine started. On the third day we boarded a train, and after two changes of trains, we arrived in Beipiao to a very warm welcome from our old friends Dr. and Mrs. Lu. From them we were surprised and gratified to learn that the South Manchurian Railway had inaugurated a daily bus service to Lingyuan and beyond. The next morning we all got aboard the bus for a one-day trip.

The busses being used were somewhat crude. Produced in a Manchurian factory, they were built onto a Japanese copy of a Chevrolet chassis, and while certainly more comfortable than an open truck, the seats were narrow and hard and built so closely together it was impossible to stretch one's legs, and we were glad when the trip was over.

The condition of the road was the biggest surprise to us. The Japanese had been in occupation of the province for only a few months, but they had used impressed labor to widen the road for most of its length, and to some extent had smoothed out the grades on the steep mountain passes. While nothing

to boast about, it was still a great improvement over the old cart road, and with the crushed-rock surface that they were applying, it would stand up fairly well to the summer rains.

However, nothing had been done to bridge the many rivers, and once or twice we got stuck and everyone had to get out and push. There was strong evidence of continued unrest in the area, with bandits suspected nearby. Despite the fact that there was a considerable amount of military truck traffic moving back and forth on the road, a truckload of Japanese soldiers accompanied our bus. We also saw a large number of SMR vehicles in evidence; it was obvious that construction of a railway line was soon to begin, and so it proved.

In Lingyuan we received a tumultuous welcome from the Sturts and the Misses Fischer and Minns, as well as all our Chinese friends, who turned out en masse to greet us, many of them waiting long hours at the bus station. To our surprise, horse-drawn Russian-style droshkies were plying the streets hauling passengers. Made in Mukden, the four-wheeled vehicles were drawn by a single horse between shafts, which were joined at the front by an arch over the horse. They were well-sprung and had hard-rubber tires on the wheels, which made for a relatively comfortable ride. There were also a number of rickshaws, and hundreds of bicycles and of course, Japanese flags everywhere, together with the new Manchukuo flag. In many ways we had a hard time recognizing the town as the same place we had left two years before.

On our way to West Street we saw many new Japanese stores as well, while Japanese civilians and Japanese soldiers filled the streets. Lingyuan, while apparently physically untouched by the fighting, was nevertheless greatly changed, and one of the very first things demanded of us after our arrival was a visit to the police station to be finger-printed and issued Manchukuo passports. Those little books, very crude copies of the British passports we carried, were to be taken with us wherever we went. I still have mine, which I brought out with me years later, and every time I look at it, it brings back unpleasant memories of encounters with arrogant and imperious Japanese officials, who never missed the chance to let us know that in their view they were the superior race and we were there purely and simply by their tolerance. Yet during those early days after our arrival, the Japanese were, for the most part, very correct in their behavior toward us, though quite obviously they distrusted our intentions and suspected that we were more than the missionaries we purported to be.

We noted very quickly after our arrival that the Japanese were trying to correct the savage image they had created for themselves, making up to the local people after their initial harsh treatment. Shortly after our arrival they held a public ceremony where the elderly men and women of the city were invited to an outdoor party. There, the Japanese "honored" them by giving every Chinese man over the age of sixty a walking cane, and the elderly women a package of cakes. However, the friendly attitude did not last very long.

From the Sturts and our Chinese friends we learned first-hand of the events surrounding the initial Japanese invasion of the province. With no advance warning, Japanese planes had flown over the city dropping leaflets, some written in Chinese and others in English, telling the populace to seek shelter and remain quiet, and announcing that the Japanese army was coming with the sole aim of putting down banditry and destroying enemy troops, and they gave assurances that all Chinese civilians and foreigners would be protected.

Subsequently, as the Japanese armored column approached, planes bombed in advance. Although some bombs fell very close behind our compound, none actually fell on the city, and the defending army of Tang Yu-lin fled in disarray, leaving a short lull before the Japanese came in.

Carrying both British and Red Cross flags, Mr. Sturt, together with a few of the leading citizens and some of the officials who had not fled the city, went outside the northern gate to meet the incoming Japanese. They stood on a high knoll overlooking the river in order to be visible from a distance, but there were a few tense moments when the advancing troops with their hundreds of camouflaged vehicles stopped their tanks and trucks on the opposite bank of the river and looked at the welcoming party through binoculars. Evidently satisfied, an armored car raced to the head of the column and approached the welcoming party. A Japanese general got out, shook hands all around, and appeared quite friendly. The welcoming party told the general the city was empty of enemy troops and thanked him for sparing the city from damage.

After instructing the local officials to carry on as usual and telling them that he would appoint new officials to take the places of those who had fled, he climbed back into his vehicle and led his column of trucks and tanks through the city, and out the western gate in pursuit of Tang Yu-lin's forces. In the following days thousands of Japanese troops poured through the city, heading west, and in a little over a week the Japanese announced that the entire province had been occupied. Hearing all that I felt considerable regret at not having been there to see all the excitement, but Mother was deeply grateful that she had missed it all.

On every occasion that I can remember when an incoming army took over the city, it invariably happened that the prison gate was opened and all the prisoners were freed. Sometimes it was done by the fleeing guards: more often by the conquerors. When the Japanese came in, it was no different. Again all the prisoners were freed, and among them were the two young ex-soldiers who had almost been shot some years before for having tried to flee the army. One of the first things they did was to come to the mission residence to express their thanks to Father once again for saving their lives, and they were most disappointed to hear that he had not returned yet. As time went on I got to know both of them well, and they frequently attended church services. I believe both of them were convinced that God had a hand in sparing their lives.

Subsequently the Japanese placed many of the freed criminals in their plainclothes network, and adopted the Chinese method of organizing the city government by means of what the Chinese called the *bao jia* administrative system, a sort of militia, where a *jia* was made up of 10 households and each *bao* consisted of ten *jia*. The Japanese placed murderers, thieves and former bandits on every street as the heads of each *bao* unit, giving them the power of life and death over 100 households. They were ordered by the Japanese to spy on their neighbors and report on any anti-Japanese activity or any expression of dissent by a Chinese citizen against the Japanese. Within days, a reign of terror began as the Chinese began reporting on each other either as a way of getting rid of old enemies or simply as a means of self-protection.

Chinese friends of mine who were eyewitnesses

told me of mass executions just outside our back wall and showed me where the victims had been buried. I was told that more than 5,000 civilians, both men and women, had been executed by the Japanese, reported by those former criminals who were not paid enough to keep quiet. The Japanese didn't waste bullets on them: they seemed to delight in showing off with their samurai swords, competing with each other to see how many they could behead before they became exhausted or their swords became so dull they would no longer cut. Many of the victims, of course, were former soldiers in Tang's army who had tried to hide in the city, but a great many innocent people known to me were also victims, and several were personal friends, as well as Christians.

By the time we arrived, sometime around April 1934, things had quieted down somewhat, and there was a semblance of law and order at least in the city itself. A week or so later I received a telegram from Dr. Lu telling me that my van had arrived in Beipiao, and I rode the bus there to retrieve it. Driving back was most enjoyable and quite uneventful, and I had the opportunity of stopping off in the city of Chaoyang to show off the van to our friends the Brewsters. I was greatly surprised to find during the entire trip that, although I saw many Japanese on the road and passed a number of checkpoints, not once was I stopped for questioning. Apparently (as far as they were concerned), my civilian automobile was on the road because someone higher up had given the necessary authorization, and there was no need to question the driver, even if he did happen to be a Westerner. From that experience I had my first lesson in how to deal with the Japanese. I found it advisable never to ask permission to do something, because it inevitably resulted in either a flat refusal or a tremendous amount of red tape. No one apparently wanted to take the responsibility of granting a request for fear of repercussions, but refusing permission was always an acceptable alternative. From that point on, I simply went ahead and did what I wanted to do until I was told to stop.

The Lingyuan to which we had returned was a very different place in many ways. As each day dawned we were reminded how different it was. At the Yamen each morning at sunrise we could hear the Manchukuo national anthem being sung lustily by a hundred or more voices. It was mandatory that all officials attend, both Chinese and Japanese, together with a large contingent of police and the children from a nearby school. The first words of the anthem were: *Tian di nei youle xin Manzhou, xin Manzhou jiushi xin tian di.* "Between heaven and earth there is a new Manchuria. The new Manchuria is a new heaven and earth." It didn't matter to the Japanese that the Chinese deliberately distorted the tune. And what the Japanese didn't know was that the Chinese had altered certain words and were singing something entirely different from the original. Even those Japanese who spoke a little Chinese failed to catch on. For example, the first line shown above was changed to: "Between heaven and earth there is now a big cauldron full of porridge." The Chinese word for "cauldron" sounded like the word for "country," and "porridge" sounded like the "chou" of Manchoukuo. There were further examples throughout the song, and in little ways like that, the Chinese found satisfaction in getting back at their conquerors, an oblique but nonetheless effective means of boosting their own morale. All Chinese officials and school children were also required to learn Japanese, so another way the Chinese found satisfaction was to distort the Japanese words that they learned, using Chinese words that sounded similar. An example was the Japanese word for goodbye, "sayonara." The Chinese made up a similar-sounding four-syllable word: "*sa you na la,*" which if said quickly sounded very much like the original, but broke down to: "(If you) spill the oil (in the lamp) then you pick up a candle." There were many other examples of their having fun with the Japanese language, most of them scatological.

Our lives were also very different. Scarcely a week passed when uninvited Japanese soldiers didn't amble into the compound. Most came out of curiosity, others looking for contraband or for Chinese soldiers in hiding. More often than not, they were very drunk. One never knew when to expect them, or what to expect from them. They always spelled trouble and they were frequently difficult to get rid of. Rarely, unless it was an official visit, were they accompanied by an interpreter. Language problems abounded.

Most often the Japanese soldiers were looking for eggs. They were afraid to eat anything from the Chinese food stalls or from restaurants. But they felt eggs were safe: when they found eggs they would, for the most part, scrupulously pay for them. However, it was some time before the Chinese learned what it was that the Japanese were looking for. Not knowing the Chinese word for eggs, the Japanese soldiers like so many American tourists abroad, believed that by shouting loudly they could make themselves understood. Their shouts of "tomago, tomago," and their attempts to cackle like a hen, at the same time putting one hand to the seat of their pants, then bringing it forward with the first finger and thumb forming a rough oval to simulate an egg, simply confused the Chinese, who saw it as some form of indecent gesture. When no eggs were forthcoming, despite the presence of hens in the yard, most often the Japanese would resort to beating the poor Chinese. As a result, it wasn't too long before every Chinese knew at least that one word of Japanese.

Chinese women, with good reason, were terrified of rape when an army of occupation came in. Generally speaking, the Chinese peasants welcomed the Japanese after their years of suffering under Tang Yu-lin. For the women, though, the fears were the same when the Japanese first came, but they need not have worried. The Japanese military showed no interest in Chinese women, nor would they visit the Chinese brothels. They brought their own women with them. Immediately behind the frontline troops were truckloads of Korean girls, widely known as "comfort girls." In every city and town the Japanese occupied they took over the first house that suited them and their brothels were in business within a matter of hours. Lingyuan sported well over a dozen such houses by the time we arrived, all populated by highly painted and pathetic young Korean women, forcibly brought into that strange and hostile environment. Because of the many years they had been under Japanese subjugation in Korea, most of the women spoke Japanese fluently, but few had any way of communicating with the Chinese. It wasn't long, though, before they hired Chinese helpers, usually men, and with gestures they made their needs known. A bastardized form of speech quickly evolved, each side learning a word or two of the other's language; mixing them, they managed to convey their ideas.

Those first weeks back in Lingyuan form a kaleidoscopic picture in my mind. It is hard to remember clearly the events as they occurred. There was much confusion as the Japanese attempted to sort things out

and colonize the people. It was an ever-changing scene, with new Japanese officials coming into town just when we had become accustomed to the old ones, and in time we learned that that was to be the fixed Japanese policy. They seldom kept any official in place for more than three months because the Chinese were so adept at bribing and corrupting their conquerors.

The Japanese promulgated new laws and regulations, set up rationing and food distribution systems, and levied new taxes. But in almost every case the Chinese found a way to get around them. When a new Japanese official arrived, the Chinese would quietly levy a small "head tax" on each family or household, then give a sizable "gift" to the incoming official, who would then turn a blind eye to whatever went on. It was a delicate balancing act for the Chinese. The Japanese wanted it to appear that it was the Chinese themselves who were running everything, so every official position was manned by a Chinese, but at the same time in every office, either government or civilian, there was always a Japanese "adviser" alongside the Chinese occupant. Although ostensibly the Chinese gave the orders, he actually dared do nothing openly without the consent of his adviser. Despite that, the Chinese weren't fazed. They went through all the motions of obeying the rules, toadying to the Japanese, but then quietly doing exactly as they wished. During the ten years or more that the Japanese occupied Manchuria, they never had any real success in colonizing the country.

Land taxes were a prime example. The Japanese pored over their maps, surveyed the land, marked out everyone's holdings, and levied their taxes, only to find themselves in a maze of lawsuits because of unclear boundaries. What happened was, as the Japanese surveyors went around, the Chinese peasants and landowners went ahead of them and overnight moved all the land markers to different positions, and moved them back when the Japanese surveyors had left. Maps were drawn and re-drawn, all in vain.

The struggle went on for months until finally the Japanese thought they had the answer. They had a fairly efficient airline that spanned the country with small planes that seated about ten people. With no warning they canceled all flights, and for several weeks they used the planes to photograph the entire province of Jehol, and pieced together the aerial maps, marking in the boundaries as they spotted them. However, the Chinese were again ahead of them. Even as the planes flew over, Chinese farmers ostensibly working in the fields were actually quietly and systematically moving every boundary stone to a new location. Ultimately it was the Chinese who won, and the Japanese had to give up in despair. They ended up levying a tax simply by taking the word of the local headman as to who owned what, accepting his word for the correct land measurements, which quite naturally always turned out in favor of the Chinese.

Rumors constantly flowed in and around the city as to what the Japanese were going to do next. Everywhere they were building something and tearing something else down. They took over Chinese stores and remodeled the storefronts to look like Japanese stores — paper and glass windows and sliding doors. Land and houses, both inside and outside the city, were requisitioned with little or no recourse for the poor owners. The Japanese military simply took what they wanted and kicked the owners out, but the Japanese businessmen paid small token amounts for properties they confiscated, leaving the owners to take it to court if they dared.

Two very exciting things happened in close succession not long after we returned to Lingyuan: first we got electricity in the city and then the railway came through. The coming of the electric light plant was not known very far in advance, and the first we knew about it was the building of a brick kiln just outside the north gate. It was modern in design and within a few weeks the Japanese were turning out small red bricks by the thousands. Then, after tearing down a number of residences on North Street, they started constructing the electric plant. The tall chimney was our first indication of what it was to be.

Well before the plant was finished, a swarm of Korean electricians came into town and started stringing wires. Not bothering to put up any poles along the streets, they simply strung the black-coated wires from house to house under the eaves, using long nails to fasten the rough ceramic insulators to the rafters, separating the wires by some six inches or so. Only at main intersections were poles erected to carry the wires across the streets.

On the outside of the front doorway of each house or place of business, a small black metal box was installed with a knife-switch inside. The wires were connected to it, then carried inside the building. Not a single meter was to be found in the entire city. They followed a simple rule of thumb: every room in every house got a single, drop-light fixture, hanging either from the inside roof beams or from any piece of wood they could conveniently find. Each wire ended with a black bakelite lamp socket, with a thumb-switch on the side and an enameled shade above it, green on top and white underneath. A flat monthly rate was charged for each fixture. Along the streets, every tenth house or so had an outdoor light, which acted as a street light. That light was not charged to the owner of the property. Throughout the city, the entire installation was basic, rough, but highly efficient. It surprised us that, despite the lack of any protective devices anywhere, we never heard of any instances of someone being electrocuted.

It was a big event for everyone when the lights were turned on for the first time. Streets that had been dark for centuries suddenly took on a new look. That first night the streets were packed with people out to enjoy the new experience of lighted streets. We enjoyed the coming of electricity as much or more than anyone else; however, the single 40-watt bulbs we were allowed in each room were totally inadequate to read by. Before long I started buying wire, receptacles, and lamps from a Japanese store in town and installing our own lights wherever we wanted them without asking for permission. Again, to have asked permission would simply have resulted in a flat refusal on general principles.

The coming of the SMR extension through our province was a much slower affair, but a great deal more spectacular. Some ten or fifteen years before, a middle-aged Japanese gentleman had arrived in Lingyuan one day riding in a mule litter; being a foreigner, he had been directed to our residence. He spoke a little English and my parents gave him a warm welcome and we put him up for several days. A most interesting man, named Tanaka, he turned out to be a university professor from Tokyo. His job was to survey the route for a railway to be built through the province at some future date.

He told us he was employed by the Chinese government, but we doubted that. Professor Tanaka was very reserved to begin with, very frightened of the

Chinese, and he was scared to death of catching some kind of illness from them. At first he would drink only the water he carried with him in sealed bottles, and he was carrying enough for several weeks. However, when he saw how healthy we were, he was persuaded to drink our tea and coffee, and once he relaxed he told us of his mission, showed us the maps he had drawn, and explained to us just exactly where he planned to put the railroad. Now, some ten or fifteen years later the exact route he had laid out was being used, and we watched with extreme interest as the line slowly crept toward us.

The coming of the railroad was heralded first by an influx of large trucks and small American Ford and Chevrolet sedans, all with canvas roofs and all carrying the very distinctive SMR logo: a cross-section of a piece of rail. The Japanese name for the SMR was *Mantetsu*, and the Chinese called it *Man Tie*, meaning "Manchurian Iron." For months we heard those words over and over again as the Japanese ruthlessly confiscated land for the railroad right-of-way and appropriated a huge parcel of fine market-garden land a half-mile or so west of the city for the station, making only token payments to the individual owners.

The trucks started hauling in vast quantities of lumber and cement, and a second large brick-kiln was built near the station site. But there were no bulldozers or earthmovers of any kind, nor even a single dump truck. Every bit of earth for the railroad embankment was moved by human labor. Day after day hundreds of local citizens were rounded up to work on the railway bed, again, with only token wages. As the line neared the city, every household was required to produce one able-bodied man each day, and he had to report with his own shovel, mattock, or carrying baskets. It proved to be a great hardship for the people, many of whom lost their livelihood for weeks, and it was particularly hard on the country peasants. Where there were long stretches of the line between villages, the villagers were taken from their homes and forced to follow the construction gangs for many miles, until new labor could be found.

We watched the building of a massive railway bridge across the North River just outside the North Gate with intense interest, and smaller ones across the several gullies behind our house. For the big bridge they chose a spot just a hundred yards or so north of the existing road crossing. Despite a high earthen embankment approach built on the far side of the river, the bridge itself had to be constructed on a gradual incline to compensate for the high bank on the near side of the river. The Japanese engineers were impressive in their efficiency. Huge wooden caissons were built in the middle of the river bed where the concrete piers were to go, the river water being diverted temporarily as they built the piers, and in a very few weeks the huge concrete towers rose inside the caissons. A few days after that, the track-laying train arrived, carrying immense girders for the bridge, and crowds of people watched in awe as those immense pieces of metal were lifted out across the chasms by a large crane, and then the track-laying train advanced behind it.

The route selected by the Japanese for the railroad right-of-way crossed the river directly in line with an ancient temple that had stood there for hundreds, perhaps thousands of years, but they tore it down despite the protests of the people. However, they were in a dilemma as to what to do with the huge earthen idols from the temple. They asked their own appointed Chinese magistrate for advice. He in turn called together a number of local priests from other temples; between them it was decided that rather than relocate the idols in another temple, they would be placed in the river just in front of the temple site, and simply be allowed to disintegrate in the water. With much fanfare and shooting off of fireworks, the statues were stood up in the shallow water in front of where the temple had been and there they gradually dissolved as hundreds of people lined the banks and watched.

From the bridge, the railway embankment came in a direct line toward our back garden wall and passed us a mere four or five hundred yards away. It barely missed the Mohammedan cemetery, and just back of our house it passed directly through a large burial ground that had probably been there for centuries. The Japanese posted notices that they were going to move the graves unless living relatives of the dead did so. Many graves had been there so long that there were no living relatives around, so the Japanese simply dumped everything in one huge grave they dug in a nearby field. One very large burial mound yielded a huge quantity of artifacts: ancient bronzes, ceramics of all kinds, pottery, and terra-cotta figures. The Japanese appropriated what they wanted and smashed much of the rest, but during the night the laborers managed to spirit away quite a quantity, and for weeks the things were secretly on sale. A lot of them were brought to our front gate by night for us to see, and Father bought several beautiful porcelain "stools" which the Chinese use to sit on in the summertime to cool off. He paid Mex. $1 for each of them, just a few cents in American money. The same things in America would have cost a small fortune.

Prior to the Japanese occupation of Jehol, the Chinese had always had a very strong feeling of sympathy toward Korean nationals. For many years the Chinese had known of Korea being enslaved by the Japanese, and the few Koreans who had visited Lingyuan had always been feted. Now, however, things were very different. From the border between Korea and Manchuria, the Japanese had enlisted the services of hundreds of Chinese-speaking Koreans who also spoke Japanese. They were used as foremen or overseers to manage the thousands of Chinese coolies used to carry earth for the railway embankment, building the bridges and digging the numerous tunnels on the line.

Those Koreans proved to be the dregs of humanity and were merciless in their treatment of the Chinese, not only beating them unmercifully, but in many cases killing them, and, since they were in charge of handing out wages, robbing them as well. Within a matter of weeks, Koreans were hated even more than the Japanese. Many times I watched as they whipped, clubbed and drove the Chinese laborers to the point of utter exhaustion. The Japanese civilian overseers were no better; they in turn used their clubs on the Koreans when the work wasn't done fast enough or wasn't to their liking.

Technically we were exempted from the demand to produce one able-bodied man each day to work on the railway. But Father didn't want to take any favors from the Japanese while the Chinese around us were made to suffer, so every day we sent a man out to work, the yard men taking turns going. Sometimes we hired a man to go when things around the house kept our own men busy. From every source we heard stories of the cruelty of both the Koreans and the Japanese, and very quickly the Chinese began to feel that they were not any better off under Japanese rule than they had been under Tang Yu-lin, and in many cases they felt they were worse off.

With typical Japanese efficiency, passenger train service was started immediately after the railway station was completed, while the building of the line continued to push westward. On the day that the first passenger train pulled in, the Japanese held a big celebration, complete with Shinto priests to dedicate the station, and it seemed as though the entire population of the city turned out to watch. It was an exciting day for us as well. To be directly linked with civilization was a strange feeling indeed. But at the same time we had mixed emotions as we saw the tremendous changes taking place, our simple and unsophisticated little city becoming a den of iniquity and vice, brought in by the Japanese and Koreans, and the demoralization of the people as the Japanese imposed ever tighter controls upon everything they did.

For us, we had to resolve a moral question with regard to the Japanese conquerors: whether or not to accept them as the lawful authority ruling the country, and, as the Bible teaches, implicitly obey the new rules and regulations being laid down. Since Manchukuo was not recognized as an official state by any major country except Japan, it was not difficult to make the decision that the Japanese were invaders and illegally in the country, and, therefore, not the lawful authority. While we, like the Chinese, gave the appearance of complying with the new laws, we had no bad conscience and no compunction whatsoever in using every opportunity to sidestep the rules and regulations whenever we felt they were unfair and harmful to the people, and in most cases we were able to get away with it just as the Chinese did.

Actually it proved to be very simple both for the Chinese and for us as well. As mentioned earlier, the Japanese made a big show of technically putting all controls into the hands of their puppet stooges. Chinese were appointed to every position of authority, but in every instance they had a Japanese alongside as an adviser, and since the adviser spoke no Chinese, there had to be interpreters as well. The interpreters made small fortunes in bribes, while the Chinese administrators made larger fortunes, and the Chinese were adept at making it look as though things were going just as the Japanese wanted them to go, while doing just what they had been doing for years before the Japanese came.

In our case we never had to resort to bribery. For the first several weeks after our return, I spent a lot of my time in getting to know every official, Chinese and Japanese. Being the only foreigners in town was an advantage. The Japanese craved recognition by our government, and at first they generally bent over backward to be friendly. Local Chinese who had been appointed as officials all knew us by sight or by reputation, and the newcomers among the Chinese were flattered that we would associate with them. In most cases, I either went ahead and did what I wanted without asking permission, or, in order to make the Japanese feel important, I would make an official request where it was not terribly important to me and where I was sure they would not object, and invariably they would comply. In turn, all I had to do to reciprocate the goodwill of the Chinese and Japanese officials was to give them an occasional ride in the van or invite them to the house for tea and cakes. I discovered that the Japanese craved fresh cow's milk, and with only two cows, we were hard put at times to satisfy them.

Although the Japanese were well aware of the activities of Christians in their own country, they were still highly suspicious of us, and, from the very beginning, we were trailed by plainclothes men wherever we went. As time went on I got to know most of them by sight, because they were not very adept at concealing their movements. I was even able to establish a good rapport with some of them. At one point, I knew of at least 28 different men who were assigned just to watch me. We became used to their slipping into the compound at all hours of the day and night, sometimes coming in over the wall. Our dogs got so used to them that they didn't even bark when they came in. For the most part we learned to ignore them, and we let them walk around wherever they wanted to. Of course, not all 28 were on duty at any one time, nor were they all assigned to watch our compound. They worked in shifts, and one would be watching the compound while another would follow me when I went out. Since I was usually either on a bicycle or driving the van, they would pass me off to the next man posted at a strategic point to observe my movements. On those occasions when they lost me, they would later question me at length as to where I had been, with whom I had talked, and generally make a nuisance of themselves. I eventually resolved that problem by frankly telling them in advance where I was going just so they could have someone waiting at the other end to observe whatever it was I did. We had nothing to hide. As time passed they slackened off to some extent, but there were some amusing incidents over the years.

I recall one evening going to my room, and just before going to bed I sat down at my desk to write a letter. As I sat there typing, I had the distinct sensation that someone was watching me, but I brushed it off after looking around the room and not seeing anyone. After about thirty minutes I distinctly heard a slight movement, and when I turned to look in that direction, I saw a very shamefaced man crawl out from under my bed. How long he'd been there I've no idea, nor did I ask him. I just treated it as though it was the most natural thing in the world. I greeted him, offered him tea as though he had just entered the room by the door, and asked him to stay awhile and chat. However, the constant watching of our every movement did nothing to calm our nerves, and the strain of having to be constantly on the alert and to be certain not to in any way involve the Chinese, who would suffer as a consequence, became very odious at times.

During those early months I made a serious effort to learn Japanese, and in time I became sufficiently proficient in the language to be able to communicate fairly freely with them when I needed to, though for the most part I concealed the fact that I understood them. It proved to be very handy to know the language, particularly on those frequent occasions when drunken Japanese soldiers would force their way into the compound. Two young soldiers came in one evening, and despite the efforts of Katie, the doorman, to dissuade them, they forced their way back to our living quarters. I heard a ruckus outside and went to see what was happening. I found Barbara's big German shepherd, Wolf, waltzing around the two soldiers with a stone in his mouth that he wanted them to throw for him. At the same time, one of the two drunken men was trying valiantly to stab the dog with his bayonet, believing the dog was about to attack. Katie, on the other hand, was trying to hold the man back and was being pummeled by the second man. I stepped in and intervened and found myself the target of their rage, and the man with the bayonet turned on me and tried to stab me. However, Katie quite sensibly took the stone from Wolf's mouth and threw it for him to get him out of the way. After that the two men were more readily pacified and I was able to escort them off the premises. That was by no means the only incident of its kind. We had to be constantly on the alert to forestall intrusions which could happen at any hour of the day or night.

The Japanese, either deliberately or purely by accident, opened a brothel directly across the street from our compound. Where there had been no door, they cut a door in the back of a large compound, (which was normally accessible only through an alley), and established about a dozen Japanese girls there exclusively for the use of officers. Quite frequently, however, ordinary soldiers would try to get in, and when barred they would come across the street to our place hoping to find women there. Most of the activity across the street occurred at night, but there was daytime activity as well, and we used to see high-ranking officers arrive in their extra-long staff cars. The cars were over twenty feet in length and seated eight comfortably. They were very odd-looking and unique in that, on both sides, placed in the middle between the doors, they had an extra wheel that normally was about six inches off the ground. It only came into use when the vehicle went over a hump, and was intended to prevent the vehicle from becoming hung up. However, they had not taken into consideration the many small dips in Chinese roads where gullies had been formed by summer freshets, and on several occasions I saw the vehicles, because of their extreme length, hung up where both ends had stuck into the opposite banks when trying to negotiate one of those dips.

When the officers didn't arrive at the brothel in their cars, they rode their Arabian horses, horses that were almost twice as tall as the little Chinese ponies and that astounded the Chinese. It was most amusing to see those diminutive Japanese officers trying to dismount the horses with dignity. They often fell off, and getting back on, particularly when they were drunk, was even more amusing. They couldn't reach the stirrups and had to have two of their men form a cradle with their hands and heave them up into the saddle. Fortunately, the Japanese troops were moved elsewhere after a relatively short period, and although there was always a Japanese presence in the city, with a large number of officers, there were not enough apparently to warrant the several officer brothels that were around, and the one across the street from us

closed after a few months.

While the intrusions by the Japanese soldiers were always an annoyance and often caused us anxious moments, it helped to be able to talk with them in their own language, and they were always surprised to find that I could communicate with them. While those young men always acted with extreme brutality toward the Chinese, or anyone else for that matter, and always adopted a ferocity of manner that was quite intimidating, for many reasons I had a great deal of sympathy for them. They were far from home in a strange land with a harsh climate that they found unbearable. They were generally fearful of the people and everything around them, and by their bluff and brutal behavior toward the Chinese, they tried to mask their fear. I had been fortunate in finding the English translation of a book written by a young Japanese gendarme in the much feared *Kempeitai*, the Japanese military police. In it he described not only the brutal training he had undergone to get into that force, and the constant beatings to which he had been subjected, but he described his dismay at finding himself in Manchuria, where everything was foreign to him, where even his own people despised him, and all he wanted to do was to get back to his beloved Japan.

The *Kempeitai* were the ones I tried to avoid as much as possible, as did both the Chinese and Japanese civilians. With the *Kempeitai*, it was the policy of both officers and men to be unapproachable, and anyone unfortunate enough to get into their hands seldom again saw the light of day. They had their headquarters near the main intersection in the center of the city, and frequently as I passed in front of the place I could hear the screams of victims being tortured inside.

The *Kempeitai* exerted their authority over Japanese civilians as well as the military and often treated their own people much worse than they treated the Chinese. I frequently saw them carrying Japanese civilians into their headquarters, bloodied and half-conscious, and more than once I saw them drag screaming Japanese women in by their hair, while Japanese males standing nearby watched with total unconcern or turned away deliberately so as not to become involved. The women were not prostitutes, but wives of businessmen who somehow had caused offense, or, in the opinion of the *Kempeitai* had brought dishonor to the Japanese race. I had many a run-in with them myself, but I usually managed to bluff my way out of any serious confrontation, and I think they were always a little puzzled as to just how to treat me.

Lingyuan was different in so many ways from the old days. It was now neither China nor was it the well-disciplined Japan, which we also knew quite well. Everything was in a constant state of flux, and conditions that were bad to begin with deteriorated as time went on, as the Japanese became more and more involved in their war against the Chinese in the central part of North China. It was something we had to learn to live with.

For me as a young man with no attachments it was easier. I could brush things off and take tremendous risks. However, it was very hard on Father. He had Mother and my two sisters to worry about, and perceptibly, his hair grew grayer as the months passed. One or two of our missionary friends found it too much for them, and they had to leave. Our beloved Ada Blackmore was one of them. She had undergone a terrifying experience shortly before our return when a gang of ruffians had broken into her place one night, roughed her up, beaten her serving woman and gateman, and taken a lot of her things. The Chinese told me that it had been a deliberate ploy instigated by the Japanese, who wanted to get rid of her. They didn't like her living by herself up on the hill outside the town and, therefore, outside of their immediate observation. In any case, after that, and with the constant harassment by Japanese soldiers wandering in and plainclothes men watching her every move, she decided to leave and went back to England shortly after our return. It was perhaps just as well she did, because during our absence, torrential rains had widened the gully next to her house to the point where the entire house and yard were in danger of being swallowed up, and I'm sure she couldn't have remained there very much longer.

Poor Miss Blackmore. Gentle and trusting as she was, she had a history of being taken in by the unscrupulous. I've mentioned the blind horse that she used to pull her cart. Her servants also robbed her blind. She found the horse was getting thinner and thinner despite the money she was paying out for corn and sorghum to feed it. One day as her woman servant left the compound, Miss Blackmore noticed a trickle of grain coming out of the bottom of the woman's trousers, where they were bound at the ankle. When she felt the woman's leg, she discovered her trousers were filled with grain and that she had been carrying the corn and sorghum out of the compound in that way.

Before we had left for America I had told Miss Blackmore of my hopes of bringing back a car, and she in turn confided in me her own hopes of one day having a small car to replace her cart. Regrettably, she greatly feared crossing rivers, and she told me she had written to both the Chevrolet and Ford people in Detroit asking them when they were going to invent a car that would be able to either fly or jump across rivers, but she had received no reply.

During the time we were away, without telling anyone, she had made a surreptitious trip to Tientsin, where she bought a very old but still serviceable English Morris Cowley two-seater, and had learned to drive it. She was away about three weeks and one day suddenly appeared back in Lingyuan with her new possession. She had not had quite enough confidence in herself to make the trip back on her own, so she had hired a Chinese driver. After he had deposited the car in a small shed at her place up on the hill, she paid him off, but later, when she attempted to get the car out, it wouldn't budge. The back wheels were locked solid and wouldn't turn, and as there was no one to whom she could turn for help, she simply abandoned it there.

One of the first things I did after returning to Lingyuan was to look at the problem for her. I discovered that four bolts holding the drive shaft to the transmission housing had worked loose, and the tension of the rear springs had forced everything backward to the point where it had stretched the emergency hand-brake cable just enough so that the brakes were locked on. The problem was that simple. However, Miss Blackmore had never once used the car she had bought with such high hopes, and now that she was leaving for England, she gave it to me to use in any way that I wanted.

Lao San helped me bring the car down from her place, but first we had to get it out of the tiny shed in which it was stored. The car had a folding canvas top and the only way to get into the driver's seat was to climb over the folded top at the back and crawl into the front seat. We managed to release the hand brake but were unable to start the engine. In the end, I used my van to tow it down the hill with Lao San proudly steering and keeping his foot on the brake most of the way.

When we got the car into our own yard, we set it up on blocks and went to work both on the drive shaft and the engine. We removed both of the back wheels, and unfortunately, while trying to get the drive shaft back into position, Lao San inadvertently placed his foot against one of the supporting blocks to gain more leverage, and the car dropped down on top of him. I was under the car on the opposite side but managed to roll out just as the car began to move. I yelled to Lao San to get out, but he was too late. I ran around to the other side and found him pinned to the ground by the left rear wheel-hub which was pressing on his right temple. I shouted for help, but in the meantime, without giving it a second thought, I turned my back, reached down and grabbed the running board with both hands and lifted the car sufficiently to free his head, and with one foot managed to push him out of the way before letting the car drop.

Lao San was semi-conscious and had lost a lot of blood from the bad gash on his temple. I carried him out to the street and fortunately found an empty droshky going by. I took him, with the horse galloping, to the young Japanese doctor whom we had in town by that time. The doctor's primary job was caring for the Japanese civilians and conducting a weekly inspection of the prostitutes. Despite his youth he was very competent, and he deftly sewed up the gash for Lao San. Apart from a bad headache for a few days and the ugly scar it left, Lao San was none the worse for the experience, but I had a sore back for about six weeks.

After getting the car operating again, I sold it to our wealthy neighbor, Mr. He, for his oldest son to drive, but it was only a month or so before the young fellow drove it into a wall and demolished it. However, the money I got for it proved very useful in buying parts to maintain my own vehicle. With the nearest garage of any sort in Peking, which was several hundred miles away, one had to be a competent mechanic. The nearest Dodge agency was in Tientsin, more than 400 road miles away, which made it very difficult to get parts. But even being a good mechanic wasn't always enough; one had to be a believer in miracles.

Bob's first van — sketch by Jim Lance

The temple had to make way for the new bridge — so idols were taken to the river to disintegrate slowly.

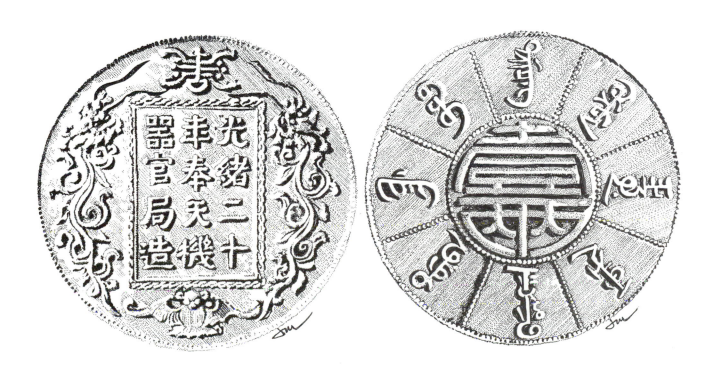

With the van at a market.

Top of Tung Ta Liang — a pass.

Stuck in mud.

Sharing the road with some heavily ladened mules.

Bob cleaning a part of the van with helper.

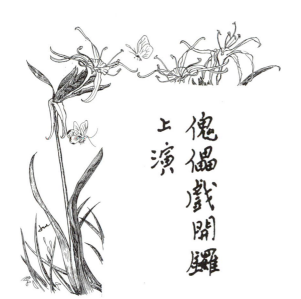

上演 傀儡戲開羅

Kui lei xi kai luo shang yan.

To the beating of gongs
the puppet show starts.

- Chinese Saying.

Chapter Twenty-One
Miles and Miracles

The third line of the Manchukuo national anthem went: *Ding tian li di, wu ku wu you,* "Supporting heaven and standing on the earth, no more bitterness and no more sorrow." In the winter of 1934-35, the irony of the words became ever more apparent as the new government increasingly tightened its control over the people. The high hopes that everyone had held that under the Japanese, justice would prevail and freedoms would be restored, all turned to naught, and the lot of the common man was definitely no better than it was before. In many cases it was much worse.

In addition to the establishment of the *bao jia* street administrative system mentioned in the previous chapter, where a former criminal was in charge of every 100 families, the Japanese enlisted Chinese nationals of the basest sort — what the Chinese call *xiadeng ren* — "bottom class people," and with them established a strong police force. But they cannily and deliberately underpaid them to ensure there

would be no complacency in the ranks. In order for the police to acquire extra income, it was expected that they bleed the people, and at the same time it forced the people into an ever greater distrust and fear of the police.

Within days after the Japanese occupation, new money had been printed and all old money was declared illegal. A deadline was set for conversion of all funds to the new currency, and any found after that was confiscated. Naturally, the exchange rate was very much in favor of the Japanese. Silver dollars, much prized by the Chinese as the only secure and tangible asset, were particularly desired by the Japanese, and, as a result, when the deadline for converting the old money had passed with almost no silver dollars showing up, the police were encouraged to start a campaign of harassment of the townspeople on the pretext of looking for anti-Japanese elements. In fact, they were only searching for dollars. Day and night, people were rousted from their homes and the houses were systematically searched. The common practice among the Chinese was to bury silver dollars — usually in large earthenware pots — and the police were well aware of that. When probing with steel rods all around the outside of the houses produced nothing, the indoor floors were dug up, and when that produced nothing, the sleeping *kang* were torn apart. Any family that failed to give up a few silver dollars was certain to be roundly beaten by the police, and as the word spread, most families managed to make sure that the police found at least a token sum of silver currency, even if they had to buy or borrow it from others. That way they kept the police off their backs for a while.

However, that didn't satisfy the voracious appetite of the police for very long. They adopted a maxim that the people were like a dirty carpet. No matter how many times you beat it, more dirt would come out, and time and again they went back to the same houses for additional searches. When silver dollars were actually found, most of them went into the pockets of the Chinese police and few got back to the Japanese who, quite naturally, continued to demand greater efforts on the part of the searchers. That made for an ongoing situation that continued for months without letup.

As foreign nationals, we had our own problems with money, but not because the police came searching our compound for silver dollars. The Japanese were so hungry for foreign exchange that they established an arbitrary exchange rate for any foreign currency that came into the country, far below what the money was actually worth. Because of that, and the fact that all of our support came from either Great Britain or the United States, we had to convert it to Manchukuo dollars at a very low rate pegged to the Japanese yen. For each U.S. dollar, we got a little over three Manchukuo yuan, and, as inflation soared, despite attempts on the part of the Japanese to control prices, we had to resort to other means to get around the Japanese monetary controls.

We very early became well aware that all our letters were censored, both incoming and outgoing, and any checks coming in from either the United States or England were noted and documented by the Japanese. When we attempted to send checks to Tientsin for deposit in banks there, at an exchange rate at least twenty times higher than in Manchukuo, our letters were returned to us by the censor, and we were told the checks could only be converted into Manchukuo currency. As a result, for a time we were forced to cash them at the official rate until we could figure some way to get around the problem.

British and American banks were still permitted to run their branches in the larger cities of Manchukuo, but every bank had to have its quota of Japanese employees, and it was obvious that all accounts were carefully monitored. It took time, but finally we hit on the idea of having all monies sent to us by way of Tientsin, which was still in Chinese hands. There, for one U.S. dollar we got as much as sixty or seventy Chinese dollars and it was possible to then convert the Chinese currency to Manchukuo yuan at par. When crossing the border back into Manchukuo, we were limited as to the amount of money that we could carry through at any one time, and anything over 500 yuan was considered suspicious and resulted in a lot of questioning.

To avoid suspicion and to keep the Japanese happy, all members of our missionary group opened bank accounts in Mukden with the British-owned Hongkong and Shanghai Banking Corporation, where we maintained a working balance with an occasional U.S. dollar check credited to the account. But in the meantime, discreet trips were made to Tientsin, where our good friends Mr. and Mrs. Lambert of the China Inland Mission agreed to do all our banking for us. From Tientsin we mailed letters to friends abroad asking that all funds be sent directly to Tientsin rather than to Lingyuan, and with Mr. Lambert we set up a simple code whereby he would inform us of what monies had reached him and from whom.

To avoid the necessity of making a trip to Tientsin each time we needed cash, we worked with our local Chinese merchants in Lingyuan, who were also in difficult straits where it came to making purchases from across the border. For them it had also been a case of getting only one Chinese yuan for each Manchukuo yuan at the border, the Japanese quite naturally wanting to discourage them from importing goods from China and to encourage them to use Manchukuo resources. But old habits die hard and the merchants did not like the local products, which they considered vastly inferior, and they continued to buy stock from Peking and Tientsin. That required sizable amounts of cash.

There was some risk involved in what we did, but we again worked out a simple code whereby we would give a merchant a slip of paper to carry to Tientsin. If he needed fifty yuan, the slip would tell Mr. Lambert to give him five pounds of sugar. If he needed five hundred, it would be five pounds of butter. In turn, the local merchants gave us Manchukuo yuan, and the scheme worked flawlessly for all the years the Japanese were in power without them catching on. Had it not been for that way of getting around the currency regulations, our work in Manchukuo would have very quickly come to a standstill.

As soon as I was issued my Manchukuo passport, I started my travels with the van. With so many Japanese businesses being set up in Lingyuan, it was not hard to find a sign painter, and I employed a young Korean who, using Chinese characters, very skillfully lettered the exterior of the van with Scripture verses, and on the front and back, in very large characters, the words "Christian Church." The Japanese used the same characters in their language, so it could be read and understood by them as well, and I made sure the Japanese saw my van on the streets as often as possible and became familiar with what we were doing.

Gasoline was readily available in Lingyuan through agents of "Socony" (the Standard Oil Co. of New York), and also Texaco. The gasoline, like kerosene, was sold in square, five-gallon cans, the empty cans being much prized by the Chinese for use in carrying water or for storing pickles, etc. Both of the American firms were permitted to operate temporarily until Japanese interests took over, after which getting gasoline became something of a problem. Lubricating oils were another matter, and I had to get those from Tientsin, where, because of the more favorable exchange rate, I also purchased spare parts as needed and occasionally took the van for major repairs or an overhaul, which I was unable to handle myself.

For the most part, during the first few months, I confined my trips out of town to villages along the east-west main highway, which the Japanese had improved, but I was anxious to try out the road to Dujiawopu, our out-station. That road, so familiar to me from the many times I had traveled over it by bicycle or in a cart, turned out to be entirely different with an automobile.

I was pleasantly surprised to find the first stage of fifteen or twenty miles to Reshuitang to be an entirely new road. In the old days it traversed the river bed or wound through narrow defiles worn down by centuries of passing cart wheels. Now, however, the Japanese had simply confiscated valuable farmland and had built the road wherever it pleased them, and although narrow, it was surfaced with crushed rock and passable in almost any kind of weather.

In Reshuitang, where the hot springs were, the road ended. But there was a lot of activity going on. The Japanese were in the process of building a huge recreational center and bathhouse for themselves. Fortunately for the Chinese, they had not touched the old bathhouses. They had gone farther up the valley, and, straddling the bubbling hot springs, had dynamited out of the rock a large pool about forty feet square and about five feet deep, and over that, using imported wood, they had built a typical Japanese building.

Out of curiosity I stopped to look at the wooden monstrosity, which was still unfinished, and the civilian Japanese workers showed no resentment at my looking around. The inside was basically one huge room, with a raised dais covered with tatami mats on all four sides of the pool, dominating the center. On one side, doors led to small changing rooms with large wooden tubs into which hot water was piped for initial mandatory wash-downs for everyone before they entered the main pool, and behind the building were quarters for the kitchen and its staff and accommodations for the geisha girls who would entertain the guests. Over the next several years the place was to become famous for the wild parties that the Japanese held there, and although I had occasion to take Japanese there numerous times in the van, I was not to see the interior again until the night before Pearl Harbor, a night I will never forget and which I will cover later.

Leaving Reshuitang that cold October day in 1934, we proceeded north and found the road to be exactly as it had always been. The Japanese had obviously not ventured beyond that point, and I am sure that my van was the first motor vehicle to traverse the mountain road. As we approached the steep slopes of the forbidding mountain range, I began to wonder if the car would make the climb, but once committed there was no turning back.

I had several Chinese with me in the van and a heavy load of books. We climbed the first mile or so of the pass without any trouble, but at one point, where the road was carved out of the sheer rock cliff, a monstrous outcrop of rock blocked the way. It was a near-vertical climb of about fifteen feet of slippery granite, with ruts deeply cut into it by the iron-bound wheels of the Chinese carts that had passed that way for decades, and with deep indentations in between the ruts worn there by the hooves of countless animals that had pulled the carts. In spots it was so narrow I had to get out and measure the width to see if my car could get by. When satisfied that I would be able to get through, I took the precaution of having my passengers get out and walk and then made the attempt by myself.

I couldn't approach it too fast because of the suddenness of the rise and the fear that my front and rear bumpers would scrape the ground. However, in low gear, much to my surprise, the car made it despite a lot of bouncing around, the wheels on both sides pretty much riding the rocky bank part of the way up. When I got to the top I stopped a short distance above the rise, where the road leveled out for a few hundred yards. At that point it was bordered by a low stone wall on one side that enclosed a tiny cultivated field that had been hacked out of the mountainside. The moment I stopped the car and got out, five bandits who had been hiding behind the wall leaped up and made a mad dash across the field to the security of a small ravine. They evidently had mistaken us for a police or military vehicle and thought they were about to be attacked.

I look back on it now with some amusement, because difficult as it was, it was nothing compared to what we routinely tackled later on, in our many trips into the countryside, but that first time was somewhat nerve-shattering. Over the next few years I made that trip on the average of twice a month, even during the summer rains. Sometimes I spent a week or more in Dujiawopu, visiting the Christians there and in the nearby villages. There were a great many small villages in that valley, and most of them were familiar to our colporteur Zhang Lan-fang. He had covered the villages on foot over the years, and as he joined with me in visiting them once again, we were joined by a new face.

During our absence from Lingyuan a young farmer named Zhao had become a Christian, and I found him to be a most extraordinary young man. The surname Zhao is the first in the list of 100 Chinese surnames, and means "to hasten or visit." I've forgotten what his given name was; however, once he became a Christian he decided to change his given name to Guang, which means "light." The reason for doing so was because another character, also pronounced Zhao, means "to shine," or "show forth." Pronouncing the two words together it sounded like "shining forth the light," and that is exactly what he wanted to do with his life. He wanted to shine the light of Christ's Gospel into the hearts and lives of his fellow Chinese wherever he went, and he used his singular name as a means of attracting the attention of strangers.

Zhao had never been outside his village before coming to Lingyuan, but had received an excellent education in the tiny village school. He had read a Bible he had bought from Zhang Lan-fang from cover to cover numerous times, and he showed an extraordinary knowledge of the Scriptures, much of which he could repeat from memory. When he moved to Lingyuan to be closer to the church, Mr. Sturt had found him to be such an earnest and sincere young man that he baptized him. Because of his great knowledge of the Bible, Mr. Sturt had enlisted him, too, as a colporteur, mainly traveling on foot into the countryside with Scripture portions just as Zhang Lan-fang did.

It didn't take me more than a day or so to find out what a jewel Zhao was, and I took him along with me on almost all of my trips into the country from then on, and it was there that he showed his true value. Among the peasant folk he was completely at ease, and they with him, and not only could he talk with them in language they understood, but a more articulate individual it would have been hard to find. He was to become my constant companion and close friend over the next several years, covering hundreds of miles in the car with me.

Zhao was a very humble and self-effacing young man, completely unflappable even under the most trying circumstances, and most even tempered. Simple in his dress, but always immaculately clean and neat, he dressed almost always in the black long gown of the teacher. After a long, hard, and dusty day, I would find myself completely exhausted and ready for bed, but Zhao would unfailingly brush out all his clothing and meticulously wash his heavy white cotton cloth socks. At the same time he wasn't afraid to get his hands dirty. When the car got stuck in mud or quicksand or fell through the ice, Zhao would be the first to whip off his shoes and socks, roll up his pant legs, and get in there with pick and shovel to dig us out. His patience and good nature were an example to everyone.

Along with everything else Zhao was an excellent storyteller, with a remarkably good sense of humor. He could hold an audience of countryfolk spellbound. One of the standard answers given by peasants when asked to accept Christianity was a pat phrase taught them by the temple priests: "The religion you are born into is the religion you stay in" (*Sheng zai na jiao jiu zai na jiao*) and Zhao's reply to that was both succinct and appropriate. Making a play on the word for religion, or church, which is *jiao*, Zhao would use another word *jiao*, which sounded exactly the same, but meant "pit," and he would say to them, "Well, my friend, suppose you were born in a vegetable pit. Would you remain a vegetable for life?" That invariably brought a laugh, but at the same time they would do some serious thinking.

Zhao had never before ridden in a car and when he and I first started out on our trips into the country he got terribly carsick, and I feared he would never get over it. However, after the first time or two, despite his obvious discomfort, he never let it get in the way of our travels, and gradually he overcame it.

After the railroad came in, the Japanese began to import all kinds of fruit, and we had fruit of some sort or another available the year-round, a new experience for us. Much of it was citrus fruit from Formosa, and one of the things we learned to like very much was the pomelo. For those who haven't seen the fruit, it looks very much like a large grapefruit. It has a very thick skin and is divided into segments that can be separated just like an orange, although each segment is contained within a very tough membrane, which has to be peeled off. The fruit tastes much like grapefruit, but sweeter, and has a texture that is considerably coarser. It was Zhao who discovered that the skin of the pomelo, held over the nose and mouth, was a sure cure for carsickness. We used it extensively in the days that followed, particularly when we had a car full of Chinese women and girls. They seemed particularly susceptible not only to the motion of the car, but to the smell of the gasoline.

In 1934 I was twenty-one and Zhao was only a year or two older than I, but he was very much of an inspiration to me, and I greatly valued his companionship and excellent advice. His humor was at times quite droll. I recall that during times when the car would have some kind of malfunction, and I was trying to carry out repairs, he would lay out the tools nearby on a piece of cloth, and he very quickly learned to hand me just what I needed. Occasionally, when he couldn't find the tool that I wanted, he would dryly mumble to himself: "Next time you buy tools, why don't you get the kind that can talk; they would then be able to tell you where they are."

During the years that Zhao and I traveled together we had many remarkable and unforgettable experiences. After we had given saturation coverage to the villages immediately along the main east-west road, we began to branch off onto the side roads to remote villages that were almost inaccessible. Usually, though, there was a rough track used by farm carts, and we held to the premise that, where a farm cart could go, we could go, too. But it wasn't always the case. We learned that it was necessary to carry quite a bit of extra equipment with us. We took along two heavy, two-inch-thick planks that were bound with iron strips on the ends to prevent their splitting, and they were used mainly to either bridge mud holes or to insert under the wheels when we got bogged down in the mud. Quite often, the roads were carved out of the side of a cliff with a deep drop on one side. Many times the trails in the mountains were so narrow and the bends so sharp, that there were spots where a farm cart, with its short wheelbase, could negotiate easily. But with my van, the front wheels would go around the bend all right, but one rear wheel tended to go over the edge. The boards we carried were useful in bridging those gaps, but frequently, when the gap was wide, the weight of the car would bend the board to the point where we were sure it would break. But it never did. Even with the boards, it was often necessary to use our pick and carve out the cliff to give us more room to maneuver, and when we had to use the boards it was always Zhao's job to place them in just the right position. I had to depend heavily on his judgment when the gap was on the off-side, which I couldn't see from where I sat. He became quite expert in placing them and in signaling my moves.

The best time of the year for our country visitation work was during the long winter months when the farmers were relatively idle, the ground frozen hard and the roads much more readily negotiated. During that period we concentrated on visiting village markets or fairs. Almost every large village had a market every five days, and they were so arranged that no matter where you went, every small village and hamlet was within eight or ten miles of a market.

The Chinese lunar calendar is divided roughly into thirty-day months, although there are a few that have only 29 days. The markets appearing on every fifth day in any given village would be named after the dates on which they fell. For example, a "three-eight" market would be held on the third, eighth, thirteenth, eighteenth, twenty-third and twenty-eighth of the month. In another direction, and within a half-day's walk, would be a "four-nine" market, and in still another direction a "two-seven." That arrangement permitted the small businessmen who made their living in those markets to have one within easy reach practically every day of the year. In the summer months, however, the markets were patronized by far fewer people.

Working with the van from our home base in Lingyuan, we could attend a large number of the markets daily, and, depending on the distance, go in a different direction each day. We charted the markets on paper, drawing rough maps of the surrounding area, and it was easy to see that the markets appeared in concentric and overlapping circles. Each of them formed a hub, with a score or more of small villages in a circle surrounding it, and each circle, in effect, meshed with another, something like a set of cog wheels.

As we gradually covered all the nearby markets, we expanded our range to reach a wider belt of markets. That frequently meant that we were on the road for two or three weeks at a time, setting up a base in one of the larger and more central market villages and only returning home to stock up on gasoline and books or to carry out repairs on the van. We carried no foodstuffs with us and depended entirely on the local economy. I did allow myself the single luxury of carrying with me condensed milk and my Lipton's black tea — something an Englishman cannot do without. At the end of a long hard day I found the English tea with milk in it much more invigorating than Chinese tea, which simply quenched the thirst.

The winter weather was at the same time our greatest friend and a bitter enemy. The advantages of the cold weather were the availability of the people and the generally good condition of the roads. The ground was frozen hard as a rock to a depth of four feet or more, and, for the most part, the rivers and streams were either crudely bridged or frozen solid. Once the first big freeze came, everything remained frozen for several months, with the daytime temperature well below zero degrees Fahrenheit sometimes for weeks on end.

As an example of how cold it was even indoors, we routinely butchered a cow at first freeze, then hung the meat in an unheated room where it remained frozen solid throughout the winter, providing us with all the beef we needed. It was a better quality than we could have bought on the market, where most often only the oldest cows, no longer good for any field work, were butchered for meat, and were thus very tough.

It was possible to wear enough clothing to keep out the cold, even when standing out in the open marketplaces for eight to ten hours at a time, but we forever had cold feet and chilblains on both hands and feet. Chilblains is one complaint that few Americans have seen or are aware of. It is an inflammation caused by exposure to cold and moisture, and it causes swelling, burning and intense itching on both the hands and feet. The affected parts, after swelling up, are split by numerous fissures, particularly on the hands, and they can be so wide and deep that one could easily stand a quarter in them, but they rarely bleed and, surprisingly, rarely become infected. Apart from soaking the affected parts in warm water, there is very little that can be done to alleviate the discomfort and intense itching.

For my cold feet, I tried every kind of felt boot that I could find on the market, but none of them worked. We finally went to the Mongolian felt boots, which are designed for people riding horses or camels, but they were intended only for that purpose and were not meant for walking and certainly not for driving a car. I had to wear one pair of shoes in the car, then change to the Mongolian boots when we arrived at our destination. The Mongolian boots looked very much like over-sized wooden Dutch clogs, extending fairly high up the ankle, rounded on the bottoms instead of having a flat sole, and approximately half an inch or more in thickness. The secret was to get them large enough so the foot was loose inside with plenty of room for air to circulate. Only when wearing those were we able to stand out in the marketplaces for hours on end and keep our feet relatively warm. Fur gloves kept our hands warm, except when we were on the road and had to remove them to patch an inner tube, dig the car out of a hole in the ice, or carry out repairs on the engine.

That first winter with the van we learned through trial and error just what it took to operate a motor vehicle in that kind of cold weather. I never used antifreeze, partly because frequent damage to the radiator or hoses caused by flying stones kicked up by the front wheels necessitated very frequent repair and replacement. However, that wasn't the main reason we didn't use antifreeze. The cold was so intense that even the thinnest or lightest weight motor oil almost solidified. Even with a hand crank, it was impossible to turn the engine over in the mornings. We quickly learned, as did the Japanese, that the only way to start a car in that weather was to place a pan of red-hot coals under the engine sump for about an hour before attempting to start the engine. That necessitated getting up extra early to light the charcoal and get it red hot. And, because of the possibility of dripping oil causing a fire, someone had to stand by during the entire period to make sure nothing untoward occurred. The Japanese, it seemed, always wanted to hurry the process and not stand for long periods out in the cold, so they often poured gasoline onto the lighted charcoal, frequently with disastrous results. The flame would follow the stream of gasoline up to the can, and the can would then explode in their faces. We saw several cases of serious injury because of that practice and, in one case, the death of a Japanese woman.

When the engine oil had thinned out sufficiently to enable one to turn the engine over with the hand crank, with radiator and engine block drain cocks open, boiling water was poured through the radiator until the engine block and radiator were somewhat warmed up. Only then could the engine be fired up, and more often than not, it had to be done, not with the self-starter, but with a bunch of men and boys pushing from behind. Fortunately, we always found a group of willing volunteers who thought it a lot of fun and something to brighten an otherwise monotonous day.

One hazard of using that method for warming the engine (apart from the danger of fire) was the need to exercise great care in draining the radiator and engine-block the night before, as well as in the mornings. We had to make certain the water from the radiator didn't get near the front wheels. Water in those temperatures (particularly warm or hot water) froze immediately on contact with the ground, and if we were not careful, we would find our front tires frozen solidly in place. When that happened, it would sometimes take hours of careful work with a pick to free them, as we discovered the first time it happened. I'll never forget my surprise when, having started and warmed the engine up one morning, I was unable to move the car and hadn't the slightest idea why, until I discovered the front wheels solidly frozen into the sheet of ice that had formed around them.

Later, another complication appeared. As the war between Japan and China got worse, the major American oil companies were no longer permitted to sell gasoline in Manchukuo, and the Japanese came out with their own substitute product, which defies description. It was a smelly mixture of an ersatz alcohol with just a touch of gasoline in it, and to start the engine when our tank was filled with it, I had to take a small pan of the mixture, heat it over a flame until it was near the boiling point, and then pour it into the carburetor. Using that fuel, only rarely could the engine be turned over and started with the self-starter, even when the weather was warm, and we usually had to depend entirely on manpower pushing the car to start. As things got worse for the Japanese and fuel became even scarcer, most of the Japanese trucks were equipped with a clumsy contraption about the size of a large water heater, which burned small blocks of wood or charcoal to produce a gas fuel for the engines, but fortunately I never had to resort to that.

On those very cold mornings, even after the engine was started, our troubles weren't over. A great deal of care had to be taken in driving for the first few miles until everything had warmed up somewhat. When the temperature is between twenty and forty below zero Fahrenheit, steel becomes extremely brittle, and a sudden jar or jolt can cause a lot of damage. One morning, we had gone only a few hundred feet from the inn when we had to go through a shallow stream where the ice had been broken by heavy carts that preceded us. The water splashed up onto the rear springs and froze instantly, and no sooner were we out of the water than one of the rear wheels bounced over a deep rut in the road and one of the rear leaf springs shattered into small pieces, none of them larger than a couple of inches in length. I couldn't believe my eyes. No spring left, and the car frame tilted down onto the wheel and axle.

Being several hundred miles from the nearest available garage and tow truck, we had to improvise and do the best we could. We cut a small log and shaped it to fit the top of the axle to support the car frame, wired it in place, then tied ropes back and front to keep the rear axle more or less in line, and limping along in low gear we headed for home. I had to go to Tientsin for a new spring, and from then on I not only always carried a spare one, but I also designed leather boots to completely cover the springs. I also packed them with heavy grease to make sure they retained maximum flexibility and were protected from immersion in water when we broke through the ice or had to cross an open stream.

Rivers and small streams were always a hazard in summer and winter, even though in winter most of the larger rivers had bridges built over them at first freeze. Despite that, because of the extreme cold and because the currents were so strong and the water so deep, there was usually some open water. Freezing would begin at the edges of a stream or river, and the ice would gradually build up until it was four or five feet thick on both sides of the stream. That would compress the flowing water into a narrow channel in the middle, which made it easier for the builders of the bridges. But when the bridges failed, as many of them did, and we had to take to the water, our problems were sometimes horrendous. Even when the bridges remained intact, the water being compressed into an ever-narrowing channel raised the water level over the tops of the ice banks. It then would spread for hundreds of feet on each side of the river or stream. Where in warm weather the expanse of water might only be fifteen or twenty feet wide, in winter, the expanse of ice might cover an entire valley floor a mile or more in width, and the open part of the stream, while perhaps less than ten feet across, would

be a rushing torrent and very deep.

To begin with, the winter bridges were extremely crude. Piers to support the bridge framework were made of loose rocks piled inside a very large, loosely woven basketwork of willow twigs about six or seven feet in height. When the freeze started men would stand in the river, holding the open-ended "baskets" in place, as other men threw rocks inside. Water was then poured over them so that they froze solidly together. When the piers were in place, large logs were laid between them, and on top of the logs were placed bundles of *shujie* stalks and then a thick layer of earth mixed with small stones, well watered to freeze it solid.

The bridges were usually constructed by nearby villagers who sometimes levied a small charge on passing vehicles to help pay for them. In other places they were built by wealthy landowners who needed the bridges for their own carts. At the same time they felt they were doing something meritorious that would gain them great favor in the afterlife.

Even though most of the bridges were fairly well maintained over the winter months, the iron-shod wheels of the carts cut deeply into them. The cartwheel gauge being about six inches narrower than that of an American car, negotiating one of those narrow bridges in a car was always extremely hazardous. There was almost always a sagging between the piers, and frequently one of the piers would have tipped slightly, leaving the bridge surface at an angle. Most times, Zhao or someone else would have to get out and walk backward ahead of the car in the exact middle of the bridge so he could watch my front wheels and be sure they stayed on the bridge.

Quite often the bridges were either too narrow or too flimsy to carry the weight of the van, in which case we would have to find a place to ford the river. That wasn't always an easy thing to do. At best it meant chopping through several feet of ice to make a slope down into the water, and then another slope on the other side in order to get out of the water.

I shall never forget the surprise I got on the first occasion we had to do that. We got through the water without difficulty and managed to climb the opposite slope without too much trouble, since we had thrown sand on it. However, the opposite bank was littered with small pebbles and as we crossed them, I had the strange sensation that the car was slowly rising beneath me. As the wet tires had met the pebbles, they froze to the tires in a near-solid mass. I stopped and after knocking the pebbles off with a hammer, I got back into the van to proceed only to find that my brakes had frozen solid and the car wouldn't budge an inch. It took me many minutes, lying on my back under the car hammering on the brake drums to dislodge the ice. After that lesson, we never stopped after going through water. We simply kept going and let the pebbles dislodge themselves, even though the loud tattoo as they hit the underside of the fenders was most disturbing. At the same time, I kept my foot lightly pressed on the brake pedal to ensure that the brake shoes would dry out.

One of my greatest challenges in repairing the car came one wintry day when we were out in the middle of a dry river bed, a mile or more from the nearest village. My right rear axle sheared off and I lost a wheel.

The reason it happened was that some weeks earlier, in late fall, the axle housing had taken a very hard rap when I plowed over a boulder submerged in deep mud. It happened one bright sunny fall day when we were on the main east-west highway on our way home and about fifty miles from Lingyuan. We had just forded a river and reached the opposite bank where the road began to climb toward a steep mountain pass. Without any warning, a sudden cloudburst swept in over the mountains and dumped so much rain on us that we couldn't see anything and had to stop until the storm passed.

When the rain lessened, we were amazed to see a river of mud oozing down the mountainside and engulfing the road ahead of us. It missed us by less than a hundred feet and covered the road for several hundred yards ahead. The mud was nearly two feet deep and very liquid, so we had to sit there and wait for more than three hours until it stabilized and the hot sun somewhat dried the surface. Even then, when the surface looked dry and I tried to walk on it, it felt like a sea of Jello beneath my feet. I knew there was no possible way of driving the car through it, even though the road base underneath was hard.

While we had been sitting by the riverbank waiting, a Japanese-owned truck had caught up to us and pulled up just in front of us before the driver saw the sea of mud and stopped. The driver was Chinese, and I knew him by sight although I had never spoken with him. He was as baffled as I was as to how to proceed, but we discussed the best way to negotiate the mud, and then an idea came to us. About half a mile up ahead, on the farther side of the stream of mud, there was a tiny village where we could see people moving around. We decided to go there and see if we could get help: perhaps horses to tow us through, or failing that, maybe some boards to lay on top of the slowly hardening crust, so as to at least enable us to get a running start in plowing through the mud.

The headman of the village was most cooperative when he heard our problem, and he took us to one of the houses where we were delighted to find a coffin-maker's establishment. Not only did they have a huge stack of roughly hewn boards in the small back yard, but the owner was quite willing to lend them to us. By that time all the men of the village had crowded around and the headman quickly organized them, giving each a board to carry, and we set off to see what we could do.

The boards were about ten feet long, two inches or so in thickness, and roughly a foot in width. We laid them in two parallel rows, end to end on top of the mud, the width of a car track, and they extended for just a little over a hundred feet. We hoped it would be enough to enable us to gain sufficient momentum to get through the mud on the other side.

Since the Chinese truck driver had suggested the boards, and was ahead of me anyway, I let him go first. He mounted the boards and set off at a good pace, built up speed, and at the point where the boards ended, plowed on through the mud. Despite some fishtailing, he managed to get through to the high ground on the other side. However, the weight of the truck caused the board track to disappear under the mud, much to the amusement of the onlookers.

I knew it was hazardous, and that the boards would be slippery under the mud, but at least there was now a discernible track through the mud, and I felt that with my chains on, if I could manage to stay on the boards, I could make it through. We started off well enough, but two-thirds of the way through, the boards proved to be too slick, and I skidded off to one side. The right wheels ended up in the shallow drainage ditch alongside the road (filled completely with mud, of course), but I managed to maintain momentum and continued to plow along. Suddenly I felt a tremendous bump as my front and rear axles went over a concealed boulder. But we made it to dry ground, helped the villagers dig out their boards, and despite their protests, gave them a little money to pay for their time and the chore of washing the mud off the boards. Although I carefully inspected both axles, no damage was visible. Nevertheless, apparently there had been some fractional distortion, which resulted in the eventual breaking of the axle shaft some weeks later.

I must have traveled some three or four hundred miles after that incident. Then, weeks later, on a cold November afternoon as I mentioned above, we were returning home from a day in one of the markets when, on level ground, plowing through a sandy river bed, the right rear axle suddenly sheared off exactly at the point where it emerged from the axle housing and was supported by the bearing. We were some twenty-five miles from home, the sun low in the sky, and the area well known for its bandit population.

No matter where you were in China, it always seemed that you were not far from a small village of some kind. While Zhao and I busied ourselves draining water from the radiator and engine block because of the freezing temperature, we spotted three villagers approaching. The car always excited great interest wherever we went, and the three men appeared quite friendly. Zhao and I had our heads under the hood, inside the engine compartment, and I overheard one of the men volubly explaining to his companions that the "electric cooking pot" in the car had broken. But then they noticed the broken axle and realized why we had stopped there.

We obviously had to abandon the car there for the night, until I could figure out a way to repair the axle. I asked the men if they had a horse I could hire to ride back to Lingyuan, but they had nothing in the village, not even a donkey. I decided that Zhao should stay in the village overnight and I would walk home. It would be necessary to dismantle the entire axle housing and somehow get it to Lingyuan. To do that we would need a vehicle and some means of dragging the car out of the riverbed to some place where it would be safe from vandalism.

The talkative villager said that Zhao could stay at his house. He then suggested that someone stay by the car and watch it overnight because "there were bad men in the area." I agreed, and the other two men said they would stay with the car. It was going to be a very cold night, so I bought a load of brush for them to maintain a fire for warmth, and told them they could sit inside the van provided they didn't touch anything and that they built the fire far enough away so it would not endanger the car. They were obviously thrilled to be involved in such an exciting event in their otherwise dull lives.

It was well after dark by that time, and although the friendly villagers urged me to eat with them, I wanted to be on my way. It was a cloudy, windy night, and without any moon to aid me in seeing the road. I trudged and stumbled my way through the night, walking between the ruts so as not to lose my way. Passing through numerous villages en route, I managed to disturb all the dogs but not the sleeping inhabitants. I carried a thick stick just in case I was attacked by dogs, but they left me alone, and as dawn broke I reached the bank of the South River a mile from Lingyuan, footsore, weary and weak with hunger.

A bitter north wind was blowing steadily by that time and getting stronger by the minute, and although within sight of home, without food of some kind I was unable to face the wide riverbed between me and the house. There were no eating places in the village, but fortunately I found a man just setting out for town with a load of freshly roasted peanuts. He let me have a pound or so, and I munched them until my jaws ached, but it gave me enough strength to cover that last mile.

Lao San was already at work when I arrived home. I explained the problem to him and together we came up with a plan for dragging the car to the village, where I could remove the axle. We proposed making a rough sled to support the end of the axle, and Lao San set to at once to make it. Katie, the gateman, was dispatched to hire a four-wheeled one-horse droshky for the day, and I lay down for a short nap. An hour later Lao San woke me. He had beveled a square piece of thick board at one end and had found some heavy wire with which to secure it to the axle housing. With that, the two of us started off in the droshky, back south toward the village.

I had promised the driver a bonus if he would make good time, and by early afternoon we were within sight of the van again, which had by that time a sizable crowd gathered around it. Zhao was in excellent spirits and told me that he had spent almost the entire night preaching to the villagers, all of whom happily went without sleep in order to listen to him. From that incident we established friendships that were to last for a number of years, and ultimately a number of them became believers.

With a will, they set to helping us get the board under the broken end of the axle. We then harnessed up the horse from the droshky to the front bumper, and with the villagers pushing from behind, we got the car to the village and into one of the small yards, where it would be safe until I could get back with a new axle. Some two hours later Lao San and I had dismantled the entire rear axle and had it in the droshky, and with Zhao aboard we three started off for home again, arriving in the early hours of the next morning.

As I had no way of getting the axle shaft out, I had to take the entire assembly down with me to Tientsin — a two-day journey by train and bus — and my good friend Bob McCann at the Dodge agency there ran a very thorough test on it to see if there was any distortion that could have caused the break. However, if there was something wrong it was so slight his instruments were unable to detect it. But just to be on the safe side, he made a couple of extra axle shafts for me to take, and it was most fortunate that he did. Although I stood there and watched them pull the bearings to remove the broken shaft, using a special tool for the purpose, both he and I overlooked the need for such a tool in the event I experienced another breakage of the shaft.

Approximately four or five hundred miles later the same thing happened again. Thereafter, again and again at approximately the same intervals for as long as I owned the vehicle it recurred, and I became an absolute expert in putting in new axle shafts. However, the second time it happened was memorable, and almost beyond belief. To this day, vivid as it is in my memory, it still seems like something that could only be dreamed up for a movie script.

Zhao and I had just crossed a high mountain range and were coming down out of the foothills. We were bowling along smoothly at about fifteen miles an hour on one of the few spots where the road was level and comparatively smooth, when we felt a sudden bump. The car stopped abruptly, and I saw my right rear wheel roll past us and continue on down the road for a hundred feet or so. After the initial shock I

thought: "No problem. Don't I have two brand new axle shafts in the van for just such an emergency?" But when I looked at the break, my heart sank. The break was once again in exactly the same spot, flush with the axle housing, and right where the bearings were tightly pressed in. Looking at it, I realized I didn't have the necessary tool to pull the bearings. How in the world was I going to get them out to replace the axle shaft?

I was very familiar with that part of the road and knew there were no villages within several miles, and even if there had been any, the most we could have hoped for was some manpower to help us move the car off the road. We would simply have to do what we could by ourselves.

The tool I had watched the mechanics use in Tientsin seemed so simple. It was a device with two short arms about ten inches long, each sharply pointed at the tip into a wedge-like shape, and each tip bent slightly outward. To pull the bearings, the tips were placed into the beveled groove where the bearing met the shaft, and gently tapped in. Then the tip of a threaded screw in the center of the tool was placed against the end of the broken shaft, and as the screw was tightened, the bearings were smoothly pulled out. But where was I to get such a tool without going to Tientsin? The nearest Japanese military truck repair depot was more than fifty miles away, and although it was possible they had such a tool, it was very questionable whether they would lend it to me.

Somehow I had to improvise my own tool, and I thought of perhaps bending the tips of two screwdrivers to pry the bearing out. But I needed heat to soften the screwdriver blades so that I could bend the tips and something hard onto which to hammer them out. I looked around for a rock, but it was hilly loess country, and apart from a few tiny pebbles, there wasn't a rock in sight.

As I stood up, facing across the top of the van and looking in the direction of the nearby hills, I prayed for the wisdom to know what to do. I stood there, my eyes focused on the V-shaped notch between two hills in the near distance, and for some moments my brain refused to take in what my eyes were seeing. There, in the notch between the two hills was a faint wisp of rising smoke, and where there was smoke, there was certain to be a habitation of some sort, and where there was a house, I was sure to find a rock or something hard and a fire to heat and bend my screwdrivers.

Instantly, as I looked at the smoke, the words of Psalm 121:1 flashed into my mind: "I will lift up mine eyes unto the hills, from whence cometh my help." I turned to Zhao and said: "See that smoke over there? I'm going to walk over there, and I know that I'm going to find just exactly what I need to fix the axle." In my own mind I was certain our problem was solved.

I suggested that Zhao stay with the car in case other traffic came by. As I walked the half-mile or so toward the hills I mulled over what I might find and how I could use it. As I topped the rise in the gap between the hills, I saw a very small two-roomed farmhouse. It stood all by itself, a *shujie* fence around it and a small plot of cultivated land nearby. As I neared the house, a dog ran out and barked fiercely, followed by a tall, well-muscled young Chinese who smiled and greeted me as though it was the most ordinary thing in the world for a foreigner to come walking in over the hills from out of nowhere. In the yard I immediately spotted a large piece of granite that he had hauled in from somewhere, and telling him my problem, I showed him my two screwdrivers and asked if I could borrow some fuel to heat the points so that I could hammer them out and make a tool to fit my need.

He smiled and said: "You won't need that. Please come inside and take a look." I followed him in, and there in a tiny room, was a fully equipped blacksmith's shop. There was everything I needed including an anvil, hammers, a fireplace with bellows, and some lengths of metal that could be used to fashion the tool.

There had been no evidence outside of the usual hitching rack for shoeing horses, so I asked him why he had a blacksmith shop so far from any customers. He simply smiled and said: "I'm a farmer, but this is what I enjoy doing. I like to work with metal and make things, and then I take them to the market and sell them."

On a scrap of paper I drew him a rough diagram of what I needed, but it looked so strange to him that he asked if he could go over and look at the car to get a better idea of the problem, and with his three small children following, we walked back. He studied it for a few minutes, then smiled and said to me: "*Mei wenti* (no problem) I can make a tool that will work for you."

Back we walked to his shop, and within thirty minutes he had fashioned a tool with the two necessary outwardly bent, hook-like wedges. Instead of using a threaded screw to provide the pulling force, he used a stiff central post with a sharp point to center it on the broken end of the axle shaft, and above the post, an offset handle, hinged, which used the post as a fulcrum so as to provide the leverage to lift both the hooks. We took it back to the car, gently tapped in the two wedge-shaped points, and applying leverage on the handle, out came the bearing as smooth as silk. That tool was to serve the same purpose on a number of occasions thereafter. I estimate that I must have had the axle shaft break at least nine times during the life of the car (some 10,000 miles), and each time I remembered that kind and generous man who not only refused to take anything for his services, but insisted that both Zhao and I go back to his house for the meal his wife had prepared while we worked on the car.

Was the whole episode sheer coincidence? Consider the fact that the axle break happened at that precise location. Had it occurred a few yards either before, or after, that particular spot, I would never have seen the column of smoke, nor would I have found the house, and humanly speaking, there was no rational reason why a man would have a complete blacksmith shop out in the middle of nowhere, so far from potential customers. I can only conclude that God had placed the man there to meet my need at the time and to strengthen my faith in Him.

That was neither the first nor the last occasion when God showed us His hand in our lives over those years. Many were the times when we were completely helpless, but God provided the way, just as I was ready to give up in despair.

Just before Christmas one year, I think it was in 1936, I had driven over to Chengde, to pick up a group of our fellow missionaries and bring them to our place in Lingyuan for the holidays. We set out early in the morning from Chengde, and shortly after sunrise were climbing the steep pass just a few miles to the east of the city. It was bitterly cold, and just as we were nearing the top and were about to start down the other side, the engine suddenly and without any warning stopped and would not start again.

I had a heavy quilted covering lined with goatskin over the entire hood and grille in front of the radiator. We had learned from experience that in weather that cold, any engine repairs had to be completed within twenty minutes, otherwise, with the hood open, there was danger of the engine block and radiator freezing up solid. So I was faced with finding the trouble quickly and fixing it, or dumping the water to save the engine — all on a mountain top with the north wind blowing so hard I thought it would blow us off!

I quickly tested the electrical system and found that, although I had a good spark from the coil, nothing was going beyond the distributor. I opened that up and examined the points and the rotor and found the problem. For those not familiar with a car engine, the rotor is a small device mounted on a central shaft inside the distributor cup. As it revolves, it distributes electrical current to the spark plugs in a definite sequence. The rotor is made of a hard Bakelite substance, and on top, it has a protruding flat metal blade that comes into near contact with a series of small brass protrusions on the inside of the distributor cup, each of which is connected to a spark plug. As the shaft rotates, a spark jumps the tiny gap between the end of the blade and each of the little brass terminals to fire the mixture of gasoline and air in the respective cylinders.

In the bottom of the distributor cup I found a deposit of gritty dust. Not only was it apparent that the tiny metal blade on the end of the rotor head had been worn down by the abrasive effect of the dust, it was also clear that the extreme cold had further shrunk the blade to the point that the spark could not jump the gap. A simple problem, and a simple solution, if one had a spare rotor, but I didn't. Could I possibly find one back in Chengde? I didn't think so, because my car was a Dodge and I knew of no other Dodges in the area; in any case, we would have to turn back. I had Mr. and Mrs. Duthie in the car, with two young single women, both of them newcomers to China. I decided to turn the car around and coast down the pass to the nearest village, where we could find shelter for my passengers, and I would walk back to Chengde.

There was room to turn the car around if everyone got out and pushed, but just as I had my hand on the spigot to drain the water out of the radiator and engine block, I heard a truck engine laboring up the pass behind us. It was not a reassuring sound. Almost all motorized vehicles in those days were operated by the Japanese military, and experience had taught us they were unpleasant people to encounter on the road at any time. I hoped they would pass and leave us alone.

The truck came into view and, sure enough, it was a Japanese army truck, with just a driver and his assistant aboard. My heart sank as, instead of passing, they pulled up beside us and stopped, and the two men got out and walked over to me.

My first surprise was in seeing their smiling faces and hearing their friendly *Ohayo gozaimasu*, "Good morning," which was so unusual from a Japanese soldier. Both of them then bowed and said they were mechanics on their way to repair a disabled truck up ahead, and they asked me what was wrong with my car. I opened up the distributor head again, showed them the rotor, and told them what the problem was. One of them took the rotor in his hand while the second man climbed in behind the wheel. Just as the first man was attempting to push the rotor back onto the top of the shaft, the man inside put his foot on the starter. The partly mounted rotor, revolving at an acute angle, struck one of the protruding contact points and promptly broke into two parts.

To me, that simply compounded my troubles, but the two men thought it a huge joke and they laughed uproariously. Taking the rotor back to their own vehicle, they opened up the hood and, in the heated air of the engine compartment, stuck the two broken parts together with tire cement, dried it, brought it back to my car and inserted it properly, and with one press of the starter my car engine sprang to life again. A small miracle perhaps, but a miracle nevertheless. Apparently the thin film of cement and the heat of the engine had increased the length of the blade on the rotor just enough that the sparks could jump the gaps, and we were ready once more to be on our way.

I shook hands and thanked the two men, neither of whom we ever met again, and we were off. We traveled all that day without further mishap, but in the late afternoon, with the sun low on the horizon, the extreme cold set in again, and a mere ten miles from Lingyuan the engine once again stopped. Once more the extreme cold had shrunk the metal blade of the rotor.

Help wasn't long in coming. Even before I could

get out of the car I saw a dilapidated bus approaching us from the opposite direction. The driver was a Chinese man I knew. The bus was empty and was being driven to Pingquan for repairs. The man immediately stopped and asked me what was wrong. I showed him the rotor and explained the problem. Without a word, he reached into an inside pocket of his coat and brought out a brand new rotor, still in its original packaging. We fitted it onto the shaft, capped the distributor, and my engine sprang to life. When I asked him where he had gotten the rotor, he told me someone had sent the wrong kind for his vehicle, and he had just stuck it in his pocket rather than throw it away. Another sheer coincidence? Not in my book it wasn't! I was again reminded of a verse in Scripture where Christ was talking to His disciples in Matthew 6:8: "...Your Father knoweth what things ye have need of, before ye ask Him."

I was not the first to use a motor vehicle successfully in missionary work in Jehol Province. Mr. Sturt, some years earlier, had bought a Dodge truck chassis and had a Chinese firm in Tientsin build a coach body onto it to his specifications. He had used it very extensively in his travels through Mongolia, but during the two years of our absence, when he had taken over the work for us in Lingyuan, he had left the coach in Hada, a town about 100 miles north of us (also known as Chifeng) where, up to that point, he had made his home base. Upon our return, he and his family had gone back to Hada, but his health was poor and the coach remained in storage, raised up on wooden blocks to protect the tires. A year or so later he was feeling better, and wrote me asking me to come up and get his vehicle into shape and drive it to the coast for him for a badly needed overhaul.

I was only too happy to help him and, after a very roundabout trip to Hada by bus and truck, I found the coach up on the blocks all right. But all the tires were flat and, of course, the battery was dead. A local Japanese army unit had a portable generator and they obligingly charged the battery. To my surprise, the engine turned over and started on the first try, despite the fact that the gasoline in the tank was at least three or four years old. With Mr. Sturt aboard, we started out on our three-day journey south to Tientsin. It was an experience I would not have missed for anything.

It was late March or early April, so the roads were not too bad, but almost the entire trip was through mountainous country until we got down close to Peking, where the terrain leveled out. The wheels were wooden-spoked, and the tires were mounted on split rims with tubes inside. We carried two spares, but we had so many flats I became expert in breaking apart the split rims and fixing the inner tubes, and in addition we had the usual quota of bogging down in mud holes and getting stuck in rivers with sandy bottoms. The greatest hazard was descending the mountain passes. The coach had brakes only on the rear wheels and they were of the old type, where the brake bands were on the outside of the brake drums, and exposed to a lot of sand and grit. They were so badly worn that the brake shoes had very little braking surface left.

Each time we descended a steep slope I used the lowest gear possible so that engine compression would hold us back, but I still had to use the brakes, and each time the brakes overheated and smoke poured from them. I was afraid of a fire occurring, so the first time it happened, I cooled the brakes with coffee we had in a thermos flask. After that, I kept the flask filled with water. By the time we reached Peking, our brakes were entirely gone, and we had absolutely no braking power left and had to depend entirely on engine compression to slow us down. That meant we had to travel very slowly all the time, and after we reached Peking, we still had another ninety miles to go to get to Tientsin and the Dodge agency. But we did eventually make it safely.

At one point on the second day of the trip we had a miraculous escape from almost certain injury or death. We had just descended a mountain pass, and, in the foothills, the road ran through plowed fields, as yet unplanted. Six or seven inches of dust covered the road. The dust was extremely fine, about the consistency of talcum powder, and it filled the entire vehicle so we could scarcely breathe and had to cover our mouths with handkerchiefs. Our maximum speed was under ten miles an hour, and, worst of all, a following wind was at the same relative speed that we were making, which meant that the huge dust cloud we raised stayed with us and completely blinded us to anything that lay ahead.

I drove with extreme caution, now and then stopping to let the dust cloud blow ahead of us, so I could see where we were. The tires on the vehicle were very narrow, and I found the only way to stay on the road was to get one front wheel into a cart rut, then let the car go more or less where it willed. We had progressed several miles in that fashion, stopping every couple of miles to clear out the dust that had collected in the air-intake oil-bath cleaner. So much dust was sucked in that, after only a mile or two, the oil level would rise to the point where it choked off all the air and the engine would overheat.

At one point where we stopped, as the dust cloud blew away to the front of us, I could see the road ahead for a short distance. It appeared to go in a fairly straight line. However, we started up again and immediately found ourselves once more in the enveloping cloud of dust. We had driven only a short distance when I sensed a different feel to the steering wheel. It seemed that we were somehow on soft ground. I started to slow down, and then I distinctly heard a voice telling me to stop at once. I cut the engine, and when the dust cloud cleared away, there was nothing in front of us but open space. We had stopped on the very brink of a 100-foot precipice, with the front bumper out over the edge. The road had made a slight bend to the left, but in the thick layer of dust, the change in direction of the rut had not been transmitted to me through the steering column, and I had kept the wheels going straight out into a plowed field, where my left front wheel had picked up a plowed furrow and followed it right up to the edge of the chasm. It was on occasions such as that when we had the realization that God was on our side and that His angels were watching over us.

Reaching the multitudes. Van in the center at the back.

Ready to spend a night or two on one of Bob's trips.

One of the new motor roads built by the Japanese.

The Christians at Dujiawopu and from surrounding villages.

On the road and through the water.

Safely over the frozen bridge.

Among the mountains toward the south.

Car waiting its turn to drive through one of the city gates in Lingyuan.

Hot water for the radiator to help warm the engine on a very cold morning.

Different stalls at the market.

Market in full swing.

Bob looking out from under his first van as he overhauled engine.

Van needed lots of careful attention.

真金不怕火煉

Zhen jin bu pa huo lian.

True gold does not fear refinement by fire.

– Chinese Saying.

Chapter Twenty-Two
Life Takes a New Turn

We were daily reminded by the Manchukuo anthem that there were 30 million people under the new Japanese-controlled regime, and that instead of the wonderful life promised by the anthem, the people were really suffering more than before and things were growing worse by the day. The Japanese in 1935 continued to tighten the screws, making it increasingly difficult for the average person to work or eat. Not only were farm products taxed, but people were told what they could and could not plant, something entirely new. Also, rationing of foodstuffs began, at first in a small way, but increasingly it became more and more difficult to feed a family.

We began to hear the word "communists" more and more frequently. The Japanese were extremely sensitive to the activities of a relatively small band of guerrillas who had infiltrated Manchukuo. Everywhere the Japanese plastered the walls of the towns and villages with huge slogans denouncing the communists and threatening dire consequences to anyone who aided them. Few people had any idea what a communist was and wouldn't have known one if they saw him.

As an initial move to identify guerrillas and at the same time control the population, the Japanese began to issue identity cards. That met with heavy opposition. Chinese don't like to be counted: they are always in fear of some ulterior motive. They were familiar with head taxes, where families were taxed according to the number of "mouths" in the family, and they suspected it was another round of the same kind of taxation. But their resistance was useless. First, everyone in the cities and larger towns were finger-printed and issued an I.D. card, then bands of police went to all the villages one by one, surrounded them, again finger-printed everyone they found, and issued more cards. Once that had been accomplished, it became a crime to go anywhere away from their immediate neighborhood without carrying the identity card.

The city gates were reinforced and closed at dusk, not to be opened again until after sunrise, making it extremely difficult for the farmers who traditionally came in before dawn with their produce for market. It was equally difficult for laborers, who had to be available for hire by dawn and be out in the fields, or on any job outside the city, by sunrise. Anyone not inside the city by dusk was simply unable to get in, until the Chinese, as usual, found ways to circumvent the ruling by using little alleys unknown to the Japanese. Before daylight, the streets near each gate were always packed with people waiting to get out of the city, with an equal number outside waiting to get in. It made the Japanese even more unpopular than before, and the new laws were enforced not only by the police, but by the new Manchukuo army of Chinese that the Japanese had recruited.

The whole business created a tremendous amount of apprehension among the peasants in particular, and everywhere I went in the countryside, they told me horror stories of individuals and families in isolated areas who had been missed by the Japanese in the initial issuance of I.D. cards. When those poor innocents tried to enter the city and were unable to produce a card, they were often stripped and beaten, and were usually thrown into jail until someone from their village could put up a bond for them and guarantee they weren't communist guerrillas.

It was only a matter of weeks before a new and very bizarre element entered the picture. The cards had been printed on a stiff white stock, but the paper was of poor quality, and on all the cards there were minuscule black specks embedded in the paper. Somehow, the rumor arose that the black specks were poison that the Japanese had deliberately implanted into the paper, and everyone was required to carry the cards at all times because the Japanese intended killing everyone off. The rumor grew in strength and became ever more widely accepted when some people began to develop severe rashes all over their bodies — quite possibly from nervous apprehension — and that was accepted as proof. The fear became so widespread that not only were the farmers fearful of carrying the cards on their person, but they were afraid to have them anywhere inside their houses as well, and the same fear began to spread to people in the city as — true or false — more and more cases of sickness were reported. Everywhere, even in the city,

the practice of hiding the cards somewhere outside the house began. They were hidden in earthenware containers buried underground; under stones in the wall; fastened to the inside of the outer gate; hidden in the crotch of trees or up under the eaves of their houses. Then it became a common sight to see the farmers coming into town, carrying their identity cards on long, cleft sticks held aloft and well out and away from their bodies or fastened to the ends of their carrying poles. No amount of persuasion on the part of the Japanese could convince them to do otherwise, even when — as I saw happen much too frequently — they were beaten unmercifully by the Japanese for carrying their cards in that manner. It was many months before the rumor died and things returned to normal.

The contempt in which the Chinese held their Japanese conquerors began to show more clearly every day. Not everyone knows that the Japanese don't call their country "Japan" in their own language, but rather use the word "Nippon," which is pronounced *nihon*. They use two Chinese characters for the word, which mean very simply, "source of the sun." For the Chinese, there was no problem as to what to call the Japanese. The Chinese initially called them *riben ren*, which means literally: "Japan person," but it wasn't long before they came up with something different. They put the word "little" in front of the term, dropped the word for "person" and started adding an "r" sound at the end, *xiao ribenr*, which at once acted as a diminutive and made the term contemptible. But even the best among the Chinese-speaking Japanese never caught onto it. It roughly translated as "little Japs."

While writing of little black spots on the I.D. cards, I'm reminded of something else that happened in January 1935, that had nothing to do with the Japanese, but is illustrative of the extreme gullibility of people the world over when it comes to questions of money or health. Before I tell of the incident, it is appropriate that I provide a little background.

In a previous chapter I wrote of the Chinese lunar calendar and the bimonthly dates that were so important to the peasants, by which they judged the time to plant their fields or when to expect rain or frost. The Winter Solstice, *Dongzhi*, is one of the most important to them. On that day, winter officially starts, and the Chinese have calculated that there are 81 days of winter starting with that date. For reasons that no one now remembers, the Chinese divide the 81 days into nine, nine-day periods, and they use that method to keep track of where they stand. To help them know what weather to expect in any given nine-day period, they have a little rhyme, which rhymes in Chinese, but not in English. In Chinese it goes like this:

Yi jiu er jiu bu chu shou
San jiu si jiu bingshang zou
Wu jiu liu jiu kan he bian yang liu
Qi jiu he kai, ba jiu yan lai
Jiu jiu wu ling jian
Jiu jiu jia yi jiu, li niu man di zou.

It translates (My comments are in parentheses):

In the first and second nine, hands don't show. (It's so cold hands are kept up the sleeves.)

In the third and fourth nine, you walk on the ice.

In the fifth and sixth nine, you look at the poplars and willows along the river's edge (to see the buds forming).

In the seventh nine, the rivers open up (ice begins to melt).

In the eighth nine, the geese come.

In the ninth nine, no ice is to be seen. (Then they add another "nine.")

(If) a nine is added to the ninth nine, everywhere in the fields (one can see) brown cows are walking (pulling plows, planting time has arrived).

In Jehol Province that system of keeping track of winter was used by everyone, even the city dwellers, but being so far north, our cold began earlier and lasted much longer than 81 days. Nonetheless, the saying was valid for the third "nine" because that was not only the coldest time of the winter, it was when the ice was at its thickest and when most people stayed at home if they could.

In the "third nine" of 1935, there was a sudden flurry of excitement in the city that completely overshadowed everything else that was going on at the time, even what the Japanese were doing. Word came that about seven miles north of the city, on the road to Reshuitang, a live serpent had been discovered, and anyone going there to burn incense would be given medicine and would immediately be cured of any ill-

ness or infirmity he might have.

For days on end, thousands of people flocked to the spot, disregarding the extreme cold, and the Japanese became thoroughly alarmed, thinking that some sort of uprising was in the making. When I heard about it, I talked to Zhao and we drove up there in the van to take advantage of the large crowds to preach to them. Of course I knew there couldn't be any snake or serpent alive in that weather, but certainly something had been seen to justify such a happening.

The morning we arrived there the crowds were so dense we couldn't get within two or three miles of the spot where the snake was supposedly spotted. Tens of thousands of people must have been there by that time. The Japanese had dispatched police and soldiers to handle the crowds, but they weren't needed. The crowds were milling about, but were entirely peaceful. They just wanted to see the snake. Eventually I was able to make my way to the spot where the snake was reputed to be. There, the crowds were packed so tightly it was almost impossible to move.

The whole affair was in the middle of the river bed where ice covered the surface from one side of the valley to the other, and the people were standing on the ice. At one point, where the river made a wide sweep around a rocky outcrop, there was a sheer rock cliff some 100 feet in height, and mid-way up that rock, there was a small opening probably four feet square, and to my disbelieving eyes, there, sure enough, was coiled a snake, its head raised as if about to strike. It seemed to be alive. However, the cliff was so sheer, it appeared no one could possibly get close enough to the small cave to verify it, and despite what I could see, I had my doubts that it actually was a live snake because of the intense cold.

The people milling around were all carrying small cups or bowls, and holes had been dug through the ice so they could get water in the cups. I soon learned the reason. The word was that if you held out a cup of water toward the snake, "medicine" would appear in the water, and if you drank it immediately, any illness you had would be cured at once. What was happening was that the dust was so thick in the air, that as people held up the cups of water, a few flecks of black "medicine" would appear instantly in the water, no matter whose cup it was, and before the water froze, they hurriedly drank it down.

Zhao and I went up there two days running to take

advantage of the huge crowds. Then, as suddenly as it had started, it was over. The word quickly spread that a shepherd boy was responsible for the whole scam. Somewhere he had discovered the snake, frozen in that coiled position, and had managed to crawl out onto the face of the cliff to the tiny cave, where he had set the snake up in a most lifelike position, and then he started the rumor about the snake "dispensing medicine."

Despite their persecution of the people. it was ironic that the Japanese suddenly became greatly concerned about sanitation and hygiene, but it was probably more out of consideration for their own welfare than that of the Chinese. At any rate, much to the consternation of the people, one of their first moves was to abolish the outdoor pissoirs that had stood on every street in Lingyuan for centuries. Not only were those outdoor urinals for the convenience of passersby, they were also a source of income for many. Owners of streetside buildings established them outside their dwellings, and regularly they raked up the saturated earth to reclaim the ammonia from it. All that was stopped by the Japanese and no substitute was provided.

Of course, that didn't stop the peasants and others from using the same spots they had used in the past; the only difference was that the low *shujie* fences that had marked the spots were no longer there. The signs posted above the various locations by the Japanese could be read only by the educated class anyway, and they were usually not the people using the facilities. But even there, the characteristic Chinese sense of humor showed itself, and as usual they had the last word. The signs written in Chinese characters read: "Traveling persons et cetera mustn't urinate here." (*Xing ren deng bu de zai ci xiao bian*). In the original form, no punctuation was required, but it wasn't long before some jokesters spotted a chance to have fun at the expense of the Japanese. They went around and on every sign they put a comma after the Chinese word *de*. The Chinese character for "et cetera" (*deng*) in other usages carries the meaning "to wait." Thus, with the comma inserted, the sentence was completely turned around and now read: "Passersby can't wait to urinate here." Once again, the Japanese never caught on to what had been done.

Another effort in hygiene backfired on the Japanese. They were very fearful of catching some kind of disease from insects, and from the common housefly and green bottle flies in particular. At one point they instituted a big campaign to do away with all flies, making it mandatory that every household should bring in one catty (a little over a pound) of dead flies each week. That didn't work out too well, because it was too difficult to supervise and keep tabs on who had and who hadn't brought in their flies, so they started paying a small bonus. The results were overwhelming. The Chinese, alert to any way of making money, not only trapped all the flies they could get, but also set about breeding them and brought them in to the Japanese by the bushel. But the campaign didn't last very long. The Chinese started a rumor that the Japanese wanted the flies because their war with China wasn't going well, there was a famine in Japan, and the flies were needed for food. The Chinese made sure the rumor got to the ears of the Japanese, and when they heard it, they abandoned the whole effort.

Culturally, judgment of the people of one race by the people of another depends to a very large extent on one's point of view. The Japanese thought the Chinese were a filthy race because they seldom, or rarely, bathed, and had no bathing facilities in their houses. The Chinese, on the other hand, thought the Japanese must be a very filthy race because they bathed daily, and every house had its bathtub. They also thought it an appalling custom for the Japanese to install toilets inside their houses in a room right next to their cooking and eating facilities.

The Japanese, having in many respects adopted Western ways, used tissues or handkerchiefs to blow their noses just as we do. That, in Chinese eyes, was another filthy habit. Where the Chinese were concerned, if one wanted to get rid of some body waste, one did so by throwing it away as far as possible, not by putting it in one's pocket. The Chinese way of blowing their noses was to alternately press one nostril and blow hard through the other, depositing everything directly on the floor or out in the open street, then wiping away any excess with a finger, which in turn was wiped on the bottom of one's shoe. To this day the custom is still very prevalent in China. My wife and I were very amused one night during President Nixon's visit to Peking in 1972. Dan Rather was doing a piece on television about the cleanliness of the streets in Peking, and how disciplined the

Chinese were in their personal habits. His camera happened to be focused on the steps of the Post Office building as he was speaking, and at that precise moment, a Chinese man walked out and blew his nose in the age-old manner, unnoticed either by Rather or his camera crew. We wondered how many watching Americans were aware of what the man was doing.

In addition to the rest of the problems the Japanese faced, banditry and communist guerrillas continued to haunt them, and large numbers of Japanese troops and the country police under Japanese direction were continuously carrying out sweeps of the countryside. The area around Hei Shan Ke, where White Snake, the brigand chief, had held out years before, was still an impregnable stronghold. A very large band of men was holed up there, and no one knew whether they were bandits or communist guerrillas. Very often they were one and the same.

The Japanese attacked the area again and again, without success. They finally decided to use planes to bomb the area, but that, too, failed. They brought in two large bombers, and one day they pressed a low-level attack with bombs and machine guns. Flying through the narrow mountain defiles, they forgot that they were overlooked by bandits on the peaks above them, and in the rain of fire that ensued, one of the bomber pilots was killed and his plane crashed with the entire crew wiped out. I later saw the salvaged wreckage as it was trucked past our front gate to the railway station as crowds of Chinese watched, smiling at the discomfort of their enemy. After that incident, the Japanese gave up aerial attacks, and the second bomber quietly disappeared.

Around that period the Japanese became distracted by other events. In the far north of Manchukuo, the Russians were making repeated armed sorties across the Amur river, which marked the border. The Japanese, fearful of a full-scale invasion, decided to build fortifications on their side of the river. For that they needed manpower, and without fanfare, they began to round up workers by the thousands, transporting them in boxcars to the far north.

Jehol Province wasn't spared. Each day for several weeks a long freight train composed entirely of boxcars passed our back wall. From our garden we could clearly hear the cries and shouts of the men locked in the boxcars, pleading for food and water. At the back end of the train were two passenger cars filled with Japanese troops, and we learned later that their practice was to pick up a quota of men at each station until the train was full, but only empty cars were opened, and the newly "recruited" men were hustled inside and the doors were locked. When the train got out into open country, "rest" stops were made at some deserted siding where few could see what was going on, and food and water would be thrown into the cars while the dead and sick were thrown out. That might occur once a day, or once in every two or three days. It depended entirely on their whim of the moment.

In the beginning, men were openly recruited with promises of good wages and good food, and many went quite willingly. As time went on and the families heard nothing from their men, people began to fear the worst and fewer volunteers were available. That didn't stop the Japanese; they simply grabbed able-bodied men off the streets wherever they found them, and kept at it until they had filled their quota for the day. When that didn't work, they used the *bao jia* "ten household" administrative system described earlier, whereby a quota was levied on every community, and men had to be supplied or the family faced dire consequences.

For almost a year none of us had the slightest idea where the men were being taken, although there were plenty of rumors. Then, in ones and twos, the survivors began to drift back and we heard the true story.

I knew three young men who went north voluntarily, and only one of them returned. The young fellow was named Tao, and when he left he was in the peak of good health; on his return, he was unrecognizable. He looked at least 20 years older, and he not only looked like an old man, he was almost completely crippled. At first he dared say nothing about his experiences because the Japanese had threatened death to anyone who talked about what they had been doing, but eventually I gained his confidence, and in strictest secrecy he told me the full story.

The journey to their work site had taken almost a week. He wasn't sure of the exact length of time, because being shut in the boxcar they saw no daylight except on those few occasions when the door was opened to give them food and water, so they lost track of days and nights. A number of his companions in the car died en route, some from being trampled, others from illness, and their bodies were simply thrown alongside the railway tracks by the Japanese. The cars were so crowded there was no room to sit or lie, and anyone who did sit down did so at the risk of being trampled by the others. There was never enough food or water to go around, and usually only those nearest the door got a share of it. Terrible fights ensued each time food was thrown in, much to the amusement of the Japanese soldiers, who stood outside and watched. As a result of the mistreatment, when they arrived at their destination, most of the men were in no condition to work.

At the particular work camp where Tao found himself, the men were herded into large, barn-like structures with open sides, where they were forced to sleep on the ground. The camp, built at the foot of a long range of steep hills, was on swampy ground adjoining the wide Amur river. The ground inside the sheds was damp, and almost everyone caught severe colds, and many died of pneumonia or malaria, carried by the millions of mosquitoes around them.

Sanitation facilities were totally inadequate, so other diseases became rampant. From his description I gathered there had been outbreaks of both typhoid and typhus, with so many deaths he was unable to give me an estimate of the numbers. Japanese doctors were there, but they treated only the Japanese soldiers guarding the camps; Chinese coolies were expendable, and when one died, there was always another train arriving with two new men to take his place.

Tao estimated that there must have been well over 100,000 men working out of that particular camp, and it was only one of many along the border. Where he was, the Japanese were building gun emplacements in the hills overlooking the river. Their most ambitious project was a fighter plane airfield built inside one of the nearby mountains. The wide, low tunnel entrance was the end of the runway. Inside, the mountain was hollowed out, with space large enough to contain not only a large number of aircraft, but everything else needed for such an operation, including repair facilities. The runway was of sufficient length to allow the fighter craft to take off as they exited the mouth of the tunnel. Tao's description of the place staggered my imagination. However, five or six years later, after Pearl Harbor, the story was confirmed to me while we were interned in Japan. A Japanese officer boasted of his part in building the project and regaled the unmarried ladies in our group by telling of his prowess in lopping off the heads of Russian prisoners.

When Tao arrived, the work was already well advanced and he worked inside the mountain for almost an entire year until he became totally disabled from rheumatism. Because he refused to die, the Japanese shipped him home with a train ticket and a few dollars as compensation for his year of suffering. He told me that at the time he left, planes were flying directly out of the tunnel mouth, which was over 100 feet above the river below.

In building the work camp the Japanese had failed to take into account the rising waters from the summer rains, and Tao told me that once the rains started, not only were the men constantly wet from exposure to the rain, but there was always two feet of standing water in the sheds where they were supposed to sleep. Since they had no beds, they had to squat in the water, which then came well over their hips. He said that many simply toppled over in their sleep and drowned. The flood conditions lasted for almost three months.

The winter months were even worse for the poor laborers, because the clothing issued to them was totally inadequate and the sheds were unheated. They were allowed to collect river grasses for small fires inside, but those were never enough to give any real warmth since the sides of the sheds were open to the elements. Had he not been working inside the mountain (he was there for twelve hours out of every twenty-four) Tao said he never would have survived the winter. But it was the squatting in the water that did him in, and when I saw him he was doubled over in the same squatting position, unable to straighten his back or legs. But he still felt he was lucky, and he estimated that fewer than one in ten survived the experience. So much for the new land with "no more bitterness and no more sorrow."

Meanwhile, Zhao and I continued our trips into the countryside, and each was an adventure, sometimes humorous and sometimes not, but always rewarding in one way or another. One trip in particular comes to mind. We were exploring new territory to the east of Lingyuan and heard of a large market fair we had not previously visited, so we planned to spend a week there. On the way, we happened to see a tiny village of about a dozen or so homes nestled between the hills, and since it wasn't far off the main road and had a narrow dirt track leading toward it, we decided to visit.

Entering the village we were met by a young man, very flashily dressed and quite obviously well-to-do, but he seemed out of place in such a poverty-stricken village. He welcomed us warmly and invited us into his home, no better than those around him and consisting only of two small rooms for himself, his wife and two small children, and his elderly mother. He called in all his neighbors to meet us, and to our surprise he asked us to preach to them. We were, of course, delighted, and we talked to them for over an hour. About noon, his wife came in and started to set up a table on the *kang* for a lunch she had prepared for us. We protested, but the young man insisted, and we were served *jiaozi*, the delicious meat-filled dumplings that the Chinese traditionally serve to honored guests.

I devoured the dumplings with relish, but noticed something a little different in their flavor that I couldn't quite place. However, I refrained from remarking on it. During lunch, and not to our surprise, the young man quite openly told us that he was a bandit, and that he had a small gang that worked an area to the north. He proudly told us of the attacks they had made on the Japanese. He also quite openly showed us his weapons and seemed completely confident that we would not expose him to the Japanese, but he was troubled by what he had heard from us as we preached and asked us if what he was doing was sinful. He added that some years before, he had been shot in the leg and my father had removed the bullet and cured him, and for that he was most grateful. We had a long talk with him and convinced him that he should change his ways, turn to God, and find some other profession. We followed up on that young man in later months and he indeed became a born-again Christian.

About an hour later we left him and proceeded to the fair, but as we traveled I became increasingly light-headed and had difficulty keeping the car on the road. By the time we arrived at our destination, I was barely able to help set up the table for our display of books, then I had to lie down in the car. My head was swimming, and I felt I was floating several feet above the ground, a not-unpleasant feeling.

Poor Zhao was greatly concerned and asked me what was wrong. When I told him, to my surprise he burst out laughing. He told me it was nothing to worry about; it was just the after-effects of the meat used in the dumplings. Apparently I had eaten donkey meat (from a donkey that had died from natural causes) that had been air-cured up in the inside rafters of the building. The meat was obviously slighted tainted, and it was that which caused my light headedness. Fortunately, the sensation wore off after an hour or so and I suffered no ill results.

I remember that particular fair well. It was in full swing when we arrived, and because of our late arrival, the only place we could find to park the van was right next to a magician who put on a show once every hour throughout the day. Although we had a front seat view of the whole thing, it wasn't the most desirable position from our standpoint, because when his show started, we simply had to shut down and wait until it was over. From his point of view, he was quite pleased to have us next to him because the van drew a large crowd without our having to do anything. When he wanted to start his performance, all he had to do was bang on a big gong and all of our crowd went over to watch him. Since we had no alternative, we lived with it, but it all worked out well in the end.

The magician was a man of about sixty, an old man by Chinese standards, and he had two young boys working as indentured apprentices. The older of the two was about nine or ten years old, and the younger not more than six or seven. The boys, who were not brothers, had been given to the old man by their parents to learn the trade, and his only responsibility was to feed and clothe them for the eight or ten years that it would take them to learn the tricks of the trade and become magicians in their own right.

The old man's performance lasted for about twenty minutes and began with some very clever juggling acts and a half dozen magic tricks that astounded the onlookers. However, his finale was an absolute masterpiece, and I have never seen anything like it performed elsewhere. He led into it with such subtlety, and so adroitly, that it always took everyone completely by surprise. It not only appeared to be both spontaneous and unrehearsed, but also a one-time thing, because what he did was murder his chief assistant, the older boy.

The action was so fast and so realistic that the first time we saw the act, both Zhao and I rushed through the crowd in an attempt to stop him, but we were too late, and later had reason to feel very foolish.

Over the next five days I must have watched that act fifty times or more and each time its realism shocked me. Even later, when I knew the secret, I still found myself wanting to believe what my eyes told me rather than what I knew to be actually happening. I even photographed it, but the man was so deft, and his two boys so well trained, that the camera saw just what I did and revealed nothing of the old man's secret.

This is what he did: his next-to-last act was the lead-in, when he took a kiln-baked brick and laid it flat on the ground, and then lay down on his side with his right cheek on top of the brick. The older boy then took a second brick and laid it flat on the old man's other cheek, and put a third brick on top of that. Then, taking a large wooden mallet from the younger boy, he hit the uppermost brick with a sharp rap. At that point the brick at the very bottom shattered into tiny fragments, and the old man leaped to his feet unhurt, but holding his cheek and pretending that he had suffered great injury.

The act always brought loud cheers from the crowd, but as the old man got to his feet, he pretended to be in a towering rage, rubbing his face and claiming that the older boy had done his part improperly and had injured him. Grabbing a shiny, six-inch-wide sword off his table, and with murder in his eyes, he set off after the boy, chasing him round and round the small enclosure, both boys screaming in pretended terror. At first the crowd laughed, and then, seeing the seriousness of the situation, lapsed into shocked silence, but no one stepped forward to stop the old man for fear of getting cut by the sword.

Inevitably, of course, he caught the boy, tied him down on a narrow bench with his head hanging over the end, and then, with one swift stroke of the sword, he beheaded the lad. Blood spurted in every direction as the severed head fell into a basket below. While everyone gasped in disbelief, the old man quickly covered the body and the sword with a cloth, then smilingly turned to the audience, bowed deeply, and held out a plate for contributions.

The crowd's first reaction was always anger, but then someone would notice not only that the "corpse" was kicking, but that there was obviously a head bobbing up and down under the cloth covering, and loud noises were coming from underneath. In the mean-

time, the younger boy, who had carried away the "severed head," came back and lifted the covering from his companion and untied him. Realizing that they had been "had," the crowd would burst into loud laughter, and would want to see the whole show over again.

The old man happened to be staying in the same inn with us and in the evenings over the next several days, I got to know him quite well, particularly since we all shared the same *kang*. Incidentally, when people share a *kang*, each person has his own set of bedding — a sleeping mat for underneath and a quilted covering in which to roll oneself — so there is no physical contact between the sleepers, although there is often very little distance between them. One very great advantage, of course, was that since the bed was made of solid brick, it did not shake when anyone turned over in his sleep.

After the second night together I asked the old man his secret. At first he was very reluctant to tell me, but ultimately, after I had assured him that I would not reveal it to anyone else at the fair and so spoil his business, he told me. Like all such tricks, once you know how it is done, it seems so simple you wonder why you didn't see it in the first place. However, in this case, the old man's sleight of hand was so superb, and the interaction of the unnoticed smaller boy so well timed, that no matter how many times I saw the trick after that, the illusion still persisted, and I momentarily felt convinced that the older boy had been killed.

The secret, of course, was in the sword, which had a half-moon cutout in the middle of the blade, and over that the old magician would paste a stiff silver-colored paper pocket, which matched the shiny blade both in shape and color. Inside the pocket he put realistic liquid "blood" of his own mixing, and when he "severed" the boy's head, the pocket on the sword blade collapsed with the exact sound one would expect to hear when a blade met a person's extended neck, the "blood" spattered, and the sword was so deftly placed beneath the cloth with the "corpse" that no one would notice the cut-out blade. The "severed head" falling into the basket was accomplished by the younger boy quietly slipping up behind the old man just as he raised his sword. Naturally, everyone's attention was on the sword, and while they watched the downward sweep of the blade, the little fellow, with perfect timing, would throw the "severed head" between the old man's legs into the basket.

The reason the old man performed only once each hour was because it took him that long to go back to the inn and prepare his sword for the next performance, and also because the older boy, who always worked with his coat off, badly needed a washdown.

The inn we shared with the old man was the scene one night of something that now, in retrospect, was amusing, although not particularly funny at the time. Zhao and I shared a room with about five or six other men, and after our evening meal the first night, I was the first to retire. During our meal we had heard a number of rats scampering around up in the paper ceiling, and as I lay back on the *kang* I noticed some holes in the ceiling directly above my face. Just as Zhao was about to turn out the light, I remarked to him that I hoped none of the rats would fall through the holes onto my face, and with that we all settled down to sleep. Not ten minutes later, just as I was getting drowsy, I heard unusual activity in the ceiling above me, and then with a big thump a large rat fell squarely onto my chest. I sat up at once and felt around my chest for the rat, thinking that perhaps it had been killed. Instantly the rat ran up the sleeve of my pajamas. I let out a yell that woke the entire inn, and at the same instant I swung my arm in a wide arc to throw the rat out of my sleeve. In that I was successful, but when Zhao got up and lit the lamp, we could not find the slightest evidence of the rat and everyone began to believe that I had just had a nightmare.

That annoyed me. But just as we were about to give up, I noticed a hole in the paper window that hadn't been there before. I pulled on my pants and went outside and there, about ten feet from the window, I found the dead rat, which I triumphantly brought in by its tail to prove my story. Needless to say, from then on I changed my position on the *kang* and let someone else have the spot under the holes. Fortunately, on succeeding nights we had no further visitors from above.

During those months of activity we had a number of weddings among the friends with whom I had grown up, and there were frequent suggestions made to me that I, too, ought to find myself a wife because I was then twenty-three. I paid no particular attention to it until one day Zhao brought up the subject. He

was happily married with two children. He started by talking about bachelors and what an unsavory reputation they had in China. The Chinese call them *guang gunr*, which means "bare stick." However, the same expression without the "r" sound on the end of it has the connotation of ruffian, rascal or scoundrel. Zhao emphasized that the Chinese are very wary of that kind of individual, and that I should avoid having myself classified with such unsavory people. The way to do it would be to find myself a wife. He added that with a wife, I would have much better access to the homes wherever I went, and he even offered to act as a go-between in finding a wife for me — a Chinese girl, of course.

I had been too busy up to that point to even give a thought to marriage. My work was occupying all my time and giving me great satisfaction and enjoyment as well; moreover, Chinese girls never had even the slightest appeal for me. Nonetheless, I was unable to forget what Zhao had said and I began to do some serious thinking on the subject. However, no matter how I racked my brains and thought of the few Western girls that I knew, none of them seemed to be right except for the one girl I had first met on the beach some eight years before. She alone seemed to be the one person that filled the bill. She, of course, was the one I thought of as "Eva." I could not, however, rid myself of the feeling that despite our casual friendship, and the one date I had had with her in Chicago, she was unattainable as far as I was concerned. I felt sure that she, for her part, couldn't possibly consider me as a potential husband. I felt her to be far above me in intellect and sophistication, and in her presence I felt clumsy and awkward.

But as the hymn says, "...God works in mysterious ways..." Just as these thoughts were going through my mind in the spring of 1936, my sister Ruth received a letter from Eva, and casually mentioned at the dinner table that Eva had finished her courses at Moody Bible Institute, had joined the China Inland Mission, and would be leaving the United States in June on her way back to China. My ears pricked up at the news, but I tried to be casual as I asked when she was due to arrive. Ruth told me Eva had named the ship she was booked on to travel to Japan, and although she had mentioned the date of her arrival in Kobe, she had not mentioned what ship she would be taking from that point to Tientsin. At that moment I began to see God's hand directing my life, because we were all leaving shortly to spend the summer at Beidaihe, and the date of Eva's arrival would coincide with our being right there on the coast. I made up my mind immediately that I would go and meet her at the boat and leave the rest in God's hands, and started to work out some good reason for going to Tientsin around the time of her arrival. But I said nothing to anyone about my thoughts or plans.

Some weeks later, at Beidaihe beach, as the date drew nearer for Eva's arrival, I casually mentioned to the family that I needed to go to Tientsin to get some parts for the van. That was the truth, but not the whole truth. Somehow I dared not confide in the family. It was all too uncertain in my mind, and I felt very mixed up about it, but I timed my visit for the week that Eva's ship was due to arrive in Kobe, and I set out for Tientsin, where I stayed at the China Inland Mission home. There I hoped to hear something about her plans, but during the several days I was there no one mentioned her name and I was afraid to bring it up for fear of arousing suspicions and starting undue gossip. But there were other ways to find out what I needed to know.

I visited the shipping line agents and found that three ships were leaving Kobe for Tientsin shortly after Eva's ship from America was due to dock there, and she could be on any one of them. That information complicated matters considerably. How was I to know which of the three she might be on? I got the names of the three ships, each of which by that time had already departed Kobe and was on the way, and sent out wireless messages to the captains of each ship asking if "Evangeline Kok" was listed as a passenger. However, I waited in vain for a reply; none of them answered. Discouraged but not dismayed, I wasn't about to give up. I decided I would meet all three of them if I had to. Eva had to be on one of them.

Two days before the first of the three ships was due to arrive in Tientsin, I said my goodbyes to the friends at the China Inland Mission and made as though I was returning to Beidaihe. Instead, I took a rickshaw down to the native quarter of Tientsin and found lodging in a Chinese inn, much to the astonishment of the proprietor and the other guests who were staying there. They were naturally curious as to why a foreigner would elect to stay there instead of at one of the fancy hotels in the concessions. I hadn't been there long before the police even came around to investigate, but I quite truthfully told them I had insufficient money to stay in one of the foreign hotels, and that appeared to satisfy them.

Tientsin is some 35 miles inland from the sea on the Hai River, which at that time was constantly dredged, and for most of the year was navigable by small coastal steamers as far as Tientsin. At that particular time of the year the water was low, and all steamers had to dock at a small town called Tanggu near the mouth of the river. Early on the day of the first ship's arrival I caught a train to Tanggu, and an hour or so later I was standing on the dock waiting for the high tide, which would allow the ship to cross the sand bar at Dagu, the actual mouth of the river, where two ancient forts guarded the entrance.

As I stood on the dock in the bright sunshine with a throng of coolies milling around me, doubts and questions raced through my mind. Had I done the right thing in coming here? What would Eva's reaction be at my meeting her? Would I embarrass her? But I had spent much time in prayer about it, and as those thoughts came to me, an inner peace prevailed and I suddenly had the firm conviction that I was indeed doing the right thing and that good would come of it.

There were several other foreigners on the dock that morning, but I recognized none of them, so I felt secure in my anonymity. At least I would not have to answer a host of questions as to why I was there. Tied up a short distance down the long riverside dock, was a U.S. submarine making a port call, and I wandered in that direction as I waited, passing the time of day with one or two of the sailors. Then, suddenly I saw someone I knew. There, from inside the conning tower, climbed Eva's older brother, Paul, obviously there to meet her. He was the very last person I wanted to see or be seen by, but as I dodged back into the crowd, a surge of joy came over me. Since it was obvious he was there to meet Eva, it was equally obvious that she must be on this first ship to arrive.

Although I knew Paul by sight, I don't think I had ever spoken to him, and I didn't think he knew me, but still I decided to play it safe and stay in the back of the crowd. I was facing a dilemma. How was I to approach Eva with her brother, of all people, on the scene? How would I be able to say anything to her in private? That was something not only totally unanticipated, it was a disaster. But I took courage and decided I would see it through to the end.

I watched as the ship slowly steamed into sight around a bend in the river, then it passed us, going upriver a short distance in order to turn around and come down with the current to tie up. My excitement grew to the point where I thought my heart would burst as I spotted Eva standing on the deck, completely unaware of me but waving to her brother.

Then came another of God's small miracles in my life. The ship turned around and started back toward the dock, but the captain had miscalculated. The current was too strong, and the ship was going too fast. It hove in against the dock sideways with a mighty bump, bounced right off again, and had to go out into the middle of the stream, turn around and go upstream once again, and repeat the whole maneuver. However, I saw what was going to happen as a God-given opportunity. Instinctively, as I saw the speed of the ship, I knew exactly what was going to occur. I ran from the back of the crowd to the dock's edge, timing my arrival there with the bumping of the ship against the dock, and at the instant the ship came into contact with the dock, I leaped upward, caught hold of the ship's rail, and, accompanied by yells of protest from both the crew and police on the dock, hauled myself aboard and found myself standing immediately in front of Eva.

It would be an understatement to say that she was surprised to see me, but there was a welcome smile on her face as she took it quite calmly, and after I had caught my breath, I greeted her as if that was the normal way of boarding a ship to meet someone when she arrived. For the next 15 or 20 minutes we had complete privacy on the crowded deck before the ship tied up and her brother Paul came aboard, and it took only those few minutes for me to know that I was deeply in love with her and that whether she knew it or not, I knew that she was God's choice to be my wife. At the same time, I felt strongly that she reciprocated my feelings. At least she didn't seem unhappy to see me.

Now, as I write this, some 55 years later, I can remember that whole scene as vividly as if it were yesterday, but I don't remember a single word we said to each other. Before Paul came aboard, I remember I had at least exacted a promise from her

that she would answer my letters if I wrote to her. When Paul appeared, she quite naturally had to turn her attention to him, and I felt jealous of the kiss she gave him. She introduced me, but Paul, while quite polite, seemed somewhat cool toward me, and although I felt my presence was unwanted, somehow I just couldn't tear myself away.

I suspected that Paul was trying to get rid of me when he suggested that perhaps I could go and send a telegram, go check on her baggage, go and hire a couple of coolies to carry her bags to the train, and so on, but at the risk of appearing rude, I ignored the suggestions and he had to go himself while I stayed with Eva until he returned. Ultimately though, the time for parting came as we all found our way over to the railway station. They boarded the train for Peking, where Eva's home was, and I somewhat forlornly stood on the platform and watched the train move out of sight, wondering to myself just what my next move should be in courting that wonderful young lady. At the same time I was exhilarated, and when I caught the next train north to Beidaihe, my brain was whirling.

My face and whole appearance must have given me away when I got home that evening, because Mother wanted to know why I was in such high spirits. I explained to the family what I had done, and what I felt my prospects were, and they were all delighted. I was, however, in for a big surprise. The very next day, shortly after lunch, a special delivery letter came to the house addressed to me. It was from Eva, and I opened it with trembling fingers. It was the first letter she had ever written to me and it was a shocker indeed.

She wrote that Paul (the dutiful son) had told her father about my meeting her on the ship at Tanggu, and that her father had called her in to ask what our intentions were. He and I had met before, and he knew me slightly and knew the missionary group with which I was associated. I know he had the very highest respect for them, but for some inexplicable reason he was extremely upset when Eva told him about our desire to correspond with each other. He immediately gave her explicit orders not to encourage my attentions in any way, and she was to write me at once and tell me that she would be unable to correspond with me. Later I learned he had added: "...or you will not be welcome in my home any longer." All of that he had told her with no explanation whatsoever.

In her letter Eva asked me what she should do, and explained that if she went against his wishes, it would be the first time she had ever done so. On the other hand she felt that as she was 22, he had no right to dictate to her with whom she could correspond. She finished the letter on a somewhat lighter note by asking me how my "cookie duster was doing," referring to the incipient mustache that I had tried to grow in order to look a little more mature and perhaps to impress her. It was little more than a bit of fuzz on my upper lip, and I shaved it off that same day.

I acted on her letter without hesitation, dashing off to the telegraph office to send her a telegram saying that I would be there the first thing the following morning to discuss the question. Having come so far, and realizing what my feelings for her were and that my feelings seemed to be reciprocated, I was not about to give up. From the telegraph office I raced to the station, caught a train almost at once, and was in Peking by ten o'clock that night checking in at the YMCA. I ascertained from the desk clerk that the first bus out to Xiang Shan (Fragrant Mountain) in the Western Hills, where the Koks had their summer home, would leave at six in the morning, and asking to be awakened at five, I headed off to bed.

The bus ride to Xiang Shan took a little over an hour and after a brief walk I found their house on a steep hillside, with a long flight of steps leading up to it. With my heart thumping I approached the gateway, and at that very moment, out walked Eva's father. He spotted me but didn't stop to talk, he just touched his hat and walked away purposefully. But Eva's reception, and that of her mother and younger sister Annie, was all that I could have desired. I found out later that Eva's mother was, God bless her, secretly quite sympathetic. After my telegram arrived and she learned I was on the way to the house, she had whispered to Eva: "Hurry up and change your dress." As I approached, she graciously came to greet me, but instead of ushering me into the house, with great diplomacy, and possibly in order not to seem to go against her husband's wishes, she directed Eva and me over to a small ornamental pavilion in the middle of the garden a short distance from the house, and brought us some coffee.

There, on a stone bench in full view of the house, Eva and I sat hand in hand and talked for a little over an hour in what amounted to complete privacy, although now and then I caught occasional glimpses of Eva's younger sister Annie. To her, it was very exciting, and she supported it fully. There was no sign of Paul at all. He had already left to return to his missionary activities in the villages about 100 miles west of Peking and behind the Western Hills. He worked there with a "lost tribe" who had been banished there by the Manchu Dynasty in 1644.

Eva told me that my telegram had been delivered to her only an hour before my arrival and that her father had become extremely angry, telling her to telephone every hotel in Peking until she found me to tell me not to come. After trying every likely place she could think of, she had remembered the YMCA and had called them, only to be told that I had left on the six o'clock bus. When she told her father that I was already on the way, he ordered her to get rid of me as soon as possible and stalked out of the house, only to run into me at the foot of the steps.

Mr. Kok was an extremely intelligent man, and I am sure that he must have been fully aware both then and later that it was his own arbitrary actions toward Eva that had precipitated my coming to Peking so quickly. Actually, I have no reason to feel anything but gratitude toward Mr. Kok. Had it not been for him, our courtship might have lasted for months instead of the less than 48 hours that had elapsed since I had met her at Tanggu, which resulted in my asking Eva then and there, that morning on the stone bench, to do me the honor of marrying me. Eva showed not the slightest hesitation in accepting, and with her acceptance came one of her kisses, albeit a most discreet one, for which I had been waiting so long.

In case her father should come back, I didn't want to embarrass Eva and her mother by overstaying my welcome. In the limited time we had together, we talked of the future and of the problems that faced us. We agreed that winning over her father was of primary importance, and until that was accomplished, we should keep our engagement secret. Never for a moment did either of us imagine that a change of heart would never happen during his lifetime, or that it would be two long years before we could make our secret public and I could give her an engagement ring. However, that is the way it turned out. Even then, the timing of our marriage was dictated by political circumstances beyond our control.

That morning, neither of us mentioned the actual word "engagement," although both of us knew that was the case. We had other problems to worry about, not the least of which was the contract Eva had with the China Inland Mission (C.I.M.), which stipulated that, should she marry within two years after joining the mission, she would have to repay all monies expended on her, not only for passage to China from the United States, but also for the period of training that followed. We knew it would be a sizable sum, and learned later that it amounted to approximately $2,000, which in 1936 dollars was the equivalent of approximately five years' income for me at the time, and in today's dollars would be equal to around $20,000.

Uppermost in our minds was the moral question of whether we owed it to her mission authorities to inform them of her intentions before she became even more deeply obligated to them. Both of us were desperately in love, and none of those things loomed very large in our thinking at the time. So we decided to simply keep our secret to ourselves, and a few weeks later, after Eva had left for the south for her period of training, she wrote to her parents to tell them that we would be corresponding with each other, and that we hoped to marry later, but that we wanted to wait for her father's consent. Both of us had the faith and confidence to wait and see how God would order our pathway.

Before I left Eva's house that day Mrs. Kok kindly invited me to stay for lunch, but, much as I wanted to, I thought it best not to irk Eva's father any more than necessary, so with Eva and Annie walking with me to the bus stop, I left to catch the bus back to Peking. Joyful as I was over having "won her hand," I nevertheless left with a heavy heart, not knowing when I would see her again. She had orders to report to the C.I.M. training school in Yangzhou, not far from Shanghai, before summer ended, and that would separate us by another thousand miles or more. Letters were going to be a very poor substitute to seeing her in person.

When I reached Peking and caught the train back to Beidaihe, the world seemed a whole different place for me. On the train I started writing my first letter to Eva, and I learned later that she was doing the very same thing at home. Those were the first of our daily

letters to each other over the next two years, years of great turbulence, violence, and unrest. And during those years, with the exception of a very select few individuals, we were unable to confide in anyone about that momentous happening in our lives.

Fall came, and with it Eva's departure for Yangzhou, a fairly large city 100 miles or so northeast of Shanghai, quite close to the Yangtze river, and only a relatively short distance from Nanking. But even though we were in the same country, Eva might just as well have been on the other side of the world as far as I was concerned.

The C.I.M. maintained a language school in Yangzhou exclusively for single ladies, and despite the fact that Eva was already fluent in spoken Chinese, the mission felt that she should be treated no differently from any other raw recruit. Besides, apart from language training, there were many other things she had to learn of life in the mission field. Eva put her heart into her studies, especially the reading and writing of Chinese characters, and was there for eight months before being assigned to a mission station for actual work. I was back in Lingyuan all that time with the family, and when Eva learned of her assigned post early in 1937, I was overjoyed to learn that it was to be a small town called Huairou in Hebei Province, the province next to Jehol. That was good news indeed. At least she would be that much nearer.

However, world-shaking events were fast overtaking us. Hardly had Eva been transferred to the north when the Japanese launched their attack on China proper, beginning with the infamous Marco Polo Bridge incident outside Peking on July 7, 1937. The Japanese then surged down the railroad toward the south, and all missionaries in the area were evacuated to Peking and Tientsin, Eva included.

While the new outbreak of war was troubling news for all of us, I personally had reason to be overjoyed because, not only did it bring Eva that much closer to me, there was also a remote chance that I would be able to see her again shortly. When Eva wrote that she had arrived in Peking and would be staying with her parents for a short time, my mother was very sympathetic toward her lovesick son and, as she needed to be fitted for some new glasses, she suggested we take a trip to Peking. I could always think of something I urgently needed for the van, so, with that as an additional excuse, when events around Peking had quieted down a bit, we drove down in the van and stayed at the Wagon Lits hotel. There, for a couple of hours one glorious afternoon, in a corner of the huge lobby, Eva and I sat together on a couch and had a wonderful visit. Her father was still unapproachable and very cool and distant toward her, and it was only her mother's poor health that had made him agree to Eva's return to her home in Peking. And, of course, he knew nothing of my visit to Peking, nor of Eva meeting me at the hotel.

Not long after, Eva was moved down to the C.I.M. home in Tientsin, where I always stayed when visiting there. Tientsin, except for the foreign concessions, was occupied by the Japanese. They set up barbed wire barricades at every entrance to the concessions and made life miserable for British and French nationals in particular whenever they entered or left the area. Since the railroad station was outside the concessions and in Japanese-occupied territory, any time one traveled, the barricades had to be negotiated. When Eva traveled down from Peking to Tientsin and was about to enter the British Concession, she had a most frightening and disturbing experience. It was pouring rain at the time, and riding in a rickshaw with the top up, she was stopped by a surly and uncouth Japanese soldier who wanted to see her papers and then searched her baggage. As a final insult he tried to search her person, even going to the extent of thrusting his hand up under her skirt. When Eva wrote me about it I was furious and vowed to do everything possible to bring about our marriage as soon as possible so as to have her under my protection, but it was still to be many months before that could come about, and our only contact was still by letter, a most unsatisfactory medium.

I have mentioned elsewhere the Japanese censorship of all the mails, and that was constantly on our mind when we wrote each other. We had to be most discreet in what we said of the political situation, and it was galling to think that someone else was reading our endearments to each other. The Japanese were extremely clever in opening letters, and it was often difficult to tell when they had been tampered with. However, occasionally they gave themselves away, such as the time when I opened an envelope from Eva only to find my own letter to her of the previous day inside it, while she got her letter to me back in my envelope. Apparently our two letters had been on the

same censor's desk at the same time, and he had slipped up.

Many people refused to believe that their mail was being censored, but some amusing stories were told by fellow foreigners that fully confirmed it. One lady writing to a friend remarked: "I'd better be careful of what I say because the little brown men will be reading this." When her friend received the letter, a penciled note had been added at the bottom: "We're not little brown men, and we don't read your letters."

On the train one day I met a young Englishman who told a classic incident that had occurred when he and another young Britisher working for the Hong Kong and Shanghai Banking Corporation were talking over a beer in Tientsin. One of them was to leave the following day for his post in Mukden, in Manchukuo, and he was unconvinced that the Japanese had the capability or the desire to read everyone's letters and insisted that it was only the occasional one that got opened. His friend insisted that the Japanese read every single letter that went through. They eventually agreed to a test, and decided that they would each write the other, and in the letters, each would state that he was enclosing something specific, but in actuality neither would do so. The test was to see what the Japanese censor would do when he read their letters.

When the letters were eventually written, the Mukden man said he was sending his friend a $10 bill to show him what Manchukuo currency looked like, but he didn't actually enclose it. However, when the letter reached Tientsin, there was a $10 bill inside. The Tientsin lad wrote his friend and remarked how fierce the mosquitoes were in Tientsin and how huge they were, and said he was enclosing one for his friend to see, but he didn't actually put one in. Nonetheless, when the letter reached Mukden, there was a flattened mosquito carefully placed inside by the censor!

The Marco Polo Bridge incident on the night of July 7, 1937, is now famous, but at the time it passed us almost unnoticed. For us it was just another in the many clashes between the Japanese and Chinese. But it is actually considered by many to be the first engagement of World War II. The Japanese had planned night maneuvers at the bridge, and had fired blank cartridges. However, Chinese troops nearby, hearing the firing, thought they were being attacked and started to shell the area, but without anyone being hit. Nonetheless, when the Japanese found a man missing at roll call, they thought he had been captured by the Chinese and an attack on the Chinese base at Wanping ensued.

What happened in the next few days caught everyone very much by surprise. We happened to be in Beidaihe at the time, and suddenly the sky each day was filled with the roar of Japanese bombers heading toward Tientsin. It seemed to us that they deliberately flew at a very low altitude over Beidaihe, perhaps to intimidate the foreign residents. All passenger train service was disrupted as Japanese troop trains monopolized the line.

One afternoon I rode my bicycle the five miles or so through the grain fields toward the main line to see what was going on. Hiding in the tall sorghum, I watched for hours as one train after another in very short intervals headed south toward Tientsin. Everything I saw appeared to be brand new: locomotives and rolling stock, tanks, trucks and heavy artillery, and thousands upon thousands of Japanese troops cheering and singing as they went by. Despondent, I rode home, wondering just how long it would be before the Japanese took over the whole of China.

We became aware much later that the invasion had been in the planning stages for well over two years, although at the time we had been unable to see it. What we had noticed was the propaganda war that lasted for many months, and the Japanese had also run a drug campaign for more than a year in which they employed hundreds of Koreans who canvassed the countryside in China, distributing heroin-laced cigarettes to young men of military age. The intention was to bring about addiction, which would neutralize the Chinese army to a large extent, and in that they were to a high degree successful.

Along with that campaign, the Japanese had also very deftly and insidiously destroyed the Chinese economy by systematically robbing the country of its silver dollars and thus bringing about tremendous inflation, as the Chinese government printed paper money in the billions of *yuan* to take its place. To accomplish that, the Japanese again employed hundreds of Korean civilians. Every passenger train coming into China from Manchukuo through Shanhaiguan had two or three extra passenger cars attached to it at Shanhaiguan exclusively for the Koreans, all loaded down with Chinese paper money. Reaching Tientsin, they bought up all the silver dollars they could, regardless of the cost, then quite openly carried them out of the country back into Manchukuo.

The Chinese government protested, but to no avail. A law was passed prohibiting anyone from carrying silver dollars out, but police and soldiers at railroad stations and border crossings were bribed and the flow of outgoing dollars continued unabated. The Japanese came up with a simple but effective ruse to mask what they were doing, although everyone knew what was happening. Each Korean was supplied with a sleeveless jacket made of coarse Chinese cotton, almost as heavy as canvas. Into each of those, back and front, were sewn narrow vertical pockets. The silver dollars were laid out on paper in rows, where each dollar overlapped the next. They were then wrapped in the paper and slid into the narrow pockets until the jacket was full. A full jacket contained several hundred dollars and weighed somewhere in excess of a hundred pounds.

I happened to be on the station platform in Tientsin one day and watched the entire procedure. Outside the station, in full view of anyone who cared to watch, busloads of Koreans arrived, carrying their loaded jackets quite openly. Then, before they walked into the railroad station where police officers were supposed to stop them, they put the jackets on. It took two men to hold up the heavy jacket while the courier stretched out his arms and slipped into it. Once the jacket was on, the man had to walk stiffly erect with tiny steps; otherwise, if he bent forward even slightly, the weight would cause him to fall flat on his face. That happened with four of the older men, one of them as he was being assisted up the steps of the railroad car, only in his case, he fell over backward, despite the efforts of the two men supporting him. The watching Chinese police, fully aware of what was going on, did nothing, even when silver dollars rolled all over the platform. I was traveling on that same train, and after I had found a seat, I walked back to see what the Koreans had done with the jackets once they were aboard. I found they had taken the jackets off and had stowed them under their seats.

That was in the summer of 1936 and I was on my way back to Lingyuan at the time. The family were in

Beidaihe for the hottest months, but I had been going back and forth to Lingyuan a number of times, and that was one time when I had made a side trip to Tientsin to pick up some parts for the van.

While in Lingyuan I somehow either ate something that disagreed with me or caught some kind of "bug." In any event, I became quite ill and spent several miserable days in bed. No matter what I took, nothing helped, and the Japanese doctor whom I consulted was unable to diagnose my problem. I decided to head for the coast and tried unsuccessfully to get a ticket on the small single-engined passenger plane the Japanese operated once a day. As things turned out, it was perhaps just as well.

Instead, I caught the first train out, and traveled all night. The following morning, as my train reached Chinhuangtao, just inside the China border, I saw a gruesome sight. More than 50 dead Koreans were laid out on the station platform. They had been riding on the train a few hours ahead of mine, the one I would have been on had I been able to take the plane the previous day. Just after their train had left Shanhaiguan, it had been hijacked by a band of Chinese bandits or soldiers, no one quite knew which. Railroad ties had been piled on the track, and when the train stopped, the attackers systematically machine-gunned the passenger cars carrying Korean couriers on their way to Tientsin with their paper money, killing quite a few of them. The attackers then went aboard the train and robbed the surviving Koreans of everything they had, after which they indiscriminately fired their guns at the passengers, leaving many more dead and wounded. But the incident in no way deterred either the Japanese or the Koreans, who continued bleeding China until no more silver dollars could be found. When the Japanese felt the Chinese had been sufficiently weakened, they created the incident at the Marco Polo Bridge, and a full-scale war with China was on. It lasted through Pearl Harbor, and continued another eight years right up until the end of World War II.

Cut Paper Art. A charm to insure prosperity and long life combining the four characters.

福 Fù (Prosperity),

寿 Shòu (Long Life),

雙(刄)全 Shuangqúan (Complete In All Respects).

Can you find them all?

(The cover reads:)
"IDENTIFICATION CERTIFICATE FOR PROPAGATOR OF RELIGION" — ID booklet Bob was required to carry at all times.

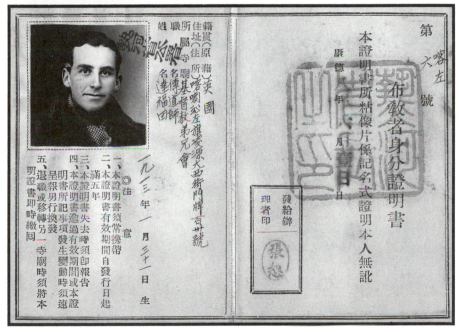

(Left-hand page:)
NATIVE PLACE: ENGLAND
RESIDENTIAL ADDRESS: DOOR NUMBER 130 GREAT WEST STREET, LINGYUAN, LEFT BANNER OF THE K'A-LA-CH'I LEAGUE. (The last part of this address is there because of the fact that this area of Jehol Province was heavily populated by Mongols and Manchus. Today in the PRC, this area is called the Harqin Zuoyi Mongolzu—Mongol Race—Autonomous County, centering around another town—Ta Ch'eng Tzu.)
MOSQUE OR TEMPLE ASSOCIATED WITH: CHRISTIAN BRETHREN SOCIETY
OCCUPATION: Preacher
NAME: TA FU-T'IEN (This is Bob's Chinese name.)
DATE OF BIRTH: JANUARY 31, 1913
(The stamp over the photograph:) PUBLIC OFFICE (YAMEN) OF JEHOL PROVINCE.
*TAKE NOTICE (OF THE FOLLOWING)
1. YOU MUST CARRY THIS CERTIFICATE WITH YOU AT ALL TIMES.
2. THIS CERTIFICATE IS IN EFFECT FOR A FULL FIVE YEARS FROM THE DATE IT WAS ISSUED.
3. YOU MUST REPORT IMMEDIATELY IF THIS CERTIFICATE IS LOST.
4. WHEN THE EFFECTIVE PERIOD FOR THIS CERTIFICATE HAS EXPIRED OR WHEN ANY CHANGES OCCUR IN THE FACTS AS NOTED ON THIS CERTIFICATE, YOU MUST IMMEDIATELY REPORT AND APPLY FOR A CHANGE.
5. WHEN YOU RESIGN OR TRANSFER TO A DIFFERENT MOSQUE OR TEMPLE, YOU MUST IMMEDIATELY HAND BACK THIS CERTIFICATE.

(Inside right-hand page:)
K'A TSO (This is an abbreviation for an area in then-Jehol Province where Lingyuan is located. The name in full appears under "Street Address" below.
NUMBER SIX (These first two lines apparently mean that this is the sixth such identification card issued for propagators of religion in the K'A TSO area of Jehol Province.)
(Large square seal with seal script characters:) SEAL OF THE PUBLIC OFFICE OF JEHOL PROVINCE
IDENTIFICATION CERTIFICATE FOR PROPAGATOR OF RELIGION
THE PERSON WHOSE PHOTOGRAPH IS ATTACHED TO THIS CERTIFICATE IS GENUINELY THE PERSON CERTIFIED
JUNE 1, 8TH YEAR OF K'ANG TE (The year and month are not clear. KANG TE was the Reign Name (in Manchukuo) of Henry Pu-Yi, the Japanese puppet emperor in Manchukuo. Henry Pu-Yi was the last emperor of China. The K'ang Te reign was from 1934 to 1945.
(In lower left corner of right-hand page:) SEAL OF ISSUER: Chang Shu

The Kok family in 1930s. The lady behind Eva's mother is her Aunt Anna—
sister to Mr. Kok. The two boys were in the States at school.

The Koks when Eva came to visit in
1936 on return from the U.S.

Yangchow—China Inland Mission Language School for new lady missionaries, where Eva spent some months.

The place we became engaged. Note lily pods on the ground.

Manchukuo 1 yuan bank note.

Eva's home in the Austrian Legation in Peking. (To the right in the background is the Grand Hotel de Pekin.)

Where Eva's parents had their summer home. (Xiangshan)

Getting ready to load the van for a trip.

The time Bob picked up pebbles that froze to his tires and springs.

Pushing through the ice.

Dropped down a steep ledge.

In trouble.

Narrow road next to an edge straight down the mountain.

A typical bridge for winters only.

After a dusty trip.

On the way to market.

A church group welcoming us on one of our return trips to Lingyuan.

Eva with friends at Chaoyang. Miss Wilks on the far right.

Our home occupied by the military.

Our two blind friends.

An unhappy visitor.

Ren xin si tie, guan fa ru lu.

Mens' hearts are like iron,
but government laws are like a furnace.

- Chinese Peasant Saying.

Chapter Twenty-Three
Twice Married in Two Days

I think I've painted a somewhat unfavorable picture of Eva's father, so I think I should tell something further about this kindly and remarkable man, and explain what he was really like.

Despite his seeming intransigence where Eva and I were concerned, I still had the highest possible respect for him and knew him to be a man of sterling character and high moral principles. He was a man of exceptionally strong convictions, and when he made up his mind on a given point, it was impossible to convince him otherwise. A great believer in the Bible, he held strongly to the Biblical injunction regarding children in Ephesians 6:1: "Children, obey your parents in the Lord, for this is right."

Mr. Kok quite naturally wanted the best for his daughter, and presumably, I didn't measure up in his eyes. And, even though Eva was 22 years old, he may have felt that she was incapable of judging for herself. Aware that Eva had disobeyed his instructions, he made it clear to her that she was unwelcome in his

home until she obeyed him, and that was that. He never mentioned the subject again over all the years that we knew him.

Mr. Kok was one of the most charming and likable men you could meet anywhere. He was quite short in stature, standing barely five feet tall, and he was soft-spoken and retiring in his manner and very dapper in his dress. At the same time, he was a giant of a man in his courage and most aggressive in expressing his beliefs and defending his Christian faith as taught in the Bible.

Born in Holland, Arie Kok entered the Dutch Civil Service as a young man and married a Dutch girl, Elsje Aldenberg. Their first son, Paul, was born in 1909 in Amsterdam. On a trip to England sometime around 1910, he attended a conference of evangelical Christians interested in missions and came to the firm conviction that God wanted him to become a missionary. He decided to go to Estonia — at that time a small republic on the Baltic, later annexed by the

Soviet Union in 1940 — to look over the mission field. He resigned from civil service and took his wife and child to Estonia, then later they lived in Moscow for a time. Two years later he felt a strong call to take the Gospel to the Tibetans, but Tibet was closed to foreigners at the time, so he decided to find a place in western China, as close as possible to the border, where he could establish a mission and still reach the many Tibetans crossing the border into China.

Their journey across Russia on the Trans-Siberian Railway to the port of Vladivostok was long and tedious. From Vladivostok they traveled by coastal steamer, first to Dairen, then Tientsin, and from there to the German-held port of Tsingtao, on the tip of the Shandong peninsula. There their second son, Gerard was born in 1912. But Tsingtao was only a jumping-off point. When Eva's mother was ready to travel once again, they left by ship for Shanghai, and from there to Foochow, then Amoy, and from there they went to Hong Kong, then Hainan Island, then on to the port of Haiphong (Vietnam), at that time known as French Indochina. From Haiphong they made a long overland trip by narrow-gauge train first to Hanoi, then by way of Kunming, capital of the province of Yunnan in west China, eventually arriving in the city of Dali.

Mr. Kok left no record of his trip, but tracing the journey through the writings of explorers and other travelers who visited Yunnan around the same period of time, it is estimated that the journey from Tsingtao alone took over 60 days, not counting the time spent on layovers at various points.

The Kok family stopped first at the China Inland Mission station in Dali, which was probably one of the most remote mission stations in China at the time, but it was still not close enough to Tibet for Arie Kok. From there he scouted around until he found the town of Lijiang, in the shadow of the Himalayan mountains, seven days' journey on muleback from Dali. There he set up his mission and in time established a small church.

The trip from Hanoi to Kunming, at that time called Yunnanfu, was unquestionably the most scenic part of their entire journey. The railway line passed through almost impassable mountains for most of the route, and, because of constant rock slides and tunnel cave-ins, trains traveled only during the daylight hours. At nightfall the passengers were put up in "railway hotels," the discomforts of which are well described in Roy Chapman Andrew's book, *Camps and Trails in China*, written after he made the same journey some four years later. The railway ran only as far as Kunming, and from there it was a three-week journey by litter or muleback to Lijiang through spectacularly beautiful scenery.

In Lijiang the Koks were joined by a Miss Scharten and later by Arie Kok's sister, Anna, the latter going there primarily to help in the schooling of young Paul and Jerry, as Gerard came to be known. Anna eventually entered missionary work herself and served there, and in other parts of China, for many years, including a number of years with Dr. and Mrs. Jonathan Goforth in Manchuria.

When Eva was born on January 26, 1914, the circumstances of her birth were so unique they bear recording. There was a small hospital in Kunming, but there was great political unrest in the province at the time, marked by a lot of fighting between the various tribes and the Chinese. Doubtless because of that, or perhaps because the 21-day journey was too daunting, instead of going to Kunming, Mr. Kok took Eva's mother to Dali, seven days' ride on muleback, for the birth of her third child. Leaving his wife there in the capable hands of a Mr. Hanna, who ran a small medical clinic there with the China Inland Mission. Mr. Kok meanwhile made the seven-day trip back to Lijiang to await a telegram announcing the birth.

Most cities in China were served by telegraph in those days. Usually, the telegraph line consisted of a single wire strung between very thin poles cut from fresh saplings, so fresh that many of them took root and sprouted branches and leaves. To have erected anything more substantial would have invited theft. Electric current to power the system was derived from bulky, glass jar water-batteries.

However, when telegraphy was first introduced into China, the Chinese faced a unique problem. Their written language consists of characters or ideographs, each unique and representing a complete word or concept. These ideographs number in the tens of thousands, and because of their complexity, they could not be conveyed by telegraphy. A novel approach was devised for transmitting them: for each individual character, a four-digit group of Arabic numerals was substituted, and code books, called the Standard Telegraphic Code, were printed and distributed to anyone who wanted them.

Sending a telegraphic message in English was possible between most of the larger cities, but apart from those relatively few places, most of the Chinese telegraphists knew no English, so the C.I.M. came up with an equally novel solution to the problem. Using the same idea as the Arabic numeral code for Chinese characters, they developed their own code book, a list of thousands of possible messages, each of which could be transmitted by Arabic numbers. Those, the Chinese telegraphists could readily handle. Should a situation arise where the code book did not contain the exact message desired, individual words could be strung together, each using its own group of digits. The code book was so successful, and filled such a long-felt need that all English-speaking missionaries in China adopted its use, but like everything else it had to be used correctly or human error could result in serious communication problems.

Can you imagine the shock that poor Mr. Kok got some weeks later when he received a telegram, which, when decoded, read: "Twin boys born, mother dead"? And the further shock he received when, after his seven-day journey to Dali to pick up the baby "twins," he discovered his wife with a healthy baby girl very much alive and well. Somewhere along the way two digits had been transposed, resulting in the wrong message being either transmitted or incorrectly transcribed at the receiving end.

In those days, all children born to Westerners in China had to be registered at birth with their respective consulates, but in Eva's case, the nearest Dutch consulate was in Canton, some six to eight weeks' journey away. Her father was unsure of the exact procedure, so he wrote to ask for instructions. Considerable time elapsed before he received an answer. Two British botanist-explorers happened to be passing through Lijiang about that time. One of them was the famous Mr. George Forrest, whose writings are well known in Britain. On their return to the coast, Eva's father entrusted them with a letter to the Dutch consulate, feeling it was safer than sending it through the regular mails. In the end it was seven months after her birth that her name was finally registered.

It wasn't until sometime in the 1960's that we learned of it. When applying for U.S. citizenship, we were required to produce our birth certificates, but Eva had none. All consular records in Canton had been lost during World War II. However, Eva's father managed to contact a friend in The Hague, and through him we received a two-page document in Dutch describing the above incident in detail. The original document and a translation made by Berlitz in New York satisfied the Immigration and Naturalization Service, but I imagine among those bureaucrats it must have aroused at least some interest and comment.

Eva's father was an amateur botanist and had quite a collection of unusual specimens he had found in the mountains of Yunnan. When the two visiting British botanists saw his collection, they were particularly excited over one very unusual flower. When they took it back to England, they discovered it was unique and had never been seen in the Western world; thereupon, it was given a Latin botanical name that included Eva's father's name. Unfortunately we've not been able to track it down, and don't remember what the name actually was.

At the termination of World War I in 1918, four years after Eva's birth, the Netherlands Legation in Peking had great need of a Chinese language specialist and wrote to Mr. Kok, asking him to rejoin the civil service in that capacity. He had been a serious student of Chinese and was not only exceptionally fluent in speaking the language, but he had a remarkable facility with the written language as well, one which very few Westerners could match. After giving the offer considerable thought, he finally accepted the post of first chancellor, with the proviso that he be given complete freedom to pursue his church and missionary activities in his free time. To that the minister (as representatives were called in those days) agreed, and in 1919 the Kok family moved to Peking and took up residence in the Legation Quarter.

Eva was four when they made the move and remembers very little of the journey from Lijiang to the coast except that her two brothers rode opposite each other in basket panniers on each side of a mule's back. As boys will, they constantly played or bickered loudly, and, Eva remembers, they had to be frequently hushed because of the fear that roving bandits might hear them and attack.

In Peking, the children were enrolled in the Peking American School, a school that had been established not only for all Western children, but which also accepted talented Chinese children. The two boys, Paul and Jerry, were later transferred to a boarding school for Western children in a town called Tongzhou, a short distance outside of Peking.

At the Peking American School Eva made lifelong friends with three of the girls who started kindergarten with her in 1919. Almost 70 years later, in September 1986, they had a reunion here in Monterey: Eva's best friend, Damaris Peck Reynolds, whose father was a diplomat in the American Legation in Peking, was there. Also Barbara Baker Loudon, whose father was in the Famine Relief Commission, and Helen Corbett Bacon, the daughter of a university professor. For years, all four girls, as well as others, enjoyed happy times together in the Peck home in the Legation Quarter and in their summer home in the Western Hills. The hospitality and kindness of the Pecks will never be forgotten.

Mr. Kok, meanwhile, became very active in Christian work with both foreigners and Chinese. He felt a deep desire to be of service to the many missionaries who visited the city from time to time, for medical or other reasons such as to visit a dentist, be fitted for eyeglasses, or for the birth of a child. Having limited funds, it was expensive for them to stay in hotels, so for several years the Koks took them into their home in the Austrian Legation, where Chancellor Kok had been invited to act as a representative of the Netherlands Legation, the Austrian Legation having been closed down because of the war. Then, when the number of visitors increased, Mr. Kok found a suitable place just outside the Legation Quarter, and there set up the "Home of Rest," which I have described in a previous chapter. Mr. and Mrs. Kok spent many hours there each day and most of their weekends, conducting devotional services for all visitors and helping them, both physically and spiritually. Mr. Kok was a special kind of man, greatly beloved by everyone, Chinese and Westerners alike, and much respected in the diplomatic community as well.

Yet when it came to his daughter marrying me, he was completely and totally inflexible and refused to even discuss the subject when we brought it up. What his real reason was for rejecting me, I shall never know, but it most certainly wasn't because Eva was marrying a missionary, as he had great interest in all missionary work.

In any event, in the fall of 1937, three things happened that made us decide we had waited long enough and that it was time to do something. First of all, Eva's parents went on home leave to the Netherlands, and Eva and I decided that his absence from the country provided us with a unique opportunity. We could now get married without causing him the public embarrassment that would have inevitably followed if he had been in China, yet conspicuously absent from our wedding. So we started making plans.

The second impelling factor was the situation in Europe, where the inevitability of World War II was even then very apparent. We knew it would eventually spill over and involve Japan, thus further complicating our lives. The third, and perhaps the most compelling factor of all was the arrival in Tientsin of Mr. Gibb, director of the China Inland Mission at that time. Both Eva and I recognized it to be another of God's miracles in our lives when I happened to be in Tientsin at the time of Mr. Gibb's very brief and unannounced visit. Immediately upon meeting him, we knew he was the man to whom we could tell our problem, and we asked for a brief interview.

When it came time for the interview, we were both very nervous, but Mr. Gibb immediately put us at ease with his gracious manner. We told him of our long secret engagement, the reasons for our having had to keep it a secret, and of our desire to get married as soon as possible, mainly because of the unstable political situation and fear of further hostilities. However, we explained, it was to take advantage of the fact that Eva's father would be out of the country. Mr. Gibb, of course, knew Mr. Kok very well and showed complete understanding of the situation. He agreed that we should go ahead with our plans. At the same time, however, he suggested that since we had now told him our story, it would be best if Eva formally resigned from the Mission at the earliest possible date. He urged us to make whatever plans we could but said we should not feel under any pressure, and promised he would keep our secret for as long as necessary. What a remarkably understanding man he was.

When I brought up the subject of reimbursing the Mission for all of Eva's travel expenses to China, and told him in some detail of my penurious situation, he told us not to worry about it. He asked me how much

I thought we would be able to pay each month. When I told him that we had figured out that with what I was averaging in income, the most we could afford to pay would be US $5, he told us that would be perfectly satisfactory, and that when the time came he would make all necessary arrangements.

I had been in Tientsin for four days prior to Mr. Gibb's arrival, staying in the same building as Eva, my room being on the same floor as hers. We ate at the same table, sitting right across from each other, and yet we might just as well have been a thousand miles apart. I dared not speak to her nor look at her directly, let alone touch her as I longed to do; prying eyes and wagging tongues were everywhere, and we had to maintain our secret. However, as so often happens in storybooks, love found a way.

Staying at the C.I.M. home at the same time was another evacuee, a young and very delightful Scottish girl, Alison Ballantyne, a close friend of Eva's from her time at the language school in Yangzhou. Sitting beside her the second morning at breakfast, I had a brilliant idea. Why not confide our secret to Alison and get her to help us?

I wrote a note to Eva suggesting the idea and managed to secretly slip it under the door of her room. Shortly afterwards, when Alison and she were together in the large living room, I walked over and joined them. The three of us together could not possibly arouse any suspicions, although many heads were turned our way. Eva, quite logically, suggested we three go out and take a walk together. Once outside, we told a very surprised and delighted Alison our secret. She could scarcely believe that we had been engaged for over a year without her having had the slightest suspicion of it.

From that moment on Alison proved a great ally. When in the company of others, she and I flirted outrageously and gave everyone the impression that we definitely had a "thing" going, and it allowed Eva to join us without attracting any undue attention. We would set out for walks together, and then Alison would discreetly go her own way, while Eva and I would wander off to some secluded restaurant or park. One such place we went to several times was a park in the former Russian Concession across the river and we had to get there by sampan ferry in the same way many years earlier I had gone across for my violin lessons. It had been well over a year since

our engagement, and up to that point I had probably not spent more than a total of two or three hours in Eva's company. Now I could have her to myself for hours at a time. It was wonderful and I was grateful for it, but at the same time we were always forced to be on the alert, constantly looking over our shoulders in case we were observed, and it was definitely not the usual tranquil sort of experience that storybook lovers are supposed to have.

Late one very hot afternoon I bought a sandwich lunch at Tientsin's famous German bakery, Kiesslings and Bader, together with some containers of ice cream, and we biked out toward the country club, a distance of several miles. We reached the club grounds just after dark and discovered we were unable to enter the grounds unless we could show a membership card. Naturally I didn't want to approach any of the people I recognized going in to ask if we could accompany them.

Instead, we found a grassy spot near the river just outside the club grounds and within range of the lights from their outdoor pool. Sad to say, the spot we picked was largely swampy, and the mosquitoes swarmed out in droves. In the near distance, through the fence, we could see the club members sitting around the pool, with their legs inside cloth bags to protect themselves from the insects, while servants circled around spraying the air with hand-held pumps. I hadn't given a thought to mosquitoes, and I couldn't care less. We were together, alone, very much in love, and the future, at least for us, looked brighter. Our sandwiches tasted delicious, but our ice cream was completely melted, but even that didn't bother us.

As well as we thought we had kept our secret, one young recently married couple wasn't fooled. Their name was Henderson, and apparently they had either seen us together at some point or had read something in our eyes as we looked at each other. Mr. Henderson was the local representative of the Scottish Bible Society and had a small apartment a short distance from the C.I.M. home. At any rate, one day when Mrs. Henderson was visiting the C.I.M. home, she came over to me and smilingly whispered: "If you want a quiet place to take your girl, you can use our apartment any afternoon that you wish." With that, she quietly slipped a key into my hand. I asked her: "Do you mean Alison?" She smiled, shook her head and whispered: "No, of course not. Take Evangeline."

Without saying anything further, we took her up on her offer, and for the rest of my two-week stay, we spent many afternoons in their lovely apartment and it was heavenly not having to worry about someone seeing us together. We still owe the Hendersons a deep debt of gratitude.

After talking to Mr. Gibb we felt as though a huge load had been lifted from our shoulders, but much remained to be done before we could set our wedding date. Most important, if Eva were to resign from the Mission, as Mr. Gibb had suggested, some place must be found for her to stay. On my way back to Lingyuan on the train, I gave it much thought, and then, just as the train was approaching Chaoyang, the next biggest town east of Lingyuan, it was as though I heard a voice telling me to leave the train. Hurriedly, I got off and dropped in unexpectedly to visit our neighbors and colleagues, Herbert and Heather Brewster. I spent the night with them and in a long private session, told them the whole story. Both were delighted to hear the news, and immediately, just as though they had been planning it all along, they suggested the perfect solution. They invited Eva to stay with them until our wedding day, no matter how long it took, and as far as the world was concerned, she would be just another of the young women missionaries under their wing.

That fall, when it came time for Eva to leave Beidaihe, she quietly announced her resignation from the China Inland Mission and told all concerned that she was joining the Brethren in Jehol Province. So much was going on at the time that it created no great stir. There were two other young ladies in Chaoyang at the time, Frances Wilks and Dorothy Flanagan, and whether or not they were let in on our secret, neither Eva nor I now remember. In any case, the secret went no further and I was overjoyed to have Eva in the same province with me and only some 90 miles away.

Our daily letters to each other continued all that winter — uncensored by the Japanese because they now crossed no border — but near as she was, I was unable to visit her without arousing comment, so I busied myself in my work and tried to plan a house for the two of us. But in that I was stymied by the Japanese. Because of their war needs, they had placed restrictions on all new construction and would only permit limited repairs to existing buildings.

In the meantime Eva was active in the medical and women's work in Chaoyang, and the time passed relatively quickly, but by early spring, despite several letters from Eva to her parents in Holland asking their approval of our marriage, she received no reply. Her mother's health was poor, but they were expected back in Peking toward the end of the year, so if we were to get married, it would have to be soon. We finally decided we could wait no longer than August, and since many things had to be done in preparation, we decided to announce our engagement in June. That we did, to the delight and astonishment of all our friends. One last letter was written to Eva's parents inviting them to the wedding, but that, too, was ignored, and unfortunately, neither of them came to the wedding.

That summer in Beidaihe was heaven on earth for us. Even though we were now openly engaged, the conventions of the time still demanded a great deal of discretion on our part. Although we could go for walks and bicycle rides together and meet on the beach for swimming, there were always dozens of people around who knew us, and we had to be most circumspect and not show our emotions openly. As chance would have it, Eva was the guest of our very good friends, Kenny and Eleanor Wilson, who lived in the house directly in front of ours. After dark, we regularly took long walks together on the beach, and during the rainy season, when few people were abroad, we relished the privacy the rain gave us as, soaked to the skin, we spent hours walking the beaches, occasionally taking shelter in one of the mat sheds during the heaviest downpours.

Our wedding plans went very smoothly as everyone pitched in to help. I had to get a suit and Eva a dress. The keynote was simplicity. On August 17, 1938, we had a memorable civil wedding in the new Community Center that had been built in East Cliff, a building that was open on all four sides to the sea breezes and that could accommodate several hundred people. Ours was the first wedding to be held there. All our friends helped to decorate the place with countless garden and wildflowers. Our very good friend the Rev. Joseph Toop officiated, and everyone we knew or who knew us was there, including many Chinese. Alison Ballantyne was Eva's bridesmaid, while another former fellow-student at Yangzhou, Mary Portway, also gave Eva a lot of help. My friend and colleague from Chengde, Leonard R. Steel was my best man, and other friends provided special music and acted as ushers. We still have a faded two-column newspaper account which was published in the *Peking and Tientsin Times* the next day, describing the wedding in great detail and declaring it a "great success." However, for us, the whole affair is pretty much of a blur in our memories. After the ceremony a lavish reception was most generously provided on their front lawn by Mr. and Mrs. James Leynse, friends of Eva's family, and Mrs. Leynse and Heather Brewster acted as hostesses. Afterwards, Eva and I left to change clothes and head for the railroad station to catch the night train to Tientsin for a second, "official" civil ceremony at the British Consulate the next morning, since church weddings were not legally binding in China. En route to the station we had to pass through the Chinese village near Rocky Point and we were surprised and delighted when the shopkeepers, many of whom knew us, came out to wave to us and show us a front-page advance story with pictures that my friend Mr. Jones had put in the newspaper that morning.

Because we were not considered to have been properly married in the religious ceremony, and wouldn't be until we appeared before the British Consul, we had to be chaperoned on the train that night, and naturally it was dear Alison Ballantyne who most graciously volunteered for the job.

We sat up for the entire night in a third-class carriage, the only Westerners there, and excited a lot of comment from our Chinese fellow passengers who evidently guessed from Eva's and my hand-holding that we had just been married. But we were happily oblivious to it all. As far as we were concerned, we had achieved our goal and nothing could separate us now — or so we thought.

We arrived in Tientsin around daybreak and had to wait for several hours at a restaurant until the British Consulate opened. Shortly after 9 a.m. we appeared before a somewhat bored consular officer at the British Consulate and in a matter of minutes the formalities were completed; we were now properly married. We thanked Alison, and she went her way with a "God bless you both," while we headed for a small Chinese hotel, where they gave us a three-room suite for the price of a single room. That was our honeymoon, and although it was the hottest time of the year, and air-conditioning was unknown — at least in

Tientsin — it made no difference to us. We spent a delightful week there, pampered by the Chinese staff, the kitchen chef doing his best to spoil us with the tastiest Chinese dishes imaginable, and all included in the price of the room. I guess it is true even in China that "everyone loves a lover."

Finally the time came to leave, and we caught a train to Lingyuan, the rest of the family having gone on ahead. It was an 18-hour trip, with a change of trains at Jinzhou. We could only afford to travel third class, and as usual the cars were packed with people, but there was much to entertain us and the time passed quickly. We had a double seat to ourselves at the end of the car and were greatly amused by a fellow passenger in the seat across the aisle. It was obviously his first train ride, but dressed in his best, he tried to appear very blasé and sophisticated and tried to give the impression of being a seasoned traveler. However, things began to fall apart when the refreshment vendor came through the car. The man was intrigued by the variety of things the vendor had in his basket, and most particularly by the cans of fruit, which obviously he had never seen before. He looked at all the pictures on the outside of the cans and finally settled for a can of pineapple.

We watched covertly with considerable amusement as he turned the can this way and that, looking for a way to open it. He shook it, putting the can up to his ear to try and hear what was inside. He then carefully peeled off the label to see if there was some sort of opening device. He decided the seam must somehow come apart, but no matter how he tried, he couldn't open it. For a considerable time he sat and mused about it, then, after looking about him, he took out a coin, and with it he carefully removed a screw from the window frame beside him. He placed the point of the screw against the top of the can in an upside-down position, and holding it in position, he banged the screw down on the wooden armrest beside him. Though the hole he had managed to make was quite tiny, he succeeded in sucking the juice out from inside the can, showing distinct pleasure with each mouthful. However, when he again shook the can, there was obviously something else inside, and he had to find a way to get it out.

All that must have taken the best part of an hour, but we finally took pity on him. It was time for our own lunch, and although we had taken sandwiches with us, we also had some canned fruit and a can opener. Since it might offend him if we offered the can opener to him directly, and then cause him to lose face if he didn't know how to operate it, we did the next best thing. We took out a can of fruit, then, after waving it around to indirectly attract his attention, I very ostentatiously opened the can and we consumed the contents. He mulled that over for a short while, then, since we had not revealed the fact that we spoke Chinese, he leaned over to us and made gestures miming what we had done with our can, pointing meanwhile to his own can. We passed over the can opener and he very deftly opened his can as though he had done it a hundred times before.

The same man was to provide us with more entertainment the following morning. We decided to have breakfast in the dining car, and, filled with curiosity, he followed us and sat at a nearby table watching to see what we ordered. We ordered bacon and eggs with toast. When his turn came, he pointed to our table and ordered the same thing. Unfortunately for him, he was so distracted with what was going on around him, he forgot to watch how we ate our eggs and toast. When his order was placed in front of him, he studied it long and hard. The toast was served dry in the English manner, with butter and jam on the side. He figured out the fork must be used to stab the toast, so he started by stabbing a slice of toast and eating it. He then tasted the butter, but he didn't seem to like the flavor particularly. However, since he had paid for it, he put the whole pat in his mouth and swallowed it. The jam came next. He used a spoon for that and ate it with gusto. However, the bacon and eggs really stymied him. Finally, using his knife and fork in one hand like chopsticks, he picked up the slices of bacon and ate them without trouble, but the eggs were something else. Eventually, after he had studied the situation for a good five minutes, he carefully separated the two eggs on the plate, slid the point of the knife blade under one of them, balanced the egg carefully on the knife, and, bending low over the plate, with one noisy slurp, the entire egg disappeared into his mouth. The second egg disappeared with the same dispatch, leaving his plate spotless. We felt like cheering.

Later that same morning the conductor came through punching tickets. Our seat was right next to the door, and as he came into the car, he was laughing

uproariously. I asked him what was so funny. He told me that in the next car, which was first class, there was a wealthy farmer's wife with her elderly serving woman. As he had entered their compartment, they had been playing with the different electrical switches, turning on the lights and a small three-bladed fan. Never having seen an electric fan before, the farmer's wife asked the woman servant what it was. Without a moment's hesitation the servant had answered: "That's three shoehorns that have been turned into celestial beings." (*Sange xie bazi cheng xianle.*)

It was Eva's first visit to Lingyuan, and when we finally arrived there the next evening, it was quite traumatic for her. To begin with, it was a strange city, she had to meet so many new faces, and she was the object of great curiosity from strangers, with everyone anxious to see what the new bride looked like. Our arrival brought about another enthusiastic reception by all the Christians, who put on a big wedding feast for us and held a meeting of thanksgiving.

Gradually, however, we settled into the routine of married life. Eva was warmly received by the Chinese womenfolk and busied herself helping Mother in the dispensary and visiting the Chinese women in their homes when she wasn't accompanying me on my trips into the countryside.

Eva and I lived in my small room for that winter and well into the following summer, eating all our meals with the family. Meanwhile I battled with the Japanese authorities, trying to get permission to build a small home in a corner of the compound. After countless meetings, I was finally able to convince them that an old dilapidated cow shed in the corner needed repairs, and bit by bit we were able to transform the place. It took so long that the Japanese officials who initially gave us permission were not there to see the final results; otherwise, they would undoubtedly have objected. We first took out the front wall, then replaced it, moving it out slightly and installing two bay windows. We then, one by one, rebuilt the end walls and the back wall and finally put on a new roof. Being a small three-*jian* building, we divided the interior into two rooms so that we had a living room and a bedroom, and both rooms were entered from a tiny vestibule just inside the front door, which was in the middle of the building. That kept the place much warmer.

We went to Mukden and bought a large Russian

stove of the type used in Siberia to heat an entire house. Those stoves were a unique Russian invention. Standing about eight feet tall and perhaps four feet in diameter, they were lined with fire brick and used a minimum amount of fuel. In Siberia, we were told, in the coldest part of the winter, people kept the fire banked for several days at a time while they did nothing but sleep, getting up only occasionally to eat and put more fuel into the stove. At any rate, we found it admirably suited for our purposes, and in the following winters our little house was the warmest place around.

We installed it in a corner of the vestibule, where the two side walls met the central dividing wall that we had put in. In that way, a large, rounded section of the stove provided a heating surface in each room as well as the vestibule, from where the stove was fed.

The Japanese frequently came to inspect our work on the house, but they didn't interfere, nor did they question the fact that we were simply "repairing" an old building. However, they showed intense interest because, as we moved along, the place began to look more and more like a Western-style house. The fact that they didn't realize we were actually building a new house rather than merely carrying out repairs was due to the policy of the Japanese government in constantly shuffling their officials around. As each new man came into office, he naturally thought that his predecessor had given us the necessary permission and made no fuss. As we got to know the Japanese better, we found that to be standard practice with them. One of the reasons was that they wanted to transfer seasoned men to new areas in China that they had captured, but it was also because they wanted to keep their men from being bribed and to prevent their succumbing to opium addiction. We took advantage of it whenever we could, with considerable success.

When we had the living quarters finished we added a lean-to shed on one end, cut a doorway through the main end wall into it, and made ourselves an indoor bathroom with a full-sized bathtub made of galvanized sheet metal. With one of the old pipes from the back well pump, I fitted a drain to a dry well out back and tied it in both to the bathtub and a Japanese porcelain washbasin that we had been able to purchase locally, but of course the faucets on it were useless since we had no piped-in water. The drain worked as well as any plumbing anywhere else except in the coldest part of the winter, when the portion just outside the house froze solid whenever we used it. We had a wooden floor and a small stove in the bathroom, but our toilet still had to be the old-fashioned kind. We placed it, however, in a separate enclosure at the north end of the building and it was serviced from the outside through a small door at the back, so, of course, we didn't have to go outdoors. The whole thing gave us a great deal of satisfaction. When eventually we moved in the following spring, we were both delighted. Of the twenty or more houses we have owned and lived in during our lifetimes since then, none has given us more pleasure. Unfortunately, we lived there for a little less than two years.

For our kitchen we modified a two-*jian* building that stood alongside the new house at a right angle and divided it into a pantry and kitchen. We bought a secondhand kitchen stove in Mukden and installed a dishwashing sink. Lily Root, Lao San's brother, the reformed thief and cured opium addict, asked if he could become our special servant, and a more loyal and dedicated man we could not have found.

The final touch to the building was a low wall with a gate in it that enclosed that corner of the yard. But from our windows we looked out onto a bare patch of brown earth, and Eva and I had the inspiration to turn part of that space into a green lawn. It would be the first of its kind in Jehol Province, perhaps in the whole of Manchuria. On one of my trips to Mukden I managed to find a bag of lawn seed, which we carefully planted and watered, and then waited for results. A few days later one of our regular windstorms blew in from the Gobi desert a few hundred miles to the north. We well knew what damage could be done, and I was sure it would pick up all our lawn seed and scatter it far and wide. I rushed to another part of the garden and got some dry earth, which I sprinkled thickly over the lawn seed, thinking I had saved the day. Some days later we were delighted to see the entire surface showing a profuse growth of green shoots, but alas, as they got a little bigger, we discovered that the dry earth I had thrown on the "lawn" had come from our portulaca bed, and instead of a green lawn, we ended up with the finest spread of multi-colored flowers one ever saw. It was just as well, since we didn't have a lawn mower anyway.

Happy as we both were, there was one thing that continued to trouble us greatly and that was our debt to the China Inland Mission. Even though no interest was being charged, our having sent them $5 a month for well over a year hadn't made much of a dent on the principal, which was still over $1,900. We prayed a lot about it and then one day another small miracle happened in our lives.

I read in the newspaper one afternoon that the Bank of Manchukuo would honor any legitimate debts owed by foreigners in the country to individuals or business concerns outside of Manchukuo, and would permit the purchase of drafts in United States currency to cover any such debts with no limit stated as to the amount. All that was needed was adequate proof that such a debt had been incurred. That gave me an idea. I wrote the finance officer of the C.I.M. in Philadelphia and asked them to provide me with a statement of the full amount that Eva had initially incurred, both for her fare across the Pacific and her schooling in Yangzhou. When they returned it to me, I took it to the Japanese bank officials at the Bank of Manchukuo in Mukden and asked them if they could give me a draft in U.S. dollars to cover it. They worked out the exchange rate, which was approximately $3 Manchukuo currency to one U.S. dollar, and they told me that if I gave them a check for approximately $6,000 in Manchukuo yuan, they would issue a draft payable to the China Inland Mission.

Back in Lingyuan I borrowed $6,000 in yuan from a Chinese businessman friend, mailed a check to the Mukden bank, and in a few weeks I had a legitimate draft in U.S. currency for the entire amount which, if I remember correctly, was about $1,980. I then sent the draft to the business manager of the C.I.M. home in Tientsin. He, in turn, deducted the amount we had already paid on the debt, giving the equivalent back to us in Chinese dollars. Because of severe inflation, the exchange rate had jumped to well over $100 Mexican dollars for one U.S. dollar in Tientsin, so with that, I was not only able to repay my $6,000 loan, but had a sizable balance left. Best of all, our debt was finally paid off in full. It was all perfectly legal, but naturally we didn't tell the Japanese what we had done.

We had been married in August 1938, and that November my parents and two sisters left for Canada where, because of Ruth's deteriorating health, they hoped to consult with a specialist on Parkinson's disease. At the time we had no young missionaries living with us, so Eva and I were left alone in Lingyuan to keep things going.

We continued our trips into the countryside all that winter and on one occasion had a most remarkable experience. Eva and I, together with Zhao the colporteur, had taken a day trip to a big country fair about thirty miles to the south of us. The entire day had been fraught with one problem after another. On our way down, the van broke through the ice when we were crossing an unbridged river, causing a considerable delay. Then, one of the extra cans of gasoline we were carrying developed a leak, which we didn't notice until we had lost most of the gasoline; it was the Japanese diluted kind, so there was very little smell in the van to alert us. And, as if that wasn't enough, when we reached our destination, the local police and a very officious Japanese gave us an endless amount of trouble before they would let us preach in the marketplace.

We left in mid-afternoon, on what should have been a relatively easy journey home, but again, trouble dogged us all the way. We got bogged down in one spot for nearly two hours, then had a flat tire shortly after that. As a result, it was after dark when we approached the big pass that we had to negotiate about ten miles south of Lingyuan.

The upward climb to the summit of the pass was about two miles in length, and the road for the most part was a narrow, winding track that over the centuries had been cut deeply into the cliff on one side of a steep ravine that began at the top of the mountain. On the one side was a sheer drop-off and on the other the high cliff, and as we wound our way up in low gear through the twists and turns of the road, I kept noticing, out of the corner of my eye, small groups of people huddled against the cliff to my right at each of the turns. It began to bother me, because the sight of so many people out on the road at night was unheard of. However, the road was so steep we didn't want to stop and ask what was going on. Farther along, about two-thirds of the way to the top, we passed a group of carts drawn over to the side of the road in a gully, and beyond them, as our headlights swept over the group, we could see a number of animals and men.

Just as I was remarking to Zhao about how unusual

it all was, a man suddenly jumped out into the road in front of us, waving his arms wildly, signaling us to stop. I did so, and he came up to my window and said quietly: "They're up there at the top and no one can get through." I asked him what he meant, and he told me that about 50 bandits had been holding the pass since noon, and no one had been allowed to come through from the other side. Seeing the lights of our vehicle, he had thought we were police or military personnel.

We turned off the lights and the engine and climbed out of the van. In the stillness of the night, we could clearly hear shouting and the occasional sound of gunfire in the far distance at the top of the pass. Now that we had stopped, the people who had been in hiding began to swarm around us. There must have been well over 100 travelers there: men, women and children. Many had been hiding behind the rocks on the cliff above us. They all feared that the bandits would come down when they had finished their work at the top, and they begged us to do something.

It was an intensely cold night and a bitter north wind swept down the pass. I feared the engine would freeze up if we stayed there too long, but it seemed folly to proceed. Standing together in the cold, the three of us prayed to God for guidance. We'd been there perhaps 30 minutes when one of the men suddenly nudged me and said, "They've started a big fire up there. They must be burning the village." Sure enough, there was a bright redness in the sky that had not been there before. As we watched, it spread and seemed to grow ever larger.

After another ten minutes or so, I could no longer hear either shouts or gunfire, and since it was impossible to turn around and equally impossible to back down the pass, we decided to head for the top. With lights off I crawled along in low gear, head out of the window studying the track ahead in the starlight. After a few hundred yards I heard the sound of feet pounding down the pass toward us. I switched on the headlights and illuminated a small crowd of people running in our direction, so I stopped to let them go by. All of them were silent and looked very much afraid, and none paused to answer our questions. I surmised they had been let go by the bandits.

As the crush of people lessened, we proceeded on up to the summit with considerable trepidation, again with our lights off, the glow of the fire becoming

brighter as we neared the summit. But as we topped the rise and came into a narrow defile between the hills, we were astonished to see no fire, but the redness in the sky was even more apparent and more widespread, only farther away. It seemed to be just over the rise on the downward side of the pass to the north.

The few houses in the village at the top were intact but there was no sign of the inhabitants. The road was littered with debris: clothing, piles of shoes, hats, and abandoned vehicles, some of them smashed. It was no place to loiter, and we continued on our way, although at times we had to stop and push carts and other debris out of the way. We feared the bandits might be hiding behind the large boulders we could see on the hillsides above us, but we reached the downward side of the pass without incident and saw no sign of bandits.

The pass was perhaps 3,500 feet high, and as we rounded a bend and started downhill, I could clearly see, outlined against the redness in the sky, the tops of a series of hills between us and Lingyuan. Now, in addition to the vast area of redness, we could see occasional flashes of light that seemed to indicate explosions of some sort exactly where the city of Lingyuan lay. If it had been in the summertime, we might have mistaken it for lightning. Thankful that we had escaped the bandits, we then began to dread that the city of Lingyuan was ablaze. Fearful and concerned for our loved ones there, we pushed ahead as fast as possible. In each village we passed through, the entire population was out in the street looking at the sky, obviously as puzzled as we were, and they seemed to be terrified.

Finally, the south gate of Lingyuan came into view, and our puzzlement grew. The extraordinarily red sky was brilliant and pulsating, but no flames or smoke were visible. Once we were inside the city it was bedlam; terrified people rushed around banging on gongs and heading for the temples to burn incense. Then as we raced up West Street from the center of town, and still saw no flames, it suddenly dawned on me that it must be the Northern Lights that I had read about but had never seen before.

It was a great relief to find everyone safe in the compound, but they were all as astonished as we were. I tried to explain the phenomenon to them, but even though the sky darkened after an hour or so, few people slept that night, and for days the city was abuzz with talk of the strange sight that no one had ever seen before. I talked with a number of elders, some in their eighties, and none of them had seen or heard of that in their lifetime. To pursue the matter further, I wrote to a scientific journal in London asking them if there was anything in their records about Northern Lights having been reported in that latitude before. They replied that it was previously unheard of in Northern China. Quite surprisingly, our neighbors in the towns to the east and west of us, as well as in Hada to the north, never saw it. It was entirely localized to the Lingyuan area.

Since then I've seen the aurora borealis on numerous occasions in northern Canada, but never so brilliant nor so spectacular as that night some 50 years ago in North China. Was it simply a coincidence that it should have happened just that night, when we were out on the road and meeting bandits? We didn't think so at all. The bandits must have seen the lights of the van coming up the pass, and, like the people below, would undoubtedly have thought we were police or soldiers. Knowing there would only be a few armed men on what they thought was a truck, they would have been prepared to do battle, well armed as they undoubtedly were. No, it wasn't our van that frightened them away. We'd been out doing God's work and He had scared the bandits off to allow us to get home unmolested, and had shown us one of His heavenly wonders at the same time.

That was one of the last trips that my beloved companion Zhao Guang took with us. With no prior warning, nor any previous indication of illness, he suddenly developed a bad cough that nothing seemed to help. Within a matter of days he was spitting blood. It was obvious he had contracted tuberculosis, that dread disease that struck down so many around us. Zhao accepted it very serenely and on one of the last Sundays that he was able to attend church, he told everyone that he was about to be called into God's presence, and he felt greatly privileged. I sat at his bedside when the end came a few days later, and he held my hand, with a smile on his face to the very last. Still in his early forties, he had served God for no more than ten years or so, but in that relatively short time he had been instrumental in carrying the Gospel to countless numbers of his fellow Chinese, and in the days that followed, as we revisited villages

and fairs, we were repeatedly asked about him by strangers. The seeds that he had sown were bearing fruit. He will long be remembered.

We lost another good friend around that same time, an elderly gentleman, a fairly well-to-do country farmer by the name of Zhang, whom, for some reason that I have since forgotten, we always called "Little Zhang." He was a delightful old chap who had been a Christian for many years, and he attended church regularly at our Dujiawopu outstation. His home was about ten miles from there in a very mountainous area to the north, very difficult to reach by car, but I had been there a few times over the years and found that he was considered an elder and was much respected by his fellow villagers.

One day he came by cart to Lingyuan complaining of a severe abdominal pain. Both Eva and I examined him, and after palpating his abdomen, we felt convinced that he had some kind of growth there. We told him he ought to take the train to Mukden and visit the Presbyterian Hospital, where they could take an X-ray and give a better diagnosis. He made the trip, accompanied by one of his four sons, and a few days later returned with a written report from the hospital confirming the diagnosis and stating that the tumor was so large and so far advanced that it was inoperable, and the prognosis was that he had only a few months to live.

Little Zhang took the news very calmly, and in fact, it seemed he was happy, if anything, to hear the verdict. But he was in so much pain that I decided to take him home in the van. When we reached his village late that evening after a deliberately slow journey to spare him as much jolting as possible, we decided to stay overnight. At once he called in all his neighbors to tell them the news, then very proudly uncovered a large coffin that he had already prepared some months beforehand and asked me to take a photograph of it. He explained to the villagers what death meant to him as a Christian, and told them that his coffin was intended only to hold his dead body, while his soul would go to heaven to be with God.

Chinese coffins, unlike American caskets, are built with what looks like, and often is, a very thick lid, sometimes six or eight inches thick, but on the cheaper ones the thickness is often faked. The sides are somewhat bellied outward. The head end is very large, then it tapers down to a smaller opposite end.

Both ends are often ornately carved with figures and symbols relating to Chinese beliefs regarding the afterlife. But the large end of Zhang's coffin was elaborately carved with an open Bible, surrounded by flowers, and a text from Scripture painted thereon. Around the outside were figures representing angels. Zhang explained to the fascinated crowd what all of it meant and how God's angels would carry his spirit to Heaven.

Eva and I returned home the next morning, but three days later one of Little Zhang's sons arrived in Lingyuan completely exhausted, having run the whole distance. He told us his father was dying and was asking for us, and for us to go there as soon as possible. We loaded up the van and started off just after dark, but we hadn't gone far when I lost my headlights. It wasn't a blown fuse, but evidently the prolonged, severe vibration had caused a short somewhere, and although I had a flashlight with me, I was unable to find the problem. We knew the road well enough, having traveled it perhaps a hundred times or more — at least as far as Dujiawopu — so I decided to continue in the dark without lights. There was no moon and we had to crawl along in low gear almost the entire distance.

With us was a young lad, Gao Yu-sheng, about 18 at the time, who was the second son of Katie, our doorman. He was an extremely intelligent young fellow who years earlier had been sold by his opium-smoking father into an apprenticeship in a bathhouse for a life of degradation and sin. The young lads employed there had a variety of duties. Among them was the drying off of the male customers with towels, and they were often required to masturbate the men. When we learned about his job from Katie, we immediately bought him out of the bathhouse, and since then, Yu-sheng had become a Christian, anxious to travel with us in the car and testify to others about his new-found life. He was also a ready learner when it came to helping me with the car.

The night was so dark that familiar landmarks were no longer visible and we frequently lost all sense of where we were. The road to Reshuitang wasn't too bad, but even so we came near to going into the ditch a number of times. After that came the mountains and the infamous pass we'd crossed so often. Finally, I asked young Gao to sit on the front fender with the flashlight so that I could see the cart ruts. Since the batteries wouldn't hold out for very long, I would spot a rut, then try to keep my left front wheel in it and feel my way along with the flashlight turned off. Now and then Gao's sharp eyes would notice that I was out of the rut, and he would bang on the hood to warn me, then use the flashlight to find the rut again. In that fashion we proceeded for the rest of the night, arriving at Little Zhang's home shortly after dawn.

We found him still alive but sinking fast. Wondering what had caused his sudden collapse, we learned that his four sons had conferred together after I had left them three days previously and had decided that, no matter what the Western doctors had said, it was their filial duty to find a Chinese herbal doctor to look at him. Perhaps Chinese medicine could cure him. By sheer happenstance the next day an itinerant acupuncturist rode into the village, and the four young men had invited him in to look at their father. The "doctor" felt the old man's pulse and stomach and told them there was no big problem, and he could effect an immediate cure. With that, he had taken two long needles and inserted them into the tumor, puncturing it and, of course, draining a large quantity of fluid into the abdominal cavity. Quite naturally Little Zhang felt immediate relief and a complete cessation of pain.

The so-called doctor got his fee and immediately left the village. But a few hours later the old man collapsed into a coma as septicemia set in. The youngest son was immediately dispatched to Lingyuan to get my help while the other three sons set out in different directions to try and find the guilty "doctor," but without success. Of course there was nothing we could do, and we watched helplessly as our dear old friend passed away without regaining consciousness. But, sad as we were, we were happy that he had been spared many possible months of pain. We buried him on his own land, and the entire village came out to watch. I gave a short sermon. Eva and young Gao and I sang a couple of hymns, and that was it.

A short time prior to our marriage, either in late 1937 or early 1938, we experienced the very welcome visit of a good friend from Canada who had learned that he could reach us by railway and had come all the way out from Canada to pay us a surprise visit. We were naturally delighted to see him, and I regret that I cannot recall his name. Although we had electricity in the house, he was appalled to learn that we didn't have a radio and were able to keep up with world news only through our three-day-old newspapers from Tientsin. Those, incidentally, more often than not were censored by the Japanese, either arriving with pages torn out or not arriving at all. Obviously they had contained news of the continuing, costly Japanese war with China, which the Japanese didn't want the people in Manchukuo to know about.

Upon his departure our friend promised us that as soon as he got back to Canada he would send us a shortwave radio, but several months went by with no radio appearing, and we thought he had either forgotten about it or the Japanese had confiscated it. Suddenly, one day, there it was: a huge wooden crate containing a cardboard box, in which we found a large table-model Stromberg-Carlson, Super-Heterodyne Console radio. (It took us a long time to find out that "Super-Heterodyne" had reference to the way in which radio waves were changed to a lower frequency.) I rigged up an electrical outlet, and like magic, we were instantly in touch with the outside world.

We only had electricity at night, but with just a short length of wire strung outside the window as an antenna, we could pick up an endless number of shortwave stations around the world, and Barbara became quite a music addict, staying up until eleven o'clock or later to listen. We were able to get some American stations, but except for one in San Francisco, they didn't come in very clearly. However, the BBC from London was marvelously clear, as was a U.S. station in Manila. Unfortunately, due to time differences and also climatic conditions, the best time to listen to the news was around 3 A.M. Father, however, faithfully got up each morning at that time and listened to the news, then passed it on to the rest of us, but none of it was good. The situation in Europe was fast deteriorating, with Hitler growing in power and threatening war, and Japan's aggression in China was detailed in a manner we would otherwise not have known. We suddenly became aware that things in China weren't going the way the Japanese had expected or were telling us, and we began to realize why, in Manchukuo, the Japanese were tightening their belts and everything was so severely rationed.

But having that shortwave access to the outside

world was too good to last. One day Japanese gendarmes, the dreaded Kempeitai, came in to inspect the radio, and finding it had shortwave reception, they took it away. We thought we had seen the last of it; however, a few days later it was returned to us, modified so that it would only receive Japanese stations, which obviously were of no use to us.

We found that very depressing, but I was curious as to what they had done to eliminate the shortwave, so I opened up the back. To my surprise I discovered they had merely cut one wire. I took a knife and peeled the insulation from the two cut ends, then took a short loop of wire and twisted it loosely to the two bare ends, and "presto," we had our shortwave back again. It would never have done to let the Japanese discover it, though, so I stretched the middle of the wire loop through an air vent in the rear panel, leaving a tiny part of the loop exposed. In that way, if any unwelcome visitor came while we were listening to it, we could twitch out the wire, and the shortwave would be once more cut off. After that, when we listened to the radio we always sat with one finger in the loop so that we could instantly pull the wire out. It wasn't a comfortable way to listen to the radio, but it was better than nothing. Much to our relief, the Japanese, confident that they had done a good job on the radio, never bothered to come back again and inspect it. However, many were the times when we spotted some Japanese soldier or nosy official coming around the spirit screen into the yard, and the wire was hastily pulled out just to be on the safe side.

That winter of 1938 Eva and I were on the road constantly, making trips to every place we could reach, but more and more being harassed by the Japanese, who were highly suspicious of our every action. I got into the habit of telling them in advance where we were going, but even then, when we reached our destination, we were often held for hours by the police and asked an unending series of questions. I finally resolved that problem by taking two or three Chinese colporteurs or preachers with us, and setting up the van in the marketplace before the police had spotted us. While the Chinese carried on with the preaching, Eva and I would walk to the police station to satisfy the suspicions of the police. But it was always nerve-wracking, and there was no way out of it. It was always good to get back to

Lingyuan and our warm little home, where we at least had a modicum of privacy, at least after darkness fell. We spent Christmas alone that year, and when the New Year dawned, our greatest hope was that things would get better, but that was not to be the case.

Bob's Chinese name: Futian
Combined with his surname Da, it means:
Having reached a happy field — or he has attained happiness

Eva's Chinese name: Fuyin
Meaning: Happy sound or good news or Gospel or Evangel: thus name given became Evangeline

Eva and her lifelong friend, Damarie Peck Reynolds (holding doll) at the Western Hills.

At Yangzhou with Eva's friend Sadie Custer. They are helping each other do up the buttons on their padded gowns.

Eva's oldest brother Paul with two Christian Tibetans. Paul was 3 years old in 1913.

Mr. Zhang—the Christian Bob tells about at the end of Ch. 23

This is a front-end view of the long rectangular coffin, which Mr. Zhang prepared before his death.

Cover of Coffin

Characters read:

"Long life" — "Waiting for the return of the Lord" — "Happiness"

"Christian Zhang Jeng-Fang, 68 years old has left the world and gone to Heaven."

Open Bible

Home of Rest where Bob and his friends stayed when visiting Peking and where he met Eva for the 2nd time. The 1st being at Beidaihe 3 years earlier.

At the China Inland Mission in Tientsin before we could openly announce our engagement of nearly 2 years.

Where the marriage took place in Beidaihe.

At Beidaihe waiting for the wedding day.

Our Wedding Picture
Aug. 17, 1938

Eva and bridesmaid go to the house to change for trip to Tientsin for the Consular marriage on Aug. 18, 1938.

Step 1 of our home — an old cowshed.

Step 2 — Working on our home.

Step 3 — The Russian stove we bought.

Step 4 — The home is completed.

The Living room and dining area.

Our bedroom.

The low wall that gave us privacy.

好了瘡，忘了疼。

Haole chuang wangle teng.

When the sore is healed
the pain is forgotten.

- Chinese Peasant Saying.

Chapter Twenty-Four
Was Married Life Ever Like This?

Early in 1939 we received word from our good friends in Methuen, Mass., that they were sending us a new vehicle to replace the earlier one. This one was also a Dodge van, but heavier, a three-quarter-ton panel truck which they also customized for us with windows in the sides and extra seats to make up into a bed. A young woman drove it from the factory to San Francisco, where it was loaded aboard a freighter for Japan, but we had to go to Japan to arrange for the shipment from there to Dairen in Southern Manchuria.

Our trip to Japan on a small coastal steamer was a most pleasant little vacation except that we ran into the edge of a typhoon the day before we reached Yokohama. It was a vicious storm, and our little ship was tossed around like a cork. Just before dark, Eva and I were out on a fairly sheltered part of the deck, enjoying the storm, when we saw the astonishing sight of a dozen or more Japanese destroyers, with their distinctive white-banded funnels, passing direct-ly across our bow and less than half a mile ahead of us. The howling wind, high waves, and pouring rain made the scene surrealistic to the point that we found it hard to believe what we saw. The destroyers looked like so many porpoises as they repeatedly appeared and disappeared in the storm-tossed seas. Our ship had to slow down to let them cross our path, and then they were gone into the murk. Little did we know that less than two years later those same ships would be attacking American and British ships in the waters nearby.

We spent two or three days in Yokohama as the new van was unloaded from one ship and put aboard the ship we had come on, and then we sailed back to Dairen aboard the same ship, passing once again through the picturesque Inland Sea of Japan, and docking in Dairen three or four days later.

Even in those days Dairen was a very modern city. The Japanese had been dominant there for many years and had done extensive work in building a large port, and the many docks and the outer harbor anchorage were thronged with freighters from all over the world. The city itself was well laid out with wide boulevards, heavy with automobile traffic. We had two days to wait while the ship unloaded its cargo and the van was passed through Customs, and we used the time to do some sight-seeing and window-shopping in the very modern and attractive Japanese department stores, which, in spite of the war with China, were well stocked with merchandise from various foreign countries.

For lunch on our first day there, we happened upon a small Russian restaurant where we found the Russian waitress spoke no English. We did manage, however, to tell her that we would like borscht, a creamy Russian soup made primarily with beets, followed by zakuska, which is supposed to be just a snack or appetizer. Those were the only two Russian dishes that we knew. We pantomimed that we each wanted a small steak and she seemed to understand.

The girl went cheerfully away and shortly thereafter returned with the largest soup tureen we'd ever seen, filled to the brim with enough soup to serve ten people. The zakuska came next, but instead of the one dish we'd expected, she brought at least ten different plates of delicious Russian delicacies. Along with the zakuska came plenty of fresh, crusty Russian bread. By the time the steaks arrived, we were so stuffed we could hardly face them, and to top it off, each steak must have weighed at least 16 ounces. However, the bill, which we expected to be horrendous, was so modest when it was brought that we thought the girl had made a mistake.

While we were eating, the door to the street opened, and in walked one of the most strikingly handsome women I've ever seen, quite obviously Russian. She was at least six feet tall, big-boned, with long blonde hair done up in a French twist. However, despite the Russian eating habits that our "modest" lunch would seem to indicate was the norm, she was in no way overweight. She seated herself at a table near us and ate a lunch that turned out to be even bigger than ours.

Following lunch we searched out the local agency for Dodge, which was a branch of the Tientsin firm, Frazer Federal, Inc. On the way, eating a piece of caramel candy that had been put on our table with the bill, I pulled a filling out of a tooth. At the Dodge

agency I asked one of the Americans where I could find a good dentist. He gave me a nearby address and we went there at once.

There was no receptionist and no one waiting in the small waiting room. We knocked on an inner door, but no one seemed to be there either, so we simply sat down and waited for the dentist to appear, presuming that he had gone off to have his lunch. After about twenty minutes, who should walk in but our handsome lady of the restaurant. We thought at first she was another patient, but she turned out to be the dentist I was supposed to see.

Eva had had some very unpleasant experiences with dentists in the past, but she felt that it was a good opportunity to have her teeth cleaned, so she went in first. When she came out half an hour later she looked shaken and pale, but she had no time to tell me what had occurred as the woman dentist, unable to speak a word of English, simply grabbed me by the arm and pulled me into her office.

I tried to indicate to her what I needed done, but she paid not the slightest attention. The minute I sat in the chair I knew what Eva had gone through. The young woman put one strong arm around my neck, held my head firmly against her ample bosom with her elbow, and proceeded to dig into my gums with gusto. I've seen potatoes treated more gently than that! And although I bled copiously, I was not allowed to spit.

I don't think she'd ever heard of novocaine, because when it came to the cavity, without a pause, she picked up her foot-operated drill and drilled away with even greater enthusiasm than she had shown in the digging and scraping. I wondered at the time if she had at some time been rejected by some young man and was taking it out on me. However, when the job was finished, it turned out to be one of the best fillings I have ever had. Since then, neither of us have gone to a dentist without remembering that very attractive lady with anything but fond memories. Not only did she speak no English, we began to wonder if she even spoke Russian, because during the entire time we were there she said not a single word to us, even when it came time to pay her. She merely wrote the amount on a scrap of paper, and it was so extraordinarily low compared to what we were used to paying in Tientsin that we could scarcely believe it. So, despite the pain we had both suffered, we felt it was well worth it.

It was exciting the next day to watch our new van unloaded from the ship. The old van had been a dark blue; this one was a rich, dark green, and it was the most beautiful thing we'd ever seen. Our Japanese Customs friend, who had helped us with the first van, was still in office, and after taking the time to show us his gorgeous collection of chrysanthemums, he swiftly gave clearance for the new van, and by the end of the day, with the help of the Americans at the Dodge agency, we had arranged for it to be shipped by rail direct to Lingyuan. The Dodge agency, in fact, was so good and so well equipped with spare parts that I decided in the future to use them rather than make the longer trip to Tientsin, as I had done in the past.

On our way down to Dairen, we had changed trains in Mukden, and from there had ridden on an ordinary express train to Dairen, and we returned by the same route. While in the station at Mukden we briefly saw on the opposite platform a most unusual train operated by the South Manchurian Railway. It was called the Asia Express, and it was the fastest and most luxurious train I have seen either before or since. At the end of that summer, Eva and I had the chance to ride that train when we went to Dairen a second time to pick up some parts for the new van.

The train had three classes of travel. I don't know just how luxurious first class was, but third class, where we rode, was superbly equipped with soft spacious seats and plenty of leg room. Every seat on the train had to be reserved in advance and, before the train entered the station, all passengers were lined up in orderly queues at the exact spot where they were to board, with the train never stopping anywhere for more than a minute or two.

The train was operated with split-second timing and we were informed that it traveled at speeds in excess of 150 miles an hour, but perhaps our informant was referring to kilometers. It was so quiet in the cars one could talk in whispers and still be heard, and the track was so well maintained and smooth that one could balance a coin on edge on the table. In the dining car there was scarcely a ripple to be seen on the drinks they served.

The dining car was open to everyone on the train and we went there for a delicious lunch, served in Western style. The car was staffed entirely by young White Russian women, working both as cooks and waitresses, all of whom had quite obviously been selected for their beauty. The freshly cooked food was equal to that of a five-star restaurant anywhere. The whole train was air-conditioned, and the dining car itself was lavishly decorated with rare woods from around the world. It was perfectly obvious from the train crew and the train itself that the whole thing was a showpiece for the Japanese, and they made certain that it was maintained in such a way that one could not fail to be impressed by it. They operated only one train a day in each direction, and they were always solidly booked.

Our ride to Dairen on that comfortable train was delightful, and, on arrival in Dairen, we immediately booked seats on the same train going back to Mukden the next day at noon. The next morning, however, picking up the spare parts I wanted took longer than we had expected, and when we arrived back at the station, it was one minute to noon. We dashed through the gate to the train, but the first car we approached was the wrong one and the car attendant wouldn't let us board. By the time we made it to the right car, the train was in motion. The Japanese made no provision whatsoever for latecomers.

The railway people honored our tickets for the next train north, which departed a few minutes later. It was a local, made up with third-class seats throughout, and one of the slowest I have ever ridden. We learned later that had we waited a half hour, we could have ridden on an express, but no one had offered us that information. Our train stopped at every single station on the line between Dairen and Mukden, sometimes standing for fifteen or twenty minutes to let a freight train pass and get ahead of us. To our disgust, we even saw the express pass us as well while we sat there in the hot sun and wilted. The hard seats were packed with people, and it was abominably hot with no overhead fans. However, when the train was in motion, with all the windows on each side open, we at least had a breeze blowing through, although, with the steam locomotive, a lot of soot and ash also blew in.

At some stops we were able to buy food from platform vendors, so we didn't mind there not being any diner on the train; also, hot tea was served whenever we wanted it. At many stops, we stayed so long we could get out and walk up and down on the platform for exercise. However, at one point we pulled into a siding where there was no station, and the train just sat there for an interminable period of time with nothing whatsoever happening and the car getting hotter and hotter under the blazing sun. We thought the engine had broken down, so we just sat there and suffered, while most of our traveling companions wisely spent the time sleeping.

On the trains of those days the conductor came through after every stop to check tickets, very much like on American commuter trains. The Chinese passengers adopted the practice of hanging their hats on an overhead hook, with their ticket stubs inserted into the hatband so the conductor could check their tickets without disturbing their sleep.

Just when we had concluded that the train was never again going to move, I heard a faint sound in the distance that grew increasingly louder. In less time than it takes to write it here, the Asia Express on its journey south to Dairen passed us on the adjoining track with a mighty "whoosh" and roar. In those few seconds as it went by, I watched with utter fascination as every single hat hanging on that side of the car was sucked out the windows in perfect sequence, carrying the ticket stubs with them. Everyone, of course, woke up, a few of them just in time to see their hats sail out the window, but as our train started up immediately, there was no chance to go outside to try and find one's hat. The arguments that followed with the harassed conductor as to points of origin and destination occupied the rest of the trip to Mukden, where we once again had to change trains.

Earlier that spring, shortly after the new van had arrived in Lingyuan, Eva and I, with Gao Yu-sheng accompanying us, had taken the old van to a small town up in the mountains west of Chengde, where our colleague Herbert Robinson and his wife had opened a small mission station. He had expressed a desire to have the old van for use in his work in that area. Despite the fact that the vehicle had only a little more than 10,000 miles on the odometer, the rough roads had played havoc with the front end, and the body had lots of squeaks and cracks that let in the dust and cold. However, the engine was still in excellent condition and, since the roads in Robinson's area were generally better than where we were, I felt he could still get several years' use out of it.

We reached the small town of Fengning on the sec-

ond day without any major incident and spent two days there showing Robinson how to maintain the vehicle; most importantly, how to change a broken rear axle. In the early afternoon of the second day we drove back to Chengde to catch a train home, taking Robinson with us so he could take over the van there and drive it back to Fengning on his own.

We started off well enough, but we hadn't gone many miles when we came to a section of the new road that had been surfaced with shale. A very sharp piece of shale was thrown up by one of the wheels and punctured the gasoline tank. That was nothing new. It happened all the time, and I always carried a piece of soft wood in the car so I could whittle a plug to drive into any holes made in the tank. But that particular day there was so much noise from the flying stones that we didn't hear the one that struck the tank. We didn't know about the puncture until our gasoline had run out.

For once I hadn't carried a spare can of gasoline with me, thinking I could fill up in Fengning, but they had no supplies there and there were no other motor vehicles in the town. We sat by the roadside for a time and waited, thinking perhaps some truck or bus might come by, but nothing appeared.

We were 20 miles from the junction with the main north-south road from Chengde to Peking, where there was fairly constant motor traffic. There I knew we could beg some gasoline from a passing vehicle, but we would have to push the car the entire distance. Eva sat behind the wheel and steered, while Robinson, Gao Yu-sheng and I pushed. There were very few villages within sight of the road — the Japanese in designing the road had deliberately bypassed them all — and only rarely did we see farmers in the fields. However, it was a relatively good road, less than a year old, and all the rivers bridged. Also, since Fengning was at a much higher altitude than Chengde and the main north-south highway, much of the road was slightly downhill, although every now and then there was a rise in the road making it very difficult to push the van. Sometimes we found willing farmers working in nearby fields who gave us a hand; other times we had to wait until some passersby came along. After a very long afternoon, and well after dark, we finally reached the junction where, in utter exhaustion, we sat and waited for a truck to come by. It was our good fortune that the very first truck was driven by a Chinese who let me siphon off enough gasoline from his tank to last us to Chengde.

Tire wear on those roads was, of course, phenomenal, and in the six years that I used that first car, I went through five complete sets of tires. All tires in those days used inner tubes, and although the tread on my tires remained in fairly good condition, the walls of the tires were very quickly damaged with deep cuts and abrasions. Some of them we could sew up but others we repaired with a "boot" cut from an old tire, which we placed inside. Blowouts were common, but since we rarely traveled at a speed above fifteen miles an hour, they posed no danger. But I shall never forget one momentous occasion when a rear tire blew out underwater when I was in the midst of crossing a deep river. The tremendous explosion and roar was so loud I thought the gasoline tank had blown up. It reverberated through the hills and brought farmers running from all directions.

Sad as we were to say goodbye to the trusty old van, the new one very quickly captured our hearts. It was an absolute delight to drive, and with much higher clearance, it could take us to places we had long wanted to visit but couldn't in the old vehicle. It had a much more powerful engine and heavy-duty tires, and for the next three years it gave us excellent service and many memorable experiences.

The Japanese, too, were enamored of the new van. Since there were no passenger cars in Lingyuan, they were constantly wanting to borrow it to convey important visitors to and from the railway station or to go to some outlying town to bring in some sick person. More than once I was asked to pick up a Japanese woman from some remote outpost who wanted her baby delivered by the Japanese doctor in Lingyuan.

Unfailingly, the Japanese always wanted to drive the van themselves, but I resolutely refused, offering instead to drive them wherever they wanted to go. But I imposed two conditions: they had to provide me with enough gasoline to make the trip there and back, and, except for their dress swords, I would permit no one in the van to carry weapons of any sort.

Beginning in 1939 all non-governmental motor vehicles were rationed one five-gallon can of gasoline per month. But because the Japanese so frequently wanted the van for some special use, I never lacked for gasoline. In fact, with what the Japanese gave me to cover their use of the car, and what I could buy on the black market, the problem was finding a place to store the gas so the nosey plainclothes police wouldn't see how much I really had.

We solved the gasoline storage problem by building our own secret storehouse in, of all places, the ceiling of the garage. I had converted a two-*jian* building next to the big meeting hall into the garage. My first move was to build a small darkroom in one corner, where, for the benefit of all Japanese visitors, I did my photography; it was one of the very first things I proudly showed them. What they didn't know was that the black-painted ceiling of the darkroom was actually a trap door.

Above the ceiling, I built a platform, using the big cross-beams as a base and running poles across, with loose boards on top. Eva and I were the only ones who knew about it, and we built it together in the dead of night, pretending to go to bed early and then getting up after midnight when everyone was sound asleep. We didn't want any of the Chinese to become involved, in the event they were tortured by the Japanese. Getting all the poles and boards up there was problem enough, but at least that made very little noise. Hoisting the gasoline cans up was something else, and some noise was inevitable, but I could do that in the daytime with the garage doors closed. I placed can after can up there until I had a reserve of some 50 or 60 cans. But one problem persisted. As the weather changed, the cans tended to expand or contract with loud bangs. I was always fearful that that would happen when some Japanese visitor was present, and in fact it did occur more than once when they were there, but fortunately none of them showed any surprise or interest. Gao Yu-sheng, who helped me with repairs on the van, often heard the noises from the ceiling and would look me in the eye with a slight smile, but said nothing. I think he had his suspicions.

The black market gasoline we bought had obviously been "liberated" from the Japanese. It was sold mainly by the Chinese drivers, usually out on the highway away from prying eyes, although occasionally it came in over the back wall at night. One day I bought a can from a civilian whom I'd never met before. The can appeared untouched, but many months later when I went to use it I discovered the can had been emptied of gasoline and filled with water. I discovered it on a trip when I was far from home and had only that one spare can in the van. It had been so cleverly opened and re-sealed that I was unable to tell from looking at the outside of the can that it had been tampered with. Fortunately, I always filtered gasoline through a piece of chamois leather, which caught all the water, as there was a slight amount of water caused by condensation in most of the cans of gasoline we bought.

The weapon restriction I placed on passengers was to ensure my safety from bandits or communist guerrillas, and I made certain that everyone knew the Japanese traveling in my vehicle were unarmed. On several occasions I picked up Chinese people in the villages with gunshot wounds and brought them in to Lingyuan for treatment. Of course, few of them would admit to what they actually were, and most of them pretended to be peasants or farmers who had been shot by the Japanese or by someone unknown. We never asked questions, even though we strongly suspected that they were communist guerrillas or bandits.

The new van seemed to have a personality of its own. Early one Sunday morning in December, I had driven out a short distance into the countryside to pick up a load of villagers to attend the Sunday services. I drove through the river on our return, and the brakes were still wet when I put the van in the garage and set the emergency brake. As it turned out, I should have put a wooden chock behind one of the rear wheels.

The garage floor was about four feet above the ground level outside, and a concrete ramp led into it. Because the new van was longer, I had been forced to add a small extension to the front of the building, and when the van was inside, the rear wheels were actually on the sloping ramp itself. When I parked the vehicle in the garage that day, it was still well below freezing and apparently the brake bands had ice on them, preventing direct contact with the wheel drums. In any case, toward noon, the warm sun on the garage doors raised the inside temperature sufficiently for the frozen brake linings to thaw. Just when the Sunday service next door was in full swing, we heard a loud crash as the van rolled backward, knocking down the garage doors and rolling over them. Seconds later, there was a second crash, louder than the first, which

actually shook the building, bringing everyone to his feet.

The van had rolled clear across the yard and knocked down about 20 feet of the mud wall adjoining the men's outdoor toilet, which happened to be in use at the time. Talk about getting caught with one's pants down! The poor man inside suddenly found himself not only in full view of more than a hundred people, but he was also staring at a huge green intruder not three feet from him, almost in his lap. The Sunday service resumed, but for everyone present it was difficult to keep a straight face for the rest of the morning.

Managing to keep on good terms with the Japanese officials was not always easy and was often frustrating. They changed so frequently that it seemed no sooner had I gotten to know one of them than he would suddenly disappear. I knew that the Japanese had a policy of leaving their officials in office for only three or four months before rotating them, but I didn't learn the real reason for that until one of the Chinese underlings told me.

One of the most lucrative sources of income for the Japanese was the opium crop. They not only permitted its growth, but openly encouraged it. But it was a government monopoly that backfired on them. The Chinese had discovered that their Japanese overlords could not only be readily bribed with gifts of raw opium, but they could also be tempted to try smoking it, and once that happened, they quickly became addicted.

I learned that in a town not far from us the Japanese had established a sanitarium for their addicts. All of the "inmates" were officials, and the cure was brutal: "cold turkey" treatment with no niceties whatsoever until they graduated, and when they did, they were immediately shipped back to Japan or transferred into the army.

Japanese civilians, too, began to adopt the habit of smoking opium, but in their case, when discovered by the Kempeitai, they were immediately locked up and brutally beaten, after which they were shipped back to Japan in disgrace. Most of them adopted the habit out of sheer boredom and the inability to cope with the harsh climate, together with their homesickness.

Although the Japanese government used every inducement to get their people to migrate to Manchukuo to stay, their success rate for colonization was very low. The newcomers didn't mind living in the big cities so much. There they had formed large Japanese communities, with their own culture, houses, entertainment and lifestyle. Apart from an occasional Chinese servant, they had no contact with the Chinese, whom they heartily disliked and actually feared. But in smaller cities like Lingyuan, things were very different. They were surrounded by the Chinese. Streets were unpaved, dust or mud was everywhere, there was little in the way of entertainment, and the terrible harshness of the climate as compared to that of their beloved Japan, all got to them.

In Lingyuan we watched one Japanese business after another fail after having been in operation for only a year or so, primarily because they dealt only in products or services that were aimed directly at Japanese consumers, and those became fewer and fewer. Only those stores that sold articles of interest to the Chinese were successful, and even in that area, the Chinese often imported the same products and undersold the Japanese, who had a much higher standard of living. As the Japanese population grew smaller, particularly the military, the brothels also closed up one by one until there were only three or four left.

Despite the large number of departures, there were still plenty of Japanese around to make things unpleasant for us and everyone else. The fewer there were, the meaner they seemed to get. From the time the Japanese first came, they demanded that the Chinese bow to them whenever they passed in the street. Not to do so resulted in being punched in the stomach or face or being hit over the head with the butt of a rifle. I saw it happen numerous times and I knew of many cases of poor ignorant farmers coming into town who were shot because they didn't bow.

The Japanese made it plain that I, too, was expected to bow to them, but from the very beginning I refused to do so on general principle. Instead, I adopted a policy of always approaching them with a big smile on my face, no matter how they glared at me. I would walk toward them with hand outstretched, talking up a storm in English, and after briefly shaking their hand, I would clap them on the back and walk away, leaving them shaking their heads over the strange antics of an Englishman. When I was called in to see Japanese officials, I adopted the same policy.

I inevitably walked in with a cheerful shout, walked around behind the desk or counter to shake their hands, and if not offered a chair I would perch on their desks, which always infuriated them. But they merely mumbled about it to themselves and wrote me off as a nut. Playing the buffoon was a dangerous game, but it paid dividends, and I got away with it.

From time to time newly arrived Japanese officials would adopt the tactic of threatening me indirectly by demonstrating on Chinese prisoners what might happen to me if I didn't toe the line. Usually it was the Japanese chief of police who would send for me. When I entered his office I would find a Chinese prisoner being tortured by the "water torture" as it was known, or being beaten on the soles of his feet with the flat of a sword. All of it was done for my benefit. The first time or two I made the mistake of interceding on the man's behalf, only to have the Japanese official treat the individual even more inhumanely while I was forced to watch until he got around to whatever business he pretended to have called me in for. When I remonstrated with them, or took the part of the victim, it made the Japanese lose face, so when I realized that, I simply pretended that nothing was going on. Hard as it was, I tried to ignore the agonized groans of the victims being tortured behind me. When the Japanese saw that it made no apparent impression on me, they dropped the tactic.

Most people have heard of the "water torture" but probably don't really know what it is. The way the Japanese conducted it was to tie the victim on his back on a narrow bench, with his head hanging over the end and tied in such a position that his nostrils were upward. Then they would suspend a large can of water directly over the victim's head after having punched a small hole in the bottom of the can, into which they inserted a small, pointed stick. By twisting the stick either in or out, the flow of water could be regulated to a drip every eight or ten seconds, or more frequently if desired; or one drip every minute or so, which was the ultimate refinement by making the victim wait for what seemed an interminable period of time for the next drop to fall. The drips were not only timed, they were directed into the victim's nostrils as well, and, with his head hanging backward, he suffered the sensation of drowning. Although few victims actually died from the torture, many went insane as the insistent drip left no hope of relief, and no victim knew how long it would last. The Japanese were masters in that and other forms of torture. One of the most commonly used was to place live cartridges between a victim's fingers and then squeeze the fingers together. It sounds simple, but it was extraordinarily painful, and many were the fingers that were broken that way.

For a period of several weeks in 1939 a situation arose on the trains that forced the Japanese into the rare position of having to apologize to the Chinese. The smuggling of opium had become so lucrative that the trains were widely used for the purpose, and women were employed as couriers. They transported the opium in bags hung inside their voluminous trousers, dangling between their legs. The Japanese learned of it through paid informers and started to search all women indiscriminately, as I saw happen again and again. The men who were accompanying the women might protest, but they would be beaten to the floor and brutally kicked, while the Japanese and Chinese train guards forced the women to publicly disrobe, or thrust their hands down the front of the women's trousers. That behavior on the part of the Japanese caused such an uproar that within a few days not a single woman could be found aboard a train in Jehol Province. The Japanese became so perturbed by that that they quickly posted notices to the effect that women would not again be molested, but it was some time before the women would again use the trains.

Over the years there were numerous amusing incidents associated with the Japanese bureaucracy and their proclivity for concocting new laws and regulations. Around 1936 the Japanese decided that there were so many motor vehicles in the province that they would have to be registered. Everyone was given a crudely hand-lettered tin license plate to attach to his vehicle, and the Japanese collected a tidy sum of money in the process. Not long after that they decided that every driver needed to have a driver's license, because there had been a number of accidents. Every single driver in the province was called to Chengde to undergo the driver's test on a given day. We were told in advance that the test would take three days but were not told what to expect.

I drove over to Chengde alone, but on the road I had the company of several trucks driven by Chinese, and at stops for meals, we got to talking about the impending tests. One of the drivers I knew very well, and some of the others I had met once or twice before. They were all extremely nervous about taking the test and asked me what to expect, but apart from what I knew of similar tests in Canada and the United States, I could tell them nothing.

As we entered the outskirts of Chengde, an hour or so before dark, I noticed a large gathering of motor vehicles in a wide-open space near a big temple. Instinctively, I felt it had to be where the testing was to be carried out, so I turned in there and the Chinese truck drivers followed me. Getting out of the van, I walked over to a group of Japanese officials standing there and asked them if that was where the driver tests were to take place. They assured me it was, and that the testing would start the next morning at 9 o'clock. They had a small tent erected for the officials, and I was puzzled to see an intricate sort of maze laid out on the ground with heavy straw rope. I asked one of the officials what it was, and he told me that it would be the first day's test. Each driver would have to drive a test car through the maze and would be disqualified if, at any point, he touched one of the straw ropes. I asked if I could walk through the maze to see just what it was, and they told me I could.

It was laid out as a pathway, with ropes on each side, and was roughly in the form of an inverted figure "5," with the straw ropes pegged down approximately eight feet apart. One entered through the short "bar" of the inverted "5" and then turned left, but just past that point, they had added a side "alley" into which one would have to back, then come out, heading back toward the entrance, stop, and then back out the rest of the way through the maze, including taking the entire curve going backward. I didn't feel it was particularly difficult and I asked how much time one had to maneuver the maze and pass the test, and was told six minutes. I was just about to leave when I overheard the Japanese laughing among themselves and mentioning me; then one of them came over to me and asked if I would like to try and drive my van through the maze. I jumped at the opportunity, of course, realizing they thought they were going to have some fun at my expense because the wheel base on my van was longer than that of the test vehicle, a beat-up old Chevrolet touring car with the top up to make visibility more difficult.

I got into my van and started into the maze while

the Japanese clocked me on a stopwatch, and in just under two minutes I had cleared the maze without touching any of the ropes. The Japanese were red-faced and furious and told me I would have to do it again; something had to be wrong. I went through it a second time, making even better time. What the Japanese had not realized, of course, was that my car had an American left-hand drive, which enabled me to simply stick my head out the window and watch my left rear wheel as I backed around the curve. When they did perhaps realize it, they insisted that I drive their test car through, with the steering wheel on the right. I had no problem with that, either. When it came to the curve, with my long legs I was able to simply slide over in the seat so I could watch out of that side, and I finished the course in just half a minute over my time in my own vehicle.

The frustration of the Japanese officials was hilarious to watch. They started blaming each other, and in turn, each of them again tried to rush their way through the maze in the test car, but not one of them could make it under four minutes, and several of them touched the ropes as they drove through. Finally, they announced that the new timing for the next day would be four minutes instead of the six that had been previously announced.

That decision met with a roar of disapproval from the fifty or more drivers who were standing around watching, and I was quite naturally blamed for what had occurred. That evening, two of the Chinese truck drivers came over to the mission house where I was staying and asked me for advice on how to negotiate the maze, so I took them out into a nearby square and roughly drew the same figure on the ground. Then, over and over again, I walked them through it backward and forward, telling them to make believe they were in the test car. Counting each move, and then drawing the whole thing on a small sketch, I told them to go by that and they wouldn't have any problem. The next day when we all undertook the test, my timing was under two minutes in their test car, and my two Chinese friends came in second and third, in just under four minutes. But apart from them, not a single individual out of the many there was able to complete the course in under four minutes, including all the Japanese drivers.

I spent the whole day there watching them, and the Japanese officials conducting the test, as well as the numerous drivers, all gave me some black looks. But the fact that the two Chinese drivers had made the grade in less than the designated time proved that it could be done, so no one could complain, least of all the Japanese officials, since none of them had managed to do it in the first place.

It was announced at the end of the day that the next day's test would be city driving, and in the narrow, crowded streets of Chengde, that would be an excellent test of any driver's abilities. However, I was sure that the officials carrying out the test would probably try to disqualify me if I wasn't extremely careful, so I decided that when my turn came, I would do the unexpected as much as possible, in order to throw them off balance.

I was, of course, quite familiar with the streets of Chengde, and had driven them numerous times. But the Japanese who rode with me in the test car added a few wrinkles by having me go into some of the narrower alleys and through some extremely narrow gates. In fact, he tried every way possible to fail me, but I kept one step ahead of him. To begin with, before I ever got into the vehicle, I carried out an itemized check of all the running gear. I checked every wheel, tested the tires, looked under the hood, checked the gasoline gauge, made sure all the springs were good and tried the steering wheel, making certain all the while that the inspector noted down everything I did. Once in the car, I started the engine, then before starting out, I ostentatiously looked all around me, stuck out my hand, blew the horn and got out into the traffic. At every intersection I stopped and looked both ways, blew the horn, and gave all the necessary signals. There was no possible way the man could fail me and he knew it, but he kept me going for almost half an hour while everyone else was through in ten minutes.

The third day was supposed to be a written test, but I was fed up with the whole thing and decided to try a bluff. I asked one of the inspectors what the test consisted of, and he told me it was composed of fifty questions that had to be answered. I asked what language the questions were written in and he told me they had Japanese, Chinese and Korean versions. I asked why there was no English version; he appeared nonplussed and couldn't give me an answer. I told him that I was very busy and couldn't afford to spend another day taking the test, but that I could read

Chinese and would take the Chinese version of the test. But I insisted that I wanted an English-language typewriter to type out my answers in my own language, which I could do much faster than it could be written in Chinese. I said I would do the test that evening if they would give me a typewriter. There happened to be one other Englishman, David M'Colm, taking the test, who was a fellow missionary from Luanping, a small town south of Chengde. It was for his sake as much as my own that I made the demand, knowing full well that they wouldn't have an English-language typewriter there, and that consequently both he and I could take the test home and do it at our leisure. After a big confab among themselves the Japanese officials agreed. I was given a copy of the test in a sealed envelope, but was told that when I actually typed the test, a policeman would have to be present to see that I did it fairly and didn't have any help. I agreed to the terms.

When I got home I contacted the police, arranged for a man to be present the next day, then sat down at my typewriter and typed 10 or 15 pages in answer to the questions, deliberately making my answers as long and as abstruse as possible, selecting the most erudite and pedantic terminology that I could manufacture. I knew they would never be able to read it, and that they would have difficulty justifying failing me unless they could come up with specifics.

I also had the satisfaction of keeping the Japanese police officer waiting there for nearly three hours while I took the test. At the moment I can only remember one specific question, which concerned coming down a mountain pass and having the brakes fail. What would I do? If I remember rightly I managed two full pages on that one question and came up with some unique improbabilities of what could be done under those circumstances. For the fun of it I kept a copy, but, like everything else we had, it was ultimately left behind.

Two or three weeks after the test the results were announced in the Chinese and Japanese newspapers, and I was amused at the results, which were all given in percentages. I don't remember now the exact figures, but I do remember that the Chinese did better than the Koreans, and I was surprised at the large number of Japanese failures. The percentage figures were something like 16 percent of the Koreans made the grade, 22 percent of the Chinese, and 34 percent

of the Japanese. However, when it came to the British who had taken the test, we came out looking terrific. Fifty percent of us had passed the test. My colleague from Luanping had failed, but I had passed. Sad to say, one of the two Chinese truck drivers I had helped, when returning home from the test, was either drunk or high on drugs, because he tried to race a freight train to one of the level crossings, and lost the race and his life as well.

In the spring and summer of 1939, my parents and sisters being in Canada, Eva and I stayed pretty much in the city except for our regular bi-weekly trips to Dujiawopu, but the rains were so heavy after July that for a time we were unable to even go that far. There was a great deal of sickness in the community, and in Mother's absence, Eva had taken over the women's dispensary and I the one downtown. We encountered some very unusual cases that taxed our limited knowledge of medicine. Eva had one case, that of a young woman with an infected hand which, had it been anywhere else, I am sure would have resulted in the immediate amputation of the entire arm.

When the young woman first came riding in on a donkey, we thought she was carrying a baby in her arms. Her right hand, wrapped in some filthy cloths, was, without the slightest exaggeration, swollen to the size of a very large ham, and was totally unrecognizable as a human hand. No fingers, as such, were recognizable. The arm itself, all the way to her shoulder, was swollen to about the thickness of a man's thigh. Her youthful husband led the donkey into the compound, and we were astonished that the woman, in that condition and suffering such obvious pain, could still manage to remain upright on the donkey, as she had been sitting astride the animal for a full 12 hours.

Our first reaction was that nothing at all could humanly be done for her outside of amputation, and we told her so, recommending to her husband that he take her by train to Mukden at once to the Presbyterian Hospital. He replied that she had already been there, and they had told her the arm would have to come off. Then the woman herself spoke up and told us that without her right arm she might just as well be dead, because she would be of no use whatsoever to her husband.

This young couple were quite remarkable for another reason. Like most Chinese marriages, theirs had been arranged by their respective families. Nevertheless, many husbands and wives became quite fond of one another, but this couple were quite obviously deeply in love. That was extremely rare in Chinese marriages, and that was only the second or third such case that we could remember. The young man was relatively well off, by Chinese standards, and had already spent a small fortune on her, what with travel to Mukden and the many Chinese doctors they had consulted. Why she wasn't already dead mystified us as we looked at her.

The young man got down on his knees and begged us to do what we could for her, and against our better judgment, we decided to try. We gave them an empty room where the husband could look after her, and there they remained for several weeks as Eva worked on her hand day after day.

At first it looked totally hopeless. The few medical journals we had gave us no clue at all as to how to approach the problem. More by instinct than anything else we decided that plain old Epsom Salts and a lot of prayer would be the best cure. We got Lao San to make up a shallow tub the length of her arm, and for hours each day her devoted husband attended her, keeping the water in the tub at a comfortably warm temperature and adding salts as needed. Within a very few days her condition improved, and in time the swelling subsided, but several times each day, Eva had to strip off dead skin and flesh and drain the immense amount of pus that was contained inside the arm. Astonishingly, during all that, the woman ran no temperature whatsoever, and by keeping the hand and arm sterile, any further infection was avoided. After four or five weeks of patient and heroic work on Eva's part and the unflagging help of the woman's husband, we saw amazing results. The swelling completely subsided, and not only was the arm back to its normal size, but also there were no signs of the skin having been stretched. The hand, which should have suffered considerable damage, was quite whole once again, and the woman was able to use it without pain.

During the course of treatment the young man showed his appreciation in the only way he could think of, and at first we suspected nothing untoward. He attended all the services he could, and apparently he had decided in his own mind that by becoming a Christian he would please us the most, and he did so with a verve and gusto that was quite breathtaking.

He bought a Bible, memorized long portions of it, and after only a few days of attending the services, he was taking part, praying aloud in the prayer meetings. We had no wish to dampen his ardor, but we began to have a very uncomfortable feeling that it was all an act put on for our benefit. But at the same time, if it was an act, it was very impressive. Since we might be wrong in our judgment, we said nothing to him and didn't try to discourage him.

When the hand and arm were once again quite normal, the young couple thanked us profusely and returned to their home. We had intended following up on them and visiting in their village, but world events caught up with us and we never saw them again. Whether he was really just a so-called "rice bowl" Christian (one that became a Christian for what he could get out of it), we shall never know.

Another activity we were involved in that year was some remodeling of some of the older buildings. Before he left, Father had talked with us about a surprise he would like to have for Mother when they came back. He and Barbara had drawn up a plan to put an indoor bathroom in one end of the room adjoining his and Mother's bedroom. He also wanted to have the small front porch glassed in to give more space in the dining room and also to add warmth in winter. Additionally, the old schoolroom and kitchen building were badly in need of repair but instead of doing that, Father suggested we build an entirely new building out in the back garden just behind the dining room and then tear down the old schoolroom and kitchen building. That would enlarge the front yard and give an unobstructed view of Guang Mountain to the east and a lot more morning sun in the wintertime.

Our carpenter friend Sun was the man chiefly involved, and he made up some double windows for the front porch, which vastly improved the place. We left the glazing of the many panes of glass for a rainy-day project and got along with the new kitchen while the weather was good. The new building we put up was immediately behind the dining room, at a right angle to it and facing the cow yard, with a triangular flower garden in between. We built a continuation of the back wall of the cow yard to separate the new building from the back garden, and put in a gate near the kitchen that could be barred at night. Out of courtesy, we had to place the building slightly forward of the property line we shared with the Zhang family next door so that the water running off the back roof wouldn't run into their courtyard. That meant that when the place was finished there was a very narrow, eighteen-inch-wide alley behind the building, blocked up at one end, and with the other end open so the water could run out. As the opening was close to the corner of the newly built dividing wall, it was practically invisible. (I mention this alley because it comes into my story again several years later).

We completed that project before the rains came, and Gao Cai started using it. Meanwhile, tearing down the old kitchen building only took a few days. However, heavy rains came early that year, before we were able to start fixing the bathroom for Mother, but since it was an indoor job, we thought it wouldn't matter.

In China one didn't build an inside wall with 2 x 4s and drywall sheets as is so easily done in the United States. There, the only materials we had to work with were mud bricks, with mud for mortar. The bricks, made in our own yard, were over a foot long, six inches wide, and almost three inches thick. When used in a wall they naturally took up a lot of space. However, the dividing wall at the north end of the room went up quickly, and the two masons did a good job. By late afternoon they were putting a coat of mud and straw on both sides, and the wall, with a door to one side, was complete. Since it would take a couple of days for the wall to dry, I was ready to pay them off, and have them come back a few days later at which time they would apply a coat of plaster inside and out to finish the job.

But one thing we hadn't taken into consideration was the high humidity indoors, together with the heavy rains outdoors. Just before dark, when I went to pay off the two masons, I discovered the entire new wall was bulging out badly at the top and in imminent danger of collapse because the wet mud used, both between the bricks and as a first coat before putting on plaster, had softened the bricks and they had begun to disintegrate. That amounted to an emergency and required instantaneous action. We hurriedly got boards and poles, and it required six or seven people to push the wall back to the perpendicular and then prop it up with the poles. We then carried in a stove to dry the place out, which meant someone staying up most of the night to keep the fire going. Despite the discomfort, the temperature being over

ninety degrees with high humidity, we had the satisfaction of saving the wall from collapse. It reminded us of a classic Chinese story of an amateur mason who, after building a wall, tells his apprentice helper to stand there and support it while he goes off to collect their pay; we had to laugh as we found ourselves in an identical situation.

When the wall was plastered and painted, we had Sun build some cabinets in the bathroom and we installed a stove for the winter months. For all the 25 years they had lived in our Lingyuan house, like everyone else my parents had been forced to use the outdoor toilet across the yard, and it was particularly hard on them during inclement weather. As a special surprise for them when they returned, we put in a toilet behind the bathroom, setting it out in the alley behind the building, with a door cut through the wall into the new bathroom. For ventilation and light it had a tiny window, high on the east wall, and it was serviced through a small door behind the commode so that the yard boy did not have to go inside. There was no way to heat the place, but by leaving the connecting door to the new bathroom open, the temperature in there would be moderated somewhat.

With the radio we were able to listen in each night to the news from the BBC in London and to another station that came in very clearly from Manila. The events surrounding Chamberlain's trip to see Hitler after his invasion of Poland, September 1, 1939, gave us momentary hope, but just two days later Britain and France declared war on Germany as Hitler showed his contempt for all other nations. Under those circumstances, one might have wondered why we would be making renovations to old buildings and making plans for the future. It was simply because, despite the bleakness of the outlook, we somehow remained optimistic, and never for a moment did it occur to us that our work in Lingyuan might somehow come to an end. We were there for life, and since we had grown up amongst wars, another one in the offing didn't, at that remote distance, seem so terribly formidable. Even though the Japanese were supporting the Axis, it was our hope that because they were so occupied with their own war with China, and so bogged down there, they couldn't possibly take on anything else.

The rains continued on and off into early September, but when they let up one weekend, and the old men who were our weather forecasters told us we would have several days of sunshine, we made a long-delayed trip to Dujiawopu. The sorghum was high on both sides of the road, but apart from a lot of mud holes we had to negotiate, and which the new van took in stride, it performed admirably and we had a very enjoyable four days up there.

When we returned, the chief of police dropped in for a chat. As he walked in, he grinned at me and said: "Do you know that the other day you interrupted a battle we were having with some bandits just south of Reshuitang?" Apparently, as we drove through one of the narrow valleys leading to Reshuitang, the police were on one hillside facing a large gang of bandits across the road on the opposite hillside. As the battle was in progress, with both sides shooting at each other, we came along. But in the noise of the battle, neither side heard us, and it wasn't until the police chief looked down and saw our green van threading its way through the tall grain below that he called for a cease-fire. When the police stopped shooting, the bandits did also, and then both sides went at it again after we had passed. The grain was so tall that we had been unable to notice anything up on the hillsides, and the noise of the engine had evidently kept us from hearing the gunfire that had gone on over our heads.

On a winter trip. Bob and Eva on a "kang" at the inn. Eva leans against their bedding roll.

Bob's second van in the background. In the foreground — moving a grinding stone.

Bob's garage.

Wedding of a young Christian when the van was the bridal carriage.

Stuck in mud. Others preparing the bank so Bob can back out.

Bob and helpers leveling the steep slope.

Bob trying to raise the van off a steep ledge.

Taking detour due to broken bridge.

Fording a deep river.

Having just negotiated a dry river bed.

Coins of Ancient China
(Circa 11th Century-221 B.C.)

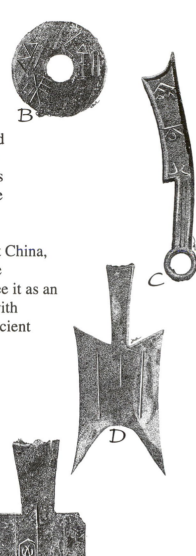

There were 17 Chinese dynasties, which began with the Xia (ca. the 21st-16th century B.C.) and ended with the Qing (1644-1911). The coins on this page were made and in circulation during what are called the Spring and Autumn Period (770-476 B.C.) and the Warring States Period (475-221 B.C.) of the Eastern Zhou Dynasty. All of these coins are made of cast bronze. All are approximately actual size. They came in various shapes:

A. Cowrie-shaped. Actual cowrie shells were highly valued in ancient China, used not only as ornaments, but also for barter. In fact, the Chinese character 貝 is a pictograph of a cowrie, and whenever you see it as an element in a character you can bet the word has something to do with money or finance. Its pictographic nature is more evident in the ancient forms, which were: 𝍓, 𝍔, 𝍕, 𝍖.

B. Circular. Like the cowrie coin, the circular coins of ancient China had a hole in the center, enabling them to be strung together. The hole in the center continued to be a feature of most Chinese coins right up into the 20th century.

C. Knife-shaped. Knife coins must have developed from the use of knives for barter in earlier times. Such coins ranged in size from 2½ to 1¾ inches long. They always had a ring at the end of the handle, which enabled them to be strung together for easier carrying.

D-G. Shovel-shaped. Shovel-shaped coins evolved from the use of actual bronze shovels for barter (one shovel for one bolt of cloth) during the Shang Dynasty (16th-11th century B.C.) and earlier in the Zhou Dynasty (11th century-221 B.C. As a general rule, the larger the shovel-shaped coin, the earlier it was put into circulation.

Bing cong kou ru, huo cong kou chu.

Diseases enter through the mouth, calamities come out of the mouth.

- Chinese Proverb.

Chapter Twenty-Five
Thin Ice and Tie Rod Bent

By harvest time in 1939, Communist guerrillas were actively operating in the countryside and the Japanese were beginning to panic. In addition to all the other restrictions they had set up regarding travel, they instituted a search of every individual entering the city. It caused a tremendous pileup at the gates, and I went out to the West gate one afternoon to watch the procedure.

There were Chinese police and Manchukuo soldiers, with one or two Japanese in charge, and all those coming in through the gate were stopped and body searched, and anything they were carrying was opened and inspected very thoroughly as the Japanese looked for weapons. The Japanese suspected Communist guerrillas were infiltrating the city, as indeed they were. I hadn't stood there very long before I noticed a man walking in carrying a load of straw on his shoulder carrying-pole. As he entered the gate he stretched his left arm down the seam of his trousers, with his first finger and thumb extended, much in the way that American children extend their finger and thumb in pretense of firing a pistol. One of the Chinese police walked over to him and after a very cursory search, let him go. Not long afterward I saw another man do the same thing, and again the policeman let him go by. Knowing what the signal conveyed, I asked one of the policemen that I knew just what the extended finger and thumb meant, wondering if he would tell me the truth. To me it was so obvious. He grinned and told me not to tell the Japanese, but that the sign (meaning "eight") was the secret signal of the *balu*, or Eighth Route Army of the Communists. He told me they had to let them into the city without exposing them, otherwise they and their families would be in danger. The sign was one of the "sleeve" signals used by the livestock brokers in the morning animal markets.

In the livestock market, anyone selling an animal would approach a broker and, inserting one hand up the broker's sleeve, would use his fingers on the bare arm to indicate the price he expected for his animal. Individual fingers meant anywhere from one to four dollars. Four fingers and a thumb pressed together on the arm was five dollars. Six was indicated by gently scratching with the tips of four fingers, seven was the thumb and first two fingers pressed tightly together, while eight was the outstretched thumb and first finger. Nine was indicated by crooking the first finger toward the inbent thumb, and ten was shown by the thumb alone. Any combination of the figures could be used to show dollars and cents.

The form of secret communication was to obviate any embarrassment to either buyer or seller, and to enable the broker to make his percentage as the go-between. For example, the seller having indicated to the broker the asking price for an animal, the broker would approach a likely buyer who was looking at the animal and would insert his hand up the man's sleeve, indicating a price two or three dollars higher than that being asked. The man would come back with a lower counter-offer, which would then be passed on to the seller via his sleeve, but reduced by a couple of dollars. That would go on, back and forth, until a price satisfactory to both could be agreed upon, and the sale would be concluded, with the broker making his bit as well.

I had first seen that *balu* signal while traveling on the train to Tientsin about three years before the incident at the gate, and at the time I guessed what it meant. I was riding third class. The train wasn't very crowded, and sitting opposite me was a well-dressed Chinese sporting Western-style clothing, with a white shirt and tie. I wanted to nap, so I hadn't started any conversation with him, and he had no idea that I understood Chinese. After one or two curious looks at me, he, too, settled down for sleep.

As we approached the border between Manchukuo and China at Shanhaiguan, a Japanese Railway Police officer came through the car with two Chinese policeman, checking everyone's travel papers. The procedure was for the two Chinese policemen to precede the Japanese officer and have all papers produced and ready by the time he got there. I was awakened by one of the Chinese police, whom I knew from previous trips. As he politely asked me to produce my passport, he jerked his chin in the direction of his Japanese superior and, using a Chinese form of circumlocutory humor, he whispered to me: "Beggar beating a dog" (*Yao fande da gou*). By that I understood him to mean that his boss, the Japanese, was a tough customer in appearance and speech only, but that I shouldn't worry too much about him because he was all bark and no bite. I arrived at that conclusion because a beggar can carry a stick and look fierce. He can hit the dog when approaching someone's house to beg for food, but his is an idle gesture, which he cannot back up because of his lowly position in life; he can only pretend to have power. As a result, when the Japanese approached me and started shouting at me, I didn't let it bother me.

While waiting for the Japanese to come, though, I noticed that as the Chinese policeman woke up the man sitting opposite me, the latter placed his outstretched hand on his knee with three fingers folded under, and his thumb and first finger extended. The policeman immediately greeted the man politely, asked for his papers, and then waited until the Japanese arrived, whereupon he told his superior that the man was OK and need not be body searched. I was very curious about it because it was the first time I had seen it done, although I had heard about it. After we had passed the border, I asked my Chinese policeman friend what the extended thumb and finger meant besides "eight," and he confirmed that it was the secret symbol used by the *balu*. He further told me that the man was probably a *balu* spy courier, but, explaining his actions, he said that because they all hated the Japanese so much, they let those men move around freely without harassing them.

Later, back in my seat, I decided to have a little fun. When the man across from me awoke from a nap, I looked around behind me in a conspiratorial manner and then, looking him straight in the eye, I crossed my legs just as he had done and laid my partly clenched hand on my knee with the first finger and thumb extended. A shocked expression came into his eyes. Having heard me talk with the policeman, he knew I spoke Chinese. For a moment he said nothing, then, as perspiration appeared on his forehead, he leaned across to me and, in a hoarse whisper, he asked, *Ni ye shi ma?* ("Are you one too?") I looked blankly at him as though I didn't understand, and then said, "What do you mean?" He didn't answer, but later I saw him talking to the policeman, who evidently told him who I was and that most certainly I wasn't a Communist guerrilla. When he returned to his seat he struck up a casual conversation, which continued until I reached my destination, and he didn't bring up the matter of my making the "eight" sign, evidently deciding it had been purely accidental on my part.

Coincidentally, I was on the same train two or three months later, and I met up with the same Chinese policeman. He sat down beside me and asked if I remembered the man who had sat opposite me dressed in Western clothes. I told him I did. He went on to tell me that the man was indeed a spy for the Communists and that he traveled back and forth across the border. However, his luck had run out just a few days before. Another Chinese policeman was substituting for him on that trip, and as the spy was sleeping, the new policeman noticed that the point of his shirt collar had remained stiffly stuck out, instead of bending as it should have when the man's chin was down. He became suspicious and hauled the man off into the nearest toilet, where he searched and interrogated him. Taking a knife, he slit the shirt collar open and found secret papers, and the man immediately admitted to being a *balu* spy, producing 4,000 yuan, which he offered as a bribe if the policeman would look the other way. The Chinese policeman, however, was more avaricious than that. He knew he had caught a big fish and turned him over to the Japanese at the border. The man was immediately shot without trial and the policeman was promoted to division chief, a position that ultimately would bring him a great deal more money than the 4,000 yuan he had been offered.

As I think back now, that visit to Tientsin was interesting in other ways. I had gone there to get a new set of tires and also a couple of new rear springs for the van. In a previous chapter I wrote of the Japanese blockade of the British concession and the harassment of everyone who went in and out. Each time I negotiated the barriers, I was reminded of the nasty experience Eva had undergone when the Japanese soldier had attempted to molest her, and each time my blood boiled and I wanted somehow to get back at them. At the time, it had become customary for all foreigners going through the barricade to offer their passports with a ten yuan note folded inside. With that, they usually got through without the slightest delay. However, that was something I refused to do. As I lined up to go through the barricade, and eventually, when I got to the head of the

line, the Japanese soldier saw that I was British and had put no money in the passport, so he sent me back to the end of the line, which had nearly 50 people in it. Twenty minutes later I was back in front of him again, and the same thing occurred. That happened over and over again for about three hours. The soldier became more and more abusive toward me, and I was sure he was about to strike me after I had appeared before him about ten times. However, at that moment he was relieved by another soldier who, just coming on duty, was in a better mood and let me through without trouble.

On my return to Lingyuan I would have to go through the same barricade again, and I knew that the auto parts I was carrying would give me a problem, so I talked with some of the rickshaw men. After gaining their confidence, I asked if there wasn't some way around the barricades, knowing full well that with the Chinese there most certainly would be a way. They assured me they could get me to the station without any trouble. I hired three rickshaws to carry my tires and auto parts, and we set off in exactly the opposite direction from the station, through the ex-German concession and out into the swamps and rice fields that bordered the city. On narrow little footpaths atop the dikes between the wet fields, barely wide enough in spots for the rickshaws, the rickshaw men followed a circuitous path that eventually led through some back alleys into the native city and from there to the station, and we didn't see a single Japanese on the entire route.

Boarding the train, I used another ploy to bypass the Japanese. I paid the station coolies extra to carry my stuff by a roundabout entry and to wait for me in one of the third-class cars, where I had them stuff it all under the seats, and then I sat down beside it. Just before the train pulled out, I got up and walked out of the car, strolling along the platform to another third-class car two or three cars ahead of the first one, and there I got in and found a seat, and the train pulled out a minute or two later.

I knew it was possible that the Japanese would find the things when they inspected the train at the border with Manchukuo at Shanhaiguan, but the Chinese sitting there could truthfully deny owning any of it, and would be able to testify that a foreigner had brought it on and then had left the train, and there was nothing about the auto parts that the Japanese could connect with me. It was bulky and heavy, and it was unlikely they would want to move it, and I gambled on the fact they would probably shrug it off and leave it there for the railway people to deal with when the train reached its final stop. Once the train was well across the border into Manchukuo, I went back to the original car and reclaimed my seat, and when we reached Jinzhou, where I had to change trains, I got off with all my stuff without having had to pay duty. As far as I was concerned, Manchukuo didn't exist; it was all part of China and the Japanese had no legal right to impose taxes or fines on me, nor had I any legal obligation to obey their rules and regulations.

It was that winter of 1939-40 that a very enthusiastic young Englishman, Harry Bishop, came out to Jehol as a missionary and joined us in Lingyuan for a year or so to learn the language. My parents and the girls were still in Canada and didn't return until early in 1940, so Eva and I, with Harry Bishop, were alone in Lingyuan that winter. During the preceding summer months, as part of all the building that was going on, we had also enlarged the small gate in our back garden wall that led out into the fields, making it into a large, two-leaved gate wide enough to admit the van. Outside, I had made a road across to the nearby threshing floor, which was not in use during the winter months, and in that way I could bring the van into the back garden. I had done that because we wanted to dig an ice pit so that we could have some refrigeration for our food during the summer.

The pit was about fourteen feet long by ten feet wide and twelve feet deep. I had put a substantial, heavy dirt roof over it, covered with a thin layer of lime plaster to shed water, but I had not protected the inside walls. That proved to be a mistake. When the third "nine" of the very cold weather arrived, and when the ice was at its thickest, Harry Bishop joined me, with Lao San and Gao Yu-sheng, and together we went down to the East River where there was a deep pool to cut the ice we wanted. I'd had the local blacksmith make me a couple of ice tongs from a picture I drew for him, but even with those it was a cold and unpleasant job and our ice-cutting methods were crude. The resulting blocks of ice lacked uniformity in size and shape, but the ice was crystal clear, although we would never dare to use it in drinks.

We filled the van over and over again, and I hauled the ice blocks back to our back garden, slid them down a wooden chute into the pit, where Lily Root and Chang Yin put them in place, and covered each layer with a thick padding of straw. It took us three days to fill the pit, then we sealed it up well. It was most satisfying the following summer to be able to have cold drinks, even though they didn't have ice in them, and we enjoyed making ice cream for the first time in Lingyuan. The ice lasted us well through the hot weather, although we lost the bottommost layer because the heavy rains soaked through the ground around the pit and eventually seeped down into the bottom, flooding it to a depth of about three feet and melting a lot of the ice.

While we were working on the ice-cutting job, a young man walked in from a village about 30 miles to the east of Lingyuan and told me he was getting married in four days, would I come to his home to perform a Christian wedding for him? I was happy to oblige, and on the appointed day we set out early in the morning. The temperature was around 40 degrees Fahrenheit below zero, and a bitterly cold north wind was blowing, but otherwise it was a fine, clear, sunny day. We knew the temperature because we had an outdoor thermometer, but another way of telling when it was forty below, or lower, was to spit. When one did so, the spittle formed a ball of ice before it reached the ground.

Since it was a relatively easy trip I had anticipated no problems and decided we could easily get back the same day after the wedding was over, so only Eva and I went, and I suggested to Harry Bishop that he join us too, as he had never seen a Chinese wedding. Since he had come to Lingyuan by train, it was also to be his first experience of travel by road. It turned out to be quite an initiation for him.

All went well until we were about six or seven miles from our destination, at which point we had to cross a deep river that ran between sheer cliffs to the crossing point, where the valley broadened out on the other side of the river while the cliffs continued on the near side. As we descended the steep defile near the river, I could see the bridge in the distance, a very long one with eight or nine spans, but as we neared it, I was dismayed to see that one or two of the spans at the mid-point were sagging badly. Although carts were still using it, I was afraid it would give way under the weight of the van. I got out and walked across it to check it out. The extreme slant, and the fact that the roadway was worn through to the *shujie* base underneath, convinced me that it was too risky to take the van across.

A few yards downstream we found where the Japanese trucks crossed. They had cut a ramp down through the four-foot-thick ice into the narrow and fast-running stream, and the opposite sloping cut slightly downstream showed that they crossed at an angle. However, the water, which was level with the top of the ice banks, appeared far too deep for my vehicle. While we debated whether to try it or not a Japanese army truck came along and went through without a pause. But I noticed that the water came up inside the body of the truck, and our vehicle was a good foot or so lower, so I knew we would drown our engine if we tried it, and would get very wet in the process.

I looked around for some other way across, but upstream the river ran too close to the cliffs on the opposite side, so downstream was our only bet. There, the riverbed widened out and perhaps we could cross there.

At that moment a young farmer walked across the bridge toward us. He stopped to look at the van, and then asked us why we weren't going across the bridge. When I told him our problem, he pointed downstream and said, "No problem. There's a ford about a mile down there where the water is shallow and the bottom hard. Our carts use it all the time. I'll show you where it is." That was great news, so we started off downstream on the glassy ice, which stretched the entire width of the valley, the young man standing on the running board of the van by my open window. I had warned him to keep a sharp lookout for cracks in the ice that sometimes appear when the ice is thick and there is no water underneath, and the ice drops from its own weight. Because the ice was so slick, I stayed in low gear, as it was dangerous to use the brakes. Otherwise, with the constant downward slope, we could easily go into a sideways skid, and from that, there was usually no recovery until you hit something solid, usually the bank, which ordinarily would cause the vehicle to capsize.

That day we found ourselves going through freezing slush every few minutes where the open water, constricted as it was in the narrow ice channel on our left, repeatedly surged up over the top of the ice banks and overflowed the ice areas nearby. It froze immediately into ripples and corrugations that, although beautiful, were dangerous to cross because they tended to throw the car wheels away from the direction in which I was trying to steer. I was also on the lookout for another phenomenon that we had experienced a number of times when traveling on ice. In previous winters we had on numerous occasions negotiated frozen rivers where there was no open water at all, sometimes traveling downstream for miles where the roads, which frequently followed a river bed, had been completely covered by the ice. In those cases we had found an additional hazard that, the first time we experienced it, almost ended in disaster.

What we had discovered was, when going downstream on a wide expanse of ice, the thickness was no guarantee of safety. Apparently, when there was any significant depth of water under the ice, the weight of a moving car on the ice above was sufficient to start a pressure ridge of compressed air and water under the ice that traveled a few yards ahead of the moving vehicle, gradually building up in strength to a point where something had to give way. When that happened, some 20 or 30 yards ahead of you the ice would suddenly erupt upward like a miniature volcano, spewing ice and water for yards around.

The first time it happened I was driving in low gear, but when I saw the ice burst open just ahead of me, there was no way I could stop. The ice was so slick that with my wheels locked, I just kept sliding toward that mound of ice with its gushing torrent of water, and I could do nothing about it. Fortunately for us, the slabs of ice that had erupted were so large and so thick that they formed a pyramid-like structure, and as the car hit that slope at a slight angle, we slid off to one side and continued on downstream. Had we hit it head-on and gone over the top, we would in all probability have ended up on the bottom of the river. That same day we experienced that phenomenon five different times before I figured out what was happening.

From that experience we learned to stop every few minutes to allow the underwater pressure ridge to dissipate. On that day, heading for the wedding, as we went downstream, I watched for just such a blowout. But something entirely different cropped up, and it was an experience probably few others have ever had.

We'd gone about half a mile downstream from the

bridge when we came to a fairly sharp downward slope on the ice. Just past the bottom of the slope, where it leveled out again, I saw something ahead that I knew meant trouble. A distinct, dark black line extended directly across the ice from right to left, and I knew it had to be a fast-flowing stream of water under the ice, coming from the mountains to our right and feeding into the main channel. It was a stream that flowed so fast that it cut deeply through the ice base but would freeze only slightly across the surface, regardless of how cold the weather was.

There wasn't the slightest possibility of our being able to stop the van's progress on the downward slope, and it was absolutely mandatory that I keep a straight course. To apply the brakes might have caused us to broach sideways onto the dark strip, which I was certain was thin ice, and that would have been disastrous if the ice gave way. But just how thin was the ice? Would it carry our weight? And how deep was the water underneath?

We learned all the answers in a matter of seconds. The dark area was indeed an open channel of water under the ice, a mere six feet or so wide, but with only about three inches of ice on top. The front wheels of the van were almost across it when it gave way. The front of the van dropped abruptly, and we jolted to a stop. However, to my intense relief, the front end of the car had dropped only a foot or so, the back wheels remaining on top of the thick ice behind us and some six feet or so back of the channel edge. Immediately I thought that the stream was only a foot or so deep and that our wheels had hit bottom. We'd been in similar situations many times before, and it had posed no problem, but that one turned out to be entirely different.

Although we'd been traveling slowly, the sudden stop catapulted the young Chinese off the running board onto the ice on the other side of the channel. Apparently unhurt, he scrambled to his feet, and without a word to us or even a look in our direction, he sprinted off over the ice as fast as his legs could carry him. I suspect he feared he would be blamed for leading us into that predicament.

I got out of the van expecting to find, at the very least, some severe damage to the front of the van, possibly the grille pushed in. The ice alongside the hole where we had broken through easily carried my weight, but when I got to the other side of the stream and looked at the front of the van, I saw nothing wrong. The front bumper had gained the far side of the channel, and was embedded deep in the four-foot-thick ice bordering the channel. The grille was untouched and the engine was still operating smoothly. I thought, "Great, we should be out of this in no time at all."

With the pick we carried, I broke some more ice to determine how deep the water was and whether we could bridge the gap with the long boards we always carried with us. If that was possible, we might be able to jack up the front end, slide the boards underneath the van and the front wheels, and then back out or even proceed straight across. But to my surprise I found the water to be a little over four feet deep, and as I bent low to see where the front wheels were, an extraordinary sight met my eyes. There, in the sparkling clear water, I could clearly see the two front wheels, but instead of being in the expected position, parallel with the rear wheels, the impact when they hit the ice wall had been such that they were splayed out at right angles to the ice bank and flat up against it. I fully expected to see the tie rod, which linked the two wheels together, to have snapped in two, but there it was, bent at each end where it touched the wheels, and with the center portion of it bent out toward the rear of the vehicle in a tight "V" shape.

Over the years we'd had many experiences of falling through the ice but never had we experienced anything like that. Thankfully I was able to keep the engine running as I studied the situation, but the longer I looked at it the greater the problem grew. Obviously, even if we could bridge the gap with the boards, we could neither back out nor go forward unless the wheels were straightened out. If we didn't first straighten out the wheels, and were able to pull the vehicle backward, the wheels, fixed in that position, would not be able to climb the ice bank on the near side. Additionally, as I studied the situation, I knew it was impossible to get a jack under the front bumper, deeply embedded as it was in the ice, and even if I had been able to do so, I feared that the slightest movement of the vehicle might cause the front end to drop off the ice bank and plunge down into the stream, thus killing the engine and making things even more difficult than they were.

It became more and more obvious that I had no alternative but to get down into the water, remove the tie rod, straighten it out, and then straighten out the wheels. Only after I had put the tie rod back on again to control the wheels could we hope to pull the vehicle out backward, provided that we could find the animals to do it.

It was equally obvious that we needed help, because on that slick ice, even with chains on the rear wheels, I would have been unable to pull the front wheels up onto the hard ice. The bridge was nearly a half mile away, and from our position it was out of sight because of the drop in the river level. Thinking it over, I realized that if I went there I might be able to prevail on some carter to lend us his animals, but it was a long shot, and mules and horses are known for their skittishness on ice. I came to the conclusion that it was highly unlikely I could get help.

In the near distance across the river I could see what looked like smoke haze, and I recalled that there was a small village there, a short distance from the highway. By way of the bridge it would be about a two-mile walk. Doubtless we could get help there, but who could go? Harry Bishop was unable to speak more than a word or two of Chinese, so there would be no point in his going. I had to stay behind and somehow straighten out the wheels or we'd never get out. Poor Eva had to make the trek!

She was dressed warmly enough, but she was wearing the clumsy Mongolian felt boots that were never intended for walking, and she would surely develop blisters. But little did we realize that blisters would be the least of her troubles. She set off toward the bridge, even though the ford was much closer, but I didn't want her trying to wade through cold unknown water. She was gone a little over two hours, and it took me all of that time to finally straighten out the wheels.

I should add at this point that I was dressed in my Sunday best for the wedding ceremony I was to perform. I had on a brand-new pair of slacks that looked fine and fit me well, but they were made of some kind of Japanese wartime ersatz material and were sewn with thread of the same sort. When I first squatted down to look under the van, all the seams on the pants suddenly split open, and I found myself left with empty pant legs dangling from my belt with only the cuffs intact around my ankles. Everything else was wide open.

Fortunately I always carried a pair of greasy over-

alls with me, and I donned those immediately, but not for long. Obviously there was no alternative. I had to get down into the water under the van, dismantle the tie rod, and straighten it and the wheels out. I stripped to my underpants, broke the thin ice that had already formed on the open water, and slid down under the van. Not surprisingly, the water felt much warmer in contrast to the outside air, and I found I had just enough room under the engine to keep my head above water, but I was limited to the space on each side in the wheel wells, the engine's oil pan being under water. I had to pull out a cotter pin on each end of the tie rod and undo a series of double bolts on each end, and because it was all under water and the running water caused distortion, I had to do it mainly by feel. At the same time I had difficulty keeping my footing, because of the swiftly flowing water.

Harry Bishop handed me the tools I needed as I called for them, and as I dismantled each part I put it up on the ice beside me, where they all promptly froze solidly to the ice surface. Later we had to hammer them free. While I was working in the water, to keep Harry warm, I set him to work carrying sand from the river bank about 100 yards away, and spreading it on the glare ice behind the van, so that when we eventually got some animals to pull the van out, there would be some footing for them. My split pants came in useful for carrying the sand.

Getting the tie rod off took me about twenty minutes, and that was the easy part. As soon as that was done I threw the tie rod up onto the ice, crawled out of the water, and dashed into the van before the water could freeze on my body. I had worn a pair of knee-high rubber boots into the water; otherwise, my feet would have frozen to the ice as I dashed the few steps to the van, and they certainly would have frozen to the running board as I stepped in. Of course the boots were full of water as I got into the van, but I kicked them off and Harry dumped the water before it could freeze solid inside them. Inside, with the heater on full blast, the van was nice and warm. I dried off as best I could and put on my outer clothing. Then, wearing gloves, Harry and I inserted one end of the bent tie rod behind the back bumper, and with both of us pulling outward on the other end, we were able to straighten it out to at least a semblance of its former self. After that it was necessary to go back down into the water to put it on again, but before I could do that, the wheels, which were tightly pressed flat against the ice wall, had to be straightened out. To accomplish that I had to, in some fashion, move the van backward a foot or more, to be able to swing the wheels around so that they were aimed forward.

That was a puzzle. If I moved the car back, then the front bumper would slip off the ice shelf and the whole front end, engine included, might dive into the water. Even though I didn't expect it to fall to the bottom, I felt sure it could fall far enough before the chassis hit the ice to drown the engine, and then we would really be in bad shape. I wasn't at all sure where the actual center of gravity might be on the van's frame. Harry and I talked it over, and then I took some rough measurements and decided that if I placed one of the boards crosswise in front of the rear wheels, near the edge of the firm ice, and then supported it at each end with a large flat rock so that it came almost into contact with the underframe of the van, we could perhaps drop the front end of the van off the ice shelf, and the board would support the chassis. But to play it safe, we also decided to weigh down the tail end of the van with some heavy rocks. We carried a dozen or so large rocks from the nearby hillside and stacked them in the back end of the van and then closed the doors. All that time we had been able to keep the engine running, which was a lifesaver, because from time to time we simply had to hop in and get warm.

Finally, we took the remaining heavy board, and after using the pick to dig out a hole in the ice in front of the front bumper, we managed, bit by bit, to wedge the board between the front bumper and the ice shelf. Using the ice as a fulcrum, we gradually edged the bumper off the shelf, expecting any moment that the front end of the van would drop into the stream. As the bumper finally slid off the shelf, the front end did drop, but only a few inches. The mid-point of the underframe of the van dropped neatly onto the board we had placed underneath the vehicle and held.

We were most thankful for that. We continued to pry the van backward inch by inch, with the board sliding along on the rock supports carrying the load of the van. When we had moved it out about a foot or more from the opposite bank, I felt sure I had enough room to get down into the water to turn the wheels. By that time our teeth were chattering with the cold, and we hastily crawled back into the van to warm up

again.

I delayed as long as I could because, although the first time I went into the water it wasn't so bad, to go back down again wasn't an attractive prospect. But it had to be done. Eventually, I again took off my clothes and back down I went to find the wheels were free of the ice bank, and they straightened out nicely. Harry handed me the tie rod, and I put it back on, taking much less time than I had to remove it, leaving a final tightening of the bolts until we got the whole thing back up on the ice. I then made another mad dash back into the warmth of the van. Thinking back, just why I wasn't overcome by hypothermia in that icy water I don't know. I was young and healthy, and at the time, going in there was the natural and only thing to do, and I gave it very little thought. Come to think of it, I had never heard of hypothermia.

From then on it was almost anticlimactic. We sat inside the van keeping warm and watching for Eva to return. From inside the van we could look across the river, and we eventually saw Eva trudging along in the distance, and behind her was a man leading a large ox, but it was a full half hour or more before she crossed the bridge and reached the van. As she came close to us I saw with dismay that she was walking in her stockinged feet and carrying what remained of her felt boots. The wet slush she trudged through on the way to the bridge had caused the soles of her Mongolian felt boots to start to disintegrate. From then on they had gradually fallen off her feet, and she had walked without shoes most of the way to the village and back. And she had no spare shoes in the van. I feared she would have frostbite, but she had walked so fast that her good circulation had kept her feet from freezing. But with the chilblains she already had on her feet, it was painful for her when she first got into the warmth of the van and her feet started to warm up again.

Eva's finding the ox was no mean achievement in itself. When she had reached the village she first had to convince the farmers that she was not Japanese and meant them no harm. One can readily imagine their surprise at seeing a lone foreign woman arriving in their midst, and not wearing any shoes at that. When she explained her problem, they led her to the only man in the village who had an ox, an ideal animal for the job. Oxen have tremendous strength, and they are so phlegmatic and docile that they are rarely spooked by a motor vehicle, and unlike horses and mules, they are not afraid of ice.

The old farmer had brought along his cart traces, and with those he hooked the ox up to the back of the van and we were ready to go. I sat behind the steering wheel to hold the front wheels straight and kept the back doors open so I could watch the ox. It was an extraordinary sight. At the urging of the farmer the ox took a few paces forward on the sanded stretch that Harry Bishop had made on the ice, moving very slowly until the traces behind him were taut. He then turned his head and looked back at the van for what seemed a full half minute as though sizing up the situation. Then he slightly tossed his head as if to say: "That little thing? No problem." With that, he reared up on his back legs, moving ahead as he did so and keeping the traces taut, and then he dropped his full weight slowly forward. Effortlessly the van rose from the water, the front wheels climbing the ice bank with no difficulty at all.

We counted that incident as another of the many miracles in our lives, and rightly so, I believe. None of us in any way suffered any aftereffects. Eva's feet were not frostbitten, although for the remainder of the trip she had only her scarf and mine to wrap around them, and neither Harry nor I caught colds. We had much to be thankful for.

We still had to cross that stream, but we managed to do so by going up close to the mountain base, where the ice was thinner and the channel of running water under it was much wider and shallower. We broke through the ice again but had no problem making the other side of the stream. When we reached the downstream ford on the main river, a wide stretch of fairly shallow water, it was equally easy to cross. It was very rocky, and with an uneven bottom, but the ice shelf on each side was not more than a foot or so thick, and with our pick we readily made ramps on each side that enabled us to get down into the stream and then up the other side without difficulty.

We arrived some three hours late for the wedding, but no one seemed to mind. The Chinese are noted for their patience. It was well into the afternoon when we arrived there, and because the wedding feast was all ready to be served, I performed the ceremony for the bride and groom without delay, and no one seemed to notice that I was dressed in a pair of greasy overalls and that Eva wasn't wearing any shoes.

A traditional Chinese wedding is a complicated affair accompanied by numerous rites and traditions, but the one that day was short and simple, and the villagers were much impressed. Because they were very poor, the bride had ridden a donkey from her home in an adjoining village, and her trousseau had been carried on the shoulders of friends. One Chinese custom for weddings is that the bride and groom must sleep their first night under a quilt provided by the bride's family, and in the corners of the mattress on which they sleep (or inside the bride's pillow), dates and chestnuts are inserted. The Chinese words for dates and chestnuts, when said closely together, sound like "raise sons quickly," so it was considered to be auspicious for the future. Another peasant tradition dictates that on their wedding night neither the bride nor groom should say a single word to the other. They believed that whichever one spoke first would be the first to die, and usually a vigil was kept outside the closed door to make certain that neither one spoke. Of course, this young couple dispensed with those and other superstitious rites.

After a very welcome feast, our journey home by the same route was quite uneventful. Surprisingly, when we got home, a close inspection revealed that, apart from the bent tie rod, no damage had been done to the van's front end, but that weakened tie rod was to play a part in an unusual experience some weeks later.

Although I managed to remain on relatively good terms with the local Japanese officials in Lingyuan and was generally treated with courtesy, that was not always the case with minor Japanese officials we ran into in the outlying areas. On several occasions when we were visiting village fairs, the resident Japanese police official would deliberately delay us by holding us for hours before inspecting our passports. However, as the political situation intensified, the Japanese in the smaller places, after inspecting our papers and finding no reason to hold us, started venting their spleen on the Chinese who accompanied us. At times they dragged them off to the police station for hours of questioning. So we decided to change our policy somewhat. As time went on, rather than expose the Chinese Christians to such abuse and degrading treatment, more and more frequently Eva and I would go out on trips into the countryside by ourselves.

The Japanese head of the police in Lingyuan at that particular time was a fairly easygoing fellow who generally showed himself quite friendly. One day he suggested that, for my own safety, I should stick to the "motor roads" that the Japanese had built throughout the province — his way of telling me not to get off the beaten path and thus out of their sight and jurisdiction. I had no intention of following his advice, but it did give me the opportunity to ask him for a map of the so-called "motor roads," and he gave me a roughly drawn sketch that showed all the roads that supposedly could be covered by police vehicles. Several of the roads I had not even known about, and as Eva and I studied the map, we found that several areas of the county that had previously been inaccessible to us were now opened up. We decided to explore them.

One morning we loaded up the van with Bible portions and religious tracts and headed southeast, intending to be away several days. When we were about 20 miles out, we came to a small village, which, according to the map, was the point from which one of the new roads branched off. But it wasn't immediately visible. We stopped to visit with the villagers, and I asked one of the men where the new road was. He replied, "Oh, you'll find it down in the river bed." Then, using a common Chinese expression he added, "It's smooth as glass and gleaming bright." (*Liu guang, zheng liang.*)

Sure enough, down in the riverbed we found his "road." It was a smoothed-off track about eight feet wide, carefully marked with a border of small stones along the edges and cleared of even the smallest rocks. As we started along it, it became quite obvious that ours was the very first vehicle to use it since there were no other tracks. We followed it for several miles, then the road swung off through plowed fields toward the crest of what looked like a range of low hills. When we reached the hills, the road turned sharply into a narrow cleft between two outcroppings of rock, where it suddenly ended. Only faint cart tracks were evident from that point on, and yet, according to the map, the road was supposed to continue for another three or four miles to a large village in the mountains.

I made the mistake of trusting the map rather than my common sense, which normally would have dictated that I walk ahead a few hundred yards to see where the road led. Instead, we followed the cart track through the narrow, winding cut, and quite unexpectedly, an extraordinary panorama opened up before us. We found ourselves high on the edge of an escarpment, with a drop ahead of us of at least two thousand feet into a small valley below, and nothing but mountains in the distance. I realized it was the area behind Heishan Ke, the infamous mountainous hangout for bandits that we had known about over the years and had always skirted with a certain degree of apprehension. In the distance below us, we could clearly see a large village, and we decided to head toward it, hoping to find an inn where we could spend the night.

The cart tracks led into a small ravine that twisted and turned as it headed downward, becoming ever more narrow, with high, steeply tapering sides of almost solid rock, and we realized it was nothing more than an ancient watercourse. However, we were committed, since there was no possibility of turning back or even backing out. We could only continue ahead and trust that where a cart could go, we could go.

The road became steeper and steeper, and the sides towered above us menacingly. From time to time we had to stop to remove large boulders that had fallen from above. The ravine increasingly narrowed, and my running boards occasionally scraped the rock on both sides, until I noticed that my wheels were riding the banks, high above the deeply cut V of the rocky floor of the ravine, and that we were actually riding the sides of the tires on the sloping walls. The road ahead dropped so steeply that the top of the engine hood blocked my view of the path. I suggested to Eva that she get out and walk backward ahead of me to guide me.

Easier said than done. The rock walls were so close we couldn't open either of the side doors, nor was there room to crawl out of the window. I opened up the back doors and found a four-foot drop to the ravine floor. Holding Eva's hands, I let her down, and bent double, she was able to walk under the van out to the front with a full three-foot clearance underneath. When she stood up, I couldn't see her head, and she had to raise her hand above her head for me to follow her. We moved down very slowly, and all the time I feared that the wheels on one side or the other would slide downward and the van would end up on its side. However, I'd only gone about 20 feet or so when we came to a jarring stop, and I saw Eva frantically waving her arms for me to halt. I had no idea what I could have hit.

I crawled out the back door and under the van, and found the reason for the sudden stop. The intense side pressure on the base of the front wheel tires had been so great that the weakened tie rod had once again given way, and again it was bent backward into a tight V just as it had been before, and once again the front wheels were splayed out sideways and jammed tightly against the rock walls.

We lost all sense of time getting out of that mess, but it must have taken us three hours or more, because the sun was very low when we finally reached the village below. It was a great deal easier than when I had to fix the tie rod under water, but even so, it was a time-consuming and very challenging job. First I had to find flat rocks and build a platform to support the jack under the front axle. With the jack finally in position, I had to solidly block the back wheels to prevent the entire van from sliding forward and down on top of me. Before doing anything else I first dismantled the bent tie rod, but trying to straighten it out in the narrow confines of the ravine, with less than a foot of clearance at each end of the back bumper, proved quite impossible. I had to insert one end of the rod under one of the rear springs and then, bit by bit, heave up on the opposite end until I got it straightened out. I then got the front end jacked up and the front wheels turned back into line. But I was afraid that as soon as the weight of the vehicle came down on the wheels, the tie rod would once again give way. To try to prevent that, I took two tire irons and, with some heavy wire that I always carried with me for emergency repairs, I put a splint around the weakened section of the tie rod, and when we let the jack down, it held.

Fortunately we were more than halfway down the mountain, and a few yards beyond that point the rocky sides petered out and were replaced by banks of clay hardpan, which soon turned into the softer loess soil as the ravine widened out. Without further trouble beyond the moving of a few more boulders out of our way here and there, we reached the bottom and entered the village completely exhausted.

There was only one inn, and we thankfully pulled in there and found the innkeeper friendly and appar-ently happy to see us. He gave us what he called his "office" to sleep in and very quickly prepared a much welcomed meal. However, we detected a note of strain in his manner and were not long in learning the reason. Within minutes of our arrival, a diminutive but very surly and arrogant Japanese police officer arrived with about ten of his men, and proceeded to interrogate us and generally to give us a hard time. He questioned us for perhaps 30 minutes, asking the same things over and over again, obviously disbeliev-ing our story that we had arrived in the village to preach. His questions seemed endless, and his Chinese interpreter was as rude and surly as he was. Finally, as our food was served and we tried to eat, he left us, but he returned a short time later. He made it quite apparent that we were unwelcome in the village, and he obviously thought we were spics. But our trav-el papers were in perfect order, and there was nothing he could do about it.

When he finally left, I questioned the innkeeper about him and learned that he was in command of a mounted police patrol that was there searching for bandits. He told me that three men accused of being bandits were actually tied up in the room next to ours. I asked to see them and went in to talk with them, but to me they looked no different than ordinary farmers, which I firmly believe they were. Terrified, all three told me they had simply come to the village to con-duct business and had been falsely accused. I told the innkeeper to feed them and put it on my account, and Eva and I went to bed.

The *kang* we were to sleep on had obviously not been in use for some time, but after a brief period, the innkeeper got a good fire going in it with some local-ly mined anthracite coal. It was slow in igniting, but once lit it gave off excellent heat, and we quickly fell into a deep sleep. Around two o'clock the next morn-ing we both awoke dripping with perspiration, and discovered the surface of the *kang* next to us was too hot to touch. I smelled something burning, and after lighting a lamp, I discovered that flames had come up through cracks in the *kang* and the underside of my bedroll was smoldering. While we were occupied with that, we became aware of some kind of distur-bance outside, a great deal of subdued talking and activity of some kind, but we paid little attention to it. A few minutes later the innkeeper came in white-faced and told us the Japanese officer had just beheaded the three prisoners next door.

After that we could sleep no longer and, heartsick, we decided to move on at daylight, feeling that the local residents would be in no mood to welcome our presence under those circumstances and with that bloodthirsty Japanese police officer in town. Despite the early hour, he was there to watch us leave, and he glared at us malevolently as we glanced up at the three severed heads hanging overhead from the inn's gateway. We found a different route home by going a considerable distance farther south, and we hoped that someday we could return to that village under better circumstances. However, world events caught up with us and the opportunity never came.

Another rather interesting event occurred late in 1939 that illustrates the idiosyncrasies of the Japanese officials with whom we had to deal. There was an announcement one day that threw the entire city into a tizzy. We were to be honored with a visit from no less a personage than the Emperor Puyi's personal representative, a high-ranking general who was considered his deputy, the second most powerful Chinese in the country. The occasion for his visit was the graduation of a class of cadet officers in the Manchukuo puppet army who had undergone training in Lingyuan, and the Emperor's representative was being sent to hand out citations and pin some medals on them.

The Chinese population couldn't have cared less who the great man was, but the Japanese were overwhelmed by the honor being done to the city. They immediately set about a cleanup campaign of the entire city, not merely the route the great man would be taking from the railway station. Every householder was required to get out and rake and sweep the street in front of his residence; the ground had to be cleared of any loose stones, and all walls on the route from the West Gate down to the local Japanese hotel where he was to stay were whitewashed. Even the tree trunks got a coat of whitewash, and never had the city looked so clean.

Normally, when some VIP came to town, the Japanese asked for the loan of the van, with me as the driver. However, on that occasion I had a visit from the chief of police the day before the great man arrived, and with some embarrassment he advised me of the forthcoming event, and in effect told me to lock our front gates and not go outside. Nor should I

allow anyone else to go out. I asked if they needed to use the van, but he told me they would have their own transportation, and, in fact, several luxury sedans arrived that afternoon on a flatcar attached to the afternoon train.

Since the streets were to be lined with soldiers and no one was allowed to move about, I told the servants who lived off the premises to take the day off, and Eva and I decided to celebrate the day by painting the kitchen and pantry.

The following morning shortly after nine a special, seven-car luxury train passed the back of our compound, pulled by a shiny new locomotive decorated with flags. We watched it pass our back wall, and a short time later, peeping through the crack between the front gates, we saw his entourage pass by, while the police and soldiers lining the streets stood with their backs turned, facing away from the caravan of cars.

Thankful for a day when we wouldn't be disturbed, Eva and I went back to our painting, stopping for a sandwich at lunchtime, and then started to paint some more. However, soon after one o'clock and without the slightest advance warning, we suddenly found the compound swarming with armed soldiers and police, a number of whom had come in over the walls. I went out to try to find out what was going on and was told that His Excellency was coming to visit us. We barely had time to change our paint-spattered clothes when he walked in around the spirit screen, accompanied by 15 or 20 high-ranking officers.

It turned out that our local Japanese, with all their forethought and careful preparation, had overlooked one point. The railway was single-tracked, and his special train had to be turned around before he could board it for his return journey, since it would never do for so distinguished a personage to ride with a locomotive pushing the train backward. So they had been forced to send the entire train several hours down the track to a point where the locomotive could be turned around to face in the opposite direction. That had taken hours, and his scheduled departure had been put off until the evening.

No preparations had been made whatsoever to entertain His August Highness in the interval. There was no local person of sufficiently high rank with whom he could converse or who could eat at the same table with him, and when the medal-awarding ceremony was completed, he had dined alone in solitary splendor. After that, they didn't know what to do with him for three or four hours. Apparently, though, someone had the bright idea of taking him up to visit the Tharps. We were foreigners, representatives of Great Britain, and apparently, at least for that particular occasion, we were considered to be his equals.

But the whole incident was more amusing to us than anything else. That high-ranking official who, as far as the Japanese were concerned, was in effect the Emperor himself, turned out to be a most engaging chap. For more than three hours he sat in our tiny living room chatting with me on a variety of subjects while Eva plied him with tea, milk and cookies. His personal staff of at least 15, none below the rank of colonel, and including several generals, were a mixed group of Chinese and Japanese, and all were crowded into our living room. Since they were too lowly in rank to sit in his presence, we pushed the dining table to one side, and they stood in three ranks at one end of the room while the Emperor's representative and I sat at the opposite end of the room near the bay window, in the only two easy chairs we owned.

After the usual preliminary courtesies, he enquired about us and wanted to know why we were able to speak Chinese like natives, and he was amazed to learn that we had both been born in China. He promptly told us that as far as he was concerned, we were White Chinese and in his opinion simply masquerading as foreigners.

I showed him a *National Geographic* magazine lying on a side table, and he turned the pages with tremendous interest, not so much for the content of the pictures but for the technique with which they had been taken. He turned out to be an amateur photographer and we talked on that subject until we had exhausted it. He then asked about our work. In replying, I used a uniquely Chinese witticism to illustrate a point, saying one thing while actually meaning something entirely different. It was the same kind of witticism that the Chinese policeman had used on the train when saying to me, "beggar beats a dog," indicating that his Japanese boss was all talk and no action.

The general's attitude changed immediately. He picked up on what I had said and replied in the same vein, using another of the same kind of witticisms, which calls for the listener to actually supply the correct ending. When I came up with the proper

response, he glanced over at his Japanese cohorts, then continued to talk, concealing his true meaning by the use of these very ambiguous phrases, and launched into a lengthy apologia for his presence there in such a patently ridiculous situation. He told me quite frankly that he couldn't stand the Japanese, that they had invaded his land and were oppressing his people, and that he was carrying on in his present position only to try and help his people with the goal of eventually getting rid of those interlopers.

Of course, it was all an attempt on his part to make himself look good in my eyes. He knew full well that he was simply a puppet of the Japanese and all the honor being done him was a charade, and that I was fully aware of the sham in which he was playing a part. But I played along with him and let him have his say, careful not to say anything myself that could be construed as anti-Japanese or that could be misinterpreted.

To me, while all that was going on, the most interesting part was to watch the faces of his Japanese staff members. Most of them spoke some Chinese and they were obviously there to monitor everything that he said or did, but it was obvious they hadn't the slightest idea of what he was saying as he and I exchanged our remarks with the ambiguities of humor. They began to surreptitiously eye each other, wondering if someone else understood what was going on, and then I noticed that several of them were showing beads of sweat on their foreheads. Meanwhile, the Chinese officers who were standing in the back row were all grinning and chuckling to themselves as they listened to our conversation. Finally, the Japanese officers could take it no longer. They obviously suspected that something improper was being done at their expense, and one of the higher-ranking generals nudged his neighbor and whispered something, and then, stepping forward, he bowed low and told my visitor that it was time to go to the station to board his train.

I know of no other language that has that form of oblique sayings. In our own language the only thing which remotely resembles it are expressions such as, "He's behind the eight ball," "He's got two strikes against him," or "He's got one foot in the grave and the other on a banana peel." With each of the above, anyone knowledgeable of our culture and mores can readily interpret them. However, the Chinese expressions are totally dissimilar in concept. They are wide ranging and cover almost every conceivable subject one can think of. The Chinese call them by three different names but the most common is *xie hou yu*, which literally means "proverb after a rest." All of them are a two-part allegorical saying of which the first part, always clearly stated, is descriptive. The second part, sometimes unstated, which follows after a short pause (the "rest"), may be supplied either by the listener or the speaker, and it is the second part that carries the actual message. As an example, where we would say of someone that "it's a case of the blind leading the blind" (perfectly obvious in its meaning), the Chinese might say: *"Ni pusa guo he (pause) zi shen nan bao."* Translated, it means "He's like an unbaked clay idol fording a river" — that is, he is hardly able to save himself from disaster (let alone anyone else). Obviously, being made of clay, the idol would dissolve in the water.

In our part of North China, where the sense of humor among the people was much more evident than elsewhere, people at all levels used those witticisms, or wisecracks, as part of their everyday speech, although some considered them rather vulgar. However, they often proved extremely useful when talking to Chinese friends in front of the Japanese when we didn't want to be understood. In later chapters I shall refer once again to the unusual form of communication, little known to Westerners, and will tell of one case where they were used to pass me a secret message, and another incident where they possibly saved the sanity of a colleague.

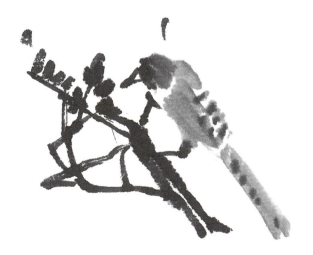

Bringing in ice for the vegetable pit.
Characters on back of van say: Lingyuan
Christian Mission

Here Bob's tie rod got bent and he had to go into the water at 40°
below zero to straighten it. Front wheels are already raised. Eva
went for the oxen and wore out her felt boots.

Really deep in the water this time.

Down a steep slope.

Bob trying to put a board under the back wheel.

Crossing a bridge.

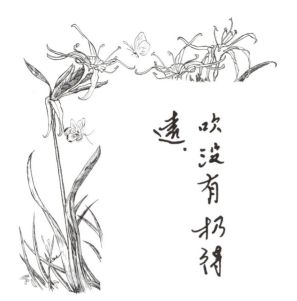

Chapter Twenty-Six

The Tension Builds

As 1940 began, the BBC news we picked up on the radio was increasingly depressing. The Germans were about to invade Holland, and the Japanese, eager to get on the bandwagon, had declared an alliance with Germany and Italy.

Closer to home, what Western nations called the "China Incident," Japan's ongoing occupation of China, had reached a stalemate. In Central China, Nanking, Free China's capital, had finally been captured in 1937 by the Japanese, who in revenge for the courageous Chinese holdout against them in the Shanghai fighting, had gone berserk once they entered the city. For seven weeks they slaughtered civilians by the thousands and captured Chinese Nationalist troops by the tens of thousands. Having watched Japanese atrocities in Manchuria for years, we were not surprised by it, but photographs of the massacre by Japanese troops shocked the rest of the world. Foreign observers estimated that female rape victims numbered 20,000; the captured Nationalist troops killed numbered 30,000; and over 12,000 civilians were murdered. Appalling as it was, the incident was remembered only briefly as events in Europe took the limelight.

Despite their victory in Nanking, the Japanese were bogged down in other parts of China. In Manchuria they were under frequent attack by Russian troops at various points along the northern borders of Manchukuo, and estimates of Japanese losses were reported at the time to be over a million men on the various fronts, with 18,000 alone lost in their battles with the Russians.

All that activity elsewhere meant that we saw fewer and fewer Japanese soldiers in Lingyuan, but the belt-tightening and war weariness that had long been a way of life in Japan extended to us throughout Jehol Province on a daily basis, with the Japanese trying to make up for the shortages of oil and raw materials for their war machine. When Holland fell to the Germans, Japan openly began to tell the world of her intentions toward the Dutch East Indies, where oil and rubber were plentiful. As Japan became ever more belligerent toward the United States, it became increasingly obvious to us that it was now only a matter of time before the Japanese widened the scope of their hostilities. Our thoughts often went to what it might mean to us, should we, too, become engulfed in the war.

Were it not for the radio, all those happenings worldwide would have seemed very far away, but they were brought home to us daily by the actions of the Japanese authorities. Increasing demands were made on the Chinese population, to the point that taxes were levied on almost everything conceivable, and almost every commodity produced by the people was declared a government monopoly: food grains, meats and vegetables, lamp oil, cotton cloth. Everything that the people needed for their daily existence became subject to rationing, and nothing could be bought or sold without government permission. Every individual was issued a ration book, and not only were limits placed on the amount each individual could get, but age limits were also established. Children under the age of five and adults over the age of 65 were given no rations at all.

In the cities it was easier for the Japanese to exert strict control; therefore, to a large extent, it was the city folk who were hit the hardest. Farmers were permitted to bring their produce in for sale, but all prices were controlled and all purchasers had to produce ration tickets in order to buy anything. Roving secret police saw to it that orders were obeyed, but there was still tremendous black market activity everywhere, with people going into the countryside to buy, then smuggling goods into the city by night. But it was the poor, as usual, who suffered the most.

Fortunately, we, as foreign nationals, were exempted and not given ration books — the Japanese feared antagonizing our various governments — but even so, there were limits to what we could get because of the shortages. One of the first things to become scarce was wheat flour, which we needed for bread, and the quality of what little was available began to decline rapidly.

When the Japanese asked us what our needs were in that regard, we anticipated increasing shortages, so we deliberately overstated our weekly requirements, and the chief of police did not quibble. He authorized just what we asked for. As a result, on those days each month when flour became available, we were able to buy much more than we could actually use, and the problem arose of where to store it. It had to be stored away from the prying eyes of the secret police who were in and out of the compound daily.

The flour came in fifty-pound cotton sacks. We managed to give some away to needy Christian families, but even that had to be done most discreetly and with extreme caution. To have given them a full sack would have endangered their lives because they were not entitled to it, so we gave it out only in limited amounts. However, like the gasoline, Eva and I finally came up with a solution, but in order to avoid endangering others, we kept it to ourselves.

Eva and I once again began living a night life of deception. Ostensibly going to bed early, we would set the alarm for midnight, when we would get up and work for several hours in our quiet corner of the compound, and we got away with it unobserved.

When building our small house, we had modified a three-*jian* building into two rooms. That meant that in the central part there were two large cross-beams inside the ceiling, as well as the dividing wall, which extended up just above the plastered ceiling. We decided to build a platform inside the ceiling just as we had done for storing the gasoline. Bridging the gap above the ceiling between the beams was easier than the job we had done in the garage ceiling, but access to it was more difficult to hide. We had to make a small trap door, which somehow had to be completely hidden. We accomplished that by cutting through the ceiling just above a large, free-standing closet that Sun had built for us, which reached almost to the ceiling. Since the trap door needed only to be large enough to admit a slimly built man, it didn't have to be very big. We cut the hole, fitted it with a door painted just like the ceiling, and then, with the closet pulled back into position, we camouflaged it by placing some eye-catching ornaments on top of the closet. When it was completed, one of the first things we did was to take several of the Chinese secret police into the room to let them look around, and we deliberately pointed out the ornaments to see if they would notice the trap door, but none of them did, so we felt safe proceeding from there.

We next cut the poles we needed to bridge the gap above. The poles had to be long enough to do the job, but short enough that we could maneuver them inside the ceiling. Since the trap door was near the dividing wall, I had a place to stand up inside, on top of the wall, as Eva handed the pre-cut poles up to me, followed by boards to lay on top of them, and we finally had a platform on which we could store our flour. Once every couple of weeks we would move stock up into the ceiling, taking care to clean up the telltale flour that inevitably showed on the floor from damaged bags so there would be no evidence in the morning. We let my parents in on the secret but no one else, and in time we had such a good supply of flour that, in the event of a siege, it would have enabled us to stay alive for several months. Sugar, too, was in short supply, and we managed to wangle a few sacks from the Japanese and store those up in the ceiling as well. When that was done, we felt a little more confident in facing a future in which we were sure nothing would be available.

Of all the restrictions the Japanese placed on the people, the one that was felt most was a complete ban on the making and selling of tofu, or *doufu*, as the Chinese call it. That beancurd, high in protein, was an extremely important part of the Chinese diet. Every small village had its *doufu* shop; and in the cities there were small *doufu* shops on almost every street, and salesman carried it around to every part of the city each morning at daybreak. Now suddenly the use of the yellow soya bean was forbidden, and the entire crop was declared a government monopoly to be shipped off to Japan, to be used in production of fuel for Japan's warships. One of the largest of Japan's battleships, the ill-fated *Yamato*, which never saw battle, had boilers specifically designed to burn soybean oil, but the fuel was so crude that they had many problems with it.

Almost immediately we began to see the effects of the ban on *doufu*. The health of the people rapidly deteriorated. Loss of hair was one of the first symptoms of failing health, while almost everyone complained of a feeling of lassitude and physical weakness. As part of the normal production of beancurd, the crushed bean husks were salvaged for animal fodder and processed by being pressed into very hard "wheels" about the diameter of a small bicycle wheel and about three inches thick. Each wheel weighed around thirty pounds and had a hole in the center to facilitate carrying. Up to the time of the ban on *doufu*,

those bean "cakes," as they were called, were used only for feeding animals, but as a sop to the population, the Japanese made them available for human consumption. But they did little good, and after about six months, the health of the people had deteriorated so badly that the Japanese lifted the ban somewhat and allowed *doufu* to be rationed, but there was never enough to go around.

Millet, the main staple of the average daily diet in our part of China, and sorghum, which was eaten by the very poor, became entirely different problems. With the strict controls on the sale of those two commodities and the severe rationing, it wasn't long before everyone found themselves in dire straits, and for all practical purposes everyone was living under famine conditions. Because of the ban against children and the elderly getting rations, it became an extreme hardship, since most families had elderly parents, and very often two or three children under the designated age living with them. Since many of the Christian families fell into that category, I felt we had to do something about it. I went to the authorities and protested the regulations, asking for help, but my pleas fell on deaf ears, so Eva and I took matters into our own hands.

Dujiawopu was in a grain-growing area, and because of its remoteness it was largely exempt from the strict regulations imposed in the cities, so I purchased a number of large burlap bags and took them up with me on one of our trips. We had a young caretaker there named Wang Bin, and I instructed him to quietly buy up as much millet as he could each market day when his actions wouldn't be noticed and then store it for me in the mission compound. Thereafter, on each trip we made up there, we brought back a dozen or so bags of grain and smuggled them into Lingyuan under the very noses of the Japanese.

Wang Bin, incidentally, was such an interesting young man that I must digress for a moment to tell something about him. He had grown up next door to us in Lingyuan, his father dying when he was only a year or so old. His widowed mother did her best by him, but he was always a weakling and badly set upon by other boys his own age. I had gotten to know him when I was about ten, and we often played together. Later we had him enrolled in Zhang Yaoting's school in the downtown hall, but he was so sickly he lost a lot of school time, and Mother was always treating him for something or other. In time, though, he seemed to grow out of it, but he remained extremely shy and retiring and almost effeminate both in his walk and speech, and he was never able to hold down a job because of his frailty. Coming so often to Mother's dispensary for treatment, he frequently saw her vaccinating people and offered to help her by holding the pan she used. That gave Mother an idea, and she told young Wang Bin to watch carefully how she did it. In time he was given the opportunity to practice giving vaccinations himself, and before long Mother had set him up with his own equipment and supply of vaccine, and she sent him out into the countryside to vaccinate the peasants, who were very susceptible to smallpox. Wang Bin thrived on his new status, being called "Doctor" by everyone, and managed to make a fairly good living for himself. Ultimately he gained so much self-confidence that he began to preach, and of his own volition he volunteered to take over care of the property at Dujiawopu so that he could practice his trade in that area and also preach in the small hall on Sundays.

I have one very strong recollection of Wang Bin that illustrates his extremely retiring and self-effacing nature. On one trip Zhao and I had made to Dujiawopu soon after Wang Bin took over up there, I had bought a load of straw for our cows and was bringing it back in the van. Wang Bin wanted to come back to visit his mother, so he rode with us, lying in the back of the van on top of the straw, which was piled almost to the roof.

It was a very cold day when we left Dujiawopu, so we had the car's engine covered with the goatskin-lined padded hood, and, for the first few miles, left down the little curtain covering the grille. Then, as the engine heated up, I stopped the car to roll the curtain up. It was snowing hard by that time, with a strong wind blowing from behind us, and Zhao, who was riding in the front seat next to me, jumped out to help. When we'd rolled up the curtain, both of us dashed back into the car to get warm again, and we sped off down the dusty road.

We'd gone about five miles or so when I realized that Wang Bin had not joined in the conversation, something that was not particularly unusual for him, but his silence on that occasion had lasted altogether

too long, so I directed some remarks to him. Receiving no answer, I looked over my shoulder only to find that he wasn't there. Both Zhao and I were astonished because we hadn't seen him get out of the car, but obviously he had done so. I turned around and drove back into the storm, and after a few miles we found Wang Bin quietly plodding along the road toward us. I asked him why he had gotten out of the car, and he said he thought something was wrong because both of us had gotten out so quickly, so he followed suit. He didn't know what we were doing at the front of the car, and when we both rushed to get back in, neither of us had seen him in the driving snow. He was so timid that he did't make a sound as we drove away.

Now, several years later, Eva and I were hauling grain on each trip in the new van. In Dujiawopu we were able to load it secretly in the small yard out of the view of prying eyes, and once inside the van the sacks couldn't be seen, so we felt fairly confident. However, we knew we were taking a very big risk every time we did it, and we never took any of the Chinese with us just in case we were stopped and searched. Fortunately, I knew all the side roads and back alleys around Lingyuan, and we were always able to bypass the main north gate and get back into the city unseen.

On the highway it was a different matter, and we feared being stopped, particularly at Reshuitang where, with the reduced number of Japanese in Lingyuan, there were no longer any geisha girls living in the bathhouse, and no caretaker. Ordinarily just one armed Japanese soldier was on duty to guard the place. Those guards seemed to rotate every week or so, and perhaps out of sheer boredom, they seemed to be over-zealous in challenging every vehicle that went by. Supposedly, they were searching for contraband, but I suspected at the time that they also used the opportunity as a means of taking some bribes on the side.

In any event, I timed our return trips from Dujiawopu to pass that point after dark, when the soldier was usually indoors. Every now and then he would hear us coming down the pass or would see our lights in the distance, and we would find him standing by the side of the road waiting to stop us. I was never sure whether he knew it was us, or whether he thought we were some official vehicle and felt he had to prove how diligent and efficient he was and how seriously he took his job. Nonetheless, the first time it happened, the man recognized us for who we were and waved us by without searching the van. The next time, however, a different man was quite belligerent and demanded to see our papers.

I knew instinctively from his attitude and behavior that his next move would be to search the van, whereupon we would be in deep trouble. Knowing the man must be extremely lonely out there by himself, and possibly afraid as well, I took a big gamble. On the spur of the moment I smiled broadly and suggested he ride back to Lingyuan with us and enjoy a night on the town. He hesitated only for a moment or two, but the temptation was too great, and without a word he climbed into the back of the van on top of the sacks of grain and rode into town with us. Quite obviously he could feel what was in the bags. It is conceivable he thought we had permission to carry the grain, but I felt it was more likely that, having committed himself and now being absent from his duty post, he knew we could turn him in if he made a fuss, so he said nothing and we kept him talking until we got back to the city. Of course we had to use the main gate with him along, but he took it on himself to shout out the window to the Chinese guards on duty and they let us by with just a wave.

Since that ruse proved so successful, we did it again on several other occasions when we were stopped. Each time the young soldiers, for whom we felt a measure of sympathy, far from home and in a hostile land as they were, fell into the trap and rode into town with us. Never once were we challenged as to what we were carrying, and none of them reported us. How they managed to get back to their posts by morning I never enquired.

Eva and I ran those grain-carrying trips for months and were able to keep all the needy Christians supplied with food. But sometimes it was very hard work. On one of our return trips to Lingyuan with a heavier load than usual, we ran into a heavy rainstorm at the top of the pass, and the road was so slick at one point that we couldn't climb a very steep incline with our load. I tried again and again but only succeeded in churning up the mud and making matters worse, and fearing we would get bogged down, I decided we had to unload the grain.

With the van almost empty we slid and bounced our way to the top, but then Eva and I somehow had to wrestle ten or twelve heavy sacks of grain, each weighing at least 100 pounds, to the top of the slope. The only thing we could use as a carrying pole was the short handle from the pick. It was well after dark when we finished, and not a soul was on the road. We slipped and fell in the mud time after time, and when we got the last bag to the top of the slope, we were covered with mud from head to foot, soaked to the skin, and completely exhausted, but we enjoyed a feeling of satisfaction over a job well done.

Writing of the mountain pass I am reminded of an incident that occurred in 1939. The road to Dujiawopu was so familiar to us and we had traveled it so many times that we thought we knew every village and hamlet along the route, and had visited most of them at one time or another. However, one day we got a big surprise. For some reason that I have now forgotten, we had to stop on the pass, and we found ourselves opposite a narrow cleft in the rocks where we could look through and see that there was an apparent opening on the other side. A footpath led up through the cleft, and I walked up through it for a short distance, finding after it made a sharp bend that it opened out onto a mountain slope. In the near distance stood a tiny, one-room shack, built entirely of stone except for the thatched roof. Only a door and a window showed, and in the foreground, working on a small patch of ground that had literally been scraped out of the mountain side, was a middle-aged Chinese woman.

We'd never seen the place before and had no idea anyone could be living on the pass. So as not to scare the woman, I called to Eva to join me, and together we approached her. When she heard us speak Chinese and knew we were not the Japanese whom she had seen on her occasional trips to Reshuitang to sell produce, she opened up to us and told us a bit about herself.

As we talked, I heard a man's voice coming from the shack and noticed movement behind the window, where I then made out the head of a young man in his early twenties. We asked the woman if he was her husband, but she told us her husband was dead and the man was her crippled son. We walked over to the house and beheld one of the strangest sights we've ever seen. The young man, who turned out to be 24 years of age, had a perfectly normal head and face, but he had the body and legs of a small child and the arms of a baby, and he stood less than eighteen inches tall. His voice was deep and resonant, so it was an eerie experience to hear him talk. He toddled around the *kang* on his short legs like a one-year-old, and his mother had to lift him onto the floor when he wanted to go outside. Most surprisingly, we found he had somehow taught himself to read, and his shouting to us had been to inquire if we had any books with us. We happily gave him a Bible and a supply of other religious reading materials and spent a pleasant hour talking with those two lonely souls.

Their poverty was beyond description, and no Westerner could possibly conceive of the conditions under which they were living. There was literally nothing of any substance inside the shack. No furniture whatsoever and only an absolute minimum of bedding on the *kang*. They had two or three clay pots near the cooking stove and a small container for water, and that was all. I asked where they got their water and the mother told us there was a mountain spring about a half mile away where she had to go each day to get what they needed. I asked if they were ever bothered by bandits, but she merely smiled, and looking at her son, she said, "With him here looking as he does, they are afraid to bother us; they think he is a devil," whereupon the young man laughed uproariously. For Eva and me it was an experience we shall never forget; the young man with absolutely nothing to live for was cheerful and completely self-assured in our presence, and we left them feeling that we'd been friends for years.

The mother told us they had come to that spot when the boy was a baby, her husband having brought them from Shandong province during the famines of the 1920s. They had discovered the hideaway in the mountains and had built the house themselves, and from then on they had scratched out a living, but she told us with tears running down her face that she dreaded the future and what would happen to her son if she were to die. She felt that it was the famine and her own lack of milk that had caused her child's malformation.

After finding them we made it a point to stop there and visit each time we went by. Our only regret was that we had not made their acquaintance years earlier. Even Zhang Lan-fang, who seemed to know every inch of the countryside, had never been aware of them. On our next trip we took the two colporteurs to meet them, and they, too, visited with them from time to time. The young man with his insatiable appetite for reading welcomed all the reading materials we could give him. On one of our visits mother and son told us they wanted to believe in our God, and they took down the paper idols from the walls and burned them. We knew them for only two years before we were forced to leave the country and I've often wondered what became of them.

With very few exceptions, the Japanese soldiery and officials were so uniformly obnoxious in their behavior toward the Chinese, and to a lesser extent to us, that looking back now over those years, "putting one over" on them became a personal obsession with me. Though extremely dangerous, at the time it seemed the natural thing to do. Certainly for every Chinese in Manchuria it was the daily norm, and they took the most unbelievable risks in circumventing Japanese rules and regulations. Many were caught and severely punished, and others were shot or beheaded, but it in no way deterred the rest, and Eva and I blatantly took much the same sort of risks.

What we found most disconcerting about the Japanese military and police was their total lack of morals and conscience. As we dealt with them from day to day they showed a complete unpredictability of behavior. One moment they would be smiling and friendly and the next they could be in a towering rage, threatening to kill for no reason at all. As I write this, numerous incidents, when we saw the military and government officials at their worst, flash through my mind. And yet we found the civilians generally to be a decent, hard-working group who were almost always friendly and civil toward us, although their behavior toward the Chinese around them was less than cordial.

Illustrative of that was an unusual experience I had a year or so before we were married. One day after returning from a trip I had very sore eyes and feared I might have been exposed to some kind of infection, so I made an eye bath, dissolving permanganate of potash crystals in warm water. I had seen Mother do it many times and thought there was nothing to it. What I didn't know was that there was a certain saturation point at which a given quantity of water would no longer dissolve the crystals that were added to it; I used too many crystals and too little water. As a result, when I used the eye glass to bathe my sore eyes, some of the undissolved crystals lodged in my eyes, where they remained and started to dissolve in the eye fluid. The concentration was so high that it burned my eyes badly and within minutes my eyelids had swollen completely shut. I could see nothing at all and was in extreme pain.

Mother was badly frightened when she saw it and immediately bathed my eyes with olive oil, which turned out to be the correct thing to do. However, I was so afraid I had lost my sight that I got Katie to lead me down to the telegraph office, where I got on the telephone to the next city to our east, Chaoyang, where there was a young Scottish doctor, Dr. Soutter, and his wife, who had joined our missionary group a year or so before.

The telephone system we had was definitely unusual. To place a call I had to tell the telegraph clerk who I wanted to contact and where he lived. The clerk then rang through and gave the name and address of the individual who was to be called down to the telegraph office at that end to take the call, while I sat and waited at my end.

I waited for nearly an hour before Dr. Soutter came on the line. When I told him the problem he asked what we had done to relieve the pain and I told him Mother had used olive oil. He said we had done the right thing, but he wanted me to catch the first train over to Chaoyang so he could look at my eyes for himself.

I had just enough time to dash out to the railway station to catch the afternoon one-car diesel train, and then I had a four- or five-hour ride over to Chaoyang, where I would spend the night. Ironically, just as so often happens when one visits a dentist with a bad toothache and the toothache disappears by the time one reaches his office, just so with my eyes. By the time I was half-way to Chaoyang, they felt completely better, and I could see as well as ever.

Those diesel cars were fast and comfortable and held some fifty or sixty passengers. They had a driver and a conductor and, always, a Japanese soldier to guard against bandits. I found the young soldier a pleasant enough chap, and as we were conversing together, we heard the car's air horn blasting repeatedly. The emergency brakes were applied, and we jolted to a halt. I thought at once that we had been held up by bandits and so did the young Japanese sol-

dier. We both leaped from the back of the car where we had been sitting and rushed up to the front to see what had happened. We discovered that an ox cart was stalled on a level crossing just ahead of us. I walked up with the soldier and found the cart driver, an elderly farmer, was feverishly trying to extricate the ox's front left foot, which had stuck in the groove between the steel rail and the wooden ties used to bridge the gap between the two rails. The ox's hoof was tightly jammed and no amount of pulling could get it out. The Japanese soldier sized up the situation and went berserk. He grabbed his bayonet and started to saw away at the ankle of the poor ox, trying to cut its foot off, while the old man knelt and knocked his head on the ground, begging him to desist.

I knew the soldier would never be able to cut through the bone, and even after several sawing motions with the bayonet it proved so dull that he hadn't drawn any blood, so I wasn't unduly concerned. However, when he started to use the bayonet to chop at the ankle I had to step in and stop him. I grabbed his hand and took the bayonet away from him as he looked up at me in astonishment, ready to punch me in the face. However, I simply grinned at him and told him to let me take care of it. He hesitated, unsure as to whether or not to hit me. But as the engineer continued to blast away with his horn, edging the car up ever closer to us, and the passengers all crowded around watching to see what would happen, I used the point of the bayonet to dig out the wood behind the ox's hoof a little at a time and within a minute or so had him freed. But the Japanese soldier, unable to take his wrath out on me, had turned on the old man and started to beat him unmercifully. Again I stepped in, and again with a big smile on my face I grabbed the fellow's two hands, pointed at the track, which was now free, and dragged him back with me toward the train. For a long time he wouldn't talk to me, he was so angry and embarrassed, but before we got to Chaoyang he had forgotten the entire incident and was smiling once more.

In Lingyuan, there was a fine young man named Li who owned a large and very successful restaurant on East Street, not far from our downtown hall, which he called *Chaoyang Lou*, or "Restaurant facing the Sun." He and his wife had been Christians for a number of years and he made certain that everyone knew it. His two-story restaurant — one of the few two-story buildings in Lingyuan — was decorated with Christian posters and he had Bibles displayed for anyone who wanted to read them. His business continued to thrive, despite the pressures and limitations brought to bear by the Japanese, none of whom ever ate in his or any other Chinese restaurant even though they liked Chinese food.

Li naturally served a tremendous amount of rice in his restaurant. The Japanese themselves, of course, also ate a great deal of rice, so that was one of the last things to be controlled, despite the fact that, with little or none coming in from Free China, most of Manchuria's rice had to be imported from Korea or Japan. However, in 1940 the Japanese decreed that no Chinese would be permitted to buy rice, and all restaurants were notified that, after a given date, they would not be permitted to serve rice with any meal, only white sorghum, one of the commonest of grains, normally only used as animal feed. Sorghum being plentiful, it was not at first rationed, but only the white variety was really palatable. A year later, the Japanese discovered that white sorghum ground into flour made relatively tasty cookies, and the Morinaga company started manufacturing them in large quantities, primarily for their front-line troops. At that time white sorghum, too, was rationed.

For ordinary folk in our area, rice was a great luxury and eaten only at New Year, so the restrictions on buying it mattered little to the average Chinese. However, for the restaurants it was a disaster. Wheat flour had long been rationed, so they were unable to serve steamed bread as a substitute, and who would eat at a restaurant if all they could get was sorghum or millet?

Li came to me with his problem and we discussed it at length. Finally, I went to the chief of police and told him quite frankly that the ruling would put a lot of restaurants out of business. Since a number of them had a sizable stock of rice on hand, unless they were permitted to sell it, they would be unfairly penalized. I suggested to him that they should be permitted to sell what they had, provided they mixed it with a little white sorghum. He thought it over for a minute or two and then said he would issue another order to the effect that existing stocks could be used despite the deadline, but he told me he would send men to inventory the stocks of rice in each of the restaurants to ensure there was no cheating. That was

enough for us. He had given us a loophole and Li and I took advantage of it.

Li made sure he had a good supply of rice in his storeroom to show the police when they went to inspect, and from that point on he complied with the ruling by mixing a little white sorghum with the rice he served, and, like the five loaves of bread and two fish that Christ used to feed the multitude in the Biblical story, Li's stock of rice never gave out. This is how he managed it.

The Japanese had confiscated a large plot of level land near the river on the east side of Lingyuan, and, under the pretense of establishing a model farm to teach horticulture to the Chinese, had brought in a large number of Korean farmers to grow rice on the land, diverting water from the river for irrigation. The displaced Chinese landowners were in no way compensated for their loss and had no legal recourse. Even though is was supposed to be a model farm, apart from being able to view the thriving rice paddies from a distance, no help was given to would-be Chinese growers. The rice that was harvested was all taken by the Japanese for their own use, with the Koreans permitted to keep just enough to feed themselves.

However, the Koreans, just as wily as the Chinese and long experienced in deceiving their Japanese masters, had their own ways of getting around the rules and regulations; and it wasn't long before large quantities of illegal rice could be found on the black market, provided one knew where to look.

Li secretly visited the Koreans one night and arranged to buy a large shipment from them, which he would pick up with my help. He promised them he would repeat his order at frequent intervals whenever they could make more rice available. The Koreans were happy because it saved them from hiding it from the Japanese, whom they hated as much or more than the Chinese did. Additionally they were not required to run the risk of carrying it into the city for sale, so they gave Li a good price. Having made his purchase, Li and I smuggled the rice into the city in the same way Eva and I brought in the millet.

We drove the van out in the dead of night without lights, using back alleys to gain access to the riverbed, from where we worked our way over to the Korean farm. Only after crossing the river, where we were out of sight of the guards at the gates, did we turn on the headlights. The Koreans loaded the van for us, and back to town we went, making two trips that first night, all within the space of a couple of hours.

That part was relatively easy. Back in the city we dared not use the front entrance of the restaurant to unload the rice because it was only a stone's throw from the new police station on East Street. Fortunately, Li had a back gate leading into a narrow alley, which was just wide enough for the van, and, risky though it was, we unloaded the rice there without even any neighbors seeing it. The few night patrols of Japanese and Chinese police normally thought it wisest to stay out of dark alleys, and that was fine with us. Li's trusted staff unloaded the van, and when the two loads of rice-filled straw sacks were moved in, the entire supply was hidden under a huge pile of coal that Li maintained in one corner of his back yard. From there, Li could discreetly withdraw a sack at a time, as needed.

Time and again the Japanese went to inspect Li's storeroom to see why his rice was lasting so long. Little by little Li reduced the amount, but managed to convince the Japanese that it was because of mixing in white sorghum that he was able to stretch out his supply, and the Japanese could find no proof to the contrary. Twice, though, he was taken into custody by the police and locked up on suspicion of having broken the law, and I had to go and bail him out. I recall that one of those times I happened to be in the middle of having a haircut when a messenger came to tell me the news. Without finishing the haircut, I rushed down to the police station. When I interceded for Li with the Japanese, they apparently felt it was not a big enough issue to risk losing what they felt to be my friendship, plus the occasional use of my van, so very reluctantly they let him go.

Eva and I frequently ate in Li's restaurant. Being close to the downtown hall, I often ate lunch there, and Eva would sometimes walk down to join me. Other times, returning late in the evening from our out-of-town trips, we would stop in there for an evening meal. Li was a most gracious host, and although we always insisted on paying, he unfailingly presented us with some special dish he had cooked for us that he wanted us to try.

On one occasion, we were sitting in his restaurant having lunch, when a well-dressed young Chinese sat down at a table near us. I happened to notice that he placed his straw hat upside down on the table, then, after wiping his face with his handkerchief, he draped that over his upturned hat, with one side hanging down over the edge of the table. It struck me as unusual behavior, but I came to the conclusion it was simply his way of drying out his handkerchief, and I gave it no further thought.

The man finished his simple meal before we did, and I was annoyed to see him get up and leave the table without paying. I quickly called Li's attention to it, hoping he could catch the man before he managed to get downstairs and out of the restaurant, but Li just smiled and told me he would tell me about it some other time.

Like many classic Chinese restaurants, the entire lower floor of Li's establishment was occupied by the kitchen, with the upper floor for guests. That is why so many Chinese restaurants have a name ending in *lou*, which means "storied building" and has become synonymous with the word "restaurant." To get upstairs in Li's restaurant, one had to traverse the length of the kitchen, then climb a rickety stairway near the back. The upstairs wooden floor was a patchwork of various-sized boards, with wide cracks between, and the cooking odors from below wafted upward throughout the meal, adding to one's appetite; however, we never went up there without my thinking what a fire trap the place was, and how most of my fellow countrymen would fear to eat in such a place. But it didn't really bother us.

The next time we went there Li asked me if I remembered the man with the hat. He then told me the man was a member of a Chinese secret society, the infamous Green Gang, which the Chinese called the *qing bang*, and which they claimed was the largest of the many Chinese secret societies. It was reputed to have members in all levels of society and was something like the Mafia, involved in every kind of illegal activity, including prostitution, opium smuggling and gambling. Li told me, as others have since, that it meant instant death to any member who revealed the inner secrets of the gang. However, the Chinese are not noted for their ability to keep secrets, so a lot was known about them, and I've met several ex-members of the gang in this country who were not reluctant to tell me about the inner workings of the group and about the many high-ranking government officials who were members.

Li told me that the kerchief in the hat was a sign that was well-known to restaurateurs, and it meant that the owner of the hat was a member of the Green Gang who was short of cash and in need of a meal. Inevitably, some other member of the gang, either working in the restaurant or eating there, would see the signal and pay his bill for him. Otherwise, the restaurant owner would simply pick up the tab and ultimately some other member of the gang would reimburse him. Li told me that he had never lost a penny giving free meals to members of the gang and that it was a frequent occurrence. It surprised me that the man was so well-dressed and yet short of money, and I asked Li if he could possibly have been abusing the system, but Li assured me that none would dare. There were too many members around, and any individual getting a free meal was carefully watched after he left the table. If for any reason he had cheated, and was then seen spending money on something else without having obviously earned it, borrowed it, or otherwise legitimately acquired it, he would be marked for death as an example to others.

Li was well informed on the gang's secrets, and, among other things, he showed me a special knot that members used when tying up their luggage with rope. Any piece of luggage so tied was absolutely safe no matter where it was left. Would-be thieves and baggage-handling coolies would immediately spot the knot and give the piece special handling and protection. Thieves and even beggars had members of the Green Gang in their own organizations and none of them wanted in any way to violate the code of ethics and find themselves involved with the enforcers of the Green Gang. To be a member of the Green Gang in China was a mark of great prestige, and Chiang Kai-shek was well known to be a member, as were most of the other high officials in the Chinese government. Or so it was widely rumored. No one would ever admit to being a member; it was not permitted.

As the year 1940 progressed, we noticed that the Japanese, who had cozied up to the Germans, were now buying quantities of goods from Germany, particularly motor vehicles. Their own production was falling off badly due to a shortage of raw materials, and one of their first imports was a number of large Mercedes-Benz diesel buses. Ten or twelve of those monsters appeared in Lingyuan, and they were used on rural routes by the S.M. Railway people, not so much for the benefit of the Chinese — although they were allowed to ride them — but primarily to keep the roads open and move troops and police forces when Communist guerrillas were reported in any given area.

That didn't in any way discourage the guerrilla bands. Dressed as they were in civilian clothes, usually in black, they readily blended in with the general populace and increasingly seemed to be everywhere, much to the dismay of the Japanese. As Eva and I traveled through the countryside on our daily trips, we came across them frequently, but they left us strictly alone. We had no difficulty recognizing them, as did the puppet police, but the latter were afraid to touch them and simply ignored them.

The *balu*, as everyone now called them, had an incomparable intelligence system and knew exactly who we were and what we were doing and, on several occasions, we became aware that a patient we were treating was a member. Visiting the more remote villages we frequently ran across them, and the Chinese peasants would proudly point them out to us and tell us how good they were to them. Their practice was to first send in two or three well-spoken young men to feel out the villagers and find out what their reaction might be to the *balu* coming in. They would then speak for housing, making certain that no one was in any way put out by their coming. They always showed extreme respect for the elderly — very important to the Chinese — and were quite satisfied to sleep on the floor of an outhouse or shed, never in any way putting their hosts to any inconvenience. That, compared to the cavalier actions of the common Chinese soldiery, impressed the peasants more than anything else.

The Chinese communists, unlike the Japanese, were experts in public relations, and their greatest strength lay in the way they won over the peasant class. The Chinese word for "communism" meant nothing to the average peasant. They looked upon the *balu* as simply nice people who had their interests at heart and who demanded nothing from them. When the Japanese had placed an embargo on all imports of cotton cloth and cotton thread from Free China, the *balu* smuggled it across the border in huge quantities, exchanging it with the peasants for raw opium that the Chinese had withheld from the Japanese. The opium was then smuggled back inside the Great Wall by the guerrillas for sale at huge profits.

Each village where the *balu* lived had a special hiding place for them in case of a police raid, and in a number of places the peasants showed us those hiding places with great pride. They had the utmost confidence in us and knew that we wouldn't give them away. In one village a farmer proudly showed us how he had dug a pit under the cooking stove in his outer room that would hold up to a dozen men. Access to the pit was through the stove itself. The fire box under the wok had been ingeniously covered with a metal plate. When an emergency arose, the wok could be lifted out, the iron plate pulled aside through a slit in the base of the stove, and a hole was revealed that led down into the pit.

In another village, which adjoined a deep ravine about two hundred yards away, another farmer showed me how they had tunneled from a hole dug in his kitchen out to the ravine. At the point where the tunnel emerged into the ravine, a piece of burlap was hung over the exit, and from a distance of ten feet away I was unable to spot it even after I was shown where it was, and not until the burlap moved slightly in the breeze could I distinguish it from the brown earth around it. The hole in the kitchen leading to the tunnel was covered with a "night pot," something that everyone recognized and no one wanted to touch.

As each day passed the *balu* became more daring, and to combat that, the Japanese established small police posts in outlying villages, supplying each one with a telephone so they could call for help if an attack was made on them. In each village where one of the police posts was established, the Japanese simply took over any farmhouse that suited their fancy, kicking the owners out with the usual lack of compensation. Three or four Chinese police would be assigned to each of those village police stations, and for the most part they lived off the people and made a nuisance of themselves.

In Lingyuan I had a very good friend, a Muslim named Han Gui-bao. We'd known the family for years because they owned several carts that we hired every time we went on one of our journeys to the coast, and we'd always found the Muslim drivers to be trustworthy and reliable.

Han Gui-bao and I were about the same age and he frequently visited us. His first visit came about when he lost the tip of one of his little fingers in an argument with someone who bit it off and spat it out. He picked up the severed tip and brought it to the downtown hall, where Father stuck it back on for him and sewed it in place. He completely recovered the use of the finger, for which he continuously showed his gratitude. He was unusually tall and slim, an extremely handsome young man with an open face and ruddy complexion and a most engaging personality. He came at least once a week to visit me, dropping in at all hours and quietly sitting in my study to wait for me if I was busy. I remember the first time he went into my room. On the wall I had a picture of Dan Baillie, a young Canadian missionary who had lived with us for a little over a year while he was learning the language, and whom I had counted as a close friend. Sadly, he developed epilepsy and was subject to violent and most frightening fits at the most unexpected times, and he had been forced to return to Canada. I kept his picture just above my desk.

Dan had been bald, and the first time Han Gui-bao came into my room he spotted the picture. Because of the bald head and the prominent position of the picture, he had thought it was a likeness of the god we worshipped and had promptly gotten down on his hands and knees to knock his head on the floor in obeisance. It was a delicate job to let him know it was only a picture of a friend and not cause him to lose face. Sometimes when Han Gui-bao came we would invite him to stay for a meal, other times I simply gave him tea and cookies, but he always ate what I gave him, trusting me not to serve him anything with pork in it. When I dropped in to visit him in his own home, his mother always made me mutton dumplings, not one of my favorite dishes, but I tried to eat them with gusto in order not to offend them. At Chinese New Year's and other festival days throughout the year, he showered us with gifts. He was a most generous person.

Han Gui-bao had a younger brother, Gui-de, who had become a policeman. He had chosen the profession primarily to avoid being conscripted into the Manchukuo army and because it would keep him near home. He was well aware of how the populace hated the police, and, being a kindly person by nature, when he was assigned to a small village called Wang Zhuang, about nine miles to the west of Lingyuan, he made up his mind that he would show the people there that he, for one, was quite different from the other policemen they knew. Very quickly he made a name for himself as being a benefactor to anyone in trouble. It was he who told me a lot about the Communist guerrillas and of their frequent visits to the villages in groups of two to six men at a time, and of the widespread commerce that was going on between them and the villagers. One night his police post was surrounded by *balu* guerrillas who caught them sleeping and had them all tied up before they knew what was happening.

That same night I was awakened around three in the morning when some geese we kept in the back yard set up such a clamor that we knew something unusual was going on. I went out with a flashlight to investigate, and the birds, intelligent as they were, led me with loud squawks to the back garden wall where the laundry drain was. From there I could clearly hear someone moaning on the outside. I called to ask who it was and Han Gui-de answered me, begging for help.

I quickly got help, and we brought him into the compound. He was indeed a sorrowful sight; his legs from the knees down were a mass of blood and torn tissue, and his feet were swollen so badly as to be almost unrecognizable. He told me he had crawled all the way from Wang Zhuang and he begged me to save his life. He had quite a story to tell.

The *balu*, after tying all four policeman with rope, had called in all the villagers and held a kangaroo court to try the four men. I've mentioned above the excellent intelligence network the *balu* maintained. In that case, they had with them a book in which every alleged misdeed of the four policemen was well documented. In their many trips to the village they had surreptitiously learned all about the four, and now it was judgment day.

After reading off the crimes that each man had committed, the guerrillas asked the villagers what should be done with them. Unanimously, the village folk called for the death sentence. However, in the case of young Han, there were far fewer so-called "crimes" documented against him. His biggest crime had been cooperating with the Japanese and wearing the police uniform, and the villagers told the *balu* that he was a good sort and didn't deserve to die. The *balu* thereupon slit the throats of three of the men (they never wasted any bullets), but they stripped off young

Han Gui-de's uniform, gave him a sound beating, and then hung him from a rafter by his big toes, leaving him there for the Japanese to find in the morning.

Han Gui-de told me he had hung there for perhaps an hour or so, not daring to move for fear the *balu* might still be around. He was nearly unconscious, with his head down and the blood flowing into it, and he was in ever-increasing pain. All the time he knew that when the Japanese came in the morning, as they inevitably would if the regular morning phone call was not made, he would be a dead man. The Japanese would shoot him without trial as being a collaborator or spy. In their thinking, why else would he have been spared by the guerrillas?

Han Gui-de's calls for help to the villagers went unanswered. They had all fled the village fearing that the Japanese would retaliate and burn the village and possibly shoot all of them as well. So, with what must have been superhuman strength and willpower, and in absolute desperation, young Han had used his hands, clawing his way up his body to the point where he could first untie one big toe, leaving his entire weight hanging from the other one, then untie that one, and finally fall to the floor. He could neither stand nor walk, but he could crawl, and crawl he did, all nine miles back to Lingyuan and our back wall.

Just how in the dark of night he was able to identify our wall from all the others that looked just the same was a marvel in itself. Not only did he find it, he found the exact spot in the wall where the laundry drain was, and he was able to shout through that; otherwise the geese would probably not have heard him. While Eva and I cleaned and bandaged his injuries, I sent Katie to fetch his older brother, and before dawn he was smuggled out of the compound and back to the Muslim quarter, where he could be safely hidden from the Japanese and then moved to another city. We never saw him again, but after that episode the older Han couldn't do enough for us, so appreciative was he that we'd saved his brother's life.

After that episode we began to see and hear of many more such instances of the *balu*'s taking justice into their own hands. One day when Eva and I were driving along one of the more well-traveled roads, we turned a sharp corner and came across one of the large diesel buses stalled there, blocking our way. A group of somber-faced and obviously frightened people surrounded it. We got out of the van to find out what had happened, and they led us to the side of the road where they showed us a fresh grave. They told us that six armed guerrillas had stopped the bus and had taken the Chinese driver off. They had then given him a shovel and told him to dig his own grave. When he had dug down about three feet, they tied him hand and foot and then proceeded to bury him alive, after which they left without saying a single word to any of the passengers.

The frightened passengers told us they had stood there helplessly watching the heaving earth as the driver inside his grave had struggled for air, but they dared not dig him out for fear the *balu* were watching, as doubtless they were. Eva and I examined the grave and could clearly see the cracks in the earth formed as the man had thrashed around in his last moments, and although our own first impulse was to dig him out, since there was no further movement, we knew it was too late to do anything to help him. It was a terrible feeling of helplessness.

In the days that followed we heard about and saw many more such instances of bus drivers being buried alive. Finally, the Japanese in desperation were able to maintain bus service only by having a truckload of armed troops accompany each bus, a very expensive way of running a bus line.

Usually the Communists were most careful never to bring any harm to the local peasants, whose goodwill they wanted to maintain at all costs, so when they made those attacks on the buses they usually did so at a spot remote from any village to discourage the Japanese from wreaking vengeance on the villagers.

But there were instances, too, where uncooperative peasants were summarily dealt with by the Communists as a lesson to others. One case was particularly revolting. Five miles south of Lingyuan was a tiny village perched on a rocky hillside at a bend in the Ling river, a spot that was in clear view of the city's South Gate. It was considered by the Japanese to be a very strategic spot, and in order to keep the road open, a small group of puppet Manchukuo soldiers was sent out there every morning to occupy the village during the day. But when night fell, they were withdrawn to the city because it was too dangerous to leave them there. At dusk, as soon as the soldiers left, the guerrillas came in and held the village until dawn when they, in turn, slipped away.

That had been going on for several months. Then one day a young man from the village came into our downtown preaching hall for medical treatment and told me quite a story. He said that both the puppet Manchukuo troops and the *balu* guerrillas had demanded to be fed each day, and that had been going on so long that in the entire village there was nothing left to eat either for them or for the villagers themselves, and many of the villagers had fled. One evening, just after the puppet soldiers had left, his wife broke into tears and started to berate him, and at the same time cursed both the Manchukuo soldiers and the *balu*. She had said to her husband, "We've nothing left to eat but that smoked ham hidden up in the rafters, and the *balu* are sure to find that tonight. Let's you and I eat it now and then kill ourselves before the *balu* come."

At that exact moment a young *balu* guerrilla walked in and sat down on the *kang*. Smiling at both of them, and in a very casual conversational manner, he asked the young man how much it would cost to buy a new wife. The young fellow had replied that one could get a good wife for as little as 300 yuan. The *balu* guerrilla had thereupon reached into his pocket, and, taking out a roll of bills, he counted out 300 yuan and handed it to the young man, telling him to buy himself a new wife forthwith, because his present wife was much too talkative. With that, he shot the young woman through the head.

That was the first such instance we had heard of, but a few years later such events were commonplace. At the time the guerrilla had warned the young man to tell no one else about it or he, too, would be killed. He was to tell the other villagers that his wife had gone home to visit her mother. He secretly buried his wife that night and none of the other villagers knew about it, but he knew he could safely tell me, and he asked me what he should do. There was no advice I could give him except to tell him to stay where he was and make the best of it.

One trip we made in the fall of 1940 stays indelibly in my memory. Eva and I, again traveling alone, had been on the road for several days, trying out new roads a good distance from Lingyuan and visiting places for the first time. The weather had been exceptionally good, and with the harvesting over, the people everywhere had been receptive to our visits.

On our way home we joined a main route that was fairly heavily traveled by Japanese military trucks and an occasional civilian truck. While the road itself was nothing to boast about, as most of it had a washboard surface, it was at least dry. Most of the rivers had either been bridged by the Japanese with low concrete structures, or in some cases where the streams were too wide and where the river constantly changed its course, they had simply laid down an eight-foot-wide concrete causeway about a foot above the river bed, with the water flowing over it, but at least providing a hard bottom for their trucks. Those causeways were, for the most part, quite effective. Frequently, though, when the rivers were in spate, rocks and sand built up on them and the going became treacherous.

At one point on our way we came to a river that normally was quite easy to cross. The crossing point was in a deep, narrow ravine with steep banks on each side. The Japanese had tried several times to bridge it without success and had eventually put in a causeway. But that summer had been very wet, and the causeway had been undermined by the water and washed out. With the causeway no longer usable, we had to cross the river the old-fashioned way.

As we drove down onto a tiny rocky beach near the river's edge, I noticed the water was running very high, with a lot of turbulence in the center of the stream, which indicated large boulders under the surface. The tracks made by passing trucks indicated the crossing point was from the extreme right of the little beach, in a diagonal line through the water, to a point about two hundred yards downstream, where there was another tiny beach on the far side. As a precaution I decided to wade in and see just how deep it was and how firm the bottom was.

Immediately I found myself thigh-deep in a very strong current, and I could barely keep my footing. It was obviously too deep for normal crossing procedures, and, although the sky above was a brilliant blue with bright sun, there was evidence that the water was actually continuing to rise and we knew there had been a rain squall somewhere upstream. However, since there were no telltale bubbles of brown foam on the surface, sure indicators of a rush of flood waters coming down, we set about preparing for a deep-water crossing.

I taped up all the spark plugs with electrical tape, took off the fan belt, covered the dip-stick hole and the air vent from the engine sump, and tied a sheet of

oiled cloth in front of the grille. As an added precaution I took off the air cleaner and taped a cardboard tube upright around the air intake of the carburetor. I then felt we were ready to make a try at it. In the meantime, just to be on the safe side, Eva had piled our bedrolls on top of a case of gasoline we were carrying in the back of the van.

While we were working on the engine, the loud rushing sound of the river drowned the sound of a Japanese army truck going in the same direction as we were. It roared past us, and without a pause, the driver plunged into the river; I was glad of the opportunity to watch its progress. As I watched, it not only bounced around over what were obviously very large boulders, but the water was deeper than I had anticipated, right up to the underside of the truck bed, and our vehicle was at least a foot or more lower. It was obvious we were in for a drenching.

Nonetheless, we decided to risk it. To wait might mean several hours or even days, and as darkness was setting in, I decided to go ahead. Praying for a safe crossing, I shifted into low gear, and with the engine at full throttle and playing the clutch bit by bit to prevent stalling, we headed out into the stream.

In those days I don't think anyone had heard of Disney World and its thrill rides, but even Disney would have had a hard time trying to duplicate the thrills of that short ride across that broiling stream. Within seconds the water in the cab was up around our waists, and the higher floor of the van behind us was eight or ten inches under water. I knew that the engine had to be at least two-thirds submerged, but the comforting sound of its roar continued unabated as we proceeded forward, and in fact our forward motion with the river surging behind us created an eddy in front of the engine that doubtless kept the water from going right over the top.

We bounced over the unseen boulders and then, crossing as we were at an angle, reached midstream, and the strong current pushing against the blunt rear of the van started to swing the back end down and around to the left. I suddenly realized that I had no traction at all in the rear wheels. The half-empty gasoline tank was so buoyant that the rear end of the van was actually up off the river bed and floating. It became a struggle to keep the front wheels on course and we could do nothing but hope for the best. I feared that the current would turn us sideways, in which case the van could overturn, or we could be turned completely around, or, facing upstream in that depth of water, the engine would be immediately swamped.

However, between the force of the river current pushing us and the occasional contact of the spinning rear wheels with submerged boulders, we continued our wild ride generally on course, praying all the way, and never in my life was I so thankful as when our front wheels finally made the opposite bank with the engine still faithfully running, although greatly overheated. Our smaller van would never have made it, but the extra height and weight of the newer van had made all the difference.

Another incident on that same trip comes to mind. Earlier I wrote of geese that we kept as watchdogs and for an occasional Sunday dinner, and I am reminded that from the time I was a boy, from year to year as the wild geese were flying over in early spring and late fall, I used to notice a man who regularly passed our front gate at those times of the year carrying, at each end of his shoulder pole, baskets filled with live wild geese, all of them appearing healthy and undamaged. Obviously he had not shot them, but how had be managed to catch them alive? It puzzled me so much that one year I ran out into the street and stopped him and asked how he did it. He merely smiled and told me he "had a way."

While on our trip into new territory we were about twelve miles from home in a small valley where there were three villages we had never previously visited. In one of them an elderly man came up to me with a badly swollen face and asked me to pull a tooth for him.

In those days there were very few dentists in our part of China, and in Lingyuan only one, and he shied away from pulling teeth unless he absolutely had to. Father and I, as was the case with most of our fellow missionaries, were constantly being called upon to pull badly rotted teeth, so almost all of us had become fairly well practiced in the art. My father had a rusty old pair of forceps he had picked up in some second-hand market, and he used them with great dexterity. I, on the other hand, used the pliers that came in the tool kit of the van.

We had, of course, no novocaine, but my patients seemed to have a very high threshold for pain and expected to suffer somewhat. They naturally made a lot of noise for the benefit of the usual crowd of onlookers. The problem that always arose was keeping the patient's head immobilized while I pulled with all my strength. The poor sufferer tended to follow the pulling and come along with me. I finally worked out a method that always worked well. The ideal way, I found, was to have the patient lie flat on his back on the *kang*, with his head and shoulders on the low windowsill. I then stood outside the opened window, and while two men held the patient's head and shoulders in position, I pulled the tooth.

The old gentleman's teeth were far gone, so in no time at all I had pulled the offending one — much to his relief. He wanted me to pull still more, but I told him to wait until they really hurt him and then he should come to Lingyuan, where I would do the job. It was at that point that I thought I recognized him and asked if he were not the man who used to come into the city with wild geese for sale. With a broad smile he admitted that he was. I then asked if he remembered coming into the city some years before and having a small foreign boy run out and ask him how he caught the geese. He replied that he did remember. I asked if he would now tell me his secret, and I promised not to reveal it to anyone who might compete against him. He put his head back and laughing heartily said, "Come with me and I'll show you. There's nothing to it."

I followed him for about a third of a mile outside the village to the bank of a small stream where, in a patch of swampy ground overgrown with tall reeds, he showed me a blind that he had built. It was just a deep hole in the ground near the edge of the swamp, in which he could stand upright, with a screen of reeds in front through which he could peek. He told me that every spring and fall when the geese were passing, that was one of their favorite feeding grounds, and he would hide in the blind just before they landed at dusk.

He then told me that the geese after feeding would go to sleep, but, intelligent as they were, they always had one of their number stay awake and stand guard. Just how he had learned that he didn't say. However, he went on to tell me that he would wait until all the geese had settled down for the night and were fully asleep, and then he would quietly light a stick of incense and wave it gently in the air over the blind for a few seconds and immediately withdraw it. The sentry goose, seeing the tiny pinpoint of light, would set up a clamor that woke the entire flock, but not seeing anything to alarm them, the other geese would give the sentry goose a couple of pecks and then go back to sleep.

The old man said he would wave the lighted incense stick like that three or four times, and get the same result each time. Eventually the flock would become so annoyed at being awakened for no apparent reason, they would thoroughly chastise the sentry goose so that ultimately, when the old man again waved the lighted incense stick, the sentry would no longer make a sound for fear of being pecked again.

The old man then laughed some more and said that was all there was to it. He added that at that point, he would quietly get up and steal around the blind to where the geese were sleeping and would grasp the sentry goose by the neck to still any cries it might make. Then he would manage to catch ten or more before their flapping wings awoke the rest of the flock and they flew away in the darkness. He told me he had been catching geese alive for over 20 years, but had now passed on the trick to his son.

The year 1940 ended on a very somber note for us. We had received word several times during the course of the year, from both the American and British consulates, that the situation was deteriorating and all who could, should consider leaving the interior for the coast. A few colleagues of ours with children had done so, but most of us had been able to continue our work with only minor interference from the Japanese, and we decided to stick it out as long as we could.

We had received intermittent messages from our good friend Reginald Sturt, whose work was about 100 miles north of us on the borders of Mongolia, and he told of continual harassment by the Japanese. It became quite obvious they wanted him out of that area, which was considered strategic and had great military significance for the Japanese. But for nearly three months we had received no word from him, and we worried for his safety.

Mr. Sturt had married for the third time, and with his wife and a young New Zealander, Douglas Broughton, had been traveling in his motor coach over the Mongolian steppes doing what they had been doing for years — visiting the Mongols wherever they could be found. Suddenly, a friendly Chinese merchant who had been traveling in that area came

down to Hada, which was Mr. Sturt's home base, and brought word to the Christians there that Mr. and Mrs. Sturt and Doug Broughton had been arrested by the Japanese as spies and had been locked up in a Chinese jail for over a month, together with the two Chinese Christians who had been accompanying them on their travels. For 35 days the five of them had been locked in individual cells with no personal possessions except their meager bedding, eating the same food as the common prisoners.

There were no other Western missionaries in Hada when the message arrived, but the Chinese Christians there quickly got word to James Duthie in Chengde, and several of us signed a telegram, which we sent to a high Japanese official named Kurimoto who had shown himself friendly in the past, asking for his intervention in the case. Within a day or two Mr. Kurimoto flew to the city of Linxi where the three were in prison, and he successfully persuaded his fellow Japanese there to at least allow them out on parole until the matter could be fully investigated. They were released from jail and permitted to live with a Chinese Christian family while charges against them were completed. Weeks later, charged with being spies in the employ of the British, they were flown to another province and handed over to the Japanese army.

That move was somewhat of an improvement insofar as living conditions were concerned, but for a period of several weeks they had to appear in court every day and were forced to stand for hours while they were interrogated. Ultimately they were allowed to return to their home in Hada for Christmas, although they were told they would have to return for further hearings after the New Year.

We were cheered by one incident that December. A young farmer came in one Sunday morning with his wife and two small children and told us he wanted to be a Christian because he knew that the God we believed in was very powerful. We had no recollection of ever having seen him before, and we asked him what he meant. He told us he had been in the city a few days previously and had bought some Scriptures at the downtown hall. On his way home to his village, his donkey had bolted when a Japanese army truck came up behind him, and he had started to chase the donkey across the fields. The Japanese, mistaking him for a bandit, started shooting at him, so he stopped and held up his hands. Instead of shooting him on the spot without further questioning, as was their usual procedure, they first searched him, and finding the Scripture portions sticking out of his pocket, they decided he couldn't be a bandit, so they let him go.

In earlier chapters I wrote of my good friend Zhao who used to travel so widely with me. The above incident of the donkey bolting reminds me of a scene that stays vividly in my memory and illustrates the kind of person Zhao was. He and I were traveling in the first Dodge van one wintry day, and after driving for some distance along one of the sunken roads that abounded in our part of China, we came to the end of the defile and a steep ramp that brought us up to the level of the farmland around us. Because of the narrowness of those sunken roads, only vehicles used them, and all other traffic, including pedestrians, used the footpaths that ran along the upper edges of the twelve- to fifteen-foot banks on each side.

As we came up out of the defile and reached the level land above, it so happened that simultaneously along the footpath, a young farmer leading a donkey with his young wife and tiny baby on it reached that point at the exact time we did. It is probable that they had either just been visiting her mother's home to show off the baby or else were on their way there. In any event, as so often was the case, the woman was sitting on the donkey's rump as near to the tail as she could get for a smoother ride. She was balanced, with her legs crossed and her feet tucked under her to keep them warm, and the baby was lying asleep in her lap.

As we drove up out of the defile, the terrified donkey leaped forward and raced off across the plowed fields with the young man in pursuit. We had come abreast of them at the exact moment when the donkey bolted and parted company with the woman and her baby. For a fraction of a second I saw the unusual sight of the young woman, seemingly suspended in mid-air as though levitated, sitting bolt upright in the exact position she had been in on the donkey. Then, like a stone, she dropped straight to the ground. But the sight of her sitting upright in space is imprinted on my brain like a photograph. The whole thing happened in just an instant, and she sat there on the ground as though in a daze, still in her upright position and with her legs crossed, not aware of what had happened to her. There was also a strange foreign vehicle alongside her just a few feet away.

It took me only seconds to stop, but even before I had done so, Zhao was out of the van and running toward her to see if she was all right. Fortunately, she had landed on relatively soft ground and was unhurt, and the baby didn't even wake up.

Cut Paper Art. "Niánnián Rúyì" — A charm to provide satisfaction every year.

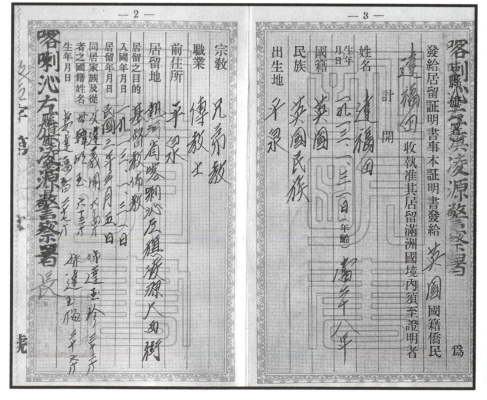

Residence Certificates for Manchukuo

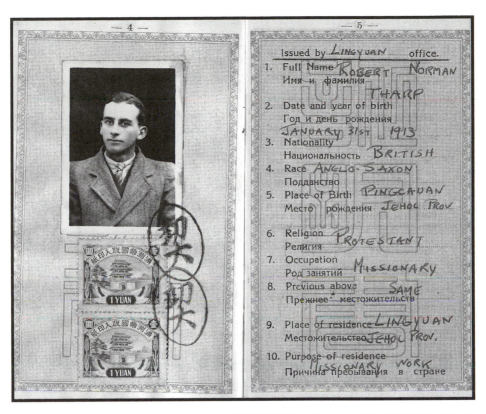

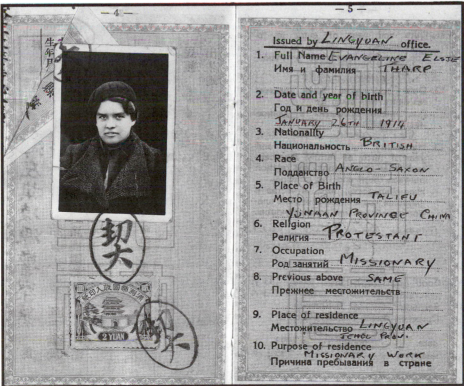

Note: 2 yuan revenue tax stamps collected from each resident.

Fuyintang
Gospel Hall Downtown

Inside Libaitang — Gospel Hall
(church) A Sunday school class

Paper gods being carried to the graveyard.

The old lady who had the crippled son.

The home of the old lady with the crippled son.

掛羊頭，賣狗肉

Gua yang tou, mai gou rou.

Hanging up a sheep's head,
but selling dogmeat.
(Doing something under false pretenses.)

- Chinese Proverb.

Chapter Twenty-Seven

Pearl Harbor

Nineteen forty-one dawned like any other year, and bleak as was the news from the battlefronts in Europe, Africa and the Atlantic, little did we, or anyone else, know what momentous events would occur before the year was out. With the arrest of the Sturts still fresh in our minds, it was as though a dark shadow hung over us, and we could only wonder if the same charges might not be brought against all of us. It was not until March, when the Sturts and Doug Broughton were cleared of all charges and allowed to return to their work, that we finally breathed more easily. In the meantime we tried to go about our normal activities, and in general we were not harassed by the Japanese any more than usual, at least for the first part of the year.

The Sturt incident, however, did not go unnoticed by the American and British consular authorities. At the time they couldn't do much about it, but subsequently they sent letters to all their nationals warning them of the possibility of hostilities and strongly advising them to leave the country as soon as possible. In fact, over the next few months we received three or four such warnings. We were told of evacuation ships that would be leaving on certain dates, and were advised to take advantage of them. A few of our colleagues did so, but we, as a family, after giving it long consideration, decided to stay on. We reasoned that no matter where we went, we were likely to run into a similar or even worse situation should a world conflagration break out.

Things were basically so peaceful in Lingyuan that we were perhaps lulled into a false sense of security. However, as a matter of record, two of the evacuation ships that we could have been on left so late in the year that they were caught up in the hostilities. One was reportedly bombed and sunk, the second was stopped by the Japanese, and everyone aboard was taken to the Philippines, where they were interned for the duration of the war. So in the end, and despite the vicissitudes along the way, everything turned out favorably for us, although at the time there were many occasions when we wondered if we had made the right decision.

The large number of sick people dependent on us was one of the most compelling reasons for our decision to stay on. Among the sick was my older sister, Ruth, whose health had deteriorated so badly that she was, to a large extent, confined to bed. Her diet was a big problem. One of the few things she could tolerate was condensed milk, and that was in increasingly short supply. It had been many months since we had been able to purchase any imported brands of milk, but the Japanese Morinaga Company produced condensed milk in cans that were identical to the American brands, even to the tiny cap one had to pull off in order to get to the milk, and it was of excellent quality. However, the Japanese would only allow sales of the milk to families with sick babies, and then only with a prescription from the local Japanese doctor. Failing that, one had to have some "pull" with the Japanese authorities. I contacted the doctor and managed to get a small supply, but the outlook for any more was bleak. I put out the word very quietly that we would pay a good price for any quantity available from anyone who had it for sale, and here and there we managed to get an occasional can from some family whose baby had needed the milk at one time but had either died or recovered before its allotment of milk had been used up, and they had a can or two left over.

That went on over a period of months, then late one night, during harvest time, a strange thing occurred. We were just about to go to bed, when Katie, the gateman, came up to tell me that a man was out in the front street selling straw and specifically asking to see me. Although Katie had told him it was too late in the day and that he should come back the following morning, the man had insisted that when I saw the straw I would most certainly want it, and he refused to leave. I was intrigued and told Katie to bring the man into the back yard.

When I went out with a flashlight to look at the straw, the man hissed at me, "No light, no light." The thought crossed my mind that perhaps he didn't want to be recognized or was afraid the Japanese might see him talking to me, although he was certainly breaking no law in selling straw. In any case, I turned off the light, but in the brief glimpse I caught of his load of straw it looked the same as any other straw we had bought, and I wondered what was so special about it.

As I got close to the man, he grabbed one of my hands and thrust it down into the center of one of the bundles of straw, and I felt the unmistakable shape of a can of condensed milk. That was indeed something I wanted, and I asked how many he had. In all he had eleven cans hidden in the straw, and he wanted five Manchukuo yuan for each of them, a prohibitive price. But for us they were worth their weight in gold, so I bought them from him without further question. I went to fetch the money, and when I returned, he threw in the straw for free and scurried off without saying a further word.

I took the milk into the house, and when I looked at them under the light, I realized why the man had been so insistent that I turn off the flashlight. The cans were covered with rust and dried mud, and the labels were almost completely illegible. However, there was enough of some of them left to determine they were a very well-known American brand. On one of the labels I was able to decipher the date of manufacture, shown in perforations, and I discovered the cans were almost as old as I was, having been manufactured in 1919, some twenty-two years earlier. Obviously they had either been buried for some considerable length of time or had been stored in a damp place. The cans looked so bad I thought the milk inside would be spoiled. I came to the conclusion that I definitely had been had.

Nonetheless, we cleaned the mud off the cans and opened one. Not surprisingly, the contents not only would not pour, but the color, instead of being a creamy white, was a dark caramel brown. I tried to dip some out with the handle of a spoon only to discover it was almost as hard as rock and completely unyielding. After I peeled away the entire can, the milk came out in one solid block, and eventually, by hacking at it with a cleaver, I managed to break off a small piece.

We unsuccessfully tried to melt it in hot water. I then tried cold water, but the hard lump of milk just sat there. Completely frustrated, I left it sitting in the water and went to bed.

Miraculously, when we looked at it in the morning, it had not only dissolved, but had reverted to the right consistency and color. Despite that, quite frankly, we were afraid to try it for fear it might poison us. I called in one of the dogs and let him lap it up. He survived and over the next several months those cans of milk made the difference between life and death for Ruth.

Some years later when we returned to the United States, I wrote an account of the incident and sent it to the milk company concerned. We were sorely in need of money at the time and I thought that a testimonial of that kind might be worth something to them for advertising purposes. Their reply was a brusque brush-off. They simply gave me the name of the firm that did their advertising; the latter declined to accept the story. Possibly they didn't believe a word of it, but the facts are exactly as I have stated them.

Toward the end of April 1941, while the Sturt affair was still very fresh in our minds, an incident occurred involving one of our colleagues, Leonard Steel of Chengde, which reminded us of how volatile the situation was. One afternoon I received an urgent telegram from him, sent from Peking, asking me to meet him at the Great Wall crossing at Gubeikou, on the Chengde-Peking road. He needed me to drive his car from there for him. The only other information he gave me was that he had been stopped and forced to leave his car there because he didn't have a valid Manchukuo driver's license. It was all rather mysterious, but I left right away by train for Chengde; from there I caught a bus and was in Gubeikou by noon of the next day, getting there before Steel arrived from Peking.

I located the inn where Steel had left his car, a Buick sedan that he had purchased used two years earlier and which he had been using in Chengde ever since, and started to prepare it for the road by pumping up two soft tires. I then thought it might be advisable to pay a courtesy visit to the local Japanese officials, to perhaps forestall any unpleasantness when it came to driving the car away.

It turned out that the only Japanese there were several members of the Kempeitai and a more unpleasant bunch of sadists it would be hard to find anywhere. I stayed clear of them if at all possible, but in that case I had no alternative.

All Japanese officials expected everyone to approach them hat in hand, showing extreme servility and humility and bowing low, something I refused to do out of principle. So, despite my inward misgiv-

ings, I adopted my usual outward show of confidence and marched in the front door of the ramshackle house in which they had set up their office. I found two Japanese officers there, one standing by the door and the second sitting behind a desk. I grabbed the hand of the first man and shook it vigorously and then did the same to the man behind the desk, all the while smiling broadly and talking a blue streak in English. Then I perched on the corner of the desk and put my hat down on the desk beside me, (a calculated discourtesy) and, in English launched into a lengthy tale as to why I was there.

For a few moments both of them stared at me blankly in a state of shock. Here was this strange foreigner bouncing into their room, and neither of them could understand a word of what he was saying. With no interpreter present, they had no way of communicating with me except in Japanese. For the moment I pretended not to understand what they were saying. The man behind the desk, who turned out to be the senior officer, muttered something to his partner to the effect that I was an ignorant oaf without manners, and my sitting on his desk and putting my hat on his desk proved it. He added that all of my kind deserved only to be shot.

I gave no indication of having understood him, and, talking all the while without giving him an opportunity to say anything to me directly, I produced my Manchukuo passport, handed it to him, and then pulled out my Manchukuo driver's permit. The way he looked at the permit gave me the impression that it was probably the first of its kind he had ever seen, despite the fact that he had demanded one from Leonard Steel. In fact, it was the very first occasion I had ever had to show my permit to anyone after having acquired it several years previously.

The officer looked at me for a few minutes, then, as was typical of the Japanese military, he started to bellow at me in Japanese in a highly discourteous manner, using what passed for expletives in the Japanese language, but I knew it was largely to try and restore his dignity in front of his underling. I paid no attention and merely kept on smiling and nodding. When he paused for breath I addressed him politely in his own language, thanked him for all he had done for me, and taking my passport and driver's permit from his hand, I shook his hand firmly, picked up my hat and started to walk out of the door.

The Japanese have very few expletives in their language, and they rarely use those unless they feel they have good reason to do so. Now, realizing I had understood all that he had said to his underling, he found himself in a very embarrassing situation. I gathered that he had come to the conclusion that he had seriously misjudged me, and that with such an impressive driver's license, I was a person deserving of respect. He did the only thing he could to restore his dignity. He leaped to his feet and saluted me, bellowing to his companion to do the same, then abjectly apologized for his behavior and begged me to overlook it. I slapped him on the back and told him to forget it. My bluff had worked, and from then on he was polite and helpful. He walked over to the inn with me, and when Leonard Steel arrived, he even apologized to him for having caused him any inconvenience. I knew that if I ever had cause to go that way again, I would have him as a friend. However, Steel told me that when he had been stopped in the first instance, the man had been most threatening and intimidating, and he had feared he would be arrested.

Steel, not surprisingly, had never heard of the need for a driver's permit. It was typical of the way the occupying force did things. They came out with so many rules and regulations that they themselves frequently lost count of them and, after a few weeks, forgot to enforce them. And, of course, the irony of the situation was that Steel was leaving Manchukuo with his car when he was stopped, and in Free China, across the border marked by the Great Wall, he would have had no need of a permit to drive. Steel's mistake was in stopping in Gubeikou for lunch. The Japanese officer had seen him and had had to demonstrate his authority in some way; had Steel driven straight on through, nothing would have happened.

While on the trip to pick up Steel's car, I had noticed that the new railroad between Chengde and Peking was almost completed, and a couple of months later it was opened for service. I needed some parts for the van, so Eva and I decided to take a trip down to Tientsin by way of Peking and try out the new line. It proved to be a most interesting experience.

We had to change trains in Chengde, staying there overnight and leaving early the next morning. At that time it was almost a full day's journey from Chengde to Peking, but I hear that nowadays it can be done in about four hours. The Communist regime has built a large number of railroads over the past 40 years since they took over in 1949, and have modified some existing lines. In fact, from maps I have seen showing the Peking-Chengde line and a timetable showing the stations en route, very few of the original station names remain. That particular line has quite obviously been redesigned and routed over a different route than the one first built by the Japanese.

When the Japanese first built that branch of the railroad, they simply paralleled the motor road they had built earlier. They needed the road to protect the railway. The motor road had originally been built along the old cart road that wound its way through the mountains. When I first traversed it in my van in 1934 it had been described by a writer of the time as "the worst motor road in the world." But at one time it had been the Imperial Highway, built exclusively for the emperors to travel on. Huttner, a member of Lord Macartney's expedition in 1790, gives this description:

"The Emperor's Road from Peking to Jehol is 418 li long (139 English miles), and is fully repaired twice a year. It runs right through the main traffic routes, and is ten feet broad, and is made of a mixture of sand and clay so evenly tamped and well packed that it becomes as hard as cement. That Emperor's Road is as smooth as the floor of one of our drawing-rooms. It is constantly swept, not only to remove leaves but also the smallest grain of dust. On either side there are reservoirs every 200 paces, from which often with great trouble the water is carried to dampen the road. Probably in the whole world there is not a more beautiful road than this one when it has been cleaned in readiness for the Emperor's journey to Tartary. Watch posts are set up along the road, and no one is allowed to step on it until the Emperor has passed."

Heading south in the train, we approached Gubeikou, the pass through the Great Wall, which was the highest point on the route. The upward climb was relatively brief, and we climbed only about 400 or 500 feet. But when we came to the Great Wall, the train passed through a breach in the wall that the Japanese engineers had hacked out close by the original gateway, and we saw spread out before us a marvelous panorama, with the terrain dropping abruptly for some 3000 or 4000 feet to the plains below, a sight that never failed to excite me.

From that point downward the Japanese had accomplished a remarkable engineering feat. They had copied an approach pioneered in the Swiss Alps and had constructed the railroad by means of a series of zigzag traverses, or switch-back "steps," all the way down the mountain slopes. How many there were I have now forgotten, but it was a slow, tedious process, going down and coming back up on our return. Each traverse dropped only a relatively few feet and ended in a tunnel that had an entrance but no exit. The train would enter the tunnel, a switch in the track behind it would be thrown and the train would then back down another traverse to a second tunnel. It would come out of that one and on down to a third, and so on, back and forth all the way to the bottom. The entire trip from top to bottom took us just over two hours if I remember correctly.

On our return trip Eva and I decided to travel second class. We found ourselves in the same car with 20 to 30 high-ranking officers of the Manchukuo puppet army who were returning from the front for a conference in Chengde. Apart from them, we were the only other occupants of the car. Eva and I sat there luxuriating in the soft seats and enjoying the scenery, but before long I began to notice the conversations around us.

In front of us, and across the aisle, was a group of about eight young officers who were exchanging details of their recent battles on various fronts in China against Chinese troops. It was most illuminating to hear them talk. From their stories, it was not at all surprising that the Japanese had run into a stalemate in their campaign to conquer China. Each battle front was basically the same story. The officers told how the so-called "battles" had been fought in their particular areas, the essence of it being that there was a mutual understanding. When a battle was joined it was usually at night. Both sides fired an immense amount of artillery shells and rifle ammunition into the air, making a horrendous noise to impress their officers, who on the side of the Manchukuo troops were Japanese. While all that was going on, soldiers on both sides surreptitiously exchanged gifts. The Chinese would hand over opium and silver dollars,

while the Manchukuo troops passed over the latest in Japanese weaponry and all the ammunition the other side could use. The young officers talked openly, and they laughed a great deal at the expense of the Japanese.

In order not to appear to be listening to them I held an open book in front of my face. However, at one point, something apparently was said that amused me and I must have smiled. One of them must have seen it, because he suddenly exclaimed and that was followed by a sudden hush. The young officers whispered among themselves, looking at each other and then over at me. Finally, one of them came over to me, saluted me and then bowed, and politely asked if I had understood what they were saying. When I acknowledged that I had, he invited me to join them, and in great agitation, all of them begged me to please keep their confidence and not pass on to the Japanese what I had heard; otherwise, their lives would be in great danger. When I assured them that their secret was quite safe with me and that I had no love for the Japanese either, they relaxed. Including Eva and myself in their conversation, they filled us in on numerous other details of how the war with China was being carried on. The incident further pointed up to us why the Japanese had been so unsuccessful in colonizing Manchukuo and winning the hearts of the people. If the army, in which they had placed so much trust, could act that way, what chance had they? The Chinese would remain essentially Chinese no matter who was in power or for whom they worked.

For the first few months of 1941 we were limited in our travels only by the availability of gasoline. We continued our regular visitation of the cycle of markets within a 40- or 50-mile radius around Lingyuan. Earlier we had been required by the Japanese to notify them where we were going each time we went out, but they had become lax and for many months had not insisted on it. But as the weeks went by they again began to tighten the screws, scrutinizing our every move and insisting on detailed advance notice of our trips. That became extremely annoying, particularly when, on reaching our destination, we were again hassled by them.

In May 1941 a group of us left Lingyuan in the van to attend the annual Daiming (Great Brightness) fair, where a Christian testimony had been presented each year for at least 20 years. Father had gone there every year for as long as I can remember, and I had visited it every year after 1934. On that May 1941 trip there were seven of us in the party: my father, Herbert Brewster from Chaoyang, three Chinese preachers, and, finally, Eva and myself. We carried with us thousands of copies of Scripture portions and tracts and other literature in both the Chinese and Mongol languages, so we had a heavy load, but the big van took it all with ease.

The fair was held at a fairly large village about 70 miles northwest of Lingyuan, a two-day journey by cart or on horseback in the old days. But with the van we could make it in one day with relative ease, although the road was one of the most difficult in the area to negotiate. It was actually the main road from Lingyuan to Hada, but it was so rugged the Japanese had not attempted to widen it for motor vehicles, and few Japanese trucks ever attempted it, preferring to go around on a longer route by way of Chaoyang.

The site of the fair was at the foot of one of the tallest pagodas in Manchuria, one that, although well over 1,100 years old, was still in a remarkable state of preservation. It stood within the ruined earthen ramparts of a city enclosing over 30 square miles. At one time the city was the capital of a noted Tartar general and robber king, Li Chin-wang, who established his rule over the Mongol tribes of that region over a hundred years before the Norman conquest of England.

The fair was held in the lunar fourth month, just after spring planting and before the seeds had sprouted, so the farmers could attend. Upward of 100,000 people swarmed to the site from as far away as Mongolia, many of them traveling for several weeks to get there. Merchants and entrepreneurs of every kind came from all over the province. The majority were Han Chinese, but there were large numbers of Muslims, and about 20 percent of those attending were Mongols dressed in their traditional costumes, while Manchus were also well represented. From time to time we even saw Tibetans.

Daiming was primarily a religious festival. The daily activities centered around the pagoda, where thousands of devotees paraded around its base in a counterclockwise direction, a distance of 480 feet. Many of them burned incense and turned the numerous prayer wheels as they went. Others, more devout, prostrated themselves after each step, knocking their heads on the hard-rock paved surface, then standing

up and taking another step and repeating the process. The prayer wheels, in varying sizes, were usually in the shape of cylindrical drums, standing on end, from a foot or so in diameter to larger ones three or four feet across. They were made of wood, richly carved with religious figures, and brightly painted, with Tibetan writings in gold leaf on most of them. Each was filled with thousands of slips of paper on which prayers were written; each turn of the wheel by a worshiper meant a massive outpouring of prayer on the part of the person doing the turning. Most of the wheels were sadly in need of lubrication and the predominant noises around the base of the pagoda were the loud squeaking of the wheels and the audible prayers of the Mongol worshipers and the lama priests repeating the prayer *Om Mani Padme Hum* — "Hail, Jewel in the Lotus." In addition sacred flags flew everywhere, each embellished with its quota of prayers or some sacred thought. The worshipers believed that each time a flag fluttered in the breeze, a prayer went forth.

The pagoda, octagonal in shape, stood on a 20-foot-high mound, and a huge representation of Buddha on the front face, beautifully carved and colored, stood high above the people's heads. Nearby was a large Buddhist temple, and after the worshipers had made their rounds of both the pagoda and the temple, they settled down to enjoying the excitement of the fair. There were activities of every sort calculated to fleece the peasants of their hard-earned money. In the village were gambling houses, opium dens and brothels, but most of the excitement and activity was out on the wide-open plain between the pagoda and the village: puppet shows, acrobats and magicians, shadow plays at night and free entertainment provided by the traditional outdoor opera, performed on a stage facing the temple.

The fair was also a businessman's dream. It was well organized, with tents and stalls of every kind laid out in long aisles. There was one long aisle of food stalls, another of "doctors," acupuncturists, and medicine sellers. One aisle held dozens of fortunetellers of every conceivable kind: card readers, hand readers, face readers and others who just listened to the client talk, and also were, in effect, "mind readers." On other aisles were hundreds of stalls selling every conceivable commodity to tempt the peasants, and there were even pawnshops and itinerant repairmen of every kind, including blacksmiths. For everyone concerned it was a wonderful way to start the year. It was also a grand holiday, particularly for the womenfolk, who got out so seldom to anything of that nature and who were there in the thousands, dressed in all their colorful finery.

On the fair's perimeter, and in the yards of the inns were livestock markets, and every year dozens of small Mongolian ponies were for sale, still as wild as when captured, with their cowboys looking after them and taming them on the spot for prospective buyers by biting the horses' ears.

Of course, sleeping accommodations were at a premium, and there was no way the inns could house everyone. All the village householders made rooms or else space in a straw shed available for a price. But the great majority slept outdoors, in makeshift tents made with *shujie* mats or with cloth awnings stretched over farm carts, many even sleeping under their carts.

To get to Daiming from Lingyuan we first headed north to Reshuitang, then a mile or so past that point we took the left-hand fork at the junction point where the Dujiawopu road began. Immediately the road climbed steeply through narrow rocky defiles, and I kept sounding the horn, hoping to ensure that anyone coming down the pass would wait until we reached the top. Negotiating that pass took the best part of an hour.

The fair normally lasted about 10 days, and we usually got there a day early to make sure we could find a room in one of the three inns in the village. Each time we went we had an adventure of some sort on the road, and they usually came toward the end of the journey, after we had negotiated all the mountains. Daiming lay in a wide and verdant valley that was perhaps 40 miles long. As we came down out of the mountains, in the far distance, some 20 miles away, we could clearly see the top of the pagoda.

As we wound our way through the fields and small villages, we could see columns of people, animals and vehicles pouring down from the hills to the right and left of us and joining the road we were on. When the roads were muddy, it created problems in the areas where the roads were deeply sunken below the level of the land, and much of the road was like that.

Being springtime, there were occasional rain squalls, which turned the roads into liquid mud, and when that didn't happen we would come across areas where the frost was still coming out of the ground. Although a person or an animal could walk across those areas without trouble, a vehicle of any weight would break through the thin, hard crust and end up in a deep bog. Many times we ran afoul of that problem, and I recall one instance when we had to cut down a tree to use as a fulcrum to lift the rear end of the vehicle sufficiently for us to insert our boards under the rear wheels. Usually there was no way to spot the danger areas in advance unless some other vehicle had broken through.

At one place, the road crossed a deep but rather narrow ravine, with a running stream at the bottom about five feet wide. The first year I went up to Daiming in the old van, when we reached that ravine, I watched a cart negotiate it ahead of us and saw that although the water wasn't too deep, the mud beneath the water was two feet deep. But I thought I would be able to make it through with no trouble.

The banks on each side were very steep, so it was basically a slide down the slope to the stream, then a dash through the water and mud and a fast climb up the other side. However, going down, the drop-off from the hard bank into the stream was so abrupt that, although my front wheels made it across and were out of the water, the tail end of the car lodged on the bank when the back wheels dropped down into the water, and we found ourselves stuck. It was absolutely impossible to get a jack under the back end, and we faced the necessity of finding rocks to place under the wheels in the mud to gradually raise the vehicle. It looked like a lengthy project.

Fortunately, just as we were about to start, a column of heavy freight carts carrying grain from one of the large wine distilleries in the area came up behind us. We had passed them earlier and had remarked on what very fine animals were harnessed to the carts. They, too, were heading for the fair and were in more of a hurry than we were, as it would take them until dark to get there. Seeing our difficulty and unable to pass until we were out of the way, the driver of the first cart volunteered to use his mules to pull us out. I doubted whether they could do it, but he had six beautifully matched, well-fed mules harnessed in two rows three abreast, ahead of the horse that was between the shafts, and he assured me the six mules would easily pull us out.

He unharnessed his mules and led them down the bank and across the stream alongside the van, and I noticed the mules were glancing at the van with some apprehension and trying to sidle away from it. However, they reached the other side, and I helped the driver tie the ropes to the front bumper, and we were ready to try it. I had to wade into the mud and water to get back into the van, and as I did so, I accidentally hit the horn with my elbow. Like jackrabbits, the six mules lunged forward simultaneously, dragging the van out of the mud as though it had been made of balsa wood and it went flying up the steep slope, with the driver vainly trying to catch up. When we reached the top I slammed on the brakes to try to stop the mules, but their panic was such that they took off in a headlong dash straight across a newly planted field, dragging the van behind them with all four wheels locked. We traveled for about 500 yards before the mules, completely exhausted, and hearing no further sound from the van, finally stopped. We had pretty well messed up the field for the owner, so I had to locate him and pay him a few dollars to compensate him. After that experience, every time we crossed that particular stream we always bridged it with our boards first.

It was during that same first trip when, sleeping out in the van in the yard of the inn, I was awakened just before dawn by a tremendous earthquake. The van was being bounced up and down and from side to side to an extraordinary degree, and as I feverishly tried to put on my pants and shoes, I kept losing my balance and falling over sideways. As I dressed, I listened closely, expecting to hear the sounds of falling buildings and the cries of the injured, but I heard nothing and was deeply worried because Father and several others in our party were asleep indoors. I finally managed to work my way out of the van and stand up, expecting to have difficulty maintaining my footing, but when I got there, holding onto the van for support, I found the ground quite still under my feet and everything around me quiet. But the van continued its insane gyrations. Looking toward the rear of the van I could make out a dim figure in the darkness, and going closer, I discovered that the "earthquake" was a large mule that had broken its tether and had found the rounded corner of the van to be an ideal rubbing-post. With a blissful look on its face, it had its shoulder against the corner of the van and was

heaving itself up and down, up and down. It paid not the slightest attention to me as I tried to shoo it away. I had to eventually grab it by the nose to get its attention and get it to move.

In 1941, however, our journey up and back was quite uneventful. Although the nights were still cold, Eva and I slept out in the van and were quite comfortable in our sleeping bags. At dawn each morning we got up and ate breakfast with the others, and by sunup we had the van out in the fairgrounds and took turns preaching to the crowds that gathered around us for the next ten hours, with barely a break for lunch. Eva, in the meantime, visited the women of the village in their homes or walked around the fairgrounds visiting with the groups of women and children sitting in their farm carts or working at the stoves in the various food stalls. There was never a want for an audience.

Each year we parked the van at the outer edge of the wide-open space near the pagoda on the bank of a dry watercourse that separated us from the tilled fields nearby. The van inevitably drew a crowd of curious onlookers, and parking it near the riverbank helped keep the curious from encircling the van and tampering with the front end while we were occupied at the back. When the crowd dwindled, I played hymn tunes on my trumpet, and You Bi-chen, our head teacher, accompanied me on a small concertina or accordion. Between us we had no difficulty drawing a crowd.

We never saw any Japanese at the fair; they studiously avoided such large gatherings. However, there were plenty of police in evidence to maintain order, and from time to time we saw a few Manchukuo soldiers. Never, in all the times we had been there, had there ever been an occasion when bandits had raided the fair, although they were often rumored to be in the vicinity, and they frequently stopped people on the roads, both coming and going. However, on the afternoon of the second or third day, as we were considering closing up for the day, we suddenly heard an ominous roar in the distance that defies description. It was a subdued sound, not loud, but insistent and increasing gradually in volume. It was not the sound of voices. As it got closer it became a pounding, thudding sound. Standing up on the platform we had at the back of the van, I saw in the near distance a cloud of dust approaching and realized the crowd of thousands of people had, for some reason, panicked, and everyone was racing in our direction. I yelled to my companions to get inside the van as quickly as possible and, ducking in, I managed to slam the back doors before the crowd reached us, pouring over and around us like a gigantic wave.

There was pandemonium everywhere. Stalls, tents, and everything that stood in their way were knocked over and flattened. People were knocked down and trampled, and as the crowd surged around and past us, with many climbing over the van itself, the weirdest part of all was the utter silence that had fallen over the mob. They were wide-eyed with fear and their faces were white and drawn. Most had their mouths open, but no sound came out.

As suddenly as it had started, the panic stopped. I opened the back doors, but no one I questioned seemed to know what had happened. Our platform was smashed flat, but it could be repaired. Then, standing on the back bumper of the van and looking over the heads of the crowd, I saw the cause of the disturbance. Coming toward us through the crowd were about a dozen policemen escorting three prisoners with their hands tied behind their backs. When they got closer we saw they were young, handsome men, but with the characteristic long hair that was usually sported by ruffians. As they were about to pass me, I went over and asked one of the policemen who the men were. He told me they were bandits who had long been sought in the area, and who had sneaked into the village to enjoy the fair, hoping they wouldn't be spotted. They had been seen gambling in one of the sporting houses. With no ceremony at all the police dragged the three men past us and down into the watercourse behind the van, and shot them in the backs of their heads in less time than it takes me to write of it. The panic had somehow been caused when people saw the prisoners and knew they were to be shot, and had started a rush to be first on the execution spot. Others, not knowing what was happening, just panicked.

Strange to say, although we had seen evidence of Communist guerrillas on most of our trips as we traveled to the fair, none were in evidence at the fair itself, although undoubtedly many were there incognito. On several occasions I was suspicious of some young men in black clothing whom I saw standing in the crowd, listening to us preach and watching us. Somehow they looked very much out of place. They were obviously too old to be students, and they didn't appear to be businessmen, so I felt fairly certain they were *balu*. I spoke to the innkeeper about them and he confirmed that *balu* were very active in the area, but he couldn't confirm that any were staying at the inn. In 1946 after the war was over, we learned that that particular area was one of their strongholds, and that they had established a presence in all the surrounding villages.

As 1941 progressed, our travels with the van became more and more limited. That was partly due to the increasing scarcity of gasoline, but also because the Japanese became increasingly more difficult to deal with. They wanted a detailed itinerary each time we went anywhere, and frequently tried to dissuade us from going because of "unruly elements" who were supposedly in the areas we wanted to visit. As a result, that spring and summer found us spending more and more time at home, producing on our printing press as large a quantity of literature as we could while paper stocks were still available.

To this point I have not mentioned the printing press, which I acquired around 1939, not long after our marriage. I got it because a total ban had been imposed by the Japanese on imports of printed matter from China proper, with the one exception of Bibles or portions of the Bible. Our newspapers were censored to the extent that we got no news of the fighting in China, and any Gospel tracts or Christian literature of any kind was stopped at the border for fear it might contain unfavorable propaganda. When that had occurred, Eva and I decided to get our own press even though we knew nothing about printing, nor had I any idea of how to go about buying a press. But we were willing to learn.

We made a trip to Mukden, where we looked up the largest Chinese printing establishment we could find, called on the Chinese owner, and explained our problem to him. He turned out to be a delightfully obliging person, open and friendly and quite as desirous as we to beat the Japanese at their own game. He threw open his entire facility for us, showed us all their equipment and how to operate it, and over a period of two days, gave me an overview of all the intricacies of the art of printing and as many of the pitfalls as he could think of. He then helped me select the right type of machine for our needs, wrote out the order to a firm in Japan that was still producing presses despite the war and the shortage of metal. Then, finally, he helped me with the most important thing of all: the amount and correct sizes of type that I would need for the press.

Before we left him, he helped us with another very important step. In order to operate a printing press we needed to have official permission, and for that we would have to go up to the new capital of Manchukuo, the old city of Changchun, "Long Spring," which the Japanese had re-named Xinjing, or "New Capital." Our friend told us which office we would have to go to, just whom to see, and he supplied us with the necessary forms we needed and even helped us fill them out. He was a remarkable person and we owed him a deep debt of gratitude, for without him I don't think we would have been able to get the printing off the ground.

As we were on the point of saying goodbye to him, Eva discovered that the diamond from her engagement ring was missing. It was only a tiny diamond — we hadn't been able to afford anything larger when we became engaged. We had bought it at a reputable Japanese jewelers in Tientsin, but like many Japanese things made in those days, the workmanship was inferior and the diamond was not very securely mounted. But small as it was, Eva loved it, and still does, even though the present diamond is not the original.

Eva remembered having seen it that morning at the hotel, so it would seem she had dropped it somewhere in the print shop. When the owner noticed us glancing around, he asked me what the problem was. Then, with his typical generosity, he stopped all work in the shop and had his entire staff join in the hunt for the diamond. As they combed the entire area, the owner suggested that Eva and I sit in the waiting room and relax, and he had tea and cakes brought to us. We sat in the same chairs we had occupied when we had first arrived at the shop that morning, and a few minutes later, as we were sitting there drinking tea, Eva happened to look down toward the floor and there, within an inch or so of her foot, was her diamond. Apparently she had pulled it off with her glove earlier that morning.

We had the diamond reset while there in Mukden, but again it wasn't too well mounted, because Eva was to lose it once again, not too long after the first incident. She discovered it missing while she was

mixing dough for bread one morning in Lingyuan. She searched through the dough without success, and as we later ate the bread, we carefully chewed each mouthful, but never found it. Lily Root, Lao San's brother, was working for us, and he, of course, knew about Eva's loss. The next morning I was awakened about three o'clock and saw a dim light across the courtyard in the kitchen. Thinking it was an intruder I crept in, only to discover that it was dear, faithful Lily Root looking for the diamond, although when I first saw him I couldn't figure out what he was doing. He had scraped the sand up from between all the bricks on the floor and had put it in a dustpan, and when I first saw him, he had the dustpan up close to his face as he meticulously went through it grain by grain.

Years before, Lily Root had lost an eye to disease. The other eye was so poor that to see anything in detail, he had to hold it about four inches from his face. As he held the pan in the light of a candle, I realized what he was doing. I was shocked to see in the dustpan, inches from his good eye, a large black scorpion he had inadvertently swept up. It stood there with its tail raised and ready to strike. Had I not gone in at that particular moment and grabbed the dustpan from him, Lily Root might well have lost his second eye.

When we left the print shop and returned to our hotel, it was with the knowledge that it would take more than a month for the new press to arrive from Japan. However, since we were so close to Xinjing, we decided to go there and get the permit, just in case there might be some delay later on. We caught a train the next morning and were in Xinjing by noon. The original name for the city, Changchun, has long since been restored, but at the time we went there, little was to be seen of the old city. The Japanese had spent millions of yuan in laying out a brand-new city in the suburbs, complete with its own new railway station.

The new part was very modern and ornate, with wide boulevards and many trees, and the palace buildings were most impressive. However, there were many buildings that were only partly finished and all work on them seemed to have stopped, presumably because the continuing war with China was using up all the resources.

We found the office we were looking for and secured our permit for the press with no difficulty, then that same afternoon we left for the city of

Harbin, a few hours to the north. Being so close, we thought it would be fun to at least see the place about which we had heard so much. Harbin is relatively close to the Russian border, and for many years it had been home to thousands of displaced White Russians, who had fled across the border at the time the Czar was overthrown. They were called "White" Russians as opposed to the "Red" Bolsheviks.

We found the place distressingly drab and filthy. Most of the buildings looked very old and decrepit and showed a strong Russian influence, and White Russians were everywhere. Since their escape from the Bolsheviks, their lot had been a hard one, and in Harbin the Chinese had treated them very harshly, looking upon them with utter disdain. However, when the Japanese took over, they suffered still worse treatment, characterized by its calculated cruelty and callousness, and almost without exception, every White Russian we saw was a pitiful sight. What struck us most were the large numbers of middle-aged and elderly Russian women sweeping the streets at daybreak, and Russian men doing the coolie labor that the Chinese usually did. Our hotel was supposed to be the best in Harbin, and at one time it probably had been quite grand. However, when we stayed there it was a disaster, with torn and dirty bed sheets, frayed carpets on the floors, and drapes that hung in tatters. The old restaurant in which we had dinner that night was so filthy that we had no appetite for what they served, and we were happy to leave for home early the next morning.

When the press finally arrived, it came extremely well packed in about twenty different wooden boxes. Assembling it posed a real challenge, particularly as all the instructions were in Japanese, which I was unable to read. By trial and error we finally got it all together, but we never could have done so had we not seen a prototype of it in the print shop in Mukden.

It was a newer model with some improvements that I was glad to note. When the printing machine was assembled, we had the job of sorting the type and placing it in little compartments in shallow trays on a number of different racks around the room, a job made more complicated for us because all the characters in the type fonts were backward, and we had to learn to read them that way. The room we had designated for the press was the one directly across from Mother's dispensary. To get the proper light we

would need, I put in glass windows front and back, and because we needed a fairly warm room for the ink and rollers to stay pliable, I put in a large stove.

When Eva and I had the type all classified by size, and in the designated order of strokes and radicals to make each character easier to find, we tried our hand at setting up a plate and running it off. As the days went by and we became more adept at it, and I felt we had fully mastered the technique, I trained two young Chinese lads to help me, and in time I was able to hand over the entire operation to them. One of them was Gao Yu-de, the youngest son of Katie, our gateman, and younger brother to Gao Yu-sheng.

Although we had electricity, it came on only at night, so the press was operated by a foot treadle. It had a large, heavy flywheel on the side, and once the flywheel started turning, it did not require a great deal of effort to operate it. In fact, Eva and Barbara frequently came in to spell us on the treadle. The trick was to stand there, partially leaning on the press for balance, keeping one leg going up and down on the treadle, with one hand feeding paper into the press as it rotated, while at the other end someone stacked the printed papers as they came off.

In winter, because we had to keep the room warm, we frequently found ourselves with a lot of company, and it became a regular gathering place. More often than not we had the company of one of our watchdog plainclothes policemen as well.

One unique aspect of the press was the rollers used to put ink on the face of the type. They were made of some composition that had the feel of a fairly spongy rubber, but which hardened and shrank in a couple of days and had to be melted down and then remolded. That was done by pouring the liquid — which was almost exactly like Chinese glue — into steel molding tubes, into the center of which a steel shaft was inserted. After pouring, the molds had to stand outside the door to cool and harden, and the whole process had to be repeated every couple of days. As we did such a large amount of printing, we eventually had one man who did little else but melt and pour rollers for the press.

When we first started, our local Japanese authorities showed a great interest in the press. They were gratified that we had bought a Japanese model, but to begin with, they demanded a copy of everything we printed before we could distribute it. In time, though, they became so overwhelmed with the quantity we put out that they lost interest, and we were left undisturbed. In a period of just three years we printed hundreds of thousands of tracts, not only for our own use, but for the other mission stations throughout the province. We also printed a variety of booklets, and toward the end of each year, we printed off hundreds of thousands of single-sheet calendars, which were greatly prized by the peasants. They were printed in almanac style in a variety of bright colors. All the lunar calendar dates of importance to farmers were included, such as when rain or snow could be expected and when cold or hot weather might begin, and although we suspected that some of the things we gave away at the markets ended up being used to repair windows and paper ceilings, we knew for certain that the calendars were preserved on walls in thousands of homes and the gospel messages printed thereon were read and reread throughout the year.

Paper, like everything else, was becoming scarce and harder to find in Lingyuan in 1941, but we bought as much as we could find and printed off huge stocks of literature against the time when nothing more would be available. As our skills grew, we produced a block calendar with a daily tear-off sheet and the block mounted on a brightly colored picture background, an innovation that was completely new to the peasants and very much prized. Each day's sheet showed a verse of Scripture and a short message.

An amusing incident occurred connected with those calendars. One Saturday morning as we were working the press, a young Chinese businessman turned up, dressed in his Sunday best and carrying his Bible. After watching us for a short time he asked why the morning service hadn't yet started. We were puzzled until we realized he thought it was Sunday, and we asked him what had happened to his calendar. Somewhat ruefully he admitted that his two little boys loved to tear the sheet off each day and took turns at it. Presumably, that particular day, they had each torn off a sheet, causing him to think it was Sunday.

When fall came and the harvest was in, Eva and I took an extended tour in the van to the east of Lingyuan, visiting areas we had not touched on before, and going as far as Chaoyang, where we visited with the Brewsters. Our map showed an entirely new road put in by the Japanese still farther to the

east of Chaoyang, circling up north to join with the main road from Chaoyang to Hada. Eva and I decided to try out the road, and visit as many as possible of the villages along it.

We had no trouble finding where the new road branched off, but not until we were well launched on it did we realize our dilemma. The road had been laid out in a straight line for miles through plowed fields, and it was quite evident it had only just been completed, because ours was obviously the first vehicle to use it. Following instructions from the Japanese, the peasants who had been forced into building it had simply dug two deep ditches, eight feet apart, and had piled the loose earth into the center of the "road" and then leveled it. It was smoothly spread, but so soft that we sank in up to the van's axles and had to stay in low gear for miles. We kept hoping that it would soon firm up, but no such luck. I watched with dismay as our gasoline gauge dropped almost visibly, and yet there was no way we could get off the road because of the deep ditches on each side, nor was there any alternate road that we knew of. We even found it impossible to visit any of the villages, which the road had bypassed.

Eventually we came to a cluster of houses and some hard ground, and I stopped to fill up with the single extra five-gallon can of gasoline I was carrying. However, that particular can was the one I mentioned earlier that had been tampered with and filled with water. As soon as I started to pour it through my chamois leather filter, I knew we were in trouble.

We learned from the villagers that there was another village a few miles ahead, where there was an inn, so we headed for there. I had just enough gas left in the tank to make it. Later that evening, a Japanese truck pulled into the inn. I approached the driver and politely asked him if he could sell me a can of gasoline because I had completely run dry. He most insolently refused and turned his back on me. Eva and I didn't lose too much sleep wondering how long we were going to have to wait for another truck to come along with, perhaps, a more obliging driver.

In the early morning I heard loud banging in the inn yard, and looked out to see the Japanese driver trying to change a flat tire on his truck, but having difficulty with the split rim. He was going about it in completely the wrong way and was getting nowhere. I went out, nodded to him, and with no protest from him, took the tire irons away from him and set about changing the tire myself. In minutes I had the old tire off and the new one on, and I left him to pump up the tire. As I turned to leave, he grabbed me by the shoulder, and with a somewhat sheepish grin, he reached up onto the truck and took down a five-gallon can of gasoline and handed it to me, refusing to take any payment for it.

We could quite easily have returned to Chaoyang from that point by the same road the truck had used, but I felt compelled to go the entire length of the new road, not only to see where it went, but to visit the various villages along it if we could. We somehow felt certain the road ahead would have to be an improvement over what we had experienced the first day, and I was sure we could make it with the five gallons of gasoline we had in the tank. Alas, the mileage shown on the map was very inaccurate, and although the road was indeed somewhat better, much of it was heavy sand, which again used up a lot of gasoline. We did manage to visit a fairly large number of villages that day. However, toward nightfall, with less than half a mile to go to join the main north-south road from Chaoyang to Hada, the engine sputtered and died.

We locked the van and left it where it was, and Eva and I walked the half mile or so to the main highway, hoping that perhaps we might find a friendly trucker who would sell us some gasoline, or we might be fortunate enough to catch the scheduled daily bus on its way to Chaoyang. When we reached the road, we were surprised to find a tiny hut there. The place was so small and ramshackle that we didn't expect to find anyone inside, but as we approached, an old man in his late seventies came out. He didn't show any surprise in seeing a foreign man and woman on foot, and greeting us very warmly, he invited us inside.

Inside, the hut measured no more than six feet by eight feet. The only thing he had by way of furniture was a rough board pallet to sleep on with a crude, mud-brick cooking stove alongside. He had us sit on his bed, and using the ubiquitous *kuai hu*, or "fast kettle," he boiled some water and quickly had a welcome cup of tea for us. I felt badly that we were using some of his precious supply of water, since it was obvious he had to go some distance to get it. However, he brushed off my apologies and said he was happy indeed that we had dropped in to visit him.

I asked the old man what he was doing living there by the roadside, and he said he made a meager living selling cigarettes and candy to the few travelers who went by on foot. We chatted with him a short while, and I kept my ears open for the sound of any motor vehicle approaching on the highway. I heard nothing, and as it began to get dark, I finally asked him if there was any likelihood of a motor vehicle passing at that time of the day. He looked at me and chuckled and told me that there were too many "bad" people in the area and that the Japanese were afraid to travel after dark. He then wondered why we had arrived there on foot and wanted to know where we were going. I told him of our problem and need for gasoline and he responded, "Why didn't you tell me sooner? I've got gasoline here. You can have it." With that, he reached under his bed and pulled out a full five-gallon can that some driver had probably given him in exchange for cigarettes.

He adamantly refused payment, but we insisted, and, learning that he could read, we left him with a supply of Christian literature and were on our way back to Chaoyang shortly thereafter, reaching there a little after midnight. That was one of the very last trips we made with the van, but not the last of the many small miracles in our lives.

In June 1941, the war in Europe became our war as well, in a very real sense, because the Japanese demonstrated exactly what they thought of British and American nationals. When Hitler launched his treacherous attack on Russia, we heard the news on the radio, and because Japan was a member of the Axis supporting Germany, it was almost immediately thereafter that we heard the news that Britain and the United States had frozen all Japanese assets in their countries. The Japanese at once retaliated by doing the same thing in Manchukuo and Japan to the assets of all British and American nationals. That meant that all bank accounts were frozen, and we could withdraw no more money. That was very bad news for us.

We picked up the report of the Japanese move on a news broadcast late Friday night, after the banks were closed for the weekend. But knowing how the Japanese worked, I guessed that the actual enforcement of the freeze on bank accounts would not become effective until sometime Monday morning, so I decided to take a chance at beating them to the punch.

It was about an 18-hour journey to Mukden, where our money was banked. If we left Lingyuan on the Sunday train, we could get there before the banks opened on Monday morning. On Saturday I contacted our neighboring colleagues along the railway line, sending them telegrams to the effect that I was going to Mukden and would be glad to get them butter if they needed it. The word "butter" was our code word for money, and I hoped they would know what I meant.

From Pingquan to our west, Kenneth Morrison arrived Saturday afternoon with his checkbook and wrote us a check for cash. He also had with him checks from two other workers in Pingquan. On Sunday, Eva and I caught the noon train from Lingyuan, and late that afternoon we were met in Chaoyang by Herbert and Heather Brewster, who had correctly interpreted my telegram and had brought blank checks for themselves and for the Misses Flanagan and Wilks, who were living with them. As the two stood on the railway platform, we spotted at least six Chinese detectives watching them, but Mr. Brewster was an old hand at the game and had anticipated that. He had brought with him an old pair of shoes that needed new heels and soles. With a broad wink he passed them to me quite ostentatiously, displaying the holes in the soles and the worn-down heels. After we were back on the train, we found their checks stuffed into the toes.

After sitting up all night, we reached Mukden around seven the next morning. We hired two rickshaws, and for the benefit of the watching plainclothes police, loudly told the men to take us to the Yamato Hotel, which was a very modern hotel run by the SMR. However, after going a few blocks, we diverted directly to the Hongkong and Shanghai Bank and camped on the top step, waiting for the doors to open at 9:30. We were gambling that the Japanese officials would not be there when the bank first opened, and we might just possibly get in under the wire.

When the bank finally did open, we were the first in a line of about 50 people to enter the bank. Although it was obvious to the Chinese tellers what was going on, we cashed all our checks with not a single question asked, nor any surprise shown at our large withdrawals. We left small amounts in each account so as not to be too obvious about it, and as I

was leaving the counter, I heard the teller next to ours telling his next customer, "I'm sorry, but we've exhausted all our cash. You must wait until ten o'clock, when we will have more sent in." As we went down the steps we passed a long line of people waiting for their money, many of them British and American nationals, and as we got into our rickshaws, a car pulled up with several Japanese officials in it. We had made it just in time.

That was the easy part. On our way up to Mukden on the train we had been questioned and searched three times by the Japanese Kempeitai, and now on our return trip, we would be carrying thousands of yuan in cash. If it were to be found, how would we explain it? We hadn't really given it any thought, but now it was time to do something about it.

We dropped the shoes off to be repaired, checked into the hotel for a nap, had our lunch, then picked up the repaired shoes, and suddenly had what turned out to be a brilliant idea. Whenever the Japanese traveled, they always carried with them lunch boxes, called "bento." Made of paper-thin wood, the boxes contained cooked rice, pickles, some vegetables, and usually some fish, and were always carried tied up in a knotted handkerchief. We bought half a dozen of them at a Japanese food store, took them back to the hotel and dumped the contents down the toilet, then packed several stacks of currency into the empty boxes. When that was done we loosely tied them into two packages with the standard kerchief and were ready to face the Kempeitai.

The first search came at Mukden station, even before we boarded our train. Two gendarmes approached us, asking for our papers, then demanded we open our overnight cases. Our coat pockets were then searched and I was patted down, but neither man even glanced at the two "bento" packages sitting on the floor at our feet. On the night train home we were again searched twice, and once again at Jinzhou where we changed trains, but the "bento" packages were never once touched.

Shifting some of the cash to the toes of the repaired shoes for our Chaoyang friends was a bit tricky, but we managed it under cover of our coats, and openly giving boxes of "bento" took care of the rest of the people for whom we had drawn money. Without that cash over the next few months we would have been in dire straits, with no way to pay our faithful servants and nothing with which to buy food and supplies.

Writing of that large amount of cash reminds me of my Chinese coin collection. From early childhood I can remember seeing Father slice bits of silver off a roughly shoe-shaped ingot of silver, called in Chinese a *yuan bao*, and known to Westerners as a "tael," although the "tael" was actually a measure of the weight of the ingot, not the ingot itself. For smaller amounts we had been accustomed to using the ancient Chinese "cash" coinage: circular coins of various sizes, each with a square hole in the center. The coins had become very commonplace to us, and were so much of a nuisance to carry or store that, when they went out of circulation as the Mexican dollar was introduced, we never gave them a second thought and were happy to see them go.

As children, it was rare to see another white man in Lingyuan except for the occasional visit of one of our missionary colleagues. But once or twice a year, other foreigners did appear in town: representatives of American or British firms such as Standard Oil (Socony), Texaco, Shell and the British and American Tobacco Company. Usually they stayed at their company branch offices and were the types of individuals who wanted nothing to do with missionaries. They were quite content to be wined and dined by their Chinese hosts and entertained in the brothels, and we were just as glad they didn't look us up.

However, there was one Socony man, an American, who always made a point of visiting us as a family and spending a night or two with us. I regret that I have forgotten his name, but he was a most charming individual and seemed to enjoy the company of children as much as that of adults. When we visited Tientsin we always stopped in to see him if he was in town, and I remember how much I admired his shiny automobile.

It was he who introduced me to coin collecting when I was about ten or twelve. It had been his hobby for years, and he showed me some of his latest purchases and got me hooked with his stories about the origins of the coins. From then on I, too, became an avid collector.

Primarily, it was a story about some Tang Dynasty coins that excited my interest. The coins were among the most common in circulation at the time and something we handled each day, but I had never noticed anything unusual about them until that gentleman pointed it out to me.

He took a handful of the coins and laid them out on the dining table, showing me first how they all appeared completely alike, but then, one by one, he pointed out a tiny imperfection on each one, which, although minute, was clearly visible as being in the shape of a small crescent. Furthermore, no two coins were exactly alike, the imperfection either being in a slightly different position or with minutely different proportions. He then told me how they came about.

He began by telling me how the coins were first minted. Skilled artisans used wax to first carve out a "tree" with trunk, branches, and twigs, and then the "leaves," which were the actual coins. Of the leaves, there might be several hundred on a "tree," each carved with raised lettering of four Chinese characters on the face side denoting the reign and title of the current emperor. (In later dynasties there was Mongol or Manchu writing on the other side.) When the wax tree was complete, it was buried in a mold consisting of a shallow box containing a mixture of fine sand and glue, dampened with water and tightly compacted. The box was then sealed, with the base of the "tree" trunk protruding from it. After that, heat was applied, melting the wax, which poured out through the base of the trunk. The molten metal was poured into the cavities thus formed inside to form the coin "leaves." When cold, they were individually broken off the branches and twigs of the solid "tree." On many of the coins it was possible to detect the slightly rough and flattened part, where it had originally been attached to the branch.

The Tang Dynasty lasted for 289 years, from 618-905 A.D., and there were not only 23 different emperors during that period, but 72 different titles given to the reigns of those emperors, some titles lasting only a year or two. Many of the different titles appeared on successive coins during the period, and the year in which a coin had been minted could be determined by the title of the reign carved on its face. That was one of the important features in collecting the coins.

The story of the tiny crescent on many of the coins of the Kai Yuan reign (718 A.D.) concerned a beautiful young concubine named Yang Gwei-fei, who was the favorite of the Emperor Tang Ming-huang. The young woman, by Chinese standards, was far ahead of her time. She was so pampered and spoiled by the emperor that she had the run of the court and went wherever her inclination took her.

According to legend, she wandered one day into the mint just in time to see a number of the wax "trees" being pressed into the sand molds. On a sudden whim, she used the little fingernail on one hand, and randomly jabbed each wax leaf on the reverse side, causing a slight indentation in the shape of a tiny crescent, thus defacing each coin. However, the workers in the mint were so in awe of her and of the emperor that they did nothing about it, and the wax coins were melted down and brass ones reproduced, each with the tiny imperfection that made the coins valuable to a collector mainly because of the different positions in which the crescents could be found. Just how many different ones there were I have never been able to ascertain, but I spent years trying to find as many different ones as possible.

Starting my collection first with the Tang coins, of which I managed to obtain quite a number, I gradually branched out, and over the years had a sizable collection of ancient coins in all shapes and sizes, including many Japanese and Korean coins that had ended up in China. I had a large collection of the earliest known metal coins called *bu qian*, or "cloth money," because each, in the shape of a spade, was the value of a bolt of cloth, the medium of exchange at the time but difficult to store or carry around. Later came the "knife" coins, where the handle was a circular coin exactly like the "cash" coins of later years and attached to a slightly crescent-shaped blade, often with an inscription down the middle of it, sometimes in gold. Those coins tended to break off where the handle joined the "coin" and that resulted in the switch to the circular "cash" coin, which lasted many years thereafter. The "cash" varied largely in size. The smallest I possessed was about the size of my small fingernail. They ranged in size on up to some that were almost as big as dinner plates, and worth 10,000 cash each.

In the long evenings in that fall of 1941, Eva and I spent many of our evenings identifying and cataloging those coins. In a Peking market I had managed to find a copy of an ancient Chinese tome called the *gu quan hui*, which was a listing of all the known coins of China, each of them illustrated with a woodcut. We had a fascinating time matching my coins to the illustrations in the book, and I was gratified to find that I had almost all of them, numbering several thousand.

Incidentally, after the occupation of Jehol in 1933, the Japanese had evinced a tremendous interest in Chinese pottery, bronzes and antiques of almost any kind. However, their chief interest seemed to have been in coins. Ancient Japanese money had been very much the same as Chinese coins and had actually devolved from them, and perhaps that was the reason for their interest. At any rate, unable to communicate with the Chinese people themselves, they hired Chinese agents to canvass the countryside buying up all the coins they could find. It became a common sight to see those buyers in the various country marketplaces. There were always several at the Daiming Fair each year. They prominently displayed a large cloth banner emblazoned with facsimiles of the various coins they wanted to purchase and showing the amount offered for each coin. They did a roaring business, and coins began to get scarcer after that as their owners discovered their value and sold them to the Japanese. Prior to that, old coins, as they went out of circulation, were either melted down by the Chinese for their metal content or used in a hundred different ways, from paperweights — not as we know them in a block form, but in long strings, which were draped over a table to hold papers down — to their use as the base for a shuttlecock made with chicken feathers that Chinese children kicked around with the sides of their heels. Still another use for the old coins was to sew them into the hem of door curtains to keep them from blowing in the breeze. But when the Japanese began to buy them, all those old coins were searched out and taken to market, where the buyers for the Japanese took almost everything that came along. For some of the rarer coins they paid the equivalent of an entire year's income for the average peasant.

In one of the inns in which I stayed one night I met one of those buyers and we became good friends. From him I learned a great deal about the value and history of different coins and how to tell the genuine from the counterfeit, because, as the demand grew, counterfeiting became very popular, and it was difficult to tell the genuine from the false. He had some coins that I badly wanted and couldn't find. In turn, I had some that he had been unable to locate and of which I had extras, so we frequently exchanged coins. I've written earlier of one particular small coin, the *ban liang* or "half ounce" coin, which was highly prized as a medication to knit broken bones. It became extremely rare in time, but I had been fortunate in acquiring a fairly large number of them, and their rarity continued to cause the price to rise.

It is of interest perhaps to mention an incident that occurred in Peking not long after the Japanese had taken over the city in 1937. At the time, the Salvation Army had a large open compound in which they wanted to erect a building. After obtaining permission from the Japanese they started excavating for the foundations, and almost with the very first shovelful of dirt they discovered one of the large four-foot-tall earthenware pots called *gang*, which the Chinese use to store water or grain. It was tightly sealed, and when opened it was found to be filled to the brim with ancient coins that apparently had been buried there centuries before.

I forget now in which dynasty those particular coins had been minted, but, unlike most ancient coins, made of brass or bronze, they were all made from iron and were almost twice the size of the usual "cash." Finding one pot full of coins was no great novelty. However, as they continued to dig, the workmen discovered that the entire compound was full of buried pots, all of them full of the same kind of coins. Since the pots were all tightly sealed, the coins were in excellent condition, but their value lay only in their use as scrap iron, and there, the Salvation Army people had a problem on their hands.

The problem was a moral one and arose over the fact that the Japanese badly needed scrap metal for their armament factories and had placed an embargo on the sale of metals of any description. Only officials of the Japanese government were permitted to buy or sell metals, and, since the Salvation Army folk didn't want to sell to the Japanese and thus help even indirectly in furthering the war in China, they were faced with the dilemma of how to get rid of those tons of iron coins. Fortunately, the problem was solved when they learned of a Chinese in the suburbs of Peking who was in the business of manufacturing iron radiators for steam heating. The man was delighted to pay top price for the coins, and transporting those large earthenware crocks through the streets of Peking aroused no suspicion among the Japanese. The proceeds from the sale went a long way toward paying for the building that was eventually erected on the site.

In early October 1941, after all the harvesting was done, there was a strange incident involving the *balu*. Japanese troop strength in Lingyuan had been reduced to an absolute minimum. The Chinese, who generally knew what was going on, reported that there were fewer than 50 Japanese soldiers in the city, although there were several hundred civilians. The Japanese continued to show considerable apprehension, fearing that the *balu* would attempt to attack the city, even though no one had actually seen any of their troops and only isolated actions against the Japanese had taken place.

However, around ten o'clock one night we suddenly heard the sound of machine gun and rifle fire and discovered that the Japanese garrison troops were madly dashing around in their trucks to different points in the city. They were apparently firing their weapons randomly into the darkness of the open countryside, attempting to give the impression that they had massive numbers of men in different parts of the city. Of course, everyone knew differently, including the *balu*.

At first we couldn't imagine why they were doing it since there was no return fire, although rumors were that the *balu* were attacking. Then, as the firing moved away from us and down to the south gate, we understood what it was. The *balu* had somehow managed to organize large numbers of peasants into an army, which was marching around the city stomping their feet as they went, but otherwise making no sound at all. That went on for several hours. They were far enough away so that the rifle and machine gun fire apparently didn't touch them, but close enough so that not only could everyone in the city hear the thudding sound of their feet, but we could actually feel the vibrations in the ground beneath our feet as they marched in formation. Of course nothing could be seen of them since there were no searchlights available, and around two in the morning the sounds died away. We calculated that they had circled the city at least five or six times. However, there were so many of them, and they appeared to have been divided into battalions or regiments, with gaps between the groups, so it was hard to determine when one group had passed and another followed.

In the morning I, together with hundreds of Chinese, went out into the fields to see where they had been and found a swath cut through the plowed fields that was over a hundred feet wide. The plowed rows had been completely flattened and showed the footprints of thousands of people. Estimates of the number of peasants involved ranged from ten thousand to fifty thousand, but there could have been far fewer and they could still have made the same noise. Some Chinese said they found spots where blood could be seen on the ground indicating that some had been hit by Japanese shots, but I didn't see any.

The Japanese were absolutely terrified that night, and we, as well as the Chinese population, were not too much at ease either. However, it was simply a propaganda tactic and was never repeated. What astounded everyone was how the *balu* had managed to organize the demonstration in such secrecy and not have a word of it get out. However, in later years the ability of the *balu* to do the unusual and unexpected became commonplace.

December rolled around, and on the evening of December 7, 1941, Eva and I were sitting at our dining room table doing the final touches in cataloging our coins. We had put a small identifying tag on each one, then strung them on thin wire to facilitate handling. We had our radio turned on and I recall that as we were congratulating ourselves on finishing the job, we heard an English-language broadcast from a Japanese station telling of the efforts of the Japanese ambassador in Washington to convince the United States government that the Japanese nation wanted only peace, and that their warlike moves in the South Pacific were not meant in any way to threaten the United States or Britain. Despite those assurances, a strong feeling of apprehension was in the air, and we somehow felt a sense of dread as to what the future would bring.

That same afternoon I had been asked by a local Japanese official to go with him in my van to the railroad station to meet a very important Japanese general who was visiting Lingyuan for two days and was to leave on the 9th. I found him to be a most agreeable old chap, extremely friendly, and when I delivered him to the Japanese hotel where he was to stay, he insisted that I go in and join him in a few cups of sake. Rather than offend him, I agreed to go in for a few minutes, but I accepted only some soda pop to drink and limited my stay to no more than 40 minutes or so. However, in that short time I received quite an

education in Japanese culture, and was not sorry that I had gone.

There were numerous Japanese officials there, and a lot of heavy drinking was going on. I sat next to the general and watched in amazement as he downed one cup of sake after another, becoming more mellow with each. However, I was more intrigued by the fact that the geisha serving him was required to match him cup for cup, as was the case with all the geishas serving the other officials. What astounded me was the fact that the fiery liquor seemed to have not the slightest effect on her or the other girls. It didn't take too long for me to find out why.

From where I sat, I was able to watch the girls, as from time to time they went into an adjoining room to fetch more sake. As each one went in, I noticed them reach into the front of their kimonos, draw out a sodden ball of thin rice paper tissues, and substitute a dry one in its place. When the general's girl returned I watched her very closely and noticed that each time she drank, she demurely covered her mouth with her left hand and raised the sake cup with her right. At the same time, with a rapid and deft twist of her right wrist she poured the contents of her sake cup down into the front of her kimono, onto the rice-paper ball. It was done so quickly and neatly that had I not been watching closely, I wouldn't have seen it. I watched the other girls doing the same thing, and not one of the Japanese men who were paying for the wine was apparently any the wiser. Later, I saw the girls squeeze the sake out of the wet balls into a container to be recycled.

Unknown to me at the time, the local Japanese had organized a huge party at the hot springs resort, Reshuitang, for the general for that evening. I was not asked to drive the general up there. Instead, they had commandeered several trucks and buses for the occasion. I learned later that almost the entire Japanese community had gone along.

After finishing with the coins, Eva and I had gone to bed sometime around 9:30, and were sound asleep when we were awakened shortly after 11 by Katie, the gateman, banging on our front door. It appeared that two of the Japanese officials had been so drunk from the afternoon session with the general that they had missed the bus to Reshuitang. Now, several hours later, having awakened from their stupor, they wanted to go and join the party and had come to ask me to drive them up there. They were most apologetic for bothering me at that late hour, but as an inducement they had brought along two five-gallon cans of precious gasoline for me, and with it being so scarce, I was in no mood to refuse them. I backed the van out of the garage, and away we went. Eva badly wanted to go along with me but I dissuaded her, and as things turned out, it was just as well that she didn't go.

The two men slept the whole way, but when we arrived there, an hour or so later, they awoke bright eyed and bushy-tailed and ready for a big evening. As I started to turn around and leave, they both grabbed at my arms and refused to let me go, insisting that I go inside with them and join the party. Against my better judgment I reluctantly agreed, and with one hanging onto each arm, they dragged me in with them.

As we entered the large main room with the big sunken pool, which I had first seen several years earlier, the party was in full swing with probably 150 to 200 Japanese present. I had taken about five steps into the room and had just caught the eye of the general, who was sitting at a low table on the raised platform to my left, when suddenly, without any warning at all, a drunken Japanese soldier rushed across the room toward me. He grabbed me around the neck with both hands, and proceeded to strangle me. I made no resistance, knowing that most of them were experts in judo, and allowed myself to go limp, thinking this might fool him into believing he had killed me.

He was well practiced in the art, and within seconds I blacked out completely. I remember only that my eyes were still fixed on those of the general, who was looking back at me in apparent recognition. Since I lived to tell the tale, presumably the old general was not so drunk that he was unaware of what was happening, and he evidently called off the soldier just in time and saved my life.

I regained consciousness a few minutes later, got up off the floor where I was lying, and found that no one was paying me the slightest attention, nor did anyone there, least of all the general, show any remorse or apologize for the incident. As far as they were concerned, nothing had happened. The general, instead, patted the cushion beside him and invited me to join him, but I'd had enough and declined, and thankfully made my departure. When I got home I

said nothing to Eva of the incident, and crawled into bed around two o'clock on the morning of December 8th. With the International Date Line we were one day ahead of the United States.

About an hour later, shortly after three o'clock, we awoke to hear Father banging on our front door. He had risen early to listen to the three o'clock BBC news and learn the latest information on the Washington talks with the Japanese ambassador. He woke us to tell us that the Japanese had attacked Pearl Harbor, and that we were at war with Japan.

Eva and I hurriedly dressed and went over to listen to the shortwave reports from Manila telling of Japanese bombing attacks there, the destruction of all American aircraft at Clark Field, and the damage to U.S. ships in the harbor. But what was of immediate interest to us was the ominous news that, in the United States and the Philippines, all Japanese nationals were to be rounded up for immediate internment.

We expected the Japanese to come momentarily and arrest us, but nothing happened all that day and no Japanese came near us. The interminable waiting for something to happen made that day one of the longest I can remember. All of us tried to busy ourselves burning up old letters and documents and photographs that we thought the Japanese might find and consider incriminating, leaving only old house and property deeds intact. Even so, we were insufficiently thorough and left a few things we should have burned, which caused us difficulties later.

The unnatural peace and quiet of that December day contrasted dramatically with the intense fighting we knew to be going on in Hong Kong and the Philippines. Every few minutes our Chinese friends would come up and tell us of wild celebrations being held by the Japanese in the center of the city, and of huge posters that were being put up telling of Japanese victories against the Americans and British on every front.

The next morning, the 9th of December, I was in somewhat of a dilemma, because on the 7th when the general had arrived in Lingyuan, I had agreed to drive him back to the railroad station on the afternoon of the 9th. Now that war with America had been declared, would they still expect me to do so? I decided to venture downtown and see for myself what was going on.

Around noon I rode my bicycle out the back way,

and using alleys and back streets wherever possible, I wound my way to the center of town. Astonishingly, all the Japanese I ran into showed themselves just as friendly as usual, and I saw nothing to alarm me. So, at three-thirty, the time agreed upon, I drove the van down to the hotel, picked up the general and his entourage, and drove him to the station. All the way he kept patting me on my knee and telling me what a good friend I was.

There was a big crowd of Japanese at the station to see him off, and I knew most of them. Again, to my surprise, they seemed to make it a special point to come over and greet me and show their friendliness. Not a single word was said about Pearl Harbor or the war that was now raging between Japan and Britain, as well as America. We all stood around and chatted until the train came in, and the old general climbed aboard. Then, as the train pulled out, it was as though a switch had been pulled. Every single Japanese man and woman there turned away from me and, completely ignoring me, they cut me dead as they went their separate ways.

It was an extraordinary experience at the time. I feel quite certain that the local Japanese had advance knowledge of the imminent outbreak of war. Admiral Tojo at his trial years later confessed that the decision to attack the United States was made on December 1st. I suspect that our visiting general had been in the know and had let out the news at the party the evening of the 7th. I am equally sure it was that that brought about the attack on me by the drunken soldier. Be that as it may, I went home from the station with a strong foreboding, knowing it wouldn't be too long before we learned our fate. As I put the van away in the garage, I stood with one hand on it and looked at it for a long moment, wondering if this was the last time I would ever see it again. It was. Soon thereafter, the Japanese were driving it around, eventually crashing it into a ravine, but I was not to learn that until after the war was over.

Nothing happened that evening, and we all worked late into the night, continuing to destroy everything we thought the Japanese might find suspicious. We were loathe to destroy our books and family photographs, but eventually we burned all the latter, and Eva and I most reluctantly destroyed the stack of love letters we had written each other over the two years of our engagement, though we left them to the very last.

We didn't quite know what to do with my coin collection, but I decided that if at all possible, the Japanese shouldn't get them. So with hammer in hand I proceeded to our bathroom and ripped up one of the floor boards, and, wrapping the coins in an old raincoat, we buried them underneath the floor and nailed the board back down again. The coins might still be there to this day except that some weeks later, when I was able to get a message to Eva, I suggested she get them out and hand them over to our restaurant friend, Mr. Li, for safekeeping. We knew he would hide them well, and he unquestionably did. However, at war's end, we learned that when the Chinese Communists took over the city, he was one of the first they executed, partly because he was a Christian and partly because he was such a successful businessman. The secret of where he had hidden our coins died with him.

One of the last things we did that night was to listen to the shortwave radio for the final time, after which I cut off the wires just as they had been when the Kempeitai first took the shortwave out. The news of Japanese successes on every front was extremely depressing, as was news of their rounding up British and American nationals for internment. We were certain our turn would come in the morning, and we finally retired to a very troubled sleep. 1941 was nearly over, but traumatic and historic events were only beginning.

Manchukuo "One Ch'ien" copper coin. This one was minted in 1938, the 5th year of K'ang Te (the Reign Title of Henry Pu Yi, Japan's puppet emperor of Manchukuo during World War II). Pu Yi, it will be remembered, was a Manchu and the last emperor of China. This drawing is from a photograph of a coin that was badly worn, and what apparently were Manchu characters on the left and right sides on the obverse side were too worn for legibility.

"Our latest press which has printed over 300,000 tracts since May. The boy standing near me is the operator, and now is able to take most of the responsibility for which I am very glad." — caption written by Bob when he wrote a friend and sent this picture.

3 years of the press. 1 for each year, showing the growth.

On the way to the Daiming Tower.

One of the Daiming Towers.

The Daiming Tower.

A priest blessing the woman on her knees.

A fortune teller. Words above say: Long Life — and Luck & Beauty. Shou Jao Fu Mei.

Crowds gather at the van to buy booklets and Gospel tracts.

Women listening to the preaching of the Gospel.

A view of Lingyuan.

Calenders and tracts printed on our press.

A blind man feeling the front of the van to know what it was like.

言必信，行必
果。

Yan bi xin, xing bi guo.

*Promises must be kept
and action must be resolute.*

- Chinese Proverb.

Chapter Twenty-Eight

Imprisonment

They came for us with a bang. More specifically, it was with a series of loud thuds, as armed men climbed the walls and dropped into our courtyard sometime before dawn on the morning of December 10, 1941. Those unfamiliar sounds, accompanied by the barking of our dogs, awakened us after a very troubled sleep, and at first we couldn't figure out what was happening. Then loud shouts from Katie, the gateman, calling my name, followed by the sounds of running feet, alerted us to the fact that the Japanese had invaded our compound and had finally come to arrest us.

I just had time to turn on a light when there came a loud banging on the front door, and a dozen or more armed men burst into our bedroom and surrounded us. A similar number invaded my parents' room and the rooms of both my sisters.

The doors wide open to the bitterly cold outdoor air, Eva and I were told to dress immediately and go with them. They did have the decency to give us a measure of privacy in the bathroom, but only when they had made sure there was no back exit from which we could escape. Then, with guns pressed against our backs, we were hustled over to my parents' dining room, where my father and mother sat at the table. A few moments later Barbara came in carrying her little dog. My sister Ruth, being confined to bed in the next room, was not made to appear. For once, and it was extremely rare for it to be so, no one else was living with us at the time, so only our family was taken.

Our captors must have numbered some 30 or 40 men in all. Most were Chinese policemen, but there were two local Japanese detectives and five Japanese policemen who were strangers to us. We later learned they had come the preceding evening by train from Chengde, the capital, specifically to arrest us. For a while it was sheer pandemonium, with police rushing in and out and a great deal of shouting going on. Then things quieted down a bit and only about a dozen or so were left in the room, their guns pointed at us the whole time. I was surprised not to see our own chief of police, a fairly decent sort and a man I knew well. I learned later he had begged off the onerous job of arresting us, and instead was across town arresting the Belgian Catholic fathers.

After what seemed an interminable wait and a lot of loud talking on the part of the five unknown Japanese, one of them, a very short, mean-looking man, stepped forward and in execrable English, told us to stand up and form a straight line. After pushing us around a bit to get us into a straighter line, simply to show his authority, he loudly said, "My name Major Miki. All same Miki Mouse. Ha, ha, ha." He then told us that Japan was at war with Great Britain and America, that we were his prisoners. We were to be taken at once to the capital for internment.

He first demanded that we hand over all our guns, cameras, photos, papers and keys. With a gun to his back, Father was escorted to his study to produce his shotgun and camera, and I was escorted back to our house to get my .22 rifle and box camera. Then, as groups of police ransacked our living quarters, others raided the store cupboards and appropriated all the foodstuffs they could stuff into their bags. The few books, papers and photographs we hadn't destroyed all merited special attention, as did the maps we had on the walls and anything that looked like a drawing. All were brought in and piled on the table for closer examination.

For three and a half hours we stood as they examined the stuff and quizzed us about people in the few photographs they found. Then a man ran in from outside carrying what he thought was a real find. He had been going through Eva's and my place and had found a rough sketch that Eva had made of our small sofa, with all the measurements she needed to make a slip cover. Miki pounced on that, certain it was a drawing of some Japanese fortification, and not until we were allowed to physically take him over there and demonstrate with a tape measure that all the measurements matched the sofa in our living room was he finally convinced. Another big find was a notebook in which Barbara had kept a daily record of the eggs her hens laid. Against each date in the book was a number. The Japanese found that highly suspicious and were certain it indicated we had been keeping a record of troop movements or something equally sin-

ister, possibly even a code. However, since they were unable to prove their point, they had to finally accept our explanation, but I don't think they were entirely satisfied.

Finally, Miki, shouted at us to dress warmly, to pack a suitcase each, with both winter and summer clothing, and to prepare a roll of bedding. We were told to be prepared to leave immediately. We packed under the scrutiny of one of the Japanese, who pointed his revolver at us the whole time. No toilet articles were allowed except for a towel, and we were not permitted to pack our Bibles. Under those conditions of extreme haste and pressure, none of us managed to pack more than the barest of necessities, including one change of underwear.

Up to that point we had not been permitted to light any of the stoves nor have any breakfast, and neither had our captors for that matter. But, around 9:30 they reluctantly agreed to allow us to eat something, and Gao Cai was allowed to cook us some oatmeal and toast, but none of us had much of an appetite. It was not made any easier with an audience of some twelve or more Chinese and Japanese police watching us and prodding us to hurry, hurry, hurry.

As we finished breakfast, Miki, who had wandered in and out of Ruth's bedroom, suddenly became belligerent and demanded that she, too, be dressed to accompany us. Father flatly refused, saying it was too dangerous to her health and might cost her life. Miki again went in to look at her and became convinced that she really couldn't get out of bed, but he refused permission for any of us to stay with her, saying that one of the young Chinese girls could come and keep her company. Poor Ruth had to lie there without the slightest idea of where we were being taken or what might happen to her in our absence, or when she might see any of us again.

We were hustled out of the house and down to the front gate, where we found that all the Chinese men and women residents of the compound had been rounded up and were standing there in the cold under guard. With them were also a number of Christians from nearby houses who had been rousted from their beds and made to stand in the cold all those hours. We foreigners were hustled down the steps out into the street and told to climb into two droshkies waiting there. With an armed guard standing on the step on each side and one sitting beside the driver, we headed downtown toward the police station. All the Chinese men and women followed behind on foot, surrounded by a small army of police, many of whom were carrying bags and suitcases full of confiscated "evidence." Of all that they took, only the photographs were returned to us; the rest we never saw again. A small, one-cylinder engine I had used to power some of my tools was also taken. The Japanese at first accused me of using it to send wireless messages, but nothing was said about it in subsequent questioning.

By that time it was midmorning. The streets, usually bustling with people at that time of the day, were singularly deserted. Word had spread of our arrest and people just stayed out of sight for fear of becoming involved. However, as we went down the main street, a few of our old friends peeked out of their doors and nodded to us, and we saw a few women crying as we went by. Also somewhat amusing to us at that point were the comments made to us by some of the Chinese police, whom we knew well. Every time they were out of earshot of their Japanese superiors they kept muttering under their breath, *duibuqi, duibuqi*, "sorry, sorry," telling us how disagreeable they found their task, and asking us not to hold it against them.

After all the hurry and rush to get us to the police station, they didn't know what to do with us once they got us there. All the Chinese Christians were locked up in barred cells at the back of the station, where they stood, packed tightly together and looking out sorrowfully at us between the bars. Many of them remained there for two or three months without ever being charged or tried for any criminal act. We, on the other hand, were kept standing in the main reception room for some time; later we were given backless benches on which to sit while our fate was decided. For four hours we waited there. At times one or the other of us was questioned, but somewhat halfheartedly.

I must digress here briefly to bring in another wonderful character who had come into our lives in Lingyuan. Of all the Chinese residents of our compound, only two had not been rounded up and taken to the police station. One of them was the beggar boy Chang Yin, of whom I have written earlier. The other was another beggar boy whom we had taken under our wing, and his was a truly remarkable story.

His name was Qian Yi. He was about the same height and build as Chang Yin and, like Chang Yin,

had been a beggar all his life. He was equally as deformed as Chang Yin, from sleeping in the outdoor cookstoves to try and keep warm, and his head and body showed the scars of disease. In addition, he had the added problems of defective eyesight and a terrible speech impediment.

I had first seen him almost a year before at the downtown hall where he was sitting talking with Zhang Yao-ting, my teacher and friend. As I listened, I was unable to understand a word he said, although from frequent contact Zhang Yao-ting had learned to communicate with him. Zhang Yao-ting told me that he came in frequently to listen to the preaching and had said that he wanted to become a believer.

A short time later he began to appear at the Sunday services at our West Street hall. They were open to everyone, and beggars were never turned away. Poor little Qian Yi always sat near the stove to keep warm, and the heat from the stove brought out the strong odors from his unwashed body and clothes, but none of the Chinese Christians protested. It wasn't long before we noticed that when hymns were being sung, Qian Yi lustily sang along, even though he couldn't read the words or carry a tune. I then discovered that Zhang Yao-ting was teaching him to read and had taught him the words to many of the hymns, which he memorized.

Qian Yi spent hours of his time at both halls, when he normally should have been out begging for food. He never once asked any of us for a handout, and, as I mentioned once before, it was our policy not to give beggars anything. However, here was a young man who was willing to make sacrifices in order to learn more about Christianity.

In time there were other developments. One day he disappeared and we didn't see him for over a month. When he came back he wore a completely new set of clothes. He told us he had walked to Pingquan, the next big city 60 miles to our west, taking several days to make the trip. There he had begged, wearing a placard asking for help to get new clothes, and apparently it had worked. By that time I had begun to understand his speech, and I asked him why he wanted new clothes. He told me he was ashamed to enter the house of God with the dirty clothes he had worn before.

A short time later he disappeared once again and was gone for about three weeks. When he returned I asked him where he had been and he told me he had gone to visit his mother, who had remarried and lived in a village about 50 miles to the northwest of Lingyuan. He said he had gone to tell her about the true God he had come to believe in, and he wanted her to believe also. He told me that the reason he had gone when he did was because a short time before, God had saved his life.

He said that returning late one evening from the railroad station, where he had gone to beg, a Japanese army truck had come up alongside him and several Japanese officers had jumped down and accosted him. He said they seemed to be drunk and wanted to have some fun with him. One of the officers pulled out his sword and forced Qian Yi to kneel down. Qian Yi knew that the man was about to cut his head off, so he asked to be allowed to pray. Putting his hands together, he raised his head, shut his eyes, and asked God to take his soul to Heaven as he died. The Japanese officer was apparently so nonplussed by that action that he let Qian Yi go, got into the truck with the others, and drove off. Qian Yi said that after that he knew God had saved his life because He wanted him to tell others about Christianity.

As the days went by Qian Yi spent more and more time studying the Bible, and one day he asked to be baptized. The church elders got together and questioned him at length, with Zhang Yao-ting acting as interpreter. They were deeply impressed by his sincerity and knowledge, and none could refuse him. When, with a number of others, he was baptized, the question arose: how could we allow a fellow believer to remain a beggar? We knew he didn't want charity and wouldn't accept it, and yet what could he do for a living in his semi-crippled state and with his speech impediment?

We finally decided that for the few dollars a month it would cost to feed him, we could offer him the job of yard boy to help Lao San and Chang Yin, and that is what he did for a couple of years, working happily without pay and quickly becoming part of our extended family. To our surprise, he made himself extremely useful and had skills we knew nothing about. Among them was a talent for making coal balls at a speed that no one could match.

Coal balls were made from coal dust that we bought by the freight car load from the Beipiao mines. The stuff resulted from the quality coal going through a washing process. The mine had mountains of the dust and very little use for it. Father thought it might burn well if made into coal balls, using a binder of our local red clay, and so it did. However, one year the mine was late in sending the carload of dust over, and being wet, it froze solid in the freight car and couldn't be unloaded when it arrived in Lingyuan. We had to hire a crew of several men to hack it out in lumps before it could be moved, a job that took several days.

On December 10th, when the police had rounded up everyone in the compound, Chang Yin and Qian Yi had wanted to be taken along as well, but the police rudely thrust them aside, telling them to stay out of the way. Left at the mission, they both felt extremely offended that they had been looked upon as non-persons and weren't worthy of being taken to jail like everyone else. As we sat in the police station waiting for something to happen, Qian Yi and Chang Yin trudged up the steps of the police station and demanded to be locked up with the others. What could the police do but somewhat shamefacedly oblige them? We were very touched, not only by their demonstration of loyalty to us, but by their bravery in identifying themselves with the rest of the Christians in a time of trouble.

Nearly an hour later, our local police chief came in with the Belgian Catholic fathers he had rounded up. They were made to sit apart from us and we were told not to talk to them. Then, after a brief confab with Major Miki, the chief came out and very politely told my parents that they could return home to take care of Ruth, but that they should remain ready to leave on the afternoon train for Chengde. Eva, Barbara and I were told to stay where we were.

When Father and Mother arrived at the house they found the place deserted, with no one there to guard it. Ruth and the little orphan girl who had been left with her were the only ones there. Father immediately set about lighting the stoves to get some heat into the house.

At the police station, after several more hours of indecision on the part of the police and numerous phone calls to his superiors in Chengde, Major Miki finally came to us and told us that we, too, could return home, and that we wouldn't be going on the afternoon train after all, but would travel on a night train instead. I knew there were no trains at night except for a freight train that went through around three in the morning. It puzzled me why they had chosen to move us that way. We came to the conclusion that they were afraid to move us in daylight for fear the Chinese might try to free us. We could think of no other reason.

It was late afternoon by the time we got home, with only Major Miki accompanying us. By that time he had thawed out somewhat and was far less aggressive when he spoke to us. At the house, we were made to sit in the dining room and were not allowed to go anywhere except to the outdoor privy. An hour or so later, just before dark, our servants were freed and Gao Cai was permitted to cook supper for us. Miki, at Father's invitation, joined us at the table, where his behavior became almost human. Obviously knowing our state of mind, he tried to amuse us by telling us in his deplorable English what he thought were jokes, though none of us were much in the mood for laughter.

Finally, well after dark, Father had a brilliant idea. We always kept a bottle of brandy in the house for medical emergencies. Somehow they had overlooked it in their search, and Father gave it to Miki. He seemed delighted and promptly ensconced himself on the couch next to the stove and happily consumed the entire bottle. It wasn't long before he was stripped to his long underwear, his revolver thrown onto the dining table and his clothes onto a chair, and soon he was fast asleep for the balance of the night.

That gave us the opportunity we had been waiting for. Together with my father, Eva and I slipped quietly down to the front of the compound, where we found most of the Christians gathered in the small meeting hall praying in the darkness. We were happy to see that only three had been kept at the police station: young Hu, the dentist; his partner Zhang, our neighbor at the back; and Zhang Yao-ting. Possibly it was because of their youth, or so we surmised, but we never did find out why they were held for weeks after everyone else was freed. They were never charged with anything. Both Qian Yi and Chang Yin had been freed, but both were in such a somber mood that we had to hug them and tell them not to worry on our behalf.

After talking for a time with the group and praying together, I called Gao Yu-sheng and his father, Katie, out into the yard, and under cover of darkness, I told them of the hiding places Eva and I had built for the gasoline in the garage ceiling and the flour in our bedroom ceiling. I told them to use the supplies whenever the need arose. In addition, there were some other hidden stores, and some things I had hidden by hanging them on ropes down the disused well in the front compound. We said our tearful goodbyes to all of them around midnight, but we slept in our clothing, and slept very little at that, and we talked of what the future might possibly hold for us.

We had been told we would leave on the night train, but then Miki had talked about a morning train, and I couldn't be sure whether he meant the freight or the eleven o'clock train. It turned out to be the freight. Just before three in the morning we were again rousted out of bed and told to get ready to leave at once. Much to our surprise, though, Miki, who was obviously nursing a big hangover, told my parents that they were to stay behind to take care of Ruth. We were deeply grateful for the news because it would have been terribly hard on Mother to have had to leave Ruth alone with untrained help and to have had to travel in that weather.

Apparently the decision for my parents to stay in Lingyuan had been made during Miki's telephone conversations with his superiors in Chengde the day before. But at the police station, when we had requested that Mother be permitted to stay with Ruth, he had told us in a loud and overbearing manner that we should count ourselves fortunate that we were being treated so well and that the request was impossible. At the same time he also told us that Japanese citizens in England and America were being subjected to much greater indignities than we were. He added that in Seattle, Japanese had been tortured. We later learned that as a result of those rumors, reprisals had been carried out against some unfortunate White Russians in the city of Tsitsihar to the north, when they had been mistaken for British or American citizens.

After telling us that Mother could stay, Miki sent Eva, Barbara and me to the railroad station in the care of two Japanese plainclothes detectives whom we'd never seen before, while he stayed behind. We never saw him again. It was a bitterly cold morning as we said good-by to my parents and Ruth, and all in the compound came to the gate to see us off. No conveyance had been arranged for us. I think the

Japanese were probably embarrassed by what they were doing and were intent on keeping our departure a secret. They also undoubtedly knew how much we were loved and respected by the Chinese in Lingyuan, and I believe they feared some sort of protest. As a result, we had to walk the mile or more to the station, carrying our suitcases and bedding rolls. We talked very little on the way. Our hearts were heavy and our faces so cold we could barely move our lips.

At the station we were told we were going to be put aboard the freight train that was due in from the east at four o'clock. However, it was late and did not appear until after eight. We were put into the caboose, unheated except for a small potbellied stove that gave off almost no warmth at all. The fast train to Chengde from Lingyuan usually took four to five hours, but we were in that caboose for nine and a half hours.

The two Japanese guarding us spoke a mixture of bastardized Chinese and English and I decided not to let them know that I understood Japanese. As our journey progressed and they saw that we were quite harmless, they dropped their arrogant manner and became almost jocular.

We had not been allowed any breakfast before leaving, and no food or drink was available at any of the stations at which we stopped. Because we were in the caboose at the end of the train and were so far out from the end of the platform, we saw nothing for sale. Fortunately, however, Gao Cai had packed some sandwiches and had given us a thermos of tea.

The two Japanese had nothing with them, and instead of going off the train at one of the many stations to buy something to eat, they helped themselves to our sandwiches when we broke them out. Still, I felt at the time that it might help them unbend a bit, and I finally screwed up enough courage to ask them where we were to be housed when we got to Chengde.

My question seemed to cause them a great deal of amusement, which made me suspicious. Then one of them said, "We're taking you to the best hotel in Chengde. You've never stayed in a place as grand as it is, and we know you'll be very comfortable." With that they both roared with laughter. I wasn't the least bit amused, and my suspicions were further aroused when I heard them talking later about taking us directly to the police station.

At one point in the long afternoon, as our train sat on a siding for an interminable period of time, the daily passenger train came up from behind and passed us. We looked enviously at the passengers sitting so comfortably in the warm carriages as it passed. Finally, just after dark, we pulled into Chengde and I felt a sense of momentary relief, if only at escaping the hard benches of the caboose. Finally we were to learn what was to become of us.

Our relief was short-lived. We were immediately surrounded by armed police who hustled Eva and Barbara away into a waiting sedan and the two detectives who had accompanied us refused to tell me where they were being taken. I felt utterly helpless and completely frustrated as, not even given a chance to say good-by, I, too, was hustled away and pushed up into the back of a truck. Obviously we were to be separately housed, but where were they taking Eva and Barbara? I felt as though the bottom had dropped out of my world.

The police left me alone momentarily on the truck. At that moment I saw the sedan containing Eva and Barbara drawing alongside as it was about to leave the station yard. I leaned over the side of the truck and called to the Korean driver of the car in colloquial Japanese, *Doko made?* ("Where are you going?") He looked around, and seeing no one standing nearby, said in a low voice, *Kirisuto Kyokai* ("the Christian church, or mission"). A tremendous sense of relief swept over me as I realized God had once again answered my prayers, and I just had time to shout good-by to them as the sedan pulled away. It was to be two weeks before I was to see Eva again, and then only for a few minutes.

As I was to learn much later, the women were indeed taken to the mission house, where Mrs. Duthie was still in residence. They were later joined by the wives of several other colleagues, together with some single missionary ladies who had been brought in from other cities throughout the province. Although the compound was fairly spacious, they were confined to the one large living room and were required to set up cots in a large bedroom they all shared, while Japanese police and soldiers occupied the rest of the house. They were permitted the help of one servant, who was allowed to buy provisions for them and to cook their meals.

Their greatest hardship was the lack of any privacy

and being under the constant observation of the Japanese. They had to share the one privy with the Japanese and Chinese police. Every time one of them went to the outhouse she was laughed at and suggestive remarks were made. That became intolerable and something had to be done about it.

There was an old open shed in the back garden, and Eva and Barbara set to work to dig an open latrine there, where they would be out of sight of the Japanese. They found some loose bricks around the yard and used them to line the edges of the latrine. The ground was frozen so hard it took them two days to dig it, but it helped pass the time as they worried about their loved ones. A day or so later they were all standing around the organ singing to cheer themselves up, and one of the group chose the hymn: "Somebody did a golden deed," at which point they all looked at Eva and Barbara and had a good laugh.

For my part, the truck took me through the dark familiar streets of Chengde until we reached the huge police station complex and prison that had been newly built by the Japanese a few years previously. That, as the Japanese detectives had gleefully told me on the train, was presumably the "modern hotel" in which I was to be housed.

I was hustled inside by two policemen, and after walking down a long corridor lined with wooden-barred cells, I was checked in at the desk, which stood at the bend of the L-shaped building. I was then pushed into one of the cells nearby, entering through a tiny doorway so small I had to crawl in. Inside I found the cell already had one occupant, an elderly Belgian priest who spoke not a word of English but did quite well in Chinese. I was left there for about 20 minutes until the two Chinese guards at the desk heard us whispering to each other after we had been told not to talk, so they dragged me out and made me stand up against the wall behind where they were sitting, and there I stood for several hours, completely ignored by them.

In the few minutes that I was in the cell with the priest we had been able to share our experiences. He had been brought in that morning, and he told me that before the Japanese had come to pick him up, he had managed to listen to his shortwave radio and had heard of the sinking, south of Singapore, of two of Britain's largest warships, the newest battleship, HMS *Prince of Wales*, and HMS *Repulse*, which was

accompanying her. Up to that point I had thought my sense of depression and foreboding could go no lower, but that piece of bad news, so soon after Pearl Harbor and so much closer to us, made me realize the magnitude of what had befallen us, and I stood there for those hours in a complete daze.

The two guards talked together all the time, smoking one cigarette after another, and from the nature of their conversation I gathered they didn't think I could understand them, so I didn't disillusion them. After some time they were served a meal by a very attractive young Japanese servant girl. They made lewd remarks about her in Chinese that she didn't understand, as she smilingly stood by and waited on them. But nothing was offered to me. I'd had nothing to eat all day except for my share of sandwiches on the train, but somehow I felt no hunger. Considerably later — I had not been permitted a watch, but I thought it had to be going on toward midnight — a Japanese officer came in. Both of the Chinese guards leapt to their feet and saluted him and then asked him where I should be put. They told him they had put me in with the Belgian priest, but they had heard us talking together and that was why they had pulled me out. The officer directed them to put me in the cell nearest the front entrance, and I was unceremoniously dragged there and again pushed in through the little entryway, not much larger than that of a dog house. That cell was to be my home for the next two weeks.

By Chinese standards, and compared with our Lingyuan prison, the prison I found myself in was modern and luxurious, but that isn't saying very much. The building was made entirely of poured concrete and was in the shape of a right angle, or an L, with both branches elongated with cells on both sides. There were some side buildings, but the main building in which I was housed occupied one corner of the police complex, and entry to the cell blocks was through an ill-fitting door, just a few feet from me at the bottom of the "L," which let in cold air day and night. However, we had reason to be thankful for that because of the atrocious stench in the building, and at least we got some fresh air.

At the other end of the building were living quarters for the numerous Japanese staff. As I mentioned, at the bend of the L was a desk at which two guards were stationed day and night. From there they could look down both branches of the prison and watch the cells. However, the one I was in was far enough away so that we were out of earshot. I say "we" because later I was joined by some colleagues.

Each cell measured just a little over six feet wide by approximately ten feet deep. The dividing walls between cells were of poured concrete and so was the floor. At the back end of the cell was a tiny, barred window near the ceiling, too high in the wall for us to be able to look out. But filthy as the window was, it did let in a little light, and for a portion of the day a shaft of sunlight came into the cell. At night we could see a star or two. We didn't feel quite so shut away from the world, and, of course, the front door next to us was being opened and closed dozens of times each hour, giving us glimpses of the outdoors.

The side of the cell that faced the open corridor was made of thick upright wooden bars. They were about four inches square and approximately eight inches apart. In addition to the two-foot-high entry door through which we had to crawl, there was a much smaller "slot" at the foot of the bars through which food and water were passed in. Several 40-watt lamps hung in the corridor, but none in the cells, and as I sat there in semi-darkness wishing for sleep, they finally brought me some food. But it was cold and of poor quality, and I had no appetite, principally because of the appalling smell all around me.

When the Japanese had designed the prison they doubtless considered it to be the latest in modern architecture, particularly since it had one unique feature. That was the "basement," which in actuality was an open septic pool under the entire main floor. At the back of each cell in one corner was a four-foot-square, eight-inch-high platform. It had a low one-foot-high wall on one side, and in the center of the platform was a ten-inch hole. That was the privy, so designed that all human waste could drop into the pool below.

The original concept, at least to Japanese thinking, was considerably superior to the open outdoor latrines in Chinese prisons, but the Japanese had not taken into account the fact that warm air rises, and each of the twenty or thirty open holes in the cells acted as a chimney to conduct the foul-smelling odor upward. That suffocating, permeating, choking smell pervaded the entire building day and night, and for the first few days we were in a state of constant nausea. Were it not for the ill-fitting door next to our cell,

we would have been in a bad way. However, like everything else, in time we learned to live with it and in the end barely noticed it.

The roof above was also of concrete. In summer it must have been appallingly hot, but when we were there, in December, it was like one huge icehouse. The only sources of heat were a couple of small stoves in the middle of each corridor, and they gave off insufficient heat to even keep the temperature above freezing. The prisoners were not permitted to talk, so the place was generally quiet except for those occasions when someone was being beaten. Of course, no provision was made for sleeping except on the bare concrete floor. It was pitch dark when I was put into my cell, and it was not until the next morning that I discovered that much of the floor was covered with dried human feces, and the walls, as high as one could reach, were black with the blood of squashed bedbugs and other filth. Since it was winter, we were fortunately spared those not-too-friendly companions, but fleas were in abundance.

After eating, I crawled into my fur-lined sleeping bag and tried to settle down to sleep, but an hour or so later the front door opened again and a draft of cold air brought me upright as a bunch of new prisoners were brought in. To my delight, five colleagues from various other cities were pushed into my cell. If the old saying, "misery loves company" is true, then we should have been ecstatic, but we had little reason to rejoice. We were loudly told by the guards that we were not permitted to talk to each other, but as the night wore on and the guards dozed, we did manage to talk in whispers without the guards hearing us.

One of the five brought in was James Duthie, and I was delighted to see him. He was a tall, lanky New Zealander, well over six feet tall, and for him to crawl through the tiny opening was a major project. Under any other circumstances it would have been hilarious to watch. He normally wore a long face and rarely seemed to smile, but when he did, his whole face lit up. He was actually a delightful fellow and a great companion. His somewhat morose appearance belied his sense of humor, and even under those depressing circumstances, he managed to find things to laugh at, even if it was only his own awkward and stumbling entry into the cell.

I was particularly pleased to see him, because I learned that Eva and Barbara were safely in his home with a number of other ladies. He also told us that one of the ladies, prior to being taken to the mission, had, for two days, occupied the same cell that we were in. By the time we had settled down for sleep it was well past midnight and none of us got much sleep that night. We had too much on our minds.

Next morning at daylight, the realities of the place really struck home, and I felt very low. My mind went to the Bible and I was reminded of the many times the Apostle Paul was imprisoned. However, the difference was that, unlike Paul, we were not there because we were Christians but because we were "enemies" of the Japanese. It was ironic to realize that, while we were physically in China, an ally of Great Britain and the United States, it was most unfortunate that we happened to be in that part of China that had been arbitrarily occupied by the Japanese. How different things might have been had the Western powers taken action against the Japanese at the time of their initial occupation of Manchuria instead of quietly letting them go their own way and do just as they pleased. But those thoughts did little to comfort me.

Around nine o'clock our first real meal was brought to us, and, like the evening before, it was unceremoniously pushed through the slot at the base of the bars onto the filthy floor. Fortunately it was on a tray, and we were pleasantly surprised to find that it was not the usual prison fare. It had been brought in from a small Chinese foodshop nearby, delivered by one of the kitchen help, who stood by as we ate, waiting for the dirty dishes. The man's filthy apron, together with the muck on the floor, didn't in any way diminish our appetites, and I, at least, ate with relish. From then on we were served three meals a day, but were never given chopsticks or any other utensil with which to eat the food, so we reluctantly had to use our dirty fingers.

Up to that point no provision had been made for us to have water to wash our faces and hands. Perhaps in anticipation of the fact that we had to eat with our fingers, the Japanese had selected small, six-inch Chinese pancakes stuffed with meat and vegetables as our daily diet. They were quite nourishing and always hot when served, and for the first two or three days all of us thoroughly enjoyed them, ignoring the dirty, gray-colored cloth that covered the tray. In time, however, the sameness of the food and the gradually dete-

riorating quality became terribly monotonous and wearisome, and to this day I find myself avoiding that particular dish in Chinese restaurants. In all, we must have eaten the same thing some 40 or more times during our 15 days there. Our requests for noodles or rice gruel or even millet went unheard. I suppose the Japanese thought we might try to commit suicide if we were given chopsticks and bowls.

We were permitted neither to stand nor to walk around our cell, not that there was any room in which to walk. Our bedding was spread across the floor, and during the daytime we either sat or reclined, mostly dozing as we waited for the long hours to pass. The pervasive, intense cold seeped through the cement floor under us, and the constantly opening door to the outside kept us in a perpetual draft, particularly when there was a wind outdoors. The indoor temperature, even with the door closed, was rarely above freezing, but at least we could breathe, and the draft from the door helped dissipate the abominable odor from the open latrine hole just a few feet from our heads.

That very first night I knew I would have to do something about that latrine in the corner. As the youngest of the party, I volunteered to take the position nearest the hole. The odor was stupefying. We soon discovered that not only was it frozen over with urine and excrement so that only a tiny hole remained, but it had also overflowed onto the surrounding floor. When an opportunity came, we told the guards about it and asked for it to be cleaned, but they did nothing until the next day. They finally sent in two men to clean and disinfect it, at the same time giving us a broom and telling us to sweep out the cell ourselves. However, everything was so badly frozen and spread about that it did little good.

With the latrine cleaned and now at least usable, and the condition of the cell floor somewhat improved, our spirits rose a little. However, that night we realized that by cleaning the latrine we had actually worsened the condition of the air in our cell. The smell was now much more potent than before, and we had nothing with which to cover the gaping hole. We tied handkerchiefs over our noses and mouths, but it was still unbearable.

The following morning we protested vigorously to the guards, asking to be allowed to use an outdoor latrine, but they adamantly refused. We then decided to go on a "toilet strike" and simply refuse to use the in-cell latrine. When we made that known to the guards, I think they were a little perturbed, because they told their superiors at once, and a Japanese official came in to talk with us. We explained to him that we were not criminals and deserved better treatment.

At first he was hostile and unyielding, but we persisted. We told him that as Westerners we were not used to that kind of open facility where we had to perform in public, and beginning that day, we definitely would not use it, even if it meant constipation and blockage of the bowels. That appeared to shock him, and he finally relented to the point that he said we could use the outdoor latrine twice a day. We felt we had won a small victory.

For some unknown reason they would only take us out under cover of darkness. Before dawn and after dark in the evening were the prescribed times, and we had to adjust accordingly. We presumed they didn't want us to be seen by the rest of the prison population and the many outsiders that thronged the main courtyard in the daytime. However, it was better than nothing.

That first evening they took us out to the latrine it was marvelous to breathe the fresh air and to see the open sky once again. We dawdled as long as we could on our visit to the big latrine at the back of the compound. It was a filthy, smelly place, with four open holes in the ground, backed up against the rear of a building. They were separated by low walls but entirely open in front, and the entire area around it was an ash heap where ashes from the many stoves in the complex were dumped each day. In summer the smell would have been intolerable, but in mid-December everything was frozen solid, so it wasn't too bad, certainly no comparison with the air inside the prison.

We walked to the latrine in single file, a policeman in the lead and another following behind. On our way, we had to pass under the windows of what I took to be the residence of either the Japanese head of the police or someone of equal or higher rank. It had Western-style glass windows, and since the Japanese suffered greatly from the cold, the place was so overheated that one window was ajar. As I went by I looked in through the six-inch-wide gap. There, close to the window, stood a small round table draped with a purple-colored velour tablecloth. An idea hit me. That was exactly what I needed to plug the latrine

hole in our cell, and I decided that somehow I simply had to get hold of it that night.

In the latrine I dawdled longer than anyone else. Only one guard had stayed with us. When he urged me to hurry I told him, truthfully, that I was badly constipated. He could go ahead without me and I'd be right along. My five cellmates, ready and waiting for me, were in a hurry to get back because of the extreme cold, so the guard had to either hold all six of us or leave me behind and then come back for me. My gamble paid off and he chose the latter, telling me to wait for his return.

No sooner had he gone than I quickly followed, staying a short distance behind. In the darkness he couldn't see me, and as I passed the open window, I reached in, snatched the tablecloth off the table, and quickly thrust it up under the back of my coat, tucking it into my waistband. I caught up with the others just as the last one was climbing into the cell, and I didn't let on to the others what I had done.

The tablecloth was too small and insufficiently bulky to block the hole by itself. I needed something to pack inside it. Each of us had only the barest of necessities of clothing with us and we needed to wear everything we had to keep out the cold, so I had to look for something else. I remembered the ash pile and decided that the next morning when we were taken to the latrine, I would fill the cloth with ashes.

The next morning we had the same Chinese guard, and on my way to the latrine, I walked in a bent-over position, hugging my stomach as though in pain in order to prepare the way for my return trip, when I would have the cloth filled with ashes hugged to my chest. Once again I dawdled, giving the guard the same excuse, and groaning the while. He seemed somewhat concerned and told me to take my time and return to the cell on my own when I was through, and he headed back to the cell with the others, who by that time were growing curious.

I stuffed the tablecloth with ashes and tied the corners together to form a rough bag. Holding the bulky bundle inside my coat, close to my chest, and in the same bent-over position, I headed back to the cell, getting there just before the guard locked the others in. When his back was turned, I took the bag of ashes out and plugged the open hole. Immediately the air in the cell was decidedly improved. My companions weren't too happy over the risks I had taken, but they appreciated the end results.

I was well aware of what a tremendous risk I had taken. There was a strong possibility that the theft would be reported by the owner, and should the guards enter our cell during our absence to search our belongings and come across the tablecloth, we all could have been in serious trouble. However, I had taken the precaution of turning the tablecloth inside out so it was not readily recognizable, particularly covered with ash as it was, and I had also thrust it well down into the hole so that not much of it was visible, unless someone was directly over the hole. Even so, I worried about it for a few days. However, as things turned out, they never discovered it. In any case, the difference in the air quality was such that we were able to dispense with the handkerchiefs that we had tied over our noses and mouths up to that point, and I in particular benefitted by it, lying as close to it as I did at night.

Our sleeping arrangements were unique. All six of us were spread out on the floor, leaving no floor space. The latrine took up about 16 square feet of space, and the small area to the left of that was useless, except to store our suitcases. Because of our shoulders, there wasn't enough room for all of us to lie side by side with our heads against the longest wall, so we tried various other ways of fitting ourselves in. We finally settled on the plan of lying alternately head to toe, thus allowing each of us a little more shoulder room. But there was little or no turning in our sleep, and the nights were so cold that the proximity of our bodies was something of an advantage.

The hardness of the cement floor didn't bother us too much. We were all quite used to sleeping on *kang* in the inns, but as the nights wore on and the stoves were left untended, the intense cold seeped up through the thin materials between us and the cement, and with the constant draft from the door, we slept only fitfully. By morning there was always a layer of hoar frost on the bedding next to our mouths, and we all awoke with stiff joints.

For me, despite the cold and discomfort, the nights passed all too quickly; it was the daylight hours that dragged by. Apart from the meals there was little or nothing to look forward to, but there were occasional distractions. On the second morning of our imprisonment, a young Chinese boy of about 12 wandered in.

He seemed to have the run of the place and was not challenged by the guards. We later learned he was the son of one of the high officials there. He had evidently heard of us and had specifically come to see us. He seemed to take a great interest in just standing outside our cell gazing at us. But after a while he grew bored, as we sat there bundled in our blankets, motionless in our misery, and he wandered off. Somewhere he got hold of a long stick, and with it he started to poke us into life, just as children will do to animals at the zoo.

I happened to be nearest the bars, and it was me he poked first. When he did so, I stared at him, but he was not to be intimidated. He then poked one of the others. I spoke to him quietly in Chinese, asking him what he was doing. We were apparently the first foreigners he had ever seen close up, and he was so thunderstruck that I could speak Chinese that he dropped the stick and just gaped at me. Once more I asked him, and at first he answered me rudely, spoiled brat that he was, but then his natural curiosity overcame his rudeness and he started asking us questions about ourselves. Before long he became quite friendly and after that became a constant visitor. But he did become a bit of a nuisance, and we started to call him "the pest." Later, however, I took advantage of his friendliness from time to time to ask him to get us a pot of hot water to drink, which he did. And since the guards evidently were afraid to stop the boy from talking with us, when he was present the restrictions against our talking among ourselves were ignored and we could talk at will.

One of our number was Reginald Sturt. He was very sick with sprue and chronic chest problems, and shouldn't have been in the jail at all. We worried constantly about him, but he maintained his cheerfulness and didn't seem greatly perturbed. With him was Doug Broughton. He, together with Mr. and Mrs. Sturt, had been imprisoned by the Japanese for three months the previous winter, so prison was in no way new to them. In fact, our prison was much more pleasant than the one they had been in when in Mongolia, where they had each been in individual cells and with far worse food. The two of them regaled us with stories of their experiences in Mongolia and the treatment the Japanese had accorded them, but it wasn't particularly encouraging.

Another member of our group was A.E. Trevor Oliver, a Welshman and one of the older missionaries in the province. We all felt pretty depressed, but Mr. Oliver was far more despondent than any of us. Despite our efforts to cheer him up, he sat, for the most part, with his eyes closed, and it was difficult to get him to participate in our desultory conversation. None of us had been permitted to bring a Bible with us, and we had nothing to read, but all of us knew a number of verses of Scripture from memory, and we passed a lot of time repeating whatever came to mind, particularly those of God's promises of help to His own when they were in need. We had to talk in whispers except when the young Chinese lad was there, otherwise the guards would shout at us to be quiet. When the lad was present, there were usually too many distractions and it was not conducive to conversation.

To while away the time when "the pest" came and stared at us, as he did most days, I started to play a game with him, challenging him with the subtle two-part allegorical sayings that I have mentioned in a previous chapter. Challenging one another to come up with the second part of a saying is a common form of entertainment with the Chinese, and the object is to stump your opponent either with one that he has not heard before or one to which he cannot figure out the proper response. The young lad entered into it with spirit, and it not only helped pass the time, it later served an additional useful purpose.

The lad eventually tired of it and left, whereupon Mr. Oliver, who up to that time had barely spoken a word unless spoken to, asked me what I had been saying to him. He said he had understood none of it, despite his many years in China. Seeing a good opening, I got him interested, and from that point on his attitude changed and he began to take an interest in life once again. I started to teach him some of the simpler sayings and the background of Chinese culture that led to their usage, and at the same time gave him illustrations of the kind of circumstances in which they might be used. It seemed to pique his interest greatly, and in the days that followed it gave him something to do, and I like to think it helped restore his sense of balance.

Near the end of that first week the attitude of the Chinese guards toward us changed considerably. Out of curiosity, or perhaps boredom, they would come and stand by to listen, and when they saw the boy was losing ground to my obviously greater knowledge of

the sayings, (I had, after all, been collecting them for years), they would join in and try to catch me out.

The trick with those sayings when used in a conversation, particularly with one that you've never heard before, is to mentally figure out the speaker's intent and then try to arrive at a logical response. It is something like this: instead of going from point A to point B by a straight line, one uses a circuitous route by way of C, a route that seemingly has no bearing whatsoever upon the statement in question.

Since we have nothing that even approximates it in our English-language culture, one simple example will perhaps help the reader to understand the concept. Suppose, for example, I make a statement to you in Chinese, and then ask if you understand it or not. To do so, I would say in Chinese *Dong bu dong*, which literally means, "Understand, not understand?" In replying you would have the obvious choice of two possibilities. You could say you understood, in which case you would just say *dong*. Or you might say you don't understand, in which case you would say *bu dong*, where *bu* is simply a negative. Choosing, however, to use the allegorical form of reply instead of one or the other of the two obvious choices above, one might say instead: *shitou diao jing* (a stone falls into the well).

That would seemingly be totally irrelevant, but, since it had to be a direct answer to my question, "Do you understand?" it has to obviously replace one or other of the normal responses, either *dong* or *bu dong*, and the job of the listener is to rationalize the phrase and come up with the answer.

The sayings vary from place to place in China; in Peking the response might be "frog jumps into the well." However, whichever form is said, one starts out by mentally visualizing either a stone falling into a well or a frog jumping in. In either case, what would happen? I would mentally see either a stone or a frog silently falling through space, then suddenly, as one or the other hit the water, a sound would be heard.

In English, we might describe the sound as "splash," or perhaps "plop," but the Chinese go far beyond us in their use of onomatopoeic words to describe sounds. In that case, a Chinese would not only hear the original "splash" sound, but he would also note the echo from the walls of the well. For the sound of the echo we don't have a word in English, but the Chinese do, and combining the two sounds in Chinese, the first, that of the "splash" when the object hits the water, would be *pu* (pooh), and the echo *tung* (toong), which gives us the correct answer, i.e., *putung*, an approximation of *bu dong*, "I don't understand." To us Westerners the whole thing may seem facetious and rather far-fetched, but to the Chinese the sayings are apt, incisive and pertinent, and are widely used in conversation. Rarely are they taught to Westerners in language schools because they require such a broad background knowledge of Chinese culture.

Another distraction in the prison was the bizarre arrival each morning of the postman. The Chinese postal service was like none other in the world. The main post office on 42nd Street in Manhattan has an inscription above the facade, well-known to Americans: "Neither snow, rain nor sleet shall... etc." But the Chinese postal service went them one better and could add many other things to the list, such as civil wars, bandits, floods, famines, earthquakes, and the invasion of foreigners, such as the Japanese. In China the postman had always been almost sacrosanct and could go anywhere at any time. Even during civil wars, dressed in their light green uniforms, they usually managed to get through the lines of the opposing armies, and bandits seldom bothered them, probably because they carried nothing of any basic value. Even with the coming of the Japanese, they had managed to keep up the tradition, and we were surprised when, in midmorning of our first full day in the prison, the man walked in with the mail. He did so each day thereafter. To his thinking, he had letters addressed to Mr. Duthie, and since Mr. Duthie wasn't at home, the next best thing was to deliver them to Mr. Duthie's temporary home, even if it was the common prison. He showed not the slightest surprise when he handed the letters through the bars. When Mr. Duthie received his mail, he asked the man to wait while he looked through it, and finding items there for the ladies at the mission, he gave them back to the postman. That became a daily routine and the guards never batted an eyelid. Apparently for the postman a little thing like a world war was minor, and to the guards the postman could do no wrong.

Being shut up in the prison behind a locked door was terrible, but it was something I could handle without too much of a problem. I didn't particularly

mind the cold, the filth, and the hardness of the floor; we were used to that kind of hardship in our travels. What bothered me most was not knowing what the future would bring, nor how long we would be there. But above all I was concerned about Eva and my other loved ones because, although I knew where they were, they most probably hadn't the faintest idea where I was or what was happening to me. And I knew that Eva and my mother would be worrying every minute of the day.

There was no way I could get a message to Mother, but with Eva in the same town and less than a mile away, somehow I had to get a message to her. The arrival of the postman gave me an idea.

Two or three days later the postman brought a magazine in a brown paper wrapper addressed to one of the ladies at the mission. But before Mr. Duthie handed it back to the postman, I whispered to him to let me have it for a few minutes and to stall the postman for a bit. Slipping the magazine out of its wrapper, I used the stub of a pencil that I had found in my pocket to scribble a note to Eva on an inside page of the magazine, telling her I was in the jail, but was well, and for her not to worry. I then slipped the wrapper back on and gave the magazine back to Mr. Duthie, who handed it to the postman. I was sure that when it got to the mission, whoever read it would find the note and tell Eva. It was risky and I would have been in trouble if what I was doing had been noticed, but I felt a great sense of relief in knowing that Eva's mind would be set at rest. Eva, however, never got the message. Quite unexpectedly, after keeping Eva and Barbara in Chengde for a week, the Japanese had sent them back to Lingyuan under escort to help take care of Ruth. It was that same night that I learned about it.

I had been sleeping heavily when I was awakened by something in the middle of the night. The prison was absolutely quiet except for some voices coming from the guards' desk, but I felt a strong draft and noticed that the front door near us was wide open. I heard the sound of an idling truck motor outside. Since none of us had watches, I had no idea of the time, but I was certain it was after midnight and I wondered what was going on. Then a terrible sense of dread overcame me. Because of that idling motor I felt sure something new and terribly unpleasant was about to happen to us. It was all-too-reminiscent of the early morning arousal a week or so before, and I began to shake all over and my teeth chattered, not only from the cold. For 15 minutes or so I sat there and shook as though I had the ague, hearing only the voices, which seemed to get louder, and the persistent sound of the truck's motor. I felt certain we were about to be taken somewhere.

Suddenly there was a burst of activity. Several armed men rushed down the corridor, went outdoors, and then almost at once brought in a file of new prisoners. There must have been 15 or 20 of them, all Westerners. Most were Catholic priests, but there were a few White Russian traders and two nuns. Then, at the end of the column, I spotted my father. It was a shock, but at the same time I felt a great sense of relief. I barely had time to call his name and see him turn his face toward me before he was gone, out of sight up the corridor.

Not knowing who he was, the guards first put him in another cell. A few minutes later, when a guard came by escorting the visiting police to the door, I accosted him, told him that one of the new prisoners was my father, and asked that he be put in with us. Tight as our quarters were, he surprisingly agreed. The two nuns were given seats out in the corridor next to the stove, where they sat the rest of the night, and in the morning they were taken elsewhere, presumably either to the Catholic mission or to Mr. Duthie's home.

Of course, with Father squeezing into our cramped space, everyone had to be awakened, but we were all old friends and it was a joyous occasion in more ways than one. At first he was so frozen from being out on top of the truck for so long that he couldn't talk, but when he had warmed up a bit he told me that Eva and Barbara had been sent home to Lingyuan for the duration and had turned up just that morning, while he was to take their place in Chengde, and had been brought over on the late afternoon single-car diesel train. I was delighted to know Eva was back home in our own little house. Father also had some late news of the war, but none of it was good. Hong Kong was about to fall, there was severe fighting in Singapore, and the Japanese were having success everywhere in Southeast Asia. Our spirits sagged.

Coincidentally with the arrival of that batch of prisoners things definitely changed for the better. We judged that the Japanese had heard how their people were being treated in Britain and the United States and had decided they had better do the same. Whether by design or by sheer coincidence, our morning walk to the latrine was now changed to just after sunrise, and in addition, we were taken to a nearby pump, where, after breaking off the ice and priming it, we were able to get cold water to wash with. We were provided with tin wash basins, filthy and battered old things, but better than nothing, and some old gray towels, plus a chunk of hard laundry soap. However, after a week of having no bathing facilities whatsoever, that was a little piece of heaven, even if the water was icy cold. The hardier among us stripped to the waist and had a good wash each morning, always with an admiring group of onlookers standing by.

We were also allowed a visitor. The morning after Father's arrival the local Japanese Protestant pastor came in to see us and spent about an hour. He was a man we had known for several years, and he spoke a little English and some Chinese and went by his Chinese name, Fu Jing. He had to stand outside our cell and talk through the bars, but he read from his Bible and prayed with us, and his visit was of great comfort to us all. Despite the fact that our countries were at war, we were all brothers in Christ, and we felt a bond of closeness that the hostilities could not affect. When he learned that we had not been allowed to bring our Bibles, he demanded that we be allowed to have them, and that afternoon a half-dozen Chinese Bibles were brought in to us.

Since the coming of Pastor Fu Jing was an official act, as was the giving to us of the Bibles, the attitude of our guards changed considerably. Their natural inclination to friendliness came to the forefront and they became quite sociable. It is normal procedure for Chinese to read almost everything aloud, so we did the same as we read our Bibles, and the guards said nothing. It was a form of relaxation for us to be able to use our voices freely without reprisal, and at the same time it gave us the opportunity to witness to those of our fellow prisoners who were Chinese, and also enabled us to provide some comfort to the Catholic priests in the nearby cell, who had not been allowed the same privilege. They told us afterward that they received great comfort in hearing the familiar texts, albeit in Chinese.

The following morning another surprise awaited us. At sunrise not only were we let out to conduct our morning ablutions, but whether by design or simply for their own convenience, the guards let all the Catholic fathers out at the same time. We were delighted, because it meant we could spend more time out in the fresh air as everyone waited their turn with the wash basins, and we were taken in batches of six to the latrines. Some of the priests we had met before, so we had a chance to renew old acquaintances, and others we met for the first time.

The majority of the priests were Belgian, although two were Dutch. Few spoke more than a few words of English, but one, an elderly bishop, was quite fluent. The guards permitted him to talk with us undisturbed, and as all of them had access to radios up until the time they were arrested, they passed on to us any news that they had heard.

After that the same procedure was carried out each morning, and I recall one very amusing incident. Now that we were allowed out in daylight, our young Chinese lad was up and about and was there every morning as part of the small crowd of curious onlookers watching the crazy foreigners with their shirts off, doing sitting-up exercises and running in place to keep warm and fit while waiting for their turn to wash.

The old bishop was standing by that morning and suddenly the young lad went over to him and started to count the red buttons on his cassock. Starting at the bottom, the boy counted upward, fingering each button and counting aloud. The old man had a long white beard that extended almost to his waist. When the boy reached the beard, he simply gathered it all in one hand and raised it high as he continued counting the buttons right up to the old man's neck. I was watching the bishop's eyes, but instead of showing any annoyance, he smiled and it was apparent he thoroughly enjoyed the whole episode.

The same lad continued to prove a bit of a nuisance to me, however. He insisted on following me each time I went to the latrine and stood there watching me as I used the wide-open facility. Several times I asked him why he was staring at me, but he simply shook his head and wouldn't answer. Eventually, when I persisted in wanting to know why he kept bothering me, he reluctantly told me that he had been told that all Westerners had a penis that was eight feet in length and we had to wrap it twice around our waists and tuck the end in. He had also heard that we could crack it like a whip. He was greatly disappointed when I assured him that he had been misinformed and that we were in no way different from Chinese men. His story didn't surprise me at all. I had heard many such wild ideas over the years. To the Chinese, we foreigners were always a mystery.

Many other happenings from day to day were not so amusing. From our position on the floor of the cell we could see through the two-inch crack of the partly opened door, and our view took in the buildings across the courtyard. Every day a long column of people lined up there, and we learned from the young Chinese lad that they were drug addicts who had come for their daily ration, whether opium, morphine or heroin. After producing a special ration card and paying the required sum of money, each person had a dose doled out to him. We had known for a long time that the Japanese would not permit the sale of drugs of any sort to the Chinese, and kept it as a monopoly for themselves and we watched the tragic evidence.

One morning we noticed quite a ruckus going on across the courtyard. A few moments later, four policemen came across the yard, dragging an elderly Chinese woman with them. They had her spread-eagled, with a man holding each leg and another two holding her arms. As they dragged her across the yard, her head bumped on the ground, and her loud screams filled the air. They brought her into the jail past our cell and dragged her down the corridor, her head bumping on the floor all the way. It must have been extremely painful for the poor soul, but all the police did was laugh uproariously. They threw her into a cell near ours, and for hours we could hear the poor woman groaning. It seemed that her crime was that the Japanese had discovered she was not an addict herself, but was buying drugs to sell to others at a profit.

Toward the end of that second week we had another visit from the pastor, who brought sensational news. He told us that a decision had been made to move all male missionaries to an internment camp someplace in northern Manchuria. We didn't know whether that was good news or bad. Bad as were the conditions of our jail, they were now at least familiar and we could manage with them. Were we going to something worse or better? That entire day our minds were in a turmoil, and we slept little that night.

I am sure you will have justifiably formed the

impression that I was always a bit devious in my dealings with the Japanese, and you wouldn't be wrong. As the pastor was talking about our imminent move, an idea came to me. If I played my cards right, I might be able to wangle a visit back to Lingyuan to see Eva. So, without giving it a second thought, I pulled up my trouser leg and showed him my bare leg under the trousers, and told him I hadn't brought along any thick woolen underwear, and asked if he thought it was possible that I might be permitted to return a day earlier to Lingyuan to get myself some warm clothing. If that was possible, I could then join the others on the train as it passed through Lingyuan.

All the Japanese wore at least one, and sometimes two or more, sets of the heaviest possible woolen long johns. The pastor was suitably shocked to see the sad condition I was in with my bare legs. What he didn't know was that I had never in my life worn any long thick underwear. I never could tolerate it because it always brought out a rash, so even in the coldest weather I wore nothing but summer underwear and regular pants.

Within the hour I was granted an interview with the senior Japanese officer in charge. It was serious business, so I didn't do my usual ebullient act; instead, I summoned up what I thought would pass for an expression of suitable humility. Entering his office, I gave His Greatness a low bow. Again, I pulled up my trouser leg and showed him my pitiable condition and was gratified to hear him exclaim, *Damedaroo* ("bad"), a term that normally comes close to profanity, but which under certain circumstances can be an expression of shock or horror. He got up from his desk, came around to where I stood, and pulled up his own trouser leg to show me he was wearing two pairs of long johns. He agreed with me that something had to be done about my "desperate" condition, and he even offered to lend me a pair of his own. However, I pointed out to him that I was much taller than he was. He promised he would work something out. I went back to our cell on top of the world, certain that something good would come of it. However, that was one time my duplicity didn't pay off.

Two days went by and nothing happened. Finally word came down, again through Pastor Fu Jing, that a decision had been made, once more through the kind intervention of the same Mr. Kurimoto who had been so helpful a year earlier, when the Sturts and Doug

Broughton had been jailed by the Japanese in Mongolia. The decision was that all the younger men would go north for internment, and we were informed that our destination would be Mukden. He further told us that for reasons of health and age, all the older men would be permitted to remain behind. Reginald Sturt, because of his poor health, would remain in Chengde with his wife and the Duthies, together with Mrs. Oliver and several single lady missionaries. Mr. Oliver, although in his sixties at the time, was evidently considered young enough to go north.

After telling us that, the pastor turned to me and told me that my father was to be permitted to return home the next day in order to carry a message to my wife so that she could prepare suitable winter clothing for me, and it would be brought to the station for me when our train went through. He added that Father would be permitted to remain in Lingyuan because of my sister Ruth's ill health, and Eva and Barbara could stay there as well. Despite my personal disappointment, it was fantastic news.

Presumably they didn't trust me enough to allow me to go back to Lingyuan on my own. That, of course, was a tremendous disappointment, because I had so looked forward to seeing Eva again, if only for one night. But it was not to be, and from the point of view of the Japanese it made sense. I was delighted that Father was to be allowed to go home for good, but why they had taken him to Chengde and put him in a cell for just five days didn't make any sense. But then, we had learned that very few things the Japanese did made any sense, so we should not have been surprised by it.

The next morning, December 24th, Father left by himself on the early morning train for Lingyuan; the rest of us were told that we would be leaving the following day. We were told to wash and shave, and hot water and razors were provided. Most of us availed ourselves of the luxury, but one or two refused on principle. I personally shaved because I wanted to be able to kiss Eva without a lot of stubble on my face, and I didn't want her to see how terrible I looked. The reason the Japanese wanted us to clean ourselves up was, of course, that they wanted us to look our best, and didn't want anyone knowing about the conditions under which we had been held. They were quite annoyed with those who refused to shave, but they didn't force the issue.

We were again lodged in our prison cell for the night and the next morning, Christmas Day. it was my turn to leave. I say "my turn" because I must here interject a misconception I have held for 50 years. Thinking back to that terribly bleak Christmas Day when I was to see Eva only briefly, and then be separated, certainly for the duration of the war, or, as I thought then, possibly forever, I have always thought I had total recall of the cataclysmic events of those dark days. It had stuck in my mind that I was taken alone to Mukden, with the others following a day or so later, but that was apparently not the case. While writing of these events I did some reading to try and refresh my memory, and came across a book written by S. G. Compton, *Children of the Wilderness*, in which he writes of that incident, presumably from notes written by Mr. Sturt. In it he states that all the younger men were taken in a group. I also came across a 42-page document I wrote in 1942 for British Intelligence, in which I documented the same thing, so I am sure it was the case. I was feeling such utter despair at the time, and my mood was so melancholy, that I must have been unaware of anyone else around me apart from the three Japanese detectives who accompanied us. However, there were actually four of us taken to Mukden together that day. Mr. Oliver was one. The others were Doug Broughton and Harry Bishop.

Loaded into the back of a truck with the three plainclothes Japanese detectives, we were taken to the railroad station and given third-class tickets, for which, incidentally, we were all later billed. We were also billed for the food that was given to us in the prison. For the next four hours I sat in a complete daze, living only for the few moments I would be able to spend with Eva on the Lingyuan station platform, and yet, paradoxically, dreading the moment because when it came, it would be over so swiftly.

It was a very cold, bleak day with gray skies and one of our rare, heavy snowfalls. I desperately hoped that the train would somehow become stalled by snowdrifts in Lingyuan, but well into the afternoon we pulled into the station and there on the platform, almost hidden by the falling snow, was my little Eva, standing alongside my father. Just seeing her again made my heart pound, and I wanted to hold onto her forever.

The train was running late and we had only brief minutes in which to say our good-bys. Eva handed me a bag she'd packed for me and we hugged and kissed briefly before one of the detectives dragged me back onto the train — and we were gone. They let me stand on the steps of the car until the train rounded a slight curve, when I could see Eva no longer. The image of her diminutive figure standing there in the falling snow, bravely trying to keep back the tears, has remained vividly in my mind all these years. Even today, when I think of it, it brings a big lump into my throat.

As the train passed within a few yards of the back garden wall, I pressed my nose against the window pane, seeing for the last time the old elm tree and the date tree in which I had perched so many times. Unknown to me at the time, Barbara was inside peering out through a wide crack in the wall, watching the train go by. Within seconds, all the places so familiar to me were out of sight.

That was the very lowest point in my entire life. At the time I was convinced that the war was going to last for years, just like the war in Europe, and as things looked then, Japan would inevitably be the victor. Would I ever see Eva again? Grief-stricken as I was, I also had a tremendous sense of relief in knowing that she was at home in familiar surroundings with my other loved ones around her to keep her company and to look after her. I at least knew where she was, but she, poor dear, only knew I was being taken somewhere in Mukden. We had no idea of what conditions would be like when we got there. I remember I had visions of being put into the Chinese prison in Mukden, which would inevitably be worse than the one in Chengde because it was a much larger city, and then I remember having a daydream that perhaps they would put us in little huts out in the middle of nowhere. The question burning my brain was, how in the world would I be able to let Eva know where I was so I could relieve her worry.

The entire trip to Mukden took more than 22 hours. We sat up all night in a crowded carriage and I slept not a wink for the entire trip. The Chinese around us, noticing the detectives and the fact that we were their prisoners, kept their distance as much as they could, so we at least had some elbow room. I have very little recollection of the trip except for my feeling of absolute misery, but I do recall that the detectives treated us humanely and with a great deal of consideration, purchasing apples for us en route and taking us into the dining car for meals and allowing us to eat whatever we wanted. But again, we were later billed for all of it. None of us had much of an appetite.

I remember, too, that they were particularly curious as to why such a high official as Mr. Kurimoto should have intervened on our behalf, and they repeatedly asked me how it was we knew such an important person.

When we transferred to the main-line train in the middle of the night, I remember how cold it was standing out on the platform waiting for the train to come in. Apart from that, however, I was a zombie, moving only when I was told to do so, and I remember little, except for one or two small incidents during the trip.

On the train the three detectives unbent to some extent, and although they all managed to sleep, one of them usually remained awake, watching us carefully. At every big stop the conductor would get off the train and collect the latest war news and would then come into the car and shout it out at the top of his voice in Japanese. To my surprise, the Japanese in the car showed little emotion beyond some desultory clapping, although I do recall that shortly before we arrived in Mukden the conductor announced that Hong Kong had fallen. At that point the three detectives showed great excitement and asked us what we thought about it. Naturally I felt deeply depressed at the news and I am sure the others did, too. The Allies were losing ground everywhere, and I recall one Japanese soldier sitting near us saying to another, "Singapore next, and then Sumatra and Java."

At one point during the night, when the three detectives were feeling in an expansive mood, I casually asked them exactly where it was in Mukden that we were to be taken. I was intensely surprised when they told me that we were to be housed in a large foreign club, the International Club, which had been turned into an internment center. I had never heard of it and had no idea where it was in Mukden, but somehow I had to get that news to Eva. I sat and schemed, knowing I would have to do it soon, before we were locked up. The news was cheering in a way, because up to that point I was sure we were simply being transferred to another prison cell.

At one point during the night all three detectives were asleep, so I took the opportunity to open the suitcase Eva had brought me. There, right on top, I found writing paper, some stamped, pre-addressed envelopes, and a pen. I sneaked a couple of sheets of paper into my pocket together with one of the envelopes and looked for the first possible opportunity to write Eva a note.

During the early hours of the morning, when the three detectives were feeling groggy and were dozing off and on, I noticed one of them wake up. As he did so, I leaned forward, hugging my stomach, and started to groan loudly. He showed some alarm and asked me what was wrong. I told him I had to go to the toilet in a hurry and got up and left. In the toilet I sat and wrote Eva two whole pages, giving her the name of the club as it had been told to me. I hoped that I would be able to find some way of mailing the letter without my three guardians seeing me, when we arrived in Mukden. Before I had finished the letter, the detective was pounding on the door asking me if I was all right. I mumbled something in reply and before long I reappeared, much to his relief. I am certain he thought I was trying to make my escape out the bathroom window.

We reached Mukden shortly after daybreak. It had ceased snowing, but it was a dark, dismal day, and very cold. Heavy smog filled the air from all the coal fires burning throughout the city, and a more dreary place I don't think I have ever seen.

I knew the Mukden station well. There were two exits, one through the main waiting room and the other through a side entrance in the high fence surrounding the place. As we left the train I hoped the detectives would take us through the latter, because I knew there was a mailbox right by the gate. My hopes were fulfilled as they followed the crowd milling around us and headed for the gate. I lagged behind a bit while they were ahead of me in the crowd, and as I came to the mailbox, I stopped, threw my bedding roll over the top of it, and bent down, pretending I was tying a shoelace. One of the three detectives immediately noticed my absence and headed back toward me, and as he did so, I stood up, turned my back to him and retrieved my bedding roll with one hand, while with the other I slipped my letter under the bedding roll and into the mailbox. That made me feel a lot better; at least Eva would now know where I had been taken and perhaps I might even hear from her.

When I started writing this chapter I had no recollection of it, but my 1942 account states that we were taken to the station buffet for a hot breakfast and then, after a two-hour wait, were loaded onto an open truck and taken to the International Club, my home for the next six months or more.

My only recollection of our arrival at the club was a vivid first impression of a long, low building, set well back away from the street in a spacious compound surrounded by a six-foot wall topped with steel spikes. Originally they were put there to keep intruders from climbing in, but doubtless were now intended by the Japanese to keep us from climbing out.

Just inside the high iron gate was a small gatehouse manned by Japanese soldiers, and when the gate was opened for our truck, we drove up a long driveway, perhaps three hundred feet long. I could see a number of Westerners peering out the windows, but none of the faces were familiar to me. We remained in the truck while the Japanese detectives went inside, and then, after a lot of discussion, we were handed over to a Japanese in civilian clothes. He turned out to be the commandant in charge of the place, a man I was to get to know extremely well.

I remember feeling a sense of great relief that we were not to be incarcerated in the common prison, but the overwhelming impression was that things would never again be quite the same for the rest of my life. How true that turned out to be.

This particular Mexican dollar is the one mentioned in Chapter 7 and Chapter 26, which was introduced to gradually replace the ancient Sycee silver tael ingot. It was most welcomed at the time because it brought some degree of sanity into the traditionally chaotic Chinese currency system that still existed in the early 20th century. By 1914, however, the Yuan Shih-k'ai dollar began replacing Mexican dollars, which were either melted down or resold to Mexico. Meanwhile, in the hinterlands of China the Mexican dollar, and even the Sycee, continued to circulate for years.

Garden helpers in our compound.

A Sunday School Class.

In the Hall — Note Bob's trumpet and hat.

光陰似箭，
日月如梭

Guang yin si jian, ri yue ru suo.

Time passes like an arrow,
days and months pass like a shuttle
(used for weaving).

- Chinese Proverb.

Book Three
1942 - 1946
Chapter Twenty-Nine
Internment

Prior to its occupation by the Japanese, the International Club in Mukden had been owned and operated by the British and American Tobacco Company for the convenience of not only their own employees and other British and American nationals, but also all consular staffs of the two countries. Although the club had a fairly large enrollment, none of the members were present that day, December 26, 1941, when I and my companions from Jehol arrived. All had been arrested and interned elsewhere in the city and the Japanese had decided to use the club as an internment camp exclusively for missionaries.

The Japanese camp commandant was named Nakamura. When he got through entering our names in his book, we were taken into what had once been the lounge and library. It was a huge room that took up over half the length of the west side of the building. Windows lined the entire western wall, and beneath them were bookcases filled with a wide variety of books, everything from novels to encyclope-

dias, and there were more bookcases on the other walls as well. A fair number of easy chairs were bunched together in the middle, and at the far end was a long table surrounded by straight-backed chairs, where meals were served.

But what caught my attention almost immediately was a long row of straw-filled mattresses covering the wooden floor next to the windows. I was taken to one, approximately in the center of the room, and that was my assigned "space" for the duration. The mattresses were placed about a foot apart, with just enough room between them to stand a suitcase upright at the far end under the windows. Unfortunately, they were so close together that occasionally in the night I would be awakened by a thrashing arm from one of my neighbors, or by being stepped on as one or another of them got up to go to the washroom.

My immediate neighbor on one side was an ebullient young American, Father Sullivan, who had one of the most cheerful dispositions I have ever seen, and he had an endless fund of stories and jokes that kept us all entertained over the dreary days that followed. Father Sullivan was a very big man, weighing well over 200 pounds, but he lost more than 40 pounds within the first month, and still more after that. On my other side was Father Quirk, a quiet, very introspective young man, thin and short of stature, but a man deeply dedicated to his calling. We three quickly became close friends.

My feelings as I first entered that room are difficult to describe. To say that they were distinctly mixed would be an understatement. I felt a tremendous sense of relief at finding we were not to be housed in the common prison as I had feared. But at the same time, it was evident from the number of people there, and the Japanese and Chinese guards around us, that there was no mistaking the fact that we were still prisoners, and that we undoubtedly would enjoy no freedom for a long time to come.

The surroundings of that room were a tremendous contrast to the prison in Chengde and a vast improvement over the cell in which we had spent the previous two weeks. It looked very much like a dormitory, with clothing draped over the bookcases that lined the walls and hanging from ropes tied between the numerous pillars that supported the roof. But, although I was very conscious of the fact that we were still prisoners, it was as unlike a prison as any place could be. My immediate impulse was to write and tell Eva how very fortunate we were. However, at the same time I could not help but feel that it was all too good to last, that someday we would be moved elsewhere.

I was impressed by the large number of people in the room. There were friendly, smiling faces everywhere, but for a moment I saw no one I knew. Then suddenly I caught sight of our very old friend Herbert Brewster from Chaoyang. I had wondered what had happened to him, and there he was, looking hale and hearty. He greeted me with a big hug and we filled each other in on the happenings of the previous two weeks. I was delighted to hear that Heather Brewster was also there, and I met her later that morning, together with Frances Wilks and Dorothy Flanagan, also of Chaoyang. They, together with two Catholic nuns, came out of their quarters to join us for lunch. They had all been there for more than a week and were well settled in.

In all, there were some 40 internees when I arrived, five of them women. But I was by no means the last to arrive, for within a few days more joined us. In May more followed until our number eventually approached 100. Four of the earlier newcomers were women, one of them a doctor, and another was Mrs. Leggate, whose husband came with her and was one of the four male missionary doctors in the camp.

Of our entire group, approximately half were Protestant missionaries, mostly British, and the remainder were Catholic Maryknoll missioners, all of them Americans. As new arrivals, we received a very warm welcome, which raised our spirits. Everyone wanted to know if we carried any late news of the war, but the news we had picked up on the train was not what they wanted to hear. We spent the next several hours exchanging stories of our experiences of the previous weeks.

I find it difficult to know where to begin in telling of the six months I spent in the International Club. I remember so much about that camp but for some reason or other I remember nothing about New Year's Day. It must have come and gone without our having paid any attention to it because most of us were in a state of deep depression those first weeks. In some respects, very little happened while we were in the camp, and yet there were many things that we eventually did to alleviate the boredom and add a little spice to life.

I remember that one of the first things I did was to tour the quarters that were allocated for our use and to learn from the first arrivals what we could or could not do, and just how rigid the regulations were. Actually, as it turned out, the Japanese had placed very few restrictions on what we could do indoors, and we were allowed considerable freedom. However, going outdoors was quite a different matter. We were only permitted to stand outside the front entrance in small groups for a few minutes each day to get a little fresh air and sunshine. To move even a few yards away would result in violent bellowing from the guards and in our being hustled back indoors.

The club was very large, with many rooms, but only a very few of them had been made available for our use. Apart from the lounge, which was perhaps 80 to 90 feet long by about 40 feet wide, and in which

20 or so of us slept at night, there was the bar, which held a few more. At the back of the building, reached through a short and very narrow corridor leading out from the center of the lounge, was a billiard room. There another group had their mattresses, some of them on the billiard table itself.

The nine ladies were housed at the extreme northerly end of the building in a room to themselves. It was a large room with an attached washroom containing just one basin and two toilets, but although the room was large, with nine mattresses spread out on the floor, there was little room left to walk around and they were very crowded. However, it never seemed to bother any of them. To reach their room, they had to go through the foyer, or entrance lobby, and then through a narrow corridor where, blocked off behind a curtain, the guards lived.

The privacy of the ladies was respected by the Japanese at all times and they were able to lock their door at night. However, I was not happy that neither Mr. Brewster nor Dr. Leggate were permitted to go near the room where their wives lived. Over the years I had seen a great deal of the Japanese military and their ways with women, and I didn't trust them one iota, particularly after they had been drinking. I determined to find some way of changing the situation in case of an emergency, and I didn't have to wait very long to come up with a solution.

There was a washroom for the men situated behind the lounge and reached through another corridor that led from the billiard room. There, for the use of some 40 of us, there were just two basins and two toilets. All the plumbing was modern, but totally inadequate for the number of people in the building and certainly not designed for the maximum daily use that we gave it. As the weeks passed the plumbing constantly failed, and the Japanese refused to do anything about it. We had to make all repairs ourselves.

On the left side of the short corridor leading from the lounge to the billiard room, there was another small wash basin in what was a very well-equipped barber shop. The wash basin was the most frequently used item in that room and, because there was a light on all night in there, those of us who couldn't sleep at night sometimes used the barber chair to sit and read. I used it on many sleepless nights.

There wasn't a single bathtub in the place. Consequently, for a considerable period of time we had to make do with sponge baths, but eventually we found a solution even for that problem.

For the first four months, food conditions were pretty grim. Two meals a day were served to us in the lounge by one of the three Chinese servants who had been retained by the Japanese. The remainder had all been fired. According to the three who were left, a number of those fired had been in the employ of the club for 20 years or longer and were entitled to better treatment than they received from the Japanese.

We learned that our food was contracted for by the local Russian Club, and it was not only inadequate, it was also of poor quality. We were told that the Russian Club was paid two yuan per day for each person — a pitifully small amount — so it was not surprising that they skimped. Our daily lunch consisted of Russian borscht soup (mostly vegetables, with an occasional small piece of meat). With the soup we got two slices of a very poor quality bread. Dinner at night was either a very small piece of meat or a small river fish, which was chiefly bones. Along with that we were given a spoonful of rice, one potato, and whatever bread had been saved from lunch.

Breakfast was usually a joke. It was more of a morning get-together than anything else. There seldom was more than a slice of bread and some hot water, and on one or two very rare occasions we got an egg that had been brought to the club by some Catholic nuns, a number of whom had been permitted to live in the local mission and were allowed the freedom of the city. We never got any coffee or tea nor any butter or jam to spread on our bread.

Within the first month almost everyone had lost weight, most 20 pounds or more. Like everyone else I was constantly hungry, but being thin to begin with, somehow I managed to maintain my weight pretty well and did not let the lack of food bother me too much. Actually, I had more on my mind than food. My worrying over Eva's welfare engaged my thoughts most of the time.

The Japanese did make one early concession to us. Since it had been their decision to put all the missionaries together, both Protestant and Catholic, we asked for one room in which we could conduct our church services. To our surprise they agreed and gave us the gymnasium. There, each day and on Sundays, we were able to gather together for worship, conducting services at different times in the day. Among the books in the library we discovered hymnals and Bibles, and beyond an initial curiosity as to what we were doing, the Japanese and Chinese guards never disturbed us at those times.

When I arrived I was in a deep depression, certain that the war would last for years and that I might never see Eva or the rest of my family again. Since there were not enough chairs to go around, most people simply sat or lay on their mattresses most of the day, and any exercise we got had to be managed in the minimal space available to us. As I lay on my mattress the second day, my eyes fell longingly on all those wonderful books locked in the bookcases around me. I decided that the books, at least, were something we could all use, and I determined to get some out. I knew the Japanese well enough to know that it was absolutely useless to ask for permission to use the books. The bookcases were locked and would stay that way if we were to ask to have the books, so I scouted around, and before long found a short piece of stiff wire. That night I experimented with the locks and with very little difficulty managed to open two of the bookcase nearest to my bed. After that, I had all the reading material I could use for as long as I wished. I told the others what I had done and offered to get them some books, too, if they would make their selections. Then, late at night, I would procure the books asked for, and before long everyone was reading. Not once were we asked by the Japanese where the books had come from. As far as they were concerned the bookcases were still locked — they checked them frequently enough — so the books couldn't have come from there. If they noticed our reading at all, they must have presumed that we had brought the books with us in our luggage.

On the third or fourth morning, I happened to be standing by the window looking out toward the street when I saw the mailman in his familiar green uniform enter the front gate and start walking up the driveway. I had an immediate hunch that he was bringing me a letter from Eva. I went out into the foyer, met him as he entered the door, and sure enough, he had a letter for me. Eva had received the letter I had posted from the station on the first day and had been given permission to send me a reply, and she said that she would be writing me once a week. Getting that letter was a tremendous boost to my morale, and the world didn't seem such a dreary place after all.

I wrote Eva a reply at once and then went in to ask Nakamura if he would mail it for me. Nakamura was indeed a strange man. He was initially quite gentlemanly in his attitude toward us, but we quickly learned that when in the presence of other Japanese, he became dictatorial and imperious. In time we learned also that he had a very strong sadistic streak. He was dressed in civilian clothes at all times, but it was in every way apparent that he had an army officer's background, and we felt it quite possible he still retained his officer's rank. Although he was quite obviously in charge of the internees, it became evident that he had absolutely no authority over the men assigned to him as guards, not even the Chinese. All of them were from a different organization.

I knew from experience that that was a technique employed by the Japanese authorities throughout Manchukuo. They almost always deliberately mixed their people on assignments, so that one group would keep an eye on what the other group was doing. Because of that, Nakamura, who spoke excellent English, would rarely talk to us in English if any of the other Japanese were around. If he had any announcement to make, he would make it in Japanese, and for any sort of official request, we had to go to him through our own interpreter, Father John Walsh, who spoke fluent Japanese. Almost always, though, our requests, however reasonable they seemed to us, were either politely refused (if he happened to be alone), or peremptorily dismissed if someone happened to be with him. Occasionally there were things that he felt he could allow us on his own authority, but we gained the impression that Nakamura was afraid of his superiors and didn't want to prejudice his job by going to them with what he obviously considered trivial requests on behalf of the internees. At the same time, he was equally nervous about those assigned to work with him, so we timed our requests (when we had any) to those times when we could get him alone, more often than not when he was on his way to the washroom that we all shared.

Anyway, on that particular day when I wanted to mail my letter, I found Nakamura alone in his office and in a good mood. When he heard I had received a letter from my wife and wanted to send an answer, he was all smiles and quite obliging. The following week, I was on the alert and intercepted the mailman and got my letter, but when I wrote a reply and went to Nakamura to mail it, another Japanese was in the office, and he flatly refused, telling me that only one letter was permitted. I was devastated and feared that Eva would worry herself sick if she didn't hear from me.

In the early months of our internment there were always three or more Chinese guards on duty, along with usually two Japanese. The Chinese fellows very quickly became quite friendly, provided they could talk to us out of earshot of the Japanese. I solicited the help of one of them while we were together in the washroom, produced my letter, and asked him to mail it for me, which he promised to do. However, he never did so, nor did he mail any of the subsequent letters I gave him, but it was a very long time before I learned that. I imagine he was too afraid of being caught with the letters on him and simply destroyed them. At the same time he was afraid of losing face with me if he refused my request.

When Eva's third letter came, I spotted the mailman coming up the driveway and was just about to take my letter from him when Nakamura came up behind me, snatched the letter out of the man's hand, and then proceeded to berate him, kick him and slap him around for his audacity in giving the letter to me directly. He told the man that when he came in the future, he was to hand all mail to the guard at the front gate and never again to enter the club itself.

The next few weeks were torture. Nakamura intercepted Eva's letters each week and would call me into his office, produce the letter, open it in front of me, and then pretend to read from it. Each time he invented something lewd and filthy to say, suggesting that Eva was enjoying herself with numerous other men and telling me that she didn't need me any longer and wanted a divorce. When he tired of baiting me, he would set a lighted match to the letter and slowly burn it in front of me. I was forced to stand there and watch him, seething but determined not to give him the satisfaction of letting him know that it bothered me. Ultimately he tired of the game, and I don't know what happened to the rest of the letters.

That went on for several weeks, well into 1942. In the meantime, I was racking my brain for other ways in which to get letters out to Eva. Several times I sneaked out of the building late at night when everyone was asleep and threw letters over the back wall. With postage on the envelopes, and the address writ-

ten in Chinese as well as English, I hoped that someone would pick them up and throw them into a mailbox. But of the eight or ten that I "posted" in that way, not one was received by Eva. Few of the Chinese who might have seen them were sufficiently sophisticated to know what to do with them or to be concerned with someone else's loss.

Finally, after more than a month of utter frustration, the youngest of the three Chinese servants, who as it happened was a devout Catholic, came to me quietly one day and told me that he was aware I was trying to send letters to my wife, but that it was dangerous to give them to the guards. He told me that if I would write to her in Chinese and address the envelope in Chinese as well, he would mail the letters for me. At the same time he suggested that I could use his home as the return address, and he would smuggle Eva's replies in to me. That was indeed an answer to prayer. I asked him to procure some Chinese writing paper and envelopes for me, and the very next day he did so.

At that time the Chinese used very thin paper for their letters, which were usually written with a brush pen. The envelopes were long and narrow, with the name and address of the recipient written vertically from top to bottom instead of horizontally, as we do. In addition, the envelopes had a very thin inner lining. I wrote Eva a page in Chinese, using her Chinese name and writing only something very general and noncommittal that wouldn't get the young fellow into trouble if the letter was intercepted. Then I carefully loosened the inner lining of the envelope, and using another of the very thin sheets of paper, I inserted a letter written in English, then resealed it.

For a number of weeks that worked perfectly. Eva, I knew, would read my mind and would examine the envelopes with extreme care, which she did. She found my concealed letters and did the same thing when she replied. The young fellow, whose name was Liu, smuggled those letters into the club, hidden inside his sock, under his foot. A very brave young man, he literally risked his life each time he did so.

That exchange of letters went on until near the end of March. Then one day, just a few minutes after Liu had produced a letter for me, one of the older servants who had a grudge against him reported him to Nakamura. Somehow the other fellow must have seen him produce a letter from inside his sock and hand it to me, because Nakamura dragged young Liu into the guard room and made him take off his shoes and socks. Although he found nothing, he gave the young fellow a savage beating. Apparently the man who acted as informer had not said to whom the letters were being smuggled, because I was not brought into it, nor was I asked anything by Nakamura. From then on, however, I hadn't the heart to involve the young man any further, and, as it so happened, the need for doing so ceased a short time later.

Years later, when we returned to Mukden, I made it a special point to go to the club and find young Liu and thank him once again for the wonderful service he had rendered me, and to give him a few small gifts and some money. He had survived the war and was anticipating being employed once again by the club. Sad to say, however, the Communists shortly thereafter took over Mukden and all Westerners left. I've often wondered what became of that extraordinary young man with a big heart.

Apart from worrying about how to get letters out to Eva, I had other things on my mind as well. As I mentioned, I was unhappy over the way the ladies were kept isolated from us at night and felt that at least one of the men should somehow be given the right to go to the ladies' room if some emergency arose during the night.

For the first several weeks, the guards made a head count several times a day and every night. They varied the time, and frequently the night head count would come when we were all sleeping. They simply counted us as we lay in our beds, but the loud noises they made as they stumped around on the wooden floor by our heads, shining their flashlights into our faces at the same time, inevitably awakened us, and it became very annoying. Fortunately for us, they tired of it and in time we were no longer bothered.

One night toward the end of my first week there, I was awakened by the head count and couldn't get back to sleep. I got up and went to the barber shop and sat shivering in the chair. Suddenly an idea came to me. I decided to put it into effect immediately, and without giving it a second thought, I headed for the washroom. I planned to sabotage the electrical system and then take it from there, and if I was caught, my excuse would be that I was merely going to the washroom.

I should mention that the Japanese imposed an arbitrary "lights out" at 10:30 each night. By that time most of us were in bed anyway, so it was no great hardship. We learned later that at a second camp for internees in Mukden, where all the local British and American businessmen were held in the Hong Kong & Shanghai Bank building, their lights were extinguished at 9:30. I don't know why we were so privileged. It was just another illustration of the lack of uniformity in the way the Japanese ran things, and in that case it was particularly strange, because the same men who supervised our camp took turns supervising the internees in the bank building as well.

In any event, the only lights left on in the club at night were those in the hallways and the one in the barber shop, and from that I deduced that there were several circuits and that the hallway lights were probably all on one circuit. Just to be safe, I unscrewed several bulbs, both in the hallways and in the main rooms, shorted out the various circuits, and then crawled back into bed and pretended to be asleep.

I didn't have very long to wait for something to happen. Apparently one of the circuits I had shorted out covered the lights in the room where the guards slept, which were always kept on. One of the guards apparently woke up, and finding the entire place in darkness, became alarmed. I heard him shouting to awaken the others, and within a few seconds, all the guards stormed into our room, rushing around to check and see that we were all in our beds.

I hadn't let on to anyone, including my fellow internees, that I understood the Japanese language. I thought I might learn more that way. As Nakamura and another Japanese entered the room, I heard them talking excitedly about a mass attempt to escape. The noise they made naturally awakened everyone. They visited every bed, shining their lights in our faces, but when they came to my bed I pretended to be still fast asleep. A not-too-gentle boot in my ribs "woke" me, and rubbing my eyes I politely asked Nakamura what was wrong. He told me that all the lights were out and then turned to go on with his inspection. I immediately sat up, looked out of the window and said: "Mr. Nakamura, it is only the lights in this building that are out. The lights in the street are still on. It must be a problem with the wiring system in this building. I'm an electrician. I can take a look at it and try to fix it if you want me to." He hesitated for a moment or two, then told me to dress and follow him. I knew then that

I had it made.

Nakamura hadn't the slightest idea where the fuse boxes were, nor had I. But that was fine with me. I made a big pretense of looking in a lot of unlikely places, just so I could see as much of the building as possible, then I told him I'd have to go outside and see where the wires came in. From that point I quickly located the fuse boxes in one of the back rooms adjacent to the servants' quarters. Before changing the blown fuses with new ones (fortunately there was a box of them on a nearby shelf), I told him I would first have to find the source of the trouble. I had him provide me with a screwdriver and a pair of pliers, and he patiently followed me around as I checked wiring and lights for a good 20 minutes. Ultimately, after opening up one of the "suspected" switch boxes I "found" a loose wire and promptly fixed it. I then went back and replaced the blown fuses and had all the lights back on again, to Nakamura's immense satisfaction.

From that point on, I had Nakamura just where I wanted him. I told him (quite truthfully) that the building and wiring were very old and that the whole system ought to be carefully inspected in case the same thing happened again. He apparently was impressed with my expertise and asked if I would carry out the inspection for him. That was just what I wanted, and I of course agreed. But I told him it would take a long time and I would need keys for all the rooms that were locked, because the wiring in them would have to be checked as well. I also told him that he would have to allow me to go wherever I thought necessary and at whatever time I thought it necessary. He immediately agreed, and from then on I was the "official" electrician and naturally had the run of the entire building, which included the women's room. Even though I was largely faking it, checking the entire electrical system kept me happily busy for two or three weeks and helped take my mind off worrying about Eva. At the same time it also opened up a lot of interesting possibilities. As I systematically checked every switch, outlet and lamp socket, I found a number of rooms that we hadn't known existed, and which I felt we could legitimately use. I decided to do something about it as soon as possible.

I was delighted to find that one of the rooms at the extreme rear of the building turned out to be a regula-

tion bowling alley with two alleys, and with all the balls and pins still in place from the last time it had been used. After checking it out, I deliberately left that door unlocked and awaited the right opportunity to move in.

We didn't have long to wait. I had noticed very early that the pattern of guard-changing followed an exact schedule. Every two weeks Nakamura was replaced by another man named Watanabe, who was also Japanese, but spoke very little English. He was a quiet, almost mousy sort of chap, very unassuming, and, I felt, very insecure. I judged that when his turn came to take over the camp, he wouldn't question whatever he found in place, but would think that Nakamura had approved it, and therefore wouldn't think to mention it to Nakamura when, two weeks later, the latter came back on duty. I was certain also that Nakamura, when he reappeared, would presume that his replacement had given us permission to use the bowling alley. In any case, it was worth a try.

I talked it over with some of the Maryknoll Fathers, and we decided to chance it. On the mornings of the regular guard change I had carefully timed just how long it took them to carry out their formal transfer of duties down by the front gate. Each time it took ten minutes. During that time we were left entirely alone in the building. When the next guard change came, we were all ready to go, and when the new guards showed up at the front gate, we went into action. In that brief period, we moved into the bowling alley and started to play. We needn't have worried, though. The new guards didn't make a head count that morning and didn't discover us in there bowling until a couple of days later. Just as I had anticipated, they apparently presumed that Nakamura had given us permission to use the place and not a word was said. When Nakamura came back on duty the following week, we had a few minutes of unease, but again, my supposition was correct. He, too, never remarked on it, presumably thinking that Watanabe had given us permission. Not only that, he would frequently come in and watch us and even bowl a few strings himself.

That bowling alley was a godsend for us younger men, who needed the exercise and needed to let off some steam. It was in use the entire day. We formed leagues, giving ourselves names reminiscent of baseball teams in the U.S., and we played serious competitions. We had a great deal of fun and became so familiar with the alleys that bowling 300 games was not at all uncommon and the alleys themselves took a severe beating from the long hours we put in. Of course, the pins were all set manually, and we took turns at that, but it was all part of the fun, and the exercise and good fellowship helped us pass those dreary days as little else could have done.

Opening up the bowling alley made me think about the billiard room that was not being properly utilized. I talked it over with the members of the committee that we had formed. They agreed that it would be a good idea if it could be used. So, with a little juggling, we moved some of the mattresses around and had the table free for play by the older members of our group. Again, nothing was said by the Japanese after we had moved in, again during one of the guard changes. As far as recreation went, we were much better off than the businessmen cooped up in the bank building. They had much better and much more comfortable quarters than we did. They were living in well-furnished flats over the bank, designed originally to be used by married staff members. However, for recreation they had nothing beyond card games, and no books, and their only exercise was walking about on the flat roof of the building, with strict injunctions not to look down into the streets below.

For our part, at the beginning we were not allowed outdoors for a number of weeks, except for that area just outside the front entrance where, under supervision, we could stand around or sit in the sun for a bit. But we weren't permitted to walk anywhere. Eventually, however, the Japanese relaxed on that point after our five doctors jointly made a request for outdoor exercise in the interests of good health, and we were allowed to use the driveway for brief periods of walking each day but were not permitted to go within 20 feet of the front gate.

Another valuable find while I was "inspecting" the electrical system was the two shower rooms intended for the use of club members using the outdoor swimming pool, now empty. When I discovered those two rooms, I brought the existence of the two showers to the attention of the committee, and our five doctors went in a body to Nakamura, on my advice approaching him when he was alone. They asked permission to use the shower facilities also in the interests of health, emphasizing the fact that the Japanese themselves placed great importance on bathing. Nakamura at first protested, saying that it was impossible, telling us there was no way we could get hot water. However, I had tagged along with them and had an answer prepared for that. I had discovered a small boiler room out in a tiny courtyard at the back of the building, which was obviously used to heat the water for the shower rooms, and I quickly volunteered to fire the boiler if Nakamura would supply the coal. I think he was flattered to some extent by the limited authority he had within the building and being able to grant us the occasional request. In any case, he apparently felt he could afford to be magnanimous in that particular case, so he agreed. A small amount of coal was moved around to the back, as needed, and from then on I heated the water four days a week, with one of those days reserved for the nine ladies. The shower rooms were unheated, but none of us complained. The luxury of a hot shower once a week was very much appreciated by all, and it was also a place where we could not only do our laundry, but hang it out to dry as well.

Apart from the tremendous feeling of satisfaction I had over getting those two rooms for our use, I was also overjoyed at having the job of firing the boiler. I was the only one permitted to go back there, and as the guards seldom visited the place, I had that tiny room all to myself whenever I wanted to be alone. It was in there that I wrote most of my letters to Eva. It was there, too, that I discovered when looking over the back wall, that the American consul's residence was immediately across the street. From time to time I saw two American men and a woman walking in the front yard, always with a Japanese guard watching them, and I managed to wave to them surreptitiously when the guard wasn't looking. I felt immensely sorry for them, being so alone as they were, with no contact with the outside world and without the companionship of others that we were enjoying.

The main lounge was not only overcrowded with about 50 of us using it during the daytime, but because it faced west, it was also cold and dismal until early afternoon, when the sun shone in. The building was steam-heated, but the Japanese were stingy with coal and the temperature indoors never went above 60 degrees in the daytime and at night dropped to near freezing. We had no alternative but to wear outdoor clothing or sweaters almost all the time, and at night we had to pile overcoats on top of our blankets. However, as I moved around the building checking out the electrical system, I discovered a delightful sun room on the southwest corner of the building. I cast envious eyes on the place and wondered how I could work it so we could get the use of it. For almost the entire day it was bathed in sunlight and would be a grand place for us. Unfortunately, the Japanese were using it as a storeroom for bags of flour and rice that originally had been intended for our use but that had been appropriated by them, and those bags were a problem.

However, with a group of the younger men I worked out a strategy by which we would move into the sun room on one of the days when the guards changed. I found another room nearby where the flour and rice could be stored, and on the designated day, we waited until the guards walked down to the front gate in a body and we immediately went to work.

We had all rehearsed what to do. Some moved the bags of flour and rice, others swept the place and dusted it, and within ten minutes, the time it took for the guards to change, the place was clean. By the time the new guards came on duty, we had people sitting in place reading and others engaged in a game of chess, while others were just calmly sitting with their eyes closed, snoozing in the sun.

I spent a few very uncomfortable minutes awaiting the guards as they came around to count us, but they never batted an eye to see us occupying the new room and asked not a single question.

I was worried that the Japanese might wonder what had happened to the store of flour and rice, so we made sure that the door to the new room where we had put it was left ajar. They found it readily enough, and quickly locked it. It was quite astonishing how naive they could be at times.

The use of that large sunny room made a big difference in our lives, but there was one "mystery" room in the place to which Nakamura would not give me the key, and when I told him I needed to go in there to check out the lights, he told me there weren't any in there. I found that highly suspicious. Every now and then we would see Nakamura or one of the others go in and lock himself in. Later they would come out with something hidden under their coats. I was very curious and decided to find out what the room contained.

By that time I had become quite adept at picking locks, but there was a problem with that particular room. It adjoined the main washroom and there was a nearly constant stream of traffic passing the door. It seemed that every few minutes one or another of the guards wanted to use the washroom also, so I had a problem getting in there unseen. I could have asked one of the Chinese servants, but I didn't want to arouse any suspicions, so I awaited the opportunity to find out for myself. I finally managed it one night when everyone was asleep, and was astonished to find it was a storeroom filled with supplies of various kinds for use in the club. There were stacks of playing cards, quantities of writing paper, boxes of pencils and pens, and all kinds of other things such as supplies of toilet paper, paper towels, and soap (a very precious commodity).

What excited me most, though, was a huge pile of used tennis and bowling shoes. They had been dumped in one corner, and I surmised that they had belonged to members of the club, and the Japanese had found them in some other part of the building and had moved them there for safekeeping. That was indeed a find of the first order. Most of us had only one pair of shoes and they were fast wearing out, and those of us who were bowling each day were very much in need of proper shoes for the slippery floor of the bowling alley. How to get the shoes out of there without the Japanese or the Chinese guards seeing us was the problem.

I told the others of my find and of my decision to get in there and find shoes for anyone who wanted them. I felt sure that the owners of the shoes wouldn't mind; there was very little chance of their ever seeing their shoes again anyway, and I was sure that it wouldn't be long before the Japanese would be helping themselves to the shoes if they were not already doing so. I felt, however, that it would be unwise to go in there again at night. That was when either Nakamura or Watanabe went in there, and there was also too great a risk of a surprise roll call. It had to be in the daytime, when my absence, if noted, could be accounted for by my being somewhere else in the building going about my checking of the electrical system.

Each time I went to the washroom I examined the door and tried to figure out a way to get in without being noticed. Unlocking the door was no problem, but once inside it would be difficult to get out again without being seen, and there was always the possibility of the Japanese deciding to go into the room while I was in there. Then I came upon a solution. By sheer coincidence there was a ceiling light hanging in the hallway immediately in front of the door to the room. It couldn't have been better placed, and that was our salvation. Nakamura had supplied me with a stepladder, and one day I enlisted the help of the next-youngest member of our group, who happened to be a doctor, and together we devised a plan that worked like a charm.

We first took the shoe measurements of all who needed shoes. I then placed the stepladder squarely in front of the door, which opened inward. I climbed the ladder, unscrewed the light fixture, and left the wires dangling, so that my job appeared unfinished. Then I very quickly picked the lock, let my young doctor friend in, and locked the door behind him. His job was to select the proper sizes of shoes, and when he was finished, he was to let me know with a light tap on the door so I could let him out if the coast was clear.

It took us the better part of an hour, and a lot of people passed me as I "worked" at the top of the ladder. Several of the guards came by, and then Nakamura himself stopped to see what I was doing. With screws held in my mouth I mumbled to him that that particular light needed special attention and would take some time to put back together again. My bluff, in case he should want me to move the ladder so that he could get into the room, would be that I couldn't safely leave the wires hanging loose like that and I wouldn't be able to move the ladder until the light was fixed. However, I needn't have worried. He gave no indication of wanting to go in the room and obviously hadn't the slightest suspicion.

That was the only time we went in there during daylight. I went in there again a number of times afterward to get more shoes, but always alone. There was a comparatively abundant supply, and we felt sure the few that we took wouldn't be missed by the Japanese. I went in during the early hours of the morning when the Japanese guards were sleeping their soundest, and nothing untoward ever occurred. However, there was one rather unpleasant incident connected with the shoes that I've never been able to

either forget or live down.

At the time we discovered the shoes, all of our Chinese guards had been replaced by Japanese army men. One of them was remarkably friendly and spent a lot of time chatting with us, me in particular, and also constantly came in to watch us bowl. One day he remarked to me that the shoes I was wearing were exceptionally nice, and he wished he could have a pair like them. He asked me where I had bought them.

I should mention at this point that on rare occasions, anyone with severe dental problems was permitted out of the camp to visit a Russian dentist, always accompanied by a guard. It was an outing that everyone relished, despite a sore tooth or a bad cavity to be filled, but not all of us could convince Nakamura or Watanabe that our teeth were sufficiently in need of care to be allowed to go. In fact, I never went there myself.

The dentist's office was in the back room of a Russian pharmacy some distance from the club, and anyone making that dental trip had the opportunity of making a few purchases there. There were various small things, such as toiletries and other odds and ends available, much like an American drugstore, and there was also a small selection of packaged candy. It wasn't very good, but at least it was a change of diet. With the variety of things available, anyone going was inevitably given a list of things that others wanted.

I reminded the Japanese guard that we occasionally went to the dentist and that it was possible for us to buy things there, letting him come to the conclusion that I had bought the shoes there. He then asked me if, when I next went there, I would buy him a pair like mine. That put me in a bit of a quandary, but without thinking it through, and without the slightest intention of doing anything for him, I told him that if and when I had the opportunity, I would do what I could. And, for want of anything else to say, I suggested that if he would tell me his size, and if I could find a pair to fit him, it would only cost him 5 yuan.

To this day I cannot figure out why I made such a stupid promise. I hadn't the slightest intention of supplying him with a pair of shoes from the storeroom that we had discovered, and it was highly unlikely that I would be making a trip to the dentist at any time in the near future, nor could I buy shoes if I did go there. Perhaps it was just sheer cussedness on my part, or I just wanted to get him off my back. In any case, I never had to do anything about it, because the very next day that particular guard was transferred elsewhere and we never saw him again.

But that wasn't the end of the story. Months later, when we were on board the repatriation exchange ship leaving Japan, I ran into one of the businessmen who had been locked up in the bank building. When I introduced myself and he heard my name, he took a hard look at me and said: "Oh, Tharp, eh? You're the chap who sold my tennis shoes to one of the Jap guards for five dollars." I was completely dumbfounded, and all my protestations of innocence were unavailing. Apparently, right after talking to me and prior to being transferred to the bank building, the guard must have mentioned my supposed offer to buy him shoes either to Nakamura or Watanabe, who must have told him that there was no need to pay for a pair of tennis shoes. He could get a pair to fit him in the storeroom, which is evidently what he did that very night. When he was transferred to the bank the next day, wearing the shoes, the owner of the shoes immediately recognized them as his own and accused the guard of stealing them from the club, whereupon the Japanese soldier had told him that "Tharp sold them to me for $5."

I've forgotten the name of the gentleman who owned the shoes. Each time I met him on board ship I tried to convince him that I had not fraternized with the enemy and tried to explain the circumstances of the whole incident, but I don't think he believed me. Perhaps somewhere in England he still remembers his shoes being "sold" by me to a Japanese. We took plenty of shoes for our own use, but never at any time were any either given or sold to any of the guards. However, I have always had a grudging admiration for the guard who so adroitly extricated himself from an embarrassing situation at my expense. But at the time, given the opportunity, I could gladly have wrung his neck for putting me in such a bind.

After the first couple of months the food situation changed somewhat, although it didn't noticeably improve. The Japanese apparently decided that contracting with the Russians was too expensive, so they hired a Chinese cook and helper, who made our food on the premises. However, the cook was not very good and was quite possibly underpaid. In any case,

although quantities of beef, chicken, fish and vegetables were brought in each day, very little of it got onto our table, and what we did get was invariably overcooked. The daily noontime Russian-style soup was changed to a thin watery soup with over-boiled bits of meat or fish in it, and the bread, although slightly better in quality, was less in quantity. It was very apparent that a lot of stealing was going on, evidently with the connivance of the Japanese. Every evening we could see the two cooks leaving the premises heavily laden with packages, and the houseboy told us they stole meat, flour and rice. The guards at the gate did nothing about it.

The Japanese were no better. They helped themselves to the rice and flour all the time, particularly the rice, of which we saw little. We were supposed to get half a pound of bread each day, but never did. The Catholic nuns and the wives of some of the internees who came to the front gate each day were themselves severely rationed, but despite their own meager supplies, they managed to bring something each time they came, usually a few eggs, some fruit, and quite often a loaf or two of bread. Without those extra supplies they so generously shared with us, we would have had a hard time surviving. As it was, our five doctors worried a lot about our health and we had more than one severe case of illness. One of the Maryknoll missioners, Father Sullivan, suffered a severe relapse of an old stomach ulcer. Although Nakamura showed some concern, it was several days before they secured the necessary medicine that our doctors had asked for. In another case, one of the elderly ladies became severely ill. Again, it was days before they permitted her to be moved to the hospital run by the Scottish Presbyterian Mission, and even then, only after she had agreed to say nothing about living conditions in the camp.

I remained in excellent health during the entire time we were there, although on one occasion I did manage to give our good doctors a scare. I woke up one morning with an extremely sore throat and had difficulty breathing and swallowing. When I looked at my throat in the mirror, my uvula was so swollen that it was almost blocking the entire throat passage. One of our doctors, Dr. Leggate of the Scotch Presbyterian Mission, was a delightful man. When he looked at my throat, he was completely baffled and said he'd never seen anything like it before. All he had available to give me were a couple of aspirin, but they helped, and the condition improved after a few hours. I have had several recurrences of the same thing and now know that it was due to nothing more serious than lying on my back, breathing in the dry air with my mouth open, and snoring.

To all outward appearances we were under the jurisdiction of the local Japanese police. However, as time passed, it became obvious that the army actually was in charge. From time to time army officers came into the club on inspection trips, and for those occasions we were required to spruce up the place in anticipation of their arrival. Our commandant, Nakamura, was always in a tizzy until the visitors left. Some of the army officers seemed friendly enough and inquired about our health. Others were quite arrogant and showed complete indifference. On one occasion they brought with them a newsreel cameraman and spent an entire morning documenting our various activities. We were made to pose for them at a "meal," conducting religious services, and engaged in recreational activities. All of us knew that the finished film would be used for propaganda purposes, but there was little we could do except comply with their demands. At least they didn't require us to smile or look cheerful.

Generally speaking, we managed to get along well with our Japanese captors. We had already had eight years or so of experience in trying to outwit them, and it wasn't hard to fool them once you knew their habits and train of thought. I usually managed to get what I wanted without too much trouble. However, I was deeply worried about Eva, and my brain was in a constant whirl with schemes and plans to somehow get her moved up to Mukden. If only I could get her brought into the camp with the other ladies. After long consideration I tried out one of my plans, which I thought to be foolproof, but it backfired and almost got me into very serious trouble.

Watanabe, our alternate commandant, a generally quiet and unassuming fellow who made very little fuss during the two weeks he was on duty, was the man I decided to approach. As I mentioned, he spoke very poor English, but I found him disposed to be friendly. But we could never get him to make any decisions on his own. One day I found him alone and volunteered to help him with his English by giving him a daily lesson of an hour or so. He was very

receptive to the idea, and during the remainder of his two-week tour I spent some time with him each day in general conversation and helped him put his ideas on paper.

After a number of such sessions, I started a conversation with him on the subject of the war, and remarked to him that I had read in the Japanese-supervised English-language newspapers that they allowed us, that the Japanese Red Cross had been very kind to British and American wounded in the battles over Hong Kong, Manila and Singapore. I went on to remark that I still had a little money in the bank, and I told him I would like to donate it to the Japanese Red Cross to show my appreciation. (Of course, I knew that the money I had in the bank, about 300 yuan, was lost anyway and I would never see it again.) I suggested to him that I give the money to him to pass on at his discretion, and the only thing I asked for in return was that he talk to the chief of police on my behalf and request that my wife be transferred from Lingyuan to Mukden to spend the rest of the war in the camp there with me.

He listened in silence, smiling all the time, and told me he would think about it and let me know. It was quite obviously a blatant attempt on my part to bribe him, and both of us knew it, but I thought it was worth the gamble. What did I have to lose? A few days later his tour of duty ended and Nakamura came back and the very first thing he did was to call John Walsh, our interpreter, into his room and tell him to send for me. As soon as I got the call I knew I was in for trouble. When I entered the guard room Nakamura harshly told me to stand at attention, and then, in the presence of two other Japanese officers, he proceeded to read me the riot act. He spoke entirely in Japanese with a lot of loud shouting and gesticulating, but I had the advantage of knowing enough Japanese to know in advance what he was saying before John translated it for me, and so had time to prepare my defense.

After making the statement that I had definitely tried to bribe his deputy, he asked me if I was guilty. I stuck to my story that I had no use for the money, that I had simply felt there was something I could do for the Japanese Red Cross to show my appreciation, and in return all I had asked for was a small favor, that I be reunited with my wife. Nakamura quite naturally didn't buy it, and told John that I ought to be shot for trying to bribe a police officer. Poor John was badly shaken by the whole event and I felt sorry I had inadvertently brought him into it. At the same time I must confess that I, too, was feeling uncomfortable. However, after a lot of ranting and raving at me (mainly, I felt certain, for the benefit of the other two Japanese officers), Nakamura dismissed me by saying: "You were born in China. You are simply a white Chinese and you don't know any better because you are no different in your thinking than them. The Chinese all feel that bribery is the way to accomplish anything they want, and for that reason I'll overlook your action at this time." I very gratefully left the room and decided not to try anything so risky again. As it turned out, there wasn't any need to.

However, for a few days after that I was in a state of deep depression and gave a lot of thought to the simplicity and ease with which I could escape from the camp. It would have been child's play because the supervision had become so slack. My thoughts didn't go as far as trying to escape the country. That would have been completely impossible and suicidal. All I wanted to do was to get out of the camp and onto the first train to Lingyuan to see Eva, if only for a couple of hours, and it would have been so easy to do. But I knew it would bring retribution down on my fellow internees and I didn't want that to happen, so I stopped thinking about it.

It was only a couple of weeks after the above incident, on April 1, 1942, that Nakamura called us all together with an earthshaking announcement. He told us that negotiations were under way for all of us to be exchanged for Japanese nationals in the United States and Great Britain, and that it wouldn't be long before we would all be freed. We found it almost impossible to believe, and wondered if it was just an April Fool's Day hoax. As the days passed and we heard nothing more about it, we tended to doubt that it could be true, and yet we noticed subtle changes in Nakamura's attitude toward us and in the behavior of the guards in general.

We were allowed much greater latitude: we were permitted to go outdoors as much as we liked, we could play volleyball and walk on the driveway anytime we wished (still only to within 20 feet of the main gate), and of still greater significance, two of the ladies were permitted to go into the kitchen at any time they wished to supervise cooking of the meals and to prepare our breakfasts. With a little flattery and some judicious bribing of the Chinese cooks, our food improved both in quality and quantity, and for breakfast we managed to get cereal occasionally, either rice or millet porridge, although there was neither milk nor sugar to go with it.

Those were exciting happenings, but when was the exchange to come about? No one could give us an answer, least of all Nakamura, who refused to say anything further about it. We surmised that he had not been told to make the announcement to us and was perhaps afraid that he had already said too much. Apparently he knew nothing further, nor was he to be told anything. Then one day he suddenly told us we were going to have an important visitor the following day, and to get ready for the occasion we had to tidy up the place and make ourselves look presentable. Around nine o'clock the next morning a strange Westerner walked up the driveway in the company of several Japanese officers. He turned out to be a representative of the Swiss government and the International Red Cross, and he was accompanied by a Major Saito of the Kuantung Army Press Section. With them was a large entourage carrying Red Cross packages of food and clothing, which we guessed had arrived long before but had not been handed out to us. They also brought some very elaborate recording equipment, which they proceeded to set up.

Major Saito, who spoke very good English, gave a flowery speech, telling us how very fortunate we had been to be guests of the Japanese army and how generous they had been in their treatment of us. He went on to say that they had come to do still more for our benefit. He told us they had arranged for us to be repatriated, and he added that he was there to take any messages that we might have for our loved ones back home. If we were willing, he would record our messages and then broadcast them over Japanese radio.

The Swiss representative then talked with our committee and asked how we were faring, after which he walked around and chatted briefly with most of us individually. At the same time, the Japanese technicians were making recordings of any messages we wanted sent. Saito told us we could say anything we wished and it would not be edited. We could use English or any other language we wished. There were to be no restrictions. Naturally, all of us knew it was simply a propaganda ploy, and some diehards among the group refused to have anything to do with it. However, cynical as most of us were, feeling that there was little likelihood of our messages being broadcast, some of us decided to give it a try just in case they might actually carry out their promise. I personally could see no harm in sending such a message, so I wrote a few lines on a scrap of paper, directed to my brother Gilbert Tharp in Toronto, giving as his address the Manufacturer's Life Insurance Company on Bloor Street. I then read it into the microphone, from which it was recorded onto a large wax disk. What I said was that we as a family were all well, that we were expecting shortly to be repatriated, and asked that anyone picking up the message please relay it to my brother in Toronto. Then I forgot about it completely, feeling certain nothing would come of it.

When everyone had finished making their recordings (one man spoke in Polish), we were asked by Major Saito to sing something together in English as a group, and have it recorded. We did so, and when it appeared to be all over, one of our number gave Major Saito a short "thank you" speech, and he was immediately asked to please repeat it into the microphone. In a way, the whole thing was a complete farce, but very entertaining, and certainly a big change from our dreary daily routine. But we still seemed no nearer to the date of repatriation, if indeed there was actually going to be one, and not even the Swiss representative could give us any idea as to when it would come about.

It wasn't until two years later that I learned the Japanese had been as good as their word, and had indeed broadcast the recordings we made. I am sure that our intelligence people picked up the broadcasts, but none of them had the courtesy to pass on my message to my brother Gil. However, about a dozen ham radio operators did, and I have a sheaf of garbled messages that Gil received in the mail that he saved for me. Not one of them show either his name or mine spelled correctly, but they all got the name of Manufacturer's Life, and since people in Gil's office all knew he had relatives in China, the messages, when received in their office, were all taken to him. That was the first word he had heard from us in almost a year and it was a delightful surprise for him.

One morning, shortly after the above event, a very strange thing happened. Nakamura had already given us much greater liberty in allowing us to go outdoors any time we wished, and it was quite evident from the laxity of the guards that all of them presumed that with the promise of our imminent freedom, it would naturally guarantee our good behavior, and so there would be little chance of any of us trying to escape. However, on that particular Sunday morning Nakamura quite inexplicably called about a dozen of us younger men and told us to accompany him outside the front entrance of the club. When we got there he lined us up, and telling us to wait, he went down to the front gate, grabbed the first passing Chinese who happened to come along, and brought him back, then stood him in front of us.

The man Nakamura had grabbed was middle-aged, quite well dressed, and minding his own business when Nakamura pulled him in. Shaking with fear, he stood there speechless, not knowing why he had been grabbed nor why he was suddenly facing a group of foreigners. Poor man. I felt so sorry for him because I had a premonition of what was about to happen. Without a word either to us or to the man, Nakamura suddenly started to use him as a foil to demonstrate his prowess in judo and karate. We stood there in a daze watching them, not sure whether it was simply an ego trip on Nakamura's part, trying to show us how good he was, or whether it was to demonstrate to us what would happen to us if we didn't behave ourselves. I personally felt it was the latter.

In any case, for about 20 minutes, Nakamura gave the poor man what was probably the worst drubbing he had ever had in his entire life. Nakamura was an expert. He repeatedly grabbed the man by his hair and threw him over his shoulder, slamming him to the ground, then picking him up and doing it again. When the man was almost senseless, Nakamura left him lying on the ground and then kicked him brutally in the head and groin. Several of our group tried to remonstrate with Nakamura, but I warned them quietly to desist as I knew it would only make him go at it all the more vehemently, which it did. We were certain he was going to kill the man, but finally, as we stood by in horror and disgust, Nakamura pulled the man to his feet, bowed deeply to him, then, giving him a few dollars, took him back down to the gate and let him go. When he came back to where we were standing, he abruptly dismissed us without a word, and never referred to the matter again. I think he had expected us to applaud his prowess and was disappointed at our indifference. The poor Chinese fellow, though, must have been in great pain. His clothing was badly torn and his face was bleeding, but beyond a few grunts and groans he never made any outcry during the entire performance, and that, too, I think, annoyed Nakamura.

About the middle of April, when I had just about given up all hope of any exchange coming about and was feeling very low indeed, there came a day that I now look back on as the single most momentous day of my entire life. Even now it seems impossible that it could have happened.

Right after breakfast one morning, most of us had gone out to enjoy the sunshine. April can still be quite cold in Manchuria, and that morning there was a strong wind blowing and a lot of dust in the air. A number of our group started a game of volleyball. Others just leisurely walked around, and I was pacing up and down the driveway, mulling over the future and wondering when I would see Eva again, and also wondering if word of the possible repatriation had reached her or not.

Suddenly, as I reached the point some 15 or 20 feet from the ironwork gate beyond which we were not permitted to go, and where I had to turn back, I thought I had started to hallucinate. As I started to turn, I had the visual impression of hundreds of rickshaws and bicycles out in the street passing the gate, and there, not 30 feet in front of me, I distinctly saw Eva riding by in a rickshaw and my father in another one close behind. I knew my eyes and brain had deceived me, and it couldn't possibly be so, but it was very real indeed and gave me a severe jolt.

Then my mind told me I actually had seen it, and I was NOT hallucinating at all. I really had seen Eva — the very last person on earth I could have expected to see there, and as she disappeared out of sight, I made a mad dash for the gate, half climbed it, and at the top of my voice yelled Eva's name. The Japanese guard rushed out from his little gatehouse and tried to pull me down off the gate, bellowing at me all the while. I think he thought I was trying to escape. Nevertheless, I continued to yell Eva's name, shouting at the guard, "Oke San, Oke San" (My wife, my wife), and unaccountably he let me be.

Astonishingly, both rickshaws had stopped just

beyond the gate. Eva had heard my call and turned her rickshaw back, and for a few precious and unbelievable minutes, we were able to converse together just a few feet apart but not close enough to touch. It was a glorious sight to see her once again after four months, but I found her greatly changed and barely recognizable because she was so thin and emaciated and her face was pale and drawn.

I learned later that Eva had been losing weight rapidly ever since I had left her on the station platform on Christmas Day. She was worrying so much about me she had no appetite at all, and my parents had become greatly concerned about her. Father had told the local Japanese officials about Eva and had badgered them repeatedly to allow him to escort her to the Scottish Mission Hospital in Mukden for a physical exam, fearing that she might have tuberculosis or cancer. Finally, after repeated efforts by my father, the Japanese had relented, and there she was. Again I was reminded that "God works in mysterious ways..." Neither Eva nor my father had the slightest idea where the International Club was, so they weren't on the lookout for me, but at the exact moment when they were passing our gate, not only was I watching the street, but their Japanese escort in his rickshaw had been held up by a traffic light at the nearby corner. Otherwise, even had I seen her, with him there I would have been unable to speak with her. Eva barely had time to tell me that she was being taken not to the mission hospital, but to a Japanese hospital for a physical exam, when their escort showed up and yelled at the rickshaw men to get going. I watched them out of sight and then I was immediately galvanized into action.

I raced into the club building and found John Walsh, and together we went to see Nakamura. I made an impassioned plea to him to get me an immediate interview with the chief of police concerning my wife, whom I had just seen pass the gate, and who, I told him, was "desperately ill" and on her way to the hospital. Nakamura for once showed some concern and was obliging. Within an hour the chief of police showed up at the club and listened to me as I implored him to take action to have my wife kept in Mukden for treatment rather than being taken back to Lingyuan. That was one time when I didn't let pride stand in my way, and I did all but get down on my knees to him. I begged him to consider the fact that all of us were soon to be repatriated, that he would not want my wife to die in the meantime, and there could be no harm in her staying on in Mukden. I suggested she could fit in with the nine women we already had in the camp, or that she could stay at the Presbyterian Mission House with the other wives. And all the time I was begging him, I was praying that God would overrule and enable her to stay on. God answered my prayers.

The police chief was evidently swayed by my eloquence and promised to do what he could. I sweated out the rest of that day. Then, near nightfall, Nakamura brought word to me that Eva's case had been looked into and that she would be allowed to stay on in Mukden until repatriation. But he said it was impossible for her to be housed at the club, and she would be kept at the mission house. What a tremendous relief I felt.

The next day, greatly to my surprise, Father was permitted to come into the camp to visit with me for a half hour before being taken back to Lingyuan, but they wouldn't let Eva come. It was so good to see him again in such good health. He told me all the latest news of Lingyuan, of the family and of their lives there over the preceding four months. They had remained unmolested, and the local Japanese authorities had generally left them alone, although confining them to the compound. They had been permitted to conduct all church services normally and the Chinese Christians had in no way been restricted from visiting them. All of that was good news.

Father also told me how deeply worried they had been about Eva, and how long it had taken him to get permission for her to go to Mukden. But he gave me the good news that the Japanese doctors at the hospital had told him there was nothing wrong with her, and that it was just worry that had caused her loss of weight. He added that on the scales at the hospital Eva had weighed in at just under 80 pounds. I couldn't believe it.

Father also told me that Eva had suffered the indignity at the hospital of having to disrobe in a roomful of men (typically Japanese), and had then been assigned to live in the Presbyterian mission compound in Mukden with a woman doctor there until repatriation day came. I was greatly relieved to hear

that, because I knew she would be well taken care of. Father was required to return to Lingyuan that evening to await word of the exact date of the repatriation, at which time all the family would be brought to Mukden. All of us hoped it would be soon, but knew there were many possibilities of delay or even cancellation, so we didn't set our hopes too high.

Before Father left I told him of the secret hiding place we had made for our coin collection under a specific board in the bathroom floor and asked him to get the coins out and hand them over to Mr. Li, the restaurant owner, for safekeeping. Father did so, and I'm quite sure that Mr. Li hid them well. Most unfortunately five years later when we were able to return to Lingyuan, we learned that during a raid by Communist guerrillas, when they had temporarily captured the city, there had been a wholesale slaughter of leading city officials and businessmen, and our dear friend Mr. Li was one of the first to be beheaded. He was the only one of the Chinese Christians killed at the time. Why it happened we shall never know, whether it was simply because he was a Christian or because he was a successful businessman. But I do know that one day we will see him again in Heaven. However, I'm equally sure that when that day comes I shall have no interest in asking him what he did with the coins. It is, however, interesting to speculate on the possibility that one day the collection will be found by someone, if it hasn't already. It will be all the more mysterious to the finder because of the English-language identifying tags Eva and I so meticulously attached to them, provided, of course, that the tags remain intact.

Eva's arrival in Mukden added a whole new dimension to my time there in the camp. It was a tremendous relief to know she was in the same city, and I was almost delirious with delight. I knew that even though we couldn't be together, I could at least briefly see her in the distance each day when she came with the other wives and nuns who brought food and laundry. I schemed as to how I could smuggle letters out to her in some way. It wasn't long before the opportunity showed itself, but it was another two months before we actually left the camp and Eva and I were together once again. Much happened during that interval.

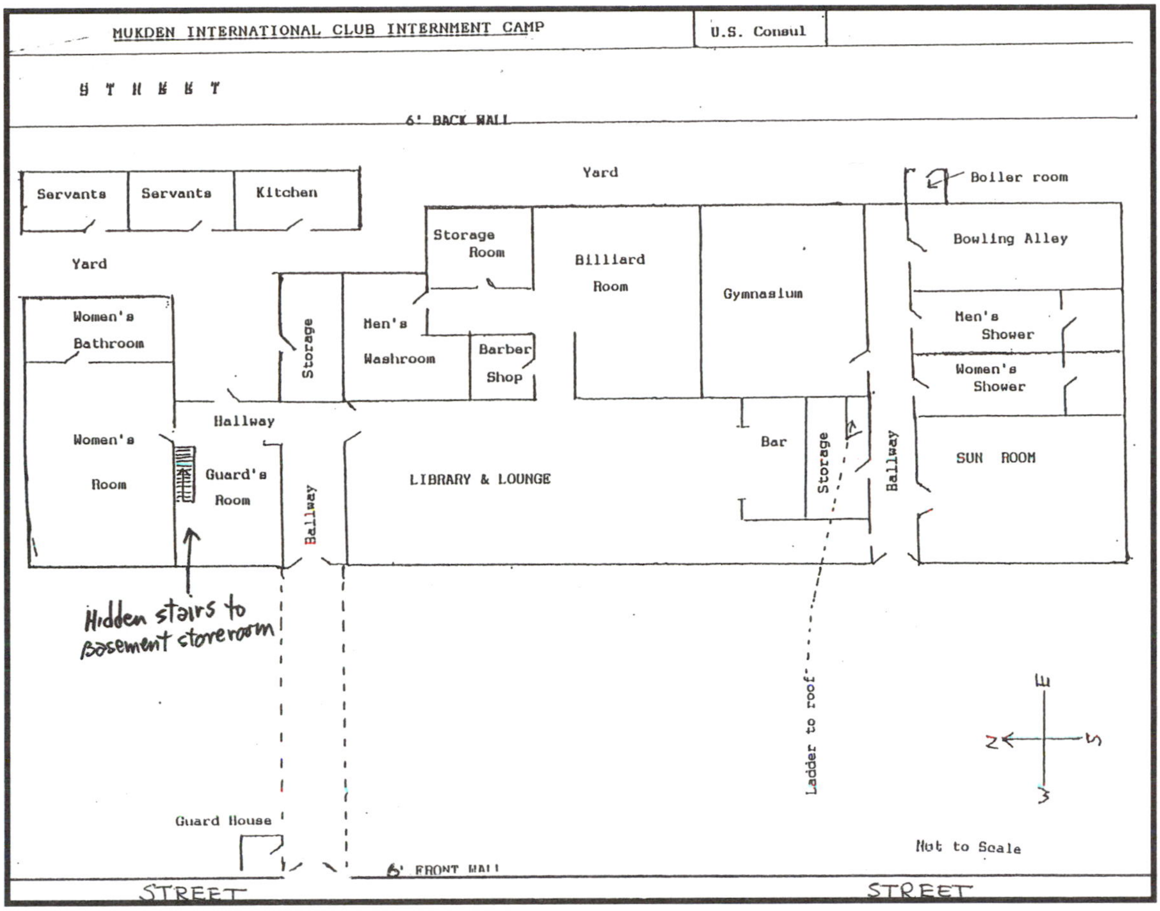
MUKDEN INTERNATIONAL CLUB INTERNMENT CAMP
U.S. Consul
STREET
6' BACK WALL
Servants
Servants
Kitchen
Yard
Boiler room
Storage Room
Billiard Room
Gymnasium
Bowling Alley
Yard
Women's Bathroom
Storage
Men's Washroom
Barber Shop
Men's Shower
Women's Shower
Hallway
Women's Room
Guard's Room
Hallway
LIBRARY & LOUNGE
Bar
Storage
Hallway
SUN ROOM
Hidden stairs to basement storeroom
Ladder to roof
E
N
S
W
Guard House
Not to Scale
6' FRONT WALL
STREET
STREET

Bob's map of Mukden International Club Internment Camp

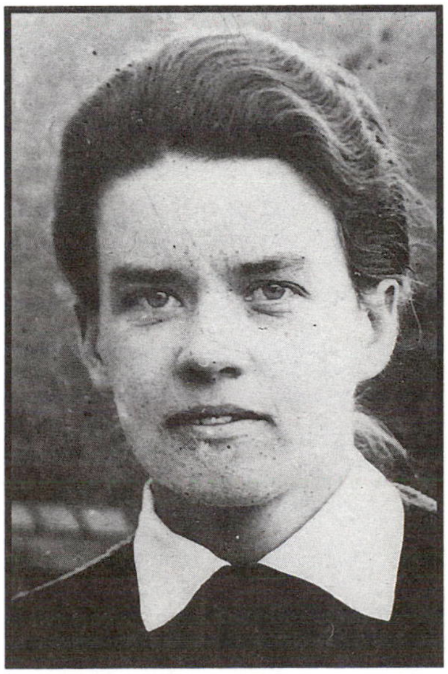

Eva as she appeared to Bob at the internment camp — 88 lbs. 1942

Photo of first visit of Swiss representatives to Mukden Internment Camp. As a result of the visit, letters home were allowed for the first time. Photo taken sometime before April, 1942. The insert photo is Monsignor Lane, who later became Bishop. Note the large number of Maryknoll Fathers in the group.

寝不言，食不
语。

Qin bu yan, shi bu yu.

One does not talk when sleeping,
nor when eating.

- Chinese Proverb.

Chapter Thirty
Japan — A Step Closer To Freedom

At the International Club internment camp in Mukden there was no specified time when visitors could come to the gate to make deliveries. However, over the weeks we had been there it had become customary for a group of ladies, some of them wives of the internees and a few of them Catholic nuns, to arrive around ten in the morning with their gifts of fruit and food, and frequently one or two would turn up in the afternoon around three. The very next morning after I had seen Eva riding by in a rickshaw I was excitedly expecting to see her once again as she came with some of the ladies from the mission, and I could hardly wait for the time to come.

Well before ten o'clock I was standing outside the front door of the club, watching for their arrival at the front gate. What a welcome sight it was to finally see her small figure there in the distance. I could barely make out her face and features under her fur hat, but since we were not allowed to approach the gate while visitors were there, I had to be satisfied with that.

Even so, she was there in the flesh, and I didn't care in the least how long it took before repatriation came about. She was safe and well, and I could see her once a day. I was ecstatic.

The daily procedure for the Japanese guard at the gate was to open the gates wide while the ladies were there, and let them stand in the entryway, out of the crush of passing foot traffic, while he carried their various bags and packages up to Nakamura for examination and then final distribution to the designated individuals inside. While that was going on, we could stand there and wave to the ladies, and as the Japanese began to be a bit more lenient in their behavior toward us, we could even manage a shouted greeting without incurring their wrath.

That first day Eva came to the gate I noticed she was carrying a small gray attache case, and I watched its progress as the guard carried it up the driveway, gave it to Nakamura, who searched it thoroughly, and then released it to me. It held only a couple of bananas that morning, but along with them was a brief and impersonal hand-written note from Eva asking me to pack my dirty laundry in the case and she would wash it for me. And so began a daily pattern that lasted for the next two months.

The attache case was Japanese-made. It was a very light, cardboard thing, with two spring catches on the outside, and a sort of plastic-like exterior. On the inside, it was loosely lined with a thin cotton-like cloth, and like most such cases, it also had a cloth pocket in the lid. It is important to describe the case because it played such a large part in our daily lives and the lives of my fellow internees over the next eight or ten weeks.

Nakamura's examination of the bags and contents was usually quite thorough. He usually paid particular attention to any written notes that were in the bags. Since that took a bit of time, the guards usually returned to the front gate after delivering the bags to him in order to pick up a second load, and when Nakamura finished, he would dump the bag or package onto the floor, where we could then take possession of it. That usually allowed us as much as ten or fifteen minutes in which to unpack it, put in anything we wanted to send out, write a brief note to go with it, and then give it back to Nakamura, who would go through it once again, reading any note that we might have included.

The whole procedure could be quite time-consuming, depending on just how many ladies happened to be down at the gate at any given time. Any written material in the bags, such as newspapers or magazines, was given special attention, and the hand-written notes were scrupulously read by Nakamura or Watanabe. If there was anything either of them considered suspicious, they would either question the recipient or simply destroy the note. But we had noticed one significant detail. When a bag or package was not accompanied by a written note, however short, that bag and its contents got a much more thorough search than one that openly carried a note.

Presumably the men doing the searching were suspicious that a note had been hidden somewhere within in the folds of a garment or bedsheet if it wasn't immediately apparent. The Japanese seemed to be greatly concerned that information might be smuggled in to us somehow, but they were not so concerned either about what we sent out or what was written in our notes. After all, dirty laundry is simply dirty laundry, and we didn't have much else to put in our outgoing bags, nor did we have much to tell our wives. Learning from experience, the ladies generally kept their notes brief and businesslike, so the note that Eva sent me that first day was no exception, and mine back to her was just as brief. However, we were at least in contact with one another once again. Just to be able to see her in the distance was a delight, and her handwriting on the notes was a bonus. Nonetheless, I found it was not enough. I simply had to figure out a way to communicate with her at length, and in a more satisfying manner. All that day and half the night I visualized the attache case she had sent in, wondering how I could manage to insert a letter to her without Nakamura managing to find it. Finally, a solution occurred to me.

The next morning, before the bag had become too familiar to Nakamura, I had time in which to make a tiny slit in the cloth lining, just inside the pocket in the lid, and I then ripped it down for three or four inches in two directions, forming a rough triangle, and making it look as though it was an accidental tear. I was sure that Eva would spot it and would read my mind. Even though we had only been married a relatively short time, she knew how deviously my mind worked when it came to the Japanese. When the case came back the next morning, the tear was still there and hadn't been sewn up, so in my return note to Eva I deliberately drew her attention to it (and Nakamura's as well), by suggesting to Eva that if possible, she should pin it up with a safety pin "to prevent the tear from becoming larger." The next day the safety pin was in place.

We left it that way for a day or two in case Nakamura became suspicious and undid the pin to peer inside the lining, but when a close examination of the pin holes showed that it had not been touched, I took the risk of putting a note inside the lining of the lid. I was very careful to use the same pin holes, and the next morning, to my joy, there was a return note from Eva. We had found a means of communication. That very obvious but quite innocent-looking tear in the cloth had excited no suspicions whatsoever, and it remained that way for as long as we used it.

For the next two months we traded letters every day. They got longer and longer, but we used the thinnest possible tissue paper so as not to create a bulge. It was most important for the case not to be empty. There had to be something for Nakamura to look at or he would become suspicious, so to allay his suspicions I had to find something every day to put in there and that began to be something of a problem. My laundry was now being washed every day instead of once every couple of weeks, and even then I was sometimes hard put to find something to put in. Eva anticipated this and suggested that I borrow clothing from some of the others who hadn't anyone to do their laundry, offering to do it for them, and that was just what we did. I even sent out socks with holes in them that needed mending. All of us had some of those, and Eva faithfully mended them and sent them back in.

But it was her daily letters that were so important and which filled me with so much joy. It was almost like having her there in the camp with me. At the end of that first week as we gained confidence, Eva started to write snippets of war news. At first it was couched in very vague and abstruse language, but progressively, as we got more daring, she wrote openly and at length, telling us news of the war that positively enthralled us. One of the first bits of exciting news Eva gave us was about the Doolittle raid on Tokyo on April 18, 1942. That was fantastic news, and we had to be careful not to betray our excitement and joy to the Japanese, in case they got suspicious. To us that was the first indication we had of a turning point in the war and the first really good news we had received since being in the camp.

A short distance from the Scottish Presbyterian Mission compound where Eva was living, the missionaries conducted a school for blind girls. At the outbreak of war, one of the missionaries with a great deal of forethought had hidden a shortwave radio there — the very last place the Japanese would think to look — and every day, one of the mission ladies would walk over there, listen to the BBC news broadcasts, and secretly pass on the news to other Westerners in the city who were free. Now we were getting all that news through Eva's letters, and what a tremendous boost that was to our morale. When I passed on the news to my fellow inmates, I didn't tell them how I had heard it, and they didn't ask any questions, although I am sure they guessed. It was best not to know. But for the first time we heard of Russian successes in the war against the Germans, of

America's huge contribution in the war against the Japanese, and then, in early June, we heard the electrifying news of the American Navy's successes in the battle of Midway. All of it gave us absolute confidence that our side would definitely win the war.

Eva and I both knew that we were taking tremendous risks, but when desperate, there is no limit to human ingenuity or daring, and we had been so successful in the past in pulling the wool over the eyes of our captors that what we were doing seemed quite commonplace to us. However, at one point our "foolproof" plan nearly met with disaster.

A new Japanese guard came on duty a week or two after Eva's arrival and he proved to be the surliest, meanest, laziest man that I had ever seen. He was very truculent to the ladies when they came. He resented having to make numerous trips up and down the long driveway with the bags and packages they brought, and he demanded that they come in a body at a specific time so that he could carry more on each trip.

That wasn't too bad, but it got worse. He was so lazy that he decided to wait beside us while we unpacked the bags and then repacked them. In that way he could return to the front gate with a full load instead of empty-handed. The first time that happened, he stood over me as I unpacked my bag and read Eva's brief cover note and then put my return load back into the bag. As he watched my every move, there wasn't the slightest chance of my unpinning the safety pin and retrieving her hidden letter, nor of putting my own back inside, and I had to let the bag go back to Eva just as it was.

That continued for three days, and I knew Eva would be desperate to know what was going on when she found her own letter still in the lid of the case day after day. I, in turn, was infuriated at not being able to take her letters out to read them. I knew, though, that Eva would eventually figure it out once she saw how rude the man was and that he did not return immediately after delivering a bag as the previous guards had done, but waited for them to be emptied and then refilled. I was determined to rectify the situation.

I tried making friends with the man, but he remained surly and would not respond to my advances. I suggested he leave the bag and I would bring it to him when I was ready, but he simply stood there and shouted at me to hurry. By the end of the third day, I had decided on a solution. It required desperate measures, which I was prepared to take whatever the outcome, and it hinged on several key factors and unwitting cooperation on his part.

Over the previous eight years or more of our dealings with the Japanese military, we had noticed that their sense of humor was mixed with a strong streak of cruelty, even sadism, in that they openly delighted in causing pain to others and took joy in seeing each other suffer. It was that peculiarity of character that I decided to take advantage of. Despite the man's unfriendliness, I had remained unfailingly cheerful at all times when dealing with him, much as I despised doing so. Despite his ferocious attitude, I decided to feel him out and see if he had a weak spot that I could attack.

Late in the afternoon of the third day I sat down at a small card table in the lounge at a spot near the entrance to the corridor leading to the toilets, where I knew the man would eventually have to pass. I placed an empty chair opposite me, hoping to entice him to sit down. I sat there, openly writing a letter to Eva, and when he finally came by, I spotted him out of the corner of my eye. As he started to pass me, I stuck out my foot playfully, pretending to trip him, looking in his face and grinning broadly as I did so, and then quickly withdrew my foot. He knew it was deliberate on my part, but for the very first time I got a laugh out of him as he stumbled and then caught his balance. It caused him to stop and ask me what I was doing.

All the Japanese guards used a bastardized form of speech when talking with us. It was part-Chinese, part-Japanese, and I laughed back at him and answered him in the same form of speech, telling him I was writing a letter to my wife. That struck him as extremely funny. Why would I be writing a letter to my wife when there was no possible way I could send it to her? I told him that I could always give it to her when I got out of the camp. He thought that was even funnier, and then, as he sat down opposite me, he began to get extremely personal, as I suspected he would, and started making lewd suggestions as to what I should write. At that, I pretended to get extremely annoyed. I stood up suddenly, shouted at him to shut up, and without any warning tipped the table over into his lap, knocking him off his chair onto the floor. That was the critical point. If he got

angry I could abjectly apologize and claim it was an accident, but I had judged him correctly. He thought what I did was very, very funny. He got up off the floor laughing uproariously, banged me on the shoulder, and went on his way.

I knew then I had a foot in the door. The next morning I carried my plan one step further. I borrowed a package of cigarettes from one of my neighbors, and when the man brought Eva's bag in to me, I was sitting on my bed, pretending to read. As he walked up to me I took the bag from him, and as he stood there waiting, I opened up the lid as if to start taking things out. Then, as though I had just thought of it, I looked him straight in the eye, reached into my pocket with my left hand and took out the pack of cigarettes, grinned at him and offered him one. I had never met a Japanese who would refuse a cigarette, and as he took the package from me, extracted a cigarette and leisurely lit it, I kept my eyes on his. All the time my right hand was busy behind the open lid, opening the safety pin and extracting Eva's letter. I kept him talking, asking him if the cigarette was okay, and how many he smoked each day, anything to give myself more time.

But I could sense he was getting impatient. I needed a moment or two more to put my own letter back inside the lid and pin up the tear, so on the spur of the moment I did something I had not planned. I reached up quickly with my left hand, making a pretense of snatching the cigarette from his mouth. He backed off, then came forward again grinning, and I actually did grab the cigarette out of his mouth, meanwhile working with my right hand to hide my letter. His response was just as I had anticipated. He tried to grab the cigarette back from me, so I waved it in front of him, then made as if to put it into his mouth. But just as he opened his lips to receive it, I quickly reversed the cigarette and put the hot end in. He spluttered and roared aloud at the pain, but true to the cruel streak so characteristic of the military, it happened just as I had expected. It struck him as absolutely hilarious, and he doubled over with laughter. By that time I had inserted my letter and pinned the safety pin again. I laughed with him, slapped him on the shoulder and handed the bag back to him. Thankfully I watched him take the bag down to the front gate and hand it to Eva. Unfortunately I could only work a trick like that one time.

In my letter to Eva I told her about the guard and how he normally was on duty in the morning. Much as I hated to do so, I suggested that she might be better off coming in the afternoon, when he usually gave the job over to someone else. But because his behavior was erratic, I had to have some means of letting Eva know before she reached the gate whether he happened to be on duty, so she could come at another time, and I had a plan for that too.

In the previous months while rambling around the building during my "electrical survey," I had discovered a door that led only into a tiny closet with a ladder leading upward. Out of curiosity I had climbed the ladder, and after opening another door, found myself out on the flat roof of the building. It had evidently been put in for maintenance purposes and I took full advantage of my discovery. I went up there frequently to be alone and to sit in the sun, sheltered from the wind by the small building that housed the ladder. It was actually a very exposed position and I could easily have been seen from the front gate or the street, but if I sat on the roof with my back against the small building, only my head showed above the parapet, and no one ever spotted me there.

Sometime in the past someone had left a large piece of lumber about the size of a railroad tie up there on the roof. I told Eva to continue to come in the morning as usual if she wanted the walk, but to be sure to look to the roof. If she saw that piece of wood standing upright against the little building that stuck up above the roof, it would be a sign that the surly guard was on duty and she should come back later in the day. She could see it from about a block away, and since she was free to move about the city as she wished, she could come when convenient. After that we had no further trouble, and I got her letters without ever being found out, right up to the last day we were there.

I actually managed to establish a sort of friendship with that particular guard and I became something of a showpiece for his companions, whom he brought in to meet me as a person who had the same sense of humor as they did. I kept up the pretense and showed them a number of Chinese tricks that were designed to cause pain. One such trick is what the Chinese call the "scorpion sting." One bends the knuckle of the first finger up against the inside of the thumb. Then, placing the thumb into the body hair of one's opponent (such as on the outer forearm or chest), the finger knuckle is lightly rolled down the inside of the thumb, pulling hairs with it. The result can be excruciatingly painful, but all it elicited from the Japanese guards was loud laughter. From then on I was "their kind of guy" and had no further trouble from them. The Chinese have dozens of other such devices to induce pain, some of which I showed the guards. I didn't mind if they wanted to practice on each other. I had gotten what I wanted.

Around the middle of May we began to see signs that our repatriation date might indeed be drawing nearer. In ones and twos the Japanese began to move other internees into our camp, increasing our numbers considerably. They were people who had been kept elsewhere for a variety of reasons, and some of them had horrendous stories to tell of barbaric treatment by the Japanese. One in particular comes to mind.

Among the first to come in were three Americans: Dr. and Mrs. Roy Byram and Bruce Hunt. Dr. and Mrs. Byram had been missionaries in the northern Manchurian city of Harbin, where they conducted a large boys' school. In October 1941 the two of them had been arrested by the Japanese for "contravention of laws governing religious activities," and had also been accused of "disseminating propaganda hurtful to the Japanese." Actually, the only evidence against them was an ordinary notebook in which one of the Chinese schoolboys had written a composition. Dr. Byram had used a red pen to correct the boy's grammar, and that was used as evidence. The statement written by the schoolboy had been to the effect: "Japanese is cruel people," and Dr. Byram had merely corrected the word "is" and added the two words "are a." The Japanese interrogators had insisted that that was evidence of their personal opinion of the Japanese and was what they had been teaching to the Chinese boys in their school.

All three Americans had been handcuffed and taken by train to the city of Andong in the south of Manchuria, on the border with Korea. There, together with a number of Chinese Christians held on similar charges, they were confined to the common prison for many weeks in particularly harsh circumstances. Finally they were tried and sentenced to deportation. But before that could be carried out, war had broken out with the United States and the Japanese had decided to take them back to Harbin, where they were thrown into a prison reserved for political prisoners. They were placed in solitary confinement, and their treatment at the hands of the Japanese was unusually severe.

They told us chilling stories of the torturing of prisoners by the Japanese. There were several other Westerners confined in the same place, including a number of British nationals, whose identity they never learned, but who were constantly being beaten and tortured. In the cell next to Mrs. Byram's was an Englishwoman who was heard crying each day in great distress, constantly begging for a Bible. She was heard only to speak in English, although the guards who interrogated her insisted on speaking to her in Russian, trying to make her admit she was Russian and not British. In another nearby cell was a Mrs. Watson, a Russian woman married to a British merchant in Harbin, who was also in the jail. Mrs. Watson was so badly treated that she temporarily lost her sanity and was later released by the Japanese. In the meantime, her daughter, who was outside, had been approached one day by the Japanese police, who asked her to supply a clean pair of pajamas for her father. She gave them to the Japanese and the next day the body of her father was brought to her, clothed in the clean pair of pajamas. There was every indication that he had been subjected to extreme torture, and marks on his wrists suggested that he had committed suicide. We met that Mrs. Watson and her daughter in June, just before repatriation, but neither of them were included in the exchange with us and I don't know if they got out later.

I shall never forget Mrs. Byram's story of her time in the Harbin prison. She was not physically tortured, but was subjected almost daily to mental torture. Her husband's cell was out of sight of her own, but the Japanese tried to break her spirit by having someone pretend to be her husband and frequently call her name, then howl in agony while sounds of beating were heard. Of course Mrs. Byram thought it was her husband, and whether that "someone" was actually being tortured, neither Dr. Byram nor his wife ever learned. Dr. Byram was given the same treatment. Almost every day he saw some woman whom he took to be his wife being dragged from a cell by her hair and taken to another cell, from where he could hear loud screams, while his name was being constantly

called. It wasn't Mrs. Byram, but possibly some poor unfortunate Russian woman dragged away to carry out the farce.

When Dr. and Mrs. Byram entered our camp, it was pathetic to see their appreciation of the very simple and scanty fare that we were getting. For nearly three months they had been existing on the poorest kind of Chinese prison food: one bowl of coarse sorghum gruel once a day and a single cup of water. I think what touched all of us most was Mrs. Byram's heroic efforts, not only to save her sanity, but to somehow improve the appallingly filthy conditions of her cell. Having been in one quite similar, I could well understand her repugnance at having to live under those conditions. She told us that from the single cup of water that she got each day, she limited herself to a few sips and used the rest of the water to carefully wash a minute section of her cell floor, until by the time she was finally released, she had the place reasonably clean. We were all much struck by her courage, perseverance, and fortitude.

Those two months after Eva's arrival in Mukden were unique in many ways. On the one hand, just catching a glimpse of her each day and getting her letters made the days pass much more pleasantly and swiftly. Now there was something to look forward to each morning. At the same time, the much-talked-about exchange of prisoners seemed very slow in coming about, and many of our group became quite cynical about it and lost hope. No one would give us a definitive date, and rumors flew daily, some good, some bad. Some of our group referred to it as the "I'll believe it when I see it exchange."

Eventually, by the last week of May, we began to see further evidence that it couldn't be much longer in coming. More and more people were brought in, our guards became ever more friendly and considerate, and we were allowed much greater freedom of action. I even had the opportunity several times to call across the street to the American consular people and exchange a few words with them. Their Japanese guard gave no indication of annoyance.

On the 29th of May, I received a wonderful surprise. With no warning my parents and two sisters were brought in from Lingyuan and we were together once again. They were all deeply saddened at having to abandon not only all their belongings, but also our many Chinese friends whom we had known since childhood, and it was particularly hard on poor Barbara, because the day they left Lingyuan, May 28th, was her birthday. Since then she has never enjoyed a birthday because of the sad memories it brings back. It isn't easy to walk away from everything you possess and the people you love, feeling certain that you'll never see any of them again.

Ruth was in very poor condition and too weak to walk. There were no such things as wheelchairs available in those days, so the Japanese had permitted one servant to accompany them to Mukden to carry her, and dear, faithful Cao Cai, our cook since babyhood, was the one to volunteer. He wept when he saw me, but we only had minutes in which to talk, since the Japanese hustled him away immediately after he had delivered Ruth to the club with my parents. They only had time to share lunch with us, because a short time later the Japanese decided that all four of them should be taken to a Chinese hotel until the day of repatriation. It was doubtless very considerate from the point of view of the Japanese, but the hotel was hot and very dirty, and they were confined to one room, with a guard standing duty outside, so the next day Father appealed to the Japanese to let them return to the club and the Japanese surprisingly agreed. I was utterly dumbfounded to see them coming in through the front gate the next afternoon, particularly because Eva was accompanying them. For some unknown reason she had been designated as their escort, but then she had to leave again almost immediately. The ladies in their already overcrowded room did a little extra squeezing together and made space for Mother and the girls, and we found space for a mattress for Father elsewhere in the building. For once, Nakamura was decent and allowed me a few minutes alone with Eva before she was escorted out the front gate, but we were in full view of everyone and we couldn't even manage a hug, let alone a kiss. In those days one always had to be very discreet.

On his previous visit to Mukden, when he had accompanied Eva to the hospital, I had told Father about some personal belongings that I wanted him to bring with him when they came, and he had them with him. The problem I then faced was what to do with them and how to smuggle them past the Japanese on our final departure day. I had about $100 in U.S. traveler's checks which, since we could not take out any U.S. currency, would be considered con-

traband and would definitely be confiscated. I didn't want that to happen. In addition, I had asked Father to convert my remaining Manchukuo yuan into Manchukuo postage stamps. I thought they might become valuable someday. I still have them, but their value has not increased to any great extent.

The Japanese told us that we would be limited to two suitcases each, and that we would have to carry them ourselves, but Eva and I limited ourselves to one suitcase each. Beyond our meager clothing, there was nothing the Japanese would let us take out anyway. On Christmas Day, as I had passed through Lingyuan, Eva had provided me with a small, trunk-like suitcase that was the sturdiest of all we possessed, and I decided to somehow create a false bottom in it to hide my checks and stamps as well as some personal papers.

I carried the suitcase out to my little boiler room, where I could work in privacy, and tried to figure out a way to construct a false bottom. That didn't prove feasible. However, I found that I could pry away the inside lining around the four sides, and, after removing the cardboard backing that was inside, I could replace it with my stamps and papers. I then pasted the lining back on again with some paste made from white flour that I "liberated" from the flour stores. When I had finished, I carried the suitcase back to the lounge and showed it to my fellow inmates and asked them if they could detect my tampering. When none of them could find anything to arouse any suspicion, I felt confident that it would pass any close scrutiny the Japanese Customs officers might give it. That eventually proved to be the case.

We were never given any definitive news on an actual departure date. All the Japanese could tell us was that it would be "soon," and the Swiss consular representative apparently could tell us no more. However, on the last day of May, the Japanese told us they were going to give us a big farewell "banquet" on June 1st to celebrate our departure.

On the day of that so-called banquet, a lot of Japanese officials and photographers turned up. The table was expanded to almost twice its length and we all sat down together in the lounge, while photographers snapped pictures of us. We had expected something out of the ordinary in the food served us, but it was exactly the same old food we had been getting each day. The only difference was that the Japanese had brought in huge quantities of beer, without which no Japanese meal was complete. Many of our number didn't drink beer at all, but for that particular occasion, even the beer drinkers refused the beer. We felt that to sit down with them to a meal was a sufficient indignity, but to drink beer with them after all we had gone through was just a bit too much. To our surprise, though, when we refused the beer they immediately provided us with quantities of a Japanese-made soft drink very much like 7-Up, which they called "cider." The Chinese servants brought in case after case of it, and even though there was no ice and it was warm, it was still most refreshing.

As we were drinking it, an idea suddenly occurred to me. We had been told by the Swiss representative that, proceeding to Japan to board the repatriation ship, we would be going by train through Korea to Pusan, and from there by ferry to Japan. He had warned us that on the two-day journey we would get nothing much in the way of food or drink, and he suggested we take with us whatever we could. What better than a bottle or two of that soft drink if we could get it?

Young Liu, the servant who had helped me with letters to Eva, was serving the table where I sat, next to my bed, and I asked him where the soda pop was coming from. I was astonished when he told me it came from a storeroom in the basement. I had been allowed the freedom of roaming the entire building for months, and I had never even known there was such a place as a storeroom or basement. How could I possibly have missed it? I felt greatly chagrined and asked Liu where it was. He told me that the stairway leading to it was behind a door in the room in which the guards lived. That still didn't explain how I could have missed seeing it. I had been in the guards' room on many occasions and had seen no door leading to any other rooms. Liu told me that the door was behind a curtain, and that was why I hadn't noticed it. I was very annoyed with myself. If only we had known about the soft drink supply earlier, we could have enjoyed some.

Anyway, I quietly passed the word around the table for everyone to ask for as many bottles of the soft drink as possible, which we pretended to drink. Actually the bottles were not opened, but were passed along under the table to me. We would save as many as possible for the trip through Korea. Since I was sit-

ting right at the end of my bed, I was able to hide the bottles under my bedclothes as they reached me. The other two Chinese servants soon figured out what we were doing and collaborated with us wholeheartedly, so it wasn't long before I felt we had a sufficient number to supply everyone with one bottle, although I hadn't been able to actually count them. Our Japanese hosts were, by that time, nearly drunk on the beer, so they noticed nothing out of the ordinary going on.

Near the end of the meal, the spokesman for the Japanese group gave us some electrifying news. We were told that we were to be divided into two groups by nationality. Because we were scheduled to travel on two different ships, the Americans would be leaving the very next day, and the British nationals two days later. It didn't bother us. The end was now so near, what did an extra day or so matter? We all cheered, and the Japanese made some flowery speeches, a spokesman for our group responded briefly, and the "banquet" was over.

We finished the meal just about an hour before dark, and the Japanese chief of police suggested, since it was a nice evening, we might all like to go outdoors and play some baseball or volleyball. We'd not been allowed out that late in the evening before, so we all trooped outside, some to play and others just to walk up and down.

When the coast was clear, I went back into the lounge and counted the bottles of soda pop we had scrounged. I was disappointed to find there were barely enough bottles to allow one each for the American contingent, who would be leaving the next day. My friend the young doctor was nearby, and I suggested to him that we give all those bottles to the Americans, and that night, after our guards had gone to sleep, he and I would steal down into the basement and get ourselves a new supply for the British group. He agreed that it would be a fun thing to do. We felt certain the guards, who would be very drunk by the time they went to bed, would be sleeping in a sound stupor by the time we were ready to make our move. But something highly unexpected occurred to spoil our plan.

I had barely joined the others outdoors when Nakamura came out and shouted to us that he had an announcement to make. We gathered around him and he asked for a show of hands as to how many of us had wives living in the city. Together with about eight or ten others, I raised my hand. He then beckoned to us and told us to accompany him inside because the police chief wanted to talk to us.

Indoors, we found the chief sitting, of all places, in the ladies' shower room. He was very drunk but in an ebullient mood. Although his speech was slurred and he was barely coherent, he leered at us and asked us how long it had been since we had slept with our wives. Then, without waiting for an answer, he told us that as a gesture of goodwill he was going to allow us out of the club to spend the night with our wives. He told us we could leave immediately, but that we had to be back at the camp by six o'clock the following morning. Otherwise we would forfeit our chance to go with the rest when they left to board the train for Japan.

That was unbelievable news. As a group, we were escorted down to the front gate. None of us stopped for even so much as a toothbrush. Outside the gate we scattered in different directions so as not to unduly attract attention, confident that we could find our way to where our wives were staying.

By that time it was almost dark. I had never been to the Scottish Presbyterian Mission compound and hadn't the slightest idea where it was, nor had I any money to hire a rickshaw. I inquired about the way from various people and discovered it was only a 20-minute walk. Once inside the compound, it was only a matter of a minute or two until I found the house where Eva was staying. But when I knocked on the door and Eva saw me, she was shocked speechless. She first thought that I had escaped from the camp, and she was very frightened for me. I had to reassure her that I was there by permission and quite legally. After six very long months of being apart, it was wonderful to be able to hold her in my arms once again.

The lady doctor with whom Eva had been staying provided us with some marvelous cocoa and cookies. I was a little uneasy though, because I feared that it was entirely possible someone in the Japanese command who was not drunk would change his mind and come after me, so we decided it was advisable to remain visible. Accordingly we sat up for the entire night in the dining room in front of uncurtained windows, just to be on the safe side. We had so much to talk about and so much to catch up on that the night

hours just flew by.

At 5:30 in the morning I decided I had better get back to the camp. I arrived there a few minutes before six, and the other men who had been let out came soon after. We were dismayed to find that an entirely new set of guards had been put on duty to cover the place, and we knew none of them, nor did they know who we were, and as a result they refused to let us in.

After about half an hour of talking it over among themselves and going back and forth to the club building to check with their commanding officer, they decided that we had "escaped" the night before and they became very angry. Apparently the chief of police and his entourage had been so drunk when we had left the club that someone had decided to change the guards, and no one had informed them of the chief's decision to let us out for the night. We tried to convince the guards at the gate that we had been allowed out quite legitimately and told them to phone their chief, but it was nearly two hours before they were able to contact him and straighten things out. Meanwhile, thinking it highly amusing, our friends stood around inside the gate poking gentle fun at us. But we had missed breakfast and a lot of sleep, and although delighted to have been able to visit our wives, we failed to see the funny side of it at the time.

By 10 o'clock all the Americans had been loaded onto trucks and were taken to the railroad station for the trip through Korea to Japan. The place seemed very empty without them, but we were all in high spirits, eager for our own turn to come. I had not forgotten my intention of raiding the basement to secure a supply of soda pop, so I approached my doctor friend and told him we ought to do it that night, just in case the Japanese moved the date of our departure forward. However, he had developed cold feet about the escapade. He told me he thought it would be much too dangerous, and at that late date he had no intention of risking being caught doing something so stupid and possibly not being allowed to leave with the others. I didn't blame him, but I did not share his views and was so confident that I could carry it off that I decided to go ahead by myself.

Around two o'clock the next morning I awoke and, in my pajamas, crept barefoot to the guards' room, where I found the light on as usual and all three guards sound asleep. I deliberately coughed a couple of times and made some noise to see if they would awaken, having a story ready to tell them in case they did, but none of them stirred. With no trouble at all I located the door behind the curtain, picked the lock, and made my way down the flight of stairs in the dark, only to find another locked door at the bottom. That, too, proved to be no problem, and when I had picked the lock and closed the door behind me, I found the light switch and turned on the light.

I was agreeably surprised to find myself in a room measuring about twenty feet square. Not only were there rack upon rack of bottles of beer, but there was also a sizable quantity of hard liquor. I found it hard to understand why, during all those months with that stuff so near at hand, the Japanese guards had not helped themselves to it. At one side there was a stack of wooden cases containing hundreds of bottles of the soda pop I was after. But I discovered something else. Everything was neatly arranged, and the Japanese had kept a meticulous account of everything that had been there when they first took over the building. They had made notations on a card on each shelf for every bottle they had removed. I knew I would have to do the same or risk detection.

Each case held 24 bottles. They were very much the same kind of partitioned wooden cases that were used for Coca Cola bottles in this country before metal cans became popular. Each stack of cases had a card carrying the number of bottles in the stack.

I decided that perhaps three cases would be sufficient to supply every member of our party with two bottles each, so I changed the record to show three cases taken away. But I had forgotten one thing. The bottles would rattle against the sides of the case as I carried them, and that would never do. I looked around for something to stuff between them, but nothing was available, so I took off my pajama top and wound that around and between the bottles and proceeded to carefully carry the boxes upstairs, one at a time.

My first trip was quite uneventful. The guards remained fast asleep and I deposited the bottles under the end of my mattress and returned with the empty case for a second load. When I came back up with the second case and entered the lounge, I suddenly sensed that I was being watched. Uncomfortable, I looked around carefully, wondering if it was one of the guards, but then I remembered that when coming up the stairs, I had carefully peeked through the curtain before entering the room where they were sleeping, and had seen all three still asleep. Then, in the dim light coming from the hallway, I discovered that all but a few of my fellow internees were awake and watching me. No one said a word. They hadn't the foggiest idea of what I was doing, but I had the feeling that they didn't like what they saw and they suspected I was doing something I shouldn't. But at the same time they didn't want to risk interfering. When I saw it was not the Japanese guards were watching me, I went down for the third time to bring up the last case.

Just as I reached the bottom of the stairway I looked across the basement room and saw something I had not previously noticed. Stacked on the very top of one of the racks were some 20 or 30 two-pound cans of genuine Maxwell House coffee. Unbelievable! I'd not seen coffee for over a year and had almost forgotten that such a thing existed, and I knew that was true for all my other friends upstairs. I felt completely chagrined to think we had lived there for six months with all that coffee right below our feet and hadn't learned of its existence until it was too late to do anything about it. However, another idea occurred to me.

Leading the group of Maryknoll fathers was a Monsignor Lane, later to become Bishop Lane. After our repatriation had been announced, he had spent the two months making impassioned pleas to the Japanese to allow him to stay behind in Manchuria to continue his missionary work, and he had finally convinced them that it was his right to do so. When, surprisingly, they agreed to let him stay, six of the young missioners volunteered to stay with him and were given permission. I thought a few cans of coffee would be a wonderful parting gift to the group staying behind, so I decided to take some upstairs with me, but it would require a fourth trip. I couldn't carry them along with a case of soda pop.

When I had put the third case of bottles under my bed, I stripped off my pillowcase and went downstairs for the final trip. After changing the record of the number of cans left, I loaded seven cans of coffee into my pillowcase, turned off the light, locked both doors, and then, after peering around the curtain again to make sure the guards were still asleep, I left the room. I returned to my bed and fell asleep. It had been a "piece of cake."

The next morning I met with a surprise. At breakfast, as I gleefully told my friends what I had done, a number of them gave me the cold shoulder. When breakfast was over, what was left of our committee called me over and proceeded to scold me in no uncertain terms for my "foolish" action, which "might have prejudiced the entire internee exchange." As I look back on it now, what I did was doubtless foolhardy. But somehow, at the time, it seemed to me imperative that I get a supply of drinks for the train trip, and, judging by my previous escapades, the risk seemed minimal. At the same time I guess I had an innate contempt for the Japanese guards and was confident that, even if I had been caught in the act, I would have been able to talk my way out of it. Anyway, such are the follies of our youth.

I spent a good part of that morning transporting the bottles, a few at a time, to my boiler-room retreat, where I washed off the incriminating labels. I then distributed them, two apiece to each of my fellow inmates, to pack in their luggage. There again I was rebuffed by several who wanted no part of the "theft." I didn't let it bother me. I found a sack and loaded the extra bottles in among some of my clothes, feeling sure that when the time came, someone would be grateful for them, and so it proved. Later, when we were on the train going through Korea, those who had refused the bottles when I first offered them came sheepishly to ask if I "happened" to have an extra bottle around that I could spare for them. It made me feel justified in what I had done.

At 7:30 on the evening of June 4th, along with our baggage we were loaded aboard several trucks and were taken to the railroad station. I don't think a single one of us gave a backward look at the International Club and our goodbyes to Nakamura were purely perfunctory. I was happy to see the last of him and couldn't forget his many unkindnesses. A taxi was provided for my parents and Ruth. At the station we were joined by the wives from the Presbyterian Mission, Eva among them, and I began to feel that we were really together once more. I vowed to myself that nothing would part us again. Ruth had to be carried onto the train, and Doug Broughton and I took turns carrying her up and down the many stairs and along the long platforms to where our train was standing. We then rushed back to pick up our luggage and to help some of the more infirm with their belongings.

Ruth was given a berth in a second-class car and Mother was permitted to stay with her. The rest of us were taken to the front of the train, where two third-class cars had been provided for us. Just before the train left we were joined by a number of other British nationals from the bank building. We were also surprised and pleased to see our old friend Mr. Fukumoto, the government official, who was going to accompany us part of the way. That night around 10 o'clock, when things had quieted down a bit, he permitted Father and Barbara to go to the rear of the train to visit with Mother and Ruth. But then, when he saw how crowded the cars were and how difficult it would be for them to walk through the train, he had them wait until the next stop and escorted them as they walked back along the platform. Later, when we reached Antong, where we crossed into Korea, Mr. Fukumoto got off to return to Mukden, but he told Father and Barbara that they could stay with Mother and Ruth until the end of the trip.

We were not overly crowded in the two cars we occupied at the front of the train. We were permitted to visit back and forth between the two cars, but not to go anywhere else on the train. Strangely enough, for the entire trip the guards in the forward car, where Eva and I were sitting, insisted that the window shades remain drawn for the entire trip; however, in the second car, they remained up. I don't know what it was they were afraid we would see. Evidently the guards on the two cars had different ideas on security.

The weather was unusually hot, and we kept the end doors on the cars open to try to get a through draft. However, despite the heat and discomfort of that long, two-day train trip, our hearts were light. As the miles rolled by, we began to feel that we were indeed actually on our way to freedom and the unhappy experiences of the previous months began to fade. At Seoul, capital of Korea, the train stopped for a considerable length of time and we were given a meal of cold rice and pickles, the traditional Japanese "bento" lunch, and those of us who had thermos flasks were allowed to go out onto the platform to fill them with hot water or tea. There were also stalls selling earthenware teapots filled with hot tea, which we were able to purchase if we wished.

After a second night on the train, again sitting up all night, we reached Pusan, on the southern tip of

Korea, around 7 a.m. At 8:30 we were put aboard a large ocean-going ferry, where we were all immediately herded below decks into a large room with a Japanese-style "tatami" floor, and were told to remove our shoes. With no chairs available, we had to either sit or lie on the mats. We were very surprised when the crew showed much consideration for Mother and Ruth, and allowed them to have chairs in the Western-style forward lounge.

Shortly after we boarded we were served a breakfast of delicious ham sandwiches. Then, although it was unbearably hot and stuffy in the room we were in, with all the portholes closed and covered, most of us managed to get some sleep, having been awake for most of the two nights on the train.

When we awoke we were well out to sea. Fortunately it was very calm, so no one got seasick. After an hour or so, members of the crew opened the portholes, and it was a tremendous relief to get some fresh air. Some time later, when we were out of sight of land, they allowed us up on deck for a couple of hours. We found it delightfully cool and refreshing, but the time passed all too quickly, and as we approached Japan, they once again confined us below decks and the portholes were again closed and covered. If anything, it was even hotter in Japan than it had been in Korea.

Around 5:30 p.m. we arrived at Shimonoseki on the island of Honshu and were taken off the ship. We had a short walk to the railroad station, each carrying his own baggage, and again Doug Broughton kindly spelled me in carrying Ruth. At the station we found two very nice, clean second-class cars reserved for us. Then, to our surprise, just before the train pulled out, our escorts approached with a number of Japanese women in tow, carrying the inevitable "bento" boxes for us. However, instead of the usual rice, fish and pickles, we opened them to find delicate little ham, sausage and cucumber sandwiches. In addition, neatly packed on a bed of crisp lettuce were some huge strawberries, each of them two or three times the size of American strawberries. They were very tasty, but with almost no juice in them. Nonetheless, they were greatly appreciated.

We had been somewhat apprehensive as to what kind of reception we would receive in Japan. We need not have worried. We found courteous and deferential treatment accorded to us by everyone we met, civil-

ians and police. It was markedly different from Manchukuo and Korea, and we were reminded that it was generally the worst element among the Japanese who manned their overseas colonies. Certainly during the eight weeks or so that we were in Japan we received nothing but kindness and consideration everywhere, and with the exception of one isolated incident, never once did any of the Japanese, either civilian or military, indicate to us in any way that they considered us their enemies. Some of that was unquestionably for propaganda purposes, but as a people, the Japanese are mostly friendly and courteous, and it showed.

We traveled all that night, again sitting up, although Ruth was provided with a berth. The train was much more comfortable than the one we rode through Korea, but it was terribly hot. However, the window shades were left up; we were able to open windows as we wished, and by leaving the doors open at each end of the car, we had air circulation that greatly helped. By 4:30 in the morning we started to line up at the washrooms, as we'd been told we were to arrive in Kobe at 7:30 a.m. There were 200 or more in the party, so it took a considerable time for all to get their turn in the washrooms.

Kobe was a city quite familiar to us as a family, as we'd been there several times previously. We were surprised, therefore, when we did not get off at the main railroad station, but instead went on several miles to a small stop in the central hotel district. Our escorts told us the train would only stop for two minutes exactly, and we had to get off quickly or the train would pull out with us still aboard. We piled all our baggage on the seats on the platform side, and before the train stopped, all windows were opened. Some of the men went outside to receive the baggage as it was passed through the windows, and everyone was off the train well before the two minutes were up. Trains in Japan leave with split-second timing and wait for no one.

Our escorts from Mukden said goodbye and handed us over to an entirely new group of people, whom we took to be police in civilian clothing. One older man assumed charge, and he asked us to line up on the platform in two rows. He spoke excellent English, and introduced himself as Mr. Tachibana, head of the Foreign Section of the local government. He told us we would be in his charge while in Kobe and then proceeded to form us into three groups: "weak and invalids," "medium," and "strong."

When all had been sorted out, Eva and I found ourselves in the "weak" group with my sisters and parents, since the Japanese apparently didn't want to separate us as a family. There were 35 of us in that group, and Tachibana had us stand to one side as he arranged for the others to go to different lodging places in the city.

Eventually, my parents and Ruth were put in a taxi and whisked away. Another man and I were asked to load the baggage onto a truck and ride with it, and the rest, including Eva and Barbara, were led away on foot by Tachibana, each carrying a small handbag. It was drizzling lightly, what the Chinese call "cow hair rain" (*niu mao yu*), but it was pleasantly cool and it was good to be out in the fresh air once again.

When we reached our destination, we were agreeably surprised to find it was a nice little Japanese hotel, the Yamato. We expected Japanese-style tatami mats on the floors, but were again pleasantly surprised to find it was furnished entirely in Western style, with beds in each room, and some with private bathrooms. We couldn't believe we were to enjoy such luxury. It was a two-story building, half of it having been built only two years previously, and although the other half was quite old, it was clean and comfortable.

The manager and staff made us feel at home immediately. They could not have been more considerate if we had been royalty. It was obvious that the Japanese government had requisitioned the entire building for us and doubtless paid much less for our lodging than the going tariff. But the hotel staff never gave the slightest indication of being unhappy about it. Instead they were courteous at all times and we became good friends with all of them over the next several weeks.

As soon as we were all inside, Tachibana lined us up and informed us that the hotel was to be our home while we were in Kobe. He told us there would be two guards on duty at all times, and if there was anything that we needed, we had only to let the guards know and they would get it for us. There were a few restrictions: we were told we could use the tiny front courtyard for exercise, but we were not to go out into the street without a guard escorting us "for our own safety," and we were not to talk to any of the other guests in the hotel. The latter rule seemed a bit super-fluous since there were only two of them, one a Japanese and the other a Westerner, but we never learned his nationality.

We were told it would only be a day or two before our ship was to sail, but it turned out to be a little over seven and a half weeks. The reason for our delay was not immediately known; in fact it was not revealed to us until we were on board the ship. At that time we learned from the British ambassador that he had refused to leave until a member of his staff, held by the Japanese as a spy, was released. The man, whose name was Redman if I remember correctly, had indeed been a member of the British Secret Service and had been so badly tortured that it appeared as though almost every bone in his body that could be broken had been. He was barely alive when the ship was due to leave, and the Japanese didn't want him to be seen in such bad shape, but they had promised to let him go on a later exchange ship. That didn't satisfy Ambassador Craigie and the tug-of-war went on for several weeks until Craigie finally won out and the man was released. I saw Redman and talked with him many times aboard ship, and he was a pitiful wreck. I am certain he would never have survived if he had been left behind.

Our rooms at the Yamato were quite comfortable but unbearably hot. Kobe is renowned for its hot weather, and that summer was no exception. We sweltered, and the only relief came from a few electric fans around the place. Eva and I had a small room in the older part of the building, directly above the kitchen. It was private, and in many ways was like a second honeymoon for us after our long separation. But it had one big disadvantage. Each morning around 4 o'clock the trash collectors came, and the noise they made never failed to waken us.

The two guards assigned to take care of us counted us twice each day, but apart from that we were almost unsupervised. They became extremely friendly and helpful, and when we begged to be allowed to go out for some exercise, they did their best to get permission for us. But it wasn't until after an unfortunate incident with our food that permission was granted.

The dining room had eight tables, with white linen tablecloths and good quality silver cutlery. Each day a small silver vase filled with fresh flowers was put on each table. We were served three meals a day in the hotel and the service was excellent, even though the food was somewhat unusual. One waiter served all of us. He was always deferential and became a good friend. The cooks, despite the food shortages in Japan, did their best to make our meals look appetizing. Breakfast, in the early days, started with fruit, followed by a macaroni and cheese dish, ham and eggs, and plenty of toast and butter —real butter that we'd not seen in almost a year. Coffee was ersatz, but palatable. When they noticed that we didn't particularly care for macaroni and cheese as a breakfast dish, a cereal was substituted. The other meals were varied. There was always an abundance of fruit, and a good variety. Loquats were in season, and we had them three times a day, which, in the end, got to be a bit too much.

Meat, of course, was very scarce in Japan and we saw little of it, but fish was served almost daily and was cooked a variety of different ways. We had a lot of "steak." It looked like beef, had the texture of beef, cut like beef, and also tasted vaguely like beef, but it was whale meat. Although at first the taste took a little getting used to, we all managed to eat it. Strangely, although very oily in appearance, it had no fishy taste.

On two occasions soon after our arrival, a number of our group suffered poisoning from the fish served. No one quite knew what caused it. The first time it happened I noticed at the first taste that my gums felt a stinging sensation. At once I called out to the rest of our group that there was something wrong with the fish and that they shouldn't eat it. However, those who noticed nothing wrong with theirs proceeded to eat it anyway, Eva included. In less than an hour she had a serious reaction. She developed a terrible headache and chills, and then from her feet upward her entire body gradually became affected with a sort of paralysis until she lost consciousness. Fortunately we had a woman doctor in our group, and even though she hadn't the slightest idea what had caused Eva's attack, through her heroic efforts Eva was finally brought around and felt none the worse for it. It happened again a few days later, but with less severe results. Eva again was not the only one to be so affected; several others were similarly struck down. In their cases it was not quite as severe, but it gave us all a bad scare.

The manager and hotel staff, as well as the guards, all showed great concern, and the poor chef was almost beside himself. No one had the slightest idea what caused the illness. The doctor speculated it might have been due to lack of proper refrigeration in handling the fish. However, it was after the fish poisoning incident that the Japanese began to take us out for daily walks, both in the city and the surrounding countryside. All of us who wanted to go could do so. We were lined up in a double column in what the British school children call crocodile-style, with one guard in front and the other at the rear, while those remaining at the hotel were left unguarded.

On one of those early walks, we met our American friends from the Mukden camp, also out on a walk. They were just about to depart from Kobe on the *Asama Maru*, and left a few days later. On other occasions we met groups of internees from several other places in Kobe. At the time, we were completely unaware of it, but just a few miles from us there were hundreds of allied prisoners of war held in a large camp in most wretched conditions, forced to work in munitions and on the docks, and subjected to all kinds of cruelty and indignities. How different our lot was from theirs. Very few of them survived that ordeal.

On one occasion during our stay in Kobe I was asked by one of the guards to accompany him somewhere to get some furniture, but he gave no indication of where we were going. We rode in a truck for some eight or ten miles to a makeshift camp outside Kobe, where there were a lot of temporary buildings. Japanese guards were at the gate, and when we got inside, I saw a considerable number of Westerners, who turned out to be Americans.

The minute we arrived the guard accompanying me left me alone in the truck and was gone for about 30 minutes while he hobnobbed with his counterparts in the camp headquarters. That gave me a wonderful chance to talk with the prisoners. They turned out to be civilians who had been captured on Wake Island soon after Pearl Harbor, and although their living conditions and food left much to be desired, they were in good spirits and had few complaints. However, I am certain they remained there for the duration of the war, and conditions most certainly got much worse for them.

There were no women among them, just 20 or 30 men, and I was the first outside person they had seen since they had been put into the camp. I was able to fill them in on news of Allied victories, which cheered them no end, and in turn they gave me vivid details, not only of their initial capture by the Japanese on Wake Island and their subsequent move to Japan. But with great excitement they told me of the Doolittle raid a few weeks earlier when they had seen several American planes fly over and drop bombs. It had done wonders for their morale, but because they cheered the planes as they flew over, the Japanese took it out on them afterward, punishing them by depriving them of food and exercise.

From what we could see in the streets of Kobe, the Doolittle raid had, in turn, destroyed Japanese morale, and it was obvious that everyone was living in fear that there would be another similar raid. We frequently saw Japanese planes fly over. On every such occasion, the minute they heard the sound of an airplane the Japanese would run out into the streets to see if they were American. We noticed that every house and shop had made extensive, yet very primitive, preparations for fighting fires. Barrels of sand and water were placed outside every shop and residence, along with long bamboo poles with hooks on the end, designed for use in tearing down burning buildings.

What interested me was that on our long walks, our guards made no attempt to prevent us from seeing all the various fortifications set up by the Japanese military. Anti-aircraft guns were on the tops of the high buildings all over the city, and all around the shipbuilding areas along the harbor shores. It was equally surprising to me that the guards seemed to take great pride in pointing to the various warships being built in the shipyards. They took us on one walk to the top of a nearby hill from which the entire harbor was visible. From there they showed us aircraft carriers being built in one shipyard and battleships in another. Possibly their idea was for us to carry the information back to our own country in order to destroy morale. Apart from that, however, they made very little reference to the war except, on one occasion, they did make reference to the big sea battle at Midway Island, implying that they had been victorious. But after that one reference, they said nothing more.

We had anticipated a great deal of hostility toward us in Japan, but it never materialized. Wherever we went, everyone was exceptionally friendly. The only exception was on one occasion when we were being walked through a large department store. Behind one of the counters a Japanese woman suddenly started to scream at us unintelligibly. Our guards quickly ushered us out of the way and explained that the poor woman had lost her son in the fighting, hence her open hostility. We really couldn't blame her.

With all the walking we did, most of our shoes were sadly in need of repair. Eva's in particular were in bad shape, but since leather was unavailable, we were unable to get them repaired. On one of the department store trips Eva was allowed to buy a new pair of shoes, but the only thing available was shoes with flat wooden soles, hinged across the instep. They were noisy as she walked, and hard to get used to, but they lasted Eva until we got to South Africa. She took a lot of ribbing from fellow internees because of the noise they made wherever she went.

Our Japanese guards at the hotel were young and very friendly. All had at one time been in the army, and possibly still were on active duty, but they dressed in civilian clothes. One of them enjoyed recounting to the ladies in our group his experiences on the Manchurian border when they had skirmishes with the Russians. He boasted of his prowess with a sword and told in vivid detail of all the Russian heads he had cut off. We had four guards who alternated the duty: one day we had Tachibana and Hamaoka, and the next day Unetto and Nakaie. Hamaoka and Nakaie, in particular, were exceptionally kind to us and gave us unlimited freedom, both in the hotel and on our walks. Because the tiny front courtyard was so confining and without any breeze, they allowed us to walk up and down on the street outside, and I was even permitted to go by myself to a Japanese barber a block or so away to get a haircut. We got to know the various shopkeepers on our block and always got a friendly nod and smile from them when we went by. Across the street from the hotel was a fruit stand. The Japanese woman who owned it formed a very strong attachment to Ruth. Whenever I carried Ruth down into the front yard for a bit of air, the woman came across the street with a gift of fruit for her. Such thoughtful actions on her part, and the friendliness of other civilians, did much to change the very bad impressions we had formed of the Japanese in China.

Now and then we had brief visits from the Swiss consul. Usually he had nothing to tell us as to when we might be leaving, nor could he tell us the reason for the delay. However, toward the end of July we began to see some movement, and one day we were told to pack our bags in preparation for leaving. We were asked to take a sheet of paper and itemize every single article in our possession, and to be prepared for a Customs examination. Two days later, the Swiss consul came again to the hotel and sadly told us that he had been informed by the Japanese authorities that the ship was too crowded and some of us were to be left behind. Our family of six was among those selected to stay until the next exchange could be arranged, one that did not come about until almost a year later. Because of Ruth's generally deteriorating condition, Father was greatly concerned when he heard the news, and he asked the Swiss consul to intercede on her behalf and allow Ruth to be examined by Japanese doctors. My parents both had good reason to doubt that she could survive many more weeks if she were to be left in Japan. The consul arranged for the examination; Father got a written statement from the hospital to the effect that Ruth's health was so poor she should be permitted to leave, and we were greatly relieved when all six of us were once again put on the list for repatriation.

Several other of our Jehol colleagues were not so fortunate. Our good friends Carrie Brixton, Mr. and Mrs. Oliver and Florence Bartlett were left behind, and together with a number of others, they were eventually moved to the port city of Nagasaki for the duration of the war, where they miraculously survived the second atomic bomb. When Eva and I learned that those older friends of ours were not to be permitted to leave, we volunteered to stay and let two of them take our places, suggesting that it be Mr. and Mrs. Oliver. But the Japanese would not hear of it. Evidently they felt that there was much propaganda value in keeping our family of six united, so they refused our request. Had that not been the case, Eva and I might well have been in Nagasaki as well when the bomb was dropped.

After the war, our friends told us of their experiences in Nagasaki. Apparently the building in which they were housed was in a tiny valley, a mile or two from the city center where the bomb fell, and was protected by a large hill. They saw the horrendous flash of light, but the immense blast and fire-storm that followed went right over their heads. The roof of the building was completely lifted off and carried away, and Carrie Brixton had her glasses blown off her nose, but none of them suffered any harm, either from the blast itself or the fallout that followed. God was indeed good to them.

On the appointed day for the Customs examination, our bags were all piled up in the hotel courtyard, and we were made to sit in rows on the steps to watch them being examined. The Customs men were exceedingly thorough and went through everything with great care. All books and photographs were thrown out, as well as a lot of little keepsakes that people had with them. I was very nervous as they went through my suitcase, fearing that when they had it entirely empty they might find the items I had secreted in the sides. But they never even glanced at the interior of the case.

The items that the Customs men took out of the baggage were all piled up on the lowest step behind the long tables on which the bags were being examined. Since the lids of the opened suitcases blocked their view of the people sitting on the next-to-the-bottom step, those folk managed to deftly filch a number of items from the pile and pass them back through the crowd to their respective owners, who promptly secreted them on their persons. These included Bibles and photographs. But many items were left behind. Ostensibly it was left in care of the Swiss consul, but to my knowledge none of us ever saw any of it again.

Barbara was particularly upset about losing all of her precious photographs and Chinese drawings, which she had brought from Lingyuan. One of the guards who had shown himself unusually sympathetic toward us saw her distress and secretly managed to get them all back. He hid them under a cushion in the lounge and then whispered to Barbara where she could find them. Some of those photographs are used to illustrate this book.

The Customs examination was held on July 26th and we were told we would be leaving either on July 29th or 30th. However, once the examination was over, all baggage was loaded on trucks and taken away and we were left with only one small handbag each. It was at that point that the Swiss consul came and announced that a number of us had been taken off the list. That, of course, gave Father very little time in which to negotiate with the authorities regarding Ruth, and I well remember how hectic and filled with uncertainty those last two days were. It must have been particularly trying for my parents.

Finally came the day of departure. On July 29th we

were given our evening meal early, and at 5:30 p.m. we were taken to the station to board a train for Tokyo. After an all-night trip, again sitting up in a second-class coach, we awoke to the early sunlight shining on Mount Fuji on our left, and shortly afterward we were in Tokyo. We were escorted to the Station Hotel through a cordon of a hundred or more police who lined the route. Behind the police barricade, a large crowd of civilians watched us in absolute silence. None showed the slightest antagonism toward us, merely curiosity.

At the hotel, what for us was a sumptuous breakfast was served in the dining room in great style and we were then allowed to rest in the lounge for an hour or more before once again being taken to the station to board the electric train for Yokohama. A 30-minute ride on a high-speed train brought us to Yokohama, where the train deposited us directly onto the pier, alongside which the *Tatuta Maru* was tied up. The 17,000-ton luxury liner was a sister ship of the *Asama Maru*, on which we had sailed a few years before and which had been used a few weeks previously to carry the American contingent to Africa. Painted black in her peacetime color, with huge white crosses painted on her sides to indicate she was carrying repatriates and to protect her from submarine attack, she looked wonderful to us. It is impossible to describe our feelings of joy and hope at that moment.

The *Tatuta Maru* (also pronounced Tatsuta) had been the last civilian liner to cross the Pacific in December 1941, just before the attack on Pearl Harbor. She had been heading for San Francisco at the time, and on December 6th, just before she reached America, she had received a radio message from Tokyo and had turned around and headed back to Japan, carrying with her a large number of disappointed American and British nationals who found themselves headed for internment. Some of them told us how they watched in dismay as, with the ship traveling at high speed, the crew set about painting the entire exterior of the ship with gray paint, which they

had carried for just such an eventuality. But as we looked at her that morning, she looked just as she had in peacetime except for the white crosses. We all hoped that our Allied submarine captains had been well informed of her identity and route, and that they, as well as Japanese submarines, would leave us alone.

After a two-hour wait for another Customs examination, which never materialized, we started to board. By that time other contingents of repatriates from Japan had joined us and there were well over 300 of us standing on the pier, so it took an appreciable amount of time. Once we were on board the ship, there was a certain amount of confusion, while we were assigned to our cabins and berths, but by 8 p.m. everyone was aboard, all portholes were closed and curtained, and we sailed out into Tokyo Bay, where, to everyone's disappointment, the ship dropped anchor for the night. I must admit that we found that disturbing, and rumors flew around the ship regarding cancellation of the exchange. We thought back to Carrie Brixton, always a realist, who had referred to our repatriation as a "wait and see" operation. She, poor dear, had waited in vain.

Although I never let on to anyone else, not even to Eva, I had been extremely nervous all the time we were in Japan. Concerned about appropriating the soft drinks and coffee from the club basement, I worried that Nakamura would discover the loss and chase me down, even as far away as Japan. However, at noon the next day the anchor was raised and we sailed for Shanghai. Not until we were actually in motion did I relax and breathe a little easier.

I am sure that at that moment there was a collective sigh of relief from all on board as we began to thread our way through the spectacularly beautiful Inland Sea of Japan, leaving behind us a lot of happy, as well as highly unpleasant, memories. Although we were finally on our way to freedom, there were many miles to be covered and many unknown dangers and uncertainties ahead.

This drawing attempts to depict a street scene in an imaginary residential area — more prosperous than most — in northeast China circa 1920. Shown are a singing mendicant, a manure collector, a horse-drawn passenger carriage, an unloaded camel caravan perhaps returning from a long journey, and a few of the many types of vehicles for transporting goods, people, and other living things. Such a scene would usually also include scores of street hawkers, peddlers, and other entrepreneurs — such as bean curd sellers, buyers and sellers of rags, repairers of porcelain, metalsmiths, cobblers, and others — each using his own distinctive call or noisemaking device to announce his presence in the neighborhood. One might also see a young foreign boy — a son of missionaries — eagerly taking in all the sights, sounds, smells, tastes and excitement of the humanity around him.

的胖子不是一口吃

Pangzi bushi yikou chide.

A fatty doesn't get that way from just one mouthful of food.

- Chinese Peasant Saying.

Chapter Thirty-One
Shanghai To Bombay

Although the *Tatuta Maru* in peacetime had been a luxury liner, our trip aboard her was far from a luxury cruise. Nonetheless, because she was carrying us to freedom, the indignities and discomforts we were subjected to aboard her in no way detracted from the happiness we felt and our enjoyment of every minute of that lengthy trip.

Normally a "four-class" ship, in our case she became "one class," at least when it came to the use of the public rooms and decks. But sleeping accommodations were another matter entirely. Cabins and berths were assigned by the Japanese on what they evidently considered a class basis. Diplomats got the luxury suites and first-class cabins, businessmen were in second class, and missionaries and "others" got third class and steerage.

When we boarded the ship on July 30, 1942, we were initially all assigned to a cabin in steerage. It was on the very lowest deck of the ship and actually on the steel floor of the forward hold, well below the waterline. As a matter of fact, we hadn't a cabin at all. It was a sort of partitioned cubicle space containing six berths, stacked three high. There was no door — just a wide doorway with a curtain hung over it. Adding to the lack of privacy, the compartment walls extended only to within a foot or so of the deck above. Anyone coming down the nearby stairway had a full view of the interior. There were no chairs or tables, and bathroom facilities were down a long hallway near the center of the ship.

Access to our quarters was down seemingly endless flights of stairs, the last of them being very steep, and it immediately became obvious that Mother and Ruth would be unable to negotiate them. Father waylaid the Swiss representative before he left the ship and explained the problem to him. He was most receptive, and after a wait of nearly three hours, we found ourselves reassigned to a second-class cabin, but with only two berths. That didn't pose a very great problem. By putting a mattress on the floor for

Ruth, my parents were able to use the two berths, and Eva, Barbara, and I went back down to the steerage compartment. However, even that turned out to be only temporary, because of the large number of people who boarded the ship in Shanghai.

August is usually the hottest month of the year in China, and as we moved ever southward, it got hotter and hotter each day. There was no air-conditioning on the ship and absolutely no air circulation at all in steerage. Those first few nights were like being in an overheated sauna and we got very little sleep. But the trip through the beautiful Inland Sea of Japan was just as spectacular as always, and we spent long hours up on deck at night, although with the wartime blackout we could see nothing of the lighthouses and other navigational lights along the shore that normally made the trip so interesting, and we were also unable to see any sign of the many towns and villages. Usually, too, there was a lot of water traffic in those narrow waters, but at night, that too was invisible for the most part. Our ship was brightly illuminated, with floodlights trained on the big white crosses on her sides. Occasionally, within the glow of light that spread several hundred yards around us, we could see a fishing boat gliding silently by, only to disappear into the blackness astern. In the past, making that trip by night had always been like a trip through fairy-land; now it was an eerie sensation to be moving so quickly through the black night, knowing that there were numerous small islands and fishing boats every-where, with land on each side only a short distance away. We marvelled at the skill of the captain or pilot who was taking such a large ship through those dangerous waters. Presumably there had to have been some sort of lighted reference points for them to steer by, something that couldn't be seen by us from the deck or from the air. Radar had just been invented, but I'm sure the *Tatuta Maru* had none.

As we moved from the Inland Sea out into the China Sea the following day, we began to see a lot of marine life: a whale or two, many schools of porpoises, and hundreds of flying fish. But again we saw very few ships. We did see the tip of a submarine periscope quite near our ship early one morning, but there was no way of knowing whether it was American or Japanese.

Early on the morning of August 3rd we sailed up the smelly Whangpoo River (*Huangpu Jiang*) to

Shanghai, and by 5:30 a.m. we were alongside the famous bund. What a change it was from the Shanghai we knew of old. The place seemed entirely devoid of life. A few Chinese policemen and a hand-ful of coolies lolled around on the dock, and some Japanese soldiers were on guard, and those were the only signs of life ashore. None of the teeming crowds of yesteryear.

Our ship was tied up across from what we were told was Hongkew Park, normally a bustling part of the international settlement. As the day progressed, there was still very little movement to be seen on shore, where normally the bund was a hive of activity. Life on the river, though, was much more like the old days: sampans and houseboats going back and forth with the usual large families aboard; ferries loaded with people crossing from one side of the river to the other; junks of all sizes carrying foodstuffs of every kind, and seemingly everything else, from coffins to live animals. There were also numerous tugs towing barges, and several police boats bustled around us all that day and the next. But there were none of the usual freighters and steamships, coming as they had from almost every country around the world and characteristic of the great port of Shanghai in the past. A few rusting hulks were tied up farther upriver, but no smoke came from their funnels. We guessed that they had been impounded and their crews interned.

All day long and well into the next day barges and lighters tied up alongside us delivering fuel, water and foodstuffs. It wasn't until around two o'clock the afternoon of August 4th that passengers started arriv-ing in trucks and buses, and, after a considerable delay, came aboard. We had great sympathy for them as they were made to stand in line for hours, tired and frightened. Not until they actually climbed the gang-way and stepped aboard were they obviously relieved and happy.

About 200 British nationals came aboard, a num-ber of them having come from the large internee camp in Shanghai depicted in the 1990 film, "Empire of the Sun." As we watched them climb the gang-plank, Eva and I were suddenly astonished to see Eva's Aunt Annie. She was with a small group of Dutch and Belgian nationals, a few of whom were diplomats, but most of whom were missionaries and businessmen released from the infamous Weihsien

(Weixian) internment camp in Shandong, where Eric Liddell was interned and later died. Just why the Japanese had decided to let them go was uncertain. We surmised that perhaps it was because the Japanese had many more diplomats in Holland and Belgium than the Dutch and Belgian governments had in China and Japan. And, since the exchange had to be on a one-for-one basis, the Japanese had been forced to find people somewhere to make up the difference in numbers, just as they had done in picking us up from Manchuria. At any rate, we were delighted to see her, but she had no word of Eva's parents, and we presumed they were interned in Peking, which later turned out to be the case. Just why they were never repatriated with the other diplomats was never explained.

When all the Westerners had been brought aboard, the activity on the dock ceased. Then, very much to our surprise, truckloads of Indians began to arrive until eventually more than 400 of them were brought aboard. Although they were British subjects and carried British passports, they had not been interned. However, most of them had been in business in Shanghai and other Chinese cities, and wartime restrictions had caused them such a loss of trade that all were anxious to get back to India. The Japanese had obliged them by giving them passage at British government expense. The Japanese were also sympathetic to the Indian nationalist cause that was trying to overthrow British rule in India. By sending back this large group of "oppressed" people, the Japanese were getting in another lick at the British. We couldn't help but feel some resentment as we saw those Indians come aboard. It was obviously because of them that our friends and colleagues had been left behind in Japan, and they had taken the places of many other British nationals from the Shanghai area as well.

The Japanese assigned almost the entire group of Indians to the forward hold, where we had been quartered, and they were so numerous that they completely overflowed the place. The majority simply camped on the steel deck, but three were assigned to our compartment to occupy the three remaining berths, while others showed an inclination to camp out on the floor of our cubicle. Seeing that our compartment was about to be overrun, we decided to move out into the open space, where we hoped to get a little more air. I found a sort of small alcove between two large steel buttresses that supported the hull, right near the prow of the ship. Being well below the water line and so near the prow, when we sat with our backs against the hull we could hear the water rushing by behind us when the ship was in motion, and it felt strange to realize that only an inch or so of steel stood between us and the ocean outside.

That hold on the other hand was cavernous, with huge spotlights high above our heads that were on day and night. From where we sat, we could look directly upward to the underside of the deck hatch covers some 70 or 80 feet above us, and although air was plentiful, it was mostly stale and motionless, and only when we were at sea was there a faint draft of fresh air sifting down through the deck ventilators. But the intense heat and humidity were a minor annoyance and didn't bother us too much, since we were only down there at night. What did annoy us was the unusual lifestyle of the Indians. That was our first introduction to them as a people, and the first time I'd seen them really close up. I'd seen them in the coastal cities of China over the years, many of them Sikhs who were employed as bank guards or policemen in the concessions, all of them bearded and with turbans around their heads. But these were an entirely different class of people. Mostly Parsees, they were mainly small businessmen with their wives and families, and we found their living habits to be very different from anything we'd seen before. The heat and high humidity didn't seem to bother them in the slightest, and they appeared to prefer it to the fresh air on deck. The majority of them slept most of the day and played most of the night: talking, shouting, singing, enjoying card games, and many of them playing musical instruments while the children raced around, climbing over obstacles (including us, as we lay there trying to sleep) and yelling their heads off. Also, all of them seemed to have brought quantities of food and drink with them, which they consumed all night long.

After two nights of that in the open hold, we could take it no longer. There was absolutely no point in asking the Japanese to assign us elsewhere. We simply took matters into our own hands. We left our bedrolls there in the daytime and when darkness came we climbed up to the highest deck, found a sheltered spot where we could spread our blankets, and spent the night there. It worked out well the first night and we were undisturbed until around three o'clock in the morning, when the deck crew came up and hosed down the decks. Fortunately the noise of their shouting to each other awakened us, and we just had time to grab our bedding and run before they sprayed the area where we had been lying. I am sure that had we not moved, they would have gladly sprayed us as well.

After that we moved frequently, seldom spending two nights in the same place. We slept in stairwells and hallways when it rained, but usually were out on the deck somewhere when we could find nothing else, and there were quite a few others who did the same thing, particularly after our next two stops, when many more people came aboard. One night we slept in the main lounge, hiding behind one of the large sofas. But the early morning cleaning crew drove us out and were quite unpleasant about it, so we didn't try that again.

Leaving Shanghai, we sailed down the coast of China, and except for the occasional island, were out of sight of land most of the time. Early on the morning of August 9th we rounded the tip of Cape St. Jacques and entered the mouth of the great Saigon River, in what was then French Indochina.

As we entered the broad lower reaches of the Mekong Delta, we saw a number of ships at anchor. One of our shipmates, a seaman formerly employed by a British shipping line, Butterfield and Swire, recognized his old ship, which he told us had been scuttled in Hong Kong harbor early in December 1941 to avoid capture. Obviously the Japanese had refloated it and put it into service once again, but they hadn't bothered to repaint it.

The trip up the river to Saigon took several hours. As we slipped through the muddy water, with jungle-lined banks close on both sides, we were surprised at the high speed the ship maintained. The river was not much wider than our ship was long, and the wash from our wake created huge waves that swept up the banks as we passed. Many small bamboo structures thatched with palm leaves lined the shores, and several of them were engulfed by our wake, while others were swept away. Several small fishing boats were either swamped or overturned.

En route we passed a number of fairly large Japanese steamers chugging downstream, all of them with heavy deck loads of tanks, artillery, trucks, sol-

diers, and war equipment of every kind, some even with airplanes on deck. All of them seemed to be traveling at the same high rate of speed. We wondered if they feared being attacked from the shore if they moved more slowly, and our suspicions seemed confirmed by the fact that on each ship numerous guards were posted, all of them standing with their rifles pointed at the jungle on either side of the ship.

Around 2 p.m. we anchored in a large, landlocked open bay in the river about 12 miles below Saigon. Within a matter of minutes, dozens of small craft laden with fruit of all kinds surrounded the ship. We had some Japanese money with us and buying fruit was a good way to get rid of it. We had our choice of bananas, plantains, pineapples, pomeloes, custard-apples, lichees, mangoes, limes, oranges and more. Long bamboo poles with a basket tied to the end were passed up to us. We put our money into the basket and let it back down, indicating with gestures the fruit we wanted. The desired fruit was then passed up to us. We hadn't seen fruit like that in a very long time, and we all gorged ourselves until we could eat no more.

Later the boats left and returned with various locally made curios and souvenir knickknacks of all kinds: baskets of all shapes and sizes, dolls, sun hats, purses, sleeping mats. There were also towels and soap, Japanese beer and whiskey, and miscellaneous shoes and clothing, all of Japanese manufacture. It was mainly the Indian passengers who bought the latter.

Toward evening more passengers were brought downriver on a launch and came aboard. They looked even more exhausted and beaten than the Shanghai bunch. Among them was a British woman carried on a stretcher. With her was her husband, a little boy of around three, and a two-day-old baby carried in a fruit basket alongside. Our ship was filling up fast, and we still had one more stop to make.

Among the Indians who had come aboard in Shanghai was an Indian maharajah, one of the ruling princes of India. Although with the group, he was not a part of it, and we were never quite sure just why he had been in China. For the most part he dressed in the uniform of a British colonel, but he quite often wore a traditional Indian costume in the evenings, and we wondered if perhaps he had not been in the British Secret Service in China. He was a big man, about 6 feet 4 inches tall, with wide shoulders and a broad chest, handsome, with piercing eyes, a prince in every sense of the word. When he became aware that the sick woman with the newborn baby had been put below decks in a third-class cabin, he immediately relinquished his luxury suite to the lady and her husband. We got to know him very well during our trip across to India, and we met him many times later in India as well.

At 2 p.m. the following day we left Saigon and made the same mad dash downriver to the open sea. As we exited the river we saw more Japanese ships at anchor, evidently forming up for a convoy, all with armed men standing guard and facing the river banks. Again, we could only wonder if they feared some kind of attack from the jungle on each side. Once we were again at sea, printed notices appeared all over the ship warning passengers that the area between Saigon and Singapore, *Shonan*, as they called it, was a danger zone with many floating mines left by the allies. Passengers were warned to be prepared for any emergency. From then on everyone carried life jackets at all times. However, we saw nothing and the trip was uneventful.

At 9:30 on August 13th we arrived off Singapore and dropped anchor in a huge bay some 30 miles from the city. We couldn't see the city, and the shoreline of what we were told was the mainland was barely visible in the hazy distance, but around us were some islands with many high mountain peaks off to one side. A large number of other ships were anchored around us, but few of them were close enough for us to see what they were carrying. They seemed to be waiting for dock space before proceeding to Singapore. Not long after we arrived, a small launch trimmed with polished brass and shining mahogany, bearing the name *Sir Hastings Anderson*, came out to meet us. Obviously it had been captured by the Japanese from the British, and they were using it. It brought very mixed feelings to all of us.

We sat at anchor all day, stewing in the humid heat, under the blazing sun in a cloudless sky. Most of the time we were out on deck despite the heat, and it wasn't at all boring because there was much to see. The water around us was clean and clear and filled with giant jellyfish: white, mauve and rust-colored, and small fish swam with them, probably feeding off the parasites and other marine life that congregated

under those huge, colored "umbrellas."

On the near shoreline we saw what we took to be an island. We were unable to make out any buildings of any kind, but saw what appeared to be the wrecks of several ships. No one had binoculars, so we couldn't tell for certain. In various directions huge plumes of heavy black smoke rose, indicating oil fires. Perhaps they had been started during the original capture of Singapore, or could it have been sabotage? We felt that Singapore wasn't a very pleasant place to be, and all of us were anxious to be out of there and away from those reminders of Japan's victorious campaign against what they called Greater East Asia.

But the Japanese weren't through with us yet. Late that afternoon they put on a show for us, a tremendously impressive display of their aerial might. Without any warning, 50 huge two-engine bombers roared over our heads at near mast height. They were flying in three groups, so low that we could clearly see the helmeted pilots looking down at us. First came 12 of them in a spearhead formation three abreast, then a second group of 18 a few minutes later, and finally a flight of 20. No doubt it was intended to impress us and give us something to tell our intelligence people when we got back to wherever it was we were going. The Japanese probably thought it would properly scare our military leaders. The planes, painted a mottled green, roared so low over head they would have indeed been a frightening sight if we hadn't seen them so often before. But with the shortage of fuel that the Japanese were so soon to experience, I wondered in later months if they had not looked back and regretted that meaningless gesture.

We finally sailed at 2 p.m. on August 14th after taking on the final group of passengers. That brought our number up to just under 1,000. As we headed toward Java, down the coast of Sumatra, we passed close to a number of islands where we could clearly see the skeletons of wrecked ships, most of them fairly small ones. Later, when we reached India, we were to hear the story of one of those small wrecked ships from a British officer who survived its bombing.

By the following morning we were passing through the Sunda Strait between Sumatra and Java. The strait varies in width between 20 and 65 miles, and at times it was relatively narrow, with the ship channel very close to the Sumatra side. Not only did we have wonderful closeup views of the waves breaking onto the rocky shore, but it also allowed us the marvelous spectacle of the gorgeous greenery of the jungle, rolling hills coming down close to the shore, and high mountains in the far distance. Adding to the beauty of the passage from the Java Sea to the Indian Ocean were the many small and large islands, some inhabited, others not.

As we exited into the Indian Ocean our last sight of land was some small islands. But it was the broad expanse of the Indian Ocean that beckoned to us and thrilled us with the realization that we were finally out of the area of Japanese control and would soon be truly free. Eva and I both felt as though a load had been taken off our shoulders and we felt a tremendous sense of relief. I am sure that almost all of the nearly 1,000 people aboard the ship felt very much the same way.

The ship was not designed to carry so many passengers. It was very crowded, not only in the public rooms, but also on the decks. The food was adequate but not very exciting. There were no menus; we had to take whatever was given to us. Fortunately, it varied from day to day, and we were not restricted as to quantity. However, again there was a lot of whale meat. We ate so much of it that I never wanted to see it again. One thing we did miss was table napkins. No provision was made for them, not even paper ones. The tablecloths were changed once a week, probably to conserve on fresh water for the laundering, and being on the second sitting, we regularly found our tablecloths filthy, the corners having obviously been used to wipe the mouths of those who had used the table before us. We never bothered to find out who they were, but we frequently wondered why they were so thoughtless about others who had to use the same table each meal.

We had taken on fresh water in Singapore, but the intense heat resulted in frequent showers being taken by everyone who could get near a bathroom. That proved a severe drain on the water capacity, and rationing was instituted a few days later. Water was turned on only for an hour each morning and once again in the afternoon. We three were able to make use of the wash basin in my parents' cabin each morning if we hurried. But for the entire trip we were unable to have a bath or shower. More annoying was the action of some of our fellow passengers in the first-class cabins; they openly boasted of filling their bathtubs each time the water was turned on, and not only enjoying a bath whenever they felt like it, but implying that it was hurting the Japanese, when in fact it was hurting their fellow passengers.

The Indian Ocean was glassily smooth for the first few days, except for huge, almost invisible swells, running at an oblique angle across our track. That caused the ship to pitch and roll abominably for days on end and resulted in many cases of seasickness. With so many aboard, the limited deck space was very crowded during daylight hours. Everyone tried to get some fresh air and feel a bit of breeze, and although a few deck chairs were available, there were never enough for all. We three, Eva, Barbara and I, were seldom off the decks, and fortunately the motion of the ship didn't trouble us at all.

The first day out of Sumatra, we were sitting on the deck with our backs up against a bulkhead when we were astonished to see a small boy of about 3 blithely walk along on top of the protective railing in front of us, totally oblivious to the ocean 40 feet below him. I leapt to my feet and grabbed him, telling him how dangerous it was, and sent him back to his mother — or at least that's where I thought he was going. Not ten minutes later we heard a commotion at the stern of the ship, and there he was, climbing out on the flagpole that extended out over the fantail. Japanese sailors were shouting to him to come back, but he continued out toward the flag. Eventually one of the sailors climbed part of the way out and was able to grab the boy by one foot and pull him to safety, struggling and yelling all the while. I took him from the sailor and that time I made sure I found his mother and told her of the danger he had been in. He led me to her cabin, where I found her lying in her berth so ill from the ship's motion that she could barely speak. At the same time I discovered that it was she whom we had seen being carried aboard the ship at Saigon with her day-old baby. The baby was there beside her, and her distraught husband, between taking care of the baby and his sick wife, had not had time for the older boy. When I told Eva about it, she went down and offered to take charge of the baby for the duration of the trip. The little boy, whenever he was on deck after that, was kept tied by a length of rope.

The second evening out of Sumatra, just at dusk, we passed the *Asama Maru* and the Italian ship *Conte*

Verdi, both returning from Lourenco Marques after having dropped off the American contingent. Horns blew and signals flashed back and forth before they faded into the gathering darkness. It gave us great pleasure to realize that our American friends were safely back in the hands of their own people. There was one more exchange of prisoners the following year in which one or more of the same three ships was involved. After that the two Japanese ships became troop carriers, and both were sunk before the war ended. I don't know what happened to the *Conte Verdi*.

A day or so later, everyone was electrified by a rumor that suddenly flew around the ship to the effect that during the night the ship had turned around and was heading back toward Japan. Someone had apparently noticed that, whereas the sun had been on the right side of the ship the previous several days, it was now on the other side. Fortunately we had as a fellow passenger an old ship's captain. When he learned of the rumor he quickly reassured everyone, telling us that we had simply crossed the equator, thus explaining why the sun had apparently changed position.

Soon after we entered the Indian Ocean, I had occasion to converse with one of the British consular officials aboard. He mentioned that they were busily engaged in compiling a list of all the passengers. I volunteered to help, telling him that I could type. He readily accepted my offer, and I ended up typing multiple copies of endless lists of the passengers, their ultimate destinations and their addresses. The Japanese had drawn up a list, but the spelling of names was atrocious, and it proved totally useless, so we had to start from scratch. The Japanese had been completely flummoxed in trying to list the many Indians who had come aboard in Shanghai. As everyone may be aware, many Indian names end in the word "Singh." The Japanese had accepted that as a common surname, which was not surprising, because it was something that I, too, had thought to be the case. We were told, however, that Singh simply meant "son of," and the spokesman for the group told us that Parsee Indians had no surname as we think of it. That made for considerable complications in sorting them out and getting their names in alphabetical order.

While working on the lists, the Japanese allowed us to work in a corner of the large first-class dining room between meals. While involved in that job, I became acquainted with the British Ambassador to Japan, Mr. Craigie. When he learned I had been born in China and spoke Chinese, he approached me one day toward the end of the trip and asked me about my plans. I told him I had no plans. Our home was in China, and although we had relatives in both England and Canada, we had made only tentative plans to go to either of those countries and would have to wait and see what shipping was available.

Ambassador Craigie told me that, should I go to England, I would be immediately drafted into the army, and he asked whether I would have any objections to going to India to work for the government of India, where I could use my knowledge of Chinese. He was certain that, because India was then connected to China by the Burma road, there would obviously be a lot of commerce between the two countries. It occurred to him that I might be of much greater use in the war effort if my knowledge of Chinese could be used than if I was simply another enlisted man. I told him I would be delighted to go to India, provided that Eva could accompany me, telling him that we had already been separated for many months and didn't want that to happen again. He assured me that he would send a cable to New Delhi as soon as we reached Africa. My parents, meanwhile, had given some thought to going on to Australia if possible, rather than to England. They thought that the climate there might be better for Ruth's health.

The Japanese crew of the *Tatuta Maru* were well trained and quite used to carrying civilian passengers. For the entire trip their attitude toward us was civil, but somewhat distant, and could be described as unfriendly. It was completely different from that of the people of Kobe, but I cannot venture to say why it was so. Possibly they resented having us aboard and felt that they ought to be doing more in the war effort than shuttling civilians around. Yet despite that seeming unfriendliness, they surprised us when, on August 25th, within a day or two of our arrival, they put on a party especially for the large number of children aboard. Members of the crew acted as clowns and performed well. There was a highly accomplished ventriloquist with two performing dolls, and they provided a lot of games and songs, followed by cake and ice cream. In the evening, a movie was staged on the boat deck, and we viewed a documentary film about whaling ships in the Antarctic and a second about Hawaii. It was obvious that they were making an effort to have us leave the ship feeling good about them. However, a few days later, after we had reached port, their attitude changed drastically. More of that later.

When we were about 500 miles off the coast of Madagascar, a very large island some 250 miles off the southeast coast of Africa, we began to see large numbers of birds, and very soon after that we could smell the unmistakable odor of rotting jungle vegetation. We never came within view of the island, but the following afternoon we were in the Mozambique Channel between the island and the mainland, still out of sight of land.

Finally, on the afternoon of August 27th, we arrived at Lourenco Marques, capital of Mozambique, then known as Portuguese East Africa. We had been aboard the ship since July 30th and were good and ready to leave her.

A heavy fog had enveloped us that morning, but as we approached the mouth of the Limpopo River the fog lifted. Ahead we could see high, red bluffs surmounted by beautiful green trees. A launch came out carrying the harbor pilot, and the black faces of the native crew were the most welcome sight we'd seen in years. It was the first convincing evidence that we were no longer in an area of Japanese domination, and we knew we'd reached the other side of the Indian Ocean.

We spent 16 days in Lourenco Marques and did not leave there until September 12th. The two British ships bringing Japanese repatriates from India and Australia had been held up by bad weather, so the exchange could not take place until they arrived, and that was well over a week after we got there. However, from the moment we docked, we were in a neutral country and thus were technically "free." The British authorities aboard advanced each of us a 10-pound note, for which we had to sign a receipt and a promise to repay, but we were then allowed to go ashore immediately.

Our feelings as we stepped on the dock are something I am quite unable to describe. For the first time in nine years we didn't have the Japanese breathing down our necks, and with light hearts, Eva and I tramped around the city exploring the stores and restaurants and marveling at the cleanliness. We went to the beaches and lay on the sand just soaking up the gorgeous weather, and we luxuriated in the lovely parks where everything was neat and precise. However, our "freedom" turned out to be strictly relative. Eva and I were sitting on a bench in one of the parks that first afternoon holding hands and occasionally indulging in a bit of hugging and kissing in the sheer joy at being alone together once again. Soon a burly Portuguese policeman approached us, and although he spoke no English, he made it plain that that sort of behavior was not permitted. We were told to sit a few inches apart and to conduct ourselves properly. But it didn't dampen our joy for long.

Each night we had to return to the ship to sleep, but there were no restrictions as to how we spent our days, and we were ashore most of the time. The only problem was that the 20 pounds we had between us didn't go very far in buying food in the restaurants. We craved chocolate and real meat, and although both were plentiful and relatively inexpensive, our money began to disappear very quickly. We also learned very quickly that food was the only thing any of us were permitted to buy in Lourenco Marques. In fact, had we even wanted to buy something else, such as clothing or shoes, we discovered that nothing whatsoever was available in the entire city. The stores had been cleaned out by the Japanese internees who had come from the United States for the exchange that had preceded ours by just a few weeks and who had been taken back to Japan on the *Asama Maru* and the *Conte Verdi*.

We looked into store after store and saw the shelves completely bare. Storekeepers who spoke English told us that when the Swedish liner *Gripsholm* had arrived from the United States with the Japanese aboard, there had been a wait of a couple of days for the ships from Japan to arrive. In that short time the Japanese, evidently operating on orders from their ambassador, had rented trucks and had gone methodically from store to store, buying up the entire stock: clothing, luggage, jewelry, furniture. Gift stores had been completely denuded of every item in stock, and we were told that the Japanese had been particularly anxious to buy up as many pairs of shoes as possible. They had even bought up huge quantities of chinaware and as many automobiles as they could. Not everyone wanted to sell his car, but those who did were paid new car prices for very old vehicles.

We even heard of one incident where a Japanese backed his truck up to a home that had large, decorative rocks on the front lawn. He offered the homeowner so much for them the man couldn't refuse, and they were trucked away to be loaded aboard the *Asama Maru* and doubtless were eventually used in some Japanese garden, but why they would bother with decorative rocks in wartime is beyond me. One men's clothing store owner told me that the Japanese had trucked away his complete stock of over 2,000 suits, and all he still had for sale were a few items that had been locally made. Many other stores were simply closed, because with the wartime shortages of transportation and manufacture, they were unable to replenish their stocks except for what they could buy from adjoining towns, so effectively they had been put out of business.

In any case, to prevent the same thing from recurring, the mayor of Lourenco Marques had issued a proclamation prohibiting the sale of anything except food to either Japanese or British nationals, in order to conserve what little was left for the local inhabitants.

To us it didn't matter much. The women of the local Portuguese ladies' society were extremely kind and set up centers to entertain the children with all kinds of food and games, and the adults at afternoon teas and lunches. There was even a Red Cross center where we could select whatever we wanted from piles of used clothing and shoes. Barbara managed to find a pair of shoes that fit Mother, but by the time Eva and I got there, we could find nothing that would fit Eva's feet. Most of the stuff had been thoroughly picked over. We eked out our limited funds by going back to the ship for the evening meal, as we had to sleep aboard anyway. But for lunches and our afternoon teas, we reveled in the huge steaks and the marvelous white bread and rolls available, and, of course, the chocolate and ice cream delicacies that we had missed for years. We had almost forgotten what white bread looked like; our bread for months had been almost gray. But I think what we found most novel was the way the Portuguese served steak: always with a poached egg on top. We discovered it to be a most delicious combination.

Those 16 days in Lourenco Marques were some of the most exciting days we have ever spent. There was so much to do and see and so much to enjoy once

again. Mozambique gained its independence in 1975 and Lourenco Marques was renamed Maputo. The country is now one of the poorest in the world, with famine and internal strife tearing it apart. Then, however, it was a bustling, prosperous city with a large European population. One thing that struck us almost immediately was the fact that all the blacks spoke fluent English, but with a strong and most noticeable Scottish accent. We were told it was because the very first English-speaking settlers had been Scottish missionaries. How true that was we don't know.

One morning we boarded a local train and took a relatively short ride through acres of cashew trees to the bank of the Limpopo River. We then rode a motor launch upriver through dense jungle on both sides until we found some hippos. It was a delightful trip that we've never forgotten. We not only saw dozens of hippos in their native habitat, some in the water with just their nostrils showing and others lying on the banks or feeding, but we also saw a tremendous variety of other animals and many different snakes and birds, most of which we'd never seen before even in zoos. It made a memorable day.

The ship coming from India with the Japanese repatriates was called the *City of Paris*. Two days before she was due in Lourenco Marques, word came by radio that there had been a number of deaths among the Japanese aboard the ship. Some were from natural causes, but several others had been suicides. There was speculation that they had apparently seen the massive buildup of the Allied war machine in India and did not want to return to Japan to face the inevitable bombings and defeat that were certain to follow. In all, some nine or ten individuals had died. When the Japanese crew on the *Tatuta Maru* heard about it, they became extremely angry, accusing the British authorities of having deliberately killed them. As a result, they started to take out their anger on those of us who had remained aboard the *Tatuta Maru*. (A few who could afford it had gone to live in hotels on shore.) Their attitude became openly hostile, with some people being pushed around or roughed up for no reason at all; in one case, an Englishman was playing the piano in the lounge when a Japanese steward came by and slammed the lid down on his fingers, crushing them. The food also became almost impossible to eat. It was cold most of the time, and was literally slammed down on the table in front of us. All water was also turned off, and the bathrooms were left in a deplorable condition.

When the *City of Paris* finally arrived, my parents and the two girls were among the first to be exchanged. Two gangways were set up on each ship, outgoing passengers using one, and incoming passengers the other. One by one the internees from opposing ships wound their way down the dock, past tables where Japanese and British officials sat. Names were carefully checked against lists and travel documents were studied with extreme care. Swiss and Portuguese officials sat at other tables nearby looking on. It was a very time-consuming process. Those of us who were not immediately involved were confined to the ship for the day and watched from the ship's railing, impatiently awaiting our turn.

The first group of Britishers off the *Tatuta Maru*, which included all our family except Eva and myself, was temporarily taken aboard the British liner *El Nil*, a very old but still serviceable passenger liner that was tied up nearby because the *City of Paris* had to be fumigated before she could take on passengers. Our turn to be exchanged came two days later, when the fumigation was complete, and Eva and I moved directly to the *City of Paris*, while the rest of the family joined us that same day. Our immediate destination was to be Durban, South Africa, the closest British possession. From there each individual could make a choice as to a final destination.

In the meantime, Eva and I had received the exciting news from Ambassador Craigie that both of us had been accepted for employment by the government of India and would be going there direct from Durban. I still have the original cable that came from India, which I kept as a souvenir. For us it was a tremendous relief to know that, at least for the duration of the war, we would not be separated again.

On September 12th, 47 days after we had boarded the *Tatuta Maru* in Yokohama, we sailed for Durban at 5:30 in the afternoon, clearing the headlands just before dark. Our ship, just like the *Tatuta Maru*, was painted black and protected with large white crosses, which were illuminated at night. When we entered the Mozambique Channel once again, we encountered very rough seas that lasted all night and all the way to Durban, where we arrived at noon the following day.

Our arrival was expected, and although we knew no one there, a huge crowd had assembled on the dock to welcome us. As we came alongside, a military band was playing and hundreds of Union Jacks were waving. It was a most moving experience. However, even before that, as we had been approaching the harbor entrance, we had been serenaded from the end of the breakwater by a middle-aged, buxom lady with a marvelous voice. She sang a medley of popular songs, and her voice carried over the three or four hundred yards of water between us without the use of a megaphone. We learned that she did that for every ship that entered or left the harbor; bolstering the morale of the soldiers on the troopships was her contribution to the war effort.

Durban harbor was so crowded with shipping that there was actually no dock space for the *City of Paris*, and we had to tie up next to another ship. It took a few hours to process us all, but we eventually all got ashore. There was no Customs examination, and a special bus whisked us away to a comfortable hotel called the Rydal Mount. Eva and I spent five days there while the *City of Paris* was repainted in her wartime camouflage-dappled colors and again readied as a troopship.

Once ashore we finally felt truly free from all Japanese influence and domination and we reveled in the feeling. We found Durban a very modern city. Transportation around the city was good, with numerous convenient bus routes. There were also clumsy-looking two-seater rickshaws pulled by Zulus, outlandishly bedecked with feathered headdresses and clothing, white socks painted on their bare feet, and with anklets of dried seed pods. We found their jerky, loping gait quite different from the smooth-running Chinese rickshawmen, and the rickshaws were not nearly as comfortable.

We had a wonderful time shopping for shoes and clothing, having been advanced more money by the British ambassador. For lunch one day we ate in a large movie theater that really intrigued us. It was a restaurant as well as a movie house. After selecting our food, we carried it to our seats, and found a wide shelf on the back of the row of seats in front of us on which to put the tray. I've never seen anything quite like it elsewhere. In China, during performances of the traditional Chinese opera, waiters would brings snacks to anyone in the audience who wanted them, but there was no tray and no convenient shelf.

During the daytime we visited the gorgeous beaches around Durban, and one evening we relaxed in an air-conditioned movie palace such as we had never seen before. We faced a gigantic stage, and before the movie began the curtains drew back, organ music swelled, and then from the center of the stage a hidden organ with an organist sitting in place playing suddenly came up on an elevator. The lyrics of patriotic and popular songs flashed on the screen, and the audience, consisting mainly of soldiers, enthusiastically sang along. It was a thrilling experience for us. I have forgotten what the movie was, but we particularly enjoyed the newsreel pictures depicting the progress of the war, including scenes of the Battle of Midway. For the very first time we realized what a tremendous war machine the allies had assembled to battle the Japanese, and it gave us the assurance that there could be no doubt as to the outcome of the war.

Because we would no longer be under the protection of the white crosses of a repatriation ship and would be carrying troops, there was great secrecy about the time our ship would sail for India. Eventually, on September 19th, with very little advance notice, Eva and I were told to board the *City of Paris* by 2 p.m. that same day. It was hard to say goodbye to our loved ones. After much thought my parents had decided to stay on in Durban for the duration of the war rather than go to either Australia or Canada. Passage by sea was fraught with danger. They had been given a comfortable flat in the Rydal Mount hotel, where they settled down, and it was there we bade them farewell.

As we left the hotel and waved our goodbyes, Mother was sitting outside on the small porch. It was the last time I was ever to see her, and that is the way I remember her. Dear Mother was brokenhearted at having had to leave her beloved China and was so looking forward to returning there after the war. But it was not to be. Three years later, in 1945, and just a short time before the war ended, my father became ill and was hospitalized. Mother worried so much over him that she, too, was hospitalized within the same week and was diagnosed as having a strangulated colon, which the doctors said was inoperable. She went to be with her Lord a few days later, at the age of 65. I have always consoled myself since then with the thought that she never had to suffer what would have been her greatest disappointment when return to China was impossible at war's end. China was going Communist, and very few missionaries were able to go back. Those who did weren't there for very long before they were forced to leave.

Life on the *City of Paris* was quite different during our second trip aboard. Eva and I had been issued diplomatic passports in Durban and were classified as "officials," and thus we rated a first-class cabin. We found a few familiar faces among the passengers — chiefly consular people who had been assigned to India. But in addition to the 400 Indians who had come from Shanghai, the ship was crammed with well over 1,000 British troops from New Zealand who were en route to Egypt, our first and only stop.

We sailed from Durban around 5:30 in the evening, and again were serenaded from the breakwater by the unknown lady with the marvelous voice. She sang unaccompanied, and, as we sailed away, we could still hear her when we were nearly a mile from shore. Everyone was thrilled by her magnificent voice, and there was scarcely a dry eye among those on board. One song that she sang, and which we heard then for the first time, was the haunting classic English song about the cliffs of Dover. One line of it went: "There'll be bluebirds over the white cliffs of Dover...," and we were to hear it sung again and again by the soldiers on board as they gathered each night on deck to escape the heat below. It was a most moving experience to hear those hundreds of voices singing in the total blackout, particularly when the night was stormy, and we knew that enemy submarines were nearby.

Once outside the harbor we were joined by a large number of other ships — mostly freighters and oil tankers — but also two or three other passenger ships of considerable size. It wasn't until the next morning that we realized we were part of a convoy of more than 30 ships. We never learned exactly how many there were, because although we could count those that were in sight around us, some others were always over the horizon behind, showing only a wisp of smoke and the tips of their masts. Accompanying us was one Royal Navy destroyer and at least six corvettes. The latter were much smaller than a destroyer: clumsy-looking, but exceedingly fast and extraordinarily maneuverable. During the next ten days or so, as we sailed up the coast of Africa, we were to see them in action many times as submarines threatened the convoy. They took fierce punishment from the very rough weather, and we felt sorry indeed for their crews.

Immediately after we left the Durban harbor we were warned that wartime conditions would prevail, and that we were no longer under international protection. Our journey up the coast was considered extremely dangerous, and we were told to wear our life jackets at all times, at meals and even in bed at night.

Our progress up the coast was painfully slow. Our speed was limited to that of the slowest ship in the convoy — a very old freighter that kept breaking down — and I don't think we ever exceeded five knots. Each time a freighter broke down, and several of them did, a corvette would detach itself from the convoy and stay with the ship until repairs were made. The rest of the convoy slowed down until the stray could catch up. Every few minutes the convoy would change course, zigzagging across the ocean.

The most dangerous spot was the Mozambique Channel, between Madagascar and the African coast. It averaged 300 miles or so in width and was the normal route for all traffic up the coast. It formed a natural bottleneck where Japanese submarines lay in wait. The channel is 950 miles long, and it took us more than three days to negotiate it. Time after time, day and night, there were constant submarine alerts. The little corvettes dashed around, seemingly without rhyme or reason, like so many water bugs, but they were obviously carrying out a well-orchestrated pattern as they dropped their depth charges. The action continued each day and well into each night that we were going through the channel; nevertheless, several of the freighters were hit by torpedoes and sunk.

Once through the channel we headed well out to sea, and things quieted for several days until we rounded the Horn of Africa and headed into the Gulf of Aden, at the mouth of the Red Sea. There again we had repeated alerts; it was obvious the enemy submarines had no intention of allowing us to enter the Red Sea unscathed. The action was fierce, and there were so many submarines around that the convoy broke up. Ships dashed madly in every direction, with the destroyer and the six corvettes tearing around in wide circles furiously dropping their depth charges. Many times ships came so close to each other that it was astonishing that there were no collisions. At one

point our ship made a direct run for the high cliffs near the port of Djibouti, across the gulf from Aden. As we drew closer and closer to shore, a corvette came parallel to us, just a couple of hundred yards away, moving at flank speed and dropping depth charges every few minutes. The explosions were so near that the shock waves shook our ship. We were traveling so fast that it seemed inevitable we would run aground. However, the captain evidently knew the waters well and knew he had sufficient depth of water in which to maneuver. Only at what seemed the last possible minute before we hit the shore did the captain execute a crash turn. We were so close to shore we heard the waves pounding on the nearby rocks.

During that engagement also, several ships in the convoy were hit by torpedoes, and several were sunk. Two freighters beached themselves on the shore. However, the action was spread over a vast expanse of ocean, with many ships involved, and we saw only what went on in our immediate vicinity.

While the sea battle with the submarines was raging, the Indian passengers milled around the forward deck of the ship in utter panic, some of them racing to the boat deck to demand that lifeboats be dropped so they could escape to shore. That caused a great deal of confusion and seriously hindered the work of the Navy men aboard our ship who were manning the guns fore and aft. At that point the Indian prince showed his true leadership. He stood on top of the bridge and shouted down at the assembled Indians through a megaphone, chiding them for their lack of courage and urging them to have patience and to keep out of the way of the crew. Within a few minutes he had quieted them down. It was an impressive performance. However, we didn't blame the Indians for being frightened; we all were.

We were near the head of the convoy, and after an hour or so when the battle moved away from us, our ship headed for the other side of the gulf and the port of Aden, in what is now known as Yemen. Several of the other large troopships followed our lead. Our ship was able to pull alongside a pier in the small harbor, but most of the other ships had to anchor. Apparently that move was part of a regular procedure. The lower end of the Red Sea was considered too dangerous for troopships to negotiate in daylight, not because of submarines, but because German bombers were constantly flying bombing runs in those narrow waters. We were told that we were too far from British fighter bases for the RAF to be able to defend us. We waited there until nightfall, but the surviving freighters and oil tankers in the convoy continued on their way to Suez with their escorts.

Aden was then a British colony and protectorate, and a more desolate and poverty-stricken place I've never seen. It was unbelievably hot there. Aboard ship it proved intolerable, what with the stench from the city and the sand blowing in our faces. We finally went ashore, walked around a bit, then took a taxi to a high peak a few miles outside the city, where we at least found a bit of clean air. But there was no way to get cool, nor were we able to find any place that served cold drinks, so we returned to the ship just before sundown.

The living conditions of the native Arab population in Aden were pitiful. Abject poverty was everywhere, and the entire city appeared to be one large slum. Most noticeable everywhere were the rope-slung beds outdoors, propped against the sides of the houses or up on the flat roofs. It seemed evident that no one ever slept indoors, and with that intense heat it was not surprising.

At dark we headed up through the Red Sea to the port of Suez, where the Suez Canal begins. We traveled at high speed, constantly zigzagging, and frequently on alert because German bombers were in the habit of flying over at night, spotting the phosphorescent wake of ships and dropping bombs with considerable accuracy. Thankfully our trip proved uneventful, and we finally docked in Suez in the early afternoon of the next day.

We were absolutely astonished by what we saw in Suez. The Gulf of Suez is the entrance to the canal, and it was a fairly wide area crammed with ships of every kind and size. I have never, before nor since, seen so many ships crammed into such a relatively small area. Everywhere on shore, where there was any open space at all, we could see acres of war equipment: tanks, trucks, guns of every size and description, airplanes, tents, stacks of ammunition boxes. Thousands of British troops marched about in formation or worked on the docks. Somehow they managed to find space for us to dock, and we disembarked immediately because we feared night bombing. The civilian passengers, including Eva and me,

were loaded onto a train and taken to Cairo for safety. The only exceptions were the Indians. I was told by one of the ship's officers that the Indians were adamant, refusing to leave the ship under any circumstances, even though German planes from Alexandria were bombing Suez nearly every night. The Indians were afraid they would be left in Egypt, never to get to India.

Security was very tight as we boarded that train, and we were questioned repeatedly before being allowed aboard. It wasn't long before we understood the reason. Cairo is not far from Suez, but that train ride was unforgettable. Despite the short distance, it was several hours of slow travel in intense heat, punctuated by lengthy, unscheduled stops in the middle of the desert. Yet what we saw along the entire route was mind-boggling and made up for the time spent on the train. Remember that we were there at the end of September 1942; just a few weeks later, on October 23rd, General Sir Bernard Montgomery, with his inimitable British Eighth Army, launched his massive and successful attack on Field Marshal Erwin Rommel's troops in the historic battle of El Alamein. General Rommel, the "Desert Fox," had succeeded in advancing toward Alexandria, just 107 miles from Suez, before he was stopped. What we saw were preparations being made to drive Rommel out of North Africa; before our eyes on both sides of the track were miles and miles of war equipment of every imaginable description, spreading as far as the eye could see.

In addition to the thousands of British troops encamped in tent cities near the tracks, there were hundreds of tanks, trucks, artillery pieces and piles of ammunition. Every now and then we saw temporary airfields covered with fighter planes and heavy bombers. Later, Sir Winston Churchill, in the fourth volume of his history of World War II, *The Hinge of Fate*, wrote: "Before Alamein we never had a victory. After Alamein we never had a defeat."

As our train headed toward Cairo, we noted that everything we saw, all the motorized equipment, the tents, and everything else in sight, had been painted the same color as the desert sands. The trucks, Jeeps and tanks racing in every direction blended in so well with the scenery that it was possible only to identify them by the rooster tail of dust they raised. Never before had we seen such a tremendous display of armed might, and we were both proud and awestruck as we contemplated the battle that was about to begin.

Cairo, a seething mass of humanity, struck us as a filthy city. Somehow the authorities had managed to reserve space for us at the famous Shepherd's Hotel, but large as the hotel was, it seemed impossible that the milling crowd of officers and soldiers in the lobby and public rooms could possibly be accommodated there. Apparently multiple beds had been placed in each room; however, Eva and I were given a room to ourselves.

We were there for just one night. As we walked the streets after dark, the scene begs description. British, American and other Allied troops, in uniforms of every branch of the services, jostled for space with the local Arab population, which in itself seemed to encompass people of every nationality. The Germans were only a few miles away in the desert, but one would never have known it from the carefree attitude of the troops and the local population. Everyone seemed to be having a wonderful time.

All the stores and restaurants were doing a booming business, and Arabs, with their street stalls selling foodstuffs and trinkets, were not far behind. The morale of the troops was obviously very high, and it was equally obvious that they were itching to get into action. Mr. Churchill, in his story of the battle that came so soon after our visit, noted that more than 13,000 men were lost in 12 days. When reading it, Eva and I could only wonder how many of the young men from New Zealand who traveled from Durban with us on the *City of Paris* were among those casualties, and I'm sure that many of those with whom we rubbed shoulders that night also died.

The next day we were back on the train heading for Suez, and the moment we arrived, we boarded the *City of Paris* and departed almost immediately. However we now sailed entirely on our own, no longer having any escort. There were only a very few military men on board, most of them officers. The rest of the passengers were civilians, including the 400 Indians, of course. Once more we traversed the Red Sea by night, and by late morning of the next day we were abreast of Aden and speeding out into the Arabian Sea for the relatively short trip across the Arabian Sea to Bombay.

We were again warned by the ship's officers to wear life jackets day and night because the area was heavily seeded with Japanese mines, and Japanese submarines were known to be very active in the area, trying to stop shipping from reaching Karachi and Bombay. Day and night, a constant watch on the sea was kept from numerous points on the ship, and all male passengers were assigned shifts of two hours each as lookouts. The responsibility weighed heavily on each of us, particularly at night. As one stared into the darkness, concentrating on the assigned direction, we were convinced that every breaking wavetop — the only thing visible — was the periscope of an enemy sub or an approaching torpedo. It took tremendous will power not to sound the alarm until one was absolutely certain. Fortunately, neither submarines nor their torpedoes were seen.

It took us three days to cross to Bombay, but it seemed an eternity. We traveled at top speed all the way, zigzagging every few minutes. All went well, and we reached Bombay without seeing any other ships, friend or foe.

It was late afternoon when we approached the shores of India. The first indications of land were the many fishing boats far out to sea and the strong smell from the land, quite different from the smell of either China or Africa. Each country seems to have its own distinctive odor.

Our ship was held outside the harbor until after dark because of crowded conditions at the piers. Just when we had about given up any hope of going ashore that night, a launch came alongside at around 9 o'clock and all diplomats and military officers were taken ashore, Eva and I included. Our baggage was checked by Customs, we were briefly interrogated by military intelligence, and finally we were taken to a large Western-style hotel for the night.

The intelligence people asked me if I had any papers with me. Aboard ship I had spent many hours in our cabin using a borrowed typewriter to type up a long report that British Intelligence in South Africa had suggested I write while our experiences with the Japanese were still fresh in my mind. I handed over a copy, then remembered my stash of traveler's checks and stamps, hidden in the lining of my suitcase. With supreme honesty and patriotism I tore open the lining of the suitcase and produced them. We were dismayed when everything was taken from us for examination, and it was to be several months before they were returned to us. That meant that we would arrive in New Delhi without a penny in our pockets. Fortunately, the consular people who were traveling with us understood our need and advanced us enough spending money to take care of our needs in Bombay.

We spent several days there while arrangements were made for us to proceed by train to New Delhi. Bombay was hot and humid, even in October. Although the nights were passable in the large hotel in which we stayed, with its high ceilings and electric fans, the days were extraordinarily hot and unpleasant. Our introduction to India that first morning was to walk along the streets, where our first impression was that either there had been a battle the night before, or everyone had tuberculosis or had had a nosebleed. Everywhere we looked, the streets and sidewalks were stained with what we took to be blood. It took us quite some time to realize that it wasn't blood, but betel nut juice. Betel was chewed by almost every Indian in sight, and they spat indiscriminately wherever they happened to be. Their blood-red mouths and stained teeth also took some getting used to.

Hotel employees informed us of a beach club on the outskirts of Bombay where we could enjoy some swimming, and told us which bus to take to get there. As we waited for the bus, a huge cow wandered down the sidewalk and took up a position alongside us. When the bus stopped, the cow attempted to get aboard, and not a soul made a move to stop it. It stood there for what seemed like several minutes, with its two front hooves on the back platform of the bus, while the conductor and driver, seemingly quite unperturbed, simply looked on and waited to see what it would do. I had never heard of India's "sacred cows," so I attempted to give it a gentle push to get it out of the way so we could climb aboard. But the minute I put my hand out to touch the animal, pandemonium broke out on the bus and among the Indians on the sidewalk. I had done the unthinkable, and I was told later by other Europeans that I was fortunate in not being beaten up by the crowd. I learned fast that in India those cows could do exactly what they wanted and no one would lay a finger on them or interfere. As the months went by and we saw more of India, we were to frequently see cows wandering through the streets at will, sometimes breaking through fences or gates and happily feeding in people's front yards, consuming flowers and vegetables alike, while the householders looked on seemingly unconcerned, possibly even feeling honored that the cow should have chosen their place in which to feed. I never ceased to be amazed at the honor and respect and even worship that the Hindus accorded them. I once asked a very well-educated young Hindu man who worked for us in New Delhi just how sacred the cows were to Indians. Without hesitation he replied that, if he were to see his father and a cow both drowning in the same pool or river, he would have no choice but to save the cow first, even at the risk of his father's life. From what we saw in the next two years, I came to fully believe that, and the two years we stayed in India proved quite an education for us in a lot of areas, not just in cultural differences.

The Bombay Beach Club, when we finally got there, was delightful. Set immediately back from a sandy ocean beach, it comprised not only spacious club buildings, open on four sides and cooled by the ocean breeze, but also a Western-style bar and coffee shop. There were also dining and dancing facilities, and a very large outdoor pool filled with ocean water. For those who preferred to swim in the ocean itself, a section of beach was protected against sharks by a wire fence in the water. However, we had to be satisfied with swimming in the pool, because being wartime the beach was guarded by Indian soldiers and no one was allowed in the water. Barbed wire barricades had been placed along the waterline either to discourage Japanese spies coming ashore, or because an invasion was feared.

Japanese spies came ashore frequently along those beaches, a fact of life that we learned about later, when we got to New Delhi and I became involved in working with British Intelligence. Each month several were captured, having come ashore at night in rubber boats from a submarine. They were easy to spot, and it is highly questionable that any of them ever managed to do any spying, because they never changed their procedure. They always dressed the same, trying to blend in with the local population by wearing Indian dress; however, because of their attire and their oriental appearance, they stood out like sore thumbs. Moreover, every single one of them came ashore with a brand new galvanized iron pail and little else. The pails had false bottoms in which small radios were concealed. Evidently the Japanese thought the pails would make them look like civilians going about some very ordinary business, whereas in fact, no Indian men were ever seen carrying pails of any kind, let alone brand new ones, so it was an immediate giveaway. British agents picked them up quickly or followed them to see who their contacts were. Yet despite the fact that presumably none of them ever reported back to their headquarters, more kept coming. They were courageous men, but with very poor leadership, and their superiors back in Japan were definitely lacking in imagination and in knowledge of India.

The Tatuta Maru carried British nationals interned under the Japanese to Portuguese East Africa for repatriation.

Chui mao qiu ci

Blowing into fur to look for flaws
(Finding fault; nitpicking.)

- Chinese Peasant Saying.

Chapter Thirty-Two
India

India might well have been another planet as it was so different from any other country we'd seen. The landscape was different, the people were different, the smell of the country was overpowering, and the climate was hot, humid, dusty and windy.

We were given second-class tickets for the train to New Delhi. The accommodations were quite comfortable, and we enjoyed the trip in spite of the heat. The scenes outside our window were fascinating but discouraging at the same time. There was such poverty among the people, their living conditions were deplorable, and they looked overworked. Unlike China, their methods of tilling the soil seemed to be from the dark ages, showing no advance at all. The more we saw of the countryside, the more we longed to be back in China.

As we neared New Delhi, the climate became drier, although it was just as hot or even hotter, even though it was October. The flat land was unbroken by hills of any significant size, and, like China, almost no trees showed except those near villages and towns. One place we stopped at was an exception. There, and for some distance on both sides of the track, a jungle grew, and we were astonished at the number of wild monkeys running around. As our train stood in the station, the monkeys climbed all over it, climbing in through the open windows and onto our laps. Exceedingly tame, they obviously were used to handouts of food. We learned that they were held in very high religious regard by the Indian populace, and, like the sacred cows, one didn't attempt to chase them off.

The train service was excellent, although trains were just as crowded as in China. In addition to hundreds of Indians, our train carried a large number of British and American officers and men. There were food stalls and hawkers at every station, but with a well-run dining car on the train, we weren't tempted to try any of the Indian snacks. There was one thing, though, that caught our attention. At almost every stop it was possible to purchase hot tea. Brewed very strong in the English style, and served with milk and sugar, it was excellent and most refreshing.

We were met at the station in New Delhi by a representative of the government of India and were assigned living quarters in what was called a "hostel." There were a number of these around the city: buildings that had been hastily built for the huge influx of military. They were simple, crudely constructed, but clean, and sparsely furnished with cane chairs and rough wooden furniture, including rope-slung beds with very thin mattresses. However, after months in the Mukden camp, I found them luxurious. The hostel we were assigned to was in Old Delhi, the original city. Our room was very small, with makeshift bathroom facilities, but we ate in a general dining room with about 50 or 60 other people, the majority of them military officers, and Eva was the only woman present. The food, although plain, was quite good.

Our first evening, Eva and I had a table to ourselves, but because of the proximity of others, we talked mainly in Chinese so as not to be overheard. We noticed a young British Army captain at a table nearby who seemed to watch us closely. At the end of the meal he came over and politely asked if he could join us for coffee. Thus began a friendship that was to last for some 25 years.

The young captain's name was George Shirras Walker, and he had an absorbing tale to tell us that evening. He'd only been in New Delhi a short time himself. Until then he'd made no friends, but hearing us talk in Chinese, he had recognized it as an oriental language and felt that we would be kindred spirits.

Born in Japan and having lived there all his life, George had a native fluency in Japanese. A short time prior to Pearl Harbor he'd gone to Shanghai for some reason that I have now forgotten. While there, as war seemed imminent, he'd enlisted in the volunteer armed force organized by the authorities in the International Settlement and was given the rank of lieutenant. He had served there for some weeks, helping with the evacuation of British and American nationals, until he, too, had been evacuated to Singapore, where he was when the Japanese struck.

Helped by the volunteers, British and Indian troops managed to hold the Japanese at bay as they attacked down the Malayan Peninsula to the causeway linking the mainland with the city of Singapore. For a little over two months the battles raged, with heavy casualties on both sides. In the thick of the fighting during that period, George was put in charge of captured Japanese prisoners. He was ordered to leave Singapore on Friday, just two days prior to the final attack launched by the Japanese that resulted in the capitulation by the British, after almost all food and water were exhausted, and hundreds lay dead or injured.

Sir Winston Churchill gave a stirring account of that period in *The Hinge of Fate*. He wrote that on the 13th of February, some 3,000 of what he called "nominated individuals" were evacuated from Singapore by sea, on some 80 "little ships," as he called them, almost all of which were lost to Japanese air attacks. Together with another young lieutenant, George Walker was on one of those ships, in charge of some 25 or 30 Japanese prisoners whom they were to take to Ceylon if possible. (Ceylon, now Sri Lanka, was then a British possession.)

A month later, George wrote a letter from Ceylon to his sister, Jennie, in Canada. George died some years ago from diabetes while still a young man, but one of his sons recently gave me a copy of that letter, which was in diary form, and it is such a stirring tale that it is worth relating here just as he wrote it.

After a few preliminary remarks of a personal nature he wrote:

Many tragic things have happened — first the fall of Hong Kong, then that of Malaya and Singapore — I had my full share of Jap bombing, shelling and machine-gunning while in Singapore, but fortunately escaped intact and am very much alive.

I was ordered to leave Singapore on Friday, 13th of February, which, as you know, was two days before the capitulation. The trip was most eventful to say the least and will make a good yarn to tell you when I see you again. My party left on a small naval craft at about 11 p.m., while shells were exploding near us. Subsequent events can be summarized as follows:

- Feb. 14th. At about 8 a.m. sighted a Japanese reconnaissance seaplane, which dropped one bomb that missed the stern of the ship. At about 10 a.m., sighted over 60 Jap bombers flying in formation overhead. They gave us a fright but seemed to ignore us completely and continued on their course southwards. At 11 a.m. saw some islands where I hoped the skipper would shelter the ship for the rest of the day and continue the trip at night.

At 11:30 a.m., when nearing islands saw much wreckage and knew then that the ships which had preceded us had got into trouble. At 11:45 a.m. observed sister ship which was accompanying us being attacked by many bombers and shortly after was set on fire and sunk. From about noon to 1:30 p.m. we were ourselves persistently attacked by a series of bombers, which dropped over 200 light bombs around us. In the early part of the attack, one hit the cookhouse and started a fire. I was crouching on the floor of the mess located next door, and the blast blew out my breath and caused tables, chairs, etc., to pile up over my back. I managed to extricate myself and was amazed to find that I had not incurred any injury.

At 1:30 p.m. the ship was beached on the shore of a small island with her stern on fire. The water was deep enough that a lifeboat had to be lowered to take the wounded ashore. I ran back to the burning mess to salvage my kitbag, containing the precious Jap books and some valuable notes I had made on the Nip army in Malaya. While trying to place the bag in the lifeboat, I was caught in the open when a final formation of bombers came over to unload its load. Bombs fell around the helpless ship, caused spray to fall on the deck like rain and a small piece of shrapnel from a near miss hit my back while I was lying flat on my face. The lifeboat, with its load of wounded, was fortunately untouched and left for shore without me. I abandoned the kitbag on the deck and swam for shore, about 30 yards away. I felt exhausted when I neared the beach, from loss of blood, but found I had more energy left in me when another formation of Nips started machine-gunning the beach and those in the water. I reached the shore and ran wildly into the woods and fell down somewhere in a semi-conscious state. I was eventually carried back by two friends to a camp which had been built in the woods. In the meantime one of our number volunteered to return to the burning ship and had brought back some

food and a little water.

The magazine of the ship was expected to blow up at any time. I lay with the wounded and slept soundly while the others were sent out in different directions in search of friendly natives and water. The search was fruitless and the search parties returned in the evening with only a few coconuts. The night was spent in the woods and was interrupted by a tremendous explosion when the ship finally blew up.

-Feb. 15. Food and water were short. Search parties were again sent out. One party eventually returned with news of a village on a nearby island. It was decided to move as quickly as possible due to shortage of medical supplies for the wounded. However, no movement could be made during the day, since the Nips were constantly over the island on reconnaissance.

-Feb. 16-19. Long and slow trek from our first camp to the other side, which was nearest for crossing over to the fishing village. The wounded were carried on rough stretchers. I was among the walking wounded, but had to be supported by two friends after I collapsed in the early stages of the journey. On several occasions we had to wade in the water and stumble over slippery rocks in complete darkness. The nights were spent on the beaches and during daytime we lay hidden in the woods. The advance party which went ahead failed to send back food and water. We survived by drinking coconut juice and eating a few ship's biscuits, with an occasional tin of sardines or sausage, which had to be divided among five or six people per meal.

I was comparatively comfortable and soon managed to wobble about with the aid of a stick. The seriously wounded suffered pitifully from lack of proper attention. One died and another became delirious. In most cases gangrene had set in and the wounds let off a horrible stench. On the last night we set off in a native prau (small boat) for the village. We found that the villagers were themselves short of food and were demanding fantastic prices. I had already had my wallet, with all my money except five cents, pinched by someone when I was asleep on the first island.

-Feb. 20-23. We reached a large Dutch island

where we heard there was a large well-equipped hospital. I was placed in the hospital with the other wounded. The hospital was fairly large, but the doctors and staff had already evacuated. Two Malay dressers who had remained did excellent work with what they had. The dressing table where they probed for my bit of shrapnel and then bandaged me gave me a shock, since the top was full of maggots from the other wounded who had been treated there before me. The hospital was short of food and we therefore had a small quantity of watery porridge for breakfast, two potatoes for tiffin [lunch] and likewise for dinner. We felt extremely happy when we received small bits of bread and scraps of pork. At night the others in the ward suffered a great deal, and being one of the least wounded, I hobbled about tending their needs since there was no one else to help them. On the second day in hospital, a doctor who had managed to escape from Singapore arrived at the Dutch island and immediately set to work on the wounded until late at night. He saved several lives by amputating.

-Feb. 24th. By now we learnt that there was no possibility of getting to Java, since the Nips had already occupied the next large island to the south and were beginning to invade southern Sumatra. It was clear that no rescue could come from that direction. It was decided to make for the eastern coast of central Sumatra and cross overland to the west coast before the Nips caught up with us. In the afternoon I was placed in a Red Cross launch with ten other walking cases and set off for the mouth of a large river in Sumatra.

-Feb. 26th. We reached our destination at noon, were fed some rice and eggs, and slept on the concrete floor of a warehouse. The mosquitoes were numerous and very busy.

-Feb. 26-27. We continued our trip up river. The boat was stranded on a sand bank for some hours. The country was very wild and primitive. The natives said that the crocodiles were abundant, but I failed to see any — I observed many families of wild monkeys on the river bank. We eventually reached a town in the centre of Sumatra and I enjoyed a good sleep on some

bags of rice in a warehouse.

-Feb. 28. We were sent to a rest camp, where I managed to wash my only suit of clothing and ate some good stew.

-March 1-2. The wounded party was sent westwards by bus. On arrival on the west coast, we were given a good meal and some money. I immediately made off to a good hotel and had my meal all over again and how I enjoyed it!

-March 3rd. We were on a ship for Ceylon. At the time we left, the Nips were already reported to be 200 miles to the south of us. We reached Ceylon on March 19th without further incident apart from the fact that the ship became desperately short of food.

George's account ended with his entering hospital to have the piece of shrapnel removed from his back and his assignment to a temporary post in Ceylon. But it made no mention of the severe case of malaria he had contracted, which was to give him much trouble over the next two years in India.

Eva and I were thrilled to hear George's story. It seemed so much more exciting than anything we had experienced. And it was all the more interesting to us because we had just come from the area where his story began. In fact, one of the many wrecked ships we had seen on the islands near Sumatra might have been his. But in telling us the story in person, he added many more details than were contained in the letter to his sister. In the letter he told of "friends" helping him. Those were the Japanese prisoners he had been guarding. His treatment of them had been so humane that they helped him in every way they could. He also told of an advance party sent ahead to find food and water, but never returning.

The leader of that small advance party was the second young lieutenant who embarked on the ship with George in Singapore. Rather than name him, I will simply call him "X". I was to see a lot of that young man in the next two years. After the war he became a very well-known and highly respected professor at a leading university. However, his actions both during the period spoken of in George's letter and subsequent to that were despicable and demonstrated a high degree of cowardice and self interest.

When X had reached the other island spoken of in the above account, he promptly forgot about his friend George and the wounded Japanese. He commandeered the only serviceable boat and made for the big Dutch island, where he got on the first available ship heading for safety, and ended up in India months before George got there. Once in India he proclaimed himself an "expert" on things Chinese, was immediately given captain's rank, and by the time we reached there in October, was already a major. The first time he saw George — just a few days prior to our arrival — he had been greatly embarrassed. He had fully expected George to have been either taken prisoner or to have died in Sumatra, and hadn't expected to meet up with him again. He made up a fanciful story to excuse his actions, but George had already learned the truth of what had happened in Sumatra and was not convinced.

A short time after Eva and I had been assigned to our new jobs, I was told to meet with this fellow X as my "opposite number" on the military side. He greeted me in a very haughty and condescending manner, and when, in the course of our conversation, I told him a bit about myself and the fact that I had been a missionary in China, he became agitated and strongly advised me never to tell another soul about it because, in his words: "it would hurt my image." I told him I was proud of having been a missionary, that it was a highly honorable calling, and that I had not the slightest intention of hiding the fact.

What he didn't know was that both Eva and I knew him well — not personally, but by reputation. He had married a good friend of Eva's from her time at the school in Yangzhou and he'd gone to China originally as a missionary himself. To give him credit, he had done a remarkable job of learning the language. However, he had become very conceited and overbearing in his manner toward his fellow missionaries and superiors, telling them how to run the mission and being critical of everyone around him. Eventually asked to leave the mission, he did so, abandoning his wife as well, and went to Shanghai, where he made a name for himself with his heavy drinking, wild behavior, and womanizing.

In India, X continued that way of life for the two years that we were there. But with the scarcity of people who were even slightly familiar with China, he became the British army's expert on how to deal with the Chinese army authorities, without having any background knowledge to support his actions or advice. I, on the other hand, was designated as the political and cultural adviser to the government of India's Foreign Office, even though I frankly admitted to them that I had no political experience whatsoever. Still, I frequently had to iron out problems that X had created by his offensive and overbearing manner in dealing with Chinese officialdom in India and also in Chungking. For some reason, he treated all Chinese, officials or otherwise, as inferiors, and became one of the most heartily disliked individuals around. But enough of him.

The day after our arrival in New Delhi, Eva and I reported to Government House for work. Our office was quite near where George worked, so he showed us the way. He rode his bicycle and we rode in New Delhi's most popular form of transport, a two-wheeled, horse-drawn cart called a "tonga."

We discovered that we had about an eight-mile ride through the filthy streets of Old Delhi before we reached the new city. In the days to follow, that daily ride became something of a nightmare because of the intense heat, the dense traffic, and the overpowering smells. Additionally, we found it to be quite expensive and time-consuming. We quickly bought bicycles, but in our poor physical condition after internment, we soon found that it was too much for us and later asked for new quarters nearer our job.

Our first day in the office was confusing, but it had its amusing moments. When we finally found the Foreign Affairs Office in the maze of corridors and rooms in the huge and imposing Government House, we walked in and discovered that our new boss was a young English woman about our own age. When we reported to her and gave her our names, she was literally speechless for a few seconds. She then told us that the cable sent by Ambassador Craigie from Lourenco Marques had given no details about us. It had simply reported us as being a married couple with "30 years of experience in China." She had been astonished at our youthful appearance, since she had been expecting to see someone much older.

We got along fine with her, and learned that our job was primarily to act as liaison between Chinese and Indian officials. Up to that point language barriers and social and cultural differences had caused a great deal of friction and misunderstanding between them, and our job was to try to iron out those differences and bring about better feelings and understanding between them.

The completion of the Burma Road had brought a large number of Chinese officials to India, many of whom were simply wealthy refugees with nothing to do except loll around and at times make a nuisance of themselves. We quickly found that the Chinese hated the Indians, calling them "black devils," the same name they gave to Negroes. In turn the Indians despised the Chinese, hating them for their ostentatious wealth and for having found a reason to come to India in the first place, and wanting them out of the country. It was readily apparent that our task was not to be an easy one.

We learned that a social/cultural center was to be set up in the new downtown area that had been built adjoining the Government House. The entire second floor of one of the new buildings had already been acquired, and was to be made over into a comfortable entertainment and information center. The place was to be called the "China Relations Office," and I was given the grandiose titles of China Relations Officer and Assistant Head. Eva was the Associate Director.

Our first job was to furnish the place, and to secure supplies of not only food and drinks, but to scrounge around for English, Indian and Chinese "cultural" exhibits as well. That made for some interesting experiences during those early days after our arrival, when there was confusion everywhere and a shortage of everything.

Three weeks after our arrival we were given temporary quarters in another hostel much nearer to our office, and were thus spared the long daily commute. But as that hostel was only for transients, a week or so later we were moved to a third location, family quarters in large tents. We had one big tent as our combined living room, bedroom and dining area. A smaller tent nearby held very basic and crude bathing facilities, and we shared a third "cook" tent and the services of an Indian servant, whose cooking left much to be desired. We lived there for several weeks enduring the heat, dust storms and innumerable insects crawling over us every night, until one day we arrived "home" to find the tent flattened. Termites had gotten into the center supporting pole, which was about six inches in diameter. They had hollowed it out to the point that the weakened shell of the pole just let go. We were glad that it hadn't occurred during the night, and at the same time we were very

thankful that it had happened, because it meant our being given better quarters elsewhere. From there we were moved back into another hostel about a mile from our job, at the far end of a long and very wide open mall or avenue, in front of Government House. The avenue was much like the one between the Capitol building and the Washington Monument in Washington, D.C. Even though our room was tiny, it was a great deal more comfortable than the tent.

While buying furniture for the new China Relations Office, I had a chance to see Indian businessmen at their worst. We shopped around in a number of places to get prices and found that attempts were being made by all concerned to bribe us. We'd return home to our tent, or later our room in the hostel, to find a case of whiskey, a basket of fruit, a fancy lamp, or some Indian commodity just outside the door, and always nearby an Indian hovered, waiting to see if we would accept it. In each case we threw it out and had nothing further to do with that particular merchant. We finally found one man who quoted fair prices, promised early delivery, and attempted no bribery, so we gave him the contract and had the satisfaction of seeing him follow through and deliver the furniture to us in a remarkably short time.

Not long after our China Relations Office was ready for business, our new boss arrived from England. He was a fascinating old gentleman, the epitome of what one would expect of a British Foreign Office "servant." Always impeccably dressed and groomed, and with a charming personality, Sir Humphrey Prideaux-Brune was a retired Foreign Office veteran who had been recalled from retirement to head up that wartime effort, and he brought to it a spirit and enthusiasm that would have been hard to find in one many years younger.

Standing no more than five feet in height, Sir Humphrey gave the initial impression of being a diminutive person whom one could easily ignore or overlook in a crowd. However, when he talked, he took on a remarkably commanding presence and dignity that evoked immediate respect from everyone. He was the perfect man for the job: a consummate diplomat, a gracious host, and a great conversationalist. We took to each other immediately and he became like a second father to us, treating Eva and me as his children, with great affection and love. We found him a most endearing individual.

Prior to Sir Humphrey's arrival our only daytime work at Government House had been the shuffling of innumerable papers and writing proposals as to how to go about improving relations between the Chinese and their Indian counterparts. About the only excitement that enlivened our days there was when a file couldn't be found. The missing file would usually turn up after an exhaustive search, and nine times out of ten it was being used as a seat cushion on one of the hard chairs used by the lowly clerks in the office, or by one of the *chaprasis*, as the humbler servants were called. But after Sir Humphrey arrived, the center formally opened and a lot of social events followed, not only at the center itself, but almost every night of the week in some potentate's palace, a large restaurant, or in one of the clubs. It seemed that nowhere in the entire world could there have been more of those parties than in New Delhi. Meanwhile, the war raged in nearby Burma, China, and the whole Far East, as well as in Europe.

During that period Mahatma Gandhi was leading his Nationalist movement against the British in an attempt to abolish colonial rule, and things were tense. Street demonstrations and bombings were a near-daily event, yet partying continued almost nightly somewhere in New Delhi, and Eva and I began to feel that in playing our part in the war effort, formal dress was our uniform. Being assigned to the government of India, we found our pay to be that of middle-range Indian government servants. Being paid in rupees, we barely had enough to get by on. In fact, our first month's pay went entirely for clothing, much of it formal.

Those were the days of the maharajahs and rajahs in India: the Indian princes who, under the British Viceroy, ruled their own great and small states and lived, for part of the year, in their palatial mansions in New Delhi, on large, beautifully landscaped estates on each side of the long, wide avenue fronting Government House. Each of them tried to outdo the others in the size and magnificence of their banquets and afternoon garden parties, to which all diplomats and high-ranking military officers were invited. Not to be outdone, the Chinese ambassador gave sumptuous Chinese banquets and parties in return, and we were invited to all of them.

With no vehicle at our disposal, we couldn't compete with the many Rolls Royces in abundance around New Delhi, which were much favored by the maharajahs. All were equipped with very dark, smoked glass windows, behind which the royal womenfolk could ride unobserved. The Chinese, on the other hand, preferred expensive American cars. We had only our bicycles, and it would hardly be seemly to ride them up to the door of a maharajah's palace, so we rode to some nearby point where we could stash them behind a fence or some bushes, lock them, and then walk the short distance to the party. In that way we tried to add some modicum of dignity to the impressive titles that had been accorded us in our humble jobs at the China Relations Office. But no one seemed to notice or comment on our lowly mode of transport. Our attendance at all those functions was mandatory, primarily to interpret between the Chinese guests and their Indian hosts, or vice versa, and try to better the understanding between the two nations. But it was an uphill job.

The dinners and afternoon garden parties were always long, drawn-out affairs, accompanied by a lot of speeches and toasts. All the high-ranking allied generals, any time they happened to be in town, were sure to be invited. In that way we got to know those men who became so famous in that theater of the war. There was General William Slim, the British general, and Brigadier General Frank Merrill, commander of the famous American "Merrill's Marauders," who made many perilous ventures into the jungles of Burma. There was also the British Brigadier Orde Wingate, whose commandos with the name "Chindits" fought valiantly in the jungles of Burma, surviving only with air drops. And then, of course, there was General Joseph Stilwell, whom we saw frequently and came to know very well. The viceroy, Lord Louis Mountbatten, also attended many of those functions. Not only was he viceroy, but he was also Commander in Chief of that entire theater of war and a very busy man indeed. All visiting Chinese dignitaries were also present, and we came to know many of them as well. In addition we met many Burmese officials who had their government in exile in New Delhi. Among them was a short, very plump woman, exuding great charm and wit, who later became a close colleague of ours when we got into another type of work.

Usually, Chinese and Indian officials would be seated together, and Eva and I would act as interpreters. Apart from their jobs, they had very little in common, and beyond the usual small talk they didn't have much to say to each other, so the atmosphere frequently became somewhat strained. When the conversation lagged, I would draw on my fund of Chinese jokes and humorous stories in an effort to liven things up a bit. But in general we found the Indians almost totally lacking in humor, as opposed to the Chinese, who were usually very witty and possessed a tremendous sense of humor. Nonetheless, my stories usually got a big laugh from everyone present and seemed to ease the tensions between the Chinese and the Indians.

After one of those big affairs, the Chinese ambassador, who in excellent English had given an after-dinner speech, drew me to one side and somewhat petulantly complained to me that my Chinese stories always made people laugh, whereas those he told always seemed to fall flat. He wanted to know why. After a few seconds, I asked him to write out a list of his favorite stories, and we would go over them together to see if we could find the problem.

A few days later he invited me to the Chinese Embassy, and I had him tell me his stories, first in Chinese and then in English. Told in Chinese, I found them to be uniformly, intensely amusing, but most of them translated poorly into English. When I examined them in detail, I realized that most of his stories required a deep knowledge of Chinese culture on the part of the listener; otherwise, the point was lost. I weeded out a few that did translate well and gave him some pointers on how to emphasize certain aspects of the stories, then I gave him a few of my own stories that also translated well into English. From then on his after-dinner speeches proved a great success, and he was unstinting in his thanks and appreciation of my help. We became good friends.

That reminds me of another high-ranking Chinese official in the embassy, who also became a good friend. We saw him frequently, and he often visited our China Relations Office. He usually wanted to talk with us about the Japanese occupation of most of China, and to exchange experiences with us as he, too, had suffered much at the hands of the Japanese. One day he confided to me that he was cataloging Japanese atrocities and tortures committed in China, and he went over many of them with me. I was able to add a number from my own experiences that he'd

never heard of.

He told me it was his intention when the war was over to give the Japanese back some of their own barbaric coinage when the opportunity came, and at the same time he intended adding some of the more infamous, fiendish Chinese tortures. He was basically a gentleman at heart and didn't at all seem the type who would carry a grudge to that extent. He was in every way an intellectual, but with an all-consuming hatred for the Japanese, something they had well earned for what they had done to his family and his country.

In addition to all the outside parties and dinners that we had to attend, at least once a week Sir Humphrey gave a cocktail party at the China Relations Office. They were always well attended, usually with well over 100 people present. Sometimes guests came by invitation; otherwise it became just a standard weekly event that was open to anyone in the military or civil service who wanted to come, and of course to all the Indian aristocracy. Neither Eva nor I knew anything about serving drinks, so we left that part of it in the capable hands of Sir Humphrey. We mixed with the guests and passed around the always plentiful appetizers and sandwiches.

As time passed, our office became the local meeting place for many of the U.S. servicemen and officers stationed in New Delhi, and those back from the front for R and R (rest and recreation). We got to know a considerable number of those men very well indeed, and quite a few of them asked us to act as their bankers. On payday they would deposit sums of money with us and ask us to guard it well, and under no circumstances to give it to them if they came in drunk and wanted more money. Amusingly enough, almost all of them who asked us to watch over their money did exactly what they had predicted. They inevitably came in drunk and penniless and demanded money from us. When we refused, they became quite indignant and in some cases frighteningly abusive. But we never gave in and the following morning would always see them come in and abjectly apologize for what they had done. A lot of our visitors were Army Air Force pilots flying the "hump" to Chungking. They told us extraordinary stories of that hazardous route over the Himalayan mountains and the jungles of Burma.

To our surprise, one of the young American pilots turned out to be Royal Grubb, whom we had last seen as a small boy in Lingyuan some 20 years before. He was flying B-24 Liberators over the Hump and every now and then after that, when he came to New Delhi, he would drop in to visit us. Shortly after meeting Royal, another young officer walked into our office. He was a British army captain, a huge, strapping fellow about 6 feet 4 inches tall, with a barrel chest and a big moustache, and weighing well over 200 pounds. Unbelievably it was John Duthie, youngest son of the Duthies of Chengde. When we had last seen him, he was a little tyke of around 8 years old. Now he was in charge of a Gurkha parachute corps fighting the Japanese. The Gurkhas came from Nepal and were famed for their *kukri* knives with long curved blades. John told us that the Japanese were terrified of his Gurkhas, but with some amusement he added that his men, all of them short of stature and none of them weighing over 100 pounds, would jump with him wherever he went, but he had to be the first one out of the plane. The problem with that was that with his size and weight he dropped like a stone, whereas the Gurkhas might drift on for a mile or two farther. That made for problems when they reached the ground, particularly in enemy territory. He solved it by draping each of his men with as much armament as they could carry, extra guns, ammunition and hand grenades. Their weight was then comparable to his. John Duthie survived the war and went back to England, only to be tragically killed in a motorcycle accident.

General Joseph Stilwell, known to everyone as "Vinegar Joe," was another frequent visitor to our office. Whenever he was in town for consultations or meetings, he would drop in to see us, usually in the mornings when things were quiet, and he seemed to avoid the afternoon cocktail parties. He liked to lie on a couch and relax, or sit with his feet up on a table drinking cup after cup of Chinese tea, talking a blue streak all the time while his Chinese aide-de-camp sat nearby listening. He sometimes would just nap or sit, deep in thought. Other times he filled me in with the latest details of his campaign against the Japanese in Burma and complained about the stodgy "Limeys" and the intransigence of the Chinese government officials. He was greatly incensed over the way Generalissimo Chiang Kai-shek acted toward him. He never called him General Chiang; it was always "Peanut," and he never had anything good to say

about him.

I got to know Stilwell so well that I used to chide him and urge tolerance on his part in all his dealings with the Chinese. I reminded him that the Chinese had their own way of doing things and had been doing it that way for centuries, that they had been fighting the Japanese for years and the Chinese Communists even longer, and would continue doing so long after both he and I were out of the picture. What bothered him most was the fact that Chiang Kai-shek had surrounded himself with relatives, making it hard to get through to him or to get anything accomplished. I assured him that nepotism was standard Chinese practice with all officialdom, that it was a form of personal life insurance as well as a guarantee against external coups by ambitious generals. He and I got along famously, and I like to think that those long chats we had together helped him to relax somewhat and forget his many problems.

While Stilwell had a problem getting along with his colleagues, both English and Chinese, he had tremendous rapport with the Chinese troops under his command and was literally worshipped by the officers and men. I met many of them in later months and years. All of them told of Stilwell's visits to the front, usually in the heat of battle, when, in complete disregard for his personal safety, he would visit the wounded and the men in the trenches, spending time hobnobbing with them. He spoke vernacular Chinese quite well and enjoyed Chinese food, and he never seemed happier than when in the thick of battle with his Chinese buddies.

Rubbing shoulders with those government people and wartime leaders brought us many interesting experiences that helped to liven the boredom we found in the social aspects of the job. It wasn't too long after our arrival that the Indian CID (Criminal Investigation Department) contacted me and asked me to help them in their clandestine investigations of the Chinese in India. Although the Americans carried the brunt of supplying the Chinese war effort with their airlift over the Hump to Kunming, the British at the same time were also active in helping to support the Chinese cause.

However, even while China was an official ally of the British, the Chinese wisely kept their options open. Quite understandably, just in case the Japanese should overrun India, they were playing both ends against the middle and secretly supporting Gandhi's Nationalist movement to the detriment of the British. I learned about that shortly after we got into our job, and what the CID people wanted from me was any information that I could glean that would confirm their suspicions.

Eva and I usually lunched in the one and only Chinese restaurant in New Delhi. It was in the same building as our office, downstairs from us. Sitting there in one of the curtained booths I would dawdle over my food and listen to the conversations of the Chinese diplomats who frequented the place as they unthinkingly talked openly in Chinese about politics and what they were doing in India. I quickly learned enough to verify the suspicions of the CID, but we needed someone who could readily infiltrate their ranks, preferably by getting a job in the Chinese Embassy. I suggested to the CID that our office be used as a cover to hire a Chinese for that purpose. They agreed, and asked me to start looking for the right person.

Around New Delhi at the time there were a number of young Chinese men who were obviously deserters from the Chinese army. Some had made their own way from China by one means or another, others had escaped from the camps in Northern India, where Chinese troops were being trained by the Americans. One day one of them sat at a table next to ours in the restaurant and I struck up a conversation with him. His name was Chen, and we chatted for a while, and I let it go at that. After seeing him there several times — sometimes he ate with us, at our invitation — I felt I had gained his confidence, so I asked him outright if he was a deserter. With some diffidence, he acknowledged that he was. I asked him if he wasn't afraid of being picked up by the Chinese military police. He told me he was in constant fear of being caught. I then suggested to him that perhaps I could find a job for him where we could guarantee his safety, provided he gave us his unswerving loyalty. The net result was that he came to work for us and proved to be an extraordinarily gifted agent. He quickly established rapport with some of the lower-ranking officials in the Chinese Embassy, and through them provided us with a remarkable amount of information. In turn, we fed him suitable disinformation to pass on in order to confuse the opposition.

However, even though our suspicions were con-firmed, we needed documentary evidence; it was not long in coming. One day Chen informed us that documents involving Chinese aid to the Indian Nationalists were being sent to Chungking the next day in the Chinese diplomatic pouch, which was carried by British aircraft and not accompanied by a courier. I passed on the information, and the next day rumor had it that the plane had crashed on its way to China and that the Chinese pouch was lost. Although I cannot vouch for the story, because I was informed only on a "need to know" basis, I do know that we had the satisfaction after that of seeing a great deal less activity on the part of the Chinese diplomats as far as the Indian Nationalists were concerned. Doubtless it was because of their uncertainty as to whether the British had acquired documentary evidence of what they were doing.

Young Chen was with us for several months and we became good friends. We had fixed him up with an apartment with a built-in escape route in case of trouble. One morning around 7 o'clock, just after I had arrived for work, he telephoned me. His voice was strained, and he was extremely distraught. He told me that two Chinese MPs were standing outside his apartment waiting to arrest him, and asked what he should do.

I reminded him of the escape route, instructing him to climb out of the skylight, cross the roof, and jump down into a back alley, and from there make his way to a nearby restaurant, where I would pick him up. I met him there and escorted him to one of the Indian police stations, where I showed my credentials and asked the officer in charge to lock Chen up until someone came for him. Late that night he was given women's clothing, and, wearing a wig, was smuggled aboard a train to Bombay, where he was put on a freighter for London. Months later I heard indirectly that he had arrived safely in England and had been given a job in another government agency.

Although Eva and I were quite used to hot weather in North China, the intense summer heat of New Delhi was quite different and hard to take. As we sweltered through our first summer there, we often thought of Kipling's line: "Only mad dogs and Englishmen go out in the noonday sun." Prior to the war, the entire government had been in the habit of moving to Simla in the Himalayan foothills for the summer, and no self-respecting Englishman would ever stay in Delhi. However, the war had changed all that, and there were far too many people in New Delhi for all to move away. Not only that, Simla itself was crowded with refugees and allied wounded sent there for recuperation. There was no alternative but to bear the exhausting heat the best we could, and in New Delhi there weren't too many ways to find any alleviation.

Apart from the maharajahs' palaces, about the only places in the city that had air-conditioning were some bars and a couple of movie houses. Just to have a few hours of relief from the heat, Eva and I went to one or another of the latter places at least one or two evenings a week when we had no other commitments. We always had to battle large crowds, and often had to stand in line for an hour or more to obtain tickets. Sometimes we would sit and watch the same film two or three times, for the pleasure of those few hours of solace from the heat, often over 110 degrees Fahrenheit.

The newsreels were the main attraction for everyone, except perhaps the Indians. Eva and I were thrilled by the reports of progress by the allies both in Europe and in our own part of the world. We were relatively close to the Burma front, and through our contact with the officers and men of the allied armies, were able to keep fairly well up-to-date on what was happening, but it was quite another thing to see it on the screen.

Every movie house was always filled to capacity, usually with a preponderance of both American and British servicemen on leave. Of course, there were always a large number of Indians, mostly middle class, and the excitement wasn't always on the screen. That was the period when Indian Nationalist agitators were frequently throwing bombs at British military installations and any place where allied troops congregated. Several times when we were watching a movie, a bomb would explode somewhere in the theater. Fortunately they were usually quite small and did little damage, even to the servicemen at whom they were aimed. However, they inevitably resulted in a melee and a lot of hand-to-hand fighting between the allied troops and the Indians. It seemed to us that more people got hurt that way than from the bombs themselves.

The bombs weren't the only cause of excitement in the movie houses. In British India, any public perfor-mance was always preceded by the playing of the national anthem, "God save the King." Naturally, all loyal Britishers and most Indians stood up for the playing of the anthem. But there were always a few Indian Nationalists in the audience who made it a point to remain seated as a form of protest. That never failed to bring about a fracas where British soldiers would seek them out and thrash them. But apart from giving the participants an opportunity to let off a little steam, it never seemed to do much good. The same thing would recur again and again, and we came to recognize some of the more prominent agitators who took their punishment, apparently subscribing to the Mahatma's doctrine of passive resistance. They were resolutely determined to speed up the demise of colonial rule.

One late afternoon after work Eva and I were waiting in line to buy tickets for a movie when an incident of a different kind occurred that turned out to be both amusing and somewhat embarrassing. We were at the Odeon Theater, where the waiting line wound in a big circle around the inside of a large rotunda. I was perhaps 50th in line, and some distance from the ticket window, while Eva was standing near one of the exits from the auditorium in an effort to catch some of the cooling draft coming out between the doors.

As the line crept ahead, a young, beautiful English woman entered the theater, pushed her way unceremoniously to the front of the line and bought two tickets. The Indians in the line said nothing, but I found her behavior annoying and discourteous. In a very loud voice I expressed my feelings to Eva across the room, speaking in Chinese. The young woman glanced my way, turned very red in the face, and left the theater. At the time, I presumed that my tone of voice had been sufficient to cause her reaction, and Eva and I forgot about the whole incident.

A day or two later I was told by my boss that a young English couple had just arrived in New Delhi, and that the young man would be joining our staff. It was suggested that I get in touch with him to welcome him to the area.

I went over to the small apartment he and his wife were occupying and he seated me in a chair, with my back to what I took to be the entrance to the kitchen. We chatted for a few minutes, then he called to his wife to come in and meet me. I heard her approaching from behind, but before I could turn my head and catch sight of her, she apparently turned around and went back in, closing the door behind her. At the time I thought it was a bit odd, but I dismissed it from my mind. As I left, I invited the two of them to join us for a Chinese meal the following evening.

When Eva and I arrived at the restaurant the next evening the young couple were waiting outside. I didn't recognize the woman, but Eva spotted her at once and told me she was the one we had seen in the theater pushing her way to the front of the line. She looked embarrassed as we greeted them, but we pretended not to notice, and she gamely bluffed her way through the meal. But Eva and I were embarrassed to learn that both of them were quite proficient in Chinese, and without a doubt she had understood what I had said about her in the theater and knew exactly what I thought of her rudeness — which might not have been a bad thing in itself.

For most of the year 1943 Eva and I got around town on our bicycles, but when the monsoon rains started, we had an experience that made us decide we needed a motor vehicle. We were on our way home after work one day when I passed a stall selling fresh strawberries in flat, shallow baskets. They were such a rare treat that I stopped to buy a basket and balanced it on the handlebars of my bicycle as we rode on home. We were living in the hostel at the end of the long, wide avenue in front of Government House. Just as we turned onto that avenue, a sudden thunderstorm hit, starting with large hailstones that battered us out there in the open. There was no place to shelter, and we had to dismount because the hail on the roadway made it too dangerous to ride. We were bareheaded, but while Eva covered her head with her hands, I, stupidly, was concerned about the strawberries, so I covered them with my outstretched hands. The net result was that both of us had severe bruises and cuts on our hands and heads from the golfball-sized hailstones. I wasn't able to save the strawberries from being mashed into a pulp, and my head was so battered by the hail that I had several severe cuts and blood was pouring down my face as we headed for home. However, we patched ourselves up and were none the worse for the experience.

Shortly after that, one of my colleagues was transferred back to England, and we had the opportunity to buy his old car, a Ford. It was one of the tiny models made in England, considerably smaller than most compact cars of today, but it had been well treated and gave us excellent service. It was to play a big part later in the making of some wonderful friends.

The third hostel we lived in, called Mundi House, was unique in that the food was appallingly bad. We were there for about six months, and the "old-timers" among us set up a committee to handle the dining room. Each month it became necessary to fire the old caterer and find a new one to contract for the dining room. But unfailingly, each turned out to be worse than the one before. The first day each new man started on the job we would get wonderful meals, and everyone felt that, at last, we were on the right track. However, the same thing happened each time. Right after that first day the food would deteriorate daily until we had to fire the man and find someone else. They were all the same; there was never any variation in the menu, and we knew the day of the week by what was served. However, that didn't particularly bother Eva and me. We were always able to compare it with what we'd had in the camp in Mukden and on board the Japanese ship, and anything was better than that. And fortunately, we always got a wide choice of fruit that made up for it.

As I said before, Eva and I started out with a table to ourselves. One morning a distinguished-looking brigadier came into the dining room, looked around, spotted us, then came over and asked if he could join us. We were delighted to have his company and learned that he had just gotten off a supply plane from England and was shortly to be joined by his staff, when air transport for them could be found.

Like all new arrivals from England, he was delighted with the abundance of fresh fruit in India, particularly the mangoes. Eva warned him to go easy on them, or he might get an upset stomach. But he ignored her advice, and within the week he was hospitalized with a bad case of what was known as "Delhi Belly." He had no sooner come back from the hospital than the first member of his staff arrived, a full colonel. The same thing happened to him. Both the general and Eva urged him to eat mangoes with moderation. But he, too, ate too many, and like his boss, ended up in the hospital. The same thing happened to each member of the general's staff as they arrived at intervals over the next several weeks. Seven different men all ignored the warnings about the mangoes, and each in turn had to be hospitalized for varying periods. The only man who heeded Eva's advice was the Scottish doctor for the team. He was a major, and about the third to arrive. Not only would he touch no fruit at all, he seemed to exist entirely on eggs and managed to stay healthy. It was ironic, though, because he was so overworked at the office, with the shortage of manpower, that he had a breakdown from sheer exhaustion and had to be hospitalized for that, despite his precautions with the food.

Eva and I managed to stay remarkably healthy during our two years in India, despite our weakened condition on arrival there. Stupidly, though, I got myself into trouble soon after getting there when I saw how cheap cashew nuts were and bought a five-gallon can of them for a mere pittance. We placed the can near the door and I grabbed a handful each time I went in or out of the room. In a few days I came down with a severe case of the hives, and was in utter misery for several weeks. Not long after that I completely lost my taste for cashew nuts when I saw what they did to the poor people who picked them. Most of the nuts came from the state of Madras, near the city of Calicut. There, hundreds of the local Indian population had lost their fingers completely, and had only stubs left. It had been caused by the extreme acidity of the outside skins of the cashew nuts, which they removed with their fingers, and, of course, gloves were far too expensive a luxury for them.

Not long after I got over the hives I developed symptoms of severe discomfort in the lower right side of my stomach, so I visited an elderly British army doctor, a colonel. He first thought my spleen was giving me trouble, but after a thorough examination, he diagnosed it as simple nervous strain brought about from the years of uncertainty living under the Japanese during the occupation of Manchuria and our subsequent internment. He said there was no medicine he could give me that would help; instead, he prescribed a cigarette each time the pain got too bad. I followed his advice and was surprised at the immediate relief it gave me. That was long before the dangers of cigarette smoking were known, and as my work in the following years became more strenuous and demanding, my reliance on cigarettes developed into a two-pack-a-day habit, which I was unable to lick until many years later. Subsequently, the adoption of a pipe served the same purpose, and since I didn't inhale the smoke, doctors told me there was little danger from it. I continued smoking a pipe until 1989.

One hot summer night Eva needed the services of our colonel doctor. She awoke in extreme pain, and I got her to the doctor with great difficulty, because we didn't have a car at the time. He X-rayed her and diagnosed a number of fairly large kidney stones. However, instead of giving her any medication, he prescribed 18 quarts of water to be drunk each day and told her that would eventually flush the stones out. Eighteen quarts sounds like a lot, but in the hot, very dry climate of New Delhi, it was not far above the normal liquid intake for all of us, who were almost always suffering from dehydration. In fact, one of the most common drinks served in the bars was called a "Nimbu Pani." It was, if my memory serves me correctly, nothing more than ice water with lime juice. Served in a very tall glass, it was not at all unusual for people to drink eight or ten of them in an evening. Eva followed the doctor's advice and in three weeks or so had no further pain, and she has never had any return of the trouble.

Toward the end of 1943 we found ourselves becoming more and more involved with activities outside the scope of the China Relations Office, many in connection with consular and other officials either in China or in remote areas such as Nepal or Afghanistan. We received frequent requests for assistance in getting supplies of one sort or another, and many of the things they wanted could only be found on the black market. In time, I became most familiar with the back streets of Old Delhi where those markets flourished, and in most cases I was able to fill the requests, even for such rare wartime items as cameras, binoculars, typewriters and bicycle parts. Some of the younger men wanted silk stockings and other ladies' wear for their girlfriends, and in that, Eva was able to help. We were happy indeed to have been of some help to those lonely people, and over the months we formed some strong friendships that lasted well beyond the end of the war.

We slowly began to see that the original purpose of the China Relations Office had been largely met, and a much better understanding between the Chinese and Indians had been achieved. One day Eva and I were approached by a British official whom we knew who suggested that we resign from our posts with the government of India and join a British wartime organization called the British Ministry of Information (BMOI), which we did. The BMOI was similar to the American wartime OWI, or Office of War Information, and had been established ostensibly to counter Japanese and Axis propaganda. But as we got to know the people around us, we learned that for many of us, our real jobs were much like those of the American OSS (Office of Strategic Services), which had been formed by Major General "Wild Bill" Donovan early in 1942, and was the predecessor of the CIA. It wasn't long before I learned that my services had been asked for specifically by Lord Louis Mountbatten, and that I was indirectly attached to his staff. My assignment at BMOI was simply a cover for more covert activities.

The work we became involved in appealed to us both much more than that we had been doing in the China Relations Office, and we began to feel we were really doing something for the war effort and seeing some results.

The new position put us on the British rather than the Indian pay scale, and not only was our income greater, we also qualified for a private residence. After two years of "institutional" food, it was a tremendous relief to once again have our own kitchen and get back to a more wholesome and simpler diet. Our social obligations were also greatly reduced, and that, too, was a relief.

We were moved to a wartime housing development built on the outskirts of New Delhi, only half a mile from the hostel we'd been living in. It was close to an old Indian burial ground, heavily overgrown with thorn trees and jungle. Our house immediately faced that jungle, with a small "lawn" in between, the grass growing almost uncontrolled since lawn mowers were non-existent during wartime.

Built of red brick, the houses were called "hutments." Their floors were concrete, and the roofs were made from the local red stone, which was very soft and something like slate. The Indians had developed a technique for cutting the rock into square slabs about two inches thick and two feet square. Those formed the roof, much like a patio layout, with the seams filled with a cement mix. There were no ceilings, and from inside we looked up to the rock roof, which was whitewashed, as were the plastered walls. That little three-room house, our home for a little over a year, seemed like a palace to us after over a

year of living in all sorts of odd places. Although even in winter it was hotter than anything we had ever before experienced, it was still a joy and delight to be on our own once again.

Naturally, with a house and both of us working long hours, we needed servants, particularly a cook. But trained servants were much in demand and hard to find because of the huge influx of foreigners. We talked it over with a young Indian clerk in our office, and he recommended a young Hindu friend, telling us that he was a "fully qualified chef." Well, he might have been fully qualified in cooking Indian food, but he knew nothing at all about English-style cooking, and we came to the conclusion that all he knew was how to boil water. However, that wasn't all bad, because Eva could train him from scratch to cook things the way we liked them.

On our second day in the house the young man turned up with his wife and four children. That was no problem, because there was lots of room in the servants' quarters out back, and we quickly became good friends with all of them. I've forgotten the young fellow's name, but he spoke excellent English and responded well to Eva's teaching. She first had to teach him how to keep the kitchen clean and tidy, and a problem arose right there. He didn't mind cleaning the stove and the table, in other words, everything above the floor. He quickly told us that sweeping the floor was not within his "job description," or words to that effect, and that we would have to get a "sweeper" — someone of a lower caste — and most fortunately, he knew just the man.

The sweeper arrived the next day with his large family; all seemed harmonious, and we thought we were in business. With the two of them, and just the two of us to take care of, we should have no problems. The "cook" would cook and serve the meals and shop for groceries, and the "sweeper" would not only sweep out the kitchen, but would sweep out the rest of the house as many times a day as was necessary, and at the same time he wasn't averse to dusting the furniture. However, it was soon obvious that we didn't know much about India. When we wanted to take a bath, neither of the men would involve themselves in heating the water. They told us we needed a "water man," someone who would not only heat the water and fill the bath, but would also empty the chemical toilets. How fortuitous it was that a neighbor had an old man employed for just that job, and he had plenty of time in which to take care of us as well. By the end of the third day we were well equipped with three servants, none of whom was in any way overworked, particularly the "water man." That old boy really had it made. Between the two houses he never worked more than two hours any day, and he had lots of time to sleep in between. But he did have to get up early in the morning to prepare the baths, because all the water had to be carried in by hand.

Having a house to ourselves was wonderful, but the house was not without its problems. For one thing, the stone slabs of the roof expanded during the heat of the day, then contracted in the relatively cooler night. In the process, they shed a fine red dust the consistency of talcum powder over everything below, and we had to rig a canopy over our bed to protect ourselves during the night, and during the daytime we covered all the furniture with sheets while we were out of the house. Because of the daily expansion and contraction of the roof slabs, none of the seams were tight, and when the monsoon rains came, the roof leaked like a sieve, and although men came and tried to patch the leaks, nothing worked.

Insects were our next greatest problem. India has possibly the world's greatest variety of insects — certainly we'd never before seen anything like them either in Africa or China. Our first night in the new house we hung our clothes in the closet; in the morning, we found holes eaten wherever there were even the smallest grease spots. My ties, for example, were full of holes. But for Eva it was worse. She had an evening dress — very classy and up-to-date at the time — where the material was interwoven with fine strips of cellophane paper. Every scrap of the cellophane had been consumed during that first night. Although the dress was completely ruined, we never saw the insects that did the job.

There were many other insects that we couldn't see. At night when we were in bed we could hear a noise that sounded vaguely like a low-powered electric drill, and we discovered there was a type of insect that bored its way up through the cement floor. In the mornings we would find tiny mounds of fine dust around the holes, but no sign of the insects that did the drilling. Another type of insect weaved its way around the walls just under the surface of the plaster, leaving minute trails that were slightly raised and

were reminiscent of the trails made in a garden by a mole or the common American gopher. Again, we never saw the insect that made the trails.

None of those or the other insects bothered us as much as the ants. There were so many varieties that we lost count. The most common ones, which bothered us the most, were very tiny, much like the common American ant, and another one even more minute, a red ant that was almost invisible to the naked eye, but which had a ferocious bite that caused intense pain and swelling. Fortunately neither kind entered the house in any great numbers. But one kind did. They were the large ants, which, without the slightest exaggeration, grew to more than an inch in length. They were larger and moved a great deal faster than cockroaches. They swarmed into the house at night in the hundreds in search of food, but they usually haunted the kitchen and pantry and became the bane of Eva's life.

The little house was built with two bedrooms and a living room on the front, with connecting doors between and a covered porch outside in front. Behind each bedroom was a small lean-to "bathroom" with a built-in concrete tub of most generous dimensions, and with a four-inch-square drain hole with a wooden stopper. No water was piped in, but behind the house was a single faucet from which all our water was drawn and carried into the house.

Adjoining the living room was a small pantry. From there one stepped outdoors and walked a few paces to the servants' quarters, which also housed the kitchen. The kitchen was about 8 by 10 feet and held only a small brick stove that burned either charcoal or coal, and a crudely built cement-lined sink for washing the dishes. A four-foot-long wooden table was the only furniture.

Although we had electricity, we had nothing in the way of refrigeration. Any leftover food was kept overnight on a table in the pantry, covered with an inverted bowl. But that didn't stop the big ants. On our second evening in the house, we were reading when we heard noises in the pantry. There was no light switch there, just an overhead hanging lamp, and one had to walk several paces into the room to turn it on. Eva went to see what the noise was and screamed when she found herself walking over a carpet of those monstrous ants, which crackled and crunched underfoot, and which, when she turned on the light, fled immediately, many crawling up her legs. Covers over the food on the table had been pushed aside and every scrap of food had been consumed.

There were no sprays on the market in those days to combat ants. The only remedy was to pour kerosene over their trails and nests where we could find them. But even that did little good. We eventually remembered an old Chinese trick, which we thought would certainly defeat them. We took four empty, shallow tin cans, about the size of small tuna-fish cans, filled them with kerosene, and put one under each of the four legs of the table. And we thought we had the problem licked. We did, but just for one night.

On the next night, we were again sitting there reading when we heard intermittent "plops" coming from the pantry, which sounded like a leaking faucet. But when I went out to investigate, unbelievably, those highly intelligent ants had solved the problem of getting to the food on the table. They were climbing up the wall, crawling across the ceiling until they were directly above the table, and then dropping down. After eating their fill, they dropped again to the floor, in a never-ending stream. I found it hard to believe what I was seeing. From then on we gave up, and any leftover food was either put into sealed containers or given to the servants to eat. We had to find a refrigerator, and find one fast. We did, but that story comes later.

Our first experience with the minute red ants came during the first monsoon rain, which fortunately lasted only one night. Even so, that first night the roof leaked so badly that nothing escaped; everything was soaked, ourselves included. Our bedding, mattresses, clothing and furniture were drenched and had to be put out in the sun the next morning to dry. That, naturally, was the sweeper's job. I explained to him what he had to do, and we went off to the office at the usual time in our damp clothing.

When we returned that evening, everything was in order, and after a day in the hot sun everything was nice and dry. However, more rain was due that night. Since we were sure the roof would leak again, we decided to sleep on the covered porch, which hadn't leaked with the earlier rain.

I slept well in spite of the noise of the rain. However, I awakened during the night feeling terribly hot, having the impression that my back was on fire.

It was just like the time in China when we had slept on the *kang* with the cracks in it and our bedding caught fire, only worse. Eva examined my back and found it to be badly swollen and almost raw, and it wasn't only my back that was affected. The backs of my legs and buttocks were in the same condition — every part of me that had been in contact with the mattress. We closely examined the bed and discovered that it was swarming with what appeared to be millions of the minuscule red ants. The servant, instead of putting the mattress on top of a couple of chairs in the yard as I had instructed him, had simply thrown it down on the lawn. Inadvertently he had put it exactly atop one of the red ant nests. For several weeks I was reminded of red ants every time I sat or lay down.

One other insect we never actually saw, although Eva certainly saw and felt the results of its visitations during the night. She usually slept with her hands outside the sheet, our only covering. One morning she awoke to find the fingers of both hands had huge, water-filled blisters between them and there were more across the backs of her hands. Her fingers remained spread out because they were swollen so badly she was unable to make a fist or hold any eating utensils.

I was greatly alarmed because of the intense pain she was suffering, so we dashed off to see our faithful old colonel-doctor friend. He merely laughed and told Eva she had been visited by a spider. What she had was called a "spider lick." We were just thankful that it hadn't crawled across our faces. It happened to Eva again several times after that, but we knew what to do to alleviate the pain and take away the blisters. Fortunately the spiders only seemed attracted to her hands and arms. For some reason the spiders never came near me even though I usually slept with my bare chest exposed. In fact, I seemed to have immunity from any kind of insect except the red ants. I attributed it to the immunity I seemed to have gained when, as a child, we visited Banff and I was so badly bitten by mosquitoes.

Of course India had its share of mosquitoes, and during the summer months we had to sleep under nets every night. But insects weren't the only pests we had to contend with. The jungle near us was full of many varieties of snakes. We followed the Indian custom of placing thick, very rough mats in front of all the doors, and lengths of thick rope in a circle around our beds when we slept outdoors in the hottest weather. The Indians also laid a trail of coarse stove-ash around the house. We were told that snakes had tender bellies and wouldn't crawl over those obstacles. Apparently it was true, because none ever entered the house.

We did, however, have one very close call with a snake. One night driving home late from a dinner party, we apparently ran over one of them right in front of our house, at the spot where I usually parked the car. In the morning the sweeper found it and brought it in to show us. It was only about eight inches in length, but it was one of the deadliest known in India and had been given the name "death in two strides," because that was as far as a man could walk after being bitten. The dead snake had been lying exactly in front of the car door on my side, and had I not first run over it with my front wheel, it doubtless would have struck at my ankle the minute I stepped from the car. God was certainly watching my footsteps, or at least my wheels, that night.

The summer heat at night was often well over 100 degrees Fahrenheit, so we frequently moved our beds out onto the so-called lawn to try and catch a rare breeze. In addition to mosquito nets, we always surrounded our beds with a coil of heavy rope to protect against the snakes. But there was nothing we could do to keep the jackals away. Each time we slept out there, we would awaken some time during the night to find ourselves ringed by an audience, only their red eyes visible. They never attacked us, but apparently they were waiting for us to die. Somehow, they sensed it when we woke up and started looking at them, even if we didn't move, because one of them would immediately start to howl. Then the entire pack would join in and all of them would quietly steal away, only to come back a short time later, as soon as we had gone to sleep again. We tried using flashlights to scare them away, and at times we even lit a smoky fire, but nothing worked.

Then there were the flies. Mosquito nets protected us during the night, but during wartime, no screening of any sort was available for windows and doors. Because of the heat, every door and window was left wide open at all times to at least give the illusion of some movement of air. The interiors of all houses were a paradise for flies, which, like humans, liked to get in out of the sun. But our Hindu servants could never be persuaded to swat them, or, for that matter, to kill any kind of living creature they might find in the house. They would simply laboriously catch them if they could, then take them outdoors and release them, whereupon they immediately either flew or crawled back into the house. Only Eva and I used a swatter on them, much to the obvious disapproval of the servants.

But I will say this of Indian flies: they were certainly much more intelligent than any I have seen elsewhere. Our milk was delivered each morning by an Indian riding his bicycle, a big can of milk strapped on the carrier at the back. At each stop he would take the large wooden stopper from the mouth of the can and ladle out whatever quantity of milk his customers wanted before resuming his route.

The man arrived faithfully just after sunup each morning, always accompanied by a swarm of hundreds of flies. The fascinating part about it to me was that the flies didn't fly from one stop to the next; they were much smarter than that. They rode on his back. The instant he stopped and stepped off his bike, the flies would take off en masse and circle around, awaiting the removal of the stopper from the mouth of the can. They would then instantly alight on the can and the ladle, in order to get their share as he filled the customer's container. The instant he was finished and put the stopper back in, the entire "flock" would settle thickly on his back for the ride to the next stop. It was an extraordinary sight that never failed to amuse and astonish us. I often wished I had a movie camera to record it.

The milk was excellent, fresh every day, but whole and untreated in any way. The very first thing Eva taught the cook was how to pasteurize the milk by scalding it — heating it to the point just below boiling — just as we had always done in Lingyuan, then setting it out to cool so the cream would rise to the top. The young man learned quickly, and after a few days of watching him do it, Eva decided he had mastered the idea and could be safely left to do it each morning on his own. However, as the days went by, we were puzzled by tiny black specks in the milk that shouldn't have been there, and Eva decided to track down the problem. She quietly watched the cook from a distance as he prepared the milk. He did everything perfectly except when it came to cooling it. Then, instead of placing it on the table to cool as Eva had instructed him, he placed the pan of milk on the dirt floor, apparently thinking that was as good a place for it as anywhere. But his next move was to call the sweeper in to sweep out the kitchen. Hence the black specks.

Among other things, Eva taught him how to make toast. He also learned to do that quickly, except he piled the slices on top of each other, so that they tended to be soggy when they reached the table. Eva showed him how to stack the slices against each other in a pyramid form; from then on the toast was nice and crisp. But a few days later Eva happened to go into the kitchen when he was toasting the bread. Ingeniously, he had gone her one better. Like all Hindu men, the only clothing he wore was the loin-cloth called a "dhoti" — a length of coarse white cotton cloth tied around the waist and between the legs, much like a diaper — and Eva found him sitting on the floor, his bare feet stretched out in front of him, toasting the bread, with the finished slices neatly placed between his outstretched toes.

I think it was while I was in the internment camp in Mukden that I read a book about India called *An American Doctor's Odyssey* by Victor Heiser. In the book he told how he had taught his Indian cook to make American-style hamburgers. His cook must have been related to ours, because one day the doctor, after having carefully taught him how to shape the hamburger patties, using both hands, found the cook shaping the patties by placing a handful of meat in his armpit, then dropping his arm to press it into shape. I was reminded of that as we ate our toast after we discovered how our cook kept it from getting soggy. At least the doctor had the satisfaction of knowing that the patties had been thoroughly cooked after being formed, so they probably carried fewer germs than did our toast. But whenever we ate toast after that, we were never quite happy in our minds. We still wondered if the cook was using his toes. It wasn't until Eva was able to find a traditional British toast rack at one of the outdoor markets one day that our minds were set at rest.

There was another story that went the rounds in New Delhi about American hamburgers. Supposedly,

an American taught his Indian cook how to make them, first chopping the meat finely, then shaping the patties and cooking them. The American was so pleased with the results that one day he invited several of his American friends to come to dinner, just to try out his hamburgers. As he left for work in the morning, he told his cook he liked the hamburgers so much that he had invited seven people for dinner, and he wanted the cook to make hamburgers for them. He was surprised when the cook appeared distinctly unhappy at the news. He asked the man what was wrong, and he replied: "But Sahib, it takes me so long to chew the tough meat before I chop it that I'll never be able to get them made in time."

The Indians didn't use their bare feet only for walking. It seemed quite natural to them to use bare feet for many of their daily chores. We found that our cook was a terrible shopper. Not only did he overcharge us for everything he bought, he never seemed able to find the right meat or a chicken that wasn't all bone. Eva finally took over all the shopping, going after work to a nearby market. The butcher, a Moslem, had an open stall with sides of beef hanging, available to all the flies. Eva would point to a cut that she wanted and the butcher would throw the entire side of beef onto the dirt floor, then, sitting down beside it, he would take a long, sharp knife, and hold the carcass between his feet. He would then grab the carcass and saw it back and forth until he had cut off the desired piece. We gained the impression, perhaps wrongly, that Indians, at least the men, were never happy working unless they were sitting. In fact, it appeared that the women did most of the work.

When we first arrived in New Delhi, many new buildings were under construction to house the incoming American troops, and almost every job on the buildings was done by women; their menfolk sat nearby in the shade, sometimes looking after the children, sometimes not. Many of the women carried babies strapped to their backs as they worked.

The GIs were incensed when they first saw that, and they rebelled, stating that they wouldn't live in barracks that had been built under such conditions. It did no good. The women continued to work just the same, and the men continued to loll in the shade.

In India — recuperating from the stress of internment.

Having tea on the "Lawn" in New Delhi.

Eva in our hutment in New Delhi.

Our first mode of transportation in New Delhi.

Sir Humphrey Prideaux-Brume and wife, our
"Boss" in India.

Our second mode of trans-
portation in New Delhi.

With our friend George
Walker.

Cha yi chi jiangjiu shi,
cha yi zhang shibushang.

If it's off by a foot,
one can make do with it.
When it's off by ten feet,
there's no way it can be used.

- Chinese Peasant Saying.

Chapter Thirty-Three
More Of India

Our move from the China Relations Office to the Far Eastern Bureau of the British Ministry of Information was smooth and uneventful. However, it was a big change to go from our relatively tiny office of six people, then find ourselves in the nearby Malhotra Building with well over a hundred people working on two floors.

We were a motley group. There were representatives of just about every one of the Allied nations there: Chinese, Burmese, French, Czechs, Poles, Belgians, Dutch, Australians, New Zealanders, Indians, Nepalese, Tibetans and more. I can recall no Americans on the staff, but that was probably because we had close relations with the OSS people, who were just around the corner from us. Some of them often visited us, and as my job called for me to visit them frequently as liaison where things Chinese were concerned, they assigned me a desk. The first time I used it, I looked across the aisle to my neighbor and discovered it was Melvyn Douglas, the movie star. I

recognized him at once, but one would never have known he was a celebrity from his appearance and his amiable and casual behavior. In his major's "pinks" he was just one more of the dashing young officers who thronged the place, friendly to everyone and always ready to give a helping hand. He was very well-liked and never presumed on the fact that he was a celebrity.

Because of the British Official Secrets Act I am unable to say much about my work at BMOI, but a few things have become public knowledge, which I can mention. I was assigned to the China Department near the front of the building, with my boss's office just behind me, next door to the director's office. My immediate boss was a tall and very distinguished-looking Englishman, Harold Braham, a really fine person and capable administrator with whom I developed a fast friendship that was to last a long time.

Ostensibly, my main assignment was to produce editorials and commentaries written in Chinese, which were broadcast to China in several dialects over All-India Radio. To do that, I had to read every Chinese newspaper available, including those published in Japanese-occupied China, as well as other parts of Greater East Asia, which were smuggled to us by our agents. At the same time I had to monitor not only the Japanese puppet radio from Nanking, but other broadcasts in Chinese from Japanese-occupied territory, as well as all British and Allied radio broadcasts in Chinese from England, America and one or two other places. Additionally I read radio scripts that were mailed to me from several sources. The purpose of all that was not only to coordinate our efforts, but to ensure that what we said did not overlap or contradict something someone else had said.

For staff I had several highly competent and gifted Chinese writers, some of whom we had recruited in New Delhi and others from Chungking. The most senior man among them spoke flawless English, and given a subject, could produce a script in a very short time. After the war he returned to China and was there when the Communists took over. The last I heard of him he was editor-in-chief of an English-language weekly magazine produced in Peking.

Among others, we had a young Chinese man named Ho, who was also a valuable asset to our organization, but we lost him under unusual circumstances a month or so after I arrived. One morning around 10 I was surprised to see ten or 15 British military police enter the building, wearing their unmistakable red caps. They barricaded all the doors, while several of them headed for Harold Braham's office behind me, and I was then called in. I learned from them that Ho was a deserter from the Chinese army and they had been asked by the Chinese authorities to pick him up.

Ho had come to us with impeccable and authentic recommendations from an American medical outfit in China with which he had worked for more than a year. When hiring him, we had checked with them and found nothing amiss. They told us he had left them for family reasons and we had not questioned his background any further. However, when I went over and asked him point blank, he admitted to me that he had been a major in the Chinese army and had indeed deserted his post in China and joined up with the Americans. He had left the Americans because he knew the MPs were not far behind him, and he had

managed to wangle his way to India aboard an American truck.

We had no alternative but to hand him over to the Chinese authorities. However, I liked and respected the man, and knowing that he would most certainly be shot if we didn't do something about it, I asked the MPs to allow me to be responsible for turning him over to the Chinese. They granted my request.

I went in person to see the highest-ranking resident Chinese general, whom I knew from formal dinners at the Chinese embassy. He greeted me cordially, and after the usual social amenities, I told him I had an unusual request, and I told him about Major Ho. He had not heard about him, but I told him Major Ho had performed invaluable services, both for us and for the Allied cause, which meant that he had also greatly helped the war against the Japanese in China. I asked the general to be lenient with him and give him a pardon, using the Chinese expression "to give me face."

The general was flattered by my visit, and I in turn had given him so much "face," he agreed to my request. Later in the day, when I turned Ho over, he was merely given a reprimand, reduced in rank to captain and reinstated into the Chinese army. I was happy to know that I had saved his life. He kept in touch with us for several months thereafter, but then was transferred elsewhere and we lost touch with him.

Another incident involving the British "Red Caps," as the MPs were called, occurred a few weeks later. Soon after I joined BMOI I was invited over to British Army GHQ to meet Lord Mountbatten's chief of staff. They were in a building next door to Government House. From then on, I went there at least once a week, either to act as interpreter or to do various Chinese translations for them. For that purpose I had been given a top security pass, which gave me immediate access to the building and to the commanding general. Some weeks after my first visit they had one of their regular security checks, and in the process came across my name as a frequent visitor to GHQ. But in trying to check my background, they could find no record of my having entered the country. That set off a tremendous flap.

I first learned about it when I again saw a large number of MPs surrounding our office one morning, and a white-faced Harold Braham called me into his office and told me that they had come to arrest me as a suspected German spy. When I heard that, I was highly amused and approached the captain in charge of the MPs. I told him how Eva and I had been hustled off the ship in Bombay at night by British Intelligence, and how we had bypassed Immigration, and only the Customs people had seen us. I suggested he telephone Bombay for confirmation. He did so, and the matter was cleared up quickly, but for an hour or two I had visions of myself once again languishing in prison, this time an Indian one.

GHQ gave me many interesting jobs, most of which I cannot discuss. However, one of them came quite early in my assignment there, and it was a direct request from Lord Louis Mountbatten to design a Chinese-style seal, or "chop" for him to use on his personal communications with the Chinese government. Lord Mountbatten had his own very definite ideas as to what he wanted: a "chop" about four inches square, with his name and title in Chinese characters. To carry out the idea of a once badly beaten Allied army now on the offensive and becoming victorious over the Japanese, he wanted a background design of a phoenix rising from flames and ashes. We drew up the design, translated his title into Chinese, and gave him a Chinese name, and the chop was skillfully cut out of rubber by some of the Royal Air Force men who specialized in faking enemy documents. Lord Mountbatten was delighted with the result, and he used the chop from then until the end of the war. I still have a badly faded sample of our first test impression of the chop, perhaps one of the few left in existence.

Another interesting and, to me, highly amusing incident comes to mind, but it doesn't involve GHQ. I received a mysterious phone call one day. The caller identified himself as General "So-and-so" and told me he needed my services immediately for a top-secret project. He told me he was sending a staff car to pick me up, and gave me specific instructions as to what I was to do. I was to go downstairs, go to a certain corner and stand on the curb with my back to the street, and I would be picked up by the car and blindfolded. I did as he had instructed. A car pulled up behind me and I was hustled inside backwards. Before a blindfold was put over my eyes I noticed the car was curtained all around, with an opaque curtain between the back and front seats, and two British Army officers sat in the back. Not a word was said on

the trip. I could tell we were going by a very round-about route, and although I knew the New Delhi area well, I haven't the slightest idea where they took me. We ended up in some super hush-hush military encampment surrounded by barbed wire, where I was taken in to see the general.

Once inside, I found myself in a room filled with a great deal of electronic gear and the general, after apologizing for the way in which I had been abducted, excitedly told me that they had picked up a broadcast in Chinese that they suspected came from some clandestine source in mainland China. He wanted me to listen to it and give my opinion. He produced one of those tubular wax cylinders that were used in those days for making recordings and gave me a pair of earphones. I only had to listen for a few seconds to know that the poor man was in for a big disappointment. My dilemma was just how to tell him diplomatically what he had picked up. What I heard was a routine news broadcast from one of our Allied stations that somehow, due to freak weather conditions, had appeared on an entirely different wavelength. The poor man was understandably quite disappointed when I told him, and he wasn't satisfied until I had given him a translation of what it was I had heard.

Eva, although working in the same office with me, was on another floor and had been assigned as assistant librarian in charge of all Chinese-language materials. One of the much-prized books in her custody was a very old and very worn copy of the *Chinese Postal Gazetteer*. It was a complete listing of all the cities, towns and villages in China served by the Chinese Post Office, and it had the place names in Chinese characters and in romanized form.

Unfortunately, the romanization of Chinese characters (sometimes called Latinization), a system where Chinese language sounds are written out phonetically in English so that English-speaking people can pronounce them, was a very imperfect art at the time. There were many variations in the spelling, and that gazetteer was a fine example. Since Westerners first set foot in China, many attempts have been made to romanize Chinese sounds, and many changes have been made over the years. The same thing happened to Pinyin, the Chinese Communist form of romanization, which came into being after they took over in 1949. It, too, has undergone many changes since it was first introduced, and although at the present time it is considered by many to be in its final form, it may yet show changes in years to come.

In any event, in 1942-43, when the correct identification of Chinese geographical names and places was very important to the war effort and there was great need for uniformity in spelling those names both for radio and in written communications between the Allied forces in the field, the *Chinese Postal Gazetteer* was at first held to be the final authority. Yet it had so many discrepancies and misspellings that confusion often resulted. As a result, a decision was made by the local British authorities to rectify the situation.

The biggest problem was that, in addition to the somewhat varied spellings that appeared in the Chinese gazetteer, there were two other widely used systems of romanization, both of them appearing on the then-current maps of China. The two systems had been developed by early and well-known Sinologists, and had been named after them. One of them, the Wade system, had been developed by Sir Thomas Francis Wade (1818-95), and the other, known as the Giles system, by Herbert Allen Giles (1845-1935). The two systems had much in common, but also a sufficient number of variations to cause additional confusion. Accordingly, in 1942 a joint British/American task force had worked on the problem and had come up with a uniform system combining the two, which became known as the Wade-Giles system. Thereafter, it was used by all British and American cartographers in making up maps of China. But the map names didn't always agree with those in the gazetteer, which made it difficult to locate places on a map.

Eva and I were asked to "volunteer" for the job of converting the hundreds of thousands of place names in the gazetteer into the Wade-Giles system, and to do the work outside of our normal working hours and our regular duties in the office. Undaunted, we set to, and for the next three months we put in long hours at night, trying to bring some kind of order out of the chaos. However, it promised to be a long job, and very early we came to the conclusion that the war would probably be long over before the two of us could complete the job.

Fortunately, before we had gotten too deeply involved, we heard quite by accident that the Americans had also recognized the problem, and in

Washington they had a team of some 50 or more people doing exactly what we were doing. Furthermore, they were well along toward completion. When I brought that to the attention of our immediate superiors, we were relieved of the task, and before long we had copies of the revised American version of the gazetteer on our desks. That was by no means the last of the extra-curricular duties that we were asked to perform in a covert capacity. There were numerous other ones, and one of them I can relate.

We were, at irregular intervals, given copies of Chinese newspapers and documents to scan, in order to identify and to translate anything we thought significant or of possible value to Allied Intelligence. We had to do it under strictest secrecy in order not to compromise the sources through which the documents were acquired. At the same time, under the "need to know" rules, we were not told the source of the documents nor how they reached us. But they proved to be invaluable, and we had strong suspicions as to how they were acquired.

Some years after WWII, I came across an enthralling book written by a retired British Army major and wish I could remember its name and author. The writer had been one of a small group of British Army Intelligence officers who had, after the capitulation of Malaya and Singapore, been deliberately left behind in Malaya to work closely with the Chinese Communist guerrillas. For the duration of hostilities, the guerrillas harassed the Japanese, but after the war was over, they proved to be a tremendous problem to the returning British authorities.

The exploits of those brave few have been documented by the BBC and were seen by many Americans on PBS television in recent years. But the book went into details that didn't appear in the television documentary. At the same time it confirmed the suspicions I had always had about the source of those most fascinating documents that Eva and I spent so many long hours translating.

The British major wrote primarily of his personal experiences: his difficulties in learning the Chinese language where, when he felt he was just attaining some degree of success in communicating with his Chinese colleagues, they would assign him a new teacher from a different part of China, with a wholly different pronunciation of the language. All of that he discovered was a ploy on their part to stymie his progress in the language and in his becoming aware of their real objectives in Malaysia.

In the course of his story he told some of the daredevil exploits carried out by their small group, particularly by the Chinese, in infiltrating the Japanese lines. They frequently made forays right into the heart of Singapore, and at his request brought back any newspapers, magazines, documents or public notices that they came across. Those documents were smuggled out to a British submarine that surfaced offshore in some secluded bay when the Japanese weren't looking, and from there found their way to Ceylon, then by air to New Delhi, where they were passed on to Eva and me to evaluate.

For reasons of total security, Eva and I had to work on those documents at night in our own home. In reading them we knew full well that they were from Malayan towns and Singapore, and because of the very recent dates we strongly suspected they had come out by submarine. But it was fascinating to read the full story in the major's book. Much of the material we had gleaned from those documents was of great importance in our counter-propaganda broadcasts. At the same time we had to be careful to a allow sufficient time to elapse before using it in order not to give away the fact that we were getting them just days after they had been printed, which would compromise our source.

Apart from the items that were of propaganda value, we also gathered a number of excellent intelligence "scoops," from the newspapers and especially from the public notices the Japanese had posted in Singapore. From the latter we gleaned a definitive picture of some of their clandestine activities that would have a bearing on any future Allied counterattack on Singapore. One in particular was considered quite a "find" at the time, but in the course of events it so happened that the war ended before there came a need to use the information we had found.

What occurred was a series of notices that the Japanese posted over a series of several weeks indicating they had closed off certain streets and areas in Singapore. By studying the pattern of the closures we were able to deduce that they had removed the famous large naval guns that had originally guarded the sea approaches to Singapore and had moved them to positions facing the causeway leading to the Malayan Peninsula, down which they had so successfully approached when they attacked Singapore in 1941, and from which they expected any Allied attack to come.

There were other excellent finds in the newspapers. One of them came when we discovered the Japanese were playing around with Chinese characters, notably those for "Britain" and "America." In order to denigrate the two names and bring ridicule on them in the eyes of Chinese readers, they had modified them. The Chinese character *ying* for Britain carries the "grass" radical above it, and *mei* for America has the "sheep" radical. What the Japanese did was to add a new radical to the left of each of the characters, that of the "dog," thus implying that both countries were in the category of dogs.

We found that move on the part of the Japanese to be a heaven-sent opportunity to get back at them. We let it lie for few days, then we put out a barrage of commentaries in Chinese accusing the Japanese of not only illegally occupying China, but also of tampering with their traditional characters, which to the Chinese are sacrosanct. It was satisfying to note that after a brief period of time the Japanese thought better of their actions and the characters reappeared in the original forms.

Earlier I wrote of the way in which the Japanese infiltrated their spies into India. In a somewhat remote way Eva and I became involved in the measures taken against them. After they were first identified, they were usually followed to their safe houses so that our side could identify their contacts. Following that, our agents would usually manage to cozy up to the men, give them "knockout" drops to put them to sleep for a few hours, and filch their identification documents so that they could be photographed and returned, after which they were frequently allowed to go their way for a period of time. In certain cases our experts duplicated their documents, substituting the names of our own agents, who then used them to infiltrate Japanese-occupied territories. Eva's and my job was to supply appropriate names in Chinese characters, see that they were properly written, and check the final results to see if they would pass inspection by the Japanese. We found that part of our work particularly nerve-racking because of the danger to our agents should the documents not be sufficiently authentic. Unfortunately, because of the "need to know" rule, we were never told whether the men using them ever ran into any trouble.

During the early months of 1944, after we had moved into our little "hutment" house, we managed to see a lot more of George Walker. He had been moved to Mundi House hostel in which we had been living, and was thus less than half a mile from us. He spent many evenings with us and we had some good times together. However, he would frequently disappear without telling us and would be absent for long periods at a time. Each time he returned, he was a very sick man with severe malarial attacks, and we worried greatly over his health and the fact that he was consuming as many as 20 or 30 aspirin tablets a day. It was pitiful to see how unable he was to control the shakes when an attack came on.

We learned that his disappearances had to do with his job, securing and interrogating Japanese prisoners. Usually he would go to the front, where the prisoners were being held, and would be responsible for bringing them back to New Delhi. But for a considerable period it became almost impossible to obtain any prisoners.

The reason was that a fairly large group of General Wingate's "Chindits" had been surrounded and captured by the Japanese in the Burmese jungle, and the Japanese, being short of men and not wanting to waste any manpower by having to guard their prisoners, had simply shot the men in each kneecap or in the calves of their legs so that they couldn't escape. Many died when their wounds were left untreated. However, about 30 of them survived, and the Japanese decided to set them free; but as an example to the British, and to discourage any further forays by the commandos, they cut out their tongues before letting them cross the lines to the British side.

When the British troops saw what had been done to their comrades, they were so incensed that no further Japanese prisoners were taken alive. All were shot the minute they were captured. But George's job was to keep up with current intelligence and learn of the whereabouts of Japanese units, and prisoners were a vital source for that information. In order to accomplish that, he decided to take his own prisoners.

George went to the front lines in the jungle, and using a loud-speaker, became extremely successful in persuading Japanese soldiers to surrender. Born in Japan, George's spoken Japanese was so authentic and impeccable that he was able to convince the soldiers he was one of them and had been given good treatment by his captors. George never came back empty-handed, but in the process of making those trips into the jungle, his malaria flared up to the point that when he returned, he looked like a walking skeleton.

One evening George surprised us by bringing along with him an extremely attractive young Scottish woman who had recently arrived from Great Britain. We saw a lot of her during the next several weeks and had great hopes that wedding bells were in the offing for George. Unhappily, a short time later the young woman was tragically killed in a freak accident.

From the way the lights flickered all the time, it was apparent that the electrical system in New Delhi was on a cyclical frequency which was slow enough to approximate that of the human heartbeat. One night as George's friend was getting into bed, she turned off her bedside light while her bare feet were still in contact with the damp concrete floor. There was only a tiny trickle of current escaping from the light fixture, but it was enough to exactly coincide with her heartbeat and to stop her heart. Her death was a tragic loss, and poor George felt it deeply and took a long time to get over it. We heard of a number of similar cases happening in New Delhi while we were there. Strangely enough it seemed to only happen to Westerners, and we heard of no instances of any Indians being electrocuted in that manner. I have no idea why that should have been so.

One memorable afternoon George was visiting us, and because it was during daylight hours, I am certain it was a weekend. Anyway, I noticed him looking at his watch frequently. Eva and I were also keeping a close watch on the time because, in the strictest of secrecy, I had been informed that at a given hour, the very first of the famous B-29 Superfortresses would fly over New Delhi on their way to China. That was to be an extremely exciting event, and we didn't want to miss it. Noticing George's unease I concluded that he, too, had heard the same information. But ridiculous as it may seem, neither of us felt he could talk to the other about it, so strict were the rules of secrecy. As the hour drew near all three of us got up casually and went out into the front yard and looked skyward. In a few minutes a large flight of those massive bombers flew over us at a great height, thrilling all of us. They were so high as to be almost invisible except for their contrails, and unless one knew of their presence, the sound that reached the ground was so faint that they were almost out of sight before we heard it. Now the Japanese were about to get a dose of their own medicine. When the flight had passed, George and I looked at each other and laughed over the irony of the situation in which we found ourselves, but such were the rules of wartime life.

Winters in New Delhi, although relatively hot, were comfortable compared to the summers, and as the summer of 1944 approached, Eva and I gave a lot of thought to the purchase of a refrigerator. Keeping leftover foodstuffs was a constant headache, and although we were able to purchase ice, it was only partially successful in keeping food from spoiling, milk in particular. Also the ants, which could smell the food, were a constant nuisance.

We could by that time readily afford a refrigerator, but there were none to be had in New Delhi, either new or used, nor were we able to find even an old-fashioned icebox, despite our widespread inquiries and the advertisements we placed in the local newspaper. Someone at the office suggested that we might have better luck in Bombay, which was a large metropolis, so we sent an advertisement to the Bombay newspaper and waited for results. A week or so later we got a letter from an Indian gentlemen telling us that he had a used refrigerator for sale. We had some leave coming to us and decided the safest way to get the refrigerator was to go down to Bombay in person to pick it up.

Air-conditioning was available in first class on some of the trains, but we were unable to get accommodations in one of those coaches, so we contented ourselves with a regular first-class compartment, which we found to be quite comfortable. By that time we had learned some of the tricks the "old hands" employed to beat the heat when traveling. Before we left New Delhi we had a huge 100-pound cake of ice delivered to the station and stood it up in the center of our compartment, with a large towel draped over it. With the two electric fans blowing over it, the compartment was delightfully cool. What astonished us was that in the extreme dryness of the climate the ice gradually vanished without leaving a trace of water on the compartment floor. Of course, the one cake didn't last too long, but we were able to purchase ice at various other large stations en route, so we enjoyed the trip despite the heat.

We didn't even have to stay overnight in Bombay. We picked up the refrigerator (an old one, but in good condition), had it hauled to the railroad station on a handcart manned by ten Indian coolies. Because it was so precious and we dared not trust it in the baggage car, we bought a first-class ticket for the refrigerator and had it placed in our compartment for the return trip to New Delhi. Sadly, though, it left no room for a cake of ice and little enough room for our feet, but we sat there and gloated over the cool drinks we were going to enjoy in future weeks, and the miles went by very quickly.

The refrigerator reached New Delhi without a scratch, and we managed to hire another handcart. It was manned by 16 men, and it took most of them to lift the refrigerator onto the cart. We had barely left the station when disaster almost struck. Another handcart manned by a similar number of men appeared. They claimed they had priority in hauling the load, and a fight started between the two groups. A bloody battle ensued, with our precious refrigerator in the middle of it and in danger of being pulled off the cart onto the ground. I had to call the police to settle the squabble.

Once we had it installed in our living room, that humble piece of equipment that we take so much for granted in this country proved a lifesaver. When we left New Delhi some months later we were able to sell it for three times the amount we had paid for it, thus covering not only the original cost, but our travel expenses as well.

For some reason, both Eva and I felt that our second summer in New Delhi was even hotter than the first. Perhaps we were more conscious of the exact temperatures. At the office Eva was given the job of keeping a daily record of the temperature inside the building, and for weeks it seldom fell below 110 degrees Fahrenheit. We've no idea what the outside temperature was. It was only when the monsoon rains came that the heat let up a bit, but then the humidity became unbearable.

Various efforts were made to try and combat the heat in the office, but the results were more psychological than actual. Normally the climate was so dry that in order to try and put a little humidity into the air, "sweepers" with goatskin bags filled with water would roam the office, spilling water onto the concrete floor. Newcomers from England were particularly affected by the heat, and cases of heat prostration were an almost daily event. Many of the ladies resorted to an ingenious solution. They stripped to their underwear and wrapped themselves in wet sheets during office hours, and the sweepers as they made their rounds poured water over them several times a day. But it was only effective for those who remained sitting at their desks. From the point of view of management, it must have been a headache because of the distraction it provided for the male employees.

The Indian method of combating the heat was slightly more scientific and effective. All windows were covered with a coarse, two-inch thick woven mat, made from a plant called the vetiver, the grasses of which the Indians called *khus-khus*. The mats absorbed and held water quite well, and the sweepers kept them wet throughout the day. Fans inside the building drew in moist air that helped one feel cool, but only if one could manage to sit within range of the fan. But electric fans were in very short supply, and most of us had to grin and bear it.

At home it wasn't any better, except that at night the temperature might drop a few degrees. But it usually stayed slightly above the 100-degree mark or higher, and did so for weeks at a time. Ironically, we couldn't even take a cool bath. Our only water supply in the hutment was a single "cold" water line that had been laid just below the surface of the ground. Day or night the water ran hotter than the body could stand, and our water bearer had to run the bath tub full the night before. However, after standing all night the temperature of the water was still higher than normal body temperature.

With our Chinese background we consumed tea in great quantities, and to bring a kettle of water to a boil was an absolute cinch, taking only a few seconds. When we wanted to add water to the teapot we simply turned on the "cold" faucet. To anyone who has not experienced the heat of New Delhi in summer, what I've just written must seem like an exaggeration, but it is the truth.

One Sunday morning a neighbor of ours fell victim to heat prostration and the doctor was called. He made the mistake of pulling his thermometer out of his bag before he got into the house, and it was so hot the glass tube burst. Fortunately we had one that we kept in the refrigerator, which we were able to lend him. Water was supplied us free by the government, which was lucky because otherwise it would have cost us a fortune. Out on our lawn was a spigot that was presumably for watering the grass, but since we had no hose, it was never used for that purpose. Nonetheless, it was constantly in use. Morning and evening there was always a long file of Indian men and women who passed our house on their way to work. They took advantage of our water spigot to have their daily baths. The women modestly covered themselves with their voluminous saris, but the men stripped down to the buff. It used to amuse us that none of them ever used any soap. Their habit was to grasp a handful of coarse sand and rub that over their wet bodies and then wash it off. And I am reminded that when the monsoon rains finally came, one thing we noticed was that the Indians bought a precious cake of scented soap, not for themselves, but to give their sacred cows a bath out in the rain.

Before the rains came, one of the weekend haunts for a large number of local European residents was the outdoor swimming pool at the Cecil Hotel. The water was far too hot to swim in, and I never once saw it being used for that purpose during the summer months. We all just sat around the pool under large sunshades looking at the water and thus deriving a small measure of comfort. Eva and I went there a few times. Afternoon tea was the big thing in those days, and the Cecil served delicious sandwiches along with the tea, but there was a catch to it. When the "bearer," or waiter, placed the plate of sandwiches on the table, one had to guard it almost with one's life, not from marauding humans, but from the huge Indian kites that swarmed in from every side.

My dictionary defines the kite as a small bird of the hawk family. But what the Indians called a kite was a very large bird with a wingspread of almost six feet. The first day we went to the Cecil we noticed a string of small boys walking around the perimeter of the hotel lawn, each carrying a long bamboo pole held upright, with a flag tied to the top of it. At first mystified, we quickly learned that it was intended to try and keep the kites at bay. But it did little good. No one had forewarned us, and the minute the sandwiches were placed on the table, a kite swooped down from behind me, knocking me on the head with its wing, and went for the sandwiches. Fortunately, perhaps because its wing had hit my head, it missed its target and grabbed the tablecloth instead, snatching it out from under the plate of sandwiches and the tea things, and flying away with it. We actually saw instances of food snatched out of a person's hand while it was on the way to their mouth, some people suffering severe scratches from the birds' sharp claws.

Eva and I usually found the Cecil Hotel too crowded for our liking. We had our own little haunt that was much more private, but we had to provide our own sandwiches. We discovered a small stream that meandered through the grain fields just on the outskirts of northern New Delhi. There was a spot on the bank where the stream took a sharp turn around a clump of thorn trees, and it made a nice place for a weekend picnic. We frequently took George Walker, as well as other friends, along with us. The thorn trees provided little or no shade since they had few leaves, but at least, as we listened to the trickling sound of the water, we had the illusion of being somewhat cooler than at home. It was very satisfying to sit there and watch the moving water and listen to the birds.

There were a few places of historical interest around New Delhi that were worth visiting. One was the ancient and famous Red Fort within the old city. It was built entirely with the local red stone and was a formidable place that was off limits most of the time we were there because it was where George Walker kept his Japanese prisoners. However, he took us there several times to see the place. Ironically, it was the same place where, at the outbreak of war in the Pacific, the local Japanese civilians had been interned. They had lived there for almost a year until they were taken to Lourenco Marques to be exchanged for people like us.

Another spot not far from New Delhi, but out in the middle of nowhere, was a unique tower called the Quatab Minar, also built entirely of stone and standing perhaps 100 feet high. From a distance it reminded us of the Chinese pagodas. Compared to them it was very plain-looking, but a closer examination revealed the highly detailed carvings on the entire exterior. At the top was an open balcony from which one had a good view of the surrounding countryside. We were told that it had been constructed several hundred years before by some maharajah for his favorite wife as a place she could go and relax in privacy without having to wear her purdah (veil). In India, the seclusion of women from the sight of men or strangers was practiced by some Muslims and certain Hindus.

There was an entrance at the bottom on the northern side, and a spiral stone stairway made it possible to climb to the top. But the climb was an eerie experience that precluded a second visit. Tiny apertures let in light, but they were so small they did little to alleviate the darkness. The air inside was hot and fetid, and the steps were so constructed that it was impossible to walk upright. In darkness we climbed the steep staircase in a bent-over position with literally millions of bats hanging from the underside of the stairs overhead, brushing the tops of our heads the entire distance. For Eva — who feared the bats would get in her hair — it was a nightmare. After we reached the top we found the view hardly worth the climb, and Eva in particular was tempted to jump down rather than face the return trip down the stairs.

No trip to India is complete without a visit to Agra, site of the famous Taj Mahal, a white marble mausoleum built between 1628 and 1638 by the Mogul emperor Shah Jahan for his favorite wife. By bus Agra was a fairly long trip from New Delhi, best undertaken in the winter months. However, it was a trip well worth taking. We stayed there overnight in a very comfortable visitors' bungalow and spent several hours viewing the Taj the following morning.

Photographs don't do the Taj Mahal justice. It has a majesty about it that defies description; the immensity of the rooms, the beautiful proportions of the edifice itself, the intricate detail in the many-colored tiles, and the random mixture of colors that reminded us of a garden of wild flowers. Unfortunately there was much evidence of general neglect with decay and evidence of vandalism everywhere. The caretakers told us it had been done by tourists seeking souvenirs; bits of tile pried out here and there or cornices broken off. The caretakers seemed more concerned about getting *baksheesh* from visitors than they were about doing their job, and outside on the street, the many stalls selling bits and pieces of colored tile made us suspicious that the vandalism inside wasn't entirely due to the visiting tourists as the caretakers alleged. Perhaps that was another source of income for them.

The blacktopped road between New Delhi and

Agra was narrow and barely wide enough for two vehicles to pass. Alongside, for most of the distance, there was a cart track, and the iron-wheeled native carts were supposedly prohibited from using the motor road because of the damage they caused. In daylight that rule was generally observed, but nighttime was a different matter.

The American army had a base in Agra, so there was a fairly constant flow of military trucks and jeeps on the road. But because of the daytime heat, most of the large convoys traveled only after dark. But so did the Indian carters, and because there were no police patrolling the motor road at night, the Indians used it at will.

Using the black-topped motor road had several advantages for them. It was smooth and hard-surfaced, so it was easier on the bullocks pulling the carts. Also it had deep ditches on each side, and no side roads entering it for the entire distance, as I recall, so it was tailor-made for the Indian carters. They usually set out in a long column of anywhere from 10 to 30 carts, and once on the road, the drivers would settle down on top of their loads and sleep the night away, undisturbed by the passing traffic. Because of the ditches on each side of the road they were supremely confident that their patient bullocks would plod steadily onward without the distraction of any vegetation on the sides of the road and would be unable to leave the road.

It was a heaven-sent opportunity for the American GIs to carry out a practical joke on the carters. Meeting a column of those carts, the GI truck drivers would quietly turn the entire column around and head them back in the opposite direction. The Indian drivers would awake the next morning back where they started from, completely at a loss to know what had happened.

That summer we had several visits from Royal Grubb, on leave from flying the Hump to China. In all, he told us he had made some 80 or 90 flights to Kunming, and each time he came to New Delhi he regaled us with his adventures on that dangerous route. He told of the terrible weather conditions over the Himalayan mountains, the surprise attacks by Japanese planes, and of the pitiable condition of the hundreds of Chinese military conscripts that he frequently ferried back to India for training in the Chinese army.

He told us how the young conscripts, mainly peasants, would be led to his plane in Kunming with their hands tied behind them and a long rope looped around their necks, linking them together in a column. They were untied only after they were safely aboard the plane. None of them had ever flown before, and most had never even seen an airplane, except perhaps high in the sky. Once on board the plane, usually a B-24 Liberator with no side windows to look out of, the Chinese peasants hadn't the slightest idea that they were up in the air and thought they were traveling on the ground.

Royal told us that on one occasion several of them opened the door and jumped out in an attempt to escape and head back home, falling several thousand feet to their deaths. On other trips some were injured when they were bounced around during turbulence over the mountains. After that Royal would only fly them when they remained tied in their seats for their own safety.

After reaching India, the Chinese were trained at huge camps set up in the northern desert area of India near Ramgarh, a remote place very distant from China, but the conscripts didn't know that. For them, the flight had been a short trip; therefore, they imagined they were less than a day's travel from home. As a result, since there were no fences around the camps and no guards to stop them, many would take off into the desert in the direction from which they had come, thinking they could make it back to China within a day or so. I was told by the American officers who trained the men that the common practice was to allow the deserters two days' head start, after which someone would go after them with a truck and bring them back, hungry and thirsty and footsore. They were never punished for running away; the two days in the desert was considered to be punishment enough, and they never tried it again, although other newcomers did, on a regular basis.

Those same American officers told me that when the Chinese conscripts first arrived in India they were so emaciated and weak from lack of food that they posed no discipline problem whatsoever. However, after a few weeks of heavy doses of vitamins and three good meals a day, they became feisty and difficult to control and constantly had to be restrained from raiding the nearby Indian villages in search of women. The American officers commented that, in the end, those conscripts turned out to be some of the toughest fighters they had ever seen, and I have good reason to believe it because I saw those same Chinese troops back in Manchuria a few years later, fighting the Chinese Communists.

One American officer told me of an incident where a number of Chinese were being trained to operate tanks, and they became so conceited and arrogant that one day they deliberately ran down a jeep carrying several American officers. The latter managed to jump out of the jeep at the last second before it was run over by the tank. I was not told whether the men were disciplined for it, or whether it was just considered a demonstration of their eagerness to get into battle.

Royal Grubb told many stories of the situation in Kunming and Chungking, and a number of them had to do with the smuggling of gold into China. I was well aware of the smuggling that was going on. In 1943 while working at the China Relations Office, I became involved several times with the CID in investigating the smuggling of gold, and I was not surprised by Royal's stories. Because of the war, there was a shortage of everything in Chungking, and with inflation, prices had skyrocketed. Clothing of any kind was greatly in demand, and Allied pilots were carrying in clothing to sell by simply wearing it — several layers of it. A pilot might have on three or four suits under his flying outfit, and it was a lucrative business to wear a new pair of shoes each time they went to Chungking, sell them there, and wear a pair of Chinese cloth shoes on their return trip. But smuggling gold paid much greater dividends. Readily available in India, it was a big temptation for both Americans and Chinese to smuggle it into China. It was naturally illegal, because the Chinese government had banned it in an attempt to try and stabilize the economy, and anyone caught smuggling gold could be executed on the spot. Many got away with small-time smuggling by wearing extra gold rings, which they sold on arrival in Chungking. However, there were many instances of big-time smuggling where people got caught.

In one such incident, two U.S. Army colonels were boarding a plane in Calcutta for Chungking. At the same time two Chinese Army officers started to board. Just as they started up the steps to the plane, the American MPs noticed something peculiar about their walk, pulled all four of them over to one side, and searched them. The two U.S. officers were found to be wearing money belts stuffed full of gold. They were returned to base and were severely reprimanded, but that was it. The two Chinese officers were also wearing money belts filled with gold. The Chinese MPs who searched them shot them on the spot. The Americans protested that harsh treatment to the Chinese government, recommending that offenders should be given a trial, so on future occasions when any Chinese was caught with gold on him, he was returned to China for "trial" and shot as soon as he stepped off the plane.

Royal Grubb told us of one occasion when a captured offender was placed on his plane. While he was on the plane, the two Chinese MPs guarding the man decided that it was safe enough to remove his handcuffs. They did so, and then both of them fell asleep. When they were flying over the large lake near Kunming, the prisoner saw what he thought was a good opportunity to escape. He opened the door and jumped down into the water several thousand feet below, and was, of course, killed. The two MPs woke up to find their prisoner gone and the door of the plane open. When they got off the plane in Kunming without their prisoner, they were promptly shot on the spot.

One other story Royal Grubb told us in connection with the smuggling of gold into China is worth relating, and to the best of my knowledge it has never appeared in print. I subsequently heard the same story from other U.S. Army Air Force personnel, so I have every reason to believe it is authentic. Royal told me that on one occasion a fairly large number of new American fighter planes flown by U.S. personnel were being ferried over to China for delivery to the Chinese government. When they left Assam in northern India, they were escorted over the Hump by a Liberator bomber, which had better navigational equipment, and because of the limited range of the radios on the fighter planes, the Liberator also served as a relay station for any messages the fighter pilots might send. In addition, the big bomber was also used to bring the American fighter pilots back to India after the planes had been delivered to Kunming.

While flying over the jungle of Japanese-occupied Burma, a significant number of the fighter pilots suddenly reported that their planes were out of control, and one after the other they nosed forward and dove straight down into the jungle below. Most of the pilots managed to bail out, but not one of them could account for the sudden loss of control. Since both planes and pilots landed in Japanese-held territory, there was no way to locate the wreckage, to rescue the pilots, or to find the possible cause. Conceivably that might have been done at the end of the war, but I've read nothing about it anywhere. At the time, the theory held by fellow pilots was that the fighter planes had a small compartment in the nose, designed to hold some tools and spare parts. It was theorized that someone had removed the tools — the weight of which was normally compensated for — and had substituted much heavier gold bars. As each plane burned off part of its load of fuel, the plane became nose-heavy and went down. The mystery may have been solved.

Royal told us another story of something he had personally witnessed. He was at a forward bomber base in Assam, northern India, the jumping-off point for Liberator bombers en route to China. The base was surrounded by high mountain peaks. Since the Liberators had a limited ceiling of around 30,000 feet — less when heavily loaded — and a very slow climbing rate, they had to circle the base repeatedly after taking off in order to gain sufficient altitude to clear the nearby mountain peaks.

One morning a large flight of planes was scheduled to leave for China. The cloud ceiling was very low that day, and the heavily loaded Liberators could not gain sufficient altitude to break out above the clouds into the clear, in order to be sure to clear the nearby peaks. The base meteorologist forecast that the cloud cover would lift before long, so from time to time the base commander sent a fighter plane aloft to report on the cloud height. When the fighter pilot reported the cloud cover was getting considerably higher, and to the point where in 30 minutes or so the Liberators would be able to top out, the base commander decided to save time and get the flight started.

The heavily loaded planes took off, one after another, and circled in the clouds at designated heights as they climbed for altitude. When a number had gone aloft, Royal and other pilots standing outside the tower watching suddenly heard an ominous sound that chilled their hearts. Out of sight, but directly above them, one of the planes had developed engine trouble and was obviously losing altitude. It was apparent that a collision with one of the other planes circling in the clouds was likely. Within minutes they heard two planes collide, and seconds later debris from the two planes dropped all over the field.

Some of the two crews parachuted to safety, and as Royal and the others rushed out onto the field to see if they could be of any help to the survivors, they suddenly saw an amazing sight. The tail section of one of the bombers was spiraling slowly downward, drifting back and forth like a falling leaf. It made a perfectly smooth landing, and out stepped a much shaken but otherwise unharmed tail gunner. I have read of only one other incident of this kind, and that occurred in the European theater.

Royal survived the war and his many dangerous flights into and out of China and returned to the United States, where he got married and went into business in California. I corresponded with him for some years and we met him once again in Monterey when he and his wife paid us a visit. Sad to say he died of cancer a few years later, still a comparatively young man.

If I remember correctly, while we were in India, Madame Chiang Kai-shek passed through more than once en route to the United States, but she didn't stop for any length of time. Many stories were written during and after the war concerning the Madame and her visits to America, primarily to drum up support for the China cause and to seek donations. Most of the stories concerned her dictatorial and imperious attitude toward underlings and employees of the hotels in which she stayed, usually demanding three floors for herself and her entourage for security reasons. She was reported to have demanded that her bed linen be changed three or four times each day whether it had been used or not. On one occasion she visited for medical reasons and spent some time in a hospital in the Washington, D.C. area. Newsmen we met said that she insisted on having three floors of the hospital, becoming quite incensed when told that it was impossible. While recuperating, she expressed a wish to see some dogwood flowers. None were available except in Connecticut, so the Chinese Embassy chartered a plane, flew up to New Haven, loaded up with a mass of flowering dogwood tree limbs, and decorated the hospital for the Madame.

I was told another story concerning the lady by an

Air Force officer and heard the same story repeated several times afterward, so I have every reason to believe it is true. When Madame Chiang returned to China, she carried so much merchandise back with her that in addition to her own private plane provided by the Americans, several other large planes were needed to transport it, much to the annoyance of the American military, who were desperately in need of supplies in China. They begrudged the use of planes to carry Madame Chiang's trinkets when there wasn't room on any of the flights to carry supplies for the PX set up in Chungking and at forward bases for General Chennault's Flying Tigers; even military requirements were in short supply. On a stopover in Karachi to refuel, Madame Chiang demanded yet another plane to carry a large quantity of rosewood furniture she had ordered made for her there. The Americans reluctantly complied, and the fleet of several planes headed toward Kunming.

Madame Chiang's plane was the first to touch down in Kunming. When she got off the plane, she stomped directly to the tower, where a U.S. colonel was in charge. Most imperiously she directed him to radio the several planes carrying her stuff to be very careful in landing so that nothing would be damaged. She particularly cautioned him to notify the pilot of the plane carrying her rosewood furniture, since it had not been packed as carefully as the stuff she had carried from America. The story goes that the colonel was so incensed by her attitude and by the fact that American planes and lives were being risked for so frivolous a cause, that he radioed the "rosewood furniture" plane and ordered the crew to bail out and abandon the plane the minute they came within sight of Kunming Lake. No one was able to tell me what the Madame had to say to the colonel when he told her that her precious cargo of rosewood furniture had been lost.

While we were living in New Delhi, we had a "pet." It was a mole, about six or seven inches in length, which came into our house every evening at exactly the same time, toured the entire house and then left again. Why it did so we had no idea. It never found anything to eat, and we never left anything out for it, primarily because we didn't know what it ate.

We first noticed the mole one evening when we were sitting reading. It came in the front door of the living room, turned left and followed the wall to the open doorway of the guest bedroom, and disappeared. A few moments later it reappeared, after having apparently circled that room, continued around the living room until it reached the pantry door, where it once again disappeared for a few minutes. Finally it came back again into the living room, completed the circuit and disappeared out the front door, where it had come in. For several months the little mole repeated that performance nightly, at exactly the same time, never once varying its routine and never straying from its path just an inch or so from the wall.

We suspected that it was blind. It had tiny eyes, but when we put something in its path it simply walked around it, not over it, and never bumped into anything. It did the same when I put my hand in front of it. It would stop for a second or two and then go around my hand. We wondered if it depended on its hearing to determine where it went and we found the nightly episode quite fascinating to watch. Why that denizen of the dark should have been attracted to our lighted rooms we were unable to fathom. We tried talking to it, but it didn't respond to our voices, and when we touched it, it never flinched. It just stood still until we stopped petting it and then continued on its way.

Shortly after the mole started visiting us, Eva and I were returning home late one night from a party when, in the pouring rain, we saw a lone figure walking down the long avenue in front of Government House. We stopped and offered him a ride, and in that way made the acquaintance of an R.A.F. Wing Commander (equivalent to the rank of lieutenant colonel in the U.S. Air Force), who was on temporary assignment to New Delhi from Calcutta. We found him to be a most congenial and engaging chap, and since he said he came up at least once a month for three or four days, we invited him to stay with us each time after that.

I have forgotten the wing commander's name, but we'll never forget him. He had a marvelous sense of humor, a fund of war stories to tell, and he regaled us with his personal experiences in a self-effacing manner that belied the many rows of ribbons he wore on his chest. One of his stories concerned the evacuation of refugees from an island the Japanese were attacking. He went in with a C-47 and picked up so many people they were packed in like sardines, and he was certain they would never make it into the air. He gunned the plane down the runway toward the beach, with the Japanese shooting at them, and the wheels were actually hitting the wave tops when the plane finally lumbered into the air.

He was always good company, and a more gracious and appreciative guest it would have been hard to find. On one visit he arrived late one afternoon, left his luggage in his room and left immediately to attend a meeting, not coming back until long after we had gone to bed. The next morning at breakfast he came in somewhat later than usual and in the course of conversation remarked: "That mole of yours is really quite extraordinary. I've never seen one so big." Eva and I thought that he had seen our diminutive nightly visitor and was being facetious, so we merely laughed and let it pass. However, he seemed to be slightly hurt by our attitude and protested: "I really mean it. He's huge. Judging by his tail, he must be all of three feet in length."

Eva and I looked at each other, and although we knew he was a teetotaller, we wondered if he had not been drinking the previous evening. But seeing his hurt expression, I asked him where he had seen it. He replied that it had been in his bathtub, and that it was still there. We knew then that it couldn't be our little pet mole.

We followed him to his bathroom, and there, sure enough, protruding from the large drain hole of the bathtub was the two-foot-long tail of what must have been the great-granddaddy of all moles from the time of creation. The tail was more than an inch thick at the base and tapered to a fine point. It was scaly and covered sparsely with short stubbly hairs and looked for all the world like an elephant's tail.

The bathtub drained into a dry-well and the mole probably had spent its entire life in the dry-well and somehow had made its way up through the drain into the bathtub. Not being able to get out it had then tried to re-enter its hole and got stuck. We gingerly pulled him out and found he was over 24 inches in length, not including the tail, which was equally as long. I don't know how long he had been stuck in the drain, but he was still alive. He didn't resist our touch, and when we let him go, out in the back yard, he made his way off in a leisurely and dignified manner, just as though it was something he did every day. Thankfully that was the last we saw of him. Our wing commander friend was shortly thereafter transferred to Ceylon, and we never saw him again, although we carried on a desultory correspondence for some months.

Another incident comes to mind involving another acquaintance. Early in 1943 a young White Russian arrived in New Delhi. He'd been in the British Army in Hong Kong, and when it fell to the Japanese, he'd been incarcerated in the infamous Changi prison, where so many Allied prisoners died. Somehow he had managed to escape, but he kept the details secret so that those left behind might have the same chance. But his story of how he had made his way overland from Hong Kong to India was epic. The fact that he spoke fluent Chinese had originally been in his favor, but his trek through Burma and other Japanese-occupied areas was nothing short of a miracle.

When he arrived, he was emaciated and in very poor health, and for some reason he came first to the China Relations Office for help. I put him in touch with the proper Army authorities, who took care of him at once. After he regained his health, he was given the rank of captain and a responsible job in British Intelligence.

The first day he was in my office I knew he was penniless, so I offered him a loan. A proud young man, he politely refused. All he would accept from me was a meal. Not long after he had been made captain, I noticed that he was living far beyond his captain's pay, was drinking heavily, and squiring the "wrong" kind of Indian girls to the various parties.

Not long afterward he came to my office one day with a story of being hard up and asked if I would lend him the 500 rupees that I had originally offered. I could hardly refuse, and he promised to repay me on his next pay day. In fact, he wrote me a check then and there to cover it, asking me not to cash it for a month. A month later, when I presented the check at the bank, it bounced. I called him on the phone, and he was most apologetic, promising that the check would be good if I would just wait another month. Unbelievably the same scenario was repeated for several months. Each time I presented the check, I was told he had no funds in his account.

I got fed up with his duplicity and finally phoned the army paymaster to learn what day of the month he got paid. On that day I went to the bank early and waited until his account had been credited with his pay for the month. I then presented my well-worn check and got my money back. Later that same day I had a telephone call from the young man, who was deeply offended at what he called my deceitfulness, and he claimed my action had made him penniless once again. From that day on he would have nothing further to do with me.

Another acquaintance, who became a good friend, was in the British Consular Service and temporarily attached to our office. He had more than ten years of experience in the consular service in China and was especially gifted in writing documents in Chinese, and he also had a good working knowledge of the spoken language. Each Sunday he took my place in monitoring the Nanking puppet radio broadcasts, and, if necessary, he prepared a rebuttal commentary for broadcast the same day.

One Sunday toward the end of my stay in India, he listened to the Nanking broadcast and then wrote a piece that was immediately put on the air, refuting what he thought the Japanese puppet report had said. Sad to say, when I read his script the following morning, and compared it with the broadcast he had heard, I found he had completely misunderstood what the Chinese had said. Not only was his rebuttal inappropriate, it made us look extremely foolish. I had the unpleasant job of telling him of his error, and although we were good friends, he became annoyed with me and asked if I was trying to take his job away from him. I patiently explained the part of the Chinese broadcast that he had misunderstood and gave him the proper version, at which point he put his head down in his hands and, to my surprise and embarrassment, burst into tears.

I was at a loss to know what to do, thinking I had somehow deeply offended him. However, when he regained his composure he told me he was utterly disappointed in himself. He confessed that although he had been a student of Chinese for more than ten years, he had to admit that when it came to listening to Chinese on the radio he was completely at sea, and half the time he really didn't know what was being said. But so far he had just bluffed his way through.

That wasn't totally true, because he had considerable talent, but it surprised me to hear him say it. At that time, few Westerners apart from the missionaries had a good knowledge of both written and spoken Chinese. The patois, or vernacular, that most people learned to speak was very different from the semi-for-

mal speech the Chinese used in radio broadcasting, where they tended to be very erudite, and very few of even the most competent Western speakers of Chinese had ever had any experience along those lines. The form of speech used in broadcasting was much akin to the abbreviated newspaper style, and employed specialized terminology that even many Chinese high-school graduates would be unable to grasp. It was no wonder my consular friend had his problems.

He wasn't the only one who was something of a misfit and in a job that was over his head. During the war, almost anyone with even the most basic knowledge of Chinese was pressed into service. A classic case was that of a senior official in San Francisco, who was responsible for a British counter-propaganda broadcast that originated there. He was an elderly man, formerly attached to the Chinese Customs Service, and although he had a working knowledge of spoken Chinese, it was very basic and he was completely unfamiliar with the semi-newspaper style that was necessary for radio work. Nor did he have the slightest knowledge of Chinese technical or military terminology that was often so much a part of the wartime news.

As part of my job I received a weekly batch of Chinese scripts from the San Francisco office and was required to read them and write a critique. I found much that disturbed me. There was considerable evidence that some of the men responsible for voicing the news were not native speakers of the Mandarin dialect, the dialect that was mandatory for use in broadcasts to North China. On the scripts, alongside the Chinese characters that were uniformly used throughout China but pronounced differently in various provinces, I found small pencilled-in tone marks where the individual who was voicing the script had to remind himself of the proper way to pronounce the word in Mandarin — something a native speaker of the Mandarin dialect would never have done. I was unable to hear the broadcasts in New Delhi and simply had to go by the scripts. but I suspected that the voicing was less than professional.

In addition, I frequently found translations that were totally wrong or inappropriate, and I found it hard to believe that the translators could be so inept. One glaring example that recurred frequently concerned news items reporting attacks made by British aircraft on the European continent. Where the U.S. Army Air Force called a significant number of aircraft in a flying formation a "flight of aircraft," the British equivalent was a "train," as in: "a train of aircraft flew across the channel." But in the scripts I read it had been translated as a "trainload of aircraft," which, since England was an island, was patently ridiculous and highly misleading. My weekly criticisms were intended to draw attention to those errors and perhaps bring about a higher standard of work from the San Francisco office. But they bore fruit in a totally unexpected way. In the latter part of September 1944, I was called in to the director's office and told that I was to be sent to San Francisco to take over that office. I should be prepared to leave immediately on the first aircraft available.

Eva and I were delighted at the prospect of getting out of India. However, when I inquired further into my assignment, I was told that Eva would not be able to accompany me, and I received a somewhat nebulous promise that she would join me as soon as sea transport could be found for her. We had already been separated so much by the war that I didn't want it to happen again, and I determined to do something about it.

My appeals to the highest levels I could contact, asking that either both of us go by air to San Francisco, or, failing that, go by sea, fell on deaf ears. So I went to our elderly doctor friend and told him of our dilemma. He was a very dear man who listened patiently to my story. I told him that apart from our three-day trip to Bombay to buy the refrigerator, neither of us had even taken one day of leave since our arrival in India. Furthermore, as he well knew, for a number of years before that we had been under great stress while living under Japanese occupation of Manchuria. I asked him whether in good conscience he could recommend a sea voyage for me to America for my health. Army man that he was, he was still a doctor and a humanitarian. Without a moment's hesitation he took out his pen and wrote a statement insisting that for reasons of health, if it was necessary to transfer me to the United States, I should be sent by sea, not by air.

Armed with that I again approached my superiors, only to be grudgingly told that in my case the request would be granted, but that it was impossible for Eva to accompany me, since the necessary American visa

could not be acquired in time. That didn't bother me. The U.S. representative in New Delhi was a close personal friend, and in less than an hour, I had the visa stamped in Eva's passport. When I presented that, our orders were cut, and we began the process of getting passage to America.

Several weeks elapsed before we heard anything. In the meantime, we had the once-in-a-lifetime opportunity to see Noel Coward perform for the troops. It was a marvelous two-hour show, with him on stage the entire time, singing, dancing and telling jokes. It was a memorable occasion. Lord Mountbatten himself made the introduction, and the troops loved it.

Not long after, we met some newsmen back from Chungking, and they had a good story to tell on one of their colleagues. A freelance reporter by the name of Martin had made his way to Chungking and not only had succeeded in antagonizing the Chinese officials and military by his negative reports about them and their conduct of the war, but he had also annoyed his colleagues to the point where they wanted desperately to get rid of him.

The English-speaking Chinese newsmen noticed that Martin was heartily disliked by his American and British colleagues, so they quietly asked a few of them if it would make them happy to see Martin leave. They all agreed that it would. The Chinese newsmen said, "Leave it to us. He won't be here very much longer."

A few days later a group of the Chinese newsmen approached Martin and told him that his work in Chungking was very much appreciated and had come to the notice of the Chinese authorities. Because he had done such a wonderful job of reporting the true situation in Chungking, the Chinese government was going to give him an award at a banquet to be held in his honor in a few days' time.

Martin was deeply flattered. On the appointed day he showed up at the temporary tent that had been erected, and found himself the center of attention as the guest of honor. He was seated at a table on a raised platform at one end of the tent, and several high-ranking government officials were there to keep him company.

Partway through the elaborate banquet there was a pause in the proceedings while Martin was toasted and a presentation was made to him by the unveiling of a large silk banner that was hanging on the wall, bearing two immense Chinese characters reading: *Ma Ding*. One of the Chinese officials gave a short speech, telling Martin how honored they were to have had him come to Chungking, and how much his work had been appreciated. As a token of their appreciation, the banner carried the honorific name they had given him in Chinese, a transliteration of his English name, "Martin." However, as the official explained, the Chinese language had no direct translation of "martin," so they had used two characters to approximate the English sound. The first character was his Chinese surname "Ma," which was a common Chinese surname meaning "horse," and the second was the closest they could come to the English sound of "tin." What they didn't tell him at the time was the meaning of the second character they had used. However, by way of the Chinese officials and newsmen present, it quickly spread through the assembled group of Western newsmen, who roared their approval. The meaning of the two characters combined was "horse's ass." Martin thought the roar of approval was for him, but before the end of the meal someone tipped him off as to what the two characters meant, and he disappeared from Chungking the next day. The event illustrated the indirect approach so typical of Chinese diplomacy.

During our stay in India, one of the things that troubled us most was the caste system. China was a poor country, and although it had a class system of sorts in which the people were divided purely by either education or their wealth and position in society, it hardly compared to the caste system of India, where a person of one caste would not dare to be seen talking with an individual of a lower caste or associate with him in any way. We saw instances of people of the next-to-the-lowest caste sitting by the roadside eating their meager meal when someone of the "untouchable" caste came by and their shadow fell across the food. Immediately and without giving it a second's thought the food was thrown away. It had been "contaminated" by the shadow falling on it, and thus couldn't be eaten.

Many incidents of that sort bothered us greatly, as did the constant strife between Hindus and Moslems. But the one incident that troubled me most occurred as I was riding my bicycle down a street in Old Delhi one day. I saw an old man kneeling on the sidewalk imploring passersby for help. At first I thought he was a beggar, but he was too well-dressed for that. I couldn't understand a word he said, but his attitude and facial expression were unmistakable, and I knew something was seriously wrong, but not one single person stopped. I stopped to see what was wrong and saw three children behind him and their mother lying on the sidewalk rolling in apparent pain. I concluded she was in labor and about to give birth.

Two well-dressed young Parsees approached, so I stopped them and asked them to find out what the old man wanted. The two men drew back in horror and told me they couldn't talk to him because he was an untouchable. Furiously, I grabbed each of them by his shirt-front and dragged them toward me, and, with my face an inch or so from theirs, I told them they would either translate for me or go to jail. They had their choice. Reluctantly they asked the old man what was wrong, and he said he had come in from the country that day and his daughter-in-law was about to have a child. He didn't know what to do or where to take her. He told us her husband had recently died.

I told the two young men to immediately hire a tonga and take the old man and his family to the nearest hospital, and I would pay all expenses. Again they refused. I told them that it was people like them, unwilling to help their fellow man, who helped keep the Indian nation as "slaves" to the British Empire, and that unless they learned to help each other, they could never be free. I verbally abused them roundly and again threatened to have them put in jail if they didn't do as I told them. Finally, reluctantly, they hired a tonga and started off to the hospital with the family. I followed on my bicycle just to make sure they carried out my orders. I felt helpless as I thought about the incident. I knew the same sort of thing was happening all over that poor country and would continue happening for years to come. And from what we see in the news from day to day it still is.

Throughout the year that we had lived in the hutment, a constant visitor in our front yard had been a female mongoose, a delicate, highly nervous creature that ambled up the path made through the grass by the daily procession of laborers. She was about 18 inches long, not including her tail, which was about another 14 inches, and she had a thin, ferret-like head and was covered with light brown fur. We always liked to see her because we felt her presence kept the snakes at bay and made it safer for us to walk in the jungle nearby. Sometimes she brought her mate, who was smaller than she was; more often than not she was alone. She would walk a few feet, then sit back on her haunches, stretching her head and neck into the air and looking carefully in every direction over the top of the grass to see if there was any danger. When she came within sight of us, either sitting on the porch or out on the grass, she would stand absolutely still about 20 feet from us and look at us for at least five minutes before moving on. We used to talk to her in a low voice, and in time we began to feel that she was almost tame.

Just two days before we were to leave New Delhi she appeared one morning with six little babies in line behind her. It was obvious she was giving them a lesson in security, because every ten feet or so she would stop, sit up on her haunches and look around, and all six of her babies sat up in exactly the same manner and looked around, too, even though they were much too small to look out over the top of the long grass. When she fell forward onto her forepaws, the babies all did the same, just like falling dominoes,

and the procession continued another few paces. When she got close to us, she sat up and looked at us for the usual length of time, meanwhile chattering quietly to her babies, all of them squeaking back to her in reply, and then they moved on. We felt she was telling her babies that we wouldn't hurt them. She always followed the same routine, passing the house in that one direction, never going back the same way she came, and we had no idea where she lived. But seeing those six babies was as nice a going away present as anyone could have given us.

On October 19, 1944, we received our train tickets to Bombay and vouchers for sea travel, and we left New Delhi on the 24th. Before we left, a number of farewell parties and dinners were held for us. We were most sorry to say goodbye to George, but just before we left he told us that he, too, was being transferred elsewhere. He was being sent to Ceylon (where it was rumored that our office also would soon be relocated), and he told us he hoped it wouldn't be too long before he found himself assigned to the Pentagon in Washington D.C. It took many months, but it eventually happened just as he predicted.

The Taj Mahal in India.

The Quatab Minar in India.

Picnicking by the water in New Delhi.

Picnicking by the water.

Tea with George Walker.

George Walker

The Royal Grubb family. (See page 494)

信神有神在，不
信是泥胎。
佳是泥胎

Chapter Thirty-Four

Sixty Days At Sea

Carrying diplomatic passports and traveling on government service, Eva and I were given a first-class compartment for the trip from New Delhi to Bombay, and we made the trip in great style and comfort. In Bombay we were lodged at the Taj Mahal Hotel. Like its namesake in Agra, it was massively built, using a great deal of white marble, with floors of colored tile. The bedrooms were huge as were all the public rooms, with high ceilings throughout. It had no air-conditioning, but there were punkahs everywhere, those large, swinging, screenlike fans hung from the ceilings and operated by a bearer pulling on a rope. They didn't do much in the way of cooling the place, but at least they moved the air around somewhat.

With the extreme secrecy surrounding all wartime ship movements, we were given no date for departure. We were simply ordered to stand by the telephone and be prepared to leave at a moment's notice. However, we presumed it would take a day or two

and that they would give us adequate notice, so we spent the whole of the next day in Bombay out at the beach club, enjoying some good swimming.

The following day we were notified to board the ship as soon as possible. But once we were on board nothing happened for two whole days. The ship remained tied up at the pier, with lots of activity going on around her. Foodstuffs and baggage were loaded, and hundreds of military personnel climbed aboard, but there was no indication of when we would leave.

The ship was a U.S. Navy transport, the *General Simms*. It was a large, two-funneled ship of the type built during the war exclusively to transport as many troops as possible with a maximum of speed and safety and a minimum of comfort. A number of those ships were built during the war, and I saw many of them in the next two years entering and leaving San Francisco harbor. Even now, many of them that survived the war can be seen "mothballed" in the upper reaches of the Hudson River, and quite a few more in Suisun Bay near San Francisco.

Eva was assigned to a cabin in what was known as "officer's country" with about a dozen Navy nurses, a large number of whom were aboard. I was given a berth in the No. 2 forward hold, where I shared space with the only other male civilians on the ship, three American engineers who were heading back to the States after finishing up some contract work for the U.S. Army. The rest of the ship was filled with several thousand U.S. troops, most of them just rotated from the front lines, and since the ship was to be the last to leave India in time to get them back home for Christmas, they were, for the most part, a happy bunch.

In addition to the American troops, I was intrigued to find 900 Chinese military men on board. They were not conscripts; all were Chinese Air Force personnel, hand-picked for advanced training at an Army Air Corps base in Santa Ana, California. They were a proud and well-disciplined group, intent on showing their U.S. counterparts that they were an elite force, the equal of soldiers in any country in the war. A few of the officers among them spoke some English, but almost none of the enlisted men did. Since we were quartered in the same area, I immediately found myself very much in demand as their interpreter, but it was fun and helped pass the time.

Our sleeping quarters were very basic and tight. Bunks were stacked three high, with only a foot-wide alleyway between each stack. The vertical space between the bunks was also tight; one could not sit up in bed, and the topmost bunk was the least desirable, because it was less than 18 inches from the steel deck above, which was criss-crossed with numerous pipes, many of them carrying hot water or steam. However, the top bunk was the one that I chose. I have never suffered from seasickness, but I had traveled enough times by ship to know that many people do, and I wanted to be in a position where someone being sick in the night would be below me rather than above.

My bunk had one big disadvantage in addition to the proximity of the overhead deck and the pipes. On the bulkhead at the foot of the bunk was a loudspeaker that seemingly blared into action every few minutes, and although during the night it happened less often, I was still repeatedly awakened until I became accustomed to it. The first time or two that I was awakened in the night it was so sudden and so loud that I sat up abruptly and banged my head on the steel overhead. To avoid permanent injury, I fastened a pillow there to cushion the shock on future occasions, and then, in time, I found myself awakened by the initial click of the speaker being turned on, before any voice was heard, and I was never again alarmed in the same way.

The Chinese airmen were naturally curious about all the announcements, but since they normally only concerned the crew, they eventually tired of asking me to translate. However, I made sure that they learned some of the calls by heart. One of them was the 4 a.m. "wake-up" call, another was the chow call, and, of most importance, the emergency calls such as "fire" and "boat drill" that came frequently, often several times a day.

Fire aboard ship is undoubtedly dreaded more than any other mishap. While we were aboard the *General Simms*, because most of the huge number of men smoked cigarettes, fire calls were almost a daily occurrence, sometimes several times a day and quite frequently at night. Fortunately, most of the fires were minor, but all resulted in the loud, and terrifying "FIRE, FIRE, FIRE" call on the speakers, followed by directions to the crew as to the location of the fire and instructions to the passengers to remain calm. No matter how often the calls came, everyone was filled with apprehension until the "stand down" call came through.

The two days we remained tied to the dock in Bombay were extremely boring, and we became impatient to be on our way. Even though it was late October, Bombay was sweltering, and below decks it was so hot that sleep was almost impossible. Eva and I spent the days on deck watching with interest all the activity on the dock below or on the off-side watching the sea birds catch fish. The ever-present kites circled the ship constantly looking for scraps, and the soldiers amused themselves by throwing bits of food to the birds, which unfailingly caught everything before it hit the water. We were amused to note how adept they were at identifying food from a balled-up piece of paper, which they ignored. Of all the sea birds, the kites were by far the most graceful and the best catchers of fish. They could spot a fish from a great height, swoop down in a graceful dive, leveling off at the last moment before touching the water, and at the last second they would skim the top of the water and catch a fish nine tries out of ten, getting only their claws wet.

In the middle of the third night, our ship quietly slipped her moorings and we woke to find ourselves well out of sight of land. We were so far forward that the starting of the ship's engines had not awakened us. One of the first things I noticed was that the air in our hold was fresh, being piped down from the huge scoops out on the decks, and from the slight motion of the ship I knew we were at sea. Not too long after we got up, the captain announced that our first stop would be Australia, our only indication of our route back to the United States, at which a mighty shout of joy went up from the American troops aboard. Most of them had spent several months in Australia before going to India, and looked forward to going ashore to renew old acquaintances. Eva and I also were excited about the prospect of seeing something of that great country, but when we finally reached there, everyone was in for a big surprise.

We were told the ship was designed to carry around 5,000 men, but being the last ship from India that could reach the U.S. before Christmas, we had many more than that aboard. By the time we picked up still more in Australia and at other stops, we ended up with more than 9,000 men and women packed into every available bit of space.

Of course, no one had the slightest idea when we would reach the U.S., nor what our exact route would be, and the Navy crew were very close-mouthed when asked. In New Delhi we'd been told that it would take two weeks, which my boss had hoped would be the case. Apart from the ship's officers, no one aboard dreamed that the journey would actually take 60 days. Almost everyone but us found the long journey tiresome, but Eva and I love shipboard life, and we enjoyed every minute of the trip. Since we were together, neither of us cared how long the journey lasted. Eva hadn't seen the United States for eight years, and I, eleven, but despite the hazards of wartime travel by sea, we somehow felt much safer aboard the *General Simms* than we had on board the *City of Paris*. For one thing, she was a much larger ship and very much faster; for another, she was run by the Navy, and they obviously knew what they were doing.

Life aboard ship quickly fell into a routine. In day-light hours I saw little of Eva, but after dark I was permitted to join her in "officer's country," and we sat out on the deck and enjoyed the balmy evenings of the Indian Ocean, and I could stay there with her as long as I wished. However, our day started at 4 a.m., so I had to get to bed by 11 p.m., and it always meant undressing in the dark.

In the mornings I had two choices when the "wake up" call came. I could either join the breakfast line or another one going to the "head," as the Navy calls the toilets. Either one meant standing in line for upward of an hour, and the "chow" line, no matter when one joined it, invariably took two hours or more. The dining area for the troops was toward the stern of the ship and on another deck. Our quarters were up in the prow of the ship, and our line was but one of several converging on the dining area.

I usually chose to wash and shave first. I hated to start the day with stubble on my face, so I seldom got to breakfast before seven or eight o'clock. I then went up on deck for an hour or so, and it was then time to join the chow line for lunch — another three hours, including the time spent eating. I then napped in my bunk for a while, spent another half hour or so on deck, and it was back to the evening chow line for supper, and that's the way the days passed, with little or no variation.

The lines wound their way through the bowels of the ship, up and down staircases and steep ladders. At times one line would cross another heading else-where. Our own chow line was so long it described a figure eight in the center of the ship. At the point where it crossed itself, an enterprising GI had set up a chair under a stairway overhang, and there, for fifty cents, one could get a haircut. He did a roaring business throughout the day. As every man on the ship had at least two haircuts during the voyage, the barber probably carried more money ashore than anyone else, save perhaps the ultimate winner of the many competing "crap" games that went on every night in the heads, the only places where lights remained lit.

By unspoken agreement, anyone who wanted a haircut could step out of line at that crossing point, then rejoin the line in his original place when the line came by again, provided, of course, that his hair had been cut. If it hadn't been cut, or if it so happened that he was still in the middle of his haircut when his place in line came by, that was his bad luck, and back to the end of the line he went.

Together with my three civilian companions, I was given no special treatment, and we ate with the troops and did everything they did. My three friends griped a lot about the food the first day or so, but for me it was a pleasant change from the food we'd been having in India, even though it was usually overcooked. I particularly enjoyed the freshly baked breads and pastries and the excellent ice cream that was served quite frequently.

We could purchase all sorts of candies, cigarettes and other oddments from a canteen on board. For years Eva and I had eaten no chocolate, and we had pined for it. Aboard the *General Simms* we could buy all the Hershey bars we wanted, but there was one thing I wanted even more. In the old days when we visited Tientsin, there was a German bakery called Kiessling and Baders. They were world famous for their pastries and ice creams, and their chocolate milkshakes were incredibly good. I'd not had one for at least five years and I began to dream of stepping off the ship when we finally got to the States and heading for the nearest drugstore for a good chocolate shake. The truth is, however, that when we did finally arrive in the U.S., it was more than six months before I could screw up enough courage to try a milkshake. In my mind I had built up such a picture of that delight that I was afraid the real thing would not match up to what I had expected and dreamed of. In fact, good as it was the first time I tried one, it still fell short of what I had imagined it would be like. Such is human nature.

Of course, for those 60 days I never saw Eva at mealtimes. She, together with the one or two other civilian women traveling on the ship, wives of military men we presumed, ate with the Navy nurses and the numerous military officers and ship's officers in a spacious dining room on one of the upper decks. Unlike us, they always had their meals at regular times and never had to stand in line. I, on the other hand, ate whenever my line happened to reach the dining area, where we picked up a tray, had our choice of a good variety of food doled out to us by sailors behind the counter, then sat 20 or 30 men to a table. Rarely did I sit at the same table twice in one day, nor with the same companions, except that we four male civilians stuck pretty much together, and, except for breakfast, always ate our meals together.

Two of the three engineers simply drank a cup of coffee for breakfast. They preferred to lie in bed, and I and the other man would bring a cup back for them from breakfast. The leader of the three was a man of about 45, whom I shall call "Smith." He was a cheerful type, full of fun and a great jokester, always pulling someone's leg, and mine in particular because I was pretty gullible and believed his tall stories. He never lost an opportunity to pull a practical joke on me whenever he could, and I was always finding all sorts of odd things in my bunk, things that he had collected around the ship.

One of his companions was a short, stocky man whom I shall call "Jones." He was much younger than Smith and bunked immediately above him, and he was frequently heard to complain that he was unable to get to sleep because Smith kept bumping him with his raised knees. It was almost a nightly complaint. The third man was a big bruiser of a chap, very quiet and introspective, but a really gentle soul. No one bothered him, nor did he bother anyone else. He sat around a lot and read paperbacks and did little else. To the three of them, I was "Limey" and fair game for Smith's jokes. I began to look for an opportunity to get back at him if I possibly could. My chance came quite suddenly one day and I acted without thinking, but it backfired on me in an unexpected way.

Our dining area was one deck above the one where we bunked, and to reach it, our line had to negotiate a very steep ladder that led to the upper deck. One day as we were step-by-step climbing that ladder on our way to lunch, I was immediately behind Smith, and I noticed that his wallet had worked its way up out of his back pocket and was in imminent danger of falling out. With no other thought in mind, I reached forward to push it back down into his pocket. That same moment, Jones, who was behind me, saw what I was about to do, grabbed my arm and whispered to me to remove the wallet as a joke. It seemed like a good idea to give Smith a bit of a scare, so I lifted the wallet gently from his pocket and stuck it in my back pocket, intending to give it to him when we reached our table. No one but Jones noticed what I had done, and once the wallet was in my pocket, so much time elapsed before we sat down for lunch that I had completely forgotten about it by the time we got there.

Later that afternoon I was out on deck when I

heard an announcement on the PA system to the effect that a wallet had been lost, and would the finder please return it to the lost-and-found department. I at once remembered Smith's wallet in my back pocket, slapped my hand back there to see if it was still there, and jumped to my feet with the intention of rushing off to find Smith and give it back to him. But I'd only gone a few steps when a heavy hand fell on my shoulder and I turned to find myself facing a stern-faced captain of the U.S. Marines, wearing an MP arm band. Without cracking a smile, he told me I had been observed stealing a wallet, and was under arrest. Astonished, I started to splutter out an explanation when over his shoulder I happened to see Smith standing a few feet away, grinning broadly, and I realized that once again I had been had.

It turned out that Smith had noticed the loss of his wallet right after lunch and had mentioned it in front of Jones, the man who had prompted me to lift it in the first place. Jones told him not to worry, that I had the wallet, and he told him the circumstances under which it had been taken. But Smith wasn't satisfied with just coming to me to ask for it. He couldn't resist playing a joke on me. He'd arranged for the announcement on the PA system and cooked up the phony "arrest" with the MP captain, much to my discomfiture. But I didn't have to wait long to get back at him.

On our way to meals we passed a point where everyone was handed two salt pills, which, in the tropics, we were required to take three times a day. As I went to breakfast the next morning an idea occurred to me. I asked for extra pills, and when I took Smith his morning cup of coffee, I put four or five pills into it. He always had to be awakened to take his coffee, and half asleep, he gulped it down without noticing the saltiness. But within seconds after swallowing it, he leapt to his feet and made a mad rush for the head, where he was violently sick. When he returned to his bunk and saw my grinning face, he caught on and realized that I had finally managed to get back at him for all the things he'd done to me, but he took it in very good humor. For my part, when I saw how sick it had made him, I felt something of a heel.

The Chinese airmen had their own dining area. At first they tolerated U.S. Navy cooking, but even though a special effort had been made to serve them rice at each meal, the rice was not cooked to their liking, and they didn't care for the way most meats and vegetables were overcooked. They finally appealed to the ship's captain for permission to cook their own food, and he granted their request. After that, the delicious aroma of Chinese food being prepared assailed our nostrils each day, and many were the times I wished I could have shared their meals. As it was, some of the men brought food back to their bunks and generously shared it.

One of my neighbors was a young Chinese lad who, quite different from the rest of the men, seemed deeply depressed. He, like most of the others, had been very seasick for the first week or so. All of them had been flown over the "Hump" and had experienced air sickness, but they found seasickness to be different and many times worse. They really suffered and wanted badly to get off the ship. After a week or so, they got over it, but not this particular fellow.

He caught my attention because he didn't seem to want to get better. He began to miss meals, simply sitting morosely on his bunk staring into space, and from time to time he would loudly shout something unintelligible, often in the middle of the night. One day he disappeared and I learned from the others that the Chinese doctor who was accompanying the group had requested he be put into sick bay. The American Navy doctors who examined him felt that he was mentally ill. For his own safety they decided to commit him to a special "section eight" ward on the topmost deck. A "section eight" is a wartime military discharge for any serviceman considered physically or mentally unfit for duty, and in time, the term was applied to any individual getting such a discharge or in apparent need of one.

Everyone had noticed that special area; it was right behind the bridge and ahead of the first funnel. It was a fairly large section of deck, completely surrounded by a high, chain-link fence with barbed wire on top, and had only one entrance, which was kept locked and usually guarded. Rumor had it there were anywhere from 60 to 600 men up there, all of them suffering either from shell shock or some other mental illness brought on by their experiences at the front. We seldom saw any of them out on the deck. If they did walk outside, they were always accompanied by an orderly, and their pallid complexions and vacant eyes made it all too apparent how sick they were.

Right after the ship left Bombay, notices had been posted throughout the ship warning everyone of wartime regulations, particularly the need for a complete blackout at night. Smoking on deck at night was totally prohibited; anyone caught stepping out on deck with a lighted cigarette could end up in the brig. We were also informed right after leaving port that we would be proceeding alone, without escort, and as there was a great danger of Japanese submarines, we would travel at high speed. Time and time again, we were warned to be careful on deck and not to fall overboard, because under no circumstances would the ship stop to pick anyone up. The danger from submarines was considered too great, and there were too many men on the ship to take any such risk for the sake of one man's life.

When we were about eight or ten days out from Bombay, I was on deck just after lunch when the dread call "Man Overboard" came over the loudspeakers. No one knew who had fallen overboard, and everyone rushed to the rails to try to spot the victim, but being up in the prow of the ship, there was little chance that we could see anything.

Then, to everyone's surprise because of the notices posted around the ship, it became evident that the captain had decided to make an effort to locate the man. We had been traveling at high speed in a constant zigzag pattern, but the captain put the ship into a crash turn, and underfoot we could feel the engines being put into reverse. Even so, the ship traveled for several miles before we came full circle and met up with our original track, which we could clearly see in the calm water ahead.

By that time we had learned that it was one of the patients from the psychiatric ward who had gone overboard. He had somehow been left unattended on their outside deck and had noticed an open gate. Someone from below had seen him calmly walk out to an open area of the deck, where he climbed the rail and deliberately jumped over the side. Life belts had been thrown over immediately, and it was toward those floating life belts that we were heading.

When the ship had slowed almost to a stop and a lifeboat was being lowered, several thousand pairs of eyes were scanning the water below, hoping to sight the missing man, but he was nowhere to be seen. When he had first jumped, due to the speed of the ship, the life belts that had been thrown over after

him had all reached the water some fifty to a hundred yards behind him. We spotted those life belts as we slowly passed them some 20 or 30 feet from the side of the ship, but there was no sign of the missing man.

I happened to be standing at the port railing near the extreme front, where the prow bends inward sharply down to the waterline. For no particular reason I looked down to where the sharp stem of the ship was cutting through the water with only a very slight bow wave. I saw the missing man, serenely paddling in the water just a foot or so from the side of the ship, looking upward with a broad grin on his face as though he was enjoying having played a joke on us. I shouted loudly and pointed downward, and a shower of life belts was thrown down to him, some of them landing within a foot or so of him and well within his reach. He ignored them completely, and with the momentum of the ship, continued to slowly drift his way along the side of the ship until we lost sight of him.

On the other side of the ship the lifeboat was in the water and the sailors quickly headed back toward the bunch of life belts that marked the spot where we had sighted the man. From where we were, at first we couldn't see the lifeboat, but gradually the ship began to describe a turn and pick up speed, and the lifeboat came into view. Doubtless the captain wasn't willing to stay too long in any one position as a possible target for a submarine. We continued to travel in wide circles around the spot where the lifeboat crew was searching, but dusk was approaching and in the failing light and the haze over the ocean we quickly lost sight of the lifeboat and began to fear for its crew. But we reassured ourselves that the captain could readily see it on radar, so it couldn't get lost, and the sea was very calm. It was well after dark when the lifeboat returned with only a bunch of life belts, and, sadly, we watched it hoisted onto the ship. We immediately continued on our way. They had found no sign of the man. Just why he had lasted so long in the water to begin with, and then disappeared so quickly after we had first sighted him, couldn't be explained, but it left a deep scar on the feelings of everyone on the ship, and for days we talked of little else.

A week or so later the young Chinese airman was back from the hospital ward. His bunk was separated from mine by just one other stack of bunks, so I went over to talk with him, but he was no better. In fact, he would talk only in monosyllables, or would answer my questions with merely a nod or shake of his head. I learned from his immediate superior that he had been extremely unhappy up in the hospital ward and that he had insisted on being brought back, because he felt that in the hospital he was losing face for the group of Chinese as a whole. The young officer told me that he was deeply worried about the man and had assigned two men on alternating shifts to guard him day and night. Indeed, from then on I noticed one or the other of the men sitting on the floor beside his bunk whenever the young man was there, or following him when he went to the head or to eat, or occasionally to the deck.

A day or so later, when we were about three days out from Australia and everyone was in very high spirits, I was once again on deck in the same small section forward of the bridge that had been allocated to us in the second hold. I was sitting on the hatch cover enjoying the sun when I saw the young Chinese airman come up on deck with his guard close behind him. He sauntered across the deck to the railing and stood there looking out to sea while his guard stood beside him; I lay back on the hatch cover and continued to enjoy the sun.

It was were well into November, but in Australia that was the beginning of summer. It was a perfectly gorgeous summer's day, with not a cloud in the sky and a perfectly delightful day to be alive. There had to have been at least 200 or more soldiers and Chinese airmen milling around on the deck beside me or just lying there enjoying the sun. Suddenly there was a lot of shouting among the Chinese and a rush toward the railing with the GIs and MPs grabbing life preservers and throwing them over the side. Seconds later we again heard the dreaded "Man Overboard" call on the loudspeakers.

I felt certain it was the young Chinese lad whom I had seen standing there not ten minutes before, and when I squeezed my way through the crowd to the railing, there was indeed no sign of him nor of his guard. I asked some of the other Chinese airmen standing there what had happened. One of them had seen him go overboard and told me that he had watched the young lad calmly climb up onto the railing where one of the huge "assault" nets was folded. He had sat there for a few moments with his back to the sea, seemingly quite at ease, and then, just as

calmly, and without a word to any of those around him, he simply pitched over backward and disappeared over the side.

All that had taken only a minute or so. Just as I was talking to the eyewitness, the young soldier who had been guarding the lad came rushing up on deck. He was terribly distraught when he learned what had happened. He told us that when he and the young man had been standing by the rail a few minutes previously, the young chap had told him he was tired and wanted to go to his bunk to lie down for a nap. The guard had accompanied him down, had watched him lie down on his bunk and then had himself sat down with his back against the bunk and had been unaware of anything until he had heard the shouting up on deck and the "Man Overboard" call. He'd then turned to look behind him and found the young fellow gone. Apparently it had all been planned. As the young fellow lay back on the bunk, he had watched his guard sit down with his back to the bunk, and in a smooth gliding movement he had simply rolled on over to the opposite side of the bunk and slipped up to the deck, all in a matter of seconds.

While the guard was telling me that, the ship had once again described a wide circle and was gradually slowing down as we approached the spot where we could see the life belts floating on the water. I was standing in almost exactly the same spot where I'd been when the first man went over, and perhaps because the first incident was so fresh in my mind, I once again looked down toward the stem of the ship, hoping to spot the man even though we hadn't yet reached the spot where the life belts floated. But what I saw wasn't in the water at all.

I should explain at this point that most if not all Navy ships have, on each side of the forward hull, a spar or boom that is attached to the side about four or five feet below the level of the deck. When the ship is at sea the spars are securely attached alongside the hull, but when the ship is at anchor, the spar is extended outward at a right angle, and from it, ropes are hung to tie up the ship's motorboats when they are not in use.

The spar on the port side was immediately below the point where I was standing. But as I glanced down toward the water, something unusual caught my eye in passing and made me look again. Because of the added height of the railing, the spar was at least eight or ten feet below me, and beneath it, the ship's hull slanted in at a very sharp angle as it curved down to the water. I had to look twice, because I thought my eyes were deceiving me, but I could clearly see the fingers of a man's two hands clinging to the outer edge of the spar, although the man himself hanging below was out of sight due to the inward bend of the ship.

I was so excited I could barely talk. I reached out and grabbed the arm of the nearest MP, and pointing downward to the spar, showed him what I had spotted. Within seconds he had stripped off his jacket and was lying over the railing on his stomach yelling to us to grab hold of his feet and slowly let him downward as he tried to grab the man.

Several of the Chinese airmen helped me as we held the young MP by his feet. He stretched his arms down as far as he could, and we lay over the railing reaching down as far as we could, holding his feet and legs. From behind, others held onto us, and all the time the young MP kept shouting "lower, lower," and we'd let him down another couple of inches. Out of the corner of my eye I could see his hands reaching nearer and nearer to the spar and the man's fingers. We redoubled our efforts to give him just a little more reach. Then I saw a flash of movement, and then clearly, below the spar, I saw the man plummeting toward the water. At that instant the young MP screamed, "He's gone, he's gone," followed by "Pull me up, pull me up."

We all felt sick over having been so close to saving the man's life, only to lose him at the last minute. But I felt desperately sorry for the young MP. He took it hard indeed, as in tears, he told me he had managed to grasp the man's wrists, but as he struggled to get a good grip on them, his own hands were sweaty, and the man's were equally wet, and he had been unable to retain his grip. The man, feeling someone grasp him by the wrists, had apparently released his grip and had fallen with no outcry, and I had seen him hit the water and disappear immediately.

As we tried to piece together the sequence of events, it was apparent, even though almost unbelievable, that as the young man had originally tipped himself over backward, his body had described a complete somersault and his outstretched hands had come into contact with the spar. Just how he had managed to grab onto the spar and retain his grip is a mystery,

nor can it be explained why, hanging there as he did for what must have been at least ten minutes, he had made no outcry whatsoever. I think he had simply not wanted to survive, and grabbing the spar had simply been a reflex when his fingers touched it. I also think that when he felt his wrists grabbed, he deliberately let himself go, and not knowing how to swim, had simply gone down like a stone.

Our ship circled the spot for almost an hour as a Navy crew in a lifeboat searched in vain for the man. Those two incidents following each other so closely depressed everyone, particularly the Chinese airmen, who normally were fatalistic about death and scarcely gave it a thought. But that young man had taken his own life while en route to America, the "Promised Land," and it seemed to stun them and for days they talked of nothing else.

The closer we got to Australia the more pleasant the weather became. In fact, for the entire 60 days we were at sea, we had excellent weather, and apart from one or two light rain squalls, it was nothing but sunshine. One morning early we finally spotted land in the distance, and before long we were approaching the mouth of the river leading to Melbourne. We were soon steaming up that beautiful stream lined with farmhouses and small hamlets, amid lush pasture land and rolling hills in the near distance. It was vastly different from anything Eva and I had imagined Australia would be like, and we reveled in the sight.

We all looked forward to going ashore in Melbourne, but we were in for a disappointment. For security reasons, none of us were allowed ashore, not even onto the wharf. Only the captain and some of his officers left the ship, but as we watched them go down the gangplank, all of us became annoyed to see one of the civilian women accompanying the captain. She was one of the women we had presumed was a military wife, and we had noticed her spending considerable time with the captain. That she should have been selected to accompany him ashore incensed everyone who saw her go, and the Navy nurses in particular were vocal about it.

The ship's holds were opened to discharge and take on mail, and that night, those of us who had bunks in the hold area got no sleep. All the bunks were dismantled and moved to one side, and even though my bunk was under an overhang and wasn't touched, so much was piled up against it that I couldn't even get near it to fetch my toilet articles. For us in the hold, there were no public rooms where we could sleep. We simply spent the night out on deck. However, the weather was perfect and the activity on the dock was ceaseless throughout the night and kept us awake and interested.

From Melbourne we steamed up the coast to Brisbane, bypassing Sydney. To that point the ocean for the entire voyage had been relatively calm, but in the Tasman Sea, although the sky was clear, the sea was as rough as we were told it usually was. But by that time almost everyone had his sea legs and didn't mind it, and with land in view most of the way, it was a pleasant trip. As we approached Brisbane, the American GIs on board grew excited. Since most of them had previously been stationed there for almost a year on their way to India, they were looking forward to going ashore to look up old girlfriends. However, when we got there, the same rule applied. No one was allowed ashore, and as we heard the announcement, the concerted groan that went up from all aboard could doubtless have been heard on shore.

We docked in midafternoon, and again the captain and his girlfriend went ashore with some of the other ship's officers, but no one else. After some hours I approached the MP at the gangplank and asked if I could walk to the shore end of the gangplank and step onto the dock just to be able to say that I had stepped onto Australian soil. To my surprise he made no objection, but that was as far as I got.

For another night, those of us who slept in the holds went without sleep, but it was a very different night from the one in Melbourne. As soon as darkness fell, the GIs by ones and twos began to sneak ashore by sliding down the hawsers or on ropes into the water, and swimming to land. The MPs were caught napping, and before they realized what was going on, more than 700 men had successfully made their escape. However, getting back aboard was to be a different matter.

When, late that night, the captain came back aboard and learned what had happened, he was furious. He ordered floodlights set up on both sides of the ship and on the dock itself, and ordered that every one of the returning men be arrested and thrown into the brig. I had a vantage point on the upper deck throughout the night and watched with intense interest as, during the early hours of the morning, the sol-

diers in their same small groups tried to sneak back aboard. However, by that time most of them were very drunk and it wasn't an easy job.

The first few to return to the ship were unaware of the precautions that had been taken, so most of them were caught. But the men who had remained aboard were siding with those trying to get back on, and the MPs didn't stand a chance. From various points on the ship, lookouts would shout to the men ashore and tell them where the MPs were, and which way to go. I watched as shadowy figures crept around the buildings ashore, keeping out of the floodlit areas, and then, either individually or in small groups, making a run for a part of the ship where no MP was on guard, and the men on board threw ropes down to them and pulled them up. As the crowd ashore became larger, new measures were taken by those on board. Fake "fights" were started in several places on the decks to create a diversion and occupy the MPs, and as the MPs rushed around, preoccupied in breaking up the fights, swarms of men got back on board, many by swimming to the opposite side of the ship, where they were pulled up on ropes. It was astonishing, considering the drunken condition some of them were in, that they didn't drown.

In all, about 40 were caught and put in the brig. The captain publicly announced that they would remain there until the ship reached the U.S., and they then would be shipped back to India. However, although the men spent the next several weeks locked up, the captain ultimately relented and rescinded his order as most of us had thought he would.

In Brisbane, impossible as it seemed, we took on more troops returning to the United States, and conditions aboard became even more crowded. There was no room left on deck to get any exercise. When everyone was up on deck, it was so packed with bodies that there was scarcely room to move, but no one seemed to mind, and we heard no complaints. Even though the food lines were longer and took much more time, no one griped about it, and a happier group of people it would have been hard to find. Everyone anticipated that after leaving Brisbane, we would be heading directly for the U.S. However, even more surprises were in store for us.

No one would tell us where we were going, but from Brisbane we headed northwest through the famed Coral Sea to Noumea, capital of New

Caledonia. We stopped there for just one night and then continued to the Fiji Islands, where we made several more short stops. Everywhere we saw U.S. warships, planes and merchant vessels carrying war supplies. It was during the period when the great assault was being made by General MacArthur to retake the Philippines, and shortly after the great battle of Leyte Gulf. Many of the ships, both civilian and military, showed signs of bomb damage.

From Fiji we unexpectedly turned north, and after a day or two reached the island of Ulithi. The island itself wasn't much to look at, but the nearby anchorage inside the reefs, with its hundreds of ships at anchor or moving about from place to place, simply boggled the mind. We attempted to count the ships, but it was hopeless. Warships of every size and kind stretched as far as the horizon, and we counted at least five aircraft carriers. The sky was filled day and night with planes from the carriers and from an air strip on shore. We were thrilled by the sight of such immense power massed against the Japanese.

At the time, beyond hearing the names of the islands, we had no access to any maps and so really hadn't the faintest idea as to where we actually were. We were ignorant of the fact that we were very close to Japanese-occupied territory. Not until we reached San Francisco and saw a map did we realize how close we had been to the Philippines without being aware of it. Not only that, but many of the islands close to Ulithi, such as Yap, only 20 miles away, and Truk, only a short distance further, were still occupied by the Japanese. General MacArthur's strategy had been simply to bypass them and press forward. It was only three months after our stop in Ulithi, on March 11, 1945, that the Japanese launched a 24-plane kamikaze suicide attack on the island. However, only 11 of the planes managed to reach the atoll, and only the carrier U.S.S. *Randolph* was hit and damaged.

At none of those island stops were we or anyone else permitted to go ashore, and even the captain's girlfriend was confined to the ship. At each stop we took on a few more men, most of them casualties of war — walking wounded — who nevertheless were a mighty cheerful bunch of men homeward bound. By then, so many were aboard we wondered where they all slept and ate, and almost every area of the ship was so packed with bodies that it was difficult to move from one point to another. However, no one seemed to mind and morale continued to be high.

Anchored a mile or so offshore at Ulithi, we were close enough to shore to see the feverish activity everywhere. Clouds of dust rose from construction work, and from the lay of the land we surmised that another airstrip was being prepared. Dozens of ships were anchored almost within a stone's throw of us, but one in particular caught our attention. It was one of the famous Liberty ships, the ugly ducklings of the war, which nevertheless contributed so tremendously to the success of the entire operation. We were on her starboard side when we dropped anchor, and at first she aroused no curiosity except for the fact that she was riding so high in the water that we presumed she was empty and waiting for a returning convoy. Then, later in the afternoon, the tide turned and both the Liberty ship and our ship turned with the tide, and we could see the other side of the ship. In the middle of her port side was a monstrous hole, which had obviously been blasted out by a torpedo. The hole was so huge we could see deep into her bowels, and it extended from well below the water line almost to the top deck. The ship itself appeared to be full of water, and the hole was fully large enough for a tugboat to enter, turn around inside and come out again. The damage was appalling, and we all wondered how she had ever managed to stay afloat and make it to port.

Anxious as all of us were by that time to finish the voyage and reach our final destination, I think that everyone was a bit sorry to say goodbye to those lovely islands. The deep azure blue of the skies and the gorgeous green of the ocean, changing color as we approached each island, the atolls with their verdant foliage and surf-covered reefs, and the variety of birds and sea life that we saw, completely defy description. But ultimately we found ourselves heading away from it all on a direct route to what we thought would be San Francisco, but which turned out to be Long Beach.

There was no room anywhere on the ship for any kind of deck sports and the only recreation for the men was gambling. It went on day and night in odd corners of the ship. At night all lights in sleeping areas were turned off at 10:30, but that didn't stop the gamblers. They congregated in the "heads" where the lights were on all night, blissfully sitting on the floor for the entire night, playing on a blanket spread in front of them. Many thousands of dollars changed hands every day, and after leaving the islands, the gambling fever grew more intense and was the subject of just about everyone's conversation.

The gambling wasn't limited to card playing or "craps." They gambled on just about everything. Several men were big winners in each of the games, and bets were placed throughout the ship as to who would be the eventual winner in the final playoff that was supposed to occur just before we reached land. The man who did finally win the last hand was reputed to have walked ashore with more than $50,000, big money in those days. He and the barber were undoubtedly the two richest men to leave the ship.

As we neared the U.S. mainland, excitement ran high throughout the ship, and bets were placed as to which day we would arrive and at which port. The crew either couldn't or wouldn't give us any hints at all, but when we were about 500 miles from shore things began to happen. It started with the crew tearing out all the bunks in our forward hold so that the mail could be unloaded as soon as we docked, and we knew then that we would be arriving the next day. Of course, we in the forward hold again got no sleep that night, but we didn't mind too much. There was so much activity and so much to watch. I was astonished to see the crew burning GI uniforms and boots in an incinerator on the top deck. That went on all night long until the incinerator was red hot. I soon noticed other members of the crew carrying out the contents of the freezers and throwing it all overboard. I watched in amazement as sailors carried complete sides of beef and great slabs of pork and threw them overboard. That was followed by what seemed like hundreds of cases of chicken. All that night the activity went on. Hundreds of pounds of butter, sugar and other foodstuffs were thrown away. I asked why they were doing it and was told that before reaching the United States the entire ship had to be emptied of foods that might have been contaminated, and before taking on new supplies for their next trip, all the old stuff had to be gotten rid of. It seemed a terrible waste, but it was understandable that the foodstuffs we had aboard, which had been purchased either in India or Australia, might be suspect, and the health authorities wanted to take no chances.

The weather that last night was cold and damp. Because it was so cold on deck with the fog and I had nowhere else to go, I spent most of the night in the vicinity of the incinerator, where it was nice and warm. Early in the afternoon we had run into heavy fog, and hour after hour the ship crept along, her horn blowing every few minutes. Suddenly we were startled by the sight of a U.S. Navy blimp looming out of the fog directly overhead, so close we could see the men in the gondola. The blimp shadowed us that night. We could see her lights above us or nearby all night long and she was still there the next morning. Then we knew we were much nearer land because coastal aircraft came out and flew over us repeatedly. We finally broke out of the fog toward noon, only a few miles out from San Pedro harbor, and when land was finally spotted, a tremendous roar went up from all on board. Our 60-day voyage was ended.

At dockside a Navy band welcomed us with a spirited rendition of a song we heard for the first time, "California, Here I Come." Every time I have heard it since, it has brought back happy memories. On the dock hundreds of well-wishers waved flags and handkerchiefs — a heartwarming sight. It took several hours before we could get ashore, but when we did, it was wonderful to feel solid ground beneath our feet once again, although at first we found it difficult to walk after being on the ship so long.

What did interest us greatly was the feverish wartime activity around us everywhere. Los Angeles, when we got there later in the day, was jammed with troops. Interestingly enough, we found ourselves assigned to a room in the Hotel Cecil, bringing back memories of the New Delhi hotel, although the two were vastly different places. When we were taken to our room, we found wall-to-wall beds. It was only a small room, but six beds had been placed in it, side by side. The door could only be opened just enough for a person to slip in, and a dressing table took up most of the remaining space, so that there was hardly room to stand and remove one's clothes. Eva and I had the room to ourselves, though, and we spent the next day in Los Angeles because tickets had to be booked in advance for the train to San Francisco. Later in the day we called on some friends whom we'd not seen in more than 11 years. When we walked in on them, they were so surprised that one of them said: "We don't see you in 11 years and you walk in as casually as though you'd come from just across the street instead of across the Pacific."

The next morning, when I stopped at the desk to

pay our bill, I was surprised by the amount. Upon examination, I saw I had been charged for six nights instead of just the two. When I drew that to the attention of the clerk he said, "You are Mr. Robert N. Tharp aren't you? And you were in room 612 weren't you?" I told him I was indeed Robert N. Tharp, but that we had been in room 432. When he checked again he found our card, but by a strange coincidence, rare as our surname is, someone with exactly the same name and initial had been staying at the same hotel. Unfortunately, we had to rush to the train station, so there was no time to make the individual's acquaintance. Although the train was crowded, our trip up the central California coast was delightful. Despite heavy rain that came later in the day, the unending panorama of the ocean on one side and the green countryside on the other was most relaxing, and we thoroughly enjoyed it.

We arrived in San Francisco long after dark in heavy rain and were immediately directed to Traveler's Aid for assignment of hotel rooms. There was a long line of people ahead of us. Finally it was our turn, and the girl at the desk gave us vouchers for a room at the "Mark Hotel."

Some years before, while in China, I had seen an article in *Life* magazine about the new "Mark Hopkins Hotel," and what a marvelous place it was. In the taxi, which we shared with several others, I told Eva that we had been given a room at the Mark Hopkins. America was indeed laying out the red carpet for us. However, after a very short ride, the taxi pulled up at a three-story hotel in an unpleasant neighborhood south of Market Street, in what is known as the Mission District. Instead of the palatial Mark Hopkins, we found ourselves in a flea-bag hotel, little better than a flop house. But we had stayed in worse places, and despite the carousing of the many servicemen with their girlfriends who thronged the place, we managed to get some sleep. The next morning, before reporting for my new assignment, I took time to walk around and find a room in another hotel.

We were fortunate in finally finding a delightful room at the Canterbury Hotel on Sutter Street, as I believe it was. It was near the center of the city and convenient for any shopping we wanted to do. We stayed there for two weeks until an apartment could be found for us through the office. Thus began a most interesting period in our lives, quite different from anything we'd had before or have since experienced, and it was to last for almost another two years.

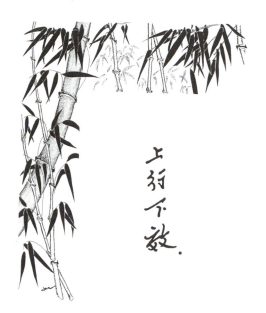

Chapter Thirty-Five
1945 — A Memorable Year

The organization I joined in San Francisco had the unwieldy name, "The British Political Warfare Mission," and had its offices on the fourth floor of 147 Montgomery Street, in the heart of San Francisco's financial district. It was within a few blocks of what is now known as North Beach, originally San Francisco's notorious Barbary Coast, an entertainment center that has always had a somewhat dubious reputation. It was no different during those war years.

I suppose it was shortly after New Year's Day, 1945, when I first reported for work, but I have no recollection whatsoever of Christmas week, nor of what we did, beyond perhaps getting to know the city a bit. I do remember going in to the office and being surprised that it was such an old building. There was a creaky old elevator to the fourth floor, where our offices occupied five or six large rooms. I remember meeting many new people, and all were most friendly, particularly the Chinese staff, who greeted me like an old friend.

The atmosphere was a little strained between me and the man I had gone there to replace. That was to be expected, particularly since I had sent in so many reports critical of his output. However, he turned out to be a friendly sort who didn't seem to hold a grudge against me. It was simply a case of an elderly man called in from retirement to do a job for which he wasn't fully qualified, but trying nonetheless to do his best with the limited amount of Chinese that he had mastered. Within those limitations he had actually done an excellent job from an organizational point of view. The staff members were all competent and well trained, and the operation was running very smoothly. However, when I initially met with the Chinese staff, they were the first to agree that their end product, the broadcasts, left much to be desired. My job was to help rectify that.

I had no difficulty settling in to work that first day. I'd been reading the news scripts from that office for over a year in India, so they were familiar to me. Now it became my job to select the news to be translated into Chinese, then to correct and edit the translations, and finally to sit in the studio as the scripts were recorded for broadcast. Along with the job, I found it exciting to be among the first to see the news as it came in hot off the wires.

There was, of course, such a plethora of news that the biggest problem was to select those items that would be of the most interest to our Chinese listeners in mainland China. Their interests, like my own, tended to be chiefly concerned with the progress of the war in the Pacific and the battle against the Japanese in Burma, the Philippines, and on the China mainland itself. At the same time, since the Pacific war was largely an American operation, even though British and Australian forces were involved, we couldn't limit ourselves to simply reporting on that. As an organ of the British government we were expected to report as much as possible of British efforts in the war, political and military. That meant reporting news of the war in Europe, as well as decisions that were being made in London. It was a bit one-sided, though, because the war in Europe was winding down so quickly that everyone speculated it would soon be over, and British and American forces would then presumably concentrate all their efforts against Japan. That, of course, was what the Chinese wanted to hear.

I had a staff of six or seven Chinese writers, only one of whom was female. I was delighted to find that despite their poor showing in the past, they were a talented and competent group and their morale was high. Their problem had been that in translating the news, they had been restricted to writing it in language that the boss could understand, and unless it was couched in the simplest of language, it just didn't get by him. Of course, to an educated Chinese listening at the other end it sounded ridiculous, and it annoyed the writers no end, because it reflected on their ability and competency. They were delighted when I gave them complete freedom to write just as they wished, and our broadcasts at once improved tremendously.

As I had suspected, several of the Chinese staff were not native Mandarin speakers, and although they did a commendable job when it came to reading the news on the air, their regional accents were quite

obvious. I diplomatically selected the best voices for making the broadcasts, alternating them night after night, and kept the others busy writing scripts and commentaries. Things settled down into a very smooth-working pattern with an absolute minimum of friction.

Because of the time difference between the United States and the China mainland, our working hours were unusual, to say the least. We went to work around 4:30 in the afternoon and got off work from two to three o'clock in the morning, seven days a week. It was a little difficult to get used to at first, but Eva and I soon adjusted to it and found it quite pleasurable in the long run, because it gave us a lot of freedom during the daylight hours.

There was a big shortage of manpower in San Francisco at the time, and Eva found a job the first week, with hours that coincided with my own. She was hired by Stanford University Hospital to work on the night shift in the nursery, something she enjoyed very much. But her first job lasted only two weeks. As part of their routine in hiring new personnel, she was given a thorough physical. Two weeks later there was a big flap when the doctors discovered she was a carrier of a particularly virulent type of intestinal disorder, even though neither she nor I had ever had the disease. Where she had picked it up was a mystery. Perhaps in India or China, but in any case the nursery was no place for her to be, and she was immediately moved to "accounts," where she spent the nights, alone most of the time, filing and posting the day's receipts.

The news that she was a carrier devastated Eva, and she was terrified that she might inadvertently have infected some of the babies. But the incubation period passed with no sign of anyone having been affected, and Eva could breathe easily once again. Stanford Hospital is a training school, and Eva was greatly amused as she was pointed out to the young medical students as the one carrying the unusual disease, something that was both rare and strange to medical personnel in the United States. It was obvious that the students were disappointed to see that Eva looked entirely normal.

About two weeks after our arrival in San Francisco we were allocated an apartment on Vallejo Street, quite near Nob Hill, the famous San Francisco district noted for its luxurious homes. Our apartment was in a building on one of San Francisco's steep hills, in an area overlooking the Marina and the Palace of Fine Arts, with the bay beyond. Vallejo Street was an area where there were many large, old mansions, a number of which had been converted by the local authorities into eight or nine small apartments. The tiny apartment we were given was in one of them. It was a three-story mansion with a large basement. Our apartment was one of three on the top floor, facing the bay, offering a wonderful, unobstructed panoramic view that extended from the Golden Gate Bridge on our left, all the way past Alcatraz Island to the Bay Bridge on the extreme right. We never tired of watching the ever-changing activities below us: the constant and seemingly never-ending parade of warships and freighters coming and going, the many smaller boats and ferries criss-crossing the busy harbor, the daily takeoffs and landings of the huge, heavily laden four-engined flying boats that raced their way along the bay past Alcatraz, then laboriously clawed their way into the air to clear the Golden Gate Bridge, seemingly by only a few feet.

I recall one morning when one of those huge planes appeared to be having a particularly hard time getting airborne. Standing by our front window, I watched it as it increased speed, throwing up a rooster tail of spume, but as it passed the point where normally it would have taken to the air, I began to worry. When it seemed to me that it would either have to abort its run or continue to taxi out under the bridge, it finally lurched into the air. It continued flying just a few feet above the water in the direction of the bridge, and from where I stood, high above it, there appeared to be no possibility that it could clear the bridge towers, or even the lower mid-point, nor did it appear to have sufficient room to circle back over the bay. Eva heard me pounding my fists on the window sill and came into the room to find me kneeling by the window praying that the plane would make it. It did finally clear the center of the bridge by just a few feet.

Our apartment was small but comfortable, and we loved the place. Ridiculously, we paid only $40 a month in rent. We had one fairly large room, which doubled as bedroom and sitting room, and there was another tiny room, little larger than a big closet, that was primarily a storage room, although it accommodated a single bed. The kitchen measured about five feet by ten feet, and the bathroom was even smaller, being exactly five feet square. A narrow hallway led to the front door.

Despite its tininess, we liked everything about the place except for the shower stall in the bathroom. It was a crudely constructed, makeshift wartime product made from plasterboard with a cement coating. It had the great disadvantage that in the foggy and damp San Francisco weather, it never completely dried out and was always moldy and foul-smelling. We longed for a tub where we could take a proper bath.

As usual, I decided to do something about it on my own. Following the practice I had perfected in dealing with the Japanese bureaucracy in Manchukuo, I decided not to complicate matters by asking permission from our landlord, the United States government, but to just go ahead and install a tub myself. It was easier thought about than accomplished. It turned out to be a sizable operation fraught with difficulties and frustrations that I could never have foreseen.

Our first priority was to locate a bathtub, and not just any tub; it had to be exactly five feet long and no more. In San Francisco, in wartime, I discovered that such a tub was nonexistent, at least on the open market. I resorted to advertising for one, and after a few days I learned to my delight that I could get one from a private party in Hayward, a small town on the other side of the bay. Sight unseen I told the owner over the phone to hold it for me and I would come at the first possible opportunity to pick it up.

Timing was critical. Our apartment being government owned, it was subject to monthly inspections, and we were expected to keep the place as spotless as when we moved in. That wasn't difficult, but we had to time the installation of the tub so the inspector didn't come in and find us in the middle of the job. Fortunately his visits were quite regular and we were always notified a day or so in advance. I waited until immediately after he came and then we set out for Hayward to get the tub.

Shortly after our arrival in San Francisco, one of the first things I had done was to purchase a car. As a government official I was given a special allocation of gasoline, more than the ration allowed the average car owner. And because of my night work, and the absence of public transportation during those hours, the car was a necessity, so my ration was even higher than that of the average official. Luckily we found a rather elderly, yet quite serviceable, Dodge two-seater, which turned out to be a real treasure. It had been well treated by its former owner, worked like a charm, and never gave us the slightest trouble during the two years that we owned it.

With only a bench seat in front that would seat three in a pinch, it had a big storage shelf behind the seat, and a huge baggage compartment in the trunk at the back. I felt sure I could get the bathtub into it, so Eva and I set off confidently for Hayward.

We found the address of the tub's owner with no trouble, mainly because we spotted the tub lying upside down on the lawn out in front of the small house. I carefully measured it and found it to be exactly five feet in length, so I paid the man. I backed the car up close to the tub, and keeping the tub upside down, Eva and I tried to get it into the car's trunk. But we discovered that it was made of cast iron, weighing something like 300 pounds or more, and I could barely lift one end of it. Eventually, with the help of the owner and two neighbors, we finally got it into the trunk, tied it securely, and with the trunk open and the bathtub protruding from it, we leisurely drove back across the Bay Bridge to San Francisco.

Unloading it in front of our apartment was a different matter. All of our neighbors were at work and there wasn't a soul we could call upon for help. We found an old blanket, and between the two of us we finally managed to slide the tub out of the car and onto the street behind the car, where we left it for the night and hurried off to our respective jobs. Given the weight of the tub, we were not the least bit concerned that anyone would steal it.

Next morning around ten we again tackled the job. With the blanket underneath, and Eva pulling on a rope in front while I pushed from the back, we managed to slide the tub across the sidewalk, then inched it up a wide flight of stone steps onto the front porch. But it took us most of the day to get it that far, and we had to leave it there for another night. With three flights of stairs facing us before we could get it to our floor, it was going to be a lengthy process.

I think of all the things we have tackled in our lives that was one of the most Herculean, and there were times when we despaired of ever being able to get it up to the third floor and into our apartment. But having gone so far, we couldn't give up. In those days there were no such things as the handy "come-along"

ratchet and steel-rope gadgets that nowadays would have made such a job mere child's play. All we could do was use a piece of 2 x 4 with which I levered the tub upwards from below, as Eva at the front used the rope we had tied around it, and wound that around the bannister supports to keep the tub from sliding backward, and we measured our progress by a few inches every hour. Day after day we made pitifully slow progress as we managed to move that monster bit by bit, flight by flight, leaving it on a landing each night for the other tenants to stumble over and wonder about, resuming our work again the next morning when everyone had left for work. It was not until four days later that we finally managed to get it onto the tiny landing outside our apartment door, only to find that it was too wide to go through the doorway unless we turned it on its side. By that time we had neither the time nor the strength to tackle it, so we had to leave it where it was for the night, partially blocking the doors to the two neighboring apartments. What our poor neighbors must have thought and said when they got home and had to clamber over it to get into their homes was something we often speculated about. However, we never heard a word from any of them.

Eventually, and without having seen a soul all that time, we lifted one side of the tub a few inches, and got it inside the hallway where it sat — still upside down — for the next two weeks, and it was our turn to have to clamber over it each time we went in or out of the front door, something we had to do countless times each day thereafter as we carted the rubble from the dismantled shower stall down to the sidewalk.

One small shower stall hadn't appeared at first glance to contain too much material. But when I began to dismantle it, there was a surprising amount of plaster board and concrete. Eva and I took turns carrying it downstairs in a pouch made by holding up the corners of the aprons we wore. It was too bulky and heavy to put into a trash can, so we piled it neatly on the sidewalk. Day by day the mound grew until we had a pile about four feet high. Again, we never saw anyone, even out on the street. Everyone was at work, and although people must have noticed the pile of rubble there when they came home at night, there apparently were no complaints made, and eventually the trash collectors carted it all away.

When we finally had the shower torn out, it left a gaping hole in the corner where the two walls joined, and a deep hole in the floor that had to be filled. I scrounged around San Francisco until I found materials. I patched the wall and floor, then had to search through a dozen or more stores until I could find ceramic tile to match that on the walls, and more particularly, the exact match of the composition tile for the floor. All building materials were so scarce that I began to think I would never be able to find what we needed.

With less than a week to go before the inspector was due again on his rounds, we finally came to the big day when we could upend the tub and maneuver it into position in the bathroom to hook up the pipes. When we finally got it right side up, we both stared at the interior in a state of shock. It was immediately apparent why the original owner had turned the tub upside down. Obviously it had been left outdoors for some years, where it had collected rain water and leaves, because the bottom and sides for a foot or more were stained a deep brown that seemingly nothing could remove. We tried every kind of scouring powder without success, and ultimately had to resort to pumice stone to remove the stain bit by bit, completing the job only on the final day before the inspector came. He walked into the apartment and glanced into the bathroom as we stood by, holding our breath. But he apparently noticed nothing out of the ordinary, and walked out with a cheerful "good-bye." We'd gotten away with it. After all that effort, each time we took a bath in that tiny tub, it was a most satisfying experience and the utmost in luxury.

During the entire month that we'd been working on the tub, we'd not met a single one of our many neighbors. Even on Saturdays none of them seemed to be around, and on Sundays we were away from the place attending church. However, a week or so later we did meet one of them.

Eva and I both had typewriters and wrote a lot of letters. Just after breakfast one morning we were both happily banging away on our typewriters when there was a knock on the door. On opening it, we met a charming lady, somewhere in her early fifties, who identified herself as Mrs. Abrams from the apartment immediately below ours. She had come to bring us a small present, which we thought was very sweet of her. We invited her in for a cup of coffee and chatted for a time, learning she was a widow who lived with her only son, who was in his thirties. After she left and we opened her gift we discovered it to be two thick felt pads to put under our typewriters. Mrs. Abrams was too much of a lady to complain about the noise we made, which must have been most annoying for her. The pads were her discreet and diplomatic way of telling us. We became good friends and were able to laugh about it later.

February 1945 was a momentous month as far as war news was concerned. In the office we were kept excited and busy trying to keep up with all the daily happenings. First came the Yalta Conference, then Gen. MacArthur liberated Manila and made us feel that the war in the Far East was really about to come to an end. Shortly after that the long battle over the island of Iwo Jima dominated the news for days. Japan was undergoing saturation bombing that convinced everyone that she would be unable to hold out much longer.

Eva and I were exhilarated by all those encouraging developments and began to discuss the possibility of returning to China before too long. My mother's letters from South Africa were also full of optimistic hopes for an early end to the war. She, too, was intensely looking forward to getting back to her beloved China. Her letters were somewhat irregular because of wartime restrictions.

Toward the end of February, Mother wrote from Durban that Dad had been taken very ill and was in the hospital. It was not until a later letter that I learned he had suffered a slight stroke. Mother's letter showed that she was deeply worried, although she tried to conceal it. Then, with no prior warning, on March 6th we received a cable from Durban saying that my beloved mother had been hospitalized and was seriously ill. A week later another cable came telling us that Mother had been taken to be with her Lord, whom she had served so faithfully in China for nearly forty years. There were no details as to what had caused her sudden death.

I was devastated by the news of Mother's death and pulled every string I could think of to try to get air transportation, military or otherwise, so that I could get to Durban to attend her funeral and take care of the family. But although all the officials I talked to were most sympathetic, it proved completely impossible, and I had to content myself with waiting for a letter from either Dad or Barbara with details. My mind went back to my childhood days in Lingyuan, where Mother loved so much to sit at the organ and sing her favorite hymn "In the Garden," with the words: "...and He walks with me and He talks with me, and He tells me I am His own." I comforted myself with the thought that Mother was now in the presence of her Lord and could indeed now walk and talk with Him.

When a letter finally came from Durban we learned that Mother had literally worried herself sick over Dad's illness and had then complained of severe stomach cramps. It became so bad she was taken to the hospital, where the doctors diagnosed her condition as strangulation of the colon and determined that in Mother's state of health it was inoperable. Dad was in another room of the same hospital, and had recovered sufficiently that he was able to visit with Mother and was at her side when the Lord took her.

For poor Barbara, Mother's sudden death had to have been a most traumatic experience, and a severe burden was thrust upon her young shoulders. Adding to the problem was the fact that my older sister, Ruth, was an invalid requiring constant attention. Eva and I felt so completely helpless thousands of miles away. But Barbara has always been a courageous individual and she bore up remarkably well under the strain, although it took her many months to get over it. She, with Dad's help, quickly took over the responsibilities thrust upon her, and for the next year or more managed the depleted household until the war was over and they were able to get transportation to America to join us.

Rationing of both gasoline and foodstuffs was in effect all over the United States during those war years, but that was nothing new to us. Eva and I found that by comparison with what we had seen under the Japanese, America was still the land of plenty. We were amused by the little red dime-sized tokens that had to be surrendered every time we bought some meat, and were disturbed by the constant complaints we heard from those around us as to the poor quality of the meat. To us, tough and stringy as it was, it was prime quality compared to what we had been getting in China for years under the Japanese, and the ration was more than ample for our requirements.

All fats were in very short supply, and, like every-one else, we saved every bit of used fat and turned it over to the nearest butcher for a few cents a pound, to be used in making armaments. The first time I took our can of used fat in to the butcher I was surprised to see him take an ice-pick and stab through the fat to the bottom of the can. I asked him why he was doing that. He told me many people put small stones in the bottom of the fat to add to the weight. I was incensed that anyone could be so unpatriotic and so avaricious, and doubly incensed that the butcher should have suspected me of doing it. However, it seemed to be a common practice.

Butter was, of course, also very scarce. On those rare occasions when it became available, one had to stand in long lines to get a single pound. The first line I stood in to get butter was so long it wound around the entire block.

Just by chance, as I got in line near the front of the store, to begin my journey around the block in the line, I noticed a Dodge panel truck exactly like the first one I had owned in China, standing against the curb in front of the store. The hood was raised and the driver was fiddling with the engine, evidently having some kind of trouble. When an hour or more later I again came within sight of the store, the man was still working on the car's engine. After I had picked up my pound of butter, I stopped beside him and asked if I could be of any help, telling him that I had owned a similar vehicle and knew something about its quirks. He was most happy to have me take a look at the problem, which actually was quite minor, and in a few minutes I was able to start the engine. He proved to be the man who had delivered the butter to the store, and he still had some left. When he saw the pound I was carrying, he was so appreciative of my help that he insisted on pressing upon me two more pounds.

The next time I stood in line for butter was the afternoon of April 12. It was a beautiful, sunny afternoon, and many people were out in the streets. Suddenly shopkeepers from nearby stores rushed out with the news they'd just heard over the radio: President Franklin D. Roosevelt had died in Warm Springs, Georgia. The butter line broke up as people started to weep, milling around in the streets trying to get more details. I, too, was deeply affected by the news and by the genuine grief that everyone showed over the loss of that great man. Even though I was still an Englishman at the time, I had come to greatly respect him and mourned his passing.

Eva and I spent two years in San Francisco and came to love the city and everything about it. Of the many cities in the world that we have visited, it is still our favorite place. Working as we did all night, we had the greater part of the day free, and we roamed the city, enjoying its beautiful parks and historic buildings. San Francisco is famed for its many restaurants serving foods from every part of the world. We got to know many of them, particularly those in Chinatown, where we could taste the flavors that brought back memories of home.

We were rationed sufficient gasoline for my trips to and from the office, but not much more than that, and we were not able to use the car much for any kind of joy riding. But there were many bus rides that we could take, and one of our favorite trips was across the Golden Gate Bridge and out into the Marin countryside. After studying the bus routes, we discovered we could get off the bus at a certain point out in the middle of nowhere, then hike through the fields and woods to another road a few miles away and catch a bus home. Bus drivers in those days were always friendly and obliging, and they thought nothing of letting people on or off at unscheduled spots.

Another bus trip we enjoyed was down the peninsula to Moffett Field Naval Air Station in Mountain View. It was a large airfield where the Navy blimps were stored in huge hangers, and from where they headed out to sea on their ceaseless rounds of submarine hunting. On one occasion we were fortunate enough to watch a demonstration of fully loaded gliders being picked up from the ground. A low-flying C-47 with a hook under its tail came in just above ground level, skimmed over the top of the loaded glider, and engaged a nylon rope strung between two upright poles. The other end of the rope was attached to the nose of the glider. As the plane caught the rope loop and gained altitude, the rope gradually played out until, with a gentle jerk, the glider started to move and then suddenly bounded into the air a few hundred feet behind the plane. It was fascinating to watch and brought home the reality of what we'd read of those gliders in action in the invasion of Normandy just a few months earlier.

My extra gasoline ration paid off in one experience we had that summer. I had returned home from work around 2 a.m. and had just gotten into bed when the telephone rang. The operator was on the line, and she first asked me if I worked for the British government. When I replied in the affirmative, she told me she had tried every number in the book for British government agencies without success, but she didn't tell me how she had learned that I worked for the British Political Warfare Mission. At any rate, her call was an example of the extent to which telephone operators went in those days to be helpful. Her call, she told me, was on behalf of a British national who was in great need of help, and she asked me to please talk with him.

I found myself talking with an officer of the Royal Air Force who had come to San Francisco along with some of his men in order to ferry a number of planes back to England. He had come into the city on business and had missed the last bus back to the airfield. He wanted to know if I would be kind enough to drive him out to the field, because they were to take off at dawn.

I was delighted to be of service, but Eva wasn't happy about my going out at that time of the morning alone, and insisted on accompanying me. We set out at once to pick him up. When we met the officer at a designated spot downtown, it turned out he had an enlisted flyer with him, and they both had to get back to a small town called Pittsburg, about 40 miles from San Francisco. With only room for three in the front seat, Eva had to climb onto the shelf behind, where fortunately, although somewhat cramped, there was room for her to lie, and we headed off for Pittsburg.

There were no freeways in those days, and once across the Bay Bridge, it was a two-lane blacktop road all the way. But it was a trip I wouldn't have missed for anything. The young officer regaled us the entire distance with exciting stories of his flying experiences during the war, all told in a self-effacing manner that made light of his bravery, quite evident from the many medals on his tunic. He had flown in the Battle of Britain and also in the invasion of Europe. Finally, after seeing much action, he'd been rewarded with the task of supervising the ferrying of new aircraft from the U.S. to Britain, and he seemed rather bored by it, even though it meant hours of dangerous flying over the open Atlantic.

One story he told was remarkably similar to that of the squadron leader in India. This man told of flying his C-47 two-engined plane onto a small island near Java at the outset of the Pacific war. There were a number of British nationals stranded there whom he was sent in to rescue — far too many for the plane's normal capacity. However, he wasn't about to leave anyone behind, and he managed to squeeze all of them aboard, men, women, and children. He told everyone to pray hard as he started his takeoff run down the short airstrip, but they ran out of runway long before the wheels left the ground. He actually ran down over the beach before he got sufficient lift to become airborne and the plane's wheels were touching the wavetops before he was able to pull the plane up. He justifiably felt that that particular trip was the best one he had ever made, but he acknowledged it could never have been done without God's help. After he got to England he dropped us a postcard, but we lost touch with him after that.

Eva, working in the hospital, had regular night hours and left for work about thirty minutes after I did, usually around 4:30 in the afternoon, and she only had a ten-minute walk to work.

She either carried a lunch with her or ate in the hospital cafeteria. However, hours at my office were irregular, and since we were always working against a deadline of getting the news out on the air, any breaks we took depended on the volume and importance of the news that was coming in.

Our deadline for recording the news was 2 a.m. and by shortly after midnight we usually had selected all the stories we wanted to use. While waiting for the translations to be completed, I could usually slip out for my "lunch," and normally one or other of the Chinese translators or voice men would accompany me.

San Francisco in 1945 seemed just as busy at night as in the daytime. Hundreds of people were always in the streets, and a wide choice of restaurants operated around the clock. Chinatown was only a couple of blocks away from us, and we frequently ate in one of the tiny places that catered to the night owls or in one of the all-night cafeterias in the North Beach area. They were always full of people.

The whirlwind of world events during 1945, particularly from April onward, made it difficult to keep up with things at the office. We were constantly in a state of turmoil, adjusting our news scripts up to the last minute to keep up with more important events as they

unfolded. On April 28th came news of Mussolini and his mistress, Clara Petacci, being executed at Lake Como in Italy. May 1st brought the astounding news of Hitler's suicide, and the following day Berlin fell to the Russians. Six days later, on May 7th, Germany signed unconditional surrender terms at Reims, and the war in Europe was over. All that was followed in July by the Potsdam conference, where Churchill, Truman and Stalin met to plan for postwar Germany. Clement Atlee joined them on July 28th, and the conference carried over into August.

The night of August 6th was one that will live in the memory of every Japanese, but unlike Pearl Harbor on December 7th, 1941 — a date that every American remembers — so many cataclysmic events were occurring one after another that year that not many Americans remember what happened on that August date. One of my Chinese colleagues and I had just finished our nightly broadcast, and returning to our office from the OWI studios just two blocks away, were about to turn off the lights and leave when bells rang on the teleprinter, indicating a bulletin. I looked to see what had occurred.

What I read made no sense at all. "Atomic bomb dropped on Hiroshima, Japan." That was followed by seemingly garbled and unbelievable reports of the tremendous damage and of the expected casualties that the single bomb had caused. Up to that time it seemed that few had ever heard the word "atomic." We'd heard of the Manhattan Project, but it was all so secret that no one really knew what was going on there. Now the reports were all using the word "atom." When we turned on the radio, we heard commentators talking of the extraordinary power of that super-bomb, which came from splitting the atom, whatever that might mean. It was such earth-shaking news that I felt we had to get it out on the air immediately, and we started to work on a script. But our first problem was how to translate the word "atomic." None of our Chinese crew had ever heard of it, nor had I.

We had a large number of dictionaries and finally found the Chinese word for "atom" in one of them, which was translated into English as "original seed," *(yuanzi)*, so we decided to simply add the word *dan* for bomb, thus coining the Chinese word *yuanzi dan* (atom bomb). However, just to be sure we were on the right track, I made a call to the Chinese Consul

General, even though it was around 3 a.m. I woke him from a deep sleep and when I told him the news, he couldn't believe it. I told him the translation we had made for atomic bomb and asked him if he agreed with it. He, too, had never heard of the atomic bomb, and he agreed there was obviously no other way to say it, so we decided to go ahead and use it.

We shared broadcast facilities with the U.S. Office of War Information (OWI), which had offices nearby on the 11th floor of a building on the corner of California and Montgomery streets. They put out their Chinese language broadcast earlier than ours and gave us air time immediately following their own. OWI had an all-night crew on duty, and just as I was about to phone them to see if we could get some special air time, they called me and asked what we planned to do about the "atomic bomb" news. I told them we were preparing a script. They said they, too, would have liked to have put out a bulletin immediately, but they had no Chinese staff on hand either to translate it or voice it. They offered to give us air time immediately, and I told them we would be right over, and after voicing our own broadcast, we would be glad to write and voice theirs as well.

For security reasons, no "live" broadcasts were made at any time, and everything was first recorded on large wax disks for later transmission. That was to prevent any of the announcers from slipping in some unauthorized comment or secret message. It was my responsibility to sit by and listen as our broadcasts were recorded in both Mandarin and Cantonese, checking the scripts as the announcers read them and making certain there was no deviation from what was written there. It was also a way to check for normal speaking errors, which could then be rectified.

Within some thirty minutes of first receiving the news of the atom bomb, we were in the OWI studio. Because the news was so momentous, an exception was made, and we made live broadcasts in Mandarin and Cantonese dialects. So far as I know, ours were the first broadcasts in Chinese to go out over the air. Our translation for "atomic" was adopted by the Chinese government as the official term, not surprisingly, because no other way could be found to translate it. The term was so new and the idea of an atomic weapon so unique that from then on we were much amused to find the Chinese naming everything "new" that came out as being "atomic." When we later went

back to China we discovered nearly a dozen products had been given the "atomic" prefix, including the ball-point pen, which to this day is still known as the "atomic pen," *(yuanzi bi).*

Events in the Far East came to a head quickly after that night. Two days after the first bomb was dropped, the U.S.S.R. declared war on Japan and began their invasion of Manchuria. A day later, August 9th, a second bomb was dropped, this time on Nagasaki, a seaport on the island of Kyushu in southwest Japan. It produced fewer casualties, but brought about the immediate surrender of Japan on August 14th, when the Emperor broadcast a message to his nation, the first time in history most Japanese people had heard the voice of their emperor.

It was not until September 2nd that Japan signed surrender terms with General MacArthur, aboard the battleship Missouri in Tokyo Bay. But August 15th was officially V-J Day in America, and in San Francisco the crowds were so enthusiastic and unruly in their celebrating that it eventually turned into a riot.

I had reported to the office as usual that afternoon around 4:30, but because of the crowds in the streets, I had to park my car about ten blocks from the downtown area and walk the rest of the way. As it happened, that same night we were expecting the arrival of a newly hired Chinese translator. He was an old friend of mine from India days, Chih Yu-ju, and around 10:30 I headed out for the bus station to meet him. Even working on the fourth floor, we had been able to hear the noise of the crowd below, but nothing I'd heard prepared me for what I ran into when I reached Market Street, which I had to cross to get to the Greyhound Bus station.

History has recorded the events of that night in San Francisco and the several days of rioting that followed, so I won't go into detail. But already by that time of the evening the crowds were out of hand. A large number of Navy recruits had been given the night off from Treasure Island and were behaving in a most unruly manner. Joined by young civilian punks, they were openly assaulting women on the street; no woman walking alone was safe. At the same time they were systematically smashing every store window on Market Street, and on many of the side streets as well, particularly liquor stores. Looting was commonplace, and the police were powerless to control the crowds.

The downtown area resembled a war zone. Even walking along the sidewalk was hazardous because of paper bags full of water being dropped from upper-story windows by enthusiastic revelers. Numerous injuries were reported in the press the next day, and at least one person was killed. Actually, things got so bad that the press avoided reporting everything, lest San Francisco receive a bad reputation. The press suffered a lot of well-deserved criticism as a result.

One of the ugliest aspects of the rioting happened when young toughs, military and civilian, started venting their anger on any Army or Navy officer who happened along in uniform. As I was standing on the corner of Market and Montgomery streets waiting to cross the street through the mob, I saw a young Army captain stagger along the sidewalk toward me. His face was bloodied and his coat was badly torn. He had been hit on the head with some sort of makeshift weapon and was thoroughly dazed and barely able to walk.

When he got close to me and I saw the state he was in, I grabbed him by the shoulders and hustled him into a nearby drugstore, where we did what we could to patch up his facial injuries. I then took off his tunic, turned it inside out, and put it on him again, at the same time removing his tie and all insignia from his shirt collar as well. I then managed to get him outside and safely into a taxi a block or so away.

Then I got back to the corner and once more tried to cross the street, where a large truck carrying oranges had been caught in the intersection. The young hoodlums, civilian and Navy, were swarming over the truck, opening the orange crates and pelting the crowd with the oranges until none were left. It was a disgraceful scene, and I was vividly reminded of mob scenes I had witnessed in China and realized that man's behavior is no different regardless of nationality.

I eventually reached the bus station to find my friend waiting for me. It took me more than two hours to get him back to the office in a cab. That was indeed a night that anyone who witnessed it will never forget.

Although World War II had officially ended, it was to be several months before the British government got around to closing our office. In the meantime the office was kept going as usual well into 1946. But even with the war ended, there was still a lot to report. Earlier in 1945, between April 25th and June 26th, an organization for the maintenance of world peace, later known as the United Nations, had been establishing itself in San Francisco and was much in the news. On June 26th the newly written charter was signed by 50 nations, and on October 24th, with visitors from all over the world in San Francisco, the charter went into effect. Those were exciting days, particularly for the people of San Francisco, as they welcomed the officials from so many different countries.

There was great excitement in our office when Sir Anthony Eden, Britain's Foreign Secretary, came to San Francisco and held a big party for all the British nationals in the city in the restaurant at the top of the Mark Hopkins Hotel. We were all invited and got to meet Sir Anthony in person, and he complimented us on the work we had done during the war.

However, Eva and I were much more interested in what was going on in China. Although little news came through, we devoured every bit that we got and started making active plans to return as soon as possible. The Russians had established themselves in Manchuria and the new country of Manchukuo was no more. That in itself was good news, but we all wondered when the Russians would leave. Japanese armies in both Manchuria and China had, for the most part, surrendered peacefully, some to the Russians and others to the Chinese. But there were ominous reports of Chinese Communist troops picking up Japanese weapons for themselves wherever they could. That boded ill for a peaceful solution to the situation in China where, up to that point, both the Communists and Nationalists under Chiang Kai-shek had ostensibly been cooperating with each other in fighting their common enemy, the Japanese. There were, however, many believable reports to the contrary.

Nonetheless we had high hopes of being able to leave for China within weeks, and I badgered the shipping offices for word of any passenger ships heading there. Almost all civilian ships, however, had been sunk or were being used to bring troops back from overseas. It was to be a long time before things got back to normal. In fact, due to a variety of circumstances beyond our control, it was to be another full year before we could get transportation to China.

Bob's *ID* for the job in San Francisco.

George Walker and Betty, before they were married.

Our cousins — Jim and Ernie Frens.

Cut Paper Art. "Húangjín Wàn Lǐang" — A charm to bring 10,000 ounces of gold.

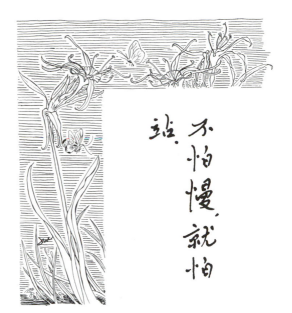

不怕慢，就怕站

Bu pa man, jiu pa zhan.

Slowness is not to be feared;
what is to be feared is standing still.

- Chinese Peasant Saying.

Chapter Thirty-Six
Slow Boat To China

Because I just couldn't wait to get started on our preparations for returning to China, I resigned from the British Political Warfare Mission in September 1945. The terms under which I had originally been sent from India to San Francisco contained a clause whereby it was clearly stipulated that at the termination of my employment with the mission, my return passage would be paid back to New Delhi or to London, whichever I chose. However, I had no wish to go to either place, and asked instead for a ticket to either Shanghai or Tientsin. I have no recollection of what response I received, but am sure that I was given the equivalent of my fare in cash.

I left the mission on friendly terms despite a tremendous amount of pressure put on me to stay longer and then go to London with the other members of the mission. In fact, I received a cablegram from London promising me a permanent job with the British Foreign Office with an attractive salary. But our minds were made up — it was back to China. Our

work there was uppermost in our minds.

Despite my leaving the mission and relinquishing my diplomatic passport, the building authorities in San Francisco told us we could remain in our apartment for as long as might be necessary. That turned out to be a real boon because housing was difficult to find. For several weeks I spent much of my time going the rounds of all the shipping offices in San Francisco trying to book passage to China. However, with the shortage of shipping and the priority movement of troops back to the U.S., I was told there would be no passenger ships for perhaps a year.

Although that was discouraging news, we learned that occasionally there were freighters that carried passengers to the Far East. Every morning we scanned the newspapers for the sailing of freighters, and one day we were rewarded. We found a news item about a Swedish cargo ship that would be calling at San Francisco en route to Shanghai that was equipped to carry a few passengers. I raced downtown to the office of the ship's agents and was most fortunate in being able to book passage for Eva and myself. If my memory serves me correctly, the ship was due to sail from San Francisco in early March 1946.

That left us little time to get together all the things we wanted to take with us, and I recall a period of feverish activity during January and early February as we tore around San Francisco buying clothing and supplies. War surplus stores had sprung up all over the city, and we frequented them, picking up some wonderful bargains. I purchased five or six large steamer trunks made by a well-known American manufacturer for a fraction of what they would normally have sold for. The only difference was that they had been designed for the military, and each was fitted inside with padded compartments of varying sizes, each with a lid. They were intended to hold fragile items of military hardware, such as cameras and camera parts, dental or medical equipment, and things of that nature. When the compartments were torn out, the trunks were no different from the civilian model, and to this day we still use the same trunks for storage.

We also bought, among other things, a warm and well-padded airman's flying suit, complete with numerous zippers and pockets, and a large patch on the back with crossed American and Chinese flags and a notice in Chinese stating that the wearer was an American airman who should be treated properly by any Chinese who found him. There was also the all-too-familiar and colorful CBI (China, Burma and India theater) shoulder patch we had seen worn by all the military in India. The notice on the back had been intended to protect any airman who had to parachute into a part of China occupied by the Japanese. I didn't need either the shoulder patch or the notice on the back, but I thought the suit would serve me well in Manchuria's cold winter weather, and it did. But at one point I had to get rid of it hastily, an incident that I will cover in a future chapter.

We also bought a large army tent, big enough to hold more than 100 people. I wanted that to use around Lingyuan in our country evangelism work in the villages, something we hoped to resume as soon as possible.

I definitely had to take some kind of a motor vehicle back with us, but that proved to be a real problem.

Although automobile manufacturers had resumed production, the type of van-like vehicle I needed was given a low priority, and I despaired of being able to get one in time for our departure. There were, however, thousands of surplus army Jeeps being sold at giveaway prices, many of them new. For around $100 each, I could have purchased as many used ones as I wanted. However, although they would have provided good transportation on our rough roads in Jehol Province, they were not equipped with good heaters and the canvas tops were not adequate to keep out the cold. In addition they could only carry four people and very little else. I worried also that parts might not be available when production of that model ceased.

Then I read somewhere that Willys Jeeps were being produced for the civilian market in a modified form. I visited one of the dealers and discovered the new models could be equipped with large heaters and they had quite substantial tops with weatherproof doors and sides. I was also delighted to find that they had a 3-foot-long extension that could be bolted onto the rear of the Jeep, making it into a small pickup truck. That would allow me to carry more people or heavier loads of one thing or another. I immediately put in an order, and since the Jeeps were less popular than sedans, I was promised delivery well before March, when our ship was to sail. Everything seemed to be falling nicely into place for our early departure. I was so confident we would be leaving soon that I rented a one-car garage a short distance from our apartment, where I intended building a shipping case for the Jeep.

While all that was going on in early January 1946, I received a surprise letter from my father in Durban, saying he and my two sisters had booked passage on a cargo ship sailing for New York on or about January 14th, and they would be arriving there approximately three weeks later. At about the same time I happened to see a notice in the newspaper's maritime section saying that the American President Lines, one of America's largest, was sending a freighter to Chinhuangtao, in North China. It was to sail just a month later than the Swedish ship on which we had booked our passage. Furthermore, it too would be carrying passengers.

That was all exciting news. We had been troubled by the fact that going to Shanghai on the Swedish freighter would have meant changing to a coastal steamer there in order to get to Tientsin, and the agents had also informed us that they were unable to book us tickets on any ship going from Shanghai to Tientsin because sailings were so irregular and there was a shortage of coastal steamers because of the heavy movement of Chinese troops northward. With the possibility of a freighter sailing direct to Chinhuangtao, our problems were greatly lessened. That was like landing in our own back yard. Not only that, but the later sailing would be compensated for by the savings in both time and money at the other end. At the same time the uncertainties regarding ongoing transportation when we got to Shanghai would be eliminated. As an added bonus it gave us more time in San Francisco to prepare for our trip. It didn't take us long to decide to try and book on the American ship.

I wasted no time getting down to the President Lines' office to try and book passage to Chinhuangtao and was happy indeed to be told that we would be given the last two spaces available. We then canceled our passage on the Swedish ship. Everything was going our way.

Since we had purchased almost everything that we needed, we decided that while we waited for the new Jeep to be delivered, we had time to go to New York to meet Father and the girls and bring them back with us to California. We felt sure that by that time the Jeep would be waiting for us. In addition, the trip to New York would give us a chance to visit some of Eva's aunts and uncles in the Boston area, whom she had not seen for many years. At the same time it would allow us to visit a number of the Christian Assemblies en route and let them know of our impending departure for China.

Unfortunately, we had been so confident of getting away in March that we had taken advantage of a good offer for the Dodge coupe that had served us so well and had sold it. We now needed another vehicle, but rather than buy one in San Francisco where prices were much higher, we decided to go by Greyhound bus to Chicago and pick up a car there.

We stayed a few days in Chicago visiting old friends and speaking at the various assemblies. I looked around for a used car and found a DeSoto sedan in good condition. Then, when I was just about to pay for it, the dealer showed me a brand new Chevrolet that had just come off the line in Detroit. It

had been turned down by the original purchaser because the front and rear bumpers, rather than being chrome covered, had been painted black. I could have purchased it for just a couple of hundred dollars more than the DeSoto, and was tempted to do so, because it obviously would give me better service than the used vehicle. However, on second thought I reluctantly bought the cheaper vehicle. To have driven around in a brand-new car while visiting our church associates would have given the impression that I didn't need their financial support in going back to China, and I couldn't afford to create that kind of misconception. Few of them were in a position at the end of the war to buy a new car. The only reason we could do so was because both Eva and I had saved almost all of our wartime pay, but we were by no means rich, and I thought it unwise to create that impression. I was to greatly regret the decision in the days that followed.

The day following the purchase of the car we were to leave Chicago after speaking at an evening service. We were to drive all night, and were due in Holland, Michigan, the next day to speak at another gathering. Before leaving Chicago, though, I took the precaution of first driving the DeSoto around to a garage, where I asked a mechanic to check it over to see if it needed any work. He told me the tires were all good, and they were not recaps (something that I could see for myself), and among other things that the generator, starter and battery were all in good condition. But there were a few minor items that needed attention, so I took it back to the dealer, who quite cheerfully agreed to make the repairs at no extra charge. Since it was then late in the afternoon and I was due on the other side of Chicago to speak at the evening service, I told the man we would pick the car up at around ten that night, and I asked him to leave it out in the lot, with the keys behind the sun visor.

It had been raining most of the day and was still coming down hard when we finally said our good-byes to our friends in Chicago. One of them kindly drove us back to the dealer's lot, where we found the car ready for us. Off we started with great confidence, on our way to Michigan.

Just outside the city limits the heavy rain turned to wet snow that packed up on the windshield, and the wipers barely made any impression on it. Driving became very difficult. We nonetheless moved along at a measured thirty miles an hour.

I began to notice a fast, distinct, intermittent yet regular "slapping" sound coming from the rear of the car. I hadn't the faintest idea what it could be and at first thought it might be snow being thrown up against the underside of the car. But then it began to sound worse. Around two o'clock in the morning, in one of the small towns we had to pass through, I pulled into the first gas station we saw open. When I got out to investigate the noise, I found to my dismay that the right rear tire was definitely not the one that had been on the car when I had paid for it. It was a recap, and the capping had been poorly done and was stripping off. The sound I had been hearing was the ever-lengthening strip coming off and slapping on the underside of the fender with each turn of the wheel. When I inspected the other three tires and the spare, I found that all of them were recaps and realized that the dealer had switched all the tires on me.

We were too far on our way to go back to Chicago, and we didn't have the time to do that anyway. We continued on our way using the spare, but were afraid to drive with any speed. Then a few miles farther, with the snow still coming down, my headlights started to go dim and I barely managed to get to an all-night garage before they went out completely. The mechanic told me that I needed a new generator. Again, the dealer had pulled a switch on me and substituted a broken-down old generator for the one that had been in there before. It cost me $50 to get a rebuilt replacement and I began to wonder what else he had changed on me. I didn't have to wait too long to find out, because a few days later the starter also went out on me. Not all used car dealers are so venal, but that one in Chicago certainly lived up to the worst reputation that any of them could have earned.

At that time in 1946, just after the war's end, it was impossible to buy a new tire without a certificate issued by the local "tire control board," which was charged with the responsibility of supervising new tire distribution. When we arrived in Holland, Michigan, we learned that Eva's uncle, Carl Frens, was a member of the tire board. Through him we were able to get a new tire, but only one. As we moved farther east we managed to get a second one, also through friends, and the other two held out until we got back to San Francisco several weeks and thousands of miles later.

From Michigan we headed across upper New York

state to Boston, battling heavy snow all the way, and over roads that had never seen a snow plow. The deep ruts in the frozen snow created by the many trucks that had been over the route made driving extremely hazardous, and I lived in fear that my tires would give out. The tires held, but the battery died when we were halfway there. It, too, had obviously been substituted.

But we made it safely to Boston. We visited for a few days with family members, and both of us spoke at dozens of assemblies in the many small towns nearby, including Methuen, where the people had been so generous in giving us the two vans for our use in China. Then, since it was getting close to the end of January, we headed for New York City, because it was about time for Father and the girls to arrive.

In New York I checked with the shipping line, Lykes Brothers, and received a shock when they told me their ship, the *Lipscomb Lykes*, was on schedule but had been diverted to Mobile, Alabama. We had to make a mad dash down there, driving day and night to get there in time, and we reached there just a few hours before the ship docked.

It was just after dawn when we reached Mobile. Without waiting to check into a motel, we headed straight for the docks. There they told us the ship was due at any minute. While waiting on the dock we became acquainted with an officer of the Immigration Service, and learned that it was he who would be inspecting the passengers once the ship arrived. He was an exceedingly affable chap, so unlike many of the INS people I had met before.

We had told the INS officer we were meeting my father and sisters on the incoming ship and that I had not seen them in four years. I was extremely nervous and afraid that he might not admit Ruth because of her disability. But I needn't have worried. He kindly offered to take us out to the ship when it anchored because it would, in all probability, be several hours before it could come alongside the pier. We gladly accepted his offer, and when the *Lipscomb Lykes* finally came into sight and dropped anchor, we accompanied him out on a small launch.

As we got closer, we could see Father and my two sisters standing by the rail with the other ten or twelve passengers the ship carried, but I felt a deep pang of regret that Mother wasn't there with them. The ship, a rather old freighter, either didn't have or didn't bother to let down the folding companionway that most ships carried. Instead they dropped a rope ladder over the side, and we had to climb some 20 feet or so to the deck. Although I had climbed a "Jacob's ladder" a few times before, it was a first-time experience for Eva. But, as one of the sailors on the launch held the bottom of the ladder to steady it, she gamely climbed to the top, where sailors on the ship helped her over the railing.

After four years it was good to see Father and the girls again. They had been on the ship for almost three weeks, with only one short stop in Trinidad, so they were not sorry to step ashore. Father decided to head straight for Boston where, as we later learned, he had been in touch with an old family friend, Isabel French, whom he married some months later. In the meantime Eva and I headed back to California in the old DeSoto with Ruth and Barbara.

Our cross-country trip along the southern route was uneventful. Once back in San Francisco we managed to fit my two sisters into our tiny apartment for a few weeks until we found a three-bedroom house for them across the bay in Alameda, an island that is now reached by bridges and tunnels. Some weeks later Father and his new bride arrived and took up residence there, and Ruth and Barbara moved in with them, although Barbara didn't stay very long. Eva and I stayed on in our apartment in San Francisco and busily packed the remainder of the stuff we wanted to take to China.

We found our new stepmother, Isabel, to be a delightful person. She was witty and vivacious, and although approaching seventy, was a person with boundless energy and enthusiasm. Although a very modest person, she nevertheless had a claim to fame, but one would never have suspected it. In her younger years she had been famous in the Boston area as a concert soprano. Born in Washington, D.C., her father, Philip Mauro, was the attorney who obtained the telephone patent for Alexander Graham Bell. In addition, she was the great-granddaughter of Pierre Duport, who had taught music to the children of Marie Antoinette. Another great-grandfather of hers, Alexander Reinagle, founded the Philadelphia Symphony Orchestra, started the first American theater, and wrote marches for George Washington and dance music for Martha Washington. None of us felt quite like calling her "Mother," so we settled for

"Moms," which she fully approved of. She immediately assumed responsibility for Ruth, who was an invalid at the time. But because of her age, Moms needed help in caring for Ruth, so Father was able to secure the services of an elderly lady, a Miss McCabe, who came as live-in help.

Barbara, who had cared for Ruth for so long, was thus freed to make a life for herself. She had very much wanted to return to China in missionary work, but since that door soon closed with the Communists taking over, she spent some weeks helping in a local orphanage in a small town not far from San Francisco. She later left for Chicago, where she took up a business career that lasted almost thirty years.

Our new Jeep was awaiting us when we got back to San Francisco and I took delivery of it a couple of days later, parking it in the rented garage a few blocks from our apartment. Then I went to a lumber yard and purchased a load of two-inch-thick, rough redwood boards, and some heavier wood for bracing, and set about building a shipping case for the Jeep and some of the other stuff we had bought. I intentionally used heavier lumber than would normally have been used, hoping to salvage it at the other end, where good wood was scarce. I also used two or three times as many nails as would normally have been required, and for the same reason. I took along a set of spare tires, which I had been able to persuade the tire board to allocate to me. I also carried spare axles and front and rear springs, together with miscellaneous parts for the engine. I had room left over to pack in some small trunks and suitcases, a keg or two of nails, and, of course, the tent I had bought, which was bulky and heavy and took up quite a lot of space.

One weekend we had a visit from two of Eva's cousins, Jim and Ernie Frens. Both were still serving in the Navy, but their ships had returned to San Francisco and the crews were about to be demobilized and their ships mothballed. We were able to fit the two lads into our apartment, where they slept head to head on the narrow corridor floor. Early on Sunday morning, we decided to get the tent down onto the street and see how big it actually was. The three of us managed to haul it down to the street and open it up in the middle of the road. Since there was no traffic to speak of, we decided to set it up and see just how many people it would hold. That may give the reader an idea of how casual things were in San Francisco in

1946.

The tent came with collapsible poles, but we naturally couldn't dig holes in the street for the end poles, so we improvised by using the large trees that grew on each side of the street. After a half hour or so we had the tent set up and found it would easily accommodate up to 200 people. It was exactly what I needed. Just what our neighbors must have thought of our Sunday morning goings on, I can only guess, but I imagine by that time they were pretty much used to my odd behavior; fortunately people in those days were much more tolerant and long-suffering than they are now.

It was on that same Sunday morning after we had packed the tent away and were heading for church in the old DeSoto that I saw some very nice wooden cases discarded on the sidewalk in front of a large apartment house not far from us. I decided I could really use them to pack some of our stuff. At church I asked around to see if I could borrow a trailer to haul them home. A young married couple told me they had an old trailer that they had just sold for $100, but the buyer wasn't picking it up until the following morning. They said I could borrow it if I could get it back to them by 9 o'clock the next day. I was sure we could manage that, so we hooked it on behind the DeSoto and headed home for lunch, intending to pick up the used packing cases in the afternoon.

So much for our plans. Exactly one block from our apartment house we had to cross a busy intersection with four-way stop signs. I stopped, as a car was waiting on my left. The driver waved, telling me to go ahead, but as I started across the street, he, too, started to move, and I noticed that he was maintaining eye contact with me rather than looking where he was going. I knew instinctively that he was going to cut too close behind my car and would hit the trailer. I was heading up a steep hill and was unable to accelerate, and sure enough, he ran right over the top of the trailer, smashing it flat.

The driver of the car was an Army major, a little the worse for drink even though it was just after noon, but very apologetic. He promised to pay for the damage he had caused and gave me his name and address and the phone number of his insurance company. Jim and Ernie Frens helped me drag the remains of the trailer back to the apartment, where we left it out on the sidewalk. I had to phone the young

couple to tell them the sad news that their trailer had been demolished.

But repairing that trailer was a challenge to us. The wheels and axle had come from an old Model T Ford. The wheels were narrow, with thin wooden spokes, and both wheels had been broken off the axle. One tire had burst and the body of the trailer was a disaster. However, we were able to buy some boards the next day and after straightening the metal frame we rebuilt the trailer body. With a liberal use of glue, we managed to put the wheels back together, and when we took the burst tire to a tire repair shop, they were able to bond a patch onto it. By week's end we had a practically brand-new trailer, all at the cost of about $10. Not only that, but the insurance company came through with a check for $150, and on the following Sunday when we returned the trailer to the young couple at church, not only were they able to sell it to the original buyer for $100 but we also gave them the $150 as well. Unfortunately, the packing crates that we had seen on the sidewalk, and which had been the reason for our borrowing the trailer in the first place, were picked up by the trash men before we could get to them.

Finally, just a few days before our ship was ready to sail, the Jeep was completely boxed and ready to go. Two days later the shipping company notified me that they were ready to load the Jeep aboard the ship. I contacted a firm that specialized in moving freight down to the docks. They arrived with a flatbed truck and a small mobile crane. In the meantime, I had jacked up the heavy crate, put short lengths of pipe crosswise under the two skids, and with very little effort Eva and I pushed it out of the garage and into the middle of the street. The crane operator, with professional nonchalance, moved his crane into position, but then, to my horror, instead of using rope slings under the crate to lift it, he started to use a huge grasping device, similar to ice tongs, and gripping the crate on each side, started to apply power. I rushed over to him and yelled to him to stop, telling him that the crate contained not only the Jeep but a lot of other stuff as well, and that it was much too heavy and not designed to be lifted in that manner. I told him that if he persisted, the bottom would fall out.

Imperiously he waved me to one side, telling me that they did it that way all the time, and everything would be all right. He again applied power and the cables started to tighten. I dutifully stood back, all the time visualizing my precious Jeep being raised ten feet into the air before the bottom dropped out. But I need not have worried. When the cables became taut, the man applied more power, and with a loud rasping sound the entire top of the crate pulled away from the platform base, leaving the Jeep and the rest of the contents of the case sitting there in the middle of the street on the undamaged bottom, with stuff spilling out on all sides.

The crane operator was both embarrassed and angry. They had to get a carpenter over to repair the damage. After a couple of hours and the eventual use of slings, the Jeep was transferred to the docks, and there, to my great relief, the stevedores were ready with metal hawsers, which they strung beneath the crate and hoisted it aboard the ship. I watched until it was safely stowed in the stern hold, and until one of the ship's officers told me the ship would definitely sail two days later. It was a wonderful feeling standing there on the dock looking up at the *President Grant* and imagining ourselves aboard her in just a couple of days.

Then the unbelievable happened. After feverishly packing up the rest of our stuff and relinquishing our apartment, we moved in with some friends for the last night, said our goodbyes to all our friends and family, and woke up to learn that dock workers on the entire West Coast had gone on strike and our ship's sailing would be delayed indefinitely. The strike, which was expected to last only a few days, continued for more than six months.

That was a period of extreme exasperation for us. We couldn't get back into our apartment because it had been snapped up the minute we relinquished it. We'd sold the car, so we had no transportation and were completely dependent on others to get around town. Furthermore, because the strike was only expected to last a few days, we started out living with friends, moving every couple of weeks to another friend's house, with our trunks and suitcases stored in three different places.

Ultimately, when it became obvious that the strike was going to go on indefinitely, we finally moved over to Alameda to share the house with the family. Although conditions were a little cramped, we all put up with it, thinking it was only temporary, but those were certainly the longest six months we have ever experienced.

We scanned the papers daily for news of the strike's end, but the days dragged by with nothing happening. Shortly before the strike started we had read in the paper one day of the arrival of the Swedish ship on which we had originally booked passage.

I spent much of my time those six months researching things that I thought might be helpful to the Chinese. I was very taken with the cinder blocks that were coming into vogue throughout the U.S. and thought how much better they would be for the Chinese to build with than their mud bricks. I went to several cinder block manufacturers and studied manufacturing techniques, hoping that some day we might perhaps set up a factory in Lingyuan. I also explored all the different kinds of well-drilling equipment, particularly the type that could be adapted to use by the Chinese without electrical power.

From childhood I had watched the Chinese dig wells, a slow and laborious process that could occupy the manpower of entire villages, sometimes with hundreds of men involved. They first dug a large circular hole and went down about 20 or 30 feet, bringing up all the earth in baskets on the end of ropes, sometimes using two or more windlasses at the top. Then they would branch outward with a ramp and carry the earth up in baskets on shoulder poles, using a small army of men. As the well got deeper, the ramp got deeper and longer, extending farther and farther out into open land. It was an extremely dangerous process because the banks on each side of the ramp were unprotected, and cave-ins were commonplace. When water was reached, they started to build up a rock lining for the well, then filled in the ramp as the work progressed. A deep well often took as long as a year to dig and could be more than 100 feet deep.

I filled those six months with many speaking engagements for church groups throughout the Bay Area. However, I couldn't keep away from the docks, and each day we studied the shipping page in the newspapers for ships arriving from China, and each time one came in, I would be down at the docks to meet it.

There were no commercial passenger ships operating across the Pacific at the time. However, the U.S. government was running regular trips from San Francisco to Shanghai with a former Navy transport, the *Lynx*, which, although it carried a few civilian passengers outward bound, was normally reserved for the military. On its return from Shanghai it carried a large number of civilians, and I always met it on arrival to glean news of what was going on in China. In that way I managed to meet a few old friends and acquaintances I'd not seen in some years and hear their stories of how they survived the war in China.

I saw some strange happenings on the piers over those several months each time the *Lynx* came in. When she came in, they always raised two gangplanks, one forward for the passengers and one at the stern for the crew, all U.S. Navy men. As they came off the ship carrying their heavy duffel bags over their shoulders, a U.S. Customs man met them at the foot of the gangplank to check their baggage. Like everything else, cigarettes were in short supply for civilians right after the war, and I noticed that most of the sailors carried a carton or two of cigarettes off the ship with them. As they walked past the Customs officer, they surreptitiously handed the cigarettes to him, and the sailors went their way without having to open a single bag for inspection. Rumors abounded as to what contraband they carried in with them.

On one occasion I was standing near the forward gangplank chatting with a Chinese traveler who had just gotten off the ship and was waiting with his bags for his Customs inspection. As we talked, the Customs officer came over and the Chinese gentleman opened his several suitcases for the officer. Most of the bags seemed to contain clothing and ordinary articles of travel, but one of them was filled to capacity with wrist watches. As I watched, the Customs officer, with no attempt at concealment, grabbed a handful of the watches, thrust them into his trouser pocket, and marked the rest of the bags without looking into a single one of them. Those are only some of the numerous instances of corruption I witnessed. Having lived almost my entire life in China, where graft and corruption were considered the normal way of life and where almost any official could be bought, I was shocked to see that it could happen in America as well. It is not my intention to impugn the integrity of the U.S. Customs Service as a whole. I know that on every occasion whenever we had to pass U.S. Customs, they always did a conscientious and thorough job. Their honesty and reputation for being unbribable is well known. However, at the end of the

war things were different, and conditions all over were in a state of flux. It was obvious that discipline was lax, and many of the regular staffers who had gone into the military services had not yet returned. In all probability, the men I saw were temporary staff members whose morale was low because they knew their jobs were soon to be terminated.

Among the many things I learned from the travelers about conditions in Shanghai was that the Chinese government was being sticky about imports. Millions of tons of war surplus supplies were in various parts of the Far East, and much of it was being given to the Chinese. A number of Chinese government officials had their own monopoly on what could be imported and what could not, and for some strange reason, among the embargoed items were suitcases. That was brought to my attention because so many of the travelers getting off the *Lynx* were carrying their possessions in wicker baskets or simply wrapped in a tarpaulin or a blanket tied with rope.

Many times I watched the *Lynx* leave for Shanghai, wishing we could sail aboard her and forget all about the other ship. However, we were committed because the Jeep was already aboard the cargo ship *President Grant*, so we simply had to wait for the strike to end. The months dragged by with no settlement, but on December 13 the situation changed.

I had gone over to San Francisco that day to conduct some business. The newspapers, as usual, were reporting a possible settlement of the strike in the offing, but I had paid little heed, because we had heard such reports before and had been disappointed every time.

Around four in the afternoon I phoned Eva to tell her that my business was finished and I was about to head for home, and she excitedly told me that the President Lines had phoned to say that the strike had been settled and that our ship would sail that very night. They gave strict instructions that we were to be aboard by 11 p.m. at the latest.

That was a shock. I had exactly seven hours in which to accomplish all that needed to be done. First, I had to get some cash from the bank, which was already closed. I went to our bank on Market Street and tried the front door, but it was locked. I banged on the door a few times without result. I could see that lights were still on and people were moving about, but no one took any notice of me. I was sure that if I could get their attention and explain the situation they would do something for me, so I continued hammering on the door.

Without warning I suddenly felt a heavy hand on my shoulder and turned to find a burly policeman who wanted to know what I was doing. I explained the situation to him, and unlikely as it must have sounded to him, he apparently believed me. He took me around to the back door where he quickly got the attention of the people inside. They let us in and as soon as I had explained my dilemma, they immediately gave me the money I needed even though I didn't have my checkbook with me.

My next job was to get in touch with the three families in San Francisco where some of our baggage had been stored and arrange for them to get it down to the pier for us. Some of it was heavy. The large steamer trunks had to go into the ship's hold and needed to be taken down to the pier immediately. I accompanied them and saw to it that they were taken aboard. The lighter stuff could wait until we went aboard that night. When all that had been accomplished it was already after 9 p.m. I dashed back to Alameda, where Eva had completed all the packing of our personal effects. We ate a late supper, said our goodbyes to the family, and friends drove us back across the bridge to the pier to board the ship.

When we arrived, conditions were quite different from what they had been a few hours earlier. We found the ship's crew and all the stevedores having a momentous party on the pier. Almost all of them were drunk, including the ship's captain. One of the stevedores enthusiastically grabbed two of our suitcases and started up the gangplank, only to fall off into the water when halfway up. Most fortunately, he threw the bags as he fell and they landed on the pier. While the rest of the crowd fished him out of the bay, we carried our own stuff aboard. There we found just one sober officer on duty. We were somewhat disappointed when he directed us to two different cabins, and didn't find out who our cabin mates were until later. It was the following morning when we learned why we hadn't been given a cabin to ourselves.

So much was going on that we abandoned any attempt to sleep and watched as departure preparations were made, hoping that the captain wouldn't be too inebriated to navigate the ship under the Golden Gate Bridge. We need not have been concerned.

Around midnight the ship pulled away from the dock amid loud shouts from the assembled stevedores and a few sightseers. After all, ours was the first American, non-military ship to sail from San Francisco in six months. Everyone was overjoyed, none more so than Eva and I. As we pulled away from the pier, our spirits rose, and we finally had the feeling that after all the frustrations of the past year or so, we were actually on our way. But more surprises were in store.

The ship slowly moved out into the bay and turned toward the Golden Gate. As we were approaching Alcatraz Island, to our surprise, the ship slowed and dropped anchor. There we stayed until the next morning. It didn't occur to us to ask anyone at the time just why we had stopped. We presumed that the captain preferred to wait until morning light, or perhaps they had been unable to get a pilot. In any case we went off to bed.

The next morning at breakfast, we were informed by the captain that during the long shutdown of the ship, the refrigeration system had deteriorated to the point where it needed repairs. Rather than stay tied to the pier where daily fees ran to thousands of dollars, the company had decided to move the ship out into the bay and have the work done there. He told us the repairs were not expected to take more than a day, but three days later we were still there.

The *President Grant* was one of the new "Victory" ships, successors to the ugly duckling of the war years, the "Liberty" class. It was a much larger and considerably faster ship, modern in all its construction, and with accommodations for exactly twelve passengers, who were housed in four identical three-berth cabins, although, as we soon discovered, only nine civilians were aboard.

Apart from ourselves, there was one other married couple, and they had a cabin to themselves. Middle-aged business people who owned their own gift shop, they were en route to China on a buying expedition. Eva and I, having bought our tickets somewhat later than the others, were separated. Eva bunked in with two somewhat elderly ladies who were on a sightseeing trip. I found myself in with two Chinese professors who were on their way home after studying in the U.S. during the war years. One of them had just graduated from Massachusetts Institute of Technology, the other from the University of

California at Berkeley. The ninth passenger was Bob McCann, an American businessman from Tientsin, whom we had met once or twice before in Tientsin. He had a cabin to himself, having been the first one to buy a ticket. He was head of Frazer Federal, Inc., the Dodge agency in China.

The accommodations were comfortable and not at all crowded. There were two bunks, stacked one above the other, and under the porthole in each cabin was a couch that was made up into a bed at night. We ate with the officers in a large dining room forward, which was right under the bridge and extended the full width of the ship. Between meals it served as a recreation room where passengers and off-duty officers could play cards or just sit and read. In one corner were some glassed-in cabinets where a limited number of books were available. In a cupboard were games such as chess, checkers, and so on, and copies of current magazines were scattered around on side tables.

Those three days at anchor in San Francisco harbor were without question the most tedious and boring I think any of us ever experienced. We were anxious to be on our way, and the delay seemed so unnecessary. The repair boat came out each morning and the men worked on the refrigeration plant. Apart from that, and the passing traffic in the bay, there was nothing much to see or do, and we were all champing at the bit by the middle of the second day.

There was very little deck space for walking, so finally, several of us went to the captain and begged him to launch a boat and put us ashore for a few hours of exercise. He was a very nice young chap in his mid-30s and was quite understanding of our boredom. However, he explained that officially we had departed the U.S. and to go ashore would entail endless red tape. Just when we thought it was a lost cause he relented, and told us that after dark he would put a boat out and drop us on a secluded beach for a few hours, but he warned us not to attract attention or get caught.

When darkness came we boarded the boat and were landed on a beach near where the San Francisco Giants baseball team's Candlestick Park now stands. There was no dock, so the ship's boat was just run up onto the beach as far as it would go. We then had to take off our shoes and socks and wade the rest of the way, but it was fun. The officer in charge of the boat

told us he would be back there at the same spot at midnight to pick us up, and he left us on our own. We walked over to Highway 101 nearby, managed to flag down some empty taxis returning to the city, and headed for downtown San Francisco. Once there, some went window shopping and others took in a movie. It was certainly a welcome change from being cooped up on a ship that was going nowhere.

Eva and I headed for Chinatown and had some Chinese food. We found a telephone booth and phoned my father in Alameda to tell him about our delay. Expecting us to be somewhere far out in the Pacific, he was at first shocked but agreeably surprised to hear our voices. When midnight came, we were all waiting at the beach, and shortly thereafter were back aboard ship without having run afoul of the authorities during our "illegal" landing on American soil. The next afternoon, December 16, 1946, the anchor was raised, and we slipped under the Golden Gate Bridge shortly before dark. The ship was to be our home for the next three weeks.

In some ways that was one of the most enjoyable of all the many sea voyages we've taken. The crew was friendly, happy to be at sea again after being tied up at a pier in San Francisco for so many months, and our fellow passengers were a sociable group with whom we found we had much in common. We soon became close friends with Bob McCann. We found him a delightful traveling companion and an interesting conversationalist, full of optimism over the future of China and his business interests there, something I was unable to agree with, although I hoped he was right. He was a healthy young man at the time, but, tragically, he was destined within a year or two to become a prisoner of the Chinese Communists, who put him into a Chinese jail, where they kept him in solitary confinement for years. He was released only after he had contracted cancer, which they did nothing to relieve. Seeing that he was dying, they dropped him off at the border between Hong Kong and China and he died a few days after reaching freedom.

My two Chinese cabin mates interested me greatly. Both were fluent in English, but we spoke in Chinese most of the time. Strange to say, both had somehow formed a very strong dislike for America and all things American, including its people, and were not the least bit hesitant in expressing their opinions. We had long conversations as I tried to give them a different view of America, but they had both become soured, and for no particular reason that I could determine. Perhaps it was partially because of the wealth and extravagance of what they considered the average American, and also because of either real or imagined discrimination while at school. One of them, I'll call him Professor Liu, was the MIT man. He and Professor Ma (not his real name), had a very low opinion of American women in general, and of American men who put up with them. Of the two, Liu was the most outspoken. He told me that his own marriage in China had been a failure because of American movies and the American way of life. He said his wife had spent most of her time watching American films and aping the ways of the American women she saw — spending money in stores, playing bridge, and never being at home to cook his meals or to take care of his needs and those of their children, leaving everything to a servant. He said he had left her for those reasons and had gone to America. But he was now sorry that he had done so.

Both men had been in the United States for more than four years, having left China just before Pearl Harbor; however, in that entire period, neither of them had been inside an American home, nor had either of them ever become friendly enough with any of their American fellow students to really understand American ways. Their judgment was based purely on what they observed in the behavior of their fellow students, men and women, at school, or watching them in the streets, in stores, or at movies. I found it discouraging trying to change their opinions and attitudes. Both planned on joining the Communist Party when they arrived in China. They felt Communism would be the only salvation for their country. I finally gave up trying to convince them otherwise.

Our first ten days at sea were pleasant and uneventful. The weather was mostly fair and the seas only moderately rough. However, my two Chinese friends were both seasick and spent almost the entire time in the cabin. Christmas came and went with only minor festivities, but some good food. Then, three days after Christmas, I was on the bridge talking with the captain when he told me that the barometer was dropping rapidly and he suspected we were in for some really bad weather. In fact, he said, he had never seen a barometer drop so quickly. He thought there was a strong possibility it might be a hurricane, or typhoon

(dafeng), as such storms are called in the Pacific. He expressed concern because, being the first and only ship to have left San Francisco, there were no other ships in the area except one other American one three days behind us. The captain was unable to get any weather reports from elsewhere. Hawaii had no reports of bad weather, and he hadn't the slightest idea from which direction the bad weather was approaching.

The sky that morning was a brilliant blue and the sea deceptively calm. It had every appearance of turning out to be a beautiful day. But within the hour the wind started up, getting stronger as the minutes passed. In no time, the wind was an incessant roar. We could still see blue skies directly overhead, but the wind was so strong, sheets of water were blowing over the ship like heavy rain, the ship was listing to one side, and in the distance heavy black clouds were starting to pile up. Shortly thereafter the clouds were overhead, and the wind was increasing in intensity every minute. We knew we were in for a sizable typhoon.

As so often happens in a typhoon at sea, the wind kept changing directions, so the captain couldn't determine the true direction of the storm. He turned the ship into the wind one minute and a few minutes later it was blowing just as heavily from another direction, and he had to turn the ship again. "Sparks," the radio operator, kept trying to raise some other ship in the vicinity to get a weather report, but we were apparently alone in the far Pacific, and the only ship to answer his calls was the American ship that was three days behind us. They reported their barometer dropping, but the weather there was still clear.

All that afternoon and through the night the wind continued to intensify until it reached 120 miles an hour, when the anemometer, a device for measuring the force of the wind, was blown away from where it was installed on top of the bridge. Through the night the movement of the ship was so violent that we made no attempt to go to bed as it would have been impossible to stay in our bunks. The ship pitched, rolled from side to side, and bounced around like a cork. Every few seconds we would hear a resounding "boom," and the ship would shudder as a huge wave would hit us from an angle. No one could sleep, and the only place we could find where we had any sense of security was a long couch amidships in the corridor just outside the dining saloon. The couch was designed to seat six, but eight of us squeezed into it, and we remained there through the night as the storm howled around us, the noise so loud we had to shout into each other's ears to be heard.

Normally one of these storms usually blows over in a few hours, but that one stayed with us for nearly fifty hours. The captain kept changing course, hoping to run out of the storm, but we were slowed down by the violence of the wind and the tremendous waves. We made very little headway, and through that first night the storm continued to get worse instead of better. At dawn the sky was still black, and by mid-morning the captain estimated that the wind had exceeded 145 miles an hour.

Early on the second morning the waves crashed over the prow of the ship so violently that the deck cargo, consisting of lumber and 50-gallon metal drums, started to break loose. From where we sat we could hear loud thuds and bangs against the heavy metal plating below the bridge and just under our dining saloon. The steel drums contained acid of some kind, either sulfuric or hydrochloric, I forget which. When I went forward to peer through one of the front portholes I could see some of the drums rolling back and forth across the deck, and every now and then, when a wave came over the prow, one would be tossed up against the bridgework below. They were obviously leaking. With each wave more and more of the lumber pile was also breaking up, and was being washed overboard.

The captain called for volunteers to go out and try to secure the drums, and several seamen trudged out with safety ropes tied around their waists. It was immediately apparent that to try and tie the drums down again would be futile. In complete disregard of the danger, and in between waves, the seamen man-handled the drums to the side and threw them overboard. But since many of them had been damaged and were leaking badly, the men suffered burns on their exposed faces and hands.

Eva and I had worked with burns before. We went to the bosun's medicine locker, but the only thing we could find was some boric acid. We poured a quantity of it into a bathtub and made a solution for the men to bathe in after they had been hosed down outside. They were in some pain, but the solution seemed to help, and none of them suffered serious aftereffects.

Just as we were finishing that job, we smelled smoke, and over the PA system came the call of "Fire!" I ran back down the corridor to the mid-point of the ship and saw smoke pouring out from under the door of the paint locker. Apparently some cans of paint thinner had crashed to the floor and broken open, and an electrical short had started a blaze. Fortunately it was confined to that one room and was quickly extinguished, but it was a scary time for everyone.

Just after "lunch" — one of the stewards bravely handed out sandwiches — and with the wind howling as badly as ever, suddenly an ominous sense of stillness pervaded the ship, and we realized that the engines had stopped. We never learned what the actual cause was, but it took nearly three hours to restart the engines. In the meantime, the ship drifted broadside to the wind, which was so strong the ship lay on her side at a fearsome angle, held there by the intensity of the wind. From where we sat we looked down sideways through the glass ports of the closed double doors directly into the ocean. Every few minutes a wave crashed up against the doors just a few feet away from us. The main deck railings were under water, and the side wing of the bridge, usually about 40 feet or more above the water, was pounded badly by the waves and suffered considerable damage.

Twice during the storm we passed through the eye of the typhoon. Anyone who has not had that experience at sea cannot conceive of the majesty of such a phenomenon. One moment there is nothing but the incessant roar of the wind, and because of the driving spume, one cannot see more than a few feet over the side of the ship. Then suddenly comes a lull and a complete stillness of the air. Most eerie of all was the total silence — no sound whatsoever except for the waves pounding against the ship and the creaks and groans caused by the incessant motion of the ship, something we'd been unable to hear before. Surrounding us and as far as we could see loomed a wall of towering black clouds, swirling around us in a circular motion, and there, directly above us, was clear blue sky, and every now and then a burst of sunshine. Altogether one was lulled into a false sense of security. Then the ship headed once again into the cloud bank on the far side of the circle and the wind was back with us again, seemingly blowing harder than ever before.

During the entire storm the captain hadn't left the bridge even to eat, and the rest of us hadn't been able to use the dining saloon either, because nothing would stay on the tables. One of the stewards staggered around with plates of sandwiches every now and then, regardless of the time of day or night, and we managed to get a drink of water when we became thirsty. Two or three times that day I went up to the bridge to offer my help if it were needed. Conditions there were, in some ways, even worse. The ship rolled so violently and the waves were so immense that several windows on both sides of the bridge had been smashed. Temporary boarding had been placed over the openings, but the howling wind made verbal communication on the bridge impossible.

The second night dragged by, and dawn finally came with no cessation of the wind. Then, around ten o'clock that morning, as we were all sitting tightly packed together on the couch, I suddenly noted the unmistakable smell of gasoline. I knew we were carrying a cargo of high-octane gasoline and new tires in one of the aft holds, so I immediately dashed up to the bridge and told the captain. He didn't hesitate for even a second, nor did he question my information. He instantly gave orders for everything electrical on the ship to be turned off immediately and for all doors and portholes to be opened to vent the ship.

The crew members raced around opening everything, and the immediate effect was mind-boggling. Anything loose that could be picked up by the wind was suddenly sucked out of every opening. In the cabins, sheets and blankets were sucked out the portholes and towels vanished off the racks. Any clothing lying around disappeared. Even those sitting on the couch felt as though their clothing was being torn off. Breathing became very difficult, and the driving spume carrying through the center of the ship between the two open doors on each side immediately soaked everyone to the skin. When trying to stand or walk, we had to hang onto the nearest solid object, and I'm sure that all the others felt as Eva and I did, that our last moment on earth had come.

I wasn't with the others on the couch. The captain couldn't leave the bridge, but the first mate, a young Irishman, stocky, but not much more than five feet in height, raced down from the bridge with an already lit electric lantern in his hand, and I gave chase as he tore down the stairways and then down a series of ladders to the very bottom of the ship, where there was an access door into the rear hold. I had watched my Jeep being loaded aboard in San Francisco, so I knew that that was the hold it was in, and I wanted to see if it was still in one piece.

There were no lights on, and in the pitch blackness I held the lantern for the first mate as, with his fist, he hammered open the metal dogs that held shut a small hatchway leading into the hold. When he'd opened it, we peered together into the blackness. It was an awesome experience, one that has lived in my memory. The motion of the ship, far down below water level where we were, was quite unlike what it had been up on the bridge and not nearly so pronounced. Even so, it was most difficult to keep our footing. The gasoline fumes pouring through the opened hatchway were so overpowering that both of us gagged and had to tie handkerchiefs over our noses and mouths. In the blackness inside, with the powerful beam of the lantern, we could see gasoline drums that had broken loose, and as we watched, some slid back and forth, crashing up against each other with each roll of the ship. One drum in particular caught our eye. It had apparently been one of those on a second level stacked on top of the others and had broken loose, and with each roll of the ship, it sailed through the air from side to side of the ship like a ping-pong ball, spouting a thin stream of gasoline. The danger of a spark setting off an explosion was so real that I was certain any second could be my last.

The first mate didn't hesitate for a moment. Sizing up the situation, he handed me the lantern and told me to stay outside, but to follow him with the beam of the lantern. He squeezed through the small opening, and despite the danger of being crushed, single-handedly moved the loose drums around until he could once again tie them down securely, but it took him the best part of an hour. From where I stood I could see the crate with my Jeep inside, and it appeared undamaged, for which I was thankful. At the same time I really didn't care, because I doubted I would ever get the chance to use it. I was certain the ship was going to blow up at any moment. Then, as the first mate continued to tie down the drums, I suddenly saw a chink of daylight far above us and realized that the captain had sent some men to open up the hatch cover to vent the hold. Within a few seconds, as more hatch covers came off, I could feel the wind sucking through the hatchway where I stood, carrying the fumes up to the open air above.

After another hour or so the captain declared the emergency over and the doors and portholes were all closed up. Everyone breathed a little more easily and thanked God for our safe deliverance, and then a sort of strange euphoria took over. We all felt reborn. We laughed and shouted to each other and even broke into song. My two Chinese professor friends had long since recovered from their seasickness, and Prof. Liu, an avid amateur photographer, said he wanted to take some pictures of the storm.

From the level of the main deck little could be seen of the waves forward, and it was much too dangerous to attempt to climb atop the bridge. However, amidships, where the single funnel was, it was high enough that we thought we could get a good view of the prow. Together with Prof. Ma, the three of us started off, one on each side of Prof. Liu, who was loaded with cameras. Holding tightly onto his arms as we battled against the wind, we made our way to a stern ladder that led up to the boat deck and approached the funnel from the rear. Up there the wind was much more pronounced, but there was less water being driven through the air. The only way we could make any headway was by hauling ourselves along the deck, grabbing onto anything that was bolted down. At the foot of the huge funnel we had a good view forward. A ladder led up to a small platform on the forward part of the funnel where it serviced the ship's horn, but Prof. Liu wasn't satisfied until we climbed the funnel itself and installed ourselves on the minuscule platform where, crowded together, we had a wonderful vantage point from which to view the prow as we plowed into the monstrous waves ahead.

Why we took such risks is hard to explain. It must have been from the sense of relief after the near disaster of the gasoline leakage. Perhaps, having survived that, we felt subconsciously that by comparison nothing could be so dangerous. I recall that as we stood there, we were filled with a sense of exhilaration. As we climbed the narrow ladder up the funnel, completely soaked by the driving spume, we laughed and shouted with joy even as the wind threatened every moment to tear us off the ladder. Once on the platform we crouched there in silent awe. With the rolling of the ship, high as we were, at one moment

we would be hanging in space, far out over the water; then, whip-like, the ship would jerk back in the opposite direction, and a second or two later we'd be looking directly down into the water on the opposite side. Simultaneously the ship was pitched forward and backward with monotonous regularity as it climbed one wave, then dropped into the trough between it and the next.

Our young captain told us later that, although he'd been at sea since he was a teenager, he'd never seen a storm like that one and had never seen waves so huge, estimating them at well over 100 feet. From where we were on the funnel, probably 100 feet higher than the surface of the water, the ship below us was diminished in size, and we marveled that she stayed afloat. I've ridden on roller coasters, and as the ship raced down the back of a wave into the deep trough behind it, the sensation was much the same. High as we were on our perch, we still had to crane our necks and look upward to see the top of the oncoming waves.

For the first few minutes on the platform, we were completely mesmerized. As we seemingly crawled up the side of one monstrous wave, then topped it, we looked downward, and the entire ship below us was foreshortened and appeared far too tiny and insubstantial to be able to face the chasm ahead. Then the ship seemed to tilt forward before beginning its rush down the back of the wave, and the next approaching wave towered far above us as we dove farther and farther down into the trough. We crouched on the platform, hanging on tightly, terrified yet exhilarated as we watched the prow of the ship bury itself directly into the base of the oncoming wave and completely disappear from view as the green water surged over the forward deck and crashed against the bridge, completely engulfing it while foaming white water swept around and above the bridge, even reaching back to the base of the funnel below us. We felt each time it happened that there was no possible way the ship could survive, but beneath us we could feel the ship tremble and then gradually pull itself up, frothing white water pouring off in all directions as slowly, the prow and forward deck would reappear from under a mass of foam, and begin to climb the monstrous wave ahead. As we clung to the platform with both feet and hands, completely speechless, another part of the unusual ride was caused by the violent side-to-side rolling of the ship, which, combined with the front-to-back pitching, resulted in a corkscrew-like motion. And the odd angles at which the prow would enter the oncoming waves, seeming sometimes to be skidding sideways instead of approaching the wave head on, was both terrifying and fascinating to watch. At times our sideways skid was so pronounced when we got down into the trough of the wave that we appeared about to broach parallel to the oncoming wave. That would have been disastrous, as the huge wave, instead of being in front of us, was suddenly alongside of us, seemingly close enough for us to reach out and touch it. Each time it happened it seemed impossible that we could avoid being sucked under. It was only at the last second that we found ourselves jerked back and then the ship was rolling and sliding in the opposite direction at breakneck speed. We timed the rolls and it took exactly nine seconds to complete each of them.

When Professor Liu finally started to use his camera, he took some magnificent pictures, copies of which he sent me later. I've never seen anything quite like them before or since; unfortunately, like everything else we owned, we lost them to the Chinese Communists.

We must have remained on the platform for almost an hour, completely fascinated with the awesome sight of nature on a rampage. We suddenly became aware that the sun was trying to break through, and the wind seemed to be abating somewhat. Instead of one continuous roar, with the wind sucking the air out of our lungs, we began to have short periods where the wind seemed to come in gusts from different directions. Then, almost as suddenly as it had started, the storm was over, and we were back in bright sunshine. Although the seas remained rough through the night, by next morning we had only moderate swells. At breakfast the radio operator told us he had been in contact with the American ship three days behind us. They had just entered the storm and already their deck cargo had been lost, and the cargo below decks had shifted so that the ship had a pronounced list. I think our captain had visions of having to go back through the storm to rescue them, but we heard nothing further from them as the day progressed.

I've experienced at least six hurricanes or typhoons since then, two of them aboard the *Queen Mary* on the Atlantic, but none approached the intensity of that particular storm on the Pacific and I never want to see one quite like it again. However, the fact that our relatively small ship lived through it gave me a sense of such utter confidence in ocean-going steamers that every trip by sea since then has been an absolute delight.

That was the last bad weather we experienced as, day by day, we came ever closer to the Chinese mainland. We made no stops in Japan, but just after dusk one day when we were still well over a thousand miles off the Japanese coast, we came across a fleet of Japanese fishing boats. Those hardy fishermen were far out in the open ocean in tiny boats, few of them carrying navigation lights, some passing so close we could see the faces of the occupants, men and women, as they waved to us in friendly greeting. How different it had been just a few months before when our ships of war had prowled those waters, sinking everything in sight.

It was then late December. New Year's Day came and went almost unnoticed, and the weather grew so cold it was only possible to stay on deck a few minutes at a time. Nevertheless, we welcomed that cold north wind because it was blowing from China. Eagerly, we followed our track on the ship's chart as we moved through the East China Sea into the Yellow Sea, which incidentally, is one of the shallowest bodies of ocean water anywhere, averaging only a little over 100 feet deep throughout. Once there we kept a sharp lookout for the first sight of our beloved homeland. Finally we saw the familiar outline of the rugged coast of the Shandong Peninsula on our left. We headed up through the Gulf of Po Hai, and by mid-morning on January 4th, we could discern the high peaks of the mountain range behind Chinhuangtao. I was on the bridge when we first spotted the tips of the mountain peaks far in the distance. As we drew closer, the captain handed me his high-powered binoculars, and I could clearly see the oft-visited section of the Great Wall near Shanhaiguan, winding its way up the sides of the mountains, and then I knew that we were really home once again. Shortly I could see, through the powerful glasses, the lookout tower on top of the bluff where I had spent so many happy hours as a boy watching ships such as ours come up over the horizon.

Late in the afternoon we dropped anchor about a mile off the harbor of Chinhuangtao. Almost before the ship had come to a stop the familiar Kailan Mining Administration's seagoing tug, the *Kailan*, on which I had ridden so many times as a boy, was hovering nearby. The harbor master, an old friend, came aboard with a warm welcome and an invitation from Mr. Chilton, KMA superintendent in Chinhuangtao, for the captain, his officers, and Eva and me, as former residents, to be his guests at the club for dinner.

We were naturally anxious for our journey to end; however, it was too late in the day for the Customs officials to come aboard, and a space alongside the pier would not be available until the next day, so everything had to wait. Instead, we boarded the tug and headed for shore as our fellow passengers watched enviously.

Stepping ashore on familiar ground after being away for more than four years was a tremendous thrill. Nothing there in Chinhuangtao had changed. It was just like old times once again. During dinner at the club we met many old friends and exchanged stories of our wartime experiences. Some of them had also been interned and later exchanged for Japanese prisoners of the allies, others had sat out the war in various internment camps. A few had managed to get away to England just before hostilities broke out and had experienced the bombing of London and other parts of England. But all of them, like ourselves, were delighted to be back in China once again.

It was after 11 p.m. when the party broke up and the tug took us back to the ship. It was a bitterly cold night, with a choppy sea and a strong wind blowing out of the north. We all huddled in the wheelhouse until we came alongside the *President Grant*, only to find there was no accommodation ladder awaiting us, no one in sight on deck, and no lookout on the bridge. We circled the ship several times with the tug's horn blowing, but the wind was making so much noise that I guess they couldn't hear us below decks, because we failed to rouse anyone. Later we learned they had all been involved in a major crap game below decks, and with the extreme cold, had closed everything up tight.

The captain was of course furious because the one junior officer he had left aboard had been so lax. We finally realized no one could hear the tug's horn, and it was either go back ashore or try somehow to climb aboard as best we could. The tug's captain, another old friend of mine, suggested we could get aboard

with no problem whatsoever. He told us he had a *fazi*, — "a way" to do it. With great aplomb he pulled the tug up close on the lee side, near the stern, but even there the waves were such that one minute we were high above the deck of the *President Grant* and the next minute we were in a trough of a wave looking up to the railing. That didn't faze the Chinese crew of the tug; they were old hands at that sort of thing.

Stored atop the tug's wheelhouse was a long wooden board, some twenty feet long and about a foot wide. Three men worked it up over the railing above the wheelhouse, pushing it upward and outward until most of its length was out over the side. The tug's captain then worked his vessel as close as possible to the *President Grant*, and, timing his move between the swells, they dropped the far end of the board onto the railing of the *President Grant*. Instantaneously, one of the Chinese seamen scampered across the board with a short piece of rope in his hand and tied the far end of the board securely to the ship's railing. The tug's captain then held the tug in position as best he could, as one by one the men made their way across the board. The precaution had been taken of tying a rope around the waist of each person as they went across, as a fall into that icy sea would have been a nasty experience.

When it came Eva's turn, one of the ship's officers stood on the far end of the board, supported by a man on each side, extending his hand as far as he could reach. I stood on the tug end of the board in the same manner, tied the rope around Eva, and helped her up. Then, holding on with one hand to the outstretched hand of one of the men who was supporting me, I handed Eva out toward the center of the board, watching in the dim glow from the ship's deck lights as the waves came toward us to see the ideal moment to let go of her so she could run across the ten feet or so in between the outstretched hands.

It was a hazardous undertaking at best, and it took a lot of nerve on Eva's part, particularly with the gusts of wind battering us and the sight and sound of the swirling waves 20 feet or more below. Eva stood in front of me as I held onto her hand, waiting for the word from me. The tug rose and fell with the swells, and then there was a very brief moment when the board was level. I shouted "go" in Eva's ear, and with the board bending ominously under the combined weight of the three of us, Eva started forward, as I watched with my heart in my mouth. But she made it safely to the other side and caught onto the officer's hand just as the tug behind her began to drop into a trough. We were all thankful to have made it safely across.

The next morning two Chinese Customs officers came aboard. Ours was the first American ship in port since the end of the war, and they were most friendly and cooperative. All of us, particularly Eva and I, had a considerable amount of baggage with us, and all of us expected to pay some duty on our belongings. But after filling out the necessary forms, we plied the two men with coffee, Cokes and sandwiches. We then gave each of them a half dozen cartons of American cigarettes, and I asked one of them what they had missed the most and had been unable to buy during the war. One of them said he had not been able to buy a decent shirt. Bob McCann and I each went to our cabins and managed to produce a shirt for each of them and our personal baggage went unopened, including all our trunks down in the hold, and not a cent of duty was levied.

But declaring the Jeep was another matter entirely. The Customs officers reluctantly informed me that I had a big problem. If I had been importing a sedan, or any other kind of passenger automobile, they could have passed it. However, a Jeep had been arbitrarily classified as a quarter-ton truck, and the import of any trucks was prohibited without a special permit. It turned out that a prominent Chinese official, a relative of Chiang Kai-shek, had taken over the monopoly of importing trucks into China, and without his specific permission, no truck could be brought in. He had fallen heir to thousands of U.S. Army surplus trucks and was bringing them in from all over the Far Eastern theater, the Philippines and other island bases.

It was a problem of the first magnitude for me. The Customs officials told me I would have to go up to Tientsin to try to get the necessary permits, but they were not optimistic. They knew of no commercial trucks having been allowed in. They did, however, tell me I could store the Jeep without charge in bond ashore for a limited time in their Customs' warehouse until a decision had been reached, and that was at least better than having it shipped back to the United States.

Later that morning we slowly pulled alongside the pier. Crowds of coolies gathered below, shouting for coins or cigarettes. As we stood by the rail with our fellow passengers, the other married couple standing next to us, I noticed the coolies immediately below us on the wharf were laughing uproariously and pointing up toward the man and wife next to us. The word soon spread and more and more coolies came. I was puzzled at first and couldn't figure out what they were pointing at nor what was amusing them. Then I heard the shouted words, *lu maozi* — "green hat" — and I looked over to see that the husband had a bright green woolen cap pulled down over his ears. Just as we sometimes refer to some poor husband "wearing horns," those imaginary projections on a cuckold's head, the Chinese use the expression "wearing a green hat" to refer to someone whose wife has been unfaithful to him. I discreetly told our friend what all the uproar was about, and he retreated to his cabin to find something more suitable in the way of headgear. I'm sure that he and his wife found that to be a rude introduction to the China they had so much looked forward to visiting for the first time.

Once we were off the ship, we deposited our hand baggage at the KMA guest house and took the ship's officers, the two Customs men and all of our fellow passengers to a Chinese restaurant we knew well. We ate a sumptuous meal that tasted all the better for the many years we had had to wait for it. Eva and I were staying over in Chinhuangtao for a few days, but the rest of the passengers were leaving for Tientsin by train the next morning. That evening, the Customs people had asked Professor Liu to give them a talk about his life in America, and Professor Liu invited Eva and me to go along, although I'm sure that later he regretted having done so.

Approximately four hundred Chinese officials gathered in the hall, and from the beginning, Liu's speech was completely anti-American. The more he talked, the more annoyed I became, because most of what he said was utter rubbish, and I could tell from the reaction of the audience around me that it wasn't what they had expected to hear. But there was nothing I could do about it until the end of his talk, when he said he would be open to questions.

During the talk, Professor Liu expounded his favorite theme: American women. How they were spendthrifts, wasting their husbands' hard-earned money; spending most of their leisure time either at the movies or playing bridge; how they were never home to welcome their husbands when they returned after a day's work, and weren't there to make their husband's meals, nor to take care of their children, and so on. He went on to elaborate on the promiscuity of American women, and stated that every American husband, when he left his house in the morning to go to work, did so with fear in his heart that his wife would have an affair with the iceman or the milkman during his absence. The professor justified his statement by telling the audience the situation was so bad in America that a play had been written on the subject, called, *The Iceman Cometh.*

Of course, the play has nothing whatsoever to do with an iceman delivering his ice. But it offered me an opportunity to challenge Liu on what he had said. He finished his talk and asked if there were any questions; I waited while one or two others asked questions first, and then I raised my hand and said I had a couple of questions that might be of interest to the audience.

I first asked him one or two innocuous questions of general interest to put him off his guard, then I asked him to comment on the dairy business in America and how milk was distributed. Falling into my trap, he told the audience that milk was packaged more and more in paper cartons and sold in stores, and that fewer and fewer dairies delivered their milk to the door. I next asked him to comment on the electrification of the American countryside. He again took the bait and informed the audience that every household in America had electricity, even those in remote areas of the countryside. He volunteered the opinion that there was probably not a single house in the entire country of America that didn't have electric lighting.

I followed that with a question asking what that electrification of every household meant to the average housewife: what time-saving equipment she had at her disposal, and, in his opinion, what percentage of American households had that sort of equipment.

Professor Liu loved the question and immediately elaborated on the fact that every single housewife had a vacuum sweeper, and he mentioned a variety of other time-saving gadgets that Americans use. I then raised my key question. I asked him to tell the audience how many households in his opinion had electric refrigerators. Poor Professor Liu. He enthusiastically answered that every single household with electricity also had an electric refrigerator, and most households had a freezer as well.

I gave the audience a moment or so for the answer to sink in, then very quickly, before another question could be asked, I said to the professor, "Well, that being the case, if every single household in America has an electric refrigerator, it doesn't leave many houses for the iceman to call at each morning to seduce the housewife, does it?"

Professor Ma, who was sitting next to me, saw what I was doing and was highly amused at his friend's discomfiture, but said nothing. The audience immediately saw the import of my statement and for a moment was stunned. Then they broke out into raucous laughter and clapping, and of course, everything that Professor Liu had told them was now suspect. The embarrassed professor subsided into a chair, and the meeting broke up with few of the audience bothering to talk with him. He came to me afterward and somewhat petulantly complained that I had set him up and made him lose face. I told him bluntly that he deserved it for not being truthful about America and for telling the audience so many lies.

The two professors and our other fellow passengers left the next morning for Tientsin, but at the railroad station they ran into trouble with two Customs men on duty who had heard of the extravagant treatment that had been accorded their colleagues aboard the *President Grant* the day before and felt that they, too, deserved a share of the booty. They demanded that every piece of baggage be opened and declarations be made out by each individual. It appeared certain that they were all going to miss their train, and it took a few minutes for Bob McCann to catch on to what was going on. When he did, he discreetly distributed some cigarettes, a shirt, and some ties, and the two officers smilingly cleared all the baggage and let them board the train without delay. It was the same old China as before, and yet there was a difference.

Before the war the Chinese had been only mildly anti-American, but now we found it to be much more pronounced. Professor Liu's anti-American speech was only the first of many such incidents we experienced during the next several months. Even though America had helped rid China of the Japanese, and China was still receiving an enormous amount of American help at the time, both financially and in moving hundreds of thousands of Chinese troops from Burma and South China up to the northeast, there was still a very strong feeling that America was not doing enough to put down the Communist threat. The situation was aggravated by the fact that General George Marshall was there at the time as head of a mission sent by President Truman to try and bring about an understanding between the Chinese Nationalists and their Communist foes, and with the faint hope of persuading the Chinese to set up a coalition government.

Marshall's attempts proved fruitless in the end, but that was to come much later. The Chinese, feeling that President Truman should have done more than just give aid to the Nationalists to fight the Communists, had fully expected to see American troops step in and obliterate them as they had the Japanese. When that didn't happen, and as the Communists became stronger by the day, eventually completely taking over China in 1949, many Americans felt the same way about it. By then it was too late.

Eva and I stayed on in Chinhuangtao for a few days. For one thing we wanted to visit Beidaihe to see how the two mission houses there had fared. Being wintertime, there was no train running to the beach station so we had to get off the train at Beidaihe Junction and ride donkeys from there. That part of the trip was fun and took about two hours. Although extremely cold, the day was sunny and we were well dressed, so we didn't suffer. We found the houses in pretty poor shape, having been neglected for four years. The exteriors were badly in need of paint and the insides of both were filthy, with all the furniture missing and considerable damage done. The Chinese caretaker told us that several Japanese families had lived in each house for the entire four-year period, and it showed. There was strong evidence that they had left in a big hurry. One locked room in each house had a police seal on the doors so we were unable to open them to determine whether any furniture at all had been saved, and the police were uncharacteristically unavailable to open the doors for us. But as things turned out later, it didn't really matter.

We spent the next two days in Chinhuangtao as I tried my best to convince the Customs people to let me unpack the Jeep and ship it to Tientsin in bond, and there negotiate the import license. They were friendly and helpful and sent off telegrams and made telephone calls, but all to no avail. The necessary permission was not forthcoming. We finally left for Tientsin with the rest of our baggage, and it was several months before we saw the Jeep again and then under most unusual circumstances.

Ancient Chinese Square-holed "Cash" Coin

京奉路

The logo of the Peking-Mukden Railway as the author remembered and described it for Jim Lance to draw. (See opposite page.)

Yi bu xie, bai bu wai.

One step in the wrong direction,
you end up 100 steps away from your
intended destination.

- Chinese Proverb.

Book Four
1946 - 1947

Chapter Thirty-Seven
A Year To Forget

Nineteen forty-seven was a year of frustration and seemingly little accomplishment. On the other hand it was a year that was filled with new and different experiences for us, many of which we could well have done without.

After arriving in Chinhuangtao our immediate inclination was to go north to Lingyuan as soon as possible, particularly since we were already halfway there. However, because I wanted to resolve the problem of how to get the Jeep into the country, the wisest move, we decided, was first to go to Tientsin, where we hoped to be able to contact the appropriate authorities in person and get the necessary import permit.

We left Chinhuangtao on the morning train, which was supposed to leave at 9 o'clock but was two hours late. As we stood on the platform and watched the train pull in, a feeling of great excitement welled up in us as we approached the starting point of what we hoped was a new beginning for our work in China. As the huge steam locomotive chuffed its way past us, the distinctive polished brass Peking-Mukden railway logo on the side of the tender came into sight. It brought back to us once again the many, many times we had seen it before and the numerous trips we had made on that railway line.

There were a number of different railway lines in China, many of them built by foreign nations in the late 1800s. Some were built by the French, as, for example, the line running into Yunnan Province. The Tsingtao-Peking line was built by the Germans and was noted for having cast-iron railway ties, which were constantly being stolen for their metal content. The Peking-Mukden railway on which we were traveling had been built by the British. Although each of the different railway lines had its own distinctive logo — one of them, for example, being a flying railway wheel, another, a cross section of a steel rail — the logo for the Peking-Mukden line was unique and showed remarkable inventiveness and imagination. I am quite certain that none of the British construction people conceived it.

To the uninitiated, the logo was simply a line drawing of the front end of a steam locomotive as one would see it when standing directly in front of it on the track. But its uniqueness lay in the fact that the outline of the locomotive's front end was, in fact, a combination of the two Chinese characters that made up the Chinese name for the line.

When the line was first built, well before my birth in 1913, and for the first twenty years or so of my life in China, the north Manchurian city of Mukden, as it was known to Westerners, was called in Chinese, Fengtian, which loosely translated as "Honor Heaven." Some time later the name was changed to Shenyang, as it is still known today. The current name has no particular meaning, but is a combination of *shen*, a Chinese surname, and *yang*, the positive or male principle in nature, which is used in a number of Chinese place names, i.e., Hengyang, Luoyang and others.

What some imaginative and enterprising individual had done was to take the *jing* of Beijing (Peking) and the *feng* of Fengtian, and place the first above the second. The dot above the *jing* character became the funnel or stack of the locomotive, the small square when rounded out became the circular front of the boiler, and the balance of the character became the platform on which the boiler rested. The character *feng* was blended into it, with the "skirt" spread out to look exactly like that triangular steel frame on the front of steam locomotives, the "cowcatcher," designed to clear the track of obstructions. Strangely enough, few Chinese and almost none of the Westerners riding the line knew the significance of the logo. To them, if they noticed it at all, it was just the front end of a locomotive.

Our trip to Tientsin was uneventful but slow because the track was in poor condition most of the way. As I chatted with the conductor he told me there was a shortage of manpower to maintain the tracks since there was so much damage up and down the line caused by frequent Communist guerrilla attacks; he cited the reluctance of the track workers to operate out in the open countryside, away from the protection of cities.

Earlier, when talking with the Kailan Mining people in Chinhuangtao, we had learned that the political situation, while not stable, seemed at least to be in a state of rest. As I mentioned in the previous chapter, General George Marshall was in China representing President Truman, heading up a mission trying to mediate the civil strife going on between the Chinese Communists and Nationalists. At the same time he was attempting to bring about a coalition government. But the outlook for that was not very bright, and few that we spoke with held out any hope that any good would result from the continuing talks. As we chatted with our fellow passengers, they were all pessimistic about the outcome of the talks, fearing that civil war would not only continue, but would get worse.

Cease-fires had been repeatedly declared and just as frequently broken, by one side or the other. But we did notice one thing. Along the entire route to Tientsin, every viaduct and bridge of any size was guarded by U.S. Marines. Usually two or three were at each end of the bridges, and as we went by we could see their tents pitched nearby. Now and then we passed supply trains operated entirely by Marines as they moved up and down the line. It was a cold, lonely and thankless job for them, and one filled with considerable danger. The United States had deliberately stayed out of the conflict in China, although the U.S. Navy had been used to help Chiang Kai-shek's government by transporting hundreds of thousands of his Chinese Nationalist troops from the Burma/India theater as well as from the southwestern part of China, up to North China and Manchuria. The guarding of the bridges by U.S. Marines was just one more effort on the part of the United States to help the Nationalists keep the vital railroads running, and indirectly to help in the war against the Communists. Even so, there were constant hit-and-run raids on the rail lines, particularly on the spur lines leading inland.

Upon reaching Tientsin we headed for the China Inland Mission home and old friends already there welcomed us warmly. We were delighted to find letters from Lingyuan awaiting us, telling us that all was peaceful there and urging us to head that way as soon as possible. We also learned that a conference of Chinese Christians from Jehol Province was being held in Peking. We hurried there, arriving on the last day of the conference, but in time to meet four of our Chinese brethren from Lingyuan and from other towns in the province. It was a heartwarming experience to see them after four years. They confirmed that it was safe to make the trip to Lingyuan, where they, too, said things were peaceful. But they warned us that the train journey, which used to take 16 to 18 hours, now required four days, since trains would not travel by night and the tracks were in such bad shape that progress was slow.

They also told us what didn't greatly surprise us, that our mission premises in Lingyuan were occupied by large numbers of Chinese Nationalist troops, and that the city magistrate was actually occupying our little house. That bit of news was hard to take. The contact with our old friends from Jehol only made us all the more anxious to head for Lingyuan immediately, but getting a permit to import the Jeep was our first priority, so we told our friends to carry back the news that we would be heading their way just as soon as I could get the permit, and back to Tientsin we went.

In Tientsin I spent a very frustrating week visiting the many officials connected with importation of goods from abroad. They were extraordinarily polite and deferential, and in typical Chinese fashion, not one of them told us it couldn't be done. They just said that up until then they had never had a similar case, and that it posed problems. I was politely shunted from one office to another, drank countless cups of tea, and made small talk with more officials than I could count. But not one of them could help me or give the necessary permission. All said permission had to come from higher up, but from whom was never clearly stated.

Someone finally suggested that I approach officials of the Bank of China. That didn't surprise me because the Bank of China was, in effect, an arm of the Chinese government. When I got there I was able to talk with one of the senior men, a vice president. He talked with me in a friendly manner and admitted that his boss, H.H. Kung, the finance minister and brother-in-law to Chiang Kai-shek, held the monopoly for the importation of all trucks into China and controlled all permits for their importation. He told me that thousands of surplus U.S. Army trucks and Jeeps were being imported each month, and when I suggested that a Jeep was hardly a truck and should be classified as a passenger vehicle, he agreed wholeheartedly and said he thought the ruling was unreasonable. But at the same time there was no way he could get around the ban on importation of vehicles other than those brought in on the government monopoly. He suggested that if I wrote a letter to the finance minister stating my case that perhaps I would get a favorable response. I left his office feeling I had reached a dead end.

Yet China being what it was, I knew that if I could reach the right man there was still a good possibility of getting the permit. Perhaps I needed to grease a few palms along the way, but that was a last resort, one I wanted to avoid because it could lead to complications down the line. We had done a lot of praying about the Jeep, and although I was disappointed, I wasn't willing to admit defeat. I felt sure that sooner or later something would give, but I had no firm idea as to where to go next.

Those thoughts were running through my mind as I walked out of his office into the main office of the bank, where possibly one or two hundred clerks were sitting at desks with abaci and brush pens, adding and subtracting figures and writing them into account books. As I passed down the long rows of desks, a hand reached out and clutched at my sleeve, stopping me. His head still bowed over his desk, a middle-aged man said to me in a low voice, "I know why you are here and that you had no success in getting what you wanted. I, too, am a Christian. Don't say that I told you, but go over to the UNRRA (United Nations Relief and Rehabilitation Administration) offices and talk to them. They have been given permission to import all the trucks and other vehicles that they need, since all of them will be left in China anyway after they have gone. They are the only ones who can do something for you. Donate your vehicle to them and then have them give it back to you." With that he nodded his head, looked at me and smiled and, with a slight wave of his hand, dismissed me and went on with his work. I never learned his name nor where he went to church, but I owe him a deep debt of gratitude. Thank God for that kind soul and his good advice.

I went immediately to see the UNRRA people, who were distributing food and clothing throughout China. I found a young American official and told him my problem, repeating the bank clerk's suggestion and showing him a letter from Zhang Yao-ting in Lingyuan in which he mentioned that UNRRA had set up a dried-milk distribution point in our mission compound. I suggested that donating the Jeep to UNRRA and their returning it to me "for work in the

Lingyuan district," might not be such a far-fetched idea after all.

The young man roared with laughter. "This is another angle of China that I've never yet seen," he said. However, he was most sympathetic and, after thinking it over for a few minutes, said he could see no reason why it couldn't be done. I borrowed a typewriter from him and wrote a letter donating the Jeep to UNRRA. Simultaneously, at another machine he typed a letter donating the Jeep back to me "for use in the Lingyuan area in connection with UNRRA activities and any other usage required." We exchanged documents, shook hands, and I was on my way.

Armed with his letter I went back to the vice president of the Bank of China. He showed no surprise in seeing me and getting the letter from UNRRA. He at once made out a permit and wished me every success. I've often wondered if he had somehow secretly passed the word to his lowly employee to waylay me and tell me about UNRRA, because for him to have done so might have jeopardized his job. China was always full of surprises.

The next problem was how to get the Jeep from Chinhuangtao up to Lingyuan. To drive it was feasible in every way except that we would not be able to carry all our stuff, and much would have to be shipped by train. Furthermore, all our sources said that going overland by any of the several available routes would be dangerous because of the pockets of Communist guerrillas in the countryside. I eventually decided to have the entire packing case shipped by rail. We would need the wood from that packing case to repair the damage done to our houses in Lingyuan.

That seemed like the best idea. However, when I checked at the railroad station, I ran into a blank wall. The railway authorities, usually sympathetic and helpful, told me that no flatcars of any size were available anywhere for civilian use. All had been commandeered by the army to transport military vehicles, guns and troops, and there were just not enough to go around. They told me that, in fact, many old boxcars were being dismantled to make flatcars in order to try and meet the demands of the military. They added that it would probably be months before any would be available for civilians.

They also told me — and I had the opportunity of seeing it for myself shortly afterward — that all trains were being equipped with a set of four or five flatcars up ahead of the locomotive. First, they were there to detect and explode any mines that might have been laid on the track before the much more valuable locomotives ran over them, and secondly, all the flatcars so used had sandbags piled around all four sides, partly to give added weight to explode the mines, but chiefly to protect the Chinese government troops inside, who were equipped with rifles, machine-guns and mortars to fend off guerrilla attacks.

I walked over to the Dodge agency to look up Bob McCann, our old friend from aboard ship. I knew he had shipped 10 or 12 Dodge and Chrysler sedans on the *President Grant*, and I wondered how he had been able to get them from Chinhuangtao to Tientsin. He told me he had run into the same problem that I had. His sedans were all still in Chinhuangtao in their original packing cases, and he had absolutely no hope whatsoever of being able to get them shipped to Tientsin in the foreseeable future.

That put pretty much of a damper on our plans of taking the Jeep with us to Lingyuan. In addition, I was unhappy that storage of the vehicle in Chinhuangtao was going to cost me a lot of money, since I could no longer store it free in the Customs shed. Then I came up with an idea. I went over to the KMA headquarters in Tientsin, and, using their private overland telephone, called Chinhuangtao and spoke with a young English bachelor whom we had met there. He was chief engineer in charge of all KMA coal trains, including locomotives and rolling stock, and supervised a large repair facility in Chinhuangtao. I knew that he got around on a motorcycle, so I told him of my problem. And rather than pay storage for an indeterminate amount of time, I offered him the use of the Jeep if he would unpack it and store the rest of the stuff, including the wooden case, without cost. He eagerly agreed, and Eva and I decided to leave at once for Lingyuan to see how things were there.

Because our entire compound was occupied by Chinese troops and our little house by the magistrate and his family, we decided to take as little as possible on the first trip. We needed to know if we could manage to get everyone moved out, to assess the damage done to the place, and to determine what other supplies we might need. As a result, we traveled very light, and it was a good thing we did.

We left Tientsin early one morning around the second week in January, approaching the coldest time of the year. The mainline train was quite comfortable, even though there were only third-class cars. The diner served only Chinese food, but that was fine with us, and although the train was solidly packed, with delays at every station because of the number of people getting off and on, we were only about two hours late in reaching Jinzhou late that night. There we had to change trains. Since there was no train until early the next morning, we simply sat in the waiting room the rest of the night.

When our train pulled into the station next morning from the yards where it had been made up, we discovered that it was already solidly packed with people who had gone out in the darkness and climbed aboard. With great difficulty we managed to find a place. But what a difference between that train and the one on the main line. Again, the train was made up of third-class carriages exclusively, thirteen of them, all in deplorable condition. Most had no seats at all, not even the frames on which the seats had once rested, and few of the cars had glass in any of the windows. Even the doors at the ends of the cars were missing, as were the doors to the lavatories. The overhead baggage racks were also missing. In some of the cars, through large holes burned through the floor, we could see the track below. Apparently soldiers being moved in the cars had lit fires to keep warm. Now, of course, when the train was in motion, dust and gravel came up through those holes. I squeezed my way through the entire train to try to find a decent place to sit, but nothing was available, and the few seats that there were had no backs or cushions. Since everyone else was standing, we had no option but to stand as well.

No conductor came through the train to punch tickets. I guessed that the railway authorities had just given it up as a bad job and as we found out later, they were catching people as they left the train and making them buy their tickets then if they didn't already have one. In conversation with those around us, we were told that during the occupation of Jehol Province by the Russians, just after the Japanese surrender, the Russians had been unable to find coal to fire the railway engines, so they had torn out all available wood from the passenger cars. We also learned from some of the railway staff that when news of the Russian advance came, many of the trains had simply been abandoned by their crews out in the open countryside as they fled for safety. As a result, the nearby farmers had started the destruction of the passenger cars by stealing the leather-like fabric that covered the seat cushions and backs to use for shoes and then taking the window glass to use in their homes. One couldn't really blame them after all they had suffered at the hands of the Japanese, having their land confiscated for the railway right of way, and the forced labor that had accompanied the building of the line. If they could have somehow moved the cars for use in some way on their farms or as dwellings, I am sure they would have done so.

That trip was unforgettable. There was no heat whatsoever on the train. All the pipes had been allowed to freeze and burst, and with most of the windows missing, we found it little different from riding in an open car. The cold was intense. A biting wind blew through the car while the train was in motion, and the smoke, soot and ashes from the engine made everyone's eyes smart.

From time to time we tried to crouch down to escape the wind, but most of the time it was useless — people were crowded too close to us. Only after several hours, when a few had gotten off the train, were we able to sit on our suitcases part of the time. Even then, the people crowded us so closely that we could scarcely breathe, and despite the cold, the odor from all those bodies jammed up against us made standing preferable. Happily, the close proximity of the 300 or more people jammed into the car at least kept our bodies warm. But our feet were particularly vulnerable, and as the day dragged on, we lost all feeling in our feet, and by nightfall both of us had severe cases of chilblains.

There had been almost no maintenance of the rail bed on that branch line, and our progress was painfully slow. The car rocked from side to side, threatening to tip over. As we slowly chugged up the long, winding valley through the mountains that led to Beipiao, I don't think we exceeded 20 miles per hour. The train stopped at every station, sometimes for an hour or so, but no one dared to get off for fear they would be unable to get on again. Now and then food vendors came to the train and we were able to buy steamed buns or deep-fried pretzel-like sticks through the windows, but we suffered from thirst. Eva, despite her fur hat, developed a terrible headache. However, a perfect stranger standing not far away from us saw her massaging her head, and from his pocket he took a bottle of aspirin and offered her a couple of tablets. It was such a gracious gesture. We had some aspirin in our suitcases, but there was no way we could get to it.

Among the many passengers on the train were the usual number of military men, most either going on leave or returning to their units, but few of them had weapons. However, on the car just ahead of ours, a number of armed soldiers guarded a group of prisoners who had their arms tied behind them. They were probably soldiers who had been captured after going AWOL and were now being taken back to their units for certain execution. We felt so very sorry for them.

Around mid-morning, as we wound our way alongside a frozen stream, the track followed the natural contours of the valley and twisted in and out between the barren hills, crossing and re-crossing the stream from time to time. Suddenly, as I stood there, out of the corner of my eye I saw something drop from the back end of the car ahead and flash by the window next to us, then roll down the railway embankment toward the stream. As I turned my head and watched, the rolling ball materialized into one of the soldier-prisoners, who had escaped. When he stopped rolling, he leaped to his feet and started running for his life. I learned later from his guards that he had apparently seen his opportunity, had asked to be allowed to go into the toilet, and since there was no door, they had untied his hands and he had gone in unguarded. He immediately smashed the frosted glass window (about the only kind of glass that remained intact), and dived out headfirst.

We watched him racing along on the ice in the opposite direction to that in which the train was going, his figure growing smaller and smaller. He had a moment or two head start before his guards noticed his absence. Then we heard the sound of shooting. His guards were leaning out the window, and from the platform at the end of the car, firing their rifles at him. We could see the bullets hitting the ice around him and raising puffs of dust in the sand on the river bank.

The man bobbed and ducked, weaving from side to side, and kept on running. Then a bend in the track hid him from sight for a few minutes. At the next outward bend in the track, the man again came into view, but now much farther away. Although the guards kept firing their rifles at him, we, as well as all the Chinese around us, were cheering him on.

Meanwhile other guards were trying to stop the train. They finally located the conductor, but since there was no emergency cord on the train, there was nothing he could do. Although the guards beat him unmercifully with their gun butts, he told them the only way to stop the train was to go up to the forward car, climb over the back of the locomotive, and notify the engineer. They eventually made him do that, but by that time we had covered perhaps ten miles. Several of the soldiers dropped off and headed back on foot to chase the fugitive. But I was confident that they would not be successful in catching up with him.

That delay and our slow progress brought us into Chaoyang, our neighboring mission station to the east, just before dusk. We hadn't let them know we were coming, so no one was at the station to meet us, and when we made our way to the mission compound, it was already well after dark. We found the place occupied by several hundred Chinese Nationalist soldiers, who weren't at all pleased to see us arrive and didn't want to let us in. The frightened gateman, who knew us, finally convinced them to admit us. We made our way to Mr. Brewster's house, where to our astonishment we found a small detachment of U.S. Army personnel encamped.

That was indeed a surprise. It was just supper time for them, and several of the soldiers were out behind the kitchen preparing the meal on portable stoves by the light of a gasoline lantern. They were mighty surprised to see us walk in. Immediately the sergeant in charge took us in to see his superiors, two elderly Army colonels. The room was lit by one flickering candle, and we found the colonels sitting on their camp beds, the only items of furniture in the room, having a pre-dinner drink. They, too, were surprised to see us and invited us to join them. They told us they were an advance observation team and their job was to see that the peace was kept between the two opposing Chinese armies while negotiations continued in Peking.

The interior of Mr. Brewster's house was a disaster. It had been looted of every stick of furniture, presumably by both the Russians and the Chinese. The two officers had chosen the only room that still had some glass in the windows. They had an oil stove for heat, but the room was still so cold that they were wearing their overcoats. Both appeared extremely unhappy about their lot and were most pessimistic about the future. When we told them the purpose of our visit, to reopen the various mission stations, they shook their heads and told us it would be an impossibility. They said they expected hostilities to break out any day. They advised us to return to Tientsin by the next train and told us that they were packing up to leave within a day or so because the situation looked so bad. We found they had one Chinese-American soldier with them acting as interpreter, and he, too, told us that the Communist guerrillas were very active in outlying areas.

In light of what happened later, perhaps it would have been wiser if we had taken their advice and returned to Tientsin. But we were young and foolish and not so easily discouraged. We stayed that night with some of the Chinese Christians, and since the purpose of our trip was simply to assess the situation, the following afternoon we caught the next train heading west to Lingyuan.

We waited on the station platform in Chaoyang for several hours before the train arrived. It was so late we doubted it would proceed west in the dark. Contrary to our expectations, they hurriedly got us on board, and we started off. The car we boarded, while less crowded than the one we had been on the day before, was in just as bad a condition, with neither window glass nor doors, and we prepared ourselves for a very cold night.

Our progress westward was over a track that was in much worse condition than anything we'd seen before, and the train seemed barely to move. There were no lights on anywhere on the train; even the locomotive had no headlight. I gathered that they had deliberately not turned on the headlight to avoid attracting gunfire from guerrillas, who might be hiding alongside the track. We stopped at every bridge while someone from the locomotive went ahead to see that there was still a bridge there. Almost all of them had been blown up and had been replaced by temporary structures made from railroad ties erected in a crisscross pattern, so flimsy that it seemed impossible they could support the weight of the train.

At one point we came to a wide riverbed, a place that I knew well, and found the long bridge totally demolished. We could dimly see piles of material strewn around, so it was evident that work was in progress to replace it; in the meantime the railway engineers had ingeniously laid down a temporary detour track through the sand and rocks, across the thick ice to the water's edge, then down a slanting ramp on the ice into the open channel of the river itself. It was a novel experience riding the train as it crawled down into the riverbed, through the two-foot deep water, then climbed up the opposite bank, all in total darkness.

By the time we reached Yebaishou, a railway junction point about an hour from Lingyuan, it was after ten o'clock. After a long delay, we learned from the train conductor that since it was too dangerous to proceed, the train would stop there for the night and passengers were to remain aboard. It was so late that no food vendors were about, so neither food nor water was available, and although small food shops were in an area down a steep bank just behind the station buildings, a military curfew was in effect and we were told that if we got off the train, we may be shot. So we settled down for a cold and hungry night.

The toilets on the train, all blocked with frozen feces and urine, were unusable, so the passengers were allowed off onto the track to answer the calls of nature. But they had to stay in the immediate proximity of the train. I looked across to the station buildings, hoping one of them might be open, but they were all dark and no railway personnel were visible anywhere.

I decided I had to do something, since spending a night under those windswept, freezing conditions was tantamount to committing suicide. I told one of the soldiers that I was going to go and look for some fuel to make a fire. But no sooner had I stepped down off the car steps than I ran into one of the railway men who was inspecting the underside of the train. He turned out to be an old friend and a fine Christian.

Mr. Liao was a most interesting man. When we had first met him five or six years before, he had two wives and several children by each of them. His first wife had been barren at the outset, and it was at her insistence that he had taken a second wife, whom she had selected, so he might have children. He no sooner married the second wife than the first one became pregnant, and she ultimately bore him three children.

That, however, didn't affect the relationship between the two wives. They got along wonderfully well together. But soon after Mr. Liao had arrived in

Yebaishou, he went to Lingyuan one Sunday and found his way to our compound, where, out of curiosity, he attended church and ultimately became a Christian. Shortly after that he was instrumental in encouraging both his wives to become Christians. The whole family came to church in Lingyuan almost every Sunday, and it wasn't long before he asked to talk to the church elders, telling them that he had a problem. He had read his Bible extensively, and St. Paul's admonitions to Timothy and Titus, that a man should be the husband of only one wife, had made him do a great deal of soul searching. He wanted to know from us whether he should divorce his second wife in order to be a true Christian.

That was a hard question to answer, and I recall we had a number of meetings with the Chinese elders to discuss the problem. It was not merely a question of whether Mr. Liao should do what he felt was the right thing before God. There was also the question of what would happen to his second wife, should he divorce her. As was the way with the Chinese at that time, her family would never have accepted her back, and a divorced woman with children would probably be unable to find another husband.

The problem was eventually resolved when the second wife, a very intelligent woman, came to the independent conclusion that her position as a second wife was not right before God and she asked her husband for a divorce. Shortly thereafter she did find another husband, a man who also worked for the railroad, and she became happily married once more. Her two children, of course, stayed with the first husband.

Mr. Liao was surprised and delighted to see us after almost five years, and insisted we go with him to his house nearby. He had only two tiny rooms, measuring approximately ten feet by twelve feet, that were provided by the railroad. One he used as the kitchen and the other for sleeping. Half the sleeping room was taken up by the *kang*, which we shared with Mr. and Mrs. Liao and their five children, spending a warm and comfortable night. The next morning after breakfast Mr. Liao told us our train would not leave for another two hours or more because they wanted to send a locomotive on a test run over the pass just in case the guerrillas had laid mines during the night, as was often the case. While we ate breakfast, Mr. Liao regaled us with stories of the Japanese surrender to the Russians when they invaded from the north

toward the end of the war. He also filled us in on the current situation regarding local Communist guerrillas.

He told many stories of the Russians, of their abuse of both their allies, the Chinese, and of the Japanese soldiers who surrendered to them, and especially of their total disregard for the rights of Japanese women, young and old, whom they raped indiscriminately. Because of the terrible way in which the Japanese had treated the Chinese population during the ten years of Manchukuo, I had fully expected to hear that the Chinese populace as a whole would have turned against them when they surrendered. But such was not the case. Mr. Liao and many other Chinese with whom I talked told us that Japanese prisoners, and Japanese women in particular, had been well treated by their Chinese captors, and I was unable to find even one instance of their having been molested by the Chinese. But that wasn't the case with the Russians.

Mr. Liao told of the wholesale destruction of property by the Russian troops, particularly railway property. He confirmed the stories of their tearing seats out of the passenger cars to fuel the engines, and showed us parts of his own home and the station buildings where wood had been torn out. Japanese prisoners and the Chinese populace alike had been pressed into service to scrounge wood wherever they could find it.

From Yebaishou a spur line leads northward to Chifeng, about 100 miles away. That line ran right behind Mr. Liao's house and he took me out to look at it. He told me that, there being no direct motor road from Chifeng to Yebaishou, the Russians, after capturing Chifeng and finding no locomotives or rolling stock there that they could use, had simply used the railway roadbed as a highway for their heavy tanks when they advanced south.

The huge tanks, (and Mr. Liao said there had been more than 50 of them), had straddled the rails, riding the outside ends of the wooden ties, crushing them in the process. Although at first glance the line appeared to be in excellent shape, Mr. Liao took me along the track and showed me where the immense weight of the tanks had crushed or snapped off the ends of every tie on each side of the rails; that had happened over the entire distance between Yebaishou and Chifeng, rendering the line unusable. It had been that way for two years or more, and with the shortage of ties and the intense guerrilla activity everywhere, there was little prospect that the line could be repaired within the foreseeable future.

I walked with Mr. Liao about half a mile or so along the track to a large bridge that spanned a nearby river. There the destruction caused by the tanks was much more evident. Although from a distance it was impossible to see anything wrong, close up I saw that the heavy spikes holding the rails down had been sheared off and most were missing, and the tie ends had been crushed completely flat. Were it not for the wide girders below them, they would have broken off and fallen into the river.

Mr. Liao also filled me in on the activity of the *balu*, the Communist guerrillas in the area. He said an estimated 300,000 of them were active throughout the province, and their strength was growing daily with defections of Nationalist troops. These were not the same *balu* that had been active back in 1941. At that time they promoted themselves as friends of the people, and everywhere the peasants accepted them with open arms. However, things had changed. The peasants were now suffering terribly under the harsh rule of the *balu*. Forced labor was the norm, and the *balu* lived off the people, yet at the same time they preached the virtues of Communism and equality.

Mr. Liao added that defecting Nationalist soldiers were extremely well treated by the *balu*, provided they surrendered without too much of a fight. But those who fought stubbornly, were, if subsequently captured, tortured and killed in a most barbaric manner. A few weeks later I had the opportunity to gain some firsthand knowledge of just exactly what that meant.

After those pleasant hours with the Liao family, he took us back to the station and saw us board the train. Our progress over the pass between Yebaishou and Lingyuan was without incident until we were on the downward side, about ten miles from Lingyuan. There, as we were traveling at about ten miles an hour, without any warning or apparent reason, the train jolted to a stop. I thought immediately of Communist guerrillas, but no one was in sight out the window. I then got off the train and walked to the front, where I discovered that the locomotive was partially derailed. The front four bogie wheels had come off the track and were well off to the side at a sharp angle.

In no time at all everyone else was off the train and pushing to see what was wrong. I estimated that there were well over 2,000 people on the train, and they milled around, offering a thousand suggestions as to what should be done. Fearing an attack from the *balu*, the soldiers, meanwhile, had been deployed to defensive positions nearby, and one of the officers sent men to the nearby peaks to stand watch.

I anticipated a long delay while someone walked to the nearest station where there would be a telephone to summon a repair train. But I had not taken into account the ingenuity and resourcefulness of the Chinese. The engineer was an older man who had been in the business for a number of years. He studied the situation, then turned to me and said, "This is no great problem. I've had this happen to me many times when I was driving trains up in Suiyuan Province. What we need are a number of flat stones." I couldn't imagine why.

Although we were up in the mountains, the pass was composed entirely of loess soil, completely devoid of rocks of any kind. Nevertheless I suspected that if we could find a watercourse, we'd probably find what we needed. With the help of the army officers and the railway police we formed several groups of men to go out as scouting parties to look for small, flat stones. In about an hour nearly all were back, most empty handed, but enough of them had managed to find flat stones in the deep gullies that abounded in the area. With those, the engineer proceeded to build small ramps behind each of the derailed wheels, each ramp leading to the steel rail on which the locomotive's drive wheels still rested.

When he had built the ramps to his satisfaction, he climbed aboard his locomotive and put it into reverse. On the first try, as he slowly backed up the train, the bogie wheels climbed the ramps and dropped back onto the track once again. Why they had derailed in the first place was anyone's guess, but the engineer thought that perhaps shepherd boys had put something on the track, although there was no evidence of anything there. As I watched the old engineer do his trick with the stones I wondered if that ingenious idea was exclusively Chinese, or whether Americans had, out of sheer necessity, perhaps used the same method in the days of America's old West, when trains first crossed the United States. Certainly I had never heard of it having been done before.

Our arrival in Lingyuan was expected, and we were met at the station by a large crowd of happy people who had been waiting for hours to welcome us back after an absence of nearly five years. But when we reached our old home, our hearts fell. From the outside the place was an absolute shambles and we hardly recognized it.

Our front street entrance, once so dignified and well kept, was completely unrecognizable. Alongside the platform that adjoined the front steps, the Chinese military, using large rocks, had built massive "pill-box" block-houses on each side of the steps. Gunports faced in each direction up and down the street, and only a narrow passageway had been left to get by them. Our two large front gates, always painted a shiny black, were now battered and worn almost beyond recognition, with almost all the paint chipped off and the brass work missing.

Armed Chinese soldiers standing at the gate challenged us, unwilling to let us in at first. When we finally did get inside, we found the compound occupied by more than 300 Chinese soldiers who had made themselves at home everywhere. The courtyards, front and back, once so tidy, were littered with military equipment of every description: battered and broken-down vehicles, horse-drawn artillery pieces, piles of empty shell cases, and everywhere litter of one kind or another. Horses and mules were either running loose or stabled or tethered indiscriminately in almost every corner, contributing to the filth and smells around the place. Many, tied to the fruit trees in our back garden, had chewed the bark off, leaving little hope that the trees could survive.

The back garden itself, once so lovely and manicured, was a wilderness that looked like a battleground. Many of the larger trees had been chopped down to be used as timbers in roofing the blockhouses: the two at the front of the compound, and two more large ones that had been built just outside our back wall that were reached by short tunnels cut through the wall. Almost every single building in the compound showed signs of damage: broken windows by the score, doors off their hinges, tiles missing from the roofs, chimneys knocked down, and temporary Chinese-style cooking stoves helter-skelter all over the place, both outdoors and inside our residences, built right on top of the wooden floors. Many of the

wooden floors had huge holes burned into them where the occupying troops had built their fires directly on the floor. That had been done either by the Russians, who threw the Japanese out; the Chinese *balu* forces, who had held the city for a brief period of time after the Russians left and had used our premises as barracks; or the Nationalist troops who were occupying it when we arrived.

Katie (Gao Zun), our loyal gateman, was one of only two or three people who had been permitted to remain in the compound. He had not been allowed to go to the back of the compound except to draw water from the back well, so he was unable to tell us which army had wreaked the most havoc. He said that all of them had done their share of damage.

Not all the damage to the buildings had been caused by occupying troops. Some of it was normal deterioration due to neglect and wear and tear over the five years of our absence. But I could hardly believe my eyes at the damage and filth, and it was hard to imagine where and how we could begin to clean things up and start repairs. I had a camera with me, and despite the protests of the soldiers, I took a lot of pictures, some of which I still have. As I looked them over prior to writing this chapter, the whole miserable scene came back vividly. Despite the great damage, it was actually less, in many ways, than we had expected. We had imagined that in the fighting back and forth over the city our houses might have been destroyed completely. Even so, it was going to take many thousands of dollars and years of work to restore the place to what it had been before.

The Chinese military men as a whole were not at all happy to see us, and at first they showed considerable hostility. It took me some time to locate the officer in charge. I told him the place was our residence and that we had come back to claim it and to live there, and that we required a room for a few days. He begrudgingly cleared his men out of one room — my former study, the room Eva and I had occupied for six months or so right after our marriage until our little house had been built — and there we stayed for the ten days we spent in Lingyuan. Chinese soldiers in the room next to us left us little quiet, day or night, and the entire compound swarmed with them wherever we went. It was a strange situation in which we found ourselves.

We didn't have the heart to go near our own little

place across the courtyard, which the magistrate had taken over. From across the yard it, too, looked a disaster. Piles of junk lay outside and clotheslines were strung from the windows to the trees Eva had so lovingly planted, and which were by then quite tall. From where we stood we could see that almost all the paint was gone from the outside of the windows and the front door. I felt so annoyed with the magistrate for having taken over our house without our permission that I decided not to pay him the usual official courtesy visit. But at the same time I thought it wise not to embarrass him, because I hoped that he would have the decency to move out as soon as he learned of our arrival. Toward the end of our stay I did eventually pay him a short visit at the Yamen, but neither he nor I brought up the subject of his occupying our house. He was a new man, not the magistrate who had been there in 1941, and he turned out to be a remarkably difficult man to deal with.

He had first moved into the compound some years before when the city was threatened by an attack from Communist guerrillas. Obviously he thought it would be safer there than in the Yamen, which would be one of the first places they would have attacked. After my visit to him in the Yamen, I let it be known to him through an intermediary (as such things are done in China), that I was going back to Tientsin to collect the rest of our things, but that I would be back before long and expected him to have moved out by then. He, however, made it abundantly clear that he had no intention whatsoever of moving. I figured he was just saying that to gain face and so I let it ride for the moment.

That first afternoon of our arrival we held a thanksgiving service in the meeting hall, which had remained intact and unmolested and was the one place not occupied by Chinese troops. More than 100 Chinese Christians were there to welcome us back, and later in the week, in true Chinese fashion, they surprised us with a feast, cooked right on the premises on temporary stoves set up in the yard. For that occasion still more Christians were present, many from the country villages, and as they greeted us there were more tears than laughter. All of them had stories to tell us: of months of imprisonment under the Japanese for some who had been arrested for no apparent reason right after my parents and sisters left the city in May 1942. Others told us of food shortages and near-starvation as the war drew to a close and the Japanese deprived the people of even the very basics of life. Hardest of all for us to bear was the absence of so many familiar faces. Many of our beloved friends had died, including our old cook, Gao Cai, and our faithful table boy, You Wang. Both had died of natural causes, neither having attained much more than middle age. I am certain that grief over our departure as well as uncertainty over their own future had played a part in their deaths. It was strange not to see them around. Those old friends who were there looked so much older; it was obvious they had been through a lot since we had last seen them. Another missing face was that of our beloved Mr. Li of the restaurant, killed by the *balu* when they had taken the city. Also gone was Mr. Yang, the incense manufacturer, and a number of women and children as well. However, we were glad to see a lot of new faces in the hall. The church elders told us they had been able to continue church services without hindrance except during the period when the *balu* had been there, and a number of new members had been added to the church in the years we had been gone.

When we got around to making a second tour of our back garden we were doubly shocked to see the immense damage done to the trees Father had so carefully nurtured over the years. The few that were left were missing branches, which had been cut for firewood. The large cedar trees were intact, as were the elms, but most of the young trees were gone, as were most of the date trees. The "bug house" near the well, where You Wang did the laundry, had collapsed and was a total ruin. But what shocked me most were the huge holes dug through the back wall leading to the block houses outside. The wall at those two points had been seriously weakened and was badly cracked. Of everything we saw, I found the blockhouses back and front to be the most objectionable. Those outside the front gate were only large enough to hold three or four men, but the ones behind our back wall could have easily held ten men each, together with their machine guns. From a purely military point of view they were ideally situated to defend that part of the city wall, of which our back wall constituted a part. But to have our mission compound converted into a military bastion, as it was, put us into an untenable position should an attack come from the *balu*, and it was obvious that we would have been one of their first objectives. The blockhouses had to go, and as soon as possible.

I somewhat reluctantly paid a courtesy call on the commanding general of the Nationalist forces and told him that we would shortly be moving back to Lingyuan permanently, and we asked him to kindly withdraw his forces from our compound and have the four blockhouses dismantled as soon as possible. When I first approached him he was all smiles and polite, but when he heard what I wanted he became hostile and aggressive and flatly refused my request. He told me there was no room anywhere else in the city for his men — an outright lie, because there were actually very few troops stationed in the city — and he stated that the blockhouses were necessary for the defense of the city and would stay where they were, no matter what I said and regardless of my coming back at any future date. I knew then that I would have to go over his head to his superiors in Mukden.

Despite the protests of the soldiers and their deliberately getting in our way, Eva and I made a detailed inspection of the interiors of all the buildings and found them in much worse condition than we had been led to believe. The ceilings and walls were all blackened with smoke and the walls in every room were covered with the blood of squashed bedbugs and lice, and it was obvious from the many holes in the walls that the place was infested with rats and mice as well. Many of the windowpanes had been broken, and where glass had once been, there was only dirty paper or nothing at all. Most heartbreaking of all were the holes burned into the floors in almost every room.

Katie, who accompanied me on my tour, told me that when, in 1942, my parents had left Lingyuan, the Japanese had, that very same day, moved in a number of Japanese families to occupy our quarters, using the rooms just as they were, with all the furniture intact. Gradually, though, things began to disappear. Then, at war's end, when the Russian troops occupied the city and the Japanese surrendered, the Russians drove all the Japanese out of our compound and occupied the place themselves for several weeks. When they left they took many of our belongings with them. What furniture they didn't take they burned. When Chinese Nationalist troops took over, they finished the job. Of course, I had my suspicions that somewhere between the various occupations by military forces, the local civilians had had a part in looting the premises. But I hadn't the heart to ask Katie about it, and I didn't really want to know. As it was, on our visits into some of the private homes we spotted some of our things that had been "dropped" by the soldiers, or so we were told. The fact was that not a single item of furniture remained, and not one single stove was left except for the one in the kitchen, which, built into a brick foundation, was still intact.

During the years of our absence, trusty Gao Zun, subjected to many beatings and often at the risk of his life, had valiantly tried to protect our property as each of the occupying forces had either looted the place or destroyed or burned what they couldn't take with them. I was so glad that my parents weren't able to see the damage done and the mess that the place was in. I was particularly sad when I saw that the dining room floor, our first wooden floor, of which we were so proud, had five large holes burned in it, one of them right near the entrance. I couldn't figure out why they had built a fire at that point, since it would have interfered with the opening and closing of the door.

After showing me the worst of the damage, Gao Zun took us to the room we used to call the "box room," where all our trunks were usually stored, and with justifiable pride he showed us that he had managed to salvage some of our possessions. The door to the room was even locked. But the sight that met our eyes when we opened it beggars description. All our old boxes and trunks were there intact, but lying in odd positions all over the floor, all with their lids open and some lying on their sides and others upside down. The contents were mostly scattered around on the floor, clothing for the most part, things the Chinese wouldn't want to wear, and not much of that. Some of our books were there, though most of them had been burned. We were happy to find some of the few family photographs that we hadn't destroyed at Pearl Harbor time when we knew the Japanese were about to arrest us.

Stacked in one corner of the room were some 40 or 50 band instruments that most certainly didn't belong to us, and I couldn't understand how they came to be there. Gao Zun told us that, for some unknown reason, they had been left behind by the Communist *balu* troops. There were ten or twelve drums of various sizes, and several different kinds of brass horns and trumpets.

Quite surprisingly, a number of our floor carpets were also there, but only the larger ones, most of them pretty well worn. Then, as we looked around, I was agreeably surprised to find that all four of our precious portable typewriters were there: Dad's, Eva's, Barbara's and my own. Quite unaccountably, there were two more that didn't belong to us. They had apparently been picked up elsewhere and for some unknown reason had been brought to Lingyuan for storage. We eventually took them back with us to Tientsin, but were never able to find out to whom they had originally belonged.

I recall that as Eva and I first entered the room, the utter chaos and disarray shocked us, and for a moment we stood there trying to take it all in. Then simultaneously, the first object that we both identified was Eva's wedding dress, still complete with faded orange blossoms. It was hanging from a nail on the wall and for some strange reason it struck both of us as hilarious, and we doubled over with laughter. Poor Gao Zun couldn't understand why we were laughing, and there was no way we could explain it. I guess it was basically a choice between laughter and tears, and the laughter won out.

Among some old papers I came across just recently was a copy of a letter dated March 5, 1947, which we had written to friends in this country shortly after that trip. In it we had described the damage and loss to our buildings as being "less than we had anticipated," and that we were "pleasantly surprised to find it was not worse." I suppose, being much younger at the time, we were filled with hope and enthusiasm and were able to accept conditions, which now, as I look back some 45 years later, were simply appalling. All one can say is that the only bright spot in the whole mess was that the houses themselves were still standing. That in itself was something to be thankful for, but little good it did us.

Toward the end of our ten-day stay in Lingyuan, rumors abounded that an attack by the *balu* was imminent. The local general and the magistrate were in a complete panic, believing it would occur within the next few days. At once they ordered that a deep moat, eight feet deep and ten feet wide, be dug around the entire perimeter of the city. Every able-bodied man in the city was ordered out to commence digging immediately, and when we left the city a day or so later, the digging was still in progress, with

thousands of people involved. But no attack materialized, and it seemed the *balu* were simply biding their time. For my part, I thought perhaps it was a rumor circulated by the *balu* strictly for propaganda purposes and in order perhaps to influence the talks then in progress in Peking. But it was a very unnerving experience, to say the least.

Our initial intention had been to pay a brief visit to all the mission stations in the province to see what the situation was, but we were told that in each of the other cities, the same thing had happened. Chinese troops had occupied mission premises everywhere. So we decided the best thing was to make a quick trip to Mukden as soon as possible to visit the headquarters of the Chinese 1st Army command to see if we could get some action in having our mission premises cleared of troops. At the same time we would report our presence to the British consulate.

We caught the morning train from Lingyuan, and at the brief stop in Chaoyang some of the Christians were there at the station to see us. They told us that the American Army men had left two or three days previously. I felt that was not a good sign.

Slow as the train was, it got us to Jinzhou junction in time to catch an evening train on the main line heading for Mukden, and we were surprised to find they continued to operate the train, even after dark. It seemed that all along the entire route U.S. Marines were still guarding the bridges, which wasn't true of our branch line to Lingyuan. Another surprise was to find a dining car on the train, where we were able to get a good meal. We were directed to a table that we shared with a Dutch Roman Catholic bishop. He was returning to his mission in Sipingkai, some distance north of Mukden. We started talking about the *balu* threat, and he described to us an attack made on that city a few weeks before. That was the period when the *balu* were making hit-and-run attacks against Nationalist strongholds, and they had attacked one night in huge numbers with heavy artillery and mortars as well as rifles and machine guns.

The bishop told us that the attack started soon after dusk and lasted till dawn, with heavy casualties on both sides and much damage inside the city from the guerrillas' shellfire. But despite their large numbers, the *balu* had been beaten back. Although it was certain they had suffered many casualties, the only evidence of *balu* losses on the battlefield in the morning were the numerous pools of blood. They had carried all their dead and wounded away with them, as was their practice. It was not long after that defeat at Sipingkai that they changed their tactics to simply bypassing Nationalist strongholds and concentrating instead on cutting their supply lines. That eventually proved effective and was so demoralizing to the Nationalists that their men started defecting by the thousands.

What interested us most in the bishop's story, apart from the details of the battle, was his account of how the fierce fighting affected the priests and nuns of his mission. Like our own compound in Lingyuan, his, too, was on the outer edge of the city, and their mission wall was, in effect, part of the city wall, just as ours was. The bishop told us that as the attack intensified, he, with his priests, lined the top of the wall to watch the fighting. It became so terrifying that the priests got panicky and several had nervous breakdowns. On the other hand, the nuns remained completely calm throughout the entire attack, taking it all in stride and busying themselves attending to the wounded, acting as though it was an everyday affair. The bishop found it hard to explain why that should have been so, and why the women showed much greater strength than the men, and he had nothing but praise for the courage of his nuns.

In Mukden we tried to check in at the Yamato Hotel as we had always done. The Yamato, originally built and operated by the South Manchurian Railway, was a luxury hotel with moderate prices. However, we found it completely occupied by Chinese Army officers and being run by one of their generals. We were directed to a former Japanese hotel nearby and learned that it, too, was operated by a Chinese general. It was almost full, but we managed at least to get a room. Sad to say, it was very run down: filthy in the extreme, with no bedding on the grimy bare mattresses, no towels in the bathroom, no hot running water, and worst of all, no heat except for one hour each day to prevent the pipes from freezing up.

Mukden was well north of Lingyuan, the weather was much colder, and for the three or four days we were there, it was well below zero the entire time. I busied myself running around seeing the authorities, but poor Eva sat in the hotel room wrapped in her sleeping bag, or lying in the bag itself in a vain effort to keep warm. I did manage to buy a hot water bottle and was able to get it filled each morning downstairs, so that she at least had that to keep her hands and feet warm. Fortunately, there were both Chinese and Russian restaurants nearby where we could eat. That first trip of ours to Lingyuan and Mukden covered around 20 days, and over the entire period and the two subsequent trips that we made, cold was our worst enemy, and Eva suffered greatly, primarily from neuralgic headaches. She had never had them before and attributed them to having had to sleep directly under the open porthole aboard the *President Grant*. The open porthole was something her two roommates had insisted upon because they wanted fresh air in the room at all times.

After reporting to the British Consul in Mukden, I went to the Chinese 1st Army Headquarters, where I was initially refused entry. I persisted, going back again and again and demanding to see the commanding general. I knew of the 1st Army from our time in India; we had heard from U.S. Army personnel who trained them about their arrogant behavior and their anti-American attitude, and the guards at the outer gate certainly lived up to their reputation as they repeatedly rebuffed my efforts to gain entrance. But on the third day I finally wore them down and managed to get one of them to carry my card in to their commanding officer.

I was given an audience with the assistant chief of staff, a very young officer named Pai (White), with the rank of lieutenant general. When he heard what I had come for, he was at first arrogant, antagonistic, and totally uncooperative. However, as I persisted in my demands for his help, he slowly became curious about me and then turned increasingly friendly.

Apologizing for his initial unfriendly attitude, he told me that he thought that I was an American spy. Otherwise, how was it that I was able to speak such fluent Chinese? I don't know what made him change his mind; perhaps it was my knowledge of local idioms and Chinese customs, or perhaps because I asked if he was any relation to a very well-known Chinese general, Pai Chung-hsi. In any case, we spent several hours together as his curiosity about me got the better of him, and we ended up becoming good friends. It took a little time, but he bent over backward to be of help and issued instructions to a junior officer to write me a number of orders to each of his several commands throughout Jehol Province.

He had learned a little English while working with the Americans in India. At first he was hesitant to use it with me, but later he showed considerable pride as he used some of the phrases he had learned. Since all the orders had to be handwritten, he suggested that I come back for them the next day. I was only too glad to do so.

What a difference when I returned the next day to pick up the orders. He had left word with the sentries at the gate, and I was admitted at once, with much deferential saluting and a junior officer escorting me to General Pai's office. The orders were all ready for me, packed in a pouch, each of them written on a large sheet of paper, stamped with his commanding officer, General Sun Li-chen's "chop," which was about six inches square. They were imposing documents. Before he would let me go he held me in conversation for another hour or two discussing America and life in this country. Toward the end, as I was about to leave, he pressed me for details as to when I was actually returning to Jehol. He said he wanted to notify his various field commanders of my coming. He then said he wanted to accompany us to assure our safety. He told me he would have a special car attached to our train, and we could ride with him. He would also take along his personal armored half-track personnel carrier so that we could travel together in safety at each of my stops, and he would accompany me to each of the different cities in Jehol Province to ensure that all the mission compounds were properly evacuated by his men. I felt he was quite sincere in his offer and thanked him profusely, at the same time declining as gracefully as I could, assuring him that we placed our trust in God and were quite sure that we would be kept safe whatever the circumstances.

I've often wondered what happened to that young man. Not many months after my contact with him, the *balu* attacked on a broad front in northern Manchuria and completely overran all the large cities, including Mukden. The Nationalist Army troops either defected en masse to the Communists or were wiped out. A relatively small number of them fled to Formosa (Taiwan) and I've wondered if that young general was among them. Years later I met and talked with some former Chinese Army officers who had escaped to Taiwan, and I asked about him, but none of them knew of his whereabouts.

From Mukden we went straight back to Tientsin, where we stayed only briefly, and then set off once again for Chaoyang and Lingyuan, armed with the papers given us by the young general. We again carried very little with us because I was certain we would have to return to the coast once again if we were successful in getting the army men out of the various compounds, and perhaps we could even get the Jeep. In any event, it would be necessary to buy a lot of supplies to effect repairs to the buildings.

Only a couple of weeks had passed since our earlier trip, but we found conditions on the railroad to be much worse. All the U.S. Marine guards had been withdrawn from protecting the railway bridges, and a number of bridges had already been destroyed. One of the first things we noted was that alongside the railroad track, for a distance of many miles, the telegraph poles had been cut night after night by the *balu* and the shortened poles replaced by repair crews the following day until they stood only about six or eight feet high, with the wires dragging on the ground. A different section of the line was hit each night, and we passed areas where the poles were still lying on the ground, the repair crews having not yet been able to get to them. That meant, of course, that there were delays with our train passing that section since the wires were all broken as well. Destruction of the poles was not only to disrupt communications, but because the *balu* had discovered that the yellow-colored composition containing sulphur that was used as an adhesive to glue the ceramic insulators onto their metal brackets contained an ingredient that was useful in making their hand grenades. As a result, the ground around each pole was littered with smashed insulators.

Instead of four days it took us six to make the journey, and it was as cold and miserable. Because no trains dared to move after dark, we spent most nights on the train, stamping our feet to try to keep them warm or walking outside on the track or the platform of some small wayside station. That second trip, knowing in advance what to expect, we had carried with us a small Coleman gasoline stove and several bottles of fuel so that we could make ourselves hot tea from time to time; we also carried with us some supplies in the way of food. Apart from long delays while bridges were repaired, our trip was relatively uneventful, and we eventually reached Chaoyang to find the Americans gone but the Chinese troops still occupying the compound and Mr. Grubb's house, while the magistrate had moved into Mr. Brewster's house as soon as the American Army men had left.

I went to the local Army headquarters, where I was able to meet with the general and show him the papers I had picked up in Mukden. With very poor grace, he issued instructions for his men to vacate the mission premises, which they did within two or three days. As soon as they had left, Eva and I moved into one of the school buildings because there was a *kang* there that could be heated, and also because Mr. Grubb's house, although empty, was both filthy and, with no glass in any of the windows, impossible to heat. It seems that the soldiers had smashed all the glass when they left as a way of expressing their annoyance. It took me ten days of constant pressuring to get the magistrate to move out of Mr. Brewster's house. When he finally left, we assessed the damage to the compound and counted some 250 panes of glass smashed either by his men or by the soldiers. Unlike Lingyuan, where the church hall had not been touched, the one in Chaoyang had been occupied by Nationalist troops and was a mess. When they left, I encouraged the local Christians to clean the place up and resume church activities there as well as restarting the two separate schools for boys and girls. Since there was little else we could do, Eva and I set out for Lingyuan.

As with the previous trip, the train from Chaoyang heading west was late in leaving. Again we traveled in darkness, which once again surprised me since they weren't doing it on the main line. But they wouldn't travel past Yebaishou. We reached Yebaishou sometime after ten o'clock, and once more all the passengers were confined to the train, with no heat. It was such a cold and windy night I was afraid we might not survive it, so I set out to find some warmer place. Although all the station buildings were boarded up, I found one room open. It was being used for communications, and there was no room for us there. I asked about Mr. Liao and was told that he, together with all the other railway staff who were not urgently needed, had been evacuated because of the fear of an imminent attack by the *balu*, so there was no place to go. I thought about walking over to the roundhouse, where the locomotives were being serviced, but we knew we wouldn't get any sleep there either. I then walked to the front of the train, where I found the baggage car full of Chinese army officers. They appeared quite friendly, and when I asked if my wife and I could move in with them for the night, they promptly agreed. We spread our sleeping bags crosswise on the floor at one end of the car with Eva closest to the one end door that remained intact. I figured that no one would use it during the night and she would be safer there. Despite the cold we both fell asleep, while the officers continued to enjoy themselves with wine they had acquired somewhere.

Several hours later I was rudely awakened by one of the officers kicking me in the ribs and ordering me to get up and get out. He turned out to be a young major, very drunk, and in an ugly mood. He thought I was a Russian, and he ranted and raved about how the Russians were supporting the *balu* and destroying China. I tried to placate him, telling him I was English and not Russian, but that seemed to make him angrier still. He said that the English were worse than the Russians because they had stolen Hong Kong from the Chinese, and he carried on about how Britain had introduced opium to China, etc. He made so much noise that he finally woke the other officers, who had been friendly toward us, and they managed to pacify him and put him to bed. The rest of the night passed uneventfully.

The next morning our train to Lingyuan was again delayed while they sent a pilot engine over the pass to check out the track, and when we finally got to Lingyuan, it was near noon. Things on the surface appeared quiet, but there was a feeling of nervousness among the people, again because of rumors of an impending guerrilla attack. We found the Chinese troops still occupying the compound, but the one room we had previously occupied had been left vacant, and I left Eva there while I went downtown to do battle, if necessary, with the local commander in order to get the troops out and the blockhouses torn down. Getting the magistrate out of our little house was of secondary importance.

I was admitted to see the general right away. He seemed nervous, and although he accepted the written orders that I handed to him and promised to have his men out within a couple of days, I could see that his mind was on something else, so I left him and went back to our compound.

Eva, in the meantime, had mixed a batch of dough and had started to bake some bread in the kitchen oven. Less than an hour later we saw a flurry of activity among the troops in the compound, with men rushing around picking up their weapons and other equipment and obviously forming up for battle. We realized that something big was about to happen.

Just then a runner came up from the Yamen with a message for us from the magistrate, telling us that an attack by the *balu* was expected before nightfall and telling us that we should get out of the city as quickly as possible. The man told us there was a train standing at the station ready to leave, and that the magistrate had called the station master and asked that the train stop behind our house and pick us up there and the station master had agreed. We were urged to leave immediately.

Neither Eva nor I panic easily, so our first inclination was to wait it out and see what would happen. However, on second thought, having heard of the atrocities committed by the *balu* at the time of their previous occupation of Lingyuan, we felt that our presence there might make it more dangerous for the Chinese Christians. So, taking our sleeping bags and Coleman stove and leaving everything else behind, including the bread in the oven, we dashed through the back garden gate and over the plowed fields, crossing the freshly dug moat on a long board at a point where a soldier stood guard, and we ran toward the railroad track to await the train.

In the distance we could hear the repeated blowing of the locomotive's whistle at the station, evidently urging people to hurry and board. The word had quickly spread around town, and there was a mad exodus toward the station of men, women and children trying to escape the city. We must have stood there waiting for an hour or more, and when we finally saw it approaching, it turned out to be a coal train with open cars loaded with coal, and every inch of space atop the coal packed with people fleeing to safety. I stood in the middle of the track waving to the engineer as the train came close and was relieved to hear him start to slow down.

When the train stopped we climbed aboard the nearest car, and the train immediately set in motion once again. We had climbed up at the front end of the car, the third one behind the locomotive. Although it was solidly packed with people, they made way for us and gave us room just behind the somewhat hi gher

steel front of the car. With our gloved hands, we burrowed our way down into the coal as best we could, wrapped our sleeping bags around our heads, and hoped for the best.

It was then around the middle of March, not the coldest time of the year, but the cold still so intense atop that open car that within minutes we were completely numb, despite our heavy clothing. The locomotive was going backwards, indicating that it had originally been going west before the train was turned back toward Chaoyang. As we were only three cars back, the smoke and ash from the locomotive's stack fell directly on us. Everyone on the car was coughing and trying to protect their eyes from the cinders, and we felt particularly sorry for the children. But there was nothing we could do. We simply tied handkerchiefs around our mouths and noses and toughed it out. Both Eva and I dimly recall the train slowly climbing the big pass on the way to Yebaishou and then stopping briefly there, with more people climbing aboard. It was a single-track line, and right after we left Yebaishou we entered a long tunnel. We both faintly remember the train entering the tunnel and the intense darkness that followed, then the suffocating smoke swirled around us and made it almost impossible for us to breathe. That is the last recollection either of us have of that part of the journey. For three days at least, and it might have been four, we somehow survived and managed to keep going. Neither of us have the slightest memory of anything that occurred during that period, nor have we any accurate estimate of how long we were in a blacked-out state. We cannot remember eating or drinking, we don't remember anything about the days or where we stopped at night, nor do we remember arriving at Jinzhou junction, where we obviously had to change trains. Somehow, though, we apparently did what had to be done, all of it as though walking in our sleep, because the next thing we remember was finding ourselves in a warm, third-class car on the main line heading toward Tientsin. Even though I wrote of the incident immediately afterward and have a copy of that letter, we are still unable to account for the exact number of days that passed between our departure from Lingyuan and our arrival in Tientsin. Whether it was the intense cold or something in the smoke that caused our loss of memory, I have no idea.

癩狗成群

Lai gou cheng qun.

Mangy dogs gather in a pack.
(Equivalent to "Birds of a feather
flock together.")

- Chinese Peasant Saying.

Chapter Thirty-Eight
Thirteen Days On The Trains

We spent a couple of weeks in Tientsin before making our third trip to Lingyuan. In the short time we'd been away, conditions there had changed beyond belief. With the failure of the Marshall Mission talks, it had become obvious no coalition government could be formed; with the withdrawal of the U.S. Marines from the railroads, the Communist guerrillas had intensified their attacks on Nationalist strongholds, particularly on the railways.

When we got off the train in Tientsin we found the huge square just in front of the Tientsin East Station packed with refugees, although we didn't recognize them at first as such. We thought they were simply people waiting for a train, as many of them were. Our rickshaw men told us that people were flocking into the city from the countryside.

When we arrived back at the China Inland Mission guest home, where we always stayed, our good friends Mr. and Mrs. Seaman told us with great regret that the home was filled to capacity, and there wasn't even a corner into which they could fit us. Feeding us would be no problem, but we'd have to find somewhere else to sleep.

Since it was already late in the evening, they invited us to put our sleeping bags on the living room floor, and that's where we spent the night. Next morning I asked Mr. Seaman if perhaps we could find a spot in the basement storage room as a makeshift place to sleep. He took us down there, but we found it to be impossible. The overpowering musty smell and the lack of any daylight quickly made us change our minds.

While trying to decide what to do, I strolled around to the back of the compound. There, in a small courtyard behind the kitchen and the servants' quarters, I found a small coal shed with a door and a window. I decided that if we removed the coal, it was large enough to meet our needs. Mr. Seaman felt badly that we should be reduced to such straits, but he had no objection to our using it. We set to with a shovel and moved the pile of coal out into the yard. I estimated it as a little over a ton. Then, after sweeping down the walls, we used a bucket of whitewash that made the walls acceptable, and by evening we had a place to sleep that was much better than many other places we had stayed.

We still have the old steamer trunks we used as a base for our bed, so from those I can give an accurate estimate of the size of the room. It measured approximately nine feet by a little over six feet. We placed bricks on the dirt floor under four of our trunks and put them together in one back corner. Then, with a borrowed double mattress on top, we were in business. The tiny window, about four feet square, didn't open — a good thing because the thin door was ill-fitting and let in plenty of cold air. The door opened inward, and our bed was so close to it that it wasn't possible to open it wider than eighteen inches or so before it hit the bed. At the end of the bed, there was just room enough in the corner for a two-burner oil-burning cooking range we'd bought in the U.S. and had brought to China with us. We also had a free-standing oil-burning heater, which, because of the fumes, we dared use only in the daytime. We had an upturned packing case on which to place a wash basin; when we needed a bath we could go inside the house, but our toilet was a Chinese-style open-air latrine just across the courtyard. What more could anyone want? That little room became our very comfortable home for our stay.

But we'd not returned to China to sit around waiting in the comparative comfort and safety of Tientsin, even if it was a coal shed. We were itching to get back up to Lingyuan. A week or so later we received a letter from Lingyuan telling us that the *balu* had attacked the night we left, but their numbers were small and they had been beaten off. The orders from my friend, the young Lt. General Pai in Mukden, had been fully effective. He had moved all his men out of our compound and things were quiet once more. The writer, Zhang Yao-ting, felt that the situation had stabilized and it was quite safe for us to return.

We waited another week to see how things would go and studied the reports of fighting in the daily papers. It seemed to us that conditions couldn't possibly get any worse, and might get better. We were eternally optimistic, and despite warnings from friends and the advice of the British consul in Tientsin, we

decided to follow the old adage, "If at first you don't succeed..." and give it one more try. The events of that memorable third trip back to Lingyuan are hard to believe and are forever etched in our memories. It was truly a miracle that we escaped with our lives.

As we fully expected to be able to stay in Lingyuan permanently, we purchased several cases of Bibles and Scripture portions from the Bible Society and had them shipped to Lingyuan by rail. We packed eight or nine boxes of foodstuffs, summer clothing and gifts for our friends, and toward the end of March 1947, we got ready to leave for Lingyuan. As the crow flies the distance was exactly 200 miles, but the zigzag railroad journey was a little over double that distance. Although in normal times it was only an 18-hour journey, we confidently expected that, judging by our two previous trips and despite the increased activity of the *balu*, it would simply be a four- or six-day journey at the most. But a great number of surprises were in store for us. The China Inland Mission home in Tientsin usually had many guests, so a group of rickshaws inevitably gathered at the corner each day trying to pick up fares. I had gotten to know several of the men and we asked four of them to come to the mission home with their rickshaws at four o'clock on the morning we wanted to leave. The train wasn't due to leave until 6:30, but we felt sure we would need the extra time. We had always found Chinese rickshaw men to be most reliable, and we had just finished an early breakfast at four o'clock when we heard the men outside the front gate. Quietly, so we wouldn't wake the rest of the guests, we loaded up the four rickshaws and started off for Tientsin East Station about four or five miles away.

The morning was cold even for Tientsin at that time of the year, and the breath of the rickshaw pullers rose in a cloud as they padded their way down the quiet streets. When we came to the river and crossed the old iron bridge, I noticed Chinese soldiers on guard, something quite unusual. When we got to the station, we again found the huge square in front of it jammed so tightly with people that we could barely make our way to the station entrance. The crowd, which a week or so before had been quiet and docile, was now rowdy and surging around the station doors demanding to be allowed on the trains. The whole thing looked pretty ominous, but the police were holding them back and we were allowed through.

I paid off the rickshaws and went over to the ticket office to buy our tickets, only to be told by the clerk behind the counter that our train, coming in from Peking, was 24 hours late. I had barely recovered from that surprise announcement when I noticed a passenger train pulling in to the station, coming from the direction of Peking. I asked the ticket clerk what train it was. He replied, quite casually, "Oh, that's yesterday's train. It, too, was 24 hours late." I told him that would be just fine for us, and he sold us our tickets. We booked most of our heavier belongings into the baggage car, hired coolies to help us with our suitcases, and went out onto the platform to board the train.

Many passengers aboard the train were going through to other destinations, but so many got off that we found seats without too much difficulty and congratulated ourselves that things weren't too bad after all. It was a long train, made up entirely of third-class carriages, sixteen of them by actual count. The seats, the narrow, slatted wooden kind with no cushions either on the seat or the back, were built in pairs, designed for two people to sit back to back with two others behind them. Furthermore, the seat backs extended only about two feet high, which meant that a good part of the time one's head was in contact with that of the person behind, particularly when that individual fell asleep. But we were used to that and hardly gave it a thought. After all, what was a mere 18 hours on the train, or even three or four days? But 24 hours later we were still sitting motionless in the same spot. Although it is hard to believe, we were still sitting in those same seats eleven days later, even though the location had changed.

For a long time after we got aboard the train, when it didn't move, I tried to get information from the railwaymen on the platform about the delay. But all they could tell me was that there was a blockage on the line ahead. At one point we did make a false start and everyone perked up, but the train merely pulled a short distance out from the platform and then backed onto a center track, where we continued to sit. Most depressingly, the locomotive was detached, leaving us without heat.

At that point I felt it was safe enough to briefly leave the train, so I found the station master and learned that a passenger train had been derailed by Communist guerrillas about 20 miles down the line near Tanggu. The whole line was blocked and much of it torn up, so we would have to wait until the wreckage was cleared and the track repaired.

We sat there that entire day, and nothing happened except that more and more people crowded onto the train. Eventually, our car and all the others were so full that three people were sitting in seats designed for two, others were sitting on their baggage in the aisles, with still others lying in the overhead luggage racks. There being no room in the luggage racks for our suitcases and bedding rolls, we had them piled up in front of us, between us and the facing seat, and we and the friends across from us sat with our legs intertwined up on top of the bags.

Our Chinese fellow passengers took it all most philosophically and with the utmost patience; it didn't seem to bother them at all. From their point of view, they were satisfied that they had managed to get onto the train at all, and eventually it would take them where they wanted to go. What was the rush? As the afternoon wore away and the sun went down, one by one people started to drift off onto the platform to buy food from vendors or went outside the station to small foodshops, and I decided I had better get something for us as well.

The French concession, where the French Bakery was famed for its tempting sandwiches, was less than a mile away. I felt that a few of those and some hot coffee would be just the thing for us. I went outside the station, jumped into a rickshaw, and thirty minutes later I was back with a tasty repast that turned out to be our last real meal for the next eleven days — the time it took us just to reach Jinzhou junction, normally a 12-hour journey.

The next morning around eleven we made another false start, but we only went a mile or so and then backed up into Tientsin station once again. We learned that a heavy crane trying to remove the wreckage of the previous day's derailment had, itself, overturned. However, we finally left Tientsin late in the afternoon of that second day, made very slow progress down the line to the point where the derailment had occurred, and found it had been caused by a mine placed by the guerrillas under a culvert, demolishing it. The overturned engine and eight passenger cars were lying beside the track, and the huge crane was lying on its side on top of the locomotive.

Our train crawled past the spot, traveled about a

mile farther down the line to a small wayside station, and stopped there for the night. We didn't even get as far as Tanggu, where we would have been able to buy something to eat, but at least we had heat provided by the locomotive, and we were able to buy hot water on the train to make our tea.

Rubbing shoulders with our fellow-passengers for eleven days, we got to know them far better than we have our neighbors here in America, even though we've lived next door to them for 12 or 15 years. We were packed so tightly together there was constant physical contact. Since the window glass on the car we were in was intact, as were the doors at each end, it actually worked to our advantage during the long cold nights, with all that body heat being given off. But the diverse body odors that had to be endured had to be experienced to be believed! By actual count more than 300 people were in our car — I counted them over and over again, just for something to do. I conservatively estimated that there were well over 4,000 people on the train.

When we stopped for any length of time on a siding or out in the open countryside, I frequently got down off the train to get in a little exercise by walking alongside on the track. Most others didn't dare get off for fear of losing their seats. Because of the bombings, a lot of armed soldiers were on the train, at least two or three in each car. At the front of the train three flatcars were coupled ahead of the locomotive, each with sandbags piled waist high around the edges and with soldiers camped inside. I estimated there were nearly 300 of them, all heavily armed with machine guns, mortars and hand grenades. With them there we felt somewhat safer in case we encountered a bomb or mine on the track. Theoretically, the flatcars were supposed to explode any mines and thus protect the more valuable locomotive. But I felt sorry for the soldiers, who were considered expendable and who must have suffered terribly from the cold.

Our progress down the line averaged at first perhaps 20 miles a day. Sometimes we went forward for a few miles, came to a blown-up bridge or a derailment, and the entire train would then back up to the nearest station or even to the same spot where we had spent the previous night. Communications along the line were non-existent, with all telegraph and telephone lines down, and all movement of trains was line-of-sight. For that reason alone we traveled extremely slowly in case another train might be approaching from the opposite direction. That happened several times, and when it did, one of the trains had to back up. More often than not it was ours, because the others were usually troop trains.

We began to lose count of the days. One day we sat in the same spot out in the open countryside for ten hours as we waited for a long viaduct ahead of us to be repaired. I walked along the track and squatted there for hours watching the Chinese engineers at work, marveling at their ingenuity. The damaged span crossed a chasm that was well over 100 feet deep. Two of the bridge's concrete piers had been blown up, with the huge steel girders down on the floor of the canyon. But the men below, looking like scurrying ants, were painstakingly rebuilding the piers using wooden railroad ties, placing them crisscross, tying them in place with straw ropes, and fastening them with huge iron staples which they formed on the spot over open fires, using sledge hammers to sharpen the red hot tips on a piece of broken rail which they used as an anvil.

When the supporting towers were complete, a railway crane came from the other side of the bridge and raised the girders into place, after which the tracks were restored. However, the result looked exactly like the well-known "Toonerville Trolley" cartoons — a wavy, uneven track that had dips and humps in it, and places where one side was quite obviously several inches lower than the opposite side. I couldn't believe that it would hold the weight of our train, but it did.

As our train crawled slowly across it, I stood on the platform of the front car, just behind the locomotive, and held my breath as the flimsy structure groaned and creaked beneath us. I tensed as the engine ahead of me tilted first to one side and then to the other, appearing in imminent danger of overturning. But far below us, on the floor of the ravine, the Chinese engineers stood looking up at us, evidently supremely confident that their work would sustain the load. They made no attempt to stand out of the way in case the train fell onto them; that, in itself, gave me a little confidence. When we finally made it to the other side, a loud cheer went up from the passengers aboard, and we puffed ahead toward the next obstacle, knowing full well that the bridge we had just crossed would probably have disappeared by the next morning.

Life aboard that train those eleven days was not boring. On a Chinese train something is always happening, and people were in motion the entire time, day or night. First, everyone had to drink tea several times a day, or all day long if at all possible. On board every Chinese train there was always a concessionaire in one car, usually in the center of the train, where he had a large, coal-fired boiler in which the water was heated, and which sold for a few pennies a potful. Normally the boiler would be refilled with water at each large stop, but we reached the larger stations only every two or three days. With 4,000 people on the train, the water didn't last very long, and sometimes two days went by with no water at all. That was hard on everyone. However, when water was available, a constant stream of people carrying their teapots, kettles or thermos flasks trudged from each end of the train to the "water" car. The going was slow and tedious because they had to climb over people and their belongings all the way down each aisle and do the same on their return trip. But no one complained, and all seemed cheerful and optimistic. When the water ran out, word got around through the train; still, an unceasing line of hopefuls headed for the water car, carrying their empty containers and hoping for the best. Sometimes the trip from their seat at either end of the train to the "water" car and back could take upwards of an hour, but still they didn't complain. I made the trip many times myself.

At times one couldn't get through a car because of an argument going on between one of the soldiers and a passenger, perhaps because the soldier had been stepped on while lying fast asleep in the middle of the aisle, or it could have been for a variety of other reasons. No one wanted to push his way past in a situation like that for fear of becoming involved. Fortunately, when the train was stationary, as was so often the case, we could get down and walk along the track. But the soldiers and railway police tried to discourage that. It was too easy for one or more of the *balu* guerrillas to mix with the crowd and get aboard the train without being noticed.

Sanitary conditions aboard the train soon became intolerable. By the third day the toilets in every car were clogged, frozen solid, and with no one to do anything about it. Eva and I usually managed to wait until nightfall and get off the train when we had to go, and because we had so little to eat or drink, that

wasn't often necessary. And at night, the soldiers guarding the train were a little more lenient about letting people off the train, knowing they wouldn't go far. It was a paradoxical situation, since in the darkness it would have been a great deal easier for any number of the *balu* to infiltrate the crowd and climb aboard the train. On the other hand, everyone in each car knew everyone else and a stranger would have stood out like the proverbial sore thumb, and when daylight came an intruder would have been noticed.

Thirst was the biggest problem for everyone, ourselves included. We had our Coleman stove and a few bottles of gasoline for it. However, getting the water to make our tea wasn't easy. Although we had plenty of canned food in our boxes in the baggage car, I was unable to get to them. The car, when I got there, was so tightly packed that I couldn't even be sure that our boxes were actually on the train.

Wherever we stopped for an hour or more, even out in the middle of nowhere, we were certain to be visited by enterprising villagers with some sort of foodstuffs for sale. If I managed to see the villagers in time, and could get to them before the mad rush by my fellow passengers, I usually managed to get a bowl of gruel or some steamed bread now and then, so, although we were always hungry, we didn't starve. At those larger stops, where food vendors were on the platform, there was never enough food to go around and people fought each other for what little there was. However, it was really surprising how long one could actually go without food provided one didn't think about it too much.

The third or fourth night after the water had run out in the "water" car we were held at one isolated location where there was no platform, no station, and no village nearby. There was just a long section of switching track used by trains to pass each other. When we came to a stop we found a troop train occupying the adjoining track. During the night the soldiers built fires on the ground between the two trains and sat around them warming themselves. Because by that time the electrical system on the entire train had ceased functioning, the light of those flickering fires was the only light we had. Batteries under each car had been exhausted, and with so little train motion, the generators were just not charging adequately.

Several things happened that night, and we got

very little sleep. Among the fellow passengers in our car was a man of around 30 who, with his vacant gaze and slack-jawed expression, gave every indication of being mentally retarded. The Chinese around us unkindly called him a *shazi*, meaning a simpleton or idiot. Strangely enough, he had shown a great interest in Eva and me and frequently had come from his seat at the far end of the car just to sit and gaze at us by the hour, never saying a word. I spoke to him numerous times but was unable to elicit any response, and I had to presume that he was both deaf and unable to speak. Some time after midnight he had apparently felt the cold and, seeing the fires outside, had slipped off the train to warm himself, without anyone noticing.

I happened to wake from an uneasy dozing when I heard a commotion, a lot of jabbering, and everyone rushing to look out the windows. There, not ten feet from me, was this unfortunate man. One soldier held him by his hair while another beat him unmercifully, and a third had a gun leveled at his head. They obviously suspected him of being a *balu* spy and were about to execute him.

Fortunately we were only two seats away from the end of the car. I scrambled over the heads of sleeping figures in the aisle, raced down the steps, and approached the soldiers, yelling at the top of my voice for them not to shoot the man, that he was a passenger from our car. At first they were disinclined to believe me, particularly because they had been unable to get anything out of him. They suspected him of the usual tactic of silence employed by captured *balu*, who would rather die than tell the enemy anything. But eventually I was able to convince them, and I dragged the shaken man back aboard our train. From that moment on, for the rest of our journey, he spent every moment of his time as close to me as he could get. We later learned that he was traveling with an older brother who, being fast asleep, hadn't noticed him leaving the car. When I gently scolded the man for getting off the car and endangering himself, he nodded his head, seeming to understand me. However, his brother insisted he was a *longya*, meaning a deaf-mute. That later proved to be incorrect.

The second event that night occurred shortly thereafter. We had just settled down again to try to get back to sleep when we heard a single rifle shot in the far distance. It was followed almost immediately by a volley of shots and feverish activity on the part of the soldiers on the adjoining train. They rushed around in every direction, firing their rifles into the darkness on both sides of the track. Everyone thought it was an attack by the *balu*, their usual practice being to attack at about that time of the night. Gradually the firing died down, and since no bullets hit the train, at least not our car, I began to wonder if it actually was an attack on the train. When all was quiet, I went and talked to one of the officers and learned that one of the soldiers on sentry duty had fallen asleep and dropped his rifle, which went off, thus providing the initial shot. That had caused a panic among the soldiers near the fires outside.

Before returning to my seat I climbed off the train to relieve myself and found, to my surprise, two long lines of people, like columns of ants, walking along a footpath below the railway embankment, where they were out of sight of the soldiers on the train. One column headed for the front of the train and the other in the opposite direction. For some unknown reason, no sentries had been placed on that side of the track.

Upon closer scrutiny I realized they were passengers from our train. Each carried a teapot or kettle or some other container. I climbed down the embankment toward them and found the ones returning were carrying boiling water. Some enterprising individual had discovered a spigot on the side of the locomotive that produced boiling water, and the word hadn't taken long to get around. Were it not for the excitement in our own car, I am sure we would have heard about it as well.

I scurried back onto the train to get our own thermos flask, told my near neighbors about it, and then dashed to the front of the train where I, too, after standing in line for 20 minutes or more, got my boiling water, and Eva and I had a refreshing middle-of-the-night cup of tea. But when morning came, we, and everyone else, had reason to regret it. When the tired engineer awoke at daylight and attempted to fire up his locomotive he found the water supply had been drained so low he couldn't raise any steam. There we were, stuck out in the middle of nowhere, and the nearest water tower was an hour's run ahead of us.

But the Chinese were never at a loss to come up with some kind of temporary solution when the need arose. As the sun came up, someone discovered a small stream nearby that was only lightly frozen over.

A line of perhaps 200 people was formed, each equipped with the ubiquitous wash basin that every Chinese traveler carried, and hand to hand, muddy water was passed from the stream to the locomotive until the engineer felt he had enough to raise the steam he needed to get to the next water tower. Detaching the locomotive from the train and pushing the three flatcars loaded with troops ahead of him, he set off, leaving our train without protection.

The few soldiers and police left on the train became very nervous. The troop train that had been next to us all night had left at dawn and we were entirely alone, with no villages in sight, and right next to a high hill that obscured the countryside in that direction. The soldiers feared the *balu* might attack from behind that hill.

The nervousness of the soldiers didn't help the civilians feel any better. However, one of the young officers aboard the train had enough sense to send a couple of soldiers to the top of the hill to act as lookouts. But that still didn't resolve the problem of what might happen should the *balu* decide we were fair game. It was with a real sense of relief that two hours later we heard our locomotive returning, and before long we were again in motion for another short run.

I very early lost count of the number of times we stopped and waited for bridges to be repaired or sections of track to be replaced where culverts had been blown up. During the long daylight hours, by invitation from our fellow passengers, who had learned that I was a missionary, I spent much of my time preaching to them, individually or in small groups at first, and then, as interest grew, to the car as a whole. Frequently we were joined by others from adjoining cars who squeezed into our already crowded car to hear what I had to say.

Eva and I taught them Scripture verses, which many learned by heart, and Gospel choruses, which they sang lustily if not tunefully. Every time I preached, my "retarded" friend was always in the front row. While I was teaching the crowd a song one morning, I was stunned to see his lips moving and hear that he, too, was among those singing the loudest. His brother, who had never once heard him speak, was amazed, unable to believe his ears. Right then everyone stopped calling him a half-wit, and before our trip ended, the man was speaking normally and seemed to have complete control of all his senses

and functions. I had long talks with him, asking him why he had never been able to talk. He could not account for it, nor could he understand why it was that he had suddenly been able to sing along with the rest of us and then start talking as though he had done so all his life. The rest of the people in the car were just as astonished as we were; immediately they attributed it to the God I had been telling them about and to the songs and Scriptures they had been learning. I wondered if the scare he had experienced when he had almost been shot had anything to do with it. But the more we thought about it, we had to believe it was just one more of the many miracles that God had shown us over the years.

When I preached, all but one individual in our car were eager listeners. The one exception was a brash young student of about 18 or 19 who occupied a seat about halfway down the car. Whenever I started to preach he would interrupt with loud, argumentative theories of his own about creation, evolution, the existence of God, and the after-life certainties of either Heaven or Hell. Whenever I mentioned the latter, he would loudly shout the common Chinese saying, *si ru deng mie*, "death is like a lamp being extinguished," i.e., there is nothing after it. He agreed with me that all Chinese gods were false gods, but claimed that the God I was preaching about was just another invention of the foreigners being forced down the throats of the Chinese people, and was of no more use than the clay gods in the temples or the paper ones they pasted on their walls. Whenever I spoke, he would heckle me unceasingly with totally irrelevant and uncomplimentary statements about foreigners in general and the British in particular, anything to cause a diversion and interrupt my preaching. He became quite a nuisance.

Most of the time I just sat there and smiled, letting him have his say. When he stopped for breath I would continue, without giving him an argument. Soon, however, the other passengers got tired of his ranting, argumentative and repetitive statements and tried to shut him up. But he was a bumptious, arrogant young fellow, and since the majority of the passengers were illiterate, he felt he was a cut above everyone else, and most of the other passengers saw him as a learned person and were afraid to contradict him or even talk to him.

A strange thing happened with that young man on

our fifth day out. After an exceptionally cold night at another small wayside station, we arrived at the city of Tangshan around ten in the morning. (Tangshan is a large city that was very much in the news in July 1976, when an earthquake measuring 8.2 on the Richter scale took the lives of some 240,000 people, as officially reported by the Chinese government. But I have met and talked with Chinese who were sent there for rescue work, and they put the number of casualties closer to 700,000.)

Tangshan, when we passed through it that morning in 1947, was the site of the British-owned and operated Kailan coal mines, then still in full operation despite the Communist guerrilla threats, with company-owned coal trains operating from there down to the port of Chinhuangtao, about 80 miles away over double tracks for the entire distance. The mines cover a tremendous area, largely under the city itself, and were in continuous operation 24 hours a day with three shifts of upwards of 10,000 miners each. (Immediately after the 1976 earthquake, the authorities had expected to find that the mine pits had collapsed, but they were so well built there was very little damage, and almost no loss of life among the miners. Most deaths occurred in the collapse of the mud-walled buildings of which the city largely consisted.)

Tangshan station in 1947 was huge by the standards of those days, with numerous tracks filled with coal trains either loaded or ready for loading, and pulled by huge, green-painted British-built locomotives that never failed to impress people with their spotless shine and polish. The guerrilla activities of the *balu* had put a crimp in the clockwork-like schedules of the KMA trains, but in spite of delays, they somehow still managed to keep their trains running most of the time, and they were never the main targets of the *balu*.

As we entered the Tangshan station, our train had to slow perceptibly to switch from the main line to a side track. As we bumped over the points at a crawl, apparently (as we surmised later) at that point a *balu* "human bomb" swung himself aboard at the end of the train. Unseen by any of the soldiers, and unnoticed by the passengers among whom he quickly hid himself, he inconspicuously started to make his way to the front of the train. With everyone engrossed in the activities on the station platform, he almost succeeded.

The "human bomb" was at that time a unique weapon of the *balu*, who used them against barbed wire defenses, blockhouses and in blowing holes in the walls of cities they were attacking. There seemed to be no lack of volunteers for the job, and the individuals concerned strapped hand grenades around their waists or carried satchels of explosives, and then simply blew themselves up against the chosen objective.

Our train stopped for nearly two hours, and everyone aboard had a chance to buy something substantial to eat for the first time in five days. Tangshan in those days was famous for its *xun ji* or smoked chickens, small but delicious, and Eva and I managed to get one apiece before the supply ran out. With it we also had steamed buns and a pot of tea.

Leaving Tangshan, we made good time on the double track line to the next big stop, Luan Xian, about 30 miles farther along, where the line crossed the Luan River on a long, high, steel bridge. As we approached Luan Xian station I saw two soldiers making their way through our car toward me with a slim young man, possibly 20 years of age and dressed entirely in black, held firmly between them by his arms. Because of all the obstructions in the aisle, their progress was slow, and I had a good look at the man. When they came closer, they stopped less than two feet in front of me, and under the young man's rucked-up coat I could see the telltale long wooden handles of perhaps a dozen of the *balu*'s famous homemade "potato masher" hand grenades strapped around his waist. I knew instantly why he had come aboard the train. It was obvious he had intended bombing the Luan River bridge just ahead of us.

As he stood there the young man looked me straight in the eye, not with any curiosity, but with a baleful, fanatical glare that seemed to say, "Just wait, I may have failed this time, but I'll get all of you yet." Then, as the two soldiers hustled him along toward the next car forward, presumably to interrogate him, I turned and watched their progress.

At the time I was sitting in our usual seat just two seats away from the end of the car and the door out onto the open platform. As the three of them moved out, someone held the door open, watching out of curiosity. I, too, watched and saw the three of them pause for a moment because people were coming from the opposite direction. The young man saw his chance, and in one fluid motion, without the slightest warning, he bent his knees and dropped to a squat and, slipping from the grasp of the two soldiers, launched himself through the air in a graceful arc, out through the open side of the platform and down onto the embankment below. I just had time to turn my head and look out the window to see him land on the back of his shoulders. Curled into a tight ball, he rolled to the bottom of the embankment, where he was instantly on his feet and running as hard as he could go. The two soldiers immediately pulled their guns and fired after him, but the train was going so fast that he was soon out of range, and as far as I could determine he was not hit.

The two soldiers, angry and exasperated at their failure to hold the man, told me they had spotted him the next car behind ours as he was working his way to the front of the train. One of the soldiers had been standing in the aisle in such a position that the young fellow had been forced to squeeze past him. In doing so, he brushed against the soldier, who felt the hardness of the hand grenades around the man's waist, and was sufficiently alert to realize what they were.

He had grabbed the young man, who put up a brief fight, but then meekly gave in and quite loudly and brazenly boasted to the two soldiers, and anyone in the car that wanted to listen, that his mission had indeed been to blow up the bridge over the Luan River. His plan had been to stand on the outside platform of the front car, just behind the locomotive, and as the train reached the middle of the bridge, he would have pulled the pin on one grenade, then jumped down between the engine and the first car, exploding all the grenades as he fell, and, of course, sacrificing his life at the same time. There is little doubt that had he succeeded, with the amount of explosive he was carrying, not only would the bridge have been severely damaged, it is highly likely that our train would have been wrecked and might possibly have plunged into the river some 50 or 60 feet below.

As Eva and I sat there and thanked God for deliverance from that near disaster, I realized the young student heckler, who had been listening as the two soldiers talked with me, had joined us and was squeezing himself onto the seat beside me. White in the face and shaking with fear, he grabbed my arm and said, "Mr. Missionary, I'm so sorry. Please forgive me for all the bad things I said to you when you were preaching. Now I believe that your God is the true God. Because of you He protected all of us on this train. Right here beside you is the safest place on the train and that's where I'm going to sit from now on." And that's exactly what he did, all the way to Jinzhou, where we had to change trains, and which we reached several days later without any further major incident.

After passing Chinhuangtao and going out through the Great Wall at Shanhaiguan, we were once more on a single track, again subject to the delays caused by lack of communication because of the destroyed telegraph and telephone lines, as well as damaged bridges and derailed trains. In addition there were also frequent troop-train movements. We continued to travel only in daylight hours, and night after night we stopped at tiny wayside stations or simply out in the open near a blown bridge while we waited for it to be repaired.

Those eleven days on the train were a wonderful opportunity to observe life in the car, and we developed a strong bond of friendship with all our fellow passengers, particularly with those in our immediate vicinity. Being cheek by jowl with them 24 hours of the day we couldn't help but become attached to them. The fixed seats were so placed that we all sat in small groups on each side of the aisle across from each other. In our four seats, seated immediately across from Eva and me, usually with our legs intertwined on top of our luggage pile, were two Chinese women, but they didn't know each other. One was a young wife returning to her husband's home near Jinzhou after a visit to her parents in Peking. The other, heading for Mukden, was middle-aged and had been with us all the way from Tientsin. She had initially aroused our curiosity because of her evident refinement, her immaculate clothing, and her overall attention to cleanliness. We had quite early noticed that her hands in particular were scrupulously clean with well-kept nails, and I suggested to Eva that she was probably a nurse or maybe even a doctor. It turned out that she was a practicing midwife.

A most interesting woman, Mrs. Wang busily knitted from morning to night and kept us amused by her fund of stories and her comments about our fellow passengers. She never seemed to stop talking, but didn't seem to mind when, at times, we dozed off, bored with listening to her. The second morning out from Tientsin I noticed her sitting placidly with her hands folded in her lap, not knitting. When I asked her why, she told me in all seriousness that it was the second day of the second lunar month, the day that the dragon raised its head from its long winter's sleep (lung tai tou). On that day, no needles or sharp knives could be used for fear of poking out the eyes of the dragon. I'd of course known of the day since childhood and of how strongly the Chinese believed that superstition. Just to tease her, I asked her if she, as an educated, intelligent woman, really believed in the dragon, and if so, where on the train was the dragon? She somewhat embarrassedly told us that it was simply a Chinese custom and a superstition. She added that she wasn't sure whether it actually was dangerous or not to use sharp instruments on that day, but she thought it better to take no chances.

Diagonally across the aisle from us, and slightly behind Eva and me, sat a young Chinese Army major with his wife and two little girls. The two children appeared to be about six or seven years of age and so much alike in height and weight that they might well have been twins. However, they differed so much in facial appearance that we had doubts as to whether they were actually even sisters.

Eva and I were particularly interested in those two little girls because twins were a very rare sight in China in those days. As a matter of fact, although on a number of occasions we had heard of the birth of twins, neither of us had ever actually seen any. Chinese peasants and middle-class people alike considered them to be very unlucky. Usually, one or both were secretly put to death at birth by the mother or midwife before the father or anyone else could see them. That was because of the general assumption that in all such cases it was a sign that the wife had not been faithful to her husband, and someone other than the father had sired the second child. At present, in modern China, where, except in rural areas, all such superstitions have been officially abolished, I am told that twins are almost as common as they are in Western countries.

The father of the two girls was a stern and taciturn man. Just before we left Tientsin an incident had occurred that had caused him much embarrassment and loss of face. It was quite obvious he'd not forgotten it nor forgiven the man who had been its inadver-

tent cause. As a result, no one was anxious to strike up a conversation with him, nor did he initiate a conversation himself with anyone. He just sat there glumly, not saying a word to anyone except his wife, and then only rarely and very roughly. Obviously, she, and the two little girls were very much afraid of him.

The incident had happened this way. After waiting all day that first day in the Tientsin station, shortly before nightfall when just about everyone in the car had gotten off the train to buy food as I did, a young farmer sitting with his wife and baby boy in the seat directly across the aisle from us had gone out and purchased a tall, three-gallon can of hot boiled noodles. He and his wife had eaten as much as they could and had even fed some to the infant, but a good half had been left over. The man had placed the half-full can on the overhead rack, but because a man lay up there immediately above his seat, the only space available had been immediately above the young army officer.

During the night, while almost everyone in the car was fast asleep, the train had been shunted around to another track, and the bumps and jerks as they hooked up a locomotive to the train had caused the can to tilt sufficiently so that the noodles started to run out. No one noticed as the long, cold noodles began to drip down onto the sleeping officer's head immediately below.

With the continued movement of the train, and as new cars were added, I awoke from a fitful sleep and glanced across at the officer. The noodles were draped all over his head, shoulders and uniform jacket. Having seen the farmer place the can on the rack I sensed there was going to be trouble, so I gently woke the young farmer and showed him what had happened. What followed was hilarious, and I woke Eva so that she, too, could enjoy it.

The young farmer, in obvious fear and distress, reached up for the noodle can. Then, with very deliberate and meticulous care, he used a pair of chopsticks and commenced to pick the noodles off the head and face of the sleeping officer, carefully placing each one in the can to be eaten later. He wasn't about to see them go to waste.

Everything would have been fine had it not been that the train made another violent jerk, and the young farmer fell into the officer's lap, waking him.

The officer, thinking he was being attacked, let out a roar that woke everyone, and the sight of him with noodles draped all over his head set everyone in the car laughing. The young major soundly slapped the farmer's face, then sat there placidly, glaring out between the dangling noodles, and for the next fifteen minutes we were entertained with the sight of the farmer patiently picking off the noodles, one by one, and bowing to the officer with each one he picked off. It was a scene that Laurel and Hardy would have thoroughly enjoyed. I had anticipated that the farmer would ultimately receive a sound beating — such was the way with Chinese army officers — but the major, after roundly cursing the man, apparently decided not to pursue the matter further. As it was, he had already attracted too much attention.

That same poor young farmer appeared to be out of his element on the train and seemed to have a knack for getting himself into trouble. More than once I had to step in and plead on his behalf with either the railway police or one of the soldiers whom he somehow managed to annoy. On one occasion he was fast asleep with his legs sticking out into the aisle, and a passing soldier tripped over them. For that he got a sound drubbing until I intervened. A day or so later, this time during the day, he again fell asleep. Partially awakening, he unthinkingly cleared his throat and spat toward the floor of the aisle instead of into one of the large spittoons that lined the aisle. Unfortunately for him, his gob of spittle landed directly on the shoe of a railway policeman passing by. Again, he was pulled from his seat and roundly cuffed, and it would have gone further had I not intervened and spoken "soft words" to the policeman and suggested that the farmer clean his shoe. That in itself, had it not been so serious, would have provided a lot of amusement for everyone, the farmer groveling on the floor, wiping the man's boot assiduously with the sleeve of his coat and at the same time bumping his head on the floor in the traditional "kowtow."

Sitting on our side of the aisle, directly across from the farmer and his wife and immediately behind our friend Mrs. Wang, the midwife, was another army officer, a young lieutenant, and his wife. She was carrying a baby boy about the same age as the one the farmer had. The two young families were directly in our view, and the contrast between the way in which they cared for their babies was a constant source of amusement to Eva and me.

The farmer and his wife were totally unsophisticated but thoroughly practical. The care of the baby was left entirely to her, although from time to time he proudly bounced the gurgling child on his knee and fed him bits of food, which he had first carefully chewed. Most of the time, though, he sat next to the window and slept. The wife, plump and loud-voiced, dressed in the traditional dark-blue trousers and jacket and nothing else, breast-fed the baby, not at any regular or stipulated time but, like most Chinese mothers, every time the child fussed even the slightest bit. Day or night, it made no difference, she seemed to be perpetually feeding the infant and it was rare indeed to hear the child cry for more than a moment or two.

It was customary and quite proper in China for a mother to breast feed her child in public, provided the top button of her jacket was kept buttoned. Buttoning the top button was a sign of modesty, and the Chinese deplored our Western women with their vulgar low-necked dresses. In the case of the farmer's wife, for her own and the child's convenience, her single upper garment, except for the top button, was left unbuttoned all the time, fully exposing her opulent, milk-filled breasts and most of her upper body. As was so typical of the peasant class, who lived always on the edge of extreme poverty with little or no access to soap and water, her torso was caked with the black soot and dirt of winter, streaked in places with sweat. Only a small area around her nipples, where the child continually sucked, looked comparatively clean.

The baby, sewn into his one-piece padded garment, was equally filthy and had in all probability not been bathed since birth. But a healthier child would have been hard to find. Like almost all Chinese children, he had never seen a diaper. His open-crotch pants allowed his mother to take instant action the moment he showed any inclination to relieve himself. She seemed to have an instinctive awareness of when something was about to happen, and the nearby spittoon served admirably. It is highly probable that she presumed it was there for that very purpose. Day after day and time after time we watched as, after feeding the child, she would hold him spread-eagled over the spittoon, and in Chinese fashion would whistle tunelessly through her teeth until the child obliged by either urinating or defecating, as the need might be.

The lieutenant and his wife were typical of the "Chinese modern class." The wife, quiet-spoken, slim and petite, always spotlessly clean, was dressed in a long, form-fitting satin gown slit up the sides to show a lot of leg, a dress which Americans have come to know as a *cheongsam*, but which Northern Chinese call a *qi pao*. She was the picture of modest gentility, and she eyed the goings on across the aisle with obvious distaste and annoyance. Her baby spent most of his time in a portable bassinet, balanced on top of their extensive pile of luggage, which, like our own, was stacked between their seats. Her baby, in contrast to the one across the aisle, appeared sickly and seemed to cry a great deal of the time. He was bottle-fed, and the young father, so unlike the average Chinese, was kept busy running back and forth getting their five or six thermos flasks refilled with hot water, which they used not only for mixing the baby's formula, but also for drinking and for washing the baby's diapers out on the platform of the car. After wringing out the diapers, he would then knot them together and string them outside the window to dry or else drape them from the baggage rack overhead. It amused us to see the farmer's wife watching all those strange antics with wide-eyed wonderment. But never a word passed between the two women during the entire eleven days they spent just a few feet from each other, nor did the two husbands compare notes. They were worlds apart.

Mrs. Wang had a direct view of the young major and his family across the aisle. As the days went by, her curiosity over the two little girls knew no bounds. Mrs. Wang was quite a talker and didn't hesitate to talk to anyone who would listen, but in the case of the army family, she was chary of talking to the mother of the two little girls because the husband was almost always there, and she was a little afraid of him. But as she continued to speculate on the subject of why the two little girls appeared to be twins, yet looked so utterly different, I grew tired of hearing her. One day when the officer had left his seat to get some hot water, I urged Mrs. Wang to satisfy her curiosity by asking the mother outright about the girls.

The poor mother was glad to have someone to talk with and told Mrs. Wang that the two girls were indeed sisters; both of them were hers, but they were not twins. Mrs. Wang asked her why the girls had no

family resemblance. The mother told her they had been born a year apart, but when giving birth to the first girl she had been very ill and was unable to nurse her, and so she had hired a wet nurse to feed the child.

We, of course, could hear the entire conversation between them and that explanation satisfied what little curiosity Eva and I had about the two children. We simply presumed that, because of the mother's ill health, the child, too, had not been well, and, fed by a wet nurse, her growth had somehow been stunted and hence she was no taller than her younger sister. But it didn't explain to us why they didn't look at all like sisters.

However, it was all quite clear to Mrs. Wang. She went one step further and said to the mother, "Aha! Now I know why their faces look so much different. The younger one looks just like you, but the older one, having been raised on the milk of a wet nurse, looks exactly like the wet nurse must have looked." And with a self-satisfied smirk on her face, she returned to her seat and proceeded to retell the whole story to us.

I'd heard so much on the topic that I was tired of it, and I couldn't resist needling Mrs. Wang a bit with her simplistic outlook. Pointing to the young military couple immediately behind her, I somewhat unkindly said, "Mrs. Wang, you know, you may be quite right. See that baby there? It has been fed out of a bottle ever since birth. In Western countries that is quite common, and many babies are fed canned milk or canned formulas or even cow's milk, and that's why that baby looks like a bottle and so many of us Westerners look either like bottles or tin cans."

Poor Mrs. Wang. For a moment she took me quite seriously and started to nod her head. But then she heard the roar of laughter from those sitting nearby, who had overheard me, and knew I was pulling her leg. She sat back somewhat chastened, and for a few hours, at least, subsided into an offended silence, never again referring to the subject. But she eventually forgave me, and when we parted at Jinzhou we were still good friends.

After we passed Shanhaiguan, the railway line ran just a few miles inland from the ocean for the 100 miles or so to Jinzhou. Because of the previous guerrilla activity in that area, I was somewhat apprehensive that they might stop our train, but their tactics continued to be simply to harass and not to attack, and we saw nothing of them. Gradually, with the ocean to our right just a few miles away and the wide open fields on our left, we began to feel a little more secure. Nonetheless, our progress was no faster. There were still the same delays for destroyed bridges and torn-up tracks. Time and time again we stood for hours as work crews feverishly made repairs or temporary detours around a destroyed bridge. Some days we traveled no more than five miles and getting something to eat or drink was a continuing problem.

Eventually, in the early afternoon of the eleventh day, we saw in the distance the distinctive, well-preserved, 1000-year-old 15-story pagoda that marked Jinzhou, and we were so thankful when our train pulled into the station. We said goodbye to our friends, most of whom were going on to Mukden or beyond, and headed for our favorite inn, only to find it had been taken over by Chinese troops. The baggage coolies from the station carrying our stuff recommended a nearby Japanese hotel, so we went there. As the coolies left us they promised they would come in the morning to help us board the branch-line train for Lingyuan. Like the coolies we had used on a previous trip, they warned us that it would be very crowded and said that although the train wasn't due to leave until 7 a.m., unless we went out to the yards where the train was made up and got there by around two in the morning, there was no guarantee that we could get on board. We knew it was going to be another short night.

The hotel, which I had never seen before, had been built during the four years we had been away, but it had been a shoddy job and the whole place was already in a bad state of disrepair. Even so, the hotel was unique in its design. Six stories high, it was built of poured concrete, and constructed in a square, built around a large, well-like inner shaft, which was open to the sky. It had no elevator and only one stairway. The rooms on each floor faced outward and were serviced from a balcony that ran around the inner shaft, behind the rooms.

The unique part about the hotel was that the inner shaft, which was at least fifty feet square, was the public toilet, the bottom an open cesspool. On each floor, at staggered intervals, small platforms extended about six feet out over the well shaft, and at the end of each was an enclosed privy, slightly larger than a

telephone booth, with a standard Japanese squat-type ceramic toilet fixture. Each fixture was set over a hole in the floor through which everything dropped straight down to the bottom of the shaft. Although the hotel had water piped throughout, fed from a tank on the roof, no water was piped to the toilets. A constant, light cloud of steam rising from the cesspool below had caused ice to form on all of the walkways out to the privies, making a trip out there hazardous in the extreme, and we used it as infrequently as possible.

When we were there in early April, the weather was still so cold that the odor from the bottom of the well was not yet intolerable, but what it must have been like in the hot summer months does not bear imagining. In our lifetime we have used many different kinds of toilet facilities, but that one, where we could look up and see various other toilets in use above us, was a remarkable experience, to say the least.

The Chinese manager told me the hotel had been taken over from the Japanese at the time of their surrender, and, like the hotels in Mukden, it was operated by a Chinese general. After we had chatted a while I asked him the same question I had asked many others — about the treatment of the Japanese by the Chinese population at the time of the surrender. He told me much the same as others had: the Chinese, despite the harsh treatment from the Japanese over so many years, had not been vindictive in return. He said he knew of only one incident; some Japanese boarding a train for evacuation to Japan had been booed by a large crowd of Chinese who threw feces at them. Other than that, he said there had been no incidents of molestation, but everything the Japanese had left behind had been thoroughly looted.

The hotel manager told me one very interesting story. He said a certain Japanese army major, upon hearing Emperor Hirohito's radio broadcast ordering all his troops to surrender, had, out of shame for his country's defeat, tried to commit *harakiri*, that ceremonial form of suicide performed in Japan by warriors who felt somehow disgraced. As he was just about to slit his belly, he was discovered by some Chinese soldiers who stopped him and took him into custody for his own safety. Later, when all the Japanese were shipped back home, the man was somehow forgotten and continued to languish in the police lockup for several months.

When the Chinese police finally let him out and told him to make his own way back to Japan, he was still so ashamed that he offered himself as a slave to a well-to-do Chinese family and elected to take the place of their donkey, working the public grindstone that the family operated nearby.

The manager offered to take me over to see the man, so I went along. In an open shed on a back street behind the hotel, I found the man, short, thick-set and sturdy-looking, harnessed to the heavy stone roller on top of the grindstone. There, his head down, a blank expression on his face, he paced in a constant circle, pulling the roller just like the usual donkey or mule. The only difference was that he was not blindfolded as the animals always were, to prevent them from getting dizzy or wanting to break away from the circle. The householder told me that the man worked there from daybreak until dusk, never saying a word to anyone, never stopping for food or water unless it was brought to him and he was forced to stop. He never rested except when a batch of grain had been properly ground into flour and had to be swept up before a new batch could be put onto the stone.

During the ten minutes or so that I stood there watching him, he never raised his eyes or looked around. Each time as he passed close to me I spoke to him in Japanese, giving him the usual salutations and greetings. But he completely ignored me and made no response. From what I could see, his eyes looked like those of a dead man or a sleep-walker, and it was obvious that what he was doing was his form of penance on behalf of the Japanese nation and his own failure to achieve victory over the Russians. I am quite sure he remained there until his death.

Sometime during the last two days on the train I had caught a very severe cold and was feeling miserable. Since there is nothing quite like a good Chinese meal to cure a cold, Eva and I went to a small restaurant that we knew well and ordered a sumptuous feast. Sad to say, my cold was at that stage where I had lost all sense of taste, and the delicious-looking food tasted just like cotton. I can still vividly recall my keen disappointment in finally getting a good meal after such a long time on the train without proper food, and then being unable to enjoy it.

Almost every large city in China was famous for some special product or commodity, and Jinzhou was no exception. Its specialty was a pickled gherkin, but much smaller than the ones with which Americans are familiar. The tiny cucumbers averaged a mere inch or so in length and smaller than a pencil in diameter. They were pickled in a mixture of dark vinegar, soya sauce and a foul-smelling shrimp oil. The pickles smelled abominable but tasted divine and were a much-sought-after delicacy throughout that area. They delighted the palates of the Chinese, but very few Westerners could stomach them. They were so widely known and so popular with people passing through on the trains that one could buy them packed in a foul-smelling brine inside small wicker baskets. The baskets were shaped like a squat, flat-sided crock, about five inches high and four or five inches wide. Both the inside and outside of the baskets had been waterproofed with oiled paper, and each container was tightly sealed with wax. Nonetheless, it was still possible to smell the contents.

I bought about two dozen as gifts for the various government officials in Lingyuan whom I would be visiting and some for our many Christian friends. The shopkeeper deftly tied them together in two bunches so that they could be easily carried onto the train. I had reason later to greatly regret my impetuosity in buying those pickles.

Our room was on the third floor of the hotel, and we slept soundly that night even though the room was not heated, and there were no beds and no carpet on the cement floor. There was a wash basin in one corner, but the pipes that led to it had frozen and burst, so there was no running water. We made do with a battered enamel basin placed on the floor, and the floor boy brought us plenty of hot water in a pail. It was great to have a wash-down after eleven days without.

A little before two in the morning we were awakened by the station coolies who, as promised, had come for our baggage. Instead of taking us to the station, we were taken to the make-up yards some distance away, where we fully expected to find the train empty. Imagine our surprise when we got there and found that about 3,000 people had beaten us to it and the train was solidly packed.

We walked up and down the one side of the train in almost total darkness but found nowhere to climb aboard. The cars were the same ones we had seen on our previous trips, with no window glass, and so many people crammed in each car that practically every window was occupied by a person sitting on the windowsill, legs either inside or outside the car. The platforms and steps were equally packed with people. Under the cars were makeshift rope slings tied to the rods, each with someone in them, and people balanced on top of the wheel-trucks under the cars, all of them oblivious of the danger to which they would be exposed once the train got under way. However, they only rode there until we got into the station, when all of them were dragged away by the police. People even covered the top of the cars, but in the darkness we couldn't see how many.

We weren't alone in trying to board the train. Hundreds of people milled about on each side of the train, all scrambling to get aboard, and fights broke out at the steps of the cars as the people below tried to pull others off the train so they could get on. It appeared to be completely hopeless. We checked out the baggage car, but that was out of the question. The doors were closed, and police were guarding it so that no one could climb in. I politely asked one of the men if there was room for us, but he told me there was so much baggage waiting on the station platform that there wouldn't even be room for all of it, and even if he did let us in, we would be ejected when the train pulled into the station for departure. Almost ready to give up, we decided to walk the length of the 13-car train for the third time, but this time on the other side.

Halfway along we came to what had once been a plush dining car but was now an empty shell. It had been stripped of everything that could be removed, except for the large iron cooking range that had simply been too big and heavy to move, and the remaining space was solidly packed with people, all standing. The rail yards were dark, with the only light coming from light poles on the perimeter, so it was not only hard to see where we were walking, but we constantly stumbled over people who had fallen or others who were climbing in and out under the cars looking for a place to ride. As we traveled through the dining car on the outside, we came to the kitchen section, where there was just a blank wooden wall and no windows. But something caught my eye and made me stop for a better look. High up on the blank wall was a tiny door, approximately two feet in width and about thirty inches high. I recognized it immediately for what it was — it was the door to the ice box that serviced the kitchen, and through which the

large, 100-pound blocks of ice could be loaded at platform level. If it was empty, then it was just the place for us.

From where we stood on the track, the door was about four feet above our heads, but when the train was alongside the station platform, the opening would be only a foot or so above ground level. Asking one of the coolies to bend over, I climbed up on his back and opened the door. It was pitch dark inside, but it appeared empty, so I had the men pass up our suitcases and other hand baggage, and, of course, our 24 crocks of pickles. I pushed them all back into the compartment as far as I could reach. Then Eva climbed up on the back of one of the other men and between us we hoisted her up, head first, through the opening. Finally I climbed in myself, but feet first, so that I could hold the door open to prevent it from closing accidentally, since there was no handle on the inside. The coolies thought it was a huge joke and laughed with glee at my discovery. They told me they would save that secret for the next time they had important guests.

Despite the blackness inside, we got to know the dimensions of that compartment very well, as well as every board on the floor on which we lay. The roof was too low for either of us to sit up. It wasn't quite wide enough for my shoulders, so I had to lie at an angle. The best we could do was to push our baggage as far as possible to the far end, then lie sideways, propped on one elbow, our feet overlapping in the middle, and an occasional change of position was the luxury of putting one of the smaller bags under our heads.

Not only was it necessary that I keep the door open because there was no latch on the inside, we also needed some fresh air. But we didn't want the cold wind blowing in once the train was in motion, nor did we want the door to open so widely that it would attract attention from others who would try to get in. Fortunately, it opened in the direction opposite to that in which the train would be traveling, but I puzzled for some time over how to keep it open without having to hold it. That would have been next to impossible. I eventually solved the problem by looping my scarf over the handle outside, then bringing the ends of it inside, where I could tie them to the handle of one of our suitcases, which we had dragged forward. The scarf was thick enough that the door wouldn't close completely, and it left just about a half-inch crack through which we got fresh air, but little or no light. We thankfully settled down for what we hoped would be only a few hours, but it was to be 14 hours before we left that ice compartment.

At 6:30 a.m. the train was backed alongside the station platform, a totally superfluous procedure, because the train was so packed that even an ant would have had difficulty climbing aboard. However, apparently some VIPs were boarding, and we were told later that the police had unceremoniously pulled people off to make way for them. I wanted to see if our other boxes had been loaded into the baggage car. But I didn't dare open our door for fear we might be kicked out. One never knew what the police might take it into their heads to do. I decided to leave things the way they were. At 7 a.m. we pulled out exactly on time. But that was the last adherence to any schedule for the remainder of the trip.

Crawling at what seemed a snail's pace, we slowly made our way in a northeasterly direction, stopping at every little station for what seemed an interminable time, sometimes for well over an hour. That gave me a chance to peek out and see where we were, but the farther north we traveled the colder the weather became. Heavy clouds rolled in, along with a bitterly cold north wind, and the sun very soon disappeared. It looked and felt very much as though it was going to snow.

When the train was stationary, we could hear the voices of people in the dining car through the thin wooden wall between us and the kitchen. Our box began to get so cold I wondered if, unable to move around, we might not freeze to death, and I tried to figure out some way of getting warm. We had our sleeping bags with us, but there wasn't room enough to get them opened up. It suddenly occurred to me that there had to be some sort of access between the kitchen and the ice box so that the cooks could get to the ice. Maybe if I could find it and open it, we might get some warmth from inside the car. At one of the stops I took a chance and opened our little entrance door wide enough so that I had light enough to see the wall beside me. Sure enough, I found a crack from top to bottom. I pushed, but nothing happened, then I figured out that it must be a sliding panel. Naturally, there was no handle on the inside. After much pushing, I managed to get it open a foot or so.

Very little light came in, but looking through it at floor level, all I could see was a forest of legs and feet. The air that reached us, warmed as it was by the bodies of the 300 or so people inside, was initially welcome. But it was so thick with the smell of perspiration and the odor of feet that combined with the smell of the shrimp oil from our pickle crocks, it was more than we could stand. Only by tying handkerchiefs over our noses and mouths were we able to endure it. In time, though, we became completely accustomed to it and no longer noticed it.

After about 30 miles we reached the village of Ni Hozi (literally "Muddy River"), just a short distance before the big town of Yixian, where the line branched off due north to Beipiao. We stopped there for so long that, peeking out, I saw people milling around on the platform and decided it was safe for me to get out to stretch my legs and perhaps find out the reason for the delay. I walked over to a group of soldiers and started chatting with them, but no sooner had we started to talk than there was a great deal of shouting and everyone was told to get back on the train at once, and we were told that the train was going back to Jinzhou. No explanation was given.

The locomotive was shunted to the rear of the train and then hooked back on. But that was it; nothing further happened for ten or fifteen minutes. Then the whistle blew. But no sooner had the train started to move than it jerked to a stop. There was a lot more shouting, and through the crack of our partially opened door, I could see soldiers running toward what was now the front of the train. Then we heard the locomotive coming back down the track again, and it was hooked up to its original position once more. It was all very baffling and mysterious.

Then came a further long wait. In all we waited there for nearly five hours. The station was so tiny that there was no waiting room, just the station master's office and a signal box. Once more I got out and walked around a bit, and then I decided it was safe for Eva to get out and walk about for awhile. Still, no one could tell me the reason for the delay except that there was "trouble up the line." After a few minutes of walking around in that freezing wind, we decided to head back to the comparative warmth of our little nest. Just as I was about to close the door, I saw a group of people in the distance coming across the plowed fields toward the train. There were so many of them that at first I thought they might be a group of *balu* guerrillas, but then I saw that they were carrying things between them on poles.

They turned out to be some enterprising villagers who had taken note of the train sitting there for such a long time, and knowing that everyone would be hungry, they had cooked up a big batch of millet gruel in large iron woks, which they carried inside large baskets. I knew at once there would be a mad rush as soon as the rest of the passengers saw them, so I made sure I was in the forefront as soon as they arrived at the station.

The soldiers wouldn't allow them onto the platform, which was perhaps just as well, because there was such a vast crowd of people on the train that things would have been difficult to control. The villagers placed their woks on the ground in a row out on the dusty road behind the station and produced a few bowls. When the soldiers began to let the passengers through the gate at the back of the platform, a furious stampede ensued as people raced to get to the food. Of course, there weren't nearly enough bowls to go around; people had to eat the stodgy gruel then and there and hand the bowls back to be refilled for someone else. With no thought for the lack of hygiene, I finally got hold of a bowl that several others had used, the same unwashed bowls passing from mouth to mouth. But who cared? I got it filled, gobbled it down, and then had it filled again for Eva. Surprisingly, the villager trusted me enough to let me take it to her in the box, and those two bowls of the commonest of simple peasant food, hot and nourishing, were as welcome as any gourmet meal we'd ever had; moreover, it was the only food we had for the rest of that day.

By the time I returned the bowl all the woks were empty. There wasn't nearly enough to feed the entire train. But then, a lot of the people had *ganliang* with them: dry solid food prepared for a journey, usually steamed buns or thin wheat or millet cakes. Some even had packages of sweet cakes.

Our thermos flask was empty by that time, and we badly needed something to drink. I knew that where the station master was, there would be tea. So I walked past the soldiers to his little office and made his acquaintance. He seldom saw a foreigner, and he was happy to chat with me. But he was worried, and finally, after I had drunk three or four cups of tea, he told me the *balu* had attacked a village up the line about 10 miles north of us and had destroyed a bridge. All railway communication was down and he'd only heard about it by way of the military, who had a radio. They told him that troops had been dispatched from Beipiao and that fighting was still in progress. He said he was awaiting word about the train coming from the north, which normally we were supposed to pass at the next station. He was afraid to let our train go on for fear we might meet the other one halfway. His idea was to wait a little longer; he could then presume that the other train had been caught on the far side of the blown bridge.

While we were talking, an army officer came in and told him the other train was indeed being held on the far side of the blown-up bridge and that the fighting had moved on away from the area, so it was safe for us to proceed. The station master told me that when we got to the area in question, we would have to detrain and walk across the river about a mile to where the other train was, and he suggested that I get back on the train because he was about to let it go. I thanked him, and filling my thermos flask with hot water, I returned to the train. A few minutes later it started up, heading in the right direction.

Shortly before we had reached the transfer point I discussed with Eva how we would get ourselves and our suitcases out and across to the other train. What with the pickles, we had more than we could carry between us. I would somehow also have to arrange for the heavy boxes in the baggage car to be carried across to the other train.

An idea came to me. Perhaps with a little incentive one of the other passengers might be willing to help. Through the opening into the dining car I tapped one of the feet that was nearest to me and asked the owner if he would be willing to carry my pickles across to the other train, offering to pay him whatever he had paid for his ticket. He showed not the slightest surprise or curiosity at hearing a voice coming from down near his feet. He didn't ask me who I was or where I was going; he just flatly refused to help. I tapped another foot and then another, and all the answers were the same. Everyone was so concerned with their own problems they weren't prepared to discuss helping anyone else.

The train chugged along at about five miles an hour and when, through the crack of the partly opened door, I saw we were nearing the area of the bridge, I opened the door wide and stuck my head out to see what was ahead of us. I feared the worst and wanted no surprises.

A few minutes later an extraordinary sight met my eyes as we rounded a bend in the track. In the near distance ahead of us a column of black smoke was rising from burning homes in a village close to the track. But what caught my immediate attention was the sight of thousands of people lining the track on each side ahead of us. At first I thought it was an army approaching us, and then I realized they were the passengers from the other train who had crossed the river and were standing there waiting for us. As we pulled abreast of the first of the waiting crowd, pandemonium broke out, and they began a mad scramble to try to board our train even before we had stopped, fighting those who were trying to get off and giving them no chance of doing so. It was a madhouse, but in time it sorted itself out.

When the train finally stopped, I jumped down onto the roadbed, and Eva, by scrunching herself up against the side of the box, was able to pull the suitcases and our bedding rolls from the far end, drag them past her and push them out the door, where I could catch them. Finally she herself jumped and I caught her, and together we made our way down the embankment out of the way of the crowd.

On the other side of the damaged bridge, a good half mile away, the second train stood in the station, smoke belching from the locomotive's stack, and repeated blasts from its whistle didn't help the panic. The engineer obviously was anxious to get away from that spot and was indicating he wanted everyone to hurry and get over there. I decided that the best thing to do was to have Eva go there as soon as possible so that she could be one of the first aboard the train. I told her that if, for any reason I was delayed while getting the boxes out of the baggage car and the train should pull out without me, she should get off at Chaoyang and make her way to the house of one of the Christians, and I would join her there later. I watched her join the stream of people, which, like a column of ants, headed under the still-smoking bridge, crossed the sand and ice to the edge of the shallow stream, which they then crossed on stepping stones. After that I could see her no longer.

The baggage car was at the rear of the train.

Carrying my two suitcases and the two bundles of pickles, I pushed toward the rear, but it was hard going since everyone else was going the opposite way. When I reached the baggage car I found the men inside were emptying the car and throwing everything down the embankment. It took me several minutes to locate our boxes, and after I had done so I piled them together and looked around to see if I could find someone to help me carry them over to the other train. I first tried some of the passengers who were less burdened than I, but they were much too panicky to be bothered with helping anyone.

Then I happened to spot six men standing idly up against a wall in the nearby village, about a hundred yards away, apparently enjoying the evening sun, which by that time was very low in the west. As I ran toward them the thought occurred to me: "These men can't be villagers. Why are they standing here while some of the houses in the village are burning, and where is everyone else?" But I stopped thinking about it.

When I got close to the men I realized they were not the usual peasants. These were hard-eyed individuals of uncertain employment, and I immediately suspected they were Communist sympathizers, hangers-on who had followed the armed forces as a cleanup group, or what was known as the "poor party." But it was too late. I was close to them and had to say something. I told them I had some boxes I wanted carried to the other train, and I offered them one Mexican dollar for each box carried. They said nothing and simply shook their heads. I raised my offer to two dollars, then three, and finally five. At that, they looked at each other, muttered something, and reluctantly agreed to help me, following me back to where our boxes were piled.

They cursed about the weight of the boxes, but hefted them up on their shoulders and started off in single file, one of them carrying one of my suitcases. With the other suitcase and the pickles, I brought up the rear. As we passed under the damaged bridge, pieces of smoldering wooden ties were still dropping to the ground, and two of the huge girders had fallen into the river. It was going to be a long time before that bridge would be operational again.

By that time, we were almost the last in the long, straggling line of people hastening toward the other train, but my six men took their time and walked ever more slowly, quite deliberately dragging their feet. After crossing the river, there was a long stretch of sand and rock, and away from the noise around the train I could now clearly hear gunfire in the distance. Looking east, I could see a village about two miles away with a column of smoke rising, indicating another house on fire. I asked the men what was going on over there, and they nonchalantly replied that the *balu* had occupied the village and the Nationalist troops were attacking them and trying to drive them out. But they showed little interest in talking about it.

As we walked I tried to hurry the men, and the constant blowing of the train whistle ahead of me made me feel certain I was going to miss the train. But when I urged them to hurry, they just turned and swore at me, and then, with no warning, threw down the boxes and said they would carry them no farther. All six started to walk back toward the place where I had found them. I realized it was a simple case of blackmail, or at least I hoped it was only that. I was tempted to abandon the boxes and just run for the train without them, but I decided to give it a try. I cajoled them, talking "good talk" as the Chinese say, and offered them double what I had promised them before, and they finally agreed to pick up the boxes, but they demanded their money in advance. What could I do but give it to them? I was absolutely at their mercy. Fortunately, though, they had some degree of the Chinese sense of honor that when a bargain is made one sticks to it.

How thankful I was when we finally reached the railway track again, and came up to the last car of the train. By that time it was almost dark. Despite the cold wind, I was sweating profusely, as were the six men, and to my tremendous relief, the last car on the train happened to be the baggage car. Throwing the boxes into the car, I let the men go, thankful to see the last of them.

Carrying my suitcases and the pickles, I hurried along the narrow path between the train and a high wire fence, very near the tail end of a long line of people, all of whom were hurrying to get aboard. But I had little hope of finding any space until I reached the front of the train. Meanwhile, I was feverishly scanning every window to try and spot Eva, and I was sure, wherever she was, she was keeping an eye out for me.

Completely exhausted, I staggered blindly along, pushed and hustled by those with lighter loads who barreled past me in their rush to try and find some space up ahead. Being taller than most of those in front of me, I could see a few yards ahead in the falling darkness, but it was already too dark to see what was underfoot. Near a tall signal pole up ahead, I dimly saw, in my befogged state of mind, that everyone ahead of me seemed to bob down as they reached that spot and then bob up again. But my benumbed brain refused to supply a reason for that phenomenon until I, too, reached the spot, where I found out the hard way what was causing it. A steel wire controlling the signal led from the signal post, crossing the path and then went under the railroad track. It was just about three inches above the ground, quite invisible in the darkness, and everyone was being tripped up. When the man immediately in front of me fell, I still didn't realize why. Then came my turn, and flat on my face I went, my suitcases falling out of my hands and my precious pickles flying ahead of me, with most of them ending up under the train or under the feet of the other passengers. Before I could scramble to my feet the man behind me fell on top of me. I was so utterly exhausted, it was the last straw. I picked myself up, grabbed the suitcases, and simply ignored the pickles. There was no sense trying to find them in the darkness, and there was no time, either.

By that time it was so dark I had difficulty distinguishing faces in the windows above me. Fortunately Eva, from her vantage point, was able to spot me. I had just passed under one window when, between blasts of the engine whistle and the shouts of the crowd, I heard Eva's voice calling me. I passed my load to her through the window, and since it would have been impossible to battle my way up the steps and into the car, using my last ounce of strength for a desperate upward leap, I caught hold of the sill of the window. With Eva and some helpful bystanders inside pulling on my arms, they dragged me through the window not a second too soon. The train was in motion before I was actually inside, leaving behind a large number who had been unable to climb aboard.

There was bedlam inside the car. Everyone was talking at once about their experience and their close call with the *balu*. Despite her fur hat, poor Eva was again suffering from a terrible neuralgic headache after walking so far, directly facing into the cold wind. She was shaking from head to foot, partly from the cold but also from nerves. She had been so afraid I would be left behind. I tried to comfort her as best I could and put my arms around her to try and shield her from the cold blast of air coming in the open windows. But there was little I could do to relieve the headache except to massage her forehead.

The car was completely dark, and we were unable to see much around us. Suddenly a man forced his way through to our side, and we found ourselves facing a tall, distinguished-looking Chinese gentleman who addressed us in excellent English. He turned out to be a Christian medical doctor, Dr. Li. Also an evangelist, he was on his way to Chaoyang by special invitation to conduct a week of services. Although we'd never met him, we knew of him by repute. He came from Peking and knew Eva's father well and had often been in their home. For the next couple of hours we much enjoyed his company. Seeing Eva's distress, he deplored the fact that he had no medications with him. Before I could protest, he ripped the fur collar off his overcoat and wrapped it around Eva's head, telling her to keep it with his compliments. We've never forgotten that kind act that meant so much to Eva that very cold night, both then on the train, and later that night as the weather got even colder.

At Chaoyang Dr. Li got off the train and promised to pass on our greetings to the Christians there, telling them they would see us very soon. Unfortunately it didn't work out that way, and that was the last we ever saw of Chaoyang. We had expected the train to stop for the night there, the danger of the *balu* being so pressing. But as a railway official later told me, it was for that very reason that the train didn't stop overnight in Chaoyang. The city authorities and the military were afraid that a trainload of some 3,000 people might attract an attack from the *balu* in order to cause panic, and it would help them enter the city under cover of fleeing refugees.

Chaoyang was the northernmost point of our journey, and from there we turned due west toward Lingyuan, about 80 miles away, normally a two-hour journey. That night it took us five hours just to reach Yebaishou, a mere 50 miles. Although it was April, in one of those freak weather patterns an extraordinary cold front came down from the north. It was so cold and windy in the windowless car that we attempted to crouch on the floor and cover ourselves with our sleeping bags. It did little good. The train moved at a very slow pace, as usual pushing ahead of it the three flat cars loaded with troops. Every now and then we thought of those men and how they must have been suffering from the cold. Everyone in our car was apprehensive, fearing every moment there might be a mine on the tracks, and as on our previous trip, the locomotive was using no headlight.

Not too long after leaving Chaoyang, at a fairly large village called Dapingfang (Large Flat-Roofed Building) the train pulled into the station, which was in complete darkness. With my head out the window, I could see nothing except one dim lantern, which shone very briefly up near where the locomotive stopped and then was extinguished. We couldn't see anyone on the platform, but as is sometimes the case, we somehow sensed, rather than saw, that there was a large crowd there, surprising for a place so small. It wasn't because of any noise they were making, because there was none. But as the train slowed down I could distinctly hear the shuffling of feet, and then with a wild rush, a mob of men started climbing in the windows and pushing their way in through the end doors.

The people in our car immediately panicked, thinking it was a *balu* attack. But then we heard the words: "Don't be afraid. We're *guo jun*" (Nationalist soldiers). Several climbed in through the window next to Eva and me, and once they were inside the car we were all packed together so tightly there was no moving any farther. After saying just those few words, the men lapsed into total silence. They would answer no questions, and their behavior was so strange I began to doubt that they really were soldiers, and I thought it might possibly be a trap.

The "soldier" next to me was short and stocky, and we stood so close together that my chin almost rested on top of his head. Surreptitiously I fingered his coat and, from the stiffness, found it to be made of new material. It was a long, thick, cotton-padded coat that came down below his knees, not part of the usual Nationalist soldier's uniform. I was more suspicious than ever, and pretending to better my position, I felt around his body and detected no weapons, so I felt somewhat relieved.

I decided to ask him some questions, and quietly I talked directly into his ear, asking him who he was and whether he was he really a Nationalist soldier. At first he stubbornly refused to answer. I then took a chance and told him I was not a Chinese but an Englishman, a *mushi* (missionary preacher), and I told him why we were on the train and where we were going, and that he could safely talk to me. For a moment he was silent. Then he reached into an inside pocket and took out a match. Lighting it with his thumbnail, he lifted the match close to my face and took a long look at me. Satisfied that I was indeed a foreigner, he began to talk.

He whispered to me that he was one of a group of more than 500 Nationalist soldiers who had been captured by the *balu* a few weeks previously, and they had just that day been released from a *balu* camp in the mountains a few miles from the station where they had boarded the train.

A couple of his companions standing immediately next to him noticed him talking to me and tried to stop him. They all feared he might be talking to a *balu* spy. But he reassured them, and for the next two hours, he and two of his friends talked with Eva and me in low tones, telling us of their experiences.

Their unit had been overrun by a large number of *balu* guerrillas in a battle not far from Chengde a month or so previously. Most of their officers had been killed in the firefight, and they had been forced to surrender. In forced night marches they had covered more than 100 miles to reach a secret *balu* encampment deep in the mountains, and there they had been put through lengthy indoctrination sessions by their captors.

They told me that, expecting to be executed, much to their surprise they had been extraordinarily well treated and well fed. But for hours every day they had been made to sit and listen to long speeches by political commissars who emphasized the evils and corruption of the Kuomintang regime and the fruitlessness of their efforts in trying to defeat Communism, which was the future of China. They were told of the glories of Communism, the equality they would enjoy in a Communist state, and the rewards that would be their lot if they had a change of heart and joined the Communist forces voluntarily. It was left unsaid what would happen to them if they didn't join.

After three weeks of political indoctrination they were all made to sit on the ground one morning while their few surviving officers were brought before them

and were made to stand at attention. It was obvious the officers had been badly tortured and all of them looked near death.

The *balu* then proceeded to put the officers on trial, holding a mock court, and after reading off the alleged crimes each officer had committed, the men's uniforms were stripped off them, and one by one they were slaughtered by the infamous "thousand knife" method, the most bestial and inhumane death conceivable.

Each of the captured soldiers was made to come forward and was handed a knife and forced, at the risk of being killed himself if he refused, to slice a piece off each of his former commanding officers, until 15 of the officers had been thus murdered.

The common soldiers, having thus proven their "conversion" to the Communist cause, were given a big feast and were then told that instead of being enrolled in the guerrilla forces, they were going to be released as evidence of the "goodness and humanity" of the Communist cause.

Each man was issued a brand-new, cotton-padded coat, the same gray color as his original uniform, which it would cover. They were told that the coats were made extra long so that they would be kept warmer. Each man was then given a Mexican ten-dollar note, and they were then strictly admonished to return to their ancestral homes, wherever they may be, and under no circumstances were they to return to their former military units on pain of being killed in the same manner as their officers should they be caught again. With that, they had been escorted to within a half-mile of the tiny railroad station and released.

The cruel irony of it was that the whole thing was a complete farce. The men were all from Yunnan Province in the far west of China, thousands of miles away, and the Communists knew it. Ten dollars wouldn't be enough to feed them for more than a day, let alone cover their rail fare home. Furthermore, dressed in the long, gray, non-uniform coats, with their old uniforms underneath, they would immediately be spotted by Nationalist military police, whereupon they would be picked up as deserters and shot. Their only recourse was to return to their old command, and that the Communists well knew.

On the part of the *balu* it was all a calculated scheme to have the men go back and spread the word among their former comrades, telling them of the humane treatment they could expect should they be captured, and at the same time letting their officers know what they could expect even if they voluntarily surrendered. As the men bitterly told me, they had no option but to go back and tell their comrades to defect while there was still time, and that they could thus save themselves from the possibility of being killed in action. They knew without any doubt that they would either be dead within a few days or back in the hands of the *balu* as soon as they could escape somehow from their units without being shot. They openly told me they would either have to kill their own officers or somehow convince them of the futility of fighting the Communists, encouraging them to flee before it was too late. But they saw little possibility of the latter.

Testing the men, I asked them why they were going through the farce of returning to their unit when they could so easily have turned around and gone back to the *balu* directly from the station where they were released and saved themselves all the trouble. They grimly laughed at my suggestion and told me the *balu* had thought of that and had told them they weren't wanted and that was why they were being released. They had been told that unless they got aboard the first train that came in they would be shot down by guerrillas who would be hiding in the darkness just outside the station and watching to see what they did. They told me that was the reason why they had been in such a hurry to climb onto the train and said it was no coincidence that they had been released just before the westbound train heading for Chengde was due.

I asked the men if there had been any medical treatment for their wounded while they were in the Communist encampment and they told me there had been. A medical unit had been attached to the guerrillas, with a doctor treating the injured and sick. I asked if they had learned the doctor's name, wondering if perchance it might have been our old friend Dr. Lu, who had been kidnapped from Beipiao some five years before. But none of them could tell me his name. They did, however, describe him to me, and their description of him as a short, well-built man of about 50 certainly closely resembled Dr. Lu.

After talking with the soldiers we felt very depressed. We had previously heard of that tactic employed by the *balu* and how very effective it was. Here was further evidence of it, and in the next few weeks we repeatedly saw Nationalist troops defecting to the Communists because of just such subtle propaganda.

It was close to midnight when choking smoke filled the car and I knew we had entered the long tunnel near Yebaishou. The train continued to travel slowly for fear the track might have been mined or that another train might be approaching from the opposite direction. Ironically a few days later that very thing had happened. On their single-track lines, the Chinese used a "key" system. The engineer of a train departing from one station for another carried with him a circular iron "key" about twice the size of a hockey puck. Until that was handed over to the station master at the next stop, no train was allowed to depart. However, the military at times ignored the protestations of the locomotive engineers and forced them at gunpoint to travel the line when it was unsafe to do so. We had been in Lingyuan only a few days when we heard that a troop train had crashed into a passenger train inside the tunnel because the military had forced the engineer to leave Yebaishou and head east when the westbound train was due. Fortunately, both trains had been traveling fairly slowly and no one was killed.

When we pulled into Yebaishou station, soldiers and railway police, starting at the front of the train and working their way back, forced all the passengers off the train. As everyone disembarked, they were herded like cattle into a barbed-wire enclosure set up a few hundred yards from the station in an open field where they were to spend the rest of the night.

Yebaishou is high in the mountains and, although it was April, the night was one of the coldest we had ever experienced. A strong wind blowing off the frozen river made it colder yet. I couldn't see taking Eva out to that barbed-wire enclosure even though the soldiers told us it was for our own safety, because in the event of a *balu* attack, we would be safer there than on the train. I stalled the soldiers as long as I could, making every excuse I could think of and dawdling behind, hoping we could hide in the darkness. They were so involved in chasing all the civilians and the released soldiers off that they stopped bothering us, and I thought we had it made. A few minutes later, though, a group of railway police came through looking for stragglers, and they, too, ordered us off for our own safety. But they were easier to deal with, and I managed to convince them that we were willing to take the risk, so they relented and let us be.

That night lives in my memory as the one that should have finished both of us off. It still seems incredible to me that we survived it, or that any of the other passengers out in the open field survived. Never have we experienced such cold.

Having made the trip twice before, we were a little better prepared and had some spare blankets in our bedding rolls. We managed to hang two of those up over the windows at the end of the car, where there was the most protection from the wind. But as the night progressed, the wind intensified and howled through the car, and the blankets didn't do a bit of good. We huddled on the floor while the wind swirled around us, and the air was so thick with dust we could scarcely breathe.

We had had nothing to eat or drink since late morning, so I violated the curfew outside. Singing at the top of my voice to let the military know I wasn't a *balu* infiltrator, I climbed down from the train and made my way to the station buildings, where I could see a light in one of the windows. I got there just as they were about to lock the door for the night, but I was able to get our thermos filled with water with which to make some tea on our Coleman stove. On my way back to the train I ran into one of the station crew I had seen going through the train earlier. For a couple of dollars he kindly consented to try and find us a few sticks of charcoal. Not too long afterward he returned with the charcoal and, thoughtfully, he also brought along an old piece of thin sheet metal. Using that, I made a small fire on the floor of the car, and that kept our hands and feet from freezing. But the charcoal didn't last very long, and eventually it got so cold even our sleeping bags couldn't keep us warm, so we decided that exercise was the only way to stay alive.

We climbed off the train and, in the blackness, walked up and down the station platform, which by that time was completely deserted. Nowhere could we see any guards, but in the far distance we could see one or two fires in the barbed-wire enclosure where the rest of the passengers were being held. We wondered how many of them would fail to survive the night.

Soon after we got off the train — it must have been close to three in the morning — the wind suddenly died. An eerie silence fell, broken every few minutes by a loud boom from the direction of the river. The first time we heard it I thought it was a hand grenade exploding. Then my old experiences with river ice came back to me, and I realized it was simply the thick ice cracking with the cold.

As we walked the platform and saw no soldiers or police to stop us, we became more daring, increasing our distance each time until we got near the extreme eastern end. By that time sheer fatigue was overtaking us, and we began to feel that it was time to get back on the car and try to keep warm in our sleeping bags until daylight came. But just as we turned to walk back, I heard a faint noise in the distance that made me stop and listen again. It sounded distinctly like steam hissing. I listened closely, determined the direction from which the noise was coming, and we stumbled over the tracks toward it. We were delighted to find a solitary locomotive parked in the yards with a single second-class passenger car coupled to it. Noting steam coming out behind the car, we realized that the interior of the car was heated. We knew someone important had to be aboard the car, but we were so cold and desperate that we decided to bluff it out and try to sneak aboard the car to enjoy the warmth.

As we neared the car's steps we could see a faint light inside at the rear of the car through the frost-covered windows, so we knew the car was occupied. We suspected it had to be army officers, since no one else had the clout to enjoy that kind of luxury. We crept quietly up the front steps, and gently turning the handle, I opened the door as slowly and as quietly as I could, and we both quickly slipped inside. The heat inside almost took our breath away. But oh, how good it felt.

As we entered, the draft from the opened door blew out the candle at the other end of the car, and a voice immediately challenged us. As the owner of the voice relit his candle, I mumbled something in Chinese about it being pretty cold to have to go outside and urinate. The man, apparently on guard duty, satisfied himself that I was just one of the occupants of the car, grunted something in reply, and presumably went back to his dozing.

Eva and I stood for a few minutes until our eyes became accustomed to the gloom of the car. Then, spotting an empty seat close to the door, we settled down to enjoy the glorious warmth. The couple of hours we spent there until daylight were possibly the two most pleasurable hours we've ever enjoyed. The outside temperature was way below zero, and we could hear the continuing booms of the cracking ice. More and more we pitied our fellow passengers out there in the open.

As dawn broke we heard a train puffing into the station, coming from the east. It drew alongside the car in which we were sitting, and we saw it was a long train consisting almost entirely of flatcars loaded with Chinese farm carts, eight or ten to a car and packed with military supplies. In addition there were a number of open coal cars filled with horses and mules. Other coal cars contained the owners of the carts: peasants who had either been forced to accompany their vehicles commandeered by the military, or had chosen to do so, since otherwise they would have had no hope whatever of getting them back. At the back of the train was an old passenger car filled with armed soldiers. The train was obviously heading for the front to supply Nationalist troops.

The poor peasants had been in those open cars all night and they looked so cold and forlorn. When the train stopped, their locomotive was detached for servicing, and one by one the men clambered down from their cars and plodded over toward us, heading for the locomotive to which "our" car was attached. They climbed up onto the engine and swarmed over it, hugging the boiler to get what little warmth they could. The engineer tried to drive them off, and, in the ensuing clamor, we decided it would perhaps be best to make a discreet departure from our car before the occupants woke up. From the uniforms hanging on the hooks around us, we deduced we had stumbled into a car reserved for a high-ranking general and his staff. If we were found there we would have had a lot of questions to answer.

We walked back to our own train and brewed another cup of tea. Then, when it was fully daylight, we crossed the tracks and went down behind the railroad station to a line of shacks where we hoped to be able to find something to eat. Nothing there even approached a food shop. But we did find an elderly woman in a one-room hovel who agreed to feed us. She sat us on low stools on the filthy earthen floor, then served us a simple peasant's meal of millet gruel with sour cabbage and pickles. It was hot and nour-

ishing, and when we had finished we felt we could face another day.

When we got back to the station we found the station master and asked when our train would leave for Lingyuan. He told us it had been canceled because, with the break in the line that we had come across the day before, there was insufficient rolling stock to make up a train to go on to Chengde. The train we had come in on would be going back eastward to meet the westbound train at the same spot where we had exchanged trains the previous day. That procedure would continue until the bridge was repaired and more rolling stock could come through.

What he said made sense, but we asked what was going to happen to all the passengers who had come in on the same train with us the previous evening. He told us that unfortunately they would simply have to wait another day or two, or else make their own arrangements to continue on by road.

The more we chatted with him, the more sympathetic with our plight he became, and he asked us why we were traveling and where we were heading. When I told him who we were, and asked if he thought it possible we could hire mules to carry us the remaining 30 miles to Lingyuan, he strongly advised against it. He told us the countryside was thick with *balu* guerrillas and that we would be in serious danger.

The situation looked pretty bleak. We removed our baggage from the train, found a sunny spot out of the wind, and sat on our luggage as the almost empty train pulled out and headed east. A small number of the passengers from the previous day, most of them merchants, had given up and gotten aboard to go back. We could have done the same, but we were so close to our destination we felt very strongly that our mission was not yet accomplished and that we should somehow try to get through. We decided to wait it out and see what would happen, so we sat in the sun and prayed.

We were there for almost five hours; then, shortly after noon, when we were beginning to think about where we should spend the night, the station master came over and quietly told us that he was sending a locomotive over the pass to Lingyuan, partly to determine whether the tracks were mined or not, but also to test the locomotive, which had been badly shot up in a guerrilla ambush a few days before. It had since been repaired, and they wanted to see if everything was in working order. He said if we wanted to, we could ride on the locomotive, sitting on top of the water tank just behind the coal bin. We jumped at the opportunity, and he told us to be ready in about 30 minutes.

An hour later the old engine wheezed into the station. We threw our boxes and suitcases up onto the water tank, climbed up through the cab and out over the coal bin on the tender, and settled down on top of the tank with our backs against a steel bulkhead that we hoped would give us a little shelter from the wind. Just as we were about to pull out, a Chinese army major joined us. He was a taciturn man, seemingly very preoccupied, and we were unable to engage him in conversation.

The decrepit engine ground its way up the pass, laboring even without a load to pull; evidently something was still seriously wrong with the boiler's combustion chamber. As we chuffed along, we were showered with hot, unburned particles of coal. We brushed them off our clothing while, at the same time, trying to prevent them from going down the backs of our necks. In no time we were black with soot and had minor burns on our hands and clothing.

Seven men were in the cab of the locomotive: the regular crew of three, plus four men from the repair shop who, in addition to working inside the cab, climbed over the outside of the engine, tinkering with the various valves and steam pipes as we slowly moved along. No one seemed to be paying the slightest attention to the track ahead for mines that might be there. They all seemed pretty well hardened to the dangers of the job.

Part way up the pass the young 17-year-old fireman, who was part of the engine crew but not needed because of the repair crew aboard, climbed back toward us over the coal. Curious about his passengers, he started a conversation with us. He wanted to know who we were and what we were doing, and after learning that we were not Russians as he had thought, he opened up and told us some of his experiences.

He said they had been shot at many times by the *balu* guerrillas, the locomotives always being the main target. Usually, he said, they had managed to outrun their attackers without sustaining serious damage. However, the week before, in broad daylight,

when they were pulling into Dapingfang, the same station where we had picked up the 500 soldiers the night before, they had been ambushed by more than 100 guerrillas who had been posing as passengers waiting to board the train.

As they had entered the station, everything had appeared quite normal. Although surprised by the large number of peasants on the platform, people whom they later learned had been rounded up by the *balu* to act as cover, they had given it very little thought, thinking perhaps the people were heading for some kind of a fair. Just as they were coming to a stop, the *balu*, hiding among the crowd, opened fire with a heavy machine gun, directing their fire at the boiler of the locomotive, which was almost immediately put out of commission.

In the resulting confusion he and his two companions in the cab had climbed over the coal, opened the lid of the water tank, and jumped down into the water, which fortunately only came up to their necks. He laughingly told us that being shorter than the other two men, he had been forced to stand on his tiptoes for more than an hour in order to keep his chin above water. Meanwhile, the *balu* robbed the passengers on the train and made off.

The worst part of the experience for him was that while they were standing in the water, the *balu*, for several minutes, had continued to spray the engine with heavy machine-gun bullets. They expected every minute to be killed, but fortunately the steel was thick enough so that none of the bullets had penetrated. On the other hand, the noise inside was so loud that all three of them were deaf for several days, and they still had a loud ringing in their ears and had difficulty hearing. I asked him if he still intended going on with his job, since it was so dangerous. He replied with a shrug: *Meiyou fazi*, "There's nothing I can do about it," and then added: "I have to eat."

After a number of stops on the pass, while the engineers fiddled with the mechanics of the locomotive, we finally came to the downward grade, and near the bottom, just about eight miles from Lingyuan, we stopped at a point where there was a siding to allow trains to pass each other. Nothing else was there, other than a tiny shack, not much larger than a telephone booth, in which a switchman kept vigil during the daytime to man the track switches.

When we stopped there was a brief conversation

between the men in the cab and the switchman, then one of the engineers came back to us and excitedly told me they were not going on to Lingyuan after all, but returning immediately to Yebaishou. He seemed highly agitated, but refused to tell me their reason for not going on. He simply gave us the option of either getting off there at once or returning to Yebaishou with them.

Since we were much closer to Lingyuan, we quickly decided to get off and find some other means of getting there on our own. But I was a little puzzled by the actions of the engineer, particularly when the switchman climbed aboard the engine to return with them, and the Chinese army major elected to return with them as well.

The door of the shack was unlocked. We stacked all our boxes outside and Eva went inside to keep out of the wind while I set off at a run to a nearby village, where a family of Christians lived. I felt sure they would have a farm cart they would lend us.

As I started across the plowed fields in a direct line to the village of Hotaugou (Walnut Gully), about a half-mile away, I looked to my right toward Lingyuan. The setting sun was shining in my eyes, but I noticed with some surprise an unusual amount of activity in the fields and an unusually large number of what I took to be farmers working there. I wondered what they could be doing when it was still so cold, and weeks away from planting time. But I gave it no further thought.

It had snowed a day or so earlier and snow still lay in the furrows, but in some of the sunny spots it had melted, then frozen to ice. It was getting close to sundown, and I knew we'd have to hurry if we were to make it to the city before dark. Puffing and out of breath, I arrived in the village and found our Chinese Christian friends at home, just about to sit down to their evening meal.

In typical Chinese fashion they showed not the slightest surprise at seeing me drop in on them without warning, even though they hadn't seen me in five years nor known where I was. They invited me to sit and rest a while and share their meal. However, when I explained the situation to them, and our urgent need of a cart to get us to the city before dark, they immediately set about harnessing an old ox to their farm cart, and I ran back across the fields to keep Eva company while we waited for the cart to come. To get to

the shack the cart had to go by a roundabout route, and as slow as the old ox was, it would not be there for fifteen or twenty minutes.

By then the sun was brushing the hills in the west, leaving less than an hour of daylight. As I looked around, the people I had taken to be farmers were now all gathered in a group about 200 yards away, apparently having some sort of conference. That was equally puzzling but not particularly ominous, so I paid no attention to it. Eva and I were extremely hungry, having had nothing to eat since the meal of millet early in the morning. I dug into our luggage and found a can of corned beef hash. Opening it with the attached key, we spooned it out with our fingers and hungrily ate it cold as we waited for the cart.

Twenty minutes later the cart arrived, and after loading it up, we headed on our way to Lingyuan. As we did so, I noticed eight men detach themselves from the group of "farmers" and start to follow us at a distance. I remarked on it to old Mr. Cao, who was driving the cart. He glanced back at them, shook his head, then said the dreaded words: *balu*. I then understood why the locomotive engineer had turned back and the switchman had deserted his post.

After a moment Mr. Cao told me that the whole countryside was swarming with guerrillas, constantly harassing their village. He used the derogatory expression *jen bushi dongxi*, about the worst thing a Chinese can say about another person. It translates literally as, "(They) really aren't things," which in English is meaningless, but to a Chinese describes another fellow human being as being lower than an animal. Certainly, coming from one of the peasant class, that was a far cry from the days in which they held the *balu* in high esteem.

As we plodded along in the springless cart, bumping our way over the rocky road, old Mr. Cao told us of all the troubles they had been put through by the Japanese right after our departure. Then, in graphic detail, he told of the coming of the Russians and the various battles that had ensued in the area of his village, which was directly on the main corridor from east to west. He then told of the hardships they had experienced with the *balu*, those "visitors," who usually came in the night. They were always wanting food or money and brutally punished anyone who didn't produce them.

After following us for about a mile, the eight men

dropped back and disappeared from sight. Relieved, I surmised that we had taken them by surprise, and not being able to make out just who those two foreigners were and why we were there, they had decided to follow us to see what we did. And in all probability, there was no one around with sufficient rank to tell them to do otherwise. But I worried that when the old man went back to his village, they would give him a hard time for helping us. When I mentioned it to him, he just shrugged it off, saying, "God has protected us so far, and He'll keep on protecting us from these evil men."

Just as it was getting too dark to see anything, another farm cart passed us coming from the city. In it was a young man whom we knew. He was escorting some female relatives back to their village. We warned him of the *balu* behind us, but he simply smiled and said, *meiyou guanxi*, "It doesn't matter," and went on his way.

As we came to the river I looked to my left, expecting to see the huge experimental farm with its dozens of buildings that the Japanese had built there. Seeing nothing, I asked the old man about it. He told me that when the Russians came in they had looted the place and had taken away all the wooden doors and windows and any machinery they could find. Then the local farmers, who had originally owned the land on which it was built and who had never been given any compensation by the Japanese, immediately set to work to tear the place down. It had been built of red brick and they were in such a hurry to demolish it and reclaim their land that they simply smashed the place completely, salvaging only the wooden timbers of the roofs. He said they didn't want the red bricks because they would remind them of the Japanese. He added that the only sign that there had ever been anything there was a slight redness of the earth, which had all been plowed over. The redness was from the pulverized bricks.

It was pitch dark as we crossed the river and approached the north gate of the city. As we got close, we came to a deep dry-moat that had been dug during our absence. I noted that it had stopped short at the river's edge and had ramps cut in it for vehicles to cross, but all of it lay within reach of rifle fire from the north gate. With the moat stopping where it did, only about two-thirds of the city had the doubtful protection of that man-made obstacle. It was equally obvious that any enemy when attacking could easily enter the city from the river side without any trouble at all. Of course, that was all open ground with no natural protection, and any invaders would be under fire from the city from the time they started to cross the river. As those thoughts crossed my mind, I hadn't the slightest premonition that within a matter of hours the very thing I was thinking about would actually be happening.

We found the north gate closed and locked as I had fully expected. There was a back way around the outside of the city, but I was reluctant to go that route. If sentries were on the outskirts, we might easily have been mistaken for intruders and become targets. I therefore banged on the gate, demanding admittance.

It was some time before we could rouse the guards, and when they finally came outside their quarters, they flatly refused to open the gates until morning and told us to go away. Shouting through the bars of the gate, I told them who we were, but they were still reluctant to take the chance of admitting someone they didn't know without authorization from their superiors. Finally, though, after some lengthy palavering through the crack between the two leaves of the gate, and their lighting a lantern to determine that I was actually the foreigner I said I was, they let us in, and half an hour later we were home. So ended our epic thirteen-day journey.

Completely worn out, we climbed into our sleeping bags and fell into a deep sleep despite the cold, barely aware that faithful Gao Zun had cleaned up our little house, and we were back in our own little bedroom, although sleeping on the floor. Little did we know at the time what surprises were in store for us, and we didn't have long to wait to find out what they were.

courtesy of Ed Bohannon

Ch'ing Dynasty (1644–1911) 1,000 cash bank note.

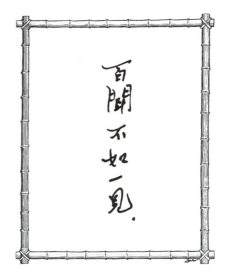

Bai wen bu ru yi jian.

Hearing about it 100 times
is not as good as seeing it one time.

- Chinese Peasant Saying.

Chapter Thirty-Nine
The City Falls

The day after our arrival in Lingyuan dawned bright and clear and it seemed strange to wake up in our own little home and find the compound completely deserted of soldiers. It was so quiet and peaceful compared to what it had been just a few weeks earlier. However, the soldiers left many reminders, what with broken windows, the piles of debris, the damage to the interior of most of the rooms, and the broken tree limbs and tree stumps in the back garden, together with horse manure everywhere.

Faithful Gao Zun and Lily Root had done their best to clean up our house as soon as the magistrate had moved out just a few days after the troops had left. We felt certain that his leaving was not because of our imminent return, but because he felt unsafe there after the troops had evacuated the compound. Looking around, we found that our little house had fared remarkably well considering the number of people who had lived in it: some Japanese civilians for several years, then the Russian troops, followed by the Chinese Communists, and then the magistrate. There had been no major damage to the floors, probably because the large Russian stove we had installed was not something that could be carried away by looters. It had been there to heat the place, so there had been no need to build fires on the floors. Despite that, the place looked far different from what it had when we left it in 1942, and it would never be quite the same again. We had slept late, but as we crawled from our sleeping bags that first morning, the sun was pouring in the front window, and that made things seem a little better.

We found our faithful Lily Root waiting patiently outside the front door. So many of our friends had died in the four years and more that we had been gone. Of our former house servants, only he was still alive. He was working as a laborer and barely eking out a living. But he had been there since before daybreak to greet us and offer his services. The first thing I wanted him to do was to tear down the blockhouses as soon as I had acquired an official permit. I suggested that he should be ready to start the following morning and told him to hire a couple of carts to haul away the rocks and other debris, and to hire several men to help him. He was also told to find a mason who could repair the holes in the back wall as soon as the blockhouses were removed.

After breakfast Eva immediately set about baking a batch of bread, and I spent most of that first morning paying courtesy calls on the magistrate and other civil officials, as well as the local army commander. I thanked the latter for pulling his troops out of the mission compound and told him my immediate priority was to remove the four blockhouses that guarded the front and rear of the compound. For that, I requested an official permit. At first he was reluctant to let me tear them down, citing the possibility that the *balu* might come again, but I insisted, and he finally gave me the permit.

I then visited the Catholic Mission in the southern part of the city to let the two Belgian fathers know I was back in town. They told me of the attack by the *balu* just after our departure on the coal train, and they expressed confidence that should another attack occur, enough Nationalist troops were in the city to beat them off once again.

Where originally there had been 30 or 40 people living in the compound at any given time, we now found the place almost entirely deserted. The two former beggar boys, Qian Yi and Chang Yin, were there, living together in one tiny room. Two other young men, one named Ho and the other óne Gao, oldest son of Gao Zun, lived there in another room. Both were completely blind, and Eva and I had taken them under our wing some years before and had sent them down to Peking where they had learned to read Chinese braille and how to knit socks so that they could earn a living. They were doing quite well at it, earning enough to partially support themselves. Gao Zun and his other son, Gao Yu-sheng, were the only other people living in the compound. It was from them, as well as from Lily Root, that we got details of the various occasions on which incoming troops had taken over the place.

Of all of the invaders, they had found the Russians to be the most frightening, mainly because of an inability to communicate with them. They had some wild stories to tell; for example, they told us that most

of the Russian troops seemed to be oriental or Asian, apparently coming from among the Russia-Mongol border region peoples who were sometimes called Turko-Tartars. They were a rough, uncouth, savage bunch of men, and almost everyone we met seemed to have a story to tell about them.

Apparently all of them had an insatiable craving for wristwatches, stripping them from the wrist of anyone who was wearing one, sometimes making payment and other times not, depending on how drunk they were. Some of the Russian troops bartered for watches, and one group stopped their truck in front of our compound because they saw a watch on the wrist of one of our neighbors who was standing on the steps in front of our gate. They asked for the watch, but when the owner was reluctant to give it to them, instead of arbitrarily taking it, they offered him a rifle in exchange. When that was refused, they took a back wheel off their truck and gave it to him, leaving the disabled truck there in the street and continuing on foot. Of course, the back wheel was of no use to our neighbor Mr. Zhang, so he threw it back on the truck, and some other Russians later came and drove the truck away.

Other stories concerned their eating habits. They ate everything with their fingers, which the Chinese thought particularly vulgar. They had also apparently never seen anything fried in deep fat, as is most common in North China. Seeing the food bubbling in the hot oil, a number of them simply reached in with their fingers to pluck the food out, suffering terrible burns as a result. In addition to bartering their weapons or vehicles, they also bartered their clothing, particularly their heavy fur coats, which they were carrying with them, despite it being August and very hot when they got there. Everyone we talked with agreed that the common soldiers showed not the slightest respect for their officers, nor appeared to pay them any heed.

Before daylight the following morning, Lily Root was there with his pick and shovel ready to start work, but the men he had hired weren't due until sunup. Eva and I were eating breakfast when he came, so I suggested he begin on the blockhouses outside the back wall. I warned him to start from the inside, and not to go outside the wall until after I had finished my breakfast and got out there to join him. I had an uneasy feeling that something might go wrong.

I continued eating, but suddenly felt a premonition that all was not as it should be. I got up from the table and told Eva I was going out to see how Lily Root was doing. When I reached the back wall, I peered through the openings into both blockhouses and found no sign of him. I shouted, but there was no answer. Noticing that the back gate was open, I raced outside, where I found Lily Root's pickax lying by the nearest blockhouse. I could see where he had managed to dislodge two of the large rocks, but Lily Root was nowhere in sight, and I feared the worst.

The sun was just coming up behind Guang Shan, and the city was still in deep shadow. As I stood atop a nearby grave and scanned the countryside, away in the distance on the far side of the deep moat, I spotted two soldiers, one of them dragging Lily Root by a rope around his neck, with his hands bound behind his back. The other man followed behind, carrying Lily Root's shovel, and even from that distance I could see that, at intervals, the soldier was using the flat of the blade to beat Lily Root over the head and back.

I shouted as loudly as I could, but they were too far off to hear me, so I gave chase. They were heading for a group of houses just outside what was known as the Little West Gate, an unprotected little island-like area with a community of perhaps a hundred or more families. I wondered why they were going there, rather than into the city. Running as fast as I could, I managed to keep the three of them in sight for a while, but they had a good ten-minute lead on me and were at least a half mile ahead and had almost reached the houses they were apparently heading for. To make things more difficult, I had to somehow first find where they had crossed the dry moat. Fortunately, I stumbled across their footsteps in the plowed field, and those led me to a footpath heading in that general direction, which I guessed they had used. I discovered a spot where people had cut a narrow, inclined path down into the moat and up the other side. When I got up on the other side of the moat, I could no longer see the soldiers or Lily Root.

When I got to the first of the group of houses I was completely out of breath. An old man was sitting on a rock outside his front door, smoking a pipe. I asked him where the soldiers had taken their prisoner. He nodded toward a small house enclosed by a tall sorghum-stalk fence. I dashed inside, yelling at the top of my voice. Lily Root knelt on the ground, his hands tied behind him, and a soldier was pointing a revolver at the back of his head. Another second or two and he would have undoubtedly pulled the trigger.

My yelling must have distracted the soldier with the gun. As I came into view, he raised his weapon and pointed it at me. I ignored it and shouted at him in Chinese, asking him what he thought he was doing arresting my servant and why was he about to shoot him. There were several other soldiers there. In unison they all started to shout back at me that their prisoner was a *balu* spy, and they had caught him tearing down a military fortification. I replied that he had merely been carrying out my orders and pulled out the official-looking permit that I was carrying in my pocket, and which I wished I had given to Lily Root earlier. But it did little good because none of them could read, so I demanded to see their commanding officer.

They said their platoon commander was sleeping and couldn't be disturbed. I ignored them; suspecting that he was inside the small building near which they were standing, I pushed my way past a trooper at the door, intending to wake the officer. I found him not only awake but smoking opium. He was mightily embarrassed. Redfaced, he bellowed loudly at me to get out, pulling his revolver to emphasize the point and asking what business I had disturbing him. I waved the permit in front of his nose, at the same time bowing politely in order to give him a little "face" in front of his men and "inviting" him politely in the Chinese manner to order his men to immediately release my servant. At first he refused to look at the paper, so I let him shout some more, then again I pressed my point, showing him the large square seal of his commanding general. Reluctantly he ordered Lily Root released, and the two of us hurried back to the compound, both of us badly shaken by the incident. It had indeed been a close call, and when we got back inside our gate we knelt and thanked God for His preserving care.

All that day as we worked to tear down those pillboxes, I had a feeling of extreme urgency that I couldn't explain, even to myself. The town seemed quite peaceful and there were no rumors of any impending *balu* attack, but somehow I just had to get the job done that day, no matter what happened. With all of us working at top speed without any significant breaks, it took almost till dark to get the job accomplished, the last of the debris hauled away and the two large holes in the back wall repaired. When we were finished, any evidence of there ever having been any blockhouses there had entirely disappeared, and I was able to relax. What we wanted was anonymity, and the compound, back and front, now looked no different from any of our neighbors. We were soon to see God's hand had been directing our efforts that day.

Eva and I went to bed soon after 8:30, but we were awakened, seemingly not too long afterward, by an insistent tapping on our window. The instant we awoke we became aware of the overwhelming sound of a loud, incessant roar, which after a moment or so I recognized as heavy gunfire in the near distance, punctuated by loud explosions from either artillery or mortar shells. I went to the door, where Gao Yusheng, Katie's youngest son, told me the city was under attack by the *balu*.

Not daring to light a lamp, we hurriedly dressed in the dark and went out into the yard, where the enormity of the attack immediately became evident. The city was being attacked from three sides. The night sky to the south, west and north was intermittently lit up by flashes from the big guns firing, as well as from exploding shells. Bullets buzzed overhead like a swarm of bees, splattering the tile roofs around us, showering us with broken bits of tile, while every now and then we heard the distinct "thup" sound of spent bullets embedding themselves in the ground and walls around us. We quickly realized the yard was a very dangerous place to be.

The city was defended by perhaps some 500 well-trained Nationalist troops and another two or three hundred militia. Most of the latter were former bandits who had received little or no training, and who had been recruited by the Nationalists. It was immediately apparent that this was no small attack, and we later learned that there were well over 6,000 men in the attacking force. There could only be one outcome: the city was doomed, and we started at once to make necessary preparations for the worst. Since the *balu* hated Americans, the first thing I did was to burn the U.S. airman's suit I had purchased in San Francisco, and we quickly hid the few U.S. dollars we had with us by burying them in the soot in one of the chim-

neys. Other than that, we could do little but wait.

As we listened to the continuous roar of battle, it appeared that the defenders were putting up stiff resistance, particularly in the area around the railway station just outside the city to the west. There, the fighting appeared to be fierce. In addition, the *balu* were concentrating on pouring heavy fire into the city itself from both north and west. It appeared they had not yet crossed the moat and were using the piled dirt on the other side of it as cover and firing over it into the city.

From what we could hear, the heavier weapons were being used against the defenders of the railway station, and fortunately none of the shells were falling on the city. It seemed, or so we hoped, that the attackers were intent on not doing any serious damage to the city.

Gradually, as we crouched behind a wall, the sounds from the west became more readily identifiable. Every now and then we could distinguish the trumpets of the *balu* repeatedly sounding the advance; then, as they got nearer, we could hear the sustained roar of hundreds of voices shouting in unison, *sha, sha, sha* — "kill, kill, kill," a sound so terrifying that even now as I write, it chills my spine. Then we noticed a similar roar of voices coming from the south, where they had obviously crossed the river and were nearing the city's outskirts. It wasn't long before the men to our north, much closer than the others, were shouting the same thing. But there, they had obviously not yet crossed the moat or they would have been up against our back wall. Perhaps the moat was going to be of some use after all.

Then a new element came into the picture. That afternoon as we were tearing down the pillboxes at the back, we had watched as the first train from the east came through and passed us heading west. When we first heard it approaching we thought it was going to be a passenger train. But it turned out to be a military train with an engine in the middle, pushing ahead of it five or six flat cars loaded with troops, and pulling more behind. A dilapidated third-class car was on the end, presumably for the officers. The locomotive was protected all around with heavy steel plates crudely welded into place; tiny slits enabled the engine crew to peer out. But apart from sandbags on the flat cars, there was no protection for the men, nor was the passenger car at the back protected in any way. I estimated about four or five hundred men were aboard the train. We had heard it stop momentarily at the Lingyuan station, then it had gone farther west. Now, suddenly, during one of the brief lulls in the fighting, we could hear the train coming back from the west toward us.

The Communist attackers heard it as well; the unmistakable blatting sound of the locomotive's stack exhaust reverberating back and forth between the mountains as the train chugged full speed through the valley leading to Lingyuan. Suddenly around us on every side was a stillness: first the firing to the west slackened off, then the same thing in the other two directions. It was obvious the *balu* attackers were getting ready to face an unexpected threat from their rear, and for a brief period we were filled with an exuberant sense of hope that perhaps the well-armed men on the train might turn the tide of battle.

The sound of the train carried clearly through the night air, and knowing the route so well, I was able to follow the train's progress as it sped closer. We heard the echoes as it passed the five-mile point, where the hills came down close to the track. Then it was a dash through relatively open country to the railway station. I followed the sound as the train entered the station at high speed, clattering over the points, then the sound echoed off the station buildings. I expected it to perhaps stop there to allow the Nationalist soldiers to attack the Communists from the rear, but that wasn't the case. Either the train's commander had no clear intelligence as to where the Communist troops were, or he was trying to make a dash for it and escape, because instead of slowing down, the locomotive gained speed as it started on the slight downward gradient toward the river crossing to our north.

As the train came beyond the station, we could clearly hear the rattling of the wheels as it crossed over the switch points where the station yard ended, the exhaust echoing back from the walls of the big temple half a mile outside the West Gate. We knew then that the Nationalist soldiers aboard the train were aware that they were greatly outnumbered and were trying to make a run for it, driving their way through the enemy lines toward the east and what they thought would be safety.

It was not to be. The Communists had anticipated just such a move. We heard the shooting slacken as the train approached within a quarter of a mile of the West Gate, where the line crossed a 15-foot-deep dry gully, which the city's defenders had incorporated as part of the moat they had dug. A steel bridge crossed it, and at the very moment we heard the roar of the first cars starting to cross the bridge, a tremendous flash lit the sky. It was followed instantly by a deafening explosion and shock wave that nearly knocked us off our feet, and we knew that the bridge had been blown up just as the train had started to cross it.

In the absolute silence that momentarily followed the explosion, we could clearly hear the locomotive and railway cars piling one on top of the other into the gully. That was followed by the sound of escaping steam from the overturned and blown-apart engine, mingled with the screams of the injured and dying soldiers. For those few seconds of eerie silence, it seemed that the entire world around us was holding its breath. Our hearts sank as we realized the enormity of the disaster and its implications for us. Then the silence was broken by a great victorious roar from three sides as the thousands of *balu* raised their voices in shouts and cheers.

Heavy shooting began again almost immediately, and within a very short time we heard from the south the distinct "crump" of hand-grenades. We guessed that the enemy was now close to what passed for a city wall and were throwing their grenades over the wall itself.

Up to that point we hadn't the faintest idea as to what time of night it was, but I assumed it was near midnight. Then, as the defenders continued to fight fiercely and more and more armed men raced past our front gate toward the west, we heard the sound of galloping horses. I could scarcely believe my ears.

Hugging the walls of the buildings to avoid the flying bullets, I slipped around to our back garden, where the sound was much more distinct — the sound of horses' hooves on hard ground, but with a strange sort of echo. Then it dawned on me; the explosion must have blown in the sides of the moat at the point where the train had dived into the gully, and a hundred or so mounted *balu* were galloping their horses down inside the moat and circling the city.

In a moment they were almost abreast of our compound and only a few hundred yards away. At that point the moat was at its closest point to the city's dwellings, and the Communist horsemen started firing their rifles over the town and over my head.

Within the high mounds of dirt on each side of the moat, they were down too low to inflict any great damage; most of their shots fortunately went high. But many hit the rooftops around us, smashing tiles, which flew in every direction. As they galloped along, they started to shout their familiar refrain, "kill, kill, kill," at the top of their voices. It was a terrifying sound — and meant to be so — and it continued for nearly an hour as the men rode back and forth along the northern perimeter of the town while the battle continued raging to the west and south. I remembered the moat ending near the river's edge outside the North Gate and felt certain that before long these same horsemen would ride out of the moat at that point and attack the North Gate, and that is exactly what happened.

It must have been around two in the morning when it occurred. We realized from the closeness of the shooting and the explosions of the hand grenades that at some point to the south the *balu* must have penetrated the city's defenses and were actually fighting in the streets to the south and southwest. However, the moat had kept the foot soldiers some distance away from the northern and western walls of the city and the smaller and less well defended gates there. But all indications were that the end was not far off.

Gao Yu-sheng kept his eye and ear to the crack between the two front gates, periodically running to the back of the compound to report to me what was going on out in the street. I patrolled the back to ensure that none of the *balu* came in over the back walls. As the noise of the fighting drew closer, Gao Yu-sheng came running back to tell me that the defending troops were panicking right and left and that he had taken a chance in going outside the front gate. He had seen soldiers entering houses all along the street demanding civilian clothes and changing into them right there on the spot, then throwing their guns and uniforms away. The householders, in turn, were throwing the guns and uniforms out into the street, where they set fire to them. I quickly ran down to the front gate, and, peering through the high window above the Gaos' *kang*, I could see the bonfires up and down the street. The fires were built as far away from their homes as possible, as no one wanted to be found with incriminating evidence in their possession.

It seemed only minutes after that when, from the rear of the compound, I heard the sounds of rifle and revolver fire approaching down our street from the west. Seconds after that young Gao raced back again to tell me that he had seen small groups of ten or twenty *balu* in camouflaged uniforms running down the street, driving terrified Nationalist troops ahead of them. Through the crack between the front gates he could see a number of dead lying in the street just across from the compound.

Gradually the sounds of battle moved toward the center of the city, and our area became quieter. Then I heard another strange and unusual noise coming from our neighbor's compound to the east, from the big garden where opium used to grow. I climbed a ladder and peeked over the wall and beheld a strange sight. In the starlight I was able to see a long file of *balu* troops carrying their dead and wounded to the rear of that compound, where someone had dug a hole through the back wall, and they were going out that way into the open countryside. I realized that someone in our neighbor's yard had been a fifth columnist and had prepared that evacuation route in advance. I felt a sense of dismay in knowing that. Whoever it was, they were well aware of our presence in the city and would inevitably pass along the word to the incoming enemy troops.

I kept watch from the wall for the best part of an hour, for fear that some of the men might stray in our direction, and dark as it was, I still found it fascinating to watch. Not twenty feet away from me the wounded were being carried out on crude stretchers. The dead, and there were seemingly hundreds of them, were carried out on the backs of fellow soldiers. I had heard of that policy; now I was seeing it in action.

Each of the elite *balu* shock troops in the attacking force had a length of light rope looped over one shoulder, a rope something like what in America would be used for hanging laundry. Should a companion fall in battle, either dead or wounded, it was the job of the man next to him to pick him up and carry him off the field by a pre-designated route. In that way, as the attacking force pushed ahead, there were no signs of dead or wounded left behind to undermine the morale of the following second-line troops, who were less highly trained and without the same experience, and thus susceptible to panic in the face of death. I must have seen upwards of 500 men file past in the darkness as I watched. For the most part I heard only the sound of shuffling feet, and only occasionally could I hear the moans of the wounded.

At daybreak, fearful that I might be seen, I climbed down from the wall. The street in front of our house was quiet except for hundreds of *balu* troops filing past in single-file columns. Fearing that we might not get a chance later, Eva and I decided it would be a good idea to get some breakfast. We anticipated that it would not be long before the inevitable house-by-house search for Nationalist soldiers began, and we wanted to be prepared.

Around 7 a.m., just as the sun was peeping over the tops of the roofs to the east, we sat down to breakfast. We had barely eaten a mouthful when, looking across the yard, I saw Gao Zun come around the spirit screen followed by three camouflaged *balu* troopers holding their guns at the ready in front of them. Gao Zun was talking loudly and gesticulating to attract our attention so that we might have an opportunity to hide. It was tempting to climb up into our ceiling hideaway where we had at one time stored the stocks of flour and rice. However, we both felt that to hide, and then perhaps be discovered, would only inflame the tempers of the *balu* and might bring retribution upon the Chinese Christians.

So we sat still, just where we were, watching them enter room after room all around the courtyard as they searched for soldiers in hiding. As they drew nearer to us, we pretended to go on eating as unconcernedly as possible, praying fervently as we did so.

Our Bible reading just before sitting down to breakfast had always been randomly chosen, but God had directed our fingers as we turned the pages and we had read about the prophet Elisha, in II Kings, Chapter Six, where he and the Israelites had been surrounded and outnumbered by a mighty host of Syrians. We had been comforted by the words Elisha spoke to his young servant: "Fear not, for they that be with us are more than they that be with them," and Elisha had prayed that God would open the eyes of the young man. Thereupon the young man saw that the nearby mountain was full of horses and chariots of fire round about.

Now, as we continued to sit inside by the window, pretending to eat, a white cloth covering the table, we had exactly the same experience as Elisha and his servant. The men advanced across the courtyard, coming to within four feet of our window, where they stopped. Just as Elisha had done, so many hundreds of years before, praying to God, "Lord, smite this people I pray thee with blindness," so Eva and I prayed fervently that the men might not see us. And just as God had done then for Elisha, He did for us.

The three men, who up to that point had entered and thoroughly searched every room in the courtyard, now stayed where they were. One of them pointed, not at us, but at the door, and we could see his lips moving, but because of the double glass, we couldn't hear what he said. We then saw Gao Zun say something back to him, then all three turned and left the way they had come.

Eva and I sat there frozen in place for a few minutes, hardly able to believe what we had witnessed. When I saw them go around the spirit screen and leave the yard, I went outside to the same spot where they had stood just seconds before, wondering, in my lack of faith, if the sun had perhaps been shining on the window in such a way that they had been unable to see us. What I saw, clearly and unmistakably through the glass, was the white tablecloth —the one thing above all others that should have attracted their attention — and there, too, sat Eva, clearly visible, and the chair where I had sat. There could be no other explanation. God had indeed blinded their eyes so that they hadn't seen us. As I learned later from Gao Zun, the man who had pointed to the door had asked, "Who lives in this place?" and Gao Zun had answered him, "Just a family that has lived here a long time." With that they had been satisfied and left.

By nine or ten o'clock, all gunfire in our part of the city had ceased. It was so quiet that people were beginning to come out into the streets out of curiosity, despite the fact that hundreds of *balu* troops were still pouring in from the west while other *balu* troops were going in the opposite direction, all seemingly somewhat aimlessly. At the same time, from the eastern side of the city we could still hear heavy gunfire, which continued well into the afternoon. It intensified after dark and continued throughout the night without letup. We were greatly puzzled as to what it all meant. It was not until two days later that we learned the truth.

At the county seat of Lingnan, some twenty miles south of Lingyuan, the county maintained a mobile force of heavily armed special police, who were used in putting down banditry and did little else. Normally they seldom visited Lingyuan, but by what most people would say was sheer coincidence, but which we knew to be God's planning, some 100 of them were in the city the night the *balu* attacked, staying at an inn at the far end of East Street.

When they heard the intensity of the attack on all three sides, they had at once retreated into the newly built, two-story bank building that overlooked the East Gate. There, from the upper floor and the roof, they had kept the *balu* at bay with a withering fire from their rifles and machine guns, despite the lavish use of mortar and artillery fire from the *balu*. The bank building had been very substantially built by the Japanese, and although heavily damaged by shell fire, the men inside sustained few injuries, and they held such a dominant position that the *balu* couldn't get close enough to take the building. As events transpired, it was indeed a godsend that that force of police held out as they did, or the story might have had a different ending.

I must interject here that the *balu* had a widely talked-about tactic when attacking a city of any size. The attacking force consisted of the elite shock troops, whose sole objective was to capture the city. When that was completed, they immediately moved on after having looted and taken prisoners, and left the temporary occupation and subjugation of the city to a second *balu* force of non-combatant men known as "The Poor Party" (*qiongdang*), probably because of their unkempt appearance and total lack of discipline. The job of that second force, led by an ugly-looking execution squad carrying wide-bladed swords, whose very appearance struck terror into everyone's hearts, was to terrorize the people into submission. They carried out mass executions, as well as roaming the streets killing in a random and most barbaric manner anyone and everyone they suspected of being pro-Nationalist. The rest of the "Poor Party" were meanwhile stripping the city of anything of value that the first group had left behind. When that was accomplished, usually within a day or so, they would generally set fire to the place and let the Nationalist troops retake it. The indiscriminate killings were intended to teach a lesson to all and sundry that they should not cooperate with the Nationalists, but it often had the opposite effect.

What had happened that morning in Lingyuan

when we heard so much shooting at the East Gate was that the "Poor Party" force was approaching the city from the south in what evidently was intended as a coordinated attack, but for some unknown reason they had come up from the south on the wrong side of the river and had mistakenly approached the city's East Gate instead of the South Gate, which was already in *balu* hands. I later surmised that since their mountain hideaway was in the same area once occupied by the bandit horde under the White Serpent leader, of whom I wrote in an earlier chapter, their approach by that route was logical. In any event, as they approached the East Gate, they met with withering fire from the roof of the bank building, and apparently, under the mistaken belief that the city had not as yet fallen into the hands of their comrades, they retreated back across the river, where they were out of range, and there they stayed for the remainder of the day to await developments. Aside from sending across small scouting parties from time to time, nothing further was seen of them. It also appeared obvious that their comrades inside the city were quite unaware of their proximity, so occupied were they in trying to dislodge the police from the bank building. But we were not aware of any of this at the time and only pieced it together later, when the whole thing was over.

But again we saw God's hand at work. Had the "Poor Party" force entered the city as planned, it would have been disastrous. As it was, the force of some 6,000 men who had entered from the other sides of the city engaged in a lot of looting, but very little of it involved the civilian population. Aside from the reported several hundred Nationalist soldiers killed in the actual fighting, there was no further taking of any lives.

In my opinion, what saved the city from mass looting was the fact that up at the far end of North Street there was a big compound where the United Nations Relief and Rehabilitation Administration had their depot filled with huge quantities of American flour and rice, together with large stocks of powdered milk, as well as used clothing, all of which the *balu* looted to the last bag and bale. Not far from there, on the same street, was the Nationalist army headquarters, where huge quantities of ammunition and artillery shells were stored, and that also claimed their attention.

Shortly after we had finished breakfast we heard the sound of drums and trumpets in various parts of the city, but had no idea what it could be. Eventually a group marched up our street from the center of town. They turned out to be teams of propagandists, groups of young men and women dressed in civilian clothes, wearing colorful headbands and jackets, and carrying flags and large banners. They had followed closely on the heels of the shock troops, and despite the continued shooting near the East Gate, before doing anything else, they whitewashed the Nationalist slogans painted on walls around town and pasted up their own posters and slogans in place of them.

At the same time, they distributed candy to the children peeping out from behind their doors and told them to bring their parents outside to listen to their lectures on the glories of Communism. When the parents didn't come out voluntarily, they were dragged out, but strangely enough, they were then treated with courtesy. However, at the same time, as an example to others, they beat any unfortunate householder whose wall had been used for Nationalist propaganda.

Within a couple of hours the entire town was plastered with their posters and slogans. But another paradox that struck us at the time was the irony of the propaganda teams telling the people such good things about Communism, and yet, under their normal procedure, the propaganda teams had no sooner finished their job than the "Poor Party" would take over and terrorize the same people who had just been assured that all would be well. To the *balu* it apparently made sense, but not to anyone else.

As the day wore on, and no more search parties came into the compound, we began to feel a little easier. Simultaneously, more and more civilians gained the courage to come out onto the streets, and a few of the Chinese Christian womenfolk came to the compound for safety, but at the same time warned us that the *balu* were openly looking for us. The *balu* had apparently been told that we were in the city, but hadn't been told our exact location. Children were being bribed with candy to tell them, and a number of adults had been questioned, but when unable or unwilling to tell, they had been roughed up. Despite that, no one told them where we were, and the womenfolk urged us to go into hiding immediately, while we still had the chance.

We had, in fact, the perfect hiding place — a place where no one would have discovered us. Behind the kitchen was a narrow two-foot-wide space with an opening at one end only. At the time the building had been erected, the space had been left so that rainwater from the back roof would not drip into our neighbor's yard. Lily Root had gathered some bricks from some other part of the compound, and the plan was for us to go inside the little alley, and he would then brick up the open end. All that morning we had given very serious consideration to going into hiding because of the urging of the Christian womenfolk, who were deeply concerned for us. We had even made some tentative preparations by moving in some canned food and blankets. But the more we thought about it, the less we liked the idea. What swayed our thinking was the fact that the *balu* obviously knew we were in the city, and it seemed certain that it was only a matter of time before someone was forced to tell them where we were. In that event, when they came looking for us and were unable to find us, it was equally obvious that they would take it out on anyone who happened to be around, and that would have put our faithful Chinese friends into a lot of danger. We decided to sit it out and trust God for His continued protection.

Throughout the entire day we could hear continuous shooting in the East Gate area, where the police force was holed up. Then, despite the large force that had captured the city, it quickly became evident they had no intention of staying very long. Through the crack between our front gates we watched an organized exodus begin in the late morning. It consisted of an unbroken column of commandeered horse-drawn carts and pack animals, loaded primarily with sacks of looted grain and flour and cartons of powdered milk, but also carrying a lot of other miscellaneous items such as furniture and household goods. Without a pause the long stream of vehicles, men and animals paraded by until well after dark, which was not surprising, because the *balu* was known to have no fear of the dark, and they usually made all their moves under cover of night.

The one interruption, however, was very exciting. Exactly at noon, while the exodus was in full swing, two American-built P-51 fighter planes belonging to the Chinese Nationalist Air Force, roared high over the city. That gave us some idea as to why the Communists were in such a hurry to get away. We surmised that their intelligence had told them a Nationalist relief force was not far behind.

When the planes appeared there was near-panic among the *balu* forces who were on the move out of the city. They knew they were an obvious target for the planes, and we were told later that they began to duck into side streets and alleys, or simply, as we could see ourselves, lined up as best they could against the walls of buildings where they would be less visible.

The two planes circled a few times at high altitude, then began to dive and strafe various parts of the city. They started with the area around the railroad station, swooping down with guns firing and then, after skimming over the ground at an altitude of about 500 feet, they climbed high into the air as small-arms fire blazed around them. After several dives in the station area, it was our turn, and it appeared that the Yamen, just a few doors to the east of us, was the target, because Gao Yu-sheng, who had ventured out onto the street, told us that the Yamen forecourt was filled with men and vehicles. However, the aim of the two pilots wasn't terribly accurate, and the 50-caliber bullets zinging down around us created a great deal of excitement. Our tile roofs took a terrible beating, and the flying bits of tile were almost as lethal as the bullets.

As we saw the planes preparing to dive toward us, Eva and I took shelter, crouching down behind a small wall abutment just inside my former study, where we happened to be at the time, but we could still watch the two planes through the open doorway. One of them roared directly toward us, and his bullets pounded the roofs, one of them smacking the wall behind which we were hiding, embedding itself not ten inches from our noses.

After several passes the planes moved on to the south, and we noticed they seemed to be concentrating their fire somewhere about a mile from the South Gate. It turned out later that they had spotted the *balu* "Poor Party" column, which had apparently discovered its mistake in approaching the East Gate, and had crossed the river well to the south and were now approaching the South Gate of the city from that direction. The strafing by the two planes evidently further discouraged them and they fell back, not to advance on the city until well after dark. By that time it was too late — the evacuation of the front-line troops was almost complete.

After about an hour of strafing the planes left and the exodus continued. Then as it neared dark we began to see large numbers of captured Nationalist soldiers, as well as students, teachers, government employees, and middle-class citizens, all tied together with ropes, walking under guard in groups, mixed in between the carts and pack animals. They were presumably being taken as prisoners either for execution or for lengthy indoctrination at the *balu* camp in the mountains.

In one such group I was shocked to see one of the Belgian Catholic fathers whom I had called on the previous day. He was quite an elderly man with a long white beard. As he was being hustled past our place with his hands tied behind his back, the men holding him by the arms suddenly stopped, knocked him to his knees, and pointing at the gates behind which I was hiding, loudly demanded of him, "Are there any Americans living in this church compound?" The old priest, knowing that Eva and I were British nationals, truthfully replied that there weren't any Americans there, and with that they appeared satisfied, and pulling him to his feet they moved on. We wondered at the time why he was alone and where his companion was, but we didn't learn the answer until late the following day.

As the sun set, the column of carts began to taper off, and we noticed large numbers of *balu* regulars beginning to assemble in the open area between us and the Yamen, many of them sitting on our front steps. Before long I could see what I estimated to be well over 1,000 men gathered there, apparently waiting for orders. Gradually, as darkness fell, we could no longer see them, but we could hear the low roar of their voices, which carried even to the rear of our large compound.

Suddenly, without warning, someone pounded on the gate and demanded to be let in. Poor, frightened Gao Zun opened the gate and three armed men came in. We feared it was another search party, but all they wanted was a drink of water, and they left a few minutes later. The men in the group immediately outside the gate were then heard talking among themselves, and Gao Yu-sheng heard one of them say, "It won't be long before the 'fire-setting gangs' reach here and set fire to this place, so perhaps we had better move on." Hearing that, our spirits dropped and we prayed as we had never prayed before.

After watching for about two hours, I decided to go to the rear of the compound again. Climbing one of the trees and looking toward the north, east, and south I could see the ominous glare of huge fires in each direction, especially in the downtown area. I was able to identify the location of several government buildings that were burning, but there were too many fires to be just the government buildings; it was obvious they were burning shops as well as private homes. I could see new fires being set, and they were advancing up West Street in our direction. I knew it would only be minutes before they set fire to the Yamen, and then it would be our turn.

Less than five hundred yards from us, and just beyond the Yamen, the big wine distillery suddenly burst into flames, burning furiously as the fire was fed by the large stock of alcohol. Then, miraculously, we heard loud shouting — quite unintelligible to us — and the entire force of armed men outside our gate started to run at full tilt toward the west, many of them firing their guns into the air as they did so. Within a matter of minutes they were all gone, the fire-setting teams apparently with them. God had again overruled, and once more we had been spared from harm.

For a short time an uneasy silence fell over the city, broken only by the shouts in the distance of the men trying to fight the fires. Suddenly I realized why the *balu* had left in such a hurry. Faintly at first, and then more clearly, I could hear to the northeast the unmistakable sound of artillery fire, with the shells gradually falling closer and closer to the city, as what we took to be a Nationalist force advanced. That went on for the rest of the night, with shells eventually falling close to the North Gate, but none of them inside the city.

Meanwhile, although it appeared that the Communists had all left, it wasn't so. All night long, a band of about fifty horsemen rode back and forth through the dark streets, firing into the air. We presumed they wanted to give the impression that the city was still occupied by the *balu*, so as to discourage the Nationalists from attacking and to allow time for the foot soldiers to get away. Then, just as dawn was breaking, the entire force on horseback rode past our gate heading west, and the city was entirely quiet once again.

A short time later the special police force, which had managed to hold out inside the bank building, emerged, and they in turn roamed the streets firing sporadically as they searched for stragglers.

As the sun came up we could see a pall of smoke over the city, but most of the fires seemed to have burned themselves out. Fortunately in Chinese houses, apart from the doors and windows and the paper ceilings, there are few flammable material unless the roofs can be set afire from underneath. But the damage was still tremendous.

Almost exactly 36 hours after it started it suddenly ended. We heard the sound of heavy motor vehicles approaching up West Street and spotted about 20 armored vehicles coming around the bend near the Yamen, with a large number of Nationalist troops following in trucks and on foot, behind.

Minutes later a young Chinese Army major climbed out of an armored personnel carrier and walked up the steps toward me, pulling out his visiting card as he came. He shook my hand heartily and congratulated us for having come through the ordeal, asking if we had been harmed in any way. I assured him that we hadn't, and, in turn, thanked him for having recaptured the city. I told him of all the prisoners that had been taken and urged him to send his men after them to try and rescue them. He assured me that his forces were already advancing westward in pursuit of the fleeing *balu*.

As commander of the mobile force, Major Liu was a most engaging young man. He was the picture of a true professional soldier: trim and spruce, with an alert manner despite his obvious exhaustion. He told me they had been on the road for three days and nights without sleep and had had very little to eat or drink. Eva and I, having been without sleep for 36 hours, could well sympathize with him. I invited him to join us for breakfast, and as Eva served him tea and toast with jam, he relaxed a bit, and I discovered that despite his professionalism he was very discouraged — just a young man who badly needed a sympathetic ear. For two solid hours he poured out his heartbreaking story.

Major Liu told us he was 30 years old and had been fighting the Communists for more than eight years. He was now convinced that it had all been fruitless and to no avail, and he was certain that the end was near, both for him and his country. Although he spoke perfect Mandarin, he told us that he came from southwest China and had fought his way across the length and breadth of the country. Although they had won many battles against the *balu*, he knew in his heart that the Nationalists had lost the war.

He told us that it hurt him deeply to be fighting fellow Chinese, but at the same time they were a newly born army of zealots who were totally un-Chinese in their behavior. Unlike most armies, where soldiers fought either out of patriotism for their country or for money, the Communists seemed to him to be driven by an almost religious fervor that was totally beyond his experience and for which he was unable to account. He didn't know what it was about Communism that made them fight the way they did, but he knew that despite the airplanes, superior firepower and mechanization of the Nationalist forces, and their training by the United States, the Communists were unstoppable and unbeatable.

I told him I had heard stories of the *balu* troops being given opium or heroin to smoke before going into battle and asked him if there was any truth in the story. He replied that he didn't rule it out, but that it wasn't the entire explanation for their seemingly total lack of fear in battle. I asked him about instances I had heard of where *balu* troops had reportedly been shot in the back by their officers for acts of cowardice in battle, of either attempting to retreat or run away. He confirmed that he had personally witnessed instances on numerous occasions, when, in the heat of battle, he had seen men turn to run, only to be immediately shot down by either their comrades or officers. However, he was convinced in his own mind that it wasn't fear alone that gave the *balu* a compulsion to fight, but just what it was he didn't know.

He described to us in graphic detail one engagement he had been in a few weeks previously. His force had been defending an outpost guarding a city in northern Manchuria. He, with 30 of his men, had been in what they thought to be an impregnable blockhouse built of concrete, one of several in a series with overlapping fields of fire that made it next to impossible for the enemy to approach close enough to throw hand grenades through the firing ports. However, he said the *balu* had attacked one night with their "human sea" (*ren hai*) tactics, pouring thousands of men into the battle until the dead were so thickly piled up in a mound on all sides and in

front of the gun ports that their field of vision and fire was blocked by a wall of dead. He said he and his men had plenty of ammunition left but had no way to fire any further at a live target because the pile of dead all around them was so high. On the other hand, the Communists were climbing the wall of dead from the other side and were shooting down at them from the top.

He told me that they then heard the sounds of men jumping onto the roof of the blockhouse. Within minutes they had used satchel charges to start a hole in the concrete, and then with pickaxes and chisels, they had finally made a small hole in the thick concrete roof, through which they had dropped several hand-grenades. Of all the men in the blockhouse, only he and one of his men had survived, and then only because, when his men saw the hole being made in the roof, they had thrown themselves on top of him to protect him. He said they lay there for hours listening to the sounds of battle outside. Then a small force of Nationalist troops had come from inside the city, and the *balu* had fallen back to regroup. Only then had they been rescued. With a bitter laugh he asked me a purely rhetorical question: "How can one fight that kind of an enemy?"

The most heart-rending part of his story came when I asked him if he was married. He looked at me for a minute or two, and then tears started to roll down his cheeks. Sobbing, in a voice choked with emotion, he told me, "My home is in Yunnan in southwest China, and I've been in the army since I was seventeen and haven't been home once in all these thirteen years. Five years ago I was briefly stationed in Peking, and one day I found a young orphan girl of thirteen abandoned on the streets, begging for a living. She was a beautiful child. Taking an interest in her, I led her to a nearby Catholic church and asked the nuns to look after her, leaving them sufficient money for her support and schooling. I planned to marry her when she was nineteen. Six months ago I went to see her. She was eighteen and more beautiful than ever, and I asked her if she would marry me. Do you know what she said? With a look of hatred she spat in my face, told me she was a Communist, that I was the enemy, and she could not marry me, an officer in the Nationalist Army. She spat in my face a second time and then turned her back on me and left. It is this kind of an enemy that I've been fighting for the past eight years, and I shall continue to fight them. I don't know anything else to do; I have no other trade. But I do know that we'll never win against them."

As Major Liu bade us farewell and headed west in pursuit of the *balu*, his story stayed with us and left us both deeply saddened, and in light of our experience over the previous 36 hours, we were much discouraged as well. After the major left, our Chinese Christian friends, together with several of the leading citizens of Lingyuan, came in one after another to greet us, using one of the very expressive Chinese sayings used after a traumatic experience, in this case, *Shou jing, shou jing*, meaning, "you (and we as well) have been badly frightened." They shared with us, and each other, stories of what had happened to them, and where they had been while the *balu* were in town. Many of them were in tears because of having lost relatives or friends, captured and taken away by the *balu*.

One of them had a somewhat humorous story. He told of a shopkeeper at the downtown crossroads who came out of his place of business at sunup and found six or eight *balu* sitting with their backs against his shop wall, resting. Not recognizing them as *balu*, he thought they were Nationalist soldiers, and he started to curse the *balu* for having given him a sleepless night. Instead of punishing him, the *balu* men thought it was amusing that he should not have recognized them and was so outspoken, and they simply told the man who they were and then watched with more amusement as he groveled at their feet and tried to make amends.

As we chatted with our friends it became quite obvious that we would have to change our plans. If the Communists continued their hit-and-run attacks, it was quite apparent that with the large forces they could muster, they could take the city again at will. It also seemed entirely likely that they would do so as soon as the Nationalist mobile forces withdrew. In that case, our staying on in Lingyuan could only be a cause of danger and embarrassment to everyone around us. We felt we should leave as soon as possible. Our Chinese friends, much as they wanted us to stay, unanimously urged us to go back to the coast for the summer and see how things developed.

We stayed on in Lingyuan for another ten days — primarily because there was no way to get out. The railway was cut on both sides of the city and no other form of transportation was available except perhaps horseback or foot. So we waited, hoping the railway line would be repaired. Meanwhile we busied ourselves trying to make the compound more secure and less inviting should the *balu* come again.

I purchased several cartloads of bricks and hired a gang of masons, and we sub-divided the compound by building a number of false walls, thus completely separating the living quarters from the church buildings. We also blocked up all doorways between the two compounds to make them separate, and made new openings, where necessary, into the residential areas, placing the openings where they would be as inconspicuous as possible. We hoped that should the *balu* be tempted to occupy the place once again, or even to set fire to it, it would be more difficult for them to do so, and some of the buildings might be saved.

When the ten days were about up, with no sign of the railway being repaired, and with the telegraph, telephone and postal services still not restored, we felt it was time for us to make some kind of move. The fact that Major Liu's mobile force had not returned from the west seemed to indicate that he had run into more trouble than he had anticipated. We began to think about possibly heading directly south on foot, since traveling by cart, litter, or horseback would attract too much attention. But before we made up our minds, I decided to sound out some of the few local officials and businessmen who had escaped capture by the *balu*.

The mood in the city was one of great fear. There were many rumors of another impending attack by the *balu*. The magistrate, when I visited him where he was then living with his family in a completely walled-in little courtyard in the back of the Yamen, also urged us to get out, telling us that his sources told of increased activity in the mountain villages held by the *balu*.

The most ominous report he had heard was brought by some farmers coming into the city that day from the west. They told of the preparation of large numbers of stretchers and the mobilization of farmers as stretcher-bearers. That was always a sure sign of impending action. The magistrate was sure the city would be attacked again in a day or so, but having nowhere to go and unable to desert his post, he was going to stay on. I asked him how he had avoided capture by the *balu* when they had occupied the city ten days previously. He smiled and pointed with his chin in an oblique gesture, remarking that there were places to hide and ways to hide. I pressed him for details, and, smiling, he ruefully admitted that he had changed into the clothing of a peasant, and with a manure-collection basket over his shoulder, had allowed himself to be discovered out in the streets when the *balu* came in and had been passed over in their search and completely ignored as being a simple peasant.

When I left the magistrate I decided to walk over to the Catholic mission to pay a quick courtesy call on the two Belgian priests and to say goodbye. At the same time I wanted to congratulate the one who had been freed by the *balu* after being held only briefly. I was also curious as to how the other priest had fared. Father Joseph, the one who had been captured, had returned after being held only two days, and a few days later the majority of the students and businessmen who had been taken prisoner had also returned.

At the mission I found Father Joseph looking well and none the worse for his traumatic experience. I told him how I had seen him knocked to his knees in front of our compound by the *balu* as they were taking him away, and asked what had happened after that. He said they had forced him to walk with them to a point about ten miles outside the city, where they had turned off to head into the mountains on a narrow cart track. At that point they had inexplicably let him go, telling him to stay in the village there for a day before returning to the city. Presumably they didn't want him carrying word back as to where they had gone, although the location of their hideout was well known. He added that they had not mistreated him in any way, but that it had been a rather frightening experience. I agreed with him and then asked the second priest, Father John, where he had been at the time of the attack.

With some embarrassment he told me that during the height of the attack he had been called to the house of one of their Chinese followers to treat someone who was sick. He had been caught there when the *balu* entered the city and had been unable to return to the mission. He said that as the *balu* started roaming the streets, firing as they went, his Chinese friends decided to hide him in a bolt-hole prepared for just such an emergency.

In the middle room of their three-room home, where the kitchen was, they had the usual large sideboard, and underneath that they had earlier dug a five-foot-deep hole, just large enough for a man. They had put him down into the hole, and had deliberately covered his head with a large, inverted earthenware bowl, the kind the Chinese called a "night pot." Their thinking was that in the event the *balu* entered the house, it was unlikely they would want to use it. There was a large nick in the rim of the pot, and that they turned to the front side. That allowed Father John enough air to breathe, and at the same time gave him a very limited view of the floor of the kitchen. He stayed in that hole without moving for two days and a night. He told me that a force of the mounted *balu* had, for some reason, selected that particular house in which to stay, probably because it had a large courtyard. The men were in and out of the kitchen the entire time he was there, walking within a foot or so of his hiding place. At night, he was in constant fear that they would take the pot and use it and thus discover him; that it looked so obviously old was probably what saved him.

He told me that the most terrifying time for him came when the two fighter planes came over. The *balu* led a number of their horses inside the room for fear the fighter pilots might spot them, and six or seven horses were lined up with their rear hooves just inches from his nose. As the planes roared low overhead, firing their guns, the horses became terrified and milled around the cramped area, kicking out in every direction. Every second he expected one of those kicks to demolish both the pot and possibly his head. But despite the unnerving experience he could still laugh as he told his story.

I mentioned to the two priests our intention of leaving Lingyuan the next day, deliberately not telling them how we intended traveling, since neither of them were leaving and I didn't want them to be in a position of being able to tell the *balu* where and how we had gone, should they be subjected to torture and asked about us. Both agreed that it was wise of us to go. They added that they were old and were confident they would not be harmed, and in any case they had to wait for instructions from their superiors before they could leave. But they, too, planned to leave before long.

After talking with our various friends, we had reluctantly reached the decision that the only way we could safely travel was to dress in Chinese clothes and make our way on foot through the mountains to the south, heading in a direct line to the coast by the footpaths and back roads that only the peasants used. We decided to take with us the two young blind men, Gao and Ho, not only because they would make good cover for us, but because we wanted to get them to Tientsin, where we could once again enroll them in a school for the blind. This time they wanted to learn the weaving trade, using newly designed machines being produced in Tientsin.

By late afternoon of that same day we had completed all our preparations and were ready to leave before daylight the following morning, leaving everything behind and carrying nothing with us but our bed rolls, made up in the manner the Chinese peasants used. But God had other plans for us.

Just before sundown we were astonished to see a Caucasian walking through the courtyard toward us. He turned out to be a young American ex-Navy lieutenant who had volunteered to join UNRRA, and he had just arrived in a Jeep with his Chinese interpreter. Since it was his first visit to Lingyuan, he hadn't known where the UNRRA depot was, and being a foreigner he had been directed to our place. He had come in from Chengde to our west and said he had not encountered any *balu* on the way, much to his disappointment. He was frankly anxious to see what they looked like after all he had heard about them.

He was a handsome, energetic, optimistically blithe young man who appeared utterly fearless and completely self-assured. He'd been driving day and night from Peking after having received word, first by a runner to Chengde, and then by telegraph, of the looting of UNRRA supplies in Lingyuan, and he had come to assess the damage. We gladly offered him a place to sleep on the floor and told him he could share meals with us. However, since all our tubs had been stolen, we were unable to offer him the bath that he badly needed.

He was obviously surprised to find us there and listened with the utmost interest to our story of the *balu* attack. When we told him of our plans to leave in the morning because of the insistent rumors of an impending attack, he laughed and pooh-poohed the whole thing and said it wouldn't change his plans. He

would be staying on for ten days or so in order to put things back into commission.

He napped on the floor for about 30 minutes, then went off to the UNRRA depot to check out the losses and damage. Within the hour he was back, and his entire attitude and manner had changed, and his interpreter's face was as white as the proverbial sheet. He was appalled by the destruction carried out by the *balu* and said that not only had everything been looted from their depot, but most of the buildings had either been burned or torn down. There was nothing left there except the second truck, which the Communists had been unable to start, and which inexplicably they had left undamaged. He did find a fairly large stock of gasoline and had managed to get the truck started despite the badly depleted battery. He had also located the two drivers who had been hiding. From them and the rest of his staff at the depot, he had heard confirmation of the rumors we had told him, and he was now convinced that we were right about an attack by the *balu* coming at any minute. That being the case, he had decided there was no point in his staying on, and he was planning to return to Chengde the following morning. He told us he would be delighted if we would share the Jeep with him. We at first declined, telling him of the two young blind men, Gao and Ho, whom we wanted to take with us. He said that was no problem. He would also be taking the truck with him, and they could ride in it.

That was certainly a God-sent solution to our problem and we happily accepted his offer. Word quickly got around about our impending departure, and quite a crowd of Christians gathered in the hall to bid us farewell. It was a sad occasion for us all, knowing full well that in all probability we would never see each other again. We prayed and sang some hymns together, committing each other to God's protecting care. I then urged them to help themselves to everything we were leaving behind, including all the clothing and rugs in the box room; otherwise, it would undoubtedly be looted by the next bunch of *balu* to take over the city. That statement convinced them of the finality of our departure, never to return again, and they wept at the thought, as did we.

Late that night, just as we were going to bed, our neighbor to the west, Mr. Yang, came over with an urgent request. His married daughter, aged 19, had been visiting them from her new home near Peking, and he begged me to allow her to accompany us on our journey, since there was no other way for her to travel except on donkeyback, and he felt that was very unsafe. Under the circumstances I was very reluctant to take responsibility for the young woman, fearing that she might be endangered en route, but I finally agreed, provided he sent a man along to escort her. He promised that her cousin, aged 16, would go along with her, and I told him to have both of them ready to leave at daybreak.

Looking back on those turbulent days, I have to smile each time I remember one aspect of our actual departure, although at the time, we, and everyone else, including our neighbors, were all in tears. Since we had originally planned on walking out, Eva and I had decided to take nothing with us but our bedrolls in order to try and pass as ordinary travelers. But now that we were going by Jeep, we could take a small quantity of food and our Coleman stove to make tea. Then, at the last minute, since there was the truck on which we could put some stuff, I thought of the six portable typewriters in the box room and decided to take them along as well. They would be absolutely useless to any of the Chinese if we left them behind. And, at that time, just after World War II, it was next to impossible to buy a new typewriter. Not only

would our own be invaluable to us, but we might even find the owners of the two extra ones we had found in the room. At least, such was my thinking at the time.

So picture us starting off. Six of us, a bedding roll over our shoulders and a thermos flask on a strap. Me with the six typewriters, which I deemed more important than anything else, one under each arm and two in each hand. Eva led the two young blind men, each with his long walking stick, one hanging onto each of her arms, both of them helpless and unable to walk by themselves in an area strange to them. At the same time Eva carried our Coleman stove and food enough for two days. As if that wasn't enough, along with us was a very young married woman, six months pregnant, carrying with her a stack of gifts her parents had given her and a generous supply of food, accompanied by her 16-year-old cousin who had never been out of the city in his entire life. A large crowd of Christians and neighbors saw us off, and we left Lingyuan for the last time, blissfully unaware of all that awaited us on the way. At the time it all seemed so ordinary and logical, but oh, how I came to loathe those six typewriters in the days ahead. We were heading for Peking by way of Chengde, a trip that used to take two days by car, but this time it was to take us well over two weeks.

Front gate of our compound where barricades were built by the troops. On our return, Bob ordered them torn down to keep the church premises from looking like a military fortress.

Troops using the Tharp family living quarters. This is the door to the living-dining room, where holes were burnt through the floors.

On our return, soldiers were using the premises. Here they are using the well.

Church Hall used by troops for registration and milk pickup place.

Troops brought in carts and broken-down equipment and stored these in corners all over the compound.

Barricades built by troops in the back garden. Trees had been stripped of branches for firewood.

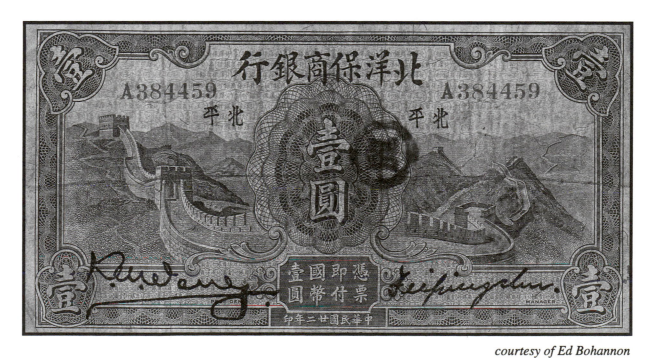

courtesy of Ed Bohannon

A Chinese one yuan bank note issued in 1933 of the Commercial Guarantee Bank of Chihli, Peiping.

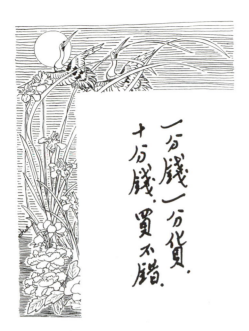

Yifen qian yifen huo, shifen qian mai bucuo.

*A penny gets you a penny's worth,
ten cents will buy something worthwhile
(i.e., you get what you pay for).*

- Chinese Peasant Saying.

Chapter Forty
Through The Lines

Dawn was breaking behind us as we drove out of the West Gate and we took one last look back at Guang mountain. We had been surprised by the large crowd there to see us off: all of our near neighbors and almost the entire church membership, together with a lot of townspeople. One after another they told us, "Now that you are going, this is the end. The *balu* will be here in no time at all." That parting was so sad. Even now, 45 years later, it is painful remembering it, and I fear that few of those who saw us off that day are still alive.

Eva and I rode in the back seat of the Jeep. The other four, the two blind lads Gao and Ho, and the young wife and her cousin, together with a dozen or so UNRRA personnel who were anxious to get away from Lingyuan, were all perched atop a heavy load of wooden boxes in the back of the UNRRA truck. Each box on the load contained two five-gallon cans of gasoline that the *balu* had unaccountably overlooked.

Both vehicles were flying large United Nations flags, but although that was protection of a sort, it was in God that we put our trust. We knew we were heading into *balu* territory, and just before leaving, as we ate a light breakfast, we once again read together Psalm 91, "The Traveler's Psalm," as my father used to call it. God's promise to us in verse 10, "There shall no evil befall thee..." had a very special meaning for us that day and in the days that followed.

We had eaten a simple supper the night before with the young American ex-Navy lieutenant who somewhat plaintively confided in us that, with all he had heard about the *balu*, he'd never managed to see any of them. He was anxious to get at least a glimpse of them to see if they were as tough as they were made out to be. That very first day he got his wish, albeit from a distance, and at first he refused to believe it.

As we headed west and began to enter the mountains, not five miles from Lingyuan, we saw, every half mile or so, the first indications of the *balu*, their youthful black-clad sentinels squatting in the fields alongside the road, posing as peasants. A few miles farther on we saw their first outpost perched high on the peak of one of the mountains, their flag brazenly flying, the men openly walking about, some using binoculars to keep the road and everything on it under surveillance. Every few miles we saw identical outposts. They had the entire road under observation and could have attacked at any time they wanted.

There was very little traffic, just a few pedestrians, all of them peasants or at least trying to look like peasants. As long as we kept on the move we felt fairly secure, but the roads were in terrible shape and we had frequent delays. It was late April; the frost was coming out of the ground, and in many places the heavily loaded truck bogged down and had to be unloaded and dug out. Each time that happened we felt terribly exposed, but the day passed without incident, and by late afternoon we reached Pingquan, my birthplace, some sixty miles from Lingyuan.

We headed straight for the mission compound. Like the others we had seen, it too had been badly looted and heavily damaged by a succession of occupying troops. The compound was empty except for a lone caretaker. He welcomed us and told us that the Nationalist troops who had occupied the place for nearly a year had only been withdrawn a few days earlier, as a result of my having forwarded a copy of the Mukden general's edict. Just as had been the case with our compound in Lingyuan, we found large blockhouses flanking both the front and rear entrances. Much as I wanted to get rid of them, it was too late in the day to go to the military headquarters to request that they be taken down. However, I gave my visiting card to the caretaker and told him to go in my place the next day to visit the local military commander and to express my regrets for not having been able to see him, and at the same time to ask for the removal of the blockhouses from the church entrance. Whether it was ever done, I have no way of knowing.

We met with the local Christians that evening. From them we heard similar stories of atrocities committed by the *balu* when the city had been taken over a short time before, in a raid almost identical to the one we experienced. They, too, anticipated another attack, which they expected to be the final takeover of the entire province. Indeed, that is exactly what happened a few weeks later.

Early the next morning we resumed our journey to Chengde. The closer we got, the more frequently we saw the *balu* on the mountain tops, their flags flying triumphantly and brazenly, and from time to time we could hear their trumpets and drums. All that while Nationalist troops, in increasing numbers, patrolled the road below on which we were traveling, but surprisingly, not in motorized vehicles. We learned later all trucks were being saved for an evacuation to the south. Although in full view of each other, both parties seemed intent on ignoring the other, and no shots were exchanged, at least not while we were there. While the Nationalists had the advantage in both men and firepower, the *balu* held the high ground, inaccessible to vehicles of any sort. Furthermore, their policy was to refuse to become involved in any engagement during daylight hours. Therein lay their strength. It was a cat-and-mouse game that they played with great skill.

In Chengde we parted company with the young ex-Navy man. He had to stay over in Chengde for a few days to close things down, and he regretfully told us that he would have too much of his own stuff to carry with him to Peking when he finally left, so he was unable to offer us a ride. We were not concerned, though. We had been told that commercial trucks were leaving daily from Chengde for Peking, and we felt that we would have no trouble getting transportation.

We again stayed at the local mission house, the same place where Eva and Barbara had stayed with Mr. and Mrs. Duthie when I was confined in the Chengde jail in 1941. If anything, the place was in a worse shambles than anything we had seen elsewhere, and I was glad that the Duthies couldn't see how their home had been systematically vandalized, with all their possessions either stolen or destroyed. The church buildings, too, had suffered badly.

Again, the only people on the premises were a caretaker, his wife, and two children. Although it was late in the afternoon, he at once went around to several of the inns at my request and finally managed to purchase six tickets for us on a truck leaving for Peking the next morning. We met with a few of the Christians that evening, had an early supper, and all six of us found a place on the floor in one of the least damaged rooms, where we put our bedrolls. Before daybreak the next morning we were at the inn, ready to board the truck and head south.

The truck was a decrepit old 1938 Ford, which in America would have long since been consigned to the scrap heap. But the Chinese driver and his mechanic had somehow managed to keep it going, although when I looked at the engine I marveled that it worked at all, there were so many odd-looking things attached here and there. The truck had a homemade wooden body on the back, with sides that extended up about three feet. It was loaded with some 50 or so empty 50-gallon gasoline drums, piled two high, and strongly roped on. We discovered that 22 people had bought tickets for the trip, and most of them were seated on top of the gasoline drums when we arrived. But they obligingly made room for the six of us, and away we went in a cloud of dust, heading for the South Gate.

We were relatively comfortable, and everything would have been fine, but when we reached the city gate the army men on guard duty demanded that all of us get down and show our identification papers. We did so and were taken to a nearby building where our papers were supposedly processed. When we were finally let out of the building, we returned to the truck to find that 18 unarmed Nationalist soldiers had climbed aboard the truck and were now occupying our places.

It was the kind of situation the commercial truckers had to put up with. A wise Chinese didn't normally argue with a soldier, armed or unarmed. And we concluded that the order for us to get down and show our papers was simply a charade carried out by the duty guards to allow their comrades an opportunity to climb on the truck. The men were all legitimately on leave, and that was their way of getting home. None of them would, of course, think of buying a ticket, nor would the driver dare demand one, and that was the way things were done. They were completely unconcerned about inconveniencing others.

The driver patiently stood by as I tried politely to reason with the soldiers to get down from the truck and make room for us since we had purchased tickets. I might just as well have talked to a stone wall. They completely ignored me, and at first I couldn't even get a word out of them. The normal procedure to get the truck under way under such circumstances, where Chinese soldiers were concerned, would have been for one or more of them to have climbed down from the truck to beat up on the driver until he got started. I

think my presence and my black looks at them discouraged that. Not only that, but to get off the truck would have weakened their position, and someone might have climbed up and taken their places. I finally broke the impasse by trying some humor, and once I got them laughing, which was followed by a considerable amount of palavering, they grudgingly allowed Eva and the young pregnant wife to climb aboard, and I then talked them into letting the two blind lads get on. That made 22 on the truck, our original number. But 18 of us were still on the ground, and I was certain that although we could squeeze a few more in, some were going to be left behind. However, it was worth a try.

I figured out a strategy, gambling that if I was the first to climb aboard, the soldiers might, to some extent, be intimidated by a foreigner and let me on. So I quietly told the rest of the ticketed passengers to simultaneously start climbing aboard as soon as they saw me do so. From four sides (some climbing up over the engine and top of the cab), we climbed up and tried to squeeze ourselves aboard. Just as I had anticipated, the soldiers, while punching at their fellow Chinese, did not attempt to stop me. Perhaps the fierce glare I was giving them had something to do with it.

But simply getting up on the truck wasn't enough for me. I squeezed myself into the center of the truck, thus making way behind me for one or two others to get aboard, and it worked quite well. With the rush from all four sides, the soldiers were so taken aback, almost everyone in our original group managed, in one way or another, to at least get themselves off the ground. But that wasn't a safe way to travel. Many had only a precarious seat, with their legs dangling over the sides, and others stood on the narrow ledge of the truck body, while still others sat on top of the hood or stood on the running boards, and everyone was terribly crowded together.

The guards at the gate who had caused the whole incident were laughing uproariously all the time, seeing it all as a huge joke. The driver, in no hurry to leave, was sitting on the ground smoking a cigarette. He had told me that that happened every time he made the trip, and he philosophically waited for things to sort themselves out.

At that point I decided to do some rearranging of the load. I first stood up in the middle of the truck and addressed the 18 soldiers who had taken our places. In very strong but polite terms I told them that we were all in it together, we all wanted to get to Peking, we civilians had paid good money for our tickets, and I was going to see to it that everyone got a safe place to ride on the truck. I added sternly that the truck was not going to move an inch until everyone was aboard. There wasn't a murmur from any of them. Then, on the pretext of making sure everyone was comfortable, I got three of the civilians to move onto the cab roof, where they sat facing backward, their legs inside the truckbed. With people leaning against their legs they would be relatively safe from sliding off. I then moved Eva and the young pregnant woman nearer to the edge of the truck where they would be more comfortable, and then I jumped to the ground, thus allowing another civilian to take my place.

I told the driver and his mechanic I was going to seat one of the older men between them on the front seat and told them all to get in. I then had two civilians stand on the running board on each side and showed them how to hold on. When all that was done, there were still five of us without a place. Because it would be unsafe to travel as they were, with people sitting on the hood, the front fenders, and one even standing on the front bumper holding on to the hood ornament, I had to find some other way.

With 35 people now on the truck, there was no possible way to pack any more in on top. There was only one thing to do. The five of us had to somehow hang onto the sides of the truck body. I spoke to young Gao and Ho and then climbed up onto the narrow two-inch-wide ledge created by the truck body, turned around so my back was up against the empty gasoline drums, and, putting my elbows back, I had Gao and Ho each hang onto one of my arms. I then bent my knees, and keeping my weight on the back of my heels, I squatted down, as they held me in place. With the truck stationary it worked fine. What it would be like with the truck in motion remained to be seen.

Having watched how I did it, the other four ticketed passengers did the same thing, each of them held in position by two men on top of the truck, some of the soldiers even helping out. Telling the driver to take his time and not drive too fast, and to go slowly over the bumps, we started off, all forty of us aboard. In that manner we traveled something over 120 miles,

over some of the worst roads I had seen in years. It was the same road the Japanese had built years before, but since the surrender, no one had maintained it. Not only was the road surface like a washboard, but in many places the rains had cut deep gullies across it, and a number of the bridges had either been blown up by the *balu* or washed out by floods.

The worst damage was between Chengde and the passage through the Great Wall at Gubeikou. Along the entire route, as we paralleled the railway track, we saw endless signs of sabotage and destruction. Almost all the railroad bridges were entirely gone, and in a great number of places the track had entirely disappeared. It was obvious there would be no trains running for many months.

After the first ten minutes in the bent-knee, hanging-by-our-elbows position, every bone in my body ached, as I am sure was the case for the other four fellows. Unfortunately we could do nothing but grit our teeth and hang on, keeping in mind that every turn of the wheels carried us that much closer to safety. We were just happy to be moving.

Now and then we had brief respites when the truck engine broke down or overheated, and we would have to stop and make repairs or fill the radiator. Also, because of the April rains a lot of water had collected in places on the road, and time after time we got bogged down in mud holes, whereupon everyone had to get off and push. Those little breaks gave us a chance to stretch our legs and arms. But getting down off the truck became something of a joke. Usually, it was simply a matter of falling, as whoever it was who was holding our arms let go. Our legs were too stiff and sore to break our fall, so we simply fell flat on our faces. It usually took a few minutes for the blood to circulate before we could walk. Fortunately, the five of us were all young men and were able to grin and bear it, but we had no kind thoughts or words for the 18 soldiers who had brought about our discomfort.

Among our problems were the bumps in the road. Our footing on the sides of the truck was so insecure that even a slight bump could dislodge us, and I lost count of the number of times I or one of the others was bounced off. When that happened, those sitting on top of the cab pounded on the cab roof, and the driver would stop and wait for us to catch up. All those delays didn't make for very good travel time, but around noon we neared the Great Wall and stopped for lunch at a small village inn. We were thankful not to have seen any signs of the *balu*. After having seen them so frequently the two previous days, I wondered why none of them were about. I asked the truck driver, and he told me it was because so many military convoys used the road each day (although we saw none of them). But he warned that the mountain pass was ahead, and we might find it to be a different story there.

Sure enough, around midafternoon as the truck started to grind its way up through a narrow defile into the pass approaching Gubeikou, where we would pass through the Great Wall, we were suddenly startled by the crack of rifle shots. A fusillade of bullets hit the rocks around us, a couple of them striking the body of the truck; fortunately no one was hit.

The driver immediately sped up, hit a bad bump that threw all five of us "hangers-on" off the truck and just kept going, totally disregarding the pounding on the roof of the cab. I didn't really blame him. While bullets continued to fly around us, we scrambled to our feet and chased after the truck, which was already out of sight. As hard as we ran, we couldn't catch up to it. Then I noticed a line of figures outlined against the sky on a nearby peak. As we ran farther into the narrow, rocky defile, we lost sight of the men on the peak, but we could hear them continuing to fire at the truck, which by that time was again within their sights. Finally, after a nasty fifteen minutes or so of uphill running we were out of range and the firing stopped. But there was no guarantee that we'd not find more of them ahead.

At the top of the pass the truck driver was finally persuaded to stop and wait for us to catch up. When we entered the village of Gubeikou, we reported the attack to the Nationalist army soldiers on guard, since it was only a few miles away. They made no comment, and their only response was to make us all get off the truck to undergo a search of our baggage and persons. The 18 soldiers aboard had to produce their travel passes. After a half-hour delay we were permitted to resume our journey and started down the precipitous southern slope, with its many hairpin bends.

I had earlier observed that the truck had almost no braking power. The only way the driver could stop was to downshift, and that caused me to worry about the pass. However, the driver fortunately had enough sense to keep the truck in low gear all the way down. Even then, on two occasions the truck attained such a high speed that he had to run it into the bank to slow it down. Each time the sudden impact threw all five of us off again. The second time, one of the men suffered an injury to his arm, fortunately not too serious. Meanwhile, those on top of the truck who were trying to hold us up by our arms were not having an easy time of it either. The strain of hanging onto us for hours at a time gave them severe backaches, but the tension and fear kept all of us going.

As the sun fell low on the mountains behind us and the shadows grew long, we finally came out onto the open plain below and felt a little more secure. We were approaching the fairly large walled city of Miyun, about 60 road miles from Peking, where the driver told us we would be spending the night and from where we hoped to be able to continue by train. But even though the city was within sight, we suffered another delay when we got stuck in a mudhole, and darkness fell before we could get going.

While working to try and get the truck out of the mud, we heard in the distance the welcome and unmistakable sound of a locomotive's whistle, and we all cheered. We had come within reach of civilization once again.

Once out of the mudhole, the driver drove headlong across the level plain toward Miyun, and we discovered that, in addition to having no brakes, he had no headlights either. It was a tense half hour before we drove up to one of the huge gates in the city wall, only to find it closed and tightly barred.

Outside every large Chinese city there was always a cluster of houses near the city gates, and it was no different at Miyun. We shouted to the soldiers inside, attracting much attention, and the locals all gathered around us, paying especial attention to Eva and me since they hadn't seen any foreigners in a long while.

Eventually, after much arguing and only after they had shone a flashlight through the crack between the two-leaved gate to confirm that I was indeed the Westerner that I claimed to be, the soldiers inside grudgingly opened the gates for us to enter. Again we had to submit to a thorough search. At the time I wondered why it was so thorough, but I didn't have to wonder for long.

The truck stopped at a fairly large inn not far from the city gate, where we fortunately got rooms for the night. After a very welcome meal I asked the innkeeper what time the train left in the morning for Peking. He looked at me and laughed. When I asked why, he told me that the railway track between Miyun and Peking had been torn up for over a week. When I asked about the train whistle we had heard, he said that one solitary locomotive and a few cars had been marooned in Miyun when the line was cut. The sound we'd heard was the engine moving around the station yards. What a bitter disappointment that was! Our truck driver was in the room next to ours, sharing it with young Gao and Ho, the blind lads, so I went and asked him what time he intended going on in the morning. Again we met with disappointment. He said the rumor was that trucks were not getting past the next big town of Huairou and none had come up from the south for several days. Reportedly, the *balu* had set up a blockade there, and all trucks were being stopped and dismantled. He'd decided to wait a few days and see what happened.

We spent a frustrating ten days at that inn in Miyun, a time full of paradoxes and far from boring. In fact, there was enough excitement in those ten days and nights to last us a lifetime. It is debatable whether anywhere else in the world one could come across a situation quite like the one in which we found ourselves.

We were greatly surprised when, just as we were about ready to settle down for sleep, the innkeeper casually came to tell us that we'd better keep our clothes on because the *balu* were due to attack at any moment. When I queried him as to how he could be so sure, he said they had been under nightly siege for the previous ten days. He added his own opinion that after another night or two of the kind of attack they had laid on, the city would fall. He suggested we had better wait a while before thinking of going to sleep.

We didn't have long to wait. The blind lads Gao and Ho came in shortly after nine o'clock to tell us that they could hear bugles in the distance. That was the first time we became aware of how keen their hearing was. That night and every night thereafter for the next ten days, around the same time, the *balu* attacked in great force. It was almost an exact repeat of the way in which their comrades had attacked Lingyuan just two weeks or so before. The big difference was that Miyun had very high, thick walls all around it, as well as a strong defense force of highly trained Nationalist troops who were well equipped and well led.

After the warning given us by Gao and Ho, the first indication of the *balu*'s attack was an ominous silence that settled over the city. Even the food vendors in the street were quiet. Then in the far distance we, too, could hear the bugles, seemingly on all four sides of the city. Not long after that we heard the beginning of the familiar chant, *sha, sha, sha,* "kill, kill, kill," which we had heard in Lingyuan as they approached the city. First it was far off, then it built to a crescendo. It rolled over us in a series of waves, first on one side of the city and then on another. Then, as the *balu* closed in to within a few hundred yards, their cries were drowned out in a hail of small arms fire, which was answered by the Nationalist troops atop the high wall surrounding the city. For hours each night thereafter the pattern was repeated, and the battles went on until near dawn, the only difference being that some nights they attacked only on one or two sides of the city, not on all four.

Intermingled with the other sounds we could hear heavy machine gun fire from the defenders, together with the explosions of hand grenades and the distinctive thump of mortars being fired by the *balu*. Every now and then a large explosion signaled that a land mine or a satchel charge had detonated somewhere at the base of the wall by men who had crept up close in the darkness, unseen from above, attempting to blow a hole in the wall. Those efforts were futile because the wall was at least fifteen to twenty feet thick at the base. I feared that they might try the same thing at one of the city gates, where they were much more likely to be successful, but the Nationalist defenders assured me they had complete control of the areas approaching the gates and could cover them with their machine guns, and that no one could get close without being seen.

Around three or four in the morning, as the cocks began to crow, the fighting would taper off. Silence would gradually reign once again, and we felt safe for another day. Night after night the entire city was terrorized, but the paradox came with daylight. The gates of the city were opened at sunrise, and life inside the city resumed its normal routine just as though nothing at all had happened. It was astonishing, unbelievable, and in one sense almost amusing. We and everyone else in the entire city had lived in fear of our lives throughout the night, but when daylight came, all seemed to go about their business as though the night of terror was simply a normal happening. No one even discussed it until evening approached once again. Everyone I spoke with, apart from the innkeeper, seemed to feel that the city was quite impregnable, and yet, while giving the impression they were not greatly worried as to what course events might take, there was still an undercurrent of uncertainty as to what the future might hold.

Of course that first night we got no sleep at all, and we were only able to doze for an hour or so after daylight before activities in the inn yard outside our paper windows awakened us. After I'd eaten I paid a courtesy call on the local military commander, apologizing for my muddy appearance and lack of a change of clothing. When I explained to him how it had come about by my repeatedly falling off the truck, we had a good laugh over it.

I learned from him that he had the best part of a full division of troops under his control, numbering in excess of 6,000 men, and he was quite confident he could keep the *balu* from taking the city. He seemed a little embarrassed to see me, and expressed concern over the responsibility he felt for our safety. I assured him he need not concern himself unduly and that we were quite content to wait until an opportunity offered itself for us to proceed south to Peking. He confidently assured me that the railway would be repaired within a matter of days, and, failing that, he was expecting a large convoy of trucks carrying troops from the Chengde area to be passing on their way south within a day or two. He said he would make sure we got seats on the trucks. I thanked him and said we would wait to hear from him, and with that I returned to the inn. There was little else we could do.

Since sleep was impossible at night, we slept when we could during the daytime and saw little of our fellow guests in the inn, all of whom were doing the same thing. When darkness fell, all the guests gathered in the yard around tables that the innkeeper had set up. Drinking tea and cracking watermelon seeds, we sat and chatted, waiting for the *balu* attack. When it came, we continued to sit and listen to the roar of battle, the cries of the *balu*, and the bullets flying high overhead.

The inn was very close to the east wall of the city,

so we were sheltered from fire from that direction. However, spent bullets from the other directions frequently hit the tile roofs around us. However, the angle was such that none that we knew of fell into the yard. Although to some extent we were in danger, for some reason everyone seemed to feel they had to be outdoors. I guess we felt safer than being inside. I believe it was because of fear that one of the mortar shells, which we could distinctly hear exploding in the distance, might land on the building and bury us alive.

Strangely enough, where the mortar fire was concerned, I quickly determined that it appeared to be a deliberate policy on the part of the *balu* not to damage any buildings inside the city itself. They seemed to be aiming all their mortar shells at the railway station and the yards around it. With the coming of daylight I frequently walked around inside the city to see what damage had been done, but I saw no instances of any buildings having been hit, except of those in and around the railway station. That was in a separate area just outside the western wall, surrounded in turn by a far less imposing wall of mud. The most vulnerable parts of that area were the points where the railway track passed through the wall, and I found those heavily barricaded and well defended.

On our third day I walked out through the main East Gate (the one by which we had originally entered) and continued on about a quarter of a mile to where the main north-south highway passed. Our young UNRRA friend had said he would be heading for Peking on that day, so I wanted to try and flag him down to warn him of the ambush the *balu* had set up just a few miles down the road. I stayed out there for several hours but saw no sign of him. I did the same thing for the next two days, but apart from a couple of commercial trucks heading south, there was no vehicular traffic whatsoever and no sign of the *balu*. I came to the conclusion that either I had missed him or he had changed his mind. I warned the two drivers who did come through of the possible ambush ahead, but they ignored my warning and continued on their way.

Another paradox of the situation was that all the cart roads and footpaths leading to the city were jammed with farmers coming and going, carrying fresh vegetables and produce of every kind: slaughtered and live pigs and sheep, other kinds of livestock, firewood, cattle feed, and all the necessities for daily life in a large city. At the city gates everyone was thoroughly searched by both police and soldiers. All packs and bundles were opened, and the bales of straw and firewood were poked thoroughly with bayonets or swords to ensure that no one was hiding inside and that they contained no bombs. Although I felt confident that every measure was being taken to prevent any weapons being carried into the city, it was perfectly obvious that any one of those peasant types could be a *balu* in disguise. Unlike Manchukuo days, no one was required to carry identification, so it was impossible to determine who any individual was or where he came from. Once or twice, though, as I watched at the gate, I saw individuals intercepted by the police as suspicious characters. The police in particular were no dummies. They inspected the "farmers'" hands to see if they had the appropriate calluses, and bared their shoulders to see if they had a callous from the carrying pole. Anyone with soft and unblemished hands or a clean shoulder was immediately suspect.

Apart from those searches of individuals entering the city, there was very little other indication of any kind of crisis afoot. But come nightfall, it was an entirely different matter. The city was sealed up tightly; yet outwardly, apart from the fear that one of the land mines might blow a hole in the wall and allow the *balu* to enter or that they might get hit by a mortar shell or the flying bullets, the people seemed little concerned.

On several occasions the city wall near our inn was hit by satchel charges, and I walked out the next morning to inspect the damage and found it to be relatively insignificant. The base of the wall was of huge, square stones, and the rest of the wall was made of kiln-fired brick. The wall seemed impervious to any really serious damage, so I doubted that the *balu* had enough in the way of explosives to be able to carry out much more than nuisance raids.

One thing they did every night was to bury land mines in the roadways leading to the gates. However, since their digging and burying was done in the dark, they weren't able to conceal their handiwork very well, and the soldiers who went out with mine detectors each morning seemed to find the mines with little difficulty. Even so, I worried that some of the peasants would be killed or maimed, but the mines seemed to have been set for vehicles rather than pedestrians.

Each day as we waited, new rumors spread that the railway line was being repaired and trains would be running within a day or so. But each day the rumors were proved false. Not only that, but we no longer heard the locomotive's whistle in the yards. I wondered if it had been hit by a mortar shell or had simply run out of fuel; later we learned that it was the latter.

On the sixth day of our stay, the entire atmosphere suddenly changed radically. We heard via the grapevine that the deputy commander of the Nationalist forces had defected to the *balu* and had sneaked out in disguise the evening before, just as the gates were closing, taking his family with him. Fortunately he had not taken any of the defending troops along, but he had carried vital information concerning the defenses of the city, including just how many troops there were and what ammunition stores existed. It was a disturbing thought, and it set everyone to worrying as to what would happen next. From what we could learn it seemed that a *balu* spy had entered the city and had approached the man with an offer he could not refuse.

Then, one day later, we heard a chilling tale that was brought in by some farmers from the south. The night before, the *balu* had rounded up more than 3,000 peasants, had lined them up alongside the railway track, shoulder to shoulder, and at a prearranged signal of a single rifle shot, the men had in unison stooped and grabbed the rail in front of them. Then, upon a second shot, they simultaneously lifted the rail and all the ties with it and flipped it over, knocked off the ties, piled them up in heaps and set fire to them. The process had been repeated all night long over a distance of several miles. It was hard to believe, but if true, our hopes of getting away by train were nil.

That same afternoon the commanding general sent one of his officers over to the inn to ask me to call on him. I accompanied the officer back to the general's quarters and found him visibly worried. He told me the situation was actually quite serious and said he had invited me over to discuss the possibility of getting us out before the situation worsened and it became even more dangerous for us.

He planned to send a small force of men south to inspect the railway line to try and confirm the rumors brought in by the farmers. He said he would make arrangements for us to go along with the troops, who would then escort us as far as Peking, if that proved necessary.

I thanked him profusely but informed him I wanted no part in any such plan if the men were being sent specifically to guard and protect us. But, I told him, if they were going to go anyway, with or without us going along, then I would take him up on his offer. I emphasized that I didn't want any of his men being put into danger on our account, and I exacted a promise from him that if and when we did go, his men should be ordered to fight only if first attacked. They were not to initiate any attacks against *balu* whom we might encounter simply in order to protect us. The general was visibly surprised and a bit amused at my insistence on those arrangements, but in the end he assured me that the commanding officer would be ordered to do exactly what I told him. He then advised us to make ourselves ready to move at a moment's notice, and said our departure would definitely be in the middle of the night or early morning, whenever the best opportunity presented itself. It was two days before anything happened.

At night, since none of us could sleep anyway, we sat around in the inn yard and chatted with the other guests, who sometimes asked me to preach to them. In all there were about thirty people staying at the inn. Among them was one very mysterious character whom we never once saw in daylight until our last day there. He came out of his room only after dark, and although he always made it a point to sit near me, he covered his face each time anyone struck a match to light a cigarette, obviously to avoid being recognized. Because we feared enemy sharpshooters climbing up onto the city wall and perhaps taking pot shots at us, no lights at all were lit at night, either inside the rooms or out in the yard. So, although the man lived in the room directly across the yard from ours, we saw nothing of him except his dim outline in the dark. Nonetheless, we came to know him well. Why he wanted to maintain complete anonymity puzzled me for some days, and I conjectured as to what the reason might be.

Despite his not wanting anyone to see who he was, the man dominated conversation in the yard. When he spoke, it was always in a cultured voice with a great deal of authority and in the language of a well-educated man. The first time I heard him speak, I concluded that he probably had at one time held a position of considerable rank. Through the tiny glass inserts in the paper window of his room he had every opportunity to study me in the daytime as I moved around in the yard. He had apparently done so and was satisfied as to whom I was. So on our third night there, very quietly he voluntarily told me that his name was Fu and that he was a colonel in the Nationalist army. But whether he was on leave, or absent without leave and on the run, he didn't say, and I didn't want to ask for fear of embarrassing him. From his behavior I suspected the latter.

Like ourselves, Colonel Fu had become marooned in Miyun and was anxious to get to Peking. Almost every evening he discussed with me various ways we might leave the city together and make our way to Peking, where he thought he would be safe. He feared making any move in daylight, and, of course, we couldn't get out of the city at night, so it was pretty much of an impasse. Colonel Fu was quite an authority on the *balu*, whom he had been fighting for years. It was obvious he was in great fear of being captured and identified by them, and we later learned from his many stories about them why that was so.

In addition to his stories about different engagements with the *balu*, he had also fought the Japanese for years, and it was his stories of those days that intrigued me the most. With very little prompting he would recount in a dry, emotionless voice, his part in various campaigns throughout northern China over a period of ten years or more, first against the Japanese and then more recently the *balu*. As his listeners hung on his every word, he was completely candid in telling of some victories and many defeats. He never boasted of his personal accomplishments and was frank in admitting his mistakes. His narrative added up to a series of frustrations, where weather, lack of support from rear echelons, the stupidity of his superiors, shortage of ammunition, the overwhelming air superiority of the Japanese, or the massive manpower and tactics of the *balu* forces had simply made it impossible for the Nationalists to succeed, and one retreat followed another.

One victory the colonel told us about I shall never forget, mainly because of the gruesome details, which he narrated without embellishment and in a completely dispassionate manner. His command of about 150 men had at one time been sent to capture a fairly large village held by a force of between 50 and 75 Japanese who had occupied the place for some months. During the time the Japanese were there, they had tortured and killed many of the men, molested and killed a number of the children, and had raped and otherwise abused almost all the women. When Colonel Fu and his men had taken the village, with very little loss of life for his own people but with a number of the Japanese killed, the villagers had surrounded the captured Japanese prisoners and had demanded that they all be put to death for their crimes. The colonel then went on to tell us in ghastly detail how that was carried out.

The villagers insisted that beheading or shooting the prisoners was much too lenient and compassionate a way for them to die. Particularly because of their mistreatment of the womenfolk, they wanted to watch the men die in a way more befitting their cruel and sadistic behavior over the previous several months. The scheme they devised is almost beyond belief, but as it was told to us by the colonel, I have every reason to believe it was in no way exaggerated.

The village bordered a small river, on the banks of which, close by the village, stood a copse of young poplar trees. The Japanese prisoners were taken to that spot, and the villagers proceeded to cut down young saplings of about one and a half to two inches in diameter, cutting them at just about knee height and then sharpening the tip.

Stripping the Japanese soldiers of their trousers but otherwise leaving them in their uniforms, they impaled each of the men on one of the sharpened stumps in a sitting position, forcing their bodies down the full length of the sharpened stump until the men were sitting on the ground, then leaving them there to die a slow and horrible death as the entire village stood around and watched. In that manner they disposed of more than 50 men. The colonel laughed dryly as he told us that the villagers had selected trees in such a way that when the job was finished, the men all faced in one direction and appeared to be in formation.

For the Japanese commander, who was forced to watch his men being slaughtered in such a barbaric manner, they had reserved a different form of death. In raping the womenfolk, as well as watching and encouraging his men to do the same, he had shown unusual cruelty, and many of the women had been maimed as a result. Accordingly, the villagers decided that the Japanese commander should be handed over to the women to do with him whatever they pleased.

The women stripped him naked and tied him to a tree in front of his dying men. Then some of the younger ones stood in front of him, exposing and flaunting themselves until they succeeded in arousing him, whereupon those who had been raped took turns taking a bite from his genitals. When there was nothing left, they stoned him into unconsciousness, then revived him by dunking him in the river. The man was bleeding profusely and near death, so they finished him off by taking one of the young poplar saplings, bending it down to ground level and slicing off the top, after which they impaled the man on it and released the tree, which, like a spring, bounced back and flung the man out into the river, where he drowned. When Colonel Fu's story was finished there was a deep hush and then quietly muttered exclamations of *Hao, hao,* "good, good," and *Gaizhao, gaizhao,* "well deserved," from many of the listeners, who themselves had suffered at the hands of the Japanese.

On our last day in Miyun I saw the colonel's face for the first time. He surprised me by coming to our room just before daylight to awaken me, telling me he'd heard that the *balu* had managed to breach the mud wall surrounding the railway yards in the northern part of the city, and he wanted to go there to see if there might be any possibility of all of us getting out through that breach after dark and then making our way to Peking. We had been sworn to secrecy by the general about our own plans to leave the city with a small number of troops, so I was unable to tell him we wouldn't be able to go with him, even if we found it possible to get out. However, since I had nothing else to do, I agreed to go with him and we set off right away.

Taking me with him was a crafty move on his part. He didn't want to be noticed or recognized, and by taking me along, he not only felt safer, but everyone would be looking at me rather than at him, so he could go unnoticed. He disguised himself in peasant clothing and an old straw hat, with a cloth wrapped around his neck and the lower part of his face, ostensibly to ward off the dust.

After a long walk through the back streets of

Miyun we exited the West Gate and climbed down a steep bank into a cut, through which the railway ran, then made our way to the station area and finally to the spot in the wall where a mine had been detonated the previous night. We found a part of the wall had indeed collapsed, leaving a gap about twenty feet wide.

A hundred or more Nationalist soldiers were there busily repairing the wall and it became immediately obvious that there would be no possibility of getting out that way. After a quick look we turned around and started back. On our return we took a slightly different route through another part of the railway yards, and we saw the lone locomotive standing there cold and silent, apparently undamaged, although buildings and some freight cars in the vicinity had been hit by mortar shells and wreckage was strewn everywhere. Dozens of men and women were there, picking up what they could find to use as fuel, but I saw no railway personnel at all and presumed they had somehow made their way out of the city to safety.

No word had come from the general that day as to when we might be leaving. That night, the *balu* attack was less intensive and was directed against the southern part of the city wall, so things were a little quieter for us, and we managed to lie down on our brick bed at around midnight. As we lay there, we could hear the familiar click of knitting needles in the next room as either Gao or Ho continued to pass the time knitting socks, the darkness making no difference for them. At the same time they were voluntarily standing a watch in case anything untoward might happen. They had been doing so from the beginning of our stay there, but I hadn't known about it until just a day or so previously.

It seemed that Eva and I had just dropped off to sleep, when around two in the morning, one of the blind lads knocked on our door and told me to get up because they had heard someone jump down into the yard from over the back wall.

To be ready for any eventuality, we had never taken our clothes off during our stay there, so I immediately jumped down off the *kang* and went out to investigate. Heading for the back of the yard, I saw a dim figure crouched at the foot of the wall. As I approached, he challenged me in a low voice. I replied, giving my Chinese name, *Da*, and telling him that I was a foreigner and asking him if he was there

looking for me. The man stood up, saluted, and told me he was a Major Liang and that he had been sent by the general to escort us back to army headquarters and that we should leave immediately.

Within a matter of minutes the six of us followed him out the front gate of the inn, which had been quietly opened for us by the innkeeper. From there we proceeded through the dark streets to a large army compound about a mile away. I was carrying the six typewriters, Eva followed with Gao and Ho, each holding onto one of her arms, while the young pregnant wife and her cousin brought up the rear.

At the army compound we were taken to a small room and served tea and cakes. Major Liang told me that the general had asked him to apologize to us for his not being there in person to welcome us. Because of the *balu* attack, he had been up all night and had just gone to bed. I told him we fully understood, and asked him to once again thank the general for us when he saw him the next day.

We waited in that small room for almost an hour until all was completely quiet outside the wall and it was apparent the *balu* had left. We were then taken to the West Gate, where a small door within one of the gates was opened, and we quietly slipped outside. There we found approximately 60 or 70 armed soldiers drawn up in formation awaiting us, and much to our surprise, a farm cart, pulled by a single mule, which thoughtfully had been made available for the ladies and the blind lads.

As we started off it was still very dark, although a faint band of light glowed to the east where the false dawn was just appearing, and we could hear the cocks starting to crow nearby. Our progress at first was very slow; three soldiers with mine detectors carefully searched the road ahead of us for the first mile or so before we could proceed. Then the young captain in charge came over and introduced himself and told me he felt it was now safe and that we need worry no more.

The young man's name was Tao. I thanked him for escorting us and asked if his commanding officer had advised him that we did not want him in any way to risk the lives of his men on our behalf. He assured me that such were his orders, and that he would do nothing to provoke an attack, nor would he attack any *balu* they might meet unless the other side fired first. With that assurance I was satisfied, and in that way we started out on another epic journey that was to last for the best part of a week.

We saw little of Captain Tao after that because he was always up ahead leading his men. But he left us in the charge of a stout, hard-bitten old sergeant who had been in the army for more than twenty years. We were only about 60 miles by road from Peking, but as it turned out, we covered only about ten or twelve miles in a day, and most of our time was spent waiting while the escorting troops felt out the territory ahead.

I was intrigued by the efficiency and alertness of our young Captain Tao. He seemed to know his business very well indeed. He deployed his men in such a way that about ten of them surrounded our cart at all times. The rest were divided into two files of about 20 men each who scouted the area on each side of us at a distance of a couple of hundred yards. In effect they formed a shield on each side of us, staying within sight most of the time. A third group stayed a few hundred yards ahead of us on the road itself, or what passed for a road, and there was an additional group of a handful who brought up the rear to protect us from any attack from that quarter.

Most of the time we weren't on the main road at all but following the railway embankment, on a muddy track alongside, in order to inspect the damage to the railway. Because of that the going was frequently very rough. From time to time there was no road at all, and the mule had to be unharnessed while the wheels on the cart were removed and the whole thing was carried across gulches or deep gullies by a dozen or so of the soldiers. Of course that always took up a lot of time.

It was an extraordinary sight to see how much damage the *balu* had managed to do to the railway. Very few undamaged sections of track remained. In some spots, where the line passed through a hilly area, huge boulders had been rolled down onto the tracks. Every bridge we came to had been destroyed, and about six miles south of Miyun we reached the section where a few nights previously the track had been entirely destroyed. We stopped for some time to examine the destruction. I stood by as Captain Tao interrogated several farmers at different points over a stretch of ground that covered two or three miles, getting details from them as to their unwilling part in the destruction and how it had been carried out.

Essentially, the story was exactly as we had heard it in Miyun. It was, of course, in the middle of the night, and the farmers said they feared they would be shot when the job was done. They showed us a series of five-foot-deep holes that had been dug at intervals of about every 200 yards along the embankment in which the *balu* riflemen had hidden.

It was from one of those holes that one of the *balu* troopers had given the signals to the farmers standing alongside the track. We asked why the riflemen had hidden in the holes and were told that they apparently were afraid that word of what they were doing might have leaked out, and they feared an attack by the Nationalist troops from Miyun. But another of the farmers told us that the *balu* were in the holes ready to shoot the civilians in the back if they failed to heed the orders they were given.

As we walked along the top of the embankment nothing remained of the track itself, but on the far side, every hundred yards or so we could see where the bonfires had been built, and the rails that had been thrown on top were now nothing but a heap of twisted metal. What astonished both me and Captain Tao was that the farmers had accomplished it by using nothing more than their bare hands and their crude mattocks to knock the ties off the rails. It was quite an achievement, and all of it carried out in complete darkness. It was hard to estimate just how much of the railway had been destroyed, but I had the impression that something over three miles of track had been ruined.

As we slowly meandered south we saw and heard many signs of the *balu*. They were everywhere around us, but they didn't molest us, and except for their lookouts they didn't come near us. I think it was more because of surprise than anything else. It was early May, and as we were much farther south than Lingyuan and at a much lower altitude, the fields had all been planted, but only in a few places were sprouts showing. Although there was obviously no work to be done in the fields, here and there men squatted along the roadside pretending to be working the land. However, in every case they were dressed not in the blue of the peasant, but in the black clothing that the *balu* favored to help make themselves invisible in the dark. As if we needed further evidence, each man we saw, although otherwise unarmed, was carrying the familiar potato-masher hand grenades around his waist, the long telltale handles protruding from under their coats as they bent or squatted, "busying" themselves as we passed and pretending to pull weeds. Meanwhile, of course, they turned their heads to covertly watch us from under the brims of their hats. True to his word, Captain Tao ignored them, although I'm sure both he and his men were itching to tangle with the *balu* who so blatantly flaunted themselves.

For the most part we bypassed the villages as we followed the track. However, when a village was very close to the line, as many of them were, our escorting troops thoroughly searched each house, just in case there might be *balu* hiding there ready to ambush us. That always took a lot of time.

At noon we stopped at a small village to feed the mule and allow everyone to relax for an hour or so and enjoy a simple meal prepared by the villagers. Captain Tao insisted on paying for everything his men ate, which was an eye-opener for me. It was rare for Nationalist troops to pay for anything, and I wondered at the time if, perhaps, it was because of our presence and they wanted to look good in front of us.

That first day, with all the delays, we covered only about ten miles. Late in the afternoon we arrived at a Nationalist army outpost close to the railway line and near a large village about halfway to the city of Huairou. I had thought we might go into the village for the night, but Captain Tao said he preferred staying at the army outpost rather than risk a possible attack on the village.

The camp was actually a fortress built with mud bricks. It had a lookout tower about 30 feet high and a six-foot wall around the several buildings adjacent to the tower. The entire complex was surrounded by barbed wire entanglements that covered a sizable piece of ground. Our group of soldiers had no radio, so, as we came within sight of the fort, we stood off while one man went ahead with semaphore flags and signalled the men in the tower that we were a friendly force. One of the soldiers came out to guide us in through complicated barbed wire barricades and along a tortuous path through a minefield. The cart was left outside and the driver was told to go to the nearby village for the night. When all of us were inside the fort the man who had led us in went out with a broom and swept away all footprints on the path we had made so that no one else could track their way in.

The mud fort had been well constructed, and although small, it held around 50 men. Despite crowded conditions, they made room for all of us, and the young officer in charge seemed delighted to have Eva and me as his guests and went out of his way to make us comfortable. They fed us well and found places for us to sleep, but they warned us not to take our clothes off in case there was a *balu* attack during the night.

When we'd finished eating, the young officer in charge came and sat on the *kang* beside us and apologized for the crowded conditions and the simple food. He appeared to be exhausted. When I remarked on it, he told us that they had experienced a heavy attack by the *balu* the previous night, and the battle had lasted until dawn. He estimated that some 2,000 men had been in the attacking force, and although some of them had penetrated the outer barbed wire perimeter, they had been blown up by the mines or had managed to get themselves hung up on the barbed wire entanglements inside, where they were then shot by his men. He had lost no men in the fight but estimated that between one and two hundred of the enemy had been killed. But following their usual practice the *balu*, although beaten off, had left no dead or wounded behind. The next morning the only evidence of casualties was the bits and pieces of clothing on the barbed wire and dried patches of blood in a number of places on the ground. But where the mines had been touched off, they did find body parts, which they had buried outside the fence.

I asked the young captain why he expected another attack would be launched again that night, and he replied that it was the usual pattern of the *balu* to quickly follow up on any attack that had not been successful. However, although we didn't sleep much due to the many activities and talking going on around us, nothing unusual happened and the night passed quietly. But the young wife traveling with us was terrified and unable to sleep, just as she had been each night in Miyun, and Eva spent most of the night trying to reassure her that all would be well.

The next morning as we ate a breakfast of millet gruel, we saw a civilian being brought into the fort. As he passed me, he stared at me, then stopped and asked if I could speak Chinese. He told me that he was a track-walker for the railway. He had been captured by the *balu* some three or four weeks before but had just been released because, he thought, they were short of food and didn't want to have to feed him.

He said that he'd been kept captive in a *balu* camp up in the nearby mountains, and while there he had seen a young foreign man, also held captive, who looked a lot like me. He wondered if I was the same man because he had not seen the foreigner for a week or more. I told him I wasn't the man and asked if he could tell me any more about the foreigner he had seen and what he looked like. He said that the *balu* suspected the man of being a government spy and had repeatedly tortured and beaten him, that the man was able to speak only a few words of Chinese, and had fair hair and was about my age. More than that I was unable to learn, but I feared it was someone I knew. He then took us outside the fort and pointed out the mountain peak where he had been held captive, and with Captain Tao's binoculars, we could clearly see the *balu* flags flying and people walking around.

As we left the fort shortly after sunrise, the young officer in charge took me over to the tower and showed me the piles of dust that had accumulated at its base, caused by the *balu* bullets hitting the tower the previous night. Then he dug out several bullets, offering them to me as souvenirs. I didn't want to carry them with me in case we should be stopped by the *balu*, so I declined. He then personally led us out through the minefield, showing us various spots where mines had blown up and large patches of dried blood on the ground. As he bade us goodbye and wished us a safe journey on to Peking, I felt a deep pang of regret that so fine a person should be in such danger, knowing in my heart that it was only a question of time before the fort would be overrun.

Our second day on the road was much like the first, except that we were going through more hilly country as we took a route that bypassed the city of Huairou. Because of the hills, our escorting troops were much more vigilant, and we moved even more slowly than the day before. Time and again we heard the sound of gunfire ahead and on both sides. Despite the squealing cart wheels and noises made by the soldiers and their jangling equipment, young Gao and Ho, with their keen sense of hearing, always heard the sounds of gunfire long before the rest of us. Whenever they warned me I passed on the word to the captain, and we would all stop while a few men were sent out to reconnoiter the road ahead or to climb a nearby hill

and look into the valley beyond. On one occasion a full-scale battle seemed to be in progress just over the hills from us, and I felt it ominous that the *balu* would be making an attack in daylight. But Captain Tao assured us that it was actually Nationalist troops conducting a foray into *balu* territory. I don't know how he knew and thought that perhaps he was saying that just to reassure us. In any event, each time we heard firing we waited until it had died out before we proceeded.

That second morning a rather frightening incident occurred that might easily have had quite serious results. Most of the time I didn't ride on the cart because there was barely room for four people; naturally the two blind lads had to ride, as did Eva and the young wife. Normally I walked a few paces in front of the cart, searching the roadway ahead for freshly turned earth that might indicate a mine had been planted overnight. However, that morning I happened to be riding on the cart when the old sergeant accompanying us decided that he, too, wanted a ride.

He was a short, heavily built, pot-bellied man, rather typical of what sergeants the world over are supposed to look like, or at least the way in which they are frequently caricatured. As he clumsily heaved himself aboard the cart just in front of me I happened to glance down. As his buttocks slid over a sack of feed that was tied on the front of the cart, I saw with a shock that a knot in the rope holding the sack had snagged the small lanyard that was tied to the pin holding down the handle of one the American-made hand grenades he carried on his belt. Before I could make a move, the pin pulled out and the handle sprang up. I knew it was only a matter of seconds before it would explode.

I had only three options. I could push the man off and let the grenade explode, in which case all of us might have been killed or injured; I could grab the grenade and throw it as far as I could, but I wasn't sure I could detach it from the man's belt in time, and I was afraid I might throw it close to some of the soldiers surrounding us and thus kill or injure them; or my third option was to depress the handle and put the pin back in. Never having handled a grenade before, I wasn't entirely sure that it would work. But that is what I did. I grabbed the handle and held it down as I reinserted the pin, praying hard that it wouldn't explode. Obviously it didn't, or I wouldn't be writing about it here.

The old sergeant hadn't noticed a thing until I brought it to his attention. He was then so shaken that he lay back on the cart, white of face, and begged me not to tell the captain because he was certain he would be shot for being so careless. I promised not to say a word, but after that I noticed he never rode on the cart again. To say that the rest of us were shaken by the incident would be an understatement, but once more we saw the protecting hand of God around us and our guardian angels there at hand to see that no harm befell us.

Other than that, and a number of incidents of shooting in the distance, nothing much happened that second day. After covering what I estimated to be only about ten miles, we again stopped in the early afternoon, around 3:30, at another fairly large village where there was a second but smaller fort, also guarded by Nationalist soldiers. Again we were led in through a minefield and met the young officer commanding the place. He showed no surprise at seeing us and welcomed us as though we were long-lost friends.

The place was much smaller than the one we had been in the previous night, and the young commandant suggested that instead of our sleeping there in very crowded conditions, we might be much more comfortable staying in a nearby temple. Even though it was outside the fort, he thought we would be quite safe. We moved over there before it got dark, had food brought in from a small inn nearby, and the six of us slept that night on benches and tables in front of a row of ten-foot-tall idols while several soldiers stood guard outside throughout the night. Several times during the night I awoke and went outside to look around and listen, but all remained peaceful.

The third morning Captain Tao surprised us by coming to say goodbye. He was returning to Miyun, but he said that another detachment of men would take us the rest of the way. We left shortly before nine o'clock, with only 18 men escorting us. They were a far less disciplined group and seemed much less alert, but we made better time, simply because they spent less time going ahead to reconnoiter.

Most of the time we again followed the railroad track or what was left of it, with high mountains on our right for a good part of the day. At one point in the late afternoon we had to cross a fairly deep river,

and on the far side we entered a small copse of willows and poplar trees. I was surprised that the soldiers escorting us had not gone ahead to scout the area.

Perhaps it was just as well, because as we passed through the belt of trees and came out into a more open area, we saw a row of abandoned civilian trucks alongside the roadside. Each had its engine and wheels missing, and one truck at the far end had several men working on it. I took one glance at them and recognized them as *balu*. We had taken them completely by surprise, but they bluffed it out, pretending to be the owners of the truck, and kept on working, with their heads down.

Before leaving that morning I had admonished the young lieutenant in charge of the soldiers not to get involved in any way with the *balu* unless we were first attacked. So we simply walked right past, ignoring them completely, and moved on unmolested. As we passed within six feet of them I noticed them eyeing us surreptitiously, with great curiosity. It must have been a strange sight for them to see a white man and woman and two blind men, together with a young Chinese woman, all traveling together under escort by Nationalist troops.

I realized at once that that was the ambush point we had heard about in Miyun. It was a well chosen spot, being in among the trees and invisible from any distance in either direction. I couldn't but wonder how our young UNRRA friend would make out when he reached that spot, but there was nothing I could do about it.

A few miles farther on we halted for the night at a small village inn, so small it didn't even have a yard, and our cart had to be left outside on the road. It had a bit of a back yard, but that was all. The innkeeper was most hospitable, welcoming us warmly, although I noticed he was a bit leery of our Nationalist escort. He whispered to me that many *balu* were nearby on a mountain peak about four miles away, but that so far he had been largely left alone and didn't expect any trouble. However, he told us he had very little in the way of food because the *balu* had been taking it. Hungry as we were, we didn't really care what we ate, and after a simple meal we were ready for bed. Just before we lay down, I went out onto the road for one last look around and ran into the innkeeper sitting outside his front gate. He drew me to one side and whispered in my ear, "Come with me." I followed him along the village street to an open area from which the nearby mountaintops were clearly visible. Pointing up to one of the peaks, he directed my attention toward some unusually bright lights, which obviously were not lanterns. He said that that was the main *balu* stronghold for the area and told me that they were using the truck engines to generate electricity for their lights and radios. I asked him how he knew, and he said it was common knowledge that the *balu* frequently came down to the village for food and boasted of what they were doing. But he was afraid to let the Nationalist soldiers know what he knew, hence the secrecy in which he told me.

After he had told me that, and seeing those lights so close, I had a strong feeling of uneasiness, knowing that the men we'd seen earlier stripping the engine from the truck had seen us and had most certainly reported it when they got back to camp. Eva and I felt very exposed that night, and expected visitors momentarily. But the night passed without incident, although neither of us slept well. Our lack of sleep, however, wasn't entirely due to the proximity of the *balu*.

The innkeeper had given us the only spare room he had, a small room in which he kept his grain. Since part of the *kang* was piled high with sacks of grain, Eva and I had barely enough room left to stretch out. The young wife who traveled with us was so frightened that Eva insisted she join us, so we were pretty crowded. Added to that, we could hear the rats and mice squealing all night, busily working on the grain. And if that wasn't enough, the warming weather had brought out the insects in the hundreds. Poor Eva was kept busy almost the entire night fending off hungry bedbugs, which we killed by the dozen. They didn't bite me; however, they kept me awake just crawling over me on their way to get to Eva. We finally got up around three in the morning, woke the soldiers, and told them we wanted to make an earlier start. It was just as well that we did.

That day was our 17th day on the road since leaving Lingyuan, counting the ten days we had spent in Miyun. I knew that if we moved as fast as we had done the day before, we could possibly make it to Peking before nightfall. The young lieutenant told us we were going by way of the city of Tongzhou, about 20 miles east of Peking and on one of the main railway lines.

Again as we moved along I was struck by the casualness of our escort as they marched ahead of us, paying little or no attention to what was around us or up ahead. I wondered if they acted so confident because they knew there was little danger, or whether it was just carelessness on their part. It turned out to be the latter.

Shortly after noon we came within sight of Tongzhou, but even when we were still several miles away both Ho and Gao excitedly told us that they could clearly hear a train whistle. No one else could hear anything, and I scarcely dared believe them. Then, a mile or two farther, both Eva and I heard it, and our spirits rose.

Tongzhou and Miyun were, at that time, both fairly large cities with populations probably in the neighborhood of 70,000. Tongzhou was known as a university town. At one time there had been an American school for boys there, which Eva's two brothers, Paul and Jerry, had attended when they were young. Tongzhou was also a busy railroad town, with numerous trains passing through it daily, and I felt sure we would be able to catch a train to Peking without much delay.

At one time Tongzhou had also been a walled city, but over the years the walls and the city gates had fallen into disrepair. The city had also expanded considerably outside the original walled area, particularly near the railroad station and on the northwest side, which we were approaching.

As we entered the outskirts of that section outside the wall, we abruptly found ourselves on a busy main street where everything around us looked perfectly normal: the usual street activities of a Chinese town, people walking in every direction, stalls alongside the street with hawkers shouting their wares, and the usual thick layer of dust in the road.

As usual, I was walking just in front of the cart, while most of our 18-soldier escort marched blithely ahead of us, forcing their way into the crowd, but a few of them were also around the cart. Although I had passed near the city many times, I had never actually been inside, so I was looking around with a good deal of curiosity. Not sure just where the railroad station was, we stopped for a moment to ask the way. At once, as was usual everywhere in China, a small crowd formed around us. One of the men in the crowd was well dressed and appeared to be a businessman, so I asked him for directions. He looked at me quizzically, then, glancing around to make sure he wasn't overheard, he said in a low voice, "Don't you know the line between here and Peking was cut last night and there are no trains running?" I asked why we could hear a locomotive whistle now and then, and he replied that a train had been caught there when the line was cut. It was a repeat of what had happened in Miyun.

It was disappointing, but I resigned myself to the thought that we were so near to Peking that it would only be another day by cart and we'd be there. Suddenly I noticed that our military escort had vanished. There wasn't a single man to be seen, and I hadn't noticed them leave. There could only be one reason, and a feeling of dread immediately came over me. Looking more closely at the crowd around us, it dawned on me why they had gone. The crowd wasn't made up of merely the townsfolk and farmers as I had first thought. There were just too many young men dressed in black, and although they were standing back and trying to look inconspicuous, I could see from those closer to the front that they were armed with revolvers and hand grenades, with a few even carrying rifles. We'd walked right into the middle of a trap and were surrounded by *balu*.

It was apparent that our escorts, being more experienced with the *balu*, had immediately spotted them, and recognizing the danger, had, without a word to us, simply melted into the crowd and disappeared. But our cart driver, a rather elderly peasant type, was a simple soul who had noticed nothing amiss. I was only thankful that a fire fight had not broken out when the *balu* spotted the Nationalist troops entering the city. Perhaps it was our presence that prevented that from happening, and of course our guardian angel was still with us. I can think of no other reason.

I knew we were in real trouble, and I had to make some quick decisions. It flashed across my mind that we could turn around and head back north out of the city, but I felt certain that if we attempted to make a run for it, we would probably be stopped right away and then would be in greater trouble. I decided the best thing to do was to bluff it out and pretend that we hadn't noticed anything. Rather than go farther into the city where we might find ourselves in a worse situation, I thought the best thing would be to duck into the nearest inn and wait for nightfall, when we might

have a chance of getting away.

Still talking with the businessman, I asked him where we could find an inn. He turned and pointed diagonally across the street to a large gate. We were almost directly in front of it. So that everyone would know our intentions, I loudly directed the driver to go to the inn across the street, where we would stop for lunch. I used the Chinese expression *da jian*, meaning to take refreshment, implying that we were continuing our journey immediately afterward. On the way to the inn I alerted Eva and the others of the situation we were in and told them to act as unconcerned as they could, and we all prayed for a miracle.

As we entered the inn yard, I concluded that we couldn't have found a better place to hide. Like so many inns that were on the edges of towns and not quite inside the city, it was the kind of inn that was attractive to travelers who wanted to make an early start and didn't want to have to make their way through city streets first thing in the morning and have the hassle of having to wait around until the city gate was opened. Consequently it was a large inn with a big courtyard, and when we entered it, I found that ours was the only vehicle there. That gave me hope that we might be the only guests.

But when we entered the large common room, I saw immediately that we had literally stepped from the frying pan into the fire. At the far end of the room we saw at least thirty men, and all but one or two of them were well armed *balu*. They were all obviously frontline troopers, with their rifles stacked on the floor in front of them, their heavily loaded bandoliers and packs lying on the *kang* beside them. It was also quite evident that they were billeted there.

Countless thoughts raced through my mind. I had no idea as to when the Communists could have occupied the city, but I guessed it had been early that morning, because otherwise word-of-mouth would have gone up the line and we would have been warned. On the other hand, the few travelers we had passed on the road coming from the Tongzhou direction had all been peasant types, and they would have been fearful of talking to Nationalist soldiers unless questions had been asked of them. So it was perhaps not surprising that we had heard nothing. But had the *balu* taken over the entire city, or just the suburb in which we found ourselves? That was the big question in my mind. If they had occupied the entire city, it was certainly very different from what had happened in Lingyuan, and it must have been a friendly takeover without fighting, because the population seemed completely unconcerned. There seemed to be no answers to these questions, and I wasn't about to ask anyone. But thinking about it, I felt certain that had we been escorted that far by Captain Tao and his men, we wouldn't have been in the fix in which we now found ourselves, because most certainly he would have sent men ahead to reconnoiter. But my main concern was how we were going to get out of there.

One thing had given me some hope as we entered the inn yard. Glancing around quickly, I had noticed that the main building of the inn backed onto the street. Opposite it, across the yard, there was another building consisting mainly of open-front sheds, and I could see a low stone wall extending out from behind it, and beyond that, open fields. Mentally I hoped that somehow we might be able to make our escape that way after dark, but that was hours away, and much could happen in the meantime.

While those thoughts were racing through my mind, the innkeeper had courteously shown us to a place on the *kang*. I decided our best bet was to continue the bluff and ignore the *balu* troopers as though they weren't there, and above all, to pretend that we didn't know who they were. As we climbed onto the *kang*, I asked the innkeeper in a loud voice to bring us hot water to wash our faces and ordered food for the six of us so we could be on our way.

The *balu* troopers were about twenty feet from us. They stopped talking when they saw us come into the room, and all eyes turned toward us. They were obviously taken aback by what they saw; then, as they stared at us, they started whispering among themselves. But none of them accosted us or even came close to us, nor did they ask us who we were.

A little later, after we had washed up and were waiting for our food to be brought, by one's and two's the men started to drift out of the room without saying a word to us, leaving behind just three of their number who immediately turned their backs on us. Not a word was said by any of the men as they walked past us, nor did they look directly at us, but when eye contact was made, as it was with several of them, I gave them a friendly nod that was returned in a rather stiff manner without a trace of a smile.

I didn't like the turn of events and suspected that the men had gone to look for one of their superiors to find out what to do with us. I whispered my suspicions to Eva and the others, and together we prayed for guidance as to what to do.

In previous years I had passed that way many times with my van, so I knew the area outside Tongzhou quite well. I knew that within a half mile or so was the main motor road to Peking, and that it was more or less in the direction outside and behind the low wall that I had seen at the back of the courtyard. An idea came to me. We had come to rely on the uncanny ability of Gao and Ho to be able to hear sounds at a great distance, so I whispered to them to listen as hard as they could and to warn me if they heard a truck approaching in the distance, particularly one coming from the north.

Not five minutes had passed when I saw by their faces that both of them had heard something. Gao leaned over to me and whispered that a truck was approaching from the north and that it was about four or five miles away. I felt immediately that that was our god-given chance, and I had a compelling urge to act on that information and make our move without delay. But we had to act fast.

Fortunately we had taken nothing into the inn with us; everything was still out in the yard on the cart. I whispered to Eva and the two blind lads that I was going to pretend to go out to the toilet, which I felt certain was behind the building facing us. Once there I was going to climb the stone wall and head across the fields to stop the truck. Eva was to give me time to get out into the yard and then, with Gao and Ho, she was to casually follow me, pretending to be doing the same thing. After them, the young man with his pregnant cousin were to come out as soon as possible.

I hurriedly placed some money under the table on the *kang* to pay for the meal we weren't going to be able to eat and jumped down onto the floor. Approaching the innkeeper who was cooking our meal just beyond the open entrance, I loudly asked him where the toilet was. He pointed across the courtyard and told me it was behind the straw shed. Going out the door, I glanced back quickly at the three *balu*. They hadn't so much as even turned their heads and were showing no interest whatsoever.

Crossing the courtyard, I grabbed my bed roll and the six typewriters from the cart — even under those circumstances I couldn't bear to part with them — and once I was around the corner of the building opposite, I climbed the four-foot-high stone wall and headed straight out across the field, running as fast as my legs could carry me.

After about a hundred yards I looked back to see if Eva was coming, ready to turn back in case she hadn't got away, and thank God, there she was, with Gao and Ho hanging onto her arms, hurrying across the field behind me. A minute or two later I looked back again and saw that the young man with his cousin had just climbed the wall, and she, tiny bound feet hobbling over the uneven furrows, was carrying all her packages with her.

By that time I, too, could hear the truck. From the sound of the laboring engine, I guessed it to be traveling at not more than about ten miles per hour. But I was still some distance from the road and it was not yet in sight. Suddenly it came into view — a very old, beat-up truck with two men in the cab, and piled high at the back with what looked like sacks of grain. Apparently they had been out in the villages to the north buying it and were heading back to Peking.

Slow as its actual progress was, to my dragging feet it seemed to be approaching at a high rate of speed, with a plume of dust behind it and black smoke pouring from the exhaust. I knew for certain I was going to miss it if I didn't run. So, dropping everything I was carrying, I made a mad dash to intercept the truck before it could pass.

But I need not have been concerned. God had everything carefully planned for us that day. Although I couldn't see it until I got there, at the exact point where I would intercept the truck, there just happened to be a small stream with a deep mud hole that extended for 40 or 50 feet on each side. As the truck approached the stream, it was forced to slow to a crawl. I continued running toward it, and as it was crossing the stream toward me in low gear, I waved furiously to the driver, indicating he should stop. When he reached my side of the mud hole and pulled up onto dry ground, I heard him accelerate and knew he had no intention of stopping. Fearing he was going to try and run me down, I stepped back until he was almost abreast of me. I then dashed to the side of the truck as he started to pass, and grabbing the mirror arm on the driver's side, jumped onto the running board and shouted to the driver through the open window, telling him we wanted a ride to Peking and would pay for it.

The poor driver and his companion were terrified. I don't know what had passed through their minds when they looked ahead and saw six strange-looking people running through the field toward them, but I can imagine how ominous we must have appeared. The driver's first reaction was to punch me in the face and try to push me off, yelling unintelligibly as he did so. But I hung on, and the thought flashed through my mind that he probably knew of the presence of the *balu* less than a half mile away and, doubtless thinking I was a Russian working with them, he continued to pummel my face and chest with his left hand. It took me a couple of minutes to calm him down, telling him I was English, not Russian, and meant him no harm.

He continued a short distance and then finally stopped the truck and listened to me. Trembling, with sweat pouring down his face, he agreed to take us aboard, but told us to hurry because there was danger. I raced back to pick up the typewriters and threw them up on top of the truck. By that time Eva and the two blind lads had arrived, and the young wife and her cousin were close behind. I glanced back toward the inn to see if we had been followed, but there was no sign of anyone chasing us.

Neither the driver nor his companion got out of the truck. They barely gave us time to climb aboard, and when all six of us were safely seated atop the load, at that minute, even before the truck began to move, it started to rain — a torrential downpour with thunder and lightning that instantaneously soaked us all to the skin. It also completely blotted out the entire landscape and effectively hid us from the view of the distant inn yard and anyone who might have noticed our departure.

It was a climactic, exhilarating, but at the same time a very depressing end, not only to our journey, but — even though we didn't know it at the time — to that aspect of our life in China. An hour later, as we slid and skidded our way toward Peking, the sun was shining. In less than two hours after that, completely dry, though all of us were caked with mud splashed up from the rear wheels, we rolled through the huge east gate of Peking, known as the Chao Yang Men, or the gate that faces the sun, our hearts rejoicing over God's protecting care and His miraculous deliverance from certain capture. Paraphrasing Psalm 91, God had indeed "...given His angels charge over us, to keep us in all our ways."

Once inside the city we stopped briefly at a small Chinese inn, thankfully paid the trucker, and dropped off Gao and Ho, together with the young woman and her cousin. Her gratitude at being safely back in Peking knew no bounds, and she wept copiously as she said goodbye to us, telling us she would never forget what we had done for her. Given the circumstances and all that had happened on the trip, I am sure she didn't.

Outside the inn we hired a couple of rickshaws and directed them to take us to the Legation Quarter and the then world-famous Wagon-Lits Hotel. We had decided that after what we'd been through, nothing was too good for us. But as we pulled up to the entrance and climbed the long flight of steps to that ornate building, with our six portable typewriters, our bedding rolls over our shoulders, and both of us with mud-streaked faces and filthy clothing, I'm sure that even our own parents would have had difficulty recognizing us. So it was not at all surprising that the gaudily dressed doorman held up his hand and attempted to stop us from entering. However, the glare I gave him and the determined look in my eyes must have convinced him to step aside at the last moment. With the promise of a hot bath and a soft bed ahead of us, I was in no mood to be stopped, and we were desperately hungry as well.

The unflappable Chinese desk clerk never turned a hair at our unusual appearance. Within minutes we were reveling in our first bath in almost six weeks. Having no change of clothing, we shook out as much dust as we could, and, dressed in the same things we had worn for the entire trip, we headed for the dining room. Our entrance created quite a stir among the many European and Chinese guests, with every head seemingly turning in our direction. What did we care! Those folks in all their finery and living their dull lives had never experienced, and never would experience, the kind of adventures we had just had. Furthermore, they wouldn't have believed us if we had told them.

Then, much to our astonishment and delight, who should get up from one of the tables and come toward us with arms outstretched in welcome but the young ex-Navy lieutenant whom we had left in Chengde.

Somehow he had beaten us to Peking. We joined him at his table and described in detail all we had been through and how I had tried to intercept him outside Miyun. He was astounded by our story. He told us he had stayed on in Chengde for three days, then had experienced an uneventful trip all the way to Peking.

I asked him if he had seen anything of the *balu* and he replied, somewhat plaintively, that he had only seen their flags on top of some of the mountain peaks and had not seen any close up. So I asked if he remembered a certain section of the road where there had been a line of abandoned trucks. He said he did indeed remember it. I asked if there happened to be any people working on the trucks as he went by, and he said yes, there had been. I smiled and said, "Don't feel too badly. Those fellows working on the trucks were your *balu*. Be thankful you didn't get any closer to them than that."

We rested two or three days in Peking before heading for Tientsin. One of the first things I did was to go to the British Embassy to report our safe return. While there, and later at several of the other Western embassies in the area, I reported what I had heard about the young Westerner in the hands of the *balu*. However, none of them knew of any of their nationals being missing, so the identity of that poor unfortunate remains a mystery.

At the American Embassy, the ambassador was so interested in our story that he called in one of the military attaches, a U.S. Marine major, and asked me to repeat what had happened when the *balu* attacked Lingyuan, and just how much warning we had had. I told him in detail, and later when we got to Tientsin I did the same at the U.S. Consulate, where another Marine major was present. I had reason to remember the occasion a few weeks later when buddies of those same Marines, in a large encampment near Tanggu, about 30 miles from Tientsin, came under heavy attack by the *balu* in exactly the same manner as we had witnessed in Lingyuan and Miyun, and were overrun, with a considerable number being wounded and quite a few killed. I could not but wonder if the officers to whom I had told our story had really paid attention to what I had told them, and had taken the necessary precautions.

Gao and Ho came to the hotel to see us before we left and told us they wanted to stay on a few days longer in Peking to look up old friends from the time when they were students at the blind school. They said they would see us in Tientsin in a few days' time. We left the next morning on a heavily guarded train for the relatively short trip between the two cities and were pleasantly surprised at how uneventful the journey was. However, the cut-down telephone and telegraph poles along the sides of the track told the story of repeated Communist attacks, and a number of the bridges had been blown up and only temporarily repaired. Other bridges out in the middle of nowhere were guarded by small contingents of Nationalist troops looking very forlorn and bedraggled as we passed. When we arrived at Tientsin East Station, a huge crowd was still gathered outside. To us, it looked as though nothing had changed since we had left there some six weeks before.

Cut Paper Art. A charm to bring wealth combining four characters.

招財 Zhaocái (Attract Wealth)

進寶 Jinbao (Receive Valuables).

Can you find all four?

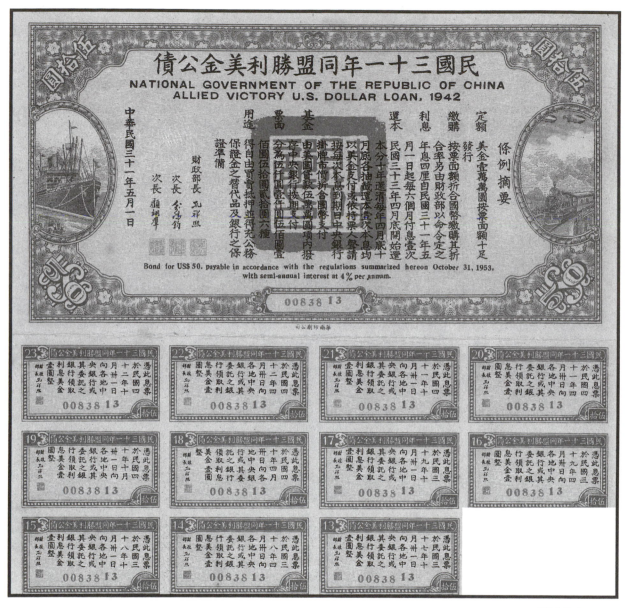

courtesy of Ed Bohannon

Nationalist Government WWII war loan bond for US $50.00 with 11 coupons left.

Chapter Forty-One
Wrapping It Up

As we entered the British concession in Tientsin we were struck by the quiet and peacefulness of the whole scene. We seemed to be in a different world, where life was going on as usual. As the days went by we found that almost no one among the Chinese or Western businessmen there seemed to be paying any attention to the war that was going on out in the countryside.

Our many friends there welcomed us back warmly, particularly those in the China Inland Mission. Their numbers had increased considerably during our absence, and some were sleeping in the public rooms. Most of the newcomers had been forced to flee before the advance of Communist guerrillas, so they were fully aware of what was going on. The local English-language newspaper printed daily reports on the fighting, but few other than the missionaries paid much attention. It all seemed so far away from the British concession. However, a small item had been printed about our having been caught in Lingyuan when the Communists had captured the city. Since our friends were unaware that all communications had been cut, they had been greatly worried as to why they had heard nothing from us. Most of them had written us off as lost, so it was quite a surprise when we turned up.

Back in our little coal shed we settled down comfortably and stayed on there for the rest of May and June. Despite the discouragements of the trip we had just completed, and the abandonment of almost all our worldly goods in Lingyuan, we found ourselves still unwilling to rule out the possibility of going back. At first, the peace and quiet of the British concession in Tientsin gave us, and everyone else, a false sense of security. But it wasn't too long before reality set in for everyone, ourselves included.

The one constant reminder of upheaval throughout the country was the ever-increasing inflation of the Chinese dollar as measured against American currency. The American dollar was greatly in demand because everyone had lost confidence in Chinese paper money, which was being printed day and night in ever-higher denominations. $10,000 bills became so commonplace that they were used there as one here would use a nickel. Because no one wanted the paper money, barter became the order of the day. And, of course, silver dollars, if they could be found at all, or gold in any form, were selling at a high premium.

I recall talking one day with Bob McCann, our friend from aboard ship, who owned the local Dodge agency. He told me he had imported an ordinary Dodge sedan into Shanghai and had it sitting in the showroom there. It was originally priced at around U.S. $4,000, but within the short space of three weeks, it had been sold many times over, had never left the showroom, and, at the time he talked with me, the price was in excess of U.S. $45,000 and the end was not in sight. He wasn't making the money. Successive buyers were simply trading the car without moving it from the showroom. He mentioned another incident in which a case of condensed milk was being used in lieu of currency. It changed hands many times over, with an ever-increasing value, until one day one of the new owners was curious enough to open a can to try it. That destroyed the value of the case as a unit, and it became relatively worthless.

Eva and I had many vivid examples of the daily depreciation in value of the Chinese dollar. One day we went out to do some grocery shopping. We selected the items we wanted, but even before the bill was totaled, the price had risen by almost half as much again. All we had with us was a U.S. $5 bill, but the shopkeeper couldn't hazard a guess as to what that day's exchange was, so we rushed off to a nearby bank to get it changed into local currency. When we left the bank, we had three rickshaw-loads of Chinese paper dollars. Bills in small denominations were counted into small packages, which were then folded in half and tied in bundles of $100,000. As closely as I could figure it, for our $5 we had several million Chinese dollars. No one bothered to count anything but the individual bundles of bills, which were about the size of a carton of cigarettes. When we returned to the store the prices had again doubled, and we had to settle for half of the items we had originally wanted.

Another example of the inflation was postage stamps. The post office tried to keep up by hand-

printing ever-greater surcharges onto the stamps, since they couldn't keep up by printing new stamps, but even that didn't work. One day I received a letter mailed from Peking from Gao and Ho. Pasted to the envelope were two sheets of newspaper, each of them covered back and front with stamps. Had I thought ahead and saved some examples of those unique covers, they would have been prized by stamp collectors outside of China, but they became so commonplace there that we ceased to be surprised at them.

Soon after our return to Tientsin I again tried several times to get the railway people to ship our Jeep down from Chinhuangtao. But each time they said it was impossible to get a flatcar since all were in use by the military. In any case, they told me that freight trains, as such, had almost ceased to be operated. In conversations with Bob McCann I learned that he had experienced the same difficulty. His shipment of about a dozen Dodge and Chrysler sedans, which had come on the same ship with us to Chinhuangtao, were still sitting there in their shipping cases. He too had been unable to find a way to get them to Tientsin and was about ready to write them off.

By sheer happenstance, about three weeks after our return to Tientsin, I read in the local paper that the Communists were active in Shandong Province, where fighting had broken out in the vicinity of the city of Yantai, known to Westerners at the time as Chefoo. The article went on to say that an UNRRA relief ship that had been making periodic trips to Chefoo had been shelled and machine-gunned from the shore on its last approach, and some of the crew had been injured. As a result, the rest of the crew had gone on strike and refused to make any further trips to Chefoo because of the danger. The ship, a surplus U.S. Navy LST (Landing Ship for Tanks), had been tied up alongside the Tientsin wharf for several weeks, and it looked as though it would be there indefinitely.

That gave me an idea. What if we could make a deal with the ship's captain to make a trip up to Chinhuangtao to bring back my Jeep and Bob McCann's cars? I made a special trip down to the wharf to see for myself that the forward ramp on the ship was still operative and vehicles could still be driven aboard it, and then I went over to talk with Bob McCann about my plan.

Bob was most receptive to my suggestion and wondered why he hadn't thought of it. Provided we could get the use of the ship, in Chinhuangtao it would be difficult to move his automobiles aboard in their packing cases, so I suggested he send a crew down to unpack them, mount the wheels, and then I could use my Jeep to tow them down to the wharf and aboard the LST. That would obviate the need to charge the batteries and get the cars' engines started.

Bob enthusiastically set off to confer with the UNRRA officials and talk to the ship's captain. That same afternoon he got word back to me that they had a deal. Both the ship's captain and the UNRRA people ashore thought it would be a good workout for the ship's engines after lying idle so long, and it would also be good for the morale of the crew, so a price was agreed upon. I forget now what the exact amount was, but although I am sure it was several million dollars in Chinese currency, in U.S. dollars it amounted to a pittance.

Once the deal was set and a date determined for the trip, I sent a telegram to the young Englishman who worked for the Kailan Mining Administration in Chinhuangtao, to whom I had lent the Jeep, letting him know we would be coming up from Tientsin on the LST on a given date and asking him to have the Jeep ready.

A day or two later, in mid-afternoon on a beautiful June day, Eva and I boarded the ship and left Tientsin to make the overnight trip northeastward up the coast, a distance of something over 330 kilometers, approximately 205 miles. Tientsin, although considered a port city, was actually about 30 road miles from the sea, but going down the winding Hai River it was a good deal farther. Normally the river was only navigable for ships of shallow draft during certain times of the year, unless it was continually dredged. But for the relatively flat-bottomed LST it was no problem at all, and we had a delightful trip down the river to its mouth. We passed Tanggu (where I had met Eva coming from the United States eleven years before, in 1936), then sailed out past the old stone forts on either side of the river's mouth at Tagu and over the sand bar that blocked the entrance to the river. Just as darkness fell, we reached the open sea.

The ship's crew was made up of nationals from at least seven different countries, and a motley group they were. The majority were, of course, Chinese, but it was hard to tell the nationality of some of the oth-

ers. The captain was a Swede, a grizzled veteran of many years at sea, and at least one of his officers was an American. The captain, a real martinet with his crew, turned out to be a friendly individual where we were concerned. He had a good sense of humor, welcomed us aboard, and told us he was delighted to be going back to sea after weeks of inactivity, even though it was to be a relatively short trip.

Crew accommodations aboard an LST are unusual, and for us they were unique. We had traveled on many types of ships, but we found those different from anything we had ever seen before. The officers' quarters were astern, over the engines and under the bridge. The ship, from the bridge forward, had a large open deck on which cargo could be stored. But the heart of the ship was under the deck, where there was a huge cavernous hold that extended almost the entire length and breadth of the ship. That immense area was designed to carry tanks and oversized motor vehicles, which were loaded over a forward ramp that could be raised and lowered and which formed the blunt prow of the ship.

Just under the main deck, on each side, a long corridor ran the full length of the ship. At intervals along the corridors ladders led both up to the deck above and into the large hold below. The corridors were wide, and on the outer side of each of them were semi-enclosed spaces for the crew to sleep. Eva and I were allotted one of the spaces, and Bob McCann and his crew of mechanics were given others.

After the evening meal, which we ate with the captain and his officers, Eva and I spent some time on deck and then decided to retire for the night. The two-tiered bunks were comfortable enough, but the problem was that, as you lay there, you were fully exposed to all the traffic along the corridor just a few feet away because there was no partition or even a curtain. Everything was wide open. Although we lay down fully clothed and attempted to sleep, there was so much activity with people passing back and forth, and with the bright lights of the corridor shining in our eyes, that sleep was impossible, so we decided to go back up on deck for an hour or so until things settled down.

It was around midnight, a gorgeous summer's night, and as we traveled along the coast just a couple of miles offshore, the mountains in the background, the occasional lights ashore, and the bright moon creating a silver path across the calm sea were an unforgettable sight. We'd only been on deck a short time when a rain squall barreled across the water toward us. But it just added to the beauty of the scene, and since we were standing under the bridge overhang, we kept dry and watched it pass. Then an extraordinary sight met our eyes, one that few people have been lucky enough to see.

With the dark bank of clouds drifting off to one side and the high mountains ashore forming a backdrop, we suddenly saw, spread across the heavens, the brightest and most perfectly formed rainbow we'd ever seen, and the first we'd ever seen in the middle of the night.

Eva and I were awed by the sight. We were alone at the stern of the ship, but we just had to tell someone about it, so we both climbed the ladder to the bridge and drew the captain's attention to it. Together we watched and marveled at its brilliance and sharpness of color. He told us that in all his years at sea, that was the first rainbow he had ever seen at night.

We waited until the rainbow had faded, then went to our bunks, but we were up again at dawn to watch the sunrise and our approach to Chinhuangtao. We arrived around 7:30 and tied up at the end of the breakwater, on one side of which was a macadamized road right out to the end. The captain dropped the ramp directly onto the roadway, and we were ready for business.

A few minutes later I saw my Jeep approaching with our young English friend at the wheel. He turned it over to me with profuse thanks for having been allowed the use of it for the five and a half months it had been there. But then, somewhat shamefacedly, he told me that he had a confession to make. He said that one night at a big party at the club, he'd had too much to drink and on his way home, as he approached a level crossing, had failed to see one of the coal trains approaching. When he spotted the train it was already too late, and the engine hit the Jeep broadside, almost cutting it in half.

Fortunately he was injured only slightly, but the Jeep was a complete wreck. Nonetheless, he had had it moved to the locomotive repair shop, where he was in charge, and his able Chinese crew had completely rebuilt the Jeep and restored it to its original condition. I walked around it and looked at it closely, but was unable to detect any sign of the damage it had

sustained. Even the paint exactly matched the original, and it was amazing what excellent work had been accomplished.

I made two trips with the Jeep to carry Bob McCann and his mechanics to where his fleet of cars was stored, and they immediately set to work opening the packing cases and mounting wheels on the vehicles. As each one was completed, I towed it back to the ship and it was stowed aboard. We broke briefly for lunch, then continued on well into the afternoon before all of them were finally loaded, and just before dark we left Chinhuangtao on our return trip to Tientsin.

I was able to salvage a few of the things from the case in which my Jeep had been shipped to China: the tent, the spare tires, and almost all of the spare parts — all that we could pack into the Jeep. But with considerable regret I had to abandon the redwood lumber with which I had built the case, lumber that I had purchased in San Francisco with such high hopes of using it in Lingyuan.

Our return trip to Tientsin was uneventful. Bob McCann was most appreciative of my help in getting all his cars safely ashore when we arrived the next morning. Because I had come up with the idea and had moved his vehicles onto the ship and off, he refused to let me pay my share for transporting the Jeep to Tientsin.

Only one letter had come from Lingyuan since our return to Tientsin, and then for several weeks we heard nothing at all and feared the worst. From time to time the newspapers reported heavy fighting all through that area, with severe setbacks for the Nationalist troops. Eventually word came that the Communists had finally taken over the entire province of Jehol and our last hopes of ever returning there were dashed. It was to be many weeks before we had any direct news from Lingyuan, and when it did come, it was all bad.

That summer in Tientsin passed very quickly for us despite the bad news from the outside. With the Jeep we were much more mobile and were able to help our China Inland Mission friends by meeting their guests at the railroad station and carrying their luggage. We also became heavily involved in Christian work among the young people in one of the large Chinese churches in what was called the "native quarter" of Tientsin, the area outside the foreign concessions. We got to know two young Chinese Christians, Mr. Yao and Mr. Wang, who were business partners in a thriving import/export business which so far had not been affected by the civil strife, and which, in spite of massive inflation, had been able to keep going.

Both men were extremely active in the Chinese branch of Youth for Christ, and they asked for our help. We spent each evening with them, and it was most gratifying to see hundreds of young people turning out every night for the services, all of them looking for some help and security in those troubled and uncertain times. Eva played the piano for the singing and I accompanied her on my cornet. Afterwards, I took a turn preaching during the services, which began around six in the evening and lasted until nearly midnight. The young people would gladly have stayed longer if we had let them.

During the course of those long summer evenings we got to know both Mr. Yao and Mr. Wang very well indeed, and in the daytime we frequently went to their place of business for conferences and prayer meetings. Both men placed their Christian activities ahead of business, and it would have been hard to find two more dedicated and hard-working individuals. Mr. Yao had his family with him in Tientsin, but Mr. Wang's home was in the city of Yantai (Chefoo) in Shandong Province. Due to guerrilla activities, he had been unable to move his wife and children to Tientsin, and he was greatly worried about their welfare.

One day a few weeks later, when we were visiting the two men, Mr. Wang told us he had finally received news about his family through a friend who had managed to make his way through the lines to Tientsin. With tears pouring down his cheeks, he told a harrowing tale of the suffering his wife and father had been put through before their deaths, and it was a story that was commonplace throughout much of the country.

Simply because Mr. Wang was known to be a successful businessman in Tientsin, the Communists had picked on his family as a likely target for possessing concealed wealth. His house in Chefoo had been searched repeatedly for hidden gold or silver dollars. The floors through the entire building had been dug up, then for some distance around the outside of the house, the cadres (the Communist officers and officials) had forced his wife and father to dig down to a depth of eight or ten feet. When nothing was found, and despite their denials that they had anything at all hidden, the cadres tortured them.

The old father, in his late sixties (which in China at that time was considered quite old), had been kept bound for days in an open outdoor shed and fed only one bowl of coarse millet gruel a day. Apart from taking the gruel to the old man, Mr. Wang's wife was not permitted to go near him. When, after repeated beatings, the father was still unable to produce any gold, they gave him the "rolling pole" treatment that I wrote of in an earlier chapter, where he was forced to kneel and a rounded pole, with two men on each end, was rolled back and forth over his bare calves. In the end, when he was still unable to tell them where the mythical gold was hidden, so much pressure was applied with the pole that the calves of both his legs were split wide open. Giving him no medical treatment at all for his injuries, the *balu* had hung him head downward from one of the rafters by his big toes, with his finger tips just out of reach of the floor below.

The old man had hung that way for several days without food or water. When the cadres came later to attempt further efforts to extract a confession from him, they found him dead. Somehow, by a supreme effort, he had apparently managed to swing his body back and forth in an arc to a point where he could reach an empty earthenware bowl that had inadvertently been left in the shed. Somehow managing to smash it, he had retained one of the sharp shards in his hand and had cut his wrists.

While torturing the old father, the Reds had not neglected to subject Wang's young wife to constant humiliation. She had been questioned for hours on end and frequently had been made to watch her father-in-law being tortured. Whenever she went out of the house to make purchases of food, she was required to wear a large placard on her back labeling her as a reactionary element, and to make sure that everybody took notice of her, she had also been forced to carry a large tin pan, banging on it with a stick as she walked.

Following the death of the old man, the *balu*, still fully convinced that there was gold hidden somewhere around the house, turned their full attention to the wife. After again subjecting her to lengthy questioning, they started to torture her. The fact that she was a Christian and endured it all without a murmur, and that throughout those long hours of punishment she never cursed or railed at them only incensed them the more. When their usual methods of pulling finger nails, breaking fingers and toes, and burning her breasts and other tender parts of her body with cigarettes failed to elicit the information they wanted, they tried more drastic ways to make her talk.

They brought water to a boil in the cooking wok, then, stripping off her pants, held her bare buttocks in the steam until she suffered excruciating burns. When that didn't work, they removed the wok and roasted her buttocks over the hot coals until the skin and flesh started to burn away.

Listening with horror to Mr. Wang's story up to that point, Eva and I thought there couldn't possibly be anything further they could have done to the poor woman, but there was. Since there had never been any hidden gold, and since she had nothing to confess, they naturally were unable to get anything out of her. Furious with what they considered her stubbornness, and as a final humiliation and a lesson to the townsfolk, they tied her wrists to her ankles, and still with her pants removed, they tied her, in a sitting position on the ground, to the tail of a horse and dragged her through the streets with a man walking behind supporting her in an upright position until her entire buttocks had been torn away down to the bare bones. In the midst of all the torture, she lost consciousness numerous times, but was revived by having cold water thrown over her. When she finally failed to respond to that treatment, they cut her loose from the horse and left her out in the street for all to see. Before lapsing into unconsciousness, she must have suffered unbelievably, and when death came it must have been a merciful release. Throughout the entire episode not a soul dared go to her assistance. The days were long past when the *balu* were trying to win the approval of the populace; now it was rule by terror.

As Mr. Wang narrated the gruesome story, he said nothing to indicate he felt the slightest bitterness or rancor against the Communists — just deep grief over the loss of his loved ones. He was particularly disturbed over the fact that his three young children had been removed from the home and taken away. To our knowledge, he never did learn what had happened to them. As he finished telling us of those terrible

events, his true faith in God showed when he quoted the words of Christ in Matthew 5:44-45: "Love your enemies, bless them that curse you, do good to them that hate you...that ye may be the children of your Father which is in heaven."

The above incident, where Christians were concerned, was only one of many similar cases we heard either directly from the persons involved or from relatives and friends. During the course of the next several months we were forced to the conclusion that there was little hope for the future of China when, as it then appeared inevitable, the entire country would be taken over by the Communists. We could only pray that other Christians would not suffer the same fate. Of course, the torture of innocent people was not limited to Christians.

Our days spent living in the coal shed were far from unpleasant — until the rainy season came. Eva cooked most of our meals on the oil-burning range, but we were often invited in to eat with our friends in the CIM home, and we formed some strong friendships with all those displaced individuals. Our little shed became a regular meeting place at afternoon teatime, and although the bed was the only place to sit, we frequently had as many as eight or nine people in to tea.

Gao and Ho, the two blind lads, had long since come down from Peking and were enrolled in a school where they were being taught how to weave cloth. They came to see us almost every weekend, eager to report on their progress in the school and to tell us of their plans to return to Lingyuan with the weaving machine we had bought them, which they were learning to use. Their goal was to go into business for themselves weaving cloth, but the big problem was how to ship the machine to Lingyuan, since the railway in both directions was out. The best alternative seemed to be to disassemble the machine and have it carried to Lingyuan on pack animals over back roads, where the *balu* were least likely to be. Both young men were optimistic that, being blind, they would be allowed to travel without hindrance.

Despite the handicap of blindness, their extraordinary talents never ceased to amaze us and any others who happened to be visiting us. As I write this I recall that while here in California in 1988 we heard about a blind woman somewhere in the United States who had been discovered with an unusual ability to detect accurately the color of any piece of thread that was handed to her. The phenomenon was widely reported by all the media and caused a mild sensation throughout the country. Eva and I smiled when we heard about it because some 41 years before that in Tientsin, Gao and Ho were visiting us one hot Sunday afternoon, and with several other visitors were sitting on our bed, which was covered with a multi-colored knitted spread. As we sat there chatting, I happened to notice that young Ho's hands were roaming over the spread from one place to another in what appeared to be a very definite pattern. Out of curiosity I asked him what he was doing, and he replied, "This spread has five major colors in it, and several other lesser colors as well."

Astonished, I exclaimed that he was quite correct and asked him what the colors were. He immediately put his fingers on a patch of red and told me the color correctly, he then moved to black and then green with the same accuracy. But he said the other colors were unfamiliar, and asked me what they were. I took his hand and placed it on each of the other colors, telling him what they were. Without the slightest hesitation he shifted his hand to another section of the spread and accurately picked out the same colors that were repeated there, naming each one flawlessly. We found it hard to believe. I happened to have a pair of argyle socks in one of the trunks under the bed. Raising the lid, I brought them out and handed them to Ho and asked him if he could tell me if there were any colors in them, and if so, how many. He ran his fingers over the varicolored diamonds and instantly told me the exact number of colors. Some he could identify, others not, but he knew they were different. When I identified each color for him, he immediately found the same color on the other sock.

Young Gao had been listening to all of that and, passing his hands over the spread, within minutes he, too, was able to identify each color, not by my telling him, but by learning from his friend, Ho. We watched in utter disbelief. As a gift I gave them the socks and suggested that they might do very well if they added multi-colored socks to their regular stock-in-trade when they finally went into business, and both agreed it would be a great idea.

We had been handling only wool, and I wondered if there was some special property in the wool that helped them identify different colors. But when we

handed them a printed cotton blouse, and even one of my ties, they were again able to determine that each had several colors. When we congratulated them on their remarkable ability, they modestly replied that there were many others among their fellow blind students far more talented than they.

They mentioned one young man who had a most remarkable gift. At the back of their school was a large courtyard used as a parking lot, surrounded on three sides by buildings. That one particular young man had the ability to stand on the steps outside the back door of one of the buildings and make a very unusual and high-pitched cry, after which he could tell exactly how many vehicles were parked there. Even their teachers, who were used to seeing remarkable talents in the blind, were astounded by that young man's gift. They tested him again and again, but never found him to fail. Apparently the young Chinese man was equipped with the same sort of remarkable hearing ability that enables bats to use echo location to navigate at night without bumping into anything as they search for food.

Around the first of August it became too hot and muggy for us to continue to live in our coal shed. We looked around for some other place to stay and found a room in a boarding house run by an elderly German lady. The room was on the third floor and there was good air circulation, so it was not uncomfortable. The only cooking facility was our trusty oil-burning range, but apart from breakfasts, Eva did little cooking on it. We had our food sent in from a small German restaurant nearby, a young Chinese lad faithfully delivering a delicious and nourishing meal twice a day, rain or shine.

About the same time, we were surprised by the sudden appearance in Tientsin of our old friend, the missionary from Chaoyang, J. Herbert Brewster. He had just arrived after a long ocean trip from Australia. My letters to him earlier in the year telling of our return to Chaoyang had led him to believe that conditions had so improved that he, too, could return. Unfortunately, during his long voyage, he had missed my letter telling of the disastrous turn of events, and we had only disappointing news to give him upon his arrival. He took a room in the same house with us, and we shared our meals together during the several weeks that he stayed.

For many weeks we had heard nothing at all from

Lingyuan. But then one day two 15-year-old Chinese schoolboys, neighbors of ours in Lingyuan, turned up on our doorstep in Tientsin, having escaped the city and made their way on foot overland through the mountains. They were tired and hungry, and the story they had to tell was one of unbelievable horror.

Not long after our departure, Lingyuan had fallen to the *balu* almost without a fight, the ragtag Nationalist troops left to guard the city putting up only token resistance before going over to the other side. No sooner was the city in *balu* hands than it was turned over to the "Poor Party," who systematically set about murdering people and wreaking havoc. Looting had been widespread with hardly a house being spared; hundreds of young women had been raped and many killed; much of the city had been torched. But the worst part was the indiscriminate killing of innocent people for no apparent reason.

The two young lads told of witnessing the hundreds, if not thousands of civilians who had either been shot or beheaded. A huge grave had been dug for them just outside the back wall of our compound. The *balu* had set up their own form of kangaroo court. For days on end accused so-called anti-Communist reactionary elements and intellectuals were "tried" by their peers at mass meetings, where attendance by the entire populace was mandatory, and where the sentence was always death. Almost everyone fell into one or both of the categories. Included were landowners, leading businessmen and wealthy citizens, whose only crimes were that they had more money than others or were educated. The Communists' greatest fear was that anyone with an education might become a leader in anti-Communist activities. Among the victims were some who were close friends and many whom I had known well.

They also told horror stories of the new government that had been set up after the initial purge had been carried out. The prison gate had been opened and every prisoner set free. From the rabble that had been released, certain men had been picked and given positions of power. Much as the Japanese had done almost 15 years before, the city was again divided into segments, where one of these ex-prisoners was given the power of life and death over all the inhabitants of the area. He, in turn, appointed men under him to supervise ten families each. Daily reports had to be made to that individual concerning all members of every family, and in each family, one family member was charged with the responsibility of reporting on the family as a whole.

One of the worst aspects of that deplorable situation concerned the way in which the *balu* controlled the children. A number of youth groups were established in each of the several areas of the city. One was for children from the age of four to ten, another for children from eleven to seventeen, at which time they were considered adults. All schooling for the children and teen-agers had been brought to a standstill. Instead, they were subjected daily to hours of political indoctrination and were quizzed individually about the conduct of their parents and relatives and encouraged to report anything done by their parents that might be considered subversive or harmful to the common interests of "the people."

Among the many stories the boys told us, one stands out in my mind. The six-year-old son of one of our neighbors was asked one morning what he had to report about his parents' behavior. For a minute or two he thought about it, and then said that his father had overslept that morning and was late reporting for work. The father was immediately dragged before the children's group and put on trial. After his "crime" had been detailed, the children were asked what punishment should be handed out. Accustomed as they were to the daily killings that had been going on, the children in unison shouted "*sha, sha, sha*." With that, the cadre in charge handed his loaded revolver to the six-year-old and told him to shoot his father in the head, which the boy did without the slightest hesitation.

That was the behavior pattern adopted by the Communists wherever they took over. At the time, it was reported in considerable detail in the Chinese and foreign press, but was generally written off by Westerners as Nationalist propaganda. However, the many reports of atrocities were later confirmed by so many witnesses that we were not surprised when, a few years later, Mao Tze-tung mobilized the youth of the country and the world learned of the appalling behavior of the infamous Red Guards, who were let loose over the entire country and who terrorized the people for a period of years. It should have surprised no one when an entire generation of children, who had been brainwashed and indoctrinated into bestiality from their very infancy, behaved in such a barbaric manner.

Asked about our church in Lingyuan, the two boys told us that the entire compound had been taken over by *balu* troops. High-ranking officers were occupying our personal living quarters, while their men were billeted in all the other buildings. Qian Yi and Chang Yin, the two beggar boys, had been permitted to stay on in the compound but were required to serve the *balu* cadres. Everyone else had been ejected from the compound, but had been unharmed. The Christians as a whole were well and had been undisturbed. But all church activities had been suspended, both halls had been closed and sealed, and any gathering of more than five people was prohibited. All Bibles and religious literature had been confiscated and burned. The Christians had also been forbidden to practice their religion in their homes. The children of Christians had been told to report on their parents if they witnessed any praying or Christian worship of any sort in the home. All that depressing news left us fearful for the safety and well-being of our many friends.

The two young schoolboys were only fifteen, but they'd seen and experienced so much since we had last seen them that they had grown up in a hurry and had become mature young men. They had left home without the knowledge of their families, and I was fearful that their parents would suffer at the hands of the Communists because of their disappearance. But the boys said it wouldn't matter. So many people were disappearing every night that no one kept count any longer. In order to curry favor with the authorities and stay alive, people were admitting their own supposed "crimes" at the daily "self confession" meetings and, at the same time, were accusing each other of similar crimes. But it was a testimony to the lives and behavior of the Christians that no one had reported on them and none had been killed.

One thing the boys told us shocked me greatly. They said that at those street meetings, young and old were required to shout the slogan: "Stalin is our father." To me that was extraordinary. The Chinese are so proud of their family lineage and heritage that an acknowledgment of any relationship to a foreigner is inconceivable and brought home to me the fact that Communism was being forced down the throats of the people more as a cult or a religion than a political doctrine. The Chinese Communists did it, of course, to humiliate and to subjugate everyone.

The two young fellows were thoroughly disenchanted with Communism, which they said was an absolute farce. They, like everyone else, had been forced to attend the daily self-confession and indoctrination sessions where they were told that all men and women were now equal, that all would share alike, and that no one would possess more than anyone else. But the lives and actions of the very cadres who were lecturing them belied what they said. In our compound the two boys had observed that when the common troopers sat down to eat their very plain food, the officers came and joined them for a few minutes, in a pretense of sharing with them. However, they then went back to their own quarters, where they ate sumptuously of only the best, with meat and chicken at every meal, something their men got only on rare occasions.

One of the first things the Communists did was take away all land and deeds from the large and wealthy landowners — our wealthy neighbor Mr. Ho lost everything, including his house and eventually his life — after which they divided it among the poor. Each adult male was given two Chinese acres, called *mu*, not to own outright but to plant and harvest for the good of all, while being allowed to take only a tiny amount of the harvest for his own use. But the Chinese acre is much smaller than ours. In fact, although the size of a *mu* varies in different provinces, it takes approximately 6.6 *mu* to equal one of our acres, so in most cases it did very little to help the individual. More often than not it became a burden, particularly in those cases where the individual was not, and never had been, a farmer.

Again, it was just another farce and a means of getting free labor to till the land and supply the cadres with grain, which they then distributed as though doing favors and expecting favors in return. An example given me was the young man named Wang, whom I've mentioned in a previous chapter, the one whom I had grown up with, and whom Mother had later taught how to vaccinate against smallpox. His mother had died and he was living alone next door to our compound. The Communists had given him charge of a piece of land several miles from the city. It took him hours to walk out there and back. He had never had the slightest experience in farming, had no equipment with which to plow and till the soil, and was completely at a loss as to what to do. Yet here he was with a piece of land assigned to him and a quota of grain expected from him by harvest time. It meant he had to give up his relatively well-paying profession of vaccinating, and being somewhat sickly and of a slight build with poor physique, he in all probability could never survive the new life. It was tragic to hear about it, and he was only one of many in similar circumstances. The two schoolboys stayed in Tientsin for about a week. However, I was greatly worried about their future and what would happen to them when Tientsin itself fell to the Communists, as was inevitable. The city was already becoming more and more crowded with refugees. There was no way they could support themselves, so I urged them to return to Lingyuan as soon as possible. There at least they would have their friends and families around them. As a cover or excuse for their absence, I helped them by purchasing a supply of salable goods to carry back to Lingyuan, and they left a few days later. We never heard whether they got back safely.

That summer we had another interesting experience in Tientsin. We were invited to dinner one night at the CIM home, where we were introduced to two American evangelists, both active in Youth for Christ. They were in China to conduct a series of special meetings for young people in various cities and had just come from Shanghai, where they had spent a week or more. They were to spend a week in Tientsin, conducting nightly services at the church where Eva and I had been helping out. Neither of them spoke Chinese, so they had to use the services of an interpreter, an elderly Christian Chinese gentleman who had been with them from the beginning of their tour and who was traveling with them.

Their coming to Tientsin had been heralded in the Chinese press and on the radio, and a local radio station had offered them free air time for a half hour every morning. To accommodate them the radio station would open half an hour early. When the evangelists learned that I spoke Chinese, one of them asked if I would interpret for them on the radio in order to allow the elderly interpreter a little more sleep after the long nightly services. I was only too glad to help them out.

The radio station put us on the air at six in the morning for the entire week. Since it was a popular station, we were guaranteed a large audience. Not only were many of the English-speaking Chinese lis-

tening, but since his sermon was being translated into Chinese, a lot of other Chinese were listening as well.

I much enjoyed the opportunity of working with them. In order to allow the English-speaking students to make the most of hearing the sermons in English, I translated sequentially instead of simultaneously, and as the preachers took turns every other morning, they broke their sermons into small segments to allow me time to render them in Chinese. That allowed the English-speaking students full opportunity to hear the English-language version.

Both men were dynamic speakers with a fund of excellent and most appropriate stories to illustrate their sermons. But one morning I was put on the spot. The story that one of them picked to use in his sermon was the well-known one of the hare and the tortoise. In effect, he made a comparison between his listeners and those two creatures, with the appropriate moral woven into his text. In the English language and to an American audience, that was entirely apt and fully acceptable. But to a Chinese audience it was entirely out of place.

The reasons were several. In China one must never compare another human being to an animal or bird unless there is a deliberate intention of slander or vilification. Consequently, expressions we commonly use, such as "eating like a horse," "appetite of a bird," "clever as a fox," and so on, should not be used. In addition, the two animals in the preacher's story share a paradoxical and somewhat ambivalent place in the lives and history of the Chinese people. On the one hand both are sacred and revered, while at the same time both are part of China's extensive vocabulary of what is generally classified by English-speaking people as profanity.

The tortoise or turtle (the Chinese don't make any particular distinction between the two) has two names. Politely it is called *gui*, and with the dragon, the unicorn and the phoenix, is revered as one of "the four spiritually endowed creatures" or *si ling*. The tortoise is also prized for its shell, which is widely used in medicine, and the Chinese at times employ tortoises to open up gutters and drains, as it is fond of burrowing in the earth. Another anomaly is the fact that the tortoise is frequently found throughout China sculptured in stone as the base or support for huge stone memorial tablets. The Chinese believed that tortoises lived for 3,000 years, so they were, and still are, a symbol of longevity.

But the tortoise has another name, which is considered very vulgar. It is called *wang ba*, or literally, "king eight," a nickname that supposedly dates back to the year A.D. 918, when it was given to a young man named Wang Jian who, after a youth spent in violence and rascality, became the founder of the Earlier Shu State. The name is said by some to be a play on a similar-sounding word, *wang ba* or "forget eight," naming the tortoise as the creature that forgets the eight rules of right and wrong, i.e., politeness, decorum, integrity, sense of shame, filial piety, fraternal duty, loyalty, and fidelity. That was because there was a superstitious belief that the female tortoise was unchaste. For that reason, the term *wang ba* is a common term of abuse, used by the Chinese as we would use SOB, bastard, or cuckold. Paradoxically, it is used by both males and females against each other, with no discrimination as to gender. One of the worst forms of abuse one Chinese can hurl at another is to call him or her a tortoise's egg *(wang ba dan)*. Chinese explain that tortoises (or turtles) lay their eggs on the bottom of a stream or river, and thus there is nothing lower than a turtle's egg. The tortoise is also commonly thought by the Chinese to be able to conceive by thought alone, hence to call someone the offspring of a tortoise is to imply that, knowing no father, the individual is a bastard.

Where the hare is concerned, (and here again the Chinese make no real distinction between the hare and the rabbit beyond saying that one is wild), it, too, is a symbol of longevity, the Chinese believing that the hare can live as long as 1,000 years. But it, as well, is a synonym of the cuckold because ancient Chinese believed that the female hare was promiscuous and able to conceive simply by gazing at the moon, while others say she did so by licking the fur of the male, and she is said to produce her young from her mouth.

In any event, neither the hare nor the tortoise are normally mentioned in polite society, a fact little known to Westerners. In Tientsin, for example, Westerners were completely unaware that Easter, with the widespread use of rabbits and eggs as decorations and gifts, was called by the Chinese, the "rabbit's egg festival," *(tuzi dan jie)*, a most derogatory term that, by implication, brought much opprobrium on the church and Christians. In short, the story of the hare and the tortoise was not an appropriate subject for a radio sermon. So when I heard the speaker start the story, I had to hurriedly come up with something that would illustrate his point without offending his listeners. I concocted a story from scratch, and of course, only the English-speaking listeners knew what I was doing and why I was doing it. The evangelist had no way of knowing that I was not telling his story word for word.

Unfortunately, my story was a little longer than his, and at one point he poked me in the arm and whispered in my ear, "This is my sermon; what are you telling them?" I shushed him and finished my story, then let him continue his sermon.

At the end, when we were leaving the studio, I told him what I had done and why. In great consternation he told me he had used that story a dozen times at other meetings in China and asked me why in the world his Chinese interpreter had not told him about the double meanings and how offensive the story could be to his audiences. I could only tell him that the Chinese are such a polite race of people that they will do anything rather than offend someone, and his interpreter was doubtless afraid that telling him about Chinese concepts of the hare and the tortoise would not only offend the American, but would demean the Chinese people as well.

Ever since the end of World War II there had been a strong U.S. military presence in Tientsin — a U.S. Marine detachment and also a small U.S. Navy craft tied up alongside one of the riverside piers. We saw a great deal of the young Marines and sailors around the British concession. There were many places in the city where they could go for recreation and amusement, but most of them had unsavory reputations.

As the *balu* became stronger and more daring and moved ever closer to Tientsin, we began to see a definite change in the mood of the Chinese people. Where previously the presence of the American military was much appreciated by the Chinese, because it not only spelled safety for them but also meant a lot of money was being spent in the city, they suddenly began to demonstrate an increasing animosity toward Americans in general, and the U.S. Marines and sailors in particular, because they were not helping the Chinese Nationalists fight the Communists.

A few days after we had moved into our room at the boarding house, I was returning home in mid-afternoon and was just unlocking the front door when I saw a huge mob of Chinese racing down the street in pursuit of a young U.S. Marine. His clothing was torn, his face was bloodied, and he was limping and running poorly, just managing to keep ahead of the mob, which obviously was in a very ugly mood. As he limped along the sidewalk toward me, perhaps fifty yards ahead of the mob, I grabbed him by the shoulders and pushed him through the open door, locked it after him, and turned to face the mob. My action had been so quick that apparently no one had noticed where the young man had gone. I had further confused the situation by moving away from the door in the direction of the mob, disarming them as they approached by asking loudly what they were running for and what it was all about. But no one seemed to know. Having lost the young Marine, the crowd, frustrated and angry, milled around for awhile and finally broke up and disappeared. From one of the few who stayed behind I learned that the young man had been drinking heavily in a certain bar, and when he was unable to pay his bill, the bar's owner had beaten him up, and as the young Marine ran out the door the commotion started. Seeing a foreigner being chased by a fellow Chinese, other Chinese had just joined in, and the crowd had become ever larger without any of them knowing what it was all about except that a hated American was to be had for a killing if they could catch up to him.

Through that small act of befriending the young Marine we came to know many of his buddies, and every Sunday night thereafter we held "open house" for as many as could be squeezed into our single room. Eva cooked bacon and eggs for them, as much as they could eat, with lots of fresh bread, and that was always followed by vanilla ice cream. The boys always brought along the latter — powdered stuff in large gallon cans of GI issue, which we simply mixed with water. With the Jeep I would run to the nearest ice house for 50 pounds of ice, then, with the boys turning the handle of the old-fashioned ice cream mixer, we produced a most delicious product. Frequently we had ten or more men in the room, many of them having had a Christian upbringing, and all of them homesick. We sang songs together, had a short period of Bible reading, and often invited a special speaker to give a short talk. Mr. Brewster participated several times and was a much-liked speaker,

and the evenings became a popular event for the boys on Sunday nights. We only wished that we had a larger place so that we could have invited more of them.

As autumn began to set in, the Tientsin Western community was greatly shocked one day to hear that the U.S. Marines were all to be withdrawn immediately. The Chinese population, despite their animosity toward Americans, was also greatly disturbed. Little as they now liked the Americans, they felt that having them there was protection against the Chinese Communists taking over the British concession, and the loss of income from the Americans would also be widely felt. Wealthy Chinese by the hundreds started to flee south or to America, if they could get a visa, and a sizable evacuation began.

As the Marines prepared to pull out, they opened their warehouses to the foreign community and told us to help ourselves. The first time Eva and I went down there, we filled three rickshaws with canned supplies. Only a few items were for ourselves; the rest were for the China Inland Mission home. As we left the warehouse, a fight started among the many rickshaw pullers there awaiting fares, and the first of our three rickshaws became involved. I went forward to try to stop the fight, and when I returned, I found that the last of our three rickshaws had been completely pilfered by the small crowd standing around. The whole thing had been a put-up job. After that I used the Jeep. Since the supplies were almost unlimited and the Marines were only too happy to get rid of them, I hauled load after load to the mission home, enough to supply them for a couple of years. Our friends there intended staying on as long as they could, and in fact, most of them did stay until the Communists took over two years later, in 1949. However, since events were taking such a rapid turn for the worse all over China, Eva and I had begun to think about leaving Tientsin for good.

Many British and American nationals were being evacuated, particularly the women and children, and it appeared obvious that it was only a matter of time before both Peking and Tientsin would fall to the Communists. However, despite widespread pessimism about the future of China as a whole, many of the Western missionaries and businessmen felt certain that, just as in the war with Japan, western China would never be conquered by the Reds; therefore many began to move toward the far western and southwestern provinces. Since the Chinese Nationalists had held that area in the west of China against the Japanese before and during World War II, we too, felt that such a generally held opinion might indeed be the case, and we gave serious consideration to moving there ourselves.

Another factor that made us decide to leave Tientsin were the letters from my father, still living in Alameda, just across the bay from San Francisco. Reading between the lines, I found his letters not at all encouraging; we could tell that looking after my invalid sister Ruth was getting to be too much for my elderly stepmother. So we planned to return to the United States, pick up Ruth, then go back to southwest China, somewhere around Chungking, an area so remote that the Communists probably would never be able to occupy it. Even if they eventually did, it would take a number of years. In theory the plan looked good, but as it turned out, everyone was wrong.

At the time, despite the heavy departure of Westerners, it was still fairly easy to book passage on a steamer from Shanghai to San Francisco, so we made a booking for early November and set about selling everything we had left in Tientsin to raise enough money for our fares. We had no problem whatsoever; the Jeep was immediately snapped up by a Swedish missionary who felt that the neutrality of his country would guarantee his ability to stay on, no matter what happened, and we were greatly surprised when he offered to pay us in U.S. dollars. Most of the rest of our belongings, including a refrigerator, were bought by White Russians who were emigrating back to the U.S.S.R. by the hundreds, but they paid us in Chinese dollars.

That phenomenon was a most interesting one. We had many friends among the White Russian community in Tientsin. Most were of the older generation who had fled Russia during the 1917 revolution and were wary of going back to the Soviet Union. However, the younger generation were tired of living in China, where they were unable to gain Chinese citizenship and were generally treated abominably by the Chinese. So when the Soviet government offered them free passage back to the Soviet Union, a great number of them jumped at the opportunities for the future that it seemed to offer.

That movement back to Soviet Russia had been going on for some months, and we had watched it with great interest. The Soviets had provided a brand-new passenger liner to carry the emigres, and all who signed up to go were encouraged to use their Chinese money to buy up everything they possibly could to take with them, particularly durable goods. As a result, those with money spent it like water, buying up everything they could find.

But as time went on, some interesting and disquieting stories began to filter back through the grapevine. Because of the suspicions and doubts held by the older White Russians, many had arranged simple codes that the younger ones could use when writing back after they had reached the "promised land." One of our friends had a son who made the trip back with his wife and two young children. His parents told him to send back a photograph of himself when he wrote and, if all was well, he would be standing in the photograph. However, if things were not what they had expected, and his advice to others would be not to make the trip, then he would be sitting down. When his letter finally arrived, with a photograph enclosed, the letter had obviously been censored, with much of it blacked out. But the photograph was there, and the young man was lying on his back! It was quite simple to deduce what he meant by that.

Another young couple had taken their infant daughter with them, but in their case no code had been arranged. However, when he wrote back to his parents, he wrote in glowing terms of how they had been welcomed on their arrival and the marvelous treatment that had been accorded them, at which point in the letter the parents became highly suspicious. Then in the very next sentence, the young man told his parents that their daughter (the infant) was about to be married, and he hoped his parents would be able to attend the wedding. The message was quite obvious: "Stay away. Don't come near this place, at least not for many years."

Through our Russian friends we heard of many such secret messages coming back. Still the younger generation could not be convinced, and more and more of them left. Then, shortly before our own departure, our friends told us of a young Russian man who had left Shanghai almost a year earlier and who had been given a job on board the ship that was being used to carry the people back to the U.S.S.R. Upon his return to Shanghai, although he had not been allowed to leave the ship, he had managed to smuggle a letter ashore that shocked the whole White Russian community. He told of each arrival of the ship at a Soviet port where everyone aboard had been stripped of everything they possessed, even the clothing they were wearing. They had then been issued the poorest quality clothes that could be found and had been assigned to hard labor and given miserable housing. In many cases, when they had protested, they had been shipped to labor camps in Siberia. He warned everyone to stay where they were and not to believe the promises being made to them, adding that they would be better off under the Chinese Communists. Despite the warning, many of the younger generation refused to believe his report and attributed it to mere rumor. They continued to believe the Soviet propaganda and climbed aboard the ship anyway. But most of our older White Russian friends tearfully told us that they had decided to stay on and face the Chinese Communists rather than the Russians.

For us, those last few weeks in Tientsin were hectic, and as we said our goodbyes to our many friends, our days were filled with emotional moments. One middle-aged Russian woman whom we'd come to know well was absolutely heartbroken by our leaving. As a young girl she had fled Russia, and the story of her life was one of extreme hardship, endless abuse by the Chinese, and later the Japanese, and then the Chinese once again. She had suffered starvation, illness and torture, and finally, as the only way to stay alive, she, like so many of her fellow White Russian women, had been forced into a life of prostitution. As a parting gift to us she wrote us the story of her life, touching only briefly on her suffering, but she ended the story by telling of how she had eventually come to know Christ and salvation. Her whole life had changed, and although still poor, she was managing to eke out a pitifully small living as a seamstress. But the future for her when the Chinese Communists eventually took over was bleak indeed. We have often wondered what happened to her and many others like her.

In order to try to control inflation the Chinese government had passed a law prohibiting any individual from carrying more than U.S. $200 out of the country. The amount of U.S. dollars we received from the sale of the Jeep far exceeded that sum. Having sold the balance of our possessions, which we left behind in Tientsin when we went north and wouldn't need back in the States, we had a fairly large sum of almost worthless Chinese dollars as well. After paying our fares to Shanghai and then on to San Francisco, we still had plenty left over. Since we were prohibited from converting the Chinese dollars into U.S. currency, we decided to spend the money any way we could.

I had a long consultation with Bob McCann about the problem, and because of our friendship, I managed to purchase a Dodge sedan with U.S. money and some of the millions of Chinese dollars. Then through a friend of his, I was also able to use more of the Chinese dollars to buy a Ford sedan. Delivery on both vehicles was to be made in the United States, the Dodge at their factory in Detroit on a stipulated date, and the Ford at an assembly plant in Hoboken, New Jersey. We only needed one car in the United States, but I was sure I could sell the other at a small profit on the West Coast and thus get our money back.

Buying the two cars was a good deal for us, and with what little Chinese money we had left after that, we bought some Chinese embroidered linens, about a dozen small Peking floor rugs, which would fit in our empty steamer trunks, and some other Chinese oddments, all of which in "real" money cost us almost nothing. When we reached the U.S., they came in handy as gifts. But we kept four of the rugs, which now, some 45 years later, are still in use and are daily reminders of "home."

Before leaving Tientsin I had several long talks with Bob McCann, who insisted that he was going to stay on no matter what happened. I tried to convince him to change his mind and urged him to pack up and pull out. I warned him that I was certain the takeover of Tientsin by the Chinese Communists would be totally unlike any of the previous takeovers by Chinese warlords or even the Japanese. But he was confident he would be able to ride it out and survive anything that came along and laughed at my concern for him. Unfortunately he was wrong. Soon after the Communists captured Tientsin, he was put in a Chinese prison and spent many years in solitary confinement. Eventually he was released and carried over the border between Hong Kong and China on a stretcher, a very ill man, dying from cancer. His wife was able to meet him there, but he died just a day or so later.

Toward the middle of August we said goodbye to Gao and Ho as they left for Lingyuan. I helped them dismantle and pack the weaving machine, watching with extreme interest as their nimble hands followed my every movement as I took the machine apart, memorizing by feel each part and where it belonged. Packed in burlap, the machine was carried by three pack animals, and Eva and I wept as we watched Gao and Ho set off on foot behind the three mules, each with a long staff in one hand and an extra pair of shoes that we had provided. They faced a walk of some 200 miles over strange mountain roads. We could only commit them to God's keeping. Mr. Brewster left for Peking about the same time for a short visit and returned to Australia soon afterward.

Then the time came for our own departure, and it was a very sad day for us when we finally left Tientsin for the last time. We had booked passage on a coastal steamer to Shanghai, but the water in the Hai River was too low for the ship to come upriver to Tientsin. Since train travel to the port of Tanggu at the mouth of the Hai River was so uncertain and dangerous, all the passengers — and there must have been about fifty of us, Westerners and wealthy Chinese — were loaded onto a large flat-topped barge with our luggage, and the barge was then towed downstream to Tanggu by a tug. It was our second trip down the river by boat, but the trip on the barge was far different from the one on the LST a few months before. On the high deck of the LST we could see the countryside as we went down the winding river. On the flat top of the barge, however, we were only two or three feet above the surface of the river, so low that the high reeds on each bank hid everything from sight. Perhaps that was just as well, because it meant that we, too, were hidden from sight of the many *balu* roaming the countryside.

The operators of the tug were extremely nervous. Fearing they would be shot at by *balu* snipers as they chugged down the river, none of them stayed on deck for more than a few minutes at a time. Our luggage was piled around the edges of the barge, and we were told to sit on the wooden deck in the middle so the baggage would provide some protection in case we were shot at. But the trip down the river turned out to be uneventful; it was simply cold, unpleasant, and monotonous.

At Tanggu we boarded a small coastal steamer for the four-day trip to Shanghai. First, however, we had to wait on the dock for some time while hundreds of Chinese refugees boarded. It was a heart-rending sight because of the many hundreds more who were left behind on the dock. Even for those who did manage to get aboard the ship, carrying their pitiful belongings, it was a terrible situation.

The ship was carrying two or three times its normal load of passengers. People were packed into all the open spaces below decks, in the holds, in the corridors, and even in the engine room. As we climbed aboard and headed for the upper deck, often less than a foot of space was left for people to walk by in the corridors, and the rest of the floor space was taken up with people lying head to foot, already having staked out their sleeping space for the night, and, in fact, for the entire trip. Hundreds more huddled on the open decks above. We prayed for good weather and a safe passage, because there were not nearly enough lifeboats to handle that many people.

While waiting on the dock we had noticed that the entire area was heavily guarded by Chinese Nationalist troops, with many military police on the dock as well. At the time we presumed that they were there to guard against Communist guerrillas. As we watched people filing up the gangplanks, we saw a sizable number of unarmed soldiers mixing in with the refugees, surreptitiously boarding the ship, then quietly disappearing. We assumed correctly that they were deserters, but what puzzled us was that the armed soldiers on the dock, as well as the military police, made no attempt to stop them. Most of the deserters were easy to spot because they were only partially disguised, usually wearing a civilian jacket but with military pants. Eva and I were standing on the top deck where the lifeboats were hanging, watching all the excitement on the dock, and every now and then one of the deserters would come up to our deck and quietly climb onto one of the lifeboats, lift a corner of the canvas cover and slip inside, then pull the canvas top back over again. We watched half a dozen or more disappear in that way.

Half an hour or so before the ship sailed, all boarding was stopped, and a large number of the Chinese military police came aboard and began to search the ship from top to bottom. They ended up capturing over a hundred of the deserters. It was heart-breaking to see so many being hauled off, inevitably to face a firing squad. Most were young men, but some were obviously teen-agers. As we watched and I snapped an occasional photograph, I heard a noise behind us and turned just in time to catch a movement in one of the lifeboats. The canvas was moving, and a head popped out. For some reason the MP's had not thought to search the lifeboats, and although some were searching the deck we were on, they were at the far end. I quickly warned the man to duck back out of sight, which he did, but not before I managed to get a snapshot of him. He was one of the few to escape the roundup. Later, after the ship sailed, he came out and thanked me. He told me he had been away from his home in the south for 12 years, but he was still facing an uncertain future. Together with about two dozen others who had managed to outwit the MPs, he was being fed by the sympathetic crew.

The trip down the coast to Shanghai was uneventful and on a relatively calm sea. That was fortunate, because the poor refugees were already suffering enough without having seasickness to contend with. We were traveling first class and had a tiny cabin to ourselves. There was just room enough in it for two berths, one above the other, and a narrow aisle alongside in which to dress and undress. It was strictly a place to sleep; there were no chairs on which to sit. However, since the door led directly onto the upper deck, we could leave the door open and lie in our bunks and watch the coastline for a good part of the way, but it was so cold we had to wrap ourselves in blankets. Our cabin steward was a man in his early 30's. His name was Huang, and he doubled as our table steward as well, so we saw quite a lot of him. He spoke English quite well and proudly told me that his English name was Jimmy. He was still of military age, and I wondered how he had managed to avoid being drafted into the army. The first time we saw him, I also noticed that he appeared to have a stiff neck. He always wore a very high collar buttoned at the throat that concealed the entire back of his neck to above the hairline, and he never turned his head. When looking to one side or the other he always turned his entire body, and I noticed further that he appeared unable to move his head up or down.

After the second day we had become quite friendly, so I asked him what was wrong with his neck. I've heard some remarkable stories over the years, but the story Jimmy Huang told us was absolutely incredible,

and is, in all probability, unique.

He told us that ten years before, in December 1937, he had been a private in the Chinese army, defending Nanking against the Japanese onslaught in their undeclared war against the Chinese. Jonathan Spence, in his book *The Search for Modern China*, graphically describes what happened in that infamous event that has been called "The Rape of Nanking." From young Huang we got a first-hand account that confirms Spence's account in every detail.

Jimmy told us that initially, Japanese planes flew over the city day after day dropping leaflets, promising humane treatment for all civilians in the city as well as for any Chinese soldiers who surrendered. However, many of the Chinese troops, who shortly before that had been involved in the Shanghai fighting against the Japanese, were highly skeptical. They began robbing the populace of civilian clothing so that they could escape the city before the Japanese captured it, in many cases killing civilians who resisted. Hundreds of those soldiers got away during the night.

On December 12, seeing that the end was near, the Nationalist commander, Gen. Tang Sheng-chih, also fled the city, leaving thousands of his troops with no leadership. When the Japanese army entered the city the next day, a reign of terror and violence followed that lasted for nearly seven weeks, and was such as the world has rarely seen. Like Pearl Harbor, though to a lesser extent, it served to catch the attention of the civilized world and was one of the first events that began to make people conscious of how savage the Japanese military could be.

There can be no excuse for what the Japanese did. However, perhaps one of the reasons for their savagery lies in the fact that, having become accustomed to overcoming Chinese resistance with relative ease, they found themselves battling for Nanking under the most severe conditions and suffering much higher casualties than they had anticipated. As a result, and as young Huang confirmed to us, when the Japanese entered the city, every Chinese became a potential victim, and thousands were slaughtered indiscriminately.

Western sources arrived at varying numbers of casualties, but most agreed that the number of women raped was in excess of 20,000, many of whom died as a result. Chinese civilians who were slaughtered for no reason at all were said to number between 12,000 and 15,000, and the number of Nationalist soldiers killed after having surrendered is variously estimated at 30,000 to 50,000, although Huang placed the figure much higher.

The slaughter began immediately after the Japanese entered the city. Anyone caught on the streets was either shot or decapitated. The Japanese systematically went from house to house looting, raping any young women they found, and killing any of their menfolk who tried to resist, setting fire to many of the houses. One of the most terrible aspects of the whole thing was the wholesale slaughter of pregnant women who were, in most cases, disemboweled. Older women, too old to be sexually attractive, were savagely violated with bayonets, tree branches, or pieces of split boards.

Huang told us that the Chinese soldiers were rounded up and placed in walled compounds, where for several days they went without food and water. Then the Japanese started to systematically slaughter them. He said that his turn came one morning when he, with several thousand others, had their shirts ripped off and their hands bound behind them. Then, walking in single file, they were driven at bayonet point to the nearby city wall and up a steep ramp to the top. The Japanese, ever health-conscious and fearful of disease that might result from thousands of unburied bodies inside the city, had devised a novel means of disposing of large numbers of the bodies outside the walls.

Huang told us that when he reached the top of the wall he could see ahead of him two Japanese officers standing up on the low, 2-foot-wide balustrade on the edge of the wall, facing each other, each holding a sword. Both men, shirtless, were blood-spattered and sweating profusely. As the Chinese soldiers shuffled toward the Japanese officers, two Japanese soldiers grabbed each man by his arms and forced him to climb onto the balustrade between the two Japanese officers, where he was forced to kneel with his head bowed forward. The Japanese officers then took turns lopping off their heads, each competing to see how many heads he could sever, laughing uproariously as they did so, and each headless body pitched forward outside the 45-foot city wall. Huang said that as he got closer and closer to them, he noticed that many of the soldiers ahead of him didn't have to be forced to climb onto the balustrade. They did so voluntarily, and having seen what went on ahead of them, they bowed their heads without being told.

Finally it was Huang's turn. He said that he, too, voluntarily climbed up between the two Japanese officers and bowed his head, and that is the last thing he remembered. He theorized that at that instant he must have fainted and started to pitch forward. He said he had no recollection of the sword hitting the back of his neck, but it must have hit at an angle, slicing upward on the back of his neck as his body moved away and downward before the sword could sever his head. As it was, the tendons and muscles at the back of his neck were cut, and his spinal column was badly bruised, but not severed.

The miracle was that he didn't bleed to death. When Huang opened his collar to show me the horrible scar on the back of his neck I could scarcely believe my eyes. It extended in a half-moon-shaped arc almost from ear to ear in an upward direction. Huang was certain that his life was spared because, with his head still attached, he had pitched farther forward than the headless bodies, and he surmised that he had somersaulted down the pile of dead below to a point where fewer bodies had fallen on top of him than might have otherwise been the case. In any event, that was all conjecture. In the middle of the night he finally recovered his senses and struggled his way upward to freedom through the pile of bodies on top of him and then climbed down the pile of dead and reached solid ground. He had an appalling headache, but the wound on the back of his neck was not bleeding. Apparently the weight of all those bodies above him had applied enough pressure to stop the bleeding, helping the blood to clot and the wound to heal.

Weak from loss of blood and with his arms still tied behind him, Huang stumbled his way in the dark out into the open countryside. After what seemed like hours, he saw a dim light ahead and found a farmhouse where the farmer was just starting his day. The farmer took pity on him, fed him and hid him from the Japanese until he was able to travel, after which he made his way to Shanghai and eventually, after learning some English, got the job on the ship as a steward.

I listened to his account with horror and astonishment, because I had seen almost every detail of his story in pictures while I was in India in 1943. The Japanese love cameras and have a strong penchant for having photographs taken of themselves in every conceivable situation. Japanese soldiers were no different. Their photographs usually showed them in groups, triumphantly celebrating a victory, waving their rifles and flags, or in pictures of themselves with girlfriends, or drinking beer. However, while in New Delhi in 1943, I was one day handed a large box full of photographs that either had been taken from the bodies of dead Japanese on the battlefield or confiscated from prisoners. The entire boxful consisted of pictures taken by Japanese during the rape of Nanking, and I was asked to sort through them and try to identify the faces of individuals who might be brought to trial at the end of the war on charges of war crimes.

Another young man was helping me with the task. There were hundreds of pictures, and it was a sickening job studying those laughing faces in the act of committing some of the most heinous and obscene crimes. Other pictures showed soldiers standing around a pile of headless corpses gloating over the physical prowess of a sword-wielding officer, standing proudly bare-chested and blood-bespattered, triumphantly waving his sword.

As Huang told his story, I recalled the photographs of long lines of shirtless soldiers, hands bound behind them, shuffling forward in the dust, with gleefully laughing Japanese soldiers on each side of them, prodding them with their bayonets. There were also close-up pictures of officers standing on the balustrade, their victim between them, and a sword in mid-air just about to decapitate a man, while other pictures showed the blur of falling corpses with the heads separate from them.

There were ghastly pictures of slain men and women, singly and in groups. But the pictures that are still most vivid in my mind were those taken outside the city wall. One in particular showed an embrasure jutting from the wall, forming a deep corner. From near the top of the wall there flowed downward what I can only describe as a "waterfall" or "cascade" of bodies, thousands of them, spreading outward for several hundred feet. By marking off a small section and examining it through a magnifying glass, we tried to estimate the number of dead in that one monstrous pile. But it was hopeless. We then tried to count the

bodies visible on the surface and reached a figure of well over three hundred, and as best we could tell, that pile was civilians only. And there were photos of numerous other such piles of dead at other points around the city wall, several of them exclusively of soldiers' bodies.

Stupidly I asked Huang why he or some of the others had not made an attempt to flee instead of mindlessly walking forward to their death. He looked at me for a long moment and then said, "We had been starved for days and had no strength left. We knew we were going to die one way or another. There were Japanese with guns all around us. Every now and then we'd hear shots when some drunken Japanese shot some of us just for the fun of it. So if they hadn't killed us with a sword, it would be some other way. It was our fate, and we were ready to die and wanted to get it done with." As he rebuttoned his collar, Huang patted his scar, and with a somewhat lopsided grin remarked, "I've something here to remember the Japanese by, and I've had a permanent headache for ten years and will have it till I die, but I'm lucky because I cannot be drafted into the Nationalist army. They don't want a soldier who cannot turn his head."

We had three or four days to wait in Shanghai before boarding the USS *Lynx*, the ship I had met so many times on the docks in San Francisco. She was still the only passenger-carrying vessel plying the run between Shanghai and San Francisco, and she had a full complement of passengers. The USS *Lynx* was basically a troopship converted for passenger use, but actually, little had been done in the way of conversion. To the best of my recollection I believe she was still at that time being operated by U.S. Navy personnel, but I could be wrong. There were few private cabins, and men and women were all housed separately, either in large cabins like the one Eva was in with some ten or twelve other women, or as in my case, in one of the holds, where several hundred men were together in the same kind of three-decker bunks as we had on the ship from India to the United States in 1944. The big difference was that we were able to eat our meals together in the common dining saloon, and some public lounges and reading rooms were available for the use of everyone.

Our fellow passengers were mostly missionaries and businessmen leaving China for good, together with a fair sprinkling of wealthy Chinese who had managed to secure passports and visas and who were overjoyed to be on their way to a life of freedom in the United States. Our trip across the Pacific was smooth. The only thing that disturbed us was the increasingly bad news of Communist advances in China published in the daily news bulletin put out by the ship's radio operator. During the two weeks that we were at sea, we began to have second thoughts about our plans to return to southwestern China with my sister, Ruth. And we were in no way encouraged by the pessimistic views of our fellow passengers.

We stopped briefly in Honolulu, where we rented an open touring car and enjoyed a tour of the island. After leaving Honolulu, three new male passengers appeared at our table the first night out, having boarded the ship in Hawaii. We didn't find out for two or three days that they were immigration officers who would be with us all the way to San Francisco, and whose job it would be to examine everyone's passports before we could leave the ship.

We found the three men to be extremely unsociable and taciturn, almost to the point of rudeness. Two were somewhat older men who barely responded when we wished them a "good morning." The third, a younger man in his late 30s, was slightly more approachable, and we managed to engage him in some limited conversation at mealtimes. Other than that, they ignored us and completely dissociated themselves from the passengers as a whole. We learned much later that it was a studied policy on their part, designed to avoid any possible accusations of favoritism or less than impartial treatment of everyone aboard. On the last day before we reached San Francisco, all passengers were notified that they would have to appear in the dining saloon to have their passports inspected. As we gradually moved forward in the long line heading for the dining saloon, we could see the three officers working at separate tables. As it turned out, when it came our turn the youngest of the three officers beckoned us over. He appeared friendly enough and very professional. He asked us a couple of questions, then, just as he was getting ready to stamp our passports, I asked him if he could give us some information.

I told him that while we had visitor's visas for a six-month stay in the United States, and our original intention had been to return to China with my invalid sister within that period of time, we now felt, after reading all the reports of rapid advances being made in China by the Communist forces, that perhaps it wasn't going to be possible to go back to China, and that we might have to stay on in the U.S. I asked if he could tell me what steps we should take upon arrival to apply for permanent residence. A simple enough question, but it nearly had grave and far-reaching consequences for us.

He paused for a moment, then laid down the rubber stamp he had been about to imprint on our passports granting us entry to the U.S., and still holding them in his hand, he said, "I'm rather busy just now. Why don't I just hang onto your passports for the present, and we'll discuss this later. I'll get in touch with you before the day is out." That seemed quite reasonable, and neither Eva nor I gave it a second thought.

That night, our last night at sea, the captain gave a semi-formal dinner and dance to which everyone was invited. But since neither Eva nor I had ever learned to dance, we left the dining saloon immediately after the meal and made our way to the boat deck where we relaxed in a couple of deck chairs, enjoying the balmy weather and the bright moonlight shining across the water. We had seen nothing of the young immigration officer, nor heard from him, but we never had the slightest doubt that he would contact us in good time.

Since there was little point in going to our bunks before the festivities ended, we were still up there around midnight when the young immigration officer suddenly turned up on the boat deck, and finding an empty chair alongside ours, he dropped into it, closed his eyes and began to snooze. We thought that perhaps he had come to discuss our problem and give us an answer to my question. But I didn't want to irritate him by asking.

He had obviously had a number of drinks, and after twenty minutes or so, he started, in a very jovial mood, to discuss the various people standing or sitting nearby. But he didn't bring up the matter that so much concerned us. Then he again lapsed into silence for an appreciable length of time. Finally, he sat up straight, and turning to me with a somewhat stern expression, he asked us why we were sitting up on deck and why we had not joined in the festivities below.

I told him neither of us had either learned to drink or dance, and we took little pleasure in watching others doing so. I said we found it much more pleasant out in the open air. He then asked us about ourselves and what we had been doing in China. We talked for about 30 minutes, telling him of our missionary work, and how and why it had so abruptly come to an end. I then repeated to him the point that we had left China with the quite honest intention of returning there and going to the southwestern part, where we thought the Communists might never reach, but that during the previous two or three weeks while we had been traveling, the situation had changed so radically that we had been forced to reconsider our position.

When I had finished, he again sat back and closed his eyes for some minutes without saying a word. Then he sat up, swung his legs over the side of the chair, and looking me straight in the eyes, he said: "You know, I have to admit that I misjudged you two when you came to me this morning with your question about applying for permanent residence in the United States. At the time, I thought you were two bums trying to get in under the wire, and that's why I withheld your passports. I had every intention of not only denying you entry into the United States, but I was going to send you back to Shanghai on this very ship. Now I've changed my mind. From what I've heard you say, I've come to the conclusion that you two are just the kind of people we need in America, and I'm going to admit you. Tomorrow morning, before we dock, I'll give you back your passports."

For a moment or two Eva and I sat there in complete shock. I then thanked him, but he said, "Don't thank me. You can thank the God whom you serve." He then continued, "Let me give you some good advice, but don't you ever quote me. Whenever you have any dealings with U.S. government officials, particularly us in the Immigration Service, never volunteer any information. Just answer any questions that they ask you, and let it go at that. We are natural-ly suspicious of everyone, and when people come to us and talk too much, we think the worst." With that, he stood up, said good night to us and headed off to bed.

We sat there stunned, wondering if we had really heard him correctly, then thoughts began to race through our heads. What if he was so drunk that in the morning he would have forgotten all about our talk and his promise to give us our passports back? We didn't sleep too well that night. The next morning, November 28, 1947, we didn't see him at breakfast, and I began to worry some more since we were fast approaching San Francisco. Around ten o'clock, amid great excitement, we passed under the Golden Gate Bridge and tied up at one of the San Francisco piers a short time later. Still there was no sign of the young immigration officer. It wasn't long before the passengers started streaming ashore, as Eva and I waited by the gangway for him to appear. We had a long wait, and it wasn't until well after noon, when everyone but us had left the ship, that he came up from his cabin, bleary-eyed and deeply apologetic. But at least he hadn't forgotten us, and he was carrying our two passports in his hand.

He wished us well, and we walked off the ship with thankful hearts. But as we landed once again on American soil, our feelings were nothing like the joy we had felt almost eleven months before when we had sailed from a nearby pier for China with such high hopes and expectations.

It was a strange feeling to be back in America again. Here, where supposedly we were "home," instead of a feeling of relief, we found ourselves filled with a sense of foreboding; the immediate future ahead of us was so uncertain. At the time, never, even for a moment, did we imagine that China would be closed for the next 30 years, not only to missionaries, but to the world as a whole.

遠水不能救近火，
遠親不如近鄰。

Yuan shui buneng jiu jin huo,
yuan qin buru jin lin.

Distant water cannot quench a nearby fire;
remote relatives are not as good
as close neighbors.

- Chinese Proverb.

Chapter Forty-Two
Immigration Woes

Most Americans, I'm sure, never give any thought to the idea of how lucky they are to be born Americans. And I venture to suggest that the average American, if asked, which of the many branches of the United States government he or she feared the most, would name the Internal Revenue Service. However, for people immigrating to the United States and arriving on America's shores for the first time, it is the Immigration and Naturalization Service (INS) with whom they first come into contact. For those many, like ourselves, coming in on a temporary visitor's visa or perhaps as a student, and then — out of choice or necessity — wishing to change their status to that of permanent resident and seeking eventual citizenship, it is the same INS that almost literally holds the power of life and death over them. Writing both from our own experience and from observation of our many friends who have entered this country, the INS holds far greater fears and uncertainties for the individual than does the IRS, at least until you get

established in this country.

An immigrant wishing to settle in the United States must first, in his own country, apply for a visa at a U.S. Consulate or Embassy and state his intentions. Getting that visa can take as little as a day; frequently it may take months or even years. If the individual is approved for permanent residence, he or she is issued on arrival in the U.S. with what is widely called a "green card," more properly known as the Alien Registration Receipt Card. Once that is secured, anyone can live and work in the United States and enjoy all the rights of a citizen except for voting privileges.

But for the person who has entered on a visitor or student visa, changing status and securing a green card usually takes several months. In our case it took almost ten years, and I know a number of other people who had to wait almost as long. Having acquired a green card, an individual need not apply for citizenship. But should he or she wish to do so, after making what is called a declaration of intention, there is usually a waiting period of five years before a citizenship hearing can be held, and if approved, the individual can usually obtain citizenship after another waiting period of several months.

The INS is doubtless one of the most overworked and harassed services in the U.S. government. Like the IRS, it is always behind in processing cases. But for the average immigrant waiting for an INS decision, it is a great deal more traumatic than simply waiting for a decision on some tax problem. In most cases with the INS, it is one's very life, livelihood and future that are in the balance.

This chapter will be largely devoted to the problems we faced with the INS after our arrival back in this country in November, 1947. It is not my intention to denigrate or tarnish the name and reputation of the INS as a whole. We have met more than our share of responsible and fine INS people. Yet our experience in gaining admittance to this country and eventual citizenship, while novel and in some ways unique, has also been shared by a number of my Chinese friends as well as people from other countries whom I have come to know, and it is a story I feel should be told.

Most Americans born in this country have no conception of what it means to go through the process of naturalization, nor can they appreciate, as we came to, the final exhilaration and sense of achievement felt upon acquiring citizenship to this great and wonderful country. But America's good name is all too often besmirched by the callous behavior, thoughtless indifference, and too often simple ignorance of the law on the part of what may be just a very limited number of individuals working for the INS. Those failings are not necessarily limited to those posted on the borders of this country.

In our case, from the time we talked to the young immigration officer aboard ship and intimated our desire to become permanent residents and eventually citizens of the U.S., it was almost exactly 15 long years before we finally got our citizenship papers. I doubt that many others can top that record. With the constant doubts and uncertainties that came with the long wait, to say nothing of the sheaves of papers we had to supply and the forms we had to complete, it is not a happy experience to look back upon.

Arriving in San Francisco on November 28, 1947, we were so vastly relieved for the reprieve we had been given by the INS officer aboard the ship that we tried to relax and not think about the relatively short period of six months that we were allowed on our visitor's visa. At first we made no move to change our status, although day by day it became ever more apparent from what was happening in China that we would be unable to go back. We settled in with my father and stepmother, Isabel, in the little house in Alameda; meanwhile, they prepared to head east right after the new year, planning to reside in the Boston area, where Isabel had lived most of her life.

We found that my sister Ruth's condition had not improved. Although not bedridden, she was unable to do much for herself because she had only the use of her right arm and hand. The doctors at that time knew very little about Parkinson's disease, and the medication she was getting did little to help her. Many years later it turned out that she had never had Parkinson's disease in the first place, but the tools for diagnosis at that time were very different from what we have today.

Eva at once realized she had a big job ahead of her caring for Ruth. Miss McCabe, an elderly neighbor who came in for several hours each day to help take care of Ruth, was herself rather frail and found it difficult to assist my sister in getting up from bed or chair. In some ways Miss McCabe's very presence seemed to complicate matters, so we made the decision to call her in only as needed.

We were not without transportation those first few weeks in Alameda. A dear Christian friend, Bain Jackson, lent us his elderly Dodge. Since it was in need of a paint job, I thought I'd try my hand at it and do Bain a favor at the same time. I rented a spray gun, although I'd never used one before, and, with the car in our little one-car garage, I got great satisfaction out of seeing the transformation into what looked like a brand-new vehicle. But my satisfaction was short-lived. The next morning when I went out to look at the car, I was stupefied to find the entire vehicle covered with a mass of tiny "pimples," which were the result of my not having provided a fan to draw out the paint-laden air, and the fine paint spray in the air had all settled onto the car. I was prepared to sand it down and do it over again, but long-suffering Bain Jackson professed to be very pleased with the results, and said he wanted it left as it was. I would classify that as one of the real measurements of a true friend and Christian.

Christmas and New Year's came and went, and Father and Isabel left for the East Coast. Since I had a January deadline to pick up the Ford in Hoboken, New Jersey, I, too, headed East soon after their departure.

I caught a train to New York, and, after arriving, found my way by bus and cab across the Hudson River to Hoboken, where Ford had their assembly plant. My car was ready and waiting for me, and by late afternoon I was on my way to Philadelphia.

Driving for a good part of the night, I reached Philadelphia and checked into a motel. I had learned that the Immigration Service had their headquarters in Philadelphia and I wanted to consult with them in regard to our status and find out whatever steps we needed to take to secure permanent residence. At the same time I wanted to learn from them the exact status Ruth held, since there was some doubt at the time that her registration card, which had been issued to her in 1946, was permanent. The people in Oakland had been unable to tell us. The next morning at the immigration office they assured me that Ruth's card was valid for as long as she wanted to stay in the United States, but in our case I was told I would have to write to a U.S. Consul abroad, either in Canada or Mexico, for the necessary information.

Without further delay I set out for California. I was in a hurry to get back to Alameda because Eva was all alone with Ruth and it was difficult for her to get out to do any grocery shopping. I drove an average of 18 hours a day, sleeping a few hours at a time either in a motel or in the car.

Once back in Alameda I was kept busy for several weeks conducting services all over the Bay area. Folks were most interested in hearing of our experiences in China, and I was much in demand two or three nights a week. However, always on my mind was the fact that time was running out on us. We only had a six-month visa, and with two months gone and only four left to go, I had to get busy making some plans.

First I visited the Immigration and Naturalization Service offices in Oakland and asked how to get an extension of our visas while we applied for permanent residence in the United States. A friendly official there told me there would be no difficulty in getting an extension, but it would only be a stop-gap measure, permitting us a longer, but still temporary, stay in the country. Sooner or later we would have to make an application for permanent residence from outside the U.S., and like the man in Philadelphia, he suggested either Canada or Mexico. He advised me to write to the U.S. Consul in Vancouver, British Columbia.

I wrote to Vancouver immediately, but the reply, although forthright, was worded in a way I found somewhat ambiguous. The consul stated that I would have to make my application outside of the United States. He didn't say whether, during the waiting period for my application to go through, we would have to reside outside of the U.S., nor did he give me any idea as to how long it would take. What I needed to know was whether we could spend the waiting time in the U.S. and thus avoid the complexities of moving temporarily to another country. But no one seemed able to give me that information, either in the Oakland or in the San Francisco office of the INS, where I later applied.

I also wrote Canadian officials in Ottawa, stating the condition of my sister's health and asking them whether she would be eligible for admission into Canada as an immigrant. The reply, when it came some weeks later, dashed any hopes of our making Canada our home should we have to move, since I was told that, considering the state of Ruth's health, it was highly unlikely that she could qualify for admittance.

We now at least knew that, failing to get permission to stay in the United States during the waiting period, which could be as long as a year or two, only two alternatives were open to us: England or Mexico. Neither was particularly attractive to us. I knew I could get a job with the British government without difficulty, but we felt strongly that the climate in England would not be favorable for Ruth's health. And the weather in Mexico was so hot that it, too, was undesirable as an alternative. We worried a lot and prayed a lot, and in no time it was the end of February, 1948.

In the first week of March I again went to the INS office in Oakland for more information. The same friendly officer answered my questions to the best of his ability, but there were still a number of points he was unable to clarify. He suggested that since Vancouver, B.C., was not that far away, I should make a trip there and talk with the U.S. Consul in person. I asked him if, with my then-current visa, it was permissible for me to leave the country briefly and then return, and he assured me that it was and that I would have no difficulty whatsoever. He further told me that the process of applying for admittance to the United States was so simple and easy that in all probability I would be able to get the whole problem cleared up with one visit, i.e., get our application in for permanent residence and then come back to Alameda for the waiting period, and in the meantime we could have our current visas extended while we waited.

All that sounded marvelous and much too good to be true. Having traveled so much, and not being unfamiliar with government officials, I was a little skeptical and thought it best to go over to the San Francisco INS office and make further inquiries, just to be sure. In San Francisco I met with another helpful officer. After I had told him our problem, he, too, quite forcefully said that the solution would be to make a trip to Vancouver to see the U.S. consul. Like his fellow officer in Oakland, he assured me that returning to the U.S. on my current visa would pose no problems at all. Armed with that information I felt doubly assured and secure in taking that step, so on the afternoon of March 7, 1948, with high hopes, I boarded a Greyhound bus and set off for Vancouver.

The bus trip took two nights and one full day, and was most enjoyable despite the lack of sleep. At around two in the morning of the second night, the bus arrived at the Canadian border, crossing from the American town of Blaine, Washington, to the Canadian village of Douglas, British Columbia. As we passed the U.S. border station, it appeared entirely dark with no one on duty, and the bus didn't stop. Had there been anyone there, and had we stopped, as is the procedure at the present time, I am sure I would have queried the border officer once again about the validity of my passport visa in returning from Canada, and would have been saved a lot of grief. As it was, it wasn't until I talked with the Canadian immigration officer that the first hint of trouble came.

When he questioned me as to the purpose of my visit to Canada, I told him exactly why I was there, and he replied, "My friend, you've been given some wrong information. There is no way you'll be able to get what you want from the U.S. consul. You would be best advised to get back into the States as soon as

you possibly can." That was disturbing news indeed, and I asked him if it would be possible for me to go back right then and there. He told me I would have to wait for the next morning's bus, and my best bet would be to go direct to Vancouver and catch the bus there.

Continuing on the bus to Vancouver, we arrived after about an hour and I checked into a small hotel for a bath and shave. Then, after a quick breakfast I inquired about bus schedules and found I had time to visit the U.S. Consul before the bus left. Maybe things would work out after all.

At the consulate, after a very short wait, I was ushered in to see one of the vice-consuls, only to be told that my trip was entirely in vain. He informed me that Eva and I, because of our China birth, fell into the category of "White Chinese" (the first time I had ever even heard of such a category). The fact that I was holding a British passport was meaningless, and in order to enter the United States, we would have to wait until our turn came on the White Chinese quota — at least 20 years!

I couldn't believe my ears, and asked him how that could possibly be the case. He pointed out that during the war years, so many China-born White Russians and German refugees had been admitted to the United States from China that the quota of 107 persons a year (if I remember the figure correctly) had been completely used up, but President Roosevelt had intervened, and the quota for the next 20 years had been "mortgaged" and also exhausted.

He advised me to return to the United States as soon as possible and explain the situation to the immigration officers at the border. He was "hopeful" that I would have no trouble there with my visa, even though, by the mere fact of having intimated my intention of changing it for permanent residence, I had technically invalidated it. He also informed me that while waiting for our turn on the quota, we would have to reside outside of the United States for the entire period, and I should make plans accordingly, because there was no possibility of our current visa being extended for that period of time. With a heavy heart I went over to the bus station just in time to catch the bus back to the U.S.A.

I arrived at the border at about 11 a.m. When the bus stopped, a short, thick-set and very grouchy immigration officer climbed aboard and started questioning the passengers. When he got to me, I held out my British passport, but instead of looking at it, he asked me the standard question, "Where were you born?" When I told him China, he then looked at my passport and asked why I had departed from the U.S. the previous evening and what was the purpose of my visit to Vancouver. With complete candor I told him briefly the purpose of my visit. He then quite politely said, "You'll have to get off the bus and go inside and wait for the next bus. We have to question you further." With that he turned to the next passenger.

I waited inside the border station until he had finished examining the rest of the passengers. I then watched the bus pull out and depart without me. When the officer came back inside, without a word he led me into the main office to a small cubicle about five feet square, containing only a chair, and told me to wait until I was called. Saying nothing further he locked me in. There were no windows in the cubicle, so I could see nothing of what was going on outside. But the walls were thin, and all around me I could hear the many different sounds of the office. For almost an hour I sat there uneasily contemplating my fate until they came to get me.

They took me to a nearby conference room and four immigration officers, including the one who had removed me from the bus, sat down on one side of the big table and offered me a chair in front of them. A young woman secretary was at the end of the table to record in shorthand the entire proceedings. With a stern face and a very formal manner one of the officers informed me that what was taking place was a Board of Special Inquiry, convened according to law to specifically examine my case, and that any decision made by the board would be legally binding. I was then required to swear that I would tell the truth and nothing but the truth, and the proceedings commenced.

At first I was not unduly alarmed. I had sat before such boards once or twice previously when crossing the border between the U.S. and Canada. Because of my birth in China they always questioned me at length, but in every case it had lasted no more than 30 minutes or so, and I had then been permitted to resume my journey. That time it was very different. The hearing lasted four full hours, and I was questioned by all four officers in great detail. The questions covered my entire past in China, my responsi-

bility for the care of my sister, my future plans, and my financial standing, which at that point, after the sale of the Ford, stood at a little over $1,000 in the bank. There were many other questions as well, including whether we had children or had any intention of having children in the future, and whether my father would be able to support us.

To me, much of the questioning seemed to be highly personal and to have little bearing on my case, but so it went, on and on interminably, without a break. At their request I recounted in great detail our experiences in China the preceding year and the years before Pearl Harbor. I detailed my sister's condition and the hardships she and my wife had been put through when the Japanese took us captive in 1941. I told of my internment by the Japanese and subsequent repatriation to India and of our life there and my work for the British government. Then of my transfer to San Francisco with a diplomatic passport. Our residence there for three years, our return to China and our abortive attempt to regain possession of our home and mission stations in China the previous year, covering all the details of the Communist takeover and our escape to Peking. I also brought them up to date by telling them I had made the trip to Vancouver specifically on the advice and suggestion of officers of their own Immigration and Naturalization Service in Oakland and San Francisco, giving the names of the officers concerned.

At several points while I told my story I noticed the young lady taking notes was emotionally upset and was surreptitiously wiping away tears. As the hours went by I became aware that their questioning revolved mainly around our decision to remain in the United States and not return to China, and they wanted to know just how I intended supporting myself, my wife and an invalid sister. Obviously I was, to some extent, at a loss in being able to satisfy them, since beyond preaching, I hadn't the slightest idea of what I would be able to do to earn a living.

Ultimately, long after everyone else in the office had left, the hearing came to an end, and I was taken back to the cubicle and told to wait until they came to a decision. I sat there, in the now quiet building, pondering my situation and wondering what it was all about. I have always been blessed with a very acute sense of hearing, and I quickly found that I was able to follow the conversation of the officers in the adjoining room because they had left the door open. I heard them discussing their findings and gained the impression that two or three of them were very much in favor of letting me proceed back to Alameda, or at least waiting until they could read the transcript before making a decision. But the fourth officer seemed to disagree, and from the voice, I concluded it was the same little man who had first pulled me off the bus. In any case, at that point one of them asked the secretary how long it would take for her to type up her notes. She replied that the hearing had taken over four hours and it would take her probably at least that long to type it up. Then to my utter disbelief, I distinctly heard one of the officers say, "We can't wait that long. Let's just deport the guy and get it all over and done with and we can go home to eat."

A moment or two later I was taken back into the conference room where I was required to stand, and one of the officers as spokesman formally informed me that my six-month visitor's visa had been invalidated by my having left the country and having intimated that it was for the specific purpose of gaining permanent residence in the United States, and that, since I had no permanent residence outside of the United States, I was therefore classified as a displaced person. Further, my financial position and lack of employment, together with insufficient funds in the bank, showed my inability to support myself, my wife and invalid sister, and all those factors being the case, I was not eligible for admission to the United States because I would become a charge on the government. For that reason I would also be barred from applying for admission for a period of at least two years. With that, they handed me a Notice of Exclusion from the United States for a minimum of two years and until such time as the "causes of rejection could be removed or overcome." With that the hearing was closed, and I was unceremoniously escorted out of the building and put aboard the next bus leaving for Vancouver, with nothing further being said by any of the four men.

To say that I was in a state of complete and utter shock would be an understatement, and for one of the few times in my life I was completely speechless. Nothing like that had ever happened to me before, and I hadn't the foggiest idea as to what steps I should take nor to whom I could turn for help. I knew not a single soul in Vancouver, although given time, I could probably have located old friends from back in the days ten or eleven years before when we had lived there for six months at the old Hotel Elysium and attended church locally. But somehow I felt it was a problem I had to resolve on my own, with God's guidance, so I checked back into the same hotel and spent the entire night sitting in front of the window praying and trying to come up with a possible solution. The feeling of utter helplessness and loneliness that overwhelmed me is impossible to describe. There I was, a single individual trying to do battle with the United States government. What chance in the world did I have of any possible success in getting back into the U.S. to pick up Eva and Ruth and get them out of the country, and how could they possibly manage without me? All those and hundreds of other questions flooded my mind. What I wanted to do most of all was to call Eva on the phone and discuss it with her. But I knew it would only worry her unduly, and although it would have been a comfort to me, I felt it would be unfair to her.

By dawn I had made my decision to fight back and not just take their decision lying down. I grabbed a cup of coffee and a doughnut, then caught the first bus back to the border and walked into the border station around 8 o'clock, just as everyone was starting work. Politely I asked to see the head man or supervising officer. I was told he was too busy to see me then, and I was asked to wait.

There was no waiting room, just a small area with a few chairs up against a partition, and I sat there throughout the entire day, completely ignored by everyone. On several occasions I saw the four officers who had questioned me. I tried to get their attention, but none would stop to talk with me. I followed them as they walked away, begging them to listen, but they just brushed me off and told me that what had been done was final and only an act of Congress could change it, and for them there was nothing further to say. I gained the impression that they were embarrassed to see me.

I determined to make a nuisance of myself, and time and again I asked to see the boss, receiving the same reply each time. He was too busy to see me. All I could do was sit and pray that God would overrule and provide me a way out.

I dared not leave the room to get anything for lunch for fear I might be called, and finally about 4:30 in the afternoon, I saw around me the obvious signs that the office was about to close for the day and I knew it would not be long before I would be ejected once again. At that point, hungry and very thirsty, I happened to go around the corner to the water cooler for a drink and found the young secretary from the previous day there getting a drink.

I stood by until she had finished, then begged her to please listen to me. I told her the very desperate situation I was in, and that I simply had to be allowed to go back to Alameda to help my wife and sister leave the country. I told her that I had noticed on the previous afternoon as she was taking notes at the hearing that she had shown great sympathy as she heard my story, and I pleaded with her to do what she could to get me in to see the head man for just a few minutes, promising that I wouldn't bother them further after that. She looked at me for a long time, her chin quivering, then she burst into tears and said, "Don't bother me with your troubles. I've enough of my own. I'm terribly sorry for you, but there is nothing I can do," and turning her back on me, she left.

I returned to my seat feeling that the situation was utterly hopeless, but I sat there praying and wondering what to do next. I didn't have long to wait. In less than five minutes the young woman came out of an inner office, still wiping her eyes, and beckoned to me, saying her boss would see me. I was led to a nearby room where, to my surprise, I found ten or twelve people standing against the walls, including the four officers who had questioned me the previous day. Behind a large desk sat a tall, good-looking young man who was apparently the officer-in-charge, but his face showed nothing but anger. He introduced himself, and I remember his name well. In fact, I could hardly forget it after what he said and did to me. However, I shall spare him and his family the embarrassment of identifying him here, because I don't consider him typical of INS officers. Furthermore, despite my problems and his insolence toward me, I was ultimately able to see the whole thing from his point of view and have since been able to understand why he acted as he did.

In a peremptory manner he told me to stand in front of him. He then proceeded to give me a "dressing down," such as a military officer might do to a private or a school principal to one of his students. With no attempt to spare my feelings, he started out by saying he had reviewed my story from the transcript and, in his opinion, it was not only a pack of lies, but I was undoubtedly the biggest and most imaginative liar he had ever come across in his career. He refused to believe my story that two different immigration officers had suggested or even condoned my making the trip to Vancouver, saying it was pure fiction on my part. Moreover, the story of our experiences in China with the Chinese Communists was just so much hogwash. He ranted on for what seemed like at least fifteen minutes, finally winding up by telling me that I was nothing but a pauper and an undesirable alien that America could well do without. He concluded by saying he wanted me to get out of his office for good, and that he never wanted to see me again. Apparently quite satisfied with himself, he stood up behind his desk and indicated that the interview was over.

All that time I hadn't said a word; indeed, I had not been given a chance to do so. But when he stopped talking, I deliberately drew up a chair and sat down in front of his desk. Leaning back in the chair and crossing one leg over the other, I told him I had a few things to say as well. He had had his turn, and I now wanted him and all the others present to listen to me for a few minutes.

He stood for a second or two completely nonplused by my audacity, then he again started to rant and rave, using foul language in telling me what he thought of me. I raised my hand and said, "Hear me out. I won't take more than a moment or two, but I've got three proposals to make to you, and I want everyone in this room to hear them." I told him it was absolutely imperative that I be allowed to return to Alameda for a few days to take care of my wife and sister and to help pack our things and get them out of the country, because there was no way my wife could manage it on her own without my help. I told him I would need about ten days to wind up our affairs and book our passages, and I told him that I was willing to go in handcuffs with one of his men if that was what it took. His immediate response was that it was completely impossible, that he couldn't spare a man, etc. I suggested that he confiscate my British passport and allow me to go back on my own with my personal guarantee that I would be out of the country within ten days. That, too, he turned down with the remark that I would "disappear into the woodwork" and they'd never find me again.

With those two suggestions shot down, I finally pulled out a $20 bill and laid it on the desk in front of him. Pointing to the telephone, I said, "I want you to call your San Francisco and Oakland offices at my expense and talk with the two men who advised me to come up here, and have them confirm my story." I went on, "If you don't do so, and persist in preventing me from going back to pick up my wife and invalid sister, I'll hold the United States government, and you personally, responsible if anything should happen to either of them as a result of my not having been permitted to go back." As I said that, I turned to face the others in the room and said, "I shall hold all of you present as witnesses to what I just said," and with that, I stood up and told him I had nothing further to say.

His face by that time had become so red I thought he was about to explode. He could barely contain himself as he picked up the $20 bill and threw it across the desk at me and shouted, "I don't want your blankety-blank money. Just get the hell out of here immediately and don't come back." He then added, "I'll give it some thought, but don't expect to hear from me again." I told him I would go back across the Canadian border to the village of Douglas, where I would stay the night in the only motel there, and he could find me there after he had made his calls and confirmed my story. I then turned and left the room, stopping only to thank the young woman for her kindness in getting me in to see her boss.

I walked out of the building into a horrendous thunderstorm, and in a few seconds I was soaked to the skin as I walked back to the Canadian side of the border. There I found the place in complete darkness because the storm had knocked out the electricity. The same friendly young border guard whom I had talked with the previous night was again on duty. He very kindly asked the driver of one of the passing cars to give me a lift as far as the village of Douglas, and there I checked into the motel, which, like the entire village, was also completely dark. With just a candle for light, I was shown my room, and exhausted both emotionally and physically after three nights without proper sleep, I collapsed onto the bed. But sleep wouldn't come. Everything that had happened in the previous 24 hours churned through my mind, and I began to wonder what would happen if the INS offi-

cer telephoned through to Alameda, as I was sure he would. I imagined him calling Eva direct and asking her if she could manage without me in the event I was delayed "for a few days." I could hear Eva courageously replying that, of course she could manage on her own, not knowing that I was being excluded from the country altogether and unable to return. It got to the point where I felt I just had to get to a telephone and call Eva to alert her to the possibility of receiving just such a call from the INS and to urge her to simply tell the truth in answering whatever she might be asked.

Easier said than done. I went to the motel office, where I found the woman manager sitting in the dark and learned from her that the storm had knocked out all the telephones in the village as well. I started back across the court to my room, feeling totally defeated, and at that moment I heard a train whistle in the near distance. Immediately my thoughts went back to Lingyuan, where on numerous occasions I had used the railway telephone system, so straight away, in the pouring rain, I headed for the railroad station about a mile away.

It was only a tiny whistle-stop station with just one man on duty. He patiently listened as I explained my problem in some detail. When I asked him if his telephone was still working, he assured me it was. I asked if it was at all possible for him to get through on his phone all the way down the line to Oakland, from where they could perhaps patch through to my home in Alameda. He seemed quite intrigued by the idea, telling me it had never been done before to his knowledge, but he was willing to try. With that he picked up the phone, told me to listen in on an extension, and step by step he began a tediously painful call down the line from one section to the next for the full 1,500 miles along the railroad to Oakland.

It took well over fifteen minutes before I finally heard the Oakland operator answer. He gave her my home number and asked her to ring it, which she did. Exuberantly I thought, "Success at last," but my hopes were dashed when all we got was a busy signal.

Few times in my life have I felt so deeply depressed and so utterly defeated. It was still pouring rain as I thanked the man and returned in a complete daze to the motel. But as I walked, a feeling of peace came over me as I thought of the many times in our lives when God had undertaken for us when everything seemed to have gone wrong, and I decided to once again leave it to Him. Entering my room, I took off my wet clothes, crawled into bed, and immediately fell into a deep sleep.

How long I slept I don't know, but I was awakened by a banging on the door and the manager telling me a man from the U.S. immigration office was outside wanting to see me. I hurriedly dressed, grabbed my things, and ran outside where I found a uniformed officer with a car, which he very politely invited me to enter, saying that his boss wanted to see me.

As we rode back over the now familiar road, a tumult of thoughts passed through my mind. But above all I felt a sense of great calmness and tremendous elation. I was certain that God had somehow overruled and that all would be well. When we reached the border station, it must have been around three in the morning. The lights were still working on the American side of the border, but the only lights in the border station were those in the office of the station chief, where the driver immediately took me.

I found the head man sitting alone, looking very tired, his hair rumpled and his clothing disheveled. As I entered the room, he got up from behind his desk and came around to meet me with both hands outstretched and a broad smile on his face. He was a totally different individual from the one I had seen and heard shouting and swearing at me just a few hours before. Taking my two hands in his, he led me to a chair and proceeded to abjectly apologize for his earlier behavior. He told me he had called both San Francisco and Oakland. He'd talked with the men whose names I had given him, and they had completely and in every detail confirmed my story. He sheepishly admitted that, when he had read the transcript, the account of my experiences had been so utterly unique and so completely out of the ordinary scope of things to which he was accustomed that he'd been unable to accept it as truth, and he asked me to please forgive him.

I held no grudge against him then, nor do I now. From his point of view I was indeed a pauper. He could see me only as a fast talker with a good line of blarney calculated to touch the heart of any listener, and as I thought about it, I found it not surprising that he and his men had been suspicious of me. When he continued it was to tell me that he was deeply sorry for what had been done. The Board of Enquiry results were now law and couldn't under any circumstances be changed, except by an act of Congress.

He told me there was only one course of action open to him, and that was to give me a temporary parole for sixty days, which would allow me to return to Alameda, settle my affairs, and leave the country with Eva and my sister. However, I was required to sign a statement to the effect that I clearly understood the terms of the parole: that it was given without the possibility of any extension being granted by the INS and that I would make no effort to have it extended, nor would I make any effort to delay my departure or try to stay on in the United States.

As I listened to him I wasn't particularly happy with the word "parole," which to me carried a connotation of criminality on my part, and I told him so. However, he assured me that as used by the Immigration Service, parole simply meant a temporary admission of an alien into the country for emergency reasons, and it carried no stigma with it. Since I had no other choice, I had to be satisfied with that.

He had the documents all prepared and ready for my signature, and I signed the agreement, with the fullest intentions of carrying it out to the letter. With the parole document in hand, I boarded the next bus heading south, and two days later was back in Alameda, where Eva, who had been kept completely ignorant of what had transpired in Blaine but had sensed that I had experienced trouble of some sort, was only too happy to see me. She told me that two immigration officers had called on her quite late one evening. They had asked only a few questions, giving her no reason as to why they were there and, to her surprise, had asked to see my sister Ruth and her passport, after which they left without saying anything further. Of course, my news of our new "parole" status and imminent departure to some place unknown was a bit of a shock, and we didn't quite know which way to turn.

The next morning I went back to the Oakland offices of the INS and asked to see the officer in charge. I was shown in to see a man who treated me most courteously. I pulled out my parole paper and showed it to him, telling him the circumstances under which I had been forced to accept it. I made a very strong protest over the misinformation that responsible officers under his command had given me, which, in my view, had been the direct cause of my present embarrassment. I knew immediately by his replies that he was well aware of the situation because of the phone call from Blaine. While not admitting that one of his men had been the cause of my problem, he was at least polite enough to express his regrets and promise to look into the matter, telling me not to worry and assuring me that all would turn out satisfactorily for me.

I was to see a great deal more of that man over the next several weeks. He told me I should make all my preparations for leaving at the end of the sixty days, but at the same time I should keep in touch with him every two or three weeks as he might have good news for me.

The following Sunday at our church services I told our many friends what had happened. They were all highly incensed and found it totally incomprehensible that such a thing could happen in America. They all agreed to pray about it. But one man, a successful businessman with strong ties in Washington and numerous contacts with members of Congress, was more than vociferous in his protests over the injustice of the situation. He said he would fly to Washington that very week and seek a bill in Congress to have the decision reversed. Moreover, he would give a full account of how it had occurred, putting the blame where it belonged. I thanked him for his concern and told him how appreciative I was. But because of the terms of my parole, and my having signed an agreement not to seek an extension of time in any way, I suggested that in all fairness I should first notify the local INS people of his intention to help me and inform them that the action proposed was not of my doing. He agreed and said he would wait to hear from me what the INS people said.

The following morning I was back at the Oakland offices of the INS asking to talk with the man I had seen earlier. I told him of the proposed action to be taken by my business friend and said I wanted him to know it was not at my instigation, since I was fully determined to carry out the terms of my parole and was making plans accordingly. However, I couldn't answer for what my friend might do.

His reaction was quite remarkable. He jumped up from his chair in obvious distress and excitement and urged me to do everything I could to dissuade my friend from taking such precipitate action. He assured me that he, personally, would undertake to get the matter resolved and that I need not have the slightest worry about having to leave the country. He further told me to go home and come back to see him again in two weeks, when he was sure he would have good news for me.

The man sounded so sincere that I began to feel some degree of encouragement. After all, who better than an INS official could directly resolve the problem? I told my businessman friend what the INS officer had promised to do. However, as a simple precaution, we continued to make plans for leaving and I again wrote the Canadian authorities in Ottawa to try and get a definitive answer as to whether or not my sister would be admitted to Canada. In reply, they asked for medical records, medical opinions from American specialists, and all sorts of information as to what means of support I would have. In the end I had to draw the conclusion that any final admittance to Canada would be up to the individual officer at the border and we would simply have to chance it, risking refusal and being sent back to the U.S. But all that gathering of information required a great deal of running around and caused poor Ruth considerable emotional distress as we took her to one doctor after another. As a further precaution we made numerous phone calls and visits to nursing homes in the area, exploring the possibility of leaving Ruth in the U.S. in one of them. But all of them showed reluctance to accept her because of her condition.

Two weeks later I returned to see my INS contact. He was ebullient in describing in detail the measures he had taken on my behalf and the phone calls he had made. He told me he was 100 percent certain of success, but said it would take another week or ten days. He told me to wait for his phone call or come back in another two weeks. That went on and on and I returned time and again at two-week intervals, each time getting the same kind of effusive assurances that all was going smoothly. As time went on and day 50 of our parole approached, I began to feel somewhat apprehensive and wondered if he was really telling me the truth.

Exactly ten days before the expiration of my parole, I went back to see the same INS officer once again and found it hard to believe he was the same man. Sternly, he ushered me into his inner office where we were entirely alone and, with no warning whatsoever, gave me a tongue-lashing much like the one given by his colleague up in Blaine a few weeks earlier. Among other things he called me a consummate liar and a conniving cheat, saying that in his opinion I was an undesirable, penniless bum whom no self-respecting officer of the INS would admit to the United States. He volunteered that he had not made any inquiries on my behalf in Washington, that he had never had the slightest intention of doing so in the first place, and that he had simply stalled me until I could be deported when my parole expired. He finished by telling me to get out of his office and not come back until ten days later when, if I did not have tickets in hand to leave the country voluntarily, I would be forcibly deported.

Again I found myself stunned and utterly speechless and could think of nothing to say. I had been able to understand the attitude of the station chief in Blaine and felt he had some justification for his actions. But this man's attitude and behavior was totally incomprehensible. What had I done to merit that kind of vindictive treatment? Why had he lied to me so repeatedly and so convincingly? Was he simply trying to save his own skin and prevent an investigation or something of that sort? And if so, what a dangerous tactic to take.

I left his office with my head swimming. After talking it over with Eva, I realized the man had deliberately left us so little time that our friend in the church would not be able to do much with his friends in Congress, and because of the delay, and the lies we had been told, we had not made any firm plans as to where we would go. I knew we would have to stall for time, and for the first time in my life I thought about getting the advice of a lawyer.

Not knowing anyone who could recommend an attorney, Eva and I prayed about it. We then opened the yellow pages of the telephone directory — or whatever the equivalent was in those days — and picked out the name of a lawyer in downtown San Francisco near the Bay Bridge Key Train depot. I called him and got an appointment for early afternoon of that day.

After lunch I headed for San Francisco. I found the lawyer to be a delightful old gentleman and he listened to my problem with considerable patience and interest. He then stopped me in the middle of a sentence, saying, "You've brought me a problem about which I know nothing at all. But I do know a man who can help you and I'll give him a call right now. His name is Zack Jackson. He was in charge of the legal department of the INS in San Francisco for 20 years and is now in private practice. If anyone knows how to help you, it will be he."

Everything seemed to be going my way that day. Zack Jackson was in and gave me an immediate appointment, and his office was only a few blocks away. And the old gentleman absolutely refused to take any payment. He said he thought it was about time we had a bit of good luck coming our way.

I found Zack to be a tall, pleasant-faced, middle-aged man with graying hair who welcomed me warmly, poured me a cup of coffee, and asked me to tell him what my problem was. He listened quietly for perhaps twenty minutes without saying anything, then stopped me abruptly and said, "Mr. Tharp, I was with the INS for over twenty years and this is positively the first time I have ever heard anything so extraordinarily bizarre, and nothing I have ever experienced even remotely compares to what you are telling me. I want you to know that my regular fee is $50 for a half hour, but in your case it won't cost you a cent. I'm going to cancel my other appointments, and I want you to keep talking for however long it takes, and please tell me every detail you can think of. I'm going to consider it a part of my education and I don't care if it takes three hours. I want to hear it all."

I'll never forget dear Zack. He listened for almost two hours without making any interruptions beyond occasionally plying me with coffee. At the end of my story he asked a few questions, then sat back in deep thought for several minutes. He finally turned to me and said, "Dear Mr. Tharp, I hate to tell you this, but they've got you over a barrel. There is absolutely no legal recourse that can be taken as far as I can see. Only an act of Congress can change the situation, and that is a very lengthy procedure that could take years, and there is no way in which your parole can be extended while that very 'iffy' thing takes place. In my opinion there are just three courses of action open to you. You can leave on your own in ten days' time, or you can just sit back and wait to be deported, which would give you some extra time, because they won't know where to send you immediately. But in my opinion it would in all probability be Shanghai, regardless of what the situation is there. But if I were in your shoes, with your knowledge of China and the Chinese, I would immediately apply to every conceivable office of the U.S. government that might be able to use your services and expertise, and perhaps you'll come up with something. I feel certain that if you get employment with the government, they can take steps to have this parole either revoked or extended in the national interest."

He then turned to his bookshelf and pulled down a volume from which he typed out a long list of addresses of various government agencies in Washington, D.C., and elsewhere. He handed it to me and advised me to get some letters out immediately. He warned me to be sure to enclose stamped, self-addressed envelopes in each one and to send them out air mail special delivery. Then, wishing me the best of luck, he shook my hand vigorously and said good-bye, refusing to even consider taking anything for his time. I've never run into anyone quite like him before or since. Even though, apart from advice, he had been unable to do anything for me, his advice gave our morale a boost and turned out to be very effective in the long run.

Since time was short, and in those days there was no such thing as a handy corner store with Xerox copiers, I sat up for the better part of the night typing individual letters to each address and took them to the all-night post office in San Francisco. After that we could do nothing but pray hard and wait for replies. But I must confess my faith was waning, and after so many letdowns, I had little confidence of success. As each day of waiting went by, and the day of our deportation loomed ever closer, our faith was sorely tried, and we spent much of our time watching and waiting for the mailman.

While waiting, just for something to do, we continued packing our belongings in anticipation of the worst possible outcome. Canada definitely appeared closed to us because of Ruth's health, and England, although a last resort, appeared to be the only course open to us if nothing transpired from the letters I had mailed out. But apart from some half-hearted packing, we did little else. How could we conceivably complete all the necessary procedures to book passage by ship to England, sell off the car and furniture, etc., then cross the continent to New York. It was just too much to contemplate. We decided after talking it over to just do as we had always done in the past:

wait upon God and do nothing until we had His clear guidance.

Slowly the replies began to trickle in, and with each one our hopes rose momentarily only to be dashed when we read the letter. I was disappointed but not surprised that, while each one of them expressed great interest, they uniformly deplored the fact that I was not a citizen of the United States, and that being the case, there was nothing they could do in the way of offering me employment. With only three full days left before we were due to report to the INS, and replies to all but one or two of my letters received, the situation looked bleak indeed. Not surprisingly we felt most discouraged.

That night our old friend George Walker came over for dinner and to commiserate with us, and he brought his fiancee, Betty, with him. George had resigned his major's commission in the British Army shortly after the Pacific war ended, and, as he had promised, he had come out to San Francisco to see us. In a very short time he had found employment. At first he stayed in our tiny apartment for two or three days, sleeping on the floor, and we then managed to find a room for him in a nearby rooming house, so we saw quite a lot of him. We learned that three delightful and very attractive young single women lived in the rooming house, and George was definitely showing great interest in at least two of them. Now, more than a year later, he had made his choice, and Betty was the one that we, too, had secretly chosen for him.

I had filled George in on our immigration troubles some time earlier, and it was very much on his mind. As we sat at the dining table, he somewhat casually remarked that he'd been discussing our problems with some of his office colleagues over lunch that day. One of them had commented that he knew of a place called Monterey, about 120 miles down the coast from San Francisco, and he'd heard there was an Army language school there where he thought Chinese was being taught. George knew of all the letters I had sent out and wondered if I had written to that school.

I had never even heard the name Monterey mentioned, although some years earlier, while working for the British Mission in San Francisco, we had gone to nearby Santa Cruz, on Monterey Bay, for a brief vacation. The Army language school had not been included on the list given me by Zack Jackson, but it looked like a possibility and was definitely worth a try. After we left the table I wrote a long letter giving details of my birth and years of residence in China. I added a few lines about my somewhat limited experience in teaching Chinese to missionaries and businessmen and asked if there was any possibility of a job opening as a teacher. Enclosing a self-addressed return envelope, I sealed the letter and without much enthusiasm asked George to mail it special delivery at the all-night post office when he went back to San Francisco that night. In the short time we had left, we had exhausted every possibility that I could think of, and our hopes had been dashed so often that I had little expectation that anything could come of that final letter or that they might consider hiring a non-citizen, and a Caucasian at that, to teach Chinese, but at least I had left no stone unturned.

The next day, knowing that two days later, at eight o'clock in the morning, we were due to report to the INS office, Eva and I felt so mentally and physically exhausted that we decided to take the day off and just do nothing at all. We called Miss McCabe to come in and keep Ruth company for the day, packed a lunch, and drove through the tunnel to the mainland and headed for Lake Merritt in the heart of Oakland. There we rented a rowboat and spent almost the entire day rowing around the lake, watching the birds, enjoying the sunshine and trying to forget the problems that faced us.

When we returned home around five o'clock that evening we found Miss McCabe in a state of excitement. She informed us that the telephone had been ringing repeatedly since noon. Someone was calling from Monterey and wanting to talk with me urgently. The last call had come just a few minutes before we entered the house, and the caller had left a number, but he had also said he would call back again the next morning at eight o'clock.

That was an exciting and astonishing development, and for the first time we began to feel there was perhaps a ray of hope. We slept very poorly that night. Promptly at eight o'clock the next morning I decided to call the number in Monterey that we had been given, thinking that since they had initiated so many calls from their end, the courteous thing for me to do would be to call them first. I picked up the telephone but found it was dead. No dial tone at all. I jiggled the hook a couple of times, then said "hello" and was astonished to hear a man's voice, with a strong Chinese accent, asking me if he could speak to Mr. Tharp. I switched to Chinese and told the caller I was Mr. Tharp, whereupon, in Chinese, he identified himself as Dr. Andrew Cheng, chairman of the Chinese Language Department at the Army Language School in Monterey. We chatted for a few moments inconsequentially in Chinese, with Dr. Cheng asking my Chinese name, and he then again asked if he could speak with Mr. Tharp. I assured him that I was Mr. Tharp and the person he wanted to talk with, but he replied, "No, that's impossible, you're Chinese; let me talk to the other man, the one I first talked with, the Englishman." It took several minutes to convince him I was one and the same individual. He then asked me to please wait a minute or so, and in the background I could hear him conversing in English with someone else.

A few minutes later an American came on the line and identified himself as Col. Barnwell of the United States Army. He told me he was the commandant of the school, that he had read my letter, and upon Dr. Cheng's strong recommendation, I met all their requirements as a teacher of the Chinese language, so when could I come to work?

Shocked, I thanked him and told him I was ready to start immediately, but there was one small problem. I explained to him in some detail our difficulties with the INS and what had brought them about, and I told him I was due to report to the INS the following morning at eight o'clock for deportation. Col, Barnwell took it in stride, as though it was an everyday affair, and simply brushed it aside with the remark, "Don't give it a second thought. I'll type up a letter right away offering you a job here in the national interest, and that'll take precedence over everything else. You'll be getting it first thing in the morning, special delivery. Just show the INS the letter and everything will be taken care of in due course."

Once again in our lives we'd seen a last-minute miracle. For that entire day Eva and I walked on clouds, our relief was so great. The next morning we watched eagerly for the mail carrier to bring the promised letter, but by the time I had to leave for the INS office, it had still not arrived. Giving Eva the number of the INS so she could call me when the letter came, I left for my appointment in Oakland.

Surprisingly, the surly INS officer was all smiles

when he saw me. He asked if we had completed our preparations for leaving the country. I replied that we were all packed but had not yet purchased our tickets to go anywhere because something else had come up. I explained that I'd been offered a job by the U.S. Army Language School in Monterey to teach Chinese. I told him that a special delivery letter, confirming my appointment, was on the way, and that I'd taken the liberty of giving his phone number to my wife, and that I expected her to call at any moment to say the letter had arrived.

The man's face underwent a dramatic change. He started to bluster and swear at me, accusing me of being up to my old tricks again, and his face and neck reddened. Suddenly he was stopped in mid-sentence by his phone ringing. After listening for a moment, he handed the phone to me, saying the call was from my wife. Eva said the letter from Monterey had been delivered, and should she open it?

I smiled at the INS officer and told him the expected letter had come and asked for an hour in which to return home and bring the letter back for him to see. There was little he could do but sullenly agree, and when I ultimately returned with the letter, he read and re-read it several times without commenting, obviously trying to think of a way out. Finally he handed the letter back to me and said the matter was now out of his hands, and without another word he turned and walked out of the room. The Department of Defense had greater clout than the Immigration and Naturalization Service, and for a time, at least, we could stay on in this country. So ended one of the most unpleasant chapters in our lives, with a conclusion so bizarre and implausible that even the most talented and adventurous novelist would have rejected such a last-minute reprieve as too improbable to be believed. Yet that is exactly what occurred. We'd learned once again that with God, all things are possible. Although our problems with the Immigration Service were far from over, we were at least spared deportation, and a new phase in our lives started the very next day.

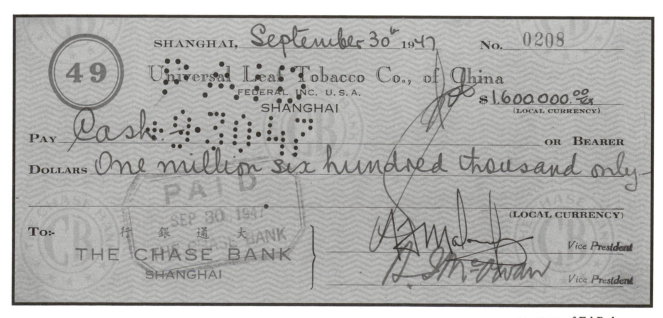

courtesy of Ed Bohannon

Bank check showing inflation in China, ca. 1947.

天上下雨地下滑,
個人摔倒個人爬.

Tianshang xia yu dixia hua,
geren shuai dao geren pa.

The ground gets slippery
after a sudden rain squall.
When you fall by yourself,
by yourself you must crawl.

(Moral: Don't expect any help
in life from others).

- Humorous Chinese Peasant Rhyme.

Book Five
1948 - 1993

Chapter Forty-Three
A New Career

The following day, May 10, 1948, I started early and drove alone down Highway 101, the 120 miles from San Francisco to Monterey. My heart was light after months of worry, and I thoroughly enjoyed the vast farm fields in the various valleys through which I passed. There were crops of all sorts, garlic near Gilroy and — new to me — the artichokes around Castroville. There were also acres upon acres of fruit trees, many in blossom; apples, cherries and plum trees predominated.

As I approached the Monterey Peninsula for the first time I was impressed by its beauty: the wide-open bay with deep blue water, the surf so close to the highway, and the spectacular background of dark green, pine-covered hills. I passed Fort Ord, bustling with activity.

The small-town atmosphere of the entire peninsula was a charming and refreshing change from the busy metropolises of San Francisco and Oakland, and I felt sure Eva and I were going to like the place.

But I began to have doubts as I entered the city of Monterey itself and was assailed by the overpowering smell of fish. Monterey at that time was the center of a thriving sardine canning business. Cannery Row, made famous by John Steinbeck's novels, was then in its heyday, its long row of canneries belching smoke and steam day and night — the source of the fish odor. May and June are the foggiest months of the year in Monterey. Under that low-hanging fog, the fish odor was particularly pungent. Fortunately the fog would usually clear around noon, and for a few hours there would be a respite from the smell. In the interior of China where I was born, we rarely ate fish, and only when we were at Beidaihe did my father sometimes catch fresh fish; therefore I never really acquired a taste for it and I found myself gagging from the powerful odor in Monterey. When I mentioned it to others they merely laughed, saying I would get used to it. I did, eventually, but it took me several months.

I found the Presidio, reported to the Army Language School, and was officially sworn in as an employee. I was hired as a Chinese language teacher, and thus began a career that was to last nearly thirty years. Immediately upon reporting at the school I met the commandant, Col. C.H. Barnwell. Tall, slender and impeccable in his uniform, he was a man I learned to admire. Over the next several months, as I got to know him, I found him to be a man of great integrity, compassion and understanding. He was a man who immediately earned the respect of everyone with whom he came in contact, and we became good friends.

While the Chinese department was only three months old, the Army Language School itself had been in existence for a number of years, although not in the same location. Established just prior to the outbreak of the war with Japan at the end of 1941, the school had initially been set up in two different locations: a classroom on the campus of the University of California at Berkeley and in an old airplane hangar at Crissy Field, near both the Presidio of San Francisco and the Golden Gate Bridge.

At the time, Army and Navy officials suddenly realized that war with Japan was imminent, and the U.S. had no Japanese-speaking linguists available. The Navy started teaching Japanese to officer students in October 1941 in Berkeley, while the Army began Japanese classes for a large number of second-generation Japanese-American recruits a month later. When, in 1942, all Japanese-American nationals were removed from the West Coast and interned, the Navy moved their school to Boulder, Colorado, while the Army went to Camp Savage, Minnesota.

During the war almost all students were trained only in Japanese. But after the war the two schools were combined and moved to Monterey, where they were housed in old pre-war wooden buildings on the historic Presidio grounds, and a number of other languages were added. But the teaching of Chinese had not been thought to be sufficiently important until early in 1948.

Col. Barnwell took me to the Chinese Language Department and introduced me to the chairman, Dr. Andrew I.S. Cheng. It was Dr. Cheng with whom I had spoken on the telephone two days previously. I also met the three or four other Chinese who comprised the staff of the department. The department,

having only been established some three months previously, had only two classes in session at the time, but new classes were scheduled to begin every two or three months.

I was temporarily quartered in the BOQ (Bachelor Officers' Quarters) for that night, and having met all the people I would need to know, asked about a place to live. I was directed to the housing authority, where I was told nothing was available in family units either on or off the base. I would have to live in the Bachelor Officers' Quarters until I could find accommodations off the base for my family. However, upon presenting my problem to the sympathetic ear of Col. Barnwell, we were allotted a two-bedroom house in what was then called Ord Village, a housing development on the southern end of the sprawling, 28,000-acre Fort Ord Army base, about six miles from the language school.

We vacated the rented house in Alameda and moved down to Monterey as soon as we could, carrying most of our belongings with us and shipping our trunks down on the railway. The house assigned to us was one of a row of identical houses, probably a hundred or so in all, on a winding street in the village. Most of the occupants were Army officers with their families, but a few civilians like us were also quartered there. We lived there for several months, enjoying the surroundings and the friendliness of our neighbors.

We were glad the house was fully furnished, because we owned no furniture. However, the house itself posed some problems for my sister Ruth. The two bedrooms were on the second floor, while the bathroom was on the ground floor, and that made it very difficult for Eva or me to help her negotiate the narrow stairway numerous times each day. But with Eva's constant care and the exercises Ruth was given as therapy, her condition improved to the extent that she was able to go out and walk the quiet streets by herself. Once or twice she fell, and having the use of only one arm, was unable to get up by herself. Neighbors, not knowing where she was from, called an ambulance, which eventually brought her back home. While Eva and I were quite concerned about it, Ruth found the incident amusing. However, because of the possibility of her falling again with no one to help her, Eva decided to teach her how to get up without assistance. In order to simulate Ruth's disability,

Eva tied one of her own hands behind her back and practiced getting up from the floor with the use of just one arm. Then she taught Ruth how to do it. After that Ruth went out by herself and became well known in the neighborhood.

As soon as we had completed moving into the house, I was thrown with no prior introduction into my new life as a teacher. I was simply handed a set of textbooks and was assigned certain hours with the two classes then in session. The first group of about seven men had been there exactly three months. The second, about the same number of men, had arrived there just a day or two before I did.

The students in those early days in the Chinese Department were predominantly Army and Air Force officers, with a sprinkling of Navy men. In each class, though, one or two lower-ranking individuals were always mixed in with the officers. There was one strict rule in the classrooms: everyone was there as a student and rank meant nothing whatsoever. All students were to be treated as equals and were to treat each other in the same way.

I started my teaching career with considerable trepidation but tremendous enthusiasm. In those days there were comparatively few women in the services and none that I knew of studying at the language school. I found it most challenging to work with those bright young men — and some of them not so young. My only prior experience in teaching had been in China, where I had worked with young missionary candidates of both sexes, but only in a very haphazard fashion. Now I had to organize my classes, develop lesson plans, devise homework assignments, and write new materials. But above all, I had to write and evaluate bi-weekly examinations, and that became extremely challenging.

Westerners had been learning Chinese in China for over a hundred years before I started to teach it. The missionaries, businessmen and diplomats had all used the old-fashioned one-on-one method with a Chinese teacher — few of whom knew any English — sitting opposite the student reading from a Chinese text while the poor student repeated after him and tried to figure out what it meant. Usually phrases and sentences were committed to memory; it had always been thus. I still have a copy of what was called *Baller's Mandarin Primer*, originally published in 1911, and as the fly leaf indicates, it was "prepared for junior members of the China Inland Mission." My copy is from the ninth edition, revised and enlarged in 1915, not long after the revolution of 1911. The author in his foreword remarked: "...the terminology consequent on the establishment of a Republic has been added, though at this writing it seems possible that terms suitable to a monarchy may supersede them ere long. No one can tell what will come out of the Witches' Cauldron of New China politics." He wasn't right about a monarchy, but certainly tremendous changes in the language took place after 1915 as the terminology of the old Chinese Empire faded from use.

It was not until the 1920s that a school for the teaching of Chinese was established in Beijing (Peking), and so far as I know it was the first of its kind. The man who started the school was W. B. Pettus of the YMCA, who had made contributions to earlier language texts. *Baller's Primer*, although covering a tremendous range of subjects, was primarily intended for missionaries, so Pettus wrote his own textbook, coming up with a methodology that more closely approached the classroom techniques of today. The text was used with considerable success at his school in Beijing for a number of years, the students coming from a wide range of society.

In 1948, although the teaching of Eastern languages in this country was relatively new, some of the larger universities, such as Yale and Harvard, had pioneered Chinese language programs during World War II. Hundreds of military men had gone through brief but intensive courses, and the teaching staffs had gained valuable experience. At the same time they had developed texts much more sophisticated and up-to-date than the Pettus text. However, neither I nor anyone else at the Army Language School had ever heard of them, so we had no recourse but to start from scratch. When the Chinese Language Department was formed at the Army Language School, the only textbook that could be found in San Francisco bookstores was the Pettus book. Although in its way it was a good basic text, the more we used it for military students, the more unsuitable we found it to be. The job requirements for servicemen were different from those of missionaries, businessmen and diplomats. As a result, as the weeks went by I found myself writing more and more adjunct materials to broaden the students' knowledge of Chinese military terminology, and at the same time I was familiarizing myself with their learning problems and the shortcomings of language textbooks, as well as finding out my own strengths and weaknesses.

In the years since 1948 I have come to know many of the widely different commandants who succeeded Col. Barnwell at the school, but I still look back to him as one of the wisest and most far-sighted of them all. He, like me, was new at the job, but unlike many of his successors, he was never afraid to try something different. He was completely flexible and ever ready to recognize and admit his mistakes. It takes a great man to do that.

To us, as teachers, it was sometimes frustrating when, as it seemed, every few weeks we were being urged to try some new method. Some techniques worked well, but many didn't. However, as I look back now, some forty years later, one of the ideas that Col. Barnwell introduced was simple and common-sense and, in my opinion, a most brilliant concept. Unfortunately, although it worked extremely well at the time — certainly as far as I personally was concerned — it was not well liked by the teaching staff as a whole. After a couple of years, when Col. Barnwell was replaced, the practice was dropped, never again to be used as far as I know.

The concept quite simply was that every new teacher, male or female, needed to be put into the position of a student in order to understand their viewpoint. To that end Col. Barnwell issued an order that all incoming teachers, as well as those already in place, would be required to spend two weeks learning a language other than the one they had been hired to teach. We were given a choice of the five different languages being taught at the school.

As I remember, the five languages were French, Japanese, Chinese, German and Arabic. Because I already knew some French, and Japanese and Chinese were both quite familiar to me, I had actually only the choice between German and Arabic. For some reason Arabic appealed to me, and for two weeks, I and my fellow teacher-students in the class were treated exactly like any of the military students. To me, and I am sure it was the same for my companions, the experiment was not only a traumatic and humbling experience, it was also an eye-opener such as one could never otherwise have encountered.

I was suddenly and relentlessly made to realize just how my students felt being exposed to a strange language. I felt a complete idiot trying to mimic those strange sounds the teacher was pronouncing; I felt an even bigger fool when called upon to respond to questions in the language and being unable to do so because I couldn't remember how to put together the odd-sounding words, nor could I remember the words themselves. Nevertheless, in every way it was a most rewarding experience; it taught me not only to have a sympathetic view toward every student who came my way, but at the same time, and more importantly perhaps, it taught me a great deal about how to teach something that was familiar to me but totally new to my students. My Arabic teacher was good at his job, but sitting in front of him as a student, I could not but find fault with much of his methodology. As I applied that knowledge and experience to myself, I realized that I, too, made many of the same mistakes in the classroom with my own students. Looking back now, some forty years later, I know that those two weeks as a student learning Arabic did more to help me become a good teacher than anything else I had experienced before or since.

A few weeks later, Col. Barnwell called me into his office and asked me to take over the job of teaching the Chinese class for all new incoming teachers. I felt it to be a great honor, and because of the rewards I had achieved through the experience, I made certain that all the teachers who were sent to me for two weeks went away feeling that they had not only acquired an introduction to Chinese, but a new insight into just how it felt to be a student and how best to get their message across in their own classes.

Over the many years since, I have been exposed to hundreds of colleagues teaching Chinese, as well as teachers of other languages, and have watched and participated in dozens of supposedly more sophisticated ways of carrying out what is euphemistically known as "teacher training." In my opinion, none even approaches the success of that very simple but straightforward process used more than forty years ago. Nowadays, in most places the new language teacher in training is pampered and babied along and given vast amounts of theory but little in the way of active participation or practice in teaching, or in what it means to the student to learn a language. From my observations, the individual conducting the training sessions usually cites examples and gives demonstrations, but all in an artificial setting. When the student-teacher is required to practice the teaching methodology that has been demonstrated, it is in the unnatural environment with fellow teachers rather than with scared and bewildered students. At the same time, although perhaps exposed briefly to some other foreign or artificial language in the training sessions, or to some supposedly novel and "innovative" approach, it is again usually in such a packaged form that the emphasis is primarily placed on the teacher's skill in making the presentation, not on the realistic problems that the students face as they sit there with a feeling of loneliness, bewilderment and incompetency, listening to something utterly beyond their comprehension.

In the months that followed, as I taught classes and met new students, I was constantly reminded of how small I had felt in trying to mouth those strange Arabic sounds. Repeating them after the teacher, I was certain at the time that I was saying them exactly as the teacher had said them, but the teacher kept correcting me, never once quite explaining just how I ought to place my tongue or shape my mouth in order to correct my pronunciation, nor was I ever told where I was going wrong. It made me feel small and insecure in front of my peers and I realized that all my students undoubtedly felt the same way those first days in class as I tried to teach them the unfamiliar Chinese words.

Above all, I think those two weeks of being a student helped me understand the student's viewpoint and gave me a deep sense of sympathy toward him and his insecurities, and impressed on me the need for not only gaining the confidence and trust of my students, but at the same time motivating him in his struggle with the newness and complexities of the Chinese language.

Working with those young men was sheer delight. Some, of course, were quite senior officers, even an occasional general, and many of them a great deal older than I. At the outset that tended to give me a feeling of insecurity myself. However, one day I happened to visit the French department and saw a sign posted prominently on the wall in one of the classrooms: "You as a student may know a great deal more than your teacher about many things, but he is the one who knows more about the language you are learning." I took that to heart and from then on had no further qualms about my youth.

Most of the incoming classes in those early days were composed of only a half dozen students at most. Their task was to learn the Chinese language: speaking, comprehending, reading, and, to a more limited extent, writing. All were destined to be assigned to posts in the Far East, either Taiwan, Korea or Thailand, where listening posts had been set up to monitor all the radio traffic from mainland China. However, directives from Washington were rather vague. No one quite knew what was wanted from the student and the situation was further complicated since the Army wanted one thing, the Navy something else, while the Air Force's needs were totally different. The end result was that in trying to please all three of the services, none of them were completely satisfied, and as the early classes graduated and went out into the field, highly unfavorable reports came back. Each branch of the services had its own specific complaints. The Air Force complained that we were not giving the men enough military or flight terminology for them to understand the Chinese pilots; the Army, that their men were not learning enough written Chinese to translate captured documents; and the Navy, from which we had only a limited number of men, naturally wanted naval terminology stressed.

Col. Barnwell was a pragmatic individual who urged us to try anything we thought would work toward meeting the goals of the different services. At the same time he was anxious to try out anything in the way of "gimmickry" that might aid the student. "Total immersion" in the language was for some time the key phrase. No English at all was to be spoken in or around the classrooms during school hours. In the classroom the teacher was not permitted to use English in the way of explanation, and naturally, with the limited grasp of Chinese that the student had, it became difficult to get across the considerable differences in Chinese sentence structure as compared with English. When it came to lexical items, new terminology that the student had to learn, hand gestures and finger pointing were mandatory.

That procedure worked well within a limited vocabulary range. Even so, it could lead to serious misunderstanding. For example, when we Caucasians speak of ourselves, we tend to point to our chests when we say "me" or "I." But it is quite characteristic of the Chinese to point to the tip of their nose when doing the same thing. As a result, many of the students formed the initial impression that the Chinese word *wo* that the teacher said while pointing to his nose meant "nose" instead of "me." Another example came when the teacher was giving the words for various military ranks. He would point to the shoulder insignia of a student and say the Chinese equivalent, but the student more often than not thought he was being taught the word for "shoulder." The obvious difficulties of that methodology soon became apparent and our instructions were modified to allow a modicum of English in the classroom in the interests of saving time and avoiding confusion.

Other experiments were tried and later abandoned. At one time half the class were given textbooks and the other half was not. The idea was to determine whether the latter group would learn more quickly if exposed only to oral instruction. The result was that neither group did well. Those with texts were jealous of the others who did not have to do any text-based homework. And those without texts quite naturally "cheated" by writing what they could on their shirt cuffs or bits of paper in order to help them remember what they had heard. As a result, they wrote the Chinese sounds incorrectly nine times out of ten. That experiment lasted only a few weeks before it, too, was abandoned.

Another much-touted theory that lasted a number of years was the idea that while asleep, the subconscious mind was still awake and was aware of all sounds. Students were supplied with phonograph records to be played continuously throughout the night as they slept; other students volunteered to change the records as necessary. In no instance that I knew of did it prove to be of any significant help. The student who was sleeping generally slept undisturbed, or was unable to get to sleep because of the noise, while other students sleeping in the same quarters complained of the disturbance. The only person who benefited from the experience was the one operating the phonograph player. He, at least, got a lot of extra exposure to the language.

As late as the 1960s that theory was still strongly advocated in many quarters. I recall two students, a husband and wife, whom we had at Yale around that time. The husband, a captain, was having a difficult time of it. His wife, on the other hand, a civilian working for the Army, was doing very well with the language.

They asked me about the theory of learning while asleep, and I told them of how unsuccessful the experiments had been years before in Monterey. However, they wanted to try it, so I supplied the wife with all she would need, and for nearly a month she sat up most of the night changing records on the player while her husband slept soundly. It did nothing for him, but the wife's comprehension ability progressed remarkably, despite her lack of sleep. In those first early classes at Monterey, a small number of the students were recruits, but most of the officers and some of the non-commissioned officers had served during World War II, a number of them in the CBI, or China-Burma-India, theater. All of the latter had interesting wartime experiences to recount, but two of those students in the third class stand out in my memory. One was a young Army Air Corps lieutenant named MacMillan, who had been an Army photographer during World War II. He had been posted in Chongqing (Chungking) with the wartime U.S. Embassy, and had some fascinating tales to tell of his assignments. One of them bears retelling.

In October 1934 a large force of Chinese Communists had become encircled in Jiangxi Province by Chinese Nationalist troops. Knowing that certain annihilation awaited them, they determined to break out and head north to a more remote part of China where they could reorganize. Headed by Mao Ze-dong and Zhou En-lai, a force of 80,000 men and 35 women started what was to become known as the "Long March." Almost exactly a year later on October 20, 1935, the march ended at Yan'an (Yen'an) in Shanxi Province with only about 8,000 to 9,000 of the original 80,000 men remaining. The rest had split off or died along the way, either in battle with the Guomindang (Kuomintang or KMT) forces, or from disease and cold.

In Yan'an Mao regrouped his forces and was joined by other Communist forces from elsewhere in China. As time went on and Chinese Nationalist forces showed less and less inclination to fight the Japanese, the large force under Mao began to look attractive to U.S. military planners because of its demonstrated aggressiveness against the Japanese. In July 1944 a small "observer group" under Col. David Barrett, a Chinese linguist, was sent in to Yan'an to explore the possibilities of rearming the Communist forces to make them even more effective against the Japanese, but nothing came of it.

In 1945 after a stream of Western visitors had visited Yan'an, among them some U.S. diplomats and news reporters, including the well-known Edgar Snow, glowing reports were written of the marvelous results that were being seen by Mao's troops in the field, and of his agricultural "reforms." Even some State Department personnel were taken in by what they saw and thought the Chinese Communists would be the saviors of the country and should be supported by the U.S. government. At the same time the Communists themselves started talking about forming a coalition government with the Nationalists. As a result, the American government gave even more attention to Mao.

By that time President Roosevelt had died and been replaced by President Truman, who dispatched Patrick Hurley to China, first as a special envoy to survey the situation, and then as ambassador to China with his embassy in Chongqing. In August 1945, Ambassador Hurley flew to Yan'an to personally escort Mao Ze-dong to Chongqing for negotiations with Chiang Kai-shek. The talks resulted in a measure of compromise between the two factions, but eventually came to naught.

It was on that trip to Yan'an by Ambassador Hurley (widely known among newsmen as "Hurley Burley"), that my young student friend MacMillan was sent along as official photographer to record the event for posterity.

Flying in a two-engined C-47 (the military version of the DC-3), the party approached the makeshift Yan'an airstrip. As the pilot flew low over the field, they could see the welcoming party gathered at a point close to the end of the air strip. However, Ambassador Hurley didn't like the arrangement so he ordered the pilot to land the plane and sent his interpreter over to tell Mao and his party to line up at a given point elsewhere on the field. The plane then took off again and circled the field until the welcoming party were in place below at the point Hurley had indicated.

When Ambassador Hurley was satisfied that all the people were in place, he directed the pilot to land and taxi to where the welcoming group of Chinese was standing, telling the pilot to stop the plane so that the door of the plane would open directly opposite the welcoming party.

My student photographer friend was told to get off the plane first and stand where he could film Ambassador Hurley coming down the steps from the plane. When all was ready, Hurley came bounding down the steps shouting his famous Choctaw war cry at the top of his voice, then he warmly embraced the first Chinese in line, taking him to be Mao Ze-dong. However, Mao was actually last in line, so the whole thing had to be repeated for the movie camera. Once more Hurley bounded down the steps voicing his war cry and on that occasion embraced the right individual. Naturally, all that didn't sit very well with the very conservative Chinese. It also caused considerable embarrassment to the State Department officials who were accompanying the ambassador. One wonders how Mao Ze-dong recorded the event in his personal journal!

In the same class with the young ex-photographer was another young Air Corps 1st Lieutenant named Delmar C. Lang, known to everyone as Del. He was a remarkably apt pupil, highly motivated and extremely intelligent. He, too, had served in the U.S. Army Air Corps during the war, and, like MacMillan, he had been in China from mid-1944 until shortly after the war ended in 1945. However, his assignment had been as a forward air controller for the Army Air Corps, which took over from General Claire Chennault and his Flying Tigers, who were in support of the Chinese fighting the Japanese. Their mission was to bomb the Japanese forces in the western part of China and later in Japan itself.

Del, with a team of two U.S. Army sergeants and a Chinese second lieutenant as an interpreter, had been stationed near a small village called Zhaoyi near the junction of the Wei and the Yellow rivers, some 90 miles east of Xi'an in what is now Shaanxi Province. Del's headquarters was just outside Xi'an, and his job had been to initiate air strikes when he saw a good opportunity or when requested by the two Chinese Army Divisions he was supporting. Del had some fabulous stories of his experiences there. By and large the Chinese and Japanese armies facing each other across the Yellow River were content to let things remain quiet for months at a time, the Chinese Guomindang forces husbanding their strength to later fight the Communist forces, which lay only a short distance to their north, and the Japanese, weary after years of fighting in China, only too glad to sit out the rest of the war.

Del told one story of a bombing strike that was called in to wipe out the officer corps of the opposing Japanese forces. His intelligence had learned that the Japanese officers gathered each noon in a certain pagoda-like structure in the middle of a village across the river to dally with the "Comfort Girls" — mainly Korean peasant girls kidnapped by the Japanese to serve as prostitutes — and to have lengthy lunches. One day a strike was timed for the lunch hour and the entire structure was destroyed together with other primary targets.

When World War II ended Del returned to the United States, left the service, and married a delightful woman named Terry. They had two children by 1948, when he re-enlisted in the Air Corps at his former rank. Because of his love for China, he asked for and got Chinese language training in Monterey, but the fact that he completed the course was a small miracle in itself. Everything seemed to be against him.

There were only five men in Del's class, and he'd been in Monterey only about three months when, for some unexplained reason, but presumably in the interests of saving money, someone in Washington decided to eliminate his entire class. No explanation was given either to Del, to us teachers, or to the commandant of the school. The order came down and that was that. All five were given orders posting them elsewhere.

I was extremely annoyed when I heard the news. In Lt. Lang I saw the potential of not only an excellent Chinese linguist, but also a leader, and I wasn't about to let him go without a fight. First I went to see Col. Barnwell and pleaded to have Lang reinstated. But the colonel told me his hands were tied and there was nothing he could do about it.

But there was something I could do. As a civilian I was not bound by military rules and protocol and I could go over the colonel's head. I drove to the Western Union office in Monterey, where I drafted a long telegram addressed simply to: "The Commanding General, United States Air Force, The Pentagon, Washington, D.C." In the telegram I detailed all the reasons why an exception should be made in the case of Lt. Lang and why, with his extraordinary potential as a Chinese linguist, I felt he should be reinstated. I felt he was an invaluable asset to the Air Force and foresaw that he would some day prove invaluable to that service.

Within 24 hours an answer came back, but not to me. It was addressed to Col. Barnwell. I was called to headquarters and a very annoyed commandant rebuked me for going over his head. He told me he had received orders for Lt. Lang to be reinstated. However, he said there was no possible way in which Lang could continue his studies as a class of one, and since no new incoming classes were due for several months, he had no option but to put Lang into the class that was three months ahead of him.

I was afraid the news would discourage Lang, since the others were so far ahead of him, but it didn't at all. His desire to learn Chinese was so strong that he jumped at the opportunity. With a wife and two small children in his small apartment, his opportunities for studying on his own were limited, but he dug in his heels and doggedly set about catching up with the others. Almost every evening after class I would either spend time at the school tutoring him or he would come over to our house after supper for a few hours. Eventually he not only caught up, but surpassed the others in his class and graduated with honors. The particular class he joined had started with six individuals, but only two survived in addition to Lang. One was a Lt. Reg Gilbert and the other a major named Matthews, of whom I shall have more to say later. In the end, though, it all appeared to have been a complete waste of both Lang's and my time and effort. After graduation he was sent to Brooks Air Force Base in San Antonio, Texas, where he was assigned as adjutant for a squadron being formed to go to Alaska, where there would not be the slightest chance of his using his extensive knowledge of Chinese. However, before the squadron moved out his wife Terry became pregnant with their third child and Del was allowed to remain in San Antonio until the child was born.

When the war in Korea started, Lang was assigned to the Personnel Section, where he was responsible for calling up reserve officers to active duty. I had kept in touch with him, and I thought at the time that my efforts on his behalf had all been in vain. However, I had underestimated Lang's persuasive abilities as well as his farsightedness. Unknown to me or to the general public at the time, a dangerous situation was coming to a head in Korea. It was then that forward-looking Lang foresaw the eventual entry of Communist Chinese forces into the Korean War and made loud noises to his superiors pointing out that before long there would be a tremendous demand for Americans with a knowledge of both Korean and Chinese. He talked himself out of the assignment to Alaska and prepared a convincing argument for his superiors that the program in Chinese at the Army Language School in Monterey was inadequate for the Air Force's needs and that an all-Air Force school for Chinese linguists should be set up elsewhere, preferably at one of the leading universities. As a direct result of his efforts, but after a very considerable delay, the Air Force started negotiations with Yale University, which resulted in a Chinese language program being established there in 1951, a program that was to continue for 15 years. I became a part of that program, also directly through Lang's intervention and efforts. But I am getting ahead of myself. In a later chapter I shall have much more to say about that remarkable individual to whom our country owes a great debt of gratitude.

In the class just ahead of Lang's was another remarkable individual, Maj. Jack McClure, from whom I learned several very important lessons in language learning and teaching that I've never forgotten. One of them concerned something to which at the time neither I nor anyone else could give a name, but which I later learned to call "language aptitude." A few years older than I, Jack was a very quiet and unassuming individual who rarely spoke unless addressed. From the very beginning he appeared to be a bright student, but in my first two weeks of contact with him I became disappointed by his attitude in class. Where with most students I was able to establish direct eye contact, with Jack McClure it was near to impossible unless I spoke directly to him and asked him a question. For almost the entire class hour he sat with his eyes closed, appearing to be asleep, apparently unaware of what was going on around him. Only when called upon to participate directly would he "wake up" and say his piece, whereupon he always did exceptionally well. On several occasions I was at the point of taking him aside to caution him to show a little more interest in class. But I desisted, thinking that perhaps with a young family he had to study late at night and perhaps wasn't getting enough sleep. How wrong I was.

At that time the program called for a major test at the end of every two-week period. When test day came I was dumbfounded to find that Jack McClure was letter-perfect in all his answers and far outshone the entire class in his overall performance. I discovered that he had what is often called a photographic memory. Sitting with his eyes closed was his way of focusing his entire attention on what he was hearing so that nothing escaped him. By the end of the course his mastery of Chinese was nothing short of phenomenal, and I realized that he was one of those rare individuals who have a natural aptitude for languages, in addition to his extraordinary mental capacity. In almost forty years of teaching I've only seen two or three others like him.

Like Lt. Lang, at the end of the course Jack McClure got his assignment. In the supreme wisdom of the Army it turned out to be the Russian desk in the Pentagon instead of someplace where his knowledge of Chinese could be used. He remained on the Russian desk for several years, even after hostilities began in Korea, and eventually became so proficient in Russian that he was more valuable in that slot than he would have been on the Chinese desk. I was deeply saddened a few years later to learn of his untimely death from what (if I remember correctly) was a brain tumor.

Maj. Matthews, the third member of Del Lang's class, was more fortunate. After graduation he was sent directly to Taiwan, where his knowledge of Chinese was well used. He remained there for several years and his several children were all enrolled in Chinese schools, where they became extremely proficient in Chinese. In later years, at least one of his daughters made a name for herself in Chinese-speaking circles.

While writing of Maj. Matthews I am reminded of an incident that occurred during those early months in Monterey that points up some of the differences between Chinese and American cultures. As the classes grew in size and frequency of admission, there was a need for more teachers. The Army brought over a man named Wu from the U.S. Embassy in Beijing after it closed down with the Communist takeover. We were all surprised at his almost flawless English.

But poor Dr. Wu arrived in this country a frustrated and disillusioned man. Something had gone wrong in the preparation of his travel documents in Beijing and the immigration people in Hawaii had yanked him off the plane and locked him up for several days until the matter could be cleared up. Not surprisingly, that soured Dr. Wu's perception of American efficiency in just about every area, and from the moment he arrived all we heard from him were complaints about everything and everyone around him.

A tall, dignified man, he wore his hair cut short and refused to wear Western clothes. He always dressed in the traditional long satin or silk gowns of the Chinese educated class, and it was rare indeed to see him crack a smile. His students tried their best to amuse him, but he apparently found their efforts childish and at all times maintained his dignified and aloof manner. Being a single man, Dr. Wu was given a room in the Bachelor Officers' Quarters on the Presidio grounds and ate in the Officers' Club. But nothing suited him. His room was unsatisfactory, the food was terrible, and every single day when he came into the teachers' office, we heard nothing but complaints. Despite his broad knowledge of English, he was an extremely conservative individual who categorically refused to learn American ways, and unlike most of his Chinese associates, he refused to mingle with the students between and after classes.

In those early days, all civilian teachers were given the same privileges on base as military officers. We had the use of the Officers' Club, where we could go for our midmorning coffee break and lunch, and could play the slot machines as much as we wished. We could also use the barber shop and the PX and commissary, where we could purchase articles for daily use a good deal cheaper than on the outside market. Additionally, we were welcomed in the base cinema theaters, both at the Presidio and at Fort Ord, and could see current films for a fraction of the price charged in the downtown theaters. There was just one rule, however, about going to the base theaters. Every man had to wear a tie.

One evening Dr. Wu was feeling a little bored and decided to go to a movie. Knowing the rule about ties, he interpreted it as meaning he should wear "formal" dress. Accordingly, he put on his most formal Chinese clothing, a long gown, topped with a short coat made of black satin, with a decorative pattern throughout, and of course buttoned up tightly at the throat. At the door to the theater he was stopped by a young military policeman, who told him he couldn't go in because he wasn't wearing a tie. For Dr. Wu, that was an insult of the highest order. He remonstrated vehemently with the military policeman, but to no avail. He was told to go back and put on a tie. Dr. Wu was so upset he marched directly to the nearby home of Col. Barnwell and lodged a complaint. The colonel was most sympathetic and personally escorted him back to the theater and gave orders to the young GI to let him in, and issued orders that thereafter any of the civilian teachers dressed in their native clothes were exempt from the "tie" order and should be admitted without questioning.

Maj. Matthews was an extremely serious individual when it came to learning the Chinese language and everything associated with it, and Dr. Wu's unhappiness with American life bothered him greatly. He made a concerted effort to try and convince Dr. Wu that there was more to the way Americans lived than was to be seen on an Army base, and as often as he could talk Dr. Wu into accepting, invited him to his home to meet his wife and two small children, where they shared a typical American meal.

On one occasion when Maj. Matthews had a two-week vacation coming up, he extended an invitation to Dr. Wu to join the family on an automobile tour of the redwood forests of Northern California. Dr. Wu eagerly accepted, and they headed north.

Toward evening of the first day they pulled into a campground and started to unpack their gear. Mrs. Matthews cooked a meal on a camp stove and they ate off a picnic table. But as darkness began to fall, Dr. Wu asked where they were going to sleep. Maj. Matthews showed him a sleeping bag he had brought along for him and told him they were going to sleep on the ground. Dr. Wu was horrified. "Not me" he said, "I have never slept on the ground and I'm not going to start now."

A compromise was reached by laying a sleeping bag on top of one of the nearby picnic tables for Dr. Wu, and they all retired for the night. Most unfortunately, during the night Dr. Wu turned in his sleep and rolled off the table onto the ground. That did it for him! It was the last straw. Furious, and without awakening the Matthews family, he dressed and strode off into the darkness to the nearby highway, where he thumbed a ride back to Monterey on the first bus that came along. Not too long after that he returned to China a thoroughly disgruntled man, and it was rumored he went to work for one of the Chinese Communist English-language publications, where, with his excellent knowledge of English, I am quite sure he was in the forefront of those writing anti-American propaganda.

But strangely, that wasn't the last we heard of Dr. Wu. Almost exactly forty years later, in 1984, a young American Navy officer and his wife were visiting Beijing. Like all tourists they took in the renowned Temple of Heaven. As they stood there admiring the architecture and the superb colorations of the building, a soft-voiced individual behind them addressed them in impeccable English, asking them where they "hailed from in the United States." When they replied that they were from Monterey, the gray-haired man told them he had been in Monterey at one time and proceeded to tell them how he had taught at the Army language school there. He happened to have a picture of himself in his wallet, which he gave to the young couple, and a week or so later when they returned to the U.S., they told me the story and showed the picture to me. It was my old friend Dr. Wu.

Despite the seeming security of having a job with the United States government, our immigration troubles were by no means over. The Army Language School could do nothing more for us than ask for an extension of my parole, and in Eva's case, an extension of her visitor's visa. Since she had not left the country as I had, she was simply overstaying her visa and was in a better position than I. As a result, every six months I had to appear before an INS Board of Inquiry for an evaluation of my status. However, each time I went, the Army always gave me a letter stating that my presence in the country was of vital importance to the national interest, particularly because of the war in Korea. Each time I got a six-month extension of my parole without any problem, and Eva as my wife got an extension of her visitor's visa. But we were not getting any further with our desire to become U.S. citizens.

Many of my colleagues at the Army Language School, both Chinese and others, were also "temporary visitors" in this country. For them, however, there was a law that allowed them, after two years of residence, to qualify for special status that would give them the coveted "green card" of a resident alien.

Unfortunately for me, as far as the INS was concerned, I was "officially" not in the country. Therefore my time of residence here counted for nothing, and the extensions of my parole did not count toward the requisite two years of residence. As such, I was at a severe disadvantage.

At that time there was an INS office in Salinas, a town about 20 miles from Monterey, so we didn't have to travel too far for our regular six-month hearings. Along about our third visit to the INS to seek our extensions, one of the younger officers took me aside and in a friendly manner suggested that if I managed to get my wife pregnant, with the baby being born in this country, our status would immediately be changed and our problems would be over. Forty years ago that was the INS ruling for parents of a child born in the United States. Today it is quite different, and not until the child is 21 are the parents able to take advantage of their child's American nationality and automatically qualify for permanent residence and citizenship.

I was not unaware of that particular loophole in the law, and another one that allowed an individual marrying an American citizen to also gain a special status leading to early citizenship. Both loopholes were greatly abused and I strongly objected to them in principle. I'd seen several of my colleagues making "marriages of convenience," often simply picking up the first woman they could find in San Francisco, be she bar girl or prostitute, and marrying her simply to get by the INS, and the idea of conceiving a child specifically for that purpose rankled with both Eva and me. If we wanted a child, we wanted one for reasons other than that.

When, on our subsequent visit to the INS in Salinas six months later, the same young man asked me point-blank if my wife was pregnant or not, I again thanked him for his suggestion, which I believed to have been made in good faith, but told him very candidly just how I felt about the law and of our desire to gain U.S. citizenship on our own merits, not on the strength of a baby conceived for that specific purpose. I am sure the poor young man was much perplexed by my seeming inflexibility.

That was the latter part of 1949 and shortly thereafter some new hope came into our lives. My father, who by that time had already become a naturalized U.S. citizen on the strength of having married Mrs.

Isabel French, happened to be visiting in Washington, D.C. At church one Sunday he met Dr. Walter Judd, a congressman from Minnesota who had himself been a missionary in China for a number of years. Father told Congressman Judd about my case, and Dr. Judd wrote me for details and subsequently introduced a bill in Congress to have the situation corrected. Unfortunately, as so often happens in those cases, with the pressure of business and so many other bills in the hopper, his bill did not manage to pass the House before adjournment at the end of the year, and thus fell by the wayside. But unknown to me at the time, other events were happening that ultimately had a significant effect on our lives and at the same time brought about a change in our position with the INS.

We had stayed on in the house the Army provided us in Ord Village for about six months, but the awkwardness of its being a two-story building with the bathroom on the ground floor and the bedrooms upstairs made it increasingly inconvenient where Ruth was concerned. As we began to feel a little more secure in our position with the school and had managed to save a little money, we started to look around and explore the possibility of buying a small, single-story house, which would be so much better all round.

One day I saw an ad in the paper for a three-room house, with no price stated, just a telephone number, but it seemed to be about the size we could afford. We called the number and a man answered, told us where to find the place, and asked us to go over and look at it, so Eva and I, full of hope, went to see the place.

The house was in the neighboring town of Seaside, high on a hilltop overlooking Monterey Bay and up against the Fort Ord military reservation fence with a magnificent, million-dollar view of the entire peninsula. It was almost completely isolated, the nearest house of any size being about four blocks away, and it was surrounded by a six-foot-high redwood fence, with a lot of pine trees growing behind it, both designed to shield the house from the strong ocean winds. It at once captured our hearts and we knew it was the place for us.

A young man answered the doorbell and showed us around, although there wasn't a great deal to see. The place was well furnished, with a large double bed in the bedroom, but apparently he was living there alone

and we were somewhat puzzled by that.

When we ventured to ask the price, the young man said we could have the house and everything in it for $3,000. He must have seen the unbelieving, astonished expressions on our faces, because he hastened to tell us that he had just been divorced, that it had been a very messy and painful experience for him, and he wanted to get away from it all as soon as possible and not take with him any reminders of his ex-wife.

I had received a small salary increase since starting with the school. Even so, with my annual salary of $3,200, it was almost a full year's pay. However, it seemed too good a bargain to pass up and we decided to take the place. I went to a bank and got a small loan to cover part of the price, and a couple of weeks later we moved in.

Eva was particularly delighted with the kitchen and all the wonderful utensils. The place, modern in every way, was equipped with cupboards full of pots and pans of the highest quality, all of which had been wedding presents to the young couple.

Ruth enjoyed the new house. In her own room she had lots of space to move around and a place for her own desk, where she loved to sit and write letters. It was a big improvement for her, and with her increased mobility and no stairs to negotiate, she could go outside unassisted and exercise in the large garden that fronted the house, and behind the fence she was sheltered from the wind that swept up the hill. I, on the other hand, was delighted to find a full set of carpentry and mason's tools and immediately started to make plans to expand the place.

After ten years of marriage that was only the second house we could call our own. In Lingyuan we had lived in our first home for barely three years before the war started, and since then had lived in a variety of prison camps and rented places. Situated as it was on top of a hill, that Seaside place was in many ways our dream house.

I must mention that very soon after we moved in, we acquired a little dog named Penny. Penny was of a nondescript breed, but she was unquestionably the smartest little dog we'd ever seen. She was originally owned by Del Lang, and when they left, they were unable to take her with them, so they gave her to us. Penny picked up new tricks with the greatest of ease. On her own she started bringing in the newspaper to us each day. She got so good at it she would sit out in the yard and listen for the paper boy to come up the hill. She then looked upward and waited for him to fling the paper over the fence, whereupon she would catch it in her mouth and bring it proudly to me. Unfortunately, in her enthusiasm, she would do the same thing when we happened to have left her home alone, and then, in frustration because we were not there, she would tear the paper to pieces. But she was good company both for Ruth and ourselves and we loved her greatly. A marvelous watchdog, she kept all strangers at bay and gave us a wonderful feeling of security.

The town of Seaside is a small community adjoining Monterey and lying between Monterey and the Army base of Fort Ord. Although Seaside had a form of city government, it was unincorporated and had no City Hall as such, no planning commission and no building inspector, nor were there any building codes, so anyone could build whatever and wherever they pleased. I drew up my plans for a two-bedroom addition to the house, with a large living room and an extra bathroom. Then I started work on it and went ahead undisturbed.

Classes were out at four in the afternoon and the teachers could go home at the same time as the students, so with the long afternoons and weekends, I was able to get quite a lot done. Off and on some of the students came out to visit us. As my extra-curricular activities became widely known, a number of the students asked if they could come out and help us. Almost every weekend we had one or two students giving us a hand, and more often than not their wives and children accompanied them. It wasn't long before the students had named our house "Tharp's Thpeak" because of its location.

Among our frequent visitors was a young captain named Raymond White and his wife, Aileen, with their two little boys, who were known as the "angels." Ray was a pilot, as were a number of the other officer students, and on weekends they frequently went out to the airport to get in some flying time. From the hill at the back of our house we overlooked the airport and could watch them take off and land, and knowing where our house was, they often buzzed low over us, waving from the cockpit windows and shouting to us.

When our Chinese language students were flying,

and several were out on the same day, it was their habit to converse with each other over the radio and practice their Chinese. On one occasion a high-ranking general was visiting Monterey and security at the airport was especially tight, with extra guards in the tower. When they heard the foreign language being spoken by our students, they panicked, thinking it was a Russian plot to shoot down the incoming general's plane. As a result they called an alert, and all planes flying in the area were warned to either land or stay away. It was only later that they discovered it was our students talking together in Chinese.

Ray and Aileen White visited us often. One sunny afternoon we sat together in the sun and chatted about their future. It was shortly before Ray's graduation and he had received orders to go to Taiwan. However, Aileen confessed that she had qualms about going; somehow she had a dread that something terrible was going to happen if she left the States and went to join her husband. We tried to reassure her, but she remained unconvinced.

Upon graduation they moved back East and Ray left a few weeks later for Taiwan. Shortly after that Aileen got a port call, but she stopped first in Monterey to talk it over with us. Again she told us she felt certain something was going to happen either to her or the boys, and in the end she panicked and refused to go. Another month or two went by and Ray, from his end, tried to reassure her as did we. Eventually she left for Taiwan, but she had only been there a few days when she came down with polio. Despite the best efforts of the American doctors in Okinawa, where she was taken, she became crippled from the waist down and was confined to a wheelchair for the rest of her life. We saw her on several occasions after she returned to the United States and she called us frequently. Always cheery and bright, she never once complained about her lot, and in fact, despite her crippled condition, gave birth to a third son shortly thereafter. We last saw her in their home in Memphis in 1984 and were saddened to see her health was failing. She passed away four years later in 1988.

With so much work to do on the exterior of the house, together with the garage, I had left the finishing of the interior of the new living room as something I could do when the rains came. I wanted to put in a fireplace and a hardwood floor, and late in 1950 I started on that project. Just about that same time things began to move in another direction at the school itself.

In the middle of June 1950, world events were coming to a head. On June 25th, some 60,000 North Korean troops, with over 100 Russian-built tanks, invaded South Korea, capturing the capital, Seoul. Five days later U.S. ground forces entered the conflict. The start of the Korean War immediately resulted in a tremendous increase in the number of students being sent to learn Chinese, among them a number of U.S. Marines.

In the early part of this chapter I mentioned that the various branches of the armed services were dissatisfied with the school's product, primarily because, although the students could all manage to speak what is often called "tea party" Chinese, they were not well enough trained in the military terminology unique to their branch of the service. They were unable to handle their assignments in the field. That was particularly true in the case of the Air Force students. They needed to know flight terminology, aircraft handling and a host of other specialized terms related to ground-to-air and air-to-air radio traffic. Because of that, toward the end of 1950, we began to hear rumors of a possible pull-out by the Air Force from the school, and early in 1951 the entire Air Force contingent of students in all languages at the Army Language School were withdrawn and sent to newly established language schools set up at different universities across the country. Chinese, Japanese and Korean courses were established at Yale, Russian at Syracuse University, and Vietnamese was to be taught at Indiana University.

Air Force students comprised about 60 percent of all the school's students, so it was a tremendous shock to the Army and to all of us teachers when those blue uniforms left. With more than half the students gone, we all began to wonder if our jobs were in jeopardy. However, because of the war in Korea, more and more Army people arrived and the school continued to function normally.

I recall one of the last graduations just before the Air Force people left. We had a young Air Force lieutenant colonel graduating. He had been a relatively good student, but was so shy that he performed poorly in oral tests. However, at the graduation party, when beer had been flowing freely for some time, he

suddenly got to his feet and in extraordinarily good Chinese, gave one of the best speeches I've ever heard. It made me wonder mildly whether a couple of beers before class might not provoke better performances from the students as a whole, but I never made the proposal. I was sure it would meet with defeat.

When we first heard about the possible move by the Air Force I was only mildly surprised to learn that my old friend and former student Delmar Lang (then a captain), had, through his aggressive and insistent demands that something be done about the inferior training being given at Monterey, spearheaded the decision by the Air Force. He wrote countless letters and proposals with solutions to the problems of language training to his superiors, pointing out that large numbers of Chinese and Korean linguists would be needed as the Korean hostilities continued. With the inevitability of Red Chinese forces coming into the fray, he succeeded where many others would have failed. It was also Del Lang who first visited Yale to explore the possibility of establishing a program there. At the same time he discovered that Eva's brother, Gerard Kok, who is known as Jerry, was director of Yale's Chinese program.

Discussing it with Jerry, Del found that the Yale Chinese program was flexible and that the university was not averse to setting up a contract to teach Air Force students. The nuts and bolts and formalities of establishing the program were commenced. While the contract with Yale was being negotiated, Jerry Kok visited Monterey to familiarize himself with what the school had been doing and to find out why it was unsatisfactory to the Air Force, so he would be better informed as to what was needed.

While in Monterey, Jerry asked me one day if I would like to join him in the program at Yale. I, of course, was delighted at the prospect, and a few weeks later I received an official invitation from Yale's personnel office inviting me to become a part of the new Chinese language program.

At the same time, I had been approached by the Air Force to go to San Antonio to work on Chinese intelligence problems, a very tempting offer as well. What finally made us decide to accept the Yale offer was that when I paid a visit to the INS people, they told me that if I went to Yale, an established educational institution, my status as a "parolee" could be changed, provided I could produce documentation that my going to Yale was in the national interest. If that were the case, the time I spent at Yale would be credited as time of domicile in the United States and would thus make the eventual resolution of my status that much easier.

Armed with that encouraging information I approached Col. Barnwell to ask his permission to resign and go to Yale. At first he was unhappy and not anxious for me to leave. He voiced various objections, chief among them that I was leaving him short-handed at a critical time — the Korean War — because of the tremendous influx of new students. At one point he as much as threatened to refuse to let me go, but then his kind heart got the better of him and he conceded that the improvement in my immigration status outweighed everything else, and he reluctantly let me go.

Much as we regretted having to leave the house we had just completed, there were so many advantages to moving to New Haven that we had no other choice. Eva's father died from a heart attack on January 8, 1951, and her mother was living alone on the outskirts of Camden, New Jersey, so in New Haven we would be closer to her. We had last seen Eva's parents in 1945 in San Francisco, when they had been brought out of Beijing by the U.S. Army at the end of World War II. At the time, we had found accommodations for them in a hotel, had driven them around in our car, and had arranged for their train trip across the continent.

At the time I thought I detected a mellowing in Mr. Kok's attitude toward me. After all, I was carrying a diplomatic passport just as he was, had a good job, and was adequately supporting his daughter. On one occasion he was greatly amused when I drove with him to a travel bureau to pick up their train tickets. Not being able to find a place to park in downtown San Francisco, I parked in a "No Parking" zone, went over to a nearby policeman, showed him my credentials, and pointed out to him that the gentleman in the car was a Dutch diplomat and I was engaged in picking up tickets for him at the travel bureau. The police officer at once came over and stood guard over the car while I went inside. Mr. Kok found that extremely amusing and apparently applauded my ingenuity. However, he had very little to say to me when we were alone together, and was distant toward both of us when visiting in our apartment and during the meals we had together. Before they left for the East Coast, his attitude had not changed, nor did he at any time refer to his initial objections to our marriage. That was the last time I saw him.

We planned to leave Monterey in the latter part of July 1951. I found a real estate agent who would handle the rental of the house, and he found a tenant for us even before we vacated the place. We packed our luggage into a trailer and we left Monterey and the Army Language School early one morning with no regrets whatsoever.

Some instructors and students at the 1949 Army Language School.

Bob with his fellow instructors of the Chinese Mandarin Department at the Army Language School in Monterey, 1949.

Army Language School students dress up for some kind of special event.

Our good friends Ray, Aileen, Doug and Paul White taken in their home in Japan after their Taiwan tour. The boys were always known as "The Angels."

牛不吃草.
圖賤買老牛.老

Tu jian mai lao niu,
lao niu bu chi cao.

Seeking to save money
he bought an old cow,
(but) old cows can't eat grass.

- Chinese Peasant Saying.

Chapter Forty-Four
The Yale Experience Begins

My first day at Yale's Institute of Far Eastern Languages (IFEL) was August 25, 1951. I was given the somewhat awesome title of senior instructor of Chinese, even though I was junior to most of the teachers already there. My salary was $6,000 a year, exactly twice as much as I had started with in Monterey just three years before.

Upon our arrival in New Haven, Eva and I received a warm welcome from her brother and his family. It was the first time we had met Jerry's wife, Ellan, and their two children, Kenny, aged six, and Grace, aged two and known to everyone then and now as Bunny.

During World War II, with the large influx of married military students, a number of Quonset huts had been set up on a grassy sward right in the shadow of Yale Bowl, each of them fitted out with two small bedrooms, a living room and a kitchen. They were still in use, and the university allocated one of them to us for as long as we needed it. We stayed there for a little over a month while we looked for something permanent.

When I first walked into the building at 215 Park Street, the very first person I met was Ida Tyrrell, the secretary of IFEL, and a key figure in running the organization. Every student who entered the building talked first to her, and for many years she was counselor and adviser to them and a good friend to everyone else. Eva and I still correspond with her.

On my first day I also met the Chinese teachers and the American staff members, and everyone gave me a warm welcome. I then met the first of the Air Force language classes, enrolled just four weeks earlier. The class consisted of sixty men, most of them just out of basic training, but it also included a number of noncommissioned officers, all with the Air Force Security Service.

I was delighted to find our old friend and former student Delmar C. Lang, wearing the bars of a captain, among the students. As mentioned earlier, it was Del who dreamed up the Yale program in the first place and who was largely instrumental in persuading the Air Force to pull their students out of Monterey and set up different language programs at various universities. Now he had been assigned as a "student" with the first class; however, his primary responsibility was to help us get the program off the ground. His expertise as a knowledgeable adviser was invaluable as we began the job of creating a new course of instruction tailored specifically to Air Force needs. What we particularly needed was his guidance and advice in the choice of military terminology for in-flight, air-to-air and air-to-ground communication procedures, as well as Air Force ground activity terms. All of them had to be incorporated into our new texts.

Yale's involvement in the teaching of languages began in 1943 during World War II, with what was called the Chinese Language School, where U.S. Army officers were taught Chinese. It was not until the spring of 1947 that the Institute of Far Eastern Languages came into being. IFEL was housed in a three-story building on the edge of campus, but right in the heart of Fraternity Row. The building had at one time been a fraternity house, lavishly built in the '20s with no thought as to expense. When the fraternity went bankrupt (as so many did), Yale had taken it over. It had remained empty for some time until IFEL came along. However, spacious as the building was, and entirely adequate for our demands in the first year or so, it wasn't long before we started to out-grow it. But that's another story.

Before I could start to teach, I had to familiarize myself with the Yale Chinese texts. I found them excitingly different from anything we had used in Monterey, not only in content, but also because they were all written in what had come to be known as the "Yale Romanization." It was the first time I had seen that particular form of the transcription of Chinese sounds. Designed by Professor George Kennedy and Jerry Kok, it used the Roman alphabet to write Chinese sounds with a strictly phonetic representation, thus making the words more easily pronounced by English-speaking people. I had been used to the Wade-Giles system since childhood, so it took me a few days to familiarize myself with the new spellings, but the more I saw of it, the more I liked it. The Pinyin system of romanization, now widely used in the People's Republic of China, was largely based on

the Yale system and differs only in a relatively few instances. A chart of the three systems is to be seen in the back of this book.

Beginning students started with a basic text, *Speak Chinese*, written by M. Gardner Tewksbury in 1942. Developed originally for the Army program during World War II, it was, then and now, considered by most Chinese language teachers to be the best basic language text of its kind. Now, fifty years later, it is still widely used both in college and high school language programs in this country and abroad. In addition to that text there was a fair amount of loose-leaf military-type teaching material also available. However, the terminology was essentially Army, useless for our purposes with the Air Force.

The need for an "intermediate" text had been recognized even before I arrived at IFEL and I found that a follow-up text to *Speak Chinese* was well on its way to completion. Of necessity it had to meet general language requirements, but since it was still incomplete, it allowed us the opportunity to include numerous basic military terms common to all branches of the services, and in common use by most civilians in general conversation. The new text would be called *Chinese Dialogues*, and was being written by Professor Fred Fang-yu Wang with the help of another Chinese professor, Pao-chen Lee. It, too, was so well received that even now, forty-five years after it was first published, it is also one of the most widely used texts in the worldwide teaching of Chinese.

In most normal university programs the undergraduate student spends, on the average, only three to six hours a week on foreign language study. Consequently, each of these two texts would have supplied enough material for a normal one-year course. Because of the relatively short tour of service that each man had, much of it taken up with other Air Force training commitments, the Air Force could only give us the students for a period of approximately eight months, or 32 weeks. In that relatively short period of time we planned to expose them to the equivalent of a three-year language course in a normal university situation. They would be studying six hours a day, five days a week.

That made for an intensive program, and it also meant we would push them through each of the two texts in about twelve weeks, thus leaving ten weeks at the end of the course for strictly military terminology suitable to their job requirements. For that, another text had to be written. All in all, we faced a formidable task, and that first year was a period of intense pressure for all concerned to produce the materials and keep ahead of the students. But we managed it.

As I studied the new textbooks, I liked them more with every page. *Speak Chinese* consisted of 24 lessons in simple conversational style, with emphasis on Chinese sentence structure — so different from English grammar — and a minimum of grammatical explanations in English. But such as there was, it was presented in a straightforward manner with multiple drills, which helped the student acquire the patterns in a natural manner.

The format chosen for the intermediate text, *Chinese Dialogues*, was somewhat different. It was largely written in a connected story form. It was the tale of a young man who went to China by ship, landing in Shanghai. From there he continued with his experiences in China in everyday situations. That format is not only logical, it is ideal both for the teacher and the student. It allows for constant review and repetition of already learned terminology, and that which comes along later in the way of new lexical items fits readily into a framework with which the student is familiar.

Writing the military text for the last ten weeks of the course proved to be a herculean job, but everyone pitched in to help. Guided in great part by Capt. Del Lang, who supplied us with long lists of Air Force jargon and practical scenarios of both ground and air activities, we tried our best to incorporate them into the text in the most natural manner possible.

We named the text *Out of the Blue*, partly to add a slightly humorous twist because of the surprise element it brought with it, and also to remind the students of the "Wild Blue Yonder" of Air Force lore and song. Again, we adopted the format of writing it in story form. A young American lad joined the Air Force, went through basic training, and then ended up as a fighter pilot in Korea. There, however, we ran into difficulties. None of us, teachers or students, had any experience with aerial warfare. We knew little of radio transmission procedures or flying tactics and largely had to "wing" it.

I spent hours reading every story of World War II aerial warfare that I could lay my hands on, and voraciously devoured *Time* and *Newsweek* accounts of air battles that had occurred in Korean skies. But we felt it wasn't enough. We appealed to the Air Force Security Service Command for help, asking for tapes of actual air engagements between U.S. and Chinese pilots as well as tapes of air-to-ground and ground-to-ground communications. The general in command was instantly obliging in promising to send them to us, but the tapes we finally received were completely worthless. Lower echelon personnel charged with maintaining security had "sanitized" them in order to avoid any compromise of U.S. Air Force tactics. The result was that every single word spoken either in English or Chinese had been obliterated. All we got were tapes full of hiss and static.

We didn't let that deter us, however, and despite those handicaps, when completed, our text and the tapes that accompanied it were apparently so realistic and true to the actual situations existing in Korea that we received a delegation of U.S. Air Force security men, who had come to investigate our sources of information. They were sure that leaks had occurred somewhere. It took me a considerable amount of time to convince them that we had made up the text out of whole cloth, and that it was entirely the product of our imaginations.

To make the tapes as realistic as possible, I had used a small microphone pressed to my throat to simulate the throat mikes used by pilots. At the same time, to provide as nearly as possible the authentic background noise, I got up at four a.m. and went to the Yale radio station, where I taped shortwave static and ambient noise, both of which we blended in on the tapes we made for student listening. At a still more advanced stage we added several different voices, some speaking Chinese and others different languages to simulate the cross-over effect that frequently occurs in shortwave radio reception. It was the student's job to recognize and follow one particular voice and write down all the information that he could. There was plenty of groaning and complaining from the students as they listened to the tapes, but in time they realized their value and developed the "ear" to hear the intended message through the noise, just as they would later have to do in the field.

But that advanced text wasn't the only thing we were writing. As we worked with each class we discovered areas of concern that needed additional emphasis. All students, without exception, had difficulties with Chinese numbers, particularly when hearing them through earphones. The Chinese numbers for one and seven *(yi, qi)* are difficult to distinguish over the radio, and the same was true for six and nine *(liu, jiu)*. Added to that, the number ten *(shi)* can readily be confused with four *(si)*, particularly when spoken by someone with a provincial dialect.

Quite early we discovered that the Chinese themselves had learned this problem the hard way. As a result they had instituted new words to eliminate the ambiguities and were using them in their radio transmissions. Those new numbers had to be taught to our students (and teachers) and incorporated into the text. And, because numbers played such an important part in Chinese communications — all codes were transmitted using numbers — we had to prepare tapes to endlessly drill the students to provide them with maximum exposure under a variety of circumstances. To do that we put together long lists of numbers in random groups and recorded them. That particular drill we called Count-Off. That drill paid huge dividends but was not the most popular by any means, particularly when students had to write the numbers they heard and have their papers checked and graded.

Because in a real-life situation in the field the student would encounter many words he had never encountered, we taught the students how to use dictionaries, creating drills where new words cropped up. The listener had to stop and look up the word(s) in a vocabulary list prepared for that purpose. We called this exercise Hi-Fi for "Hear it, Find it." Geographical names also proved a stumbling block to students. Chinese place names — like our own — tend to be multi-syllabic and, just as we do, the Chinese tend to slur the middle syllable(s) when saying them. That is particularly true when spoken at high speed, and the emphasis, or stress, is placed either on the first or last syllable. Since the students in the field would be hearing many new and strange place names on the air, we devised a practice drill we called Timing, the romanized (Wade-Giles) Chinese spelling for "place names." The student hearing the name had to locate it either from a list of geographical names or on a map.

As the students advanced we added simulated "action" drills we called Listening-In. The Chinese word for this was spelled Shouting, and these drills encompassed everything we could think of in field

conditions: air battles, aircraft emergencies, emergency landings, sighting of enemy aircraft either from the ground or from another plane, together with a wide variety of other scenarios. Visitors to the school who perused the schedules posted in the hallways were much bemused by the "subject matter" of scheduled classes judging by the odd names that showed up. Toward the end of my time at Yale, when a new non-Chinese-speaking director came aboard, I happened to be in his office one day when I overheard him talking to someone on the telephone. I heard him say: "I don't know what I've got myself into here. They teach weird things like timing, hifi, count-off and there's even one class where they apparently practice shouting." I realized I had to educate him in a hurry.

It is safe to say that Yale's Institute of Far Eastern Languages was among the first to pioneer the so-called "Language Laboratory," now so familiar in all language programs. The institute had gained much experience from the wartime teaching of languages and had acquired a few somewhat crude recording devices, which, however, were usable by the students only on a one-to-one basis. The teacher would make a recording in the presence of the student, then allow the student to play back the recording as many times as he wished. Another way was to have the student himself make a recording in Chinese and play it back to listen and correct any mistakes he might have made.

That, of course, was not cost effective in either manpower or time. Also, the wax-coated discs — designed originally for office use where busy executives used them for dictating letters and which were listened to, for the most part, just once or twice by his secretary when typing up the document — could not be erased and re-used. Our students needed to listen over and over again, perhaps as many as 100 times, so the sound quality on the discs quickly deteriorated. That required the constant replenishment of the supply, and reproducing discs in quantity became a high priority.

The recording and listening machines in use when I got to IFEL were the trusty Soundscriber, manufactured in Bridgeport, Connecticut. Encased in a sturdy wooden box, they were small, portable, very durable, and seldom broke down; when they did, they were easy to repair. To begin, we had only a dozen or so, but later, as the need arose, we had more than 300. A young woman named Elaine was in charge of the sound recordings. She worked in the basement, where someone had devised a primitive, but nevertheless quite effective, means of making multiple copies of the small, green wax discs. Six of the machines had been lined up and linked together on a table so that with the flip of a switch, all six started up simultaneously. With a tape from a standard tape-recorder fed into them, six discs were recorded at the same time. However, there was one large drawback. Making the duplicate copies took an excessive amount of time because they could only record at the same speed as the original recording.

To remedy that, the obvious solution was to increase the number of the recorders. I built a table with three shelves above it in tiers, each one a little farther back than the first, and on those we hooked 30 recorders together. Even so, with the ever-increasing student load, the demand for recordings grew greater by the day. It wasn't too long before we had to look for another solution.

Magnetic recording devices were invented as far back as 1889, and by the early 1950s they had progressed a long way from the early wire recorders so widely used by the military in World War II. The sound quality was fairly good but far inferior to the more sophisticated machines that came along in the early '50s, all of them reel-to-reel tape machines. At first they used magnetic-coated paper tape, which tended to break under the slightest strain. The first plastic tape appeared soon after that, but both the machines and tapes were once again designed primarily for use by professionals in the field of music, radio, or other entertainment; few were sold for private use.

Although we purchased several of those early tape recorders, they were unsuitable, not only because of the high cost, but more importantly because the first plastic magnetic tape, like its earlier paper predecessor, tended to break readily when exposed to the slightest stress, as when it was stopped and hurriedly switched back again to "play." Although the tape could be repaired, the ends had to be cut evenly. As a result, something was always lost, and the patch caused an audible "click." Also, repairs took time. At a later stage when unbreakable tape appeared, it, too, had drawbacks; it stretched under certain circumstances, which made for some most disconcerting moments for the listener as the recorded voice dropped and became drawn out, something like listening to someone talking in the bottom of a barrel.

But the sound quality of the new machines and the plastic tape provided a vast improvement over the old wax or paper-tape recordings, so we used the machines primarily for master recordings from which we made multiple copies of the wax discs. We had to make do with those until something better came along.

A month or so after our arrival in New Haven we purchased a home in the small town of Branford, nine miles to the east of New Haven and right on Long Island Sound.

When first looking for a house we had searched the entire area around New Haven. The particular house we finally bought was actually the first one we had looked at, and it was only three houses away from where Jerry Kok and his family lived. At the time, I didn't know Jerry and Ellan very well and we were hesitant about living so close, for fear that with working together on a daily basis at the school, then living nearby, it might bring about frictions.

We needn't have worried. We found Jerry and Ellan to be wonderful people, and with their family, consisting eventually of four children, they have, over the years, been closer to us in every way than anyone else in our immediate family. It was also Jerry's sage observation that when driving to and from work each day we would always have the sun at our backs. How true that was, and we learned to appreciate it on our daily commute.

Some few months after we moved into our new house, we came to know a young auto mechanic named Raymond Mazzarella who lived nearby. He was a stocky, good-looking and strong young man, but modest and self-effacing. Highly skilled in his profession, he was also a man of all trades. Because the workload in making recordings had become too heavy for Elaine alone (and we needed her services elsewhere in reproducing lesson copies in their hundreds on the "Ditto" machine), I persuaded Ray to join our staff as our "sound man." Neither he nor I knew anything much about the business, but we were both willing to learn.

In the basement "sound room," we built into one corner a sound-proof recording studio, so small that the recording "artist" could just barely squeeze in and sit down. It had no ventilation and was unbearably hot in summer, but it served its purpose. From then on our recordings were free of ambient noise.

Because of the demands of the Korean War, students were arriving in ever-increasing numbers, and at odd intervals. Sometimes there would be a class of four or six, then perhaps 15 or 20, but four times a year we had classes of at least 60 or more. Because of those increases, we had to rethink our "listening" facilities for the students.

When I had first arrived at IFEL the language laboratory had consisted of a six-person carousel-type installation in the center of one of the large basement rooms. The students sat in a circle facing inward around a circular table partitioned into tiny compartments, each with a Soundscriber machine. As they worked with the machines, the teacher circulated behind them monitoring their work. But obviously, six positions were totally inadequate when we had such large classes coming in. Because of the war and the demands being made on the manufacturer by the armed forces in Korea, we had extreme difficulty in purchasing new machines.

As a stop-gap measure we designed junction boxes with four outlets into which earphones could be plugged. One of those boxes plugged into each listening machine immediately enabled us to take care of four students, and in that way 24 students could be handled with the same carousel. That, however, had the significant drawback of forcing all four students on any given machine to work at the speed of the slowest student in the group. That became very frustrating for those who learned more quickly.

Eventually, as more of the purely listening machines became available, we gradually expanded our facilities to narrow tables backed against the walls with an eventual 100 or more positions around the two rooms in the basement. That worked exceptionally well for a year or two, but there was a great deal of wasted space in the center of the room. It also meant a lot of walking around for the teacher.

One of those long tables happened to be directly under a window. The five or six positions there were, for some reason, immensely popular and always in demand, and I couldn't figure out why the students always made a rush for them. But I noticed one day that the students appeared to be so "enraptured" with

what they were supposed to be listening to that they had ceased writing. I noticed further that there was some foot-tapping going on, with body gyrations as well, and I became highly suspicious. Plugging in my headset to one of the machines, I discovered that the students were listening to music. For some unexplained reason, those six machines were picking up a local radio station, loud and clear. We were unable to find any way to eliminate it, so I had to move the machines to another location, and for a time my popularity with certain of the students dropped a number of points.

As we gained more experience in language teaching, particularly in the audio-lingual field, it became more and more apparent that it was necessary for the teacher to exert maximum control over what the student was doing, specifically in listening to taped materials. We discovered that many students lacked self-confidence and would waste an inordinate amount of time listening over and over again to a specific segment on the disc, fairly certain all the time that they knew what it meant, but lacking the confidence to write it down. Accordingly they fell behind.

I experimented first in the large auditorium on the top floor, where we had installed about 100 folding chairs, the type with a writing-table arm. I started by "force feeding" the students with live voice classes, giving them short segments of material in spoken Chinese, which they were required to translate after hearing it only twice. The results proved spectacular, with the vast majority of the students grasping the material content on the first hearing and confidently writing down a translation after the second hearing gave them confirmation. There were, however, a number of inherent disadvantages and inequities for some. Echoes in the room, rustling of paper, movements by fellow students, coughing and sneezing, etc., all proved to be distractions, and those in the back of the room were obviously at a disadvantage. I discussed the problem with Ray Mazzarella, and we came up with our first so-called "passive" listening laboratory early in 1953, and so far as I know it was the first of its kind in America.

We took long lengths of 1-inch by 4-inch boards and bolted one to the backs of a row of chairs, and two others to the chair legs. Thus we had a row of chairs firmly linked. In conduits, on the board along the backs of the chairs, we strung low-impedance wiring, with a jack outlet behind each chair. We then ran the wiring through additional conduits along the floor to a master console at the front of the room. From there we were able to pipe "live" voice or tape-recorded material to each of the chairs. When a student plugged in his headset he could hear with absolute clarity and minimal outside disturbance. An instant success, it paid huge dividends.

Our language laboratories (or "electronic classrooms" as they were sometimes called at the time), were among the very first such installations in this country. Because they excited considerable interest among educators from other institutions, we had frequent visitors. Then businessmen, interested in getting into the language laboratory market, began to visit us, together with manufacturers of sound equipment. At one time I was an unofficial, unpaid adviser to five or six such firms. My particular interest was in passing on to them our findings on the shortcomings of their equipment on the one hand, so that they might improve them, and on the other, if language laboratories were indeed the wave of the future, to help them develop something much better than the relatively crude systems we were employing.

One manufacturer of sound equipment in New York, Dr. Paul King, came to me one day with a refinement of a 1940 invention in sound reproduction, and I was immediately struck with its simplicity, high fidelity, and relative inexpensiveness. The system, which he had named "Magnicord," was invented either in Germany or Austria, and, like the Soundscriber, used a flexible disc. However, there the likeness ended. The new disc was twice as large, paper-thin and made of plastic, and coated on one side with the same substance containing iron oxide particles as were the standard magnetic tapes. They were pre-grooved and self-tracking, and played at a very slow speed, which allowed the recording of two or three times as much material as could be recorded on the earlier wax discs. Furthermore, an added and very significant advantage was the fact that the plastic discs could be played over and over again, not merely hundreds of times, but for at least 5,000 playings with no noticeable wear or loss of fidelity. In addition, they had the tremendous advantage of being erasable and could be reused without showing undue wear.

The machines to record and play the discs were equally ingenious. They were contained in small, lightweight, compact metal cases about a foot square, and used a playing arm with a simple, easily replaceable needle. They were, in fact, miniatures of the conventional phonograph, familiar to almost everyone. To replay anything was a simple matter of lifting the player arm and moving it back a few grooves. I was so struck with the practicality of the system and its performance that I was determined to convert our entire operation to that more modern approach, and had little difficulty in persuading the Yale purchasing agent to approve our switching over to the new system.

We worked out a contract with Dr. King, and he and his staff, working mostly nights and weekends, installed a modern language laboratory of over a hundred positions in individual booths placed in readily accessible rows. Each partially enclosed booth contained its own listening machine, and the student had an unobstructed forward view toward the control console and the teacher. The entire laboratory was installed without disturbing our teaching schedule.

Together we also devised a master-recording bank of machines to make multiple copies of the discs. Dr. King came up with a model of the recorder that produced discs at twice the normal speed, but which sounded perfect when played back at the slower speed of the student machines. That cut down tremendously on the time required to make the hundreds of recordings we needed. The new installation was a tremendous improvement over our previous system. It not only allowed the teacher in charge of the class to move around and monitor each student's work with much greater ease, it also solved many of our other problems at the same time.

The new machines were sturdy and breakdowns were infrequent, but the wear and tear on the needles was severe, and they needed constant replacement. Students frequently and inadvertently placed their books on top of the playing arm, crushing the needle and sometimes damaging the disc. We partially rectified that problem by adding small shelves on the side wall of the booth above the desk, thus giving the student more desk surface for his books and papers.

With the enlargement of our lab and the increase in the number of recordings being made as new text materials were developed, we had to hire a second maintenance man. Leo Szalamacha, a young master welder, was a close friend of Ray Mazzarella's. Even though we paid Leo much less than he could earn as a welder, he was happy to become part of the IFEL staff and stayed with us right to the end.

As the Air Force language requirements continued to grow and as more civilian students came as well, so did the need arise for still more language laboratories. They continued to increase in number and size until we finally had six of them scattered through the various buildings into which our program eventually expanded. By 1963 there were well over 250 listening positions.

Ray and Leo will long be remembered by the thousands of students who passed through the courses at IFEL over the 15 years the Air Force program remained in existence. Not only were both of them highly efficient in maintaining the language laboratories, and always available when needed, but they both had outgoing personalities, unending good humor, and a fund of stories, and each established an extraordinary camaraderie with the students. Ray, in particular, will be remembered as the manager and catcher of the softball teams he organized, and which he ran with supreme enthusiasm over a period of years.

The coming of more and larger classes was accompanied by our need for more and more small rooms for individual classes. The original rooms at 215 Park Street were so large that I came up with the idea of doubling our capacity by subdividing them. With the help of Ray and Leo, I drew up plans and submitted them to the Yale building management people, but they were unwilling to take the necessary steps to have the work done. I finally persuaded them to supply us with the materials and let us do the work ourselves. We would use volunteer student labor where necessary and do the entire job in after-school hours so as not to disrupt the program. By the time we had finished we had managed to more than double the capacity of the building without disturbing the daytime programs. But even that was only a stop-gap measure. As time passed and the success of the Chinese program spread far and wide, we soon found ourselves expanding into adjoining buildings and even other buildings far on the other side of the sprawling Yale campus.

Special programs for missionaries had been established in 1946, with more than 60 in the first class. However, after the war was over and the Pettus language school in Beijing reopened in 1948, registra-tion of civilians at IFEL dropped off radically. But that lasted for only a little over a year until the Communist takeover was completed in 1949, when Westerners had to leave China. Even so, when I first arrived at Yale in 1951, there were only one or two civilians studying Chinese.

But in a short time that aspect of the program increased to a point where we had well over 100 civilians a year: businessmen, diplomats from a dozen different countries, newspapermen, missionaries, and for a number of years, until the State Department set up its own language school, we had all of their Chinese language students. Since all of those different people had to learn basic Chinese, we mixed them in with the airmen for the first twelve weeks. After that, however, special courses had to be written for each category of student, and we had so many requests for specialized instruction in Chinese that a copy of the Yale Directory that I have for 1963 offers some 40 different courses in Mandarin Chinese and six in Cantonese. The institute also taught Japanese, Korean and Indonesian, and, for a time, Vietnamese.

I've written about our language laboratories. They are essentially of three basic types. The first is called a passive or listening laboratory, where the student is supplied with a set of headphones and perhaps a volume control, but has no control over what he is hearing. He simply listens and perhaps repeats aloud the material that is fed to him or translates it into English.

The second type of laboratory is called an active or listen-speak laboratory, in which the student has absolute freedom in what he wants to do. He has equipment on which he can play anything he wants, and he can listen to it as many times as he wishes. He can also voice and record segments of the language being learned, or answer questions in that language and voice them aloud, recording them in the privacy of his own booth without disturbing others.

The third type is still more sophisticated, and is sometimes known as a listen-speak-record laboratory. Here, the student sits in a booth equipped with a recorder-playback machine that offers a much wider scope of possibilities in language learning. It is linked to a console where the teacher can flip a switch and listen to what each student is working on and can talk directly to him. At the same time the teacher can offer advice, give assistance or answer questions. Upon request, a different program can be fed from the console to one or all positions.

When we started putting in language laboratories, tape recorders were expensive and not too reliable, so our labs consisted only of the first two types. For civilian use, instead of tape recorders, we at first used magnetic disc machines, which had recording capability. Our Air Force students were required to become totally proficient in comprehending the Chinese language, while the ability to speak the language was of secondary importance, so they did not require recording facilities.

Within a matter of weeks after installing our first listening laboratory, we improved our techniques to the point where it in actuality became a semi-active laboratory. We accomplished that by writing and recording materials in Chinese that we played to the students, then required from them immediate confirmation that they had understood what they heard by means of test questions. At first, we played a five- or ten-minute tape in story form. We then asked a series of questions orally in Chinese, with the students required to write their answers in English. However, through trial and error we quickly realized that there were certain inequities in that system. Many students quite obviously understood what they had heard at the time they heard it, but were unable to remember the story in sufficient detail in order to answer the questions. We realized we were confusing the issue by introducing a memory factor that was patently unfair to some.

Our next step was to print question sheets in romanized Chinese, give them to the students when the class started, and have them write their answers in English as they listened to the story. That proved to be an improvement, but there again we came to realize that we had introduced a negative factor that bore no relationship to the basic task in hand, i.e., did the student understand what he was hearing? The questions written in Chinese seemed a logical approach, but, in fact, we were introducing an unrelated problem for the student, that of being able to read and understand the question itself. In many cases that turned out to be confusing for the student. After trying different methods we settled on one that was entirely satisfactory. Our goal was to determine that the student understood what he heard in Chinese, and prove it by answering questions about it. The answer was to provide the question in English, and when we did that, the results were spectacular. We got from the students exactly what we were looking for.

That exercise became a daily feature at all levels in the course. We gave it the straightforward name Comprehension, and all the teachers were put to work writing stories on a wide variety of subjects, each of them tailored to the particular level of the lessons as the students progressed. After voicing the story — and we varied the diet for the student by having as many teachers as possible do the writing and voicing — questions were prepared in English and printed. Question sheets were given to the students before the class started so they could read them through and understand just what was being asked.

Each story was approximately eight to ten minutes in length, with 50 questions on each. A partially correct answer could earn as little as a quarter point to a point and a half, and after the class, papers were collected and immediately corrected and graded by a special team, with the papers being handed back to the students an hour or so later. In that way they could see their results and have immediate confirmation as to their success or failure while the story was still fresh in their minds. The speed with which papers were returned proved a tremendous boost to morale.

Then there was Rapid Fire — the class that former students remember most vividly. It did not begin as Rapid Fire. The students needed more listening material for homework, so sentences were made up using daily lesson vocabulary as well as review material. They were recorded clearly and deliberately, and the students would listen to each sentence twice and then try to write down in English what they remembered and understood. Papers were turned in the next morning and checked but not graded. There seemed to be little challenge in that exercise, so it was decided to offer the same recordings at the speed a Chinese would normally speak. We let the students decide which version they wanted. Before long, the demand for the faster recordings far surpassed those of the slower. The students said it was easier to understand and to remember when trying to write whole sentences in English, so the slow recordings were discontinued. As the students advanced in the course, the material was spoken even faster and mixed with all kinds of background noises to challenge them to hear and follow what was said. Excitement, alarm, panic, and slurring were introduced in the voice; improbable statements were recorded interspersed with English words here and there to measure how alert the student was. By that time, the exercises were no longer homework assignments, to be done at the student's own pace, but were presented in a controlled class situation with the recordings getting more and more difficult and the sentences longer. The papers were handed in and graded. The students named the class "Rapid Fire," as it seemed that fast to them, and they dubbed me "Rapid Fire Robert," a name I carry still. The class was dreaded by students, but the challenge kept them plugging away at it with a zeal to conquer it. And conquer it most of them did. Looking back, many now say that Rapid Fire contributed most to their overall comprehension of Chinese and competency in the spoken language as well, and that it was well worth the effort they put into it. Moreover, the training and discipline has helped them in their life work, whether in the Chinese language or otherwise.

Experience such as that described above showed us that students needed to know test results immediately not only to see how well they did, but also to remember the content of the test. If errors were made, they could correct their mistakes and avoid making the same error later. The method proved so successful that we adopted it with every aspect of the course.

Each lesson in the textbook covered a twelve-hour cycle, starting with the introduction of a new lesson the first hour in the afternoon of day one, with emphasis placed on any new grammatical patterns that appeared. That was followed by a rigorous drill period in small groups, with a native instructor. The third hour was a review, test-type exercise, covering the preceding lesson, usually given in the lab. The student then had all evening to work on the new lesson and be prepared for various drills and exercises and tests on the following day. A second night of study on the same lesson was followed by still more rigorous tests until we were certain the lesson had been mastered. Classes alternated between working with a native instructor and an hour spent in the language laboratory listening to tapes of one form or another.

Since the correcting and grading of every exercise paper was a measure of the student's capabilities, we called our system of instruction "Teaching through Testing," and for a period of some 15 years at Yale it worked like a charm, with ever more satisfactory results. However, for the people whose job it was to correct and grade that flood of papers, it was horrendous, requiring great dedication in addition to an across-the-board knowledge of the entire course.

With a new class coming in every three months and three different levels of classes in session at the same time, each class having at least two lab sessions a day, there were literally hundreds of papers to be corrected every day. We weren't always able to achieve our goal of having all papers corrected and the results posted one hour after the class, but we did our best. We felt strongly that to delay returning the papers would result in students forgetting the material as they moved on rapidly to other things.

Initially, we had made the teacher of each class responsible for correcting the papers, but the results were mixed and proved quite unsatisfactory. All students tended quite naturally to scribble their answers in a hurry, and their handwriting was, at best, hard to decipher. For most of our Chinese teachers that proved such a hardship that we had to devise the method of having a special team do the work to ensure uniformity.

The last class each day at every level was invariably a lab class with another flood of papers. That meant someone had to take the papers home to correct them, an additional burden. Initially I took it on myself to handle all papers from those last classes. Night after night I took home stacks of papers, which Eva and I corrected and graded, posting the results the next morning before classes started.

Eva more than did her share of the work in helping me with the papers and proved such a natural at the job that the logical step was to hire her to do the job full-time at the school, even though it smacked of nepotism. At first she was able to keep up with the demand by herself, but as more students came in and the workload grew, we hired two young American women to help her, both of them having had a year or so of Chinese. One was Doris Seely and the other Joan Rebman. For several years that team of three worked together in the back-breaking, thankless task of grinding out hundreds of papers each working day. Their only reward — and a most satisfying one — was to see the excitement and gratification on the part of the students who, an hour after each test, would rush to the bulletin board to see how well or poorly they had done. On the part of the "test team" as we called them (Eva and her assistants), it meant not only a high degree of dedication, but also an intimate knowledge of the Chinese language and an ability to switch gears several times a day between elementary and very basic material, to materials of ever-increasing sophistication, including the highly technical military matter coming from the upper level classes. Former students who may have the opportunity of reading this will remember those three young women and their great contribution to the success of our course at Yale.

There were other members of the team, such as Pauline Brooks at first, then Mary Schloeman and Carolyn Lockhart. None knew any Chinese, but their job was to take the corrected papers and log the individual's grades, then fill out a name sheet to post on the board. Then, since students were encouraged to go in and examine their corrected papers to see where the mistakes were, one of them had to locate their papers and produce them quickly. Our highly motivated students — and most of them fell into that category — usually used their lunch hours or coffee breaks for that purpose, and the ladies were always there to help them and to offer some words of encouragement or praise. In cases where a student was having severe or unusual problems with the course, Eva called him in at the end of the day to go over his papers and advise him as to where he went wrong and what it was that was causing difficulties.

For years, Eva and I took home with us the last papers of the day, usually some three or four sets. After dinner we would sit down to correct and grade them, working frequently until midnight. To keep ourselves awake and alert, we played recordings of ragtime songs and music. The fast-moving, toe-tapping tempo of those timeless pieces kept us going, and singing along as we plowed through those nightly stacks of papers made the job enjoyable.

Naturally it wasn't all work and no play for us during those years at Yale. We did manage to get in some recreation of a sort. But it usually took the form of work of a different kind. Early in 1952, as soon as the ground thawed, just for fun we started to build a two-bedroom house on the rear part of our lot. Eva and I started the job with shovels and a wheelbarrow, first digging out the basement. We had our share of curious onlookers, and from time to time neighborhood children came over to watch us. One day one of them loudly proclaimed to me, "My dad says you're crazy not to have a bulldozer do this for you." For us, however, digging was part of the fun and a big change from school work. Besides, we weren't in any hurry.

Eva and I were invariably the first to get to school in the morning, around 7 o'clock, with Ray Mazzarella normally accompanying us. We had to unlock the doors and, in winter, start the furnace. The early-bird students were there soon afterward, even though classes didn't begin until eight.

Getting out of school soon after four in the afternoon allowed us time for a cup of tea, and we could then work on the house until dark and sometimes later with lights. Once the basement was dug we poured the footings, and I started to build the walls with concrete blocks. I used my old-fashioned Chinese method of a bowl of water and a floating stick to sight for the proper elevation, keeping constant tabs on it as the walls slowly went up. When we finally topped out, I was gratified to find that only on one corner was I off by a mere three-eighths of an inch. Not too bad for a thousand-year-old method and an amateur builder.

Our students were enthusiastic helpers on weekends, making a picnic of it and enjoying the country air. By early fall we had the roof on, but the house was far from ready for occupancy. I had miscalculated somewhat on the time it would take us, and early in the year, when a young Army captain and his wife, Ken and Betty Kochel, wrote us asking for help in finding a place to live, I had confidently told them they could have our house in October. By then I was sure we would be able to move into the one we were building. Alas, when October arrived, and with it the Kochel family, we had several months of work still to do and had to find somewhere to stay until the house was livable.

We rented a large house trailer, parked it on the back lawn just behind the house we were building, and spent the better part of the winter there. It wasn't possible to keep it very warm, but it was healthy living, and by early spring even though the floors weren't finished, nor the interior painted, we were able to move into the new place. We lived in that little house for about a year, adding finishing touches inside. In July 1953, Ray Mazzarella needed a house for his growing family, so we sold it to him, still not completely finished, and moved back into our old house, since the Kochels had long since moved on.

A year later, July 1954, I bought the house directly across the street from the new house we had built. It was an exact twin of the first house we had purchased and were living in, and not more than 100 feet away from it. But it sat on a much larger piece of land, well over an acre, most of which was tidal marsh.

Moving across the street to that house was accomplished in two or three hours one morning with the help of about a dozen students who volunteered for the job. Never did a move go so smoothly or so quickly. Afterward, we had a big hamburger luncheon together in the new place.

Looking out our side and back windows, we watched each day as the tide came in and covered a large section of our new property with about eight feet of water. To fill that all in and build another house there was my goal. But to buy that much fill would have cost a fortune, so I had to find a better way.

Less than a quarter of a mile from us in Branford was a large iron-working factory that produced galvanized pipe. They had several large foundries from which molten metal was poured each day, and daily, the coal-burning fire boxes had to be cleaned out and the resulting ash and huge clinkers were hauled several miles to the city dump. Clinkers, for the uninitiated, are large lumps of incombustible matter fused together in varying shapes. In many cases they looked much like lumps of black glass, and, like glass, had extremely sharp edges.

I saw a possibility in all that throw-away ash and clinkers, so I went over to the factory and talked to the manager, offering to take all the cinders and clinkers he could supply. He was delighted to find a nearby dump site, and for months thereafter his trucks brought their daily loads to our swamp; all it cost me was fifty cents a load.

At first, the trucks could dump their loads directly from the road into the swamp. But as time went on, and the piles of ash built up, I had to have some way of leveling them off each day of pushing the material farther out into the water. For that purpose I bought a Willys Jeep equipped with a snow plow, and each afternoon after school I leveled out the piles and spread the material through the swamp. The sharp edges of the clinkers played havoc with the Jeep tires, though, and after a few weeks my tires had worn

down to the point where I had to replace them.

The cost of tires made it impractical to continue using it for that purpose; however, I was fortunate in being able to buy a small bulldozer for just over $100. That it was rusty and wouldn't run was a minor problem. Ray Mazzarella was just the person to put it back into working condition, which he did after considerable improvisation and finding suitable parts. I also bought a used front-end loader and a used dump truck, all of which gave me endless hours of pleasure on weekends. Granted, these were "adult" toys, but I hold to the premise that every man should have a bulldozer at least once in his life. There is no better way to relax and work out the stress and frustrations of daily life than to sit atop a noisy bulldozer moving dirt around on a large vacant lot. No telephones can bother you and nothing and no one can break in to interrupt your thoughts.

Eventually the entire swamp area was filled, and with an additional few loads of topsoil I ended up with a sizable piece of reclaimed land. Unfortunately it wasn't until 1971 that we were able to place a four-bedroom house on it. But that is another story.

While all that was going on, my mind was working on a problem we faced in our language laboratories. In my contacts with the manufacturers of recording equipment, particularly tape recorders, I constantly ran into the dominant theme from all of them that language students had an interest span of a maximum of twenty minutes. That theory had been picked up by a large number of educators as well, and at the meetings of educators I attended all over the country I heard the same thing: "No recorded teaching materials should exceed twenty minutes in length." But from our own experience I strongly disputed it, and pointed to the fact that children — and some adults as well — would sit in front of the television screen for hours on end with no lag in interest. My theory, borne out by experience, was that when learning tools were made sufficiently interesting, there was no limit to the so-called interest span of any given student. In fact, a large percentage of the materials we prepared for our own students at IFEL were in excess of 20 minutes.

As I studied the matter, I became more than ever convinced that I was right. Then one day I discovered the real reason for the "20-minute" theory. It turned out that a majority of the magnetic recordings, particularly the disc-type, could only hold approximately twenty minutes of material. It suited the convenience of the manufacturers to tout their theory rather than try to develop longer-playing tapes and records. Since long-playing tapes were already available, the answer to the problem was obviously to produce a better tape recorder, one that was simple for students to handle and was "idiot-proof," as the saying goes. It also had to be one that would stand up to the wear and tear of daily schoolroom use.

A tape recorder suitable for students had, of necessity, not only to be reliable, it also had to be smaller and more compact in order to fit into the limited space of a language laboratory booth and allow space for the student's books and writing materials. Around 1958 I discussed the problem with one of the local businessmen involved in supplying audio-visual aids, and he encouraged me to design a booth of my own that would be an improvement over anything then on the market; he, in turn, would work on the tape recorder to go in it. With that in mind, I set out to design a booth that would meet all the objectives and resolve the problems that kept cropping up.

I conceived the idea of eliminating the bulky case in which all tape recorders were housed and making the case or housing a part of the booth. In order to use the minimum amount of space in the booth, the logical conclusion was to build a slanting "case" at the back of the booth, in direct view and easy reach of the student. Moreover, it would be completely out of his way and allow maximum working space on his desk, but it had to be low enough not to block his forward vision.

With the support, advice, and constant help of Ray Mazzarella, we produced five different models, one of which finally met all our requirements, and we also produced a number of miniature models to use as demonstrators. Aware of what I was doing, one of the tape-recorder manufacturers came up with a simplified tape-deck without a case, and with simplified controls that would stand up to unlimited wear and tear. A cut-out in the face of the slanting "case" at the back of my booth provided a convenient and workable method of housing the deck, and the booth itself was complete with a fold-down cover that could be locked, protecting the tape machine when not in use. In addition, the desk top was hinged with a compartment beneath it for the student's books.

The entire booth was at least one-third smaller than any other then on the market, and for the design I was able to get the very first U.S. patent for a "Language Listening Booth," Patent No. 190,081. Applying for the patent was a lengthy and expensive process that took more than two years, and long before the patent was issued in 1960, I had been encouraged to get into the business of supplying the booths for the burgeoning language laboratory market, then fast approaching its peak. I worked out a contract with a local distributor, giving him exclusive rights to the sale of the booth, then found a large furniture manufacturer in Bridgeport, Connecticut, where I was able to get the booths made. In the first year more than 1,000 were manufactured and installed in colleges, universities and high schools throughout the East Coast of the United States.

Initially, the side panels of the booth were made of a high quality plywood, which after being well sanded were stained and varnished. The result was a very attractive piece of furniture, but those heavy panels proved to be a problem. Even though they were packed well in cardboard cases, the panels tended to become scratched or otherwise damaged during shipment or at the site because of improper installation. I discovered that by using a cheaper plywood, I could get them covered with wood-grained Formica for approximately the same price, and we ended up covering the entire booth in that durable and attractive product. The newer model was an instant success, and many more were produced over the next year or two.

I bought a small Volkswagen truck to haul the finished products from Bridgeport to our house, where we used the garage as a packing and storage depot. Then, as orders came in, I took them to the distributor. After about a year of that after-hours business I learned that my distributor was undercutting my price to him by having identical booths manufactured in California to supply the demand there. It was obviously cheaper for him than shipping mine across country. He went a step further and found a manufacturer in New Jersey to whom he gave one of my booths as a model, and although the man was something of a competitor of his, they worked out a deal where he was able to get the booths considerably cheaper than I could produce them; however, it was much inferior in quality. That manufacturer made the mistake of printing up some advertising brochures, displaying a picture of a booth identical to mine on the cover, and sent me a copy in the mail, not knowing who I was.

I went to my distributor with that evidence, protested his unethical conduct, and told him I reserved the right to claim royalties for every booth he was having manufactured elsewhere. He flatly denied purchasing booths from others, even though he had some stacked nearby in plain sight. When I pointed that out to him and asked where they had come from, he said he was "storing" them for someone else, brushing off my complaint with the remark that "business was slow" and that was the reason why he had not been ordering any from me of late.

However, I was also producing teacher consoles, and the fact that he had been ordering those from me convinced me that he was lying, that he was still doing plenty of business but buying his booths elsewhere. I finally had to take legal action against him and his two other suppliers in order to protect my patent. Although I was successful in stopping those two manufacturers, others began to copy the booth, and that, together with other events in the early '60s made me decide to give up the business, since it was consuming too much of my time, and the cost for legal expenses was mounting. It wasn't worth the hassle.

In the meantime, at IFEL, the demands made by the Air Force and the ever-increasing numbers of new students had caused us to further expand our language laboratory facilities into several other buildings on the Yale campus. Because my booth and the built-in tape recorder concept were by then acknowledged by everyone in the business to be the best on the market,

I had little trouble in convincing the Yale purchasing agent not only to buy my product for the new installations, but also to convert all of our labs to the new model and install tape recorders in every booth. In order to avoid any conflict of interest, I provided the booths at cost, and had them delivered directly from the manufacturer.

Although I made nothing on the deal, I had the immense satisfaction of seeing several hundred of my booths installed in the various labs at Yale. After the students started using them, I had much greater gratification, seeing a marked improvement in student achievement using the new tape recorders. Furthermore, student interest increased as we were able to give them more material on the tapes, and that led to greater interest in doing after-hours homework. The labs were in use for two or three hours each evening, and that led me to another idea.

I discovered some small, cheap Japanese tape recorders and purchased more than 100 of them as rental units, which we supplied to the students for $5 a month. They were in constant demand, the students renting them for use beside their beds for listening well into the night and to use on weekends when the school was closed.

In this chapter I've covered mostly the mechanical aspects of language learning, with little reference to the people involved. In the next chapter I'll touch on the human side of the Yale experience — our own, that of our colleagues, both Chinese and American, and most of all the students, without whom there would never have been a course at Yale.

Chinese characters for Yale (Yelu)

BULLETIN OF YALE UNIVERSITY

Institute of Far Eastern Languages

SERIES 55, NUMBER 7. 1 APRIL 1959

Far Eastern Languages
for Practical Use of
Scholar and Traveler
Merchant and Missionary
Diplomat and Journalist

Officers

A. Whitney Griswold, *President of the University.*
Norman S. Buck, *Provost of the University.*

EXECUTIVE COMMITTEE

Reuben A. Holden, *Secretary of the University (Chairman).*
Harry R. Rudin, *Colgate Professor of History.*
David N. Rowe, *Professor of Political Science.*
George A. Kennedy, *Professor of the Chinese Language and Literature.*
Chitoshi Yanaga, *Associate Professor of Political Science.*

ADMINISTRATION

Henry C. Fenn, *Director of the Institute.*
Gerard P. Kok, *Associate Director.*
Robert P. Miller, *Chairman of Japanese and Korean Program.*
Robert N. Tharp, *Chairman of Audio Visual Laboratory and Program.*
Raymond Scungio, *Administrative Assistant.*

Cover and page one of *IFEL* Bulletin, 1959

Henry Fenn explaining patterns of spoken Chinese to a beginning class.

"Rapid Fire" exercise in the sound laboratory.

Charlie Chu's cartoon, characters saying: "Kuai ting."

Bob sitting in back of room monitoring students.

Bob in front of *IFEL* at Yale.

Faculty, staff and students at *IFEL* taken before we got our classes of 70-75 students.

Parker Huang, Bob and Henry Fenn.

YMCA class "A" Runner-up 1965

Air Force students relax at *IFEL.*

Gerard (Jerry) Kok, Henry Fenn, Bob Tharp.

Ida Tyrrell without whom the school could not have functioned.

Del Lang, Jerry Kok, Bob Tharp.

Bob taking time off to throw some snowballs.

Major Del Lang, Taiwan, 1957

With a Yale building in background.

Del Lang and his wife, Terry, visit us in 1969.

Bob found time to go sailing in his boat only a few times, but he loved it.

IFEL Student Bulletin "Shouting". Class of 1955.

ITELPOOF SONG

From the tables in our classrooms
To the place where we take tests
To the dear old record room
We love so well.

Sing we Airmen here assembled
With our earphones all plugged in
And the static on the disc
Is really hell.

Oh the static on the records
And the awful rapid fire
Mingled with a few loud grunts
Of Robert Tharp
We must listen to these records
With head and eardrums torn
Or we'll all be sent to Thule
In the morn.

We're poor little Airmen here at Yale
Blah, blah, blah
With a bullwhip waiting if we should fail
Hah, hah, hah.

Blue suited linguists so constantly
Mixing up Chinese grammatically
Tharp have mercy on such as we
Blah, blah, blah.

Harry J. Sweeney

ITELPOOF SONG

"Then we sing, 'Tharp have mercy on such as we)...'"

—José Pallazola

Institute of Technology

Air University

United States Air Force

presents this symbol of appreciation to

ROBERT N. THARP

this ___17TH___ day of ___MARCH___ in the year ___1960___

for outstanding contributions to

Air Force Education

through support and guidance of

AIR FORCE FOREIGN LANGUAGE PROGRAMS

sponsored by the Institute of Technology and

conducted by ___YALE UNIVERSITY___

as a service to the defense of the United States

_____
Commandant

Fan hou yikou yan shengguo dang shenxian.

A mouthful of (tobacco) smoke after a meal surpasses becoming an immortal.

- Chinese Peasant Saying.

Chapter Forty-Five
Can Everyone Learn Chinese?

In the previous chapter I wrote about the equipment, materials, and techniques we used at the Institute of Far Eastern Languages. But no matter how well equipped a school may be, or how good its teachers, without the student a school is nothing. All of us felt that not only were our students our most important asset, but everything we had, or did, was for their benefit. Our goal was to produce the best possible results with the students sent to us. However, we soon discovered that it was to be no easy task because of the heavy curriculum requirements set by the Air Force.

Can everyone learn Chinese? During my almost 30 years as a teacher of the language, I have been asked that question numerous times and the answer has always been a qualified "yes." Almost every individual learns at a different pace, creating problems in classes of anywhere from 60 to 90 students. Some are slow starters but pick up speed as they go along. Others start slowly and progress even more slowly as

they plow ahead. Some start well, then fall off quickly as the work becomes more difficult. Others do well for weeks, then seem to reach a saturation point, after which they seem unable to absorb any more. Then there were the precious few to whom learning Chinese, or any new language, was an absolute breeze.

That first class of 60 men who started in July 1951 were all hand-picked by Captain Lang. All were highly motivated, extremely intelligent, and anxious to make good in the course. However, due to the intensity of the course, only 25 of the 60 eventually graduated, including Capt. Lang, who had already gone through a year of Chinese in Monterey. It was clear to us at the end of the first twelve weeks that despite the high motivation and intelligence of the group, at least half were not going to make it. To be more exact, they fell into the various categories mentioned in the preceding paragraph, and far too many of them were not able to keep up with the rest of the class. At the same time, of those who eventually graduated, the majority were having no trouble at all.

When the same thing occurred with the next two classes, we seriously examined the reasons for such heavy attrition. Many questions came to mind. Were we asking too much of them? Was the course really that difficult? Was the pace too fast? Were we being allowed insufficient time with the men? Were the teachers or our methodology at fault?

It is well recognized that when every member of a class can pass a given test and get a score of 100, something is wrong with the test. When no single individual in a class can get a score of 100, then something is equally wrong. In any given group there must always be a spread in grades known as a "curve." A curve is described in *The Random House Dictionary* as "a system of grading based on the scale of performance of a group, so that those performing better, regardless of their actual knowledge of the subject, receive better grades."

What we found with those first three classes, however, was that although more than half the class were at the extreme bottom end of the grade curve, a disproportionate and limited number were bunched at the high end, with scarcely anyone in between. Furthermore, those on the high end of the curve were not only breezing through the course, they could have absorbed a great deal more than we gave them, and, in fact, most of them were asking for more.

We began to realize two wholly divergent facts about the course: If we were to fulfill the demands of the Air Force to produce a student qualified in Chinese to meet their stated requirements, our course was, on the one hand, much too difficult for a certain type of student. On the other hand, in order to attain our goals, we had to make it even more intense and rounded out than it already was for the type of student at the top of the curve. That meant we needed some method of finding the type of student who could hack the course with relative ease and at the same time weed out those who should never be allowed to even start the course. It was obvious we needed a much better selection process in order to identify the gifted individuals who were obviously out there, but of whom we were only finding a pitifully small number.

The big question was how to identify them. The three of us, our director Jerry Kok, the deputy director Henry Fenn, and I, put our heads together and for

days on end did some heavy thinking. The Air Force was doing its best to find qualified candidates for us. Two young Chinese-speaking lieutenants were doing the selecting. We had met and talked with them and made a few suggestions as to what to look for. Both men were well qualified and were enthusiastic in carrying out their job, but it wasn't working. It was also obvious that the battery of psychological and other tests they were administering wasn't adequate to weed out those who didn't have the stamina to stand up to the pace of the course or didn't have the mental capacity to absorb the material quickly enough. Something had to be done about it, and done quickly. The word "aptitude" began to appear in our conversation, something that had not been discussed in connection with language learning before that, and what we needed was to find some method of determining whether an individual had the aptitude, not merely for languages, but specifically for Chinese.

In many respects spoken Chinese is one of the simplest of all modern languages. Rudolph Flesch in his book *How to Write, Speak and Think More Effectively*, stated that Chinese is a "grammarless" tongue. In one sense he was correct, because the list of things spoken Chinese doesn't have is truly amazing. No inflections, no cases, no persons, no genders, no tenses, no voices or moods, no infinitives, no participles, gerunds or irregular verbs, and no articles, such as "the" and "a." In its spoken form Chinese is multisyllabic, but in the written form there are no words of more than one syllable. Yet to say the language is grammarless is not entirely correct. Although grammar is never taught in Chinese schools — indeed, I grew up in China thinking there was no grammar in the language — I discovered when I got to Yale that Gardner Tewksbury, Jerry Kok and Professor Kennedy, in preparing the Yale texts, had isolated and defined a specific and highly detailed form of grammar, or what we called sentence structure.

Chinese has in it many of our grammar components, but some are used quite differently and so they had to be given different names. For example, some Chinese verbs differ from ours and were given names such as stative verbs, which describe a quality or condition. In addition there were compound verbs and auxiliary verbs and nouns that we called specified, numbered and measured, and there were other variations that had to be taken into account.

Despite the seeming simplicity of the language and its lack of grammar as we know it, too many of the students were finding it beyond their capabilities. Being a tonal language made it difficult for a large number of them. American English tends to be spoken in a monotone, with very little inflection in the voice, and not much in the way of stress being placed on any specific words or parts of a sentence, certainly not as much as is the case in Chinese. In Chinese, where tones are so important, an inability to distinguish between them is a serious matter. But for some students, the very simplicity of the Chinese language word order created problems. American students, tending to think in their native language, wanted to put into Chinese more than was required, or in other words, they wanted to try and literally translate Americanisms into Chinese.

To give a couple of examples, a common American idiom, used when agreeing to another person's statement is: "me too." Those two words are readily translated into Chinese as "wo ye," but in Chinese it makes no sense whatsoever, and they cannot be used the same way. In Chinese one must repeat the verb and say, in effect, "I also wish to go," or "I also think the same way you do," and so on. Another example is our way of saying, "I don't think I want any." What we actually mean, and the way the Chinese say it is: "I think I don't want any." In other words, when you make the statement, you have, from the Chinese point of view, already thought the thought, so you say, "I think I don't..." And when you think about it, it makes a lot more sense. There are numerous other examples, but I'll offer just one more. We frequently say: "I wonder...such and such..." In Chinese there is no such word as "wonder," and it is impossible, for example, to say, "I wonder who's kissing her now." However, if a Chinese were to think that and want to express it, he would properly phrase it: "I know (or I'm sure) someone is kissing her now and I'd very much like to know who it is." Hence the differences between the two languages, English and Chinese, have something to do with the problems in learning the language, and not simply because Chinese is, despite its simplicity, a difficult language to learn. I once heard of an individual who spoke 54 different languages, and someone made the remark that he played the same tune on 54 different violins. That is

often the case. Everyone, it seems, can learn a few words in any language, while others become highly proficient. What was it that made the difference? We have never really been able to answer that question, except that some people seem to have a natural aptitude for languages, which also includes a high motivation for learning.

In general, the Air Force students were not lacking in motivation. Every single man seemed eager to tackle the job and proud of having been chosen to go to Yale. But the high hopes with which many of them started the course soon fell as the pace increased and hard work took its toll. We weren't sure what the answer was, but since it appeared that it was a week or two of exposure to Chinese that separated the sheep from the goats, as it were, we began to explore the possibility of screening the students in advance by using a condensed or shortened version of the initial Chinese text.

In the latter part of 1951 we decided to broach the subject to the Air Force as a possible way of cutting down the attrition rate and suggested that we go personally to the nearest Air Force training base to make the selection of prospective students. Whatever we might do certainly couldn't produce any worse results than we were currently seeing.

When we talked with the Air Force top brass, we found them equally concerned, and they most enthusiastically endorsed our idea of going to the air base to recruit our own students. We asked them to continue using their current testing methods to make an initial selection of men, but to test a much larger group than they normally did in order to form a pool approximately three times as great as the number actually needed to form the class. We then scheduled a date to go to the base three weeks in advance of the day on which the class was due to be admitted at Yale.

With our idea approved, we set about preparing our screening test. Knowing the most pressing problems for the students in learning the language, we decided to select some very basic Chinese vocabulary items, together with sentence patterns that caused problems. We put them into lesson form, printed some booklets, and wrote a series of tests to be given every few hours as our screening program progressed. We wanted to find out as soon as possible just where every man stood.

When that had been completed we wondered if there were some refinements we might include. How about a basic English grammar test to see if those high school graduates could identify common English grammatical terms, such as verbs, nouns, adjectives, adverbs, etc., and how they were used? Since Chinese is a tonal language, where a slight difference in the way a word or sound is said can change its meaning, another idea occurred to us. How about testing the students to see if they could carry a tune? Ultimately those and a number of other ideas were tried out, but most of them were eventually discarded because they didn't really prove anything.

The nearest Air Force training base in those days was Sampson Air Force Base near the small town of Geneva, at the tip of Lake Seneca, one of the largest of the finger lakes in upper New York state, roughly between Syracuse and Rochester. To reach Sampson AFB from New Haven was almost a day's drive over the two-lane highways of those days. On our first trip, Henry Fenn and I went along, neither of us quite sure how it would turn out. With us we took two of the top men from our soon-to-graduate class. We did that partly as a reward to them for their hard work and accomplishments and partly to provide us with some clerical help. But there was one other important reason. We felt that those two young men, with whom we could chat in Chinese in front of the candidates, would provide a strong motivating factor for the young recruits and show them that Chinese had indeed been mastered by two of their own kind. In addition they could see that it had earned the two men a second stripe on their sleeves.

As it turned out, taking those two men with us turned out to have been a wise move. From then on, and for the next 14 years, we went four times a year to Sampson, and later to Lackland AFB in San Antonio, Texas, to make our selection, invariably taking two of the top students with us. They not only helped us tremendously in dealing with Air Force "underlings," who at times could be very officious and difficult, but their assistance proved invaluable in organizing the classes we held, passing out books and papers, correcting tests and compiling grades, and generally making for a smooth operation.

But perhaps most important of all was their very presence before those large groups of anxious and almost always scared would-be finalists. As the two students chatted together in Chinese, or followed our instructions, which were always given in Chinese, the young airmen were vastly impressed. Then, during breaks or in the evenings, they were able to answer the inevitable questions about Yale: living conditions in New Haven, the course itself, and a host of other subjects. We found their presence to be a highly motivating factor, and for the two men it proved a welcome break away from the drudgery of classes.

As time went on, the chance of being selected to accompany us on our "Aptitude Screening" trip became a much-sought-after honor in every class. For us, on the other hand, it became an increasingly difficult task to select which two men we should take. We had to be perfectly fair in making our choice; we didn't want to hurt anyone's feelings. We had to choose on the basis of the men having earned the privilege; and at the same time we had to be sure the two could work well together.

I recall that on one occasion we did make an exception. In one class two men were quite outstanding and the obvious choice. However, they were bitter rivals academically, were never seen speaking together, and could not abide each other's presence. In fact, when put in a small class together, each had asked to be transferred elsewhere, a request that was not unusual, but which I never approved. As I told them, when they got out into the field it was highly likely they would find themselves sitting elbow to elbow listening to the enemy radio, and if they couldn't get along with each other in school, it boded ill for their relationship later.

Much as those two young men desired to go, when I told them they had been selected to accompany me, each said he would not go if the other went. I told them it was not up to them to decide. They would go and do the job I wanted of them, and they would get along with each other, or they would have to do some tall explaining to me.

We started off early one morning in my car with the two young men in the back seat, and for many miles they refused to either look at or talk to each other. Eventually, as the day wore on, the absurdity of the situation dawned on them. They grinned sheepishly and not only started talking to each other, but worked well together when we got to the base and ended up becoming fast friends.

On our first trip to Sampson we received a warm

welcome from the base commander and his staff. The general talked a long time with us about our selection process, then provided us with several non-commissioned officers to assist us in any way they could. As we sat there, I noticed a large sign on the wall reading — in pseudo Latin — "Illigitimus Non Carborundum." The general noticed me looking at it and with a smile asked me if I knew what it meant. When I said no, he said: "That's my motto here. It means, `Don't let the bastards grind you down.'" Despite that seemingly callous attitude toward the men he was there to train, he proved actually to be an exceptionally warm-hearted individual who was most sympathetic and understanding of the young airmen temporarily under his command.

Henry Fenn and I were assigned comfortable rooms in the BOQ and were given the freedom of the base: the Officers' Club, post exchange, and any other facility we cared to use. Our visit lasted two full weeks, simply because we were not entirely sure of what we were doing. In that time we covered the equivalent of several lessons in the first Chinese text. In the two weeks we screened well over 200 men to select the 40 or 50 we felt were most qualified for the course, and in the process learned a great deal about how to do it on subsequent trips.

We had tried to anticipate and take with us all that we would need in the way of supplies: paper, pencils, etc. However, there were things we had overlooked, so we sent our two airmen "helpers" into a nearby office to ask for certain items. While waiting at the desk, as young men will, the two lads started commenting (in Chinese) on the attractive young ladies working in the office. As they were talking together, a somewhat older woman, apparently the supervisor, came over to them and loudly told them, "Let's have none of that French language around here please. Tell us in English what you want and then get out of here." From then on we always warned our assistants not to talk "French" when they went into that office!

Initially, we had planned to teach the recruits some basic Chinese for an hour or so, give them some time for study and review, and after drilling them on what they had learned, we would give them a test at the end of each day. Gradually we would eliminate those who were obviously not doing well and were unlikely to survive the course. But an unusual situation awaited us when we started the screening.

Word had spread as to what we were doing and several Air Force psychologists were there waiting for us, together with two civilians, one of them a professor from one of the Ivy League universities. All were quite excited about what we were attempting and wanted to observe the experiment to see how it went. Over dinner at the Officers' Club that first night they asked us how we intended making our selection. When we told them of our plan to make a cut at the end of every day, they were horrified. All of them agreed that a policy of that sort would be likely to "de-motivate" the rest of the student candidates and would tend to discourage them greatly as they watched their numbers being slowly whittled down. They suggested that we should make the earliest possible selection of the men who showed promise, then pull them out of the group and publicize the results. That, they said, would encourage the rest to greater effort.

Not having any training in psychology, we could not dispute them, and it sounded quite reasonable. However, we doubted the practicality of that procedure, particularly since those so chosen would have had only a minimal exposure to the language. Nonetheless, against personal inclinations, we agreed to do as they suggested, and at the end of the first day we picked two or three men who were at the top of the list, the second day another one or two, and so on for the ten days we were there until we had the number of men we needed.

Interestingly enough, the psychologists were wrong where it came to the quality of the men we had picked, and the method they had suggested proved to be a serious mistake. When the men started classes at Yale, those who had been picked first, in almost every case, turned out to be less than adequate. They did little in the way of studying at night and acted like prima donnas, boasting that they were the best in the class because of their having been selected first. All but one or two of them failed the course. It taught us a lesson, and from then on we followed our instincts and eliminated the poorest performers early, with a daily "cut." We found that not only to be highly motivating to those who remained as they saw the crowd of contenders daily reduced in size, thus giving them more of a chance to be selected, but at the same time it allowed us to step up the pressure and really challenge the men to do their best.

The results of our "screening" trips were immediately apparent. The academic attrition rate immediately dropped from over 50 percent to under 3 percent, where it remained for as long as we continued the process, although at one point a year or so later, things changed for a short period because of an unusual event.

The professor who had observed our first screening session also attended two or three more with us. He then wrote and told us that after watching our process, he had developed his own aptitude screening test, which he thought to be much simpler, easier to administer and evaluate, and which he thought would be applicable for any language. He asked for our permission to try it out on the pool of students we would be testing on our next visit to Sampson AFB, hoping there might be some way we could somehow incorporate his test along with ours to see how they matched up.

Seeing no reason to discourage him, we invited him to join us. It would naturally take a little longer, but the students would not know the difference and would simply consider his material to be part of the overall testing. We thought we might also learn something at the same time.

His method of screening, not being specifically designed to determine aptitude for learning Chinese, consisted of a fictitious language he had created, with a few simple words and phrases and some basic grammatical rules that the students would have to learn, and the tests that he gave were a series of multiple-choice questions based on cartoon-like drawings. We fed his material in with ours and all went smoothly, and at the end we compared results.

The professor was convinced there was a sufficiently strong correlation to justify his streamlined methodology as opposed to our lengthier and more tedious approach, but although his "best" men were the same ones we had chosen as being the best, we found wide discrepancies when it came to the remainder of the group, and we had strong doubts that his test would effectively find the type of individual we needed.

But the Air Force thought differently. After running two or three more of his trial tests to refine his procedure he was able to sell his idea to the Air Force as being a valid means of determining language aptitude per se, and since it covered all languages, it

seemed to be just what the Air Force wanted. Not only that, it would be much cheaper because it could be administered individually instead of in large groups and would take much less time. In the third year of our course at Yale, the Air Force notified us that they would no longer need our services in selecting students and that they would be using the new commercially available test to find the men they would send us. We were not overly surprised.

When the first class selected by that alternate method eventually came in, we were somewhat in a quandary. Previously, our methodology and approach upon the entry of a new class, which we had screened ourselves, was based on the fact that the men had already had some intensive exposure to Chinese. After a brief review we pushed right ahead into the course. Now, however, the situation had changed. The men coming in from the new screening procedure had received no exposure whatsoever to Chinese.

We had only one alternative. By that time, 1954 or thereabouts, we had refined our own screening process to a two-day procedure, which covered approximately two lessons in Chinese. We therefore decided to take a few hours and put the new men through our regular screening process as soon as they arrived and then go on from there with the regular course. We did that with each successive class in that year.

The results we got after putting them through our own screening in no way surprised us. We again found huge discrepancies in the caliber of the men who supposedly had aptitude for Chinese. From our own test results it was obvious, judging by our past record of the two previous years, that we would lose a lot of them during the course year. But we kept the test results to ourselves, not telling anyone on the staff, not even the Chinese teachers, to avoid in any way prejudicing them, and we certainly couldn't tell the Air Force authorities at the time or it would have sounded self-serving.

With each class that came in we took our test results, sealed them in an envelope with signatures of witnesses on the outside, and put the envelopes into a safe. It wasn't long before we began to see that our projections were quite valid. With that first class, by the end of the first 12 weeks there was a significant gap between the men who were breezing through the course and those who obviously were not going to make the grade.

Halfway through that year the Air Force, which had been monitoring the progress of "their" first class, began to note the wide discrepancy in the performance of the men compared to other classes that had gone through the course in the two previous years, and the heavily increased attrition rate. Representatives came to Yale and started to ask questions, and there were indications that they thought we were being less than fair, perhaps because of pique that our test was not being used. We responded by pulling out the sealed envelopes and showing them the results of our own screening when each class of men had first arrived, the grades we had given each man, and our evaluation of their chances of making the course. In every case, those initial screening test results tallied with the subsequent performance of the men as they went through the course. The Air Force was convinced, and from then on we reverted to our old method of going to the base and screening each class in person.

As time went on and we refined our methodology, the aptitude test became so accurate that we could anticipate, within two or three points, the grade with which each man would eventually graduate. Naturally there were exceptions: a "slow" man would pick up and do remarkably well by the end of the course, or a "good" man would fall by the wayside, but in general the test became an excellent tool to measure expected performance, and it helped us greatly in the initial placing of men in the small classes where, by means of the test grades, we were able to select an across-the-board representative group in each classroom.

Despite the failure of the university professor's test in selecting men for our Chinese course, we hadn't heard the last of him. To give him credit, his test had shown good results in selecting men for Russian and the Romance languages, and a year or so later he approached us telling us he had produced a proficiency test designed to measure a given student's progress at any stage in language learning, and a Chinese version was available. He hoped we would try it on our students. I agreed, and we gave the test a fair trial.

Three classes were simultaneously in session at the time: one that was just about to graduate, another that had been there for around four months, and the third consisting of men who had not had more than two or three weeks' exposure to Chinese. The results were most interesting. We found there was a surprising overlap between the three groups. The test, like its predecessor, was a multiple-choice test based on a series of cartoon-like pictures, and it used a fair number of lexical items to which our students had not been exposed. Despite that, most of the men did extraordinarily well, but the resultant grades bore very little correlation to our own evaluation of the various students' current achievement.

What surprised me most was that many of the men who had been in the course only two or three weeks were correctly answering questions that contained terminology totally unknown to them, and in a surprising number of cases were doing better than some of the men who were three months or more ahead of them. The same thing was true in the class ahead of them, where many of the men who had four months of work behind them were doing better than those nearing the end of the course. There had to be a logical explanation.

The test, recorded on tape in Chinese, gave a series of questions or statements. The student was required to make a choice from a group of four pictures, one of which was supposed to depict the correct answer. The test results were so bizarre that I took time out to evaluate the results with every single man who had taken it, asking them why they had given the answer they did, and what it was about the picture that had given them their answer. Their replies were most illuminating and showed the fallacy of trying to take short-cuts in language learning, and how difficult it is to try to compare Chinese with any other language when it comes to testing, or even writing lesson materials. At the same time it pointed up the high degree of native intelligence of our students.

After all these years I don't remember the specifics, but I do remember one example very clearly. One question involved a series of pictures, each showing an individual carrying different objects under his arm. The purpose of the question was for the student to identify the objects. The terms for the objects were well beyond the scope of the newly arrived students who had not been exposed to them, but all of them had learned the numbers one through ten. In one question the number "four" was mentioned. The smart students picked up that single word and correctly identified a man who was carrying four books, even though none of them knew the term for books, nor did they understand the question being asked. And there were several other similar instances.

That didn't necessarily prove that the test was invalid, but because of the frequency of that sort of thing, and the results being so varied, I felt it was a poor measure of specific language competency. As I questioned the students individually, almost all of them told me they had simply done a lot of guessing. To me the test was further proof of the haphazard nature of multiple-choice tests in general, where a smart student can make an educated guess based on a single word in a sentence that he otherwise did not understand.

As a general rule, we avoided both multiple-choice and true-or-false tests, employing them only as drills to keep the students on their toes and to give them a rough evaluation of their progress rather than a definitive measurement of their total proficiency. There are too many variables in tests of that sort, and we gave much less value to grades from that type of tests, relying more on our regular daily tests where the student was required to answer a question by writing the answer out in full.

Although that latter type took much longer to correct and grade, it gave us a much better picture of each student's achievement. At the same time, since the student could look over his corrected paper and see where he had gone wrong, it provided him with much more satisfaction and helped him avoid the same error a second time.

I attribute the success of our course at IFEL to that method of testing, laborious as it was, and that was borne out very clearly when the students graduated and each man completed a mandatory self-evaluation of his personal achievement, together with a critique of both the course and the teachers. The majority of students reported favorably on the type of testing we gave them.

With a new class coming in every three months, I began to notice a phenomenon that recurred time and again and held true for every class. Within the first week I was able to spot one individual in the class who stood out as the class leader. Sometimes he was a man of great charm and personality. At other times he might be a quiet and unassuming individual. But always he quickly assumed a position in which the other students looked up to him, and I made it a point to study those individuals carefully. In time I was able

to spot the potential leader during initial screening at the Air Force base with considerable accuracy.

It became apparent from the beginning that the leaders fell into two general categories. One was the type who provided positive leadership, and the other was just the opposite. When there were officers in the class, it was usually one of them who stood out at once as a leader, and in most cases that was just what we wanted. The maturity and experience of such an individual provided an excellent balance.

However, I remember more than one occasion when officers were in the class and things didn't quite work out that way. One incident I remember well, that of a young Air Force captain who gained instant popularity because of his engaging personality and his "daredevil" style of dress. He was short of stature, always wore his cap crushed and set at a rakish angle, and was a "fly boy" with a lot of experience in fighter aircraft in the Korean War and lots of hair-raising stories. He immediately became a hero to the younger men. Unfortunately, he hadn't been there a week before I discovered at least one of the reasons for his tremendous popularity and loyal following. I happened to go into the men's room one day and found him showing his collection of dirty pictures to an enthusiastic group of young airmen. I called him into my office for a private talk, and it wasn't long before his popularity waned and another leader emerged who had the right qualifications to guide the class in the proper direction.

Homosexuality has always been a significant factor in the armed services, where large groups of men live and work together closely for months or even years at a time, and we had our share from time to time. Since almost all of our men were in the Security Service, their work was most secret, and high security clearances were demanded. Any homosexual was regarded as a big risk in those days because of the possibility of blackmail. From time to time we became suspicious of certain individuals, but for the most part we had to leave the elimination of homosexuals to the experts.

In one class of 90 men we screened for the course, one man stood out most noticeably, not because we thought he might be gay, nor for any leadership qualities he had, but because he was at least ten years older than the average one-striper just out of basic training, yet he still had only one stripe. During the screening he passed all our tests with flying colors, and his motivation appeared to be excellent, so there was no reason for us not to accept him. However, when he arrived at Yale and his class got to work, he turned out to be a loner who never made friends with anyone in the entire class. He studied hard, his work was more than adequate, and I found him to be polite but reserved. He asked no favors and minded his own business, but I often wondered what his motivation really was in signing up for the hard grind of learning Chinese in the first place. The only reason I ever had to take him to task was his consistently slovenly appearance and failure to take showers when they were so obviously needed.

At the end of the course that man graduated well toward the top of the class, and then the true reason for his presence emerged. At the graduation ceremony, instead of his Airman First Class uniform, to everyone's surprise he turned up in the uniform of a 1st lieutenant, and it developed that he was with the Office of Special Investigations (OSI) and the Air Force had planted him in the class to identify any homosexuals. In that class of 90 men he identified 22, none of whom had at any time given us the slightest indication of their being gay. I have always had the highest admiration for that young lieutenant. He not only took the grueling punishment of the screening, where competition was exceptionally high, but endured for eight months the ridicule and opprobrium of his classmates and the stresses of the course. He laughingly told me that his slovenly habits and failure to take showers were all part of his act and were meant to discourage others from getting close to him.

With such a large number of men in the program, often around 300 at a time, it was necessary they have logistical support and administrative supervision while at Yale. For that reason a small detachment of regular Air Force personnel maintained an office quite near the school. They were charged with supervising the men's housing, pay, discipline and physical training, and the detachment was usually led by a captain or a major.

We had excellent rapport with each of the officers and men in the detachment, and they fully cooperated in helping us in our mission. We had made it clear to the Air Force that during school hours the men were our responsibility. They were there to learn Chinese; that came first, and there was to be absolutely no interruption of the airmen's school life for military activities of any sort. All that was required of the men was to wear their uniforms and maintain a tidy appearance; other than that they were treated just as any civilian student. After school hours, the airmen were the responsibility of the detachment. In that way as students they were able to devote their entire time and energies to learning the language. Those whose grades were not up to our standard, for whom there was a mandatory two-hour study period in the evenings, were automatically exempt from any military activity that might have been planned for the evening. Yale also made their huge gymnasium available for the students and regular athletic activities were scheduled there. When the weather was good, they were encouraged to participate in outdoor activities such as hiking or baseball.

Among the different officers who ran the Air Force detachment at Yale over those years, one man stood out above all the others. Major Matteo Salemi will long be remembered by all those who came under his command during the several years he was there. He was an exceptional man, with great empathy for his men. He proved to be a father-figure who earned the respect of everyone with whom he came into contact. We became great friends, and have maintained that friendship over the years since his retirement from the service.

The Air Force students were for the most part serious young men, and their motivation was seldom in question. Yet they were young and frisky, and occasionally they got into serious trouble and Maj. Matt Salemi had to discipline them. I recall one of the students who was a budding inventor. Out of a wire coat hanger he designed an ingenious tool that would beat coin telephones. He did a roaring business renting it out to other students to make their long-distance calls, but it wasn't long before he was caught. Not too long after that another man used his tape recorder to tape the gong-like sounds of coins dropping into the coin box. When the operator asked for coins to be deposited, he would play the sounds through the mouthpiece, and he and his friends managed to fool the telephone company for a considerable period of time. Other students from time to time were caught siphoning off gasoline from cars late at night. Another student had a telescope that he rented out to others so they could watch the windows of the Taft Hotel across the street from their dormitory or the windows of a nearby apartment building.

One wintry, snowy night a bunch of the boys quartered in the "tower" in the freshman quadrangle thought it would be a great night to light a fire in the fireplace in their room. Most of the Yale buildings were old and the fireplaces hadn't been used in years; in fact, the dampers were all rusted in the closed position and the chimneys were likely filled with broken bricks or birds' nests, but the lads didn't know that. Having no firewood, they looked around for something to burn and spotted some plastic model planes belonging to one of their number who was out for the evening. They didn't last long. Next, they broke up some chairs and a desk, but by that time the room was full of smoke and the fire department was on its way. That little adventure cost the residents of that room a pretty penny, and it didn't endear them to the top sergeant.

On another night, a group in the same building started an impromptu water fight in the hall of the dorm and were doing well when the other side cheated. They freed the fire hose and wiped the first group out. The next morning they had to answer a lot of questions when the Air Force and university authorities discovered the badly warped floor. Fortunately for them it had rained heavily during the night and they logically pointed to an open window at the end of the hall as the source of the trouble and that got them off the hook, although no one believed them.

For the most part, however, the students' escapades were relatively harmless. More than once, some of them had to be rescued by the police or fire department after attempting to scale East Rock, a precipitous mountain landmark on the north side of New Haven. Also, since there was always rivalry between them and the regular "Yalies," there was the occasional party-crashing and coming to blows where the police had to intervene. But those instances were few and far between.

During school hours I kept a tight reign on the students and discipline was strict. Consequently it was not surprising that occasionally they wanted to let off a little steam and more often than not that took the form of playing a practical joke on me. Eva and I owned one of the first Volkswagen bugs during the 1950s and I used to park it out in a back alley behind the school, near a flight of steps that led down into the basement. At the top of the flight of steps there was a slight indentation in the wall of the building, the exact width of the steps, and about ten feet in length. Several times each year I would go out at the end of the day and find my Volkswagen had been bodily lifted into that tiny space, with the tail end hanging over the steps, and no way for me to drive it out. On each occasion, though, the culprits would be hanging out of the upper windows watching to see what I would do, and I had the satisfaction of calling them down to lift the car out for me.

When we switched to a larger car, I couldn't park it in the alley. During the winter months, a favorite trick of the airmen was to pack snow under the car to the extent that the body of the car was actually lifted. I could spin my wheels but get nowhere. Again, I merely had to look up at the windows to see the gleeful faces watching my discomfort. But it was all in good fun, and I enjoyed the jokes as much as they did.

On one occasion they outdid themselves. As I drove home one evening the car seemed to want to veer to the left all the time, and I was greatly puzzled. After I got home I raised the lid of the trunk and discovered that somehow the lads had managed to lift a huge 400-pound ornamental rock from one of the fraternity houses and had placed it in the trunk. It was a little off center, causing the car to veer to the left. There was no way I could get it out by myself, so I had to take it back to the school the next morning and round up a bunch of laughing volunteers and make them put it back where they found it. They weren't necessarily the original culprits, but the whole school was aware of the prank and all enjoyed the episode.

In addition to the practical jokes, there were always the class artists who drew caricatures of me, and scarcely a week went by that there wasn't one on the general bulletin board. I saved a large number of them and they are among my most prized possessions. None were drawn with malice even though most of them showed me in an unflattering light, usually smoking a pipe or numerous cigarettes. I always enjoyed them as much as everyone else.

After about two years of screening the students at Sampson AFB, the base was closed. After that, all Air Force training was conducted at Lackland AFB in San Antonio, Texas. We had to travel some 1,900 miles four times a year, and the obvious way, of course, was to fly. However, growing up in China as I had, I had never flown, and I had not the slightest intention of ever doing so. The very idea terrified me. I guess I was too used to the slow pace of mule- or ox-drawn carts, and leaving terra firma just didn't appeal to me.

The first trip to Lackland fell to Jerry Kok and Dr. Fenn, but when my turn came, I elected to go by train, a long, roundabout and tedious journey. I did that twice, then decided I would prefer to drive my own car.

At least three or four times I did just that, driving the 1,900 miles non-stop each way except for gasoline and food stops. Eva accompanied me on at least two occasions, and each time I took two airmen as usual. Finally, I managed to screw up enough courage to try the plane, but that first trip was a traumatic experience that I will never forget.

My first flight coincided with a fatal crash that same morning of a four-engined Electra plane, at Boston's Logan Airport, when the plane ran into a flock of birds and everyone aboard was killed. I heard the reports on the radio as I was driving from New Haven to New York's Idlewild Airport, now known as the John F. Kennedy Airport. As I boarded the plane, the agent at the gate happened to be reading a copy of the *New York Daily News* with a front page picture of two victims of the Boston crash still strapped in their seats. That didn't help restore my confidence in any way. On board the plane I discovered it also was an Electra, and apart from me there were only five other passengers aboard. I came very near to chickening out and leaving the plane then and there, but it was too late. The door was closed and we were moving.

For the first hour or so I clung to the arms of my seat, fearful of moving lest I disturb the balance of the plane, and when I had to go to the washroom, I was sure my weight at the rear of the plane would bring about disaster. However, the flight was uneventful, and after a while I began to relax and thoroughly enjoy it. Ever since then I have never had the slightest hesitation about flying, though I don't particularly enjoy the tedium of sitting for such long periods of time.

In 1953 Jerry Kok left Yale to take a position in Monterey at the Army Language School. Because of the success of the Air Force program at Yale, he had been approached by the Army to head up and completely re-organize the various oriental language courses and to introduce the newly developed Yale Chinese-language texts. I was made assistant director at IFEL, with Henry Fenn as director. With just the two of us in administrative positions, things got so hectic during the two years that Jerry was away in Monterey that it became impossible for us to go together on the screening trips to Lackland, so most of the time I went by myself.

We had sufficient experience by that time to have refined our methodology and approach. From the statistics amassed, we had learned that two days of language instruction was fully adequate to give us the data we needed to make our selections. Although we were well satisfied that we were finding the right men with language aptitude, there was one area in which we were having problems, and that was student motivation. There were no known tests to ascertain that then, and to my knowledge there are none now.

It wasn't a question of the men not being well motivated to go to Yale. Every single one of them would have gladly given his left arm for the honor of being chosen to go to such a prestigious university. Our problem was that once they arrived in New Haven and discovered that it wasn't all "fun and games," their motivation often fell off, and poor grades resulted.

I did a great deal of statistical research on the students who did poorly, as well as those who did well in the course. I took a great number of things into account, such as age, marital status, place of origin and birth, the proximity of their homes to New Haven, their reading habits, hobbies, general interests in such things as music, and so on, and among other things, did they own a car?

After several months of work I came up with some surprising facts. Among those who did well, age was an extremely important factor. We found that the ideal age group for learning Chinese was between the ages of 18 and 22. Those over 30 always seemed to have an exceptionally difficult time acquiring the language, particularly if they had a family, either with them or somewhere else. Interestingly enough, in almost every case it wasn't because of any lack of motivation to succeed, but due most frequently to the vicissitudes of married life, difficulties with landlords and rents, and the near-impossibility of being able to study when there were small children around.

In my research concerning the problems of student behavior and achievement, I found that among the younger ones who did poorly in the course, the vast majority were in the 17-year-old group. The next highest group were those who owned automobiles and had girlfriends, and the third most unsuccessful ones were those whose homes were within a short driving distance of New Haven, which tempted them to go home each weekend. From those statistics I worked out a program to conduct a brief interview with each man personally before making my final choice after screening them at the air base.

After that, those aged 17, regardless of their apparent proficiency in the Chinese language, were seldom selected for the Yale course. There was just too much of a risk in taking them. They were too immature and without a sense of direction, and going to college was just a big joke to most of them. In rare cases I made an exception, but there had to be compelling reasons. As for those who owned automobiles, or intended buying one after they got to New Haven, they were counseled and strongly warned that they would be dropped from the course if excessive use of their cars interfered with their studies. And those whose home addresses fell within 200 miles of New Haven were given particularly close scrutiny when I made it a point to delve into their real motivation for wanting the course. Were they really serious about wanting to learn Chinese, or was it just so they would be near their homes and families for a year?

Other would-be students whom we checked closely were those who had already had six months to one or two years of college, but had dropped out. I wanted to know from them exactly why that had happened. If the answer was simply a problem of finances, we questioned them no further. However, if it was a matter of poor grades, we delved deeper. What had been the problem? Was it bad study habits? Girlfriends? Drinking? And so on. Another question we always asked anyone who had been to college was what major they had taken and how many times they had changed their major. That I found to be one of the most relevant questions and extremely pertinent to our goals in the course. If an individual had changed his major a number of times it frequently meant he had a lack of direction or purpose, and to accept such an individual might lead to his deciding halfway

through the course that it was not for him.

For the student candidates, that personal interview with me became a nightmare. Over the years since then many of them have confessed to me that the entire screening process was itself a traumatic experience such as they had never in their entire lives experienced, but the interview with me, which to them spelled "life or death," was the worst part of all, and to this day those who went through it have never forgotten it. I recall one young man who during the interview told me he had finished college, and gave me his grade-point average. He was a bright, clean-cut young chap, and I had no problem accepting him because he showed excellent aptitude for Chinese. However, he had not mentioned where he went to college, and I had not asked. Just as he left the room he returned, and with tears in his eyes he confessed to me that he had majored in music at Harvard. He felt he had to tell me then and there in case I found out later, after he got to Yale, whereupon he was sure I would kick him out. When I reassured him that I had nothing against Harvard, he went away a happy man.

As the course progressed, another phenomenon came to light and it puzzled me greatly. I began to sense differences between the classes. One would show up with the entire class seemingly very bright, with minimal disciplinary problems. The next would, as a whole, have lower motivation and proportionately lower grades, and more problems among the men, either emotional or physical. I began to study the class grade curves over a period of years, making comparisons and drawing detailed graphs of comparative class averages. A most interesting pattern emerged. Although the grade curves for each class were consistent, with the normal two or three straight-A students at the top, then a large number of A- and B+ students bunched together, followed by a few lower grades tailing off to the bottom, there was a difference with every alternate class that came in. One would always be a few points higher or lower in the overall grade averages for the entire class.

I next started to compare entry dates and found to my intense interest that the January or February classes, as well as those that arrived in late July or August, were, as a class, uniformly lower in the class averages compared to classes that entered at other times of the year. The pattern was so uniform and consistent, with its alternate highs and lows, that it was both astonishing and highly puzzling. I could think of no reason why it should have been so.

I continued to study the phenomenon, going over the background notes I had made during the individual interviews. In some cases that gave me a few clues. But in the end I was able to arrive at only one conclusion, and it was in no way scientific. I knew that students arriving at Yale during the first two months of the year had to have joined the Air Force sometime shortly before Christmas in order to undergo their twelve weeks or so of training. That led me to wonder why they had made such a momentous decision to leave home at that particular time. Were the reasons financial or something else? Perhaps an unhappy home? That seemed to be a partial answer to the January/February classes. But what about those who arrived in mid-year? Although in a roundabout way I questioned many of the students as to why they had joined up at that particular time, I could come up with nothing definite except that a number of them had quit college for various reasons and joined up. Others had failed to finish high school the previous year and had tried to find a job, but when nothing came their way, they had joined the Air Force. Of course we insisted that only high school graduates were acceptable, but in many cases of dropouts we found that they had completed their high school requirements after joining the Air Force and were issued a certificate of completion. Still others had been looking for jobs but had been drafted against their will.

None of those answers were really satisfying, and I continued studying the phenomenon right up into the 1980s, when I retired. I found the pattern to be absolutely consistent even at the Defense Language Institute in Monterey. To this day I can offer no answers other than the suppositions above.

To wrap up this somewhat unique subject of finding people with what is now widely recognized as "language aptitude," I must jump ahead a bit in my narrative to 1976. After my second retirement we were living in Branford, Connecticut, and with time on my hands I decided to make a detailed study of the thousands of students we had tested and interviewed at the Air Force bases over the years, using the actual tests we had given, which I had retained, and studying the errors made by each man.

I broke everything down into the precise number of hours of Chinese to which each man had been exposed for any given test, and I was able to graph the exact point at which any individual began to show a decline in retention and response during the screening process. As a result of that study, I concluded that the same test could be packaged into a two-hour test instead of the two days we had been using, and I was certain that with such a shortened test I would come up with the same results.

After a few months of working on it, I felt the shortened test was complete. I arranged to field test it in several high schools and junior colleges in the state, where the authorities were happy to participate in the experiment. I had no lack of volunteers, who ranged in age from 17 through 25, as well as several groups of older people, some well into their sixties. Working with civilians was not new to me; I had already had some experience in that area during the '60s at Yale, when we had such a large number of civilians coming in for the course. Many of them had heard of the aptitude test, and when first applying for the course, they asked if they could be tested just to satisfy their curiosity as to whether they would make it or not. Motivation with them was no problem. They were all paying a handsome fee for the privilege of learning Chinese, so for those that asked for it, I gave them a "mini" aptitude test with about two hours of instruction and then time for them to study on their own. Each time I was surprised at the accuracy of the results and the possibility of being able to pinpoint not only the areas in which the students-to-be showed weaknesses and needed to concentrate their future efforts, but also to project their expected achievement through the course.

The abbreviated test consisted of two parts, each covering one hour. The first hour exposed the students to Chinese vowel sounds, the four tones of Mandarin, and a representative 100 or more of the 400-plus sounds in the Chinese language. The second hour was exposure to, and required learning of a mere 30 words in Chinese, which included pronouns, both singular and plural, adverbs, what we called "stative" verbs, as well as "regular" verbs, and in addition there were nouns, and the question words "Who, whom?" and "What?" There was also the word used to form negatives, and an additional one to form general questions. My choice of vocabulary included all four tones, and the choice of lexical items was made to allow coverage of the major aspects of Chinese word order and sentence structure.

After making my final decision on the words to include in the test, I made a study of the number of "meaningful" phrases or sentences that could be made using these 30 words. When I reached the figure of 2,000 I stopped trying, even though there were possibly more. At the beginning of the test, when I told the prospective students that they would be able to express themselves in at least 2,000 statements in the language, it was always a tremendous boost to their morale.

I printed an 18-page booklet for the students to "sight" read as they listened to the tapes and recorded the entire booklet and the five built-in tests on two 60-minute cassettes. To administer the test, all that was required was a tape recorder and a pair of headphones, and the student was left on his own for a two-hour period.

During the field testing, which covered a period of several weeks and was primarily a fun thing for all concerned, I made a number of refinements. When the results were tallied, I felt that I had a valid test that was entirely comparable with the two days of instruction and testing that we had used at Lackland. However, I felt the shortened test needed to be tried out with students who were actually planning to learn Chinese, not just people interested in an experiment.

I approached the Defense Language Institute in Monterey, which by that time had long since dropped my "aptitude" testing as being too expensive and time-consuming. Since the experiment I was proposing was actually only two hours of Chinese language instruction, they cooperated by allowing me to give the test to all of their incoming students in the Chinese program before they were exposed to the actual language.

Over the two-year period when the test was given to the hundreds of students who entered the Monterey Chinese course, I was given continuing status reports by one of my former students, Carl Povilaitis, who administered the test for me. As a result, even though I was on the other side of the continent, I was able to study the lists of names, their test results after the "screening," and their subsequent success or failure in the course itself. Most gratifyingly, at the end of that period it became clearly apparent that within a margin of a maximum of five points one way or the other, the

test given on that first day of school accurately predicted the student's final grade some twelve months later. Moreover, in all but a handful of cases each year, it also clearly identified those who would fail the course along the way.

Short as the entire test was, the five built-in tests, consisting of true and false questions, as well as multiple-choice items, required manual grading and a certain degree of analysis and judgment by a person competent in the language. Despite the test's proven accuracy, and the fact that it could save the Army possibly hundreds of thousands of dollars each year by predicting success or failure in the Chinese course, the Army opted against using it, preferring to use a test they had developed on their own. Their test used a fictitious language, with the entire business of test grading handled by computers. Their test was also used for all students across the board entering the school, regardless of the language being taken. Exactly like the test I wrote about that was developed by the university professor many years before, it, too, failed to project or identify people who would have problems with Chinese, and the attrition rate remained exorbitantly high when it could have been cut to a mere 3 or 4 percent. I don't know about other languages, but several senior Army officers conceded privately to me that my test had proven to be far and away more accurate than theirs in predicting the end results for any given student learning Chinese, but their word had not carried enough weight further up the line. Such is the Army way.

The FBI, however, was more open-minded, sending a number of their male and female agents to Monterey for Chinese each year. Mr. William H. Webster, then head of the FBI, wrote and asked if they could use my test to pre-screen candidates for Chinese before sending them out for training. I was happy to let them use it. During the number of years it was applied, it produced results that they considered more than satisfactory. Unfortunately, there again, as in all bureaucracies, when someone at the top was changed, things happened down the line, and someone, somewhere, decided to drop the test. But it still remains a valid test for determining aptitude in learning the Chinese language, and is the only one of its kind that I know of.

In the last few years of the program before it ended in 1965 we regularly had to select at least 90 men and sometimes more to fill a class. That meant that we usually had to screen a pool of between 400 and 500 men to find the ones we felt to be qualified. It was always an exciting and challenging event, for the candidates as well as ourselves, and I look back on those days as being among the most pleasurable and satisfying of our time at Yale, despite the long hours and hard work. On more than one occasion our baggage went astray and we arrived with nothing to work with and simply had to wing it, but with the two airmen helping us, we always managed to mimeograph something in a hurry to fill the void.

At this late date I feel I owe something of an apology to the 10,000 or more young men who over those 14 years formed the pools from which we selected our students. We put them under a tremendous amount of pressure and realized as we were doing so that there were inequities in what we were doing. But it had to be done in the interests of weeding out those who would be unable to stand the pressure of the course once they reached Yale. As I told them at the time, the fact they were not selected for the course in no way meant they were unable to learn Chinese; it just meant that they needed to go at it at a slower pace and with less pressure. To the many young men who tried so hard yet were not selected, I want to say "thank you."

Bob monitoring his students.

Bob giving recorded test in Language Lab.

Happy memories at Yale.

Major Salemi and Eva.

One of the graduations at *IFEL*.

Gone screening! At Sampson AFB.

Major Salemi, Jerry Kok, Bob Tharp, Henry Fenn. *IFEL* in good hands.

Bob and Eva at one of the class picnics.

Ready for a trip to the U.N.

Instructors and Staff at *IFEL*

Bob and some of the men.

Barber shop somewhere on an overseas base.

Airman Fandel in Japan.

Overseas duty.

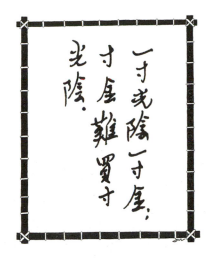

Yicun guangyin yicun jin,
cun jin nan mai cun guangyin.

A moment in time is worth an inch of gold,
but an inch of gold cannot buy a moment in time.

- Chinese Peasant Saying.

Chapter Forty-Six
Citizens At Last!

Much as we had hoped to the contrary, our move from Monterey to Yale by no means solved our problems with the INS. For another two years we still had to go through the regular routine of visiting their offices every six months (this time in Hartford, about 40 minutes' drive from New Haven), to reapply for a continuance and a stay of the expulsion order against me. But as time went on, and 1953 came, things slowly began to look better.

The bill introduced in Congress on my behalf by Congressman Walter Judd, to have me admitted as an immigrant, had bogged down and the year had ended with no action taken. However, perhaps because there was a bill pending in Congress, the INS appeared to take a more lenient view of my case. But the real breakthrough came through the kind efforts of a Christian gentleman in the INS office in Philadelphia. My father had run into him and mentioned my problems. He discovered a loophole in the law and my position suddenly changed drastically.

The INS made the decision that my permanent employment at Yale made me eligible to apply for a special category of "desirable immigrants" who could be admitted into the United States under a special provision for teachers. This was known as the Professors' Non-Quota Status, Section 4(d) of the 1924 Immigration Act. That provision required that an individual applying for admittance as a "professor" needed to have had at least five years of experience as a teacher at a qualifying university. It was not specified as to whether the university in question had to be in a foreign country. Consequently, in my case, Yale was, of course, recognized as qualifying, but the INS quite surprisingly went a step further and decided that my time at the Army Language School in Monterey would also be credited toward the required five years. Apparently they recognized the fact that I had been teaching essentially the same thing there.

That was good news indeed; it meant that with my three years in Monterey, and the almost two years already spent at Yale, I was about to be qualified for admittance, and my troubles seemed to be about over. But that was not to be the case. Once the decision had been made by the INS, one would have thought it would be a simple process to go through with the necessary paperwork. But bureaucracy has its own ways of going about things and a great deal of red tape remained. I have several inch-thick files containing copies of my correspondence with the INS from 1949 to 1962, and they make most interesting reading now, although they caused me tremendous frustration at the time.

In short, among other things, both Eva and I were required to submit evidence of every place we had ever lived, with supporting documents covering any property we had owned, what monies we had had in the banks, clean records from the various police departments of every city we had ever lived in, and a host of other things.

Naturally, our marriage certificate and birth certificates were also required. In my case that was no problem. I had managed to smuggle both our marriage certificate and my birth certificate out of China, hidden in the lining of my suitcase. However, due to the unusual circumstances of Eva's birth in Yunnan, she had never been issued a birth certificate. All records of her birth, originally kept in the Dutch consulate in Canton (now called Guangzhou, its original Chinese name), had been destroyed during World War II. Fortunately, that was where Eva's father and his connections with the Dutch Foreign Office came to the rescue. Having been employed in the Dutch diplomatic service, he had friends at The Hague. Through them, a search was made of old records, and finally, after many months, we received a lengthy two-page document in Dutch, detailing the circumstances of Eva's birth in 1914. It described the unusual conditions at the time, the remoteness of her place of birth, the very slow and insecure mail service, and that her father, having been unfamiliar with the necessary procedures for reporting her birth, had elected to delay reporting it until such time as an important document of that nature could be hand-carried by some reliable person directly to Canton.

What Eva's father had done in 1914 was to wait patiently for some six months until two English botanists happened to pass through the region, and to one of those gentlemen he gave a letter that estab-

lished the date and place of Eva's birth. That was hand-carried to the Dutch consulate in Canton, a journey of some six to eight weeks.

In the strange coincidences of life, and further evidence of the smallness of the world we live in, some 20 years after we received that document from The Hague, we learned the name of the English botanist who carried the letter. Our family doctor in Branford, Dr. Nicholas Nickou, himself an amateur botanist, had made a trip to England, and while there, he met with the famous George Forrest, whose books on plant life are world-renowned. When Dr. Nickou told Mr. Forrest about his desire to visit Yunnan Province to study the floral life there, Mr. Forrest gave him a copy of his own book covering his travels through Yunnan in 1914. He also gave him a copy of a photograph of himself taken in 1914, standing alongside a very young-looking Arie Kok in the city of Lijiang in Yunnan! Mr. Kok had shown Mr. Forrest a rare plant he had discovered, which was eventually named after him. Unfortunately we've not been able to track down the Latin name, but it incorporated the name "Kok."

Translating the document from The Hague into English proved to be quite a problem. Eva could, of course, read it, but her translation would not be accepted by the INS. After several fruitless trips into New York City I finally found an individual working for Berlitz who had the necessary qualifications to make a translation, and the INS accepted the original and the translation in lieu of a birth certificate.

That was one hurdle successfully surmounted, but others remained, and one of the biggest was providing proof of my educational background. I wrote to Wolsey Hall in Oxford, England, the place from which I had taken my correspondence course some thirty years previously. I detailed the circumstances of my having been enrolled in their courses during the years 1925-30, adding the fact that due to civil disturbances I had been unable to proceed to the coast to take the necessary examinations at the end of my studies. I further stated that my own records of the regular tests successfully passed during those years had all been destroyed when the Japanese occupied our family home in 1941, and I asked them if they could provide me with the proof I needed for the immigration people.

The bursar at Wolsey Hall graciously wrote me a

reply saying that they had not retained any records from that long ago, but he took my word for it, and supplied me with documents attesting to the fact that I had indeed "taken courses with a view to taking examinations for the College of Preceptors, Senior Oxford, and Matriculation Examinations, but had been prevented from taking the Examinations at the time, due to internal warfare." To my great relief that document, too, was accepted by the INS as being satisfactory proof that I met their educational requirements and was not totally illiterate.

When all the necessary documents had been collected, copied and filed, we again mistakenly thought that our problems were all behind us and that it would be clear sailing ahead. But we were in for another surprise. The year was 1953, but it was to be another full year before things were straightened out.

We were directed by the INS to contact the U.S. Consul in Montreal, to whom our papers had been sent, to ask for a hearing. As though our birth certificates were not enough, the consul wrote back saying he needed evidence of our having been in China, as well as evidence to support my claim that I spoke Chinese! That necessitated my writing a number of letters to our former mission board, or its equivalent, to friends and colleagues we had known in China, who were now scattered worldwide, as well as to Chinese associates in this country who could vouch for my ability to speak Chinese. In the end we must have submitted about 100 documents of one sort or another.

The wheels of government turn slowly, but in June 1954 we finally received notification from the U.S. Consulate in Montreal stating that our papers had been given preliminary approval, and giving us an appointment to appear in person at the consulate on August 3, 1954. After the previous fiasco of my leaving the country and being denied readmittance, it was with many misgivings that we drove up to Montreal. Leaving the United States, we had been told, was simply a formality, but to us, after all we had been through, as we crossed the border and entered Canada, we could not help but wonder if we would ever see the United States again. We need not have worried. The hearing at the U.S. Consulate was quite perfunctory. Within a matter of minutes our passports had been stamped with a visa admitting us to the United States as immigrants, and without spending any more time out of the country we headed back to New Haven with thankful hearts.

Within a few weeks after that we received our alien registration cards, the sought-after "green cards," without which no alien can legally hold a job in the United States. For the first time in seven years we felt a sense of relief that we were here to stay and were well on our way to acquiring U.S. citizenship. Almost immediately we filed the necessary papers declaring our intention of becoming U.S. citizens, a process that normally takes five years after the initial filing. But in our case it was to take eight long years before we finally saw the end of our troubles.

About that time, the Institute of Far Eastern Languages, which had been in existence since 1946 and had run smoothly the entire time with no problems whatsoever regarding its Asian staff, suddenly found itself embroiled in deep problems with the Chinese, whose numbers had grown considerably.

The institute, as a self-supporting and entirely autonomous adjunct entity within the university, enabled us to hire (and fire) our staff quite independently of the unions within the university itself. All our teachers had been hired on a "temporary" basis, a fact that was made known to them at the time of their employment, with the proviso that their employment was only for such time as the institute was needed to train students in the Chinese language. There was no guarantee of any permanence as Yale employees. That understanding had been quite satisfactory to our Chinese friends when they came aboard, but when the Korean War ended, although more students than ever were sent to us, everyone had some doubt in their minds that the Air Force would continue to need Chinese linguists. That troubling thought perhaps was uppermost in the minds of our Chinese colleagues when they quietly formed an association with a view to being able, by force of numbers, to put pressure on the institute and on Yale University to give them tenure.

Of the thirty-odd Chinese instructors, 99 percent of them were serious, hard-working and dependable people who had a real interest in the students and enjoyed teaching. Unfortunately, but not unusual in such a large group, there were one or two who were less than enthusiastic about their jobs. After I had found them either reading newspapers in class when they should have been teaching, or worse yet, sleeping while the students did as they pleased, they had been given fair warning. After repeated flouting of the institute's rules, they were asked for their resignations.

Because I was the one most closely involved with the teachers in assigning them their duties, visiting classes, and generally running the show as far as they were concerned, agitators among them set out to get rid of me in an organized campaign calculated to defame me and to destroy my credibility as a teacher. One man even went so far as to accuse me of homosexual conduct toward him. That was just after the period when McCarthyism had been at its height, and many people in government had lost their jobs as a result of unproven and unsubstantiated allegations that they were either Communists or homosexuals. That man, by accusing me, apparently thought it would be a sure way of having me fired.

The campaign against me continued for weeks, with "poison-pen" letters against me anonymously mailed to just about every government agency in the U.S., to the heads of every leading university, and to Drew Pearson, a muckraker whose column was then popular in almost every major newspaper in the country. I first got word of those letters when they started dribbling back to us from various universities where we had friends. From the content of the letters and the way in which they were written, it was obvious they were the work of just one or two people. I showed them to some of my loyal Chinese friends, who deplored the action by their fellow teachers and did everything they could to counteract the rumors. However, the damage had been done.

In the letters, of which I have numerous copies, I was not alone in being accused of a variety of supposed misdeeds. Mr. Fenn, our director, and Jerry Kok also came in for their share. But in their cases the accusations were brushed off by everyone as quite obviously being the work of a disgruntled employee. In my case it was a different matter. I was the chief target, and being an alien and having applied for citizenship, government agencies receiving the letters had to take note of them and conduct their private investigations accordingly.

Coincidentally, that all happened at the very time I was being investigated by various security agencies for top-secret clearances requested by the Air Force because of the sensitivity of much of the material I handled in preparing Chinese language teaching materials for our students. As a result, I was inundated with visits by intelligence personnel from all investigative branches of the government: FBI, CIA, Air Force Security, and the Office of Naval Intelligence, among others.

It was a somewhat nerve-wracking time that lasted for months and consumed many hours of my time. But in all cases I had not the slightest difficulty in clearing my name and satisfying the investigators, although one or two of them were especially assiduous in their inquiries. In at least two such investigations, the results were not without a degree of humor.

I was, of course, not unfamiliar with that kind of security investigation, having gone through them on previous occasions, and in no way did I find the investigators to be intimidating. In almost every case the officers making inquiries were gentlemanly and friendly, and the proceedings were short and to the point, although filling out the many forms took a lot of my time.

In most cases, their duties largely involved questioning friends, neighbors, relatives and former employers, and they avoided coming into direct contact with me until the very last. Of course, after their visits, our neighbors and friends all told us about having been interviewed and questioned about me, and I was well aware of what was going on. One of our neighbors in Branford was a Polish gentleman with a rather limited grasp of English. Subsequent to one of these inquiries he came to me and whispered: "I know you are in some kind of trouble with the police because they came and questioned me. But it's all right. I didn't tell them anything. I just told them you were a good man."

Another day, two plainclothes officers from the Office of Naval Intelligence came to IFEL and wanted to talk with me. They asked if there was somewhere private where we could talk, so I took them downstairs to our "sound room," where one of them immediately locked the door behind us.

They settled down for what appeared to be just a friendly chat, but after about twenty minutes of desultory questioning, one of them asked me if I had ever been in England. I replied in the affirmative and told him the dates and circumstances. The other then asked if I had ever been to Canada and I told him that I'd been there also on a number of occasions, both as a child and more recently to try to gain admittance to the United States, and even more recently than that to visit my brother in Toronto.

Suddenly, and in unison, both of them leaned forward in their chairs with their faces just inches from mine, and with a steely-eyed glare the two of them shouted a series of questions at me: "What happened there? What trouble did you have with the police? What is there about these trips to England and Canada that you are trying to hide? What is it you don't want us to know about your having been to England and Canada?"

I was thunderstruck and hadn't the faintest idea of what they meant. When I asked them, one of them replied: "Here in this questionnaire you filled out for us, you've mentioned a dozen different countries that you've visited, but there's no mention of either Canada or England. You must have had a good reason for leaving them out. What is it? We know that you went there, so tell us what happened."

I was so surprised that for a moment I had to stop and collect my thoughts. I told them nothing untoward had happened and at no time had I in any way been involved with the police. Furthermore, there certainly was no secret about my having visited both countries. In fact, I told them that if they would give me an hour, I would go home and collect copies of letters I had written the Immigration Service and forms I had filled out for them, in which I had detailed not only my visits to both countries, but the addresses of people with whom I had stayed.

I asked them if they would let me look at the form I had filled out for them. When I studied the question, the answer suddenly came to me and I said to them: "This form asks: `What foreign countries have you visited?'" I continued: "You gentlemen must remember that I am not a citizen of the United States, but a British subject. I am not aware of my having consciously done so, but I can only presume that while filling out this form, the word 'foreign' meant to me countries other than those ruled by Great Britain. To me, Canada and England are not 'foreign,' but part of Great Britain."

Both men looked a little sheepish and let the matter go, but they still required me to write a 32-page statement answering the charges that had been brought against me in the anonymous letters they had received. But that was the end of the affair, and I got my security clearances shortly thereafter.

Another result of those anonymous letters was a request one day by the IRS for me to visit their offices at a designated time. At first I thought it was just a routine income-tax audit, and it started out as such. However, when I had satisfactorily answered all their questions, one of the examiners casually asked me: "What about your profits from the coffee shop you run?" At first I hadn't the slightest idea what he was referring to, but then I suddenly remembered that in one of the anonymous letters I had been accused of using "slave labor" in running a coffee shop in the school basement for the students and profiting from the proceeds. I smilingly looked at the IRS examiner and said: "So you, too, got one of those anonymous letters?"

He got a bit red in the face, stumbled over his words for a second or two, then told me they were not permitted to discuss their reasons for calling for an audit. I told him it was quite all right with me. I knew that a lot of letters had been sent out, and from memory I started to quote to him the exact contents of the letters, using the very Chinese-oriented language in which they were written. At that, he was forced to smile, and without hesitation brought out the letter and showed it to me.

I explained to him the circumstances of our so-called "coffee shop." Our Air Force students were at that time given a daily food allowance of $2.57 a day (if I remember correctly). Out of that they had to buy their own meals, wherever they could, or they could eat in the university dining rooms, but their food allowance had to go toward the cost. As a result many of them preferred keeping their money and skipping breakfast, to eat just one big meal a day. That meant that they frequently appeared in class in the mornings groggy and without any enthusiasm for work. We had a midmorning break in classes for 20 minutes, so they could go out for coffee and doughnuts, but there were only three coffee shops in the immediate vicinity of the school, and not enough seating to handle the flood of students we let out at one time. As a result, the 20-minute break was never long enough, and many students had to return to school without having had anything to eat or drink, and classes were often delayed.

Because of that situation I came up with the idea of serving coffee in the basement of the school. With my own money I bought a big coffee urn and made arrangements with a large bakery a mile or so from the school to let me have all their day-old pastries, which I picked up first thing in the morning before school started. We bought the pastries at such a low price that I could let the boys have a doughnut or a Danish pastry for a nickel, and the same for a large cup of coffee. It was a simple matter to make the coffee each day, a chore which I and others on the staff shared. But for the cleanup afterwards, we had a roster posted where the students would take turns, two of them at a time, to tidy up the room and put things away before it was used once again as a classroom. That was my use of "slave labor."

I told the IRS agent that if he cared to stop in around 9:30 any weekday morning, he could watch the procedure for himself and I would also show him my books. He elected to come the next morning, and coincidentally, the two Chinese teachers whom I suspected of being the writers of at least some of the "poison pen" letters were themselves present there for the first and only time. The IRS officer saw what we were doing, examined my books, where a daily record of expenditures and intake was kept, noted that it was definitely a non-profit organization, and that was the end of that.

As a result of that run-in with the IRS, that particular officer and I became close friends, and over the next several years I had the pleasure of taking him out a number of times onto Long Island Sound on my sailboat.

Another result of those anonymous letters was a long-distance call from Washington one evening just as we were sitting down to dinner. The caller identified himself as Jack Anderson, working for Drew Pearson. He asked me if it was true that I was teaching at Yale, that I had no degrees whatsoever, yet nevertheless, in the Yale catalogue, which came out each year, my name was shown with a B.A. behind it. I told him it was indeed true, and that I had repeatedly notified the people who compiled the catalogue and had attempted to have the matter corrected, but to no avail. I told Jack Anderson that one year they had even given me an M.A., and I further told him that at the time I joined the staff at Yale, I had fully informed the authorities of my educational background and lack of degrees, and they had accepted me on the basis of my knowledge of Chinese.

Mr. Anderson told me he had received a letter in the mail about me, but under the circumstances he didn't think the item was particularly newsworthy and would not make use of it. I thanked him for his call and told him I would report it to the secretary of the university, Ben Holden, and that he would be receiving a letter in the mail attesting to the facts surrounding my being hired by Yale. He agreed to wait for the letter.

I contacted Ben Holden the next morning and he immediately wrote a letter to Mr. Anderson completely exonerating me. However, somehow Mr. Anderson must have forgotten to withdraw the item, or he had no intention of doing so, because without waiting for the letter, the very next day a short piece appeared in Drew Pearson's column headed: "Chinese puzzle at Yale." It elaborated on the fact that supposedly, when I joined the faculty at Yale, I had claimed to have degrees from a leading university in China, but that my claims were false, and the Chinese university when contacted had stated they had no knowledge of my ever having been there, as was indeed the case. I was disappointed that there was no subsequent publication of the letter from Ben Holden clearing my name, but perhaps that was to be expected.

The item drew a lot of laughs from friends all over the country who knew me and knew the allegations to be untrue, and I received many copies of the item in the mail. But we wondered how the story had started in the first place. When we looked in the confidential personnel files we found that someone had gained access to it, and in a handwriting completely different from mine, had doctored my initial application form and had added the fictitious information concerning my alleged degrees. That was obviously the basis of the allegations made to Mr. Anderson.

On top of everything else, without warning of any kind, two of the Chinese who had been dismissed brought suit against our director, Mr. Fenn and me, charging us with collusion in unlawfully firing them, and we were sued for $50,000 in damages, a big sum in those days. Liens were immediately attached to our properties, and for more than four years the suit hung over our heads. Of course, Yale undertook our defense and it cost us nothing except a lot of headaches. However, the case was so patently ludicrous that the two Chinese who had brought the charges against us had a hard time finding lawyers to handle the case. Reportedly they were turned down by seven different attorneys until finally they found a young man just out of law school to take the case.

Ultimately the case came to trial, and the whole thing was over in a matter of minutes. While waiting in the courthouse for the trial to begin, the young lawyer who had taken their case had to undergo a lot of good-natured ribbing from the various lawyers standing around. He was asked if he was getting his laundry done free, whether he enjoyed eating in Chinese restaurants, etc. From what our lawyers said, we gathered it was the young man's first time in court.

In any event, we went into the courtroom before a Superior Court judge and the trial began. Just after the jury had been seated, the judge started out by addressing the two Chinese, telling them that he was a Yale Law School graduate, that he frequently handled cases both for and against Yale University, that he was totally unprejudiced, and that Yale sometimes won and at other times lost. He added that he would treat this case in the same manner without forming any opinions until he had heard all the evidence. However, he suggested that if either of them had any doubts as to his being able to give them a fair trial, they were welcome to disqualify him and find another judge.

The two conferred briefly with their young lawyer, and apparently he either suggested it, or agreed with his clients' decision to go for another judge. That annoyed the judge considerably and he scolded them for implying that he could be prejudiced against them or had prejudged the case. Nonetheless, he let them go and dismissed the jury.

Their lawyer took the two of them next door to the only other judge available. When the latter heard the circumstances, he, too, blew up. He told the two Chinese that by distrusting his colleague, a Superior Court judge, they were automatically distrusting him and he would have nothing to do with the case, and he promptly threw the whole thing out of court.

The two Chinese were left with no recourse but to come to our lawyers and try to get the original generous settlement that Yale had promised them four years previously. Now, however, the Yale lawyers had the upper hand, and a much smaller settlement was finally agreed upon. The whole thing was my first experience with American justice, and I was greatly impressed, not only by the intricacies of the law, but by the competence of the lawyers handling the case for us.

Readers at this point who have noted that Eva was on the staff at IFEL may have wondered how she was able to do that and care for my sister Ruth at the same time. In 1952, the year after we got to Yale, Ruth's condition had improved to the point where she had learned to do a great deal more for herself. But because of the weather, she was housebound much of the time, and it was hard on both her and Eva. Moreover, she had an increasing need for medication at odd hours of the day and night. The ideal situation for her was to be in a home where she would get round-the-clock care, but it was almost impossible to find one that would accept her and that we could afford. Then, miraculously, we received a letter from Rest Haven Homes in Grand Rapids, Michigan, a home operated by the Pell brothers and sisters, a family known throughout the United States for their Christian devotion in helping the sick and elderly. Somehow they had heard of Ruth's condition and wrote to say they had an opening, and if Ruth would be happy to come and live with them, they would be delighted to take her in. We felt it to be an answer to our many prayers, so I flew to Grand Rapids to make the necessary arrangements; shortly thereafter we took Ruth there. She was warmly welcomed, and there, for the next eight years, she lived happily in surroundings where she had good company, excellent care, and a great deal of love. Being fairly close to Chicago, my younger sister, Barbara, was able to visit her from time to time, and I, too, dropped in that way every time I could.

Immediately after that we started to build the house on our back lot. Eva, helping out while I was in school, got busy one day pouring some concrete steps. Carrying a bucket of cement, she strained her back. After numerous chiropractic treatments, first by a Dr. White and then Dr. Scott Isaacson — my swimming companion at the beach and fellow "polar bear" as we called ourselves because of our cold-weather swimming — her back seemed to be back to normal again. Later, with Ruth gone and the little house sold, Eva decided she wanted to take up nursing, so she enrolled in a course for licensed practical nurses at Yale Hospital.

Near the culmination of the course, when the students were assigned to work in the hospital wards for practice, one of her jobs was to deliver food trays, each marked with the patient's last name. Brought up in China, neither she nor I were familiar with the word "kosher," and when that word appeared on one of the trays, Eva went through ward after ward looking at the bed charts, trying to find Mr. Kosher.

Another of her jobs was to occasionally push one of the heavy beds from one room to another, or from one floor to another. The building was old, the doors for the elevator were old and heavy, and the beds were clumsy and difficult to manipulate. One day, trying to push a bed into the elevator and hold back the door at the same time, she again twisted her back, and no amount of treatment seemed to help it. She gamely went to school each day despite the pain; however, when taking eight or ten aspirins a day had no effect on the pain, she regretfully had to withdraw from the course without getting her diploma — a great disappointment to her.

Immediately thereafter, in 1954, she was helping me so much with correcting test papers at night that she was hired for full-time work at IFEL. She taught one or two daily classes in comprehension and spent the rest of the time correcting papers and evaluating grades.

In the meantime, in 1953, the Army Language School in Monterey, having heard of the success of our course at Yale, decided to adopt the Yale texts, and one of the senior Chinese teachers, P.C. Li, was invited to take the post of chairman of the Chinese department to introduce the new texts. At the same time Jerry Kok was also invited to go to Monterey as dean of the Division of Far Eastern Languages to reorganize the Chinese, Japanese and Korean language departments, and he remained there until February 1955, when he returned to Yale.

Quite apart from events at the school, in our personal lives there had also been some changes. After the death of Eva's father in 1951, her mother continued to live in an apartment by herself in Collingswood, New Jersey. We managed to see her every month or so, but we noticed her health beginning to deteriorate and decided to bring her up to New Haven to live with us.

Coincidentally, Ray Mazzarella, who had bought the house across the street from us, decided to build a larger house a few blocks away. He wanted to sell the little house we'd built, so we bought it back from him

for Eva's mother, and installed her there in 1958, since she wanted to continue to live by herself. With an intercom plugged into the electrical circuit we were able to monitor her day and night, and for the next two or three years her health improved and she was able to happily care for herself without outside help.

Eva's mother was a great student of the Bible and took special note of the number 7, which is frequently referred to as being the "perfect number." She felt that the number had great significance for her; one time she told Eva that every seven years there had been a great change in her life. Among other events, seven years after her husband died, she had moved to Branford. Seven years after that, in 1965, she moved with us to California, and it is rather remarkable that after another seven years, in 1972, when we were again back in Branford, she passed away after a long period of illness.

Nineteen hundred and sixty was another year we shall not easily forget. Among other things, Eva had to undergo a hysterectomy, which, hard as it was on her, left me a physical wreck until it was all over. Then, one morning in early October 1960, we got a phone call from Grand Rapids telling us that during the night, Ruth had fallen, hitting her head against the bathtub and sustaining a severe injury. I flew there immediately and found her in the hospital, conscious but in an obviously deteriorating condition. The doctors, while doing everything they could, held out little hope for her recovery.

Barbara joined me there, and we sat at Ruth's bedside watching her fade away, aware that she was dying but happy in the knowledge that she would soon be with her Lord, whom she loved so dearly. On October 6, at age 51, she passed into the presence of the Lord.

At the time my father and stepmother were living in the small town of Rockport, Massachusetts, near Gloucester and the Cape. It was the area my stepmother loved best and where she had grown up. They had lived in uncomfortable apartments for several years, and I felt it was time they had a house of their own. When I had broached the subject of a house to them, my stepmother was most enthusiastic and said she would look for the ideal place and would let me know. Unfortunately, her idea of the ideal place was a house that was at least 100 years old. Time and again

I got excited calls from her to come and look at a house she had discovered, only to find it to be totally impractical for two elderly people. It was either too large or too dilapidated.

Finally, after several such futile trips to view her "finds," I instructed a real estate agent to find me a place in the center of Rockport, her favorite town, that was within walking distance of stores and within my price range.

The agent finally found a place that I thought to be just perfect for them, both as to location and size, and I bought it. Although it looked modern, my stepmother learned from her neighbors that the place was more than 120 years old, and that made it absolutely perfect! Since they were only about three hours' driving time from New Haven, I visited them frequently, and Father on his travels, which even at that age he was still making, dropped in to stay with us when en route to New York and points south.

1962 was a momentous year indeed. During the first part of the year there were indications that we might be nearing the point when we would be granted citizenship. Then one day we were called in for an examination, and both Eva and I, examined separately, were asked a number of questions on American history, government and personalities. How was Congress run and how were congressmen and senators elected. Name the first president, and who was the current president, and so on. We had done a lot of studying, so we passed the test easily and were elated when told we had finally surmounted the last hurdle. All we had to do was await a day when enough people were ready for the swearing-in ceremony.

In 1962 my father's health began to fail. A severe stroke left him unable to write or speak clearly. The first week in October I had to attend an important language conference in upper New York state, north of Syracuse, where I was to be one of the principal speakers. The conference was held in a large mansion on the edge of a lake, in a tiny rural community with only one telephone in the village and none at all in the mansion.

Arriving early, I spent that first afternoon down by the lake going over my speech. Early the next morning, before breakfast, someone from the village came up to the mansion to say there was an urgent telephone call for me. I walked the mile or so to the village and found Eva waiting on the line. She had just heard from my stepmother that my father had failed to come downstairs at his usual early hour. Alarmed, she had gone upstairs, where she found him sitting up in bed, Bible in hand, just as though he had prepared himself for his daily early morning reading of God's Word. In that way the Lord, whom my Father had loved and served so faithfully for 65 years, gently and quietly took him to His side. Father had attained the age of 86, and, because of his ill health, his death was not unexpected. Nonetheless, as these things always are, it was a great shock to all of us. The date was October 6, 1962, exactly two years to the day after my sister Ruth had died.

In November 1962, despite the ups and downs of just over 15 years, our immigration problems finally ended. On November 21st, in City Hall, we were sworn in as American citizens together with a large crowd of many different nationalities. It was a stirring moment. When we got back to IFEL after the ceremony, we were greeted by the entire student enrollment, who presented us with an American flag that had been flown over the U.S. Capitol building in Washington. At the same time they gave us a beautifully inscribed plaque, which has a prominent place in our home.

Suddenly, a student burst into the room bearing a fake telegram supposedly from draft headquarters, purporting to tell me that I was now eligible for the draft and should report at once! Then the students gave us a standing ovation. We were moved by their display of affection, and over the years we've prized the expression of their goodwill and the spirit in which it was given.

At school interesting things were always happening. In July 1954 a student named Charles Richardson came to me with a request that the students be permitted to publish a school paper once a month. I thought it was an excellent idea, and we provided them with a duplicating machine and gave them a free hand in what they wanted to write. My sole proviso was that I be shown the final copy prior to printing so as to avoid any infringement on the tight security that surrounded our students' future jobs in the field. For example, we were not permitted to publish the full names of students nor mention anything specific about their training.

The paper was called "Shouting" (listening in), in honor of one of the least-liked aspects of the course, which was listening to simulated tapes of field radio traffic with a loud static background. Many of the students were quite gifted in their writing, and humorous articles appeared about school life, well illustrated with cleverly drawn cartoons, pictures of the students themselves, as well as their teachers, with the subjects often quite recognizable. At one point the students decided it would be a good idea to include a short piece each month written by or about one of the teachers or staff, telling something about themselves. I still have a file of some of those old Shouting issues and they make nostalgic reading. The lads who wrote and illustrated them are now all men in their sixties, busy in all walks of life. Some day I would like to publish them once again. Perhaps some of the original writers would recognize what they wrote.

I have mentioned the tight security that attended our school and the students. We hadn't been long in the business when we realized that unfriendly countries were making every effort to identify our students and learn what they could about the course and its content. As each new class came in, I became aware of a car with tinted windows parked near the school entrance. The occupants were invisible, but I could see the lens of a movie camera poking out of a partly opened window, filming the men as they left the school at the end of the day. I reported it to the FBI, who apparently followed up on it, because the surveillance quickly ceased. However, when the next class came in, I happened to overhear some of the students talking among themselves about an attractive blonde who seemed interested in them. She was taking pictures of them just outside the school but would not respond to any of their overtures. I looked into the matter, saw the young lady, and again reported it to the FBI as being highly suspicious. She was found to be in the employ of a "foreign national," but was quite unaware of why she had been given the assignment or who her employer was.

When our students went to the field, either Japan, Taiwan, South Korea, Thailand or Vietnam, they were not permitted to take their Chinese textbooks with them, to avoid compromising their jobs, nor were they permitted to discuss the fact that they had undergone Chinese language training at Yale. However, the extent and thoroughness of Chinese Communist intelligence in those days was well illustrated by one incident that occurred on a remote island off the South

Korean coast where the U.S. Air Force had an advance base.

Several of our students had been assigned there, and shortly after their arrival, they were given leave to go off base to a Chinese tailor to have some work done on their uniforms. As they entered the tiny establishment, the Chinese tailor took one look at them and greeted them in Chinese. They pretended not to understand. The man laughed and said in excellent English, "You can talk Chinese with me. I know who you are and where you went to school. I also know that you had Mr. Kok and Mr. and Mrs. Tharp as your teachers." He might not have been a Communist agent, but the circumstances were highly suspicious to say the least.

The secrecy surrounding the job our students were trained to do was such that when they returned from the field, they were unable to go into any detail as to what their specific work entailed. They were allowed to say where they had been stationed, but that was about all. From time to time we had students come back to see us and most of them had interesting stories to tell of their travels and, occasionally, of something very different from their assigned jobs.

I recall one man in particular telling us about his arrival at a transit base in Japan, where he was to await transportation to a forward base. One cloudy and rainy day, he heard an announcement on the P.A. system asking if there was a Chinese linguist on the base, and if so, to report at once to the airfield tower. Thinking that there might be others around who could speak Chinese, he slowly ambled over to the tower to see if he could be of any help. It turned out he was the only man available, and they immediately put him to work.

A flight of Chinese bombers from Taiwan had flown over to Japan on a training mission and were scheduled to land at that base. However, because of the heavy cloud cover, they couldn't see the ground, and none of the pilots had any experience in instrument flying. They were unable to land and were running out of fuel. The tower personnel wanted to talk them down, but the Chinese pilots had a limited knowledge of English and were beginning to panic. I don't remember the name of the student concerned, but that was not something he had been trained to do at Yale. Nonetheless, he manfully took on the job of translating the tower's instructions and eventually brought the entire flight down safely. It was an experience of which any man could be proud, and the Chinese airmen, after landing, swarmed around him showing their gratitude.

Chinese "small talk" or "party language" was another area in which we did not have the time to train our students, nor was it required for their jobs. It was a luxury that had to wait while more important things were covered. I recall one student writing me a lengthy letter after he reached Taiwan, castigating me and the course for not covering that important area. He had married shortly before being sent to Taiwan, and because his wife was independently wealthy, he had been able to take her with him. They had rented a house and hired several servants. Specifically he blamed me for not having taught him how to deal with servants nor covering the day-to-day terminology necessary for running a house. I remember one sentence in his letter, where he bitterly complained, "I can't even say something as simple as 'I cut my hand off.'"

I let his letter lie for a week or so before answering it, and then wrote him, commiserating with him in his difficulties but pointing out that our responsibility had been to teach him enough to handle his job for the Air Force. Without question, in the normal course of events, it was hardly likely that he would have the need to say anything about cutting his hand off, nor would the Air Force attach too much importance to any such happening.

My letter crossed another from him in the mail, and in his second letter, he said that he owed me an apology, that he was even then sitting on the couch between his amah and cook, and they were able to chat together freely in Chinese. He recognized that his training at Yale, while not covering the specific terminology needed, had nevertheless given him the structural background on which he had been able to build everything he needed to say after quickly learning the few necessary basic terms for things around the house. I regret to report that he was among the first casualties among our former students who went abroad, although not in the line of duty. Returning from a trip to Hong Kong for a weekend, his plane crashed upon landing in Taipei, with all aboard killed.

In a previous chapter I mentioned our having to drop certain students from the course for failure to meet our objectives, always an unpleasant job for me.

Those young men had come to Yale with high hopes, and then, for one reason or another, had been unable to keep up with the rigid discipline and intensity of the course. I always gave them fair warning and bent over backwards to give them a second and even a third chance. And the spirit among their classmates was so high that inevitably their roommates or fellow students would pitch in to try to help bring the weaker ones up to snuff. They didn't always succeed. When eventually I had to give any student the bad news that we couldn't keep him any longer, more often than not there were tears and begging for another chance. Fellow students frequently came in to see me on behalf of the unfortunate men. And that wasn't the end of it. Even after students had left we would get letters from them or their families begging for reinstatement. But the Air Force had a firm policy in that regard and refused to consider any such requests, and we had to agree that it was highly unlikely that a student failing badly the first time around could make it on a second try.

There are the occasional exceptions to any rule, and I clearly recall the incident of two young men who, after four months, failed the course and were transferred to Keesler Air Force Base in southern Mississippi, near Biloxi. There the USAF was training Chinese Air Force personnel from Taiwan, and the two lads were given a job where even with their limited knowledge of Chinese they would be useful in dealing with the incoming Chinese recruits.

Edwin Bohannon and Robert Lipe found the job very much to their liking, and while working closely with the Chinese, they found the basic Chinese they had learned at Yale made them many friends, and their language ability continued to improve tremendously as they talked with the Chinese airmen. Their interest in the language grew day by day, and both had a burning desire to return to Yale.

A few months after they'd been there I received several letters from high-ranking Chinese Air Force officers who were in command of the Chinese airmen at Keesler. Each of them spoke highly of Lipe and Bohannon and how they were of such great help to the Chinese airmen. They urged me to reconsider and take the two men back for further training. These letters were followed by a joint letter from Lipe and Bohannon in which they begged to be given another chance.

I was impressed by the letters from the Chinese officers and felt that, considering the circumstances, it was not unlikely that the two men might do well on a second try. I approached the Air Force with a strong recommendation that the two be reinstated. It took many months, but two years later they reappeared at Yale. I lectured both of them as to the importance of making good the second time around, and told them I would ride them hard all the way. But the two years and their experience at Keesler had matured them, and the second time around they did an excellent job. Both graduated near the top in a class of some 76 men and later enjoyed satisfying tours in the field using the language.

Since they left the service, we've maintained contact over the years and have become fast friends. Their interest in things Chinese remained unflagging, although neither of them are actually using the language in their careers. Ed Bohannon has a sizable collection of Chinese stamps, coins, and paper money, and a large library of books on China. That incident gave me considerable satisfaction, and, like many others of our former students who wrote to us in later years, they gave credit for their ultimate successes in life to the rigid discipline we imposed upon them at Yale and thanked us for our part in shaping their lives. It gives me great satisfaction to note that it is Ed Bohannon who is going to print this book.

I had reason to be proud of almost every man who went through IFEL, but there were a very few who, after they reached the field, allowed themselves to fall in with the wrong kind of company and ended up badly. There was one young man of whom I was not at all proud, and I deeply regret having been in any way associated with his Air Force career because of what resulted.

At Yale he was a near-brilliant student, with great potential and usually excellent grades. However, he was forever organizing something in the way of parties for the rest of the class and was always himself the life of the party. But on at least one occasion he showed his true colors when, after crashing a party given by the Yalies at one of their college houses, he was approached by one of the Yale students and his date, was challenged and asked to leave. He vented his anger by attacking the girl and pulling her dress down to her waist in front of the assembled crowd.

After graduation he was sent to Vietnam while the war was still on there, and after picking up a smattering of Vietnamese, he was assigned to a group whose job it was to interrogate Vietcong prisoners. He met a violent death as a result of it.

A technique employed by some of the American interrogators when dealing with the Vietcong prisoners who refused to cooperate was to take them up in a helicopter and threaten to throw them out the open door unless they answered the questions put to them. One day, that young man took five or six Vietcong prisoners up in a helicopter a few hundred feet above the base, and as each man refused to answer his questions — conceivably because they didn't understand his fractured use of the Vietnamese language — he dragged them to the open door of the helicopter and threw them out in the hope of intimidating the others into cooperating. When he came to the last man, he again met with no response, and grabbing the man, dragged him to the door. But while he was attempting to throw the man out, the young prisoner wrapped his legs around his interrogator and dragged him out with him. I heard that story directly from former students who were there at the time and cannot but feel that the young man richly deserved the same death he had so callously dealt out to others.

Our relations with the Yale administrators was most cordial at all times, and we made some good friends among them. However, we got to know very few of the faculty. There were a few exceptions, but I think that most of them looked on us as an unfortunate sort of "poor cousin" — people who were necessary, and were to be tolerated, but who were not quite in their academic league. A few of the professors in the somewhat small Oriental Language department looked more kindly upon us and from time to time showed interest in what we were doing. Once in a while they would accept an invitation to come over and talk to our students in a program we called "Area Studies," in which they lectured the men on Chinese art, poetry, culture and history. Of President Griswold we saw very little except for an initial invitation to his mansion on Hillhouse Avenue very early in the program to meet the rest of the faculty.

When we first started the course the provost was a Mr. Furniss. We didn't see much of him, but he appeared to be a genial sort of man who welcomed us and was particularly friendly as time went on and the

Institute showed a profit — not the case with most of the other departments of the university. The provost at a university is probably the most important man on the campus, and it is he who runs the place on a day-to-day basis. Mr. Furniss did his job very well indeed and was always most cooperative when we had need of his help in resolving certain issues.

However, things changed drastically for us in 1961, when Yale got a new provost, Kingman Brewster. Brewster was an efficient administrator, but arrogant, dictatorial, and unapproachable most of the time, and it wasn't long before he earned the nickname, "The King." He rose meteorically, and in two years became president of Yale.

In our relationship with him he made it quite clear that he was unhappy that the Institute was earning such a name for itself worldwide. He didn't seem to feel that a prestigious university like Yale should be widely known for its language courses rather than something more academic. However, he was unable to dispute the fact that we were costing the university nothing and, indeed, were making a profit. He was also annoyed by the sight of so many blue Air Force uniforms on the campus. That was in the '60s, when military personnel were not popular on any university campus and were a constant reminder of the war in Vietnam, and Brewster decided that the Air Force had to leave.

One day in 1962 he peremptorily called me into his office and, without even asking me to sit down, bluntly told me that he had decided to terminate the Air Force contract after two more years. Patronizingly, he added that although he was well satisfied with the job I was doing for the Air Force and for Yale, I should begin to look for employment elsewhere as there was not the slightest possibility of my being retained by the university in either the language field or any other capacity when the Air Force program was terminated. At the same time, to demonstrate that my job was solely connected with the Air Force program and not Yale, he changed my title from assistant director to coordinator of military programs. It didn't matter one whit to me. I was still paid the same salary and still had supervision of all the IFEL students, military or otherwise, but the incident was something of a shock, and it should have indicated to us the way the wind was blowing.

The Institute at the time was at the height of its popularity world wide. We had a large number of civilians in the courses, a number of whom were diplomats from other countries, as well as various U.S. State Department personnel slated for overseas duties. Even Jay Rockefeller came to study Chinese for a brief time. The more I thought about Brewster's statement, the more I felt sure he was bluffing and gave it no further thought, and, as time went by, I forgot the incident completely.

However, Brewster's antipathy toward the presence of Air Force personnel became more evident as the days went by. It is of interest to note that in the Yale Bulletin of February 1963, which featured the Institute of Far Eastern Languages and which Brewster must have approved before publication, there is an admission on the first page that the Institute: "...at present enjoys a worldwide reputation in the teaching of spoken and written non-Western languages..." At the same time, in the entire 23 pages of text, there was no mention of the Air Force program, and the only concession to mentioning the military at all was a short description of two military courses.

Another notable event in 1962 was a visit by President John F. Kennedy on June 11 to give the commencement address. For days before his arrival, extensive preparations were made to welcome him, including sprucing up the entire campus as well as the city streets. Probably the best-known building on the Yale campus was Woolsey Hall, and a special area of the mezzanine there was set aside as a rest area for President and Mrs. Kennedy. The entire place was repainted and carpeted, with couches and easy chairs placed all around, and tables on which various refreshments were to be served.

We canceled all classes for that day so that our IFEL Air Force and civilian students would have a chance to hear the President's address and also to see something of the pomp and historical pageantry of a Yale commencement. In fact, a number of the Air Force students in uniform had their hands shaken by President Kennedy, who made it a point to seek them out in the crowd.

President Kennedy's address made news at the time for its daring statement on new economic principles, and many people remember him starting his address by saying he had the best of two worlds: he had graduated from Harvard and now had an honorary degree from Yale.

Our own graduation ceremonies for the Air Force students, held at least four times a year, were modest by comparison; nonetheless, we made sure each student would remember the occasion with pride. We secured the use of one of the large halls at the university — usually Sprague Hall — and canceled all classes for that morning. I made sure that every teacher and staff member at IFEL was there at the ceremony to show respect and appreciation for each student's achievement and, at the same time, to say goodbye.

The students always entered into the spirit of the occasion. For every graduation we had a valedictorian who gave his well-rehearsed speech in what passed for "fluent" Chinese and which, in fact, was always remarkably good, considering the men had only been there for 32 weeks. A second student stood by to translate it into English so that the visitors could understand it. On each occasion we also invited an outside speaker to address the graduates. Sometimes it was a member of the Yale faculty, or a notable from another leading university, but more often than not it was a USAF general or colonel. In 1957 it was the late Mike Todd — who fielded more questions about Elizabeth Taylor than about his travels around the world. Quite frequently the boys put on skits, performed entirely in Chinese, while they were dressed in pseudo-Chinese clothing, A running translation was given for the benefit of the audience. At other times they performed with group singing of Chinese folk songs, led by Jerry Kok or P.C. Li, one of the musically gifted Chinese teachers.

An important feature of each graduation was what we called the "moving up" ceremony. Our classes were designated by a letter of the alphabet. The senior, outgoing class was known as the "A" class. The one behind them was the "B" class, and the newcomers, at the time of a graduation usually having only been in the school for a few weeks, were the lowly "C" class.

At the graduation, we kept several rows of seats empty at the front of the hall. After all guests, visitors and school staff had been seated to the traditional strains of "Pomp and Circumstance," the three classes marched into the hall attired in their dress uniforms and took their places, one behind the other, in the center of the hall. When the speeches and other activities had been completed, diplomas or certificates of accomplishment were handed to each man as he mounted the stage, and then one by one they took their places in the empty seats in the front of the hall. When that was completed, I made a formal announcement designating the "B" class as the new "A" class, and the entire class moved forward to the seats that had been vacated by the outgoing class, and that was followed by the "C" class moving forward to become the new "B" class. It was a simple thing, but it did a great deal for student morale. My insistence that all members of all classes be present at a graduation was also a morale booster. For the newcomers to see fellow airmen performing on the stage in apparently fluent Chinese was always an encouraging experience. It gave them hope that in time they, too, would attain that proficiency. For the benefit of family members and invited guests, I invariably put on a brief show with the graduating class by having them stand and perform various maneuvers as I gave the commands from the stage in Chinese, speaking at a very high rate of speed. "Face left," "Face right," "Face forward," "Put your hands on top of your head," and so on, followed by the ultimate command that always brought a roar of laughter and approval, "Face to the rear and look at all the pretty girls sitting there."

It had become a tradition, a few days prior to each graduation, for me to take the entire graduating class to New York for a visit to the United Nations, where the students could sit and listen to the various delegates speaking and hear a simultaneous translation in Chinese. Of course, there was much that they were unable to understand, but the fact that they could get the gist of what was going on was always an exciting experience for them. Following our visit to the UN, we had a big Chinese lunch at one of the better Chinese restaurants, and then, in the afternoon we all went to a Broadway show. As an added bonus, students who had made straight "As" throughout the course were permitted to stay overnight in New York if they desired.

We made the trip back and forth from New Haven in chartered city buses, while a few of the students used their own cars. Both going and coming back, it had become a tradition to make a pit stop at a certain restaurant/gas station complex on the border between New York state and Connecticut. At that particular stopping point, beer could be purchased, and the younger students who were not permitted to purchase beer in Connecticut made certain that they got their fill. Of course, having taken on so much liquid, it became necessary to make another pit stop later, before reaching New Haven. On one occasion the bus driver, a surly chap who was anxious to get home, flatly refused to make a second stop, and I could not persuade him otherwise. As the need became more pressing, the students in the back of the bus set up a chant demanding a stop, but the driver ignored them. Then quiet fell, and I heard nothing more. Immediately afterward, riding as we were in the fast lane and passing cars on our right, I happened to notice a surprised look on the faces of certain drivers as we passed them, and looking to the back of the bus I discovered the reason. Our enterprising students had rolled up a copy of *Time* magazine and had thrust it between the rubber bumpers on the double back door of the bus and were using it to relieve themselves, much to the dismay of passing drivers. When I drew our bus driver's attention to what was going on, he hurriedly made a stop at the next gas station. On all trips after that I made it a point to inform the drivers that two stops each trip were part of the bargain.

Early in 1964 I received a letter from Berlin inviting me to be a participant at the International Conference of Modern Foreign Language Teaching, which was to be held in Berlin in September. I was asked to give a paper describing our courses and participate also in a number of seminars. It was made clear in the invitation that I was one of only two or three participants invited from the United States, and that it was expected that in each case the home institution should foot the bill for all travel and living expenses while in Berlin.

I approached Mr. Brewster with the invitation. Instead of showing some pride that Yale should be one of only two American universities chosen to be represented at the conference, he flatly refused to have any part in it and bluntly told me that if I went I would have to charge the time to my vacation time and pay all my own expenses.

Reluctantly I wrote the German conference hosts, telling them the circumstances and of my inability to attend because I could not afford the cost of the trip. However, to my great surprise they responded almost immediately that, in my case, an exception would be made, and they would pay all expenses for me and my wife. They expressed themselves as most anxious to hear about our program.

The language conference in Berlin was a huge affair, with hundreds of educators from every part of the world. It was held in a magnificent new building, modern in every respect, with simultaneous translation available on headsets at every seat in a variety of languages. My presentation was well received and I was then asked to join various panels of professors who questioned me as to the best methods for teaching a foreign language. I divided my time between those sessions and listening to other speakers in the main forum.

Our five days in Berlin passed all too swiftly. Amusingly enough, although we were quartered at the Hilton Hotel, except for breakfast, we ate all our other meals outside. Knowing very little about German food, we elected to eat in the many Chinese restaurants, where we found the food to be superb. I've never tasted better Chinese food anywhere outside of China. Apparently the Germans liked it so well that the Chinese were challenged to produce only the best and the competition between restaurants was intense.

In this chapter I have detailed some of the unhappy events of those years at Yale. However, the happy times were by far in the majority and we thoroughly enjoyed those years at IFEL. We look back on that period as one of the most rewarding in our entire lives. To work daily with those bright young men and have a small part in shaping their lives was both exhilarating and challenging, and we like to feel that every man who went through the school became a close friend of ours for life.

The months of October and November 1964 passed without any major developments at IFEL, but 1964 wasn't over yet, and before the year was out, we were hit with a momentous happening that was to completely change the lives of all of us who were connected with IFEL.

Certified Copy of an Entry of BIRTH within the District of the British Consul General at Tientsin

Application Number B.R.90/46

1913 BIRTH within the District of the British Consul General at Tientsin

No.	When and Where Born.	Name.	Sex.	Name and Surname of Father.	Rank or Profession of Father.	Name and Maiden Surname of Mother.	Signature, Description, and Residence of Informant.	When Registered.	Signature of Diplomatic or Consular Officer.
70	31 January 1913 Paku Chihli	Robert Norman	M.	Boris Jiff Thorp	Missionary		Dennis J. Mills Acting Vice Consul 10/2/13 British Consulate Tientsin	February 3 1913	J.P. Brenan Pro Consul

CERTIFIED to be a true Copy of an Entry in the Certified Copy of a Register of Births in the District above mentioned.

Given at the GENERAL REGISTER OFFICE, SOMERSET HOUSE, LONDON, under the Seal of the said Office, the 7th day of January 1946.

Cons. B 1425

This Certificate is issued in pursuance of and subject to the following Acts:—6 & 7 Will. IV, c. 86, sec. 38; 24 & 25 Vic., c. 98, sec. 38; 1 & 2 Geo. V. c. 27, sec. 3, 5, & 6. The Act 6 & 7 Will. IV, c. 86, sec. 38, enacts "That all Certified Copies of Entries, purporting to be Sealed or Stamped with the seal of the General Register Office, shall be received as evidence of the Birth," "Death or Marriage to which it relates, without any further or other proof of such Entry; and no Certified Copy purporting to be given in the said Office shall be of any force or effect which is not Sealed" "or Stamped as aforesaid."

Any person who (1) falsifies any of the particulars on this Certificate, or (2) uses a falsified certificate as true, knowing it to be false, is liable to Prosecution.

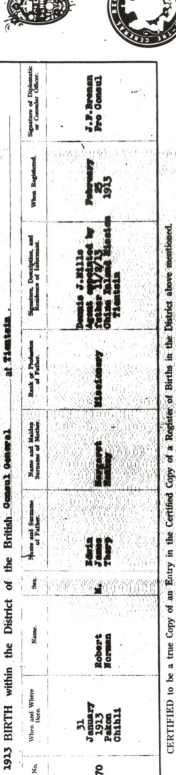

District of the British Consul General at Tientsin

1938. MARRIAGE solemnized at British Consulate General at Tientsin

No.	When Married	Name and Surname	Age	Condition	Rank or Profession	Residence at the time of Marriage	Father's Name and Surname	Rank or Profession of Father
41	Eighteen August 1938	Robert Norman THORP	25	Bachelor	Missionary	Pakaiho	Elvin James Thorp	Missionary
		Evangeline Elsje KOK	24	Spinster	Missionary	Pakaiho	Arie Kok	Netherlands Diplomatic Service

Married in the British Consulate General according to the provisions of the Foreign Marriages by me,

This Marriage was solemnized between us, Robert Norman Thorp / Evangeline Elsje Kok in the Presence of us, Alison F. Ballantyne / Leslie T. Egan, Consul General

I, Norman Richard Shaw, Acting British Consul at Tientsin do hereby certify

That this is a true Copy of the Entry of the Marriage of Robert Norman Thorp and Evangeline Elsje Kok Number 41 in the Register Book of Marriages kept at this Consulate General

Witness my Hand and Seal this 18th day of August 1938.

Thomas Pelham Acting Consul

Plaque presented by the basic class of Jan. '64 with the inscription: Isn't it amazing how much Chinese you taught us!

Bob, Leo (?), Jim Plessinger, Ray Mazzarella.

Bob in center back, last two on bottom row are: Ray Mazzarella, lab technician, and Winston Sun, instructor.

Ray Mazzarella — one of the lab technicians.

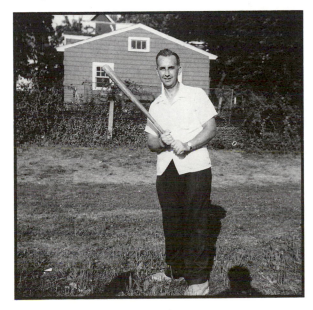

"Slugger Tharp"

Ball game fun — at least Bob has some shade.

Whereas: This twenty-first day of November in the year of Our Lord, 1962 is the most solemn occasion of granting United States citizenship to

Mr. and Mrs. Robert N. Tharp

and

Whereas: It is seldom that attaining citizenship is so difficult an undertaking, or that the honor is so richly deserved; and

Whereas: The devotion and services they have rendered to this country could scarcely have been exceeded; therefore

Be It Resolved: That we, the Basic Chinese class of July, 1962, hereby extend our most heartfelt congratulations and greetings, both on behalf of ourselves and the enlisted men and Officers of the Armed Forces of the United States, who for more than a decade have been so greatly privileged to receive their instruction in the field of Chinese language studies; and

Be It Resolved: That in this spirit of gratitude and admiration we hereby express our deepest joy that they have now become, in fact, what they have been so long in spirit.

Fellow citizens, we salute you!

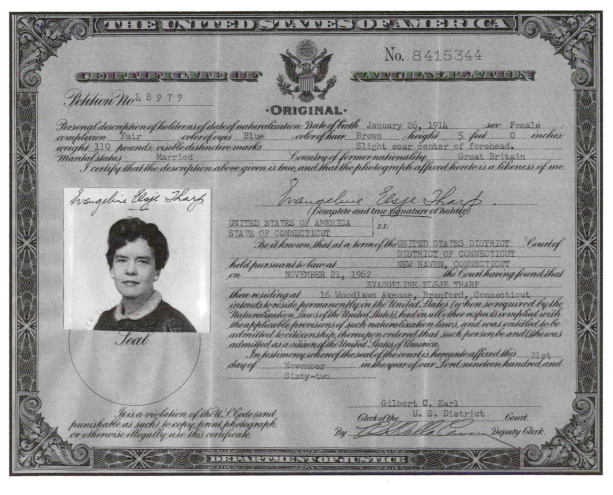

Sycee ("Shoe") Money

These drawings show typical Sycee ingots (also widely called "shoe" money among foreigners (or "boat" money by some) because it resembled a shoe or a boat. Sycee, a term originating from the Cantonese pronunciation of characters meaning "fine silk" (Mandarin *xi si*), was a small silver ingot varying in size, weight and fineness. These ingots commonly weighed anywhere from ½ to 50 tael (Chinese ounces), and sometimes 100 tael. They were used only by very wealthy households or by large business establishments. These were used in China as early as the Han Dynasty (226 B.C.-220 A.D.) right up to about 1935. The Chinese term for the Sycee was "yuan bao" (元 寶).

Characters at
upper left are
"fine silk"
in cursive script.

Gunzi tour chu xiao zi.

From the end of a stick comes a filial son.

- Chinese Peasant Saying.

Chapter Forty-Seven
The Ax Falls

A few days before Christmas in 1964, Kingman Brewster made good his threat to cancel the contract for training Air Force students at Yale. However, the circumstances were unusual, to say the least. For him, perhaps, it was a well-chosen moment, but for everyone at IFEL it brought about a very bleak Christmas.

During the previous year the Defense Department, to coordinate more effectively its overall language training requirements, had established a new agency, the Defense Language Institute (DLI). It was originally staffed by a commandant, a full colonel in the Army. Under him were a small number of military officers who represented the different branches of the military services, as well as a handful of civilians.

The Navy Language School at the Anacostia Naval Annex in Washington housed DLI Headquarters and the East Coast branch and the Army Language School in Monterey was named the West Coast branch. In addition, there was an English-language school in San Antonio for officers from allied nations, as well as

numerous small language schools overseas. The whole thing came about as a bit of a surprise, but for us at Yale, the only real change was that we now had to deal primarily with people in Washington and the Army, as DLI's executive agent, instead of Air Force officials. As a matter of fact, the Air Force and the other services from that point on had little say in the matter of how or where their students were to be trained.

Our Christmas break had started, and I was alone in the office one day catching up on some work when I got a telephone call from the commandant of DLI in Washington asking me if I could come down the next day for a conference. In strictest confidence he told me that in an attempt to save money, they were seriously considering pulling all language training for Air Force students out of the various universities and moving them to the DLI facilities in Monterey. He wanted me to give serious thought to accompanying the program to Monterey, should it move.

In the back of my mind I still remembered Mr. Brewster's statement two years previously about the inevitable termination of the program at IFEL, and it had become increasingly obvious that it would come about sooner or later. So, even though the news from DLI was unexpected, I was not surprised, given the overall controls that were already being exercised from Washington. One side or the other was going to have to give.

I wasn't happy about the thought of the program being moved to Monterey; nonetheless, I left for Washington the next day with mixed feelings, aware that our days at IFEL were numbered. As I thought over the probability of the return to Monterey, my experiences 15 years earlier at the Army's Monterey school made me seriously doubt that, should the course be moved there, it would prove to be successful. I thought it highly unlikely we could ever be afforded the same freedom in Monterey that we experienced at Yale, but I intended to make that freedom of action a strong point in any negotiations I might have with DLI in Washington.

When I reached Washington and was invited in for a private talk with the commandant, I found myself having an increasingly difficult time following his line of thought. He appeared to be talking about something entirely different from what he had said to me on the telephone the previous day. I finally asked him, "Do you know something that I don't? What you are talking about seems to bear no relationship to what the DLI intends doing."

For a moment the colonel was taken aback, then he blurted out, "Of course! They said you weren't to be told, so you obviously know nothing about it. They were afraid that if you were informed, it would get back to the Chinese staff at Yale and then there might be serious problems."

He went on to tell me that, since talking with me on the phone the previous day, he had received a phone call from Mr. Brewster telling him that the contract with the Air Force would not be renewed, and DLI had been told that it should make plans for withdrawing the program as soon as possible. He, in turn, had not let on to Mr. Brewster that he already intended to do just exactly that.

It was now a whole new ball game. Now it was not the Army's decision to move the program, but Yale's. From Yale's point of view DLI's hand had been forced, and so, to a certain extent, had mine. Little as I wanted to return to Monterey I decided then and there that for the sake of the program, and in order to try and retain its integrity, I would do so. After briefly discussing it with the commandant, I told him I would go, but under certain conditions.

I insisted that in order to maintain the current high degree of success our program enjoyed, it should be treated as an entirely separate department from the existing Chinese department there. I also insisted that as far as it was possible to do so, I would be permitted to take my own staff with me, depending, of course, on their individual desires, and in the event that none of my Chinese staff wanted to go to Monterey, I would have the authority to choose my own Chinese staff once we reached Monterey.

I further told him that, knowing well the inner workings of the Monterey school and the civil service system, I would go only if I were given the rank of a GS-13, which was one grade higher than all the other department heads. That demand was not for financial considerations, but because I wanted to be able to have direct access to the commandant of the Monterey branch without having to go through someone higher in rank than myself. Without that, I felt sure the program would have no chance of success.

To my surprise, and without the slightest hesitation, he agreed to all my demands (not that it did me much good in the end), and we began discussing the logistics of the move. I wanted the facilities for the program to remain as similar as possible to what we had at Yale, including at least two large language laboratories and an auditorium, preferably in a building remote from the existing Chinese department, since ours was a totally different sort of program. He told me they already had a building picked out for our use, and it would be converted in any way that I wished. What more could I ask?

Because remodeling the building and equipping the language laboratories would take some time, we realized it would obviously take the better part of a year to make the move. In addition, to preserve the continuity of the program and meet the needs of the Air Force, we would have to gradually phase out the three classes then in session at IFEL. We would have to take aboard the class already selected for January, and possibly another one in April. Then at some point we would have to start a new class in Monterey to avoid having any break in the scheduled input, otherwise it would create havoc all the way down the line. For those reasons, for a good part of the year, we would, in effect, be running two separate programs on opposite sides of the continent.

The logistics of all that were staggering. After we agreed that the class scheduled for April 1965 at IFEL would be the last, since it would graduate in November, and that we would shoot for the first class in Monterey to begin in June 1965, I felt we had done all we could at that point. I left the commandant and his staff to work out the details and I returned to New Haven with a heavy heart.

Immediately on my return I went to see our director, Mr. Fenn, to break the news to him. He, too, had been kept completely in the dark and was greatly perturbed to hear the unexpected development. For him, it was the end of the road; his services would not be required by DLI in Monterey, and since Yale was cutting out all but a small civilian program in Chinese, it was unlikely that Mr. Fenn's help would be needed there. And so it proved. I felt deeply disturbed for him.

After talking it over, we decided that it was only fair to let the entire Chinese staff know as soon as possible about the decision by Yale, since it would affect their lives and futures. I felt that it was important to give them a chance to think it over during the Christmas holidays and make whatever plans they could. Consequently, I called every Chinese teacher and all the Caucasian staff members with the saddest Christmas present anyone could bring them. I told them I had the authority to pick my own staff for Monterey, but we all knew that despite that, it was highly doubtful that all would be required in the new arrangement; moreover, I doubted that many of them would want to make the long trek to California. All of us faced the new year with a tremendous sense of foreboding.

Early in January 1965 I flew to Monterey, where I spent several days inspecting the building we were to use and consulting with the engineers over the changes that would have to be made. It was one of the old barracks buildings put up during World War II, and although in fair condition, it needed numerous changes. It had many small rooms that lent themselves to use as classrooms, but we needed at least two large rooms for the language laboratories and another for the auditorium. But it appeared possible, and the engineers set to work drawing up their plans.

I had a number of meetings with the commandant and his immediate staff, and I spent a lot of time with personnel discussing my teaching staff. But after I returned to Yale, as I had suspected from the beginning, none of our Chinese teachers wanted to move to Monterey. Because of the civil service system they, despite their long experience at Yale, would be treated as beginners with no seniority whatsoever, and the pay would be less than they were getting at Yale. Also, many of them had previously worked at the school in Monterey and had no desire to return, and almost all felt that the future there would be much too uncertain. At the same time, most of the teachers had houses and property in New Haven that they didn't want to sell in a hurry. At the end, only one of my Chinese staff eventually elected to go, and when he got there he only lasted a few weeks.

As for my own staff, who were mostly Caucasian, it was a little better. A number of former students had worked for me who had had at least one or two overseas tours and had taken advanced courses in Chinese. They were extremely knowledgeable regarding the needs of the Air Force and worked with me daily on the highly specialized military aspects of the course. Some of them, including Rick Richardson, Burt Hutchings, and Dick Williams were taking university courses and would help out during the summers or whenever they were free. David McCord had been with me since 1962 but had left in 1964 to go to San Francisco State to get his degree. After his graduation in 1965, at my request, he went to Monterey to help set up the program there. Abraham Yang, who had helped with class material as well as recordings, left to go to one of the agencies of the federal government.

Although good jobs had been offered them, the remainder of my staff decided to go to Monterey. They consisted of Carl Povilaitis and his wife, the former Joan Rebman of the grading and evaluation team, and Bill Harris. Doris Seely also decided to go to Monterey. But Jim Lance elected to go to work for the federal government. I was very sorry to lose that young man because of his extreme competency and ability as a teacher. In fact, he was quite unique. He had taught himself Chinese by listening to gramophone records and had acquired an extraordinary grasp of not only the spoken language, but the written language as well — something most unusual, considering the circumstances. Unlike the others on my staff, he had not been in the Air Force, but had spent two years in the Army during the Korean War. He had joined IFEL several years earlier, when I hired him after hearing him speak Chinese over the phone. He was among the first to leave for Washington, and it was some time before I saw him again.

My team in the recording studio, Raymond Mazzarella and Leo Szalamacha, did not wish to move because of family commitments and because their roots were in New England. Furthermore, even had they wanted to go, the pay would have been much less. It made me sad to learn that Yale would not continue to use the language labs and had no further use for those two loyal and hardworking men.

However, as things turned out, Yale's decision to get rid of the program turned out to be a blessing in disguise for most of the Chinese staff. When word spread of the demise of IFEL, our reputation was such that we were flooded with demands from universities throughout the country for the services of our Chinese teachers. Almost without exception, they found niches somewhere, in most cases with better pay and in charge of newly formed Chinese language departments.

Two or three of the teachers elected to go into business for themselves, one of them opening a restaurant. Various agencies and departments of the federal government in Washington were also on the lookout for promising candidates, and one of the agencies was so anxious to get good people that they sent a recruiting team to IFEL to interview the entire staff and to offer good positions to all who wanted to join. Eight or nine of the native Chinese teachers did so.

Nineteen sixty-five was one of the most hectic years I can remember. I was on the road a good part of the time: trips to Washington to iron out the details of the move and several trips to California to give advice regarding changes to be made in the building and selection of equipment for the language labs. Unfortunately, in the case of the language lab equipment, they did not take my advice but bought from the lowest bidder. From the beginning we had endless malfunctions and breakdowns with the inferior equipment. DLI had a repair team that was endlessly occupied with repairs. Unfortunately, they only worked in

daylight hours and were frequently working in the lab while a class was in progress, something that everyone found disturbing.

There were also numerous conferences regarding the personnel I would take with me and new teachers who would have to be hired there. I also had to spend a tremendous amount of time writing job descriptions for all of my staff and for the people to be hired by DLI in Monterey. Written job descriptions had been unnecessary at IFEL, but the Army bureaucracy lived on that sort of thing, and it had to be done. Then I had to write a detailed description of the course, its methodology and techniques, and at the same time I had to justify our unusual way of doing things.

In addition, I had to make two trips to Lackland Air Force Base to select the April class for Yale, our last there; later, a second trip was necessary to pick the first class to enter Monterey in June, a task that turned out to be quite difficult because it was not easy to motivate the applicants to attend a language school on a military base. They had already had their fill at Lackland and anticipated nothing better in Monterey.

Meanwhile, we had to arrange for all of our materials to be duplicated, because we would be running two programs simultaneously for half the year, in Monterey and at Yale. Every tape and piece of written material that we used had to be copied in sufficient quantity so that we would have a complete set for use in Monterey. We then began the arduous job of packing everything for the move, and every vacant bit of space in our basement rooms was piled high with cardboard boxes filled with everything we would need to make the new program a success. Eventually, when the move was actually made, we required two huge moving vans to haul all our stuff.

With the staff at IFEL anxious to take up their new positions elsewhere as quickly as possible, we became shorthanded there as the year progressed, as one by one they resigned. I badly needed someone to help me start the program in Monterey, but could spare no one from my IFEL staff, so I had to try to find someone from outside. David McCord was just graduating from San Francisco State when I approached him and asked him if he would take over the job of running the language labs in Monterey and supervising the program during my absences, at least for the few months that it would require for us to phase out the program at Yale. To my great relief he agreed, and by early June all was in readiness for the Monterey effort to begin. A nucleus of Chinese teachers were grudgingly supplied by the Chinese department, the majority of whom turned out to be those they judged to be least competent.

Eva and I moved to Monterey a week or two before the course was to start. I had not had time to find a house there, so we rented an apartment, and after packing all our household belongings for shipment, we stored them on the back porch of our house in Branford until such time as we could move Eva's mother out to Monterey and could include her belongings in the same van. Meanwhile, she remained in Branford by herself, with a couple of good neighbors to keep an eye on her. We found a tenant to rent our house, and early one morning we packed the car and were ready for the road.

Eva had been experiencing back problems for a number of years. She first hurt her back while we were building our first house in 1954, but with periodic visits to her immensely capable chiropractor, Dr. Scott Isaacson, she had managed to keep the problem under control. Now, probably from bending and packing not only ours and her mother's belongings but also IFEL's, at the very last minute, as Eva bent over to pick up her purse before we headed out the door, she had a back spasm and was unable to straighten up.

We called Dr. Isaacson, who was able to relieve some of her pain. However, she would need complete bed rest for at least 24 hours before she would be ready to leave the following morning.

By the next morning Eva could walk again, albeit with considerable pain, and because time was running out for us, we decided to start on the trip. Although she never complained, I could see that she was suffering.

By the time we reached the vicinity of Rochester, N.Y., she was in agony, and I was barely able to get her into the motel and put her to bed. It seemed obvious that we would be unable to continue our journey with her in that condition, and I began to think about putting her on a stretcher and somehow flying her to Monterey. But first I decided to try a local chiropractor.

I picked the first name that I saw in the telephone directory and telephoned him. An hour or so later he turned up, and a more patient, considerate and dedicated man it would have been impossible to find. Regretfully, I have forgotten his name, but he was an exceptionally competent young man, and for more than three hours he worked on Eva's back, trying to relieve the spasms she was having, giving her brief rests in between his treatments. Finally he resolved the problem, and she was able to walk once again.

The doctor felt that for a few days she ought to wear a support belt, and he went to Rochester to pick one up for her at an all-night pharmacy. He returned near midnight, at the end of what must have been for him a very long and tiring day. He charged us only his regular fee, but I insisted he take $100 for his time and trouble. We were deeply grateful for his skill and most gracious assistance. From that point on Eva's back continued to improve. Ultimately, by the time we reached Monterey, about eight days later, she was feeling herself again.

With Eva's mother coming to join us within a few weeks, we had to find two houses near each other. We finally found a house in what was known as the "sun belt" of Monterey near the airport, a newly developed area called "Fisherman's Flats." The Monterey sardine fishermen had for years dried their nets on the open flat spots there between the oak trees. When the sardines mysteriously left the bay a few years earlier, they sold the acreage to a developer who had built about 100 houses there. We managed to find two for sale, a block apart, and bought them.

Ironically, a week or two after we had moved into the first house, and I had flown back to Branford and brought Eva's mother out and installed her in the second house, we got to know our immediate neighbor, and discovered that his house, too, was for sale, and had been all along. We bought that house and moved Eva's mother there, where she was much happier being closer to us. Sad to say, I had great difficulty selling the first house a block away.

That first class of Air Force men we started in Monterey in June proved a huge success. Dave McCord had done an excellent job in getting ready, and with the help of some former students, still in the Air Force who were sent from Kelly AFB to help us, we began on schedule, and, at first, had the fullest possible cooperation from the Army authorities at the school.

Our curriculum called for a number of either aural or written tests every day, with more detailed comprehensive examinations every two weeks. The comprehensive examinations had been my responsibility from the inception. Since we still had two classes in session at IFEL, I flew back there every two weeks for a couple of days to give the examinations, grade them, and give the men their test results. To save valuable time, I traveled mostly by night on the "redeye" flights. With those trips, together with my regular trips to Lackland to select new classes and an occasional trip to Washington to report on progress or iron out some minor problems, in the course of that year I flew well over 100,000 miles.

After a smooth beginning, the first hint of trouble in Monterey came shortly after the first class started, when the Army started pulling men out of class for KP duties or for cleanup duties around the base. Nowadays, that is contracted out to civilians. I protested vigorously to the commandant that it was detrimental to my students, but to no avail. That was the Army way, and that was that. The procedure was for the lowest-ranking men to get the KP duties, and since most of our Air Force students came in with only one stripe, they were called most often.

I found the whole thing most annoying and disruptive to our schedule. It not only penalized the students, who lost class time during the day, but their evenings also were frequently taken up with chores around their quarters, which kept them from doing their homework.

There were many other minor but disruptive features of the Monterey school. Military discipline and military activities took precedence over language learning; academic achievement seemed to be of secondary importance. Several times a week the men had to report for drills, route marches, barracks inspections, cleanup details on the base, and a variety of other activities, all of which tended to interfere with the study habits that we had tried to instill and that had worked so successfully at Yale.

Another problem arose two months after the first class started, when it came time for me to fly to Lackland AFB to select the next class to be enrolled in September. In Washington, when I had originally agreed to take the job in Monterey, the commandant had wholeheartedly approved of my continuing the screening process at Lackland. He had agreed that those trips would not be a part of my official job, but would be paid for on a consultant basis as they had

been all along. However, the Monterey commandant decided that it was definitely a part of my job and that there were no funds to give me any additional pay to carry it out.

I found that extremely annoying because the screening test was something we had developed ourselves, and we had unquestionable proprietary rights to it. Furthermore, for nearly 15 years we had carried out the screening tests under an agreement with the Air Force. We were paid by the trip, and each class we selected had, according to the Air Force authorities, saved them tens of thousands of dollars, not only because of the extremely low attrition rate, but also because of our selection of men who were less likely to be dropped for reasons of security.

Now suddenly the rules were changed. Because of the shortness of time, I could do nothing about it with Washington, even though I phoned the commandant there and protested. He said he would see what he could do, and in order to preserve the integrity and continuity of the course, I agreed, under protest, to make the trip as part of my job. When I returned after having selected the new class, I again took up the matter with the DLI commandant in Washington, but he flatly said there were no funds available and no precedent for any such consultative travel.

Three months later, when it again came time to make the trip to Lackland, I found to my surprise that my services were no longer required. They had made other arrangements; someone else would do the screening. I suppose the idea was to teach me a lesson and to show me that I and my test were not indispensable. But if that were the case, it backfired badly on those who had thought up the idea.

To go back a bit, when the move to Monterey had been made, Washington had assigned an Air Force major to be my "liaison assistant," and, as stated to me at the time, his job was to assist me in every possible way in coordinating things with the Army and making sure the course ran smoothly. Later I learned that other motives had also been involved.

I knew the man well, and he was the last person I would have chosen for the job. He had been one of my officer students some six years before and had done poorly in the course, graduating near the bottom of the class. Moreover, he was a troublemaker, and on a number of occasions I had caught him cheating and had called him into my office. Of course, he denied everything. In addition to cheating, he took an overbearing attitude toward the lower-ranking airmen, and on one occasion when I entered the classroom a few minutes late, I heard him lecturing them and threatening that they should remember that if they did better in the course than he did and made him look bad, that when they got out into the field they would be under his command, and he would see to it that they had a hard time. Because of those and other incidents, I recommended to the Air Force that he be withdrawn. The Air Force, however, indicated that he had some special skills that they needed in the field and asked me to do my best to put up with him and let him graduate.

Undoubtedly he knew how I felt about him and I am sure he was not overly fond of me. Nonetheless, I did not protest when he was assigned as my "assistant," and I managed to get along with him without any difficulty when he first arrived in Monterey to help establish the new course. In fact, to give credit where it is due, for the first few weeks he worked indefatigably and gave me inestimable help in smoothing the way and getting things done, and I was very grateful for his assistance.

However, it wasn't long before he began to show his true colors. When time came for the trip to Lackland to select a new class, and the flap arose about there being no money to pay me, he was in the thick of it and gave me no support whatsoever. When, for the sake of the course, I gave in and went down to Lackland as part of my job, the major accompanied me, telling me he wanted to acquaint himself with the procedure and to see if he could be of any help. He watched my every move, studied my technique, took a copy of my test, and when we got back to Monterey, he secretly wrote his own version of the test. When, three months later, I was due to go down again to select a new class, he told me of the test he had written, which was "much better" than mine, and said he was going down personally to make the selection and I need not go. He assured me that he would do a better job than I could.

He took two of the senior students with him, just as I had always done, and came back with the names of 75 men whom he had chosen. He wrote a glowing report to the commandant on how successful he had been and what an outstanding class his 75 men would make. He assured the commandant that they would all graduate without any attrition whatsoever.

A few weeks later when the 75 men arrived, I was put in very much the same dilemma I had faced at Yale some years before when the Air Force had temporarily dispensed with my screening test and had used the one developed by the Harvard professor. The major had shown me a copy of his "improved" test and I found it to be totally inadequate for the purpose and knew that many of his 75 men were doomed, because the test he had given was utterly simplistic, and, unlike my test, did not touch on the first two lessons of the text that the men would be using in class. So, since our course was designed to start the men off with the prior passing of my test — the equivalent of the first two lessons in the text, and with a considerably larger vocabulary than the major's test — I decided to give them my test anyway on their first day as an introduction to the course. I would not say anything about it to anyone, least of all the major, who was so busy boasting to the commandant that he didn't show up until well after the test was completed.

Not surprisingly I found that more than two-thirds of the 75 men were unable to satisfactorily complete my test and would never have been selected had I gone to Lackland. However, there I was, stuck with them, knowing that most of them would fall by the wayside and that I could do nothing about it.

Just as I had done at Yale, I sealed the results of the test in an envelope, got the signatures of several witnesses, and put the envelope in a safe place. I then started the men with the same procedure as with any other class, with the major watching my every move over my shoulder. Within a week the results began to show what my test had predicted; a mere handful of the men showed some promise, while the rest quite obviously were unable to hack the course. The major was furious and accused me of trying to sabotage the class simply because I had not been allowed to go and select the men. He further accused me of being jealous of his test, which had proved to be so much better than mine and simpler to evaluate.

I knew the time had come to show him what we had done on the first day. In the presence of the witnesses who had signed the sealed envelope, I took out the test results, told him what I had done and why, and showed him how indisputably two-thirds of the class were doomed to failure. Enraged, he accused me and my team of lab assistants of conspiring against him to make him look a fool, said that my test results proved nothing, that he would see to it that I taught the entire class just as I would any class, and that he personally guaranteed they would all graduate.

From then on he rarely left the building, watching our every move and trying to find some aspect of the course that would prove that we were deliberately sabotaging his beloved class. Each day he harangued the men, urging them to greater effort, but it did no good, and as each scheduled test period came along, more and more men failed. The major even went so far as to accuse Eva of being in league with me and deliberately tampering with the test results so that he would look bad. He insisted on taking all the test papers to his room, where he pored over them, trying to find some place where Eva had deliberately tried to fail his men.

Eventually, he had to concede that some of the men were "slow learners" and insisted that I divide the class into three groups and teach them separately. Those who had failed the tests would start over from the beginning; the next group would repeat some of the work at a slower pace, and the few remaining ones who were better qualified would proceed with the normal schedule. However, the weaker ones, with no competition whatsoever, became weaker by the day, and knowing why they were made to repeat the material, became ever more discouraged. At times, the major even sat in class alongside the students, trying to coax them to greater effort, and with his own brand of Chinese tried to coach them in the tests. The men did their best. All of them wanted to succeed, but they simply did not have the aptitude, and all but about one-third of them were eventually dropped as being unsalvageable.

The relatively few survivors had a good sense of humor, though. The major, whom I will call "Louis," found himself being immortalized by the class. They called themselves "Louie's Losers." To this day when I hear from one of them, they remind me of the old name and identify themselves with that ill-chosen class. Finally he had to admit defeat and he never referred to the subject again.

Needless to say, when the next time came to screen a new class, the major was pointedly left out of the picture, and again I was asked to go. However, even then he interfered. When I boarded the plane I found myself accompanied by a young Army lieutenant whom I had never met and who knew not a word of Chinese. I was puzzled as to why he had been sent along. I soon found out.

For the first hour or so we chatted together. Suddenly he fell silent, and after a few minutes he turned to me and said he had a confession to make. He told me he had been sent by the major specifically to spy on my every action at Lackland, and he was to report back the names of every one of the Air Force officers or civilians with whom I talked. The young man was obviously a man of principle and said that he found the job he had been assigned to do extremely distasteful, and he had decided not to go through with it. A decent young fellow, he told me that it galled him to be asked to do that kind of a job, and after meeting me and getting to know me, he had decided that he would risk a reprimand and possible demotion by disobeying the major's orders. He further assured me that he had not the slightest intention of spying on me or reporting on anything I did, and he told me to feel perfectly free to do exactly as I had always done; he would stay out of my way. I was disturbed to think that the major would stoop so low. But the young man was a man of his word, and I saw nothing further of him until it was time to return to Monterey. Just what he told the major on his return I never learned, but each time I met him after that he always gave me a big wink.

The situation continued to worsen as the months went by. In November 1965, I flew back to New Haven for the last time to graduate the final class, and that was the end of the IFEL program as such. After that, Yale maintained a small Chinese department, but it never amounted to much. The two or three Chinese teachers who had remained behind confessed to me that their students were low in morale and not really interested in learning the language. One teacher told me that she had seven students in her class, but she had never seen all seven in class together. Discipline was so lax they came and went as they pleased, and testing was a thing of the past.

It was only a few years later that Mr. Brewster publicly acknowledged in an interview with a nationally read weekly magazine that he very much regretted having abolished the hugely successful Chinese program, and that he had now changed his mind and realized that foreign language training definitely had a place in the university setting. Of course, it was then too late to remedy the matter.

The few Caucasian members of my staff who had remained at Yale now joined me in Monterey and we plugged away despite the numerous obstacles that were placed in our path. The main problem arose when our first class graduated; the men were so superior to the graduates of the regular Army course, and their grades so uniformly higher, that the Army was deeply embarrassed. However, instead of trying to improve their own program, they tried to bring us down to their level, and I was ordered to change our grading system. I protested vigorously, but eventually was forced to concede. Meanwhile, the various innovations I had instituted to motivate the students were withdrawn one by one.

For example, we had long used Friday afternoons as a "catch-up" period for the weaker students to review the week's work. All students with a passing grade were exempted. At Yale, they had been given a half day off to do as they wished. The Army stopped that, telling me the men would have to remain at school simply because none of the other language departments permitted such a procedure and it would create a bad precedent. I countered by setting up a reading room, which I stocked with magazines and books from my own library, and the qualified students were allowed to go there to spend the afternoon. But even that was frowned upon and eventually abolished.

Whether all that was done with the knowledge and approval of the commandant, I never learned. From the beginning his attitude toward me had been ambivalent. He was always courteous but never friendly, and from our initial meeting it had been obvious that he resented being saddled with the program. He also made clear at the start that my demanding a higher civil service grade than other department heads had been an embarrassment to him and had created a precedent that could only cause trouble. Nonetheless, a few months after the course began and he saw the results, he called me into his office and bluntly told me that as a senior officer at the school it was my responsibility to have some sort of supervisory control over the various department heads who were one grade below me. Then, without in any way conceding that the course was a good one, he said I could fulfill that part of my duties by going around to

the various departments — there were some 30 different language departments — and giving them a lecture on just what my course consisted of and what techniques and methodology we used.

For a number of weeks I had to take time out from my busy schedule to give those lectures, usually two hours in length; however, the results were quite rewarding. Several of the department heads adopted some of our methodology, while others copied our specialized materials, albeit in a rather limited manner. The course from the beginning had been generally known around the base as the Yale Course. However, that wasn't good enough for the Army. Loving acronyms as they do, we became the MAFAC program, Mandarin Air Force Aural Comprehension, and that name stuck until they changed it to something else a few years later.

The major, meanwhile, after his fiasco in selecting a class at Lackland, began to interfere more and more in our program. He made an analysis of what we did and wanted detailed explanations as to why we did it and then made arbitrary decisions as to how it ought to be changed. He even eliminated certain aspects of the course that he felt were superfluous but that I knew to be essential to the training that the men needed for work in the field, where they would be monitoring radio transmissions from the Chinese mainland. Daily, he wasted hours of my time with his petty interference, but when things got too bad I went over his head to complain to the commandant, stating that what the major wanted to change or eliminate was either essential or mandatory. The commandant always replied, "that's debatable," and that was the end of that. He would not support my decisions against those of the major.

The situation became increasingly intolerable, and heated arguments with the major became almost a daily occurrence, not only with me, but with the Caucasian members of my lab team, and before long it began to take its toll. Carl Povilaitis, one of my most trusted helpers, was the first to resign in frustration, after only a few months there, and he was quickly followed by Dave McCord, who had taken the brunt of the major's wrath. I feared that he was developing ulcers and finally urged him to go back to college. After those two left, it wasn't long before others began to follow as they saw the program beginning to fall apart. Eventually, less than three years after we moved to Monterey, every single one of the Caucasian staff I had taken to Monterey from Yale had left. It was at that point, in 1968, that Eva and I, too, decided we had had enough and made up our minds to leave.

When I gave notice that I was resigning, I told the commandant that I would gladly stay on for an additional six months to train my successor if he so wished. He accepted my offer, and for the first time unbent to the extent that he told me no one except another Westerner could have done the job that I had done, and that under no circumstances would he allow the course to fall into the hands of anyone but another Westerner. He insisted that he wanted me to find a Caucasian for the job and that he would settle for nothing else. He was quite convinced that, comparing our course to the regular Army course, no Chinese would be able to handle it with any success. I agreed but told him I doubted that a suitable replacement could be found. Despite that, he asked me to write to all whom I thought might be qualified and offer them the job at the same salary I was getting.

I wrote many letters explaining the program and inviting prospective candidates to apply for the job. I was quite sure we would not get any favorable responses. I also knew full well that if no satisfactory replies to my letters were received, the major would accuse me of trying to sabotage the program. He would argue that I must have written something disparaging about the program in order to prove my point. Therefore, I wrote the letters and left them unsealed on his desk for him to read, which I am sure he did. Just as I had anticipated, from nearly 50 letters that I sent out, we got just one reply. The writer was quite uncomplimentary about having even been offered the job.

As I had anticipated, the school was left with no other option, and my job was made available to any senior Chinese teacher who wanted to apply for it. One was eventually selected; his primary qualification was that he spoke better English than the others. I spent the next six months showing him the ropes and then retired at the age of 55, the first of four retirements.

Before I left, one of the senior officers from DLI headquarters in Washington came to Monterey and expressed great regret over my decision to leave. I told him how the ground had been cut out from under

me, and it was then that he told me why they had assigned the major to be my so-called assistant: they feared I would antagonize the Army people and wanted him to keep me in check. He admitted it had been a great mistake on their part, and one he and his boss greatly regretted. They obviously had no idea that the major in his enthusiasm to butter up the Monterey commandant and secure his promotion to lieutenant colonel would all but destroy our program in the process.

During the latter part of 1965, as we were phasing out the program at Yale, I made a detour to Washington, D.C., to attend a conference at DLI headquarters. Prior to the trip one of my former Caucasian staff members at IFEL wrote, telling me that because the current head was reported to be about to retire, his department was looking for a new man to head up their Chinese section. He asked me to call him the next time I was in Washington if I was at all interested.

With the situation in Monterey growing unpleasant, I was not averse to exploring the possibilities of a job in Washington, so when I arrived, I called him. He told me he would set up a meeting with his superiors. He apologized that tight security prohibited their seeing me at his place of work, but he designated a Chinese restaurant in the Rock Creek area, where I was to meet him and his boss at noon.

I was there at noon, and a few minutes later he and his boss arrived. We had a long discussion, after which I was advised that I would be informed later of their decision. Later, my former staff member advised me that there was no way for their people to investigate my activities while in China, so they could not hire me.

There was another incident I had with people in the federal government associated with national security. My security clearance was undergoing a periodic review, and following their usual procedure, one of their plainclothes men had been sent to the area of Monterey where we lived to interview my neighbors about me. The day he came, I was working next door mowing the lawn for Eva's mother. A strange car drove up and parked halfway up the next block. A young man got out, and I immediately recognized him for what he was. Seeing me on the lawn he walked over, greeted me, and in a jovial manner said, "Do you happen to know a Mr. Tharp who lives around here? I hear he owns half the neighborhood." I smiled and told him I not only knew the man but that he was actually talking with him. I've never seen anyone as embarrassed as he was. He stuttered and mumbled something under his breath, but I tried to put him at his ease by inviting him in for a cold drink. He accepted, apologized profusely for the manner in which he had spoken to me, and then confessed the reason for his being in the area and begged me not to tell his superiors. I never saw him again after that.

As I have mentioned, my retirement from DLI in Monterey was my first retirement. I was to have three more. I was 55 at the time, had no prospects elsewhere, and had decided to just take a day at a time until something came along. Meanwhile I busied myself working on Chinese language teaching materials and doing some odd jobs around the house.

The husband of my former secretary at the school was a retired Navy petty officer who had left the service for health reasons. A relatively young man, he started the first handyman service in the area. He did extremely well and was kept so busy that from time to time, knowing of my interest in building houses, he asked me to come and help him.

I enjoyed the varied jobs that came my way and the challenges that each one offered. They ran the gamut of everything that was needed in the upkeep of houses: cleaning drains, replacing roof shingles, stringing doorbells, putting in electric wiring, piping new water lines, fixing gas stoves, and even taking care of furnaces.

At about the same time I started thinking about building a house on one of the two lots I had bought a block away from our house, lots that had previously been owned by an airline pilot named Fred Dahler, who flew for United Airlines. Eva and I very much liked the house we were living in. And the two lots, backing up against a hill, got very little in the way of sunshine, particularly in the winter months, so we had no intention of living in any house that we might build there. The whole idea was to simply build one for speculation.

While the work on the house was in progress I received a number of feelers from the National Security Agency near Washington, asking if I was interested in a job with them. That was followed by visits from one of their representatives who outlined what they wanted me to do. I was to act primarily as a sort of overall program planner and "watchdog," keeping an eye on their in-house Chinese language program, as well as monitoring student progress at the Navy's DLI East Coast school, and in particular at the Defense Language Institute in Monterey. They also wanted me to evaluate all textbooks and materials currently in use. Furthermore, they wanted me to be situated in the Washington area, at NSA headquarters in Fort Meade.

I found the offer extremely attractive and agreed to go whenever they were ready for me. On a final visit by their representative in the latter half of 1969, I was told that it was now 99 percent certain that I would get the job. He suggested that I move to the East Coast in anticipation of it. That made sense to us, because there were other good reasons for us to pull up stakes and leave Monterey. Eva's mother had moved to a retirement home in Collingswood, New Jersey, primarily to be close to her old friends there. But her health wasn't at all good, and Eva wanted to be a little closer to her.

George Sing, whom I had known for a number of years, was the NSA representative who had been largely instrumental in negotiating the job for me, although Del Lang had also been considerably involved. George lived in the newly created city of Columbia, just outside Baltimore, and suggested that I get a house there so as to be near Fort Meade. In fact, he told us of a newly built two-bedroom house not far from his own that was available. The owner, a salesman for the developers, was moving on and wanted to get rid of it. We then and there called the man on the phone, and, since the price was right, I bought the house over the phone, sight unseen.

We sold all of our properties in Monterey and set out for the East Coast once again with all our furniture and belongings loaded on a U-Haul truck. Unfortunately, the promised job at NSA suddenly fell through only a matter of days after our arrival. Until then there had been complete secrecy about their plan to hire me, but one of the NSA people visiting the DLI in Monterey had inadvertently mentioned my name and what I was expected to be doing. The Chinese department, hearing that I would be put in charge of monitoring them and what they would teach, apparently panicked, and, fearing that with me at NSA their jobs would be in jeopardy, they threatened to go on strike if I were appointed to the proposed job. Both NSA and the DLI authorities feared the threat was real and reluctantly gave up the idea of using me, and that was the end of that.

I, quite frankly, wasn't overly concerned. I had visited the NSA complex on several occasions, and although I had many friends there, mostly former students, the place was so vast and intimidating that I was not the least bit sorry the job had not materialized. I had had my fill of government rules and regulations and the limitations of bureaucracy, and I was quite happy to continue in my retirement.

We hadn't been in Columbia more than a few days when I was called by a local construction company to give them a hand. George Sing, knowing I had built a house in Monterey, had given them my name. They were desperately short of qualified help and needed a man with a variety of skills to be part of a team that made minor repairs to newly sold houses. Our job was to answer calls from the new owners, take care of their problems, and spot any other discrepancies that there might be. A few of the houses had been built by private contractors, but most had been built on a production-line basis with different teams doing different jobs on each house. In nearly every house that had been built, something had been either left out or was improperly installed. I found it interesting work.

From Columbia we made several trips up to Collingswood to see Eva's mother. Her health continued to deteriorate, and she was unhappy in the retirement home, although it was some time before she would admit to it. At one point she was hospitalized

for about six weeks. We decided that the best thing was to have her come and live with us, and we moved her down to Columbia as soon as she was well enough to travel.

As Christmas of 1969 approached, I received a letter one day from my old friend Dr. Paul King in New York, telling me that I was badly needed to do some evaluative work for a new bilingual program that was being started in Chinatown. Although in no way related to what I had been doing previously in teaching Chinese, it sounded interesting. After visiting New York to explore the possibilities and then going to the Department of Health, Education and Welfare in Washington, D.C., to learn more, I decided to take the job.

The program was an experimental pilot program at P.S. 1 in Chinatown, the first school to have been established in that area. The student population was about equally divided between Chinese and Puerto Rican children, so a dual program in both languages covering several grades was to be established. The man chosen to direct the program was a young Puerto Rican. Several Spanish-speaking teachers had been hired, as well as a number of Chinese teachers. My job was to advise on the overall teaching methodology and teaching materials, and then to test and evaluate the program. Weekly reports were required as the program progressed. The job called for me to spend two or three days a week in New York, so I decided to commute from Baltimore by train. So began a job that was to last for nearly six years.

Bob playing with nieces and nephews.

Chinese New Year dinner, 1964.

Chinese New Year, 1964.

Hai qun zhi ma.

The horse that brings harm to the herd
(i.e. one who brings disgrace on the group;
bad apple; black sheep).

- Chinese Proverb.

Chapter Forty-Eight
Chinatown – New York

I became a part of the Building Bilingual Bridges program, the name given to the bilingual program in New York's Chinatown early in January 1970. The school chosen for the experimental program, P.S. 1, on Henry Street just off Broadway, was one of the oldest elementary schools in New York City and the first to have been established in Chinatown. The school was in the heart of Chinatown, in the general area known as "Two Bridges," so named because it lay between two large bridges across the East River to Long Island, the Williamsburg Bridge and the Manhattan Bridge.

Nearby on one side was Little Italy, and on the other an area largely inhabited by Jewish people. However, the three areas blended with no discernible boundaries, and the residents seemed to get along extremely well. In the Jewish area it was not unusual to see a Chinese restaurant offering kosher food and numerous Jewish and Italian shops in the Chinese area. But Chinatown had had an influx of Puerto Rican immigrants, and a large number of them lived side by side with the Chinese.

P.S. 1 had originally been selected because its ethnic makeup was supposedly about evenly divided between Chinese and Puerto Rican children, with a sprinkling of other nationalities. However, when we actually became involved in the project and took a census, it turned out that some 68 percent of the children were Chinese and only about 22 percent Spanish-speaking. Because our effort was to jointly serve both the Chinese and Puerto Rican populations, the discrepancy in numbers led to our moving to another school, P.S. 2, a year later. Just three blocks away the balance between the nationalities was more evenly divided.

P.S. 1 was part of New York's School District 2, with headquarters in midtown Manhattan on 33rd Street. It was headed by an extremely active and capable woman, a strictly no-nonsense person who ran the district with an iron hand, but who was nevertheless highly respected and liked by nearly everyone. Like most schools in the New York area, P.S. 1 was staffed by Caucasians, even to the janitorial help. The principal was a man, with a woman as assistant principal.

Bilingualism, the object of our project, was in its infancy at the time, and like almost everything else that was new, very little was known about it by the general public. The idea, however, was strongly supported in Washington, and plenty of money was available through Title VII grants to any school district that wanted to apply for it and could show adequate justification.

The whole idea of bilingualism was new to me as well, but the arguments in favor of teaching newly arrived immigrant children in their native language as an aid to learning English, and thus more quickly becoming a part of the life of the school and community, at first made a lot of sense, and I started out supporting the whole idea. In time, though, I began to change my thinking. Considering the overall results, I now look back on those six years as the least enjoyable and productive period of my life, and the most unsatisfying.

Initially the idea was so new to both the Chinese and Puerto Rican parents that it met with a surprisingly mixed reception. The Chinese in particular strongly opposed the idea at first. They wanted their children to become proficient in English as soon as possible and believed that any time spent in class using their native tongue was not only a waste of time, but would delay their children in the acquisition of English. Arguments that the program would keep Chinese culture alive carried no weight. The Chinese parents had no fear that their children would lose touch with their native culture, because at the end of the school day the majority of them went immediately to Chinese-language schools in the area, where they spent several hours studying traditional Chinese subjects and textbooks in their native tongue. The parents felt that experience, and the use of the Chinese language in the home, was enough of a link with their cultural background. The Chinese parents also felt strongly that American schools had no business mixing the two languages, and in that viewpoint they were, at first, joined by the Chinese leadership in Chinatown. But things quickly changed. It wasn't long before the Chinese saw what a lot of money was involved in the

project, and they wanted a piece of it. In a relatively short period all the schools in the area wanted a bilingual program, more Chinese teachers, and more Chinese administrators to run the programs.

The Puerto Rican parents, on the other hand, were largely indifferent to anything the schools might suggest. Their attitude was that once outside the home, their children were the responsibility of the schools, and they were totally unconcerned that Spanish was to be used in the school. In fact, most of them saw little reason in the first place to learn English at all and were quite content to let the schools do as they wished.

For the first several weeks my job consisted of visiting the parents in their homes or places of business and explaining what we were attempting to do. We emphasized that once the children were able to function in English and keep up with English-speaking children of their own age, their use of their native tongue in school would be dropped. That seemed to satisfy the parents, and, in time, the majority were won over and opposition ceased. We found that once we were able to persuade the parents to visit the school and watch their children at work, each using his native language as well as English, they usually seemed well satisfied.

At the start of the program my job as evaluator was largely peripheral. I accompanied the Chinese and Spanish teachers to the homes of the children to watch and listen. Later, my role was to advise the teachers on better approaches and on subtler techniques in talking to the parents. I then began to spend a considerable amount of time in the classrooms watching the teachers in action and assessing the results with the children by means of simple tests. That was followed by endless reports, usually done on the train or at home in Columbia.

The first three months I wasn't away from home much because I averaged only about 18 hours of work each week. But my time in New York quickly began to mount as the district office wanted my help in writing a new proposal for the following year. That was a painstaking task that required all kinds of analysis, charts, graphs, statistics, descriptions, and justification both for more money and for details on proposed expansions into other schools. It then became necessary to create more detailed tests for the children and to administer them, and, as the weeks went by, to find new teaching materials suitable for use in a bilingual setting.

That latter proved the most difficult. We searched the market, not only in this country but also in Taiwan and Hong Kong, and found almost nothing available. Eventually we had to write our own. Finding writers to produce the small booklets didn't prove much of a problem. Written in English and copiously illustrated, we quickly produced a dozen or so booklets, but translating them into Chinese and Spanish did raise a few eyebrows. The Chinese translation was, supposedly, Mandarin; however, because most of our teachers and the majority of the Chinese children were Cantonese, some Cantonese influence crept into the translations. The Chinese parents, however, seemed quite unconcerned about that. What did bother them, and the teachers as well, was the fact that the drawings, done by a Caucasian, portrayed orientals with slanted eyes. That the Chinese rejected out of hand, and we had to re-draw all the pictures.

Where the Spanish-speaking population was concerned, the problems were much greater in one respect. Our teachers came from different parts of the Spanish-speaking world, resulting in constant arguments among them — and the parents — over the language used in the translations. Some wanted pure Castilian Spanish, others Cuban Spanish. Still others felt that Mexican Spanish was more appropriate, but since the majority of the parents were from Puerto Rico, it was Puerto Rican Spanish that was mostly in demand. We found it impossible to satisfy everyone and finally settled on a compromise.

Once the booklets were written, I kept busy finding a printing firm to produce them for us and supervising the production of the texts every step of the way. However, when finally put into use, they were generally well received and certainly took care of a big gap in the program. I found the work interesting and challenging at first, but as time went by, I began to realize that vast sums of money were being spent by the school board in areas that actually had little or nothing to do with the children's needs, and that bothered me greatly.

I also made several trips to the Department of Health, Education and Welfare (HEW) to report on the program, and at one point I asked them outright whether they wanted me to be a sort of watchdog and report on any misuse of funds. They responded affir-

matively, and from then on I gave them detailed reports on how much of the money was spent on things such as cameras, filing cabinets, typewriters, adding machines and various other office equipment, none of which was used in our program. But to my disgust they did nothing about it.

In New York I usually stayed overnight at a hotel in Manhattan and then returned to Columbia the next day. But by early June, I was so swamped with work and spending so many nights away from home, with no let-up in sight, that we began to think of moving closer to the city.

We still owned two houses in Branford, Connecticut, only 90 miles from New York. Although it again would require two hours by train to make the trip, in actual mileage Branford was a lot closer to New York than Columbia, and the idea of moving back there became increasingly attractive as time went by, particularly because we had so many friends there.

In late September 1970, we made our move from Columbia up to Branford. I then started my daily commute to Manhattan on the New Haven and Hartford railroad. There were frequent commuter trains leaving from New Haven, and to catch the first one out at 5 o'clock meant getting up at around 3:30 so that I could get to work by 8. Of course, Eva got up every morning at the same time to make my breakfast.

The train trip seldom took less than two hours, and once in New York I had a half-hour ride, either by bus or subway, to Chinatown. I usually returned home by one of the many trains that ran after 4:30 in the afternoon, and although it made for very long days, at least I was able to spend each night at home, a great consolation to Eva.

Meanwhile, as the weeks went by, my job at the school in Chinatown became ever more demanding. By the end of the first year the parents felt so much antagonism toward the director, whose arrogance and blatant display of favoritism among the teachers had caused such constant discord, that the parents and district representatives met and voted him out. No immediate replacement was found, so the senior Chinese teacher, a Mrs. Fok, was appointed acting director.

For the following year Mrs. Fok did a creditable job of managing the project. That coincided with the controversial move to the new school about three blocks away, where the Chinese children were in a more balanced proportion with Puerto Rican children, and where the school principal and staff were friendlier and more receptive to the program.

All of us in the project welcomed the move to the new school. We found the parents much more cooperative, the school modern, clean and comfortable, and, as a bonus, we were given classrooms and office space on the ground floor. In the first school we'd had our office on the third floor and classrooms on the main floor, which meant much climbing of stairs.

Things moved along fairly quietly that year, but Mrs. Fok was finding it a great strain. At the same time, there was definitely an undercurrent of antagonism toward her by the Puerto Rican parents, simply because she was Chinese. By the end of the year she indicated that she no longer wanted the job of director. Another meeting was called, and to my surprise, I found that I was voted in unanimously as the new director. It wasn't a job I had sought, nor one that I relished, but apparently both the school authorities and the parents had gotten to know me, liked what they saw, and decided that being neither Chinese nor Puerto Rican, I could be neutral in the numerous confrontations.

Along with my new job, in the third year our project had enlarged considerably. A new proposal had been accepted by the Title VII people, and we were funded for bilingual classes in seven different schools in the Chinatown area. That required more staffing and detailed scheduling. Even though the schools were relatively close, considerable time was spent in going from one to the other, and frequent meetings between parents and staff members also occupied much of my time.

I gained considerable satisfaction in being able to direct the course of instruction in ways I thought would be most beneficial to the children, but at the same time there were many frustrations in the job. Although I was ostensibly project director, I found that I had no say whatsoever in the way funds were used; that was in the hands of the district director and the various school principals. More and more I began to see a great waste of funds over which I had no control whatsoever. Each school suddenly seemed to require new filing cabinets, typewriters, tape recorders and mountains of office supplies, and only

a very small proportion of the items purchased bore any relationship to the bilingual project. On my occasional visits to Washington to report to HEW on the project, my detailed accounts of the misuse of funds went unheeded, and I came to the conclusion that the entire effort was a colossal boondoggle and waste of public funds, while relatively little was done to benefit the children.

Each week I had to visit the district office on 33rd Street at least twice. A good part of my time there was spent consulting with staffers and working up new proposals for even more money, a job that I found increasingly repugnant. On one of my trips, I noticed a young and attractive woman sitting in an armchair in the hallway just outside the director's office. Beside her was a small table covered with magazines and a big ashtray, and a wastebasket sat nearby, half-filled with empty Coke cans.

On subsequent visits to the district office over the next several months I found her still sitting there, seemingly a permanent fixture, and finally my curiosity got the better of me. I asked who she was, but none of the staffers would tell me anything. I eventually learned that she was a grade-school teacher who had shown abnormal behavior in class and had appeared very disturbed at times. The principal of her school had refused to allow her to teach any longer, but the union was so strong that he was unable to fire her. So she was assigned to sit for eight hours a day outside the office of the district director, drawing her full pay. For all I know she may be sitting there still.

Usually my visits to the district office were depressing, but one balancing factor was a man about my own age in whose company I found myself a good part of the time. He was charged with doing most of the paperwork for new proposals, and the better I got to know him the more delightful I found his company. Harold Braunstein had been in the school system for a number of years, both as a teacher and as a school principal, and he knew the system backward and forward. We became close friends, and as we discussed the "system," he agreed that there was too much graft and abuse of public monies. However, it was so cleverly concealed, with so much apparent legal justification, that there was nothing anyone could do about it.

Harold, in addition to his other great talents, was a pragmatist. During one of our discussions on the morality of what we found ourselves doing, he came up with a humorous and most apt description of the way in which the New York Board of Education appeared to operate. He called it "Braunstein's Law," and it went as follows:

"Pedagogical problems are always resolved administratively.

Administrative problems are always resolved politically.

Political problems are always resolved criminally."

The truth of his "law" seemed ever more apparent to us as time went by. But Harold never let it get him down. He was an extremely gifted man, with an immense sense of humor. His greatest love was the bouncy ragtime music of the Roaring '20s, a love that I also shared, and it was he who first introduced me to the incomparable music of Scott Joplin, his "Entertainer," and other great songs, for which I shall be eternally grateful to him.

In addition to being a gifted writer, Harold Braunstein had the unique talent of being able to see everything multi-dimensionally. When in deep thought, he would doodle on a sheet of paper or on the blackboard. But unlike most people's doodles, his took the form of precise lettering. He would absent-mindedly pick a short phrase, neatly letter it across the page, then proceed to draw or write the same thing upside down. That would then lead to his drawing it as though looking at it from back to front, then from the top looking down on it, or from underneath looking up, and even from the inside looking out. Harold seemed to be able to get inside as well as outside of whatever it was he was writing or drawing, and to look at it from every conceivable angle. I've never seen anyone else do anything quite like that. When I eventually left New York, Harold Braunstein was the one man I was most sorry to say goodbye to.

While the year 1972 brought me increased responsibilities as director of the program, and kept me busier than ever, for Eva at home things were not going at all well because of her mother's increasingly poor health.

One night in late July, Eva's mother, then 84 years of age, got up from the couch to go to bed, said good-night to us, and started across the room. She had taken only two or three steps when she suddenly fell forward against the wall, then fell backward onto the floor, banging her head against a china cabinet in the process. We called an ambulance and rushed her to the hospital. She was put to bed and shortly thereafter fell into a deep sleep. We sat with her all night and well into the morning, but she didn't wake up. Finally, when the doctor came in to see her, he realized she was in a deep coma, from which she never recovered. They discovered a blood clot on her brain, operated and tried to relieve the pressure, but nothing did any good, and for 42 days she remained in a coma.

Ultimately her kidneys failed, and the doctors told us nothing further could be done for her. They suggested removing her from the life support equipment that had been keeping her alive. We consented, then we moved her to a nearby nursing home, where for two days there was no change at all in her condition. Eva, who had been sitting by her bedside around the clock, was persuaded to go home for a few hours' sleep. Around 3 in the morning the doctor called to say her mother had finally breathed her last, passing into the presence of her Lord on August 14, 1972. Eva has always regretted that she was not at her bedside at the time of her death.

Each year Harold and I wrote new proposals to be submitted to Washington for ever-increasing amounts of funding, and our proposals continued to be accepted. The project increased and by 1975 we were operating in six elementary schools, one junior high school and three non-public Catholic schools.

Our student enrollment had increased to more than 1,200, and we had 21 teachers involved in the program. Classes were conducted in all grades from kindergarten through ninth grade. However, our curriculum was much more diversified than in the initial years. Although we covered all subjects bilingually in most of the lower grades, in the higher grades we concentrated on cross-cultural areas as well as teaching English as-a-Second-Language (ESL). That was because many of the immigrant children in that age group were newcomers to the country, totally unprepared to enter high school and study subjects useful to them in adult life.

While I derived great satisfaction from being able to help the children, and at the same time provide gainful employment to a good number of both Chinese and Puerto Rican nationals, I still felt strongly that too much money was being siphoned off by the school board and district offices for things unrelated to the project. Although I continued to protest, the expenditures ballooned out of all proportion to the number of children and teachers actually involved.

Thefts from the school were one big factor in keeping costs high. Over the weekends we became the frequent target of burglars and I lost count of the number of times I went to work on a Monday morning to find all our typewriters and tape recorders stolen and the room a complete shambles. We leased a large and bulky Xerox machine, which was too big to be stolen, but it was frequently damaged, causing long delays while repairs were made. Ironically, just around the corner from our school was a sort of flea market where stolen goods were sold. On several occasions when I went there, I saw equipment of all sorts that had been stolen from the schools, still clearly marked: "N.Y. Board of Education." Yet nothing was ever done by the police or other authorities about retrieving it.

My immediate office staff consisted of Elizabeth Kwong, a young Chinese-American woman who was my typist and secretary, two course evaluators, and several consultants who came in two or three days a week. Some of the latter doubled as ESL teachers and were well qualified for their jobs, but at least one of them was not of my choosing and had been "planted" by the district office, simply because he was a close friend of the director and was unemployed. He had no qualifications for the job and proved a considerable nuisance.

Elizabeth Kwong had lived all her life in New York's Chinatown and had never traveled farther than New Jersey. One summer she decided to use her vacation time to visit some distant relatives in Hong Kong. At one point on the trip she accidentally banged her head quite severely when emerging from the door of the aircraft, but she thought little of it. Shortly after returning to work she began to suffer severe headaches, and I would frequently find her bowed over her desk in great pain. Finally I was able to convince her to go and see a doctor. They discovered a blood clot on her brain and decided to operate. That probably saved her life, but when she came out of surgery she was blind and unable to speak.

For weeks I visited her daily in the hospital and watched her slow recovery. Eventually she was allowed to go home, but for nearly six months there was little improvement, and the doctors held out no hope of her recovering either her sight or her speech. She and her husband and two children lived in a tiny apartment on the fourth floor of a tenement building in Chinatown. Several times a week I went to do what I could to help with family problems, because her husband worked two jobs and was home only a few hours each night.

On one of my visits, Elizabeth picked up a copy of the *New York Post* and, to my astonishment, read the large-print headlines. Then, in barely intelligible speech, she told me that for some time she had been able to see blurred and flickering images on the television screen. When I left New York not long after that, she was still physically disabled but much improved. A few months later I received a card from her saying that her husband had suffered a massive heart attack climbing the stairs on his way home. He died before they could get him to a hospital. I kept in touch with Elizabeth for some months after that, and then my letters were returned to me "address unknown," and I was unable to ascertain what had happened to her.

Nineteen seventy-five was the final year of the Building Bilingual Bridges program, not because of any failure on the part of those running it, but simply because the Board of Education got too greedy. That last year I was asked to help write a new proposal for a grandiose scheme encompassing even more schools over a much wider territory of District 2. The grant requested in excess of $2 million. I told Harold at the outset that I was sure it would not be granted because the number of Chinese and Puerto Rican children involved was far too small to justify the expenditure. Sure enough, the program was canceled, and, to the best of my knowledge, the only effort made thereafter to help Chinese children was a half-hearted effort in a single high school in the area.

With that, my job and those of all the others associated with the project ended. I was asked to write a comprehensive final report, which took three months, and I had to make frequent trips to New York City to collect data and confer with the various school principals. I was told to keep a record of my time and expenses, but when the time came for me to submit the report and be reimbursed for my time, I was told that no more funds were available. I ended up being short-changed around $5,000.

So ended another episode in our lives. I was eligible for unemployment insurance, and for some weeks I collected $90 a week from the office in New Haven. However, I was required to submit proof each week that I was making a serious effort to find a new job, and although I wrote numerous letters to various universities and colleges around the country, language programs were being cut back, and my efforts met with no success. Ultimately, I found myself spending so much time in that fruitless effort that I gave it up and settled down to do some serious writing of my own.

First I spent several weeks refining my aptitude test, cutting it to two hours and testing it out in several high schools and junior colleges, where I had no trouble finding groups of enthusiastic volunteers. Partly because of the interest shown by those individuals, I decided to work on a self-study course in Chinese, essentially for those who were unable to attend a formal course on a regular basis.

I had long felt the need for such a course. However, after spending several satisfying months working on the project, I learned that the State Department's FSI school in Washington was also involved in the same type of project, although with a slightly different approach, and Eva's brother, Jerry, was in charge of it. A large team of people were involved in the effort and naturally produced at a much faster rate than I could, working alone. I was shown copies of what they had developed up to that point and it looked so promising that I felt I could more profitably spend my time on something else.

My experience with the minority groups in New York had convinced me that the current approach to teaching ESL left much to be desired. In many ways it was clumsy and ill-planned, particularly for the Chinese immigrants, because it was not adapted to their cultural background. I started to work on a self-study modular course that approached the problem not from the teacher's point of view, but from that of the Chinese student.

All ESL courses start with very basic sentences in English, usually involving questions such as: "What is your name?" "Where do you live?" and so on. However, Chinese sentence structure is such that that immediately poses a problem to the beginner. In the Chinese language, questions are asked in the format "Your name is what?" "Your home is where?" and answered in exactly the same pattern, and not turned around as they are in English. So for the Chinese, the English form required an immediate reversal in thinking. Added to that is the ambiguity of the very questions themselves. We expect the answer in the first case to be either one's given name, "John," for example, or one's surname, "Smith," or even a full name, "John Smith." There might even be a middle name or initial thrown in as well. When the Chinese ask that type of question they are quite specific and it comes out as, "What is your surname?" or "What is your given name?"

In addition to learning sentence structure and grammar, for a Chinese student, merely pronouncing the English sounds is problem enough. So rather than involve the beginning student in reversing his thinking at the outset, I instead selected basic sentence patterns identical in structure to the Chinese. At the same time I initially chose only those English word sounds that were identical to or that closely approximated Chinese.

I recorded each lesson on a cassette tape with explanations in Chinese. At the same time, rather than burden the student with learning the entire alphabet, on the printed text I displayed the letters of the alphabet at the top of each lesson sheet so that the student would acquire visual familiarity with them. I taught only those letters necessary to the lesson itself.

Few people realize the complexities of the English language for someone learning it as an adult. Taking just two of our letters of the alphabet as an example, our dictionaries give four distinct ways to pronounce the letter "a," and seven different ways to pronounce "o," depending upon the usage in a given word. For the Chinese, who are used to one single sound and meaning for all but a handful of their characters, the problem of pronouncing English words, and, in addition, learning all the multiple meanings of certain words that are pronounced in exactly the same manner, is daunting.

Thinking as a Chinese would think when speaking, I selected Chinese words with sounds identical, or nearly identical, to the English words or letter sounds, and with those I made up short sentences, concentrating on teaching grammar in traditional Chinese word order. That was, of course, radically different from the usual approach to teaching English.

When ten lessons had been completed, with accompanying instructions in Chinese, I made a number of copies of the cassettes and the lesson material and took them to New York. I located several new arrivals from the China mainland who spoke no English and asked them to try the lessons and give me their opinions. The results were extremely gratifying. All were most enthusiastic about the idea and seemed to have no difficulty at all in assimilating the material, and all of them wanted more.

Shortly thereafter I contacted a publisher of ESL materials who showed great interest. I gave him a set to look over, and, without my knowledge, he took them with him to an ESL conference in San Francisco, where he showed them to the conferees. Had I known what he was going to do, I could have predicted the results. The concept was so totally foreign to the teachers, and so radically different from the established way of teaching English, that they unanimously dismissed the idea as impracticable and unworkable, and the publisher lost interest. However, I still think the idea has merit, and someday I hope to do further work on it.

As the year 1975 drew to a close and winter set in, Eva and I began to wonder why we continued to stay on in Connecticut when there was actually nothing to hold us there. We remembered the balmy weather of Monterey in wintertime and the year-round pleasantness of the climate there, which contrasted sharply with the cold and snow of Connecticut and the hot summers and abundance of mosquitoes and other pests not so common in California. Twice before we had lived in Monterey, but because of the many frustrations associated with teaching at the Army Language School, it had not been a pleasant experience. But to retire there would be an entirely different matter. We considered moving there once again, and although leaving our many friends in Connecticut would not be easy, we also had a number of friends in Monterey. I was 62 years old at the time, a good time to retire for good — or so I thought.

Audio-visual
bilingual class, New York.

Another of the bilingual classes.
New York.

A bilingual class using earphones.
New York.

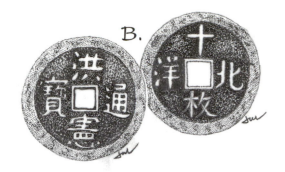

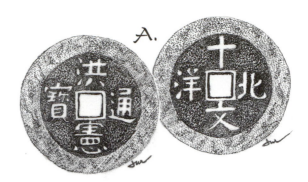

These are some of the coins *Yuan Shih-kai* had minted to commemorate his coronation as emperor in 1916. Due to failure of his plans and his early death, none of his imperial coins were actually put into circulation.

A. 10 Cash Coin (called a Copper) made of copper, showing Yuan's "reign title" of Hongxian (Hung Hsien) on obverse. On reverse, the characters translate as "10 Cash" and "Beiyang (Peiyang)," where it was minted.

B. 100 Cash Coin made of copper, showing Yuan's "reign title" of Hongxian (Hung Hsien) on obverse. On reverse, the characters translate as "10 Coppers."

C. Silver Dollar, showing Yuan in his imperial finery. The characters on the obverse read "Commemorating the First Year of the Chinese Empire in the reign of Hongxian (1916)." The dragon design on the other side is exactly as on the dragon series circulated during the Qing (Ch'ing) Dynasty.

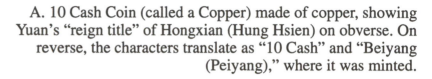

D. Silver Commemorative Dollar Coin. The characters on the reverse read "In Commemoration of 1916," the year Yuan planned to be made emperor. 1916 is expressed here in another traditional way, using the Sexagenery Cycles.

E. Silver Dollar Coin, minted in Hubei (Hupei) Province. The center characters read "Silver Currency of China," and the outside characters read "Year One in the Reign of Hongxian" and "In Commemoration of the Founding of the Country." The characters with the dragon read "One Yuan" (Dollar).

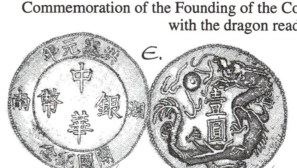

十天賣不了一斤真，一天賣了十斤假。

Shi tian maibuliao yijin zhen,
yitian maile shijin jia.

In ten days you cannot sell one catty of
the genuine, but in one day you can sell
ten catties of the false.

- Chinese Peasant Saying.

Chapter Forty-Nine
Restaurateurs

With my 63rd birthday on January 31, 1976, I became eligible for Social Security and decided to sign up. Since my employment with the military had been based on yearly contracts, I was not eligible for a pension of any sort. So when the Social Security checks came in each month, I began to feel really retired. The winter weather dragged on into spring, and we felt more and more strongly about moving out to the West Coast, but we delayed leaving until early June.

After driving cross country, we arrived in Monterey in the middle of what was, for Monterey, a heat wave, the daily temperature reaching a high of over 90 degrees each day for an entire week. Added to that, Northern California was in the middle of a bad drought, and water was severely rationed. I am afraid I unknowingly embarrassed some friends when I decided to wash the car in their driveway, something that was strictly forbidden. Fortunately no one seemed to notice.

Finding a house to purchase was a simple matter; however, the prices were about three times what they were in Branford and at least twice what they had been when we were in Monterey during the '60s. We looked at a number of new houses in several newly developed housing tracts but eventually gravitated back to the locality in which we had formerly owned three homes, Fisherman's Flats. To our surprise we had the choice of about seven different homes; however, none of them appealed to us. They were either too large or badly situated or the back gardens were unattractive and needed too much work.

At the very last house we looked at, the owners told us that a house two doors up the street was also for sale, although there was no sign out front. We walked over and found no one at home. We were, however, able to peer through the windows and also inspect the back garden; the place looked ideal. We decided to return later when the occupants were home, but upon inquiring at a neighbor's, we learned that they had been renters and had already moved out.

That evening we saw an ad in the newspaper that obviously referred to that particular house. The price was $67,500 — a little more than we had wanted to pay, but early the next morning we were at the real estate agent's office. He gave us a key to the place, we looked it over, and although it was in need of some repairs, we found it very much to our liking. Back at the agent's I made him an offer of $65,000, just about twice the amount I had received for an almost identical house just a block away that we had sold some seven years earlier.

The agent, Don Campbell, was an old friend of ours. A delightful old gentleman, well into his 70s, he was still very active and recognized by all as doyen in the real estate business on the Monterey Peninsula. He told me he would pass on my offer to the owner, but five other people were waiting in his office for the key to view the place, and he doubted that my offer would be adequate. Having already looked at so many houses, and taking Don's advice, we felt that we could not do better elsewhere, so I agreed to pay the price listed in the newspaper ad and gave Don a check for $1,000 to seal the bargain.

Our job accomplished, we left our Volvo with Carl Povilaitis, who had returned to Monterey and was again working in the Chinese program at DLI, and asked him to keep an eye on the place until we came back in the fall with all our belongings.

While we were signing the necessary papers in Don Campbell's office, he asked me what we intended doing after we moved into the house. I told him that I had retired and had nothing particular in mind. He laughed and said, "Don't be ridiculous. You're much too young to retire and spend your time in a rocking chair. What we need around here is a good Chinese restaurant, and you're the person to open one. I'll look around and find a suitable place for you before you get back." We knew it was true that a good Chinese restaurant was needed, but thought he was just joking. He wasn't.

Back in Branford we spent July and August winding up our affairs and packing. By September we were ready to leave and once again head West. We had rented the largest rental truck we could find, and in it was all of our furniture and everything else we owned, and we started off towing our Mercedes.

It was pouring rain the day we left, so we were soaked to the skin by the time we got the last items into the truck. Our old friend Dave McCord, the young man who had helped me start the Monterey program in 1965, was now working for one of the airlines. Having some vacation time coming, he decided he'd enjoy an overland trip to the West Coast and offered to help me with driving the truck. We gladly accepted, and thoroughly enjoyed his company throughout the trip, although our habit of making very early morning departures was something of a trial to him.

A few days later as we were going through the desert, Eva started to get severe stomach cramps accompanied by diarrhea. We had to make frequent stops, and she got weaker and weaker. By midmorning I realized we had to stop somewhere and get some help for her. The first tiny town we came to had a motel, but there was no doctor in town. There was, however, a small drugstore, and the pharmacist gave Eva some Kaopectate, and after taking a dose or two and sleeping for most of the day, she was ready to resume the trip by late afternoon. We went on for a hundred miles or so before stopping for the night. The significance of that stomach problem of Eva's didn't become apparent until some time later.

We reached Monterey without further incident and moved into our "new" house the following day. A sizable group of former students and friends gathered to help us and in a few hours we were unpacked and well settled.

In the three months since we had bought the house we had given some thought to what Don Campbell had said about opening a restaurant, but were not very serious about it. We wanted to get involved in something that would not be too strenuous and would allow us time for some leisure.

Now, back again in Monterey, when I saw Don he told me he had found the perfect place for us to start a Chinese restaurant, and the price was right. To humor him, I went to see the place, without any real intention of going through with it. However, the more we thought about the idea the more we liked it. At the time there were several Cantonese-American restaurants in the area, but none served the kind of Northern Chinese food that we liked. To make sure that we could eat some good Chinese food from time to time, why not start a Mandarin-style restaurant for ourselves?

We talked it over with Carl and Joan Povilaitis, the young couple who had been good friends of ours for many years, both of them having worked in the Chinese programs at Yale and DLI. Neither they nor the two of us had the slightest experience in running a restaurant. But they enthusiastically agreed to go into it with us and give it a try.

The existing business had been a fast-food establishment where they sold deep-fried squid, known to Italians as calamari, a popular food on the Monterey Peninsula. The owner, wife of a prominent lawyer in the San Francisco Bay area, had lost a lot of money in the business. She was asking $15,000 but happily accepted our offer of $13,000, and the deal was closed.

Since practically all of the existing kitchen equipment was designed for a fast-food operation, little of it was suitable for a Chinese restaurant. In addition, the place had been badly neglected for years and was filthy. Our first job was to strip everything down, wash and scrub the entire place from top to bottom, and throw out what we couldn't use.

We spent weeks just scraping grease off the floors, walls and ceilings. In the center of the kitchen was a large walk-in cooler covered with accumulated grease nearly an inch thick. It took Eva almost an entire day just to scrape it all off. All in all it was about two months before we got the whole place into shape.

After our arrival in Monterey in September, Eva felt so well that we thought her stomach problems were over. But a short time after starting work on the restaurant, her stomach cramps returned, and early in November she went to see her doctor, Dr. David Thorngate, an old China hand himself. He determined that she had some sort of intestinal growth and ordered X-rays. They showed a distinct growth in her colon. Eva would need surgery. We feared it was cancer.

Eva was operated on the day before Thanksgiving. Her surgeon, Dr. Zug, was a remarkably gifted man. I sat in the waiting room for several hours waiting for the verdict, and then Dr. Zug came out with a big smile on his face and told me the operation had been a complete success. He said he had been forced to remove over a foot of her colon, and that it was indeed cancerous. However, he was sure it had been caught sufficiently early, before the cancer had had time to eat through the wall of her colon. Had that not been the case it would have been a great deal more serious.

I thanked God for the good news and realized how He had planned our pathway for us. Had we not come out to Monterey when we did, and had it not been for the bumpy ride in the truck, the symptoms might not have occurred for months, and then it could have been too late. It was just one more of the many miracles in our lives.

Eva was home within a few days, and after a month of recuperation was back at work scrubbing down walls and floors in the restaurant, albeit, for the most part, sitting on a stool as she worked.

The central part of any Chinese restaurant is the cooking range, which consists of a row of cooking pots that the Cantonese call *wok* and the Northern Chinese call *guo*. In the San Francisco Bay area two Chinese firms specialized in building those ranges, made entirely of stainless steel, and I visited both of them to price a range that would meet our requirements. However, the prices were staggering; they cost well over $6,000 for the size we would need, more than we could face at the time.

We gave it a lot of thought and prayer. A few days later, while shopping for some other supplies at a restaurant supply house in the neighboring town of Salinas, I overheard a Chinese man and his wife talking in Mandarin in the next aisle. I introduced myself and learned that they owned a small Chinese restaurant in the nearby town of Watsonville. I told them we were starting a Chinese restaurant in Monterey and needed a range. Did he happen to know where I might be able to buy a good second-hand one? I shouldn't have been surprised, but I was. God indeed moves in mysterious ways, because the man told me he did indeed know of one, and it was right in Monterey and immediately available.

Unfortunately, although he was able to tell me the name of the Chinese lady who owned it, he didn't know her address. He simply knew she lived in the vicinity of the airport and gave me a rough idea of the general area. The name he gave us was not in the telephone directory, so that afternoon Eva and I circled through the area the man had indicated, and by chance met a newspaper boy. We asked him if he knew of a Chinese lady living in the area. He immediately pointed to a house just across the street from where we were standing.

Mrs. Liu welcomed us warmly. After serving tea she took us into her back yard to see the range, which was in a makeshift, open shed. It was exactly the size we wanted, but it was a discouraging sight. It was quite old — some 25 years old as we later learned, having been used by her husband for more than ten years, and in another restaurant before that — and was badly rusted through in spots. In addition, it was encrusted with baked-on grease. She said we could have it for $300. Whatever the condition, provided it worked, it was something we couldn't refuse.

We rented a forklift and a truck and hauled the range to an outfit that sand-blasted it down to the bare metal. Then, before the fog could move in and start the rust once again, we hurriedly gave it a coat of black paint. The next day I took it to a welder's shop, where we had the rusted spots patched, and a day or so later we installed it in our restaurant kitchen looking almost like new.

Finding a chef proved to be somewhat more difficult. A few weeks earlier I'd gone to San Francisco to visit some of the employment agencies in Chinatown. There were plenty of chefs available, but the salaries they wanted seemed extraordinarily high, over $2,500 a month, and each of them demanded, as is the custom in a lot of Chinese restaurants, to have part of his pay in cash so that he would not have to report so much to the IRS. In a Chinese restaurant a good chef is paramount, and normally he runs the show, dictating to the owner — unless the latter happens to be a chef himself — just how the place should be run. Not only that, they usually wanted a share of the profits, and I didn't particularly want that to happen.

Even though we were complete amateurs in the business, we knew that if we got into the hands of an unscrupulous chef, he could ruin us from the start, so I tried a different tactic. I went to one of the Chinese newspaper offices and inserted an ad asking for the services of a man and wife to cook simple Northern Chinese food. I felt that Monterey wasn't yet ready for a classic Chinese restaurant and the more sophisticated and exotic dishes that one normally finds in a high-class place. I wanted to keep it simple. Chinese friends told me that putting an advertisement in the paper was a waste of time and would bring no results, but we prayed, sat back, and waited.

The very next day we received our first phone call in answer to the ad, followed by a total of 42 more replies, some from as far away as Los Angeles and Salt Lake City. The first to call was a woman, speaking in Mandarin. She told me that her name was Sun (pronounced something like swun), and she said her husband had worked in restaurants for five years and knew how to cook simple dishes, and that she, too, knew how to cook. We chatted for a short while, and from her accent I knew she was from Manchuria. I told her that I, too, had been born in Manchuria, and that I was a Westerner, not Chinese. I told her that we wanted to start a restaurant and were interested in finding a couple to do the cooking and help us run it.

I then chatted for a short time with her husband and found that he came from the province of Shandong. That was good news, because Shandong people are renowned for their ability to cook. The couple lived in San Jose, about 70 miles from Monterey, so I told them we'd drive up the next morning to visit. Following the directions Mr. Sun had given me, Eva and I, with Joan and Carl, quickly found their house the next morning. As we approached we saw a Chinese gentleman standing out in front on the sidewalk, scanning the cars as they went by. When we parked the car and approached him, he took no notice of us. I stepped up close, and, addressing him in Chinese, asked if he was Mr. Sun. He replied in the affirmative, but continued to watch the street and paid no attention to me at all. I realized he wasn't even aware that I had spoken to him in Chinese, nor did he realize I was the person he was expecting. His wife had apparently not told him that I was a Westerner, and he was looking for a Chinese.

When I finally convinced him I was the person who had talked with him on the phone, he seemed shocked. He took us upstairs to meet his wife, and she was even more flustered than he was. Despite what I had told her on the phone, she had jumped to the conclusion that I was an American-born Chinese, and that was why I spoke Chinese like a native. To find that I was a white man was something totally unexpected.

We found the couple genuinely friendly and very obviously simple, honest folk, who were not making any exaggerated claims as to their abilities. Mr. Sun, formerly a colonel in the Chinese Army, had come to this country as a newspaper reporter. As I got to know him he told me he had fought in the Burma campaign in World War II under General Stilwell, for whom he had the highest regard. He told me how the general had visited his troops in the jungle and had gone right up to the very front lines to talk to his men. As I well knew, General Stilwell preferred the company of the common soldier and was generally contemptuous of officers.

Mr. Sun was a well-educated man and a good writer, but the newspaper paid him so little that he had been forced to supplement his income by taking jobs at several different Chinese restaurants, and that was how he had learned to cook.

We discussed the type of food that I felt we should serve in our restaurant, and I named a number of dishes I would like to introduce to Americans. He indicated he knew how to make all of them and told me the exact ingredients that should go into each one. The couple were obviously just what we were looking for, so we hired them on the spot and returned to Monterey. Within a few days we had found an apartment for the Suns and they moved down a short time later.

Both Mr. and Mrs. Sun pitched in and helped us with the last of the cleanup of the restaurant. The big job that we had left until the last was to clean the 12-foot-high ceiling, which was made of tongue-and-groove varnished wood. We had to rent a scaffold to scour every square inch of the ceiling. Covered with grease and blackened by smoke and soot, it took several days of back-breaking, neck-aching work. Putting down new tile on the floor of the kitchen was a relaxing job by comparison, and when the walls of the dining room had been repapered under Joan's supervision, our job was done.

For many weeks we and our partners had mulled over an appropriate name for the restaurant. It had to be something easily remembered and also had to indicate the type of food we were serving. So as not to hurt the feelings of either pro-communists or anti-communists, we settled on the name "Old Peking." We had a big, back-lit sign made, with Mr. Sun writing large Chinese characters to go on each side of the English words. Without our realizing it, the sign attracted a lot of attention.

We set a date in December 1976 for our opening but decided to keep it low-key and not advertise. We wanted to do a little practicing first, so we simply put a small notice in the window indicating we would open on a given date at 5:30 in the evening and we set

about making preparations.

I rented a panel truck, and Mr. Sun and I drove up to San Francisco and purchased large quantities of rice and other staples as well as a wide variety of all the Chinese spices and other ingredients we would need. On the day before we were to open, we all got together and made over 1,500 jiaozi, a traditional Chinese food that we wanted to introduce to the Monterey Peninsula. Jiaozi, for those who don't know them, are a meat and vegetable-filled sort of dumpling, wrapped in a pasta-like dough. Chinese usually prefer to eat them boiled, but they may also be steamed, partially boiled and then deep-fat fried, or, in the form now generally known as potstickers, from the Chinese name guo tie, which literally means "stick to the pot," they are fried on the bottoms and then steamed.

Jiaozi are shaped in a traditional form, roughly the form of a small boat, with both ends high and low in the middle, which is meant to approximate the ancient silver ingot or "tael," the form of currency in early China. They were always eaten by the Northern Chinese on New Year's Eve and thus represented the coming of wealth into the house. However, they may be served on any special occasion, particularly when unexpected guests arrive, and because of the work involved in making them, they demonstrate to guests just how honored they are. Jiaozi are now available in almost all Mandarin-type restaurants.

Our two-page menu, typed and run off on a duplicator, featured these jiaozi cooked in four different ways. In addition, we listed 30 or more different dishes that were entirely new to Monterey.

Our expectations for that first night were not very high. The restaurant seated about 60 people, and we anticipated that perhaps 30 or so might show up. Just to be on the safe side we prepared enough food for around 50. We had hired just one waitress, but no dishwasher, and we were all set to go. Imagine our shock and surprise when, about 5 o'clock, a line started to form outside, and by opening time it stretched halfway up the block. We have no accurate count of the number of people who came that first night, but we estimate it was probably well in excess of 400. By the time we fed them all and closed up, it was well past midnight.

Our supply of jiaozi were gone in no time, and time and again we ran out of food and I had to dash to an all-night grocery store to stock up again on meat and vegetables. Our customers were most patient and delighted with the food. As each group finished and went out the front door, many were heard to remark to those waiting outside, "Be patient. It's well worth waiting for!" Other customers, seeing how short-handed we were, pitched in and helped. Some waited on or cleared tables, and others went out into the kitchen and volunteered to wash dishes. It was a wild evening, but exciting, and we made some wonderful friends who still remind us of that first night. Although succeeding days weren't quite so hectic, business continued to be good for as long as we operated the restaurant. However, the work was exhausting.

We kept the restaurant for about six months. It was just too successful, and the work too much for us to keep up with. Eva and I were up every morning at 5 and, after a hurried breakfast, we left for the restaurant. We shared the early morning cleaning up for the day, and I then went out shopping for fresh vegetables and meats, while Eva, ensconced in a tiny section of the storage area, made *jiaozi*, spring rolls and *wonton* by the hundreds. Usually we worked a 16-hour day, sometimes even longer, and rarely found time to eat at normal mealtimes. Frequently we went without food for the entire day and ended up buying a hamburger on the way home. By the time we were ready to sell the restaurant I had lost 35 pounds.

One reason we decided to sell was that less than a month after we had started our operation, a Chinese competitor, also serving "Mandarin" food of exceptionally good quality, had opened a small restaurant in the adjoining town of Seaside, not more than five miles from us. The opening of Chef Lee's restaurant was quickly followed by two other Mandarin-style restaurants, as the Chinese saw how popular the food was, and although it didn't noticeably hurt our business, it obviated the need for our having our own place in which to eat Chinese food — the primary reason for having started the restaurant in the first place. Now, as I write this, some 16 years later, there are 23 such restaurants, all serving Mandarin-style food, and competition is fierce.

Our original intention when starting the restaurant was to turn it over to our partners in the event Eva and I decided not to continue with it any longer. However, since the young Povilaitis couple had two small children and were unable to face handling the restaurant on their own, we all decided to sell it. We planned to advertise the sale in one of the several Chinese newspapers in San Francisco.

Each Tuesday a young Cantonese man had driven his truck down from San Francisco, delivering Chinese food supplies to the various restaurants in all the small towns en route and along the coast. We wrote a small advertisement in Chinese for him to insert in the paper for us. It described our restaurant and the good business we were doing, but named no price.

At the time we put the restaurant up for sale, two of the original Cantonese restaurants, both only about a mile from our place, started serving what they euphemistically called "Mandarin" food. However, it was more Cantonese than anything else, and both were apparently suffering from our competition. About ten minutes after I had given the ad to the delivery man the owner of one of those restaurants came running in to see me. He had learned from the delivery man that we were about to sell, and he wanted to buy it. How much were we asking?

I was caught somewhat off guard. Up to that point we had not decided on the value of the place, and I didn't know what to tell him. Not only that, we were in the middle of the busy dinner hour, and I wanted time to consult with our partners. So to stall him, I told him that since the advertisement was going to be put into the paper, and we couldn't stop it, he would have to wait and see what replies we got, although I promised to give him preference because he had been the first to approach us. However, he insisted on knowing our price. Without giving it any serious thought I came up with what I thought was a preposterous figure, $45,000. That was approximately three times what we had paid for it, including all the additional equipment we had added and modifications we had made to the building. I thought that would stop him cold, but to my utter amazement he told me he'd take it.

We reached an agreement with him that he would retain Mr. and Mrs. Sun to handle the cooking, as well as the three or four waitresses we employed. He wanted the restaurant for a nephew of his who knew nothing at all about restaurants, and asked me if I would stay on for a few weeks to act as manager and to train his nephew to run the place. At the same time he wanted Eva to teach her skills in making pastries to someone he would bring in. We agreed to those terms and the sale went through.

A few days later a Frenchman came in for lunch. Well known to me, he was one of the higher-ranking administrative staff members at the Defense Language Institute. He told me that the commandant of DLI, Col. Sam Stapleton, wanted to talk with me, and, if it was all right, he would come into the restaurant the next day at noon. As he was leaving he rather pointedly told me that I should dress appropriately when meeting the colonel. I somewhat testily replied that I was a man working most of the time in a kitchen, and the colonel would have to take me as he found me.

When the colonel came in the next day I served him his lunch, and he immediately got down to business. He told me the Chinese department was a disaster and he desperately needed my services to help revitalize the program and restore the sagging morale. He had just returned from an extended trip to the Far East, where, in each of the places he had visited, former students of mine with whom he had consulted about the deficiencies in the Chinese program had, one after the other, told him to "get Tharp" back into the program. He had never heard of me before that, and jokingly told me that, in his opinion, I had "brainwashed a whole generation of American males."

He went on to tell me of efforts he'd made to improve the program. He had brought in quantities of books and other materials smuggled out of mainland China for the teachers to use in trying to update the terminology currently being used in China. But on every side he had met with frustrations. The instructors, all of them loyal to the Nationalist government in Taiwan and fearful of reprisals should they teach any communist terminology, refused to use the materials.

I was struck with his sincerity and humility. In the previous experiences I had had with several different commandants of the school, they had, for the most part, consistently put the blame on someone else. Col. Stapleton was refreshingly different. He blamed himself and said his approach had been wrong from the beginning and he alone was at fault.

We talked for perhaps an hour, and he was most persuasive. Knowing the Chinese department well, and also the civil service, and the difficulties of hiring new personnel or trying to get rid of someone who proved unsatisfactory, I had strong doubts that my going there could make any difference. However, I assured him that I would think it over, discuss it with Eva, and give him my answer the following day. His final word to me was that, if I agreed to go, I was to write my own job description, set my own priorities, and name my own salary.

When leaving Branford for California the previous year, I had told Eva that under no circumstances would I have anything further to do with the Defense Language Institute. But here I was faced with a situation that was totally unexpected. It was not of my seeking, but here was a man who believed I could be of help to him. He had learned of my great interest in teaching Chinese and of my dedication to the students and had offered me his unqualified support in anything I might decide to do. I felt it would be wrong if I refused to help him, and as I talked it over with Eva, we both agreed that I ought to give it a try.

The following day I went to see Col. Stapleton and told him of my decision, but I added one stipulation. I said I was unconcerned about my salary and would accept anything he thought fair. However, I would agree to join him only if I could work directly under him, without any intermediaries, and have an office next door to his, so I could have access to him any time I wished. Without that, I felt that I would be stymied in anything I might try to do in bringing about any changes.

The colonel was overjoyed and immediately agreed to my terms. He showed me a small office adjoining his that would be mine, and promised, in addition, that I would also have another office in the Chinese department. He started immediately to set the wheels in motion and accompanied me to see the director of personnel in order to get things rolling.

It wasn't long before the Chinese department got wind of my being hired, and certain factions there protested vigorously and tried to block it, even getting the union to register a protest. But Col. Stapleton was not to be stopped, and he adamantly pushed my application through with his characteristic enthusiasm and his commanding personality. Meanwhile he sent over a staff car loaded with some 40 volumes of books he had acquired from Hong Kong and mainland China and asked me to go over them and recommend any that I thought might be of value. He also asked me to write my own job description, which he approved without any questions.

But the government works in strange ways, and it was some months before my appointment was approved and confirmed. The delay in part was due to two or three Chinese instructors who had become incensed when they heard I was to be hired once again, and who were well known to me. In fact, they were mediocre instructors, although they had the potential for excellence. Their classroom performance had long been criticized by the students and fellow teachers. They brought newspapers into class to read, fell asleep in class, and frequently left the students by themselves while they went outside to conduct private business.

However, the individuals concerned had strong personalities and although they were not in any supervisory capacity, for the most part they still dominated the other instructors and generally got away with whatever they set about doing. They circulated several petitions to the commandant demanding that I not be hired and coerced all the other Chinese instructors into signing them.

One wrote a long and scurrilous letter to the commandant accusing me of a variety of misdeeds and portraying me as totally uneducated, able to speak Chinese only at the level of a country villager, and generally unfit for the job. Of course, among the 30 or 40 instructors I had many friends, and they came to the restaurant secretly to tell me of those events and to declare their support, despite the fact that they had signed the petition. Copies of the documents were also anonymously given to me. Col. Stapleton also showed me everything he had received. He simply laughed it off, taking no notice of it. Applying for a civil service job is an extremely complicated procedure. Although I had taught at the school on two previous occasions for a total of something like six years, and they had files on me an inch or more thick, complete with several letters of commendation and flattering performance ratings, I still had to apply as though for the first time. Besides filling out in great detail numerous forms covering background information, both on educational and teaching experience, I had to provide information on all places of residence for at least five years prior to the date of application so that a security check could be made.

In addition, in applying as a teacher, I, like every-

one else, was required to write an essay to prove that I could write English, and another in the language I wanted to teach, in my case Chinese. The essays had to be hand-written, and at the same time I had to submit a short tape recording, choosing any subject I wished, and voice it both in English and Chinese, speaking at normal conversational speed.

The procedure from that point on was for the language department concerned to review the material, listen to the tape, and make a decision as to whether to hire me or declare me incompetent.

In principle it seemed like a sound policy. Those who were actually teaching the language were theoretically the experts who should be able to determine the qualifications of a candidate. However, in actual practice, the choice of teachers by that means was far from foolproof and frequently broke down.

Usually a committee of four or five senior individuals in the department were selected by the chairman to listen to the tape and to judge the essays submitted. Those individuals were usually supervisory personnel, and quite often the chairman himself was part of the proceedings. Only after listening to the tape was the candidate called in for a personal interview, providing he or she was judged to be qualified up to that point. What the committee had no way of knowing when listening to the tape was whether the voice they were listening to was actually that of the applicant or someone else standing in for him. It was common knowledge in the Chinese department that three individuals were teaching there who had managed to get aboard apparently through using a stand-in. That the same thing occurred in other departments is also not unlikely.

Since, during the personal interview, they might be found out, cronyism and national pride came into play. It would never do at that point to admit that one's fellow national had resorted to deceit, so the person was usually hired. As a result, in some cases teachers who supposedly spoke standard Mandarin actually spoke it with strong provincial overtones, which, for an advanced student, was good exposure to something that would be encountered in the field, but which was highly confusing to the beginning student in whose classes the teacher was often to be found.

In my case, having had previous experience at the school, having been personally selected and recommended by the commandant, and having had 15 years' teaching experience at Yale, one would have thought that the above procedure would have been waived. Not so. The personnel department had an inflexible rule, and I had to go through the entire procedure.

I wrote my essay in both Chinese and English and recorded my voice on tape, reading in Chinese an article and its translation. Knowing, however, the procedure from that point on, I alerted Col. Stapleton to the fact that the final decision would be resting with the Chinese department. Since he had already had a lot of opposition to my being hired, I felt it was highly unlikely that they would approve my appointment. Col. Stapleton agreed and asked my advice. I suggested that my essay and tape be submitted to some neutral party outside the department, someone well known to the department, whose decision they could not refute. The colonel thought that was indeed the answer, and my tape and essay were submitted to a Chinese professor teaching at San Francisco State College, a man who at one time had been a member of the DLI Chinese department and was highly respected. Professor K.Y. Hsu knew me well, and without the slightest hesitation gave me a glowing recommendation, stating that I spoke flawless and impeccable Chinese. That report satisfied the personnel department but infuriated the people in the Chinese department. What mattered to the school was that the rules had been strictly adhered to, and all was well.

Although the delays dragged on for several months, Eva and I made good use of the time. At the restaurant, my time for helping out the new owner came to an end, and Eva, who was still recuperating from her surgery, had revisited her doctor. He was encouraged by her progress, but said that although he was certain all the cancerous cells had been removed, it would be five years before he could safely say that she was absolutely cured. He urged her to take up some activity that would keep her busy so she would not dwell on the possibilities of a recurrence of the disease.

Eva, who has always been a very active individual, had no intention of staying home doing housework while I worked at the Defense Language Institute, and she began to look for ways to utilize her time.

Foremost in her thoughts was the possibility of going into business for herself; opening an establishment where she could sell jiaozi, which had received such acclaim at the Old Peking restaurant. With that in mind, we began to look for a suitable site.

We found a place about four blocks from the restaurant and on the same street. It was a small shop that at one time had been a bookstore and later a beauty shop, but was now empty. The monthly rental was a mere $150, but the place required some modification before it could be used for the purpose we envisaged.

We visited City Hall and inquired about licenses, signs, various permits, etc., and spent several weeks acquiring all that we would need. The officials in charge of issuing licenses had difficulty in classifying the category under which to issue a license. Eva intended to produce jiaozi and a few other typical Chinese specialties, then fast-freeze them and sell them ready for cooking in the home or, in some cases, pre-cooked and requiring only heating up before serving. For that she needed only a hot plate, an electric wok and a steamer. Since she had no intention of serving food on the premises, her place could not be considered a restaurant, nor was it a delicatessen. Needing no kitchen, the requirements for a use permit were less stringent, but even though she had no stove or oven, the licensing authority decided that the classification that fit her enterprise was a bakery.

We spent a couple of weeks fixing up the place. It was quite tiny, measuring only ten feet wide by sixteen feet long, with a small washroom in back. I put in cupboards and had a sink installed. We purchased a couple of freezers, moved in a refrigerator and several work tables, and she was ready to go.

We mulled over several names for the place. Because most Americans have a problem pronouncing the Chinese word jiaozi, I thought that perhaps we should call Eva's end product a "chivoli," a shortened form for the two words "Chinese ravioli." However, in the end we decided we would educate the public to calling them exactly what they were, and so our hand-lettered sign read, "Eva's Jyaudz Factory," and because it was more phonetic and more easily pronounced, we used the Yale romanization for the word.

The word "factory" was a bit of a joke, but small as the place was, it was indeed a factory of sorts. And so the name of Eva's shop was born, although it led to some amusing incidents; customers came in and addressed Eva as "Mrs. Jyaudz." Others thought the spelling of the word *jiaozi* was Spanish and so pronounced it using the letter "h" for the "j" and came up with some wild pronunciations of the word. But in time her customers came to recognize the word, and the popularity of the product, as well as her fame, spread.

Before my appointment to DLI came through, I had time to help Eva get established. We first produced a large quantity of *jiaozi*, which we fast-froze and packaged, then Eva made Chinese spring rolls, which most Americans know as egg rolls. Eva's were made with a small quantity of ground pork and a large variety of vegetables, and became very popular. In addition she produced the traditional Chinese *won-ton*, which many people bought for homemade *won-ton* soups. With those three items she opened for business.

After one or two small advertisements the first year, Eva never had to advertise again. By word of mouth her reputation spread, and as the only institution of its kind in the entire United States, she was besieged with requests to ship *jiaozi* to various parts of the country, something we were unable to do because of the difficulty in acquiring dry ice and because of limitations on shipping them by air if we used dry ice. However, many purchasers had us pack the *jiaozi* in multiple layers of paper, or they packed them in an insulated container and carried them onto the planes themselves. Some went as far as Virginia, and, of course, many places up and down the West Coast.

As time went by Eva's customers wanted party items such as finger foods that could be readily heated and served, and by the end of her first year in business she was producing 30 to 40 different delicacies and working ten or more hours a day. However, she enjoyed every minute of it, never giving a thought to the possibilities of cancer reasserting itself.

After my new job started I was able to help Eva occasionally. My office hours started at 8 o'clock, while Eva was usually at work by 6:30. That gave me time to help her package items that had been frozen overnight. I was also able to visit her during my lunch hour, shop for her, and help her in the evenings. She could easily have expanded the business by hiring and training help and moving to a larger store, but Eva wasn't in it for the money, and the small place satisfied her. Although she frequently had to refuse large orders from restaurants and caterers, she was able to keep up with the retail demand and satisfy dozens of customers, many of whom had first tasted her products at the Old Peking restaurant.

With my going to work for the DLI, I started once again on a new career and had to cancel my Social Security checks. With the opposition that had been shown by the few individuals in the Chinese department, my job promised to be both interesting and challenging, and it certainly turned out that way. It was October 1977.

Eva's Jyaudz Factory: ready for business.

A newly found Chinese friend and Eva having fun conversing in Mandarin.

Tea break at Eva's Jyaudz Factory, 1982.

Mr. Cheer takes over working at the Jyaudz Factory while we have a vacation and go to the East Coast, 1964. Note the number of jyaudz made to date. That doubled before Eva retired in 1987.

Shan you shan bao, e you e bao,
bushi bubao, shichen wei dao.

Good will be rewarded with good,
and evil with evil;
if there are no results,
then the time hasn't come.

- Chinese Proverb.

Chapter Fifty
A Job Unfinished

My reappointment to the Defense Language Institute carried with it some heavy responsibilities. I was expected to revitalize the Chinese department, modernize the course, and re-motivate both the teachers and students. It was a tall order, one that no one else had been able to accomplish, but I would give it a try. I looked forward to the challenge; in particular, I couldn't wait to get back into contact with the students once again.

My first two weeks at the school were disappointing. The little office Col. Stapleton had given me next to his proved comfortable and pleasant, and he supplied me with a secretary to take care of any typing that might be necessary. It must have been terribly boring for the young lady, though, because she saw little of me for the next several weeks. All she could do was busy herself sorting and arranging my books.

Col. Stapleton felt that I should first get an overview of the entire school so that I could put the problems of the Chinese department into proper per-

spective, and perhaps he was right in thinking that. But it was a tedious job visiting all the different language departments and, after going through the initial niceties, familiarizing myself with what they were doing.

Somewhere along the line an educational publisher had produced a book on supposedly modern language teaching that an over-zealous administrator at DLI had decided was just the thing for the entire school. When I arrived, each department was adopting the principles of that new textbook. Mandatory classes were in progress for all teachers, who were required to familiarize themselves with the new technique, and I was asked to attend one of them as well, just to see what was going on.

More than anything else I found it rather sad. The idea wasn't new to me at all. We had tried the same principle many years before and had discarded it as being completely impracticable. Without belaboring the point, the principle was simply "free speech" in the classroom; the teacher could bring into his lecture anything that came into his mind, provided it had some bearing on the text then being studied, however remote it might be. For a majority of the teachers it was a heaven-sent opportunity to relieve the boredom of going over the same old text day after day, and they relished the idea of being able to talk about anything at all, just as it occurred to them. For the students it was a decidedly new experience, and they were encouraged to make suggestions as to what they would like to hear discussed. The general feeling was that it was a lot more fun than following the boring text in their books. But what was lost sight of was that they weren't there to have fun.

The principle behind the idea, as it was explained to us, was that even if the student was able to assimilate just one out of 100 new terms he might hear during the course of a class, it would be a plus. It was indeed, for the students and teachers, a vastly entertaining experience. However, as they all quickly discovered, their progress in the course itself was not only not accelerated, it was definitely retarded, mainly because they hadn't the time to devote to the new terminology of the text being studied, and when it came to examination time, they tended to fall flat on their faces.

After watching the process in action I expressed my views to the commandant, telling him that as far as I was concerned, the theory would not work where Chinese was to be taught. There had to be a structural integrity in the course and in the introduction and teaching of any new terminology. It couldn't be done haphazardly. The student learning a new term not only had to acquire the meaning, but at the same time he needed to know how, when, and where to use it properly. Like many other such ideas that had been introduced at DLI, it was short-lived and was soon dropped.

By the end of the fourth week I had just about finished visiting most of the 30 or so language departments and started visiting the Chinese department. I began by first "sitting in" on classes, then conducting individual and group meetings with the teachers, and generally getting a picture of what was going on. Col. Stapleton had paved the way for me with a strongly worded and lengthy directive outlining my duties and responsibilities, stating that he expected the fullest cooperation from all concerned. Nonetheless, a defi-

nite underlying current of animosity and resentment existed on the part of several of the Chinese teachers, who doubtless feared for their jobs. But the rest of them, most of whom I had known for years, welcomed me warmly.

The students were another matter. To them I was an unknown quantity and they reserved judgment until they saw what I would do. A few came to me and expressed dissatisfaction with the program then in progress and hoped I would bring about changes, others seemed quite happy with the slow progress they were making, and still others apparently cared little about learning Chinese in the first place. For them it was just a job. I found the new breed of volunteer soldiers to be quite different from the students of the old days.

The curriculum was basically the same as that which I had introduced to DLI back in 1965, although numerous changes had been made. Many aspects of the course had been dropped or modified, and some of the techniques that I had found to be so effective at Yale were no longer in evidence. Most important, the end result, the achievement level of the student at the end of the course, was considerably inferior to what I knew to be possible and within the students' potential.

Col. Stapleton had given me carte blanche to draw up my own list of priorities and tackle them as I saw fit. I felt that teacher morale was the first and most important item and set about improving it. Many teachers complained they had not had a promotion in years, others that they had been on a temporary status for an interminable length of time. Complaints of favoritism and vindictiveness in the assignment of duties were all too common.

I drew up a list of those whom I felt most needed and deserved promotion and gave it to Col. Stapleton. I was gratified to find that he took immediate action; within a matter of weeks, people who had lost all hope suddenly found themselves promoted, while others were moved from temporary status to permanent positions.

In one case, a highly talented young man, one of my former students at Yale, had resigned some years earlier because of a dispute with one of his superiors over the course content and the manner in which it was being conducted. Now that I was in charge he sought reinstatement but found his way blocked at every turn. I felt his qualifications and past record deserved recognition, and a word to Col. Stapleton was sufficient to bring about his rehiring. Currently, Harry Olsen is the chairman of a second Chinese department that has been recently added and has become a tremendous asset to the Chinese course, so there exists some promise of changes for the better in the future.

Within the Chinese department itself I found a strong ally in the person of an Army officer, Maj. Perry Cabot. He was a gifted individual with an open and charming personality. Among his many talents was the ability to speak excellent Chinese. One aspect of his job was to act as a liaison between the department and administration and, at the same time, act as a counselor to both teachers and students. Anyone could go to him at any time with their complaints, all of which he dealt with fairly, expeditiously, and with extraordinary diplomacy.

I had long talks with Maj. Cabot about the curriculum and the low morale among both students and teachers. We both agreed strongly with Col. Stapleton that there was an immediate need to introduce into the program new terminology from mainland China that, up to that point, the teachers had been reluctant to implement. Most of the teachers were formerly from the mainland and, like myself, had been away a long time and had bitter memories of the way in which the Communist Party had taken over and destroyed so many lives to bring about their new regime. However, there was a nucleus of people from Taiwan with strong Nationalist feelings who supported Chiang Kai-shek's government. As mentioned before, they feared that if they became involved in teaching the newly coined mainland terminology, they would become tainted in the eyes of their Taiwan compatriots.

Despite all that, with Col. Stapleton's strong support we managed to push through a program of new writing materials for the more advanced student, which contained a fair representation of mainland terminology. Unfortunately, only one man on the staff had experienced life under the Communists, and he'd escaped the mainland a number of years before by swimming across to Hong Kong with his girlfriend under the most harrowing of circumstances. He had been away from the scene so long that he was not fully competent to validate the materials written nor to authenticate the manner in which the terminology should be used. So the writers simply gleaned new terminology from mainland newspapers and other publications that we were able to acquire and formulated them into lesson materials the students could handle.

I felt we needed new blood in the department and strongly urged Col. Stapleton to begin hiring some new teachers from among recent arrivals from the mainland, and in that he soon was successful. Three or four highly competent people were hired, among them one outstanding individual with the unlikely name of Ewald Cheer, whose story is worth telling.

When I first met Ewald, I thought his name intriguing because it wasn't a Chinese name. I discovered that his Chinese family name was Qi, pronounced Chi, as it sounds in the first part of the word "cheese." His parents, both doctors, had been American-trained, and for many years had practiced in Peking at the Rockefeller-endowed Peking Union Medical College (shortened by everyone to PUMC), where his father had been the senior staff doctor. They came to the United States in the early 1940s and acquired citizenship for themselves, but not immediately for their four children.

Cheer had two brothers and a sister. The parents decided that at least one of their children should be given a traditional Chinese education, so young Ewald, then in his early teens, was sent to Hong Kong and enrolled in a British-operated school. There, at the age of 16, he became involved with a cell of highly pro-Communist fellow students, all of them Chinese. They convinced him that they would receive a much better education on the mainland under the new regime, so the entire group defected to the mainland, Cheer included.

For the next 30 years Ewald Cheer was not heard from by his parents or anyone else outside of China. He got an excellent education all right, but soon he became disillusioned with the Communists, although he didn't let it show. Learning Russian was mandatory in the schools, and he became proficient in that language, so, with that and his fluency in English, he soon became noticed and was given a highly responsible position in the Academy of Sciences in Beijing, where he was feted and enjoyed many privileges not available to the common man.

In the next few years Cheer made various efforts to

leave China for the United States, giving the advanced age of his parents as his reason for wanting to leave. That, however, only drew unwanted attention from the authorities who, thereupon, labeled him a CIA spy.

Even before the Cultural Revolution in 1966, Cheer had been manhandled by the Red Guards, his apartment ransacked and everything he owned stolen or irreparably damaged, including what he prized most, his collection of books. He spent the next several years in various prisons or in a camp for dissidents and reactionaries in the far northwest of China. Living conditions were base, and few survived the hardships, nor were they expected to. Beaten repeatedly, he had so many bones broken that he lost count. He once showed me a deep cavity in his chest where several broken ribs had not been set and had healed improperly.

When he was transferred to a prison in Beijing he was used as a guinea pig in some medical experiments so bizarre they boggle the mind. To distract the people from the poverty and starvation that accompanied the Cultural Revolution, Chairman Mao encouraged his medical cohorts to come up with some startling new "cures" for a variety of diseases. Cheer suffered from severe asthma, and, according to him, the cure was a once-a-week injection of a quantity of blood drawn from a live rooster.

He told me that for 14 weeks, amid great publicity, he was given that weekly injection of rooster's blood. He said it wasn't painful. In fact, he said it resulted in a pleasant afterglow of warmth over his entire body, and for a period of time seemed to alleviate the asthmatic condition. However, when he went in for the 15th treatment, something went terribly wrong. He lapsed into a coma, and the doctors were ready to give him up for dead. Several weeks later he came around and realized what had happened.

His doctor, a military officer in the hospital to which he had been admitted in great secrecy, was a young woman with whom he fell in love. She eventually divorced her husband and was ready to marry Cheer, but he was classified as a "black hat," a classification worse than that of a criminal, while she was a "white hat," the purest of the pure. For her to have married him would only have brought her great trouble. They decided to bide their time and see what developed.

Cheer's fortunes paralleled to some extent those of Deng Xiaoping, probably the best known of China's Communist leaders. When Deng was ousted from power, Cheer was imprisoned. When Deng was reinstated, Cheer was released, and to his great surprise was given back his former position in the Academy of Sciences. However, when President Nixon made his surprise trip to Beijing on February 1, 1972, Cheer was once again put into jail for the duration of his visit. They were afraid he might try to contact Nixon and bring about some unfavorable publicity. Finally, in 1976 he was permitted to leave China for the United States after convincing his superiors that his mother, then in her early 90s, needed him, his father having died some years before. In 1978 he was hired by Col. Stapleton.

Cheer had no teaching experience but was a born teacher. A prolific writer, and fiercely anti-Communist and not afraid that anyone should know it, he churned out articles and books detailing what was going on in Communist China. With his background he was a natural to teach the "in house" text on Communist China that had been prepared by the local teachers, who, as I remarked before, had gleaned all their knowledge from newspapers and magazines. Cheer was handed the two volumes and told to teach them to the intermediate classes. Examining them carefully he noticed such an excessive amount of misinformation and misuse of terminology that he went back to his supervisor and complained, telling him the book was worthless. Unfortunately he had chosen the wrong person — his supervisor was the very man who had been primarily responsible for the text, and was, of course, vastly offended. Cheer had made an enemy who would never forgive him.

Cheer and I had numerous conversations that first year he was at DLI. He was an affable person whose friends were legion, but he made many enemies because he became such a popular teacher and was so highly educated. His story doesn't end here and I will add more to it later, as it coincided to a large extent with what happened to me.

Meanwhile, I, with Major Cabot and the team of several Caucasian language lab experts, many of whom had gone through my course some years before, were struggling to do what we could with the remnants of the Yale course for beginners. However, little could be done to change the way in which the materials were being taught because so much had been lost. I began to feel strongly that the best thing to do was to start over with an entirely new course.

While in Branford I had been shown advance materials of a Chinese course being written under the auspices of the State Department's Foreign Service Institute, where their own linguists were taught. The course was sponsored by agencies of the U.S. and Canadian governments and was designed to fit the needs of all agencies with language needs in both countries, as well as to meet the needs of academic institutions both in Canada and the United States.

A representative group of people had been assembled from various agencies and universities to plan the texts, and some able writers, both Chinese and American, had been acquired to do the actual writing. One was a young Chinese woman whose father, an American, had deserted her mother when she was a baby. That was just prior to the Communist takeover in China and she and her mother had returned to China, where she was raised. Because of her mixed blood both she and her mother suffered considerably the next 20 years or so. The young girl was considered highly suspect because of having had an American father. She was shunted from one part of China to another and given a series of menial jobs, from working on the railroads and digging ditches to jobs in factories and in communes. Despite that, she managed to acquire a good education, and as a young adult, when she and her mother managed to emigrate back to the United States, her extensive travels and job experiences in China made her an ideal source for firsthand authentic information on the terminology then being used in almost every aspect of life there.

Three Chinese teachers from DLI were sent to Washington to look at that part of the course that had been completed and to give their evaluation. When they returned a week later, two of them gave glowing reports on the materials they had seen, feeling they were eminently suitable for use at DLI. The third was much less enthusiastic; in fact, he was totally against using the course. However, knowing his conservative nature, I discounted what he had to say, and in consultation with Col. Stapleton, decided that we would go ahead and use the materials once they had been printed and were made available in book form as well as on tape.

By the end of 1979 several modules of the course had been printed and recorded, and shortly thereafter, Jerry Kok, the project coordinator for the course from its inception, was sent to Monterey to supervise its implementation, initially only as a field trial.

As we contemplated using the new course in its entirety as a substitute for what we then had, we were assured by FSI that subsequent modules would be off the press in time for us to implement them without delay, so we decided to start with a new class then about to begin.

Jerry Kok stayed in Monterey for some 18 months and he and I moved into an office in the Chinese department, where we could be close to the action. Before the new class arrived, a group of volunteer teachers offered their services, and Jerry started a series of orientation workshops on how to use the new material. It was gratifying that the majority were enthusiastic about the course, and it began to look as though we might be able to turn things around and begin once again to have a viable course of instruction in Chinese at DLI.

Everything went smoothly under the able directorship of Col. Stapleton. A few teachers remained unhappy about the change in direction and heartily disliked the text, making their dislike and complaints known to the students, which was not acceptable behavior. But it was not surprising, because it meant more work for them. They were now required to do considerable preparation in advance of each class as opposed to relying on the old texts they had used for many years and with which they were comfortable and thoroughly familiar. Now, having to learn something new, it was both a challenge and a chore.

Some of the Chinese teachers openly spoke of me as a spy for the commandant and clearly resented my presence. Col. Stapleton brushed it off and laughingly referred to me as his "Chinese Buddha." He was delighted with the smooth progress of the new course, even though it was marred to some extent by the attitude of a few of the teachers and then later by the failure on the part of FSI in Washington, for reasons beyond their control, to come up with follow-up material within the time frame they had previously mentioned. However, those were all minor problems and we were able to fill in with other materials to bridge the gaps.

The good times came to an end with the termination of Col. Stapleton's three-year tenure at DLI. With his retirement came a new commandant, a man of totally different caliber. It was not long before a decision was made for the Chinese department to write its own language text, and I was transferred to a building some two miles away and put to work on writing the text with the help of several Chinese teachers. A good friend, Dr. C.K. Wu was in charge of the operation.

I was sorry to lose immediate contact with the students and deplored the decision to write a new text when the one on which so much time and money had been spent was proving to be so promising. However, the Chinese department was overjoyed at the prospect, and peace reigned once again, albeit briefly.

Of what happened over the next few months perhaps the less said the better. Dr. Wu and I jointly came up with a comprehensive plan for the new course we were to write. We drew up an outline that exhaustively detailed the grammatical presentation of the Chinese language in a sequential form that could be readily assimilated by the students, and created a story outline for the planned 30-lesson text that had continuity, thus providing for repetition of vocabulary learned along the way. When finished it was submitted to the Chinese department for final approval.

In the department a small committee had been formed to evaluate our plan. They mulled it over, and as is so often the case with such committees, the results were less than desirable. They did not flatly reject it at first, but as they brought out various objections, a young Army officer with a superficial knowledge of Chinese who had been invited to sit in on the discussions decided to voice his objections to the way things were going. Despite the directives from above, that young man felt that the expenditure of so much time and labor on creating a new course was unjustified. He had gone through the Chinese course some years earlier, and not only considered himself an expert on the subject, but at that time had seen some materials written by one of the teachers that he thought were ideal. He proposed resurrecting those forgotten drafts and using them.

Internal politics then took over, and his plan was adopted by the committee and our plan was discarded. We were thereupon directed to use the materials to be supplied us by the teacher involved and to write the text around the bare outlines she would give us.

It proved a frustrating job. The materials she had written so many years before were sketchy and lacked organization. At the same time they had nothing of the content we felt was needed, that of terminology then current on the China mainland. Added to that, the lady concerned was extremely slow in producing scripts for us to build on, and the pace, which started very slowly, began to drag even more as time went on.

At the same time we were faced with another problem. Finished drafts had to be submitted to an editorial board composed of people who knew not one word of Chinese, yet they were supposedly experts in the teaching of languages per se, and their job was to edit what we had written. Not unexpectedly we were told that what we had produced did not meet the specified criteria for course writing that had been approved for DLI. A course in German had been written a few years previously. It had proved so successful that it was designated as the approved model, and we were told to base our text on that.

Following their instructions, everything that we put into the new course had to be in specified percentages: a certain percentage of grammar in each lesson, a percentage of military terms starting from lesson one, another percentage of mainland terms, and then a final percentage of general Mandarin Chinese. The entire concept was ridiculous, because no two languages are alike, and most certainly, Chinese has little in common with German. We explored the possibilities of trying to follow the directive, but found it to be out of the question. Knowing that our protests would be futile, we simply ignored the directive and wrote what we thought was appropriate.

For more than a year we struggled with the new course. Neither Dr. Wu nor I were happy with the materials that were presented to us to work on, nor were we satisfied with our finished product. Everything was labored, and each lesson outline that we received was progressively heavy in new vocabulary, much more than a student could digest in the limited time assigned for each lesson, but there was little we could do about it. Frequently when we arbitrarily inserted the new mainland terms we felt to be of great importance, the drafts came back to us with the terms deleted.

Fortunately, in the beginning we still had the strong backing of Maj. Cabot, who exerted a strong influence in our favor. Unfortunately, not too long after we started, his tour ended. He was promoted to lieutenant colonel and assigned initially to a post in Washington, D.C., and then to Hawaii, and we lost a good friend at court. Despite his departure our personal relationship has continued over the years with frequent letters, but I sorely missed his cheerful and enthusiastic counseling and encouragement as we struggled ahead.

Thirty lessons had been planned for the basic text, which would supply material for the first 12 weeks of the course. After that would come an intermediate text and then advanced material. The situation, though, at DLI had become so uncomfortable for me that I had made up my mind to retire when the 30th lesson was completed. I felt that the all-important part of the text would have been accomplished. I'd had enough of both the place and the administration.

Meanwhile another new commandant had come on the scene, and it wasn't long before questions about the delay began to be asked by higher-ups in the administration. About one-third through the first text, Dr. Wu fell ill with severe diabetes and decided to retire. Shortly afterward he had to have both legs amputated. His successor was a younger man, quite able and very ambitious as well.

In the early part of 1984, when we had completed just 18 of the 30 lessons required for the elementary text, I was called in to see one of the upper echelon men for whom, up to that point, I had had great respect. In a rather unctuous manner he thanked me for all that I had done on the project and then with feigned regret informed me that a decision had been reached to terminate all work on the new text project. It would be shelved permanently because there were insufficient funds to continue. That being the case, there was no further need for my services, and I was given a week's notice to clear out my desk and leave. Shortly thereafter I was told the same thing by his superior.

I was disappointed but not surprised at not being able to finish the job. That shelving of a project had occurred in the past with other language texts. However, imagine my surprise and annoyance when even before the week was out I learned from some Chinese friends that the project staff had been called to a meeting that same day. One of the administrative staff members informed them of my imminent departure and said that the work would continue without

me. There would be a change in policy as far as the writing of the new text was concerned. They were told that "from here on the motto will be 'lean and clean' as far as all supporting materials are concerned." That I felt simply meant that there would, in effect, be none at all, and that is what took place.

I was not at all unhappy about severing all connections with DLI, but I was incensed at being so blatantly lied to by individuals who were supposed to be role models for the school. I was sorely tempted to go in and face them with my knowledge of what had occurred, but what they had done was beneath contempt and I would not demean myself by even acknowledging the problem.

About a year after I left, a classic example of that feverish desire to finalize a project came out. DLI published an 80-page general catalog describing the institute and the many language courses being taught. It was printed on glossy paper and lavishly illustrated with photographs of happy students and teachers at work in the classrooms, or other students dressed in colorful native costumes and singing native songs of the country whose language they were studying.

All that was fine, and well produced. However, they also wanted to display how up-to-date they were in the language laboratory field. Almost every department by that time had been equipped with the latest state-of-the-art language laboratory, and to feature that, two photographs were included. Unfortunately the editors had not done their homework. The photos they had selected were not of language laboratories at DLI at all but of Yale some 33 years earlier when we had first installed our new labs. They were publicity shots we had sent out to various schools across the country! In the first one, in our passive lab, Henry Fenn, the director of IFEL, is shown at the blackboard, and the chair backs show the wiring and earphone hookups I described in an earlier chapter. The second photo was taken in our downstairs active lab at IFEL, showing the then-latest in recording devices, the magnetic disks, which can be clearly seen in the picture. Not only that, but I am visible in the center background, in the second row in from the aisle on the left and fourth from the back. I was conducting the class and monitoring the program from that seat. Mr. Fenn, meanwhile had passed away some 15 or more years before the pictures were reproduced by DLI. Thousands of copies of that publication were sent out across the country and overseas before the ridiculous mistake was brought to the commandant's notice.

My summary dismissal from the school was in stark contrast to the accolades that were directed my way by a previous administration of the 1966-67 period when I was given a citation of achievement for meritorious service, and a performance appraisal that covered several pages and was extraordinarily detailed and effusive in praise of my work. Things had changed considerably in 18 years.

My retirement that fourth and last time in 1984 gave me ample time and opportunity to do the many things I had wanted to do for years. I was able to devote a lot of time to helping Eva in her little factory. Later in the year we took a two-week cruise through the Panama Canal and then drove back across the continent in our own car, which I'd had shipped to Miami to await our debarkation there. During our absence, Ewald Cheer, who himself had just been terminated from DLI together with several other excellent teachers, took over Eva's little shop after Eva had given him a three-week "crash" course in how to prepare all the pastries she was making and selling at the time. When Cheer was dropped from the Chinese department, the reason given was that there had been a drop in student enrollment, but it was ironic that it was mainly the teachers most recently arrived from the mainland who were dropped.

Cheer, however, soon found work. Our back yard here in Monterey drops off rapidly toward a small canyon and a green belt. Originally there had been three stepped-down levels of wooden retaining walls, which over the years had rotted out. I decided to replace them with a single retaining wall built of concrete blocks, move it out a little farther, and thus enlarge our back garden. Because of the terrain sloping off to the right as well, the wall would be only two feet high at one end, but around 12 feet high at the other. The job required the laying of some 600 blocks, considerable reinforcing with steel bars and "anchors," then backfilling with five 40-foot truckloads of earth when it was finally completed. Since the trucks couldn't get close to where we were working, the earth had to be dumped on the driveway in front of the house and then moved, one wheelbarrowfull at a time. I was 71 years of age but felt very energetic, and I surprised myself by being able to put in 8 or 10 hours a day with only a few minor aches and pains.

Ewald Cheer was without a job and sorely in need of money. I told him what I was doing and offered him minimum wage if he would help me with the menial work on the wall. He gladly accepted, saying he'd often done that sort of work in China as a prisoner. He was a great help and delightful company. His first job was digging trenches for the footings of the wall, and he tackled the job with great enthusiasm despite the quantity of hard rock he encountered. I teased him by telling him that this was one job where the individual started from the top rather than the bottom as is the case in most jobs. After the blocks had been laid he wheeled the dirt back to backfill. We estimated it required over 6,000 barrow loads.

As we worked together, Cheer little by little told me his life story and filled in the details of his existence under the Communist regime that he so passionately hated. He gave a first-hand account of the horrendous rampaging of the infamous Red Guards, the young people whom Mao Ze-dong had let loose on the country. He saw many of the appalling atrocities that those young teenagers carried out, things that have never appeared in print. The Red Guards seemed to have had a particular hatred for their teachers, and the indignities they heaped upon them were legion. In one case a male teacher was stripped naked and forced to crawl like a dog everywhere he went. As if that wasn't enough they made him crawl up and down a flight of concrete steps day and night, without being permitted to stop for food or drink, until he finally collapsed, his knees and legs worn to the bone. Cheer also witnessed an incident where a female teacher was stripped nude and bound on top of a table in full view of thousands of villagers. The Red Guards boiled water in huge woks alongside her, then ladled the boiling water over her until she was cooked, a form of cooking widely used in the Canton area for cooking young donkeys. They then ate her. That barbaric behavior is just now, in 1993, being reported in the press in this country.

Those were by no means isolated incidents. He spoke of a huge collection of photographs covering the Red Guards' activities, which he had been assigned to review after he had been restored to his original job. They showed other hideous incidents, some of which were too terrible to describe.

As he worked alongside me he would, from time to time, stop and laugh as he was reminded by what he was doing of certain incidents in his life after having been accused of being a CIA spy. For months, in the worst kind of weather, he was made to do forced labor, and at night he was cooped up in an open-sided shed with his leg chained to a post. Every couple of days, for no apparent reason, the guards would select one of the men for a beating, and his turn came regularly. However, all of that, he said, paled beside his experiences in the prison camp in the far northwest of China, where a huge number of former Kuomintang soldier prisoners were kept. Their job was to build dikes and dams with little but their bare hands, while some worked on highways and railroads. Life expectancy was short and he, like so many others of his fellow prisoners, constantly fell ill with pneumonia and rheumatic problems. There was no provision whatsoever made for medical treatment and the dead were simply cremated and forgotten. In fact, he said the authorities basically expected none of the prisoners to survive.

When we finished the retaining wall, I felt so good and had lost so much unwanted weight that I decided to start another project. Cheer, in the meantime, had actively been pursuing every lead for another teaching job but had met with failure at every turn. He wrote letters to numerous universities and colleges throughout the country, but no one was hiring language teachers.

My younger sister, Barbara, had written in her letters of her growing dissatisfaction with life in Chicago and her intention of moving out to California. Eva and I decided to buy an old duplex and fix it up for her, and Cheer was most willing to help me until something permanent came along for him. Through a friend in the real estate business, I found the perfect place: a run-down, neglected duplex in the neighboring town of Pacific Grove. It was two blocks from the ocean and within a block of a shopping area, which made it ideal for Barbara, who had never learned to drive a car. Although the price was steep, I knew that once I had remodeled the place, its value would double.

The tenants were not sorry about moving out, because the previous owner had not only raised their rent, but had refused to do more than just token repairs to the place. I moved Cheer into one of the apartments while we set to work on the other one. It took us several months to complete the job.

When the job was finally finished, Barbara moved to California and Cheer found a temporary job as a gardener and handyman at one of the prestigious schools for upper-crust children in the area. He also purchased a used mobile home in order to save on rent. Ironically, less than two months later he was offered a job in San Angelo, Texas, where his tremendous potential in Chinese could be used. He happily moved down there, initially for only six months, but eventually he was there for a year and a half. His mobile home remained vacant because the mobile park owners would not permit renters. When I suggested that he sell the place, he told me he was hoping to get married as soon as he got his American citizenship and wanted to keep the unit so he could bring his wife there. Sad to say, that never came about.

In all the time I worked with Cheer, he had never made any mention of a wife and family, and I had no idea whether he had ever been married. One day I asked him outright. He paused a moment in his digging, and a very pained expression came over his face. He looked off into the distance, then said to me in a very quiet voice, "That's a very difficult subject for me to discuss. Someday I'll tell you all about it." It was to be two years before I learned the full story, and then it was not from his lips.

On January 30, 1987, the day before my birthday, Cheer phoned me excitedly from Texas to tell me he had just acquired American citizenship and was applying immediately for a passport to go to China to marry his longtime sweetheart, the woman he had met 20 years before. I strongly urged him to reconsider and not risk going back to China, where he had suffered so much at the hands of the Communists, but he laughed and said that with an American passport in his hand, he'd be perfectly safe. As it turned out, he was badly mistaken.

Invited to a graduating class picnic Sept. 1987 at Monterey. Two Chinese instructors in the foreground: Mr. Fu Ch'i, Mr. Chang Tamu.

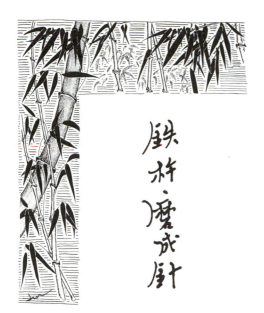

Tiechu mocheng zhen.

An iron pestle ground down to a needle.
(Perseverance will prevail;
little strokes fell great oaks).

- Chinese Proverb.

Chapter Fifty-One
China, Then and Now

Why was I so concerned about Ewald Cheer going back to China? Why was I uneasy and fearful that something might happen to him? Simply because China today is not what it used to be. Its government is corrupt and totally contemptuous of world opinion where human rights are concerned. It is a police state where the authorities stop at nothing to accomplish anything they wish, and Ewald Cheer, although an American in name, was a Chinese national pure and simple as far as the Chinese government was concerned. His American passport would mean nothing where his safety was at stake. All it would earn him in China would be the extra expenses that are levied on American and other foreign tourists.

Much has been written and said about what China was like before the Communist revolution and what it is like now. Generally speaking, the American press and the numerous books that have appeared on the market, as well as television news and documentaries, all give a glowing portrayal of what the "New China"

is like — how different and how much better things are than they were before. That is only partly true. There is much more that Westerners know little about.

Since the Communists came to power in China in 1949, every book I have read on the subject gave the reader the impression that the Chinese people were ready for Communism when the takeover came and welcomed it with open arms. That, too, is far from the truth.

It is true that the people were ready for a change in government. They were fed up with internal warfare, corruption and greed on the part of the Nationalist Kuomintang rulers and underlings, and anything was better — they thought — than what they then had. However, "communism" to them was merely a word — the name of an ideology the average man in the street knew nothing at all about, and they certainly weren't ready for what it turned out to be.

In Manchuria where the Communists were first

most active during the decade or more from 1931 to 1942, the Japanese then in power had thoroughly indoctrinated the people as to what to expect from communism, but the warnings went unheeded. Most Chinese thought it was just more Japanese propaganda. Not only that, most of them thought that what the Japanese hated and were afraid of must be something beneficial to the Chinese. Also, the Communists had been most careful with their Eighth Route Army, the famous *balu*, in showing only a benign face: placating the common people, helping the poor, harassing the Japanese at every turn and, in general, showing themselves as the saviors of the nation. In the countryside among the peasants, the Communists earned themselves a host of sympathizers, but none of the people, particularly the illiterate who formed 85 percent of the population, really knew what Communism was all about.

As each town, city and village fell to the Communists, the initial fear on the part of the inhabitants (generated by rumors of reprisals carried out by the conquerors), turned immediately to enthusiasm when the front-line *balu* troops behaved most circumspectly and did their utmost to win the confidence of the people.

In the propaganda films shown to the people — the first moving pictures most of the people had ever seen — the Nationalist KMT troops were depicted as cowardly villains, robbing, pillaging, and raping wherever they went. In contrast, the Communists were shown as saviors and benefactors who wanted nothing in return for their good deeds. They "loved the people" and had come to "serve the people." That was the message.

One film I remember particularly well. It showed the *balu* as open-faced, kindly young men, billeted with a peasant family. They did all the chores around the tiny farm, brought in kindling for the fires, cooked their own food, gave candy to the children, and brought tidbits to the elderly grandparents. One young soldier was shown borrowing a needle and thread from the farmer's wife to mend his own clothes, even doing some of her sewing for her. The viewers were quite naturally impressed.

How different things became once the initial occupation was accomplished and the front-line men moved on. When the political arm, known as the "Poor Party," took over, a blood bath began such as

the people had never before witnessed. Longtime sympathizers turned informants. Children were encouraged to report on their parents and wives on their husbands. Nationalist KMT officials and soldiers in hiding were rounded up and slaughtered.

The next step was to identify the intelligentsia and gentry and in that the local Communist sympathizers were only too happy to help. Landowners and city housing landlords became fair game. In fact, anyone who was wealthy was considered suspect. Those who owned a business, such as a winery, a restaurant, or even a pawn shop, were depicted as oppressors of the poor. Churches, both Protestant and Catholic, were taken over and used to billet troops. Christians and anyone known to have a connection with Westerners were rounded up, questioned and usually imprisoned. Then those hundreds of people from all walks of life were paraded before crowds of the cheering populace, where they were accused of being counter-revolutionaries, and all but a few were beheaded or shot.

Who were those people that the Communists killed all over China? From my own personal knowledge of friends who were killed in Lingyuan, they were certainly not criminals. Criminals, in fact, were spared and released from prison to become, for the most part, docile and obedient leaders. They were most often designated as block captains, responsible for ten households, while others were in charge of 100 households and the 10 block captains under them. They spied on everyone, bled everyone, forced everyone to spy and report on his neighbors, and demanded bribes for even the smallest favor. The majority of those criminals became the cadres of the future. Anyone suspected of the slightest infraction of their inflexible and often capricious rules was hauled before a "People's Court." There the crowd, forced to attend and fearing that they in turn might be next to be accused of something, shouted in unison for the accused to confess his or her crimes, and when the victim — guilty or not — inevitably did so, the crowd called for death. The process was known as *tan bai*, to make a clean breast of one's crimes, and that went on for many months.

The Chinese had seen a great deal of that type of behavior when the Japanese had conquered Manchuria ten years before. But the Japanese were foreigners, so it was not unexpected. But the new conquerors were Chinese, not foreigners. They knew their own people well and knew just who were likely to become potential leaders against them, and their goal was to eliminate them as soon as possible.

The exact number of people exterminated by the Communists will probably never be known, but the figure most often quoted is 50 million. I believe that to be a conservative figure. Eyewitnesses who escaped from the town of Lingyuan, where we lived so many years, told me that at least 5,000 people were killed during the first few weeks of the Communist occupation. That was approximately one-sixth of the total population of the city.

A good friend of mine was a missionary in the city of Changsha in China's Southwest. He decided to stay on when the Communists took over the place. For a short while they let him continue his work, but then they threw him into prison. He was placed in an underground cell with a tiny window high up on the wall at ground level, out of which, when he stood on tiptoe, he could see the big parade ground that was part of the prison complex. During the two years of his incarceration, he witnessed the execution of 250,000 people. He secretly kept a daily tally, but when the number reached 250,000, his mind gave out. He lived through it, only to be shipped out of the country dying of cancer, and he only survived a few days of freedom.

Communism is, by nature, totally alien to the Chinese character. It is true they were fed up with the so-called democratic form of government that had been in place since the overthrow of the emperors: a central government ruled by a self-appointed president, the warlords governing each province as though it was an independent country, the endless taxation, lack of food, and ever-increasing inflation. But Communism? To begin with no one really knew what the name meant. The Chinese term used for Communism is *gong chan*, literally meaning "common property." That was explained to them as meaning that everyone would share whatever they owned with everyone else. Men and women were to be equal. There were to be no class distinctions, a concept that frightened most, although it elated others. The Chinese had always been used to having leaders and workers, with a middleclass in between. What little they had been able to obtain for themselves had always been exclusively their own. Now they were supposed to share it with others? It just didn't make sense.

The parceling out of a small piece of land to every individual proved an absolute farce. No one got a deed to prove the land was his. They found they only had the doubtful privilege of working it, and on top of that, they had no say in what they could plant nor any choice as to where and how to sell it. They were required to produce a certain quota, often impossible where the land was poor, and they were allowed to keep only a small percentage for themselves.

When that system failed and the communes were set up, it was an even more alien concept, and life became still worse. Their homes and villages were demolished, and the peasants were forced to move into communal, barrack-like buildings where, although food was relatively plentiful, they had no say in what they could eat nor did they own anything anymore beyond the clothes they wore. "Eating out of one big pot," it was called, and the family concept was completely abolished.

It was catastrophic for the Chinese, for whom the family has always been central to their lives. Families were divided; husbands and wives were separated and living in different quarters, or husbands were sent off to work in one part of the country while the wife was sent elsewhere. Children were taken from their parents and put into nurseries. Husbands and wives were allowed only one conjugal visit each year, Mao's method of birth control.

Then Mao suddenly changed his mind and decided there were not enough workers, so families were allowed to be together once again and were encouraged to have more children. The commune, for the most part, had failed completely, although a few still survive. A few years of that and the pendulum swung in the other direction once again, as the population grew by leaps and bounds and food became scarce.

Currently, the number of children a couple wants to have is not a matter of choice. Each married couple in China is officially allowed only one child. In rural areas where children are needed to help with the farming, enforcement of the law is not as strict, and the people of the numerous, small minority tribes are not involved. In the larger cities, however, the law is strictly enforced. A pregnancy must be reported to the block committee that exists on every street. Then, if a child is born, the woman must thereafter report her monthly periods to the block committee and, if she becomes pregnant again, must submit to an abortion. Many women try to conceal their condition to give birth to a second or third child elsewhere, while visiting relatives in a distant city, for example, but few get away with it. Should an additional child be born, the couple are fined or denied commodity rations and made to feel like pariahs.

For many years atheism was the rule. Neither deities nor temples were permitted. The Chinese have always been religious; all of them believed in some kind of a god, not just one, but many, and then suddenly no gods were permitted at all. Rather, they discovered that Chairman Mao himself was actually their new deity, the one they were required to worship, not with the usual incense and burned paper, but with a picture or a bust of him in the home to which they had to bow several times each day. They had to study and memorize his speeches and be able to quote an appropriate passage from his little red book to meet every occasion. They were also required to sing a song of praise to Mao before every meal — and sing it loudly enough so that their neighbors could hear. If they didn't they risked being reported to the block committee and accused of being counter-revolutionaries, or something equally bad. The slightest infraction, or suspicion of the same, and they would be paraded before their peers, judged, and punished severely.

That, they discovered, was what Communism was really all about. Most of them wanted no part of it, but what could they do but follow orders and suffer in silence?

Every few years brought something new. When the communes failed and families were allowed to live together once again, things seemed to be a little better. People were allowed to have their own dwellings and were allotted a piece of land to build on at their own expense — though no one could own his land. They were also permitted to have their own little garden plots or to keep a few chickens and pigs. Then when they had just managed to get back on their feet, Mao unleashed the Cultural Revolution and his Red Guards on the countryside and all was in turmoil once more. It wasn't only the households of the ex-rich that were devastated; every house was visited, and the over-zealous young students, millions of them, each anxious to outdo his companions and prove himself a better Communist and disciple of Mao, smashed everything they could find that bore the slightest resemblance to anything foreign or "decadent," and almost anything that was old fell into the second category. At the same time, women and girls all over the country were raped and molested in a manner never seen before.

When Mao was finally convinced that the Red Guards had gotten out of hand, he consented to control them by sending in the army. The youths, instead of being sent back to school, were made to go into the countryside for hard labor; thus, a whole generation lost the opportunity for education. The Great Cultural Revolution had caused nearly ten years of utter turmoil and such a breakdown in communications that there was nationwide starvation such as had not been seen since the great famines of the 1920s. Reports smuggled out of China said that millions perished from lack of food.

Meanwhile, the promises of equality for all had been nowhere in evidence. The cadres were the new rulers, little dictators, all-powerful, a law unto themselves and rich beyond anyone's dreams. A new term sprang up and spread into wide usage: "back door." The concept wasn't new, because the Chinese had always been used to bribery, but it was bribery in a new and most blatant form. Nothing could be accomplished unless one fed the cadres via the "back door."

Eva and I have not been back to China since we left there in 1947, but in the four decades since the Communists took over, we've kept in close touch with events there. I've read practically every book that has been written by the few visitors who managed to get in during the years of isolation and those written by Chinese authors that were smuggled out. Since the country opened up somewhat after President Nixon's visit in 1972, I've talked personally with dozens of Americans who've made the trip to China. More importantly, we've lost count of the number of Chinese students and refugees who have immigrated to this country and with whom I've talked at length. Most of the students who came to this country either voluntarily or those sent by the Communist government have failed to return to China and have no intention of ever doing so. That gives some indication of what they thought of their own government.

At times we've been tempted to return and see the land of our birth, the places we loved so well, and the people who were so dear to us. But every time the urge becomes strong and we become nostalgic, we are reminded of the terrible cost that brought about the so-called New China, and it is something we are unable to forget. Almost without exception every one of the young Chinese who've come to America and whom we have met and talked with have been willing to admit that they were at one time part of the Red Guard movement. Most state that they had no choice and simply followed the crowds, but almost all of them show remorse and shame over the whole episode and are unwilling to talk about it. That depressing period seems to be very much on everyone's conscience.

While I was still working at the Defense Language Institute in Monterey, we were visited by the first large People's Liberation Army delegation, some 20 high-ranking Chinese military officers from the mainland, led by Xiao Ke. All were connected with Chinese service academies and were royally entertained by the U.S. Army as they traveled around the United States. I was asked to join in their entertainment when they came to Monterey, but I did so with great ambivalence and considerable reluctance. In one way I was curious enough to meet and talk with them just because they were Chinese. At the same time I couldn't help but feel that those senior officers of the People's Liberation Army all had blood on their hands.

During the introductory meeting, the commandant gave a welcoming message, but their young interpreter was having some difficulty translating it into Chinese. The deputy leader of the Chinese group, with whom I had chatted briefly before the formal meeting, suddenly broke into the commandant's speech and asked if I could do the interpreting. He rudely remarked that their own interpreter was incompetent. I found that strange, when the Chinese attach so much importance to "face," but the young man seemed to take it in stride. When the formal session was over the general sought me out and took me aside. From my accent he knew I had been brought up in Manchuria, and it turned out he was from Jinzhou, not far from our home in Lingyuan. That made us what the Chinese call *tong xiang*, people from the same village, town or province, and thus closer than mere friends.

As we talked he told me he had been the general in command at the time our province had been "liberated." Despite his geniality and unquestionable friendliness, a feeling of revulsion swept over me. Here was the man responsible for the killing of so many of my friends and neighbors in Lingyuan, and here was I, hobnobbing with him as though nothing at all had occurred, and there was nothing I could say to him about it nor could I gracefully get away from him.

Such is the background of the beginning of the Communist government in China. As time passed and the authorities deemed that all who might oppose them had been done away with, the situation began to stabilize somewhat. But the people always lived with the fear that the same kind of bloodbath would recur. Even now the recent arrivals from China that I talk with here in America all tell me that, in their opinion, the current "openness" cannot last, and when Deng Xiaoping dies they fear there will be another change in policy, and it is more than likely to revert to the repression of the early days of Communism. That there will be a political upheaval when all the oldsters die off is inevitable. My personal fear is that the military commanders, the old-line generals who survived the Long March and were rewarded with high commands — the rule of entire provinces — will do just as their predecessors did in the days of the warlords and start fighting each other for power and personal gain. As it is, they hold tremendous power in the provinces that they, in effect, govern.

One salient point that deters us from ever going back to China is that very little, apart from the scenery, is as it was when we knew it. We would like to see our old friends again, but the likelihood of any of them still being alive after these 40 trouble-filled years is extremely remote. Even if any of them are still alive, for us to visit them might bring them endless trouble. The local cadres would be all too happy to be able to identify anyone who had previously had contact with Westerners, and thus win points with their superiors. Furthermore, the area in which we lived is still off limits for foreign visitors, perhaps because it is so poverty stricken. Another possibility for the restriction on foreign visitors may be the fact that Lingyuan was recently identified in a press release from Beijing, (and printed in the *Toronto Star*), as being the location of the prison where dissidents captured at the time of the Tiananmen incident are being held. The actual number being held there is unknown but was quoted as being "several dozen." If they are being kept in the old prison that was next door to our old compound, they are in living hell, but it is conceivable that some new facility has been built there. Jehol, or Rehe as it should be spelled, is no longer a province but has been incorporated into the province of Liaoning, one of the three northeastern provinces; and Chengde, the old capital, where the old Imperial Summer Palace is located, is as far as tourists are allowed to go. I do, however, know of one American girl who got on the wrong train in Jinzhou and was not discovered until the train was well on its way through the forbidden area. The train guards simply pulled down the window shades and allowed her to continue her journey, seeing nothing of the passing countryside.

And Peking, or Beijing as everyone is now expected to call it, is quite a different place from what it was when Eva grew up there and when I frequently visited. Gone is the huge wall that encircled the city, with its ornate and massive gates — just one or two have been left as show places. Gone, too, are most of the familiar landmarks in the city streets, the famous *pailou*: ornamental, decorative archways that were scattered through the city. Considered hazards for modern traffic, they were torn down. In their place are ugly apartment buildings, ornate skyscrapers, huge office buildings, and modern hotels to make the tourists happy and comfortable. What troubles us is the thought of how many thousands of civilian houses were leveled to make way for those monstrosities and for the freeways that are now part of the landscape. Where were the residents placed? In the new apartment buildings?

The apartment buildings that now form a background where the wall once stood are a story in themselves. Many of them are 15 to 20 stories high. They were shoddily built. I've been told by people who lived in them that the water pressure in the pipes is so low that there is no water higher than the third floor, and the residents have to climb the stairs with buckets of water because the elevators don't work. The heating in winter is totally inadequate; residents have had to set up charcoal or coal stoves in their apartments to keep warm.

Nonetheless, China still has a great fascination for Westerners. Americans and Europeans, as well as Japanese, are going to China every year in the hun-

dreds of thousands. We've talked with a number of Americans who have made the trip, and their comments have been most interesting. Some who are seriously interested in China have given glowing reports of what they saw on the carefully guided tours they took. Others, and they are in the majority, were largely disappointed. Their memories are not of the beauty of the scenic spots but of the crowds that milled around them, making it difficult for them to see anything. They were not concerned with the uniqueness of anything they witnessed. All they could talk about were the hordes of grasping vendors trying to sell them worthless trinkets or of not being able to take a bath when they wanted one, and of how filthy the toilets were, not only on the trains and planes, but in the hotels, and particularly in the various restaurants they visited. Most also complained about the food, badly served and of poorer quality than it used to be in the old days. Not only that, but almost everyone who visited China developed stomach trouble of one sort or another. Whether that was due to the change in water or the difference in food is difficult to determine.

A feeling of hopelessness and resentment against the government was clearly demonstrated to the world during the Tiananmen demonstrations in the summer of 1989. Students interviewed by Western reporters at the time talked openly of the graft and corruption in the government and of their own feelings about the uselessness of an education since, once they graduate, the only jobs open to them are those designated by the government, unless, of course, they have access to a "back door."

I talked with one young American woman who was in China during the 1989 demonstrations. She said that one of the students she talked with told her that college students in China fall into three categories: "those with a back door, those without a back door, and those whose only goal was to learn English so that they had a better chance of finding a job with a future and the possibility of travel abroad." Another student told her that for students there were only "three empties." "Empty heads, empty pockets and an empty future."

More recently China has turned toward capitalism, and it is now "correct" to become rich. But as one student was heard to remark, "we study hard for years, earn our degrees, then find ourselves arbitrarily placed by the authorities in some remote unit where the most we can earn is some 30 or 40 dollars a month. The bus drivers are paid more than that, and taxi drivers are making ten times that much as tourists flood the country. We see peasants coming in from the countryside and setting up a stall by the roadside and making small fortunes. What is the use of our concentrating on books?"

With the government's change in direction, and where becoming rich is not only fashionable but encouraged by the leaders, a situation has been created where the "have nots" far outnumber the "haves," and that is causing dissension and a great deal of hard feeling among all classes of people in China. One Chinese recently told me that everyone has the "red eye disease," a euphemism for jealousy, and for most of the people, the increase in money being circulated has merely brought about further hardship because of rising prices and increased inflation.

Chinese periodicals reaching this country report a tremendous upsurge in every kind of criminal activity in China: murder, rape, extortion, robberies, prostitution, the use of drugs, as well as muggings on the streets of the big cities, sometimes in broad daylight. One young American friend of mine who recently visited China was nearly mugged on two occasions and only escaped because he could speak Chinese and talked himself out of the situation. He was also accosted by prostitutes a number of times and saw beggars traveling the streets in groups of anywhere from 20 to 50 who, by their sheer numbers, intimidated the merchants and householders. He also watched gangs of youths invading shops and places of business demanding protection money. Organized tour groups would never see that kind of thing; it is only those who can speak the language and are allowed relative freedom of travel who see the real thing.

I've written above of the prevalence of bribery in modern-day China, but, as I said before, that is nothing new. "Going by the back door" or *zou houmen* as it is called, is simply a newly coined phrase for something that has always existed in China, although never before quite so blatantly. There is an old saying in China that I learned as a boy. It is actually a rhyme: *Yamen men chao nan kai. You li mei li na qian lai.* "The doors to the Yamen (the magistrate's residence) face south. Whether or not you have right on your side, bring money." But the big difference is that in the old days bribery was limited, to a very large

extent, to officialdom at all levels, and most particularly to the courts of justice. Today bribery exists at every level in Chinese society, whether in industry, commerce or agriculture, because everyone, even in the lowest positions of authority, has been put there by the government, and to accomplish anything at all, bribery has to be resorted to.

Farmers have to produce bribes in order to get the fertilizer they need. To get bricks to build their houses, they have to use the "back door." The same holds true in trying to get medicine for the sick, a seat in a good restaurant, tickets to a theater. All these have been reported openly in Chinese publications, and although officially frowned upon, the practice persists. Despite arrests, it continues to grow without noticeable restraint.

A fairly recent issue of the English-language weekly *Beijing Review* reported the arrest of some 5,000 individuals accused of extortion or embezzlement, and over half those arrested were party members. No wonder the average Chinese wonders who is watching the watchers!

But the "back door" business is subtle, and seldom does it take the form of a cash payment. That would be illegal. The giving of a present, on the other hand, is not against the law, and usually the bribe is some sort of commodity: a carton or a few packs of cigarettes, a few pounds of pork, a bottle of scarce cooking oil or perhaps wine, a bolt of cloth, a couple of live chickens, or even a pound of tea — anything that is in short supply and generally difficult to acquire.

On the other hand, at higher levels of officialdom, where the risks are not as great, the rewards are much higher. It may take the form of a new car. I've heard of instances where a brand new Mercedes Benz has paved the way for a businessman to succeed where others failed, and in that area, Japanese and French businessmen are reported to be particularly expert.

Even though treatment in the hospitals is supposedly available and free to everyone, Chinese have told me that to get the services of a good doctor, one must go in with presents. To buy a train or plane ticket, one had better have a few packages of cigarettes to hand over, and the same is true in trying to book a room in all but the largest hotels. Cadres at all levels will do nothing unless the way is paved with appropriate gifts.

It doesn't surprise me to see the youth of China

rebelling as they did in the spring of 1989, demanding a democratic government, with leaders chosen by the people, and an end put to "back-door" activities. At the same time, a somewhat cynical corollary exists: in large part, it is not so much the "back door" principle that Chinese students and others are objecting to. It is more the fact that people they see around them have their "back doors," or what is actually access to powerful friends, and the money to use those "back doors," whereas they themselves do not. And, if the opportunity presented itself, they would in no way be averse to using it.

If all that "back door" bribery is officially illegal, where are the much vaunted police while all that is going on? China probably has more police than any country in the world. In the large cities uniformed police are very much in evidence everywhere, but for every man in uniform, there are probably two more in plain clothes circulating among the people. Not only do they know what is going on, but sad to say the Chinese police are among the worst offenders when it comes to taking bribes. The arrests that they make and that make the newspapers are either instances where they are politically forced into making the move or are of individuals who feel they are above paying bribes and have sufficient pull to avoid conviction and imprisonment.

Last year a young Chinese woman stayed with us for a week or more. She had come to Monterey to spend some time learning English, and we put her up while we found an apartment for her and her young baby. The circumstances of her coming were interesting. Both she and her husband were doctors practicing in Beijing, and her husband had achieved considerable fame with his treatment of cancer, particularly cancer of the liver. His fame had spread to the United States, and he had been asked to come to deliver a paper on the subject. However, his unit and the Chinese authorities would not let him leave China. They said he was too valuable and the work in his clinic was far too important. They possibly feared that he would never return to China. They did, however, allow his wife to make the trip and deliver a paper at the seminar.

While staying with us, that young woman, an intelligent and well-educated individual, filled us in with her accounts of life in Beijing and also what she saw at the time of the Tiananmen incident. She had noth-

ing good to say about the police and told us story after story of their cruelty, their disregard for human rights, and their rapaciousness for bribes. She described the police in typical Chinese terms, "Going around with one eye open and the other eye closed," meaning that they kept an eye out for the slightest infraction of the law and pounced on the individual with threats of imprisonment and/or torture, but kept the other eye closed as the victim handed over a sizable bribe, any sum that the policeman demanded.

The young woman, whom I shall call Mrs. Zhang, told of police brutality and false imprisonment of people who were completely innocent. However, since most of her stories concerned people she knew of rather than those directly related to her, I shall tell only of two incidents, one that concerned a relative of hers, and the other that directly affected her and her husband.

Her uncle, a man in his late 50s, had nothing to do with the events during the Tiananmen incident in June 1989 and was nowhere near the place at any time. However, on the day following the massacre in the square he unknowingly visited a friend of his who had been directly involved and who was in hiding. While he was chatting with his friend, the police came and arrested the other man and took our friend's uncle along at the same time.

He was kept for months without his family knowing where he was, and during that time was beaten and tortured to make him confess to having been involved in the struggle for democracy. He would not confess and suffered the consequences. The last thing the police did to him was to thrust an electric baton into his mouth, tie his jaws together, and turn on the electricity. The shock waves from the baton shook every single tooth loose in his mouth and most of them fell out. When he was finally released he was catatonic, unable to talk and unable to function in any normal manner.

A second story she told was not quite so heart-rending when it came to mistreatment of a fellow human being, but it was still bizarre and almost beyond belief. Her husband had applied for a permit to keep a dog in the clinic he ran. The dog would be used in experiments with new medications that he was constantly devising, and he would try them out on the dog before giving them to patients. He got the permit and acquired a young puppy. Since no one in

Beijing is allowed to keep a dog without a permit, very few people have one, and everyone fell in love with the little dog. On weekends when the clinic was closed, the dog couldn't be left alone, so the various workers took turns taking the dog home with them on Sunday, their day off.

There was a 16-year-old boy who did odd jobs around the clinic, and one weekend it was his turn to take the dog home with him. On Monday morning when he was returning to the clinic with the dog sitting up in a cardboard box on the carrier at the back of his bicycle, he was spotted by a Chinese policeman who was, even that early in the morning, the worse off for drink. The policeman stopped the lad and demanded to know where he was going with the dog, how he happened to have one, and where his permit was to have the dog. The boy, terrified, blurted out that it belong to Dr. Zhang at the medical clinic, and that they had a permit to keep the dog. The policeman refused to believe the boy and dragged him off to the police station.

In China when an incident of that sort occurs, a crowd always gathers to watch, and someone in the crowd went to the clinic and informed Dr. Zhang. He hurried over to the police station to demand his dog back but was met with open hostility from the police, who told him he had no right to the dog. Even though he was carrying the permit in his hand, they repudiated it and told him they had carried out orders and killed the dog. Dr. Zhang was infuriated, and a shouting match ensued in which he told the police lieutenant that the dog was "worth more than you are." The lieutenant couldn't allow that kind of talk in front of his men, so he locked the doctor up. In the meantime someone had gotten word to Mrs. Zhang, and when she turned up at the police station and was told what her husband had said, she explained it by saying her husband had intended to say that the dog, being so valuable at the clinic in the medical experiments they were carrying out for the benefit of mankind as a whole, was more valuable in many ways than any one single individual might be. The lieutenant, somewhat mollified and seeing a way out of his dilemma, let Dr. Zhang out of the cell and told the two of them to go home.

However, Dr. Zhang demanded the carcass of the dog because he had been carrying out experiments the previous week and wanted to conduct an autopsy to see how the medication had worked on the dog. The police refused to give him the dog's body. Somehow, someone inadvertently left the back door to the police station open, and Dr. and Mrs. Zhang suddenly noticed their dog very much alive and tied to a post out in the yard. Drawing that to the attention of the lieutenant, they again demanded the dog, but the police said they couldn't have it, and they proceeded then and there to try and kill the dog.

Two policeman took a piece of rope and tied it around the dog's neck and each pulled on one end, trying to strangle the dog. It thrashed around for some time and then fell still, but as soon as they released the rope the dog revived and started jumping around. They then got a bucket of water and took turns holding the dog's head under water until no further movement was detected. At that point they threw the body to Dr. Zhang and told him to take it and get out fast.

Outside the police station Dr. and Mrs. Zhang rented a taxi and placed the dead dog on the floor in the back. Mrs. Zhang told us that she sat there weeping, when suddenly the dog coughed, shook its head and stood up, wagging its tail, seeming none the worse for wear.

Mrs. Zhang also told numerous stories of the PLA, the People's Liberation Army. A few years ago the army men were at the top of the list of heroes in China and were greatly loved and respected. However, after the Tiananmen incident, when they callously shot and killed hundreds, if not thousands, of their fellow Chinese, the army now is heartily disliked. Moreover, she said that now the men are undisciplined and have been responsible for the rape of many young women.

She told us of an incident in which she and two other young women, one of them her sister, were riding their bicycles on their way home when, at a somewhat deserted point in the road, three soldiers stopped them and made them get off their bikes. The soldiers made lewd remarks about them and demanded they disrobe. The women were terrified and stood together in a group with their bicycles between them and the soldiers, but they knew they couldn't hold out for long. Fortunately, Mrs. Zhang's mother, worried because they were so late getting home, rode out on her own bicycle to try to find them. Coming upon the group in the road unexpectedly, she first shouted at the soldiers to distract them. Then she diplomatically defused the situation and appealed to their honor as PLA members, shaming them into leaving the girls alone. Such action on the part of Chinese soldiers was unheard of a few years ago, but is now quite common, according to Mrs. Zhang. The soldiers are poorly paid in comparison to what others are earning today, and there is general dissatisfaction among them. In addition to assaulting young women they frequently invade private homes or places of business demanding money or valuables. None of that is reported in the press.

Furthermore, Mrs. Zhang told us that a few of the Beijing police have organized brothels where they have secured the services of a number of young women and girls who speak a little English or some other foreign language. In Beijing there are at all times a large number of young Western men of different nationalities, all or most of them trying to drum up business with Chinese business firms or with the government. Usually they have to wait for months to accomplish their objectives, and these young women go out and make their acquaintance, then invite the young men to go back with them to their hotel or place of business. When they have the young man in a compromising position, a policeman in full uniform crashes into the room and arrests the young Westerner, threatening to take him to jail on the charge that visiting a prostitute is illegal. The young men, terrified of losing their jobs and reputations, are willing to pay whatever is asked. That form of extortion is so popular in Beijing that, according to Mrs. Zhang, the newspapers have reported it on numerous occasions, but they always state that the policemen involved are actually not really police but scoundrels masquerading in police uniforms. Mrs. Zhang assured us that it was widely known that they were definitely policemen, but the newspapers would be unable to print the story if they told the truth.

What of the women's lot in the so-called New China? What has Communism done for them? I've asked that question of dozens of elderly as well as young women who've come to this country. Unanimously they tell me that women are less oppressed and have greater freedom than in the old days. Younger women who have grown up knowing nothing of the old days are enthusiastic about their roles in Chinese life: equality in the workplace with men and equal pay for the same work. Their ability to

choose their own husbands is the official position, although in actual practice, according to a recent issue of the *Beijing Review*, the old system of parents selecting husbands or wives for their young is still widely practiced, particularly in the rural areas.

Supposedly, and this is generally the case in the cities, young wives no longer have to live with their in-laws as was practically mandatory in the old days. Unfortunately, housing is in such short supply that young newlyweds cannot find a place to live by themselves and usually have to be content with a curtained-off section of the room in which the rest of the family sleeps.

Older women have complained bitterly to me that the new ways in China overlook the needs of the elderly. No longer does the daughter-in-law take care of her mother-in-law. She goes to work every day, and the elderly are left at home by themselves and often have to take care of the young children as well. Of course, they all admit that they are eating better, that they regularly get enough to eat, but that they have to shop, cook and clean house for themselves. And they all say that the official food ration of important basics is never enough, and they have to buy extras at inflated prices on the open market, where profiteering is ever on the increase.

Where housing in the cities is allocated, Chinese people, regardless of age, usually find themselves ending up with one or, at best, two small rooms, and they often have to wait for months or even years to get that. But for the most part the elderly seem resigned to their lot, and although they will admit that many things have changed for the better, they still look back on the old days as being a better life in many ways. They could make decisions for themselves, and, as the elders, ruled the family and had more leisure time to themselves.

When the Communists first came to power in China in 1949, women were given the right to seek divorce. That was greeted with great enthusiasm, but so many divorces followed that the government had to put a stop to it. Divorce is still permitted, but it has become a much more difficult process. The woman, much more often than the man, is held to be the "culprit" in the case, and she must appear before her block committee to be questioned as to her behavior with her husband. If the problem cannot be resolved by the block committee, then it goes step by step higher, until a decision is finally reached. Those seeking divorce are made to feel like outcasts, and divorce is becoming rarer as a result of it.

In China today, one child per family is the policy. Chinese women I've talked with admit openly that girl children are still not wanted or held to be of any value. That is just as it has always been. With only one child permitted, killing girl babies is very common, particularly in rural areas. When a girl baby dies, few questions are asked, and the mother is permitted to try again for a boy.

The way deaths in China are handled has changed greatly. When the Communist regime started, in many areas all the old graves were plowed over. That was the same as it used to be in the days of the emperors when a new dynasty came into power. Graves were leveled to conserve the land, and everything started over once again, and in those days the people took it in stride. However, in the large cities at least, no longer are the people permitted to bury their dead in the ground. Cremation is the official method of disposing of corpses, and it is something that is completely foreign to the old Chinese way of thinking.

In large cities like Beijing, there are seldom big funerals such as there were in the old days. The remains are taken to a crematorium on the outskirts of the city, often in a taxi. More often than not, a long queue of people are waiting with their dead. The crematoriums work around the clock, and ten or more corpses are disposed of at a time. The waiting relatives are then handed a plain wooden or metal container with a handful of the ashes of their loved one, although the wealthier go prepared with ornately carved boxes or intricately designed metal containers, much like those used in this country. The ashes can be taken home or can be deposited in ornate structures called "Memorial Halls" that have been built to house them, where friends and relatives can place photographs of the deceased and bring flowers or offerings of food, although the burning of incense, as was done in the old days, is not permitted. Most Chinese I have talked with seem able to live with that. In rural areas, burial in the ground is still allowed.

One elderly Chinese lady we talked with not long ago told us that after her husband had been cremated she carried the ashes home in a container and then, partly out of curiosity and partly because she missed him so much, she opened the container and started to sift through the ashes. With tears pouring down her cheeks she told us how in the ashes she came across the small bones of a human hand, but to her dismay, on one of the fingers she found the melted remains of a Chinese thimble; a wide brass band with dimples in it which only a woman would have worn. Obviously the ashes were not those of her husband at all. It was a traumatic experience that she naturally found difficult to talk about.

A gruesome story concerning a crematorium in China came over the news wires a few months ago and was passed on to me by a friend. I doubt if any American newspaper printed it, partly because it seemed so utterly incredible. However, knowing the Chinese as I do and having heard similar stories in the past concerning the eating of human flesh, I found it completely believable.

The story was that an employee of a crematorium was in league with a partner who ran a *jiaozi* shop and secretly provided him with the fleshy parts of corpses brought in to be disposed of, which the man used for the fillings of the dumplings. The shop did a thriving business and no one knows how long it had been going on before it was accidentally discovered.

One day the body of a young woman was brought in for cremation, and a few seconds after the corpse had been handed over to the employees of the crematorium, a relative arrived and wanted to see the body before it was disposed of. The relatives asked that the remains be produced for the relative to see, but the crematorium employee refused, saying it was too late. The relatives insisted that in the few seconds that had elapsed since they passed the corpse over, it could not have been cremated. Eventually when the employee of the crematorium was forced to produce the body, the relatives found it to have been hacked to pieces and the secret was out.

There is much greater freedom of speech in China now than has been the case since the Communists came into power, although the press is still tightly controlled. Despite that, the people feel freer to talk publicly among themselves about conditions, and they even occasionally talk to foreigners about their hardships, shortages and dissatisfaction with the government. To some extent they still fear being overheard and reported, and many are not comfortable unless they are talking out in the open air.

In the past few years China has been making big money with tourism, and the official policy is to welcome people from all countries, particularly Americans. But how do the Chinese actually feel about Americans? Is it any different from the way they have always felt about Americans, or for that matter, any foreigner?

Americans for centuries have talked of the Chinese as being "inscrutable," but at the same time Americans have always thought of Chinese as being their friends. Likewise, most Americans, if asked their opinion, feel that they are loved (or at least liked) by the Chinese. That is not necessarily the case. The Chinese have no love for any race but their own and are quite openly contemptuous of their fellow orientals, the nationals of the various countries that adjoin China.

When one comes to know a Chinese well, and he develops a trust in you, he will quite frankly admit that the Chinese are racist in their thinking. They will tell you no other race of people is really comparable in any way to the Chinese, nor does any other race have a comparable culture to the Chinese. Theirs is the only acceptable way.

They do, of course, have a grudging respect for some foreign nationals and for their respective countries, but it is limited, and Americans are not high on the list. It is true that almost every Chinese would like to come to America to live, but only because it is the country that offers the greatest opportunity to make a lot of money and to live in a style that no other place on earth can match. However, that doesn't mean that they love America, or the American people.

Actually, although they will vehemently deny it, they secretly despise Americans for a number of reasons. They despise what they consider America's weakness in foreign and domestic policies. Once they arrive in the United States, it is paradoxical that while they espouse the freedom to do what they wish, at the same time they despise the American people for the excesses to which they carry that freedom: among other things, blatant pornography, the widespread use of drugs, the tolerance for the use of guns, and the leniency with which (in their opinion) convicted criminals are treated, together with the short sentences handed out by judges to criminals in general.

Singapore, with its harsh laws about the use of drugs and capital punishment for offenders, together with the near absence of crime in the country, is, to them, the model of how a country should be run. Israel has also won their respect with its tough attitude toward its enemies and immediate retaliation for any attack made on its people. America, on the other hand, seems, to their way of thinking, to tolerate every insult from other nations and to leave its citizens abroad completely unprotected.

In China, both in the old days and now, a proper education has always been considered paramount, and great sacrifices are made by parents to enable their children to attend school. In the schools, discipline is rigid. The students showed the utmost respect toward their teachers (in the old days, at least), always standing when the teacher entered or left the room. At the same time they were taught respect for each other. However, here again things are changing in China, perhaps because of Western influences, or maybe even because of the tremendous increase in population. In a recent issue of a Chinese publication I read of a surge of what they called "teacher bashing," where in cities, and in rural areas as well, teachers have been assaulted and in some cases killed, both inside and out of the classroom.

The reasons they give for that are varied. On occasion it was because the teacher had disciplined a child and the parents took offense. In others, the teacher found the child inattentive and undisciplined and had refused to have him in the school. But in many other cases, it is a growing dissatisfaction and loss of respect nationwide in China over education as a whole, and the negligible results it may bring.

The Chinese have always had great respect for Germany and for anything produced in Germany. They respect the German people as a whole but often dislike them as individuals, considering them arrogant and pettish in their behavior. The British, with their very conservative manners and dress, their ultra-correct attitude, and their apparent standoffishness or reserve, have a much greater appeal for the Chinese. To the Chinese, the British appear to be much more like them, but few Chinese want to immigrate to England because the standard of living is not as lavish as in the United States and they cannot make as much money there. The same is largely true of Canada. The Chinese also find Canada boring because there are no places to gamble.

Americans, and particularly American tourists in China, although seemingly welcomed with the smiles and courtesy that are second nature to the Chinese, are generally privately thought of as crude oafs with their superior attitude, their habit of using first names on short acquaintance, their back-slapping, and their casual, sloppy dress. Only their lavish expenditure of money is welcome to the Chinese.

However, that previously concealed feeling on the part of the Chinese is beginning to show. American travelers returning from China tell of price gouging by taxi drivers who refuse to give change for any large bill tendered them. I am told of boorish and contemptuous behavior on the part of restaurant and hotel employees who demand tips in advance, as well as the arrogance of petty officials and railway employees. That is not so often seen when the traveler is on a conducted tour. The tour guide — usually a government-appointed "official" — is in a position to report such behavior and bring unpleasant consequences as a result, but sometimes even the tour guides themselves can be unpleasant in their attitude toward their charges.

What I've written above is a generalization about the Chinese character. Of course there are many exceptions. A great number of Chinese think differently and, after meeting with Americans, show genuine friendliness. But even when that is the case there are frequently strings attached. Many Americans who have visited China, and some who have lived there for extended periods of time, tell of Chinese friends who invited them to their homes and gave them royal treatment and lavish meals. But in all but a few cases the Chinese ultimately asked for a favor from the new-found American acquaintances. Most frequently it is for assistance in getting a visa to immigrate to America, to act as a guarantor with the Immigration Service, or to intercede with the U.S. Consulate in whatever city in China they happened to be in. When that wasn't the case, the Chinese would ask the Americans to make purchases for them in the Friendship Stores, where only Westerners could shop. However, whatever the result, the Chinese always reciprocate with generous gifts. They are never indebted to anyone.

Other ingenious uses are made of Americans. One young American told me how, when he was walking back to his hotel one evening, a young Chinese woman approached him near the entrance to the hotel, grabbed him by the arm, and blatantly walked with him into the hotel, where she promptly deserted him. That was her way of getting past the police at the entrance who were there to prohibit any Chinese from entering. Other Americans have told me that when they were lined up to buy tickets at the railroad station or airport, a young Chinese would offer to buy their tickets for them. With the American in tow, the young Chinese would barge ahead of the line. While the American obtained his ticket without trouble, at the same time the Chinese, using the foreign visitor as his excuse, would purchase extra tickets for himself without having had to wait in line.

The name Bette Bao Lord is fairly well known to Americans because of her books on China and her appearances on television during the 1989 Tiananmen incident. The wife of the former U.S. ambassador to China, she is a native Chinese, born in Shanghai, where she lived until the age of six, when her family moved to the United States.

Writing in an article in a Chinese magazine of her experiences in China as wife of the ambassador, she expressed her disappointment over the way in which the Chinese attempted, through the use of hospitality and apparent friendliness, to use her to press their case and secure visas to enter the United States. What surprised me was that this was new to her, and she implied it was new to China. Actually it is not. Again there are exceptions, of course, but it is characteristic of the Chinese to use their friends, and they expect to be used in return, and it has always been so.

And what about travel in China? Is it safe for Americans and other foreign nationals? The answer depends largely on what the Chinese government knows about your background and past history. For the most part, the Chinese government is anxious for the tourist trade, and almost anyone, except missionaries, can get into the country without trouble, although former missionaries generally have no trouble going back to visit their old mission stations. Tour groups, of course, are highly welcome. They obediently follow the beaten track, seeing the sights most likely to favorably impress them.

Individuals with a knowledge of the Chinese language are, to a limited extent, allowed to travel relatively freely and to visit most places without restriction. But they are continually watched and reported to the authorities, if not by actual plainclothes police, then by the myriad of watchers set up throughout the countryside: old men and women, shopkeepers, restaurant owners. Almost everyone is responsible for reporting on any foreigner straying into their neighborhood.

There are still a number of areas in the country where foreigners are not permitted to go, either because the places are militarily important or perhaps because they are so backward and poverty-stricken that the government doesn't want the world to know about them. On occasion Americans have either knowingly or inadvertently wandered into some of those areas and found themselves in serious trouble.

Occasionally, people who have come back from China and reported unfavorably on the Chinese government's way of handling things have been denied visas when wanting to return for a second visit. I know several who have been in that position. Others allowed into China have done things and gone places without government approval, and immediate action was taken against them. Still others have either mysteriously disappeared or died under suspicious circumstances.

A close friend of mine was in the U.S. Marine Corps during and after the Korean War. He was very skilled in the Chinese language and in Korea interrogated captured Chinese Communist prisoners. When the war was over he became a professor in one of our leading universities. Because of his knowledge of China and the Chinese, he was invited by the State Department to participate in an official visit to China some years ago. When his name was submitted in advance to the Chinese government, they refused to give him a visa. The State Department protested and told the Chinese that unless he was permitted to go with the group, the entire visit would be called off. The Chinese backed down, and my friend accompanied the group to Beijing.

On the first day they were taken on a sightseeing tour. Soon after my friend boarded the bus, he happened to glance down at his camera bag and noticed a thick roll of something that had not been there previously. Pulling it out he discovered it was a roll of Taiwan currency, absolutely forbidden in the PRC. At once alert that incriminating evidence had been planted on him, he informed their group leader, and the bus was diverted to the U.S. Attache's office, where

an official protest was made to the Chinese authorities. The money was quite obviously intended to be "found" by someone along the way and thus discredit my friend, and it very nearly became an international incident.

Another friend of mine, a Chinese professor in a well-known West Coast university, wrote a book that was acclaimed worldwide, which earned him the respect and gratitude of the Chinese government. He was invited to China and given the red carpet treatment, with a private plane put at his disposal.

Some years later he decided to return to China so as to bring his book up to date. He was asked to submit in advance a list of the places he wanted to visit and the people he wanted to meet. He gave the names of a number of old acquaintances, most of whom were members of the intelligentsia who had fallen out of favor with the government and were, in effect, under house arrest. His request to meet with them was denied. He was still permitted to make his trip, although he was told he was not allowed to visit some of the places he had listed.

Arriving in China accompanied by his Caucasian wife and two children, he presumptuously counted on his earlier popularity and foolishly proceeded to ignore the restrictions placed upon him. He openly visited all the people he had first indicated he wanted to see, including Madame Sun Yat-sen, who was then still living, and being Chinese, managed (leaving his wife in Beijing), to get into areas of the country where Westerners were not permitted.

Additionally, as he traveled widely through the country he took hundreds of photographs, and everywhere he went he collected the local provincial newspapers and publications. Although they were clearly marked as not to be carried out of the province, he openly carried them when he returned to Beijing.

Until his last day in that city, the authorities gave no hint whatsoever of their displeasure. However, at two in the morning on the day of his departure, his hotel room was invaded by plainclothes security police. He and his wife and children were bound hand and foot, and except for their clothing, everything they possessed was confiscated. The four of them were roughly hustled aboard a special plane and flown to the border, where they were expelled to Hong Kong with orders never to return to China.

Another close Chinese friend, a professor in one of

the leading East Coast Ivy League universities, also went to China and was well received. He, too, was invited back, and, like my other friend, was feted wherever he went. He wanted permission to visit his aged mother who lived in a remote part of the country that was closed to Westerners, and although he was ethnic Chinese, he carried an American passport and permission was denied. The Chinese did, however, tell him that they would fly his mother out to a midway point, where he could visit with her for a few days.

He met with his mother who, because of her age, had been accompanied by a younger brother of his, and he spent two or three days visiting with them in the hotel where they were lodged. During the visit his younger brother inquired extensively into conditions in the United States, and my friend told him of his highly respected status in American intellectual circles, of the big salary he earned, the large house he lived in, his two cars, and assorted properties elsewhere in the country. The younger man was greatly impressed.

When the visit concluded and the mother and younger brother returned home, the young man inadvisably boasted to all and sundry about his very successful "American" brother and of his own ambitions to go to the United States. The authorities apparently could not tolerate that, and the younger brother was suddenly spirited away and was never heard from again. The elderly mother was so distraught she died shortly thereafter, and my friend, feeling responsible for her death, never forgave himself. He became a recluse, gave up his job, and appeared only occasionally at a Chinese restaurant where the owner was a friend and from the same province. It was a case of three lives being destroyed.

Still another case came to my attention. It concerned a Chinese-American who owned a large and successful Chinese restaurant in New York City, and although I didn't know him personally, he was a close friend of another of my Chinese friends, so I know the story to be true.

This man had a cheerful disposition, was happily married with several children, and was wealthy by Chinese standards. He decided he would visit relatives in China whom he had not seen in over 40 years. Without securing the proper permission from the authorities in China, he made his way to his old home town in a restricted area. The second day after he arrived there he was seen to "jump" from a window in one of the tallest buildings in town. His death was reported in the Chinese press as a suicide, but his friends in this country refused to accept that theory. He had every reason to live, and they believe he was murdered because, presumably, he had seen what he wasn't supposed to have seen.

These incidents occurred in the late 1970s, not too long after China reopened her doors to the world, and the reader may be inclined to brush them off with the opinion that things have now changed for the better. There have indeed been big changes in the government of China since then, and one might think that such a thing couldn't happen again. Yet China is still a police state, and the government will stop at nothing to accomplish its goals. Witness the Tiananmen massacre in 1989.

As I ended my last chapter I wrote of how my friend Ewald Cheer had phoned me January 30th, 1987, telling me he had acquired U.S. citizenship and was applying for a U.S. passport so he could go to China to marry the PLA doctor he had met when he was hospitalized some 20 years previously.

I was disturbed by his intention of going to China. They had a record on him, and I was sure the Communist authorities had followed his movements while he was in the United States, writing against them and publicly denouncing them in newspaper interviews. I warned him that in my opinion it was dangerous for him to go and told him to use extreme care if he persisted in going. He laughed and said that with an American passport he would be as safe as he was in this country, and two or three weeks later, in mid-February, he left for Beijing.

In mid-March he phoned from Beijing to say he had married his friend on March 3rd, that all had gone well, but that he was having difficulties getting a visa for his wife, and he might be delayed for some weeks. Near the end of May he phoned again saying that the visa still had not been granted, and unless it came by the 15th of June he would be returning by himself to continue with his job in Texas, and his wife would follow later. He promised to telephone from Hong Kong when he got there on or about the 16th of June.

That date came and passed with no word from him, and I became worried. Around two in the morning of

June 21st, I was awakened by a collect phone call from Beijing, and heard an unknown woman's voice, obviously distraught, saying my name in broken English. When I switched to Chinese, she identified herself as Ewald Cheer's wife, and then, amid hysterical sobbing, I thought I heard her say that Ewald was dead. I couldn't believe my ears!

She told me that Cheer had left Beijing the previous afternoon by train, on his way to Guangzhou (Canton) and then to Hong Kong, and she had just received word that during the night he had been brutally murdered by two "hoodlums" who had occupied the same compartment as he and one other passenger. The other passenger, a Chinese teacher, had been stabbed a number of times in the attack and was severely injured, but he had survived.

A number of U.S. newspapers, including the *New York Times*, published brief accounts of the incident, but in each case they identified the victim only as Ewald Cheer, an American citizen from Texas, apparently unaware that he was a native Chinese. Even his Chinese friends in this country, knowing him only by his Chinese name of Qi, were unaware of the true identity of the man who been killed until I informed them.

Cheer had told me on the telephone in May that during the three-month waiting period, he and his wife had traveled widely in China, and knowing him so well, I was certain that during that period he had followed his usual habit of taking lots of photographs and collecting as much information as possible for future articles on China, but that he had been watched by the security police all the time. That presumption was later confirmed by U.S. Embassy authorities, who wrote Cheer's sister in Australia telling her they had been aware that Cheer had been watched all the time he was in China. However, some months later, when his wife arrived in California with his ashes and stayed with us for about ten days, she stated that neither she nor Cheer had been aware that they had been watched.

The full story of his death as I later pieced it together was full of loopholes. The two men who carried out the attack were later captured and put on trial, and it was stated at the trial that as the train was about to leave the Beijing station, two of the berths in the compartment occupied by Mr. Cheer were vacant, so at the last minute, when the train was already in

motion, they were taken by the two former railroad "laborers" from Liaoning Province in China's northeastern area.

The train was a limited express, and around two o'clock the following morning, while crossing a rickety old iron bridge over the Yellow River, the two men went into action, using the noise of the train and the rattling of the bridge to cover any cries their victims might make.

Mr. Cheer was occupying a lower berth and the Chinese teacher the one above him. Both were fast asleep. One of the assailants stabbed the teacher several times, while the second simultaneously attacked Cheer with a hammer. The teacher, although seriously injured and bleeding profusely, had enough sense to play dead. It was from him that the police later learned the rest of the story.

Cheer was bashed on the head with the heavy hammer, causing severe injuries. When the first blow was struck, Cheer partly rose from the bed, but was then quickly subdued with further blows. His skull was smashed almost beyond recognition. When the two assailants thought the two men were dead, they calmly robbed the teacher of 1,000 Yuan (about U.S.$300), and from Mr. Cheer's briefcase they took $186 in U.S. travelers' checks, his passport, and other documents. Then, as the train entered the station at Zhengzhou, the two men smashed the plate glass window and jumped down onto the station platform before the train came to a stop.

One of the men broke his leg when he jumped, but the second got away. A policeman spotted the injured man but at first had no suspicion as to his being anything other than an ordinary passenger in a hurry to get off the train. After the train stopped, the attendant walking along the corridor of the car happened to hear cries from one of the compartments. He unlocked the door and found the injured teacher and Cheer's body.

The police put two and two together and took the man with the broken leg into custody. He was forced to admit his crime and to incriminate his partner, who was conveniently found two days later with some of Mr. Cheer's possessions. Both confessed that it was purely a robbery attempt on their part and they had not intended killing anyone. However, both were summarily shot, and, as far as the Chinese police and the American authorities were concerned, the incident was closed.

Personally I don't believe it was that cut and dried. Cheer was riding in what is known in China as "soft seat" class, equivalent to first class on an American train. It is never a simple matter in China to get a ticket for a soft seat, particularly on those through trains, which are normally crowded to capacity. Reservations have to be made sometimes weeks in advance. For Cheer, with an American passport, it was a relatively simple matter to get a ticket. For the Chinese teacher, with proper credentials and friends in the right places, it wouldn't have been too difficult. But for two laborers to have been able to buy soft class tickets, particularly at the last moment, is just too much to believe, as is the fact that those two berths happened to be conveniently vacant.

I've known of incidents in the past where government agents recruited known criminals to carry out murders with the promise of amnesty for their previous crimes. I believe that something of the same nature occurred in this instance. Mr. Cheer just knew too much, and someone in authority decided it was too great a risk to let him return to the United States. Traveling alone as he was, he made a perfect target, and the two men, probably with known criminal backgrounds, were recruited for the job, possibly from some prison, and doubtless were promised their freedom if they carried it out satisfactorily, even if they were caught in the process.

That one of them broke his leg during the escape changed the picture. The local police in Zhengzhou had not been let in on the secret, and once one of the men was captured it was obvious to all concerned that through him the authorities could learn the identity of the second man, as was the case, and both were then put on trial. Even then, I am sure that both men probably expected their eventual freedom, so they said nothing during the trial. It must have been an unpleasant surprise when they actually faced the firing squad.

Poor Ewald Cheer. In his death he gained greater fame than during his lifetime. Besides mention in many U.S. newspapers, he was immortalized in Paul Theroux's bestseller, *Riding the Iron Rooster*. The author was writing about the safety of train travel in China, and on page 288 he adds a footnote describing Cheer's murder and gives it the dubious distinction of being the first murder of an American in China in forty years. It seems apparent that Theroux was unaware that Cheer was a Chinese with U.S. citizenship.

Should the reader decide to pay a visit to China, try not to get sick while you are there. Medical science, and the availability of medical services throughout China, have made great advances since we were last there in 1947. During the past 40 years of Communist rule the people have unquestionably benefited tremendously from improvements in medical facilities, made available with only nominal charges to almost everyone. In many cases, however, they are crude by American standards, and I've heard some real horror stories of conditions in Chinese hospitals.

A Chinese acquaintance of mine, a restaurant owner, went there a year or two ago. His brother, who had been an interpreter for U.S. forces during the Korean War, had been captured by the Chinese Communists and held prisoner for more than 30 years. He had just been released, seriously ill with a liver ailment, and was in one of the large hospitals in the city of Qingdao (Tsingtao). On his return from China a few weeks later, my Chinese friend said that conditions in the hospital were deplorable. The place was so crowded that even the corridors were lined with beds filled with sick and dying people. Sanitary conditions were crude and almost nonexistent. He told with revulsion how gray and filthy the towels and bedding were and remarked that he would not have used anything that filthy to clean his restaurant floor.

His mother had accompanied him to China to see her oldest son for the last time. Because they were overseas Chinese, the hospital authorities gave them preferential treatment and not only housed the patient in a private room until he died but gave his mother a room nearby, providing her with a young servant girl to cook and take care of her and her son. However, my friend said that in his opinion the medical treatment and nursing care given his brother were far below the standards of the United States. I have heard similar stories from Americans who, visiting China and being taken sick, were lodged in hospitals. One American woman told me she was extremely ill when hospitalized, but the first thing the nurse did was to give her an apple and insist that she eat it.

Much has been written about the so-called "barefoot" doctors who take care of the peasants in rural areas. For the most part those men and women are serious and dedicated but have had only minimal medical training, sometimes less than two years, and a number of Chinese, including Cheer, have reported that they sometimes tend to overestimate their knowledge and skills, frequently misdiagnosing an illness that then proves fatal.

Earlier in chapter 50 I wrote of the rooster blood treatment given to Ewald Cheer to cure his asthma. Cheer, in his position in the Academy of Sciences, was in a unique position to know what was going on in the country, and he reported that one after another, "miracle" cures were foisted off on the people, most of them consisting of simple, everyday substances put into fancy bottles and touted as cures of every disease known to man. One of them was a little more exotic and consisted of pulverized tortoise shell that was injected into the patient. Cheer claimed that all of them were totally useless and nothing more than sops handed out to the populace to keep their minds off their empty stomachs and purses.

Now that American and other Western doctors and scientists are welcomed there, the Chinese medical profession is no doubt more back on track, with many of the American-trained doctors of earlier years who were purged now restored to their original positions. Unquestionably, China has some very fine scientists who, if left alone by the government and allowed to practice their professions undisturbed, can and will undoubtedly make big contributions to medical knowledge from which the entire world may someday benefit. But I doubt if the "rooster blood" cure will be one of them.

Another interesting phenomenon in the "New" China is the extraordinary growth in Christianity. In 1949 when most Protestant missionaries and Catholic priests left China for the last time, there were approximately 2 million Christian converts in the country. Now the press variously reports an increase of anywhere from a low of 4 million to a high of 50 million new converts. The actual figures are difficult to ascertain.

It is well known that the Christian church went through a period of sore trial and persecution after the Communist takeover. Churches in many places were closed and commandeered for use either by the military or as storehouses. In some cases they were made into living quarters for the populace or officials. At the few churches that were permitted to remain open,

attendance was severely limited. Young people were forcibly kept away by the police or by the local street committees, and only the elderly were allowed to gather.

All the various Protestant denominations were ignored by the government authorities; Catholics were permitted to remain Catholics, but all Protestant denominations were lumped together and forced to meet in the same church. Furthermore, they were told what they could and could not preach, and their sermons had to be submitted in advance for censorship.

The Chinese, always flexible, managed to get along fairly well under those conditions. The pastors of different denominations alternated in conducting the Sunday services, and the Church was kept alive. But they were mostly showplaces in the large cities, for the benefit of visiting foreigners.

During the rampaging of the Red Guards, all Christians were targets, pastors in particular, and many were tortured and killed. Some were imprisoned and I know of several who were in prison for more than 20 years and only released when their health was so poor that death was almost inevitable. I'm told that despite the harsh treatment by the authorities, Christians continued to gather secretly and illegally in their homes, risking imprisonment and death. Within the past five to ten years, conditions have become vastly different. Christians until very recently have enjoyed comparative freedom to worship, and not only are old churches being reopened but new ones are being built. Every church is said to be filled to capacity for Sunday services, and in many of the larger cities, multiple services have to be held to accommodate the huge crowds, which now consist largely of the younger generation. In a country that has prided itself for the past 40 years on not recognizing any superior authority other than Mao, that is truly remarkable. Many Buddhist and Taoist temples have also been restored, and their religions have been given equal freedom, However, the growth there in new followers is infinitesimal compared with that of the Protestant and Catholic churches. Why is that? Are the people really turning to God, or is there some other reason for the phenomenon?

I have talked with dozens of Chinese Christians, young and old, who have recently come to the United States from China. I have also talked with many former missionaries who have been allowed back to

China to visit their old stations. I've talked, too, with American tourists, and I've met a number of young Americans, themselves active Christians, who have spent longer periods in China. The story from all is the same, that of an increasing interest on the part of young Chinese in joining the Christian church.

One common theme is a great dissatisfaction with the emptiness of their lives under the Communist government, the sameness of everyday life, the lack of real leadership in the country, the upsurge of bribery and corruption among government officials. Then, for many, it has just been a simple desire for entertainment — something different to do on a Sunday, when a walk in the streets or in a park was the only other thing to do.

In the old days it was common for critics to claim that Chinese joined the Christian churches to be associated with the foreigner who could give protection in time of trouble, and such Christians were commonly known as "rice Christians." Today, however, no foreigners are connected with the churches. They are wholly and entirely Chinese. However, the aura of the Protestant and Catholic churches is still that of a Western religion, and that may well be partially responsible for drawing a great number of the young to join the church.

A young Chinese woman, a very devout Christian whom Eva and I had in our home for some weeks about a year ago, tearfully told us that she was greatly worried about the phenomenal growth in the church. She said that in her experience, in a number of different cities in China, the churches were indeed accepting new members at an unprecedented rate. But what concerned her was that the pastors seemed more preoccupied with being able to report growth in membership than insuring that souls were being converted to Christianity. She told us in detail of various people whom she personally knew, people who were worldly, dishonest in their daily lives, and heartily disliked by all who knew them. Yet the same people had been immediately accepted as members of the church on their very first visit, and thereafter, in the majority of cases, their lives showed no signs whatever of any Christian behavior.

It would appear from those accounts and the many news reports we've read that joining the Christian church is the "in" thing to do, just as it is to wear Western clothes, play Western music on radios and tape recorders, and ride motorcycles. Church attendees who have been questioned by news reporters have given varying answers as to why they go to a Christian church. Some have said that such a quiet place, with a solemn atmosphere and friendly people, appeals to them, and they like the Western rituals and the Western music of the hymns. Others have said that Christianity is part of Western culture, and a famous religion about which they wish to learn more. Hence, judging the true growth of Christianity in China at present simply by the reported numbers would be a mistake.

Despite all the negative things that can be said about it, there can be no gainsaying the fact that a tremendous number of new converts are indeed turning away from the vaunted idealism of atheistic Communism and looking for a God they can trust and worship. In their newly found sophistication, they know the answer is not in Buddhism or Taoism, with idols of clay and paper, but that there is indeed a living Deity in heaven, unseen, but truly felt, One that can guide and protect and rule their lives and Who must be worshiped in the heart and mind rather than with incense and outward show.

This freedom of religion has continued until quite recently. But it has been disturbing to note that with the fall of Communism in the Soviet Union, the Chinese government attributed it to Christian activity, and in recent months extreme pressure has once again been put on Chinese Christians throughout the country. Many pastors are again being imprisoned, and all church services in private homes are again prohibited. Little wonder the Chinese feel that life under Communism is much like a roller coaster.

Chinese Charm

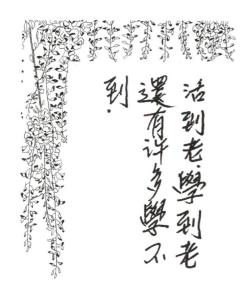

Huodao lao, xuedao lao,
huan you xuduo xuebudao.

Live to old age and study to old age,
there's still much you'll never learn.

- Ancient Chinese Saying.

Chapter Fifty-Two
The Chinese In America

"Inscrutable" is the word that most Americans have used for decades in describing the Chinese people. For the majority of Americans, the only Chinese with whom they've come in contact have been — in earlier years — the corner laundryman, and more recently the waiters and waitresses in Chinese restaurants. It is not surprising, therefore, that to many Americans, Chinese nationals were always associated with one of those two professions, and since few of the Chinese spoke or understood English, they gave the impression of being uncommunicative or even surly. When we ran our own Chinese restaurant a great number of our customers told me they were intimidated by Chinese waiters or waitresses who were unable to offer them any guidance on what was especially good on the menu and who often seemed blunt and impersonal in the way they took an order.

In the last two or three decades Chinese have had a much higher profile in the United States, and more Americans have gotten to know some of them, either in school or in their professional lives. Chinese have become quite famous as architects, artists, doctors, and scientists, while a large number of them have become particularly successful in the fields of computers and finance. The name of Wang Computers is well known, but not everyone knows that Wang is a company founded by a Chinese-American.

During the 45 years that Eva and I have been in the United States we've had the unique opportunity of getting to know hundreds of Chinese in all walks of life, and we count a considerable number of them as our close personal friends. They, in turn, have accepted us as one of themselves, not only because we understand their language, but also because, being born in China and living there for 30 years, we know their culture as well. They are aware of our sympathy and understanding and most of them have revealed to us their true feelings about life as they see it in America and how it affects them.

To begin with, when they first arrive here they

undergo a tremendous culture shock. They've heard about America from fellow Chinese and they've seen American movies, but nothing can quite prepare them for what they find when they get here.

One of the things that shocks Chinese the most is our school system. Those who bring their families to this country are appalled by the American school system as a whole and by the way most American parents neglect to discipline their young. They cite the disrespect shown to teachers, the lack of control in the classrooms, and particularly the almost total neglect of American children once they become teenagers. It worries them because their own children become infected with the behavior of their peers.

The Chinese find it difficult to understand why teachers are among the lowest paid of all professions and why the profession is not more highly regarded. While attendance at school is theoretically mandatory in America, to the Chinese way of thinking it is far too loosely controlled, with students being excused from class seemingly for the slightest reason. By Chinese standards school hours are short and vacations so plentiful that the Chinese wonder how Americans get any education at all. Homework, to their way of thinking, is haphazardly assigned and so ridiculously easy as to be almost nonexistent. Add to that the casual way American children dress and the way they are allowed to wear their hair. Those things are, to the Chinese, extremely shocking.

Chinese in America generally fall into a number of different categories. There are the Chinese-Americans — "ABC's" as they call themselves in San Francisco — American-born Chinese, or "bananas" as the New York Chinatown Chinese refer to them: yellow on the outside but white inside. Many of the American-born Chinese are descendants of Chinese laborers who came to this country several generations back during the Gold Rush days to build railroads. Others trace their lineage back to forebears who came to the United States after World War I, when thousands of coolies from France settled in America instead of returning to China. ABCs, by and large, tend to think of themselves as true Americans. A large number of them speak no Chinese at all, and many have intermarried with Caucasians. The majority are of Cantonese descent.

A second group are often referred to as "mainlanders." They came more recently, fleeing to this coun-try during the war with Japan that preceded World War II, or later, when the Chinese Communists overran their country. They are first-generation Chinese, and although most have acquired U.S. citizenship and a few have married white Americans, almost without exception they tend to think of themselves first and foremost as Chinese.

A third group are still more recent arrivals, those who've come to the United States within the past 15 or 20 years. They immigrated from Korea, Vietnam, Europe, South America and Taiwan, countries to which they or their forebears fled initially to escape famines in China, as was the case of most Chinese in Korea, or to escape the Japanese occupation of China, or later the Chinese Communists. They had to flee, to any country that would take them in. Those Chinese coming from Vietnam, the famous "boat people," originally went there because of good business opportunities and they fled when the Communist government took over. Although officially classified as Vietnamese, many of them also cling to their Chinese heritage and are proud of the fact that they are Chinese. However, these immigrants from other countries are generally despised by almost all of the old-time mainlanders, and there is very little contact between them.

Finally, there are the relative newcomers: students and visitors from mainland China and Taiwan. Officially admitted to the U.S. as temporary visitors, or for their schooling, a large number of them deliberately overstay their visas and disappear into the woodwork, something quite easy to do in the United States. Some stay with relatives or friends or make it by themselves in as remote a spot as they can find.

They usually speak very little English, but many of them inevitably start some kind of small business: a restaurant, a produce market, a gift shop, or a business specializing in Chinese products. Through sheer hard work, long hours and perseverance, they generally manage to do well for themselves, and few get caught by the immigration people. Another way they avoid detection is to get employment in some large Chinese concern, such as a large restaurant, where they can remain anonymous. But it is a strange anomaly that although those individuals can be hired for less than the basic hourly rate, most Chinese employers in this country are reluctant to hire people from the mainland who have grown up under the

Communist regime, where employment and wages, small as they may be, are guaranteed by the government whether one works hard or does nothing at all. There are exceptions, of course, but in general they have earned the unfortunate reputation of being undependable and lazy when working for others. Even those who are in this country legally fall under the same shadow, and the illegals all live in constant fear of being discovered by the INS and being deported back to China. On a number of occasions, both in New York City and in San Francisco, I have eaten in large Chinese restaurants where, after my meal, I went to the kitchen to congratulate the chefs. Time after time my appearance has caused a sudden evacuation of the help out the back door of the kitchen. They thought because I spoke Chinese that I had to be an INS agent.

The Chinese in America give the outward appearance of being a happy, hard-working, contented and law-abiding group, minding their own business and not in any way dependent upon others. The older members are, of course, drawing their Social Security checks, but apart from that, it would be difficult to find a Chinese drawing welfare or standing in an unemployment line. Where they are unemployed, it is usually by choice — young men who are members of the gangs of toughs who thrive in any large city and generally prey on their own people.

But are the Chinese really happy with their lives in America? For them, happiness and contentment are purely relative terms. Success in business, owning property and having large bank accounts naturally brings a certain degree of satisfaction. With money to spend, a nice house to live in, a good car to drive, and their children going to college, they have prestige in the eyes of their fellow countrymen. But with few exceptions they feel out of place with American society in general, rarely mixing with Americans around them. Although they may have many American acquaintances, they generally count few of them as close personal friends.

The language barrier is of course their biggest problem. Almost all of them acquire a smattering of spoken English, enough to get by, but not sufficient to be able to converse freely with Americans. Broadly speaking, only a small percentage of immigrants can read English with any degree of competency or for enjoyment, and working with a dictionary all the time

is a tremendous drawback.

Watching television is, for them, often frustrating. The dialogue is too fast for them to get more than the gist of what it is all about, so they can only watch the action and guess at what is going on. Most utilize a VCR on which they play video tapes from Taiwan or the mainland: Chinese soap operas, comedy routines, or classical Chinese operas. Rarely do they spend money on what we call entertainment, such as a movie or a concert. Eating at a Chinese restaurant either alone or with friends is one of the few luxuries they enjoy. Going on a picnic is almost unheard of.

The Chinese have a penchant for gambling that is probably greater than that of any other ethnic group. For most of them a gambling trip to Lake Tahoe, Reno, Las Vegas or Atlantic City is an annual event, and in every city of any size where there is a Chinese population there are clandestine gambling houses, which are extremely popular among the men. For the Chinese women, weekly, and sometimes nightly, mahjong parties are common. At such places language is not a barrier.

Happiness in the home among the Chinese is again relative. They enjoy their children when they are small and tend to spoil them with gifts of every sort, letting the children have their own way in just about everything. However, when the children attain school age, the problems begin. Chinese children in America tend to shy away from their cultural heritage; not surprisingly, they want to be exactly like their American counterparts and they tend to want to associate with American friends rather than with other Chinese children. They avoid speaking Chinese in the home, usually understanding what their parents say to them in Chinese but answering in English. In school or associating with their peers they resent being identified as Chinese or being different in any way from an American child, and that hurts their parents greatly.

That Chinese children generally do well in school is all the more surprising considering that they have little or no opportunity to speak English outside of school, and, for the most part, their parents are unable to assist them with their homework. Most Chinese want their children to go on to college and learn a profession, preferably law or medicine, or to excel in mathematics so they can make a name for themselves in the field of computers or science.

The Chinese don't make a big fuss about it, but the

fact is that the majority of the older generation of Chinese who've been here for a number of years, many with a fairly good knowledge of English, constantly feel that they are victims of discrimination. I know dozens of cases where there have been disputes with tradesmen — a purchase by a Chinese proves faulty and cannot be returned for cash, or the work of painters, carpenters or contractors was not acceptable to the Chinese or the Chinese felt they did not live up to the contract or what the Chinese understood the contract to mean. Too often the Chinese run into surly or arrogant behavior (just as we do) on the part of clerks, policemen, waitresses or city government employees. Of course many of the problems were simply caused by a language gap, and by the fact that neither side completely understood the other. However, I've been called to help in many cases where it was obvious that an unscrupulous American tried to take advantage of the fact that the Chinese he was dealing with did not clearly understand English.

In Monterey, where we've lived now since 1976, there is a volunteer association with a unique language bank where one can, on short notice, call for the services of translators and interpreters in a large number of different languages. Even before I retired from DLI, my name was submitted to the association by Chinese friends and I was asked to become a member. As a result I received a number of assignments helping Chinese with legal and other difficulties. The word spread among the Chinese population here, and I began to receive private calls for help in a great variety of domestic problems where the English language itself was not involved, but because I knew Chinese culture and customs, my impartial advice was sought.

I've been called to help in numerous cases where the police were involved, but in almost every instance I found them willing to bend over backward to give the Chinese the benefit of the doubt because of language misunderstandings, and that the Chinese greatly appreciate. But some of the contractors, landlords, and a few less-than-reputable businessmen, with their obvious sharp practice in dealing with Chinese customers, left a very bad taste in the mouths of the Chinese.

Ironically, the Chinese are quite accustomed to being cheated by their own people, but they tend to think that Americans should be different. I have to constantly assure them that, unfortunately in many cases, American shopkeepers and businessmen can be just as unscrupulous as their Chinese counterparts and will take advantage of the elderly or the uneducated in just the same way.

I've been involved in more than one case where the Chinese have come to grief with the IRS simply because they were unfamiliar with the need to retain all bank accounts, bank statements, receipts and canceled checks, and were unable to properly decipher the convoluted forms of the annual income tax return. Nevertheless, the Chinese are renowned for their patience and perseverance, and time and again I've seen a Chinese spend a week or so patiently, with the help of a dictionary, reading through the multitudinous IRS forms or the applications necessary for the purchase of a piece of land, or a house, or in the securing of a bank loan.

While most Chinese newcomers manage to acquire a working knowledge of spoken English within a year or so, few manage to master written English and most cannot begin to understand the highly complex double-talk of government-issued pamphlets or notices. A case in point is the test conducted by the Department of Motor Vehicles before an individual can acquire a driver's license. Fortunately in California a handbook of rules is published in Chinese as well as in other minority languages. Ironically the written test is given in English, and even native English speakers know how confusing it can be. For a Chinese it can be next to impossible.

But the Chinese have managed to find an ingenious way to circumvent that. The policy of the DMV in California is to hand back to the applicant the completed test with all the errors clearly marked. There are a half-dozen or so different test versions, with approximately 18 questions on each, and the applicant is allowed no more than three errors. Of course no applicant knows in advance which of those tests he may be given. Their solution is to save all the test sheets and circulate a complete set to any Chinese friend who is planning to take the driving test. That person then meticulously memorizes the location on each test sheet of all the questions marked as incorrect, identifying one or two words therein, and when it comes to taking the test they usually manage to get by with a passing grade even though they were unable to read the questions. Once they acquire the coveted driver's license they know the rules of the road from having studied the handbook in Chinese, and beyond getting an occasional speeding ticket, they seldom violate traffic rules and, by and large, are among the safest and most careful drivers on the roads, particularly because few of them are addicted to alcohol.

Fortunately for the non-English-speaking Chinese, most of their basic needs are met in the larger cities in this country where there are always Chinese who specialize in handling official documents for their fellow nationals, and they do an excellent business. Insurance agents help them with life, property, health and automobile insurance. Chinese lawyers take their legal cases, while some specialize in immigration problems. As a result, within the confines of the Chinatowns of America, there is actually no need for the newcomer to bother learning English. For a very large number of the elderly that is exactly what happens. They are simply transplanted from one China to another.

Now, however, the Chinatowns of America are so overcrowded that new ones are springing up. In New York, Chinatown has gradually expanded into the neighboring Italian and Jewish areas, and in San Francisco a completely new area has opened up. There is also a Japantown, and large numbers of Vietnamese immigrants congregate in their own distinct enclaves. Because of crowded conditions and the increase in population with resultant difficulties of doing business in the larger cities, many Chinese are moving to smaller communities across the United States. Restaurants are always popular and welcomed, and they invariably prosper. It is rare now to find a town of even moderate size where there are no restaurants run by Chinese or Vietnamese of Chinese descent.

Typically a young man in the family is the first to immigrate to this country. He usually starts as a kitchen helper in a Chinese restaurant, a menial job that demands a minimum of ten hours a day, seven days a week, with very low pay, but his meals are provided and he has a bed to sleep in, even if sometimes it is in the attic in the restaurant or in a room with eight or ten other men. If he works hard and is observant, after a year or two of surreptitiously watching the chefs at work he feels competent enough to apply for a job as assistant cook some-

where else. Then, after scrimping and saving every cent he can for the next few years, his next move is to open his own little restaurant, and in another year or so he can bring his wife and children over from China or wherever else they may be. Aside from a wife and children, immigration laws limit him to bringing one relative over every two years, so ultimately, perhaps five or six years elapse before he can bring his or his wife's parents over, usually one at a time. For those families it means long periods of separation.

The usual practice is for restaurant owners to provide a dormitory for their help. In New York and San Francisco, for example, it is a common sight to see mini-busloads of Chinese arriving in the early morning from some out-of-town residence where they live packed eight or ten in a room, sleeping on the floor. I knew one enterprising young Chinese who specialized in renting large, single-family dwellings, where he rented out rooms to as many as 12 or 15 fellow Chinese. They arrived late at night and left early in the morning, so the neighbors rarely saw the occupants of the house, and no complaints were made.

Unless a Chinese restaurant is family owned and members of the family do the cooking, each restaurant of any size employs a master chef, and those men are generally prima donnas. They can make or break a restaurant and are treated by the restaurant owners as dignitaries with very special privileges. Most often, the master chef is part-owner of the concern. Where there is a partnership of several individuals, the master chef has two shares, while everyone else has one. That ensures his putting the restaurant's interests first and foremost.

I used to dine frequently at one very successful restaurant in Chinatown in New York, where the master chef had at one time been chief chef to Generalissimo Chiang Kai-shek. He was so pampered that in the kitchen he primarily did supervisory work. In addition to his salary of several thousand dollars a month, on top of his shares in the restaurant, he lived in a mansion on Long Island, and the restaurant paid for his taxi fare to and from his home each day, a distance of some 25 miles.

The Chinese are very property conscious, and after they buy a car, one of their first investments is a house, then more houses as they can afford them. Quite frequently, however, furnishing the house is of secondary importance, and apart from the barest necessities to make the living room presentable, in many cases the rest of the house remains bare. I have been to a number of homes where the occupants slept on the floor. A wall-to-wall carpet is, to them, as comfortable and acceptable as the *kang* they used to use in China. In fact, most of the Chinese I know speak of their bedrooms as *kangs*.

There are definitely exceptions, especially among the wealthier Chinese and those educated in American colleges, but generally speaking, the Chinese in America, apart from professional people, rarely make close friends among their American neighbors. Again it is language that causes the biggest problem, and they have little in common to talk about. Almost without exception they are respected by their American neighbors; they are law-abiding, not given to noisy parties, and they are seldom in evidence.

For the working Chinese in California, particularly those in the restaurant business, on the few occasions when they close their establishments for a day, such as Thanksgiving or Christmas Day, the big event is a trip to Reno, Las Vegas, or to Lake Tahoe, where they can gamble to their heart's content. They travel all night to get there, gamble all the next day, and travel again by night to be back at work the following morning. Several times Eva and I have been in Las Vegas over the Christmas holidays, and on Christmas Day we saw dozens of busloads of Orientals, predominantly Chinese, arrive from Los Angeles, dressed in their finest. It was a big day for them, and winning at the gaming tables or on the slot machines was purely secondary. They were there to have fun, and they were in one place where knowledge of English was totally unnecessary.

The saddest and most pitiful among the Chinese in America are the elderly relatives. Brought over with the best of intentions, they have nothing in common with Americans, are too old to learn the language, and find themselves left alone in a large house all day while the young people either go to school or to work. Eva and I have come to know a number of those unfortunates. They live well, but their lives are very bleak. Unable to drive a car, unless they live on or very near a bus line they cannot visit their friends, and when they go out for a walk in their immediate neighborhood, they see no one else out walking. Everyone is at work, or so it seems. They've told us

of the terror they experience every time the telephone rings and they cannot understand the person on the other end of the line. When the doorbell rings they are afraid to open the door for fear it will be the police or someone in uniform, which to them spells authority. All tell us that it is exactly as though they were deaf and dumb. Were they in China, or even living in one of the large city Chinatowns, things would be different; they could at least gossip with other Chinese and do their shopping in stores where they could talk with the help.

One of the saddest cases we came across was that of an elderly man brought to this country by his son, who thought he was being most filial in taking care of his father. The old man was in good physical condition and didn't like sitting around the house all day, so he asked the son to find him some work to do. The son, a bartender, couldn't find work for his father in the bar where he worked. Instead, he got his father a job as a gardener, something the old man enjoyed. Each morning he packed a lunch for the old man, took him to work, then picked him up at night. The old man worked at the job for about two months, but in the end he could no longer stand the utter loneliness of his life in this country, so he went back to China.

The Chinese are quite frank in telling us how appalling they find the American custom of putting old folks into retirement or convalescent homes. In China it is the duty of the young to take care of the old, and they do so not only with good grace but usually with happiness, except in some cases where the daughter-in-law finds her husband's mother too bossy. Except for one in Toronto, to my knowledge there are no other retirement homes run by Chinese exclusively for Chinese, although I've known of both retirement and convalescent homes operated by Chinese where only Westerners were welcome. I've known of several cases where Chinese, through force of circumstances, have been unable to keep their parents at home and have put them in the best retirement home they could find, but in almost every case, within a month the individual died or pleaded to be sent back to China. They cannot tolerate American food and have nothing in common with their fellow inmates, with whom they cannot communicate, so they prefer going back to China even though it often means living in a tiny room in comparative squalor with just a servant girl to look after them. They face the fact that they probably will never again see their children, but even that is preferable to banishment in an institution.

Even when the elderly manage to live fairly comfortably with their children, problems arise when illness occurs. Taken to an American doctor, they are unable to describe their symptoms and are terrified of what the doctors will do to them. More and more I have found myself being asked to accompany elderly folk to doctor's offices. I explain to them in advance just what the doctor will want them to do and, in turn, describe their symptoms to the doctor and tell them what he prescribes and how to use the medication. When surgery is called for, they often plead for some other way, fearing the knife, and the placating words of the doctor and his assurances that all will be well certainly lose something in the translation.

Over the past several years I have maintained very close ties with the Chinese community in the surrounding area. For most of them, limited in their outside contacts and interests, their entire lives revolve around themselves and the few other Chinese they know, and since, not unlike ourselves, they tend to gossip about each other, one learns everything about everyone else. But there are always things they don't want others to know, so they come tell their troubles to me and seek my advice, knowing that it will go no further.

I don't like to become involved in being asked to resolve family disputes, but I've been called upon in more cases than I can remember. Quarrels between husbands and wives are the most difficult to mediate. In two cases their mutual misunderstandings and lack of communication almost led to divorce. Both cases were settled temporarily but then in one of them, the woman, who was the wife of a restaurant owner, complained to me that her husband was treating her badly and paying no attention to her, and she eventually ran away with an American and filed for divorce.

For a Chinese man, divorce (unless he is the one to initiate it), is a traumatic experience beyond his comprehension. But it is not unusual in America, and I know of half a dozen cases where the wife — at least temporarily — left her husband for an American who paid a lot of attention to her, something Chinese husbands traditionally rarely do. One restaurant owner's wife complained to me that she saw the young waitresses being wooed by Americans who brought them candy and flowers, met them after work and held the car door open for them. Their birthdays were always remembered and their husbands and boyfriends gave them special gifts on Valentine's Day and other holidays, but her husband had never once remembered her birthday nor had he ever given her flowers or candy. I reminded her that she was Chinese, and that that treatment was commonplace in China. At the same time I asked her how many of her waitresses were driving a $50,000 Mercedes and wearing a $10,000 watch and a $15,000 necklace, as well as lots of other jewelry. She contemptuously replied that her husband had only given her those things to show his competitors how well he was doing.

When death comes to a Chinese family in America, they are torn as to what to do. If the deceased was elderly and originally from the China mainland, most of them feel it is imperative they return the remains to China for burial. Things are considerably different now than they were some fifty or sixty years ago. In San Francisco in the 1930s I visited a Chinese cemetery where I saw hundreds of coffins stored above ground in temporary mausoleums, awaiting shipment to China. Once a year the Chinese community in the San Francisco area chartered one of the American President Lines luxury liners exclusively to carry their dead back to Canton. The shipping company usually gave a variety of excuses for pulling the ship out of service but never mentioned the actual reason. Nowadays it is commonplace and much simpler to cremate the remains and take the ashes back to China for burial.

To sum up, the Chinese in America, in many ways, are not unlike their American neighbors, but in other ways they are totally different, closely adhering to their ancestral customs and beliefs. The younger generation, those born in this country or coming here when very young, become completely Americanized, and often outstrip other Americans in their zeal to conform to American ways.

When I first wrote this draft in late May of 1989, the book itself was supposed to have ended at about this point. However, 1989 proved to be a memorable year, and I am compelled to chronicle some of the events here in the hope that what I have to tell may be of help to someone down the road.

In early June there was, of course, the Tiananmen

incident in Beijing. Millions of Americans saw for themselves on television the ruthlessness of the Chinese authorities in putting down student demonstrations in their bid for democracy. Like others I spent many hours watching the screen, and for me it was an extremely stressful period. At the same time I was also involved in helping a Chinese friend in his divorce case, which had become extremely messy; the custody of a minor child was at stake, both sides were tearing at each other, and I was in the middle.

Almost exactly a month later, on July 15, 1989, I suffered a massive heart attack that nearly ended my life. There is some reason to believe that the hectic schedule and stresses I was undergoing at the time were to some extent responsible, because my cholesterol was low, I had only marginally high blood pressure, and was not excessively overweight. Also I had no history of heart trouble prior to the attack. Whatever it was that caused the problem, the end result, like so many other things in my life, had to be unique and certainly different from just about every other heart attack one hears about.

It happened on a Saturday morning just as I got up from the breakfast table. We've all read about or seen people having heart attacks in the movies or on television, and the usual scenario is that the victim suddenly grabs at the left side of his chest and then, in apparent great pain, falls to the ground or the floor. But, as I said above, my heart attack was quite different.

In home medical books one reads of a variety of possible symptoms, such as intense pain in the chest often described as feeling as though the chest was being gripped in a vise, where others have described it as though an elephant had stepped onto their chest. Severe pain in the left arm extending up through the shoulder and neck to the jaws is another common symptom. The victim also frequently feels nausea, and either vomits or has a severe stomachache accompanied by diarrhea. A heart attack is also usually accompanied by a dread feeling of panic and doom, and the victim sweats intensely. In still other cases the victim believes that the discomfort being experienced is nothing more than a case of severe indigestion. I experienced nothing of the kind, and not one of the above symptoms was present in my case.

As I stood up from my chair at the table, I suddenly felt as though someone had lightly punched me in the chest, or more accurately, it felt as though someone had bounced a football off my chest. It was not in any way painful, it simply surprised me and made me sit down again, wondering what it could possibly be. The thought "heart attack" flashed across my mind, and I waited for some of the expected symptoms to appear, but none did.

Instead, I felt a strange sensation in my chest as though a small volcano had erupted there. The illusion was so vivid in my mind that I could clearly visualize a hole about the size of a quarter with a spray of debris spewing up through it and piling up around the perimeter of the hole. But it was totally painless, and, in fact, the sensation was both interesting and pleasant more than anything else.

That sensation stopped after a minute or two, and I then felt as though a warm, wet blanket or bag was being pulled up over my heart and the entire interior of my chest. The feeling was one of complete euphoria, and I had not the slightest sensation of apprehension or doom. I took a couple of deep breaths and felt just great, and the only unusual feeling I was left with was what felt like two short match sticks poking into my side, just under my left ribs. It was more annoying than painful, and I dismissed it as just another variant of simple indigestion.

I concluded that because the previous evening I had been invited to talk about our experiences in China at a gathering of some 60 people at a potluck supper. The supply of food was plentiful and delicious, but, as is usually the case with those affairs, much of the food had been cooked well in advance and then was reheated on the spot or just before being brought in. In some cases that amounted to a second cooking, which invariably gives me indigestion or heartburn. But back to the next morning.

After taking a couple of antacid tablets, I went to the bedroom, lay down, and promptly dozed off. I awoke around lunchtime and felt just fine except for the two "sticks" in my side, which again were not painful, just annoying. I ate lunch, then had another nap. Later in the afternoon I did some odd jobs. We went to bed around 10:30. But there came the rub. I couldn't get to sleep, having napped so much during the day, and the longer I lay there the more discomfort I felt from the two "sticks" in my side. By early morning the two sticks felt like two pieces of jagged metal and were then causing me considerable discomfort.

I still didn't say anything to Eva for fear of unduly alarming her, but after breakfast that Sunday morning I picked up one of our home medical books to read up on heart attacks, just to be on the safe side. Through the entire article, none of the symptoms described in detail in any way fit with what I had experienced the previous day. But the last line in the article stated that in some elderly individuals none of the usual symptoms are present.

That statement came as quite a shock, and I decided to call my doctor at once. Dr. Robert Frost, who was filling in for our regular doctor who was on vacation, suggested I go immediately to the hospital emergency room. At that point I told Eva what had occurred but didn't tell her I suspected a heart attack. She accompanied me to the hospital. I drove and parked in the lower parking lot and then walked up a slight incline a few hundred yards to the emergency room, where I stood in line waiting my turn and then reported in. From then on everything was out of my hands.

Within seconds, the nurses had me in a wheelchair and rushed me into emergency, placed me on a gurney and wheeled me into a cubicle, where three nurses started to work on me. One immediately started popping nitroglycerin tablets under my tongue every three minutes to relieve the discomfort in my side, and asking me on a scale of one to ten just how I felt. A second nurse hooked me up to an EKG machine and was taking a reading of my heart, while a third was attaching IV tubes to my right arm. Meanwhile, the doctor on duty came by every few minutes to look at the EKG reading, then in a jovial tone of voice he assured me that I had indeed had a heart attack, and he went away. Dr. Frost arrived a few minutes later and confirmed the diagnosis, telling me that the attack had been quite severe.

My greatest concern was not for myself. I felt very relaxed and comfortable, but I knew that Eva, sitting out in the waiting room, would be most apprehensive, and I kept begging the nurses to go out and tell her that I was all right, and if possible, to let her come in. They did so after about 15 minutes, and then quickly they had me moved to the Intensive Care Unit, where I spent the next six days.

At that point Dr. Frost, seeing how pale and upset Eva was, took her aside and tried to reassure her that I would come through it all right. He asked a little about our background and then told Eva, "The two of you are survivors and I'm sure your husband will survive this, so don't worry unduly." Those words were of great comfort to her.

I was not unfamiliar with the ICU, having been there on numerous occasions with Chinese patients for whom I had translated. From the beginning I was very comfortable, and Eva was permitted to sit with me for as long as she wished, but it was hard on her, particularly when the doctor told her that the first three or four days were the most critical. How right he was.

On the morning of the third day I woke at 4 and turned onto my right side so that the light wouldn't be in my eyes. At that moment I suddenly felt my heart give a lurch and go into an extremely rapid fluttering rhythm, which the doctor later told me was called fibrillation and was caused by the muscles in the upper chamber of the heart fluttering uselessly without pumping blood. The condition can prove fatal if not immediately corrected.

Within seconds a nurse was at my side, having noted it on her monitor. She assured me that I had no need to worry, that everything was under control and that the doctor would be summoned immediately. I remember telling her not to bother the poor man at that early hour of the morning.

Dr. Frost appeared soon afterward. I don't know what he did to control the condition, but by 6, some two hours later, I was able to call Eva on the phone and joke about it, although she didn't feel that it was a bit funny. In fact, when she came to the hospital a short time later, Dr. Frost told her that I had only a 50-50 chance of surviving, but neither he nor anyone else told me how serious my condition was. I felt totally at ease and knew that a lot of people were praying for me. I felt confident that the Lord would bring me through.

Dr. Frost evidently felt that he needed some expert advice, because by midmorning he brought in a cardiologist, Dr. Basil Allaire, and told me that he would be taking over all responsibility. Dr. Allaire immediately struck me as a man who knew exactly what he was doing by the way he examined me and issued instructions to the nurses. He checked my heart over and over again, using his spread-out palm as he "listened" with his hand. When I remarked on it, saying I had never seen that done before, he told me he had learned it as a young student from an Indian doctor. He said he could "hear" more with the palm of his hand than with the stethoscope, even though he used the latter as well.

From then on I saw nothing further of Dr. Frost, because our regular doctor, David Thorngate, came back on duty. I regret that I never had an opportunity to thank Dr. Frost for all his help, particularly when a few weeks later I heard that he had died from a heart attack. He had been swimming with his son and apparently died the minute he climbed out of the pool and before they could get him to the hospital.

On the first day in ICU one of the heart doctors who had treated one of my Chinese friends came by. He spotted me and came over to commiserate with me and told me that it would be four to six months before I would be back on my feet again. I couldn't believe it at the time because I felt so well, but he was absolutely right; in fact, it was closer to eight months before I felt myself again.

The hospital had a relaxed policy about visitors, and I had a constant stream of them, even in ICU, where technically only immediate family members were supposed to be allowed, and then only one at a time. It was astonishing how many "nieces" and "nephews" I suddenly acquired, most of them Chinese. The poor volunteer worker at the desk in the waiting room must have been thoroughly confused.

As I got to know Dr. Allaire better I found him to be a thoroughly caring individual who had his patients' interests at heart, and on my visits to his office in later months, he gave me all the time I could ask for and showed great patience with my endless questions and helped me with my fears. I asked him one day just exactly what had happened to me. He told me that I had suffered a massive heart attack, which they called "congestive heart failure." My condition was known as "anterior myocardial infarction," which meant that the large artery leading to the front part of my heart had become totally blocked, and the loss of blood to that part of the heart had destroyed a considerable portion of it. However, he assured me that the other arteries would take over, and, in time, new capillaries would form a network over the damaged portion of the heart, although that section of the heart would never return to normal. It would, howev-

er, in effect, remain alive.

I was in the hospital a total of 18 days. Toward the end of my stay Dr. Allaire told me of an exercise program in the hospital called Cardio Rehabilitation and suggested I should take advantage of it. He notified the nurses in charge, and I had a visit from two of them, Kathleen Alarid-Burke and Monica Casas. The program covers a variety of exercises on stationary bicycles, treadmills, stair machines and rowing devices. The patient is carefully monitored for the first 12 weeks, wearing a small radio device that shows a picture of the heart action on a screen. I joined the program as soon as I got some of my strength back, and now, three and a half years later, I am still attending the program three days a week and finding it most helpful.

As I now sit and write this, the year is 1993, and little of note happened in the years 1990 and 1991. I spent as much time as possible in writing this book, and my health remained fairly constant as I continued my thrice-weekly stints at exercise at the hospital. But the year 1992 brought several events of note. Early in January I was greatly surprised to receive letters from several former students, all of whom are fairly high-ranking officials in the National Security Agency outside Washington, telling me that the agency was about to give me an award in recognition of my help over the years in teaching Chinese to the large number of students who had eventually gone into the agency. I realized full well that the gesture on the part of the agency was unique, and that I owed it to pressures that had been brought to bear by my loyal former students and friends.

A week or two later I received a phone call from the protocol officer at the Defense Language Institute here in Monterey asking me to keep an hour or two free on the morning of February 7, 1992, at which time an award was to be presented to me, but no further details were added. I was simply told that it was to be a private ceremony to be held in the office of the commandant at 9 a.m. I have never sought public recognition for anything I've ever done and don't particularly enjoy formal ceremonies. I suggested through my ex-student friends that the award, if it was to be given, simply be mailed to me. But they would have none of it.

As the day approached I got further calls from the protocol officer and was told that the ceremony had been moved to the Officers' Club because of the large number of people who wanted to attend. I was also told that the presentation was to be made by a high-ranking official of NSA, Whitney E. Reed, commandant of the National Cryptologic School, whose civilian rank placed him in the category equivalent to a three-star general, and he would be accompanied by several members of his staff.

On the day previous to the event our good friend Judie Telfer, night editor for our local newspaper, *The Monterey County Herald*, published a short item announcing the award, so I was not surprised when I got to the Officers' Club the next morning to find about 50 people there, a number of whom were my former Chinese colleagues, and several former students who have attained positions of high responsibility in the school, including David Olney, dean of the Asian division, and Harry Olsen, chairman of one of the two Chinese departments. Many other friendly faces were there, including neighbors and family members.

The ceremony itself was very military and quite formal. It was conducted by the commandant, Col. Fischer, who in his introductory speech made some very flattering statements about the contributions I had made to DLI over the years. He was followed by Whitney Reed, who also had a lot of nice things to say, and I was then given the award, a wooden plaque with a thick lucite face, beneath which was a colored photograph of the National Security Building at Fort Meade, between Washington and Baltimore, and the seal of the agency, with the inscription:

This Certificate is Presented To
ROBERT N. THARP
On behalf of the National Security Agency, and the many, many students you taught so well and influenced so deeply during your long years of dedicated and truly outstanding service, we extend sincere appreciation and heartfelt gratitude for unheralded, though widely acknowledged, contributions to the United States of America which inspired several generations of our best and brightest professionals.

The citation was signed by Whitney E. Reed and Vice Admiral William O. Studeman, director of NSA.

Following the presentation of the award, another of my former students, Luther Deese, a member of Mr. Reed's party, presented me with a Chinese scroll, with excellent Chinese calligraphy done by a former colleague, Chang Ta Mu. Five large characters read: "Peaches and plums cover the entire earth," an ancient Chinese saying, where peaches and plums are symbolic of the students and/or disciples of a great teacher.

The entire ceremony was a very proud moment for me and after I had given a short thank-you speech the assembled group gave me a standing ovation, which I felt was undeserved, but which I much appreciated.

In May of 1992 I suffered some angina pain and after reporting in at our own hospital here, my cardiologist, Dr. Allaire, determined that one of the two remaining arteries leading to the heart was almost entirely blocked. I was rushed by ambulance to a hospital in the nearby town of Salinas, where they have an excellent heart program. There I had an angiogram, a procedure where a device is threaded up through one's artery to locate the blockage.

The blockage was found, together with a large blood clot sitting on top of it. That was dissolved with a "clot buster" medication. I then had to lie in bed for six days, taking medication to thin my blood so that no further blood clots could develop. After that an angioplasty procedure was performed, where the doctors went in with plastic tubes, one of which was equipped with a small balloon that was used to press down on the plaque blocking my artery. It took several hours and eight balloons to accomplish the job, but ever since then I've had no further trouble, and apparently the artery was cleared and has remained clear for over six months. The doctors expect the plaque to grow back again, so from time to time I have to take treadmill tests to determine how things are, but I have much to thank God for, and my health has remained fairly good. What I most regret is the lost time when I could have been working on this book.

Now that we are up to date it seems like a good place to end this book. However, since I promised in an earlier chapter that I would tell something of Chinese humor, and the tradition of the great comedians of our past is to "always leave them laughing," I'll add another chapter to give you some idea of what it is that makes the Chinese laugh.

NSA award presented to Bob by Whitney E. Reed, Commandant of the National Cryptologic School. Feb. 2, 1992.

At the NSA award ceremony, Bob was presented a scroll with calligraphy by Mr. Chang Ta Mu. Presenting the scroll was Mr. Luther Deese — member of Mr. Reed's party and former student of Bob's. Scroll says: "Peaches and Plums cover the entire earth." (Peaches and plums symbolize students or disciples.) Tau Li Man Tian Xia.

National Security Agency

This Certificate Is Presented To

Robert N. Tharp

On behalf of the National Security Agency, and the many, many students you taught so well and influenced so deeply during your long years of dedicated and truly outstanding service, we extend sincere appreciation and heartfelt gratitude for unheralded, though widely acknowledged, contributions to the United States of America which inspired several generations of our best and brightest professionals.

Whitney E. Reed
Deputy Director for Education
and Training

VADM William O. Studeman, USN
Director NSA/Chief CSS

Chinese Charm

打是亲，骂是爱．
大母娘喜欢拿
脚踹．

Da shi qin, ma shi ai,
zhangmuniang xihan na jiao chuai.

When she beats you it shows intimacy,
when she curses you it shows love,
and when your mother-in-law cherishes you,
she kicks you with her foot.

- Humorous Chinese Saying.

Chapter Fifty-Three
What Makes The Chinese Laugh

If, as *Reader's Digest* has been telling us for years, laughter is the best medicine, then the Chinese, at least those in Northern China, should be among the healthiest people in the world because of their marvelously well developed sense of humor and their ability to laugh under the most adverse of circumstances.

The Chinese word for a joke is *xiao hua*, literally "laugh talk," and their word for humor sounds a lot like ours, *youmo*. However, the meaning of these two syllables seems to belie the concept of humor because the word *you* means deep and remote, secluded, dim; while *mo* means silent or tacit. The word has been in use so long no one seems to quite remember its origin, but like so many Chinese words, it in all probability was simply arbitrarily created to sound like our English word "humor."

A number of books have been written on Chinese humor and jokes, but without exception — at least those that I have read — they are dry and dull and fail completely to convey the Chinese concept of what is funny in the Chinese language. In so many cases the humorous aspect of Chinese jokes or stories is dependent on a knowledge of Chinese culture and mores, and unless one is familiar with Chinese life, telling the joke in English leaves the listener unaffected.

Chinese humor falls into a number of categories. Where joking and laughter are concerned, nothing is sacred with the Chinese and everyone and everything is fair game to be joked about. The language being tonal, with so many spoken words sounding exactly the same, it lends itself to punning, even more so than English. An example of punning is a play made on the name of China's famous leader Deng Xiaoping. His full name when written is *Deng*, (the surname), while the *xiao* means small and the *ping* literally means level, flat or smooth. Thus the two words combined with his surname have no particular meaning, they are just a name. However, the two words *xiao ping* when spoken sound exactly the same as Deng's order to stay alive.

One morning when it came time for breakfast the husband demanded something to eat, and his wife told him there was nothing in the house and no money with which to buy anything. The man insisted that she get him his breakfast and wouldn't listen to her pleas for money, saying he had none to give her anyway.

The poor woman looked around and finally discovered two copper cash — as pennies were called in those days — which had been sewn into the hem of the curtain to weigh it down and keep it from being blown upward by the wind. Taking them out, she straightened her hair, dabbed some color on her cheeks, then went and stood just inside the front gate to await the arrival of the gruel seller, who came by that way each morning, selling not only hot gruel but freshly baked sesame cakes and deep-fried fritters. Finally, hearing his call as he came up the street, she went out to meet him.

Smiling broadly at the man, she said, "Mr. Gruel-seller, I would like two cash worth of gruel this morning," and with that she held out a very large bowl and showed him the two cash. He dutifully ladled two large spoonfuls into her bowl and held out his hand for the cash.

Before handing him the money, though, the woman was already talking again. "Mr. Gruel-seller, I see you come this way every day, and I've always wanted to talk to you and ask you your name. What is it? You're so handsome, and you have such a loud and manly voice as you call out your wares, and you always dress so well and look so smart, and I love to watch the muscles on your arm ripple as you ladle out the gruel." The merchant felt so overcome by her flattery that with each of her compliments, "plop, plop" (or *dong, dong,* as the comedian voices the sound effect), two more ladlefuls went into her bowl until it was almost filled.

The man, expecting momentarily to be invited into the house for some dalliance, was stunned when the woman blithely smiled at him, and patting him on the arm, said, "We'll have to talk another day. I must hurry in with this to my husband before it gets cold." With that she dashed into her yard, bolting the gate behind her and the poor gruel-seller realized he had been had.

One form of Chinese humor that baffles most stu-

dents of the Chinese language is probably unique to China. Although I've made inquiries from people of various nationalities I've never found any other country in the world that has anything quite the same; certainly in the English language we haven't anything that even closely approaches it.

It is known by three names. One is *diao kanr,* a purely peasant-type vernacularism that literally means falling off a cliff. A second name is *qiaopihua,* meaning a witticism, witty remark, or wisecrack as it would be called in America. However, the proper term for it, and one that definitively describes the genre is the name *xiehouyu,* literally meaning "words after a rest."

The expressions themselves are sometimes described as allegorical, and in Northern China literally thousands of them are in use. They always come in two parts; the first part is descriptive, but when used it seemingly has little or nothing to do with the topic of conversation at the time and may not necessarily be either witty or amusing by itself. It is the second part, said after a brief pause or sometimes left unstated, together with the context in which the sayings are used, that provide the humor.

To demonstrate that form of humor I shall have to, in each case, set up a short scenario where a speaker is talking to someone else and says something that requires a reply. To the American mind the expressions may seem vague, oblique, and totally unrelated to the subject under discussion, as indeed they frequently are, but to the Chinese mind they are completely appropriate. In one sense they probably fit more closely under the heading of riddles. In fact in the old days a group of men would frequently gather together and challenge each other with these sayings. One person would come up with one of them and wait to see if anyone could give the matching couplet, and many of them, of course, were so common that the second part would often be shouted before the first part was even finished. Essentially, they are a challenge to the mind. One that is very well known can be used in a variety of circumstances: where an individual is boasting of his prowess in a given area or is making wild statements as to what he intends doing with regard to a certain situation. The saying is, *Ni pusa guo he,* "a clay idol fording a river." This was explained at the end of chapter twenty-five.

A large number of the sayings seemingly bear no

obvious relationship to what is being said or seem so utterly out of place in a conversation that one is taken aback. To try to reason out the correlation becomes a real challenge. I gave you a sample of this in chapter twenty-eight with the question "dong budong" literally "understand, not understand?"

A common breakfast food in China is gruel or porridge, made from rice, millet, sorghum or some other grain, and it is called *zhou*. Suppose I was to ask you what you had for breakfast, and instead of telling me you had porridge, you said: *Lao taitai shangbuqu kang* — the old lady cannot climb up onto the brick bed.

I must figure out what kind of breakfast food would fit the situation, so I start thinking about what would happen to the old lady. Obviously someone has to either lift her up or boost her up from behind, and the colloquial Chinese word for "boost" is identical in sound to their word for gruel, i.e., *zhou*. So in other words, to help the old lady up onto the bed you would boost her from behind; you had porridge for breakfast.

The majority of these expressions are descriptive of something quite commonplace, and they fall into distinct categories. For example, dozens of them concern blind people, a very common sight in old China. One of them describes shutting the door to beat the blind man (there is no escape for him). Another speaks of a blind man selling eye medicine (a person you cannot trust when he says his product is good). A third one describes the blind man lighting a lamp (an utterly useless procedure).

Animals enter into many of the sayings. One of the most obvious concerns the polecat or stoat going to wish the hens a happy New Year. Obviously he has no good intentions. Another concerns the pack rat, which decides to haul a shovel down into its hole or burrow. Pulling it by the handle he gets along just fine until the blade part of the shovel hits the entrance to his hole, so the corollary is "the big problem comes later," and has reference to someone biting off more than he can chew.

You may recall that at the beginning of chapter twenty five, the conductor used the expression "Yao fande da gou," "beggar beating a dog." That too was a good example of such sayings.

One more in this category is similar to our expression "damned if you do and damned if you don't," or describing a no-win situation. The Chinese expression for that is, "the old sow with her head through the fence — to move forward or backward is equally difficult." *Lao mu zhu zuan zhangzi — jin tui liang nan.*

Another common form of humor is the short story the Chinese tell with great gusto and appropriate gestures, the simplicity and yet piquant humor of which I have always found quite delightful. One of them concerns a most unlikely subject, a beggar, yet it was a subject common to the everyday scene and humorous by its very unlikelihood.

The beggar had a tiny shack in the village. At one time he had been married, but his wife had died in childbirth, leaving him with a baby son whom he tried to raise by himself. Before he fell on hard times, the beggar had been a man of means and was fairly well educated, and he wanted to bring up his son to be a man of honor, polite and well behaved, so from infancy he had drummed into the boy all the proper behavior expected from a well-to-do family member so that it reflected well on the family as a whole. Chief among the things he had taught the boy was how to behave when visitors came.

Their sole possessions were the clothes they wore, a couple of pieces of ragged bedding, and the two tin cans that they carried daily in which to collect their food. Nothing else. Not a single item of furniture nor anything in the way of cooking or eating utensils. That, however, didn't daunt the father. Daily he would instruct his son in proper manners. The boy was told that when a visitor arrived, the proper thing to do was to invite the person to be seated, and the father showed the boy where, in the tiny room, was the position of greatest honor, the place farthest from the entrance. Most important was how to serve tea properly.

The child remonstrated at the seeming stupidity of what his father was telling him to do. "But father," he said, "we don't have any cups and no teapot in which to brew the tea and we don't have a chair for the visitor to sit on, and no table. How can I ask him to sit down when there is no chair?" and questions like that.

The father would patiently reply. "What is important is that you go through the motions. Pretend a chair is against the wall and invite our visitor to sit there. Tell him you are going to make tea and go through the motions of firing up a kettle of water and making the tea, and then bring the imaginary cups here to this imaginary table and put them down, then bring the pot of tea and let it brew for a few minutes while you chat with him. After that you can pour the tea, but remember one very important thing. Pour your own cupful first or pour a little out on the ground, and after that pour tea for the guest."

"That sounds strange," said the boy, "and not very polite. Why should I pour my own tea first or pour some on the ground?"

"Ah," said the father, "it is not only the custom, but there is a very important reason for it. The teapot sits on a shelf with the open spout pointing upward, where it will collect dust. You don't want to pour that dust into your guest's cup, do you? Also, the liquid that is in the spout of the teapot is not fully brewed tea, it is mostly water, and you want to give your guest the best tea possible."

"After that what should I do?" asked the boy. "When you've poured his tea you should take it to him carefully, with both your hands held out in front of you as though you were carrying a filled cup of tea, and even though there is no cup and no tea, your visitor will accept the gesture as one of great politeness and courtesy and know that you have been well brought up."

"And what is the importance of holding the cup in both hands?" asked the boy.

"Ah ha!" said the father. "I thought you would ask that. This is a custom that dates back to the times of the emperors. Whenever anyone came in and offered a gift or any object to an emperor, he had to do so with both hands. It was a matter of his security. Should something be handed to the emperor with one hand, it was too easy to conceal a weapon in the other hand, and with two hands showing, the emperor could see that he was not threatened." That and other lessons in propriety and good manners went on each day.

One day the father announced to his son that he was going to a neighboring village to beg for food and would be spending the day there because pickings had become pretty lean in their own village. Up to that point they had never had a visitor, but before he left he admonished the boy to remember his instructions in the event a visitor came.

By sheer happenstance a visitor did come that day. Beggar Wang from the other end of the village came by. He came looking for the boy's father and was surprised to find him absent. However, the boy welcomed him and went through the motions his father had taught him, greatly impressing Beggar Wang.

When the boy's father returned home that evening he asked his son how he had spent the day. The boy excitedly replied that they had had a visitor, Beggar Wang from the other end of the village. "And what did you do for him?" asked the father.

The boy proudly told his father how he had invited Beggar Wang to come into the shack and had led him over to the far wall, where he had invited him to sit in the chair, all of it, of course, in mime. He then told his father how he had informed the visitor that he would prepare him some tea. However, when he got over into the corner he decided it was such a hot day that to light a fire and make boiling water for tea would only make the shack that much hotter, so he had asked Beggar Wang if he would like a piece of watermelon. Beggar Wang had agreed, saying it was a wonderful idea for such a hot day, so the boy pretended to cut a large watermelon lengthwise, and then demonstrated to his father, with both hands outstretched in front of him and a foot or so apart, how he had carried the half watermelon over to Beggar Wang and had given it to him.

The father, instead of praising the boy for his astuteness and good behavior, was incensed. Slapping the boy across the face he shouted, "You miserable, stupid boy. Haven't I taught you to be frugal and not wasteful? Why did you give him a whole half of a watermelon when you could have placed your hands close together like this, and pretended you were giving him just a slice?"

Another cute story concerns a young country girl who was betrothed to a man from the city. He was a businessman who did a lot of traveling, and a few weeks after their wedding the husband left on a trip that would keep him away for several months. Not wanting to leave his young wife all alone in the big city, he sent the girl home to her village to stay with her mother.

Some weeks later the postman stopped at her farmhouse and dropped off a letter addressed to her, telling her it was from her husband. She had never had any schooling, so she couldn't read even what was written on the envelope, but knowing it was from her husband, she pondered how to find out what her husband had written. She finally came up with a solution.

In almost every village, a man who has had a year or two of schooling sets himself up as the village school teacher, at the same time often doubling as the village letter writer. She set out one morning to find him, and when she finally found him, she timidly approached him and asked if he could read a letter for her. He replied that he most definitely could. "Well" she said, "here's the letter. It's from my husband, and what he says in it he says to me alone and to no one else. I want you to read it aloud to me, but I want you to be sure to cover your ears so you don't hear what you are reading."

Although I've mentioned a number of different forms of Chinese humor, these are the spoken forms, and we've barely scratched the surface of Chinese humor as a whole, because there are many other types that are either sung or chanted, and they differ from province to province. "Rap" music, which came into being fairly recently in the United States, has been a form of entertainment in China for hundreds of years, and it was usually performed by itinerant mendicants.

When I was a boy I used to follow those mendicants as they practiced their art. They were sort of sophisticated beggars, and each town or city had at least one or two resident ones who walked the streets each day. They always drew a small crowd, usually peasants visiting the city, because their repertoire was somewhat "old hat" to the local residents. However, when an out-of-town mendicant came, and several were quite famous and visited Lingyuan at least once or twice a year, they drew hundreds of people. Their practice was to keep on the go, and in the course of a year they covered large areas of the countryside.

That art form is called *Shulaibao*, literally "count and precious things will come," and it is a form of Chinese art culture that has been around for centuries. The traveling mendicants who practiced it were usually fairly well educated and were definitely a cut above the ordinary beggars. Those men were constantly on the road, moving from village to village and city to city, usually traveling with two or three young apprentices who were learning the art. They were characterized by their tremendous sense of humor, their sharp wit, and their ability to ad lib whenever the occasion demanded. Just why the art form is called *Shulaibao*, or what it actually means, is anyone's guess.

Delivery of the rap was always, in Northern China, in the form of a chant and followed a completely stylized format, usually six or seven words to a line, and each pair of lines not only had to rhyme, but the tone on the last word of each line had to be exactly the same. For that reason it was often necessary to insert a nonsense line in order to find an appropriate word, but that is where much of the humor came in. The performer accompanied himself by using bamboo clappers held in each hand, which provided a syncopated beat.

The mendicants practicing the art usually concentrated on business establishments, going from shop to shop in each town they visited, and they were followed by a large crowd of people anxious to see the fun and the frequent discomfiture of the businessmen who were foolish enough not to cooperate with the mendicant. Generally speaking, the men practiced a gentle form of blackmail.

As they moved from one shop to another their chant would always start afresh and followed the format: *Wang qian zou mai da bu, yan qian daole yige_____pu*. "Walking forward taking large strides I come to the _____shop." That format would allow them to name the type of business they were approaching and, at the same time, rely on a vast store of standard phrases describing the type of shop they were about to "attack." Their introductory remarks would be followed by some flattering comments about the owner or manager, in the hopes that he would give a generous handout. But if the shopkeeper didn't cooperate or was niggardly in what he handed out, the mendicant would quickly switch to defamatory language, couched in what was generally lewd humor, and designed to make the shopkeeper lose face. The wise shopkeeper, seeing the mendicant approaching with his crowd of followers, would place a table outside his establishment and serve tea and cakes and hand out a generous cash donation in a red envelope or perhaps a bolt of cotton or silk or some other commodity. Some shopkeepers, fearing the worst, would close up shop, putting up the wooden boarding that covered their windows at night. However, that wouldn't stop the mendicant. He would stand outside the boarded-up shop and pour out a stream of vilification, greatly to the amusement of the crowd and the embarrassment of the shopkeepers crouching inside. That behavior on the part of the shopkeeper was always poor public relations, and the local people never let him forget it.

Shulaibao was a form of entertainment for everyone who listened to it. As a boy when I followed those men around I was always astonished by their versatility and incredible fund of seemingly impromptu remarks to fit every occasion and every place at which they stopped. In all the years I spent in China I only saw one occasion where one of the men was stumped and that was when we were out in a marketplace one day preaching from the back of our Dodge van and the mendicant approached us. But never having seen a Westerner before, and not having the slightest idea of what we were doing, he was completely speechless, much to the amusement of the crowd that was following him.

In other parts of China, notably in Shandong Province, rap art is done with a musical accompaniment, usually a two-stringed Chinese fiddle, and the words are sung rather than chanted, and always at a very high rate of speed. After the Communist takeover in China the men and their art were banned, or so I am informed, but recent arrivals from China have told me that there has been a revival of the art, mostly by professional comedians who perform it as part of their act. Whether the traveling mendicant will ever be seen again is highly doubtful. Of all the forms of Chinese humor that is one of the most interesting.

Other than the above there are the skits and short plays performed by professional comedians; also there are shadow plays — always performed after dark — where behind a white cloth screen actors perform with tiny figures cut out of donkey hide and manipulated on sticks and with strings, much like our Punch and Judy shows, but in China they were generally considered very vulgar and would, in this country, be X-rated. Despite the misery and poverty in which the people lived, China was still a land of laughter.

Finally, although I have by no means exhausted the subject, there is the ability of the Chinese to laugh at themselves, particularly in their efforts to learn English. My last story was told to me by a Chinese friend, and it aptly demonstrates the difficulties Chinese have with the English language.

An elderly Chinese couple were coming to the United States, but although the husband was very enthusiastic about it, his wife was not. She complained to him that with no knowledge of the English language she would never be able to find the restrooms.

Her husband assured her she would have no problem, and on a piece of paper he wrote the two words: "Men," and "Women." Then, showing them to his wife, he said: "It's all very simple. When you see doors with words like these marked on them, just count the letters. The restroom for men has just three letters, and the one for women has five. All you have to remember is to go into the room that shows the largest number of letters."

The old lady was much comforted and remembered her husband's instructions. However, when they got off the plane in New York, she saw two doors with lettering on them, but instead of "Men" and "Women," they read, "Gentlemen" and "Ladies." Remembering what her husband had said, she dutifully counted "Gentlemen" as having the most letters and promptly entered.

Wánle

("The end."
or
"It is finished.")

This statement was made by Mr. Tharp at the completion of all of his classes, tests, at graduations, and other functions. It has great significance to all of his students.

Epilogue

After some months of slow decline, my beloved Bob passed away on April 13, 1993. All his energy for the preceding four years had gone into writing this book. No matter how sick he felt, he worked on it, willing himself to finish the final draft. Halfway through the final draft, he experienced great difficulty breathing, so I took him to the emergency room. After a few days in the intensive care unit, I believe he realized it was to be his last illness. One of the hardest things he had to endure at the end was that while he was on the ventilator, he was unable to talk and too weak to write. As Bob had unwittingly stated toward the end of the book, he had told his last story.

In tribute to the thousands of students Bob loved and nurtured, I chose Air Force blue as the color of the coffin covering. With them in mind, and as a testimony to God's guidance in our lives, I knew it was my duty to continue Bob's work. Although severely daunted by the increasingly complex task, the encouragement and promises of help from all over the U.S. have buoyed my spirits immensely. I owe it to those former students and friends and to the Lord's help that our ultimate goal has survived the numerous obstacles.

Some months ago a good friend wrote, "As my wife and I read the biography, we frequently asked ourselves what drove Bob and Eva to such activities, to endure such hardship, to smile in the face of adversity? From what did they garner such confidence, wherewithal and courage? Straightforward faith in the Almighty? Many have that faith, but have not lived such lives."

Let me try to answer. When we were very young, both of us accepted Christ as our personal Savior and dedicated our lives to serve Him wherever He led us. In my case, I remember clearly that I knew it would be China. As you have read, that was also the case with Bob. We both were very well aware of what missionary life would be like, but that did not discourage us. And when God led us to fall in love, we felt His blessing on us in a special way and together we rededicated our lives to Him for whatever the future would hold.

You have read of the little and big miracles in our lives, and with each, our faith was strengthened. Though we had our times of weakness, God never failed us, and many a time we found that, "With God, all things are possible." At times in the past year, after 54 years together, I did not think I could go on without Bob, let alone complete the book. But here I am, on this New Year's Eve, with the assurance that soon we will see Bob's book in print. I am grateful to all those who made it possible. May God richly bless you and yours.

Evangeline E. Tharp
"Eva"

Monterey, California
December 31, 1993

About the Illustrations

Charles Chu, M.A. — Chinese Brush Paintings

The dust cover illustration and delightful brush paintings found throughout this book are the work of this renowned calligrapher and painter, who was born in China. Charles is an old friend and former associate of the author from The Institute of Far Eastern Languages at Yale University. He is Professor Emeritus of Chinese at Connecticut College, and presently curator of its Chu-Griffis Art Collection, which was established in his honor. It was founded by Hughes Griffis to give the western world the opportunity to enjoy a greater awareness and share in the appreciation of China's artistic contributions over the centuries and in the years to come.

James W. Lance, B.J. — Line Drawings, Sketches, Diagrams, Maps

The fascinating "pen and ink" images are the work of the author's friend and former associate at Yale University's Institute of Far Eastern Languages. An example of his attention to intricate detail is the drawing of the mission compound, created entirely from the author's description. His early interest in the culture of China, the oldest continuous civilization in the history of mankind, led him to teach himself Chinese by listening to gramaphone records. He later attended classes at the Institute, specializing in its written form. He had an extraordinary grasp of the language and became a highly competent and gifted instructor.

Kathleen Bennett Biersteker, A.A., B.A. — Copper Plate Engraving, Pen and Ink Drawings

Kathleen, the Publish Assistant for Eva E. Tharp, has had a strong influence on this book's design, and created many of the little drawings used as text endings and the "Iris" engraving on page 17. A graduate of UCSC, she has a multi-faceted artistic background in graphic art, photography, stained glass, metal work, ceramics, sculpture, watercolor, printmaking, and book arts. Combining hand printed text with her own intaglio imagery, she has created limited edition fine press books. She enjoys living on the beautiful Monterey Penisula with her family, exploring her environment, and expressing herself in her artwork.

Chang Ta-mu — Calligraphy

The beautiful scroll at the beginning of this book and on page 826 is the work of the author's friend and fellow Chinese instructor at the Defense Language Institute in Monterey, California. The five characters read: "Peaches and plums cover the entire earth," — an ancient Chinese saying where peaches and plums are symbolic of the students and/or disciples of a great teacher.

A Good Friend — Calligraphy

The characters that appear on the cover of this book and most of the proverbs and sayings in Chinese characters that make up each chapter heading were created by this long-time friend, who wishes to remain anonymous. The cover reads: Ban Sheng Hua Xia Yi Dang Nian. Translated roughly they say: "Recollections Of Half A Lifetime Spent In China".

The Photographs in this book were taken mostly by the author, by family, or friends. As all personal possessions of the author were confiscated in China and his own photographic collection destroyed, those included here have been returned by friends who received them in letters over the years. They have been selected and captioned by Bob's wife, Eva.

Dover Publications, Inc., 31 E. 2nd St. Mineola, N.Y. 11501 has allowed us to use their outstanding sourcebooks for the designs shown with the characters in the chapter heading, and for design inserts throughout this book including traditional Chinese cut paper art and other motifs.

Acknowledgements

I know that if my husband Bob were still alive, he would have no difficulty in expressing his thanks to those who encouraged him to write this book and who then stood by to help him complete it. Among those were professional writers, editors, educators, doctors, missionaries, China hands, former students, including those still in military service or in Government service, and naturally, family members. He also chose several who had not had any contact with China. All were enthusiastic in their encouragement, support and help. I know he would want me to mention Dr. Fred C. Boom, Director of The Michigan State University Press, who gave invaluable advice, and the following for thoroughly editing Bob's third draft: Judie Telfer (who also edited the final computer disks before printing), James Plessinger, James Pauley, John Mollick, Perry Cabot, Ronald Aucutt, Dr. Matthew Kaufman and David McCord. Likewise he received considerable help from his brother Gilbert, and his sister Barbara. Bob also consulted my sister Annie and her husband John Brady concerning things Japanese. He was most grateful for the time these folks and many others, unselfishly and freely, gave for so long despite the many delays due to his ill health. Bob would especially thank his good friend and former student, Ed Bohannon, for printing and distributing; our artist friends and former colleagues, Charles Chu, for the cover painting, and James Lance for the illustrations and maps to guide the readers.

After Bob passed away, all the above friends lovingly rallied around me and together we set out to complete his work. Others came to my aid as well, for which I shall be eternally grateful. I want to especially thank my brother Jerry Kok and his wife, Ellan, for their loving support, as well as that of my nephew Kenneth Kok. I add my thanks to Jim Plessinger for accepting without hesitation the task of completing the editing of the final draft, also Carl Povilaitis for insuring the proper Chinese romanization; Mr. Chang Ta Mu for permission to reproduce his scroll dedicated to Bob, as well as others who supplied beautiful calligraphy of Chinese characters; Jim Frazier for technical support in converting the word processor disks; his wife Marsha for many years of assistance in accounting and finances; Daisy Kwoh for being willing to do anything I asked her to do. I also want to thank Kathleen Biersteker, my Publishing Assistant, for her work in the many aspects of this project; and also Duan Wu and her family for help in many practical ways. This has indeed been a united labor of deep respect and love for Bob as a teacher and a human being. I cannot close without gratefulness to all the wives of the above men who also sacrificed to make this project such a special thing. May God richly bless you all. Likewise heartfelt thanks to Pastor and Mrs. Wayne Adams and all the members of the Cypress Community Church for their prayerful support through the events of the past few years.

October 1993
Evangeline E. Tharp
Monterey, California

The Team

This book could not have been completed without the help of the Lord and these friends, thirteen of whom are former students and colleagues.

John Mollick

Jim Pauley

Perry Cabot

Gilbert Tharp

Jim Plessinger

Judie Telfer

Ed Bohannon

Ron Aucutt

David McCord

Charlie Chu

Eva Tharp

Jim Lance

Carl Povilaitis

Jerry Kok

Marsha Frazier

Jim Frazier

Ken Kok

Matt Kaufman

Wade Giles Pinyin and Yale Systems of Romanization *
Comparative Tables of Romanization

WG	PY	Y	WG	PY	Y	WG	PY	Y
A	a	a	chüeh	jue	jywe	jun	run	rwun
ai	ai	ai	ch'üeh	que	chywe	jung	rong	rung
an	an	an	chün	jun	jyun			
ang	ang	ang	ch'ün	qun	chyun	KA	ga	ga
ao	ao	au				k'a	ka	ka
			E, O	e	e	kai	gai	gai
CHA	zha	ja	en	en	en	k'ai	kai	kai
ch'a	cha	cha	eng	eng	eng	kan	gan	gan
chai	zhai	jai	erh	er	er	k'an	kan	kan
ch'ai	chai	chai				kang	gang	gang
chan	zhan	jan	FA	fa	fa	k'ang	kang	kang
ch'an	chan	chan	fan	fan	fan	kao	gao	gau
chang	zhang	jang	fang	fang	fang	k'ao	kao	kau
ch'ang	chang	chang	fei	fei	fei	ke,ko	ge	ge
chao	zhao	jau	fen	fen	fen	k'e,k'o	ke	ke
ch'ao	chao	chau	feng	feng	feng	kei	gei	gei
che	zhe	jc	fo	fo	fwo	ken	gen	gen
ch'e	che	che	fou	fou	fou	k'en	ken	ken
chei	zhei	jei	fu	fu	fu	keng	geng	geng
chen	zhen	jen				k'eng	keng	keng
ch'en	chen	chen	HA	ha	ha	ko,ke	ge	ge
cheng	zheng	jeng	hai	hai	hai	k'o,k'e	ke	ke
ch'eng	cheng	cheng	han	han	han	kou	gou	gou
chi	ji	ji	hang	hang	hang	k'ou	kou	kou
ch'i	qi	chi	hao	hao	hau	ku	gu	gu
chia	jia	jya	hei	hei	hei	k'u	ku	ku
ch'ia	qia	chya	hen	hen	hen	kua	gua	gwa
chiang	jiang	jyang	heng	heng	heng	k'ua	kua	kwa
ch'iang	qiang	chyang	ho	he	he	kuai	guai	gwai
ch'iao	qiao	chyau	hou	hou	hou	k'uai	kuai	kwai
chieh	jie	jye	hsi	xi	syi	kuan	guan	gwan
ch'ieh	qie	chye	hsia	xia	sya	k'uan	kuan	kwan
chien	jian	jyan	hsiang	xiang	syang	kuang	guang	gwang
ch'ien	qian	chyan	hsiao	xiao	syau	k'uang	kuang	kwang
chih	zhi	jr	hsieh	xie	sye	kuei	gui	gwei
ch'ih	chi	chr	hsien	xian	syan	k'uei	kui	kwei
chin	jin	jin	hsin	xin	syin	kun	gun	gwur.
ch'in	qin	chin	hsing	xing	sying	k'un	kun	kwun
ching	jing	jing	hsiu	xiu	syou	kung	gong	gung
ch'ing	qing	ching	hsiung	xiong	syung	k'ung	kong	kung
chiu	jiu	jyou	hsü	xu	syu	kuo	guo	gwo
ch'iu	qiu	chyou	hsüan	xuan	sywan	k'uo	kuo	kwo
chiung	jiong	jyung	hsüeh	xue	sywe			
ch'iung	qiong	chyung	hsün	xun	syun	LA	la	la
cho	zhuo	jwo	hu	hu	hu	lai	lai	lai
ch'o	chuo	chwo	hua	hua	hwa	lan	lan	lan
chou	zhou	jou	huai	huai	hwai	lang	lang	lang
ch'ou	chou	chou	huan	huan	hwan	lao	lao	lau
chu	zhu	ju	huang	huang	hwang	le	le	le
ch'u	chu	chu	hui	hui	hwei	lei	lei	lei
chua	zhua	jwa	hun	hun	hwun	leng	leng	leng
ch'ua	chua	chwa	hung	hong	hung	li	li	li
chuai	zhuai	jwai	huo	huo	hwo	lia	lia	lya
ch'uai	chuai	chwai				liang	liang	lyang
chuan	zhuan	jwan	I, YI	yi	yi	liao	liao	lyau
ch'uan	chuan	chwan				lieh	lie	lye
chuang	zhuang	jwang	JAN	ran	ran	lien	lian	lyan
ch'uang	chuang	chwang	jang	rang	rang	lin	lin	lin
chui	zhui	jwei	jao	rao	rau	ling	ling	ling
ch'ui	chui	chwei	je	re	re	liu	liu	lyou
chun	zhun	jwun	jen	ren	ren	lo	luo	lwo
ch'un	chun	chwun	jeng	reng	reng	lou	lou	lou
chung	zhong	jung	jih	ri	r	lu	lu	lu
ch'ung	chong	chung	jo	ruo	rwo	luan	luan	lwan
chü	ju	jyu	jou	rou	rou	lun,lün	lun	lwun
ch'ü	qu	chyu	ju	ru	ru	lung	long	lung
chüan	juan	jywan	juan	ruan	rwan	lü	lü	lyu
ch'üan	quan	chywan	jui	rui	rwei			

WG	PY	Y
lüan	lüan	lywan
Lüeh	lüe	lywe
MA	ma	ma
mai	mai	mai
man	man	man
mang	mang	mang
mao	mao	mau
mei	mei	mei
men	men	men
meng	meng	meng
mi	mi	mi
miao	miao	myau
mieh	mie	mye
mien	mian	myan
min	min	min
ming	ming	ming
miu	miu	myou
mo	mo	mwo
mou	mou	mou
mu	mu	mu
NA	na	na
nai	nai	nai
nan	nan	nan
nang	nang	nang
nao	nao	nau
nei	nei	nei
nen	nen	nen
neng	neng	neng
ni	ni	ni
niang	niang	nyang
niao	niao	nyau
neih	nie	nye
nien	nian	nyan
nin	nin	nin
ning	ning	ning
niu	niu	nyou
no	no	nwo
nou	nou	nou
nu	nu	nu
nuan	nuan	nwan
nun	nun	nwun
nung	nong	nung
nü	nü	nyu
nüeh	nüe	nywe
O, E	e	e
ou	ou	ou
PA	ba	ba
p'a	pa	pa
pai	bai	bai
p'ai	pai	pai
pan	ban	ban
p'an	pan	pan
pang	bang	bang
p'ang	pang	pang
pao	bao	bau
p'ao	pao	pau
pei	bei	bei
p'ei	pei	pei
pen	ben	ben
p'en	pen	pen
peng	beng	beng
p'eng	peng	peng
pi	bi	bi
p'i	pi	pi
piao	biao	byau
p'iao	piao	pyau
pieh	bie	bye
p'ieh	pie	pye
pien	bian	byan
p'ien	pian	pyan

WG	PY	Y
pin	bin	bin
p'in	pin	pin
ping	bing	bing
p'ing	ping	ping
po	bo	bwo
p'o	po	pwo
pou	bou	bou
p'ou	pou	pou
pu	bu	bu
p'u	pu	pu
SA	sa	sa
sai	sai	sai
san	san	san
sang	sang	sang
sao	sao	sau
se	se	se
sen	sen	sen
seng	seng	seng
sha	sha	sha
shai	shai	shai
shan	shan	shan
shang	shang	shang
shao	shao	shau
she	she	she
shei	shei	shei
shen	shen	shen
sheng	sheng	sheng
shih	shi	shr
shou	shou	shou
shu	shu	shu
shua	shua	shwa
shuai	shuai	shwai
shuan	shuan	shwan
shuang	shuang	shwang
shui	shui	shwei
shun	shun	shwun
shuo	shuo	shwo
so	suo	swo
sou	sou	sou
ssu,szu	si	sz
su	su	su
suan	suan	swan
sui	sui	swei
sun	sun	swun
sung	song	sung
szu,ssu	si	sz
TA	da	da
t'a	ta	ta
tai	dai	dai
t'ai	tai	tai
tan	dan	dan
t'an	tan	tan
tang	dang	dang
t'ang	tang	tang
tao	dao	dau
t'ao	tau	tao
te	de	de
t'e	te	te
tei	dei	dei
teng	deng	deng
t'eng	teng	teng
ti	di	di
t'i	ti	ti
tiao	diao	dyau
t'iao	tiao	tyau
tieh	die	dye
t'ieh	tie	tye
tien	dian	dyan
t'ien	tian	tyan
ting	ding	ding
t'ing	ting	ting
tiu	diu	dyou

WG	PY	Y
to	duo	dwo
t'o	tuo	two
tou	dou	dou
t'ou	tou	tou
tsa	za	dza
ts'a	ca	tsa
tsai	zai	dzai
ts'ai	cai	tsai
tsan	zan	dzan
ts'an	can	tsan
tsang	zang	dzang
ts'ang	cang	tsang
tsao	zao	dzau
ts'ao	cao	t au
tse	ze	dze
ts'e	ce	tse
tsei	zei	dzei
tsen	zen	dzen
ts'en	cen	tsen
tseng	zeng	dzeng
ts'eng	ceng	tseng
tso	zuo	dzwo
ts'o	cuo	tswo
tsou	zou	dzou
ts'ou	cou	tsou
tsu	zu	dzu
ts'u	cu	tsu
tsuan	zuan	dzwan
ts'uan	cuan	tswan
tsui	zui	dzwei
ts'ui	cui	tswei
tsun	zun	dzwun
ts'un	cun	tswun
tsung	zong	dzung
tsung	cong	tsung
tu	du	du
t'u	tu	tu
tuan	duan	dwan
t'uan	tuan	twan
tui	dui	dwei
t'ui	tui	twei
tun	dun	dwun
t'un	tun	twun
tung	dong	dung
t'ung	tong	tung
tzu	zi	dz
tz'u	ci	tsz
WA	wa	wa
wai	wai	wai
wan	wan	wan
wang	wang	wang
wei	wei	wei
wen	wen	wen
weng	weng	weng
wo	wo	wo
wu	wu	wu
YA	ya	ya
yai	yai	yai
yang	yang	yang
yao	yao	yau
yeh	ye	ye
yen	yan	yan
yi, i	yi	yi
yin	yin	yin
ying	ying	ying
yu	you	you
yung	yong	yung
yü	yu	yu
yüan	yuan	ywan
yüeh	yue	ywe
yün	yun	yun

* Above chart is a copy of IFEL instruction hand-outs.